P9-DHS-516

DICTIONARY
of
WORLD LITERARY TERMS

DICTIONARY
OF
WORLD LITERARY TERMS

FORMS • TECHNIQUE • CRITICISM

Completely Revised and Enlarged Edition

Edited by

JOSEPH T. SHIPLEY

with contributions
by 260 authorities

Boston THE WRITER, INC. ***Publishers***

Reprinted 1979

Library of Congress Catalog Card No.: 75–91879
International Standard Book Number: 0–87116–012–9

Printed in the United States of America

CONTENTS

Preface to the Revised and Enlarged Third Edition

The *Dictionary of World Literary Terms* (originally called *Dictionary of World Literature*) has been completely re-examined for this new edition. Many entries have been altered, revised, and brought up to date; a large number of new terms have been added; the bibliographies have been enlarged with recent works; and hundreds of cross-references have been inserted to increase the book's usefulness. Major historical surveys of criticism have been placed in Part Two.

In addition to the contributors (the new ones listed below; the original ones at the back of the volume), I wish to thank Abraham S. and Sylvia K. Burack, whose keen interest, warm encouragement, and informed counsel have been of substantial assistance in bringing the work to such final competence as it may have achieved.

Joseph T. Shipley

CONTRIBUTORS

To contributors to the original edition (see pages 464–466), and to new contributors listed below, I extend thanks for their counsel and writings for this third edition:

E. M. Adams, Univ. of N. Carolina
Richard Armour, Scripps Col. (Emeritus)
Isaac Asimov, Boston Univ. School of Medicine
Monroe C. Beardsley, Swarthmore
George J. Becker, Swarthmore
Carol Blum, State Univ. of N.Y. (Stony Brook)
Herbert Brean, former Pres., Mystery Writers of America
Crane Brinton, Harvard (deceased)
David Daiches, Sussex Univ., England
Bryllion Fagin, Johns Hopkins
John Gassner, Yale (deceased)
Baxter Hathaway, Cornell
Ruth King (for translation from Spanish)
Murray Krieger, Univ. of California (Irvine)
Richmond Lattimore, Bryn Mawr
Harry Levin, Harvard
Oleg Maslenikov, Univ. of California (Berkeley)
Charles Morris, Univ. of Florida
Lewis Mumford
Allardyce Nicoll
Henri Peyre, Yale
Olga Ragusa, Columbia
John Burke Shipley, Univ. of Illinois (Chicago Circle)
Gonzalo Sobejano, Columbia
Harry Steinhauer, Univ. of California (Santa Barbara)
Eliseo Vivas, Northwestern
Frederic Will, Univ. of Iowa

ABBREVIATIONS and SYMBOLS

After the initial word of an item, abbreviations indicate the language. Of the many rhetorical terms, the fullest English Renaissance listing is in Puttenham's Arte of English Poesie, 1589 (**E.** Arber, 1869); this is indicated by P., often with Puttenham's paraphrase of the term quoted. **See** and **q.v.** refer to items in the Dictionary; **cf.** may refer to other works.

BOOKS

Atkins—J. W. H. Atkins, Literary Criticism in Antiquity, 2 v., 1934.
Brandes—Georg Brandes, Main Currents in Nineteenth Century Literature (Eng. 1924).
Butcher—S. H. Butcher, Aristotle's Theory of Poetry and Fine Art, 4th ed., 1923.
Cambib (or **CBEL**)—Cambridge Bibliography of English Literature, ed. F. W. Bateson, 4 v., 1940.
CBFL—Critical Bibliography of French Literature, 1947–61.
Chad.—H. M. and N. K. Chadwick, The Growth of Literature, 3 v., 1932–40.
Christ—Wilhelm Christ, Griechische Literaturgeschichte, 6th ed., 3 v., 1912–24.
Christ's Metrik—W. Christ, Metrik der Griechen und Romer, 1879.
D'Alton—J. F. D'Alton, Roman Literary Theory and Criticism, 1931.
Eppel.—H. W. Eppelsheimer, Handbuch der Weltliteratur (1937).
FFC—Folklore Fellows Communications.
Flickinger—R. C. Flickinger, The Greek Theatre and its Drama, 1926.
Gay.—C. M. Gayley and F. N. Scott, Introduction to the Methods and Materials of Literary Criticism, 1899; enlarged (with B. P. Kurtz), 1920.
H & R—Hefling and Richards, Index to Contemporary Biography and Criticism, 1929–34.
Hammer—C. Hammer, Rhetorik, 1901.
Hof.—J. B. Hoffmann, Lateinische Grammatik, 1928.
Holmes—John Holmes, The Art of Rhetoric Made Easy, 1755.
Krumbacher—Karl Krumbacher, Byzantinische Literaturgeschichte, 2d ed., 1897.
Mantz (or **Mantzius**)—Karl Mantzius, A History of Theatrical Art (Eng. 6 v., 1903–21).
Merker—P. Merker and W. Stammler, Reallexikon der deutschen Literaturgeschichte, 1925 f.
Mueller—L. Mueller, De Re Metrica, 1894.
Murray—Gilbert Murray, The Classical Tradition in Poetry, 1927.
Norden—Eduard Norden, Die antike Kunstprosa, 2 v., 1909.
OED—Oxford English Dictionary.
P—Puttenham, Arte of English Poesie, 1589 (E. Arber, 1869).
Pauly—A. Pauly, Real Encyclopädie der classischen Altertumswissenschaft, 7 v., 1839–52.
Pauly-Wissowa—Pauly-Wissowa, Real Encyclopädie der classischen Altertumswissenschaft, 31 v., 1894–1939; Supp. 1903–35.
RE—Realencyclopädie der Altertumswissenschaft, ed. G. Wissowa, W. Kroll, K. Mittelhaus, 60 v., 1894–1940.
Saints—George Saintsbury, History of Criticism and Literary Taste in Europe, 3 v., 1900–04.
Sandys—J. E. Sandys, History of Classical Scholarship, 1906.
Schanz—Martin Schanz, Geschichte der römischen Literatur, 4 v. in 8 pts., 1907–20.
Schanz-Hosius—M. Schanz, Carl Hosius, 4th ed. of work above, 2 v., 1927–35.
Schmid—Wilhelm Schmid, Der Atticismus, 5 v., 1887–97.

Schmid-Stahlin—W. Schmid, Otto Stählin, Griechische Literaturgeschichte, 2 v., 1929–34.
Ship—Joseph T. Shipley, The Quest For Literature, 1931; Trends in Literature, 1949.
Smith—G. Gregory Smith, Elizabethan Critical Essays, 2 v., 1904.
Sping—J. E. Spingarn, A History of Literary Criticism in the Renaissance, 1899; 2d ed., 1908.
Volkmann—R. Volkmann, Rhetorik der Griechen und Römer, 1885.

PERIODICALS

AES—Abstracts of English Studies
AJP—American Journal of Philology
AS—American Speech
BJ of Psych—British Journal of Psychology
CJ—Classical Journal
CP—Classical Philology
CQ—Classical Quarterly
CR—Classical Review
CW—Classical Weekly
ELH—Journal of English Literary History
HSCP—Harvard Studies in Classical Philology
JA—Journal of Æsthetics
JAFL—Journal of American Folklore
JEGP—Journal of English and German Philology
JHI—Journal of the History of Ideas
JP—Journal of Philosophy
JPPSM—Journal of Philosophy, Psychology, and Scientific Method
JUS—Journal of United Science
Lang—Language
MLN—Modern Language Notes
MLQ—Modern Language Quarterly
MLR—Modern Language Review
MP—Modern Philology
Phil—Philologus
PhQ—Philological Quarterly
PhW—Philologische Wochenschrift
PMLA—Publications of the Modern Language Association of America
PR Philosophical Review
PSc—Philosophy of Science
QJS—Quarterly Journal of Speech
RdDM—Revue des Deux Mondes
RES—Review of English Studies
RLC—Revue de Littérature Comparée
RR—Romanic Review
SP—Studies in Philology
TAPA—Transactions of the American Philological Association

OTHER SYMBOLS

A.S.—Anglo-Saxon
assoc.—association; associated (with)
bib (bibliog).—bibliography
ca.—about
contrib.—contributed (by); contributor(s)
crit.—criticism; critical
dimin.—diminutive
e.g.—for example
ed.—editor(s); edited (by); edition
E.E.T.S.—Early English Text Society
emph.—put(s) emphasis on
Eng.—English; England
esp.—especially
f.—and the following (singular or plural)
F.—French; France
fl.—flourished
G.—German; Germany
Gc.—Germanic
Gr.—Greek; Greece
hist.—history; histories; historical
introd.—introduced (by); introduction
L. (alone)—Latin
L. (with following letters)—late
M.A.—Middle Ages
ME (MEng)—Middle English
Med.—Medieval
MHG—Middle High German
No.—North
OE (OEng.)—Old English
OHG—Old High German
opp.—opposite; opposed to
p.—page(s)
posth.—posthumous(ly)
Port.—Portuguese; Portugal
prep.—preparation
pros.—prosody
Prov.—Provençal, Provence
pseud.—pseudonym (of)
pub.—published (by); publisher
q.v.—which see
R.—Roman; Rome
Ren.—Renaissance
rep.—reprint(ed); reproduction
Shak.—Shakespeare (his plays may be indicated by initials)
So.—South

spec.—specifically
supp.—supplement(ary)
Swe.—Swedish
syn.—synonym
trans.—translated (by); translation
v.—volume(s)
( )—Unless otherwise indicated, authors and titles in parentheses are representative, not exhaustive

In indicating verse form, a repeated letter means a rhyme; an *x* means an unrhymed line; a capital (*ababB*) means a repeated line.

PART I

DICTIONARY
of
WORLD LITERARY TERMS

A

A B C; *Absey.* (1) A poem of which the successive lines or, usually, stanzas (Chaucer) begin with the successive letters of the alphabet. The 119th *Psalm* has 22 stanzas, for the 22 letters of the Hebrew alphabet; each stanza has 8 couplets, the first line of which begins with the same letter. (2) A book of the alphabet, or of the rudiments of a subject, *e.g.,* Leo Stein, *The A B C of Aesthetics,* 1927.

abecedarius. *See* Acrostic.

ab ovo (L., from the egg). From the beginning, in great detail. Used by Horace (*Ars Poetica* 147) in his description of a dull account of the Trojan War, beginning with the egg of Leda from which Helen was born. Contrasted with a vivid narrative such as that of the *Odyssey,* which begins *in medias res,* in the midst of things. Not related to the proverbial expression *ab ovo usque ad mala,* "from egg to apples," which corresponds to our "from soup to nuts." *Cf.* Epic.

absolutism. The doctrine that holds that there are basic values residing in the work of art itself, or basic standards by which a work is to be judged. Opp. relativism, *q.v.*

abstract. (1) An abridgement; a brief summary of the essentials of a work. (2) Considered apart from any concrete object or reality, or application to particular entities (*e.g.,* redness, beauty). The particular, or singular, term names a specific object or event (*e.g.,* Bucephalus). The general term denotes a class of objects, or an object as belonging to a class (*e.g.,* horse). The concrete term (which may be either singular or general) refers to the object itself, either as specified (*e.g.,* Bucephalus) or as a member of a class (*e.g.,* horse), *i.e.,* possessing a certain quality or complex of qualities. The abstract term refers to the quality considered by itself, apart from the object (*e.g.,* equinity). (The term abstract is sometimes extended to the sense that here is reserved for "general.") And indeed the more general the concrete term, the more likely there is to be an abstract term corresponding to it; "equinity" is more likely to be a manageable abstraction than "white-spotted colthood." (W. E. Johnson, *Logic* Pt I, 1921, ch. 6, 7; A. Wolf, *Textbook of Logic,* 1930, p. 118–119).

In the arts, "abstract" is equivalent to "non-representational" and refers to an absence of similarity to things in the world of nature; the abstract is therefore to be distinguished from the conventional or stylized (H. Read, *Art Now,* 1933, p. 97–116). Certain kinds of writing may be said to be general or abstract in the sense that in them certain abstract qualities exemplify the whole individual (as in personal caricature) or the individual represents the qualities generally (as in the morality play or the comedy of types). On the other hand, a description may be called concrete in the sense that it contains a sufficient amount of circumstantial detail to achieve verisimilitude or a degree of sensory realization (*see* Realism). Aristotle contrasted poetry with history partly on the ground that poetry (but not history) deals with what is general or universal in human experience (*Poetics* IX); this conception was exaggerated by neo-classic theorists and creative writers. Pope's *Essay on Man* and Johnson's *Ramblers,* for example, are in harmony with Johnson's theory of "the grandeur of generality," his injunctions against numbering "the streaks of the tulip," and the concern of Reynolds for "the invariable general form which nature frequently produces, and always seems to intend in her productions" (*Idler,* 82; *cf.* W. K. Wimsatt, Jr., *The Prose Style of Samuel Johnson,* 1941, p. 52–4, 93–103; A. O. Lovejoy, *The Great Chain of Being,* 1936, p. 290–4).

As a stylistic phenomenon, abstraction is often found in close conjunction with concreteness ("unregarded age in corners thrown," Shak. *AYLI* II iii 42; "Laughter holding both her sides," Milton, *L'Allegro*; "With hope of freedom hanging by a thread," Marianne Moore, "In the Public Garden"). Eighteenth c. neo-classic style and recent imagism are endeavors toward extreme generality and extreme concreteness respectively, but most successful literary works lie between the poles. *Cf.* Realism; Objectivity. W. K. Wimsatt, Jr. and Monroe C. Beardsley.

absurd, theatre of the. Expression in plays

of the purposelessness, lack of harmony, and sense of futility that characterized post-World War II existentialism, *q.v.* Playwrights in the the theatre of the absurd—including notably Jean Genêt (*The Balcony*), Edward Albee (*The Sandbox, The American Dream*), Eugene Ionesco (*Rhinoceros*), Samuel Beckett (*Krapp's Last Tape*)—see no logic in life and feel that only the presentation of absurdity can make sense. Their plays, a succession of random or aimless bodily movements—or no movement, as of the two characters in garbage pails in Beckett's *End Game*—sometimes have incomprehensible dialogue, at times (as in Beckett's *Waiting for Godot,* 1952) have a semblance of symbolic thought. Ionesco describes his plays with such terms as anti-play and anti-theatre; he pictures the world as presenting both "an unreal transparency and an opacity," source of euphoria or anguish. In his play *The Chairs* (1951) a senile man and his wife arrange chairs for a lecture which, before an imaginary audience, consists of a series of grunts. In *The Birthday Party* (1959) Harold Pinter uses black humor, *q.v.,* and sinister urgings to lead his character to unexplained and unmotivated disaster. Beginning in little and off-Broadway playhouses, seldom attracting large audiences, these plays of the absurd have challenged traditional playwrights. (Murray Schisgal's play *Luv,* 1965, seems a burlesque of the theatre of the absurd.)

The philosophical basis for the theatre of the absurd was summarized by Albert Camus in his essay *The Myth of Sisyphus* (1942, trans. 1955). Believing that the universe is irrational and illogical, he wrote: "There are some words I do not understand; one of them is sin." Later he adopted a more moderate attitude, opposing violence and demanding responsibility, even in an absurd universe. Other absurdists state that the revolt against comprehensible discourse is a revolt against abstraction, against authority. Sartre maintains that a universe without God is absurd. As far back as the third century Tertullian said, in effect, "I believe because it is absurd"; today, belief is widely rejected. In an absurd universe without belief there are no ethical standards, no moral judgments, no perceptible or valid motives; one thing or one action is as good as another. The equalizing endeavor of Whitman's social egalitarianism is carried into the realms of behavior and art. Thus the literature of the absurd, though strengthened by French existentialism, had roots in America. Contrast Ernest Hemingway's *A Farewell to Arms* (1929) of the "lost generation" with Norman Mailer's *The Naked and the Dead* (1948): "Behind Hemingway's irony and his celebrated *nadir*" (P. Michelson, *New Republic,* Sept. 9, 1967) "there is the energy born of anger. A sentimental anger at being cosmically cheated of his beautiful image of love. Not so with Mailer. There is no indignation because there is no expectation. And Mailer's vision is too exhausted to be angry at what has become commonplace—cosmic fraud. Absurdity has supplanted idealism."

The theatre of the absurd, in some aspects of technique and presentation, resembles surrealism, but the impulse behind the plays is different. Surrealism turns away from life, while the "absurd" claims to be a reflection of life. Some of its proponents, however, state that such drama is not intended to express ideas, but seeks only theatricality, the "essence" of the theatre. It therefore discards organized plot, consistency of character, and motivation, aiming solely at the immediate excitement roused in the audience by happenings onstage. It seeks to play directly upon the passions. Traditionalists may echo Kipling's query: "But is it art?"—to which devotees of the absurd retort that the question is, rather: "Does it work?". They reject, among other things, conventional labels and æsthetic evaluations. Albee (quoted by W. Wager) says his work is "meant to be taken into the unconscious almost directly, without being filtered through the brain cells." *Cf.* Anti-hero; Modernism; Off-Broadway; Beat Generation; Comedy; Black humor; Happening; Surrealism; Short story.

M. Esslin, *The Theatre of the Absurd,* 1961; L. C. Pronko, *Avant-Garde,* 1962; G. E. Wellwarth, *The Theatre of Protest and Paradox,* 1964; D. Grossvogel, *The Blasphemers,* 1965; J. G. Bernay and R. Kuhn, ed. *Panorame du Théâtre Nouveau,* 4 v., 1967; J. Guicharnaud, *Modern French Theatre,* 1967; W. Wager, ed. *The Playwrights Speak,* 1967; L. Kampf, *On Modernism,* 1967; A. Kernan, ed. *The Modern Am. Theatre,* 1967; R. Kostelanitz, *The Theatre of Mixed Means,* 1968.

abuse. Poems of abuse are frequent among primitive peoples, especially as taunting before a fight. The abuse may include imprecation, and be combined with boasting. This is a special genre among African peoples, such as the Galla, the Tuareg, and the Abyssinians. Women as well as men chanted these often impromptu verses, ridiculing enemies or unpopular leaders. Leaden imprecatory tablets were buried by Athenian peasants, 4th c. B.C., calling upon the gods to destroy a neighbor's crops, or to render his flocks and his wife sterile. Early English (esp. Scots) poems of abuse were called flytings, as William Dunbar's "The Flyting of Dunbar and Kennedie" (1508). Similar abuse is found today in campaign cries and slogans.

academic. (1) of the school of thought of Plato. (2) scholarly, learned. Originally a term of praise; often now derogatory, from attacks on the Academies' conservatism and emphasis on form; hence (3) concerned with rules of making rather than with things made; motivated by a desire to teach a technique rather than to do, or to explain rather than observe. (4) without practical consequence, as an academic question.

acatalectic. In poetry, a line metrically complete, carrying through the basic pattern of the line or poem. Catalectic: lacking one syllable of the pattern. Brachycatalectic: lacking two syllables. Hypercatalectic: with an extra syllable (or foot). The noun is acatalexis.

accent. The stress placed upon certain syllables of a line; the metrical basis of accentual verse as opposed to that based on the length of the word, on syllable counting, or on other devices. The stress itself is called ictus: often this metrical ictus does not correspond with the normal word accent. This lack of accord was a bugbear with the Elizabethans, who listed words of "indifferencie" (corresponding to L. *syllaba anceps*) that might shift their accent. Gabriel Harvey (letter to Spenser) protested against turning *carpenter* into *carpen'ter*; such shifting is wrenched accent. Poets use the conflict between metrical and word accent to break metrical monotony, *e.g.* (Kunitz):

> Within the city of the burning cloud,
> Dragging my life behind me in a sack,
> Naked I prowl. . . .

where the meter is iambic pentameter.

In addition to word accent and metrical accent, rhetorical accent may be a factor in pronunciation, as determined by intention. Thus "We have' our work done" means we secure someone to do it; "We have our work done'" means it is completed. W. S. Gilbert (*Patience*) accents four different words in as many uses of the line "He was a little boy." Within a word, the syllable most heavily stressed receives the tonic accent; atonic syllables are unstressed; these are also called strong and weak, respectively. *Cf.* Arsis; Meter; Prosody; Caesura.

acmeism. A movement in 20th c. Russian poetry (N. Gumilev, S. Gorodetski, O. Mandelshtam, Anna Akhmatova). It rejected the "other world" of the symbolists for the visible, sensate world with its colors, sounds, odors. It insisted that poetry be more concrete. *Apollon* 1, 1913; 1, 1928; O. Mandelshtam, *On Poetry,* 1928. *Cf.* Russ. Criticism in Part II.

acroama (Gr., thing heard). (1) An entertainment, esp. a musical or declamatory recital at mealtime; later, a dramatic presentation. (2) A lecture to the initiate, esp. (plural) acroamata, the esoteric discourses of Aristotle.

acrostic. (1) A symbolic word made from first letters, *e.g., Ichthys* (Gr., fish) from the first letters of the Gr. words for Jesus Christ, Son of God, Saviour. Modern advertising and governmental terms are often formed in this fashion. (2) Poem in which certain letters of successive lines (paragraphs or chapters in the rare prose acrostics) form a definite pattern or word. If the letters of the alphabet appear in order thus, the poem is an abecedarius, or alphabetical acrostic. If initial letters make the word, it is a true acrostic; if medial letters, a mesostich; if final letters, a telestich. First letter of line 1, second letter (or first letter of second word) of line 2, etc., a cross acrostic, *e.g.* Poe, "A Valentine." The oldest type is apparently the abecedarian: *Lamentations* 1–4; *Proverbs* 31, 10–31 and twelve of the Psalms (*e.g.,* 34, 37, 111, 119). Mystical significance was ascribed to such lyrics; Cicero says they appear in Sibylline verse, though the original purpose of the device may have been mnemonic. The arguments to Plautus' comedies are acrostic. Sir John Davies wrote 26 "Hymns to Astraea," each an acrostic of Elizabetha Regina. Addison lists the acrostic as a form of false wit. E. A. Knox, *Book of Acrostics,* 1924; M. Gardner, *The Numerology of Dr. Matrix,* ch. 8, 1967.

act. A major division of a play. The division indicated by Aristotle and the Greek choral movements suggested 5 acts. This was generally maintained until the late 19th c., when compression of the last two stages of the conflict produced the 4-act play (Ibsen). The 20th century began to compress the action into 3 acts; in the past decade, even two. A short drama is often called a one-act play. Occasionally a work is divided into episodes or scenes, without act-division. *See* Freytag's pyramid.

action. (1) The movement of a performer. (2) The main story, as opposed to an incidental episode or digression. (3) The series of events that together form the plot of a play or narrative. The action (sense 3) of a play may be conveyed by physical movement, by the clash of dialogue, or by the narration of events supposed to have taken place off-stage (as with violence in ancient Greek tragedy). Aristotle says that action is basic in the drama; Vanbrugh makes the opposition clear: "I believe I could show that the chief entertainment as well as the moral lies more in the Character and the Diction than in the Business and the Event." The argument can no more be concluded than that about which of the bodily members is most important.

It is generally agreed that a play or novel should have one main line of action, leading from a recognizable beginning to an appropriate end. Recent writing, however, as in anti-novel and anti-drama, at times overlooks such restrictions, and indeed may display only occasional and casual action, without any interlinked chain of events. *Cf.* Anti-hero; Characterization; Plot; Unities. A. Cook, *Prisms,* 1967.

activism. An attitude and policy developed mainly in Germany after the first World War. Franz Pfemfert published a weekly, *Die Aktion*; Kurt Hiller a yearbook, *The Aim*; Ludwig Rubiner a volume, *Man in the Middle.* They demanded active participation in human affairs. As Hiller wrote in Pfemfert's magazine: "Although we may not understand the world, we have the obligation to better it." But the change must be in the spirit, and not through violence. The movement included Heinrich Mann, Carl Sternheim, Ernst Toller. W. Paulsen, *Expressionismus und Aktivismus,* 1935.

acyrology. Overdelicate euphemism, as the Victorian "limbs" of the table; "I have to see a man about a dog." *Cf.* Euphemism; Periphrasis.

Addisonian (Joseph Addison, 1672–1719). (1) Of style: equable, judicial, unruffled. *The Spectator* promised to attack not the faults of one man but those common to a thousand. A favorite remark of Sir Roger de Coverley's is "There is much to be said on both sides." (2) Addisonian termination (Bishop Hurd): one using a preposition to end a sentence with.

address. The indication given in a work as to the nature of the intended receptor (first, second, or third person). The writer may be communing with himself, or addressing a specific person or group or anyone at all. *See* Narrator.

adonic (Adonius versus). A line consisting of a dactyl followed by a spondee or trochee: — ∪ ∪ — ⏓. It is used as the 4th line of the Sapphic strophe. Thus *lambit Hydaspes*; There, on the hilltop.

adynaton. Magnifying an actual event by reference to an impossibility; a form of hyperbole, *q.v.* Thus: My love will last "Till the sun grows cold, and the stars are old" (B. Taylor, "Bedouin Love Song"). H. V. Cantor, "Adynaton in Gr. and L. Poetry," *AJP* 51, 1930.

aeolic (Gr. dialect in which Alcaeus and Sappho wrote their poems). A meter combining dactyls or iambs and trochees, thus producing choriambs. Special forms of it are adonic, alcaic, glyconic, sapphic. Christ, 508–68; D. Page, Sappho and Alcaeus, 1955. *See* Classical Versification.

Æschylean (Æschylus, 525–456 B.C., first of the Gr. tragic poets). Of a sombre, granite grandeur.

æsthetics (or esthetics). **Definition.** (Gr., *aisthesis,* sense-perception.) The first author to use the word æsthetic in its modern sense was Alexander Baumgarten (1714–62) [The investigation of its problems, of course, goes much farther back; the field is often referred to as "the philosophy of beauty" or "of art," where the term "philosophy" means no more than "theory," whether arrived at purely speculatively or more or less empirically.] Æsthetics, since Baumgarten's time, has been defined as "the study of the beautiful in nature and art, of its character, of its conditions, and of its conformity to law." Thus defined, it has a broad scope, including at least two major modes of approach, the philosophical and the psychological. Philosophers since Plato have been intensively concerned with problems of art and of beauty. They have been pursuing questions like the following: What is art? What is beauty? Is beauty objective? What is the relation of beauty to other values, *i.e.,* what is the relation of the beautiful to the true and to the good? For centuries philosophers adopted the deductive method. The nature of the æsthetic categories, *e.g.,* the ideally beautiful, the graceful, the worthy, the sublime, the tragic, the comical, and the grotesque, has been inferred from their alleged relation to fundamental *a priori* concepts, ideas or postulates.

Psychological æsthetics has held as its aim the inquiry into two great problems, *viz.,* æsthetic enjoyment or experience of beauty, and æsthetic creation or the art-impulse.

æsthetic attitude. From the psychological

standpoint the experience of beauty has been considered by most writers as resulting from the viewing of certain perceptual patterns under a special attitude of mind, "the æsthetic attitude." Thus, the problem of æsthetic appreciation resolves itself into two interdependent inquiries, *viz.,* (a) the analysis of those patterns of the art-object which, viewed in the æsthetic attitude, give rise to the experience of beauty; and (b) the analysis of the æsthetic attitude as compared with the attitudes men are likely to adopt in non-æsthetic situations.

(a) The analysis of the art-object has led to the recognition of its formal or abstract properties, on the one hand, and its thematic or concrete properties on the other. By the latter is meant the concretely meaningful content that the art-object represents; the story it tells, the event it depicts. Such factors as rhythm, balance, proportion, harmony and, above all, unity, are mentioned as abstract formal properties. Insofar as these properties are quantifiable, attempts have been made to express them mathematically (Zeising, Birkhoff). The concept of unity refers not only to the unity of the abstract patterns *per se,* but also to the final unity of abstract and thematic properties. Such unity has been considered a necessary criterion of all art (unity in the multitude). The successful apprehension of that unity is considered to result in a peculiar pleasure which is the æsthetic enjoyment (Alexander, Helge Lundholm). Hedonistic æsthetics holds æsthetic pleasure to be simply the pleasure associated with perceptual impressions in the fields of vision and audition (Marshall, Grant Allen).

(b) Many suggestions have been offered as to the nature of the æsthetic attitude. In modern times it has been fairly generally claimed that art lacks utility and purpose. Such characterization of art implies that our attitude in æsthetic contemplation is fundamentally different from the practical attitudes of life, in which we view things essentially as goals, as obstacles to goal-attainment, and as auxiliaries in the overcoming of obstacles. Specific qualifications of the æsthetic attitude have been attempted as follows: (1) Essential in the æsthetic attitude is the fact that we animate the art-object, *i.e.,* that we project into it something of our own nature (*see* Empathy). (2) In the æsthetic attitude is implicit the illusionary character of the art-object (Lange). Of similar significance is the criterion of æsthetic or psychic distance (*q.v.*) and the suggestion that the æsthetic attitude is relatively devoid of "reality concern," being an attitude in which you neither affirm, nor deny, nor doubt, the reality of the art-object (Stout, Lundholm). Thus Münsterberg thinks that the æsthetic attitude is one of "detachment of the subject" and "isolation of the object"; Puffer declares that it is one of "complete repose in the object of beauty." (3) Demanding, on the contrary, full alertness of being are such theories as that of I. A. Richards—which pictures a concordant and balanced organization of impulses (*see* Synæsthesis)—and of John Dewey, who posits a "dynamic organization" and declares (*Art as Experience,* 1934) that "in a distinctively æsthetic experience, characteristics that are subdued in other experiences are dominant; those that are subordinate are controlling—namely, the characteristics in virtue of which the experience is an integrated complete experience on its own account." Helge Lundholm.

This theory, that the æsthetic attitude is perception conceived as an end, enables one immediately to distinguish it from the attitudes commonly recognized as distinct from it, *e.g.,* the practical and the scientific attitudes. Both use perception as a means, not as an end.

The æsthetic attitude may occur at various levels, from a bare sensation, such as a sour taste or a sudden flash of pink which holds perception by its intrinsic quality, to the experience of amazingly complex and powerful works of art. But in all cases the æsthetic attitude has two aspects—attention and interest.

The attention aspect is constituted by the powers operating in perception to discriminate the object, *e.g.* in more complex cases, sensation, intuition, imagination, feeling, intellect. Suppose one is witnessing a drama. One has myriad sensations of lights, colors, sounds, objects. One responds to the drama imaginatively, entering empathically into the actions portrayed, imagining the people and things before one as many things which "really" they are not, *e.g.* that they are John Doe and Molly Pitcher violently in love. Furthermore, one perceives the spectacle as embodying all sorts of feeling-qualities: it is gay, tiresome, erotic, bombastic, delicate, coarse. Finally, one constantly interprets the sensory, intuitive, imaginative, affective factors of the drama, and builds up, critically or uncritically, a complex conception of the whole.

The interest aspect of the æsthetic attitude underlies and operates through these attentive powers. Thus, one senses, one intuits, one imagines, one feels, one interprets, insofar as the object is or promises to be something of interest. The interests here may be of the most diverse sorts. They may be interests in lighting and technical stage craft, in love and droll characters and other human content, in dramatic form or deeply evoked feeling, in anything from the barest sensations to the most subtle overtones of commentary on human life and fate. But if the attitude of the receptor is æsthetic, there will be a further interest present. This is the interest in perceiving the object for what it has to offer, *i.e.,* for its intrinsic values to perception whatever these may be. Only insofar as this interest is present, is the attitude of the receptor æsthetic.

The same theory has been presented in a different form by Eliseo Vivas ("A Definition of the Æsthetic Experience," *JP* 34), who defines the æsthetic attitude as one of "intransitive attention." *Cf.* Beauty. D. W. Gotshalk.

art impulse. The second problem of psychological æsthetics, *viz.,* the art-impulse, has turned attention upon: (1) the study of child drawings, (2) the anthropological study of primitive art, and (3) the testimony of great artists.

The most important theories of the nature of the art-impulse are the following: (1) The art-impulse is a derivative of the play-impulse (Schiller, Spencer). (2) It derives from a desire to attract attention by pleasing others (Marshall), (3) It derives from a desire of self-display (Baldwin), (4) It appears when the impulse prompting play is at the same time prompted by a desire for self-display, *i.e.,* a desire for an audience (Langfeld). (5) It is a sublimation of the constructive impulse; the same impulse, as, on the animal level, prompts the building of a nest, on the level of man prompts the construction of various extrinsic auxiliaries. On the level of artistic creation it prompts the construction of extrinsic permanent things which are beyond adaptive necessity (Alexander). (6) It is a substitutive outlet for the energies of the Œdipus-complex, *i.e.,* a sublimated outlet of frustrated sexuality (Freud). (7) It might be a sublimation of any one crude impulse (McDougall, Lundholm). (8) Many forms of so-called primitive art were not originally created for the purpose of ornamentation or beautification but, rather, for utilitarian reasons, *e.g.,* sexual attraction, facilitation of cooperative labor, the frightening of enemies and the effecting of magic. However, it has been held that at some indeterminate stage in cultural evolution men began to create objects for the sheer purpose of contemplation, *i.e.,* independently of any auxiliary aim (Hirn).

The concept of art as a means of information or of stirring religious or other sentiments, though studied by many, does not belong to æsthetics proper; in fact, such considerations allege to art properties quite extraneous to its beauty. Helge Lundholm.

æsthetics, experimental. The investigation of æsthetics by experimental methods embraces any type of observation in which the conditions are prearranged by the experimenter with the aim of controlling the factors upon which the occurrence of the observed æsthetic effect depends.

G. T. Fechner (1801–87) observed the affective preferences of various persons for certain simple and abstracted elements of æsthetic perception (*e.g.,* rectangles; the sounds of spoken vowels). His more significant contributions were to methodology: the particular psychophysical procedures by which materials may be arranged and presented by the experimenter for preferential discrimination by each experimental subject. His methods of choice (*Wahl*), of construction (*Herstellung*), and measurement of æsthetic proportions in existing objects (*Verwendung*), coupled with simple statistical treatment of the data, are still basic.

Observational methods have shown an evolution from those applicable only to the strictly laboratory situation to those which can be utilized in ordinary life situations or approximations of them. Electrical, mechanical, and photographic recording and reproducing apparatus now increases the accuracy and range of observations, and also provides means of repeated presentation of complex stimuli. Statistical methods of treating observed data have advanced, too, from the simple averaging and ranking of several decades ago, to the use of modern methods of psychophysical scaling, small sample technique, correlation, and factor analysis, which have proved capable of more direct application to the intrinsically complex data of æsthetics, with the added advantage of providing estimates of observational or predictive error. Finally, with the aid of the improved tests of fundamental abilities and processes in the creation and appreciation of art, it has become possible to apply the results of experimental æsthetics to the discovery and more effective education of individuals with artistic aptitudes. John Todd Cowles.

B. Croce, *Æsthetic,* trans. 1929; B. Bosanquet, *Hist. of Æsthetic,* 1892; E. F. Carritt, *Phil. of Beauty,* 1931; F. P. Chambers, *The Hist. of Taste,* 1932; E. Vivas and M. Krieger, *The Problems of Æsthetics,* 1953; M. C. Beardsley, *Æsthetics* (Problems) 1958; *Æsthetics* (History) 1966; M. Levich, *Æsthetics and the Phil. of Criticism,* 1963. *See* Beauty.

affectation. The assumption of a method or style that does not fit the person, subject, or occasion. In the 18th c. applied mainly to diction and order; since, also to tone and spirit. Spec., the assumption of elegance. Marked in periods of exuberance (as the Renaissance) or of decadence (as the late 19th c.). Satirized in *Patience,* by W. S. Gilbert.

affective fallacy. The error (according to W. K. Wimsatt, Jr., and Monroe C. Beardsley) of criticizing a work in terms of its results, esp. its emotional effect. This is the converse of the "fallacy" of judging it in the light of the author's intention (*q.v.*). Aristotle's "catharsis" and Longinus' "transport" are examples of the affective approach.

afflatus (L., blown upon). (1) Miraculous communication of supernatural knowledge or power. (2) Inspiration, *q.v.* Frequently "divine afflatus."

agon (Gr. contest, conflict). A portion of a Greek play, esp. of a comedy, devoted conventionally to debate or verbal combat between two actors, each supported by half the chorus, *e.g.,* quarrel between Just Discourse (typifying the average Athenian citizen) and Unjust Discourse (representing subversive ideas) in Aristophanes' *Clouds. Cf.* Protagonist.

agrarian movement. Early 20th c. praise of "back to the soil" in Germany and esp. in the U.S. South; mainly conservative. Sherwood Anderson went to edit a paper in a small town; the Fugitive group hailed virtues of the countryside in the symposium *I'll Take My Stand* (1930) against "the new barbarism of science and technology controlled and directed by the modern power state." In literature, this group spearheaded the "new criticism." *Cf.* Criticism, the new; Regionalism. J. M. Bradbury, *The Fugitives,* 1958.

aischrologia. *See* cacophony.

akhyana (Ind. tale form). Beast-fable or folk tale in prose, with climax or essential part of dialogue in verse. The verse (in the *jātaka,* story of the past) is the canonical part, the utterance of the Bodhisatta (the future Buddha). The *jātaka* is always preceded by a story of the present (an incident in the life of the historical Buddha) that prompts him to tell the story of the past; then comes the identification of the characters in previous births with those of the present story.

alazon (Gr., braggart). The impostor of Old Comedy. Aristotle states that if the mean under consideration is truthfulness he who exaggerates that mean is an *alazon,* he who depreciates it is an *eiron.* The boaster pretends to possess traits generally admired, or to have been a participant in marvellous adventures. The *Tractatus Coislinianus* enumerates as the three comedy character types: the buffoon, the ironical, and the impostor (the "scientists" in Aristophanes' *Birds*; Tartuffe; the delightful menage of *The School for Scandal*; the *Miles gloriosus* of Plautus).

alba (Prov.), *aubade* (Fr.), *Tagelied* (G.). A song of the parting of lovers at the break of dawn, a theme which, in the albas of the troubadors, grew to a distinct literary genre. The medieval albas were inspired in large part by Ovid. R. Schevill, *Ovid and the Renaissance in Sp.,* 1913. Occasionally religious, to the Virgin. The French aubade, instead of a lament, might be a joyous welcome to the dawn. Such an English song is "Pack clouds away and welcome day" in Heywood's *The Rape of Lucrece.*

alcaic. A strophe first found in the work of Alcaeus (of Lesbos, early 6th c. B.C.), frequently used by Horace, of the pattern

∪ — ∪ — — — ∪ ∪ — ∪ ⏓
∪ — ∪ — — — ∪ ∪ — ∪ ⏓
— — ∪ — — — ∪ — —
— ∪ ∪ — ∪ ∪ — ∪ — —

The first two lines (hendecasyllabic) are greater alcaics; the last line (decasyllabic) is a lesser alcaic. Occasionally attempted in English, notably by Tennyson, whose "Milton" begins "O mighty-mouthed inventor of harmonies."

alcmanic verse. A dactylic tetrameter line, used by Alcman, 7th c. B.C. Used in Greek, and occasionally Latin dramatic poetry. The alcmanic strophe is an archilochian verse combined with a dactylic hexameter. W.J.W. Koster, *Traité de métrique grecque,* 1936. *Cf.* Classical Versification.

Alexandrianism. The ornate style (or an instance thereof) of the Greek poets of the Alexandrian period, 323–120 B.C. The medieval chroniclers labeled everything from the east Alexandrian, as Alexandria was the gateway to the Orient.

alexandrine. Fr. heroic verse of 12 syllables, named from the OFr. developments of the Alexander cycle, 12th and 13th c. Ronsard and the Pléiade brought it back into use in the 16th c.; in the 17th it became, and has remained, the preferred Fr. form (like the L. hexameter and the Eng. pentameter) for serious and elevated poetry. The alexandrine has normally 4 rhythmic beats; except for (since the Romantics) 3-beat *alexandrin ternaire* (Victor Hugo). The caesura regularly comes after the 6th syllable, but may be varied. The Eng. "alexandrine" with its 6 iambic feet is really longer than the Fr. 4-beat *alexandrin.* Hence the error (Edna St. V. Millay with Baudelaire) of translating *alexandrins* into hexameters; hence Pope's characterization of the most familiar instance in Eng., the last line of the Spenserian stanza: "a needless alexandrine . . . That, like a wounded snake, drags its slow length along." Bridges' *Testament of Beauty* is in what he calls "my loose alexandrines." *Cf.* Romance Versification, Spenserian stanza. H. P. Thieme, *The Technique of the Fr. Alexandrine,* 1899.

alienation. (1) The deliberate withdrawal of the artist from society and its concerns. Often assumption of superiority or scorn, as with the Fr. poet Baudelaire, or of indifference, as with poets that retire to an "ivory tower." Condemned by those in this century (*e.g.,* Sartre) who insist that the writer must be committed, *engagé,* involved in the affairs of the world. (2) The removal of the receptor from the emotions of a work, so that he can be taught by it, convinced by its meaning and message. A practice of some Soviet writers and esp. the German playwright Brecht, who (as earlier, Plato) wished the citizen not to be swayed by sentiment. Similarly in France Charles Dullin hated "*l'horrible naturel*"; and Roger Planchon has followed Brecht's technique in productions of Marlowe's *Edward II,* Shakespeare's *Henry IV,* and a free adaptation of *The Three Musketeers.* Joan Littlewood in England also reacted against the spell cast upon the audience by "the witchcraft of realistic producers" and used many devices to jerk the audience to awareness of the fraud and fiction of the theatre. Devices—directly addressing the audience; interrupting the stage action with song, pageant, posters, motion pictures; deliberately unreal characters, grotesque costumes, masks, and more—remind the receptor that he is not watching real life, should not become involved in the characters' emotions, but should observe intellectually and draw the appropriate conclusions and programs for action. A play of this sort is often called anti-drama. The term estrangement (used by the surrealists in a different sense) is sometimes applied to this second form of alienation. Note that this alienation from the work of art is usually for the sake of involvement in life. With Brecht and others, esp. Communists, this desired commitment means advocacy of a specific program of action; more balanced proponents of commitment (*e.g.,* Northrop Frye) mean by it an imaginative readiness to participate, a reasoned activity, rather than blanket enlistment in a cause. *Cf.* Anti-hero; Psychic distance; Estrangement; Epic theatre; Surrealism. S. W. Finkelstein, *Existentialism and Alienation in Am. Literature,* 1965, 1967; E. N. Lee and M. Mandelbaum, *Phenomenology and Existentialism,* 1967; Ernest Becker, *Beyond Alienation,* 1967.

allegory. A trope in which a second meaning is to be read beneath and concurrent with the surface story. Distinguished from metaphor and parable as an extended story that may hold interest for the surface tale (*The Faerie Queene; Pilgrim's Progress; Idylls of the King*) as well as for the (usually ethical) meaning borne along. A mixed allegory is one that explains the buried thought. E. Honig, *Dark Conceit,* 1959; C. S. Lewis, *The Allegory of Love,* 1936, 1953; L. Broussard, *Am. Drama,* 1962; A. Fletcher, *Allegory,* 1964; A. D. Nuttall, *Two Concepts of Allegory,* 1967; A. Cook, *Prisms,* 1967.

alliteration. The recurrence of an initial sound. Frequent in most early poetry, save the Greek; basis of early Germanic versification, *q.v.* Frequent in Latin (Ennius, Lucretius); a popular device in modern poetry. Occasionally accidental and cacophonous (*e.g.* Voltaire, "*Non, il n'est rien que Nanine n'honore*"), though such harsh juxtaposition may be sought for special effects (Browning). Apt alliteration's artful aid is also an occasional ornament in prose, or for emphasis, as in reduplicate words (flimflam, tittle-tattle), epithets (fickle fortune, likely lass, primrose path), phrases (bed and board, prunes and prisms) and saws and slogans (Look before you leap). Alliteration may be simple (who *l*oves to *l*ie with me) or cross ("the *w*ay*w*ardness of man's *d*esires and the *d*ivagations of his *w*ill": note the a-b-b-a order not only of the initial letters but of the numbers, singular and plural), or complex (The *f*urrow *f*ollows *f*ree: Coleridge; O his *n*imble fi*n*ger, his *gn*arled *gr*ip: Hopkins). Swinburne's "Dolores" presents intricate and subtle intertwinings. Sometimes the device is sought for itself: in one medieval Christian poem of 1,000 lines, every word begins with *c*. There are a number of jingles of alphabetical alliteration; most familiar is that beginning

> An Austrian army, awfully arrayed,
> Boldly by battle besieged Belgrade.

Cf. Assonance; Consonance; Repetition; *see* Tone.

allusion. Originally, a parable. Now, an indication of something without direct mention of it. Direct mention is reference. A common type of allusion in poetry is quotation of a word or so from another work without identifying or acknowledging it; Eliot identifies some such in his Notes to *The Waste Land*. O. C. Johnson, *Literary Allusions in Contemporary Am. Literature*, 1928; E. C. Brewer, *Dictionary of Phrase and Fable*, 1963; W. B. Fulgham, *A Dictionary of Biblical Allusions in Eng. Literature*, 1965.

alphabet. The set of letters used in a language. In the beginning was the word; the letter is a corruption of a pictogram or other word form. In many tongues, each letter is a name (*e.g.*, Runic *h*, hail, *i*, ice). Alphabet poems (*see* Abecedarius) were written in many tongues (Norse, Hebrew). Kallias in ancient Athens wrote an alphabet drama, a grammatical play: the comic chorus of 24 represented the 24 letters of the Ionic alphabet; in the songs, each consonant is mated with every vowel. Southey wrote a lament for the passing of the alphabet hornbook through which children learnt to read. O. Ogg, *The 26 Letters*, 1948; D. Diringer, *The Alphabet*, 1948.

als ob (G. as if, theory of). Notion advanced by Hans Vaihinger, 1876, as basic in mankind's idealistic activity, that one must act on the assumption that the things essential to a desired attitude or point of view are as they seem. This is akin to the "willing suspension of disbelief," which Coleridge thinks must be granted by the receptor of a work of art, but which that work must induce in the receptor. Thus tragedy usually assumes freedom of the will. *Cf.* Determinism; Tragedy.

altercatio. L. Originally that part of a Roman legal or forensic argumentation devoted to cross-questioning, with rapid give and take of question and answer, *e.g.*, in Cicero's letter to Atticus 1, 16, 9. By the 3d c. it was a type of popular literature in the form of a dialogue of brief questions and answers. Frequent in medieval church literature in this form, it may have been the model for the catechisms. *Cf.* Débat. L. W. Daly, *Altercatio . . . and the Question-and-Answer Dialogue*, 1939.

ambiguity. A passage of, or the fact of, doubtful meaning; the possibility of more than one interpretation. Ambiguity may of course be most dangerous in legal documents, laws. It may rise from dual possibilities of word-division, of accent, of grammatical form (amphiboly), of punctuation; or from the existence of homonyms. Hermogenes cites the Greek *hetaira khrysia ei phoroie, demosia esto*: accent *demosia* on the antepenult; this means "If a courtesan wears gold ornaments, they are to become public property"; accent *demosia* on the penult, "she is to become public property." Amphiboly (*q.v.*) is an occasional device in literature, for irony or humor, as in the letter in N. Udall's *Ralph Roister Doister* (ca. 1533), which is first read:

> Sweet mistress whereas I love you nothing at all,
> Regarding your substance and richese chiefe of all,
> For your personage, beauty . . .

but when the dismissed lover, bewildered at its effect, comes to complain to the scrivener, he hears it, instead:

> Sweet mistress, whereas I love you, nothing at all
> Regarding your substance and richess: chiefe of all
> For your personage, beauty . . .

Other forms of ambiguity may obviously turn upon a pun. Ambiguity may be a fault; it is also considered (I. A. Richards, *The Philosophy of Rhetoric*, 1936) an inevitable and basic aspect of language. In *Seven Types of Ambiguity* (1930, 1953), William Empson broadens the concept to include "any consequence of language which adds some nuance to the direct statement of prose." His first type, "a word or syntax effective in several ways at once," is the archetypal ambiguity, of which the succeeding six are reflections from different angles.

Other times had different values. Fielding, in *A Journey from This World to the Next* (ch. 8, 1743) has Shakespeare say: "Certainly the greatest and most pregnant beauties are ever the plainest and most evidently striking; and when two meanings of a passage can in the least balance our judgment which to prefer, I hold it matter of unquestionable certainty that neither of them is worth a farthing." Our more complicated period wraps ambiguity in other phrases. Philip Wheelwright (*The Burning Fountain,* 1954) speaks of *plurisignation,* when the proper meaning of a symbol "is a tension between two or more directions of semantic stress"; and speaks of *paralogical dimensionality* when a passage conveys meanings "beyond those of logical universality and existential particularity." Ernst Kris (*Psychoanalytic Explorations in Art,* 1952), on the other hand, stresses *stringency,* preciseness of reference, and declares that "Art is likely to be characterized by low stringency (*i.e.,* high ambiguity) where systems of conduct or ideals are in doubt"—which looks beyond the merely ambiguous to the absurd, *q.v.* While Empson's seven types are not all clearly distinguished, the concept of ambiguity permits a fresh examination of a literary work.

Ambiguity in a word must be distinguished from two other types of connotation. Thus, with *table*: (ambiguity) piece of furniture, multiplication, of contents, postpone a motion; (implication) flat surface, sitting around; (association) dinner, thirteen (Empson limits "associations" to private, individual linkages.) *Cf.* Connotation; Clearness; Obscurity; Association of Ideas; Spontaneity; Meaning; Pivot word. W. Empson, *The Structure of Complex Words,* 1951; James J. Y. Liu, *The Art of Chinese Poetry,* 1962, 1966. JOHN L. SWEENEY.

amblysia (Gr., blunting). Speech so phrased as to make gentle preparation for a coming dire announcement—though its effect often is to stir alarm. Used by a bearer of ill tidings to soften the blow (which in olden times was repaid upon his own back). Common in early drama, when violent deeds were kept offstage, and reported by messenger. *Cf.* Euphemism.

amphiboly. (1) Ambiguity resulting from unclear construction, when the words themselves are clear; *e.g.,* "I sat by my lady soundly sleeping"—who was asleep? (2) An expression with an obvious and accepted meaning, but with a less apparent and real significance; *e.g.,* (*Macbeth*) the prophecies regarding "man born of woman" and "Birnam wood come to Dunsinane." Often put in the mouths of oracles. *See* Ambiguity; *cf.* Dilogy.

amphibrach. A metrical foot of three syllables, one long between two short (◡ — ◡); *e.g.,* according. Doubtful, however, whether such a unit was recognized by classical poets.

amphigory. Verse that sounds right but lacks sense, such as nonsense verse of the Edward Lear type, which lures with the promise of meaning. Swinburne's self-parody, *Nephelidia,* is a notable instance.

amphimacer. A metrical foot of three syllables, one short between two long (— ◡ —); *e.g.,* attitude. Also called cretic.

amplification. A figure of speech in which language is used to enlarge, magnify, or emphasize a statement, thought, idea, or expression by (1) choice of word: they "murdered" him for they "beat" him; (2) successive contrast: "not a thief but a plunderer, not an adulterer but a ravisher"; (3) the incremental building up of emphasis. This is equivalent to the modern climax, but not to the classical, for which *see* Gradation; (4) comparison with something less (or more) striking, to make it seem greater (or less) by contrast; (5) enlarging an incidental matter. Cicero about to reproach Antony with drunkenness: "You with such a throat, such flanks, such burly strength in every limb of your prize-fighter's frame," to prepare the hearers to judge the colossal quantities of wine imbibed; (6) accumulation (congeries), repetition by synonyms. Amplification was overdeveloped (esp. in Biblical paraphrase) by Johnson, Blackmore, Prior, then scorned; in the 18th c. Pope called it "the spinning-wheel of the bathos." It is used to excellent effect by Rabelais (also in Eng. translation by Urquhart) and Joyce.

anachorism. Setting an event, scene, person, or word in a place where it does not belong, as on the seacoast of Bohemia.

anachronism. Setting an event, scene, person, or word in the wrong time period; usually a slip, as with the clock in Shakespeare's *Julius Caesar,* or cannon in *King John.* Sometimes a literary device, as in Mark Twain's *A Connecticut Yankee in King Arthur's Court,* and much science fiction.

anaclasis. A metrical readjustment (for fluidity or variety) wherein a final long syllable of a foot changes place with the initial short syllable of the following foot. *Cf.* Ionic.

anacoluthon. Change of grammatical construction within a sentence or passage. Though often an error, it may be deliberate, as a device for emphasis and rhetorical effects, esp. in dialogue: "If you fail to do your duty—we'll not speak of that." Thus Milton:

Both turned, and under the open sky adored
The God that made both sky, earth, air, and
heaven,
A starry pole. Thou also madest the night. . .

Anacreontic poetry (Gr. lyric poet Anacreon, late 6th c. B.C.) Graceful lyric usually in praise of love or wine, characterized by an erotic, sensual spirit. For Anacreontic meter, *see* Ionic.

anacrusis. An extra unaccented syllable at the beginning of a line of verse, preceding the first syllable of the regular rhythm; used (Hermann, *Elementa Doctrinae Metricae,* 1816) to reduce all classical verse to a descending rhythm, *i.e.,* with stress on the initial syllable; now virtually disregarded. The term may still be applied to a method of variety in modern verse, as in the second line here:

Clearer loves sound other ways,
I miss my little human praise.

anadiplosis. *See* Repetition.

anagram. A word formed by transposition of the letters of another word. Often used as a game (love to ruin > revolution; elegant > neat leg; penitentiary > nay I repent it). Writers have thus chosen pen names (Voltaire), characters' names (Dickens), or titles (Butler, *Erewhon*). As usual with word-play, some ages have seen in it a mystical significance. Pilate's question, *Quid est veritas?* (What is truth?, *John* xviii, 38) is an anagram of *Est vir qui adest* (The man that's here: Christ). The error of transposed letters is metagrammatism; *cf.* Spoonerism. *See* Palindrome. H. B. Wheatley, *Of Anagrams,* 1862.

analects. Literary gleanings or collections of extracts; usually now as a title, *e.g., Analects of Confucius.*

analogy. (1) A stated likeness. Frequent as an explained simile, *e.g.* (Bacon): Money is like muck, not good unless it is spread. (2) Inference that things alike in some (supposed basic) respects are alike in others. A frequent device in argument. Ribot (*Essai sur l'imagination créatrice,* 6th ed., 1921) states that "the psychological mechanism of the moment of creation" is thought working through analogy. *Cf.* Argument.

analysis. The discrimination and detailed consideration of the separate parts or elements of a work and the relationship between them. *Cf.* Synthesis; Coherence; Unity.

analytical criticism. The process of distinguishing and making explicit elements of meaning and structure in a work, the several meanings that are synthesized by a particular symbol or metaphorical statement, or the various ways in which a particular group of words may be syntactically construed. This sort of verbal analysis, or "close reading," is constantly under attack from those who claim that it "falsifies" literature, that it interferes with the unified intuitive understanding of poetry. Its defenders reply that it provides the necessary conditions of full understanding, and hence of full enjoyment, and that it has thrown considerable light on the way poetry works. *Cf.* Explication; Ambiguity. W. Empson, *Seven Types of Ambiguity,* 1947; I. A. Richards, *How to Read a Page,* 1942.

anamnesis. The recalling of ideas, events, or persons. It may color an entire work (reminiscences; Proust, *A la recherche du temps perdu*) or be employed for special effects, as of contrast, as with the juxtapositions in Eliot's *The Waste Land.*

ananym. A word or name written backward, as Los, the creative spirit in Blake's mystical poems (Sol, the sun). *See* Anagram.

anapest. A metrical foot, two short syllables followed by one long (◡ ◡ —), as in Byron's "The Assyrian came down like a wolf on the fold."

anaphonema. A cry of grief. *Cf.* Ecphonema.

anaphora. Repetition of a word at the beginning of lines of poetry or clauses or sentences of prose. *Cf.* Repetition.

anastrophe. Withholding expected words, esp. verb or preposition, for suspense or stress.

anatomy. Logical analysis of a subject, with examination of its several parts. Used as a title: Lyly, *Euphues or the Anatomy of Wit,* 1579; Burton, *Anatomy of Melancholy,* 1621; Northrop Frye, *An Anatomy of Criticism,* 1957; Rosamond Harding, *An Anatomy of Inspiration,* 1940, 1967. *Cf.* Satire.

Ancients and Moderns, quarrel of the (1687–1716; but hardly to be separated from cross-currents in the revival of learning, and from over a century of consequences). The Italians and French came in the 16th c. to a rather general belief, fostered by religion and patriotism, in the worth of native letters. Boileau, Racine, La Fontaine, Bossuet, La Bruyère, Fénelon, held that judicious imitation of the Ancients is imitation of Nature and therefore proper; even the subjects should be drawn or imitated from the Ancients though made fresh in meaning and invention; the rules of Aristotle must be followed because genius needs discipline and the old rules are still the best; the Moderns have often equalled the Ancients and should always strive to outdo them.

Saint-Evremond in exile brought the quarrel to England, whence in 1690 Sir William Temple raked the French Moderns with inaccurate fire. He wrote ignorantly of modern science and literature, resting much of his defense on Aesop and the *Epistles of Phalaris,* which he assumed to be genuine. This blunder shifted attention to minor issues, and forced Wotton and Bentley, accurate scholars and liberal partisans of antiquity, to discredit its defender. Swift's *Battle of the Books* stumbled over Phalaris but combined praise of the Ancients with intelligent views on imitation and the nature of poetry. Written in 1697, when Dryden was defending the *Aeneid* against Desmarets and Perrault, the *Battle* was published in 1704 after the triumph of Bentley, and ends the English quarrel—though it continued in France, esp. between Mme Dacier, who wrote a faithful prose *Iliad,* and Houdard de la Motte, who without knowing Greek "improved" Homer with a versified version of her prose. Fénelon, a convinced but liberal Ancient, tried to please both sides, and with the reconciliation of Mme. Dacier and La Motte, the quarrel ended.

The Moderns cared mainly for ideas, especially Descartes' exaltation of reason, and the theory of progress. As literary critics, the Ancients had learning and judgment on their side. They narrowed the scope of art by deference to authority, and made too much ado about reason and good sense in poetry; but they generally knew good work from bad. The Moderns confused mediocrity with genius, salon elegance with beauty; they looked upon poetry as a kind of lesser science; but their official and popular triumph put an end to uncreative imitation and their faith in progress begot the Enlightenment. Both sides respected rules; but the Romantics (in Fr. the preface to Hugo's *Cromwell,* 1827) swept all rules away and left imagination free. This is a logical result of the Quarrel, but the Moderns themselves were not fighting for imagination (which was stronger in the Ancients) nor for freedom from rules; rather, for reason unclouded by tradition, and for the glory of a new age. *Cf.* French Criticism, in Part Two. H. Rigault, *Hist. de la querelle des anciens et des modernes,* 1859; H. Gillot, *La Querelle des Anciens et des Modernes,* 1914; J. B. Bury, *The Idea of Progress,* 1920. LUCIEN DEAN PEARSON.

anecdote (Gr., unpublished). (1) Portion of ancient writer published for the first time. (2) Individual incident (at first, item of gossip) told as inherently interesting or striking. Ancient equivalents of the second meaning are diatribe, *exemplum,* apophthegm, *testimonium.* Anecdotal fiction is that which proceeds through a succession of episodes (What next?) instead of by the development of an organic plot (How? Why?). Elizabeth H. Haight, *The Roman Use of Anecdotes,* 1940.

angry young man. One of a group of British writers whose works, beginning with Kingsley Amis' novel *Lucky Jim* (1954), picture disillusion and rebellion against conventions and middle-class society. John Osborne and John Wain are others prominent in the presentation of working-class background and protest. Osborne, whose play *Look Back in Anger* (1956) contains tirades against "the Establishment," defines his aims in *They Call It Cricket* (1957). *Cf.* Absurd; Black Comedy; Anti-hero. J. R. Taylor, *Anger and After,* 1962, 1964; John R. Brown, ed., *Modern British Dramatists,* 1968.

annal. *See* Chronicle.

anomoiosis. Contrast, *q.v.*

antanaclasis. *See* Repetition.

anthem. (1) a hymn of patriotism or praise (2) A song with words from the Scriptures (3) A hymn for alternate sets of voices. *See* Hymn.

anthology (Gr. cluster of flowers; L. *florilegium*). A collection of short poems, esp. epigrams; occasionally of prose. Now used of any collection of literary passages. The *Greek Anthology*—of ca. 4100 epigrams and over 2000 other pieces, mostly in elegiac verse: amatory, dedicatory, sepulchral, epideictic, hortatory, convivial, humorous—is a compilation of the collections of Meleager, first c. B.C.; Philippus, first c. A.D.; Agathias, 6th c., combined with a Cephalas ms. (the *Palatine Anthology*) found in 1606; it comprises works by more than 300 writers from the 5th c. B.C. to the 6th c. A.D.

anthropopathia. Speaking of deity, or of animals or lifeless things, as though endowed with human feeling, *e.g.,* "and the Lord was wroth." *See* Personification.

anthypophora. An answer to an argument one has raised oneself in order to refute it. Often one erects a "straw man," easily overthrown, to suggest the weakness of the opposing point of view. *Cf.* Erotesis; Procatalepsis.

antibacchius. A metrical foot of three syllables, two long followed by a short (— — ◡), *e.g.,* "Climb down the high mountain." Sometimes called palimbacchius or hypobacchius. *Cf.* Bacchius.

anticlimax. (1) A series in descending order of importance. (2) A sudden disappointment of roused expectancy. At times the result of ineptitude, it can be very effective in humor, as with Oliver Goldsmith, "On a Cat, Drowned in a Bowl of Goldfish." *Cf.* Climax; Bathos.

anti-hero. The anti-novel might be regarded as protest against the conventions of novelistic form, while the anti-hero usually represents defiance of novelistic content. The novel stimulated its own antithesis from the very beginning. Cervantes says in his preface to *Don Quixote* (1605) that "the entire work is an attack upon the books of chivalry." Honoré d'Urfé's *Astrée* (1607), usually called the first French novel, features an anti-hero, Hylas, satirizing its romantic hero, Céladon. As early as 1627 works were appearing in France that were explicitly in defiance of novelistic convention. Some, like Charles Sorel's *Extravagant Shepherd,* even bore the subtitle *anti-roman*. Perhaps England's most important anti-novel is Laurence Sterne's *Tristram Shandy* (1759), which had wide influence on both sides of the Channel, especially reflected in Denis Diderot's *Jacques the Fatalist* (1796). Tristram has been called a *hero manqué.*

Although various kinds of anti-hero were developed in the 19th c. (especially the young-man-from-the-provinces, who was eventually accepted as hero), less interest was shown in ironic narrative positions. Dostoevsky's *Notes from the Underground* (1846) and the Brazilian Machado de Assis' *Epitaph of a Small Winner* (1880), exceptions to the prevailing realistic and naturalistic trends, pointed toward the revival of the anti-novel in the 20th c. Attention in recent years has been focussed on the *nouveaux romans* of Alain Robbe-Grillet (*Jealousy*), Nathalie Sarraute (*The Planetarium*), Marguérite Duras (*The Square*), and Claude Mauriac (*The Dinner Party*), in France; Max Frisch (*I'm not Stiller*), Jurgen Becker (*Fields*), and Klaus Henneberg (*Monologue*) in Germany; Junchiro Tanizaki (*The Key*) in Japan; Vladimir Nabokov (*Pale Fire*), and Samuel Beckett (*Malloy; Malone*). The first modern Japanese novel, *Ukigumo* (1886, by Hasegawa Tatsunosuke writing as Futabatei Shimei) has a bumbling, ineffective anti-hero, Bunzō, a minor civil servant who loses both his job and his girl.

Whereas the traditional novel deliberately moves to suspend the reader's disbelief and permit him to enjoy fantasy elaborations with projected pseudo-emotions, the anti-novel attempts to thwart the reader by forcing him to confront his desires for "experience" without personal involvement. Thus, in such blunt anti-novels as *Tristram Shandy* and *Jacques the Fatalist,* exciting or titillating scenes are repeatedly evoked only to be destroyed by the author's direct remarks to the reader. Diderot tells the "Reader" to finish the story of Jacques' loves himself, he knows as much about it as the author, in this way deliberately undermining the assumption of the narrator's infallibility. Some novels (and plays) have been presented with alternative endings, usually one happy, one sad. Flann O'Brien (in *At Swim-Two-Birds,* 1939) declared: "One beginning and one ending for a book was a thing I did not agree with. A good book may have three openings entirely dissimilar and interrelated only in the prescience of the author, or for that matter one hundred times as many endings."

More subtle anti-novels use purposely ambiguous "documents" arranged so as to force the reader, as Nathalie Sarraute puts it, "to participate in his real life and not merely in his vicarious life." In *Dangerous Liaisons* Choderlos de Laclos uses letters in this way; Dostoevsky makes use of an annotated memoir in *Notes from the Underground*; and Nabokov's *Pale Fire* consists of an Introduction, a poem, and "notes" to the poem.

The anti-hero, on the other hand, is often found in novels of conventional form. He also emerged very early in the history of the genre, and usually embodies some deviation from the heroic standards of the day. He may be an oaf, remarkable for his boorishness in an era doting on politesse, as in Furetière's

Bourgeois Novel, or morally degenerate like Richardson's Lovelace in *Clarissa,* or uneducated and lower-class, like Jérosme Dubois in Vadé's *Letters of the Grenouillère.* In the 18th c. Benjamin Constant introduced a new kind of anti-hero in *Adolphe,* who seduced the woman of his dreams only to collapse from boredom in her company. In the life of Gustave Flaubert's anti-heroine, Emma Bovary, novelistic sentiments are systematically mocked. As more leeway was permitted proper heroes, authors have had to go farther afield in search of striking anti-heroes. From Joyce's dubious Leopold Bloom we have risen, or fallen, to Camus' affect-free stranger, Genêt's homosexual pickpockets, Céline's psychopaths and Hesse's hallucination-ridden Harry Haller; in this hemisphere, Martin in Clarice Pispector's Brazilian *The Apple in the Dark,* Sebastien in J. P. Donleavy's *The Ginger Man,* and Saul Bellow's *Herzog.* Even in popular espionage fiction, we are now given bumbling, ineffectual "heroes," surprised at their own success.

The term anti-roman has also been applied to various experimental works, which play tricks with the language, or abandon plot for almost unattached episodes or successive psychological states or mental moods, or seek to capture the aimless and depressing drift their authors see in life. More generally and historically, whatever their form, we may call anti-novels those in which the author attempts to make the reader not merely spectator but participant. The anti-novel continues to be dependent upon a large novel-reading public for the conventions it sets out to destroy, its nature that of the necessarily exceptional tour de force; whereas the anti-hero, the less-than-ordinary man, is becoming more and more the rule as fictional protagonist. *Cf.* Novel; Narrator; Hero; Spontaneity; Fabulation; Absurd; Existentialism; Surrealism. N. Sarraute, *L'Ere du soupçon,* 1965; Wayne Booth, *The Rhetoric of Fiction,* 1961; P. West, *The Modern Novel,* 1963; L. C. Pronko, *Avante-Garde,* 1962; F. J. Hoffman, *Samuel Beckett,* 1962; A. Robbe-Grillet, *For a New Novel,* 1965; A. Burgess, *The Novel Now,* 1967; R. Rabinovitz, *The Reaction Against Experiment in the Eng. Novel,* 1967; R. Scholes, *The Fabulators,* 1967; J. Ricardou, *Problèmes du nouveau roman,* 1967. CAROL BLUM.

antilogy. A contradiction in terms; an illogicality.

antimasque. A grotesque or farcical interlude between the acts of a masque. Often it is a burlesque of the masque itself, with revelers dressed as satyrs, fauns, and nymphs, or more mockingly as beggars and cripples. Because of its nature, sometimes called antic-masque. *Cf.* Masque.

antinomy. A contradiction between two laws or logical conclusions that seem equally binding and necessary. To those that suggest synaesthesis as an explanation of beauty, art involves the resolution of what elsewhere in life are basic antinomies: intellectual and emotional stimulation; the universal and the particular; the rest of the world, and I. Kant's "antinomy of taste" (*Critique of Judgment,* Sec. 55–7) states that there both can, and cannot, be a reasonable argument about taste.

anti-novel. *See* Anti-hero; *cf.* Novel; Anti-play.

antiphon. (1) A hymn sung in alternate parts. (2) A verse sung before or at the end of a religious service. *See* Hymn.

antiphrasis. The use of a word to mean its opposite. This may be in irony: "See yonder giant!" as a dwarf comes on; the "honorable men" of *Julius Caesar*; or to ward off evil, as superstitious folk speak disparagingly of what they prize. *Cf.* Euphemism; Opposition.

anti-play. A dramatic work—esp. of Eugene Ionesco, who speaks of the anti-theatre: *The Bald Soprano,* 1948; *Victims of Duty,* 1952—which does not follow the usual play pattern with a recognizable plot, consistent characters, and concordant dialogue. Instead, it is often built on the conversation of two persons who neither understand one another nor are comprehensible to the audience. It may, however, attempt to find emotional arousal or symbolical significance through the static dialogue. Anti-plays seek to evoke maximum excitement with minimum information. Sex and scatology are prominent; *e.g.,* Pablo Picasso's *Desire Caught by the Tail* (1941, performed 1967), with such characters as Big Toe and Fat Anxiety, has a stage direction for an actress to come front, face the audience, and "urinate for a good five minutes." Such works are not only anti-drama but anti-audience. *Cf.* Absurd; Modernism; Drama; *Nouvelle vague;* Anti-hero; Happening.

antistoichon. Balanced opposition of ideas, with equal structure: "The good shall flourish, but the evil shall die."

antistrophe. (1) The second of a pair of strophes, often (in Gr. dramatic chorus) a reply to the first, and in the same meter. The classical ode consists of strophe, antistrophe, and epode. (2) Repetition (a) in reverse order; (b) ending successive clauses (not at ends of lines) with the same word. *See* Repetition.

antisyzygy. Union of opposites, *e.g.* (Milton) "darkness visible." *Cf.* Oxymoron.

antithesis. Opposition of ideas emphasized by balance of sharply opposed words. An instance of this is called antitheton. The first clause or sentence is called the thesis; the second, the counterthesis—sometimes, more narrowly, the antithesis. It is esp. effective with repetition: "A juggler is a wit in things; a wit is a juggler in words."

Antithesis is associated with the rise of classicism and conscious art in modern literature. The prose of Caxton yields few clear antitheses; that of Lyly abounds in them, artfully re-enforced by transverse alliteration: "Althoughe hetherto *Euphues* I have shrined thee in my heart for a trustie friende, I will shunne thee heerafter as a trothles foe." In the curt form of Senecan prose antithesis is sharp and deft, though often asymmetrical and hence very natural in tone: "Children sweeten labours, but they make misfortune more bitter" (Bacon, *Essays,* VII). The antithesis extended into two or more parallel words and made precise by abstraction is characteristic of the later 18th c.; *e.g.,* Johnson: "If you are pleased with prognostics of good, you will be terrified likewise with tokens of evil" (*Rasselas,* chap. XIII). Antithesis appears to good advantage in verse, where rhyme adds the complexity of a counter pattern and accents inversion or ellipsis, esp. in the heroic couplet:

Favours to none, to all she smiles extends;
Oft she rejects, but never once offends.
(*Rape of the Lock,* II, 11)

Alliteration often presses the contrast home. Demetrius, differing from most classic rhetoricians, disapproved of antithesis because of its artificiality (§§247,250), and in the 20th c. it has, along with the rest of Graeco-Roman rhetoric, fallen into neglect. Macaulay is the last English writer to employ it with conspicuous success. Yet all thoughtful writing tells what one means and what one does not mean, what is and what should be or might be; positive and negative make for mutual clarity. When antithesis is not concentrated into nicely opposed words or phrases, it is expressed in longer and approximately balanced phrases or sentences, or often it lurks implied in comparisons, exceptions, or concessions. Verbal antithesis is the formal epitome of what in a broader sense is usually called contrast. *See* Oxymoron. W. K. Wimsatt, Jr., *The Verbal Icon,* 1954, 1967. W. K. WIMSATT, JR.

antonomasia. The substitution of an epithet for a proper name, as "the Bard of Avon"; or the use of a proper name as a common noun, as "a modern Nero." A form of synecdoche; *cf.* Epithet; Metonymy.

antonym. A word directly opposite in meaning to another. A common form of periphrasis, *q.v.,* used for emphasis, to affirm something by denying the opposite.

apheresis. Omission of letter or syllable at the beginning of a word, *e.g.,* (tele)phone. When gradual, in the development of a language—(e)squire; (a)down—it is called aphesis. *Cf.* Hyphaeresis.

aphorism. First employed in *Aphorisms* of Hippocrates, the term signified a concise scientific principle, primarily medical, synthesized from experience. The book opens with the famous "Life is short, art is long, opportunity fleeting, experimentation dangerous, reasoning difficult . . ." Later the term was applied to statements of principles in a variety of practical fields, law, politics, agriculture, art. Legal aphorisms, according to Charles-François Oudot (1755–1841), French politician and judge, are not principles but mnemonic devices that facilitate legalistic communication, such as *"le mari est seigneur et maître de la communauté."* Because of these enlargements of application, "aphorism" is now synonymous with "maxim": any principle or statement generally received as true.

apocalyptic literature. Dealing with revelation, esp. of the next world; *e.g., The Book of Revelation* to John; Lord Dunsany, *The Glittering Gate*; William Blake, *Jerusalem*; M. Connelly, *The Green Pastures.*

apocope. Dropping of the last letter or syllable of a word, *e.g.,* taxi(cab). *Cf.* Apheresis.

apodosis. The clause stating the conclusion in a conditional sentence. *Cf.* Protasis.

apo koinos (Gr.). Use of a word or phrase to relate to both what goes before and what comes after. *See* Pivot word; *cf.* Ambiguity.

Apollonian—Dionysian. Terms used by Friedrich Nietzsche in *The Birth of Tragedy out of the Spirit of Music* (1872) to contrast reason and instinct, culture and primitive nature, and other such associated but contrasted ideas. Nietzsche felt that these poles were joined in Greek tragedy, with its reflective (Apollonian) dialogue and the dithyrambic (Dionysian) music of its chorus. The general opposition is much the same as in the wider terms classicism and romanticism (*q.v.*). Matthew Arnold similarly spoke of Hellenism (*q.v.*) and Hebraism; Friedrich Schiller, of *naiv* and *sentimentalisch;* Shipley, of aristocratic and democratic. The terms have led to endless (and fruitless) dispute when regarded as mutually exclusive modes, but may be fruitful if recognized as marking tendencies present, in different degrees of emphasis, in many periods of works. Recent discussions (*e.g., The Science of Art,* R. E. Mueller, 1967) have set the contrast in other terms: stasis and kinesis; zero entropy (the pure order of perfect classicism, exemplified *e.g.* by the dramas of Sophocles) and maximum entropy for the system (the pure randomness to which romanticism leads, as in surrealist writing and shuffled word-cards). *Cf.* Surrealism; Form.

apologue. A narrative of fictitious events about animals or inanimate objects (thus not limited to probability) acting like human beings and reflecting human weaknesses and foibles, intended to present useful truths, as in the works of C. S. Lewis, esp. *Chronicles of Narnai;* Samuel Johnson's *Rasselas;* Aesop. Often used in sermons. *Cf.* Allegory, Fable; Parable; Fiction.

apology. Stems from the *Apology* of Plato and a number of other speeches ascribed to Socrates. It represents a defense with no admission of wrongdoing or regret. The Epicureans, Stoics, Cynics, Academics, and Cicero (*de natura deorum*) discussed the existence and nature of God, influencing Christian Apologetics. In modern literature the apology persists: Sidney, *Apologie for Poetrie,* 1595; Newman, *Apologia pro vita sua,* 1864; G. K. Chesterton, *The Defendant,* 1902.

apophasis. Seeming to deny what is really affirmed. Feigning to pass it by while really stressing it: paralepsis. Touching on it casually: metastasis. Pretending to shield or conceal while really displaying (as Antony with Caesar's will in Shakespeare's play): parasiopesis. *See* Autoclesis; *cf.* Anthypophora.

apostrophe. (1) An invocation; an exclamatory address within a work, to a god, muse, or person (often dead or absent). (2) A diversion: breaking off to make a direct address to a judge, or attack on an adversary. Often a device to divert the attention from the main question. Also frequent in poetry, to heighten interest or for metrical convenience.

apothegm. Originally, an anecdote telling of a famous person's using a maxim as a retort. Now, a terse, pointed maxim; a *bon mot* frequently involving a proverb and usually ascribed to an individual. The most famous collection of ancient apothegms is by Plutarch. Also, apophthegm. *Cf.* Gnome.

apotheosis. Deification; exalting a human to the ranks of the gods, as the Caesars.

aptronym(ic). [Coined by a columnist, F. P. A(dams).] A name that fits the nature or occupation: Mr. Glass, the glazier. In many lands, as the variety of Smiths attests, names were originally thus bestowed. Frequent in literature (1) as a label: direct in the moralities, Bunyan; often slightly disguised: Spenser, *Grantorto* (Great Wrong, the tyrant). Named from an event or characteristic: the Bible, *passim,* many figures being renamed after an important incident; Homer (*Telemachus,* the far-fighter); Shakespeare (of the minor figures) and esp. Restoration drama (of the major): Mouldy, Lydia Languish; Mrs. Malaprop. Plato was so named from his broad shoulders; his real name was Aristocles. (2) As a grotesquerie, Fielding: *Blifil*; Swift. (3) Conveying the character, but with an air of reality, Scott: *Dr. Heavysterne; Dr. Dryasdust; Kennaquhair;* Thackeray: *Newcome; Becky Sharp.* Dickens and Balzac drew most of their names from real life. Dickens: *Weller; Snodgrass; Pecksniff; Cherryble;* but also *Lord Verisopht; Dotheboys Hall.* Even with names in realistic fiction, there is a tendency to select those that seem to accord with the natures. *Cf.* Anagram; Etymology.

Arabic poetry. Arabic metric is quantitative. The word-accent probably contributed to the rhythm of the verse. Practically all verses consist of two half-verses (*miṣrâ'*). The last word of the second miṣrâ' contains the rhyme (minimum rhyme: [vowel +] consonant [+ vowel]) which is considered indispensable in any poetical composition and which is retained unchanged throughout the poem. The earliest poetry shows a considerable variety of meters, two of which (*mutaqârib* and *ramal*) may have developed under Sassanian influence (*see* Persian prosody.) Halîl b. Ahmad (d. ca. 788) is credited with the invention of the science of prosody (*'arûḍ*) and its terminology. He seems to have introduced the method of representing the different meters with forms derived from the root *f'l*. Thus the basic formula of *ṭawîl*, the most frequent meter of the earlier period, reads (for one *miṣrâ'*): *fa'ûlun mâfâ'ilun fa'ûlun mafâ'ilun;* that of *hazaj*, popular in post-classical days: *malfâ'îlun mafâ'îlun.*

The characteristic use of *bait* (tent, house) for 'verse' occurs in Syriac as early as the 6th c. Halîl specifies 16 meters, most of them occurring in classical poetry. The etymology of *shâ'ir*, poet, the "knower," points to the religious or magic origin of his art. The standard form of the classical poem was the *qaṣîda*, whose compass and composition were strictly conventionalized: an amatory prelude (*nasîb*) is followed by a journey undertaken to assuage the poet's love-pains and providing ample opportunities for descriptions of the desert, of the poet's mount, of certain animals (camel, horse, wild ass, gazelle, ostrich) and of hunting. In the end, the poet either acts as the political mouthpiece of his group, indulges in self-glorification, or praises the chieftain to whose tents the perilous journey had been directed. Convivial scenes occur. Although the poets frequently use short forms (*qiṭa*, fragment), the *qaṣîda* (primarily represented by the *mu'allaqât*, outstanding poems by classical poets, Imru'ulqais, Tarafa, Zuhair) theoretically remain the normative pattern even for the later court-poets, amongst whom al-Mutanabbi (d. 965) is most highly esteemed by the Arabs. Side by side with this artistic poetry flourished the semi-popular *rajaz* (*mustaf'ilun mustaf'ilun mustaf'ilun;* not divided into *miṣrâ'*) and a vernacular art with its own strophic forms in which word and verse tones coincide. Ibn Haldûn (d. 1406) refers to some of the popular song-types of his time: *muwashshah, zajal, dû-bait* ("two verses"; synonymous with *rubâ'i*, plural *ruba'iyyat*), *ḳân-wa-ḳân*, and the *mawâliyâ* (generally used in present-day folksong). The poetry suggests a connection with the Arabic strophic forms as perfected in Spain. This formal dependence of the Provençal troubadour song provides the strongest argument in favor of the assumption of Arabic influence on the European minnesang. In modern times European stimuli have helped to remodel Arabic lyrics, but classical tradition has by no means disappeared. G. E. von Grunebaum.

Arcadia. Referring originally to a mountainous region in the Peloponnesus inhabited by primitive shepherds and hunters, Arcadia became synonymous in the Virgilian pastoral with an ideal land where peace and simplicity ruled as in the Golden Age. In the pastoral romance *Arcadia* (1590), Sir Philip Sidney developed a highly metaphorical style (called Arcadianism) distinct from the current euphuism of John Lyly. *Cf.* Euphuism; Pastoral poetry.

archaism. The use of words or expressions appropriate to an older period. Used in Bible translations to lend reverence or dignity: "He hath holpen his servant Israel." Poetically, for various effects, as in Spenser. Its affectation in 19th c. Eng. has been called Wardour Street English, from the many shops of spurious antiques on that London Street. There is danger in the use of archaisms; when Charles Lamb read the opening of Wordsworth's *The Force of Prayer*: "What is good for a bootless bene?" his sister Mary cried "A shoeless pea!" *Cf.* Etymology; Fitness.

archetype. A basic situation, character, or image seen as constantly recurring in life and therefore in literature. The concept developed since J. G. Frazer's *The Golden Bough* (1915), which seeks the interrelations of the myths of all peoples, and Carl G. Jung's *Psychology of the Unconscious* (1916), suggesting a "collective unconscious," the storehouse of mankind's primordial experiences. Jung uses *myth* for the story, *archetype* for the single (constantly repeated) episode or motif.

Archetypal studies may follow two paths: (1) relating elements of a literary work to basic impulses or images in all men, with the thought that the work gains power through appealing to or playing upon the deep-rooted forces or desires; (2) relating a work to all other works in which a similar situation (*e.g.*, parent and child antagonism), character (*e.g.*, the woman scorned), or image (*e.g.*, the lily for purity, the number 3) occurs, as a pervasive symbol. The most comprehensive study of this kind has been made with the folktale, through the work of Antti Aarne in Finland and the Motif-Index of Stith Thompson (1937). While the recognition of an archetype enables one to establish interesting links in comparative studies, some critics warn that no two cultures, times, or works of art are alike, so that emphasis on similarities, and the extraction of archetypes, may lead one to overlook essential differences, or to substitute psychological for aesthetic considerations in examining a work of art, or may draw one from literary concerns to anthropology. There are also dangers of cataloguing. Anyone that goes looking for anything may be labeled a participant in the "quest-myth," along with the Argonauts. There was a game children used to play: "What do these have in common?" Try cobblers, meat pie bakers, bottle babies, veterinarians, and Hindus. They are all involved with the "archetypal figure" of the cow. *Cf.* Symbolism; Metaphor; Folktale; Plot. M. Bodkin, *Archetypal Patterns in Poetry,* 1934; E. Cassirer, *Language and Myth,* trans. 1946; P. Wheelwright, *Metaphor and Reality,* 1962; B. Slote, ed., *Myth and Symbol,* 1963.

Archilochian verse (Gr. poet Archilochus, ca. 700 B.C.). A dactylic tetrameter catalectic. The Lesser Archilochian is a dactylic trimeter catalectic. The Greater Archilochian is a dactylic tetrameter plus a trochaic tripody. Other variants are the Iambelegus, a trochaic diameter catalectic with anacrusis plus a Lesser Archilochian; and the Elegiambus, an Iambelegus reversed.

There are also four classes of Archilochian strophes: the 1st, a dactylic hexameter followed by a Lesser Archilochian; the 2d, a dactylic hexameter followed by an Iambelegus; the 3d, an iambic trimeter followed by an Elegiambus; the 4th, a Greater Archilochian followed by an iambic trimeter catalectic. All these forms are found in Horace.

architectonics. The principle of good design, considered as a branch of learning (Ezra Pound): the process of so ordering the elements of a work of art as to give them meaning only through the organism, in the companionship of the whole. *Cf.* Gestalt.

argot. Idiomatic speech of a class, esp. of the socially disapproved, as thieves or homosexuals. *Cf.* Slang.

argument. (1) The idea or story of a work expressed in brief summary. Acrostic arguments precede many of the Latin plays. Addison wrote an argument for each book of Dryden's translation of Vergil's *Aeneid. Cf.* Acrostic. (2) The L. *argumentum* and *argumentatio,* Eng. argument and argumentation, originally the means of establishing proof and the discourse or activity of proving, were soon used interchangeably. Either term includes both attempts to convince and attempts to persuade. As the former seek belief and the latter action, the former appeal primarily to the reason; the latter, to the emotions. The methods and devices of the two modes of argument differ correspondingly. *See* Question of fact. M. C. Beardsley, *Modes of Argument,* 1967.

argumentation. See Argument; Composition, 4 forms of.

argumentum ad (L., appeal to). Used in various phrases: *Arg. ad baculum* (L., stick): use of force. *Arg. ad crumenam* (L., wallet): appeal to the receptor's material interests. *Arg. ad hominem:* (1) appeal to the individual receptor's emotions; (2) more often, personal attack upon one's opponent. *Arg. ad ignorantium:* reliance upon the receptor's being uninformed. Misrepresentative quotations are common. *Arg. ad populum:* appeal to crowd passions. *Arg. ad verecundiam* (L., modesty): argument so turned that its answer risks breach of propriety.

ars est celare artem (L., The art consists in concealing the art). Aphoristic phrasing of Ovid's expression (*The Art of Love*): *Si latet ars, prodest,* "If the art is hidden, it succeeds." Quoted often as an indication that the best art seems spontaneous. Many have phrased similar thoughts, *e.g.,* Stevenson: "Your easy reading is your damned hard writing." Developed by Ruskin to the idea that great works carry us on wings of fancy till in the vision we forget the magic carpet whereon we fly: "they make themselves be forgotten in what they represent."

arsis. L. The stressed or emphasized syllable of a foot, opposed to thesis. The Greeks, however, meant by arsis the raising of the foot in a march or dance step, and by thesis the setting down of the foot. This would result in the thesis receiving the stress. In view of such confusion, the modern writer who uses these terms must be careful to define them. Hardie, *Res Metrica,* 1920.

art. (1) As process, art denotes the skill or dexterity, or appropriateness of manipulation, in the handling of tools and materials. One possessing this skill is artistic, one aping it is arty. The derogatory suggestion of contrivance is caught in the word *artifice,* while *artful* includes that measure of deliberate deception we call sly. (2) As product, the work of art is distinguished by something more than, or other than, utility. We may place words upon a page to give news, or into a poem to stir us so that we may wish to renew the experience again and again. This quality beyond usefulness we generally term beauty. Not natural beauty, but *homo additus naturae,* beauty created by man. *See* Beauty.

art for art's sake. The idea that the work of art is intrinsically valuable, not to be prized for any purpose outside itself, such as propaganda or teaching. First suggested in Lessing's *Laokoön* (1766); became a slogan in France after the Preface of Gautier's *Mlle. de Maupin* (1835). Poe (*The Poetic Principle,* 1848) spoke of "the heresy of the didactic": man's ultimate goal is happiness, or heightened awareness; teaching merely points the way, the arts lift us directly to the goal. Baudelaire declared that naturally all things are uncontrolled, therefore tend to be ugly or evil; in every age mankind has needed artists and seers to point the way to good: all virtue is the product of art. Oscar Wilde developed this thought into the notion that life strives to imitate art. Remy de Gourmont made the strongest claim: "To accept art because it can uplift the individual is like accepting the rose because from it we can extract a medicine for the eyes." Despite the cogency of such considerations, in the battles of the world today "art for art's sake"—like "the ivory tower"—has become a term with which to dismiss a person or work as insignificant.

Earnest moralists view art either as a sort of play or game that mature mankind will outgrow (Shaw, *Back to Methusaleh*) or as having extrinsic ends, *e.g.,* it embodies and preserves ideals, giving each generation a sense of the past of mankind (Paul Elmer More). Thus art not only informs us but forms us, our attitudes and goals; it helps us to test our goals and organize our means to their attainment. Another use is to quicken and intensify our awareness of character and emotion, thus making us richer individuals, more fully competent to pass on a heritage worthy of the best of mankind. These values, however, *are* intrinsic; they come to us only when we accept the work of art for its own sake, and do not try to direct it to didactic or propagandistic ends. *Cf.* Autotelic.

arte menor (real) and **arte mayor:** two types of Sp. verse first treated theoretically by Juan del Encina (1469–1529) in his *Arte de la poesía Castellana.* The first, minor or kingly type is, according to him, the octosyllabic line (reduced by Encina erroneously to the Church-hymn type: *Jam lucis orto sidere;* the Sp. normal verse comes from the trochaic tetrameter and not from the iambic dimeter). The second or greater type, in reality the 12-syllable verse corresponding to the Fr. Alexandrine, is identified by Encina with Horatian verse-types. Encina, however, does not recognize that the troubadours of the peninsula understood by *Arte de maestría mayor* quite another thing, *viz.,* the artful repetition of the same rhymes in all the strophes of a poem (Prov. form), whereas by *Arte de maestría menor* they meant the varying of the rhymes from strophe to strophe (Fr. form).

artificial comedy. (Lamb) Comedy of manners, *q.v.*

arts, the seven liberal (L., *liber,* free). The program of study that constituted the basis of general culture in antiquity and the Middle Ages—the *encyclios paideia* of the Greeks. As liberal, they were distinguished from the illiberal or mechanical arts in that they alone befit a free man and make a liberal culture—a distinction found as early as Solon (6th c. B.C.). Later, the term was also derived from L. *liber,* book.

Basically, the program consisted of the literary and the mathematic arts, the medieval trivium (grammar, rhetoric, dialectic) and quadrivium (arithmetic, music, geometry, astronomy). Grammar included the study of literature; rhetoric, persuasion and eloquence; through these, the classics of antiquity were preserved for us. Dialectic comprised the science of reasoning (logic) and the art of disputation. The quadrivium was for those (said Boethius, 6th c. A.D.) who would rise from things of sense to the greater certitudes of intelligence. Arithmetic considered the properties of numbers; music, the proportions of numbers; geometry, magnitudes at rest; astronomy, magnitudes in motion. Beyond these lies the realm of philosophy. Cicero (*De Orat.,* III, 15–16) complained that the downfall of learning began when Socrates, by separating knowledge from eloquence, destroyed the union between speaking and knowing. They have too seldom been conjoined since.

ascending rhythm. Flow of verse from unaccented to accented syllables; opp. descending rhythm. *See* Foot.

asclepiad (Asclepiades, poet of Samos, 2d c. B.C.). A meter: one spondee, 2 (or three) choriambs, one iambus (— — | — ∪ ∪ — | — ∪ ∪ — | ∪ —); *e.g.,* "Look now! Over the hill, speeding beyond, lost in the cloud, it flies!"

Asianism. A style of Gr. and L. oratory and prose writing, characterized by a fulsomeness in both conception and expression. Emotional appeal, expressed in an excess of short periods, marked rhythms, copious figures, antitheses and parallelisms, assonance, and general sententiousness. Found in Asia Minor after that part of the Greek world was freed from Persia by Alexander the Great, esp. in the works of Hegesias of Magnesia, a sophist of the 3d c. B.C. One of the chief centers of its dissemination was the great school of Rhodes, founded ca. 100 B.C., where Cicero studied under Apollonius Molo. During the 2d and first c. B.C. it was of greatest importance. In spite of Cicero's condemnation of the excesses of both schools, Atticism won the day, save for a brief revival of Asianism in the second Sophistic movement of the first c. A.D. *Cf.* Atticism; Hellenism.

aside. A remark that others onstage are assumed not to hear, intended to give information to the audience. Used in Eliz. drama and more extensively later (Sheridan, *The School for Scandal*), it became in the 19th c. a device of melodrama, now used only for comic effect. A subtler form, in which the character seemingly thinks aloud (akin to the soliloquy), was revived for serious use in O'Neill's *Dynamo*—where the actions or regular dialogue are often the result of such vocal thoughts—and *Strange Interlude,* analogous to the stream-of-consciousness flow in the novel. Earlier in the 20th c. modifications of the form developed. In the 1-act *Overtones* (A. Gerstenberg) veiled figures walk beside the characters, after each remark giving the suppressed thoughts; in *Lucrece* (Obey) a narrator discusses motives of the action seen in pantomime, or tells other, unseen, parts of the story. *See* Soliloquy; Monologue.

association of ideas. A psychological process in which the individual tends to connect or link an idea, word, emotion or perception with another, each acquiring the capacity to evoke the other: for example, if we often see a particular person wearing a certain hat, the sight or recollection of the hat on some future occasion will "remind" us of the person. That all psychological phenomena can be explained in terms of such a tendency was a cardinal principle of the associationist doctrine in psychology, first formulated by Hartley and Hume, and later developed by various 19th c. psychologists. It is now usual to distinguish the "free" association of ideas (*e.g.,* Alice's thoughts while falling down the hole; the recollections evoked by the cake and tea in *Swann's Way*) from the logical connection of ideas (as in deductive or inductive inference); the former is exploited by certain literary methods, such as "stream of consciousness" (*q.v.*) and symbolist poetry (*q.v.*). Associations are of four general sorts. (1) Notional. Roused by the object the word denotes, usually through custom or general belief or myth. Thus the mistletoe suggests Christmas. (2) Auditory, from the sound. (3) Contextual. From familiar context. Thus *multitudinous* with *incarnadine,* because we have read *Macbeth.* This is what has led some critics to speak of the necessity of the dissociation of ideas, the breaking of common linkages. (4) Private, sprung from one's personal history. Proust follows many of these in *A la recherche du temps perdu* (1913–27); *see* Modern Poetry. *Cf.* Dissociation; Ambiguity; Obscurity; Connotation, Originality.

assonance. Recurrence (esp. at line-ends) of the accented vowel-sound of a word with different following consonants, *e.g.,* frame, fate: vowel rhyme. A characteristic of much Provençal, O Fr. (*Chanson de Roland*), Sp., Portuguese, and Gaelic verse; Eng. ballads and nursery jingles. It occurs occasionally in all verse, and is a definite device in the late 19th and 20th c. (*e.g.,* Emily Dickinson). It abounds in spirituals and in popular song. Double assonance (argues, cargoes; penny, merry) and triple assonance (mincingly, trippingly) are also found. *See* Consonance; Quantity; Rhyme.

asteism. Civil and ingenious mockery. Thus, when pardon was asked for a thief because he had stolen only 16 shillings, the judge remarked: "I warrant you he wished it were 16 pounds!" *See* Irony.

asynartete. A poem the divisions of which have different rhythms, *e.g.,* the archilochian; or the fact of such difference.

asyndeton. Omission of conjunctions. A series of single words within a sentence, linked with commas: brachiology. If succinct and short: dialyton, *e.g., Veni, vidi, vici;* "Sighted sub, sank same." The succession of many conjunctions: polysyndeton. Asyndetic antithesis: opposition with the connectives omitted, *e.g,* Shaw is a practitioner, not a professor.

asyntactic. Loose, ungrammatical in structure. *See* Anacoluthon.

Atellan fables. *See Fabula Atellana.*

atonic. *See* Accent.

Attic. *See* Atticism; Gr. Criticism and Rom. Criticism (Part Two).

Attic salt (Cicero, *De Oratore* 2; Eng. ca. 1600; now rare). Intellectual sharpness; refined but stinging wit: *sal Atticum,* opp. *acetum Italicum,* Italic vinegar, an acrid, more insolent, mordant wit.

Atticism. A style affected esp. by Gr. and Rom. orators, marked by simplicity, directness, and avoidance of rhetorical adornment. Atticism appeared at Rome in the 2nd c. B.C., partially as a reaction to Asianism, partially as an outgrowth of tendencies already active. Hellenism, a cult of grammatical purism and correctness, which tended naturally to become simple archaism, was made familiar to the Romans through Stoic teachers. In the Scipionic circle Latinity was substituted for Hellenism, and Terence is later praised by Julius Caesar for the purity of his Latin. Under the Empire, archaism returned, and Atticism became a fetish amounting to an aping of Attic diction, carried on with the aid of lexica of old Attic words. This travesty of classicism is satirized in Lucian's *Lexiphanes*. Schmid; Norden; G. L. Hendrickson, *CP* 1 (1906). *Cf.* Asianism; Hellenism.

aubade. Prov. A morning serenade (not related to *aube,* a May festival dance). *See* Alba.

aube. *See* Old Fr. forms.

Augustan. The age of Emperor Augustus of Rome, of Horace, Virgil, and the correct and conscious style. Hence, the classical period of any national literature, esp. 18th c. Eng. of Pope, Addison, Steele, and Swift.

auto sacramental. 1-act sacramental play, performed on Corpus Christi Day in Sp. towns, 13th to 17th c. The play, of symbolical character, could represent religious, mythical, historical, and allegorical subjects. The only condition was a more or less veiled relation to the Eucharist, with the praise of which the play ended. One of the greatest writers of this type of play was Calderón de la Barca.

autobiography. Memoir, journal, diary, letter; may be grouped together as literature of personal revelation; in each instance, a large part of the interest resides in a conscious or unconscious self-portrayal by the author. Within this group, epistolary writing (*q.v.*) is marked off by the interplay between composer and intended reader, the delicate "give and take" essential to all good correspondence.

Autobiography and memoirs, though the terms are often used as if interchangeable, are properly distinguished by the relative emphasis placed on character and on external events. Memoirs customarily give some prominence to personalities and actions other than the writer's own; some are hardly more than accounts of historical occurrences that have come directly within the view of their recorders. The autobiography proper is a connected narrative of the author's life, with stress laid on introspection, or on the significance of his life against a wider background. Journals and diaries are by their very nature less connected, less refashioned by retrospective analysis of events. They give us the inestimable boon of personal impressions while these are still fresh, yet often, too, provide reappraisals in the light of later experience. What they lose in artistic shape and coherence, they gain in frankness and immediacy, many of the most famous having been kept with little if any thought of subsequent publication. The two terms, identical in derivation and in primary meaning, have acquired a slight differentiation, "journal" being used for a more detached or reflective record than "diary."

There are several reasons why such personal writings appeal to readers and survive: (1) The mere contact with great historical events or movements may ensure a memoir-writer's or diarist's being consulted by later generations; here the purely personal element may be reduced to an unconscious revelation of a mental frame fairly prevalent in the age concerned. (2) The writer may have played an important part in shaping history. He may be a notable conqueror, religious leader, or statesman. People will always be interested in hearing his own comments on himself and his world. (3) There may be something particular in his point of view, the special angle from which he surveys persons and events; he may be in advance of the age, or otherwise out of step. (4) Although the autobiographer or diarist may have lived centuries ago, he has, through the detailed exploration of his own personality, achieved an affinity with contemporary readers. Some at any rate of these qualities are to be found in all the world's great self-portrayals.

Since the official adoption of Christianity provided the people of Western Europe with a fresh impulse towards self-scrutiny and gave autobiography its first masterpiece in St. Augustine's *Confessions,* the number of such personal records has been immense. Their authors, however, fall generally into a few easily-recognizable types:

A. Those who have been converted to a religious belief or some doctrine having the stimulus of a religion, *e.g.,* George Fox, the Quaker (1624–90), John Wesley (1703–91), Cardinal Newman (1801–90), Prince Kropotkin (1842–1921).

B. Those suffering from a persistent sense of persecution and misunderstanding, causing a "defensive" attitude towards life, *e.g.*, Saint-Simon (1675–1755), Rousseau (1712–78), Marie Bashkirtseff (1860–94), Malcolm X (1925–1965).

C. Sportsmen, professional soldiers and sailors, journalists, usually writers of breezy, chatty accounts with a minimum of introspection, *e.g.*, Ousâma ibn Munkidh (1095–1188), Blaise de Monluc (1502–77), Benjamin Franklin (1706–90), Dwight D. Eisenhower (1890–1969). There are a large number of autobiographies—of sports figures, politicians, actors, industrialists—written in "as-told-to" form by professionals, with the by-lines often shared between subject and writer.

D. Actors, writers, musicians, artists, *e.g.*, Benvenuto Cellini (1500–1571); Carlo Boldoni (1707–93); Jean Jacques Rousseau (1712–88); Hector Berlioz (1803–69); Gertrude Stein (1874–1946), written as if by her companion, Alice B. Toklas; Henry Adams (1838–1918).

E. Those shining in reflected glory because they were present on famous occasions or attendant upon great men or women, *e.g.*, Joinville (1224–1319, St. Louis), Robert Cary (1550–1639, Queen Elizabeth), Mme. de Rémusat (1780–1821) and the Duchess d'Abrantès (1784–1838)—both associated with Napoleon.

This rule of thumb classification will serve in grouping the vast majority of autobiographical works. Some of the best, however, do not fall into any of the classes, *e.g.*, the life of Baber the Mongol (1483–1530), one of the few great conquerors and monarchs to leave a full length self-portrait; the diary of the immortal Samuel Pepys (1633–1703), gossip and amorist, but also naval expert and man of action; and the several volumes of the soldier and statesman Winston Churchill, recounting his life and times. *Cf.* Biography. Ann R. Burr, *The Autobiog.*, 1909; E. Stuart Bates, *Inside Out,* 1936; A. Ponsonby, *Eng. Diaries,* 1923; A. T. Boisen, *The Exploration of the Inner World,* 1936; Wayne Shumaker, *Eng. Autobiog.,* 1954; Roy Pascal, *Design and Truth in Autobiog.,* 1960; A. Girard, *Le Journal intime,* 1963; Maurianne Adams, *Autobiog.,* 1967. ALGY SMILLIE NOAD.

autoclesis (P. The self-inviter). Introduction of an idea by refusing before requested, intending thus to awaken (and respond to) a demand, as Antony with the will in *Julius Caesar*. *Cf.* Apophasis.

automatic writing. Writing as the fingers move, without conscious intervention. Gertrude Stein approached her work through studies of the rambling writing of asylum inmates. With the dadaists, automatic writing became a credo; the surrealists gave formulas for achieving it. In the 1960's, shuffling of word cards, scrambling lines of a group of sonnets, and other devices were used to create fortuitous "literary" products. Having dismissed causality and motivation as non-operative in life, such writers may rely (as some collage makers with "found" objects) upon "accident" or "chance" for the development of their works. *Cf.* Absurd; Concrete; Spontaneity; Dadaism; Surrealism; Self-expression; Futurism.

autotelic. A new term used by the New Critics for the old idea that the purpose of a work of art is not external to it, but within, non-didactic. "A poem should not mean but be," in the words of the poet Archibald MacLeish. The purpose of a work of art is not as a lesson (didactic), nor for a specific purpose (propagandistic), but it is contained wholly within itself; the work is solely to be contemplated, appreciated, enjoyed. That as a consequence one is exalted, or made more fully aware of life's feelings and meanings, is a happy irrelevance, which may justify the role of art in life but does not affect one's attitude toward the particular work. *Cf.* Art for art's sake; Beauty.

auxesis. Amplification, *q.v.*

He lost, besides his children and his wife,
His realm, renown, liege, liberty, and life.

axiology. The study of ethical or aesthetic value.

B

BACCHIUS. A metrical foot, of three syllables, one short followed by two long ($\cup$ — —), *e.g.,* "About face!" *Cf.* Antibacchius.

ballad. Has various meanings in literary or musical usage. Its literary use is restricted primarily to short simple narratives told lyrically. Popularly, any short song that appeals to sentiment may be termed a ballad; its content may be religious, political, amoristic, comic or tragic. Swinburne's "A Ballad of Dreamland" and similar pieces, having no narrative element, are really ballades. In musical nomenclature, a ballad may be solo, choral or instrumental, a song of praise or blame, a dance song, or merely something singable. Chopin, Liszt, Brahms, wrote ballads or ballades for piano and orchestra. Some musical ballads were supposed to suggest a story, but this is no longer essential.

The names ballad, ballade, ballet are derived from the late Latin and Italian *ballare,* to dance; hence it was long assumed that the lyrical story so named was bound up with dance origin. The intricate ballades of Fr. lyric verse, arising in the 12th and 13th c., were artistic dance songs, without a narrative element, and the Eng. ballades of Chaucer's time might serve as courtly dance songs. In the 16th c. the name, having by this time recessive accent, came to be used for light simple verses and music of nearly any content. It was not till the 18th c. that "ballad" began to be restricted to the narrative lyric. The word therefore affords no testimony as to the origin of this type of song.

Among the poetic ballads, two leading types may be distinguished: the popular traditional songs such as the Eng. and Scot. ballads, orally transmitted, with shifting texts, which have held the foreground of interest since the Romantic Revival; and literary ballads by known authors. Some of the latter imitate the traditional type (Longfellow, *The Wreck of the Hesperus*; Swinburne, *May Janet, The Witch Mother*); others (Scott, *Young Lochinvar*; Browning, *How They Brought the Good News*) do not.

Ballads are often termed the oldest and most universal form of poetry. This is untrue if the name is set apart for narrative lyrics. The song proper is the primitive form. Early poetry suggests happenings by allusion rather than in more direct and dramatic form. The ballad, as a species of lyric, emerged rather late in literary history; the fragmentary *Judas* of the 13th c. is often termed the oldest Eng. ballad. The early Robin Hood poems are long for ballads and suggest, like the epic or romantic narratives to which they are affiliated, oral rather than musical or choral delivery. Ballads reached their height in the 16th and 17th c.

Contrary to older belief, these ballads were not the creation of the peasantry, with an origin different from that of other lyrics, and preserved among the unlettered. Their high quality testifies to their emergence from skilful hands.

The ballad style varies with time and place and singers. Its essential characteristics are the narrative presentation, simplicity, lack of self-consciousness. The most usual Eng. ballad measure is the quatrain stanza, with rhyme at the end of the 2d and 4th lines, a singable form based on the L. septenarius. This consisted of 2 long lines of 7 accents, which might be printed as rhyming couplets or as a 4 line stanza alternating 4 and 3 beat accentuation. This form has been handed down in the hymn as well as the ballad. Sometimes inner rhyme is supplied, sometimes the quatrain is lengthened to 6 lines or doubled to 8. There is regularized form in literary imitative ballads (*The Ancient Mariner, Sister Helen*), or some independent verse form may be adopted (*Skipper Ireson's Ride, Hervé Riel*).

All European countries, small as well as large, are rich in balladry. Of special interest are the Scandinavian, Sp. for the epic ballad, Eng., G., and Slavic. F. J. Child, *Eng. and Scott. Popular Ballads,* 1882–98; F. B.

Gummere, *The Popular Ballad,* 1907; Louise Pound, *Poetic Origins and the Ballad,* 1919; G. H. Gerould, *The Ballad of Tradition,* 1932; W. J. Entwistle, *European Balladry,* 1939; J. A. and Alan Lomax's *Am. Ballads and Folksongs,* 1934; *Our Singing Country,* 1941; MacE. Leach and Tristram B. Coffin, ed. *The Critics and the Ballad,* 1961; M. J. C. Hodgart, *The Ballads,* 1962; D. C. Fowler, *Lit. Hist. of the Popular Ballad,* 1968. Louise Pound.

ballade. The Prov. *ballada* was mostly refrain. From it the Fr. *ballade* was adopted for a poem with the strophe form *a b a b b c b C*. In the 14th c. the ballade had 3 strophes, often octosyllabic lines, with an envoi, *q.v.* The chant royal was similar, but of 5 strophes. There was also a double ballade. *Cf.* Old French Forms; Rondeau; Virelais.

barbarism. A mistake in the form of a word, including, according to Quintilian, the use of a foreign term; distinguished from solecism, or fault in syntax.

bard. (1) Originally, a poet among ancient Celts and Welsh, whose occupation was to compose and sing (generally accompanied by the harp) of the deeds of chiefs, warriors, of facts of history and religion. In Scots, a strolling minstrel (against whom special laws were enacted). Term of contempt in 16th c. (2) In modern usage (a) the early Celtic and Welsh poets, *e.g.,* Taliesin and Aneiren (ca. 6th c.); (b) specifically, Shakespeare; (c) generally, a poet.

baroque (of controversial origin). First applied to art by classicist critics of the late 18th c. to denounce the non-classical taste in which the preceding period had indulged. As objective interpretation replaced academic dogmatism, the term baroque lost its derogatory meaning. The Ger. art historian H. Woelfflin described Renaissance and Baroque as two perpetually alternating principles of style, neither of which can be considered superior to the other. Others following F. Strich and O. Welzel adapted the principles of baroque philosophy to literature. This comparison with art threw new light on what had been known by such terms as Conceptivism, Euphuism, *Gongorismo,* Metaphysical Poetry, *Préciosité, Secentismo, q.v.*

Baroque style in literature is one that deliberately rejects the finite for the infinite and the indefinite, that sacrifices harmony and proportion to dynamism, that chooses the antithetical and the explosive, the playful and the obscure. This dualism inherent in baroque thought renews late medievalism and contrasts violently with the monism of the Renaissance and the Enlightenment. Baroque man accordingly is characterized as unbalanced, staggering between sensuality and spirituality, driven by violent impulses, inextricably caught between lust and death. The Sp. "Golden Age" has produced the most extreme baroque forms: thus it could be argued (S. Sitwell) that Sp. national character is baroque by predestination.

In such references, baroque is no longer a purely stylistic concept. With the revaluation of baroque art arose the awareness that phenomena like Counter-reformation, Absolutism, and Court Culture constitute a distinct period. "Baroque" in a broader sense is employed widely as a historical term without stylistic implications. As a period, baroque begins with the decline of the Ren. in the late 16th c. and ends with rococo in the 18th. Its features are not equally distributed. (1) Generally speaking, baroque is more developed in Catholic countries than in Protestant parts of Europe where such unbaroque attitudes as classicism, realism, and rationalism prevailed. Thus baroque could be described by W. Weisbach as the "Art of Counter-reformation." (2) Socially, baroque rests upon non-bourgeois classes (aristocracy, clergy, peasantry), whereas the urban citizenry maintained a clearly antibaroque attitude. To some extent baroque can be defined as the art of Absolutism. Baroque reveals itself more abundantly in the visual arts (including the theatre) and in music than in literature. Perhaps the effort to produce effects properly belonging to the sensuous arts is responsible for much of the seeming artificiality of baroque literature. The word, however, has been used so loosely that today it ranges from a total rejection of form to ultra-formalism. Five main usages are described in *Le Mirage baroque* (P. Charpentrat, 1967). J. Mark, "The Uses of the Term Baroque," *MLR,* 23, 1938; Lowry Nelson, *Baroque Lyric Poetry,* 1961; John M. Cohen, *The Baroque Lyric,* 1963; Margarite Baur-Heinhold, *Baroque Theatre,* trans. 1967. Richard Alewyn.

bas bleu (Fr.). Bluestocking, *q.v.*

basis (Gr. step). A verse of 2 feet, recited to the choric dance.

batch (amount baked at one time). Early Eng. word for stanza, *q.v.*

bathos (Gr., depth). The sudden collapse of high expectancy; a toppling from the lofty to the ludicrous. This is not the sense of the (ambiguous) use in Longinus' *On the Sublime* (first c. A.D.?) but became so after Pope's essay *Peri Bathos, or the Art of Sinking in Poetry* (1728), for example:

And thou Dalhousy, the great god of war,
Lieutenant-Colonel to the Earl of Mar.

Bathos may be an effective device in satire and humor, *e.g.* the cause of the Lilliput-Blefesco war in *Gulliver's Travels.* Other writers have often achieved this effect unintentionally. *Cf.* Anticlimax.

Battle of the Books. *See* Ancients and Moderns.

battology. Needless and wearisome repetition, *q.v.*

beat. The accent, stress, or ictus, in a rhythmical unit of poetry. Used esp. for a strong and regular emphasis, as in Poe's *The Raven* and *The Bells,* Longfellow's *Hiawatha,* and much primitive song. Anglo-Saxon alliterative verse, with four stressed syllables in every line but no fixed number unstressed, is called four-beat verse. The pronounced regular beat of primitive song can have a strong emotional effect, as has even the wordless beat of the drum in O'Neill's *The Emperor Jones. See* Rhythm; *cf.* German versification.

beat generation. A group (one member of which is called a beatnik) which after World War II rejected the society into which they were born. Led by New Yorkers Jack Kerouac (novel *On the Road,* 1957), Allen Ginsberg, and Gregory Corso, who had separately gone to San Francisco, they abandoned American "sentimentalities" for Oriental ones, disavowed any social responsibility, tried to live without conventional careers. Their writing (as in the anthology *The Beats,* 1960. ed. Seymour Krim) is, on the whole, simple but rebellious, and increasingly sensual and sexual. The beats claim to be not retreating from life but seeking a true life of the spirit.

Riding on the crest of the beat vogue was the musical quartet of the Beatles, whose members also wrote books, lyrics, and films, *e.g.,* John Lennon, *In His Own Write,* 1964. Most persisting of the beat writers is poet Lawrence Ferlinghetti (*Pictures of the Gone World,* 1955; *A Coney Island of the Mind,* 1958; *Starting from San Francisco,* 1961; *The Secret Meaning of Things,* 1969; his *Howl of the Censor,* 1961, is a discussion of his trial for obscenity). One proffered explanation of the beat writings is that they seek the expression of vitality—assurance that one is alive—and that this assurance is more important than consistency or form. And of course the fullest confirmation of vitality is in sex, the direct expression of which also marks rebellion against "the establishment." Also, in an absurd world, says John C. Holmes (in *The Beats*), crime is essential, crime "which the cruel absence of God made obligatory if a man were to prove that he was a man, not a mere blot of matter." Such crime, he avers, springs not from hatred, but from "a longing for values." Without lessening of violence or sex, but with more protestation of peacefulness and love, the beatniks were in the mid-60's displaced by the hippies—joined by beat poet Allen Ginsberg, who declared that his poem *Howl* found inspiration in the "Hebraic-Melvillian bardic breath" for its "affirmation by individual experience of God, sex, drugs, and absurdity." *See* Hippie. Thos. Parkinson, ed. *A Casebook on the Beat,* 1961.

beauty. Theories of beauty may be grouped into four classes, considering beauty as (1) essence, (2) relation, (3) cause, (4) effect. (1) *Essence.* (a) Simply, all things are beautiful that possess the quality of beauty. Thus Plato (*Phaedo* 100 C, D): "If anything is beautiful it is beautiful for no other reason than that it partakes of absolute beauty." This cannot be analyzed, it is just recognized, and enjoyed. Essences, however, have also been distilled from the three other groups. (b) Relation: seeking to find the "common quality" in all works of art, Clive Bell (*Art,* 1913) hit upon "significant form." One cannot ask: Significant of what?—the meaning lies in the organic inter-relationship of parts, again undefined, just observed. (c) Cause: beauty is that which rouses the "æsthetic emotion." Psychologists may not list this, but Roger Fry tells them: "For the moment I must be dogmatic and declare that the æsthetic emotion is an emotion about form"—again not to be analyzed, just felt. T. S. Eliot, telescoping two phrases, writes: "Very few know when there is expression of significant emotion, emotion which has its life in the poem and not in the history of the poet." (d) Effect: one definition of poetry is "the writings of a poet or poets"; similarly (Bergson) beauty is (marks) the product of the genius. First catch your seer. (2) *Relation.* (a) The earliest and most popular theory sees art as an imitation of nature. This shifts the problem of beauty from art to nature, unless the beauty be held to reside in the fact of imitation. Aristotle speaks of the pleasure of recognition, but even before the development of the camera Dryden and Coleridge objected to "too near a resemblance." Dryden wanted an improving (Aristotle: idealizing) imitation. Ruskin held straight, however, when he inquired "whether, if scorpion, it have poison enough . . . to sustain rightly its place in creation, and come up to the perfect idea of . . . scorpion." Art holds the mirror up to nature—only, adds Hugo, if it be a "concentrating mirror" that "makes of a mere gleam a light, and of a light a flame." Coleridge, however, found it folly to seek to rival nature's perfection; Nietzsche quite to the contrary bluntly declares "from an artistic point of view, nature is no model"; while the modern (Rebecca West) exclaims: "One of the damned thing is ample." . . . Linked to this theory, beyond need of further elaboration, are the notions that beauty is that which reveals truth, or goodness, or other presumably worth-while or fundamental aspects of reality. "The function of art," (Helen H. Parkhurst, *Beauty,* 1930) "of all art, is to echo in its own terms the universal conflict." (b) Anything is beautiful that results from successful exploitation of a medium, that exhibits (Irwin Edman, *The World, The Arts, and the Artist,* 1928) a nice adaptation to its function. This, of course, can more accurately be tested of a church than of a sonnet; though Kant sets here his notion that "beauty is the character of adaptation to a purpose without any actual purpose." (3) *Cause.* This and the next division introduce a subjective element into the definition. Beauty (Hume) "is no quality in things themselves; it exists merely in the mind that contemplates them." Agree then as men may on these definitions, the application (attribution of "beauty" to a specific work) will vary with the individual. (a) Anything is beautiful that causes pleasure. Ruskin, "any object is beautiful which in some degree gives us pleasure"; Santayana, "Beauty is pleasure regarded as a quality of a thing"; Haydon, "The beautiful has its origin altogether in woman." Others extend this idea to declare that anything is beautiful that rouses emotion. We scarcely need Kenneth Burke's reminder that "a mere headache is more 'authentic' than a great tragedy" to note the fallacy of assuming, since all art rouses emotion, that anything that rouses emotion is art. (b) Anything is beautiful that produces illusion. Coleridge speaks of our willing suspension of disbelief; Konrad Lange makes this statement: "The essence of æsthetic appreciation is conscious self-deception." Artistic illusion is of two sorts. One carries the receptor into the world of deliberate fantasy, with the Ancient Mariner to life-in-death, more lightly with Alice through the looking-glass, with Peter Pan to Never-Never Land. The other illusion takes him into his own daily world, but so intensely that for the time he forgets he is beholding merely a resemblance, a semblance. This thought carries us to (c) the concept of empathy (*q.v.*): anything is beautiful that draws us into its being. This innerness seems to preclude any objective consideration of the work as art; it fits the notion of books, plays, and films as escape. (d) Beauty is that which stimulates an individual in harmony and equilibrium of all his being. This doctrine of synæsthesis (*q.v.*) balances reason and emotion, absorption and detached contemplation; it sees beauty as lifting at once both ends of the see-saw polarities of being. This seems to many today the most adequate explanation of what beauty causes in us. (4) *Effect.* This group of definitions reverses the third, and considers our effect upon the object. (a) Most that have viewed beauty as a product have considered it in terms of the artist's skill. Beauty results from proper handling of the tools; from mastery of the technique; from "the removal of superfluity," as the sculptor reveals the statue within the stone. Whether *homo additus naturae,* or as in recent theory (Arno Holz) nature minus *x, x* being the limitations of the individual artist, beauty in this view is the effect of man's activity upon nature. (b) Widest in scope of all the theories, and among the most influential in recent thinking, is Croce's notion that all expression is art. If one expects something more, Croce rejoins: "No one has ever been able to indicate in what the something more consists." (*See* Revelation.) Such widening of the definition, however, narrows the usefulness of the term. Limits have therefore been suggested, as (c) (Leo Stein, *The A B C of Æsthetics,* 1927): beauty is "the perfect expression of a felt interest." Thus a surgeon may speak of a beautiful operation; a man on shore, of a beautiful ship and storm; but what a "perfect expression of a felt interest" many an urchin achieves by thumbing his nose! (d) Considering beauty as the gift of the artist, to the perfect artist there is beauty in all things; so also each receptor in the measure of his capacity finds beauty around. Shakespeare expressed this thought in *A Midsummer Night's Dream:*

Theseus: The best in the kind are but shadows; and the worst are no worse, if imagination amend them.
Hippolyta: It must be your imagination, then, and not theirs.

Beauty (Gilbert Murray) "is that which when seen is loved." Rebecca West suggests that the "bridge between love and art" is that art makes universal what love has kept personal. Love is an intense awareness, plus desire. In the presence of beauty, as Thomas Aquinas noted, desire is stilled. Beauty may thus be seen as love intransitive, not eager to possess but content to contemplate. Dante, one of our greatest poets, makes it plain:

. . . I am one who, when Love
Inspires me, note, and in the way that he
Dictates within, I give the outward form.

For both the creator and the receptor of a work, beauty is the form love gives to things. See *Æsthetics*. C. K. Ogden, I. A. Richards, and J. Wood, *The Foundations of Æsthetics,* 1925; John Laird, *Modern Problems in Philosophy,* 1928; Ship.; I. Edman, *Arts and the Man,* 1939; Yves Vincent, *Signification du beau,* 1962.

beginning rhyme. Recurrence of sound at start of successive lines. Rare:

We weave in the mills and heave in the kilns,
We sieve mine-meshes under the hills,
And thieve . . .
To relieve. . . . Lanier, *The Symphony.*

See Rhyme.

belief, problem of. This problem, which is a psychological form of the problem of truth (*q.v.*) in literature, arises because literary works sometimes contain implicit or explicit theses (or doctrines) that readers may believe or disbelieve. It may be formulated in the following way: What is the connection between (a) the æsthetic value (for a given reader) of a literary work and (b) the acceptability (to that reader) of its doctrine?

The problem arises most seriously in the critical evaluation of philosophical and religious poetry, *e.g.,* that of Lucretius, Dante, Milton, Shelley, Eliot. It has been discussed throughout the history of criticism, but most thoroughly in recent years. Traditionally, the tendency among literary theorists was to say that the acceptability of the doctrine in a poem is at least one of the important factors upon which its value depends (Plato's *Phaedrus*; for a modern statement, *See* C. S. Lewis, *Rehabilitations and other essays,* 1939). In the twentieth century there have been strong defenses of the extreme opposite position, according to which æsthetic value and doctrinal acceptability are completely independent of each other (*See* Richards, *Science and Poetry,* 1926, esp. ch. 6; compare Plato's *Ion*).

Many critics have felt, however, that even if a reader can place high value on a poem whose doctrine is unacceptable to him (for example, a Christian upon Hardy's "Nature's Questioning"), the unacceptable doctrine will spoil the poem if it is too "shallow," "ridiculous," or "delusive" (charges often made against Shelley). Thus a good deal of contemporary discussion has turned around the attempt to discover a criterion of suitability of doctrine (that is, a principle for distinguishing those doctrines that can be part of a good poem and those that cannot): *e.g.,* "sincerity" (Karl Shapiro, Ezra Pound); "plausibility" (Daiches, Eliot); "maturity" (Eliot, W. K. Wimsatt). *See* bibliography in R. W. Stallman, *The Critic's Notebook,* 1950; also W. K. Wimsatt, "The Structure of the 'Concrete Universal' in Literature," *PMLA* LXII; M. H. Adams, ed., *Literature and Belief,* 1958; A. Isenberg, "The Problem of Belief" and H. D. Aiken, "Some Notes . . . Cognitive," *JA,* 1955. MONROE C. BEARDSLEY.

belles-lettres (Fr. fine letters; similarly *beaux arts*). Refers to grammar, eloquence or rhetoric, and poetry, those activities the Romans designated *humaniores litterae,* the most human of letters. Through debasement of meaning the term was applied to elegant, polished literary works. Though now in use for (a) lighter aspects of literary endeavor, (b) critical studies and those of æsthetics, the term is also applied to literature in general. As H. Reed put it in 1878, "that vapid, half-naturalized term belles-lettres . . . has had some currency as a substitute for the term literature." Leigh Hunt had employed it so, as had Swift in *Tatler* 230 (1710): "The Traders in History and Politicks, and the Belles lettres," apparently its first use in English.

bergette (Fr. 15th c.). A rondeau of one strophe, without refrain, used today as a light verse form. *Cf.* Old Fr. Forms; Rondeau.

bibliography. I. Systematic bibliography brings together in list form material (books, perhaps magazine and newspaper articles, and manuscripts) relating to a particular author or subject, usually giving at least author, title, and date of publication. Such lists may be comprehensive, as the *Cambridge Bibliog.*

of Eng. Lit., or devoted to a period, as J. E. Wells' *Manual of the Writings in Middle Eng., 1050–1400*; or to a type, as A. Esdaile's *List of Eng. Tales and Prose Romances Printed Before 1740*; or to a man, as E. P. Hammond's *Chaucer, A Bibliographical Manual*. The Modern Humanities Research Association issues an *Annual Bibliog. of Eng. Lang. and Lit.*; PMLA does the same for its field. Such work is useful as a basis for investigation of a literary topic, or as indicating what has already been done. II. Analytical or critical bibliography studies a manuscript or book as a material object produced by mechanical means. Through examination of format, paper, binding, ink, of various printings and editions, bibliographers have established, *e.g.* (a) the fact that William Caxton was the first English printer; (b) the true authorship of the *Testament of Love*; (c) the falsity of dates on various Shakespeare quartos and on over 40 books by eminent 19th c. authors, including the once-accepted "first" edition of Elizabeth Barrett Browning. *See* Criticism, textual. W. W. Greg, "The Function of Bibliog. in Lit. Crit." *Neophilologus* XVIII, 1933; R. B. McKerrow, *Introd. to Bibliog. for Lit. Students*, 1927; A. Esdaile, *A Student's Manual of Bibliog.*, 1954; F. T. Bowers, *Principles of Bibliographical Description*, 1949, 1962; R. F. Downs and F. B. Jenkins, ed. *Bibliog.*, 1967; T. H. Horne, *An Introd. to the Study of Bibliog.*, 2 v., 1967.

Biedermeier. Term borrowed from a style of furniture and used (first by Paul Kluckhohn, 1931) to describe the German literary period from 1815 to 1848. This was a time of bourgeois expansion, of complacent acceptance of the status quo, with lyrics and novels (Adalbert Stifter, Gottfried Keller, Raabe, Freytag, Mörike) extolling cultivated gardens and domestic tranquility and virtue.

bienséances, les. Fr. A sub-principle under *vraisemblance* (*q.v.*), related directly to decorum. Two kinds were distinguished: *bienséances* (1) *externes* and (2) *internes*. (1) applied the mores of the time to the actions of fictional or dramatic characters (*i.e.*, a prince must behave as a prince), while (2) stipulated that actions be in accord with the character as depicted *within* the play or novel. *Cf.* Decorum.

Bildungsroman (G. education novel). A novel, such as Goethe's *Wilhelm Meisters Lehrjahre* (1796), presenting a person's formative years and awakening. *Cf.* Epiphany; Novel.

biography is the record of a particular man's life. As an ideal form it should be a deliberate history and should treat the whole, or at least a considerable part, of a man's career. These requirements define it conveniently as a literary form; any further theoretical limits disregard actual important and successful biographies. A distinction between biography and autobiography, *e.g.*, is descriptively convenient, provided that it points merely to the technical difference between a life written by the subject and a life written by someone else.

Before the Renaissance, biographies were composed to illustrate theses not primarily biographical. Until a surprisingly late date every biography was a *biographie à thèse*. What we know of Socrates as a person is attached to his memorable opinions; the Four Gospels, though they are short biographies, are first of all accounts of God's new testament to fallen man; and Plutarch in his *Parallel Lives* of Greeks and Romans obviously uses human careers in order to develop his great theme in comparative statecraft. In antiquity such biographies as Suetonius's *Roman Emperors* or Tacitus's *Agricola* are rare, and even these subjects are overshadowed by the Roman state.

The Middle Ages developed what may be called Generalized Biography, that is, the biography of Man in some typical role. The two commonest forms were the *saint's life* and the *royal chronicle*, the first devotional in purpose, the second historical. In the voluminous hagiographical collections and legendaries, the qualities of a Christian saint, reduced to a pattern, were illustrated in each particular life through a series of actions and miracles. In the secular world, only the life of a man in high position was recorded, and the biography of a king (Einhard's *Charlemagne*; Asser's *Alfred*) appeared as the succession of events during his reign, plus a brief summary of his traits in the form of a *character sketch*. Boccaccio gives a mournful theme to these secular lives in his *De Casibus Virorum Illustrium*, a theme that continues in Eng. in Lydgate's *Fall of Princes* and, as late as the 16th c., in the *Mirror for Magistrates*. The subjects of medieval lives are so undifferentiated that in 16th-c. England a history could still be published in which a few woodcuts were used in repeated rotation as satisfactory portraits of all the English kings. Unique personalities appear almost by accident. Philippe de Commines's subtle sketch of Louis XI cannot obscure the fact that his *Memoirs* are closer in spirit to Froissart's

Chronicles or to Machiavelli's political philosophy than to biography.

The importance attached to men considered as individuals accounts for the constantly accelerating production of biographies from the Renaissance to the present. The protestant and independent spirit of the Reformation differentiated individuals: Walton's lives of Donne, Hooker, Herbert, Wotton, and Sanderson are distinct. The Reformation conception of each man in direct relation to his God increases the importance of each individual and makes Protestant Biography a recognizable form.

The growth of imaginative literature, the increase in leisure and contemplation outside the church, the greater availability of raw materials for biography—letters, diaries, memoirs, documents—developed the new form of Intimate Biography. Lives in this type can best be written by relatives, close friends, or dependents (Roper, *Thomas More*; Cavendish, *Wolsey*). Biographers adopt all available means to live within the minds of their subjects; and what Goethe or Wordsworth accomplish for themselves in *Dichtung und Wahrheit* and *The Prelude,* William Mason and James Boswell accomplish for their subjects in their lives of Thomas Gray and Samuel Johnson, using all possible material to give the thoughts and utterances as well as the actions of a man's life.

In the 18th c. the growth of a new and larger reading public, under political and economic pressures, created fresh styles in Popular Biography. Biography became amusing; curiosity was satisfied concerning one's neighbor; commercial success and shocking crime grew to be popular themes. Biography also at times turned malicious; the picaresque replaced the pious. The growing democratic spirit led to the belief that any man's life was worthy of record, as Doctor Johnson said; and Rousseau is merely the major example of biography growing out of the feeling that each man is at least as good as his fellow.

The development of the historical sense made biography more just in its re-creations of men long dead. Antiquarianism, the encyclopedists, and scientific research instituted Scholarly Biography, the exact, dispassionate marshalling of verifiable details, often in large collections, such as the various national dictionaries of biography. The basic requisites for all true biographies must naturally lie in a certain zeal in discovering, and rectitude in presenting, facts. Such exact knowledge and its sources may be well concealed; but without it biography is merely impure fiction.

Romantic subjectivity, and the increasing study of the human mind, help to explain the characteristic modern type, which for convenience may be called Psychological or Interpretative Biography. Its seed is at least as old as Plutarch. It holds that external acts, facts, and dates cannot reproduce truly or completely the significant actual career of any man. Particularly since the popularization of Freudian theory, even the deliberate or rational utterances and opinions of a man are held to be no more than evidence toward the interpretation of hidden motives and subconscious values that govern his life. The biographies by Van Wyck Brooks, the psychographs of Gamaliel Bradford, the re-writings of existing materials in order to present the *real* Samuel Pepys, the *true* Doctor Johnson, or the *private life* of some public figure, illustrate this emphasis upon psychological interpretation.

Closely connected and overlapping is the form of Artistic Biography. The autonomy of æsthetic theory, the concept of the relativity of truth, and the prevalence of varied fictional forms of literature partially account for this new development, which is built on the conscious principle of creating the illusion of a life as it is lived, employing all the devices of fiction—soliloquy, imagined or expanded conversations, selection, heightening and massing of materials—in order to transform a few dull and dusty facts into an imitation of an actual life, with all its changes, meditations, and shifts of mood, its memories and hopes, and its progress through time. In this form, biography is an art, rather than a branch of history; as such its style and proportions are as carefully considered as if it were a novel or a drama. Often, as in the works of André Maurois, the impulses of biographer and novelist are almost equally balanced. Or again, the art of fiction has influenced the biographical writings of Philip Guedella as deeply as biography has influenced the novels of Virginia Woolf. David Cecil, who writes a life of Cowper under the title *The Stricken Deer,* furnishes one example among hundreds of recent biographers who construct their lives around a central theme, and give their heroes' careers imaginative significance.

The great force in modern biography is Lytton Strachey, who represents both the interpretative and the artistic approach. In reaction to the many-volumed and solemn Official Biography of the 19th c., his work is terse, highly selective, deliberately stylized. His mood is ironic and Olympian; he punctures pretensions, and instead of raising memorials, he strips away the decencies and reveals the poor forked animal, man himself. In his own person he has created for his imitators the modern form of Satiric Biography. But satire implies merely one new subdivision of the form into which most lives, in one respect or another, have always fallen: the Didactic Biography. *Cf.* Autobiography; Novel. Sidney Lee, *Principles of Biog.,* 1911; W. E. Thayer, *The Art of Biog.,* 1920; M. Balch, *Modern Short Biog. and Autobiog.,* 1940, introd.; W. H. Dunn, *Eng. Biog.,* 1916; Edgar Johnson, *One Mighty Torrent,* 1937; André Maurois, *Aspects of Biog.,* Harold Nicholson, *The Develop. of Eng. Biog.,* 1928; Donald A. Stauffer, *Eng. Biog. Before 1700,* 1930; *The Art of Biog. in 18th c. Eng.,* 1941; J. A. Garraty, *The Nature of Biog.,* 1957; James L. Clifford, ed. *Biog. as an Art,* 1962; R. B. Altick, *Lives and Letters,* 1965; Leon Edel, *Literary Biog.,* 1957; P. M. Kendall, *The Art of Biog.,* 1965; D. R. Stuart, *Epochs of Gr. and Rom. Biog.,* 1928, 1967; Catherine D. Bowen, *Biography: The Craft and the Calling,* 1969. DONALD A. STAUFFER.

black comedy. A type of drama without affirmation, based upon the belief that nothing is to be believed, that all ends are illusions, that man is adrift on a courseless ocean, driven by forces either fortuitous or beyond his understanding and control. Hence, the characters act without motive, the events occur without cause. Emphasis is on the sordid; sex is self-centered and cruel; no moral standards hold. Examples are *The Maids* (1954) and *The Blacks* (1958, trans. 1960) by Jean Genêt; *The Homecoming* (1965), by Harold Pinter; Joe Orton's *Entertaining Mr. Sloane* (1965), in which a brother and sister connive at the murder of their father, to share the embraces of the murderer; F. Marcus, *The Killing of Sister George. Cf.* Absurd, Theatre of the; Black humor. J. L. Styon, *The Dark Comedy,* 1962, 1968. (Note that some of Shakespeare's plays, *e.g., Measure for Measure, All's Well That Ends Well,* have been called dark comedy.)

black humor. Humor that seeks its fun in cruelty, turning moral values topsy-turvy, evoking "the grin from the grim." Found in 19th c. light verse, as in W. S. Gilbert's *Bab Ballads*: robbery and murder treated casually in "Gentle Alice Brown," cannibalism in "The Yarn of the *Nancy Bell*"; then in verse about children: of the boy that threw his sister into the fire: "Ain't he cute, he's only six!"; advice to parents: "And beat him when he sneezes." The English call these "the gruesomes." By way of jokes and short stories, black humor in the mid 20th c. moved into serious literature, although before that the Gothic (*q.v.*) mixture of horror and cruel passion had been called the *roman noir.*

Today the more pervasive black humor, attacked by many, is called healthy by those who defend it. To the questioning, disregard, or denial of ethical values, to the unreason or emptiness or evil some see in life, there are three usual reactions: cynical acceptance (and pursuit of pleasure, profit, or power); rebellion; or withdrawal—and laughter. The horrors one sees cannot be escaped by acquiescence, or ameliorated by despair; but they can be defied, perhaps defeated, by laughter. In this fashion black humor is regarded as fulfilling the function served in less ominous days by comedy: we laugh at the forces that threaten to overwhelm us, and by our laughter rise above them. Black humor brings laughter where others turn to tears. It is perhaps in this sense that Walter Kerr remarked: "Evil is fun." *Cf.* Black comedy; Cruelty, Anti-hero. B. J. Friedman, ed. *Black Humor,* 1965; R. Scholes, *The Fabulators,* 1967; J. L. Styon, *The Dark Comedy,* 1962, 1968.

blank verse. Successive unrhymed lines (rarely divided into stanzas); most frequently iambic pentameter. *See* Eng. versification.

blazon (Fr. shield, coat-of-arms). A record of virtues or excellences. Used by the followers of Petrarchism (*q.v.*) of verses celebrating in detail parts of the feminine body.

blue book (from the cover). A six-penny shocker; a short tale in the style of the long Gothic sentimental or terror romance sold by the millions in Eng. in late 18th and early 19th c., between the chapbook and the penny dreadful. *See* Dime Novel; Melodrama.

blue flower, the (G. *blaue Blume*). A symbol for romantic longing; esp., for romantic poetry, first used by Novalis (Friedrich von Hardenberg) in his novel *Heinrich von Ofterdingen* (1799).

Bluestocking or *bas bleu.* A learned or scholarly woman; often used pejoratively today to describe a woman of literary or intellectual pretensions. The term originated in 1750 and refers to those who frequented Mrs. Elizabeth Montagu's salon in London. Among them was Benjamin Stillingfleet, who wore blue worsted stockings. *Cf. Préciosité.*

blurb. A jacket description of the contents of a book, extolling its merits. The term was coined in 1914 (*Burgess Unlimited*) by

F. Gelett Burgess, who defined it as "a sound like a publisher." The earlier term for flattery from interested motives was puffery (there is a character Puff in Sheridan's play *The Critic,* 1779), which was rampant in reviewing through the early 19th c., esp. in the *Literary Gazette* (1817–62) in Eng. Today it is less frequent, though publishers seek quotable remarks among reviews, and reviewers may seek the prominence of their names in such quotation. *Cf.* Puff; Fame.

boasting poem. Widespread in oral literatures, and as part of longer works (*Beowulf*). Common among the ancient Gauls; Tartars (*Kara Tygan Khan and Suksagal Khan*); in Polynesia often of great formality; in Abyssinia often with challenge to battle (men or animals, *e.g.* hippopotamus). The Tuareg of Africa boast of the havoc among the enemy and the plunder carried off; thus also the *Bible*: David has slain his ten thousands. In the drama, *e.g.,* J. Heywood's farce *Thersites,* ca. 1537. Cf. *Farsa;* Abuse.

body. (1) The main division of a work, between the introduction and the conclusion. (2) As a characteristic of style, solidity, substance (by analogy with sculpture and potation).

bombast (OFr., cotton padding; *cf.* Farce; Satire). Inflated, exaggerated language, such as unsuccessful hyperbole. Diction more grandiose than the emotion warrants. Attacked by Longinus; frequent in Eliz. tragedy and later melodrama; burlesqued by Shakespeare (the play in *Hamlet*) and William B. Rhodes, *Bombastes Furioso,* 1810. Occasionally used for humorous effect, *e.g.,* Falstaff; Fielding's *Tom Thumb,* 1730; Pooh-Bah in W. S. Gilbert's *The Mikado.*

bomphilogy. Words "as seem farced full of wind"; pompous speech; bombast.

boulevard, *boulevardier* (Fr.). Spirit, man, or work that flourished during the Fr. Second Empire. The material, pleasure-seeking, irreverent and prankish but basically practical spirit of the young bloods of Paris. In this spirit was built the Opera House (1861–74) and were produced the plays of Labiche and other writers of boulevard drama, and esp. the operettas of J. Offenbach, with books by the playwrights Meilhac and Halévy. *Cf.* Savoyard. The term was applied to melodrama, *q.v.,* whence the Fr. theatre row was for a time called the *Boulevard de Crime.*

bourgeoisie. (Fr., middle class). A social class between the aristocracy and the proletariat or laboring class, which came into prominence as a force during the French Revolution; also a term used by Karl Marx and his followers in the 19th and 20th centuries to describe the ruling class in a capitalistic system. Jules Laforgue (1860–87) said that the one justification of the bourgeoisie is that out of the dung-heap spring roses. As used by the Fr. diabolists, *bourgeois* was a disparaging term, as in the phrase *épater le bourgeois,* and is often used interchangeably with Philistine. Yet it is this middle class whose desires and capacities determine a nation's government, whose tastes establish its art.

boustrophedon (Gr., ox-turning). Written alternately from right to left and left to right, as in some ancient inscriptions (Gr., Hittite).

bouts-rimés (Fr., rimes without lines). The poet Gilles Menage (1613–92) spread the story that one Dulot declared he'd lost 300 sonnets; being asked how he had that many, he explained, "only the rimes." From a jest the idea became a vogue; from the salons of Fr. to Eng. drawing-rooms précieuses and blue-stockings set their gallants to supplying lines for rime-tags. By the early 19th c. there were contests and clubs even in Scotland. More recent party games have included the fashioning of limericks and clerihews, *q.v.* More seriously, it may be pointed out that poets (Byron) have used a rhyming dictionary; often the challenge of a rhyme-word has evoked a felicitous figure. The practice of impromptu versifying was cultivated, and widespread (Johnson; Dumas; Hook; Burns). Leigh Hunt declared that much verse might be reduced to bouts-rimés, as the rhymes indicate the substance: moon, above, June. . . *Cf.* Rhyme.

bowdlerize (Rev. Thomas Bowdler, 1754–1825). A direct application of censorship, *q.v.* The pious editor expurgated passages from *The Family Shakespeare* (1818), to free the English from "whatever is unfit to be read by a gentleman in a company of ladies." The term is now used of any act of literary expurgation directed toward decency, often with implication of prudery. As such censorious editors are seldom scholars, their omissions and retentions depend upon their scraps of knowledge; thus Hamlet's "Get thee to a nunnery" passes safely, and in most of the school editions of *Henry V* the bilingual puns remain. M. J. Quinlan, *The Victorian Prelude,* 1941.

brachiology. (1) Condensed expression, often resulting in obscurity, *q.v.* (2) "Detachment without loss of connection" (Quintilian), *e.g.,* (Cicero): "I ordered those summoned, guarded, brought before the senate: they were led into the senate." *Cf.* Asyndeton; Zeugma.

brachycatalectic. Metrically incomplete: lacking two syllables, or a foot, of the basic pattern of the lines of a poem. *Cf.* Acatalectic.

braggadocio. A braggart, or his brags. A swaggerer, usually coward at heart. Frequent in drama, from the L. *miles gloriosus.* The Capitano of the *commedia dell'arte; Ralph Roister Doister* (earliest Eng. comedy, 1553); Falstaff. The type persists, *e.g., The Show-off* (Geo. Kelly, U.S. 1924). Frequent also in other literary forms, *e.g.,* Braggadochio, *The Faerie Queene;* Bully Dawson, *Tom Brown's School Days.*

brief. (1) A summary or epitome: "Each woman is a brief of womankind." (2) A list, a memorandum: Shakespeare, *M.N.Dr.*V 1,42. (3) A letter. (4) A communication of the Pope on matters of discipline; less formal than a bull. (5) A summary of a case at law, drawn up for counsel or for presentation to a (higher) court. R. P. Sokol, in *Language and Litigation* (1967), contends that the brief is a form of literature, its writing subject to the principles of art.

Apart from the principle of Occam's razor (*q.v.*) for all literature, brevity is a requisite for the short story, defined (Poe) as one that can be read at a single sitting. If more time is required, the affairs of the world intervene, and unity of effect may be destroyed. Very few plays (exceptions are some of Shaw's and of O'Neill's) require more than one evening; a few are still performed without any intermission. Poe warns, however, that undue brevity may degenerate into mere epigrammatism. Yet brevity (*Hamlet*) "is the soul of wit." *Cf.* Qualities of expression.

broadside. Also broadsheet. A large sheet of paper with print on one side. Used, esp. in 16–18th c. Eng., for publishing decrees. Also for "confessions" of criminals, sold to the crowd at their execution; and for short comic tales and poems, including many ballads. The term now includes what is printed on the sheet.

brut. A chronicle. Generalized from the frequent title: *Roman de Brut*; Layamon's *Brut* (ca. 1200), stories of Eng. history that go back to a legendary Brutus. (Layamon's is the first Eng. telling of Arthur's story, also Lear, Cymbeline. Its verse often drops the alliteration, occasionally uses rhyme.)

bucolic (L. herdsman). A highly stylized form, involving the conversation or songs of shepherds, with or without narrative frame. The Gr. word for individual bucolic poems, *eidyllion,* is a dim. of *eidos,* picture. Theocritus probably used Sicilian shepherd songs; with Virgil in L. comes a partial shift in locale to Arcadia, and freer use of allegory. Later writers imitate Virgil. Bucolic denoted the species, "eclogue," the poetic form. Petrarch and Boccaccio both called their eclogues *Bucolicum Carmen.* Bucolic was thus applied to any pastoral poem; also, in general to any rural association. W. P. Mustard, *CW,* 1915; G. Norlin, *AJP,* 1911; H. W. Garrod, "Varus and Varius," *CP,* 1916. *Cf.* Pastoral poetry.

bucolic diaeresis. Diaeresis (*q.v.*) as in Homer and the Gr. bucolic poets: the fifth foot of a dactylic hexameter begins a word, so that the last two feet make a phrase of one or more complete words; *e.g.,* Virgil, *Æn.* 1, 119; *arma virum tabulaeque et Troia gaza per undas.*

bugarštice. Poem of the long line, in Serbo-Croatian heroic verse: 15 syllables, usually with a cæsura after the 7th; sometimes with a refrain of three trochees. Main theme is combat, esp. with the Turks. Now replaced by the poem of the short line, for which *see* Gusla.

bull. (1) The lead seal on an official document, esp. of the Pope; hence, the pronouncement itself. (2) A grossly exaggerated tale, a tale of cock and bull. (3) "A mental juxtaposition of incongruous ideas, with a sensation, but without the sense, of connection" (Coleridge). An unintentional contradiction in terms, with mental associations where none are apparent. Sometimes (perhaps by false etymology) called Irish bull. Asked to define "an Irish bull," an Irish M.P. who was famous for them replied, "If you see three cows standing in a field, the one that's lying down is the bull." The following is of Sp. origin: "An author should always make his own index, let who will write the book." As a literary device, for humor; in serious passages for various effects, from pompous self-satisfaction to the compression of impassioned utterance, *e.g.,* Shakespeare: "Caesar did never wrong but with just cause"; Milton: "Adam, the goodliest man of men since born His sons, the fairest of her daughters Eve." *Cf.* Pun, Humor. W. Jerrold, *Bulls, Blunders, and Howlers,* 1928.

burlesque (Fr.<It.<L. *burra,* tuft of wool; *cf.* Bombast; Farce). The term appeared in Eng. in the decade before the Restoration; first denoted a robust spirit of humor rather than a literary method. Synonymous with "droll," it implied the strongly ludicrous. Applied to literary form by Scarron, 1643, and to his travesty of Virgil, 1648; Charles Cotton's Eng. imitation (first part 1664) bore the title: *Scarronides, or Virgile Travestie. A Mock-Poem, Being the First Book of Virgils Aeneis in English, Burlesque.* Similarly applied to *Hudibras,* the doggerel couplet of which became a favorite burlesque meter.

Burlesque is now used for poetry, fiction, and drama in which customs, institutions, persons, or literary works—individually or as types—are made to appear ridiculous by incongruous imitation. The comic effect is produced by a deliberate "disproportion between the style and the sentiments" (Johnson), presenting the trivial with ironic seriousness (high burlesque) or the serious with grotesque levity (low burlesque). Frequently its purpose is critical or satirical, but it may aim to amuse by extravagant incongruity. (Such a purely fantastic piece is called an extravaganza.) Its main aspects are parody, caricature, and travesty. Burlesque is parody (*q.v.*) when the imitation humorously parallels the style or mannerisms of a particular work or author or school, but with a trivial or ludicrous purpose. Caricature (Fr.<It. *caricare,* to overload, exaggerate) is the method of burlesque that aims at definite portraiture by distortion of easily recognizable features. Travesty (Fr. *travestir,* to change dress, disguise) limits burlesque closely to the original subject matter, which remains essentially unchanged, but is treated with grotesque extravagance or with incongruously trivial language. A single burlesque composition may combine all three methods—or dispense with them all, as when general ideas or common aspects of life are extravagantly presented (Byron, *Don Juan*). But since the pleasure derived from burlesque is due largely to the recognition of the subject of the ridicule, indirectly presented, some degree of parody, travesty, or caricature is almost inevitable.

Burns meter (Robert Burns, 1759–96). A 6-line stanza, rhymed *a a a b a b,* as in "Address to the Deil," "To a Louse."

bylina (or *starina*). A Russian narrative folksong arranged for chanting; tales of the early mythical heroes and of those at the Court of the Prince Vladimir (Fair Sun Vladimir) at Kiev. Collected in the 18th and 19th c., they seem to contain much older material. In style and subject matter, some of the versions merge with historical songs of events in the 16th c. *Cf.* Dumi.

Byron(ic) stanza. *Ottava rima, q.v.*

Byzantine Age (Byzantium: Constantinople; 527 to 1453). A period marked by encyclopedic and pedantic scholarship, lack of force and originality; yet the highest expression of late Gr. literature and learning. *Cf.* Classicism. K. Krumbacher, *Gesch. der byzantinische Lit.,* 1897.

C

CACEMPHATON. (1) An ill-sounding word. (2) A lewd allusion or *double entendre;* foul play on meaning or sound, *e.g.,* the husband's words repeated by the Nurse, *Romeo and Juliet,* I, iii. *See* Cacophony.

cacoethes scribendi (L., Juvenal: incurable itch of writing). Scribbler's itch. An infectious and chronic disorder, frequent among those of strong will but weak mind. Pandemic in periods of compulsory education, as forecast by Johnson: "a corrupt society has many laws . . . an ignorant age has many books. . . . Compilers and plagiaries are encouraged who give us again what we had before, and grow great by setting before us what our own sloth had hidden from our view."

cacophony. Harsh sound; esp. combinations of words that produce inharmonious noise. Browning sometimes seeks such harsh conjunction; T. S. Eliot, "anfractuous rocks."

cacozelia. Fond affectation. Exaggerated diction or decoration of style.

cadence. The flow of the language; esp. the rise and fall produced by the alternation of louder and softer syllables in accentual tongues. Specif., the fall of the voice at a pause. *See* Prosody, Free verse, *q.v.*

caesura. A perceptible break in the metrical line, properly described as an expressional pause. It is essentially an instrument not of metrics but of prose, persisting in the artificial pattern of verse, cutting across the metrical flow with a secondary rhythmic movement of normal speech. In prose this expressional pause marks off the speech phrase (speech centroid), which is dominated by a heavily stressed word and further fixed in attention by a secondary pitch pattern. In Eng. speech this phrase is usually about three words in length. The caesura in a verse line brings forward in consciousness the normal speech movement, at once enriching the simpler pattern of meter and holding the regularly recurring beat of the foot from complete control of the movement of the line. Normally, there is one caesura in a line; but a secondary is not uncommon and a third not especially rare.

In OE. and MEng. verse, where the movement of the line was dominated by a definite pattern of alliteration in half-lines, the caesura was almost as distinct as an end-pause—as which, indeed, some prosodists regard it.

Prosodists have fixed many rules for the use of the caesura. Sometimes a pause at the end of a line is termed final or terminal caesura; then that within is internal or medial. In L. verse, it always occurs within the foot, coincidence of foot ending and word ending being called diaeresis. In the hexameter, it occurs between words in the 3d foot (penthemimeral) or the 4th (hephthemimeral); in the pentameter, always between words after two and a half feet. In Romance versification, caesura is irregular in the hendecasyllable: *a maiori* if the first part of the line is longer, *a minori* if shorter. In the alexandrine it occurs precisely in the middle of the line, until the romantics introduced variety (including two caesuras) in the *alexandrin ternaire. Cf.* Alexandrine. In English, the practice has always been freer.

If the caesura follows an accented syllable, it is called masculine; if it follows an unaccented syllable, feminine. If it occurs within the foot, it is called lyric; if an extra syllable is added to the metrical pattern before the pause, it is called epic caesura. The artistic use of the caesura is one of the surest tests of an artist's skill. In general, the more the poet adjusts his phrasing by normal speech cadences and the less by prosodic rule, the richer will be the interlacing pattern. The iambic pentameter line, rhymed or unrhymed, owes much of its versatility to the lack of regularity in the placing of the expressional pause, which is another way of saying that the line lends itself readily to artistic enrichment through the patterns of normal speech. *Cf.* Prosody. F. W. Shipley, "Hiatus, Elision, Caesura . . ." *TAPA* 55, 1924; E. H. Sturtevent, "The Doctrine of Caesura," *ALP* 45, 1924; O. J. Todd, "Caesura Rediviva," *CP* 37, 1942. A. R. Morris.

Canaanite poetry (a group of West Semitic languages whose main surviving representatives are Hebrew, Phœnician, and the recently unearthed Ugaritic, in North Syria, ca. 1380 B.C.). Canaanite literature may yet shed light on the origins of Gr. drama, of which the Ugaritic *Birth of the Beautiful and Gracious Gods,* a dramatic composition, is highly suggestive. The Hebrew *Song of Songs* is also in large measure dramatic.

The essence of Canaanite poetic form is parallelism; two or more stichoi, approximating each other primarily in meaning and secondarily in length, form a verse. The following curse from the Phœnician inscription of Ahirom illustrates this principle:

Snatched be the scepter of his sovereignty
  Upset be the throne of his kingship!

The parallelism may embody a contrast:

A wise son gladdens a father
But a foolish son is the bane of his mother.
  (*Proverbs* 10:1)

The stichoi may begin identically and end differently with climactic effect (*Psalms* 29:1–2a):

Ascribe to Yahweh, O gods,
Ascribe to Yahweh glory and might
Ascribe to Yahweh the glory of His name!

Compare the Ugaritic tristich in Text 68:8–9 (C. H. Gordon, *Ugaritic Grammar,* 1940) for the structural similarity between the branches of Canaanite poetry:

Lo thine enemies, O Baal,
Lo thine enemies shalt thou smite
Lo thou shalt destroy thy foes.

Note also the inversion of verb and object. Chiasm is quite common in Canaanite poetry.

There is considerable variety in parallelistic forms and metric length. Thus *Psalm* 27:1 has the parallel structure (a-b-c)–(d-e) || (a′-b′-c′)–(d′-e′) with the length 3–2 || 3–2:

Yahweh is my light and my salvation;
  Whom should I fear?
Yahweh is the stronghold of my life;
  Of whom should I be afraid?

If a major word in the first stichos is not paralleled in the second, then one or more words (ballast variants) in the second stichos tend to be longer than their counterparts in the first stichos:

And I set against the sea his hand
And against the rivers his right hand.

The number of fixed ballast variants is greater in Ugaritic than in Hebrew. Canaanite meter is less rigid than the familiar European meters, for it reckons only with accented syllables. In considering examples, it must be remembered that many words in the translations (*e.g.,* conjunctions, articles, pronouns, prepositions, auxiliary verbs) are not separate words in Canaanite.

Verses may be grouped into strophes, esp. when a refrain is employed. The following Ugaritic example (49:VI:16–22) incidentally shows the tendency to vary the final repetition of the refrain for climactic effect (Mot is the god of death):

They fight (?) like ?-animals,
  Mot is strong, Baal is strong;
They gore like buffaloes,
  Mot is strong, Baal is strong;
They bite like serpents,
  Mot is strong, Baal is strong;
They kick (?) like steeds,
  Mot falls, Baal falls.

Canaanite poetry does not demand a uniformity of length or of parallelistic type within a given composition. Variation of verse forms appears constantly within a given poem in Ugaritic; it is therefore unsound to attribute similar variety in the Old Testament to the blending of different poems. S. R. Driver, *An Introd. to the Lit. of the Old Testament,* 1931; W. O. E. Oesterly, *An Introd. to the Books of the Old Testament,* 1934. C. H. Gordon, *The Loves and Wars of Baal . . . Poems From Ugaritic,* 1943. CYRUS H. GORDON.

cancionero. Sp. collection of songs and lyrical poetry of a particular epoch. The most famous are the Cancionero of Alonso de Bæna (1445) and the Cancionero of Lope de Stúñiga. The first contains more courtly, the second more popular poetry. There are also 13th c. *cancioneros* of poems in the Gallego-Portuguese dialect, the oldest being that of King Don Denis de Portugal; the most famous, *O Cancioneiro Geral de Resende* (1516). Karl Vollmöller, *Les Cancioneros et Romanceros Esp.,* 1909.

cancrine (L., crab-like). Verse that reads the same backward as forward; a palindrome, *q.v.*

canson. Prov. The oldest Provençal lyrics were called *vers.* Later, this term was replaced by *chanson* or *canson.* The typical *vers* employed only masculine rhymes (*mascles motz*), in lines of 8 syllables and usually in stanzas of 7 lines. The melody was called *so* or *son.* The *canson* used masculine or feminine rhymes; its lines were equal in length; it generally contained from 5 to 7 stanzas, followed by an *envoi* (called a *tornada.*)

cant. First applied (in Latin: *cantare,* to sing; about 1180) contemptuously to the church services; used first in Eng. of the special wheedling language of beggars, the "canting crew," *cant* from the 18th c. has been used to mean (1) the special turns of language of a class, trade, profession; (2) an affected fashionable or conventional phraseology without genuine feeling. Its use overlaps that of jargon, *q.v.*

canticle. *See* Hymn.

canticum. In L. drama, those parts of the play to be sung or chanted, opp. to *diverbium* or dialogue verse. In Plautus the cantica are very frequent, amazingly varied in rhythm and metrically complex; while in Terence, whose practices are closer to those of the Gr. New Comedy, they are rare. W. M. Lindsay, *Early Latin Verse,* 1922.

cantiga (L. *canticula,* short song). Old song of popular Port. origin, mainly in the Gallego-Port. dialect, most used for lyric poetry in the whole peninsula. In Sp. opposed to the *Cantares* (*de gesta*). There are three types: 1. *Cantigas de amor,* love-songs in which knights complain about their unrequited love; 2. *Cantigas de amigo,* in which girls are supposed to sing longing refrains for their boy-friends; 3. *Cantigas de escarnio,* rhymed satires. There are also religious *cantigas* (*Las Cantigas de Santa Maria,* Alfonso el Sabio, 13th c.). Ramón Menéndez-Pidal, *La primitiva lirica española,* 1919.

canzone. It. A series of stanzaic verses without refrain, usually thought of as accompanied by music, mainly in hendecasyllabic lines with end-rhyme. In 3 styles: tragic (elevated), comic (middle), elegiac (low). The worthiest subjects are *salus* (safety or war), *venus* (love), and *virtus* (virtue or religion). Dante (*De Vulgari Eloquentia,* 1306) declared that the highest type of vernacular poetry is the canzone of tragic style written on the worthiest subjects in the illustrious vernacular (the *si* dialect of the Romance tongue, which is *illustrious* because exalted, *cardinal* as the basis of local dialects, *courtly* as the language of rulers, and *curial* as the language of courts of justice).

caricature. A humorous or satirical picture or description, exaggerating distinctive features or peculiarities. *Cf.* Burlesque.

Carlylean. Of the style of Thomas Carlyle (1795–1881), marked by irregular sentence construction, neologisms, striking figures, and Germanisms. Those who dislike it call it Carlylese.

carmen (L.). (1) Originally, anything ritually or formally uttered (incantation; hence Fr. *charme,* Eng. charm). (2) Song, in the wide sense, including wordless melodies. (3) Poetry, as opposed to prose.

carmen figuratum. Emblem verse. Verses so arranged on the paper that each stanza, or the poem as a whole, takes the shape of an object, usually (cross, altar, wine-glass) the theme of the poem. First used by Simias of Rhodes (fl. 324: *Gr. Anthology* bk 15: wings, hatchet, egg). Popular in the Renaissance: F. Quarles, 1638, "Behold how short a span;" every stanza is a pyramid. Satirized by S. Butler, "Character of a Small Poet"; classed by Addison as false wit. Renewed recently in concrete verse, *q.v.* N. W. Helm, "The Carmen Figuratum," *TAPA* 33, 1902.

Caroline. Of the time of Charles I of Eng. (1625–49). Following the Eliz., this period continues the lyric grace in poetry; prose takes a neater form; declining drama (less often in verse) depends more upon noble patronage. Loyalty grows brittle in gallantry, devotion hardens to duty, as Cavalier (*q.v.*) and Roundhead shape sides for the war ahead. A grimmer note appears in the Puritan prose, while the courtiers dally and the clergy grows metaphysical.

carpe diem (L. Horace: seize the day). Applied to works, esp. lyric poems, that urge the joys of the moment, heedless of the morrow. Omar Khayyam; in the Ren., many love lyrics; in Eng., *e.g.,* Herrick: Gather ye rosebuds while ye may.

catachresis. Improper application of a term; usually in error, or as an unsuccessful figure. At times intentional, as in the safety slogan, "Children should be seen and not hurt." Occasionally effective in emotional condensation, *e.g.* (Milton, *Lycidas*) "blind mouths," which Johnson attacked and Ruskin admirably defended. Also, *see* Periphrasis.

catalectic (n., catalexis). Of a line of poetry lacking one syllable of the established pattern. *Cf.* Acatalectic.

catalects. Detached literary pieces; esp., a group of short poems attributed to Vergil. *Cf.* Analects.

catalogue verse. Lists qualities of objects, or names, at length. Common among primitive peoples (*e.g.,* Galla in Africa), tribal boasting poems. Enjoyment in the mere naming, perhaps originally with a sense of power over the thing named. A widespread genre, of many uses: the *Bible* genealogy of Jesus; L. and Ren. poems cataloguing the physical charms of the beloved: Whitman; Sandburg, *Chicago*; V. Lindsay, *The Santa Fe Trail.*

catastasis. (1) The narrative part of the introduction of a speech. (2) Third of the four parts of a tragedy (protasis, epitasis, – –, catastrophe), heightening the action to its climax.

catastrophe. The unhappy end of a tragedy, *q.v. Cf.* Denouement.

catharsis. The 16th c. commentators on Aristotle's *Poetics* made an important critical question out of a concept briefly referred to by Aristotle: the tragic catharsis. The pertinent passage in the *Poetics* reads, "Tragedy through pity and fear effects a purgation of such emotions." Further explanation cannot be found in the *Poetics*; those who have attempted to explain Aristotle's meaning have relied on another short passage in the 8th book of his *Politics,* on the definitions of pity (*q.v.*) and fear in his *Rhetoric,* on random short passages in the writings of Plato, Proclus, Plotinus, and Iamblichus of Chalcis. Few literary problems have occasioned so much controversy as this one. The discussions have taken two directions: (1) what did Aristotle mean? and (2) what usefulness has the concept in explaining the function of tragedy and of other poetic forms? 16th c. It. introduced three important interpretations. Two, closely affiliated with Neo-Stoicism, had moral connotations; the third was an application of humoral psychology. Robortelli (1548), Castelvetro (1570), Heinsius (1611), Vossius (1647), advanced the "hardening" theory, by which tragedy was said to accustom the spectator to scenes of misery and violence, hence to harden his weak inclinations to fear and to pity. Corneille's forceful, if sceptical, exposition in his 2d *discours* (1660), maintained that tragic pity leads the spectator to fear for his own well-being when he compares his weaknesses with those that caused the downfall of the tragic character; his determination to control his passions leads him to purge himself. The third view, the homœopathic conception, which attracted such men as Minturno and Milton, closely resembles the modern view of the catharsis as a relieving of emotions. Like emotions drive out like.

According to critics of the 18th c. (Batteux, Lessing, Blair) tragedy purifies the spectator by increasing his natural and good capacity for pitying by exercising his sensibilities. In the 19th c. Goethe said Aristotle meant the reconciling adjustment of fear and pity within the play (Creon in *Antigone*; Theseus in *Hippolytus*: "calm of mind, all passion spent"); Hegel saw tragedy as reconciling discordant cosmic truths; Jacob Bernays first clearly advanced the psychopathological theory, basis of most since (W. Stekel, *Dichtung und Neurose*). Bywater, *Aristotle on the Art of Poetry,* 1909; Butcher, *Aristotle's Theory of Poetry and Fine Art,* 1927; J. C. Ransom, *The World's Body,* 1938. Baxter Hathaway.

Objections of two sorts have been taken to the notion of catharsis. The first indicates that the definition is rooted in its time; the Greeks wished to be purged of pity, as disturbing reason's calm judgment; the humanitarian deems it a wholesome feeling. More trenchant is the declaration that Aristotle does not mention the major and essential effect of tragedy: exaltation; we go to the theatre not to be purged but to be roused. Shakespeare sometimes (*King Lear, Macbeth*) uses pity as relief from an awesome sense of heroic grandeur—which we yet may share; as we feel that, despite the inevitable hour of death, life thus lived is warrant for man's being. Beyond the quickening of all his powers that is the gift of every art, tragedy gives man a pride and an assurance, an inner song to sing against despair.

caudate (L., tailed). A metrical or stanzaic pattern with some extra lines added. Esp. of the sonnet, to which Francesco Berni (d. 1536) in It. added a half line followed by a rhyming couplet. Milton in Eng. wrote some caudate sonnets (with two extra lines), *e.g.,* "On the New Forcers of Conscience." *Cf.* Tail rhyme.

cavalier. A supporter of the Stuarts in 17th c. Eng. Applied by the Roundheads as a term of reproach (and still in one application meaning high-handed), it designates in the Cavalier lyric a form of dalliant verse written mainly by the courtiers (Herrick is an exception) and marked by gallantry and devotion, and the use of wine, woman, and song as subjects of their poetry, plus an attitude of living for the moment (*carpe diem, q.v.,* "Gather ye rosebuds while ye may"). Carew; Suckling; Lovelace. Browning sought to recapture the mood in his *Cavalier Tunes. Cf.* Caroline.

censorship. The suppression of books, plays, or passages therein, as sacrilegious, immoral, seditious, or otherwise objectionable. Despite puritan blue-laws and watchfulness in Eng. (esp. under Cromwell, 1642–60, when the theatres were closed) and in the U.S., censorship has been more frequently religious and political than moral. The attacks on

Cleon the tyrant of Athens in Aristophanes' *The Acharnians* led (521 B.C.) to a restrictive law—from which the chorus with its ritualistic tradition was exempt. Protagoras' treatise *Concerning the Gods* (5th c. B.C.) was burned in Athens. Antiochus Epiphanes in 168 B.C. burned Jewish books in Palestine; in that century (and later by Augustus) books on soothsaying and politically "dangerous" books were burned. These were, however, individual and sporadic attacks; there was no systematic ancient censorship. Despite the Roman office of "censor," the only recorded instance of such exercise is an edict (Cn. Domitius and L. Licinius, 92 B.C.) against the new schools of rhetoric. The early Christian church had its religious battle to wage, but even today the overwhelming majority of books on the *Index* are anti-Catholic tracts. In the first printing of *Les Etats et empires de la lune et du soleil* (Cyrano de Bergerac, 1619–55), *e.g.*, the committee of birds on the sun decide that the intruder is a man because at sight of him they are "filled with instinctive disgust"; immediately censored, and then changed so that they know he is a man because of his lying insistence that he is not.

In England, a license for printing was required from 1538 to 1694; plays had to be approved, in 1545 by the Master of the Revels, from 1737 to 1968, by the Lord Chamberlain. In the U.S. there is no prior censorship save in the motion picture field, which sought to avoid statutory regulation by establishing its own reviewing board. A book or play, in any country, is after issuance or production liable to prosecution for various reasons, usually obscenity and libel. In totalitarian countries a rigid censorship not only binds the press and stage but works retroactively by banning or burning older works. There are frequent charges in many lands of an unofficial censorship exerted by publishers, and on publishers and press by "vested interests"; detailed, *e.g.*, in Upton Sinclair's study of Am. journalism, *The Brass Check*, 1919, which incidentally gives instances of "outraged morality" (sex charges) used as pretext to censorship for more "practical" ends.

Regular, as opposed to sporadic, censorship on the ground of obscenity began, in both Eng. and the U.S., in 1868. Then Lord Chief Justice Sir Alexander Cockburn set the test of obscenity: "whether the tendency of the material is to deprave and corrupt those whose minds are open to such immoral influences and into whose hands a publication of this sort may fall." A similar standard was set by a N.Y. State law the same year, under which Anthony Comstock, organizing the Society for the Suppression of Vice, maintained constant watch and frequent prosecution that came to be mocked by the more liberal as Comstockery. The basic law remained the same, with varied and confusing phraseology in different states, until the U.S. Circuit Court in 1933 in the case of *Ulysses* ruled that a work's obscenity depends upon whether "to the average person"—no longer the susceptible minor—"the dominant theme of the material taken as a whole appeals to the prurient interest." While this introduced another disputable term, prurient, it barred condemnation of isolated words or passages; it opened the door to "four-letter words." Nevertheless authors, publishers, and booksellers continued to be prosecuted until in 1966, in "the Roth case," Supreme Court Justice Brennan declared that three things must be established: that (1) "the dominant theme taken as a whole appeals to a prurient interest in sex; (2) the material is patently offensive because it affronts contemporary community standards; and (3) the material is utterly without redeeming social value." The same attitude seems to prevail in England. Publishers are now openly issuing such works as *Fanny Hill*, and the more or less autobiographical books of Frank Harris, Henry Miller, and the anonymous author of the 11-volume *My Secret Life*; but many communities continue to try to keep these from their bookstores and library shelves. The Supreme Court, however, has recently reversed over twenty lower court obscenity convictions.

The censorship powers of the Lord Chamberlain in Eng. were withdrawn in 1968; but France under Charles de Gaulle became more restrictive. *Cf.* Pornography. E. N. S. Thompson, *Controversy Between the Puritans and the Stage*, 1903; R. A. Burke, *What is the Index?*, 1952; M. L. Ernst, *To the Pure*, 1928; with A. U. Schwartz, *Censorship*, 1964; Baron Cyril J. Radcliffe, *Censors*, 1961; A. P. Klausler, *Censorship, Obscenity, and Sex*, 1967; G. S. M. McClellan, ed. *Censorship in the U.S.*, 1967; P. Coleman, *Obscenity . . . in Australia*, 1962; C. Rembar, *The End of Obscenity*, 1968; E. Gracia, *Censorship Landmarks*, 1969.

cento (L., patched cloth). A literary patchwork, usually verse, made of lines taken from the classics, *e.g., Homerocentones*, a life of Christ by the Empress Eudoxia (5th c.), every line from Homer. Most frequently drawn upon has been Vergil. Delapierre, *Tableau de la lit. du centon,* 1875.

chain verse. Linked stanzas. By rhyme, as the *terza rima, q.v.* By words repeated. Sometimes the last line of a stanza becomes the first line of the next; or other patterns of repetition are used, as in the pantoum, *q.v.*

chair ode. *See* Eisteddfod.

chançon (Fr.). A poetic work; in OFr. and Prov. lyric poetry, spec. the love poem, often addressed to a lady but sometimes just a lament. The common form is a series of stanzas of regular meter plus an *envoi.* Probably in origin a dance poem at the May festival. *See* Canson; Old Fr. forms.

chanson. See Old Fr. forms. *Chanson de geste, see* Gesta.

chant. *See* Hymn.

chant royal. *See* Old Fr. Forms; Ballade.

chantefable. Developed from the chanson: a prose tale with *laisses* of verse, *e.g.,* 12th c., *Aucassin et Nicolette.*

chapbook (OEng., *céap,* barter). A pamphlet sold by street hawkers, esp. London 16th through 18th c. Contents from nursery rhymes and ballads through fairy tales and romances to strange events and lives of criminals. Used as title for a miscellany (Chicago 1894–98) and for a series of miscellaneous booklets, *e.g.,* Univ. of Washington Chapbooks, ca. 1930.

character, the. Dates from the *Characters* of Theophrastus (d. 278 B.C.), a series of sketches probably designed to amuse and instruct students of rhetoric (G. S. Gordon; R. C. Jebb; Christ-Schmid). All the sketches follow the same pattern: a definition of some undesirable social quality, then a description of how a man embodying such a quality will talk and act, *e.g.,* "Flattery may be considered as a mode of companionship degrading but profitable to him who flatters. The flatterer is a person who will say . . ." With the simplicity and conciseness of his method, using the language of the streets of Athens, he combines wit, clever description, shrewd psychological insight. The *Characters* gave rise to a distinct literary genre. After Casaubon's edition of the *Characters* (1529), came the 17th c. vogue: Hall; Overbury; Earle, in Eng.; La Bruyère in Fr.

"The relation of the Eng. Character to its Gr. Prototype," *PMLA* 18, 1903; G. S. Gordon, "Theophrastus and His Imitators," *Eng. Lit. and the Classics,* 1912.

characterization. Making known the appearance and nature of a person. Arnold Bennett, contrary to Aristotle's primacy on action in drama, states: "The foundation of good fiction is character creating and nothing else." (*Cf.* Plot; Action.) It is generally agreed that in most good stories the events follow logically from the natures of the persons involved. The writer may present his persons in two general ways: (1) directly, telling the reader the person's qualities; (2) through action, showing the person's deeds, by which his character may be known. The first method is most frequent for minor figures; for the main figures both are usually employed. Direct description or exposition has the advantage of instant clarity; though sometimes it is used cumulatively, gradually building up a full portrait. The cumulative method is more frequent, indeed is almost inescapable, in characterization through action. This has the further advantage of allowing the receptor to form his own conclusions, which are firmer and seem more real than any given him by the author. This sense of self-activity also draws the receptor more fully into the flow of the tale. Occasionally, esp. in first person narrative or in drama, the two methods present opposite pictures, so that the receptor must decide whether actions speak louder than words; neither John Ridd (*Lorna Doone*) nor Antony (*Julius Caesar*), *e.g.,* is so simple as he would have us believe; nor Jim Hawkins (*Treasure Island*; note the tricky words of the one-legged man at the tavern), so smart.

The minor figures in most stories are presented in only one aspect, as "flat," "thin," "disc" characters. Sometimes (esp. in romances; Scott) even the main figures are "stationary," static, the same at the finish as at the start; but they may be more fully shown, "thick," "round." A full characterization will present concrete detail, is likely to emphasize a dominant trait—one quality that colors all the rest, as the weak will in the well-intentioned Godfrey Cass, or the self-centered drive of his brother (*Silas Marner*) —and will build within the person a synthesis of individual, typical and universal characteristics (*see* Distances, the three). But the main figures of a work are likely to be "developing," dynamic characters; the conflict within the story, within their spirit, wreaks its effect upon their souls. This may, of course, be for the better or for the worse, as in the two persons, Paphnutius and Thaïs, of Anatole France's *Thaïs,* or successively as events drive within the one man, Silas Marner. Any such changes, of course, must be consistent with the potentialities shown. Such dynamic characters appear in most great fiction; in tragedy, often a final recognition brings a calm meeting of the doom that cuts off the possibility of the change that might otherwise come. *Cf.* Tragedy; Anti-hero. C. Gillie, *Character in Eng. Lit.,* 1965; W. J. Harvey, *Character and the Novel,* 1965; C. C. Walcutt, *Man's Changing Masks,* 1968.

charientism. An attack or insult so phrased that the recipient must take it as not intended. *See* Irony.

Chaucer stanza. Septet, *q.v.*

cheville (Fr.). An expression used solely to round off a sentence or verse.

Chevy Chase stanza. Ballad stanza. K. Nessler, *Gesch. d. Ballade Chevy Chase. See* Ballad.

chiasm (Gr., cross). A balanced passage whereof the second part reverses the order of the first; esp. one in which forms of the same word are used, *e.g.* (Coleridge) "Flowers are lovely, love is flowerlike." Frequent in Gr. Combined with mixed metaphor in (Pope): "See Pan with flocks, with fruits Pomona crowned." *See* Oxymoron.

chimerat. *See* Folktale.

Chinese poetry. Chinese verse is distinguished from familiar types of Occidental verse by its insistence upon rhyme and its use of tone contrast in place of meter. There is, strictly speaking, no word for "verse" in the Chinese language. The word *shih* is sometimes used in this sense (and sometimes used in the sense of the "poetic"), but it is more generally used to designate a specific form of verse. The Chinese equivalent for "verse" is "rhymed writing" as against "unrhymed writing." The reason for this insistence upon rhyme lies in the nature of the language; for the character, the unit of the Chinese language, being a simple vocable consisting of at most one initial and one final consonant (in modern Mandarin the final can be only a vowel or a nasal), it follows that the number of rhyming characters is very great and rhyming is not only easy to achieve but often difficult to avoid.

The apparent analogy to meter in Chinese verse is the number of characters that the line contains, but this analogy is misleading because the character has no stress inherent in itself.

A closer analogy to meter in Chinese verse is tone or pitch contrast, since its purpose is the same as that of meter, *i.e.,* to avoid monotony. It should be noted, however, that whereas in Western verse the tendency is to strive for contrast between the stress or quantity of the syllables within the group (that is, the foot), the Chinese tendency is to strive for contrast between the successive pairs within the line and between the corresponding pairs of the coupling lines.

Tone scheme for "modern style" poem (— even tone; ∪ sharp or deflected tone):

∪	∪	—	—		∪
—	—	∪	∪		—
—	—	—	∪		∪
∪	∪	∪	—		—

Thus in Chinese verse rhyme is obligatory; tone contrast, optional; in Occidental verse meter is obligatory; rhyme, optional.

Traditionally the Chinese distinguish 4 types of verse, in order of their historical emergence: the *shih,* the *fu,* the *tz'u* and the *ch'ü.* Of these the *shih* is the most important as a living medium of expression. It is the form of folk songs and popular ballads as well as the bulk of literary verse from the earliest times to the present. Its importance so overshadows all the other forms that the word *shih* is, as pointed out before, sometimes used to designate all verse and to suggest the poetic. There are three principal line-lengths. The 4-character line is characteristic of the *Shih Ching* (or *She King*; known in Waley's translation as *The Book of Songs*). The *Songs* employed the 4-character line because it was admirably suited to the character of ancient Chinese music, which, as far as we can judge from modern reconstructions, was slow and solemn in measure and intended to edify rather than to delight. With the vogue for foreign music from the 2d c. B.C., a more varied meter became necessary and from this demand evolved 5- and 7-character lines. The *shih* proper, which had by this time lost its musical association, adopted the new forms but followed the native tendency to employ lines of the same length throughout the poem, whereas the *yo fu* followed the verbal patterns that resulted from the music. Without reference to music, therefore, the *yo fu* is distinguished from the *shih* proper in that it does not necessarily employ lines of the same length for the entire poem. The *shih,* as distinguished from the *yo fu,* is divided into "ancient" and "modern" styles with reference to whether it follows certain arbitrary rules and conventions. Besides rhyme and uniformity in the length of the lines, the modern style requires also absolute parallelism of the coupling lines, fixed tone patterns and a fixed number of lines for the poem (eight 5- or 7-character lines). Chinese poetry is primarily lyrical; it has no epic compositions; the average poem runs only from 4 to 12 lines; the longest narrative poem extant ("Chiao Chung-ch'ing's wife," Arthur Waley, *The Temple* and other poems) contains ca. 350 lines. The type of fiction known as *t'an tz'u* and written in rhymed doggerel is of course excluded, as are Buddhist gathas, which some regard as verse because the lines are of equal length but which are not verse according to Chinese tradition because they are not rhymed.

The *tz'u* can be described as a new form of music school verse, for it originated in the 9th c. as song words to the prevailing tunes. The process of *tz'u* composition is known as *t'ien tz'u,* or "filling in the words," *i.e.,* fitting words to a given tune, of which there are several hundred known. It is like writing new songs to the tune of "Swanee River" and so on *ad nauseam,* the only difference being that in later times the *tz'u* writer has only the verbal pattern of the original song to guide him, the original tune in most cases having been lost. The most notable thing about the *tz'u* is the irregularity in the length of lines, the lines being bound together by the reiteration of the same rhyme throughout the poem. This irregularity would suggest greater freedom, but the reverse is the case, since the *verbal* pattern of the original song must be strictly followed in the total number of lines for the entire poem, the number of characters in each line and the tonal pattern (which takes into consideration all the four classical tones instead of grouping them into "even" and "deflected" as in the case of modern style *shih*) for each. The *tz'u* is largely used for sentimental lyrics and is still indulged in by the more sophisticated literati.

When divorced from its music conventions, the *ch'ü* is indistinguishable from the *tz'u.* There are two principal types: the independent *ch'ü* and *ch'ü* cycles that form the arias of the Chinese play.

From purely formal considerations, there are thus only two principal types of Chinese verse, *viz.,* the *shih* and *fu* on the one hand and the *tz'u* and *ch'ü* on the other. Rhyme is the common characteristic of both but whereas in the one uniformity in the length of line is the general rule, in the other it is irregularity. If we exclude from the field of poetry the later *fu* writers and eliminate the unnecessary distinction between *tz'u* and *ch'ü,* we may say that we have only two distinct forms of Chinese verse—the *shih* and the *tz'u.*

Diagram showing the formal elements of the historical types of Chinese verse (based upon T'ang Yüeh's "Elements of Chinese Style" in *Kuo ku hsin t'an,* 1926).

x = required; o = tendency;
blank = element absent.

TYPE	ELEMENTS						
	Rhyme	Coupling of Lines	Uniformity in Length of Coupled Lines	Uniformity in Line Length for Entire Poem	Parallelism for Coupled Lines	Fixed Tone Pattern	Fixed Length for Poem
SHIH Ancient Style	x	x	x	o	o		
Music School	x	x	x	o	o		
Modern Style	x	x	x	x	x	x	x
FU Early	x	x	x	x	o		
Middle	x	x	x	x	o		
Modern	x	x	x	x	x	x	
TZ'U	x					x	x
CH'Ü	x					x	x

Arthur Waley, *170 Chinese Poems,* 1946; W. Bynner, Introd. *The Jade Mountain,* 1929; James T. Y. Liu, *The Art of Chinese Poetry,* 1962, 1966. Chi-Chen Wang.

choliamb (Gr., "lame iambic"). An iambic trimeter in which a trochee or spondee has been substituted for the final iambus, reversing the rhythm, thus ∪ — | ∪ — | — — or ∪ — | ∪ — | — ∪. Generally in satirical, invective, or humorous verse. Also called scazon.

choree. A metrical foot, a long syllable followed by a short one (— ∪), *e.g.,* Longfellow's *Hiawatha:* "By the shores of Gitchee Gumee." The reverse of an iamb. Also called trochee.

choriambus. A metrical foot, one long syllable, then two short, then another long (— ∪ ∪ —), *e.g.,* "over the hill." Leonard, "The Choriambic," *CJ* 11, 1915–16. *Cf.* Aeolic.

chorus (Gr., dance; band of dancers and singers; place for dancing). In Gr. tragedy and satyr-play, the chorus represented a group of men or women, of lower social rank than the chief characters, interested in their destinies. Æschylus used a chorus of 12; Sophocles and subsequent tragedians, 15. The group was led by a *coryphaeus* (Gr., head man), who spoke the transitional passages between dialogue-scenes and choral odes. The odes were sung by the entire chorus, in strophes and antistrophes (Gr., turnings, counter-turnings). The metrical scheme of the antistrophe corresponded to that of the preceding strophe, as did the dance movements therewith. In Gr. comedy, the chorus numbered 24, and often appeared in symbolic guises, as animals, birds, clouds. A special feature of the comic chorus was the revue-like *parabasis* (Gr., coming forward): usually after the *agon* (*q.v.*), a series of speeches or songs, with topical jokes and comment on public affairs. In Æschylus' plays, the chorus often took part in the action (*e.g.*, at end of *Agamemnon*; throughout *Eumenides*); it always represented a specific force potentially affecting the characters, besides commenting on the action and interpreting its moral significance, which were its chief functions in Sophocles. After Euripides, who used choral odes primarily for lyric variety, they became mere intermezzos, sometimes entirely irrelevant to the play, as in New Comedy (Menander, 4th c. B.C.). In drama since Gr., except for periods of direct imitation (Rom. tragedy), the chorus is very seldom used, appearing chiefly in other forms (opera, oratorio, musical comedy) where singing and dancing are essential. It is sometimes employed in poetic plays of a highly lyrical, symbolic, or religious character (*e.g.*, Racine's *Athalie*, O'Casey's *Within the Gates*, Eliot's *Murder in the Cathedral*), or with satirical elements like those of Aristophanic comedy (*e.g.*, Auden-Isherwood: *Ascent of F6*). The function of the chorus as "ideal spectator" is sometimes carried out by the *confident(e)* of the Fr. Classical drama, or by type-figures designed for this purpose (*e.g.*, Seth Beckwith in O'Neill's *Mourning Becomes Electra*; the beggar in Giraudoux' *Electre*). P. C. Wilson, *Wagner's Dramas and Gr. Tragedy*, 1919; A. W. Pickard-Cambridge, *Dithyramb, Tragedy and Comedy*, 1927; E. G. Griffin, *The Dramatic Chorus*, 1960. FRANK W. JONES.

chronicle, annal. As the words indicate, chronicles (Gr. *chrónos*, time) and annals (L. *annus*, year) are closely related to time and the calendar. It is easiest to think of annals as marginal or interlinear historical notations attached to calendars, and of chronicles as any comprehensive gathering of annals with additions from other sources.

A calendar by nature is a long and narrow list of dates or fixed points of reference, bounded by margins which tempt the owner to insert notices of memorable events. Wherever there are written calendars there is apt to be annalistic writing. Early in the history of pagan Rome annals were inserted in the consular lists, and the Hebrews attached annals to their genealogies (*Chronicles* 9,1; *Nehemiah* 12,23).

The mediæval practice of chronicle-writing developed from the *Chronicon* of Eusebius of Caesarea (d. ca. 340)—a listing in parallel columns of events in the history of the Greeks, Hebrews, Persians, Romans, etc. As translated and extended by Jerome, this became the primary source of historical knowledge for the mediæval reader. Concurrent with the spread of the *Chronicon* was the development of annalistic writing. The liturgical year became the calendar of the West: for every religious foundation, no matter how poverty-stricken, a calendar was a *sine qua non*, and the chronicle became the depository for local records. This calendar contained an annual or solar cycle, giving the days of the year, and an extensive Easter-cycle which generally covered 532 years. On the 1st, anniversaries were noted (holidays and saints-days, seasonal regimen); out of it developed the martyrology. On the 2d, historical events (births and deaths, coronations, appointments, battles, fires, dedications) were noted. The earliest extant entry of this sort is of 501 A.D. The Eng. have left us the earliest vernacular collection in the several compilations which bear the name Anglo-Saxon Chronicle.

As communication expanded after the night of the 6th c., historians gathered together annals from separate libraries, still anchored to the Easter-tables, often appending the material to some form of the Eusebius-Jerome *Chronicon*. Thus the characteristic mediæval chronicle came into being, a form which to a notable extent determined subsequent methods of historical writing.

Some especial qualities of the form result from the method of composition. Because of inherent limitations of space in marginal notations, annalists' language was terse. Because of attachment to the calendar, dates were especially important; for instance, use of the Christian Era by historians developed from the Easter-tables. Since the annalist was usually keeper of the calendar and therefore an astronomer of sorts, astronomical notices (comets, eclipses, etc.) were disproportionately emphasized. Because of the method of notation, the chronicles recorded concrete physical action, especially single and isolated events; no long-range view was possible; and the events of single years or series of years occupied equal space despite their unequal value. Because the annals were designed for local consumption under patronage, they display a local bias; judicial discrimination is not a hallmark of the chronicler. Anglo-Normans, to exalt the deeds of the Norman conquerors, created long works that indiscriminately bore the name of chronicle or history; though occasionally legendary or fictional in content, as with Geoffrey of Monmouth, they adhered to the chronological pattern established. At the same time, Crusaders recorded their experiences in chronicles. From such background developed the late mediæval and Renaissance feeling that a chronicle was a source of romantic gestes. In Sp., *e.g.*, the *Cronica* (13–16 c.) narrate the story of the Cid as well as the antiquities, traditions, and fables of the people.

The mediæval habit of turning any material into verse brought the metrical chronicle into being. None had lasting literary importance, though they may have influenced the chronicle-epics of Warner, Daniel, Drayton, and others in Elizabethan times. In the 1580's the Eng. historical drama or chronicle-play suddenly became widely popular; even with its culmination in Shakespeare, the type is marked by civil warfare, isolated events, and national bias. Raphael Holinshed's *Chronicles of England, Scotland, and Ireland* (1578) greatly influenced Elizabethan drama. Even to the Restoration the pattern of historical thinking, despite wide reading and imitating of classical historians, was largely determined by the form and approach of the mediæval chronicle. Milton's *History of Britain, e.g.*, is a chronological chain of deaths, coronations, and battles, with never a mention of a poet. Even the mediæval chroniclers were seldom that extreme. *See* Autobiography; History.

Reginald Lane Poole, *Chronicles and Annals,* 1926; J. C. McDonald, *Chronologies and Calendars,* 1927; Harry Elmer Barnes, *A Hist. of Historical Writing,* 1937. Charles W. Jones.

chronicle play. Distinguished from a history (in early English drama) as more a succession of episodes than a well-knit story. *E.g.,* Marlowe's *Edward II,* Shakespeare's *King John.* The term was influenced by the popular *Chronicles,* 1578, of Raphael Holinshed, from which many play plots (*Macbeth, King Lear, Cymbeline*) were taken.

chronogram. Writing in which certain letters (in special position or type) form a date in Roman numerals. Listed by Addison as false wit. The initial letters of "My Day Closed Is In Immortality," MDCIII, signify 1603, the year of the death of Queen Elizabeth I. James Hilton published two volumes (1882, 1885) of and on the chronogram.

Ciceronian. Of the style of the Roman orator Marcus Tullius Cicero (160–43 B.C.). His style was long accepted as the standard; some Medieval and Renaissance writers in Latin used no word not found in Cicero. His works are melodious, clear, figurative, and marked by balanced periods; they achieved flexibility and precision. "Ciceronian invective" is powerful yet polished.

Two styles have been labeled anti-Ciceronian: (1) curt: aphoristic, with no syntactic connectives between clauses; (2) loose: informal, with digressions, parentheses, etc. Cicero's influence has been so pervasive that Ciceronian prose (J. W. Mackail, *L. Lit.,* 1923) "is practically the prose of the human race."

cinquain. A lyric form invented by the Am. poet, Adelaide Crapsey (1878–1914). It consists of five iambic lines containing respectively two, four, six, eight, and two syllables. The rigid pattern of 22 syllables was used for the concentration and swift communication of emotion. The form is distinguished by elegance, but tends to be precious. The idea was probably derived from Oriental **poetry,** esp. the Japanese *tanka* and *hokku.* Adelaide Crapsey, *Verse,* 1915; *A Study in Eng. Metrics,* 1918.

circumambages. Methods or devices of periphrasis, *q.v.*

circumlocution. Roundabout speech or expression. Circumlocution office (Dickens, *Little Dorrit*): the typical government bureau, where the red tape is tied in a Gordian knot. *Cf.* Periphrasis.

circumstance, tragedy of. That in which an external force—fate; life's irony—brings undeserved doom.

As flies to wanton boys are we to the gods;
They kill us for their sport. (*Lear* IV,1, 38)

Opposed by F. L. Lucas (*Tragedy,* 1928) to the tragedy of recoil. *See* Tragedy.

clarity. *See* Clearness; Qualities of Expression.

classic. Most commonly, a work that merits lasting interest. Marked by individuality and universality: "always somewhere in the great classic comes the stage direction, often implied: Enter the gods." (F. L. Pattee, "The Shot of Acestes," *Lit. Rev.* Dec. 1, 1923). *See* Distances, the three. For other senses, *see* Classicism.

classical versification. Many of the problems of classical versification rise from failure to distinguish the various approaches, *viz.,* (1) historical, seeking the origin of the meters; (2) descriptive or æsthetic, establishing the nature of a meter or verse-form as given; (3) practical, formulating schemes that will enable us to scan classical verse acceptably.

Ancient writers on metrical questions divide into two groups. The statements of early practitioners (Pindar, Aristophanes, Plato) have high authority, but are generally vague and always fragmentary. The metrical critics (Hephaestion) are full and explicit, and to them we owe much of our terminology; but they are late; and they were not poets but grammarians, whose sense of the realities of poetical effect leaves much to be desired.

Modern critics who have been interested in the historical approach (Schroeder, White, v. Wilamowitz) have tended to revive the ancient metricians and have used their language. Others work on an æsthetic-practical basis. No theory can be said to give a final account of all types of classical verse. Perhaps different principles should be applied in the interpretation of stichic verses (*see stichos*), which were mainly spoken or declaimed (iambic trimeter, dactylic hexameter, etc.) and of melic or lyric stanzas, which were sung. The theory of anacrusis, *e.g.,* is far more acceptable for lyric than for stichic forms; the reverse is true of caesura. Again, the logaoedic (or "musical") theory rests on the assumption that the feet of a given meter are equal in time and, if apparently unequal, must be adjusted by the lengthening or shortening of syllables. But this assumption rests on no clear ancient authority, and tends to break down when applied to iambic or trochaic rhythms, and the term logaoedic has largely been replaced by aeolic, *q.v.* Again, anaclasis, which is self-evident in certain ionic measures of Anacreon (*see* Ionic), leads only to confusion when applied to other types of meter.

The following principles, while mainly negative in bearing, may be of some value:

1. A system which allows free substitution of quantities will produce a verse-reading which at times will be so chaotic as to be useless. "The *ionicus* has so many forms that with Schroeder's *Ionicum maius* — — ◡ ◡, *minus* ◡ ◡ — —, and *medium* — ◡ ◡ —, *syllaba anceps,* and anaclasis, you can make anything out of anything" (Gildersleeve, *AJP* 29, 1908). This objection applies also to the "Æolic" theory (Blass, Schroeder).

2. Certain Latin writers are more strict in their observance of metrical principles than their Gr. models. Horace observes rules ignored by Alcæus and Sappho. Plautus, on the other hand, treats Gr. meters with extraordinary freedom. This suggests that the standards of classical composition vary from age to age and from author to author.

3. Certain classical meters do not submit to the same treatment as the majority; most notably the Saturnian, for which an accentual rather than a quantitative scansion has been urged.

4. The critic must use his own taste and experience in determining a credible procedure for a working poet to follow; but must also be aware of the extremely subjective character of such standards. In this respect, analogies drawn from modern verse must be used with extreme caution.

5. It is not clear how far the major poets of antiquity were aware of the rules which first the ancient, then the modern, critics have deduced from their works. Nor can one always make inferences safely from one poet for another. What passes now as a metrical law may have been dictated by the poet's personal feeling. *An Introd. to the Rhythmic and Metric of the Classical Languages,* trans. from Schmidt's summary of his long work by J. W. White, 1878; J. W. White, *The Verse of Greek Comedy,* 1912; Christ's *Metrik*; D. S. Raven, *Greek Metre,* 1962; P. Maas, *Greek Metre,* trans. 1962; A. M. Dale, *The Lyric Metres of Gr. Drama,* 1968. *See* Quantity; Caesura. RICHMOND LATTIMORE.

classicism. A Latin writer of the 2d c. A.D., Aulus Gellius, in his book *Noctes Atticae* coined the expression *scriptor classicus,* which he opposed to *scriptor proletarius.* Thus the term meant an aristocratic writer, an author for the "happy few," not, as is often fancied, one that is read in the classes, *i.e.,* in the schools. Many centuries later, an erroneous interpretation applied the adjective to an author or work considered worthy of permanent study in the colleges or academies; this meaning was dominant in medieval and Renaissance Latin, from which the word passed to the modern tongues. The humanists considered the Græco-Roman masterpieces the only works worthy of such study; hence the notion that the great authors of Greece and Rome constitute the classics. But thanks to them and in spite of them, national literatures in vulgar tongues produced great works, which in turn were also regarded as classics. From this conception sprang the idea that both ancient and modern classics are such insofar as they have given concrete realization to abstract and supreme ideals of beauty, to eternal standards of proportion and perfection. This idea, of both rationalistic and metaphysical content, grew slowly but surely from the Renaissance to the threshold of Romanticism; it is alive even now in Babbitt's definition: "classical is everything that is representative of a class." Here is the second false interpretation of the etymology of "classical," for Babbitt uses the word "class" in the philosophical sense of "category," *i.e.*, a metaphysical (or transcendent) entity that represents the generalization of a series of events or group of specific things.

If we accept this last viewpoint, Greek literature alone is truly classical; for Greece created, in concrete works, the abstract and rational standards of æsthetic perfection that Rome followed and left in legacy to the literature of later times. But the fact that Greece produced these works and created these standards not by following preceding models but by obeying her own cultural experience, gives substance to the claim of German Romanticists that Greek literature was the national, original manifestation of the Hellenic spirit, while both Latin and modern classicism were based on imitation of Greek models: therefore Greek literature is not classical in the sense of Latin, Renaissance, or French classicism.

The turning point in the concept of the classical occurs when its standards are applied to writing not only in Greek and Latin, but also in the vulgar tongues. Despite the new classics, however, it was felt that literature in the vulgar tongue lacked the noble creations of Greece and Rome: didactic and pastoral poetry, comedy and satire, especially tragedy and the epic. The codification of Boccaccio and Petrarch was *a posteriori;* new standards were now set *a priori.* Thus, oblivious of Ariosto's chivalric romance, Trissino proclaimed for the moderns the rules of the classical epic; equally scornful of the Christian drama, he elaborated the canons of classical tragedy (though Ariosto himself had earlier provided the first regular comedies, modeled on Plautus and Terence). Castelvetro and others gave diffusion to the *Poetics* of Aristotle, read by few, discussed by many, misunderstood by all. As a result, Italian Renaissance literature assumed the magnificent but dangerous role of "the classical literature in the vulgar tongue."

In the 17th c., this role was inherited by France. But whereas the Italians had emphasized the Latin authors, the French concentrated their attention on the Greeks. Racine wanted to be not a modern Seneca, but a modern Sophocles; even the most Latinizing writer of the time, Boileau, not only imitated Horace's *Ars Poetica* but translated the Pseudo-Longinus Gr. treatise *On the Sublime.* With the partial exceptions of Corneille and Molière, the French Golden Age is marked by its sense that it is the only literature worthy of Greece and the classical ideal, and by a consequent scorn of other modern literatures (*e.g.,* Boileau's disparaging remarks on the Italians and the Spaniards).

As for England, Shakespeare has been for too long considered both a "barbarian of genius" and a banner of Romanticism for the attribution of academic labels to his age. But even in Shakespeare's time there is an aspect of classicism, if this word implies the theory or practice of imitation, though the models were mainly (except for Francis Bacon and Ben Jonson) classics in the vulgar tongue, producing the Elizabethan Petrarchism and the Italianate Englishman. This was, however, more a pervasive mode than a concrete literary pattern, hence hardly of the classical type. But the greatest epoch of Spanish literature is called the Classical Age. Here again, however, Italianism is stronger than Latin or Greek influence; and the national spirit stronger still. The linguistic theories of the Italian Renaissance led to *culteranismo;* but the Cervantes of the *Quixote,* and Lope de Vega and Calderón, like Shakespeare and Molière, created in freedom from such bonds; wherefore this period of Spanish literature has also been characterized as romantic, each misnomer indicating the insufficiency of the other.

The center of interest for the French literature of the 18th c. was thought; it is the age of the Enlightenment and the Encyclopædia; its writers were not artists, but *philosophes;* while in the purely literary and æsthetic fields, the classical ideal became so conventionalized and frigid that it is labeled pseudo-classicism. This influence spread over Europe. In England, Dryden and Pope succeed Shakespeare and Milton. In Spain, Germany, Italy, flock the mediocre followers of this literature of France. There are many *artes poeticæ* in the spirit of Horace and Boileau: Gravina's *Ragion Poetica,* Pope's *Essay on Criticism,* Luzán's *Poetica,* Gottsched's *Versuch einer kritischen Dichtkunst.* Even Lessing's *Laokoön* is but the last, though the most intelligent, of the type. German literary historians call Gottsched's age pseudoclassical, a transplantation of French classicism; but the following epoch, of Schiller and Goethe, they consider a classical age in its own right. They evidently use the term because of the distinction that, traditionally but arbitrarily, it confers. But the formula and its implications are dangerous, because the Goethe-Schiller generation is in immediate contact with the first generation of Romanticism, which hailed the two great old men as its own masters. Thus non-German literary historians, following a tradition that begins with Mme. de Staël, label them romantics. But between *Sturm und Drang* and romanticism there sprang forth in Germany a movement that swept over Europe, triumphing in the epoch of the French Empire. Its center was no longer literature, but rather the plastic arts, especially architecture and sculpture; in the field of the applied arts and fashion, it was named *style empire.* Its theorist was Winckelmann; its greatest artist, Canova; its Maecenas, Napoleon. This is neoclassicism proper. Specific imitation of the models of the past, though more significant than in 17th c. pseudoclassicism, is not paramount; rather, the extreme elaboration of classicism considered as the quest of and obedience to the abstract standards, intellectual and spiritual, of Beauty. Sentimental, even mystical, elements loom large in Winckelmann; in concordance with these factors, both Christian and Platonic, neoclassicism appears as a religion of form, as a plastic idealism. Although the romantic potentialities of such an attitude are evident, it belongs to the classical tradition.

It is to the romantics that we owe a better understanding of the classical idea. At first, they regarded classicism and romanticism not as fluid historical concepts, but as permanent attitudes, or inflexible categories of the mind. But they understood that there were deep spiritual differences between the civilizations that had produced a Boileau, a Racine; and a Shakespeare, a Calderón. Though some of them objected strongly even to Greek literature, others saw that all the ancient works could not be grouped under the one label, to them derogatory, of classicism; that the Greek was largely of a different order from the Latin. In addition to these discoveries, and beyond all their errors, the romantics gave us a key to the unifying concept or rather the common basis of so many and such different applications of the term classic. Romantic æsthetics strongly and consistently affirms that art, poetry, is an independent creation, an autonomous activity, fresh and original. In this light, it may be said that the classical ages are those in which (regardless of their products) there was dominant the æsthetic belief that art is produced by imitating concrete works of great masters or by equating one's work to an abstract ideal of rational beauty.

Thus considered, despite its evident romantic tendencies, neoclassicism is but the last manifestation of the classical idea. After it, the æsthetics of originality triumphed everywhere; hence romantic Hellenism is but an aspect of romanticism, not a classical revival. It is vain to ask whether Chénier and Hölderlin, Foscolo and Leopardi, Shelley and Keats, or more recent poets with the same sympathy for the ancient world, are romantic or classical: even if they continue to share surviving classical beliefs, the air they breathe is new. As Chénier said for them all: *Sur des pensers nouveaux faisons des vers antiques.* (By *pensers nouveaux* he meant not so much new ideas as a new sensibility.)

Romanticism also quickened the historical approach, which makes it clear that a categorical definition of classicism is unattainable, since it is neither a noumenon nor a single phenomenon, but a series of phenomena, which are realized differently according to various historical attitudes. The term, however, has had for certain writers so pleasing a connotation (Goethe: "we may call the classic healthy; the romantic, diseased") that they would reserve it for the great periods of their literature, allowing it, *e.g.,* to Racine, with but grudging "pseudoclassical" to Voltaire or Delille. Such cultural prejudice, such injection of a judgment of value into the term, has created further confusion and contradiction, as when in French literary terminology, the classical age precedes the pseudoclassical, whereas in Germany the order is reversed.

Looking back over the various applications of the term classical, we note that the first, denoting an art or a literature for the upper classes, disappeared almost immediately, and is therefore of little present concern. The second meaning, the pedagogical one, according to which the classics are the authors worthy of lasting interest and study, survives in modern use, but in a purely practical or technical application. The important misunderstanding to avoid in this case is supposing that such a classic is necessarily classicist. The third use, the commonest, in which classical means Græco-Roman, need not be confusing if we remember that Greece produced a classical culture only in the terminology of later times. The fourth meaning, which extends the concept to ages that produced a literature worthy of the ancients, opens the way to misunderstanding. Originally applied to works imitating the ancients, it has been used of any great work, even contrary to its spirit or form. And it generates (the fifth sense) an even more troubling concept, that of permanent and absolute standards of literary perfection, attained only by certain periods, which are thus the truly classical ages. This conception is only the rationalization of the theory of imitation. Classicism, thus, must be understood not as a philosophical or psychological concept, but an historical one. It refers to the lengthy series of æsthetic principles drawn from or imitated in the Greek literature, logically almost identical and historically continuously subjected to new interpretations that Western æsthetic and literary thought has repeated through a tradition of some 2,000 years, from Hellenistic Alexandria to the Frenchified Europe of the 18th c. With the partial exception of the middle ages, and of the Spanish and English 17th c., it includes the entire history of western culture, with the significant exclusion of the ancient Greeks and ourselves. Athens (spontaneous and before standards) was pre-classic; romanticism (reestablishing spontaneity and destroying standards) begins the post-classic period. But each classical period, and each classic emphasis that despite its denial persists, must be examined for its especial qualification of the general historical term.

Sainte-Beuve, *Qu'est-ce qu'un Classique?* 1860; H. J. C. Grierson, *Classical and Romantic,* 1923; J. Körner, *Romantiker und Klassiker,* 1924; L. P. Smith, *Four Words,* 1924; H. P. Collins, "Notes on the Classical Principle in Poetry," *Criterion,* April 1925; W. Folkierski, *Entre le Classicisme et le Romantisme,* 1925; A. Guérard, *The Life and Death of an Ideal,* 1928; Ship; H. Peyre, *Qu'est-ce que le Classicisme?,* 1933, 1965; Gilbert Highet, *The Classical Tradition,* 1949, 1953; R. R. Bolgar, *The Classical Heritage . . . ,* 1964; Ed. P. Corbett, *Classical Rhetoric,* 1965; G. Seferis, *On the Gr. Style,* 1966.
Renato Poggioli.

classification, literary. Literary phenomena, like all other phenomena, can be classified or arranged in groups according to their similarities and differences. The purpose of the careful examination of literary works and processes, which is a large part of the critic's business, is to disengage and note specific elements or characteristics of those things. Some of these elements are unique in the single work or process; some reappear in others. To note that a given element appears in more than one work or process, and to group together the works or processes in which this element appears, is to distinguish a class. Some modern critics and philosophers, notably B. Croce and his followers, argue that the whole essence of a work of art is inevitably individual and unique; hence apprehension of it can produce no concept, and therefore, no truly logical class; and works of art, being entirely unique, individually exhaust the classes of which they would be specimens, so that no two can possibly belong to the same class; and thus, class and individual being one, there are as many classes as individuals, and the idea of a class is superfluous and absurd. The objection is actually not that one cannot observe similarities and differences in artistic as in other objects, but that in artistic objects the elements which are not unique, *i.e.,* those upon which classifications are founded, are inessential and so irrelevant for criticism. To this the obvious reply is that for a complete criticism no aspect of the object is irrelevant. What is unique in a work of art may indeed be what is most significant and valuable in it, and most important for the critic to seize and indicate; but its indication is not the critic's only task. To note what is not unique, and that it is not, is in itself a legitimate task, and a necessary and often crucial part of the complete description of an object; and to classify objects according to common qualities is a natural and inevitable operation of the mind in knowing, an operation that requires no ulterior justification. But if justification were needed, it is to be found in the fact that to note what is not unique in a thing or an experience is one way of arriving at a clear perception of what is. Croce and most of his followers, while denying the general philosophical validity of the notion of "kinds" of literature, acknowledge the "convenience" of classes conceived as loose unphilosophical assortments of superficially related phenomena. The compromising implications of this admission are plain; for the Crocean theory provides no means of accounting for this convenience, which is not logically disposed of by the condescending treatment it gets from Crocean hands. Actually, classifications are convenient because it is helpful and necessary to include within the process of criticism operations that are excluded from it by the æsthetics of extreme expressionism. The fact that these operations have often been badly performed—that definitions of general literary concepts have been unsatisfactory, or that from false or inadequate concepts there have been drawn unwarranted precepts for practise or norms for judgment—does not justify a general assertion of their uselessness or eternal impossibility. Such assertions imply a false, mechanical notion of the traditional distinction between the general and the individual. Distortion results not from seeing the genera, but from mistaking the genera one sees; *e.g.,* from mistaking a work of art for a personality. A song of Shakespeare or Campion does not seem less the song it is because we know it is a song. Since it is a song, it could not be whatever it in fact most individually is without being a song; and if the fact that it is a song escapes us, we do not fully know it as it actually is.

Literary works can be classified according to four basic principles (which correspond to the four "causes" of Aristotle; *see* Form), *viz.,* (1) the agent or agencies that produce them, (2) the end for which they are produced, (3) the material out of which they are produced, and (4) the characteristics that analysis discovers in them as objects. [A single classification may of course involve application of more than one of these principles, as in description of poetry as produced, *e.g.,* (1) by an inspired madman, (2) for the purpose of delighting, (3) of poetic language or diction, (4) in verse, etc. Confusion often results from combination of the principles without awareness of their difference; *e.g.,* the discrimination of "four forms of discourse" seems to arise from an awkward blend of distinctions as to ends with distinctions as to certain formal characteristics of compositions (*see* Composition).]

(1) Applying the first of these principles (that of the agent or producer; Aristotle's *efficient* cause), we group together all the works of a single author, and distinguish further classes among these as we observe variation in the author from period to period in his career; so too we may group together all the works of all the authors of a single period or place, or of all who felt a common influence or belonged to the same "school," etc.

(2) The end or purpose for which a work is produced (Aristotle's *final* cause) provides a principle of classification more objective than that of the productive agency; according to such a principle the ancients divided the whole field of rhetorical composition into (a) contemplative or deliberative, (b) juridic or judicial, and (c) epideictic or demonstrative (Aristotle, *Rhet.,* 1, 3), and to this principle they related their distinctions among the "characters" of style, as each conformed to a specific end (usually a plain style to inform, a grand to move, a "middle" to delight; Cicero, *Orator,* 76-112; St. Augustine, *Doctr. christ.,* 4, 34). Modern distinctions between propaganda and literature of "escape," *e.g.,* are of this kind. (3) The immediate material out of which a literary work is made (Aristotle's *matter* or material cause), *viz.,* its language, naturally provides the most obvious and the least differentiating of classifications, *e.g.,* that by which we distinguish writing in French from writing in English (as we distinguish sculpture in marble from sculpture in wood). But, though the distinction between two languages is, from the point of view of the literature produced in them, a distinction as to material, yet the difference between literature in French and literature in English is not wholly a material difference. Since both languages are conventional constructs, and both are constructed of the same sounds, the difference between them consists in the different forms the two peoples have given the sound by selection and structure, and these forms appear as characteristic though minor elements in literary works.

(4) The more significant of such characteristic elements in the object as such (Aristotle's *forms* or formal causes) provide the most important principle for literary classification, and much the most objective and useful, since in fact our awareness of the others is largely derived from our knowledge of aspects of artistic works simply as objects in which we can differentiate one element from another. These formal or characteristic elements in a literary object may themselves be classified as either structures (of sound or of meaning) or meanings, and according to their foundation upon one or another of these and their combination of them we may group the literary classes that result from discrimination among such elements in literary works. Of distinctions founded on difference in *structure of sound* as such, the chief is that which divides all literature into (a) *verse* and (b) *prose,* as relatively more or less highly patterned phonetically. Distinctions founded on differences in *meaning* and *struc-*

ture of meaning are more complex. Here however a line may be drawn between (A) the classes that distinguish the most general *forms* of literature and (B) those that distinguish what are usually referred to as *genres.* (A) The classification of the general literary *forms,* (a) expository, *e.g.,* essay; (b) narrative, *e.g.,* novel; and (c) dramatic, *e.g.,* play, dialogue, is based on a combination of distinctions as to kinds of reference to objects (the dynamic reference of story to event, the static reference of discourse to idea) with structural distinction as to voice and modes of address (*see* Narrator). (B) The classification of the *genres* is wholly concerned with the nature, not at all with the structure, of the meanings in a work, the *genre* of which is determined by the kind of object (*i.e.,* the "subject") referred to (shepherds, etc., in *pastoral,* heroes in *epic,* the marvelous in *romance*), or by the subjective mood or attitude (*satiric, comic,* etc.) taken toward the object, or by both of these (as in the *tragic,* where objective calamity and seriousness of mood are equally required). It is an advantage to keep these two types of classification apart and, though we fuse the two in speaking, *e.g.,* of a *tragedy,* to remember that what is meant is a work the form of which is dramatic, the genre tragic; thus we provide, as logic demands, for clear reference to a work the form of which is *not* dramatic (*e.g.,* a novel) but the genre of which is equally tragic. There are only 3 basic types of literary *form;* there are as many *genres* as there are "subjects" to which literary works can refer and attitudes which may inform their reference—and adjectives by which a Polonius may refer to them.

One other common literary classification requires mention here, that which divides *oral* from *written* "literature." This is founded on a distinction as to the process, not of composition, but of transmission of literary works; the distinction becomes important in the many cases in which the composition, and so the characteristic form, of a work is affected by the fact that it is to be transmitted by one means rather than the other, as in ballads or traditional epics. (This distinction is sometimes related to another drawn between *folk*-literature and literature of *art;* but the latter is now generally avoided as unscientific, since so far as it means anything concrete it is identical with the distinction between oral and written literature. Scientific distinction between a literature of the people and other literature will not deny art to the former. Distinction between communal and individual composition is of course a simple distinction of agents.) For the distinction between *poetry* and *prose, see* Poetry and prose.

M. Cohen and E. Nagel, *Introd. to logic and scientific method,* 1934; P. Coffey, *Science of logic,* 1912, I, 112–134; W. P. Ker, *Form and style,* 1928, 104 f., 146 f.; R. K. Hack, *Harvard studies in cl. phil.,* XXVII (1916), 1 f.; D. A. G. Hinks, *CQ* XXX (1936), 170 f.; A. Warren, *Theories of genres from the Ren. to the present.* JAMES CRAIG LADRIÈRE.

clearness. Lucidity of expression, so that the meaning and mood may be readily understood. First of the three essential qualities (*q.v.*) of expression. It may be due to (1) grammatical construction; (2) correspondence with fact; (3) logical ordering (esp. in 18th c.); (4) graphic imagery (esp. in 19th c.). The man that sarcastically observes: "I can only give you the facts, but not the intelligence to grasp them" should recognize that it is not always easy to give "the facts" clearly. The famous French clarity is the product of a long process, traced by Daniel Mornet in *Hist. de la clarté fr.,* 1929. Also, one must distinguish between a clear but potent liquid and a clear but empty glass. *Cf.* Simplicity; Ambiguity; Obscurity.

clef. *See Livre à clef.*

clench. A play on words, a quibble. Used from the 17th to the mid-19th c. Dryden (1668) said of Shakespeare: "He is many times flat, his comic wit degenerating into clenches, his serious swelling into bombast." A clencher (clincher) is a statement that settles a point being argued. *Cf.* Wit.

clerihew. A four-line, blunt, irregular stanza, used for humorous characterization. Said to have been originated by Edmund Clerihew Bentley (Eng., 1875–1956; *Biography for Beginners,* 1905; *Baseless Biography,* 1939) during the dull moments of a chemistry class:

> Sir Humphry Davy
> Abominated gravy.
> He lived in the odium
> Of having discovered sodium.

Fashioning clerihews, as a parlor game, has joined bouts-rimés, limericks, and double-dactyls, *q.v.*

climax. (1) The presentation of ideas or events in ascending order of importance, least first. Now generally used to refer to the highest or culminating point of this series. *Cf.* Gradation. (2) In a play or story, the act or moment of action that determines the reversal; the decisive moment in the dramatic conflict. In the 5-act play, it usually occurs near the end of Act III, *e.g.,* the play scene in *Hamlet.* In Shaw's *Saint Joan,* the Inquisition scene. In the novel, *e.g.,* the confession episode, ch. 34, Hardy's *Tess.* The term, applied to such scenes, bears the implication that what follows is anticlimactic, as indeed it sometimes is, even in Shakespeare. But a subdued or low-toned denouement is sometimes intended, with a rhythm of rising and falling excitement, which need not involve a slackening of interest before the final curtain. Impatience of reader and audience has helped to shorten this "falling action" (esp. since the advent of the motion picture); the current three- or two-act play form permits a growing emotional tension to the very end. Once the decisive moment—the climax—is past, the struggle is over, and so is the story. Application of the term "climax" to an earlier moment is thus historical, save when a work is described as presenting a series of minor climaxes, with the "main climax" at the close. Such a pattern distinguishes the episodic (epic) from the dramatic form. *Cf.* Freytag's pyramid; Tragedy; Drama. W. Archer, *Playmaking,* 1912; G. P. Baker, *Dramatic Technique,* 1919.

closed couplet. A set of two metrical lines, usually rhyming, in which the sense (and grammar) ends with the second line. Common in the heroic couplet, esp. in Pope, *e.g.:*

Know then thyself, presume not God to scan,
The proper study of mankind is man . . .
Sole judge of truth, in endless error hurled,
The glory, jest, and riddle of the world!

closet drama (often derogatory). A play or dramatic poem written for reading, not performance. A loose expression, for many plays written to be produced failed in performance but are read as literature (Shelley's *Prometheus Unbound*); while others not written primarily for stage presentation (Ibsen's *Peer Gynt*) have been theatrically effective.

clou (Fr., peg). A situation upon which the remainder of a story hangs—or upon which the receptor hangs with bated breath. Loosely applied to the climax or the generating circumstance.

cockney rhymes. False rhymes, as due to the London pronunciation, *e.g.,* (Keats) grass, farce; weakened, spike-end.

coherence. The logical interrelation of successive parts, so that a work holds together as a unit. Often linked with unity and emphasis as the basic qualities of a composition. *Cf.* Qualities; Rhetoric; Transition.

coincidence. Concurrence without apparent connection. "The long arm of coincidence" is a term applied to the seemingly artificial tying together of persons or events in a story, usually to effect an ending. (Dickens prepares for the ending of his *Tale of Two Cities* by placing early in the story the coincidence of the likeness of Darnay and Carton.) Coincidence makes the possible do service for the likely; Aristotle condemned this, preferring the probable-impossible to the improbable-possible. While the ends of Shakespeare's tragedies may be inevitable, the means are often coincidental: the dropped handkerchief is pat for Iago's plotting (*Othello*); the delayed friar (*Romeo and Juliet*); the exchange of swords in *Hamlet.* The phrase has special relevance to 19th c. melodrama, farce, and fiction, where the ending often involves the reunion of long separated kin, or the readjusting of a confused pair (*Box and Cox;* Mark Twain, *The Prince and the Pauper*), identified by a "strawberry mark," an amulet, an old nurse, or (*Pudd'nhead Wilson*) a fingerprint. Parodied by Gilbert in *H.M.S. Pinafore* and *The Gondoliers. Cf.* Fate, finger of.

colloquial. *See* Slang.

colloquy. (L., speaking together). A dialogue; an informal discussion, meeting, a colloquium. Sometimes a title, as the *Colloquies* (ca. 1520) of Erasmus and of Southey (1829). *See* Dialogue.

color. Term borrowed from the visual arts, in several literary applications. (1) Eliz. Figurative use of a word, or the expression so used. *See* Rhetoric. (2) Vividness, esp. through imagery, as in the early romantics. (3) bias; exaggeration; as though looking through glasses tinted by a special point of view. (4) local color. Details of the scene; emphasis on the environment, either to enrich the background of a story, or as a pervasive atmosphere, or as a determinant of the action (Poe; Kipling). Always essential, to provide solid ground on which the characters can move; in some stories this becomes the dominant aspect. (5) color and sound. Psychologists and the symbolists (*q.v.*) have in various ways interlinked the senses, esp. color and sound. *See* Correspondence of the arts.

comedia de capa y espada. Sp. comedy of mantle (cape, cloak) and sword, prototype of the Sp. classical mixed play, fostered by Lope de Vega, in which cavaliers have love-affairs with noble ladies, fight duels for them, and make an idol of Honor, so that they often are obliged to kill their innocent wives in order to wipe out even the slightest suspicion of a smudge upon the family escutcheon (*pundonor*). A special kind of gallantry, taste for adventure, grace, elegance, wit of servants, spirited tricks of beautiful veiled women, make the atmosphere of these plays unique.

comédie. Formerly used in Fr. in a more general sense than to indicate a *comic* play. It might apply to a serious portrayal of manners and customs not cast in the form of classical *tragédie*. Thus Diderot's *Le Père de famille* (1758), though what is now called a bourgeois *drame,* bears the subtitle *comédie*.

comédie de moeurs (Fr., comedy of manners *q.v.*). Applied to the problem play (A. Dumas fils, *La Dame aux camélias,* 1852), from which grew the more realistically presented thesis play, as E. Brieux' *Les Avariés,* trans. *Damaged Goods* (1901).

comédie larmoyante. Fr. The tearful and sentimental drama strongly influenced by the growing importance of the middle class (and Richardson's novels from Eng.) and best represented by Nivelle de la Chausée (*Fausse antipathie,* 1733) and Diderot in Fr. and Gellert (*Die zärtlichen Schwestern,* 1747) in G. It led (Lessing, *Miss Sara Simpson,* 1755) to the bourgeois or middle-class drama.

comedy. I. NON-DRAMATIC. A work of less exalted style than a tragedy, and usually with a happy ending. Dante's poem, the *Comedy* (later called *Divine*); Balzac's novels, grouped as *La Comédie humaine*. II. DRAMATIC. According to Aristotle, comedy deals with "some defect or ugliness that is not painful or destructive"; it pictures men worse than the average, and is thus distinguished from tragedy, which portrays the sufferings of men better than those in actual life. Comedy emphasizes intelligence and judgment, although sympathy is not excluded from its range. Its characters may be drawn from observation and experience, but they are the result of the generalizing faculty rather than the individualizing one. For this reason the characters in comedy tend to be realistic in externals, but in essence to become types or even caricatures of actual human beings. They may be stupid, and ridiculous, as in low comedy. This often verges on satire, when the absurdity of dullness or the no less flagrant absurdity of superficial brilliance predominates over the simplicity of natural human emotions.

Emotions generate a driving power that stimulates action; comedy, on the other hand, is often comparatively static in quality, placing little reliance upon the complications of plot. On the lowest physical level its plots are farcical, filled with horseplay; misunderstandings, mistaken identity, often figure prominently in them; romantic complications are sometimes introduced to give body to the narrative; at their most sophisticated they are concerned with clashes of personality rather than with obvious external action. In any case the plot of a comedy is usually a thread on which to hang a number of diverting incidents that illustrate the varieties of human weakness observed with dry detachment. With all its ribaldry and gaiety, a good comedy penetrates deeply into the roots of human nature, makes the observer intensely aware of man's possibilities as well as of his limitations. Comedy is frequently marked by both cheerfulness and seriousness; it is not mere entertainment, but reinvigoration, even rebirth.

Like tragedy, comedy is probably religious in origin. Its name seems to come from the song at a village festival in honor of Dionysus, the god of fruitfulness. It was sung by an organized group of revellers (the *comos*), which replied to the mockery of the bystanders. The give and take of argument, often abusive of specific individuals in the crowd, was resolved into a unified pæan of praise to the god. A feast was then held in honor of the reconciliation, in which wine, women, and song took their appropriate parts. The whole activity was a tribute to the physical universe from people glad to be alive; the joy of living was merged with thankfulness to the creative power in a union of the sexes, which would itself beget new life. Zest and eagerness were the order of the day; death and its terrors were forgotten. The outlines of this ritual can be clearly discerned in the earliest literary comedy of the Greeks. The 11 existing plays of Aristophanes (425–388 B.C.) make up the corpus of the so-called Old Comedy with its magisterial chorus and its personal invective. Aristophanes attacked the institutions and individuals of which he disapproved because he felt that they were antagonistic to the best ideals of human society. He made fun of local wars, of degenerate city life, of an excessive love for lawsuits, of a pretentious communistic theory. He attacked Cleon the demagogue, Socrates the sophist, Euripides the romanticist, ridiculing them as well as their ideas. The objects of Aristophanes' indignation are all defeated and dismissed with ignominy, to the satisfaction of the better elements in society represented by the Chorus. The *Birds* is perhaps Aristophanes' greatest comedy, because it rises above private considerations without losing the concentrated power that comes from a vitriolic denunciation of particular evils.

The plays of Aristophanes that follow the *Birds* tend to become more general in their attack and less vigorous in their texture. They mark the significant change that came over comedy when the Chorus, the manifestation of the divine will, receded into the background and specific individuals ceased to be as important as abstract issues. The last of Aristophanes' comedies, the *Plutus,* is concerned with the subject of wealth and poverty, which appear as concrete characters in the play. The fact that Plutus is a god connects this play with religious ritual, but the fact that he represents the physical distribution of material property brings him from the sphere of divinity to that of all too human wisdom.

This degradation of the gods must have been characteristic of Middle Comedy, no pure examples of which have come down to us, but of which we can obtain a fairly good idea from the *Amphitryon* of the Latin playwright Plautus. Here Jupiter and Mercury indulge in a series of undignified love adventures that result in the begetting of Hercules, the demi-god. The legendary world combining the activities of gods and men seems to have been the normal sphere of Middle Comedy, just as New Comedy devoted itself to the relations between fallible human beings. With one set of them, including hero and heroine, the dramatists are inclined to sympathize, the final union of male and female providing a refined equivalent of the phallic element in more primitive comedy. Such appears to have been the source of the convention of the happy ending, the orgy of the original wedding feast giving way to the milder and more civilized ceremony of a betrothal. Still there persists the idea that the principle of life is sacred and must be properly reverenced. The joining of the hands of young people causes universal rejoicing; its use here foreshadows the indiscriminate marrying and giving in marriage that later characterizes the close of a traditional comedy.

The earliest plays we know built around this formula are the dramatic fragments of Menander, written presumably about 300 B.C. In them, and still more in the Latin plays imitated from them, are presented difficulties besetting the path of young people held in the power of romantic love. The 20 extant comedies by Plautus and the 6 by Terence (214–160 B.C.) all use this thread of plot as an excuse on which to hang pictures of the absurdities of contemporary life. The scene of these plays is always a public street, usually surrounded by the houses of the principal characters. Very little is ordinarily seen of the heroines, because respectable young women were not permitted to mingle freely in the life of the outside world; sometimes this technical difficulty is overcome by having the heroine appear as a slave-girl, real or supposed. The efforts of the hero to secure the young lady's affection and person, with or without benefit of marriage, provide the core of the play and serve as an excuse to bring on the stage a number of contrasting types. The opponents of the lovers most frequently portrayed are: the wealthy rival, sometimes in the form of the *miles gloriosus* or boasting soldier; the *leno* or slave-merchant, who may own the young lady in question, and acts as a procurer for his own selfish interests; the old parents of the young people with their minds more devoted to practical considerations than to romantic love. The lovers are commonly aided by a wily slave or parasite; in the end, in spite of powerful opposition, they are united by the combined forces of ingenuity and good intentions.

Plautus is more rigid than Terence in handling these stock characters, who appear under a multitude of shapes, but with a marked similarity of execution, in the work of both dramatists. Plautus' humor is lusty and unrestrained, his standards of conduct are precise, his judgment is sane but sometimes ruthless. Terence, author of the famous line, "I am a man; I consider nothing human foreign to me," was more kindly and sympathetic. At his best, as in the comedy of the *Brothers,* he successfully combines understanding and judgment. The two brothers, of whom one favors a strict upbringing for children, while the other is all for tolerance and lack of discipline, are by the end of the comedy both proved to have been foolish in their extreme ideas. The spirit of classic comedy, whether Greek or Roman, Old or New, tends to take a definite philosophic position, subordinating the good of the individual to the good of the community in which he lives. The motto "nothing too much," dominant in Greek thought, gave a quality of intellectual firmness to social comedy, which, although often greatly modified, has never been entirely lost.

After the fall of the Roman Empire this standard was applied in many different civilizations, widely separated by space and time. Comedies of various sorts present various interpretations of the same underlying principle: in India, in the 5th or 6th c. A.D., under the influence of the Buddhistic doctrine of *nirvana,* it produced the delicately poetic *Shakuntala* of Kalidasa; in medieval Europe, in the 14th and 15th c., it combined with Jewish and Christian legends in the naïve and sometimes boisterous Miracle Plays; in Italy, in the 15th and 16th centuries, it became an active part of the Renaissance movement with the ribald comedies of Ariosto and Machiavelli, of Aretino and Giordano Bruno. These Italian writers were affected by the literary revival of learning and also by the *commedia dell'arte* tradition of the popular stage. The characters of Harlequin and Columbine, Pantaloon and the Doctor, were debased versions of the humorous types in classical drama, to fit the irregular improvised comedy flourishing in Italy during the early Renaissance. They are a sign that the Greek and Roman writers had found a formula for social comedy that fulfilled the continual demands of human nature for artistic experience. Like the ludicrous Vice of the Morality Plays, they were absorbed in a new kind of drama which arose in the modern world dominated by scientific discovery and organization.

The development of comedy in England is a particularly striking example of how the diverse elements in drama were reworked and fused into an altered pattern. The secularization of the theater, begun when the religious Miracle Plays were transformed into the more worldly Moralities, was continued with the frankly earthy Interludes written by John Heywood and others at the court of Henry VIII. The rediscovery of Plautus resulted in imitations (*Ralph Roister Doister*) and modifications (*Gammer Gurton's Needle*) of classical comedy in the reigns of Edward VI and Queen Mary. The Elizabethan flowering of this form came with the court comedies of John Lyly, the fanciful romances of Robert Greene, and the infinite variety of Shakespeare's creativeness. In his early days the master wrote a farcical comedy on the classic model, *The Comedy of Errors*; a sophisticated study of the relation between the sexes, *Love's Labour's Lost*; and a moving story of emotional confusion, capped by a somewhat artificial happy ending, *The Two Gentlemen of Verona.* In his maturer work he deepened and enriched these three facets of his comic genius, respectively in *Twelfth Night, Much Ado About Nothing,* and *As You Like It.* Between these two sets of plays he had created the titanic figure of Falstaff, in whose person he embodied the comic joy of life, both physical and intellectual, and in whose pathetic death he set forth the limitations of an unmoral vitality. Shakespeare could not continue his work indefinitely upon the plane of comedy, because he felt too intensely the deeper strands in human nature, which he wove into the great tragedies that crown his career; in his last plays he sublimated the tragic moods and created philosophical tragicomedies like *The Winter's Tale* and *The Tempest,* packed with thoughts that often lie too deep for tears.

The problem of the relationship between comedy and tragedy became active with the breaking down of formal classic categories. Romantic comedy was the evidence that the modern world was not to be confined within the strict limits set by logical consistency. During the period in which the Elizabethans were struggling with the enlargement of the dramatic fabric to include the varied elements of human experience in a single play, a somewhat similar process was going on in the Spanish peninsula. There Lope de Vega and Calderón combined medieval chivalry with a realistic awareness of practical life in the innumerable and diverse comedies which seemed to flow inexhaustibly from their pens. Tirso de Molina gave the world the character of Don Juan, profligate and libertine, who ends by going the primrose way to the everlasting bonfire, and Calderón in *Life is a Dream* approached the Shakespearean conclusion, "We are such stuff as dreams are made on." Yet among these poetic and almost tragic renderings of human existence, there is to be found the shrewd and greedy servant, known here as the *gracioso,* who never lets one forget that man has a stomach and a body as well as an imagination and a soul. The aspiring idealism and the materialism of Spanish comedy present in effective contrast the contradictory strains that run through the spirit and history of Spain.

The logical French nation succeeded in keeping comedy well within its proper bounds, although the greatest of French comic dramatists, in the 17th c., Jean Baptiste Poquelin (Molière) greatly enlarged the comic domain. He wrote light farces and *comédie-ballets,* social satires and philosophical dramas, among the 22 distinguished comedies that he composed from 1659 to 1673. Beginning with a critical attitude towards the society dominated by ridiculous *précieuses,* he went on to consider the subjects of marriage, religious hypocrisy, and social classification. His plays often present a *raisonneur,* who expounds the rational point of view on the subject under discussion, and generally a deluded, bewildered central figure, acted by Molière and infused with the bitterness of his own personal experience. Like Arnolphe in *The School for Wives,* Molière was inclined to suspicion and jealousy; like Alceste in *The Misanthrope,* he realized his intellectual superiority to the people that surrounded him; like M. Jourdain, the *bourgeois gentilhomme,* he was a victim of the caste system at the court of Louis XIV. In each of these cases, and in many more, Molière realized how absurdly he was prone to deviate from the golden mean of which he approved but which his human weaknesses made it impossible for him to approximate. "Perfect intelligence avoids all excess and counsels that one should be wise with moderation," says Philinte in *The Misanthrope,* but Alceste knows that passion, not intelligence, is the dominating element in human life.

Molière set the standard for social comedy in the late 17th and early 18th c. The English dramatists of the Restoration, Etherege and Wycherley, Congreve and Vanbrugh, moved in his direction when they softened Ben Jonson's comedy of humours, or human foibles, into the comedy of manners, or social deportment; the father of Danish comedy, Ludwig Holberg, adapted Molière's formula to changing social conditions in his country, where French culture was just beginning to make itself felt; in France itself, Regnard wrote comedies more superficial than those of Molière, and Le Sage wrote comedies more brittle than those of Regnard. Marivaux kept the external form of the comedy of common sense, but he added to it a subtle analysis of human feelings, which paved the way for the sentimental comedy that triumphed throughout Europe in the second half of the 18th c. A rising belief in the perfectibility of man, which indicated a revolt against rationalism and heralded the French Revolution, permeates the comic plays of Goldoni in Italy and Lessing in Germany. Beaumarchais in France and Goldsmith and Sheridan in England present a curious combination of intelligent and emotional comedy; their plays lack the consistency of either distinct type of drama, but they have an immense popularity because they skillfully present the two aspects of life and art, side by side, without doing violence to either ingredient in the mixture.

No complete fusion of these opposing currents was achieved in the literature of the early 19th c., when romanticism under various national forms prevailed in western Europe. The dominance of the imagination tended to subdue the sense of reality, which is an important factor in comedy, although a criticism of actual life sometimes rears its head in the fairy world of Raimund's Viennese extravaganzas or in the dream world of Alfred de Musset's Parisian fantasies. Dramatic comedy throve most vigorously in the Scandinavian countries and in Russia, which was belatedly following the precedent that had been set by western Europe in the two preceding centuries. The most original dramatist of this period was the Norwegian, Henrik Ibsen, who, although primarily the author of serious plays, is more and more recognized as a comic as well as a tragic genius. His deep feeling about social problems could not withstand his probing intelligence, which pierced into the psychological roots of human nature. He pictured life as he saw it, with its inconsistencies and its cross-purposes; the more he thought about people and their conduct, the more clearly he perceived that morals are relative and that no definite conclusions can be reached as to abstract ethical values. He pilloried his own zeal as a reformer in *The Wild Duck*; a tinge of irony suffuses all of his maturest plays. He broke down the artificial boundaries between tragedy and comedy, making it clear that in the modern world of flux and confusion hard and fast categories are no more valid in art than in life.

Something firm and stable was lost in this process, but much variety and richness were gained. Ibsen's example was soon followed, with numerous modifications, throughout Europe; no man was so influential as he in the resurgence of creative activity in comedy as well as tragedy at the end of the 19th c. In Russia, Chekhov painted pictures of a decaying aristocratic society which are without peer for subtlety and deftness; in Austria, Schnitzler presented a brilliant façade of sophistication and wit that cannot quite conceal the intense suffering behind its cynical mask; in Italy, Pirandello emphasized by uncanny means the incongruous gap between external appearance and inner reality; in Ireland, Synge added the wild poetry of a Celtic imagination to the superficially prosaic happenings of everyday life; in England, Shaw mocked at existing institutions because they fell so far short of the ideals which his heated intelligence could conceive of as possible under a socialistic regime; in America, no first-rate writer of comedy has yet arisen, but a nation that has produced the best work of S. N. Behrman, Elmer Rice, and Philip Barry need not feel unduly discouraged by its present lack of superlative distinction in the sphere of comic drama.

The development of comedy may be viewed in the light of tragedy, which comedy follows and—as in the Greek satyr play, after the three dramas of the tragic trilogy—mocks. (Even the so-called happy ending is usually arbitrary; sometimes it is wrought by an actual or implicit "god from the machine"; sometimes it is as casual as the couplings made by Hymen, for example, of *As You Like It.* "Comedy ends with the marriage, because that's where the tragedy begins.") But even as does tragedy, comedy makes a final affirmation. Tragedy is rooted in the belief in man's freedom; comedy mirrors the many limitations of free man. Lofty in his spiritual aspirations, man is held in check by his earth-bound body, which strains toward sexual release, which must eat and must excrete, which must have clothing and shelter. The woman-hunter, the glutton, the shabby vagabond, are therefore eternal comic types. Comedy, while laughing at the excesses of lust and greed, may yet be warm with indulgence for our enjoyment of our physical needs. When it turns upon the intellect, comedy shows how minds work for the satisfaction of their bodies. Often one source of comedy is the automatic nature of man's actions, the inelasticity of his mind, which gives the stock response to the expected stimulus. But comedy, too, presupposes man's free will, man's aspiration toward the ideal.

In our day, comedy has shot off along two tangents. The first has developed the theatre of the absurd, *q.v.,* where incomprehensible figures exchange meaningless repetitive words to no clear end, as Picasso (*Desire Caught by the Tail*), Beckett (*Waiting for Godot*), Ionesco, and others emphasize the excretory functions of the body amid whimperings for a soul. The second path results from the fact that, with free will abolished, comedy has nothing tragic to laugh at; with ideals brushed aside, it has no pretensions to mock. The absence of tragic aspiration has led to the black comedy of indifference. There is no affirmation to smile away; no standards are upheld to generate hypocrisy or excessive zeal, the usual butts of ridicule. Universal venality and self-concern being taken for granted, such plays as Edward Albee's *Who's Afraid of Virginia Woolf?* (1964) and Frank Marcus's *The Killing of Sister George* (1966) show us persons who are less persons than automata, who act as their desires pull the strings. Such laughter as we offer them may be derisive. Walter Kerr, however, says that such "comedy" wins our laughter by its contrast to the life we know outside the play, life in which we somehow cling to standards and ideals, life in which we accept the paradox that, while we must refrain from judging others, who are driven to their deeds by forces (within and without) stronger than their conscious powers, we must for our own actions recognize our power of free choice and free will, must at least act "as if" we are free. (*Cf. als ob.*)

At their best, both tragedy and comedy bring exaltation to the spirit of man. Tragedy shows man defying his limitations, bearing even to his own destruction the banner of the ideal. And comedy shows man laughing at his limitations, accepting his bodily shackles and mental strains, and ever beyond these winking at his fellows and fashioning wings toward the stars. *Cf.* Black Comedy; Tragedy; Drama. H. T. E. Perry, *Masters of Dramatic Comedy and Their Social Themes,* 1939; H. Thorndike, *Eng. Comedy,* 1929; F. Conford, *The Origin of Attic Comedy,* 1914; G. Murray, *Aristophanes,* 1933; P. Duchartre, *The It. Comedy,* 1929; H. A. Rennert, *The Sp. Stage in the Time of Lope de Vega,* 1909; A. Tilley, *Molière,* 1921; B. Dobrée, *Restoration Comedy,* 1924; P. Lauter, *Theories of Comedy,* 1964; M. Vos, *The Drama of Comedy,* 1966; R. W. Corrigan, ed. *Comedy, Meaning and Form,* 1965; J. J. Enck, E. T. Forter and A. Whitley, ed. *The Comic in Theory and Practice,* 1960; M. Vos, *For God's Sake Laugh,* 1967; Walter Kerr, *Tragedy and Comedy,* 1967; Elder Olson, *The Theory of Comedy,* 1968. HENRY TEN-EYCK PERRY +.

comedy of common sense. That in which a nice balance is maintained between theoretical standards of human conduct and the practical demands of the society in which individuals find themselves.

comedy of humours. That which considers the dominant traits in human nature, embodies them in typical figures (often given characterizing names), and subjects them to severe analysis. Written especially by Jonson and Shadwell (17th and 18th c.).

comedy of manners. That which is concerned with the conventional deportment of men and women under a specific social code. Polished behavior is here of greater importance than fundamental morality. Written by Molière, Congreve, Wycherley.

comic relief (—episode, —interlude). A comic scene in a serious play. Its most obvious purpose is to relax the receptor's tension, so as to permit the emotional surge to be later renewed. Such comic episodes range widely, from complete absence (*Tamburlaine*) to loose irrelevancies (*Dr. Faustus*). They may be of two sorts (a) organic: part of the play's action, taking color from the flowing with the main scenes (Shak., the commoners in *Julius Caesar*; servants, Mercutio, in *Romeo and Juliet*); (b) inorganic: a comic figure (servant, countryman) touching the outermost fringe of the action, then disappearing. (Shak., the grave diggers, *Hamlet*; the peasant that brings the asp, *Antony and Cleopatra*; the porter, *Macbeth*). The second type is often censured: Voltaire attacks it in *Hamlet*; Coleridge decries "the disgusting scene of the Porter, which I dare undertake to demonstrate to be an interpolation of the Players." De Quincey (*On the Knocking at the Gate in "Macbeth"*) shows its value, in deepening our consciousness of what's gone before. Note also, that in all this group (b) the "comic" figure is one that, introduced at a crisis, is off the plane of the action, has no sense of the impending doom. So, all around *us,* momentous things are brewing while we are unaware. What Hawthorne (*David Swan*) presents in an apologue, Shakespeare makes real.

Other things than comedy may be used for "relief." In *Lear,* the tragedy is eased by sentimental pathos; it is rather heightened by the brave folly of the Fool. Music may be used, as Ophelia's songs; this too may add to the dramatic irony, as when in Heywood's *Lucrece* the beautiful

> Pack cares way and welcome day,
> With night we banish sorrow

heralds the dawn-break over the ravished matron. Philo Buck (*The Golden Thread,* 1931) says the comic episode is not relief, but by life's senseless juxtaposition strengthens the irony. The porter ushering imaginary souls along the primrose path to the eternal bonfire; Macbeth already scorched with its flames. "The bitter smile with which we greet the comic interlude is almost the grin of the death's head." The relief, however, may come as a reminder this is not actual, but art. *See* Psychic distance. W. H. Hadow, Eng. Assn. Pamphlet 31.

commedia dell'arte (It.) Comedy of the guild (*arte:* guild); comedy of masks. A largely improvised kind of play created ca. 1550 by professional actors, organized into small groups under the patronage of powerful lords or academies. These actors composed skeleton plots (*scenari*) which they filled out with improvised dialogue, jokes and tricks (*lazzi*), often spurred by audience response, and into which they inserted poems and speeches culled from literary sources. Each company consisted of eight or nine men and three or four women, cast to type, *e.g.:* two or three old men, the principal two called Pantalone and Dottore Graziano; two or three young lovers (Pierrot and Columbine); two or three clowns, *zanni* (probably from Giovanni), one bright and lively (Arlecchino, Harlequin), one stupider (Brighella or Pulcinella, Punch); a cowardly braggart (Scaramouche or Il Capitano, a satire on Spanish soldiers). The leading woman (Isabella, Celia, etc.) had a maid (*servetta*) to pair with Arlecchino when the play ended with the marriages of the principal couples. The many surviving mss. scenarios have very similar plots, mostly derived from Plautus, Terence and their Italian imitators. The young lovers outwit their miserly elders, helped by their ingenious servants who provide disguises, arrange elopements and distract the old men by their tricks. Masks were worn by clowns and old men, whose costumes were also generally stylized; Pantalone wore the red and black long trousers, cloak and cap of a rich Venetian merchant (*Magnifico*); Arlecchino's habit was patched in many colors, his cap had a rabbit's tail in front, his sword was wooden. Il Capitano bore weapons he was afraid to use; the Doctor appeared in a university gown and a wine-stained mask. The young lovers always dressed fashionably. Speech was also typed: dialects for the comic characters, elegant Tuscan for the lovers. Oaths and obscenities abounded in the clown's talk, delighting the groundlings and shocking the pious and refined in the audiences. The principal companies—*Confidenti, Uniti, Gelosi*—influenced contemporary dramatists, Shakespeare, Ben Jonson, Molière, Goldoni, and others by their lively art. Even today their shadows are visible in the English pantomimes, the European puppet plays, ballets like *Petrouchka* and operas like *I Pagliacci. Cf.* Fabula Atellana; Happening. K. M. Lea, *Italian Popular Comedy; 1560–1620,* 2 v., 1934; Winifred Smith, *The Commedia dell'arte,* 1912, 1964; *It. Actors of the Renaissance,* 1930; P. Duchartre, *It. Comedy,* 1929, 1966; A. Nicoll, *Masks, Mimes, and Miracles,* 1931; *Scenarios of the Commedia dell'arte,* trans. H. F. Salerno, 1967. WINIFRED SMITH.

commitment. *See* Alienation. Eric Bentley, *The Theatre of Commitment,* 1967; C. W. E. Bigsby, *Confrontation and Commitment,* 1968; M. Adereth, *Commitment in Modern Fr. Lit.,* 1968.

common. (1) In verse: (a) of a syllable that may be construed as either short or long, to fit the meter; (b) — meter; so called from its frequent use in hymns; ballad meter, *q.v.* (2) Of diction: (a) ordinary; in everyday use; (b) esp. 18th c., mean, low, vulgar; unseemly.

commonplace (Gr. koinos topos). (1) A general topic, *i.e.,* one widely useful in argument. Aristotle lists four types: (a) The possible and impossible: if a man can be cured, he can also fall ill. (b) Past fact: if a man has forgotten a thing, he once knew it. (c) Future fact: rain clouds presage rain. (d) Size; relative greatness or importance of things. To Cicero and the later Romans *communes loci* was a wider concept, including any commonly accepted point of view. Hence the Ren. use: a notable passage, such as might be preserved in a "commonplace book." (2) By growth from the above: of everyday occurrence, in all times and climes; thought and said by everybody.

communication. The process of transferring thought from the writer to the reader, as through the printed word. There are natural difficulties that interfere with direct connection. To overcome such difficulties, the author often must adjust his writing to the readers, attempting from the outset to establish an intimacy between himself and the reader. Very often (Dickens) this intimacy is accomplished by chattiness; it may be by taking the reader into one's confidence, with the promise that the tale is well worth hearing.

Intimacy and promise are the two main forces in establishing communication. But the bridge between writer and reader is made up of words on a page of paper. The meaning of the words should transfer the author's intent, as nearly as possible, to the mind of the reader. Thus, in translating the Bible for the Eskimos, wherever the word "lamb" occurs, the word "baby-seal" must be substituted; for no Eskimo has any consciousness of a lamb.

Another type of adjustment is for simplification, *e.g.,* Einstein's popular book on physics; Wells' *Outline of History.* If the reader is held by the words on the page, he believes in the writing, and feels friendly to an author; if all these are accomplished, then direct and satisfactory communication has been established. If on the other hand the reader is bored, thinks the work either meaningless or not convincing, or does not feel friendly to the ideas or words of the author, then communication may be said to have broken down.

Current criticism speaks of the fallacy (Allen Tate) and of the heresy (Cleanth Brooks) of communication. The fallacy consists in the communication of the emotions that certain words may bear, without any proper relation between those emotions and their objects, as when one calls on "democracy" to cloak a totalitarian deed. The heresy consists in the notion that a work communicates an idea, when what is (or should be) communicated is the experience of the work as a whole. A work of art is a many-sided experience, all of which, in ideal communication, is enjoyed by the reader.

Some critics today state that each human being lives in his own universe, and no universes are the same; that the function of art is to establish communication among them. Thus, thanks to art, instead of seeing only one world, our own, we have at our disposal as many worlds as there are original artists. Others declare, however, that not all art aims at communication; art may instead seek to arouse in the receptor not an idea, nor a specific æsthetic appreciation, but either a particular emotion, or a vague excitation, or some sort of kinetic or even hypnotic response. (These responses, however, are also communications.) There are also a few who say that artists—esp. poets—create solely for themselves; to them may be put the question: Then, why do they publish?

For the writer, the initial problem of communication is the transference of his primary thoughts and feelings and experiences into the secondary order of "metasensory" feeling-thoughts to which he gives linguistic expression. In this process he both clarifies his thoughts for himself and carries them over (in what he hopes is appropriate form) to the reader. Communication, however, has basic limitations set by time, the medium, and the human brain, in addition to accidental disturbances such as outside sound and other distractions, fatigue, faults in the medium (misprints; piano out of tune; poor type; inept performers of a play, etc.).

Current concentration on the problems of communication may be said to have begun with Claude S. Shannon's *A Mathematical Theory of Communication* in 1948 and in the same year Norbert Wiener's *Cybernetics*. They examine—as between a source and a receiver—the aspects of Information, Message, Meaning, Noise (non-meaningful information; irrelevant interference), Entropy (measure of uncertainty), Compression, and Efficiency. Contributions have come from many fields, and the study of communication has become a significant aspect of today's global thinking. The current importance of communication is manifest in the fact that more persons see and hear a single broadcast of a popular television show than have attended every performance of *Hamlet,* in all countries and tongues, since Shakespeare first spoke the words of the ghost upon the stage. *Cf.* Semantics; Objective Correlative; Linguistics; Computational Stylistics; Persuasion; Oratory. C. Cheery, ed. *Information Theory,* 1956; W. Kees and J. Ruesch, *Nonverbal Communication,* 1956; A. A. Moles, *Théorie de l'information et perception esthétique,* 1958, trans. 1966; *Communications et langages,* 1963; E. S. Carpenter, ed. *Explorations in Communication,* 1960; H. Marshall McLuhan, *Understanding Media,* 1964; Y. Bar-Hillel, *Lang. and Information,* 1964; L. A. Dexter, *People, Society, and Mass Communications,* 1964; D. K. Berlo, *The Process of Communication,* 1966; W. C. Minnick, *The Art of Persuasion,* 1957, 1968; Mario Pei, ed. *Language Today,* 1967; F. E. X. Dance, ed. *Human Communication Theory,* 1967; R. E. Mueller, *The Science of Art,* 1967; W. L. Rivers and W. Schramm, *Responsibility in Mass Communication,* 1969. MANUEL KOMROFF.

comparative literature. The study of the interrelationships of the literatures of various peoples. Until the 18th c. all literature was conceived as one great stream. The growth of national consciousness in literature was at once countered by the reassertion of this broad unity, as in Goethe's idea of a *Weltliteratur*. Soon scientific comparison was drawn from the natural sciences into linguistics (Bopp, Dietz; Littré about 1830) and into literature. Villemain, 1829, first used the term *littérature comparée;* Sainte-Beuve popularized it. Whether with individual authors or with broad currents of thought and style, and the major literary schools, the comparative study of literature is one of the most fruitful methods of literary exploration.

comparison. *See* Amplification.

complaint. A lyric genre frequent in the Renaissance; usually a monologue in which the poet (1) bemoans the unresponsiveness of his beloved (Gr. Anthology; Villon; Surrey, "A Complaint by Night of the Lover Not Beloved") or (2) seeks relief from his unhappy lot (Chaucer, *Complaint to Pité*) or (3) pictures the sorry state of the world (Spenser, *Complaints*).

composition, the four forms of. Modern handbooks of rhetoric frequently classify written prose into four forms of composition (or discourse): exposition, argument, description, and narration. The basis for this classification is usually the function and kind of material appropriate to each form. The attempts to distinguish among these forms follow roughly the same pattern: prose that deals with definitions, processes, generalizations, that clarifies ideas, principles, with the intent of presenting meanings in readily communicable and unemotive language, is expository; prose involving an issue upon which a stand is taken and defended, and aiming at conviction (moving the mind to believe) or persuasion (moving the will to act), is argumentative; prose restricting itself to the objects of sense-experience and directed at evoking a sensuous effect is descriptive; and prose detailing actual or fictitious events arranged in time-space sequences is narrative. Contrasts are occasionally drawn. Exposition and argument appeal to the intellect (except persuasion, which appeals to the emotions), but description and narration appeal to the imagination. Exposition and argument are often considered as specifically practical forms, *i.e.,* they increase knowledge and concern themselves with subjects of material value in the world of prudence. In contrast, description and narration, though they may be utilized for ulterior ends of a practical kind, are artistic forms, for their effectiveness largely depends on inducing imaginative states enjoyable in themselves.

This classification is probably the result of an effort to organize into a simple pattern the increasing number of literary forms since the Renaissance. It does not appear before the 19th c. In 1808 George Gregory (*Letters on Literature, Taste, and Composition*, I, 201–202) employed it; but he included oratory (anything written or spoken in "declamatory form") as an additional form. Poetry was often added to make the classification of literary forms exhaustive, but the four forms themselves have been associated exclusively with prose writing. It is generally agreed that the distinctions among these forms are theoretical and that normally a composition is a mixture of the forms, but it should be observed that even on a theoretical basis the distinctions are questionable. A discussion of the nature of argument, *e.g.*, inevitably leads to the conclusion that exposition is an integral part of it. It is difficult to speak intelligently of pure narrative (*i.e.*, the mere skeleton of successive happenings) without recognizing that narrative by nature functions through a description of characters and circumstances. It is equally difficult to discuss exposition on a theoretical level without reference to description and narrative as important ingredients. In practice, a subject in its totality presents itself in terms of its concepts (exposition), its values (argument), its percepts (description), and its history (narration). Moreover, the four forms of composition function indifferently in poetry and prose. These observations lead to the conclusion that they are not in themselves forms, but modes of approaching a subject and elements contributing to the various literary forms—epic, drama, history, novel, essay. Much of the dissatisfaction with the classification is no doubt caused by the awareness that modes of approaching a subject are translated into forms.

In antiquity, what we call the four forms were particulars of two classes of composition, poetry and rhetoric. Aristotle (*Poet.* I, 10–12; IX, 1–3, and *Rhet.* I, iv, 6–7) suggests a third class, scientific composition. These three classes admit of a clear differentiation: poetry deals with imitation; rhetoric, with matters of opinion; science, with things amenable to the methods of exact demonstration. In other terms, they correspond to imaginative (or creative), persuasive, and informative composition, each with its own end: the first, to give pleasure; the second, to secure action; and the third, to increase knowledge. All compositions, whether in verse or in prose, can be organized under this pattern, in which the four "forms" have a legitimate place as techniques of presentation; but the techniques should be completed by the inclusion of dialogue (Aristotle, *Poet.* III, 1–3). *Cf.* Rhetoric and Poetic; Signs; Narration; Description; Argument. H. Gifford, *Comparative Literature*, 1969. G. GIOVANNINI.

computational stylistics. The analysis of an author's writing in terms of mathematics and the computer; basically, through the checking of measurable elements of style. Among these are: frequency of recurrence of words and of parts of speech; analysis of grammatical structure; variations from normal order or structure; length of words (by letters, by syllables); length of sentences; juxtaposition and grouping of words; occurrence of series, of clusters (such as Shakespeare's frequent linking of spaniel, fawning, licking, candy, and sweets). A Sanskrit grammar of ca. 500 B.C. gives the number of verses, words, and syllables in the *Rig-Veda.* In 1859 mathematician Augustus de Morgan suggested that counting the number of letters in an author's words would reveal personal characteristics of style; in 1887 T. C. Mendenhall studied word length in Dickens and Thackeray. The use of computers has increased such study, and led to the formulation of specific devices: the "Poisson model," based on the average occurrence of a word and the independence of each occurrence; the "Bayes theorem," a study of the probabilities of occurrence; and the recognition that in a series the *lexis* (vocabulary) is individual for each author, while the *taxis* (arrangement) may be set in a formula. Basic to this approach is the fact that these elements in a work are usually not fashioned deliberately by an author, and therefore may be more revealing than the consciously sought elements of style.

Another service of the computer has been in the determination of disputed readings, or the restoration of lost words. By calculating for the various letters of a language, their frequency as the first letter of a word, as the second letter, etc., blurred or missing passages, *e.g.*, in the Dead Sea Scrolls, have been reconstructed. Studies of this sort have also proved helpful in cases of disputed authorship or date. Their value for criticism is less immediately apparent; but the computer provides apparatus for detailed study, when critics find avenues for fruitful search.

Search for a new rhetoric based on mathematics has been undertaken in Fr. by the Oulipo (*Ou*vroir de *li*ttérature *po*tentielle, Workshop for Potential Literature) founded by Raymond Queneau and F. Le Lionnais, working mainly with syntactic but somewhat with semantic aspects of literature; also Max Bense in Germany. A. A. Mullin in the U.S. has suggested a mathematicized tanka (*See* Japanese poetry), and computer poetry has been composed, as by John R. Pierce, *Electrons, Waves, and Messages* (1956). It is still too early to see what creative efforts along these lines will achieve. *Cf.* Communication. Caroline Spurgeon, *Shakespeare's Imagery,* 1935; I. de Sola Pool, *Trends in Content Analysis,* 1959; H. Kreuzer and R. Gunsenhaüser, ed. *Mathematik und Dichtung,* 1966; J. Reed, ed. *The Computer and Literary Style,* 1966.

comstockery. *See* Censorship.

conceit. (It. *concetto;* Fr. *pointe;* Sp. *agudeza*). Originally, that which is conceived in the mind; an idea. In literature, applied to associations, in imagery and figure; later, esp. to an over-elaborated analogy. Hence, in the 18th and 19th c., a too fanciful, outworn, or otherwise unsuccessful figure. Thus Wordsworth attacked the picture of morning dewdrops as "the tears of the sky for the loss of the sun," but praised Milton's

Sky lowered, and, muttering thunder, some
sad drops
Wept, at completing of the mortal sin.

Taste has now changed, moreover, and with Donne (to whom in Eng. the term was chiefly applied) restored to critical favor, the term has lost its derogatory connotations. Even Shakespeare, however, had satirized the excessive use of conceits: "My mistress' eyes are nothing like the sun . . ." Two types of conceit are distinguished. (1) The Petrarchan; external, degenerating into preciosity: Quarles says, *e.g.,* that Christ's humanity is an umbrella to his divinity. (2) the metaphysical; more brooding, frequently extended (Donne, passim, *e.g.* "Love's Progress"), often far-fetched, e.g. (Dryden, of a young man that died of the smallpox):

Each little pimple had a tear in it,
To wail the fault its rising did commit.

conclusion. Last of three parts (introduction, body,—) of a literary composition, in which the thesis or conflict is brought to its end, or the main point is pressed home. *Cf.* Plot; Triad.

concrete. Referring to an actual substance or thing, as George Washington; my younger sister (concrete particular); horse, airplane (concrete general). *See* Abstract.

concrete universal. Term used in current criticism to indicate the long-accepted thought that the work of art achieves the union of the particular and the general, the individual and the universal, that beyond the specific person or event there are world-wide implications. *Cf.* Distances, the three; Abstract. "The Structure of the 'Concrete Universal' in Literature," Wimsatt, *PMLA,* March 1947.

concrete verse. A current development of the carmen figuratum, *q.v.,* stimulated in the 1950's by the Swiss Eugen Gomringer and the Brazilian Decio Pignatari. Thus a poem may (Ian H. Finlay) repeat the words "au pair girl" until the letters *au pair girl* have formed the shape of a pear. In Emmett Williams's volume *Sweethearts,* 1968, every page contains just a different design using nothing but the letters (each once, some or all) of the word "sweetheart." Word play, various type fonts, and random juxtapositions ("found poetry") are set upon posters, wallpaper, rubber stamps and stranger media. Concrete poetry, which has appeared in countries as far apart as Iceland, Turkey, and Japan, seems a writer's endeavor to match Mod art and modern music. It must be seen as well as heard. E. Williams, ed. *An Anthology of Concrete Poetry,* 1968; Marshall McLuhan, *Verbi-Voco-Visual Explorations,* 1968; Mary E. Solt, *Concrete Poetry,* 1969.

confession. A type of autobiography (*q.v.*), sometimes honestly intended, sometimes (Rousseau, *Confessions,* pub. posth. 1781–88) painting the portrait one would like posterity to hold. Common as a title from St. Augustine (354–430); in a flood among the romantics after Rousseau (De Quincey, *Confessions of an Eng. Opium-Eater,* 1821; A. de Musset, *Confession d'un enfant du siècle,* 1836; Chateaubriand, *Mémoires d'outre-tombe,* 1811–36, pub. posth. 1849–50); on to the fiction of the "true confessions" pulp magazines of today. We may distinguish (1) reminiscences: what a man might tell a room-full; their value depends upon the interest of the events he has shared and persons known; (2) autobiography: what he might tell his friends; its value hinges on his character in relation to persons he has known and things done; (3) confessions: what he'd not tell even his friends; its value springs from the intensity of his inner life.

confessional novel. The idea of St. Augustine's *Confessions,* reinforced by the autobiographical *The Seven Storey Mountain* (1948) of the Trappist monk Thomas Merton, gave scope to writers of fiction, from Dostoevsky (*Notes From the Underground; Crime and Punishment* was first written as a confession) to Gide (*The Immoralist*), Sartre (*Nausea*), Camus (*The Fall*), Bellow (*Herzog*). The confessional anti-hero introduces himself as afflicted, disillusioned, groping for meaning in a dark and brutal world. He may embrace pain and trouble as a way of being aware he is alive. He turns from rebellion to self-laceration, in search of self-understanding—though he may ultimately question the possibility of self-knowledge.

A variation of the confessional novel is the story within which a novelist is writing the story we are reading. André Gide used this device in his first novel (*Tentative amoureuse,* 1891) and more fully in *The Counterfeiters* (1926), for which in addition he published the *Journal* he had kept during the six years of the writing. *Cf.* Narrator; Anti-hero.

conflict. Seen by F. Brunetière as the basic element in determining the action of a play (or story). Wm. Archer prefers the term "crisis," Clayton Hamilton, "contrast." "Struggle" and "opposition" have also been suggested. It involves two opposing forces; not more, for the emotional flow of the receptor is drawn with one, and all others surge to support or to retard this. These forces may be embodied (1) in two individuals, hero and villain (*Treasure Island;* all melodramas); (2) in one person and society (Dickens' social novels; most fiction spanning a whole life); (3) within one individual, the protagonist, as when love and duty (Sp. drama) are at odds, or faith and disillusion vie (*Silas Marner*); most great works are of this type. *A Tale of Two Cities* combines the inner and the outer conflict. There must also be a cause of opposition, or a goal. The events of the conflict form the plot; their decisive moment marks the climax of the play or story. *See* Drama; Plot; Climax.

connotation. The cloud, or crowd, of ideas and associations linked with a word, because of the individual's past experience with that word. Such experience may be (1) individual: linkage of gardenias with a disliked woman may make every reference to the flower distasteful; (2) group: professional, racial, etc. Thus to those well read in Eng. lit., "albatross" will suggest the burden of the Ancient Mariner; in Fr., Baudelaire's sonnet of the poet like the bird, majestic while soaring, but on earth "its giant wings are weights that keep it low"; (3) general, widely shared: mother; fatherland; rose; snake; (4) linked with contingent properties: with the rock, its hardness, with the ice, the cold; the cunning of the fox. The scientist tries to hold a term to its precise meaning (denotation), to the thought of which it is a sign; the artist relies upon the connotations, and by his work extends them. The fact that the cluster of connotations is unique in each individual is a major argument against T. S. Eliot's objective correlative, *q.v. Cf.* Meaning; Diction.

consciousness, stream of. *See* Stream of consciousness; monologue.

consonance. (1) Harmony of sound; opposed to dissonance. Hence, accord, mutual fitness in idea or style. (2) Recurrence at the ends of lines or words of the same consonantal sounds after different accented vowels (like assonance, half-rhyme, but the other half); *e.g.,* pressed, past; shadow, meadow. When the vowels are the same, but sounded differently, called eye-rhyme (good, blood; earth, hearth). Consonance is frequent in ballad, folk and popular song. *Cf.* Assonance; Rhyme; Diction, poetic.

constructivism. Attitude of Soviet literary group formed in 1924, which tried to coordinate the ideological conceptions of a literary work with "the character of modern technical development . . . speed, economy, and capacity." Chief theoretician, K. Zelinski; most gifted poets, I. L. Selvinski and Vera Inber. Most fully developed in stage-design, it used (Meyerhold; less thoroughgoing, Tairov) non-representational settings of scaffolding, movable platforms, framework suggesting house or factory or merely levels of movement. *Gosplan literatury* (*State plan for lit.*), 1925; *Bizness* (Business), 1928.

contamination. Method of dramatic composition or adaptation, esp. in the *fabula palliata;* fusing two or more Gr. originals, or parts of them, for the production of one Rom. comedy. Terence defends the practice.

conte. Fr. Originally, any kind of short fictional tale. Now, a short-story, in the technical sense, as distinguished from the *nouvelle* and the *roman.* The *conte* is generally notable for its concision and the concentration of its plot-structure.

contextualism. The approach, developed by some of the "new critics" and named by Murray Krieger (1956), that sees the æsthetic experience (ideally, seldom if ever actually) as rapt, utterly intransitive contemplation, and the work of art as a uniquely complex, self-contained work or world. The work possesses "the all-containing, mutually opposing energies of a tension-filled object that blocks our escape from its context and thus from its world." Its unity lies in the context of the object itself, regardless of the varying idiosyncratic responses. This involves, however, no art-for-art's-sake evasion of life, contextualists claim, for the world within the work, while unique, is at the same time "an intensified, endlessly organized simulacrum of our own." M. Krieger, *The New Apologists for Poetry,* 1956; *The Play and the Place of Crit.,* 1967.

contrast. Juxtaposition of opposed ideas or images; considered important in many literary fields. (1) As a device in composition, for clarity; two things considered together become clearer than either alone. (2) As an intensifying figure:

> Rather will it
> The multitudinous seas incarnadine
> Making the green one red.

"How far that little candle throws its beams" suggests the depth of surrounding dark. (3) As a mood in creation (*cf.* chiaroscuro): Antitheses are frequent esp. among the romantics (Hugo, *e.g., Transfiguration:* the grave and the rose; *To L—*) either as images or as basic ideas, life itself being to them a contrast of desire and disillusion. (4) As an element in organization. Hazlitt, in the "thinking principle" that adapts and reconciles ideas, sees both association and contrast. (5) As an ingredient in wit (Addison): poetry finds unsuspected similarities; wit exposes the contrasts in apparently like things. (6) As a basic element in drama. *See* Conflict.

conundrum. A riddle the answer to which involves a play on words. "What is the difference between a blind man and a sailor in prison?" "The one can't see to go, the other can't go to sea." *Cf.* Pun.

convention. "A rule or practice based upon general consent, or accepted and upheld by society at large; an arbitrary rule or practice recognized as valid in any particular art or study." This O.E.D. definition takes account of three levels of convention, which tend to merge into one another. In character, conventions vary greatly, from the relatively broad, basic, unchanging to the superficial, arbitrary and highly variable. Those peculiar to literature are to be found in its language, word patterns, imagery, technical devices, the structure of the various literary types. The great literary genres—lyric and epic poetry, tragedy, comedy, the tale and the long narrative—are in themselves conventions, of the basic sort. Every literary work will be found to embody conventions at different levels. The masterpieces are those in which the conventions of a particular time and place are the least obtrusive and artificial.

Conventions of life and of literature interflow. Literary conventions may become outmoded because of technical or other modifications in social life (*e.g.,* the art of letter-writing; the "three-decker" novel). Obsolete conventions may sometimes be infused with a new vitality (*e.g.,* the classical revival ushered in by the Renaissance; François Villon's revival of the ballade; Eugene O'Neill's renewal of the soliloquy).

In the growth of a literary tradition two opposing forces are constantly found at work: convention and revolt—convention, which may be said to constitute the social molding of literature and which tends to the establishment of fixed and unyielding forms; and revolt, whereby the individual writer attempts to give his personal imprint to the medium handed to him by tradition, which always offers a degree of resistance to originality. John Livingston Lowes, *Convention and Revolt in Poetry,* 1922; F. Knebel and C. W. Bailey, *Convention,* 1964. HAAKON M. CHEVALIER.

copla (Sp., couplet). A Sp. ballad, originally of couplet stanzas, popular in origin. Its normal form extends to four stanzas of four octosyllabic lines, with rhyme or assonance in the even lines. The syllables may be varied, to eleven or twelve; the lines, to three or five.

coq-à-l'âne. Fr. A discourse, usually a dramatic monologue, in which irrelevancy, often founded on linguistic transposition or pretended misunderstanding, is used for comic or satiric effect. Flourished 16th c., esp. in Rabelais and Burchiello.

coronach. An Irish or Scots (Highland) dirge, *e.g.,* Scott, *The Lady of the Lake,* Canto 3, beginning "He is gone on the mountain."

correctness. Conformity to a standard or norm, a principle or rule. Strictly, the idea of correctness involves that of some relatively definite measure of conformity, such as the norm or rule itself supplies when it is explicit and concrete. But as the concrete norm implies an abstract standard, and the defined rule a principle or uniformity of nature or convention which it specifically formulates, correctness is used to denote not only (1) conformity with rule, or regularity, but also more freely (2) conformity, perhaps in violation of relevant existing rule, with a standard or principle imperfectly represented by the rule, or with a principle for which in the circumstances no rule has been formulated. In language, the latter correctness is conformity with usage (custom, convention); the former, conformity with rules derived from usage. In literary art, the 2nd correctness is conformity with nature or reality (as in the 18th c. "correctness of sentiment") or with accepted but unformulated convention or habit; the 1st is observance of the existing rules of rhetoric and poetics. Most practical questions concerning correctness arise from conflict between these two conformities, or between principle and rule. Theoretically, the existence of such conflict implies the failure of the rule and should suffice to render it inoperative; but in practise there are always the problems of whether the apparent conflict is a real one and if so, what acknowledged norm other than the inadequate rule may be applied to supersede it; for the specific implications of a general principle are hard to establish unless formulated as concrete and evidently applicable rules, and in fact the only thing that can effectively supplant a rule is another rule.

Where there is no felt conflict between principle and rule, correctness is simply observance of rules. This ideal singleness is never perfectly attained; but it was approached in Europe during the period of classicism, in Eng. most nearly in the earlier 18th c., and then correctness in the strict sense was more, perhaps, than at any other time, a primary concern of good writers. Walsh's exhortation to the young Pope ("He . . . used to tell me, that there was one way left of excelling: for though we had several great poets, we never had any one great poet that was correct; and he desired me to make that my study and aim." Spence, *Anecdotes, ed.* Singer, 1820, p. 280), significant as its influence doubtless was on Pope and through him on others, embodied rather than determined the aspiration of the literary society of that age. It is in connection with verse that the word *correctness* most often occurs in the 18th c., esp. in Johnson, who makes its use intelligible when he says, "the essence of verse is regularity. . . . To write verse is to dispose syllables and sounds harmonically by some known and settled rule . . ." (*Life of Dryden,* 349). Much as they esteemed correctness, however, Pope and Johnson regarded it as a negative virtue, rather avoidance of faults (by observing rules) than achievement of notable graces (which might involve breaking or transcending rules); so Pope describes mediocrity as "correctly cold, and regularly low." Correctness was the product of judgment and diligence; for great poetry this was required, but more was essential. *See* Rules; *cf.* Convention; Fitness; Decorum. J. CRAIG LADRIÈRE.

correlative verse. That in which words of the same classification are placed together. *e.g.,* (Milton) "air, water, earth, By fowl, fish, beast, was flown, was swum, was walked."

correspondence of the arts. Although the ancients believed that all the arts, esp. poetry and painting, had the common aim of imitating nature, they considered each of the arts a distinct field. Horace did say *ut pictura poesis* (Poetry resembles painting); Lessing in *Laokoon* (1766) set about to show their difference. Not until the Romantic period did it come to be felt that impressions received through one of the senses could be transmuted through any other sense. Narcotics, as DeQuincey and Baudelaire noted and many today declare, seem to blend the receptive powers of the senses. In Germany, the linkage grew from Novalis and Hoffmann to Ludwig Tieck; in France, it was most fully expressed in Baudelaire's sonnet *Correspondances* (ca. 1855). It was exploited in symbolism with "colored hearing," with Rimbaud's association of sounds and colors in his sonnet *"Voyelles"* (Vowels, 1871) and Huysman's blending of perfumes and sounds and tastes in the novel *A Rebours* (1884). After lapsing from vogue, the idea of the correspondence of the arts was revived in surrealist works and the literature of psychoanalysis. *See* Synaesthesia; *cf.* Diabolism.

counter-turn. (1) Antistrophe, in both senses: (a) response to the strophe, in choral song; (b) reverse repetition, or repetition of a word at the end of successive clauses. (2) A development, at the climax of a play or story, not expected by the characters (or, sometimes, by the receptors); *e.g.,* Macbeth's learning that Macduff was not "born of woman"; Hedda Gabler's discovery that she is in Judge Brack's power, and her quick escape. The short story type associated with O. Henry builds entirely for this final counter-turn.

couplet. Two lines of verse, usually rhymed. Most often, two of a series of lines rhyming in pairs, in stanzas and poems of various lengths. Sometimes occurs in blank verse drama, marking the close of a scene or other important moment, *e.g.* (*Macbeth* II, i):

Hear it not, Duncan, for it is a knell
That summons you to heaven or to hell.

The commonest form in Eng. versification is the heroic couplet, *q.v.*

crambe (Two syllables. Juvenal: *crambe repetita:* cabbage dished up again). (1) distasteful repetition. (2) crambo.

crambo. A game in which a word or line of verse is given, for which every player must supply a rhyme (or rhyming line). There is a forfeit for suggesting a rhyme already given. Popular in the 17th and 18th c.; Samuel Pepys played it while riding in a coach. Dumb crambo: a game in which a group is given a word rhyming with a word hidden on a folded paper; the group enacts (as in charades) one word after another until it hits upon the hidden word. Hence crambo is used to mean bad rhyming; crambo-rhyme: a mere jingle.

cretic. A metrical foot, a short syllable between two long (— ◡ —), *e.g.,* winding sheet.

creticism (from the Roman opinion of Crete). A bald lie. To creticize is to tell lies. There are a riddle and a noted paradox based on the assumption that all Cretans always lie.

crisis (Gr. *crinein,* to judge, decide). The point at which the opposing forces in a play or story interlock for the last time, moving toward the decisive moment, the climax. *See* Conflict. Drama of crisis: a play in which the fateful act occurs at the beginning or before the opening (*Oedipus Rex*; many plays of incest) and is revealed to the characters at the climax; opposed to drama of development (*Romeo and Juliet*), which presents a conflict from an early point to the close.

criterion. A principle, rule, or standard (*q.v.*) by which a thing may be judged. *Cf.* Convention; Correctness; Tradition.

criticism (Word used only since 17th c., but the judgment it represents is recorded among the Athenians, 5th c. B.C.). The conscious evaluation or appreciation of a work of art, either according to the critic's personal taste or according to some accepted æsthetic ideas. The word has been used in many senses, from "fault-finding" (*O.E.D.*) to (E. B. Browning) "the distinguishing of beauty." Victor Hugo declared: "Is the work good or bad?—that's criticism's domain." This leaves unanswered the immediate question as to the source of the standards by which to measure good and bad. Increasingly it is stated (T. S. Eliot), as it was almost always (save among the Romantics) implied, that (I. A. Richards) "to set up as a critic is to set up as a judge of values." Thus, when J. E. Spingarn (following Croce) makes the sole task of criticism to answer (1) what has the author tried to express? and (2) how has he succeeded in expressing it? There soon crowds in the third question: was it worth expressing? Observe that the earlier questions are circular; we can rarely ask the artist about his intention (*q.v.*); this must be judged only in the work; whereupon the two questions are answered together but really not at all.

Criticism, however developed, may serve in various ways. It has, first of all, for the critic the value of all self-expression that is bound in self-control. It may chasten or guide an author (not necessarily the one whose work is examined), checking too rigid adherence to or too radical departure from the tradition; it may more specifically aid in details of the work. For the public it provides both entertainment and instruction, at its best (in the hope of Matthew Arnold) helping maintain a high level of general culture, a fertile field for genius. (Henri Peyre, *The Failures of Criticism,* 1967.)

Criticism is often contrasted with creation, which refers to writing that is not about other literature. In its analytical aspect, however, criticism is an inevitable part of the creative process, as even the Romantics (Keats) recognized; and in its synthetical aspect it is as much creation as the production of any other work. The confusion arises perhaps from the fact that criticism is at once a science and an art. As a science, it involves examination of particular works, observation of their faults and excellences, and (insofar as may be) the induction of general principles. As an art, it engages in the production of stimulating works.

Accepting the distinction between criticism and other works of creation (poetry, drama, novel), it may be asked to what degree they are found together: do they tend to occur in one person? in one period? Those that have written important critical works and have at the same time been outstanding in other literary fields are comparatively few (*e.g.,* Dante, Goethe, Coleridge); but trenchant criticism has occurred in many periods. We may note, however, that in the Renaissance, in general, criticism preached law, which creation did not heed; during the Augustan age, the law was fortified in precept and observed in practice; the Romantics, in both theory and practice, broke free. (A. Koestler, *The Act of Creation,* 1964; F. P. W. McDowell, ed. *The Poet as Critic,* 1967; P. Denetz, Greene, and Nelson, ed., *The Disciplines of Criticism,* 1968; S. P. Zitner, Kissane and Liberman, ed., *A Preface to Literary Analysis,* 1964; *The Practice of Criticism,* 1966.)

Essays on the nature and function of criticism do not appear in the works of our earliest critics. One may seriously question, however, whether there has ever been a great critic who did not have some sort of philosophy of his art. Thus, Plato and Aristotle obviously had ideas about the function of criticism. Plato's conception was plainly moralistic with some leanings toward the æsthetic-interpretative. Aristotle's may be broadly characterized as scientific, ethical, judicial, basically humanistic. He sought, through observation and analysis, to know and explain poetry as an activity of man, to disengage its uniqueness in its relation to other human disciplines. With the audience always in mind he studied the problem of valid effects, and the causes of these effects. He examined and arrived at generalizations upon questions of subject matter, of plot, character, and language, of structure and specific handling, of style and diction, and of such logical qualities as probability, consistency, and decorum.

Since Aristotle's day, criticism has been written with an eye to many and diverse functions. Some of these are secondary, falling under the dubious head of the teleological and expedient. Such, *e.g.,* is *criticism to justify and explain* one's own practice (Boccaccio, Tasso, Dante, Dryden, Hugo, Wordsworth, T. S. Eliot). But this is an end that, whatever incidental values may accrue, is practical rather than philosophic. Somewhat related to such a purpose is that of *criticism to justify imaginative literature,* of which there has been a vast amount. It is possible that one of Aristotle's aims in the *Poetics* was to reply to Plato's animadversions. Much Medieval and Renaissance criticism was a defense against the attacks of the moralists, and in modern times critics have often felt impelled to justify imaginative writings to a sceptical world. Contrary to the spirit of Aristotle, criticism in the hand of his so-called followers often took the form of *prescription for writers* and *legislation for the taste of the multitude.* The ideal of prescriptive criticism, held to an extent by Horace and widely current in the Renaissance, is aptly expressed in Scaliger's boast, "We undertake, therefore, to create a poet." In recent times it has asserted itself mildly in the Freudians and in the obscurantists, more vigorously in the Marxian "leftists." The idea of legislation for the taste of readers assumed as its concern not what the public liked but what it ought to like. It asserted itself in the reiterated demand from Horace to Voltaire that the unities and the other conventions into which Aristotle's observations had unfortunately hardened be scrupulously respected. It reached its height in Chapelain and later Fr. formalists; but practice of the theory survived neo-classicism—in the judgments of Jeffrey, in Romantic attacks on Pope and Boileau, in certain recent dissections of Romantic poetry, and in neo-Marxist attempts to legislate on the basis of the presence or absence of "socialist realism." In sharp contrast to this idea is the modern notion of criticism as mere appreciation, or as expression, which in the practice of such writers as H. L. Mencken has received sharp castigation at the hands of Babbitt and More.

Allied to the foregoing are theories of *criticism as a service to writers* and *criticism as a service to the public.* The first, in its narrower sense, lies in the injunctions of Horace, Vida, Boileau, and Pope to seek out the advice of a good critic; in its broader sense, in Sainte-Beuve's idea that public evaluation should aid an author in knowing himself, and in Arnold's theory that a great critical effort must precede creative achievement. The second notion is inherent in all legislative criticism, in its zeal to protect the public from the bad and to recommend the good. It is broadly present, in more positive form, in non-legislative judicial and in interpretative criticism; and it receives specific formulation in Sainte-Beuve's idea that criticism should ameliorate society by restoring morals, by promoting healthy tastes, and by cultivating the best traditions in literature. Arnold's idea of propagating the best that has been known and thought is a conspicuous example. More recently Auden has restated the view in his theory that the critic's duty is both "to spread a knowledge of past cultures" and to show the reader the unity that is in human life, the relevance of a work of art to his own experience, and the relation of artistic values to other values.

In its principal manifestations, criticism is likely to be interpretative or judicial, though in practice the types merge. The idea that the critic should stand between literature and the reader as an interpreter of the author and his work is at least as old as the Homeric allegorists. But the specific theory of criticism as to know and to make known was definitely developed in the 19th c. (Hegel, Carlyle), and has been maintained in recent times (Spingarn; J. M. Murry; Cazamian; Edmund Wilson). The interpretative function has been variously described. The main question in criticism, declares Carlyle, is one "of the essence and peculiar life of poetry itself . . . Criticism stands like an interpreter between the inspired and uninspired; between the prophet and those who hear the melody of his words, and catch some glimpse of their material meaning, but understand not their deeper import." P. E. More holds that at least a part of the critic's work is "conscious creation of the present out of the past." And Cazamian argues for criticism as a rich creative activity: "To criticize a work . . . is to understand and interpret as fully as possible the urge of energy that produced it; to live again the stages of its development, and partake of the impulse and intentions with which it is still pregnant."

That the art of criticism is to judge well is implicit—through practice—in the earliest criticism, and explicit in the latest. "To set up as a critic," says I. A. Richards, "is to set up as a judge of values." True judicial criticism is, however, more than merely passing judgment. The judicial critic is not a legislative dogmatist; his aim is rather to reach evaluations based upon knowledge, analysis, and comparison. Since he is to analyze he must know his materials intimately; if he is to compare wisely he must know the works of the past as well as of the present, the products of other nations and cultures as well as his own—the best that has been known and written in the world. Nor does the good judicial critic rely on the reason alone. Criticism, writes T. S. Eliot, a judicial as well as an interpretative critic, "is a development of sensibility." Sainte-Beuve, Dryden, Johnson, Arnold would concur. As Johnson asserts, "The beauties of writing" are "often such as cannot . . . be evinced by evidence; they are therefore wholly subject to the imagination." To Arnold judging is important; "but," he explains, "the judgment which almost insensibly forms itself in a fair and clear mind, along with fresh knowledge, is the valuable one; . . . and it is by communicating fresh knowledge, and letting his own judgment pass along with it,—but insensibly, . . . as a sort of companion and clue, not as an abstract lawgiver—that he will generally do most good to his readers."

Arnold is here close in spirit to a kind of judicial criticism which merits especial emphasis. It may be called *criticism as the discovery and application of the principles of good writing*. In the constant effort to find more valid standards, good critics from Aristotle down—Dryden, Johnson, Lessing, Coleridge, Brunetière; in recent times Croce, Richards, Eliot, Tate, Ransom, Foerster—have regarded this as an important function of criticism. H. M. Jones has recently made an appeal for more "general ideas" in current criticism. To have right general ideas would be to know what poetry is ("to know what it is we are talking about," in the words of Thorkild); to know the processes by which poetry is created; to know the principles by which it affects the mind; to know in sum the principles by which it should be written. There is no better illustration of this ideal than Coleridge.

Believing it is as impossible for a man to be a true critic without finding "some central point from which he may command the whole" as for an astronomer to "explain the movements of the solar system without taking his stand in the sun," Coleridge declares: "The ultimate end of criticism is much more to establish principles of writing than to furnish *rules* how to pass judgment on what has been written by others; if needed . . . the two could be separated." Again he writes:

> But I should call that investigation fair and philosophical, in which the critic announces and endeavors to establish the principles, which he holds for the foundation of poetry in general, with the specification of these in their application to the different classes of poetry. Having thus prepared his canons of criticism . . . he would proceed to particularize the most striking passages to which he deems them applicable . . .

This is the empirical ideal of Aristotle. It is the ideal by which Dryden wrote his great "Essay of Dramatic Poesy"; Addison, his "Pleasures of the Imagination." Samuel Johnson shows at his best something of this temper. The end of criticism, he says (*Rambler* 3), is truth; and (*Rambler* 158) examining the principles of good writing, he maintains that "practice has introduced rules, rather than rules have directed practice." *See* Aesthetics. I. A. Richards, *Principles of Lit. Crit.*, 1926; *Science and Poetry*, 1926; Ship.; C-A. Sainte-Beuve, *Causeries du Lundi*, 15 v., 1856–69; A. Thorkild, "A Critique of Critics," (1791), in *Literary Criticism: Pope to Croce*, 1941; M. C. Beardsley, *Æsthetics*, 1958; Yvor Winters, *The Function of Criticism*, 1962; S. P. Zitner, Kissane, and Liberman, ed. *A Preface to Literary Analysis*, 1964; *The Practice of Criticism*, 1966; P. Denetz, Greene, and Nelson, ed. *The Disciplines of Criticism*,

1968; P. Salm, *Three Modes of Criticism,* 1968. CLARENCE DE WITT THORPE.

criticism, the new. After the flourishing of poetry in the second decade of the 20th c., the new criticism devoted itself mainly to that art, being distinguished from precedent consideration in its exclusive attention to the work, regardless of the author's life, background, or social leaning. Its first tendency was to make use of scientific devices, esp. graphs and statistics. Vernon Lee (Violet Paget) counted the proportions of parts of speech in various works. Thus a "sliced pie" graph showed that writings of William Sharp and "Fiona Macleod" have the same percentage of references to various colors, despite the pseudonym. Frequency of phonic symbols, of tone and of thought patterns, of images, of content and structural words, was laboriously charted. Caroline Spurgeon prepared elaborate graphs of the images in the plays of Shakespeare and some of his contemporaries. Edith Rickert, in *New Methods for the Study of Literature,* 1927, presents detailed methods for such study.

Most of this seemed to the next decade at best a drudgery background to criticism, although Laura Riding and Robert Graves (*A Study of Modernist Poetry,* 1929) soundly consider how spelling and punctuation affect appreciation of a Shakespeare sonnet. Supplanting such methods, there came out of semantics an interest in the problems of the word, with an erudite touch from T. S. Eliot, but mainly stimulated by I. A. Richards (*The Meaning of Meaning,* 1923, with C. K. Ogden; *Principles of Literary Criticism,* 1924—considered along with works of Beard, Boas, Freud, Lenin, Spengler, in *Books That Changed Our Minds,* ed. M. Cowley, 1939; *Science and Poetry,* 1926; *Practical Criticism,* 1939; *How to Read a Page,* 1924). Like Demetrius and Gellius in the first and second c. (Ship. p. 79–82) our new critics examined the interactions of words; they probed with all the tools of contemporary psychology the connotations and permutations of word and image, showing *e.g.* the general sweep but vagueness of Dryden and the richness and precision of the metaphysical Donne—naturally a favorite with this group.

The label given this attitude was the title of a controversial 1910 lecture by Joel E. Spingarn, *The New Criticism,* and was also used by John Crowe Ransom in 1941. Its ideas were most fully embraced by the group of southern writers who edited the literary magazine *Fugitive* (1922–25), and who turned from the agrarian movement (*q.v.*) back to literature, esp. in the popular textbooks *Understanding Poetry* (Cleanth Brooks and Robert Penn Warren, 1938), *The Language of Poetry* (ed. Allen Tate, 1942), and *The Well-Wrought Urn* (Brooks, 1947). They stressed the structural complexity yet inner consistency of the work, and insisted upon the close reading of the individual text. Of these formalists, René Wellek declared in 1961: "The New Criticism has, no doubt, reached a point of exhaustion."

Since then, some critics (H. Levin, M. Krieger) have applied the label to a cluster of professors at Yale: R. Wellek, C. Brooks, W. K. Wimsatt, Charles Feidelson.

The trend of the past decade has been toward a renewed emphasis on historicism and linguistics, and further attempts to apply methods of mechanical, esp. computer, analysis. In the 1960's in France, criticism has tended to emphasize an "intellectualistic humanism," and the multivalence of symbols in works of art, their complexity, ambiguity, and indirection. *See* New; Formalism; Ambiguity; and the Part Two surveys of criticism. John Crowe Ransom, *The New Criticism,* 1941; William Elton, *A Glossary of the New Criticism,* 1949; R. S. Crane, *Critics and Criticism,* 1952; L. S. Cowan, *The Fugitive Group,* 1959; W. J. Handy, *Kant and the Southern New Critics,* 1963; W. Van O'Connor, *The New University Wits,* 1963; R. Picard, *Nouvelle critique ou nouvelle imposture?,* 1965; Romain Gary, *Pour Sganarelle,* 1965; S. Doubrovsky, *Pourquoi la nouvelle critique?,* 1966; S. N. Grebstein, ed. *Perspectives in Contemporary Criticism,* 1968.

criticism, the polarities of. (1) *The poles of systematic criticism and individual works.* Literary criticism is a process applied to a subject. When the critic is too keenly aware of the process, he systematizes at the expense of individual works of art; when he is too sensitive to his subject matter, disparate or conflicting individual pieces of literature blur or render almost undiscoverable the critic's organizing principles. A balance should be struck between respect for each work of art in itself and respect for personal standards of judgment and belief, coherent in themselves, carefully thought out, and preferably expressed explicitly. Somewhere on the line between the poles of extreme imposition of standards of criticism and extreme passivity in reflecting each work of literature, all critics must take their stand.

The tendency toward absolute critical standards often results in general critical theories (Aristotle on tragedy, Boileau or Wordsworth or Poe on poetry). These are quests for general principles, based often on actual illustrations drawn at large from literature, but rarely on a single work of art completely considered. Such writing formally belongs in the domain of philosophy rather than of criticism, which is an art, a practice. The æsthetic philosopher may never have written a line of literary criticism. One should be aware of the difference between theorists on criticism and practising literary critics.

(2) *The poles of literature and life, of form and content.* Today the most obvious split between types of critics springs from the nature of literature itself. Literature is linguistic form given to a vast body of raw material which might be defined as the experience or consciousness of man. Some critics delight in the expression; others find the prime value in the experience. The former, therefore, concentrate on technical and formal studies of poem, novel, or play; the latter are not so much concerned with the magic of literary casements—their hinges, their proportions, and their panes—as with the seas and lands on which the casements open. If literature is expression of experience, then both the critic that holds to form and the critic that holds to experience are limited. A partial approach is inevitable in practical criticism; it is dangerous only when it is held as the complete or solely proper method. The formalist *l'art pour l'art* critics are right in emphasizing that they are dealing with the distinguishing aspects of literature; the experiential critics are most powerful in their claim that artists have usually felt that literature is about something, that it has human value, and that those critics are mistaken who shut it off from life in the lonely tower of ivory.

This polarity between literature and life bears no fixed relation to the first polarity between literature and criticism. A critic may be formal and relative (Croce); formal and absolute (John Crowe Ransom); vital and absolute (Sidney); or vital and relative (Sainte-Beuve). Indeed, every pair of polarities in the types of critic increases the possible traits of individual critics by geometrical progression. The most common type of critic —the moralistic—is usually a blend (M. Arnold; Paul Elmer More): he is loose in refusing to distinguish sharply between literature and life; he is inclined to be rigid in applying his own moral standards to the judgment of any particular work of art.

(3) *The poles of objectivity and subjectivity.* The last separation of critics into types depends upon where and how a work of literature exists. Does it exist static in the text itself? In the glowing conceptions of its creator, conceptions reflected only dimly in the work? In its understanding by its contemporaries? In the average reader's consciousness? In the trained modern critic's consciousness? An affirmative answer to each of these questions will produce a particular type of critic: the textual critic, the genetic or biographical critic, the historical critic, the popular book reviewer, the exponent of current psychology, sociology, or æsthetics. And, of course, by arranging the above simple answers in complex combinations, by admitting the truth or partial truth of various responses each critic may determine a basis of belief where he as an individual may stand comfortably.

These are the great polarities. They present the questions: What is the relation of criticism to literature? What is the relation of literature to life? What is the relation of the physical work of art to the æsthetic experience? Most critics do not front these questions head on, do not make their answers explicit. But they cannot proceed far in the process of actual criticism without revealing their assumptions. Realizing the importance of these questions and the variety of the possible answers, a reader who determines in his own mind the presuppositions of any critic he encounters may find that classification by types renders his own understanding of literary judgments more precise and more satisfying. The reader must, however, recognize that such categories, although they may be useful and illuminating, are theoretical and partial: each critic is unique. DONALD A. STAUFFER.

criticism, textual. Aims to reconstitute from the evidence of MSS the original text of a work, and to present the evidence to the critical reader in such a way that he may determine at any particular point the kind of testimony upon which the text is based and the soundness of the editor's judgment of that testimony.

Until ca. mid 19th c. the habits of textual criticism, at their best, consisted in the search for good MSS and the conjectural emendation (see below) of texts on the basis of the "best" MS. This entirely ignored the way in which the "best" MS came by either truth or error; and although divination might in many cases arrive at true readings, it also substituted many false. The modern improvements in technique are due to the application of the methods of Karl Lachmann (1793–1851), set forth in his edition of the *New Testament* (1842) and best illustrated in his edition of Lucretius (1850). The principal merit of Lachmann's system lies in the recognition of two distinct stages of judgment of a text and preparation of an edition: Recension and Emendation.

In the first stage of his work (Recension), the editor will search for all existing MSS or all MSS which by date and text offer hope of ancient variants, provide them with a dating as secure as possible, collate them, noting all variations, even the most minute, such as erasures, lacunæ, letters or words scratched out and rewritten, in such detail that his collation might serve as a copy of the MS itself. In actual practice such a high degree of accuracy seldom occurs, so that the editor normally provides himself with photographs by which he may verify his collations. The next step, classification of the MSS, involves the determination of their lines of descent by comparison of common faults, omissions, additions and so on. A MS which, by this process, may be proved to be copied from another existing MS must then be discarded, since any conflicting testimony it may offer is without value for the tradition. MSS, however, which closely resemble each other in their readings but are not copies of any extant MS are assumed to have been drawn from a common ancestor, either immediately or through other copies. When this process is completely successful (and except in those rare cases where two editions from the hand or the period of the author are in question) the editor will be able to represent the filiation of his MSS by a family tree (*stemma codicum*) with an assumed remote ancestor, or archetype. Good samples of such work may be seen in R. P. Robinson's edition of the *Germania* of Tacitus (1935) and, for a text involving extreme complications, B. E. Perry, *Studies in the Text History of the Life and Fables of Aesop* (1936). The editor will then attempt to determine the character of that archetype, from the letter confusions, faulty expansion of contractions and similar mistakes in the MSS before him: *i.e.,* whether it was in majuscule or minuscule, whether written in a continuous script or with divisions of the words, whether provided with marginal and interlinear notes and, if the data seem to warrant it, the pagination and lineation (stichometry) of the archetype.

When these processes have been completed, the editor may be able to recover the original reading of the archetype by determining which MS reading in each case is a corruption or correction, which original, as by the principle of *lectio difficilior* (*q.v.*). But the archetype so reconstructed, although it is as far as Recension can go, will still not be the author's copy, and it will be the editor's task next to discover when the text of the MSS, or implied by the MSS, is true, and if it is faulty to correct it. This is the process of Emendation, *i.e.,* the attempt to bridge the gap between the earliest accurate witnesses to an author's text and that text itself. In a passage which is meaningless, ungrammatical (*i.e.,* contrary to an invariable habit of the particular author, or of the author and his contemporaries) or, in the case of a poet, unmetrical, the editor, after making a determined effort to interpret the passage, will attempt to isolate the corruption and remedy it by conjectural emendation. This emendation, when proposed, should be intrinsically probable, it must be something which the author could have written in this particular context, and it should be palæographically probable, *i.e.,* it should be such a form as could reasonably be deduced from the corruption in the MSS; it should not, for example, assume in an archetype written in capitals a confusion of letters occurring only in minuscule hands (such as *n* and *u*) or a misinterpretation of an abbreviation that was not employed at the date at which the archetype was probably written.

The types of error which an editor may normally expect to be represented in his text are: confusion of similar letters, errors through general resemblance (in L. *voluntas* and *voluptas*); wrong combinations or separations of words; transposition of letters, words, sentences; substitution of late L. homonyms, *e.g., que* and *quae, aequus* and *equus, agit* and *ait* were homonyms to the scribes—*cf.* the frequent English substitution of "there" for "their," "lead" (noun) for "led," "bridal" for "bridle"; substitution of familiar words for unfamiliar, as English "till death us *do part*" for *depart;* false accommodation of endings, as *illos animos* for *illos animo;* intrusion of explanatory matter from the margin; repetition of letters or syllables (dittography); omission of words, syllables, or lines with the same beginning (*homœoarcta*), or the same ending (*homœoteleuta*)—as in Plautus, *Miles Gloriosus* 727–9, where two manuscripts omit different material for this reason. It must, however, be granted that not all errors fit within these classifications, and that mere blunders in the MSS, disarrangements of word order, and dislocations of lines or passages still lie within the province of divination rather than textual criticism. Any edition of a classical author, in consequence, which deals extensively in transpositions should not be regarded by the general reader as definitive; under present circumstances this is a game that anyone can play, but it should be left until all other methods have failed.

The methods of textual criticism are, however, not to be taken as absolute rules; they are intended to guide the informed judgment and do not in themselves lead to truth. Scholars of the 19th c. were inclined to be reckless in departing from MS readings, while scholars of the 20th c. are inclined to be gullible in abiding by them. To this extent the famous and vastly entertaining diatribes of A. E. Housman (pref. Lucan, *Bellum Civile,* 1926, and Manilius, *Astronomica,* 1937) are partially justified, although his opinion regarding his own attainments and those of Richard Bentley is grossly exaggerated.

In a few fields (especially the *Bible,* its *Apocrypha,* a good many works of the earlier Fathers, parts of Aristotle), to secure the evidence of early translations is part of the process of recension. Many of these translations are almost as old as the originals themselves, and although in the main derived from inferior MSS, they still constitute an important check upon the tradition as it is contained in MSS of the works themselves. *Cf.* Scientific method. F. W. Hall, *Companion to Classical Texts,* 1913; L. Havet, *Manuel de critique verbale appliqué aux textes latins,* 1911; Fredson Bowers, *Textual and Literary Criticism,* 1959, 1966; D. V. Erdman and E. G. Fogel, ed. *Evidence for Authorship,* 1966. KENNETH MORGAN ABBOTT.

criticism, types. All criticism is based on an individual's response to a work of art. Yet Impressionistic Criticism, "the adventures of a soul among masterpieces," is a recent type, the product of romantic individualism and modern self-consciousness. Logically, individual response is the first requisite for criticism; chronologically, criticism centering on personal sensitivities is a late-comer.

The intuitive response comes first, the instinctive, personal reaction in the presence of a work of art. If a critic—and all men who read are rudimentary critics—is responsible as well as responsive, the next step is fuller understanding: the movement toward the ideal and unattainable goal of complete, clear, faithful comprehension. The final step is judgment. This is the ideal order: instinctive response, voluntary understanding, final evaluation. History, however, reverses this order: the moral evaluation of literature was common in early criticism; techniques for comprehending literature by methods of rational analysis and historical study developed later in all their multiplicity; finally, now that we have come to realize that each critic is a unique and complex registering instrument, criticism has gained in delicacy and precision while losing the calm certainty of its general judgments.

Much of the best and most psychologically sensitive modern writing might be termed Relativistic Criticism. Its arguments are *ad hoc*: one man looks at one poem or novel. Criticism must spring from personal belief. This becomes dangerous only when sincere individual convictions are taken as universal laws. Absolutistic Criticism, characteristically excluding all middle ground, assumes that the only alternative to critical law is anarchy; that if each critic judges for himself, chaos must follow. Experience proves this position false. Although each critic must judge personally, human individuals have enough in common so that communication is usually possible, and enough agreement develops to justify the critical enterprise.

The field of Interpretative Criticism, for instance, affords opportunities for introducing relatively impersonal standards. The poem or play exists as an actual document. The actions and sequence of the past do not alter with personal whims. In establishing facts that clarify a work of art, historical scholars are serving as critics of literature. Textual Criticism brings the reader closer to what was actually written. Linguistic Criticism may keep him from misapprehensions, such as the assumption that a word has always meant the same thing. Biographical Criticism may establish significant relations between the creator and his work, may indicate the genesis, the driving force, or the conscious purpose (as distinguished from the achieved effect) of a work of art. Historical Criticism may set a work in its place, may restore its first true colors, so that we see its values more clearly. Enabling us to see a poem or play in its original state is perhaps as demonstrably valuable a critical service—certainly as dispassionate a service—as can be rendered.

Historical criticism may, of course, build up relevant background in any field—political, social, theological, philosophical, scientific. It is of particular relevance in reconstructing the literary background. Euripides considered as an isolated phenomenon makes less sense than Euripides considered as a dramatist, as a Greek dramatist, as the third in a trilogy of great tragic dramatists.

Today, historical criticism, characteristic of the nineteenth century, is supplemented by Comparative Criticism. Many of the juxtapositions in comparative criticism are illuminating and fresh; they achieve pattern not from accidents of time but from purposeful groupings by genres and dominant ideas. Such criticism, however, needs one steady rule: only comparables should be compared. This applies to tone, purpose, and manner, even more than to subject matter. More difficult in practice is comparative criticism that goes beyond the bounds of literature, seeking to avoid purely mechanical and artificial parallels in an attempt to get at the inner organizing forms. Poussin, the painter, and Racine, the argument would run, may be more profitably compared than Racine and La Fontaine. The History of Ideas, as distinct from traditional political or social history, opens new possibilities for the literary critic. In criticism of this type, literature is more than a technique of expression; it is a reflection of man's mind in one of its characteristic aspects, or, more frequently, it is a mirror of the spirit of the times.

The clear and full understanding of a work of literature is most frequently minimized in Judicial Criticism. Evaluative standards, implicit or explicit, are at work in all types of criticism, even at its most impersonal. When, however, one seeks a final evaluation, standards increase in importance, often in practice tend to warp or destroy the very work they are supposedly measuring. Usually judicial criticism is Ethical Criticism. This seems reasonable, since most literature contains moral elements; the danger is that the standards may be extraneous. When a moral critic is acting ideally as a literary critic, he will apply only those moral standards that are present in the work itself. At next remove, he will apply relevant, sympathetic standards. He will not judge *Laus Veneris* by the standards of *Pilgrim's Progress,* Sophocles by John the Evangelist, or Rousseau by Aristotle. If he judges a writer on the basis of ethical beliefs radically opposed to those of his original—as the Romantics judged the Augustans, or the New Metaphysicals judge the Romantics—then he should state his own beliefs sharply and clearly, so that his reader may decide whether he is acting really as judge or as prosecutor. On the other side, enthusiasts should set up their own roseate standards, when they can detect them, as counsels for the defense. Encomiums and jeremiads may be in themselves excellent examples of literary art; they are seldom true types of criticism. There is no reason why a poem, a play, or a novel may not afford the occasion for a sermon, provided the sermon is neither offered nor received as literary criticism.

Since the 18th c., with the development of periodicals and newspapers, all of the above types of criticism have been practised in the popular form now termed Book Reviewing. Here commercial considerations may dictate insincere judgments; topicality may destroy all perspective; deadlines may lead to ill-considered, hasty appraisals; sheer press of work may preclude responsible criticism; the demand for information may reduce the review to a description or an abridgement. Above all, the necessity of pleasing the reading public may make the public the ultimate critic rather than the book reviewer himself. These are merely lamentable general truths; individual book reviewers, now as well as in the past, conquer the perils of periodical publication; the *Causeries de Lundi* remain among the treasures and models of literary criticism, as though Mondays were seminal for Sainte-Beuve's ideas, and even their perpetual recurrence could not make his criticism weak. G. Boas, *A Primer For Critics,* 1937; T. S. Eliot, *The Use of Poetry and the Use of Criticism,* 1933; T. M. Greene, *The Arts and the Art of Criticism,* 1940; D. A. Stauffer, ed. *The Intent of the Critic,* 1941; W. Righter, *Logic and Criticism,* 1963; John Casey, *The Lang. of Criticism,* 1966; R. H. Pearce, *Historicism Once More,* 1969. DONALD A. STAUFFER.

cross order. Inversion, chiasm, *q.v.* Sometimes with repetition, *e.g.,* "The earth is at war with the sky; the heavens are battling the earth."

crown of sonnets. Interlinked poem of 7 (usually It.) sonnets: last line of each of the first six is the first line of the next; last line of the seventh repeats the first line of the first. Other rhymes are used but once in the entire poem. *e.g.,* Donne, *La Corona.*

crown poem. *See* Eisteddfod.

cruelty, theatre of. The recent emphasis on violence and sadism in the theatre may be traced to *Ubu Roi* (1896) by Alfred Jarry, and back to Elizabethan tragedies and the "sanguifulminous" blood and thunder melodramas, but today's theatre reflects esp. the violence in the world since World War II.

It was made precise by Antonin Artaud in *Le Théâtre et son double* (1938) with two "Manifestos of the Theatre of Cruelty," which emphasize the power of evil in the world. To Artaud, the theatre of cruelty was a theatre of myth and magic; its function was to liberate forces in the audience's subconscious by giving direct expression to their dreams and obsessions. Dialogue has a subordinate role, and depends upon gesture and movement. It is the purpose of such drama to express things that cannot be put into words, and the words used are intended to be ritualistic and incantatory. In this mood is Peter Weiss' *The Persecution and Assassination of Marat as Performed by the Inmates of the Asylum of Charenton under the Direction of the Marquis de Sade* (1965), which combines insanity, violence, and sex. Sex itself, far from being lasciviously stimulating, is in these plays distorted or extreme. The 19th c. French Grand Guignol illustrated the theatre of cruelty before the term was used. In a typical Grand Guignol play, a murderer leans over his sweetheart victim to make sure she is dead; the hands of the corpse, tightening in rigor mortis, close around the neck of the killer and choke him to death. Note, however, the distinction: the Guignol instance is cruel, not casually cruel but peaked with horror, therefore Gothic; in today's theatre of cruelty, the cruelty is casual, matter-of-fact. In current plays, the cruelty is not ironical, not laid on, not external; it is part of the natural scheme of things. It should be observed, however, that even in Artaud, cruelty does not necessarily imply physical violence; it is often psychic; and it may spring from what these writers deem the inevitable and therefore to us essential, educational, exposure to "the existential horror behind all social and psychological façades." *Cf.* Black comedy; Black humor; Comedy; Gothic. A different aspect, in Fr. literature, is discussed in Wallace Fowlie's *Climate of Violence,* 1967. C. Marowitz (and S. Trussler, ed.) *Theatre at Work,* 1967, 1968; John Russell Brown, ed. *Modern British Dramatists,* 1968; Bettina L. Knapp, *Antonin Artaud,* 1969.

cultures, the two. Opposition emphasized in the controversial book of that title (1959; "a second look," 1964) by C. P. Snow, claiming that the fields of science and the humanities have expanded so widely that they "can't or don't communicate." More critics believe that the impulses at work in both fields are the same, and that acquaintance with the other field is valuable for both. Some, however (*e.g.,* Wylie Sypher, *Am. Scholar,* Winter 1967–68) emphasize that there is a basic opposition between technology and poetry. A technician tends to become a bureaucrat; the methods of technology weigh opposition and "unreliability" and provide formulas to absorb these; hence technology promotes conformity and uniformity. The poet is the eternal individual, the ever-dissident. *See* Science and literature; Literature and Society. G. Bachelard, *Poetics of Space,* 1958; F. R. Leavis, *Two Cultures?,* 1962; L. A. White, *The Science of Culture,* 1949, 1969.

cursus. A pattern or segment of the flow of prose rhythm, *q.v.*

cycle. A series of poems centered around an epoch or personage of history or legend. First developed by the cycle poets of late classical times, supplementing Homer, the cycle grew extensively through the medieval romances. There were 3 main groups (listed by Jehan Bodel, 13th c.): of France (Charlemagne); of Britain (Arthur); of Rome the great (Troy, Alexander, and the offshoots). To these should be added the Norse cycle (*Beowulf*; the *Nibelungenlied*), which mingled later. While the main features of the various cycles were usually kept distinct, the manner of presentation, modeled on Homer and Virgil, was much the same, and in details they became widely intermingled: their heroes were as great as "Paris of Troy, or Absalom or Partenopex"; the sons of Rome (Brut) became the fathers of Britain; and classical demigods, oriental heroes, and Christian paladins hobnobbed with Celtic fairies. *Cf.* Epic.

cyclic foot. A foot of more than 2 syllables, speeded (according to one theory of Gr. verse) to make it equal in time to an iamb or trochee, and therefore used as an alternative to these. *See* Mora.

D

DACTYL. A metrical foot, one long syllable followed by two short (— ◡ ◡), *e.g.,* swimmingly; Longfellow, *Evangeline.* Dactylic hexameter is used in classical epic; in Eng., most frequent as a variant.

dadaism. School of art and literature dating from ca. 1917, characterized by the effort to suppress ordinary logical relationships between thought and expression. In general, it conceived of its major function as destruction of everything tending to hamper absolute freedom and spontaneity of form and content in art, and it used violent humor and devastating irony as means to this end. Tristan Tzara was prominent in the origin of the movement, which developed, ca. 1924, into surrealism, *q.v. Cf.* Absurd; Futurism; Automatic writing. T. Tzara, *7 Manifestes dada,* 1920.

daina. A form of folk poetry common to the Lithuanians and Latvians. Probably composed by the women, it deals in a simple form with all aspects of life and the relations of the people toward nature and superstition, with traces of the old paganism. Rhyme is present but not compulsory; the prevailing meter, in accordance with the accentual laws of the language, is either trochaic or dactylic. The Latvian daina is of four lines, although some may be joined to produce a longer song. It is usually accompanied on the kanklys, a peasant harp. U. Katzenelenbogen, *The Daina,* 1935.

dark comedy. *See* Black comedy.

dead metaphor. A figure so often used as to have become accepted as the normal manner of expression, thus losing its figurative power, *e.g.,* the head of the firm; a drop in the market. *See* Metaphor.

débat (*Certamen, conflictus, contentio, contradictio, disputatio; disputoison, estrif, plet; Streitgedicht*). A contest in verse in which a question is argued by two persons, personifications, or abstractions, the decision then being referred to a judge. *Débat* belongs to the great body of allegorical literature of the Middle Ages and is usually didactic, satiric, or both in purpose, although some later *débats* are literary exercises written solely to entertain. Contests in verse abound in medieval literature, but the *débat* is distinct in origin and form both from the usually impromptu folk contests (flytings *q.v.; Schnaderhüpfl, coblas*) and from the literary disputes of the Provençal poets and their imitators, such as the *tenson* and the *partimen.* The *débat* treats of varied subjects, impersonally and in the abstract, or metaphysically; the courtly dispute, purporting to deal with personal experience, treats solely of questions of love. Structurally the *débat* consists of a short introduction or description of the scene and circumstances of the dispute followed by the discussion proper, often enlivened by dramatic incident, and concluding with the reference of the case to an appointed judge. The themes vary with the interest of the writer and period; earlier *débats* drew on folk themes that reach as far back as the fables of Æsop, contests between the seasons, flowers, animals, and the like; from the later 12th c. theological, moral, political, social, and courtly questions afforded the material for dispute.

As a literary form the *débat* has a definite and clearly marked history. The tradition of those eclogues of Theocritus and Vergil that present a contest of wit, "a pastoral contest between shepherds for the prize of rustic song," survived through the 4th c. in the works of Calpurnius, Nemesianus, Vespa. The Carolingian poets in their imitations of Vergil and Calpurnius, although faithful to the pattern of the eclogue, by a shift of emphasis to the contest itself, evolved a new type, the *conflictus* (Hanford, Jeanroy). The contest of wit in the eclogue is personal, the interest lies primarily in the contestants' skill in presentation, not in the content of the argument. The anonymous *conflictus Veris et Hiemis,* attributed to Alcuin, preserves the narrative element, the song contest, and the judgment in the manner of Vergil's 7th eclogue, but strengthens the character of the disputants and the consistency of the argument. In the *Rosae Liliique Certamen* of Sedulius Scotus the framework of the eclogue is preserved but the pastoral element has disappeared. This is the literary ancestor of the L. and vernacular *débats,* which with the *chansons de geste,* the *fabliaux,* and Prov. lyrics were among the most popular literary forms of the 12th and 13th c., and survived through the 15th c. The sudden emergence and great popularity of the *débat* were undoubtedly due to the interest throughout the schools in dialectic and in poetry and to the rise of the courtly vernacular, in which the form soon made its appearance (early M.E., *Owl and Nightingale*). Except for a greater freedom in style, the use of accentual verse in both L. and vernacular versions, and the introduction of parody and satire, the *débat* differs in no essential from the *conflictus.* The matter of earlier dialogue and of scholastic disputes, such as the *Address of the Soul to the Body* and the *Four Daughters of God,* was recast into *débat* form. The dramatic and didactic character of the moral and theological *débat* brought about its incorporation into the religious drama. Versions of the *Debate of the Four Daughters of God, e.g.,* appear in Eng. drama in both cycle and moral plays. The main plot of the first secular drama in Eng. literature, Medwall's *Fulgens and Lucres,* is a dramatized *débat.* J. H. Hanford, "Classical Eclogue and Medieval Débat," *R.R.* II, 1911; A. Jeanroy, *Les Origines de la poésie lyrique en Fr. au moyen age,* 1925; F. J. E. Raby, *A Hist. of Secular L. Poetry in the Middle Ages,* 1934.

decadence. First found its modern expression in the "Ossian" poems of James Macpherson (1760–63) and the poetry of ruins. Normally a term of derogation, "the process of lapsing into an inferior condition," as in Nisard's attack on Hugo (*Latin Poets of the Decadent Era,* 1834), it was taken up boastfully by Baudelaire, who linked the spirit of modern life with the decadent literature of the past. He found its charm in the æsthetic consciousness of decay and nostalgia for ages of innocence and youth. With Mallarmé and Francis Thompson (*Ode to the Setting Sun*), but especially in France, there was emphasis on the beauty of the decline of things; and with Verlaine the term decadence became less a criticism than a banner. The review *Le Décadent,* 1886, however, was short-lived, yielding to the magazine *Le Symboliste,* founded the same year, as decadence was supplanted by symbolism (*q.v.*). Chief figure of the decadents is Des Esseintes, the aristocratic hero of Huysmans' novel, *A Rebours,* 1884, which influenced Wilde (*The Picture of Dorian Grey,* 1891) and D'Annunzio (*Il Piacere,* 1889). Their main tenet was that art is superior to nature, that human life should be lived as an art. The more pallid, nostalgic aspects of decadence, with its frail, languid, and condescending artificiality, are sometimes (with particular reference to the 19th c.) called *fin de siècle.* Today, many bewail the "decadence" of many modern novels and plays. Peyre remarks that the one type of "decadence" that is dangerous in literature "consists in being conventional and imitative, in tritely expressing cheap and superficial emotions." Henri Peyre, *The Failures of Criticism,* pp. 176–90, 1967; B. Charlesworth, *Dark Passages,* 1965.

decastich. Poem of 10 lines. *See* Stanza.

decasyllable. Line of 10 syllables. *See* Romance; Eng. versification.

décima. One of the most frequent classical Sp. stanza-forms, consisting of 10 verses, each of 8 syllables, with the rhyme scheme *abbaaccddc,* used in drama by Lope de Vega. This strophe is also called *espinela* (from the supposed inventor, Vicente Espinel). M. Milá y Fontanals, *Compendio del arte poética,* 1884.

decorum (L.; Gr. *prepon,* linked with the conception of beauty as dependent on order and fitness). In the *Rhetoric* (1404b) Aristotle says style should be neither humble nor too lofty but *prepousa.* In the *Poetics* (1455a25) the dramatist is urged to get so clear a view of all the parts of his work that they will fit properly together. With Cicero, the idea "became the all-embracing critical doctrine characteristic of the Latin genius" (Atkins, II, 31).

Hence it passed into the Renaissance; *e.g.,* Giraldi Cinthio writes: "Decorum is nothing other than grace and fitness of things, and should be thought of not merely as to actions, but as to speech and reply between men. Nor should this be considered only in the work as a whole, but in every part of it" (*Discorso intorno al comporre dei romanzi,* 1554). Milton speaks of it in *Of Education* as "the grand masterpiece to observe." Puttenham deals with it at length in his *Arte of English Poesie* (III, 23–24), calling it *decencie* and *comelynesse.*

The earlier 18th c. was familiar with it; *e.g.,* Goldsmith: "What must be the entire perversion of scenical decorum, when for instance we see an actress . . . unwieldly with fat endeavoring to convince the audience that she is dying with hunger!" (*The Bee,* Oct. 6, 1759). But the shift of *decency* and *decorum* to their later meaning had already begun; an early stage in the process appears when Addison speaks of Milton as making Adam "speak the most endearing things without descending from his natural dignity, and the woman receiving them without departing from the modesty of her character" (*On Paradise Lost* 4). Given a rigid standard of female behavior, the Victorian conception of decorum as respectable propriety was sure to follow. *Cf.* Beauty; Fitness; Correctness. Atkins; Ship; Rosemond Tuve, *Elizabethan and Metaphysical Imagery,* 1947. ALLAN H. GILBERT.

definition. When a discourse is based upon a relatively specialized and organized body of theory, such as literary criticism, it generally contains certain sentences whose function it is to supply, or stabilize, or clarify the meaning of its key terms. Such sentences are called definitions.

Definitions are divided into two fundamental types: (1) Some definitions (for example, those in a dictionary or technical glossary) are descriptions of actual usage; they state what the word means to speakers of the language in general ("pin"), or to a sub-class of its speakers ("paradox" as used by a certain group of literary critics). These definitions are called "reported definitions," "descriptive definitions," and "lexical definitions." Their usefulness depends upon the accuracy with which they describe linguistic facts. (2) Some definitions establish a *new,* though perhaps temporary usage, by assigning a new designation to a term, or introducing a newly-coined term, for the special purpose of a particular discourse or a particular field of study (for example, a critic may explain the way *he* proposes to use the term "tension" in an essay, and he may or may not go on to recommend that other critics follow suit). These definitions are called "stipulated definitions," "prescriptive definitions," "legislative definitions," "voluntary definitions," "impromptu definitions." It is usually held that they are not statements, but imperatives (recommendations or requests), and are therefore neither true nor false; in that case, their usefulness would depend upon the clarity they introduce and upon the consistency with which they are adhered to.

Whenever technical terms are used in inquiry, and especially in fields like criticism, where the crucial vocabulary is, for various reasons, likely to be misleading (*see* Terminology, technical), it is important to observe two general rules: (1) Every definition must carry a clear indication of its type; a great deal of serious misunderstanding arises because legitimate stipulated definitions ("I intend to use the word 'form' . . .") are taken to be false reported definitions ("The word 'form' generally means . . ."). (2) Every general statement must carry a clear indication of its function: that is, whether it is a definition or not. Definitions are sentences about words ("The word 'form' *means* . . ."); other statements are about the things to which the words refer ("Form *is* . . ."); and it is essential to keep them distinct, for the acceptance or rejection of a definition involves very different considerations from the acceptance or rejection of non-definitional statements. *Cf.* Meaning. R. Robinson, *Definition,* 1950; M. Scriven, "Definitions, Explanations, and Theories," *Minnesota Studies in the Phil. of Sc.* II, 1958; M. C. Beardsley, *Thinking Straight,* ch. 6, 3d ed., 1966; R. Borsodi, *The Definition of Definition,* 1967. MONROE C. BEARDSLEY.

denotation. The precise reference, or basic meaning, of a term. Opp. connotation, *q.v.*

dénouement (Fr., unknotting). The unraveling of the complications of a plot; immediately after the climax, the catastrophe (of a tragedy) or other event that brings the story to its end.

descort. Sometimes used as a synonym of the Prov. *lai;* more properly, a poem the stanzas of which are in different languages. Thus in a noted descort of the troubadour Raimbaut de Vaqueiras, a stanza of Provençal is followed by one in Genoese Italian, one in Old French, one in Gascon, and one in Galician Portuguese; the closing stanza has two lines in each of these languages.

description. Verbal portraiture; depiction of the appearance or characteristics of an object or scene, person or group. Though queen of lyric poetry, description has often been the Cinderella of prose fiction, the unconsidered servant who, except for infrequent but exquisite triumphs in portraiture or landscape painting, has merely kept the narrative house in order. Even so, this employment has been most important; for not only, in its own right, does description as setting fix the time, place, and social atmosphere of the story, but beyond this private function it assists character by suggesting or changing it (for better or worse) and plot by furnishing or removing obstacles to its progress. Thus description plays a major part in giving body to a story, in bringing about that "willing suspension of disbelief" which in a world of space and time creates objective reality.

Description may be either direct or indirect (by suggestion), enumerative (by cumulative details), or impressionistic (by few, but striking, details). The general method in any extended description, whether of place or person, may be thus indicated: (a) To fix upon the dominant impression to be conveyed. (b) To choose the most advantageous point of view, physical or mental (or both). (c) To choose the characterizing details that will most effectively create the dominant impression. (d) To appeal to as many of the senses as is feasible. (e) To link these details in spatial, chronological, rhetorical, or associational (the subtlest) order. (f) To end the passage with the dominant tone (or contrast tone), either by statement or (better) by suggestion (by means of the most characteristic detail). For specific purposes, of course, other methods are employed, *e.g.,* the disjunctive impressionism of the stream-of-consciousness novel. The usual method for brief description is to blend the individualizing details of setting with those of character and action in the forward movement of the story, as in, *e.g.,* Stevenson's "Markheim" and Katherine Mansfield's "A Cup of Tea." Modern practice leans strongly toward this incidental method of assimilation—away from setting (or characterization) in "chunks."

Devices add to both clearness and vividness, *e.g.,* (a) Fundamental image, commonly at the beginning (Thoreau's "bare and bended arm" of Cape Cod). (b) Contrast, as in Stevenson's *Night Among the Pines.* (c) Intentional repetition (the fog in *Bleak House*). (d) Direct and characterizing verbs (Kipling). (e) Putting a character in motion (cinematic rather than static photograph: Henry James).

Problems of handling description in fiction have increased in number and subtlety. To achieve picturesqueness, wonderment, or terror, the Romantic School brought setting into prominence. For the resuscitation of the storied past, background (Scott; Hugo) became a necessity; for the shift of interest from neo-classic generalization to modern individualization, places (landscape and social atmosphere) as well as persons grew in importance. Editors check stories for accuracy in such details as street names and building locations. To support their respective philosophies of life, realists and naturalists during the scientific second half of the 19th c. exploited environment, or (George Eliot; Flaubert; Zola) turned to the study of milieu. More recently, realists interested in social change or Freudian psychology (*e.g.,* memories of childhood) have assiduously studied and presented environment. Description as setting is thus no longer the neglected maidservant of narrative, but rather the fostering mother, from whom both plot and character draw ultimately their very being and sustenance. *Cf.* Composition; Milieu. For the idea of "spatial form" in recent literature, *see* J. Frank, *The Widening Gyre,* 1963, 1968. E. A. Baker, *The Hist. of the Eng. Novel,* 10 v., 1924–36; 1960–61; C. S. Baldwin, *Specimens of Prose Description,* 1895; Marjorie H. Nicolson, *The Art of Description,* 1925; Evelyn M. Albright, *Descriptive Writing,* 1925; P. Zinkernagel, *Conditions for Description,* 1962. FREDERIC THOMAS BLANCHARD.

detective story, the. A narrative in which a specific problem (commonly murder) is solved by the wit and energy of a detective. The form is one of the narrowest in popular fiction, yet it admits of astonishing variety. The detective may be a public servant supported on a police budget, a professional who lives off fees, or an amateur *sans peur et sans reproche.* The essential is that someone in the story engage in detection. In this technical sense, detection is hard to define. It is a shorthand symbol for the talents of a dozen different mechanisms: the nose of a setter, the engrams of a white rat, the bright correct bowels of an adding machine. *To detect* means to recognize intuitively, but this alone is not enough, for the reader must be let in on the process and an intuition cannot easily be displayed in print. Thus to detect means also to assemble data and make logical findings, to indulge in a kind of practical mathematics that can be reduced to premises, inferences, and conclusions, a process Poe calls ratiocination.

It is generally agreed that Poe was the first to make clearly defined use of the form, in *The Murders in the Rue Morgue* (1841). At least six elements that were at once to become fixed conventions may be found in this story. These are: (1) the apparently perfect crime (the sealed room, etc.); (2) the wrongly accused suspect at whom obvious evidence points; (3) the pedestrian bungling of the police; (4) the brighter eye and quicker mind of the detective, whose talents are advertised by eccentric manner and habits; (5) the admiring and slower-witted associate who tells the story; (6) the axiom that superficially convincing evidence is always irrelevant.

Dorothy Sayers suggests that the two main lines of development in the later detective story both stem from Poe. In one, the Sensational, as Miss Sayers puts it, "thrill is piled on thrill . . . till everything is explained in a lump in the last chapter." In the other, the Intellectual, "the action mostly takes place in the first chapter or so; the detective then follows up quietly from clue to clue till the problem is solved," keeping the reader informed throughout.

Broadly speaking, the distinction just made may be said to hold between American and British detective stories. There are exceptions enough to riddle any rule, but for the most part, British authors have been primarily concerned with niceties of deductive technique, American with dramatic incident and character.

The conventions established by Poe were carried forward intact by A. Conan Doyle in his long intermittent biography of Sherlock Holmes, beginning with *A Study in Scarlet* (1887). Doyle deepened and humanized the tradition, enriched the basic scheme by giving color to the narrator, Dr. Watson, and added at least one important element to the formula: a dramatizing of what we may call technology.

Medical science had already been used with excellent effect, but it remained for Holmes to popularize the more abstract values of chemistry, physics, and above all objective psychology. Detection itself became a science in the hands of the Master, and from the 1880's on, the method and subject-matter of the sciences play an ever more important part in the development of the detective story.

Because of the highly conventionalized nature of the form itself, there has been a tendency to conventionalize character and incident as well, to make the detective story merely a puzzle involving abstract counters. Since a premium must be placed on plot, many writers—and readers—have been led to ignore everything but plot. Pure plot stories, however, are the ephemera of the type. Those who live for more than a bookseller's month will be found, despite the restrictions of their formulæ, to have many qualities in common with the full-blooded novel.

This was pointedly illustrated in the excellent work that appeared when the espionage or spy story burst into full bloom in the early 1960's. As it proliferated, the detective story had displayed many forms, of which the espionage tale, often with more of suspense than of mystery, had been rather a minor one. The suspense story, the psychological, the supernatural, the straight mystery, and the mystery-adventure types (which include the hardboiled, often mistakenly attributed to Dashiell Hammett), all had developed capable practitioners and wide audiences. Among the most prolific, widely-read, and influential writers in the field are Agatha Christie, Erle Stanley Gardner, and Raymond Chandler. But relatively few major names had tried the espionage field. An important fragment of the Holmesian saga concerns spy activity; E. Phillips Oppenheim wrote of spying and intrigue in high places, and W. Somerset Maugham produced in the 20's a book of realistic short stories based on his own experiences as a British secret agent in World War I. (Spy stories seldom appear in time of war, when spying is presumably at its height.) Bridging the immediate past and present, Eric Ambler has produced a succession of espionage and foreign-intrigue novels that have won world-wide readership.

Then, in the early 1960's, the espionage story suddenly made itself felt, tending to be either wildly romantic and melodramatic (Ian Fleming) or bitingly true to life (John Le Carré). These two authors led the spy-pack, Fleming receiving a powerful assist from the late President John F. Kennedy, who found welcome relaxation in the derring-do of Fleming's James Bond, perhaps better known as 007. Le Carré (real name David Cornwell) in *The Spy Who Came in From the Cold* combined espionage and mystery suspense with neat unfolding of plot and solution.

Such successes encouraged a flood of spy and "military intelligence" novels, some crackling with excitement and movement and brimful of secret codes and coded secrets. Often, however, they consisted only of thrill piled on unrelated thrill; the influence of television's unreal and confusing imagism was obvious. The better writers, who repeatedly helped boost the mystery-espionage novel into the best seller lists (at times the genre occupied three of the coveted Top Ten positions), also include Len Deighton, Hans Hellmut Kirst, Donald Hamilton, Derek Marlowe, and the perennial Helen MacInnes.

What causes such new waves is seldom easy to pinpoint, but superior writing, credible backgrounds, and three-dimensional characters surely helped, as did the realization, brought home by major scientific advances and the frequent exposure of actual spy rings, that the enemy is ever near and steadily at work in Cold War or Hot. As a result, the mystery has again been advanced and refined, and its audience greatly widened—another giant step for a literary genre that had its beginnings as recently as 1841.

The detective story has been almost entirely an Anglo-American phenomenon. France has produced Gaboriau, Gaston Leroux, Maurice Leblanc (creator of Arsène Lupin) and many run-of-the-mill *romans policiers;* Belgium (and France) is responsible for the wit of Georges Simenon (creator of Maigret); but the Continent has never been fertile ground for the genre, despite the outstanding exception of Nicholas Freeling (Holland). *Cf.* Mystery II; Novel, types of; Short story; Viewpoint. A. S. Burack, ed. *Writing Detective and Mystery Fiction,* 1967; Howard Haycraft, *The Art of the Mystery Story,* 1946, 1961; *Murder for Pleasure,* 1951, 1968; G. de Traz, *Hist. et technique du roman policier,* 1937; *Les Romans policiers,* 1964; H. Brean, *Mystery Writer's Handbook,* 1956; A. E. Murch, *The Devel. of the Detective Novel,* 1958; T. Szobotka, *Aufzeichungen über des Kriminalroman,* 1961; J. Symons, *The Detective Story in Britain,* 1962; D. Madden, ed. *Tough Guy Writers of the Thirties,* 1968; R. Harper, *The World of the Thriller,* 1969; O. A. Hagen, comp. (bibliography) *Who Done It,* 1969. KURT STEEL and HERBERT BREAN.

determinism. The philosophical doctrine that nature is lawful, that is, that every event has a cause. Since the doctrine applies to human acts of choice, as well as physical events, it is opposed to one conception of free will, according to which some acts of choice are not lawful, in that a person who has made a free choice could have chosen differently under exactly the same antecedent conditions. The term "determinism" is sometimes used for two other doctrines that ought to be distinguished from it: (a) *fatalism* (of which predestination is one species), according to which some future events will necessarily occur, no matter what causal conditions happen to prevail at the time; and (b) *mechanism,* or materialistic determinism, according to which all causation is of the type that occurs in molecular physical systems.

The long-standing and wide-ranging controversies over determinism have impinged upon the field of literary theory as part of the conflict between science and the humanities. For example, determinism has been said, by the New Humanists, to be especially characteristic of naturalistic and realistic literature. What is meant and deplored here is apparently not determinism as such, but (a) the belief that men's choices are largely caused by irrational feelings, instinctual drives, or the unconscious (Zola, Dreiser, Lawrence); and (b) the belief that men's choices play little or no part in determining what happens to them, since their decisions are overwhelmed by natural or social forces (Hardy). In this sense, "determinism" means a particular theory of what is involved in the causation, and the outcome, of human choices.

It is held by some philosophers (for example, Wilber M. Urban, *Language and Reality,* ch. 10, 1939) that freedom of the will is a presupposition of tragedy in that the significance of the protagonist's actions, his responsibility and the justification of his destruction, require that his decisions be undetermined. It is held by other philosophers that literature presupposes psychological lawfulness, because it deals with the mutual influence of character and choice; and that the achievement of dramatic unity, plausibility, and inevitability in the development of a plot, as well as the revelation of character through action, depends upon adequacy of motivation. P. Macherey, *Pour une théorie de la production littéraire,* 1966. For bibliography, *see* Freedom. *Cf.* Naturalism. MONROE C. BEARDSLEY.

deus ex machina (L., God from the machine). The introduction of a god or other personage in a play, usually by a mechanical contrivance, in order to untangle the plot. Soon after its first appearance, the *deus ex machina* was criticized as an unnatural stage device. Aristotle's criticism is trenchant. Assuming a broader definition of *deus ex machina,* as including not only divine intervention but also accident, he argues that the unravelling of the plot must arise out of the plot itself; there must be nothing irrational within the scope of the tragedy. In this sense, the term is applied today to an artificial trick or coincidence for resolving the action. The Virgin Mary was thus used in some medieval mysteries. Modern instances: *Tartuffe,* King Louis XIV; *The Pirates of Penzance,* Queen Victoria. Modern scholars (T. S. Duncan) suggest that the classical use should be attributed not to poor workmanship but to an attempt on the part of the Gr. dramatists to analyze the causes and results of human action. And W. N. Bates has argued that Euripides used the *deus ex machina* deliberately to produce striking effects.

deuteragonist. *See* Protagonist.

diabolism. Works containing what is called diabolism, or Satanism, are of three general sorts: (1) books of diabolism, the *grimoires* or manuals of the theory and practice of black magic; (2) books about diabolism, chiefly histories and polemics; (3) creative literature that in some way expresses or uses diabolism.

Diabolism in creative literature is usually marked by a theme of devil worship; if this be taken as definitive, Calderon's *Magico Prodigioso,* Gautier's *Albertus,* and Marlowe's *Dr. Faustus* show diabolism. This is, however, an adventitious diabolism, for in these works and many like them, sympathy lies with heaven; at the end good is (Stephen Vincent Benét, *The Devil and Daniel Webster*) wholly victorious, or (*Dr. Faustus*) seems, in spite of disaster to the protagonist, still in arms, essentially unshaken, and destined to a wider triumph.

In what may be called essential diabolism, there is a manifest sympathy with evil for its own sake, and a chilling intensity of horror and conviction in the presentation of demonic phenomena. In English, the terror tales of Poe and such Gothic novels as *The Monk* by Matthew Gregory Lewis (known as "Monk" Lewis) show this diabolism. The poet Blake suggests it, with "the hoary figure of Nobodaddy sitting in the clouds." In Fr. it grows through Hugo and Gautier, with the romantic imagery of snakes, bats, ravens, cats, female demons, and the sinister "black sun". Vigny in his poem "Eloa" pictures Satan as the "consolateur" of oppressed man. But it is in the works of Poe's Fr. admirer, Baudelaire, and his contemporaries Villiers de l'Isle-Adam, Huysmans, and Barbey d'Aurevilly, that a literary diabolism closest to reflecting a veritable worship on the author's part shows itself. In them is a deliberate emphasizing and exaltation of evil for the sake of the extreme effects to be attained by it and as a sort of unsurpassable revolt against bourgeois morality.

Diabolism in the west has usually been linked with its essential opposite, Christianity. Baudelaire and his fellows were professed Catholics, but to extremists such as they, piety was almost as much an incitement to evil as a deterrent since it heightened the horror of perverse sin, a thing pathologically irresistible to them in their craving for the lurid. Baudelaire's famous sonnet, "Correspondances" has in his "Alchimie de la douleur" a demonic counterpart. Villiers de l'Isle-Adam said of Baudelaire that he was a Catholic possessed by a demon. The statement has some applicability to them all. It should be noted that blasphemy recognizes a god; Baudelaire was in a deeply devout mood when he spoke of Christ as the divine prostitute, soliciting all men that they take Him into their bosoms; his wildest impiety was tinged with the bravado of the sinner secretly yearning for God. Similarly in the neo-Platonic æsthetics of the Renaissance: the principal effect of the divine beauty is to commit a pleasing rape upon the soul: "grace ravishes the mind to love" (Cesare Ripa, *Iconologia,* 1613). *Cf.* Correspondence; Grotesque; Melodrama. A. Symons, *The Symbolist Movement in Lit.,* 1919; A. E. Waite, *Devil Worship in Fr.,* 1896; J. P. Houston, *The Demonic Imagination,* 1969. Robert H. West.

diacope (four syllables). Separation of a compound word, *e.g.,* to us ward. Also, tmesis. A type of transposition; *cf.* Hyperbaton.

diaeresis. In poetry, the break or pause that occurs when the end of a metric foot and the end of a word coincide; *cf.* Caesura. Bucolic diaeresis, in the fourth foot, as often in pastoral poetry.

dialectic. A philosophical method, illustrated by the Socratic dialogue of Plato, which consists in the critical examination of concepts and propositions. The Socratic dialectician takes up seriatim proposed definitions of a term (*e.g.,* "justice"), in search of that which gives the correct analysis of the concept meant by the term; and he examines proposed propositions (*e.g.,* "virtue is knowledge") and attempts to show their one-sidedness or inadequacy by deriving contradictions and absurdities from them.

In a looser, but derivative, sense, the term "dialectical" is applied to a procession of ideas in which, by contrast and comparison, they are corrected, refined, and revealed at deeper stages of significance. It is in this sense that we may speak of a dialectical development of ideas in a single work of literature, as in a "contrapuntal novel" of Aldous Huxley, or in an essay by Emerson or Montaigne, or in a series of works by the same author: for example, the plays of Ibsen and the novels of Dostoyevsky.

Aristotle called dialectics "the method of probable reasoning," as opposed to the demonstrative (later, experimental) method of science. The word was thus used (esp. in the Middle Ages) as equivalent to "logic". When a hypothesis, a suggested explanation, is presented for examination, it becomes a thesis (Gr. thing placed, laid down). Kant (1724–1804) declared that scientific principles and metaphysical concepts prove mutually contradictory, leading to antithesis. Hegel (1770–1831) retorted that they merge in a higher synthesis. The pattern of the dialectic (question and answer) from Zeno (4th c. B.C.) and Socrates (470–399 B.C.) persists in our time, combining in the ideas of Karl Marx (1818–1883) as dialectical materialism, examining interaction and change, embraced by the Communists and supposedly animating the Socialist Realism of their writings. *Cf.* Materialism.

dialogue (in novel or play). Does more than present persons as actually speaking. Their words may reveal their natures, being adapted in rhythm, in color, in diction—even in quantity—to their various characters. Through the dialogue, the persons are balanced one against another, thus each the more fully portrayed. At the same time (though no speech need come from life verbatim) it gives an air of actuality to the action—which it also carries along, growing out of and forwarding the basic struggle.

In fiction, furthermore, it adds variety, relief, and greater naturalness; by the necessary shift to the present tense, it brings the action nearer, makes it seem more swift and more intense.

In the drama, dialogue is more conventionalized, in at least 3 ways. (1) Until the present c., dialogue has been predominantly in verse, although we find prose, in Eng., in parts of Elizabethan plays (usually where commoners appear, or in comic scenes), and soon prose prevailed, despite a strain of poetry continuing to our day (Stephen Phillips, T. S. Eliot, Maxwell Anderson, W. H. Auden). (2) Speeches are much longer, or more neatly balanced, than in life. In the classical drama the speeches seem often as long as the choral songs; in the Eliz. theatre rhetoric seems to pour upon the platform stage. More often in Fr., and in Eng. Restoration high comedy, on the other hand (sometimes before: Hamlet's and Gertrude's opening words, in her closet; *Richard III,* IV, iv, 33f), the speeches are balanced: a couplet or a line by one character gaining equal response from another (*see* Stichomythia) or (*As You Like It*; Molière) the dialogue presents a succession of witty challenges and retorts. (3) The pretense and semblance of naturalness may be abandoned. The more intense the emotions of Shakespeare's characters, the more rugged the rhythm of their speeches, the more nearly their diction and its flow approximate the patterns of life; at other times he may seek deliberate ornamentation. The dialogue of many of Shaw's plays presents long-winded discussions, probing or flashing; in comedies of Wilde there may even be no effort to fit the dialogue to the speaker, both His Lordship and his lackey conversing in the same sparkling style. The plays of Shaw have, indeed, been called "discussion drama"; but in most effective plays, the dialogue is not only suited to the speaker, but carries along the conflict more than any physical action on the stage. In realistic drama, an effort is made to make the dialogue seem like conversation, which in the novel it is usually intended to represent. Tristram Shandy (in Sterne's novel, 1759–67), indeed, states that "writing when properly managed is but a different name for conversation"; the novelist in such works chats with his readers. Conversely, Samuel Johnson tried to give to his talk the qualities of his writing.

As a separate literary form, the dialogue by invented conversation usually explores philosophical positions or moral attitudes. The earliest such are the Sicilian mimes of Sophron of Syracuse (ca. 430 B.C.), of which but fragments survive. The verse mimes of Herondas (Alexandrian, third c. B.C.) present realistic scenes of ordinary persons. The dialogues of Plato (427?–347 B.C.), more formal and lengthy—some 26, including *Republic*; *Laws*; *Symposium*; *Apology* (story of Socrates)—had many imitators in the Renaissance (Spain, Juan de Valdes, 1528; Italy, Tasso, 1580). The more satiric Greek *Dialogues of the Dead* of Lucian (second c. A.D.) were imitated in the 17th and 18th c. (*Dialogues des morts*: Fontenelle, 1693; Fénelon, 1712). The *Imaginary Conversations* (5 v., 1824–29) of Walter Savage Landor range widely, *e.g.,* "Dante and Beatrice"; "Princess Mary and Princess Elizabeth"; "Calvin and Melanchthon." More recently, André Gide has used the form, which may also seek to probe the psychology of the supposed participants. R. Hirzel, *Der Dialog,* 2 v., 1895; G. L. Dickinson, "Dialogue as a Literary Form," *Royal Society of Lit n.s.,* 11, 1932; B. W. Cottrell, *Conversation Piece,* 1956; M. Ruch, *Le Préambule . . . l'art du dialogue,* 1958; G. N. Garmonsway, "The Devel. of the Colloquy," *The Anglo-Saxons,* 1959.

dialysis. (1) "the dismemberer." Sets down all possible reasons, then reasons them away. (2) Hyperbaton, *q.v.*

dialyton. *See* Asyndeton.

diary. *See* Autobiography.

diatribe. A minor genre, instrument of the Stoic and Cynic preachers of virtue. Akin to the Socratic dialogue: a limited treatment of a single philosophical, usually ethical, proposition in an informal conversational tone, simple and lively (often with abusiveness, the connotation that has survived in modern parlance). Freely used figures, citations from favorite poets, apothegms, anecdotes, witty turns of phrase, antithesis, apostrophe. Euripides exhibited a fondness for the rhetorical question, which is one of the formal characteristics of the style. Elizabeth H. Haight, *The Roman Use of Anecdotes,* etc., 1940.

dibrach. A metrical foot of 2 short syllables. Also, pyrrhic.

dicatalectic. Doubly catalectic: a line lacking a syllable of the established meter in the middle and at the end.

dichoree. A metrical foot, 2 chorees (trochees) treated as a unit (— ∪ — ∪).

dictamen. The art of writing prose, esp. letter writing. The many *Artes Dictaminis* of the 12th and 13th c. are manuals of rhetoric as applied to the writing of prose.

diction. The wording of a work; the style of phrasing. The name of an object, it was believed, gave one command of it, and something of the magic persists, as in fairy tales (*St. Olaf and the Troll,* Scand.; *Rumpelstiltskin,* G.) and in the power of slogans (*see* Hypostatization). Words are the clothes that thoughts wear. Longinus: "Beautiful words are in deed and in fact the very light of the spirit." Such an attitude, in many periods, led to a concern for words themselves, which early provoked a counter-warning. Aristophanes jibes at Aeschylus: "Let us at least use the language of men." Cato's *Rem tene, verba sequentur* is translated by Alice's Duchess: "Take care of the sense, and the sounds will take care of themselves." "The question is," says Humpty-Dumpty, "which is to be master—that's all."

Fundamentally, diction need observe but two criteria: fitness (to theme, mood, purpose, receptor, user) and—to sustain interest—variety. The problem is to determine which words fit. Here, Occam's razor may be of service: unless there is a sufficient reason for an unusual word, the familiar term is best. A rare word, however otherwise apt, may call attention to itself, away from the idea (though it must be noted that in poetry the word itself is part of what one wants to say; *see* Poetry and Prose). On the other hand, common terms may become commonplace; the words slip into a ready groove, and habit takes the place of thought. Keeping in mind this danger, note the advantages listed by Joubert: "It's through familiar words that the style bites into the reader. It's through them that great thoughts gain currency and are taken in good faith, as gold and silver of a known stamp. They inspire confidence in him that uses them to make his ideas plain; for such a use of the common parlance marks a man that knows life and keeps close to it. Such words, furthermore, make the style frank. They announce that the writer has long been nourished on this thought or feeling, that he has made it so intimate a part of himself that the most ordinary words suffice him to express the ideas, become his own through long conception. What he says, finally, is more likely to seem true; for no other diction is as clear as what we term familiar, and clarity is so fundamental a characteristic of truth as often to be taken for truth itself."

Other forces than our unthinking acceptance, however, work against the power of familiar words. They have been used so often (Drinkwater, *Victorian Poetry,* 1924) that they may seem not simple but over-naive, or imitative. Chaucer could say "Ther sprang the violet all new" and it was beauty. (Yet any period may have its Burns.) Many words and phrases have gathered associations around them. Shakespeare said:

> . . . not poppy nor mandragora
> Nor all the drowsy syrups of this world. . .

Keats dared speak of autumn "drowsed with the fume of poppies"; the third will be bold indeed. (Yet writers deliberately build upon such connotations; all, on the general store of associations words have accumulated; some —T. S. Eliot—on their more literary, more recondite, ties.) Some words bear other dangers: they have become obsolete or archaic; they are technical; they have been used so often that even newspapers list them as taboo —which in turn may lead to the deliberate seeking of unusual words that marks the tyro and the columnist, and speeds the birth and death of slang. (Yet these special attributes may be drawn to special effects, in the writer's blend of sound, sense, and suggestion.) The basic material of all writing is the familiar word; this is varied or spiced according to the purpose. *See* Meaning; Semantics.

diction, poetic. A poem is spoken or written in words. What words should be used? Many of the subsequent critical answers exist as hints in Aristotle, who in his *Poetics* gives closest scrutiny to diction, which he considers as conscious, formal embellishment. Furthermore, in suggesting that literature may portray life as better than it is, worse than it is, or as it is, he lays the groundwork for later theories of the high, the low, and the middle styles.

Diction was viewed grammatically and rhetorically; turns of speech and formal figures were therefore arranged systematically and serially; and language was considered technically as an external garment applied to an idea in order to achieve a desired effect. Dante in his *De Vulgari Eloquentia* exemplifies the medieval modification of the classical observations on the language of poetry. His analysis of diction is detailed, if somewhat mechanical: words are childish, feminine, or manly; combed or shaggy, etc. He earmarks a language for poetic purposes, and classifies appropriate types of words for particular poetic forms or effects.

In the main, as national literature developed, the critics tended to impose on poetry a high, dignified, generalized language copied from accepted models; the poets themselves, particularly in early or aureate Renaissance periods before principles were popularly codified, tended to create a language of their own regardless of the rules—witness in Eng. Spenser and Shakespeare. The Pléiade in Fr., Jonson and the tribe of Ben in Eng., polished the language to meet classical criteria. Doctor Johnson gives classic statement to the idea that poetry must be generalized, universalized in the sense that it may be readily understood by any age, race, or class: "The business of a poet is to examine, not the individual, but the species; to remark general properties and large appearances; he does not number the streaks of the tulip. He must write as the interpreter of nature and the legislator of mankind, and consider himself as presiding over the thoughts and manners of future generations, as a being superior to time and place." And the conception of clarity, dignity, regularity, polish, "the refinement of our language," is sufficiently evident in Johnson's admiring epigram on Dryden and the language of Eng. poetry: "He found it brick, and he left it marble."

The following stanza by Thomas Gray shows typical 18th c. diction. Fine as it is, it accounts in part for the layman's notion of "poetic diction" as archaic, inverted, circumlocutory, unreal, and filled with personifications.

Say, Father Thames, for thou hast seen
Full many a sprightly race
Disporting on thy margent green
The paths of pleasure trace;
Who foremost now delight to cleave
With pliant arm thy glassy wave?
The captive linnet which enthrall?
What idle progeny succeed
To chase the rolling circle's speed,
Or urge the flying ball?

Neo-classical theory and practice must not be too simply considered rigid and strait-laced. No more telling attack on the weak, conventional diction of second-rate poets has been delivered than by Pope in the *Essay on Criticism* at the height of the Augustan Age (1711). In his Preface to the second edition of *Lyrical Ballads* (1800), which became the manifesto of English Romanticism, William Wordsworth turned the spotlight on what he terms "vicious poetic diction" and declared that "there neither is, nor can be, any essential difference between the language of prose and metrical composition," and that he intends to adopt and imitate "the very language of men." If these statements were taken as general rules, they would outlaw most of the poetry before Wordsworth's time, and much of his own; they should be understood in their place, as prefatory explanation of his particular purpose in writing "lyrical ballads." In the *Biographia Literaria,* Coleridge corrected his friend's overstatements.

In recent times, variety in poetic language has been so great—from Hopkins to Yeats, from Machado to Guillén, from Frost to Eliot, from Rilke to Auden, from Masefield to Pound—that scarcely any rule can encompass it. Perhaps the best has been suggested by Robert Bridges: any words are allowable if they are in key. The line

And, O ye Dolphins, waft the hapless youth

and the line

And never lifted up a single stone

are both excellent in their places; the diction of one is not "better" than that of the other; but the languages of *Lycidas* and of *Michael* are not interchangeable. In Dryden's phrase, "Propriety of thought is that fancy which arises naturally from the subject, or which the poet adapts to it. Propriety of words is the clothing of those thoughts with such expressions as are naturally proper to them; and from both these, if they are judiciously performed, the delight of poetry results."

This principle of consonance, demanding

that the effect of each word in relation to its companions be calculated, leads to the further conclusion that the diction of poetry is by nature more conventional than that of ordinary speech. (In critical analysis, conventions in diction should not be confused with the conventions dictated by metre, stanzas, and other rhythmical and formal organizing devices, though in a poem their interplay is natural. Word order and inversion, for example, may be influenced by prosody and by rhetoric as well as by theories of diction. Is, *e.g.*, Milton's "human face divine" determined by the thought, the metre, or the desire to secure overtones from a word order natural to the inflected languages of antiquity?) Convention and control of diction result from the form and purpose of each particular poem. *The Faerie Queene* would not employ the rich imagery of a short ode by Keats or the compressed energy of a sonnet by Hopkins. The principle of consonance or propriety is always at work in good poetry, although its language varies, with times and persons, to fit closely the changing basic conceptions of the purpose and effect of poetry. For example, the *surréalistes* or the imagists hold certain fundamental beliefs concerning man, nature, and art that modify their vocabulary. In the metaphysicals and modern poets that practice the "shock technique" of juxtaposing incongruous words and images, the principle of consonance is violated in local instances in order to secure a larger consistent effect of intensity and complexity; the dissonance is not accidental but designed. Again, the vocabulary of Mallarmé or Valéry depends upon the growing autonomy of æsthetics and the progress of the conception of *la poésie pure.* Each poet or school has peculiar conventions and self-imposed limitations.

Words are inadequate instruments to present even the simplest subject directly and completely. This leads to a further observation: the diction of poetry suggests rather than states. Hence the importance of symbol, image, metaphor. The language of poetry is connotative rather than denotative. It shifts rapidly from one manner of apprehending to another; it blends various fields of consciousness; it plays simultaneously on many planes of meaning. And at its best, the language of poetry is not obscure but multiple in suggestion, so that its implications convey rich, exact, complete, and intense human experience.

Although the term "poetic diction" is now usually derogatory, the words of poetry differ from those of prose in that they are more frequently selected (from the entire range of the language) because of aspects other than mere meaning: conciseness, connotations, intertwining sound. *Cf.* Style. C. S. Baldwin, *Ancient Rhetoric and Poetic,* 1924; *Medieval Rhetoric and Poetic,* 1928; B. Groom, "Some Kinds of Poetic Diction," *Essays Eng. Assn. XV,* 1929; *The Diction of Poetry from Spenser to Bridges,* 1955; F. W. Bateson, *Eng. Poetry and the Eng. Language,* 1934, 1961. DONALD A. STAUFFER.

didactic (Gr., teaching). The lengthy discussions, from Plato to our own time, as to the purpose of art, usually employ the term didactic without noticing that it has different applications: (1) should the writer try to teach? (2) should the work of art be instructive? In certain cases (Virgil, *Georgics*; Longfellow, *Psalm of Life*) the poet clearly sets out to give information so that it may be used; such works are classified as didactic. More widely, it may be maintained that every author and every work of art (willy-nilly) is of some benefit to man; thus, all art is didactic. So great a span, however, deprives the term of value. (*Cf.* Propaganda.) Yet Aristotle neatly noted that the immature mind views everything didactically. Since not every writer who hopes to teach (sway one to specific actions) announces his intention, and since in any case the purpose must be judged from the work, a further application of the term has been suggested: if it seems that the idea existed before the form, the work is didactic; if the form before the idea, the work is precious; if idea and form took shape together, the work is art. Thus "didactic" may be used (1) as a (subjective) and usually derogatory term; (2) to mark an all-embracing characteristic; (3) to describe a kind or category of work. *Cf.* Precious.

didacticism. The belief that the first function of poetry is to teach has prevailed throughout the ages. It apparently was well rooted in Greece in Plato's time; to Hesiod (8th c. B.C.) only verse is conceivable for anything to be remembered save mere official records. Poetry occupied a high place in Greek education because it was believed that from it children learned about the gods, that poetical characters were worthy of imitation, and that many subjects, such as generalship, were admirably taught by Homer. Plato pointed out that Homer often represented the gods as immoral, that the complaining and weeping of Achilles is not to be imitated, that no man was ever chosen general because he was educated through poetry. As a result of this, and the judgment-disturbing emotional stimulation, Homer was banished from Plato's republic. Croce has spoken of Plato's theory as a negation of art; it seems quite as likely, however, that he was attempting to show the absurdity of an elementary didactic theory, and to suggest that Homer wrote not a textbook on generalship but a poem.

At any rate, Aristotle in the *Poetics* assumes that the position of poetry may be taken for granted and that he may discuss it as an æsthetic phenomenon, without regard to its didactic qualities. He abandons the notion that the characters of tragedy are subjects for imitation; indeed he rejects the perfect character as a tragic hero, and substitutes one who is morally like men as they are. Likewise Aristotle swept away the minor didactic by declaring (ch. 25) that errors in fact do not touch the essence of poetry.

Horace, nevertheless, with Roman practicality, made the didactic motive important, though not exclusive. In the *Ars Poetica,* he asserts that the poet is to teach, to please, or to do both. Lucretius had already written the charter of the didactic theory: "Even as healers, when they essay to give loathsome wormwood to children, first touch the rim all round the cup with the sweet golden moisture of honey, so that the unwitting age of children may be beguiled as far as the lips, and meanwhile may drink the bitter draught of wormwood, and though charmed may not be harmed, but rather by such means may be restored and come to health; so now, since this philosophy full often seems too bitter to those who have not tasted it, and the multitude shrinks back away from it, I have desired to set forth to you my reasoning in the sweet-tongued song of the muses, as though to touch it with the pleasant honey of poetry, if perchance I might avail by such means to keep your mind set upon my verses, while you take in the whole nature of things, and their usefulness." (*De rerum natura,* bk I, 925f; bk IV, 1–25). Through the ages since, poetry has been deemed the gilt on the philosophic pill.

Ruskin indicated a three-fold function of literature: to enforce the religious sentiments of men; to perfect their ethical state; to do them material service. Pleasure is merely the avenue and sign of their proper functioning; a byproduct, not the goal. Tolstoy stressed the first two aspects; Morris, the last two (which led to much wrought iron work, new printing fonts, the Morris chair).

After the turn of the 20th c., most liberals looked upon "Art for Art's Sake" as a slogan to free them from prudery and philistinism; didacticism became a crude schoolhouse affair, for the "transmission of conduct ideals" through proper reading. As early as 1901 A. C. Bradley (*Poetry For Poetry's Sake*) attempted constructive application of the valuable tenets, and avoidance of the errors, of the theory of Art for Art's Sake and in 1933 T. S. Eliot (*The Use of Poetry and the Use of Criticism,* p. 152) called the theory "a mistaken one, and more advertised than practised." His words, however, snag on a duality in the phrase, which may refer to the intention of the poet, but more probably is directed to the effect of the work of art itself. In this regard, two other modifications of crude didacticism have been advanced: the idea that art produces a general exaltation of spirit, and thus—without direct teaching—is wholesome and uplifting; and the suggestion that art is (like exercise and play for the body) a mental exhilarant, a recreation for the soul. The neohumanists (Paul Elmer More; Irving Babbitt) see the writer as responsible to the law of man as distinct from the law of thing; and the most loud-spoken, if not the most influential, school of critics, novelists, playwrights, poets—the sociological—carry on their work (and carry it over into the radio and cinema) with a didacticism as elementary as that of Plato's *Protagoras,* in the conception of art as document, or as "a weapon in the class war," but in any event as an intrinsic means of rousing and directing moral conduct and ideals. *See* Receptor.

R. F. Egan, *The Genesis of Theory of "Art for Art's Sake,"* 1921; I. Babbitt, *The New Laokoon,* 1910; C. R. Decker, "The Æsthetic Revolt . . . ," *PMLA,* liii, 1938; Allan H. Gilbert, *Literary Criticism from Plato to Dryden,* 1940. Allan H. Gilbert.

diffusion. A spreading of references and images through many fields, often with vague or no reference to the putative subject of the work. Frequent in the writings of "the absurd"; also, a characteristic of much modern poetry. Hinted at by Baudelaire (*My Heart Laid Bare*) as "the vaporization of the Ego"; found in the cataloguing verses of Whitman; also Eliot; Pound; Rilke; William Carlos Williams. Manifests "the manysidedness of the one," multeity in unity. Diffusion, as a deliberate literary device, is not to be confused with diffusiveness, which is a long-winded, prolix, wordy meandering or maundering. A. Cook, *Prisms,* 1967.

digression (Gr. *parekbasis*). A type of embellishment consisting in the insertion of material of only indirect relevance. Such material might serve to win sympathy, to arouse animosity towards the opposition, or to weaken adverse argument. Digressions consist in denunciation, criticism, ridicule, eulogy, appeals to pride or patriotism, or any subject matter that may effectively sustain (or relax) the mood, and maintain interest. Popular in 17th and 18th c. Eng. writings, *e.g.,* Sterne's digression on digressions in *Tristram Shandy. See* Speech, Divisions of a; Ecbasis; Excursus.

diiamb. Two iambic feet (◡ — ◡ —) considered as a unit. Thus in classical scansion, an iambic dimeter consists of two diiambs.

dilemma. A balance between two choices (the "horns") equally unfavorable, so that either way the person is impaled. Most of the traditional dilemmas (Morris R. Cohen, *Reason and Nature,* 1931), however, rest not on real contradictions, but on various, sometimes verbal, difficulties. The dilemma is an effective device in argumentation.

dilogy. An equivocal expression, or the use thereof. In amphiboly (*q.v.*) the second meaning is concealed; here, two meanings are apparent but only one is (on the surface) intended, *e.g.* "Friends—I know you too well to call you Ladies and Gentlemen."

dime novel (from the cost: also penny dreadful, serial in newspaper; shilling shocker, bound; blue book, *q.v.;* yellow back). Series, begun by E. F. Beadle, 1860, with reprint of Ann S. W. Stephens' *Malaeska.* Thrilling tale of violent action, usually bound in paper, until the days (ca. 1895) of the even cheaper Nick Carter and Frank Merriwell series and the pulp magazines. Fostered patriotism and conventional morality, but was frowned upon because of its exciting incidents. Usually crudely written, but stilted rather than vulgar. E. L. Pearson, *Dime Novels,* 1929; F. Gruber, *The Pulp Jungle,* 1967, gives 11 "basic" elements of the mystery, and 7 "basic" plots for the western. *See* Melodrama; Detective story.

dimeter. A verse of two feet. Iambic, trochaic, and anapaestic feet were (Gr. and L.) counted in pairs (*see* dipody); *e.g.,* trochaic dimeter contains 4 trochees.

Dionysian (Classical god of fertility and wine, Dionysus). Uninhibited, emotionally uncontrolled; orgiastic. Opp. Apollonian, *q.v.*

dipody. Any pair of feet treated as a unit. *See* English versification.

dirge. A song of lamentation. In the Rom. funeral processions, the *nenia,* song of praise for the departed, corresponding to the Greek threnody and *epicedium,* was chanted, with the playing of flutes. Originally sung at funeral banquets by members of the family, they were later recited by hired wailing-women, *praeficae,* and became insipid, and unintelligible. The funeral oration (Fr. *oraison funèbre*) grew to a more elaborate form. In later literatures, the dirge appears as a simple, mournful lyric, with folk-song qualities, *e.g.,* Shak., *Cymbeline*: "Fear no more the heat of the sun;" *The Tempest*: "Full fathom five thy father lies." *See* Elegy; Pastoral.

disbelief, willing suspension of. *See als ob.*

discovery. Revelation of a fact that produces a decisive turn in the dramatic action, *e.g.,* to Œdipus that he had slain his father and married his mother. Said by Aristotle to be, along with the consequent overturning, the most powerful element of emotional interest, "the thing with which tragedy leads souls."

disposition. Second faculty in the construction of a speech (first, invention, *q.v.*). In the typical medieval treatise, disposition has six parts: (1) Exordium, a (clear, modest, concise) opening. (2) Narration, a (plain, credible, brief, pleasing) statement of initial facts. (3) Proposition, presents the case; if issues are given, called partition. (4) Confirmation, presents the arguments. (5) Refutation, tries to show that objections are absurd, false, inconsistent, or irrelevant. (6) Peroration, sums up, with emotional appeal. For ancient grouping, *see* Speech, divisions of.

dissociation of ideas (an exercise pictured by Remy de Gourmont as sorely needed). (1) The refraining from irrelevant allusion, *e.g.,* from saying "There's method in his madness" when there is display of method, perhaps, but no madness there. (2) By extension, as a method in art, the successive following of tangential ideas from a central theme, *e.g.,* Proust, *A la recherche du temps perdu,* passim. *Cf.* Association; Ambiguity.

dissonance. Harsh and inharmonious rhythm or juxtaposition of sound, sometimes used (Browning) for special poetic effects. *Cf.* Consonance, Assonance.

distance. *See* Psychic distance.

distances, the three. Explicit or implied in all works of wide scope. On the physical plane (Hugh Walpole): (1) The immediate setting, *e.g.,* Wall Street today; (2) the wide background of similar marts, the Bourse, the Rialto, of other countries, other times; (3) the rest of the physical world, interested in the same things (the slums, the bourgeoisie, the park bench) or contrasted (science, art), *e.g.,* in medicine, *Arrowsmith.* On the psychological plane: (1) the character as a unique individual, his particular responses; (2) within him too, the attitudes and actions typical of his class, gentleman, lawyer, Scotsman; (3) deeper within him, the tendencies, impulses, affections, common to all mankind, *e.g., The Way of All Flesh.* Sometimes a fourth, transcendent distance completes the expanse; even on the material plane, *e.g.,* (1) a particular couch; (2) other rests of this type or social level; (3) all chairs; (4) the weariness of mankind, need of slumber, of repose, which can be satisfied with a head on a log in the forest (womb of the chair), *e.g., Moby Dick.*

distich. A couplet consisting of two dissimilar lines. In Gr. and L. by far the most common is the elegiac, *q.v.*

dit. *See* Old Fr . . . forms.

dithyramb. Most popular early Gr. lyric form; yet not a single indisputably dithyrambic poem survives in entirety. In origin, probably a song at the sacrifice to Dionysus. Sung in competition at the festivals by a chorus of 50. Music was in the Phrygian mode, orgiastic (Aristotle) and passionate; the tone was bold, the diction lush, the meters varied. Even by the 5th c. B.C. interest had begun to shift from the poem to the music until in such as Timotheos we recognize virtuosi whose lyrics were so empty they justify the proverb, "You have even less sense than the dithyrambs." Chief reason for interest in the form is Aristotle's statement (*Poetics*) that in origin, tragedy is related to the dithyramb. This is disputed in A. W. Pickard-Cambridge, *Dithyramb, Tragedy, and Comedy,* 1927.

divan (Persian, Arabic: a council of state, hence a couch, hence also an account book). Applied to a collection of poems, usually by one author, often with the rhymes running through the alphabet. Most noted are those of Hafiz, Saadi, Jami, Gabirol, Jehuda Halevi. Imitated by Goethe, *West-Östlicher Divan. Cf.* ghazel.

divisional pause. Caesura, *q.v.*

dizain. A poem or stanza of ten lines.

dochmiac. A metrical foot of 3 long and 2 short syllables, arranged ◡ — — ◡ —, often resolved. Dochmiac passages are often interspersed with iambic lines; they are almost always confined to Gr. dramatic verse, to represent intense emotion.

document. Something written that furnishes information or evidence on a subject. Hence, in literature, a work drawn directly from life and reproduced as exactly as the medium permits. The novels of the naturalists were referred to as *documents humains.* The story in which the environment is background, or even is prominent as local color, increasingly since Zola's *Roman expérimental* (1880) and his *Histoire naturelle et sociale d'une famille sous le second Empire,* the Rougon-Macquart series (1871–93), but esp. in the U.S. in the "social thirties," gave way to the work in which characters and incidents as well are taken directly from life. Sinclair Lewis had a physician consultant for his novel of a doctor, *Arrowsmith* (1925); Dreiser used the court records almost verbatim in *An American Tragedy* (1925); playwright Sidney Howard collaborated with the author of *Microbe Hunters* to "translate heroes of science" into his drama *Yellow Jack* (1934).

Such works, drawn from the immediate scene, lose perspective, but gain intensity from the receptor's involvement in the concerns and in the passions of the day. This is taken by some as a sign that such works will also die with the day, except for the historian; that they cannot live as art. Dickens stands as a reminder that this need not be; document and art are not mutually exclusive and, indeed, most books of any type are soon forgotten. The documentary work, however, is peculiarly dependent, even for its appearance, upon day-to-day changes. Novelists now hurry into print lest their material become stale; Shaw, during the run of his play *Geneva,* sent fresh dialogue as the world situation changed; two plays readying for production on Broadway were withdrawn when Japan attacked Pearl Harbor. Some novels draw their material directly from specific events given newspaper prominence: beyond Dreiser, Truman Capote built his *In Cold Blood* (1966), which he called a "non-fiction novel," not merely out of newspaper reports but out of many interviews with the murderers. For the mellowing effect of time, contrast the anger of Maxwell Anderson's play *Gods of the Lightning* (with Harold Hickerson, 1928) about the 1927 execution of Sacco and Vanzetti with his sober though still grim *Win-*

terset, looking back at the same story in 1935.

A more permanent sort of document, perhaps, is that which presents no single violent deed but a lasting feature of the landscape (Pearl Buck, *The Good Earth*) or aspect of human failure (E. Caldwell, *Tobacco Road*), or phase of psychological weakness (J. Steinbeck, *Of Mice and Men*). The document springs from journalism, but seeks to capture the essentials as well as the surface of a condition or a deed. N. M. Blake, *Novelists' America: Fiction as History, 1910–1940,* 1969.

documentary theatre. *See* Epic theatre.

doggerel. 1. Undignified, trivial verse. 2. Verse of a rough rhythm, burlesque in intent, or otherwise humorous, *e.g.,* the short-line tumbling stanzas of J. Skelton's *The Tunning of Elynour Rumming.* As he says (*Colyn Cloute*):

> . . . though my ryme be ragged,
> Tattered and iagged,
> Rudely rayne beaten,
> Rusty and mothe eaten;
> If ye take well therwith,
> It hath in it some pyth!

dogmatic. Proceeding on the basis of *a priori* principles; stating with no corroboration save one's own authority. *See* Criticism, types. Santayana declares that a measure of dogmatism in art and criticism is inevitable; it is initially justified by its sincerity, but to remain so must recognize its basis, and fortify itself with reason—or change. Similarly, taste is initially autonomous, then should be pondered and compared with the tastes of others.

dolce stil nuovo (It., sweet new style). Dante's characterization (*Purg.* XXIV, 57) of his poetry and his immediate predecessors', esp. Guido Guinicelli (1230?–1276?; *Purg.* XXVI 97, 112): symbolical, intricate. It influenced Petrarchism, and it carried Sicilian poetry to the wider It. Renaissance.

doric. (Gr. Doris, south of Thessaly). 1. Rustic, uncouth; as opposed to Attic. 2. Simple, pastoral: (*Lycidas*) "with eager thought warbling his Doric lay."

double dactyl (A metrical form, two dactyls, — ᴗ ᴗ — ᴗ ᴗ). A fixed form of light verse, which has joined the limerick and the clerihew for parlor games. It consists of two stanzas, each of 4 double dactyl lines, the last lines truncated and rhyming. The first line of the poem is a nonsense jingle like "higgledy-piggledy," the second line is a name; one line in the second stanza, preferably the antepenultimate, consists of one word. *E.g.,*

> Welladay lackaday
> Emily Dickinson
> Hid from all suitors and
> Lingered at home;
>
> Never was maiden so
> Anthropophobiac
> Snug in her garden while
> Writing a pome.

Jiggery-Pokery, ed. A. Hecht and J. Hollander, 1967.

double entendre (Fr., *double entente,* ambiguity). A word or expression so used that it can have either of two meanings, often one meaning being indelicate. Thus, when actress Sarah Bernhardt was asked where she was married, she replied: *"Naturellement, à l'autel."* (at the altar, or, at the hotel). *Cf.* Ambiguity; Irony; Pun.

double rhyme. Feminine rhyme, *q.v.*

drama (Gr., action). The word "drama" may be interpreted in a variety of senses. Most widely, it means any kind of mimetic performance, from a production of *Hamlet* to the clowning of vaudeville comedians, to wordless pantomime or to a primitive ritual ceremony. More specifically, it designates a play written for interpretation by actors; more narrowly still, a serious, and generally realistic play that does not aim at tragic grandeur but that cannot be put in the category of comedy. [This interpretation arose in 18th c. France, when Diderot (*De la poésie dramatique,* 1758), Beaumarchais (*Essai sur le genre dramatique sérieux,* 1767) and others found *drame* a convenient label for the sentimental plays dealing with contemporary problems.]

In the broadest sense, drama is simply "play"—whereby a group of persons (primitive savages, amateurs belonging to medieval guilds, modern professionals) *impersonate* certain characters before a group of their fellows. This impersonation may be intended mainly for a ritualistic or religious purpose, or entirely for entertainment, but, whatever its purpose, it is the first and cardinal element in drama. The second element is the presence of an audience. Novel and poetry make their appeals to solitary readers; the dramatist must ever have the crowd in his mind's eye as he writes.

"Drama" is most commonly employed in its middle sense—something to be interpreted by actors, and, in the modern period, this something is dialogue to be spoken (as distinct from the lyric drama of opera, where the dialogue is sung). This general field of drama ranges from tragedy to melodrama, from high comedy to farce. In other fields, clear distinctions are in practice drawn between the "art" proper and the technique of the art form used for non-æsthetic ends. Thus, not everything written in verse is accepted as poetry; an ordinary detective novel is recognized for what it is, not confused with a work by Hardy or Dostoievsky. In the modern theatre, on the contrary, there is a frequent tendency to lose sight of the fact that some dramas (farce, melodrama) may exist for the single purpose of providing entertainment, but that alongside of these entertainment-dramas are others, which have an additional aim. Drama, as an art form, looks towards immediate physical representation on the stage. While direct appeal to audiences is thus the first demand made on a dramatist, we must not fall into the mistake of assessing value quantitatively. *Abie's Irish Rose* and *The Mouse Trap* may have a longer run than *Winterset* or *Ah! Wilderness,* but the former are not, because of that, to be esteemed better plays. A juster criterion may be found in estimating the revivable quality of a drama; *Hamlet*'s greatness is partly revealed by the way in which it has held the stage from 1601 to the current season.

Being presented by actors before an audience, drama has generally tended to be conventional in form. The knowledge that the actors are not the persons they pretend to be provides a basis for this conventionalism. Thus, whereas in narrative fiction the chief critical divisions fall according to subject-matter (historical novel, domestic novel), the drama may be classified according to the conventional attitude adopted by the playwright: one tragedy (*Hamlet*) may deal with legendary or historical action, another (*Winterset*) may be contemporary in theme, but both agree in exhibiting a common spirit that we call tragic. Although we may laugh at Polonius' list of dramatic kinds, there is ample justification for speaking of tragedy, comedy, farce, melodrama, comedy of manners, comedy of humour, and the like.

The conventional form of early drama was prevailingly poetic. Prose intruded first into comedy in the 16th c.; then, in the 18th c., with the rise of a middle-class audience that demanded the more frequent treatment of contemporary themes, it came to be more often used, leading to the modern realistic prose play. Despite the popularity of the prose form, however, the theatre has never lost its leaning towards poetry. (*See* Dialogue.)

During the past few decades, in a period when previously accepted values have been challenged, numerous attacks have been made against established dramatic forms. The plot element has been discarded by some authors; others have denied the existence of character; the various dramatic categories have been dismissed, and sometimes others have been set up in their place; occasionally even the use of dialogue has been replaced by action and the term "poetry" is applied to actors' movements, not to dramatists' lines. All these contemporary experiments might seem to suggest that for the modern world the older critical standards and values have lost their significance; yet the fact remains that the most notable plays produced within recent years have exhibited, both in form and in content, qualities that, however bizarre they may seem at first sight, can be related to the qualities apparent in memorable plays from the past. *Cf.* Comedy; Tragedy; Melodrama; Farce; Black Comedy; Epic Theatre; Theatre. The library of works on drama is vast. Recent works include S. Barnet, ed. *Aspects of the Drama,* 1962; Eric Bentley, *The Life of the Drama,* 1964; R. W. Corrigan, *The Context and Craft of Drama,* 1964; John Gassner, ed. *Ideas in the Drama,* 1964; with R. C. Allen, *Theatre and Drama in the Making,* 1964; M. G. O'Leary, ed. *Dramatic Arts and the Modern Mind,* 1964; B. H. Clark, *European Theories of the Drama,* 1947, 1966; A. Nicoll, *The Development of the Theatre,* 1937, 1966; W. V. Spanos, *The Christian Tradition in Modern Verse Drama,* 1967; W. E. Taylor, ed. *Modern Am. Drama,* 1968; Raymond Williams, *Drama from Ibsen to Brecht,* 1969. ALLARDYCE NICOLL.

dramatic irony. *See* Irony; *cf.* Comic relief.

dramatic lyric. Term used by Browning for his dramatic monologues. *Cf.* Monologue.

drame. Fr. Serious, often tragic play with some mingling of the comic, in contrast to the unity of tragic tone characteristic of classic *tragédie.* The genre originated in France, in the first half of the 18th c., with the *comédie larmoyante* of La Chausée; it continued in the *drame bourgeois* of Diderot, to culminate in the romantic *drames* of Hugo and his contemporaries. Hugo's *Préface de*

Cromwell (1827) is an important literary manifesto laying down the principles of the genre.

dream. The dream has been considered a source, or used as a device, for works of art. I. Either as a waking-dream, reverie, or as the inspiration that comes in sleep, the dream has been considered, and by the romantics even cultivated, as a source of poetry. Drugs and other means of inducing wisp-fancies were sought. Coleridge tells us *Kubla Khan* was dream-born (though John Livingston Lowes has traced a longer *Road to Xanadu*). Coleridge again (*Notebook xvi*, 6–13 Dec. 1803) tells of a dream voyage: "O then what visions have I had!—*and yet my reason at the rudder*." After the romantics, objections rose to the dream as inspiration. Mallarmé pictures Gautier watching over the garden of poetry, "from which he banishes the dream, the enemy of his charge"; and in our time Roger Fry declares bluntly: "Nothing is more contrary to the essential æsthetic faculty than the dream." In the meantime Thoreau had exalted the dream not as inspiration but as aspiration: "Our dreams are the solidest facts we know." The dream not as ideal but of the earth real was brought again into the creative impulse in the Freudian picture: dreams manifest disguisedly either our desires or our dreads; awake, these betray themselves in slips of the tongue, conceal themselves in word play, in art: art is a waking dream in which we hide from ourselves our improper or impotent longings, realizing in art a goal, or at least a harmony, unattained in life. The Freudian dream theory is roundly attacked (E. Rignano, *The Psychology of Reasoning*, 1923; M. R. Cohen, *Reason and Nature*, 1931), but its general tenets, and its emphasis on sex, are too valuable to the artist for his disavowal. II. The dream as a device, esp. for launching a story on its way, came widely into European literature after Macrobius (fl. 400 A.D.), who commented on, and issued, Cicero's *Somnium Scipionis*. The vision has always been associated with religion, but the secular expression of the vision in the widely-read *Romance of the Rose* (1237, 1277), (with initial reference to Macrobius) with its dream of young love in May popularized its secular use. It has been followed in a great variety of works: Chaucer, trans. *Romance of the Rose*; *Boke of the Duchesse*; *Legend of Good Women*; *Parlement of Foules*; Langland, *Vision of Piers Plowman*; Bunyan, *Pilgrim's Progress*; Carroll, *Alice in Wonderland*. In many such works, the sleeper is taken in hand by a guide, often allegorical: Chaucer in *Hous of Fame*, an eagle; Dante, in the greatest of such visions, Vergil, then Beatrice. In the drama, the dream (or the analogous delirium of illness) permits phantasmagorian variations from reality, as in Barrie's *A Kiss for Cinderella*, 1916; the Kaufman-Connelly *Beggar on Horseback*, 1924. Effective as an opening, esp. for a supernatural journey, the dream is less fortunately used at the close (*e.g.*, St. J. Ervine-H. G. Wells, *The Wonderful Visit*, 1921) to explain otherwise unaccountable incidents: by that time either the story has held us through its own merits and the dream is an unnecessary intrusion, or interest has vanished that no dream-explanation can restore.

droll (also drollery. Eng., 17th to mid 19th c.). A facetious story or tale. A comic or farcical composition or representation. Usually a spoken or enacted piece of buffoonery, sometimes a puppet-show, performed in a droll-booth or droll-house. Also offered by itinerant entertainers; in 1860 we read that "the droll-teller went his rounds from hall to cottage."

drowned-in-tears, school of the. Term applied in scorn of the early Romantics, who, in the mood of Goethe's young Werther, seemed always bleeding from the thorns of life, albatross-hung with the heavy and the weary weight of all this unintelligible world, making songs out of their own pain, the *Weltschmerz*. *See* Graveyard School.

dualism. A metaphysics is said to be "dualistic" (a) if it divides reality into two irreducibly different types of substance, as in the Cartesian dualism of mind and matter, or (b) if it describes nature as merely phenomenal, in contrast to reality, as in the Platonist opposition of the "world of becoming" to the "realm of being." Metaphysical dualisms usually extend to a dualistic view of human nature, in which man, as in the traditional Christian conception, is regarded as a creature of two worlds, and therefore as the battleground of irreconcilable drives: the "higher" against the "lower," soul against body, transcendental self against empirical self. Thus, dualism is opposed to naturalism (*q.v.*).

The dualistic view of human nature is associated with a dualistic ethics in the philosophy of the New Humanists (*q.v.*), which centers on the distinction: "Law for man, and law for thing" (Emerson, *Ode, Inscribed to W. H. Channing*; see Irving Babbitt, introduction to *Rousseau and Romanticism,* 1919). The New Humanists have argued that the dualistic view of human nature lies behind the conflict in all great fiction, either implicitly (as claimed for Shakespeare), or explicitly (as in Dostoievsky's use of the "double" and in his conception of the "Karamazov" personality).

duan. Gaelic. A poem; or a canto thereof. (Ossian).

dumb-show. Early Eng. theatre: part of a play given in action without speech. Sometimes it presents new parts of the story; sometimes (as in the dumb-show before the Players speak their play in *Hamlet*) it pre-enacts an episode to be shown after it with dialogue. The first sort of dumb-show was interestingly revived in 1967, in Tom Stoppard's *Rosencrantz and Guildenstern Are Dead,* performing in silence the scene between Hamlet and Ophelia that in Shakespeare's play she merely reports to her father, the exchange of letters on the boat by Hamlet, and the final duel and death scene of *Hamlet.* Used, *e.g.,* in *Gorboduc,* 1561; *The Duchess of Malfi,* 1614. A variation of the dumb-show was employed in *Le Viol de Lucrèce* (1931) by André Obey: silent players enact the ravishing while a Narrator tells the story. Some modern dances use a similar technique. Dieter Mehl, *The Elizabethan Dumb-Show,* 1965.

dumi. Ukrainian folksong of irregular meter. It reflects the hard life of the Kozac military order, and its ideas of freedom and legal equality. *Cf.* Bylina.

dyad. Distich, *q.v.*

dyslogism (*cf.* eulogism). A term having a derogatory or opprobrious connotation; esp. one coined for an attack, *e.g.,* the *Impuritans.*

dysphemism (*cf.* euphemism). The use of a term (or the term so used) to emphasize a failing or blemish, instead of glossing it over; to call a spade a dirty shovel.

E

ECHO. (1) The regular recurrence of a sound (word or phrase) as at the end of successive stanzas; a refrain, *e.g.,* in the ballade (Chaucer, *Truth*) in free verse (Sandburg, "in the dust, in the cool tombs"). (2) The looser (and subtler) intertwining of such sound throughout a poem, *e.g.,* "O sister swallow" in *Itylus* (Swinburne). (3) Echo rhyme: coincidence likewise of the consonant before the accented vowel (meet, mete, meat), normal in Fr. if the meanings are different, rare in Eng. Also called perfect and identical rhyme. (4) Recurrences of a sound in rapid succession, *e.g.,* Shak., "In spring time, the only merry ring time, when birds do sing hey ding a ding ding." Attacked in 19th c. verse by Nordau (*Degeneration,* 1893) as echolalia; defended by Shaw (*Sanity and Art,* 1895). Developed by Gertrude Stein (*Tender Buttons,* 1914; *Four Saints in Three Acts,* 1934) and the surrealists. *See* Repetend.

echo verse. A line followed by an "echo," repeating with different intention its last syllables (or a poem of such lines); usually for humor. *E.g.,* (sestina by Barnaby Barnes, 1559–1609):

What shall I do to my Nymph when I go to
 behold her? Hold her.

echoism; echoic word. Onomatopœia, *q.v.*

eclipsis. P. "The figure of default." Omitting essential grammatical elements, *e.g.,* "So early come?"

eclogue. In addition to the conventional pastoral of the 16th c., with which it came to be identified, the word *eclogue* also designated any rustic dialogue in verse. With the growth of pastoral drama and romance, gradually the distinction arose between "pastoral," referring to content and "eclogue," referring to form. Thus the 18th c. produced town eclogues and others having no association with shepherd life. As successor, then, to the idyll (first written by Theocritus, 3d c. B.C.) "eclogue" preserved its similar dramatic character. It may be loosely defined as a dramatic poem which, without appreciable action or characterization, includes (1) an objective setting, described by the poet or one of his characters, and (2) appropriate sentiments expressed in dialogue or soliloquy.

R. F. Jones, "Eclogue Types in Eng. Poetry of the 18th C.," *JEGP* 24, 1925; T. P. Harrison, Jr. and H. J. Leon, *The Pastoral Elegy, an Anthology,* 1939. *See* Bucolic; Pastoral.

ecphonema. "The outcry." Exclamation. Paeanism, in joy. Anaphonema, in grief. Thaumasm, in wonder. Euche, for desired good. Votum, with a promise made, a vow. Ara, with evil wished; more emphatically, misos; with abuse piled on abuse, execration. Deesis, with entreaty. Obsecration, with prayer for evil upon one's enemies; abomination, to avert evil from oneself.

ecplexis (Gr., enthralment). According to Aristotle, the aim or effect of poetry. The achievement of every great work is to afford the receptor entertainment, enlightenment, exaltation. *Cf.* Catharsis; Poetry and Prose; Triad.

Edwardian. Applied esp. to the reign of Edward VII (1901–1910), when reaction against Victorianism led to more critical examination and depiction of life, as by Arnold Bennett, and advocacy of change as by H. G. Wells and Bernard Shaw. *Cf.* Victorian. S. Hynes, *The Edwardian Turn of Mind,* 1968.

eidyllion. A short descriptive poem, since Theocritus (Gr., 3rd c. B.C.), mainly in pastoral mood. *See* Idyll.

eight-and-six-meter. The OEng. fourteener broken into two lines, one of 8 syllables followed by one of six. This became the typical ballad meter, *e.g.,*

John Gilpin was a citizen
Of credit and renown,
A train-band captain eke was he
Of famous London town.

Einfühlung. G. Empathy, *q.v.*

eisteddfod. Welsh. A musical, literary, and dramatic gathering. Contests, from massed choirs of 200 voices to individuals. The chief literary prizes are an appropriately carved oaken chair for the best poem in the strict meters (the chair ode), and a silver crown for the best poem in the free meters (the crown poem); the subjects for the poems are usually assigned beforehand. There are also prizes for drama (for both writing and presenting), for essays, for translations and recitations, and for arts and crafts. Local *eisteddfodau* (besides the annual ones, alternately in N. and in So. Wales) are held among the Welsh in Eng., the U.S., Australia, So. Africa, and Patagonia. *Cf.* Welsh Versification.

elaboration (L., worked out). (1) Development of a subject beyond an initial statement, for clearness or emphasis. By further details; by example; by comparison, contrast, analogy; by repetition through synonyms; by definition or explication; by examining the etymology, connotations, other senses of the term; by considering various applications or uses. (2) The careful working out of a complex style, usually with balanced structure and polished phrase, as in Pater.

elegant variation. A term employed by H. W. and F. G. Fowler (*The King's English,* 1906; *A Dictionary of Modern English Usage,* 1965) to denote a fault of style that consists of carefully not repeating a word in similar applications. *E.g.:* They spend a few weeks longer in their winter *home* than in their summer *habitat.* Variation may be of two sorts: (1) a single object is successively given different names or denoted under different class concepts; (2) two physically separable objects are thought of as belonging to one class but are given different names. One-thing variation is a form of cumulative predication or description; often it does not deserve the derogatory name "elegant." It abounds in poetry, in all imaginative or excited writing; *e.g.,* in *Beowulf,* a boat is called "sea-boat," "wave-floater," "sea-goer," "foamy-necked vessel," "well-fashioned vessel," "wave-goer," "broad-bosomed vessel," and "ocean-wood winsome" within the space of thirteen lines (XXVIII, 17–30). The more intellectual or expository the writing, the more offensive even less obtrusive and pronominal forms of one-thing variation are likely to be.

The second form, two-thing variation, is of more frequent occurrence and almost always offensive, the "elegant" result of blind adherence to a misunderstood rule. Two-thing variation readily invades all the parts of speech. "France is now *going through* a similar experience *with regard to* Morocco to that which England had *to undergo with reference to* Egypt."

In simpler forms of two-thing variation, such as the "home"–"habitat" example quoted above, a degree of antithesis, expressed in two contrasting words, "winter" and "summer," is extended falsely into words, "home" and "habitat," that should denote in what respects the contrasted objects are similar. W. K. Wimsatt, Jr., *The Verbal Icon,* 1954, 1967. W. K. Wimsatt.

elegantia. L. One of the three basic attributes of ancient Roman discourse, with *compositio* and *dignitas.* It has 2 divisions, *Latinitas* and *explanatio. Latinitas* restrains the speech from solecisms and barbarisms, while *explanatio* makes it clear by the use of words *usitata et propria.* In the early Renaissance the principle of *elegantia* was revived, for purity of the vernacular. Martin Opitz and Boileau urged it in its original sense, of that which is carefully selected.

elegiac meter. That used in the elegiac distich: a dactylic hexameter followed by a dactylic pentameter. First used by Archilochus, 7th c. B.C., for personal, reflective, or didactic poetry. The early sepulchral inscription was commonly written in this form. The meter has been adopted widely by G. but not by Eng. poets. Coleridge, however, has neatly illustrated its use:

In the hexameter rises the fountain's silvery column,
In the pentameter aye falling in melody back.

Cf. Elegy.

elegiambus. *See* Archilochian.

elegy. A poem of lament or mourning for the dead; also, a meditative poem in a solemn or sorrowful mood, sometimes about unrequited love. Propertius in his *Cynthia* (25 B.C.) fixed the type of Latin elegy (*see* Elegiac meter). From the early 16th c., the elegy was employed in Eng. as a funeral song or lament. Spenser's *Daphnaida* (1591) is an early example of the form. In 1637 (long before Johnson's inadequate definition, in 1755, of elegy as "a short poem without points or turns"), Milton's great elegy, *Lycidas,* had been produced. Its idyllic conventions of referring to the dead man as a shepherd; pagan mythology; all earth mourning, with flowers for the hearse (even though Milton's friend was lost at sea), led Johnson to condemn the "inherent improbability" of the poem. Shelley's elegy on Keats, *Adonais,* and that of Arnold on his friend Clough, *Thyrsis,* have been considered among the greatest in the language. The most famous one, Gray's *Elegy Written in a Country Churchyard* (1751), differs from the others in that it mourns not a person, but a way of life. Lamartine's elegy *Le Lac* has achieved renown in Fr. equal to that which Gray's has enjoyed in Eng. The elegy has also been cultivated with much success by Camoëns (Port.), and the Italians Chiabrera, Filicaia and, more recently, Leopardi. As a poem of lamentation, the elegy does not exist in G.: those of Goethe, who followed the form and themes of Ovid, are not plaintive in character; Coleridge called the elegy "the form of poetry natural to the reflective mind." M. Lloyd, ed. *Elegies,* 1903; T. B. Harrison, *The Pastoral Elegy,* 1939; A. F. Potts, *The Elegiac Mode,* 1967. *See* Pastoral poetry. JOHN BURKE SHIPLEY.

elision. Dropping the final sound of a word, for metrical or rhythmic effect. In Gr., mainly when one word ends with a short vowel and the next begins with a vowel. In L., any final vowel, and *m* with the preceding vowel, are elided before a vowel or *h.* In Romance versification the practice is more strictly regulated. In Eng., usually indicated by an apostrophe, *e.g.,* th' everlasting. Extensively applied in 18th c. Eng. to "regularize" pentameter lines; until John Mason, 1749, declared that the line,

And many an amorous, many a humorous lay

has 14 syllables, but "the ear finds nothing in it redundant, defective, or disagreeable, but is sensible of a sweetness not ordinarily found in the common iambic verse." Poets since have tended to disregard elision in favor of the variety of effect. *See* Romance versification.

Elizabethan. A loose term applied to Eng. writing of the late 16th and early 17th c. Some extend it from the accession of Elizabeth I in 1558 to the closing of the theatres in 1642. More precisely: The Tudor period runs from the accession of Henry VII (1485) to the death of Elizabeth (1603). The Jacobean: James I, 1603–1625; the Caroline: Charles I, 1625–1649—both together called the Stuart, the period of the later Stuarts (Charles II, 1660–1685; James II, 1685–1688) being known as the Restoration. The Elizabethan Age in literature was marked by the flowering of poetry (introduction of blank verse, sonnet, Spenserian stanza), the greatest body of dramatists of any age in any land, and in prose as well the widest range of the language. The variety of styles is too great for any single aspect to be known as Elizabethan; the term suggests, rather, the fullness and richness of achievement and national pride. Hiram Haydn, *The Counter-Renaissance,* 1950; L. B. Smith, *The Horizon Book of the Elizabethan World,* 1967.

elocution. Third division of ancient and medieval rhetoric, *q.v.* Its three parts are: Composition, clarity and propriety of speech; Elegance, purity, perspicuity, and politeness of language; and Dignity, adornment of the thought with rhetorical flowers. By mid-19th c., elocution had lost this meaning, preempting that of pronunciation, a division of medieval rhetoric dealing with delivery.

emblem book. A volume of woodcuts (emblems) mainly on such subjects as the vanity of life, illustrated by proverbs, fables, brief reflections (first, Alciati, *Emblematus Libellus,* 1522) originally in L. and in elegiac meter. Popular, esp. in Dutch literature, 16th and 17th c.; Spenser's first poems are sonnets trans. for an Eng. version of a Dutch emblem book (*A Theatre for Worldlings,* 1569). Also Quarles; Wither. Blake (*The Gates of Paradise,* 1793) revived the form.

emendation. Improvement (or the product thereof) by which an alternate reading is supplied where a text seems faulty. It should explain in a reasonable manner how the error came into being, and the change should fit the context, in the language of the book's period. The emendation is "conjectural" when evidence for it is lacking. Revision: the process (or its product) by which one improves; rephrasing, rearranging, including new facts, and correcting errors. Recension: the process (or its product) by which a text is completely revised according to definite standards. Correction: the process (or its product) by which errors are removed. Redaction: the process (or its product) by which material already composed is put into the form proper for its purpose. Editing is one form of redaction. *See* Criticism, textual.

emotion. *See* Feeling; Objective correlative. P. Knapp, ed. *Expression of Emotions in Man,* 1963.

emotive use of words. Bertrand Russell (*Mysticism and Logic,* 1914) stated that all language is either propositional (cognitive) or emotive. For a time I. A. Richards and others stressed as basic the distinction between words (1) as emotive: expressions or stimulants of attitudes; and (2) as symbolic: supports or vehicles of reference. The former is the more primitive. It is related in phylogeny to the danger calls and love calls of animals, in ontogeny to the affective coos and cries of infants; communication through gesture is probably, in the main, emotive. Words may thus serve, however, (a) as outlet for or indication of the subjective state of the speaker; or (b) to play upon the feelings of the receptor. In the latter sense, it is the basic function of language in the arts, and may be a deft and dangerous weapon in propaganda (satirized in Lawson's *Processional*: two guards are beating a striker; a third draws a picture from the man's purse, cries, "His mother!" The three stop, salute, then resume their thrashing).

This two-fold division, in the light of recent semantic study, came to seem limited. Richards speaks of the four kinds of meaning (*q.v.*) and declares (*How To Read a Page,* 1942; p. 100 and bibliog. there) that language "has as many jobs as we find it convenient to distinguish." *Cf.* Language; Meaning. C. K. Ogden and I. A. Richards, *The Meaning of Meaning,* 1923; Karl Bühler, *Sprachtheorie,* 1934; J. R. Kantor, *An Objective Psychology of Grammar,* 1936; G. Stern, *Meaning and Change of Meaning,* 1931; H. Werner, *Grundfragen der Sprachphysiognomik,* 1932; B. M. Charleston, *Studies in the Emotional and Affective Means of Expression in Modern Eng.,* 1960; P. H. Knapp, *Expression of Emotions in Man,* 1963.

empathy. The idea—developed in Germany (Hermann Lotze, *Mikrokosmus,* 1858) as *Einfühlung,* feeling into—that a work of art induces the projection of the receptor into the mood and impulses of the work. Thus, before the statue Discobolus, one's muscles flex to hurl the discus. Aristotle noted such an impulse (*Rhetoric* III, 2, 1411b). Titchener first used the word empathy in 1909, translating *Einfühlung.* The idea is widely current in psychology; many situations in life evoke an empathetic response. Some (Theodor Lipps, Vernon Lee) have found in empathy the explanation of the appeal of a work of art, hence would use it as an æsthetic criterion. *Cf.* synaesthesis; beauty. Vernon Lee, *The Beautiful,* 1913; Ship; C. D. Thorpe; "Some Notices of Empathy before Lipps," *Mich. Acad. XXIII,* 1938; A. B. Barshay, *Empathy,* 1964.

emphasis. "The reenforcer." Stress laid upon the main element of a passage. Secured in many ways, *e.g.:* (1) Using words in a special sense, or an unusual order; choosing unusual words (Homer: "We *went down into* the horse") or striking figures. (2) Varying the sentence order or form; interrupting the structure; using short sentences, balanced sentences, rhetorical questions. (3) Building the idea to be emphasized: comparison, contrast; repetition (synonym); by adding details or by significant selection of detail; seeming to pass over a point in such a way as to draw attention to it. There are also mechanical devices; such as underlining, italics, different type font, illustrations. In speech, raising the voice, but also lowering the voice; placing greater stress on an individual word. The three qualities rhetorics often set as basic for sentence, paragraph, or composition are unity, coherence, and emphasis.

encomium. A laudatory speech or poem (Pindar; Theocritus). A subdivision (Aristotle) of epideictic oratory. Usually distinguished from panegyric—praise of a city or nation, before a full assembly—as praise of a living man before a select group. It grew very popular, esp. in the second Sophistic movement; Polybius and Lucian complain that it takes the name of history (which should be free of praise or bias) or of biography (which should give a rounded account). The subjects also widened, with unbridled extravagance (*e.g.,* Lucian, *Encomium of a Fly*). Burgess, *Epideictic Literature,* 1902.

endecha. Sp. dirge or doleful ditty; a literary genre corresponding to the elegy of the ancients. It consisted generally of four lines of 6 or 7 syllables; might be enlarged to the *endecha real, i.e.,* two such strophes, with the 4th and the 8th lines of 11 syllables.

ending. (1) The fact or manner of bringing a piece of writing or pattern to a close. In the theatre, the "curtain line" is of major importance. The almost universal "happy ending" of comedy is often achieved by artificial devices, such as the god from the machine, *q.v.* (2) Various degrees of stress on the final syllable of a line of verse have been distinguished: (a) light ending: an unaccented syllable, usually a separate word, that calls for only a slight pause, *e.g.,*

> Ah, Psyche, from the regions which
> Are Holy Land!

(b) weak: an unaccented syllable that calls for no pause at all, *e.g.,*

Upon the cry assembled, hastened to

The foe's fierce onslaught with upgathered rage,

(c) strong: an accented syllable, demanding a pause, as in the second lines of the two examples above. (d) feminine: an extra unaccented syllable, as at the end of a line of iambic pentameter, *e.g.,* "To be or not to be, that is the question." *Cf.* Prosody. Fr. Kermode, *The Sense of an Ending,* 1967; B. H. Smith, *Poetic Closure,* 1968.

end rhyme. Term used to mark normal rhyme (*q.v.*), from (1) alliteration, beginning likeness in words; (2) beginning or middle rhyme, according to its position in the line.

end-stopped. Of a line in which the sense (grammar) and the meter end together, as most frequently in the 18th c. heroic couplet (partial pause at end of first line; complete at end of couplet), *e.g.,*

Hope springs eternal in the human breast;
Man never is, but always to be, blessed.

So mainly in the Fr. alexandrine, until the Romantics. Opp. to run-on, enjambment (*q.v.*), which marks the flow of blank verse and most Romantic poetry. *Cf.* Rejet.

English versification. Every English sentence is a series of sounds each of which has a certain length or duration, a relative emphasis or stress, and a certain pitch. Every sentence is therefore a series of events in a constant flow of time, marked for our attention by the ways in which the sounds are spoken. When the intervals of time between the emphases are, or seem to be, approximately equal, the sentence is rhythmical. When there is superimposed on this natural rhythm of prose a fixed artificial pattern (meter) the result is verse rhythm—a harmonious blend of the inherent or potential rhythms of speech and the predetermined metrical pattern. There are thus 3 different phenomena: (1) the natural flow of speech sounds, tending to occur in rhythmical sequences; (2) the formal arrangement of stressed and unstressed syllables, or meter; and (3) the combined result when the normal arrangements of prose, always potentially rhythmical, are fitted to the metrical design. The first is very complex and has not yet been properly analysed. The second is very simple and can be clearly indicated, but is often confused with the third, which is infinitely complex and cannot be adequately represented by any symbols hitherto proposed. Thus, if Gray's line, "The lowing herd winds slowly o'er the lea," be read naturally as prose, it is a series of 10 syllables some of which receive more emphasis or stress than others (*slow-ly*) and some of which occupy more time than others (*winds; the*). The meter is 5 groups or feet each containing an unstressed syllable followed by a stressed syllable (*e.g. the lea*) and each occupying approximately the same time to pronounce. The natural reading of the words and the metrical pattern do not closely match: *winds* must somehow be taken as an unstressed and *o'er* as a stressed element; the group *winds slow-* must somehow be taken as equal in length to *-ly o'er*. Different readers manage the necessary compromise differently. Some resort to a mechanical singsong; others go to the opposite extreme of nearly obliterating the metrical movement. Some of us prefer to read the words with their natural emphasis, at the same time hearing the regular beat of the meter underneath, even though we do not make it heard when we read aloud.

Historically considered, English versification is the result of the merging of two traditions, the Germanic or accentual, brought to England from the continent in the 6th c., and the syllabic or syllable-counting, introduced after the Norman Conquest. Much later came a third, never wholly naturalized, influence, the classical or quantitative system. All combine to produce the effects of English verse. Whichever is regarded as the determinant, stress or time, they both work together to produce the rhythm of verse; and either can be made the basis of a plausible explanation of "the facts." In the case, *e.g.,* of Milton (who was probably the last of our poets to make the number of syllables a leading principle in his prosody) it is demonstrable that syllable counting yielded the same result as the accentual or temporal system. As a theory of metrics, each presents difficulties. The poets themselves have apparently almost always counted stresses, relying on various conventions for making occasional "half-stresses" serve for full stresses; and they have trusted their ear for guidance in making the time element come right. On the other hand, many recent analysts contend very properly that the basis of all sound rhythms is equal or approximately equal periods of time, in other words, that the feet or sections of the line are determined by their duration; they must, however, admit that each foot usually contains a stress (or half-stress) together with one or more unstressed syllables; moreover, they have never discovered any rules for ascertaining the length of syllables in English. The sense of time is quite variable in most of us and the assumption of an elastic time-unit works to the advantage of either theory. It is safe to say that the differences between "timers" and "stressers" are theoretical; practically, they agree. The foot is marked to the ear and recognized by its stressed syllable, but the length of the foot largely determines the rhythm of the line.

Modern English versification begins with Chaucer, and it is surprising how few chords have been added to the harmony of English verse since his death. Chaucer's verse is predominantly iambic, in spite of the feminine endings. How far this choice determined that of nearly all later poets would be difficult to determine; but something in the pattern of English words makes them fit easily into iambic meters. It was another choice, however, made by Chaucer, that affected the subsequent form of three-fourths of English verse. This is the so-called heroic line of five iambs, which he used, in rime, with nearly all the variety, freedom, and flexibility it has later shown. His favorite groups were the "Troilus" stanza, *ababbcc* (called rime royal from its later use in "The Kingis Quair") and the couplet, which he may have adapted from the French poets but which was already at hand in the last four lines of the "Troilus" stanza. But the point is not so much Chaucer's invention or introduction of these forms as his skill in handling them.

In the 15th c., Lydgate made a temporary contribution of doubtful value: the broken-backed line, in which one light syllable near the middle is designedly lacking. At the turn of the next c. the Scottish Chaucerians made a long step forward in lyrical measures. Henryson's "Robene and Makyne" (*abababab* in alternating 3's and 4's) gave us for the first time in English—his Scots is of course only Northern English—a poem whose poignancy is largely dependent on its balance of genuine feeling and a delicate artificiality sustained by careful rhythms; and Dunbar adapted the mediæval lyrical stanzas (which had hitherto been used for religious or amorous subjects) to all kinds of other uses—narrative, personal ("On his Heid-ake"), topical, satirical, conventional moralizing, and serious commentary on life. In such pieces as "Lament for the Makaris" and "Meditation in Winter" Dunbar may be fairly greeted as father of the reflective lyric. In a few pieces like "Ane Ballat of Our Lady" (7 stanzas of 12 lines *ababababxbab*—the *b* lines of 3 feet; the *a* lines of 4 feet with 3 rimes in each line "Haile, bricht the sicht in hevyn on hicht!", the *x* the refrain *"Ave Maria gracia plena"* in every stanza), he carried technical dexterity indeed far; though Chaucer's "Compleynte" of Anelida gave him a partial model. The famous "Flyting" is in a modification of Chaucer's Monk's Tale stanza, $ababbccb_5$, handled with considerable metrical as well as vituperative skill. At about the same time, Skelton introduced his saucy, heavily-accented jingles—"ragged" and "breathless" they have been called—eminently suited to his pithy and earthy matter, but little practiced by later poets.

In the early 16th c. Wyatt and Surrey imported the sonnet, and Surrey introduced blank verse (ca. 1540), perhaps taking a hint from classical models and the Italian *versi sciolti*. Its first use was for translating the rimeless long poems of antiquity. Four years after Tottell (1557) it was employed, stiffly to be sure, in drama (*Gorboduc*); 30 years after Tottell it became the mighty line of Marlowe's *Tamburlaine*; and ever since, both for long narrative and for poetic drama, it has hardly known a rival, and has proved itself for many other sorts of poetry. Because of its freedom from rime it has even greater fluidity and malleability than Chaucer could give the line in his couplets or stanzas; and when one thinks of the long roll of those who have employed it—Shakespeare, Milton, Wordsworth, Keats, Shelley, Tennyson, Browning, Swinburne, to name only the greatest—and the immense variety of effects they have achieved with it, one might call it the English measure *par excellence*. Something like three-fourths of English poetry is written in blank verse. Yet in its long history it has undergone great changes. After the rigidity of its first appearances it at once adapted itself to Marlowe's rhetoric and Shakespeare's poetry. Then the Jacobean dramatists broke it down to something very near prose; the Restoration playwrights displaced it by the heroic couplets for a few years, but presently even Dryden "grew weary of his love-loved mistress rime" and wrote in blank verse his one real tragedy (1677). Already with his learned diction and involved grammar Milton was making it a new thing, and by his elaborately worked out system of elisions combined the effects of an accentual and a syllable-counting measure. After Milton its development had to be in the direction of simplicity, and Wordsworth freed it and Landor brought it to a fine conversational level (followed but yesterday by E. A. Robinson). With Tennyson and Swinburne it became elaborate again and over-mannered; more recently, it has employed rhythms (T. S.

Eliot; Frost) nearer those of daily speech.

Another contribution of the Elizabethans was the song-lyric, as in the many miscellanies or anthologies from 1584 onwards. These lyrics are notable for grace and dexterity and variety of stanzas; they were frequently written to music, *i.e.,* are songs in both senses of the word; and though the influence of music on versification is difficult to define it is unquestionable, and here led to a consciousness of the lyric as a form. The poems of Donne and Herrick, Herbert and Vaughan, take over these lyric forms, and add meaning to the music; and this tradition, flourishing through Housman and Hardy, has virtually redefined the word lyric. Burns is the one great exception.

The influence of the popular ballad should also be mentioned. The ballads also were composed to music: they are easy to sing and notoriously difficult to read. Their accumulation of light syllables and forcing of accent natural to sung verse must have had an effect on the poets' versification.

When drama abandoned blank verse for the couplet (and then for prose until it went "poetical" again) the couplet also carried on independently; it became the staple for nearly all poetry in the 18th c. that was not under Milton's sway. Even Gray's "Elegy," though in *abab* quatrains, has an air of the couplet about it. Chaucer's fluent handling of it was forgotten; it was forged anew on stricter lines by Waller and Dryden, and hammered into a sharp instrument (rather brittle) by Pope — a tool for wit and satire. But as the subject-matter put into it changed, it became freer and easier with Goldsmith, still freer with Keats and Browning, and reached an ultimate in Swinburne's "Anactoria."

The short couplet, octosyllabic, has had a longer history than any other single English verse form: from the late 12th c. Yet in spite of its popularity it has never been a first-rate meter. When it is smooth and regular it quickly becomes monotonous; when it is handled freely, it develops an almost ametrical roughness. The rimes come so rapidly, pell-mell, that the ear is dinned by them; and the necessity of frequent rimes results in constant piercing and padding. Chaucer abandoned it after "The House of Fame"; Milton gave it a new life in "L'Allegro" and "Il Penseroso"; the early Romantics (Scott, who praised it excessively; Byron) adopted it, sometimes with variations resembling ballad quatrains, for rapid narration; Coleridge thought he was revising it in "Christabel." Its greatest success has been in short pieces, though Masefield has made effective use of it ("The Everlasting Mercy"; "Reynard the Fox").

Among many experiments in verse was Edmund Spenser's Spenserian stanza, *q.v.,* created by altering Chaucer's 7-line iambic pentameter, *ababbcc,* to *ababbcbcc,* the last line being a hexameter. The combination of the heroic line and an alexandrine gave birth to a great number of variations and imitations, varying the rime scheme or changing the number of lines (aba_5b_6) or shortening the first lines (as in Shelley's "To a Skylark," $abab_3b_6$ and Swinburne's "Hertha," $abab_2b_6$ with trisyllabic feet) or otherwise as in Milton's "Nativity Hymn," $aa_3b_5cc_3b_5d_4d_6$. Another of Spenser's inventions was the "Epithalamium" stanza of 17 and 19 lines on 8 or 9 rimes, with refrain, which was well suited to his "trailing vine" style, and gave rise to several adaptations associated with the "irregular ode." One of the peculiarities of the stanza was the presence of a 3-beat line among the prevailing 5's; it was a natural extension to add other short lines, as did Donne and Milton. The form won general recognition in Cowley's paraphrases of Pindar; the result is seen both in such poems as Dryden's "Alexander's Feast" and Wordsworth's "Immortality" ode (where there is an assumed arcane relation between the subject-matter and the length of line and the placing of rime) and in the regular stanzas of Keats's odes and Arnold's "Scholar Gypsy." Cowley's paraphrases sent the poets back (Congreve first) to the truer form of Pindar's odes, with strophe, antistrophe, and epode.

All this predominantly iambic verse was varied with occasional trochaic substitution. Poems entirely trochaic have always been rare. Tennyson composed "Locksley Hall" in trochees because Arthur Hallam told him they were popular; but this could only have meant that emphasis on the first syllable of a line tends to strengthen the accents throughout, and "the people" like strongly marked tunes. Efforts to write all in trochees produce a forcing of natural stress (*e.g., Hiawatha; "And* the hollow ocean-ridges. . .") which soon becomes unpleasing. Another means of varying the iambic rhythm, the use of trisyllabic feet, was long discouraged by the syllable-counting tradition. Such feet were introduced—hardly ever more than one to a line—in dramatic blank verse, but they have never gained a foothold because too many of them would distinctly alter the pattern. Whole short poems in trisyllabic, or mostly trisyllabic, feet occur sporadically among the Elizabethans, often in connection with musical forms, and they appear again in the 18th c. but generally for light or even comic effect. Long trisyllabic poems are rare (Clough). It remained for the 19th c. to develop a line of mingled iambs and trisyllables (dactyls, anapests) at once smooth and dignified and not too tripping or facetious in tone. The song writers tried it first (Tom Moore), then Shelley ('The Cloud') and Tennyson; Swinburne employed it with such balance that one can hardly say whether disyllabic or trisyllabic feet predominate. Together with this development came a larger attention to the spondee and a clearer reliance on time values, in opposition to syllable counting, so that the old bondage was completely dissolved. Verse had finally discovered how to take advantage of all the subtle variations of prose rhythm while retaining its inherent regularity.

From this to free verse (*q.v.*) was not a long leap. The beginnings had been made by Milton in "Samson" and Shelley in "Queen Mab": metrical lines of different lengths without rime. Matthew Arnold made experimental advances on this plan; Patmore and Henley (it is not always the greatest poets who are the best metrists) struck a very satisfactory balance between meter and prose; then in the present c.—though Whitman was fifty years in the lead—the last step was taken, the abandonment of meter for a 'higher law' of rhythm, not formally distinguishable from prose. *Cf.* Poetry and prose; Prosody.

G. Saints. *A Hist. of Eng. Prosody,* 3 v., 1906–10; *Hist. Manual of Eng. Prosody,* 1910; T. S. Omond, *Eng. Metrists,* 1921; Eg. Smith, *The Principles of Eng. Metre,* 1923; G. R. Stewart, *The Technique of Eng. Verse,* 1930; Cambib. PAULL F. BAUM.

enjambment. The carrying of sense (grammatical form) in a poem past the end of a line, couplet, or stanza. Run-on; opp. end-stopped, *q.v.; cf.* Rejet.

Enlightenment, the. A 17th and 18th c. trend in philosophy and literature, rooted in faith in the power of human reason. In G. Lessing and Moses Mendelssohn; in Fr. Voltaire, Diderot (*l'Encyclopédie*), and Rousseau; in Eng. Locke, Newton, Johnson. The prose of these thinkers is generally lucid, dignified, and formal. *Cf.* Augustan; Ancients and Moderns. Sir Isaiah Berlin, ed. *The Age of Enlightenment,* 1957; L. G. Crocker, *Nature and Culture,* 1963; P. Gay, *The Party of Humanity,* 1964, *The Age of Enlightenment,* 1966; G. R. Cragg, *Reason and Authority in the 18th C.,* 1964.

environment. *See* milieu.

envoy. Originally, a dedication, postscript to a poem. Now used of a shorter stanza at the end, esp. of a ballade, usually beginning with the name or title of the person to whom the poem is addressed, and continuing the metrical pattern (and the rhymes) of the last half stanza before, *e.g.,* Villon, *Ballade of those Condemned to be Hanged. Cf.* Ballade.

epanados, epanalepsis, epanaphora. *See* Repetition.

epanorthosis. Correction of a statement during the process of making it, *e.g.* (*Job*) "In six troubles, yea, in seven." Frequent in *Proverbs.*

épater le bourgeois (Fr., stamp on, stupefy, the middle class). 19th c. expression indicating the scorn of the bohemian artist for the conventional citizen. Note that these artists did not ignore those they scorned; they went out of their way to try to shock them. *Cf.* Decadence.

epenthesis. Addition of a letter, syllable, or sound in the middle of a word. Sometimes an error (*e.g.,* elum for elm), sometimes an aspect of language growth (blackamoor), sometimes for rhythm in refrains and nursery rhymes (Handy spandy, Jack-a-Dandy). Prosthesis: addition at the beginning of a word (beloved, yclad). Paragoge: at the end (often in Hebrew; Eng. dearie; peasant, *cf.* Fr. *paysan*).

epic poetry (as exemplified in the two Homeric poems, the *Iliad* and the *Odyssey,* and reckoned as oldest and ranked highest of the Gr. literary types. *Epos* meant word; then a speech or tale; a song; a heroic poem).

To this day the *Iliad* and the *Odyssey* serve as the chief models of epic composition wherever the literary tradition of Mediterranean culture obtains. The Æneid of Vergil, the chief L. epic, was done in strict imitation of Homer, even to the use of the Troy story. In medieval times, when the Gr. epics were not read in Western Europe, the influence of Vergil kept the Homeric tradition alive; but the men of the Middle Ages felt free to compose epics irrespective of classical models: *Beowulf,* the *Song of Roland,* the *Nibelungenlied.* The later epic poets (*Lusiads,* Camoëns; *Jerusalem Delivered,* Tasso; *Paradise Lost,* Milton) kept much of this freedom.

Many definitions of the epic have been advanced. All would agree that an epic is a narrative poem large in effect, in the characters, the events, the setting. The epic scale of being transcends at every point that of ordinary life. Trivial details (*e.g.*, dressing, undressing), presented leisurely and in detail, take on dignity and importance because they make part of an existence ampler than our own. Moreover, the chief character or hero does not tower alone, a solitary mountain in a plain of mediocrity. He has fellows of like stature, foemen worthy of his steel. The natural and usual setting for an epic is a time commonly thought of as marked by greatness of achievement: "there were giants in those days." Such was the period of discovery and exploration which began in the late 15th c., and the great Port. epic of the next c., the *Lusiads,* celebrates its achievements. But the immediate past rarely serves as matter for an epic. Camoëns' contemporary, Tasso, set his epic in the period of the Crusades, while the author of the *Song of Roland* (ca. 1100) thought of the reign of Charlemagne as the heroic age of Fr. The heroic age of the Gr. is legendary. (But epic poets have always reckoned legend a branch of history.) In general, then, a setting historical but remote in time or place is a mark of the epic. With this remoteness goes a freedom in the treatment of the epic stuff (the historical and traditional or legendary matter). In the *Song of Roland, e.g.,* a rearguard skirmish becomes the central event, fraught with meaning.

The introduction of supernatural characters has had much attention in epic theory, chiefly because of the conspicuous part which the gods play in Homer and Vergil. Supernatural machinery has even been held a *sine qua non,* so that Camoëns makes classical divinities play an active part in his epic of 15th c. Port. voyaging. While there has been considerable controversy over pagan vs. Christian material, the epic, since its scale is larger than life, readily admits the supernatural. Beowulf shows himself an overman when he slays a monster. In *Paradise Lost,* where epic grandeur reaches its peak, all the characters, except Adam and Eve, are supernatural beings.

The poet's freedom in dealing with his matter is limited, however, by the fact that his prospective audience knows the story and would resent radical changes. The epic is an outgrowth of traditional story-telling; throughout its development heroes and deeds have been chosen for celebration because of their fame among men. Invention is restricted to shift of stress, elaboration, variation of details. The poet's powers are devoted, not to making a story, but to making an epic out of a famous story. The epic form, furthermore, is highly traditional; it abounds in conventional features from which the poet departs at his peril. Even so arbitrary a convention as that of plunging *in medias res* at the start is rarely disregarded, though Homer himself made no use of it in the *Iliad* (if the theme of that poem really is the wrath of Achilles).

The epic name is sometimes given to poems radically different from those discussed above. Thus, the *Divine Comedy* of Dante has been called an epic. This poem has no hero; its chief character is the poet himself, who speaks in the first person throughout. Moreover, the poet's journey, which makes the narrative, is merely a device to enable him to map out the world we go to when we die. The journey itself has epic connections: it is based upon the familiar epic device of the hero's descent into hell, a journey which Dante has transferred to himself and extended to purgatory and heaven. In this way an episodic feature of epic tradition has become a whole poem. The scale, style, weight of the *Divine Comedy,* are what tempt critics to call it an epic. Long didactic poems, *e.g.,* Hesiod's *Works and Days,* have also been called epics; and even prose works of "heroic" proportions, through this aspect of resemblance to the epic proper.

The distinction has been made (esp. in neo-romantic criticism) between epics handed down by word of mouth and those composed for written circulation. The former are anonymous, apparently intended for entertainment only; they reflect an early stage of civilization (*e.g.,* the *Iliad,* as contrasted with Vergil's *Æneid*). In structure, the epic is presented in uniform lines, not broken into stanzas (except in the early Yugoslav epics). The diction is rich in static epithets, circumlocutions (the Germanic Kenning), recurrent formulas; speeches often occupy a considerable portion of the poem. The action usually covers but a short time; either the events of other years are narrated (as by Odysseus at the Phaeacian court), or the action is concentrated in a few scenes, with the intervals covered in a few lines. The *Iliad* covers forty-nine days, twenty-one of these being in Book One. The first part of *Beowulf* takes five days; most of the second part passes in one day. Although in the *Iliad* the similes are often drawn from humbler life, the main themes are the adventures, exploits and sufferings of princes and their followers, on battlefields and in courts (where there may be considerable feasting, minstrelsy, and drinking). Warfare is usually central to the epic mode of life. J. Clark, *A Hist. of Epic Poetry* (post-Vergilian), 1900; G. Murray, *The Rise of Gr. Epic,* 1924, 1968; L. Abercrombie, *The Epic,* 1914; W. P. Ker, *Epic and Romance,* 1908; E. M. W. Tillyard, *The Eng. Epic Tradition,* 1926; *The Epic Strain in the Eng. Novel,* 1958; D. M. Foerster, *The Fortunes of Epic Poetry,* 1962; T. M. Green, *The Descent from Heaven,* 1963; W. Calin, *The Epic Quest,* 1966. KEMP MALONE.

The non-European epics manifest the same qualities. Toward the end of the 3d millennium B.C. the Accadian epic *Gilgamesh* was composed; about half of its 3000 lines survive. A little later came the *Enuma Elish* (so called from its first words, "When above"), almost all of its one thousand lines surviving. The even earlier Sumerian epic tales also tell stories of the hero Gilgamesh, with the usual trip to the nether world, and battles of gods and heroes.

Much later, about 500 B.C., came the two great epics of India. The national epic of India, the *Mahabharata,* attributed to a legendary Vyasa, grew through various poets into 100,000 stanzas of the šloka meter, over eight times the length of the *Odyssey* and the *Iliad* combined. From its stories of the gods (especially Krishna) and the royal family of the Bharata come the plots of the classical Indian drama, the tales still told in every Indian village, and many of the motion pictures still being filmed. The *Ramayana,* almost as familiar, is mainly the work of one poet, Vālmīki. In it the exiled king Rama defeats the southern demons; beneath the stories some scholars trace the Aryan expansion to the south; also, the Indian myth of the beginning of agriculture. The *Puranas* are a series of minor Sanskrit epics, which include ten incarnations of Vishnu, and present the creation of the universe, genealogies of gods, and histories of royal families. In their mingling of myth, legend, and history, and their building of minor events to heroic proportions, the Eastern epics—whether of personal romance and battle of heroes and gods, of creation myths and religion, or of more didactic end—resemble those of the Western world. J. T. Shipley, ed. *Encyclopedia of Literature,* 1946.

epic simile. Homeric simile, *q.v.*

epic theatre. A theatrical movement in which content comes before form, and truth before illusion. It is essentially narrative and didactic; hence the adjective "epic." Its technique involves narrator, monologue, chorus, film, radio, projection, treadmill and other stage devices. The epic theatre took shape in Germany after World War I, as a platform for political ideas. Its most important exponent was playwright Bertolt Brecht, who described it as appealing "less to the spectator's feelings than to his reason." Founder was director Erwin Piscator: *Flags,* 1924; *Hoopla, We're Living!* (Toller, 1927); *The Good Soldier Schweik,* 1928; *War and Peace* (Piscator's dramatization, N.Y., 1942); Brecht's *Three-Penny Opera* (1929, from Gay's *The Beggar's Opera,* 1728). The epic theatre embraces several (overlapping) varieties: the reportorial theatre, which is merely journalistic; the documentary theatre, which uses report and document to make the meaning of history transparent (Odets, *Waiting for Lefty,* 1935); the Living Newspaper, which uses headlines to impress a social lesson on its audience; the theatre of action, including the Agit Prop and the Fighting Theatre (and such plays as Genêt's *The Blacks,* 1960), of violent propaganda; the dialectic theatre, which makes the stage a tribunal and accuses the defects of society; the didactic theatre, *Lehrtheater,* which tries to develop logical thinking and social consciousness; the political theatre, as the servant of the *polis,* the full community. *Cf.* Drama; Document; Theatre. M. Gorelik, *New Theatres for Old,* 1940; E. Piscator, *Das Politische Theater,* 1930; *Brecht on Theatre,* 1964; Maria Ley-Piscator, *The Piscator Experiment,* 1967; M. Spalter, *Brecht's Tradition,* 1967. ERWIN PISCATOR [Documentary theatre has had a recent surge in such plays as Rolf Hochhuth's *The Deputy* (1966, about Pope Pius XII and the Nazis) and *Soldiers* (1967, about Churchill), and Heinar Kipphardt's *In the Matter of J. Robert Oppenheimer* (1968, using transcripts of the U.S. Atomic Energy Commission's security investigation.]

epideictic. A formal speech, usually of praise or blame, showing the skill of the orator. *See* Encomium.

epigram. Originally, an inscription. Later (Boileau): "a *bon mot* set off with a couple of rhymes." Coleridge:

What is an epigram? A dwarfish whole,
Its body brevity, and wit its soul.

Yet one epigram of Johnson contains 196 lines. The above definitions spring from a too strict reading of Marcus Valerius Martial's epigrams (first c. A.D.). Many of Martial's 1500 short poems, however, many of the 4000 odd in the *Greek Anthology,* and of the modern poets are otherwise: solemn epitaphs, savage travesties; a neat compliment or satirical thrust; occasional poems, love lyrics, amusing incidents—diverse enough for a Renaissance critic to classify the epigram as sweet, sour, bitter, and salt.

Generally, the epigram is a short, polished poem ending with some graceful, ingenious, pointed, weighty, witty, or satirical turn of thought; more personal and specific than a proverb, less profound and more superficially ingenious than an apothegm. Two main trends are noticeable: the polished, mordant, witty epigram stemming from the "satires in brief" of Martial; and those—polished, but gracious and ingenious—deriving from the *Anthology.* In Fr., Eng., G. (Logau was best of some forty) but not Sp., the Martial epigram predominated; yet poets like Jonson and Herrick could borrow handily from the *Anthology.* Pope's wit, keenness, precision, polish make him Martial's closest stylistic successor. Since the Fr. Revolution, however, the term "epigram" has been applied to any pointed, pithy saying, in prose or verse. What remains poetic is "the epigram of the *Anthology,*" our humorous verse, our lyric. *Cf.* Light verse; Essay; Apothegm. P. Nixon, *Martial and the Modern Epigram,* 1963. John Burke Shipley.

epilogue. (1) Last of the five ancient and medieval divisions of a speech, equivalent to the (now more commonly used) term peroration. It included the *enumeratio,* recapitulation; and the *amplificatio,* against the accused, or the *commiseratio,* for the accused. (2) The conclusion of a fable, where the practical application, the point, is pressed. (3) In the drama, a plea at the end, usually delivered by one of the cast, for the good will of the audience. Sometimes in jest; Aristophanes in *The Birds* has the chorus of birds promise the judges all sorts of benefits if they award the play the prize, and warns them, if they do not, to keep their heads covered when they go abroad. (It won the second prize in 414 B.C.) Shakespeare gives the boy that plays Rosalind in *As You Like It* an amusing epilogue. Most 17th and 18th c. plays had both prologue and epilogue, sometimes written not by the author but by a distinguished friend.

epimythium. A concise statement of the moral of a fable, at the end (epimythium) or at the beginning (promythium); not a part of the earliest fables. B. E. Perry (*Trans. Am. Philol. Assn.* 71, 1940) has formulated a scheme of the development. When Demetrius of Phalerum made his collection as a writers' source book (before the emergence of the fable collection as an independent literary genre), the promythium was intended as an index-heading. Believing it, instead, explanatory or hortatory, later writers, feeling the end of the fable the more logical position, shifted it there. Later the epimythium became a tradition, often added or altered by later hands, as in medieval mss. *See* Fable.

epiphany [Gr., a showing. The Christian holy day, Twelfth Day (Twelfth Night), January 6, celebrating the first manifestation of Jesus as divine]. Applied by James Joyce to a moment of revelation, generally toward the end of a story, that quickens awareness and changes attitudes or events. It is usually sparked by a simple or commonplace occurrence. Joyce's Stephen Hero defines it as "a sudden spiritual manifestation;" Pater called such illuminating moments "exquisite pauses in time." Epiphany occurs in the *G. Erziehungsroman* (education novel), as Goethe's *Wilhelm Meister's Apprenticeship;* in Butler's *The Way of All Flesh,* and in stories of initiation, where the *rite de passage* leads through the usual three stages (separation, isolation, aggregation) to a renewed communion with society on a higher and more informed plane of living. Other anticipations of Joyce are discussed in J. H. Buckley's "The Eternal Now," in *The Triumph of Time,* 1966; S. Givens, ed. *James Joyce,* 1948.

epiplexis. Argument by censure or shame, implying that a sensible person would see the truth (as the speaker sees it). Often a question to the adversary, the answer to which is clear, and shaming.

episode. An incident; esp. one within a longer story. This may be a digression within an otherwise well-knit struggle, *e.g.,* the founding of Wilmington in Charles Reade's *The Disinherited Heir*; or one of a series of loosely connected events in a long tale, as the picaresque or the It. romantic epic (*Orlando Furioso*). In the drama, according to Aristotle, episodic plays "are the worst"; *i.e.,* those with incidents that do not rise directly from the basic conflict, as Evadne's throwing herself on her husband's pyre, in Euripides'

Suppliant Women. G. Murray, *The Classical Tradition in Poetry*, p. 160 f., 1927.

epistle. No longer in normal use as a more formal alternate for *letter;* now only as a facetious or sarcastic affectation, except to designate letters produced when the term was in natural use and so became attached to them, esp. letters distinguished by care or art, whether in prose or in verse. In the Renaissance, from the custom of casting prefatory matter into the form of a (usually dedicatory) letter, the word *epistle* (or a variant, *e.g., pistell*) had often the meaning of *preface,* and was applied even to nonepistolary preliminaries; so too from the ME. period, since the lesson at Mass was usually from a biblical epistle, the word is applied to all lessons whether epistolary or not. The adj. *epistolary* remains in use, without connotation of either formality or quaintness. *See* Letter; Letter in verse; Epistolary fiction.

epistolary fiction. The popularity of the novel in the form of letters in the 18th c., and its virtual disappearance in later fiction, are interesting phenomena in the art of narrative.

For more than a century before Samuel Richardson established the vogue in *Pamela* (1740), the epistolary method had been used to heighten the sense of actuality in didactic and facetious tales (Nicholas Breton, *A Poste with a Packet of Mad Letters,* 1630), to gratify the taste for travels, scandals, and pseudo-histories (Madame Dunoyer, *Letters from a Lady at Paris to a Lady at Avignon,* 1716), and to serve as a vehicle for sentimental analyses of the feminine heart (Mrs. Aphra Behn, *Love Letters between a Nobleman and his Sister,* 1683).

Richardson varied and perfected the technique. His epistolary practices fall into two general categories: (1) the letters are written by the chief character at the time of the occurrence of the events (*Pamela*), and (2) the letters are exchanged by several pairs of characters (*Clarissa,* 1747–48; *Sir Charles Grandison,* 1753–54). Variations of the device by Richardson's followers include: (1) the inclusion of the whole narrative in a single letter (Charlotte Lennox, *Harriot Stuart,* 1751), (2) the development of the story by means of letters from a number of correspondents to friends whose replies are often suppressed to avoid repetition (Tobias Smollett, *Humphry Clinker,* 1771), (3) the enclosure of the narrative in a journal or diary (Henry Mackenzie, *Julia de Roubigne,* 1777), (4) the unfolding of the tale by a letter writer in possession of the "facts" about the hero's adventures (Susanna Rowson, *Sarah,* 1813), (5) the exchange of letters between two characters whose stories are of equal importance (John Davis, *The Original Letters of Ferdinand and Elizabeth,* 1798), and (6) the incidental use of letters in stories carried forward mainly by direct narration (Rowson's *Reuben and Rachel,* 1798).

The epistolary method was superior to the go-as-you-please narrative procedures before *Pamela:* characters were enabled to reveal their thoughts and feelings while they were in the thick of the action; contrasting points of view were presented when letter writers of different levels of sophistication described the same occurrences; an air of charming ingenuousness was imparted by the easy circumstantiality of the letter form; sentimentalists were provided with ample scope for the dissection of their emotions; and the common accomplishment of letter-writing was an aid to verisimilitude for those readers who preferred fiction to be "genuine" or disguised as "fact."

Richardson's success in realizing these advantages and the simplicity (more apparent than real) of epistolary composition contributed to the extensive production of letter fiction, which reached its climax in the 1780's. Of the various types of fiction employing the epistolary technique, novels of the sentimental school form the largest group. Letter fiction was also peculiarly fitted for the morbidly romantic depiction of passion (Goethe, *Die Leiden des jungen Werthers,* 1774). The minute and voluminous detail of the familiar letter form helped to establish the popularity of the domestic novel of manners (Fanny Burney, *Evelina,* 1778). Epistolary devices also did yeoman service in novels of doctrine and propaganda, where letters were used to inculcate educational theories (Rousseau, *La Nouvelle Héloïse,* 1761; Enos Hitchcock, *Memoirs of the Bloomsgrove Family,* 1790), and to propagate liberal ideas (Robert Bage, *Mount Henneth,* 1781).

The decline of the epistolary method coincided with the rise of historical and Gothic fiction. The artificiality of the letter device with its assumption of indefatigable scribblers and tireless readers was apparent even in the expert handling of Richardson. Moreover, the epistolary exchange involved many repetitions, it denied the author a close association with his readers; it did not permit him to comment upon his story and characters. Defects of this kind led Jane Austen, a disciple of Richardson, to discard the epistolary for a more flexible point of view, that of the omniscient author. The disuse of the letter form in modern fiction has not obscured its service in the craft of the novel. By emphasizing the importance of the point of view in fiction, it raised significant questions of form and structure. There has been some measure of continuing use of the epistolary form in fiction. It is employed in Thomas Bailey Aldrich's best known story, *Marjorie Daw* (1873), and more recently in the novels *The Ides of March* (Thornton Wilder, 1942) and *A Meeting by the River* (Christopher Isherwood, 1967); and even a work by "Una Stannard," called *The New Pamela,* 1969. *See* Narrator. F. G. Black, *The Epistolary Novel in the Late 18th C.,* 1940; H. S. Hughes, "Eng. Epistolary Fiction before Pamela," in *Manly Anniversary Studies,* 1923; C. E. Kany, *The Beginnings of the Epistolary Novel,* 1937; G. F. Singer, *The Epistolary Novel,* 1923; N. Würzbach, ed. *The Novel in Letters,* 1968. HERBERT ROSS BROWN.

epistrophe. *See* Repetition.

epitasis. The movement of a drama toward the climax; the intensifying of the conflict, where "the plot thickens." *Cf.* Freytag's pyramid.

epithalamium (Gr., marriage song or hymeneal, sung or thought of as sung by young men and women before the bridal chamber after the bride and groom have retired). Its popular origin is evidenced by its informal tone of good-natured banter, reminiscent of the noisier charivari. Employs a refrain in which "Hymen" is the burden. A book of Sappho's poetry is devoted to epithalamia. Solomon's *Song of Songs;* Spenser. H. W. Smith, *Gr. Melic Poets,* 1900; *RE* 9.

epithet (Gr., something added; L. *appositum*). Eng. since 16th c. An appellation; also an adjective expressing a characteristic. A Homeric epithet (*bolt-hurling* Zeus, *rosy-fingered* dawn) is a compound of a poetic nature; it is considered bad taste in the Romance languages: Guillaume du Bartas was rebuked for its use in his *Première Semaine,* 1578. A static epithet is one that is descriptive but conventional: Hugh *the Strong;* Eric *the Red.* A dynamic epithet strikes for immediate, strong effect: *lying* Munchhausen; Lorenzo *the Magnificent.* A transferred epithet is one with which another word has been substituted for the appropriate noun: "the *boiling* kettle." In poetry, an epithet may be used merely for embellishment: the *wet* sea; *hollow* ships (both Homer); in prose, if it adds nothing to the thought, it is deemed redundant. An epithet was regarded as a figure; often it embodied another figure: *pale* death; *unbridled* desire. If the noun is omitted (*"The destroyer of Carthage"*—Scipio understood; *"The Bard of Avon"*), the figure is antonomasia. Epithets include (grammatically) the appositive adjunct; the tramp, *hungry and tattered,* knocked at the door; the adjunct term: Peter *the Hermit;* and the phrase in apposition: Cicero, *the Prince of Roman Eloquence.*

epitome. An abridgment or summary of a work. In classical times, a compendium of excerpts on a particular topic taken from different works, *e.g.,* of Herodotus by Theopompus, 4th c. B.C. An increased interest in science demanded short, concise expositions, such as Galen's epitome of his own longer treatise *On the Pulse.* Later, epitomes of epitomes were made, *e.g.,* Pamphilus' *Peri Glosson* (ca. 50 A.D.) in 95 books was reduced to 30 books by Vestinus in Hadrian's time and later to five books of Diogenian (in Hesychius' *Lexicon*). The 12 volumes of Frazer's *The Golden Bough* (1890–1915), which influenced T. S. Eliot's *The Waste Land* and Joyce's *Finnegans Wake,* were epitomized in one volume, as have been other lengthy modern works (Toynbee's 12 v. *A Study of History,* 1934–61).

epitrite. A metrical foot, one short syllable and three long: first: ∪ — — —; second: — ∪ — —; third; — — ∪ —; fourth: — — — ∪. *Cf.* Paeon.

epode. (1) A (non-elegiac) poem composed in distichs, most frequently iambic, or iambic and dactylic, of unequal length (Archilochus, 7th c. B.C.; Horace). (2) The third member of the choral triad; *see* Strophe.

epopee. Epic, *q.v.*

epyllion (Gr. diminutive of epos). Applied in modern times to a poem in dactylic hexameters, of the Alexandrian and Rom. period, similar in tone to the elegy, *q.v.;* often with a mythological digression. M. M. Crump, *The Epyllion . . . ,* 1931; W. Allen, Jr., "The Epyllion," *Trans. Am. Philol. Assn., 71,* 1940.

equivalence. The assumption that, in verse, one long (or accented) syllable is equal to two short (or unaccented) syllables, and that on this basis one kind of foot can be substituted for another. *Cf.* Mora; Substitution.

equivocation (L., with equal voice). Using a word with two different senses in one passage. This may be unconscious, or with deliberate attempt to mislead, or as a source of irony or humor. An expression thus used is an equivoque. It is a form of ambiguity, *q.v. Cf.* Pivot word; Pun.

erotesis. Interrogation to rouse a specific answer, usually negative; a rhetorical question for instant effect. Anthypophora: asking, then giving the answer. Erotema: with the answer obvious. Pusma: as a protest, *e.g.,* "Am I my brother's keeper?" Anacoenosis: addressed specifically, as to an adversary, a judge, or one absent or imagined. Symbouleusis: consulting, as though seeking counsel.

erotic. Of literature, mainly poetry, that treats of love, esp. the physical aspects or the psychological problems involved. Shakespeare, *Venus and Adonis. Cf.* Pornography.

error. The tragic error, or flaw (*hamartia, q.v.*), in the otherwise noble figure, whose consequent downfall makes the catastrophe. In most tragedies the opposition is within the central figure (as in the early ritual where the god himself was at once the destroyer and the saviour—perhaps in two manifestations: father and son; winter and spring—just as Judas, ordained to his role for the redemption of man, has won the obsecration of the ages). The error may be (1) unconscious, *Œdipus Rex*; Otway, *The Orphan*; (2) conscious but thoughtless, *Lear*; (3) deliberate, *Macbeth*; Shaw, *Saint Joan.* It may spring from (a) the disproportion between man's desire and his grasp, with strong characters, Marlowe; weaklings, Galsworthy, *The Pigeon*; (b) the tug of opposed ideals or desires, honor and love, the Sp. drama; Dryden, *All For Love*; (c) the pressure or inflexibility of social forces, Galsworthy, *Justice*; Hauptmann. In all of these cases, there is usually an emotional strain that bears the character off reason's charted course; rarely in the drama (Joyce, *Exiles*) does rigid reason lead a man astray. *Cf.* Tragedy.

Erziehungsroman. G. *See* Epiphany.

escape. Certain works, often called escape-literature—detective stories, musical comedies, many motion pictures—are designed or are sought as diversion (L., turning away). What is often overlooked is that the receptor is not always running from life; he may be seeking life: he turns from a drab monotony that "is no existence at all" in quest of a fullness of experience, of arousal, that alone deserves the name of living. Often these works offer garish, overdrawn, superficial absurdities; at their best (Gilbert and Sullivan; the circus clown) they present the rounded stimulation of all art.

essay. What the essay is has never been precisely determined. In general, it is a composition, usually in prose, of moderate length and on a restricted topic. If one draws a "line of similar materials," divides it in the middle, and along it to the left assigns the characteristics of formality, objectivity, and interest in what is intellectual, and along it to the right the characteristics of informality, subjectivity, and interest in what is imaginative: at the extreme left such writings as treatises and monographs will place themselves; at the extreme right, such compositions as familiar essays and sketches. From left to right will be strung formal essays—biographical, historical, critical, general expository—and about midway editorials, book reviews, magazine and newspaper articles. After the midmark to the right will appear "characters," impressionistic writings, personal essays, playful essays, sketches.

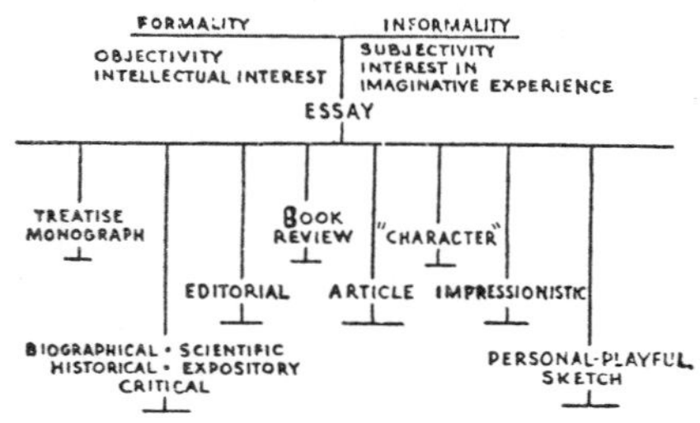

A less wide and more literary conception of the essay eliminates all but formal biographical, historical, critical essays, and personal or familiar essays, playful essays, and sketches. All of these writings are characterized by brevity and by restriction of topic, those in the formal group developing the subject logically, those in the informal group associating ideas freely, often on the basis of sentiment, imagination, whimsy. Concern for, or excellence in, manner of expression, is also a common characteristic. Formal studies, however, may be quite long.

Writers of the ancient world wrote similar compositions, but did not call them essays. The dialogues of Plato, the characters of Theophrastus, the epistles of Pliny and of Seneca, the moral writings of Plutarch, the disputations of Cicero, the meditations of Marcus Aurelius, the treatises of Aristotle, might well today be classed under the general conception of essay.

The word, its meaning of "attempt" indicating incompleteness and tentativeness, was first used by Michel de Montaigne, who pub.,

1580, his confessional comments under the title *Essais*. Their conversational tone, their intimacy, determined the tone and manner that the familiar or personal essay has historically assumed. Among the topics he discussed are "That our desires are augmented by difficulties," "Of the affections of fathers to their children," "Of idleness," "Of vanity," "Of conscience."

Francis Bacon's *Essays,* 1597, are brief, aphoristic, dogmatic, and usually lack the charm of Montaigne's. They are almost pure exposition. Both writers relied upon quotations, examples, figures of speech (Bacon more heavily).

The periodical essay began with Defoe (1704), was developed by Richard Steele in *The Tatler* (1709–11), and used by Addison and Steele in *The Spectator* (1711–12; 1714), the influence of which spread widely in Europe. Addison divided the *Spectator* writings into serious essays and occasional papers. In the latter he employed whimsy, humor, light satire, urbanity, easy elegance, which ever since have been characterizing qualities of the personal and the playful essay. In these, the reader senses the writer's spontaneity, feels as if he had caught the writer off his guard and were overhearing him. This quality allows for intimacy, which, though it seems impromptu, is often subtly arranged. The personal essay uses experience as much as knowledge, and reveals judgment, taste, originality.

In the 19th c., periodicals and the modern magazine developed, and soon came to be the most popular vehicle for the essay. In Fr., this type of essay has been the most developed in the field of literary criticism. Since 1900 the essay has been written by many in Sp. (Unamuno, with his paradoxical streak and his searching of himself; Ortega y Gasset, with penetrating thought and careful style; Salvador de Madariaga). In our crowded times, formal political essays—analyses, excoriations, prophecies, programs—are abundant; the leisurely personal essay is seen less frequently. Harold G. Merriam.

estampie. Fr. Medieval song, with dancing; accentual rhythm with tapping feet.

esthetics. *See* æsthetics.

estrangement (1) A practice among the surrealists, of inducing (as with drugs) or simulating certain forms of mental disturbance, so as to attain a different view of reality. (2) The alienation (*q.v.*) of the receptor from emotional involvement in a work, so that it may be accepted as a lesson. (3) Some early Soviet writers used estrangement (*ostranenie*) for a different purpose. They maintained that with a work of art the receptive process is a *self-aim* and should be prolonged; to increase its duration they increased the difficulty of receptivity, that is, made the work harder to understand. Constant nerve-tensing receptivity—for the sake of the tension itself, the "overload," regardless of the quality of what is received—is also a goal of some writers today, as in the theatre of the absurd (*q.v.*) and in psychedelic productions and some works of mixed media.

estribillo (Sp., little stirrup). The thematic introductory lines of a song, which in the song itself are developed (*glosados,* wherefore the commenting part of the song is called *glosa*). Corresponds to the refrain of other literatures; *refrán* in Sp. means a rhymed proverb.

etymology. Giving the primitive form of a word; or tracing it to its origin, whether in the same language or in one from which it has been borrowed. The conception of the correct method of procedure has changed greatly from ancient to modern times. The idea of a natural association of word and meaning dominated most etymological speculation in ancient times, so that philosophers hoped thereby to obtain an insight into the true (*etymos*) origin of things (whence the name *etymologia* for such speculation).

This type of etymology (often called Platonic from Plato's use of the procedure in his *Cratylus*) led to fanciful results, being based upon a wholly non-comparative, non-historical, and subjective view of one's own language alone, with no guiding concept of historical development, especially in phonetics. For example, such derivations were proposed as *Our-an-os* "heaven" from *Oran to ano* "looking at things above," or *merula* "blackbird" from *mera* "unmixed" (because it flies unmixed, that is, alone). Mere resemblance was considered of prime importance, even if the etymology obtained by such comparison were to involve words with opposite meanings, as in the derivation of *Parcae* (Fates) from the fact that *nemini parcunt,* "they spare no one."

Protests against this cavalier way of dealing with words were of course not absent. Aristotle's more objective method of describing human speech served as the basis for a viewpoint (usually called Aristotelian in opposition to the Platonic) which laid emphasis upon the conventional element in human speech, particularly in the meanings of words. This doctrine was to some extent adopted by scholastic theology, in the principle that "it is given by nature to man to speak, but any specific form of language is created *ab arbitrio hominis* or *ad placitum*."

A satisfactory underlying principle of analysis was finally furnished in the 19th c., after the discovery of Sanskrit, by the establishment of regular correspondences between the sounds of related languages, as in the Indo-European family, or in the Romance or Germanic languages, and the realization that the sounds of a language, as they change, do so regularly and following definite patterns, such as the consonantal shifts of Western Romance speech. In this way it became possible to trace a word to its origin, by establishing its phonetic relations with other words in the same or genetically related languages. In recent years, the concept of etymology has been extended to cover not only the immediate derivation of a word, but its development in meaning and its spread in time and space, thus becoming what may be termed word-history and word-geography.

Untutored persons, when they come in contact with a word of unfamiliar sound or meaning, often remodel it, changing a part or the whole of the word to resemble some better known word. As this type of contamination involves a (quite naïve and usually unconscious) reinterpretation of the word, it has been termed popular etymology. Thus *sparrow-grass* for *asparagus; G. Felleisen* for Fr. *valise*. Such transformations are frequent in names, *e.g.,* the old Eng. tavern *Bag o' Nails* from *Bacchanals*. Robert A. Hall, Jr.

In the formation of words and development of meanings, various processes may be involved: (1) Radiation. New meanings develop, related to the basic sense. Thus *head* comes to mean leader, top, mind, beginning. (2) Borrowing from another language. Gr. *aggelos* became L. *angelus,* then Eng. *angel.* This is the usual quest when one asks the derivation of a word. (3) Gradation. A consonantal framework for a general idea is made more specific by different medial vowels: ride, road, raid. (4) Composition (also, compounding). Two words put together, meaning other than the sum of their parts: *day's eye* becomes *daisy;* skyscraper. This process is frequent in Gr. and G. (5) Affixture, by adding prefix or suffix: happy, unhappy, happiness. (6) Echoism (also, onomatopoeia). Word in imitation of sound: hiss; boing. (7) Suggestion. Use of parts of words, or initials (acrostics): *Nazi* from *NA*tionalso*ZI*alistich; I.O.U. (8) Invention. Cicero coined L. words to match the Gr. Darwin coined *atoll;* Huxley, *agnostic;* Churchill, *the Iron Curtain.* By sound, as Gr. *chaos* suggested *gas* to Van Helmont. By analogy, as *margarine* because the manufacture forms drops like pearls (Gr. *margaron*). The *blimp* was the second (*B*) attempt at a *limp* (non-rigid) dirigible airship. (9) Association, with person or place: volcano; sandwich; tuxedo from Tuxedo Park, where first worn. (10) Conversion. Use as another part of speech. Boat; stomach: noun used as verb. Kill; break: verb used as noun. This is also called functional shift. (11) Blending (also telescope word; portmanteau word). A pressing of two words into one: *chortle* from *chuckle* and *snort; motel* from *motorcar* and *hotel.* This device is frequent in dadaist writing, in Joyce and in later experimenters in "the revolution of the word." (12) Back-formation (through error). *Groveling,* an adverb, was interpreted as present participle of the thence manufactured verb *grovel.* (13) Shortening. This may be back clipping (*orate* from *oration; taxi* from *taximeter cabriolet*) or front clipping (*phone* from *telephone*). (14) Folk etymology. A strange-sounding word is replaced by more familiar elements. *Pentis* became penthouse. *Samblind,* with a first part meaning "wholly," became *sand-blind,* whence by analogy (Shakespeare) *gravelblind,* on the way to *stoneblind.* (15) Generalization. *Dog* was originally a sort of mastiff. (16) Specialization (opp. 15). *Hound* was originally any kind of dog. (17) Elevation. *Pretty* originally meant sly. (18) Degeneration (opp. 17). *Silly* originally meant blessed. (19) Concentration (also, slide). A word originally indicating the entire scale of a polarity becomes limited to one point (usually one end) of the scale. "He has temperature": it's high; "He has a temper": it's bad; *humorous.* (20) Concatenation. Progression by analogy. *Cardinal* originally meant hinge; then, the thing on which matters hinge, *e.g.,* the important church official (who elected the Pope); from his robe, the color; from the color, the bird. (21) Jingling. Rhyme combinations of word or phrase: claptrap; humdrum; hankypanky; even Steven; boogie-woogie; go-go. *Cf.* Ambiguity; Meaning. C. D. Buck, *Dictionary of Selected Synonyms in the Principal Indo-European Languages,* 1949; R. W. Brown, *Composition of Scientific Words,* 1954; Alan S. C. Ross, *Etymology,* 1958; H. A. Skinner, *The Origin of Medical Terms,* 1961; H. Marchand, *The Categories and Types of Present-Day Eng. Word Formation,* 1966; H. Wentworth and S. B. Flexner, *Dictionary of Am. Slang*

(Introd. to the Appendix), 1967. FRANK SULLIVAN.

eulogism. A term used in praise. Opp. dyslogism.

euphemism. A pleasant way of referring to something unpleasant. Thus *burier* became *undertaker,* then *mortician;* when *opium* became too odious, *morphine* ("dream-bringer") came into use; later *heroin* was coined as more attractive than *diamorphine* (die o' morphine!). E. Partridge, *Words, Words, Words,* 1933.

euphony. Smooth flow of sound, an effect of choice and arrangement of words. *See* rhythm.

euphuism. Applied (G. Harvey, *Advertisement for Papp-Hatchet,* 1589) to the style developed by John Lyly in *Euphues,* 1579, and widely influential in the next decade. Originally applied to the elaborate comparisons and similes (from mythology and natural history), *e.g.,* "The rich apparel maketh their beauty more seen, your disguising causeth your faces to be more suspected, they resemble in their raiment the Ostrich who being gazed on, closeth her wings and hideth her feathers, you in your robes are not unlike the peacock, who being praised spreadeth her tail, and betrayeth her pride." Then used also for the style as a whole, with its balanced construction, rhetorical questions, antitheses with alliteration, its mainly verbal devices. Frequently condemned, undoubtedly excessive, euphuism nonetheless made Eng. writers conscious of the powers of prose. A. Feuillerat, *John Lyly,* 1910; H. Clemens and M. W. Croll, *Euphues,* 1916. *See Secentismo;* Baroque.

eupolidian. A form of polyschematic classical verse, the choriambic trochaic tetrameter.

exaltation. Suggested as the effect of tragedy. Clear or implicit in every tragedy is the sense of grandeur, the assertion of man's dignity, the stand of his courage against forces that overwhelm. A pride and an assurance well from these, a song to sing against despair. A sense that, despite inevitable death, such moments are warrant for man's being. All great works rouse in the receptor the triad of ease: entertainment, enlightenment, exaltation. *Cf.* Catharsis.

exargasia. P., "the gorgeous." "Copious and pleasant amplifications and much variety of sentences all running upon one point and to one interest." A galaxy of figurative forms applied to the enhancing of a work.

excursus. L. A detailed discussion of some point, treated more fully than can be done in a note; a digression in which some incidental point is discussed at length.

H. V. Canter, "Excursus in Gr. and Rom. Historians" *PQ* 8, 1929.

exegesis. (1) Explanation. In Rome, the exegetes were officials interpreting sacred law, dreams, omens, oracles. Hence, esp. making clear a passage in the Bible. (2) An explanatory digression. Epexegesis: an added explanation. Ecphrasis: a word or two, to make something clearer. Proecthesis: pausing to explain what has gone before.

exemplum. An illustrative story, common in sermons, esp. in middle ages. There were many collections of *exempla,* and protests (Dante, Wycliffe) against their use. Used in several of the *Canterbury Tales,* ca. 1387.

existentialism. The name applied to a loosely interrelated group of modern philosophies (post-1850) for which in varying degrees the central metaphysical fact is the existing individual. Accordingly, stress is placed on what is often called the priority of existence over essence, the existent's ability and responsibility to create his own world, and the centrality of anxiety (*Angst*) and death as experiences in such a creation.

Dostoyevsky and Kierkegaard are two of the models for this thought. The narrator of *Notes from the Underground* rages against the substantial identities provided for him by the naming and classifying society in which he finds himself; yet simultaneously he struggles to create an identity for himself. The weight of this responsibility, on himself, is increased rather than alleviated by his consciousness of his problem. This consciousness promotes endless anxiety. Kierkegaard applies the same analysis directly to his own struggle to exist as an "authentically" religious individual. As far as the truth goes, this is a life and death struggle: "The communicator of the truth can only be a single individual."

The notions here wrapped into narrative texture are unfolded and analyzed in the main systematic texts of existentialism: Heidegger's *Sein und Zeit* (1927); Marcel's *Etre et avoir* (journal covering the years 1928–33); Jasper's *Vernunft und Existenz* (1935); Sartre's *L'Etre et le néant* (1943); Merleau-Ponty's *Phénoménologie de la perception* (1945). All of these texts develop, from the kinds of concern prominent in Kierkegaard and Dostoyevsky, a radical reintroduction of the whole human person into the center of philosophic concern. They are self-reflections of that person, worked out, made explicit, in an exhaustive act of awareness.

Sein und Zeit is probably the most comprehensive document of this effort. For the Heidegger of that period, man's existence, his *Dasein,* is an anxious turning forward, through *Sorge* (care), into the temporality out of which he is to make himself. On every side, in Being, lies the temptation of *Das Man,* the impersonal *"on dit,"* "one says" or "one does," into which the individual is forever lured, in his willingness to lay down the burden of his own "authenticity." The world in which human *Dasein* deploys is in that sense always a fallen world, *verfallene Welt,* lived inadequately to the demands of human existence. The merits of authenticity, in fact, are simply those of tentative transcendence of the "fallen state," for ahead is only death, the supreme but unrepeatable possibility, which even in our authenticity we can do no more than accept.

The atheistic version of existentialism, of which there is reason to consider the early Heidegger an exponent, repeated itself in Sartre and Morleau-Ponty, offering itself as an account of human existence with which the best fiction of the past decades shows tacit agreement. (Sartre, like other existentialists, is himself one of these fiction writers; his fiction rather blackly exhorts man to courage in the face of despair.) This fact facilitates a confusion, among students of literature, between the existential and the atheistic perspectives. It is crucial to remember that what we call existentialism had its origins simply in an unsparing analysis of the human situation, and in an extension, to that analysis, of methods drawn from Husserl's phenomenology, which centered on a neutral, and non-reductive introspection. The attribution of meaninglessness and absurdity to *Angst* is no necessary part of the existential analysis; the popular influence of Sartre's humanism has stressed such a necessity, but Marcel, for instance, shows how adroitly the whole direction of this analysis can be turned, how reasonably the fullness of Being can be taken as the goal of our anxiety. And no writer of our century has claimed more than Heidegger for poetry as a holding open of Being, in readiness for the *kommende Götter,* the coming gods. In him, literary creation becomes the aperture through which escape is envisioned. *Cf.* Humanism; Beat; Absurd. J. P. Sartre, *Nausea,* 1938, trans. 1949; *Existentialism,* 1946, trans. 1948; R. Jolivet, *Sartre: The Theology of the Absurd,* 1967; W. Kaufman, ed. *Existentialism from Dostoyevsky to Sartre,* 1956; W. Barrett, *Irrational Man,* 1958; A. B. Fallico, *Art and Existentialism,* 1962; D. D. McElroy, *Existentialism and Modern Lit.,* 1963; M. Friedman, ed. *The Worlds of Existentialism,* 1964; *To Deny Our Nothingness,* 1967; J. Maritain, *Court traité de l'existence et de l'existent,* 1964; Colin Wilson, *Introd. to the New Existentialism* (but see review in London *Times Lit. Supplement,* Feb. 26, 1967); E. N. Less and M. Mandelbaum, *Phenomenology and Existentialism,* 1967; H. Peyre, *French Novelists of Today,* 1967; S. Lawall, *Critics of Consciousness,* 1968; Patricia F. Sanborn, *Existentialism,* 1968; W. Barnes, *The Phil. and Lit. of Existentialism,* 1968; Ernest Becker, *Angel in Armor,* 1969. FREDERIC WILL.

exordium. The first part of a speech, the introduction. Roman rhetoricians noted two types: *principium,* the direct opening, in which the speaker sought good will by his straightforwardness and the apparent merits of his cause; and *insinuatio,* the indirect opening, in language veiled and suggestive, through which the speaker sought to insinuate himself into the favor of the audience before venturing to present the facts of his case. *See* Disposition; Speech, divisions.

explication. A detailed examination and explanation of a work, or of a minute passage thereof. It may seek (a) to elucidate the author's meaning, as by clearing away difficulties; (b) to disclose latent meanings, perhaps not conscious in the author, or fresh for the critic's time. Partly a practice carried over from the study of works in a foreign language, or the Fr. *explication de texte,* it was given prominence in the "new criticism" (*q.v.*): I. A. Richards, *Practical Criticism,* 1929, which presents for examination passages or short poems without identifying the author; Cleanth Brooks and Robert Penn Warren, *Understanding Poetry,* 1939; and the magazine *The Explicator,* founded in 1942. The value of explication lies in the fact that understanding improves appreciation and judgment. *Cf.* Interpretation. W. K. Wimsatt, Jr., ed. *Explication as Criticism,* 1963.

exposition. *See* Composition.

exposition in drama. One of the playwright's most difficult tasks is to convey, while holding audience interest, essential information as to events before the play, as to what the situation is at curtain-rise. This is a modern problem (made more difficult by the habit of late arrival at theatre, so that the first 15 minutes may be lost); the Greeks used familiar stories, or gave the whole plot in the prologue, as perhaps the Eliz. dumb-show gave it in pantomime. Often essential prior facts are just lumped, *e.g.* (*As You Like It*) "What's the new news at the new court?" "No news but the old news"—whereupon the old news is repeated for the audience; the catechistic questioning of Caliban in *The Tempest.* In the 18th c., esp. in Fr., the confidant was always ready to hear what the audience must learn. In the 19th c. drawing-room comedy, the inevitable butler and maid open the play with relevant talk about their master and mistress. More subtle is the giving of information in the course of the action, *e.g., Hamlet.* Ibsen developed this (*A Doll's House, Ghosts*) so that items slip in one at a time, just before they are needed for understanding of the action. The problem is similar to, and as perplexing as, that of description in the novel; many writers find as effective a way as the theme and their ingenuity permit, to present it all together near the start, and have done. *See* Protatic character.

expression. In modern use the word *expression* means either the externalization of some inner reality or the manifestation, representation, or signification in general of one thing by another.

Besides an apprehending mind, to recognize expressiveness where it appears, there are three principal elements which may be involved in any process of expression: (1) that which is to be expressed (the *exprimend;* when expressed this becomes an *expressum*), (2) that which is expressive (the *expriment, e.g.* a word), and (3) the agency which produces the expression (the *expressor, e.g.* a man who speaks a word). Opinions vary as to the precise relations and functions of these elements in the accomplishment of expression. Santayana interprets the relation of expriment to exprimend as one of associative suggestion or cognitive reference (meaning) simply. This seems wise, as at once giving the word *expression* a concrete sense and conforming with the normal present intent of its use; for whatever else may be implied by *expression,* this at least is always involved in its meaning, and we may say generally that to express any thing is to make another thing suggest or refer to it. The Greeks used for the relation in question the word *imitation,* which implies not only reference, but some kind of correspondence, and a likeness to or participation in the character of the exprimend on the part of the expriment.

A common modern conception which implies that the externalization of expression involves real ontological transition of exprimend into the expressive matter, of which it becomes informing principle (*see* Form), seems demonstrably crude and erroneous. For on the one hand it is plain that a tree does not take up existence in the word *tree* when it is expressed by that word; and it seems equally absurd to suppose that the idea of the tree, or feeling about it, if that be the exprimend, passes from the mind that conceives it, to exist in the word. What happens is simply that the sounds composing the word *refer* to the idea in the mind and through it to the tree, or to the tree directly, or to the idea or feeling alone; this reference of the sound is a *signification* (part of a *meaning*); the signification exists in the word, as part and formal element of its constitution; but the exprimend, the tree or the idea or feeling, remains entirely outside the word that expresses it by so referring to it, and entirely distinct from it in its ontological constitution.

For expression, however conceived, some such real externalization of the exprimend as can be provided only by an expriment is strictly required. But externalization is relative. The expriment, though regarded as external and capable of giving externalization to the exprimend, may itself be conceived as existing wholly or primarily within the mind. It is so regarded in the mediæval use of the term *express* to refer to the operation by which the mind evolves its concepts and images, which are called *species expressae* (in contrast to the *species impressae* presented by sense); and in the very analogous usage of B. Croce, which makes intuition a process in which the mind expresses within itself the reality it experiences. In the Crocean theory, though expression strictly involves an exprimend and an expriment, the existence of the exprimend as such is wholly dependent upon that of a corresponding expriment; it is only as expressum that an exprimend can exist as exprimend, for it is only in the act of expression, *i.e.* only by producing an expressum, that the mind arrives at its knowledge of an exprimend.

Expression has always been considered a principal element in the process, and expressiveness in the work, of art. In classical poetic theory (not equally in rhetorical, of course) the place of expressiveness as such is usually subordinate to that of structure (or "form" regarded as excluding expressiveness), the constant implication of classical theory and practise being that, important as expression of idea or feeling may be in art, it is impossible without a structure which can be expressive, and that reference which is not thoroughly assimilated into the structure of an object is not truly reference at all. The problem of expressiveness as such *versus* structure as such, doubtless the chief problem of modern æsthetics, is the point of departure of Lessing's *Laokoön* (1776). After Lessing, European theory, esp. G., tends increasingly to emphasize the importance of expressiveness, arriving finally at a position from which fine art is viewed not primarily as the making of an object, but as the expression of an idea, or in practise the report of an experience (*i.e.,* in traditional terms, as essentially a rhetorical rather than a poetic process). This conception of fine art prevailed throughout Europe during the 19th c., and though it has been subjected to much criticism in the 20th it remains the commonest unconscious æsthetic prejudice of our time. Its principal systematic advocate is Croce, the foundation of whose theory is the contention that expression and fine art are absolutely identical, so that, as all fine art is expression, all expression is fine art.

Almost as many characteristics of valid expression have been advanced as there have been schools of critics. The most common require that it be clear, concise, correct, or, as the ancients emphasized for the *narratio* of an oration, that it possess clarity, brevity, and verisimilitude (interpreted as both apparently concordant with reality and self-consistent). To these was frequently added *enargeia,* vividness. *Cf.* Brief.

G. Santayana, *Sense of beauty,* 1896; C. W. Morris, *Foundations of theory of signs,* 1938; B. Bosanquet, *Hist. of æsthetic,* 1892; E. F. Carritt, *Theory of beauty,* 2d ed. 1923, 179 f.; B. Croce, *Estetica,* 1901; *La poesia,* 1935; J. E. Spingarn, *Creative criticism,* 1917. *See* Signs; Form; Revelation. J. Craig LaDrière.

expressionism. A form of artistic expression that seeks to externalize the essential emotion of a situation. Thus in Elmer Rice's play *The Adding Machine,* 1923, when Mr. Zero learns that, instead of getting a raise after his twenty-five years with one firm, he is fired, that part of the stage on which he is standing suddenly spins around. Galsworthy neatly caught the expressionists when he said that they try to show the inside of things without showing their outside. Anticipated in such plays as Frank Wedekind's *Awakening of Spring* (1891, performed 1906) and August Strindberg's *The Spook Sonata* (1907), expressionism flourished in the drama, esp. in Germany after World War I. It deals in dreamlike distortions, with characters perhaps shadowy, perhaps gigantesque. The language is likely to be clipped, breathless; yet there may be self-revealing monologues. The action may be abrupt, fantastic, many-leveled, with tricky devices and weird effects. In fiction, expressionistic devices are frequent in such works as Joyce's *Finnegans Wake* and the stories of Franz Kafka; they proliferate in such anti-novels as Robert Pinguet's *L'Inquisitoire,* Andy Warhol's *a* (1968) and the "concrete" explorations of Willar Bain's *Informed Sources* (1968). In the main, however, expressionism survives as an exciting element in a work, rather than as a method employed throughout. (For Croce's theory, *see* entry above.) *Cf.* Baroque; Concrete; Anti-hero; Narrator. W. H. Sokel, *Expressionism in G. Lit.,* 1954; P. Raabe, *Expressionismus,* 1965; E. Krispyn, *Style and Society in G. Literary Expressionism,* 1964; P. Bouland, *The Hooded Eagle,* 1968.

expressor. *See* Signs.

eye-rhyme. Rhyme that is correct according to the spelling but not according to the sound, *e.g.,* watch, catch; misery, eye:

If these delights thy mind may move,
Come live with me and be my love.

Sometimes with wrenched accent, effected by a change in spelling: see, countree (old ballads; *The Ancient Mariner*). In older poems, however, what seems to us a mere eye-rhyme may once have been correct, the pronunciation having changed: Cathay, tea. *Cf.* Consonance: Assonance: Rhyme.

F

FABLE. Several uses, now rare, led to present conception of the word, for which *see* below, Æsopic. (a) Myth or legend; a fictitious narrative of supernatural or unusual persons, more or less associated with folklore (Milton, Goldsmith). (b) Any foolish story composed of nonsense; an old wife's fable (Wyclif, Bacon). (c) An actual fabrication or falsehood, also a thing falsely supposed to exist. (Marlowe, Shakespeare, Dryden). (d) An individual or thing that has become proverbial (Ben Jonson, Tennyson, Thackeray). (e) The plot of a play or poem (Dryden, Addison, Johnson). *See* Fabliau.

fable, Æsopic. Certain traditions, combined with the discovery in recent times of typical fables in early cuneiform texts, make it probable that Greece was indebted in some measure to the Babylonians and Assyrians for the type of fable associated with Æsop, himself a native of Asia Minor in the 6th c. B.C. Prose collections, partly extant, of greatly expanded content, and ascribed to Æsop by their unknown compilers, were made throughout antiquity and later. Not until the verse compositions of Phædrus and Babrius in the 1st c. A.D. did fable-writing attain rank as belles lettres. The L. tradition of western Europe stems largely from Phædrus and his paraphrasers. Æsop himself wrote nothing; he was famed for using fables, partly in lieu of free speech, in the intercourse of real life.

With some exceptions, wherein wit or amusement is uppermost, Æsopic fables are exhortatory in aim and spirit. They convey a principle of behaviour through the transparent analogy of frankly fictitious, though plausible, actions of animals, men, gods or inanimate things. Animals act according to their nature, save that they have speech. The motifs are numerous and derive partly from folklore, partly from sophistic invention. The outlook is realistic and ironical. (*Cf.* Fairy-tale.) Typical themes are: the folly of sacrificing a small gain already achieved in the hope of winning a larger one, of never being satisfied, of trying to appease the ruthless, of showing mercy to the merciless, of the weak expecting to deal on equal terms with the strong; the irony of setting a snare for others and falling into it one's self, of the small and clever triumphing over the physically strong.

In structure, the fable is always epigrammatic; it frequently ends with a significant utterance by one of the characters. The application of fables used in a context is usually, and in the early period always, specific or personal; whereas the generalized "moral," or epimythium, introduced at the end by such phrases as "this fable teaches," originated in collections of fables without context, and therein mainly through confusion with the promythium, the purpose of which, as a prefatory statement of the fable's meaning and potential use, was not to explain but only to classify, the fable collection being originally a work of reference. In a considerable number of fables (*A Hundred Mery Tales,* 1526; *Fables for Our Time,* James Thurber, 1940) the "moral" is amoral or ironic. *Cf.* Fairy tale; Folklore; Primitivism. B. E. Perry, *TAPA* 71, 1940; *Studies in . . . Aesop,* 1936; George Boas, *The Happy Beast in the Fr. Thought of the 17th C.,* 1933, 1966. B. E. Perry.

fabliau (flourished Fr. 11th–13th c., though earlier: Egbert's *Poenitentiale,* 8th c., warns against delighting in them). A short tale (not over 400 lines) in verse (esp. octosyllabic rhymed couplets), treating comically an incident of middle-class life. Keen, gaily satiric (esp. vs. clergy: *Richeut,* 1159), often coarse; full of *l'esprit gaulois.* Moved from the aloof and adored heroine of romance and *lai* to the rough and always ready woman of the people (*Chicheface et Bicorne*). The tradition was renewed, though merged with that of the fable, by La Fontaine (*Fables,* 1668, 1678), by C. F. Gellert and more in the 18th c., by the Russ. I. A. Krylov (9 v., 1843). A. de Montaiglon and G. Raynaud,

Les Fabliaux, 6 v. 1872–90 (the texts); J. Bedier, *Les Fabliaux,* 1925. *See* Old Fr. . . . forms.

fabula Atellana (<Atella, an Oscan town in Campania). The ancient south It. farce, developed from improvisation, was early introduced to Rome and played there in the Oscan tongue until the time of Augustus. A few typical masks represented stock characters: Maccus, the fool; Bucco (big mouth) the clown; Pappus (grandpappy) the stupid old man; Dossennus (hunchback) the shrewd fellow; Manducus (gobbler) the glutton; the acting was marked by much pantomime and obscenity. These farces (ca. 2d c. B.C.) were adapted to Latin and played as after-pieces to tragedies; given fixed plots and literary form of a sort, they achieved some popularity during the period of Sulla, only to yield place to the mime. Revived, perhaps in the time of Augustus, they continued to be played until late antiquity, when the mime again drove the Atellana from the stage. The titles, such as *Maccus copo* (Maccus as Innkeeper); *Maccus miles* (Maccus in the army); *Pappus præteritus* (Grandpappy loses the election); *sponsa Pappi* (Grandpappy's bride), show the general tone and wide range of subject; a few, *e.g., Mortis et Vitae iudicium* (Life and Death come to trial) indicate plots of a more ambitious kind. The fragments are collected in O. Ribback, *Scaenicae Romanorum Poesis Fragmenta,* 3rd ed. 1897–98, v. 2. W. Beare, "Plautus and the Fabula Atellana," *CR,* 1930. Kenneth Morgan Abbott.

fabula crepidata (Gr. *crepis,* boot). Rom. tragedy based on Gr. models.

fabula motoria. *See* Fabula stataria.

fabula palliata (L. *pallium,* cloak). The principal type of Latin comedy, introduced to Rome by Livius Andronicus (fl. 240 B.C.). (The last composer of *palliatæ* known to us, Turpilius, died in 103 B.C.) The *palliata* depended throughout its history upon the adaptation or free trans. of Gr. New Comedy. In the comedies of Plautus and Terence, the only complete *palliatæ* remaining to us, the setting and characters are Gr.; the customs are a mixture of Gr. and Rom. The L. authors, however, did far more than merely translate. (*See* Contamination.) Plautus (ca. 254–ca. 184) with his exuberant tone, his boisterous and often obscene humor, his eye to the immediate dramatic effect in defiance of consistent construction, is non-Greek. Cæcilius (fl. 179), whose methods of adaptation were studied in antiquity by Aulus Gellius (*Attic Nights* 2, 23—the whole passage is significant for the methods of later Rom. criticism), borrows no more than the bare plot. With Terence (ca. 190–159) is to be found a relatively new doctrine, that of realism and consistency in plot construction (as in his protest against allowing the defendant to speak first in a court of law) which leads him to substitute dialogue for monologue, to withdraw exposition from the prologue into the play itself. He also reacts against excessive variation from the line of composition, such as too much business offstage, or flights into the tragic and lapses into the vulgar. Toward the end of the 2nd c., partly from the apathy of audiences, poets turned to forms such as the *togata* or even the *Atellana,* with a wider range of subject, fewer restraints in style, and a freer field of national characters and points of view. Kenneth Morgan Abbott.

fabula praetexta (Rom. senatorial toga; later *praetextata*). Historical Roman drama, first written by Gn. Naevius, imprisoned for political references therein. *Octavia,* author unknown, is extant entire.

fabula saltica (L., leaping). Rom. ballet pantomime. Lucan (d. 65 A.D.) wrote a partly preserved libretto: the actor gesticulates and dances; the chorus chants the text.

(fabula) stataria (Terence, Prol. *Heautontimoroumenos, The Self-Tormentor*). A static comedy, as opposed to the swift-moving (*motoria*) with stock figures: slave on the run; old man in a fury. Comments (Evanthius *De Comœdia,* 4, 4; Donatus on Terence' *Adelphæ* 24) discuss the difference as mainly one of liveliness of staging. The farce of rapid movement, always popular, developed into the chase (E. Labiche, *Le Chapeau de paille d'Italie,* 1851; adapted W. S. Gilbert, *The Wedding March*), which ran on a golden track with the "movies." Except for comedy (Mack Sennett, Charlie Chaplin) the early chase, mainly of the wild west, favored the hunters; later, sympathy has often been with the hunted. The pattern of the chase has continued in fiction, esp. in stories of espionage. *Cf.* Detective story.

(fabula) togata. (L., toga, *i.e.,* on Rom. themes.) First attempted by Nævius (325–204); revived mid 2d c. B.C. in an effort to displace the Gr. *fabula palliata* by a truly national Rom. comedy representing actual characters in the current scene (bakers, tailors, hair-dressers, freedmen, and parasites; not, as in the *palliata,* soldiers, cooks, panders, and the cunning slaves who cheat their masters). The tone of the plays, as Seneca (*Ep.* 8, 8) remarks, lay between that of tragedy and that of comedy. The *togata* fell back into the influence of the *palliata*.

fabulation. A word brought back (from Caxton: 8th Fable of Alfonce, of "The King and His Fabulator," 1484) to apply to a development in the post-realistic anti-novel. Explained by Robert Scholes (*The Fabulators,* 1967) as involving a delight in formal and verbal dexterity, and a concern less with things than with ideas and ideals. Durrell's *Alexandrian Quartet* (1957–60), an anti-novel as Cervantes' *Don Quixote* was an anti-romance, is a fabulation. Other fabulators are Iris Murdoch and John Barth. Fabulation uses allegory; it may assume a (black) comic attitude; it "springs from the collision between the philosophical and mythic perspectives on the meaning and value of existence, with their opposed dogmas of struggle and acquiescence." *Cf.* Black humor; Anti-hero; Allegory; Spontaneity; Surrealism.

fact. *See* Question of fact.

fairy tale. Rising from folk tales and gathered legends from the orient (*The 1,001 Nights*) or the native land, the fairy tale was given its modern form in three countries. In Fr. the *conte bleu* of Chas. Perrault (1628–1703) pub. 1696–97; in G. the *Kinder- and Haus-Märchen* of the brothers Grimm (philologists: Wilhelm, 1786–1859; Jacob, 1785–1863, *Deutsche Grammatik,* "Grimm's law" of consonantal shift); in Denm. Hans Christian Andersen (1805–75), *Eventyr,* 1835, and successive Christmas seasons. The fairy tale's miracles occur on the material plane; on the spiritual plane (affections, characters, justice, love) law abides: Prince Charming, changed to a bird, flies to his love and sings to her. In the fable, a shrewd or practical realism reigns: the cheese drops, the fox cannot reach the grapes, persuasion is better than force: the best policy reaps its reward. In the fairy tale, the youngest son, the ugly duckling, the Cinderella, submits patiently until heaven (in the shape of the fairy godmother) stoops to virtue's aid. Fairyland is the happy hunting ground of children; the fable warns them they must grow in the real world. *Cf.* Fable.

Falkentheorie. The theory of the *Novelle* was formulated by Paul Heyse, one of the Munich Circle (1871–76). The 9th tale of the 5th day of Boccaccio's *Decameron* (1350) tells how Federigo impoverished himself in vain wooing of his wealthy mistress until, with nothing left but his favorite falcon, he sacrifices the bird to entertain her and thereby softens her heart and wins her hand. Heyse makes the falcon stand for that unique and concrete symbol, that *starke Silhouette,* which differentiates any given *Novelle* from all others and imprints it unforgettably on the reader's mind. The falcon, furthermore, illustrates the turning point, the *Wendepunkt,* demanded theoretically by Tieck. *Cf.* Epiphany; Fiction; *Novelle.* R. M. Mitchell, *Heyse and his Predecessors in the Theory of the Novelle,* 1915; E. K. Bennett, *The G. Novelle,* 1934.

fame. The collective, perspective criticism of an author, which may be regarded as a species of literary biography, consists in an interpretation and assessment of the man and his works as they are mirrored in the minds and hearts of his readers, contemporary or posthumous. It deals with what Renan called an author's afterlife, with that essential part of his accomplishment which has received or bids fair to receive some measure of earthly immortality. The distinction between fame and influence should be kept in mind.

Typical patterns of reputation are: Contemporary success and subsequent near-oblivion (Young of the *Night Thoughts*); Contemporary undervaluation (say, of Euripides by Aristophanes) and subsequent lasting esteem; Contemporary praise for one *genre;* and subsequently, praise for another, in both of which the author has won success (Byron's poetry: romantic and satiric); Praise or dispraise for different aspects or values of the same work in different periods (Homer; Virgil). Not fewer than three periods are desirable in the study of fame: (a) Contemporary indifference, approval, or disparagement; (b) Slow growth or exaggerated reaction; (c) A more balanced judgment.

In such patterns one may observe the operation of the Test of Time, which, according to Dr. Johnson, is based not upon mere reverence for venerability but upon the opportunity afforded for varied comparison and disinterested analysis, "length of duration and continuance of esteem." (But *cf.* H. Peyre, *The Failures of Criticism,* 1967.) Usually the voice of the people as well as the *dicta* of approved critics should be carefully considered; for, by their insistence upon keeping a book alive, the reading public may influence its assessments by the writing few.

Among multifarious determining influences, for good or ill, in the building of a reputation are: (a) The character of the age itself: social, political,—but above all literary (The "spacious times of great Elizabeth").

(b) The impress of individual authority; not only of critics, favorable and unfavorable, but of powerful friends or enemies (The quarrels of Pope). (c) Accounts in reference books, textbooks (The bias of Taine), public lectures (Thackeray on Swift). (d) Inclusion in curricula of school or college (Scott's *Lady of the Lake*). Pronouncements of taste (what one likes) as well as of judgment (what is worth liking) should be recorded; the most important of these *dicta* should be carefully studied in the light of context, attendant circumstances, and previous or later utterances by the same authority. Only thus may the perplexed skein of reputation be unravelled.

The general outline of the study of a reputation will vary according to the author's purpose and the materials available. Since it deals with a time-sequence, it will usually be in the main design chronological; within this structure, however, it may be topical. The advantage in the use of the chronological pattern throughout is that of detailed, comprehensive documentation; its danger, that of uninterrupted heterogeneity. The advantage of the interior topical pattern is that of expository simplification; its danger, that of sketchiness. Although even the mere assembling of critical utterances (allusion books) has its value, the proper goal of the scholar is just and illuminating interpretation.

The services rendered by an extended and competent study of an important individual reputation are many and valuable; *e.g.,* (a) A better understanding and assessment of an author and his works. Unmerited obloquy or neglect due to ignorance or malice may eventually be remedied by the proper detective diligence and effective refutation. (Note Dryden's ignorance regarding the final *e* of Chaucer; Macaulay's disparagement of Boswell; Richardson's malignity toward Fielding.) (b) A better understanding of any *genre* in which the author has been particularly successful. (The vicissitudes of Homer's fame as a powerful aid in a study of the Epic.) (c) A contribution to the general literary (and often non-literary) history of the period (the vogue of Molière). (d) Important data for testing the acumen and catholicity of many individual critics; the book, *en revanche,* takes the measure of the critic (Hazlitt on Richardson's *Lovelace*). (e) An invaluable storehouse of materials which, properly examined and compared, must in the end throw light not only on histories of criticism and æsthetics but upon the bases of critical and æsthetic theory (The evolution of *genres;* form and significance).

Oddly enough the study of fame, as distinguished from that of influence, despite certain notable exceptions, is still an almost undiscovered country. Expressed opinions on individual reputation abound, but full-length, well-documented studies are singularly few. (*See* the interesting collectanea of Amy Cruse on the reader's share in the development of Eng. literature.) This tardiness on the part of scholars has unquestionably impeded the clarification of many important questions both in criticism and in æsthetics. *Cf.* Literature and Society. C. Spurgeon, *500 Years of Chaucer Criticism and Allusion,* 3 v., 1914–25; Ship; Amy Cruse, *The Shaping of Eng. Lit.,* 1927; *The Englishman and His Books in the Early 19th C.,* 1930; *The Victorians and their Reading,* 1935; Arnold Bennett, *Fame and Fiction,* 1901; F. L. Mott, *Golden Multitudes,* 1947, 1960; L. Marder, *His Exits and His Entrances* (Shakespeare), 1963; Alice P. Hackett, *Seventy Years of Best Sellers,* 1968. FREDERIC THOMAS BLANCHARD.

familiar verse. *See* Light verse.

fancy (Gr. *phantasia,* appearance, subjective impression, and in psychology, imagination). In late L. *imaginatio* became a synonym of *phantasia* and persisted as such throughout the Middle Ages, save for the occasional differentiation of *phantasia* (a capacity for new combinations of images) from the reproductive imagination. The frequent association in the Renaissance of fancy with love, hallucination, and madness led to the differentiation of fantasticality and fantasy (Ronsard; Sidney; Puttenham). The term was also coupled with invention. In the 17th c. it was synonymous with wit and like that power demanded the control of judgment. In the 18th c. there was a growing use of fancy as a lighter, less serious play of imagination, a distinction adopted by the Romantic critics, esp. Wordsworth. Subsequent attempts to differentiate (*e.g.* Leigh Hunt, *What is Poetry?,* 1844) have, on the whole, merely elaborated or modified Wordsworth's distinction. *Cf.* Imagination. L. Abercrombie, *The Theory of Poetry: Note on Fancy and Imagination,* 1926; C. D. Thorpe, "The Imagination: Coleridge vs. Wordsworth." *PG* 18, 1939.

fantasy (L., *phantasia,* an apparition, <Gr. *phainein,* to show). Neither etymological roots nor early uses explain the meaning "fantasy" has acquired in modern literary

practice and criticism. Among literary genres fantasy alone disregards the principle that literature should present not the possible, but the probable, unless Aristotle's "probable impossibility" be taken to countenance its realm. For fantasy includes, in the action, the characters, or the setting, things that are impossible under ordinary conditions or in the normal course of human events. In the case of no other genre is the willing suspension of disbelief so requisite. Not every work containing strange or supernatural features is a fantasy. If it deals with religious beliefs or treats the mysterious but nevertheless actual phenomena of abnormal psychology, it is not fantasy. Only purely imaginary phenomena, accepted as such by the author and his intelligent adult readers, constitute the characteristic matter of fantasy. Once the author has aimed his fancy's flight, however, its farthest range must be in the same imagined world, must seem consistent; the reader will ride but one "magic carpet" at a time.

Fantasy is an occasional element in ancient works; also later, as in Shakespeare (*M.N.Dr.; Tempest*). By Rabelais and by Swift it was used to satirize social evils and intellectual absurdities. Although it may be horrible or (Lord Dunsany) gruesomely thrilling, modern writers more frequently use it for light satire of manners or for mere indulgence of playful fancy. Some of their fantasies belong to the literature of escape. They give the mind welcome relief from the matter-of-factness of a prosaic industrial world and an over-realistic literature. They release some of the mental tensions caused by the sense of individual frustration in a regimented society. To children, to whom the suspension of disbelief is as natural as breathing, they are an unfailing delight. Some fantasies, however, have merits that only adults can fully appreciate. Beneath a deceptive air of triviality, they may conceal a stern intent. The *saeva indignatio* of Swift, his scorn of man's failure to use the powers of reason, is nowhere stronger than in *Gulliver's Travels*; and behind the apparent insouciance of Stevenson is revealed the horrible conclusion of *Dr. Jekyll and Mr. Hyde*. Beneath the seeming nonsense of Lewis Carroll, there are stinging intellectual barbs, felt also in the light operettas of W. S. Gilbert. Fantasy is often as intellectual and humane as it is amusing. It combines humor, whimsicality, and imaginative perceptiveness in a peculiarly Anglo-American blend which, as a foreign critic has said, is "a mystery, a despair, and a delight to Latin nations."

There have also been a large number of books in the tradition of Swift, by such writers as E. R. Eddison, *The Worm Ouroboros,* 1926, 1952, and its two successors; J. R. R. Tolkien, *The Hobbit,* 1937, 1966, with riddles and jingles and other suggestions of elfin and goblin days, the three books of the hobbits in the Third Age of Middle Earth, *The Lord of the Rings,* 1965; and the shuddery *Gormenghast Trilogy* of the House of Groan, by Marvyn Peake, 1946, 1967—not to mention the wide range of science fiction.

French writer Jules Verne (1828–1905) carried fantasy into the pseudo-scientific world with his boldly imaginative, and amazingly prophetic books: *A Voyage to the Center of the Earth* (1864); *The Mysterious Island* (1870); and *Twenty Thousand Leagues Under the Sea* (1869). Verne's work was the precursor of the enormously popular science fiction, a genre of fantasy which is based either on scientific fact or on plausible pseudo-science. The 1940's and 1950's saw a tremendous growth in this form of fantasy, with the publication of a large number of books and magazines devoted entirely to science fiction (*q.v.*).

One of the most sustained fantastic or mythical worlds was that created by James Branch Cabell (1879–1958), the medieval French province of Poictesme. His novels traced the history of this imaginary place from the mid-13th to the mid-18th century, describing the people, laws, habits, morals, and manners.

The motion picture and television, media which can transcend time and space, and, therefore, lend themselves to successful fantasy, have almost since their invention produced fantasy for pure entertainment, suspense, and shock (as in the horror films *King Kong, Dr. Jekyll,* etc.). *Lost Horizons* (from James Hilton's famous book) created a mythical but believable world on film, and this was followed by the successful filming of the stage fantasy, *Blithe Spirit,* by Noel Coward, and many others. With the great interest in fantasy in the late 1960's, the motion picture industry produced *Rosemary's Baby,* a filming of a book in which witchcraft is the dominant theme; and space fantasies like *2001: A Space Odyssey.*

Television also reflected the widespread interest in fantasy and produced during the 60's a number of successful series: the influential *Star Trek*; *Voyage to the Bottom of the Sea*;

and again fantasy which dealt with the supernatural in series like *The Munsters, The Addams Family, I Dream of Jeanie,* and *Bewitched*. *Cf.* Gothic.

H. Reed, *Eng. Prose Style,* 1934, p. 136–151; S. O'Faolain, "A Plea for a New Kind of Novel," *Spectator* 51, 1933; G. K. Chesterton, "Magic and Fantasy in Fiction," *Bookman* 77, 1929; J. B. Tharp, "The Fantastic Short Story in Fr.," *So. Atlantic Q.* 29, 1930; M. Summers, *The Gothic Novel,* 1939, p. 384–94; M. Brion, *Art fantastique,* 1961. ERNEST BERNBAUM.

farce generally means low comedy, intended solely to provoke laughter through gestures, buffoonery, action, or situation, as opposed to comedy of character or manners. Farce may, however, be considered the elemental quality in comic drama. As such it is not restricted by local or temporal circumstances; and in its pantomimic phases it is free from the limitations imposed by language upon more sophisticated forms of comedy. In its most elementary form it is found in the gestures and tricks of the circus clown and the buffoonery of pantomime, which provoke ready laughter among the greatest number of people. As the action becomes increasingly subtle its audience grows correspondingly limited. When words are required to convey the idea, thoughtless laughter is gradually displaced by the smile of comprehension; the appeal is further restricted to smaller groups.

Originally the term "farce," which means "stuffing," indicated an interpolation into the liturgy of the medieval Church. By analogy, it was applied to scenes of broad humor introduced into the *mystères* in France. Similar scenes are found in some English cyclic plays, moralities, and saints' plays, *e.g.,* the scenes at Mak's home in the Towneley *Secunda Pastorum*. After the suppression of the *mystères* in the 16th c., the farces and sotties, in the form of short comic pieces resembling interludes, found their way into serious plays.

In Eng. by 1800 it was not uncommon to apply the designation *farce* to any short piece that was performed after the main play, regardless of its character; and, with the general confusion of dramatic terminology in the 19th c., farce lost its identity and became indistinguishable, except for its brevity, from decadent comedy of manners on one hand and from vaudeville, extravaganza, pantomime, and burlesque on the other. These forms depended upon buffoonery and the costumes, gestures, and improvisations of actors; when dialogue was added, it was likely to consist of puns, gags, and topical allusions. Farce during the 19th and 20th c. has thus, in effect, resumed its original status as elemental comedy of physical action. *Cf.* Melodrama; Comedy. Leo Hughes, "Attitudes of Some Restoration Dramatists toward Farce," *PQ* 19, 1940; *A Century of English Farce,* 1956; H. C. Lancaster, ed. *Five Fr. Farces, 1655–94,* 1937. DOUGALD MACMILLAN.

fârsā. Tribal boasting poem among the Galla of Africa; often long, including a catalogue of the heroes of the tribe, their deeds and powers. *Giĕrása*: a personal boasting poem in that tribe. Chadwick; E. Cerulli, *Folk Lit. of the Galla,* 1922.

fate, finger of. A term expressing (a) the sense of inevitability in a happening (the mid-Eastern Kismet), as though the events of a play or novel were set by predestination; or (b) the occurrence of an arbitrary event, usually at the climax or close of a story, as though some force, exterior and superior to the characters involved, intervened to bring about the turn. *Cf.* Coincidence, long arm of; *Deus ex machina.*

fatrasie. Fr. A medieval verse composition, usually of 11 lines, in which confusion produces comical absurdities. Often written in macaronics, *q.v.* Probably sprang from the mock-religious celebrations of the *Fête des Fous* (Feast of Fools) and continued in the Renaissance comedy of masks, esp. in the doctor's monologues. *See* Masque.

feeling. Sensation or emotion, as opposed to perception or thought. Following psychoanalytical study of pseudo-entities like the subconscious and the unconscious, an emphasis on feeling as the basis of art has increased. Susanne Langer's influential studies (following the earlier work of Ernst Cassirer) conclude that "art is the creation of forms symbolic of human feeling"; the work of art is an isomorph of feeling. Some recent writers (*e.g.,* Yeats) have felt the same way; Gertrude Stein: "Passion determines the art form."

Although Langer speaks of human feeling, man of course shares feeling with other forms of life; it is in the various processes of thought that the human distinction and the human progress lie. To base a theory of art on feeling is therefore to look on art as a regression, at least toward the primitive, *q.v.* Ernst Cassirer, *The Philosophy of Symbolic Form,* 1925, trans. 1953; Susanne Langer, *Feeling and Form,* 1953; *Mind,* v. 1, 1967.

feigning. Term used in Renaissance (Boccaccio; Ronsard) by those defending poetry against the reechoing of the charge (Plato; the medieval church) that it is wedded to falsehood. Lying (ethics) is to deceive; feigning (æsthetics) is to teach. The poet must embroider and cloak the truth, is the claim; poetry is allegorical theology, which, bare, would not be comprehended. Stephen Hawes, *A Pastime of Pleasure*:

For often under a fayre fayned fable
A truth appeareth greatly profitable.

Touchstone (*AYLI*) plays on the idea: "the truest poetry is the most feigning."

feminine rhyme. Correspondence in sound of two or more sets of two syllables, the first syllable accented, the second unaccented, with different consonants before the accented vowel, *e.g.,* slender, offender, contender; after, laughter; make it, break it. In Eng. heroic couplet, feminine rhymes may be introduced to lower the style, as in Dryden's *Absalom and Achitophel.* In the Fr. *alexandrin,* masculine and feminine couplets usually alternate. *See* Rhyme.

fescennine verse (L. *fascinum,* phallic emblem worn as charm?). The most primitive of the three types of verse (satura: Atellana) serving as a background for Roman drama. Originated in the harvest and vintage festivals; they were impromptu, crude, licentious. Popular at weddings and triumphs, with rivalry in rough banter among the celebrants. Livy (7,2,7) tells that professional actors replaced the rude, extempore Fescennine verses, by dancing and singing to the flute. The two forms were blended in the theatrical *satura,* which preceded the Greek *fabula.* The literary form of the *satura,* the Rom. satire, retained elements of abuse and obscenity characteristic of the fescennines. The question of their influence on the drama is, however, controversial.

fiction (L. *fingere, fictum,* to fashion, form —whence also *feign*). The general term for imaginative narration; a work—however closely related to life or to actual persons or events—in which the imagination of the author shapes the material. Fiction is opposed to fact, as being not actual but an invention, to deceive, to entertain, or by its suggestions of reality to teach. Thus it has been said (Aristotle, of poetry versus history) that a fiction may approximate a general truth more closely than a particular (and perhaps unique) fact. The term is now usually limited to the prose novel and short story. Three main types of fiction have been differentiated. A *satire* is a work so organized that it attacks or ridicules matters external to the fictional world within it; *e.g., Gulliver's Travels*; *1984.* An *apologue* is a fictional example of the truth of a formulable statement; *e.g., Pilgrim's Progress*; *Candida.* A *novel* is a fictional work that introduces characters (about whose fates we should be made to care) in unstable relationships that are further complicated until—usually—the removal of the represented instability. Historical fiction is simply a novel woven about an actual person or period; often, the well-known historical figures play a minor part in the story. Fictional, or fictionalized, biography, on the other hand, attempts to give a true portrait of an actual person, by using devices of the novel, such as invented dialogue and presentation of the characters' feelings, and in other ways employing the author's imagination to seek out the inner self of his subject. There is also documentary fiction, which is drawn directly from (usually current) news or transcripts of trials and investigations; such books as Arthur Hailey's *Airport* (1968) and Aleksandr I. Solzhenitsyn's *The First Circle* (1968) and *Cancer Ward* (1969) have been called not "fiction" but "faction."

Fiction, as opposed to most poetry and drama, is intended to be seen, not heard. Thus Sterne in *Tristram Shandy* (1760) uses asterisks, pointing hands, black squares, empty pages, blank chapters. (Yet the poetry of e.e. cummings avoids capitals, and delights in punctuation perversities and word-wracking.) Marshall McLuhan in *The Medium is the Massage* (1967) states that "the book is an extension of the eye"; and by many photographs and printing tricks seeks to demonstrate this idea. *Cf.* Feigning; Novel; Apologue; Satire; Biography; Short story; Documentary. J. W. Aldridge, ed. *Critiques and Essays in Modern Fiction,* 1952; *Time to Murder and Create,* 1966; A. Cook, *The Meaning of Fiction,* 1960; Wayne C. Booth, *The Rhetoric of Fiction,* 1964; D. Lodge, *The Language of Fiction,* 1966; Sheldon Sachs, *Fiction and the Shape of Belief,* 1964, 1967; Ernest A. Baker, *The Hist. of the Eng. Novel,* 10 v., 1924–36, 1960–61; John C. Dunlop, *The Hist. of Fiction,* 1842, 1906; J. E. Miller and P. D. Herring, ed. *The Arts and the Public,* 1967; S. O. Lesser, *Fiction and the Unconscious,* 1957.

figura causae (Gr. *Schematismos; L. Ductus*). The stylistic pattern of a speech in relation to the speaker's purpose; the rhetorical tenor of his words in relation to his intentions. The later Gr. and Rom. distinguished various types. (1) *Ductus simplex:* straightforward; the intention is plainly and honestly stated; (2) *Ductus figuratus:* the purpose is expressed indirectly, but the real intentions are made clear in figurative ways, as by irony; (a) *Ductus subtilis:* intending the opposite of what it says, as when Demosthenes urges that he be surrendered to Philip; (b) *Ductus obliquus:* seeking an objective in addition to the opposite of what it says, as in Swift's *Modest Proposal* that to relieve the famine the Irish sell their children to be eaten at English tables; (c) *Ductus figuratus* (specif.): implying an end that (for ethical or other reasons) cannot be openly declared, *e.g.,* Cicero's fourth speech vs. Catiline wherein he does not urge but clearly desires the man's death. . . If only a part of the speech is thus affected by the intention, it is regarded as a *Chroma,* or Color, of the speech. *Cf.* Narrator.

figurate poem. One so arranged in writing or printing that it takes a shape (*e.g.* bottle, cross), usually related to its theme. Also *carmen figuratum, q.v.; cf.* Concrete poetry.

figure, figure of speech. An intentional deviation from the normal (1) spelling, (2) formation, (3) construction, or (4) application of a term. Therefore correspondingly called a figure of (1) orthography, (2) etymology, (3) syntax, or (4) rhetoric. The term figure usually includes tropes and repetitions. Figures are as old as language. They lie buried in many words of current use. They are the backbone of slang. They occur constantly in both prose and poetry. Language may be said to express four stages of thought, two of which are figurative: animism, the belief in a world of associated spirits; metaphor, this belief lapsed into symbol; simile, the symbol analyzed to analogy; concrete image, the symbol or figure rejected in favor of fact—*e.g.,* "the wet sea" (Homer). Puttenham otherwise sorts figures into 3 groups: those that serve (1) the ear alone: auricular; (2) the conceit (mind) alone: sensable; (3) both together: sententious.

Figures of speech possess various functions. They may be used to clarify, to illustrate, to energize, to animate inanimate objects, to stimulate associations, to raise laughter, to ornament. More important, they may have an æsthetic function. Thus Aristotle, who rightly called all figures of speech essentially metaphorical, pointed out that to coin good metaphors is to perceive similitudes in dissimilitudes, which he declared the chief power of the poet.

Medieval rhetoricians, devoting themselves to the "colors" of rhetoric, emphasized in great detail the ornamental function of figures of speech under "Ornament." Nevertheless, Renaissance writers must have sensed an æsthetic function of the trope, as their use of the "conceit" testifies. Often a poem of Petrarch, of Ronsard, of Donne, is the figure of speech. Remove the figure and you destroy the poem. At least one Renaissance critic, Puttenham, had some theoretical conception of this æsthetic function. He said that poetry is a "skill to speak and write harmoniously;" that the use of figures makes language "tunable to the ear," or "harmonical." In the 17th c. common sense and reason drove out the conceit. Boileau and Dryden spoke of figures of speech as graceful ornaments. Hobbes called all metaphors *ignes fatui,* fanciful, equivocal, deceitful. Dr. Johnson called figures of speech "rhetorical exornations." Wordsworth and Coleridge had some conception of an æsthetic use of metaphor, but they also relegated most figurative language to the fancy. A. E. Housman said that all metaphors and similes are ornamental, "things inessential to poetry."

Nowadays, however, many English and American critics, and poets, have returned to an æsthetic conception of figures of speech that is in accord with Aristotle's theory and with Renaissance practice. The figure, as now viewed, may be an ornament, but is more. It may serve for more than clarification or illustration, which are its commonest functions in prose discourse. It not only stimulates the formation of images with their various associations, but may also assist our imaginations to arrange these associations in a coherent, æsthetic pattern. It facilitates the transfer of an idea not merely from one experience to another, but specifically in the direction of a particular, comprehensible experience that is coherent and harmonious. When Huxley speaks of a man's "singular inward laboratory," he is figuratively illustrating and clarifying the idea of human digestion. When Milton speaks of Chaos as "the womb of Nature and perhaps her grave" he offers his reader much more than illustration and clarification. His figure not only advances the indescribable toward the particular and comprehensible, but evokes a harmonious and coherent perception of similitudes in apparent dissimilitudes, evoking thought beyond thought in an æsthetic frame. *Cf.* Image; Trope; Repetition. Richard Sherry, *A Treatise of Schemes and Tropes,* 1550; *A Treatise of the Figures of Grammar and Rhetorike,* 1555; George Puttenham, *The Arte of Eng. Poesie,*

1589; Sister Miriam Joseph, *Shak.'s Use of the Arts of Language,* 1947. MARVIN THEODORE HERRICK.

fin de siècle (Fr., end of the century). Term used (esp. of the closing years of the 19th c.) to indicate an emphasis on the decline of things, a concern with the overblown, the overbrightness, and the luxuriance of decay. *Cf.* Decadence.

Finnish method. An organization of folktales by types and motifs, according to geographical and chronological distribution. First developed by Kaarle Krohn and Antti Aarne (1867–1925) in Finland. *Cf.* Historical-Geographical Method. Archer Taylor, *General Subject-Indexes Since 1548,* 1966.

fit (1) (Old Norse *fit,* hem; G. *Fitze,* skein of yarn; also, a thread with which weavers marked off a day's work). A separate division or canto of a poem. Byron (1812): "Here is one fytte of Harold's pilgrimage." *The Ballad of Chevy Chase* is divided into fits; so too—perhaps for the humor of the word—is *The Hunting of the Snark.* (2) Appropriate; conformed to its context. *See* next item.

fitness. Conformity of related things to each other; conformity in a relation to some recognized ideal for such relation; coincidence, in matters of relatedness, of what is with what ought to be. Since everything in the universe stands in some relation to other things, the idea of fitness, under this name or another (propriety, congruity, aptness, harmony) is involved in all normative or evaluatory speculation; it is esp. important in the normative theory of art and of æsthetic experience, which is concerned with judgment of relations in general, and simply as such. The idea of fitness is so simple and abstract that attempts to reduce it to any concrete formula are likely to produce either mere tautology or a description of some other idea. Upon empirical grounds we can certainly relate it to the idea of unity (*q.v.*). But fitness seems to be prior to unity; it is rather because its internal relations are fit that a structure presents itself as unified than because it is unified that its relations seem fit. And fitness is an idea of more extension than is unity, for it applies equally to relations within an object and to relations between the object and other things, *e.g.,* the end or purpose of a process in which the object serves as instrument or means (functional fitness). Puttenham (Smith, *Eliz. crit. essays,* II, 175), following ancient masters, well summarizes the complexity of fitness in speech: "by reason of the sundry circumstances that man's affaires are, as it were, wrapt in, this *decencie* comes to be very much alterable and subject to *varietie,* insomuch as our speach asketh one manner of *decencie* in respect of the person who speakes, another of his to whom it is spoken, another of whom we speake, another of what we speake, and in what place and time and to what purpose." (*Cf.* Narrator.) The search for general norms of fitness is naturally much complicated by these problems of the relative and the particular. "For as in life," says Cicero (*Orator,* 70), "so in art, nothing is harder than to see what is fit."

Of possible objective norms of fitness the only sources are evidently (1) nature and (2) convention or custom, the latter presumably founded upon the former and only so far valid as adequate correspondence is felt to exist between the two. Norms supplied by convention are objective enough, and indisputable as long as the convention continues in effect; indeed, even where a discrepancy has been felt between nature and convention, a conventional norm may for a time persist as an acceptable alternative for a natural one. So Bacon (*Of innovation*) says, "What is setled by Custome, though it be not good, yet at least it is fit." Natural norms of fitness are harder to establish. More or less definite norms of fitness in relation to a single and definite end are sometimes plainly supplied by the end itself; but ends may be variously complicated, and in judgment of æsthetic objects as such, considerations of external finality are in any case at most only incidental. In the internal structure of such objects we may certainly require that there be manifest relevance or consistency among all related elements, that there be no unresolved conflict or contradiction; but it is hard to say whether this is really more concrete specification or tautological repetition of the requirement of fitness. In any case there remains always the problem of determining whether in a specific relation there is actual conformity to general prescriptions; for in æsthetic as in moral evaluation judgment is always ultimately of the special case and the special case is always unique. To make this ultimate judgment is not to apply a formula (though to express it may be to find a formula for it); one is here at the bare experiential ground of all knowledge and judgment, and for the critic or the reader as for the artist, or indeed for the scientist when he enters this region, the only recourse is to direct intuition, and the only ultimate test of one intuition is corroboration by others (spontaneous or induced by discriminating examination and discussion). The intuition ideally required here is of course that of the Gr. *pepaideumenos* or *phronimos,* Arnold's "judicious" man (*On tr. Homer,* I); if it refers to "taste," Dante (*Conv.,* I, i, 12) reminds us that this involves not only a sensitive palate, but also sound teeth and a competent tongue—and wide experience with a variety of foods. *Cf.* Decorum; Correctness; Form. J. Craig LaDrière.

fixed forms. *See* Old Fr.

flaw, tragic. Hamartia, *q.v.*

Fleshly School. Name given the Pre-Raphaelites in a controversy begun by article of that title, in *Contemporary Rev.,* Oct. 1871, by Robert Buchanan (using pseud. Robert Maitland).

flyting (also fliting; mainly Scots, 16th c.). Poetical invective; esp. an exchange of abusive verse by two poets, as *The Flyting of Dunbar and Kennedie,* 1508. Occurs as dispute in epics, *e.g.,* that between Beowulf and Unferth. King James I urged "tumbling verse for flyting." *Cf.* Doggerel; Débat; Abuse.

folklore. Until the mid-19th c. popular antiquities comprised all those interests and activities now denoted by the term folklore. The new term, proposed by W. J. Thomas, has been adopted in practically all modern languages. It has, however, acquired a variety of meanings. In Fr. and Scand. esp., folklore is employed to embrace such matters as traditional house forms, agricultural practices, textile methods and other aspects of material culture usually assigned to anthropology. The term, in Eng., is normally confined to the spoken or written traditions of a people, to traditional æsthetic expressions. Even within this definition, folklore approaches anthropology at many points, both in subject matter and in method.

Midway between purely anthropological studies and folklore lie such activities as feasts and ceremonies, folk dances, folk dramas. All ceremonies possess a considerable amount of traditional æsthetic expression, in the form of tales, didactic speeches, songs. Similarly, sand paintings, such as those of the Navaho, are handed down from the past and are thus properly a part of tribal folklore. The text of a traditional folk drama is undoubtedly folklore. Is the traditional acting also folklore? If so, shall we consider the traditions of the acting of Shakespeare's plays, as handed down for 300 years from actor to actor, a bit of folklore? Such are some of the marginal uses of the term.

There would seem to be no disagreement about its use to include all kinds of folksong, folktales, superstitions, local legends, proverbs, riddles.

The essential quality of folklore is that it is traditional. Persons whose lives are most affected by a folkloristic point of view see no virtue in originality. The old is always the authoritative, and is accepted without question because of its age. Weather is predicted by ancient proverbs, diseases are treated by methods learned from old people rather than from the hospital, crops are planted in the light or dark of the moon, not as advised in the agricultural bulletin. Old songs, old tales, old legends, are preferred.

From the end of the 18th c., folklore has been increasingly studied by humanistic scholars. The greatest spur to the study of folksong was the publication, 1765, of Percy's *Reliques of Ancient English Poetry;* it led to the collecting of folksongs throughout Europe and eventually almost all the U.S., and also to considerable theorizing about the origin of the folksongs themselves, and of folksong as a human activity. The fact that it is an attractive form of entertainment, associated with festive gatherings, or at least with community meetings, gives the folksong a wide popular appeal. Moreover, to the romantic scholars, the popular ballad seemed to come so directly from the soil and to be so pleasing both to the common man and to the sophisticated, that it formed a bond between the man of letters and the "folk." Thus, the folksong was supposed to lead one directly to an appreciation and understanding of ideas and poetic processes grounded in centuries of successful traditional practice. If later scholars have largely given up this romantic approach, they have nevertheless continued collecting folksongs and making an increasingly scientific evaluation of the collections.

A somewhat smaller group of men have interested themselves in the folktale. Since this is worldwide in its scope, collecting has increased rapidly and within the last c. methods and proper organization have been assiduously cultivated. Perhaps the most important such development has been the Historical-Geographical Method (*q.v.*).

It is a moot question whether traditional literary tales should be considered folklore. In practice, it is extremely difficult to separate oral from written traditions. But the methods of study of the two kinds are essentially different. Oral tradition (the usual conception of folklore), handed down by word of mouth and subject to the hazards of memory, presents different problems from those of literary history, where the emphasis is on manuscripts and printed editions and known authors. When the two kinds of tradition influence one another, the scholarly problem becomes extraordinarily complicated.

Since folklore is primarily recorded from the speech or other actions of the people themselves, it is likely to be lost unless great care is taken in its collection and proper preservation. A number of the European lands, especially those which preserve a rich oral tradition, maintain elaborate folklore archives under state subsidy, where carefully organized collecting is planned and directed and where folklore materials are properly preserved, catalogued, and studied. In America this movement has taken form slowly, but the Archive of American Folk Song in the Library of Congress has made a good start.

Folklore makes an appeal to many amateur collectors. School teachers, doctors, and lawyers in close contact with "the folk" interest themselves in collecting traditional material. Their approach is primarily sociological; the fact that these traditions are widely held in all parts of the world is frequently of little interest to such collectors. On the other hand, the folklore scholar sometimes becomes so interested in world-wide resemblances that he loses sight of the individual bearer of traditions as he is known by his fellows. Between them folklore has largely remained at the anecdotal stage that botany and chemistry occupied in the 17th c. Within our generation a considerable group of young folklore scholars, in America and abroad, have helped to put the study of folklore on a sounder basis and to interest the layman in making his collection according to better standards of accuracy. *Cf.* Ballad; Folksong; Folktale; Fairy tale; Fable; Primitivism. A. H. Krappe, *The Science of Folklore,* 1930; H. P. Beck, *Folklore in Action,* 1962; Bruce Jackson, ed. *Folklore and Society,* 1966; Tristram P. Coffin, *Our Living Tradition: An Introd. to Am. Folklore,* 1968; E. K. Chambers, *The Eng. Folk Play,* 1933, 1964. STITH THOMPSON.

folksong. In general, of two kinds. One consists of such well-known songs, many of them patriotic, as the Am. "The Star Spangled Banner," "Dixie," "America the Beautiful," or the popular "Over There" and "The Long Long Trail," from the First World War. Such songs come from known authors; people join in their singing everywhere. The Scots' "Auld Lang Syne," J. H. Payne's "Home, Sweet Home," the songs of Stephen Foster, are of this static type. Folksongs of the second kind depend for vitality on oral, not printed, transmission. They are known to singers in scattered places; some of them, in varying forms, roam widely, while other folk groups do not know them at all. The latter kind, esp. the traditional ballad, has interested the literary and scholarly world more than the former.

The basic distinction, however, does not depend upon currency among the people nor on origin. Folksongs transmitted in printed form are static. Folksongs passed on from mouth to mouth are unstable. They have no fixed text-form but are continually shifting. They have survived through a generation at the least; all sense of their authorship and history has been lost by their singers. Such songs are genuinely folklore, as differentiated from book or literary verse. Certain tests of origin once set up, such as F. B. Gummere's ring-dance improvisation of the Eng. and Scot. ballads, or insistence that traditional folksong begins orally among the unlettered, are invalid. A body of folksong is increased by pieces of many origins, often by the adaptation of old pieces and by the absorption and metamorphosis into the stream of tradition of popular texts and melodies by known composers. The nursery song of "The Frog and the Mouse" has an Elizabethan ancestor. In the popular "Hinky-Dinky Parlez-Vous," a creation of the soldiers of the First World War, the borrowed tune to which the words are sung remains constant, as does the refrain, but no stable text or narrative has established itself. W. S. Hay's "The Old Log Cabin in the Lane" of Civil War days reappears as the Western "The Little Old Sod Shanty on My Claim;" "Ocean Burial" by W. H. Saunders and G. N. Allen ("O Bury me not in the Deep Sea"), as the "O Bury Me not on the Lone Prairee" of Western cowboys.

Now and then certain poets of literary standing are credited with the production of folksong, in that their lyrics seem to voice group feeling and group life, to exhibit mass rather than individual character (Sir Walter Scott, *"Hail to the Chief," Coronach;* Kipling, *Barrack Room Ballads*).

The genus folksong has many species. Among primitive peoples, hunting and medicine or conjuring songs may be largely individual; but there are choral laments for the dead, victory songs, satires, dance songs; there are choral improvisations. The latter were long termed the germ of ballads, but they might better be thought of as ancestral for all lyrics, or for poetry in general. Contrary to older belief, too, individual utterance of song probably precedes or is at least as old as group song. A survey of contemporary American folksong of the traditional type reveals the persistence of many early kinds and the emergence of new: game songs, play or play-party songs, work songs, humorous pieces, sentimental pieces, satires, political songs, soldiers' and sailors' songs, railroad songs, prison songs, songs of popular heroes and of criminals, dialogue songs, nursery songs. Negro and Indian songs are also of diverse types. Religious songs entered into American folk tradition and so for a time did temperance songs. Every new movement, such as Civil Rights, quickly develops its folksongs, *e.g.,* "We shall overcome."

When the great collectors of the Romantic period sought out traditional songs, they hunted for the most attractive ones, often piecing together various texts, and they disregarded others. They looked for songs having lyrical quality or appeal, focussing their endeavors especially on story pieces or ballads. These have most human interest; the incidents they narrate make them more memorable. Present-day collectors, on the other hand, seek all types of songs: comic, tragic, or sentimental pieces, lampoons, fragments, whether good or bad. If they have entered into oral tradition, it is not asked that they show high literary quality.

During the 19th and 20th c. folksongs, like ballads, have been gathered in European countries, large or small, for comparison and analysis. The assembling of material from divergent areas and groups helps to clear up many problems of interest to the folklorist, such as the geographical wanderings of individual songs or groups of songs, their relative vitality, their textual variations, their impairment, their occasional improvement. Such material interests the sociologist, historian, and psychologist, as well as the student of poetry. In Am., regional collections have brought together miscellaneous traditional pieces from N. Eng., the Appalachian region, Miss., many of the central states, Nova Scotia, Newfoundland, Canada, and Mexico. Attention is now given also to the songs of special groups, such as miners, soldiers, sailors, hoboes, loggers, to Negro spirituals, work songs, blues, songs of dust bowl refugees, and WPA workers. American Bohemians, Scand., G., Fr., It., Russ., and other peoples have their own songs. Groups of mixed racial backgrounds have no folksongs, only individual songs.

As time passes, there will probably be fewer songs of the traditional type and fewer groups will sing them. Their great days seem already to have gone by. The phonograph, radio, and television, universalized, have lessened group singing for entertainment. Penetrating to remote places, they have cheapened and multiplied the output of available song. Music is turned on where formerly it was sung. One song has hardly achieved currency before others supplant it. The static type of folksong, on the other hand, may be expected to maintain its popularity indefinitely.

W. J. Entwistle, *European Balladry,* 1939; M. E. Henry, *A Bibliog. for the Study of Am. Folk-Songs,* 1937; J. A. and Alan Lomax, *Am. Ballads and Folksongs,* 1934; *Our Singing Country,* 1941; L. Pound, *Am. Ballads and Songs,* 1922. Louise Pound.

folktale. The Eng. term folktale appears in a wide variety of usages. It is much more general than the term *Märchen,* thus has escaped bitter disputes as to its meaning. The quality that determines whether a particular story is a folktale or not would seem to be the fact that it is handed down traditionally, whether by word of mouth or on the written or printed page. An animal tale or creation myth of a Central African tribe, a fairy tale like *Snow White* or *Jack the Giant Killer,* a literary tale like Andersen's *The Ugly Duckling* (provided it keeps being told), the stories of Æsop tradition—all these are at times called folktales, especially if attention is directed to the fact that they have established themselves as a part of a traditional store of tales of some group of people, whether literate or illiterate.

With this broad definition, it will be seen that the study of the folktale is concerned with both the literary and the oral tradition. No sharp line of demarcation can be drawn between the two, for the material flows freely from one channel into the other.

For the student of comparative literature the folktale is of extraordinary interest. He is able to examine the same narrative processes, the same æsthetic interests, often the same motifs and plots, among peoples of every type of cultural development. While he will undoubtedly be amazed at the universality of story telling and even of some of its detailed manifestations, he will also be able to recognize and perhaps explain significant differences as he moves from the primitive to the "civilized" or from the illiterate to the literate.

The bibliography of the folktale is enormous,[1] for much of the material is found in journals and in fugitive publications. Broadly speaking, it consists of three classes of material. (1) Within the past c. ethnologists and anthropologists have taken down collections of tales from a very large part of those primitive and half civilized peoples to which they have given their principal attention. In only a few cases have these tales been subjected to comprehensive comparative treatment, on the basis either of geography or of narrative themes.[2] (2) For most of the narrative material of antiquity and the older civilizations of the Orient, the folktales have been handed down in literary documents. These sometimes form a part of recognized tale collections, which often have elaborate frameworks and an extremely complicated literary history. Such are the papyrus manuscripts of the 13th c. B.C. containing the Egyptian story of *The Two Brothers;* the *Panchatantra;* the *Seven Sages;* the *Thousand and One Nights;* the *Gesta Romanorum.*[3] Many others of these literary tales are imbedded in some of the older literary monuments: the Homeric poems; the *Bible*; medieval romances. (3) The collecting and publishing of oral tales of Europe and the Near East is a matter of the last few c. Though Straparola[4] in the 16th and esp. Basile[5] in the 17th included a number in their collections, they rewrote them with such a revolutionary change of style as to render them of little value for comparative study except for plot content. The same may be said of all the collections made until the 19th c. But beginning with the world-famous *Household Tales* of the Brothers Grimm (1812 f.) a more and more conscientious attempt was made to record tales exactly as they are current orally among the people, esp. in countries (Ireland) where conditions of tale telling are favorable. The archives in Dublin contain above a million pages of folktale manuscript.

These tales, which exist in the memory of people all over the world, usually fall into a very few easily recognizable categories. Under "myth" the present tendency is to group all tales having to do with an imaginary world existing before the present order was created. Stories concerning the gods, creation, the establishment of the present characteristics of men or animals or of the earth or the heavenly bodies, and stories that assume a passage to and from some sort of otherworld, are usually called myths. The hero tale may be a myth, *e.g.,* the stories of Hercules, but it may be no more than an ordinary folktale of wonder, which we generally know as the fairy tale (G. *Märchen*). Our term is inaccurate, since most of the tales thus described have nothing to do with fairies but only with marvels of all kinds. C. W. von Sydow distinguishes between the *chimerat* (tale of indefinite time and place) of the Indo-European peoples and the *novellat* (definite in time and place) of the Semitic folk,[6] but this difference in precision of locale extends over the entire earth. The fairy tale is more nearly pure fiction than any other folktale form, since it is not bound by religious belief or any demands of truth to life. For the growth of fiction, especially on the primitive and illiterate levels, it has been of prime importance.

Some other folktale forms are the local tradition (G. *Sage*), often of extraordinary vitality and wide distribution; the jest or anecdote, that folktale form which has persisted longest among the sophisticated, which flashes even today in the conversation at polite dinner tables; the fable, known to everybody from the Æsop collection; the animal tale, perhaps the most universal of all narrative forms, best known to modern literary readers through the tales of Uncle Remus; finally the cumulative story, especially dear to the Orientals and to children, *e.g.,* the Jewish Passover Service verses; *The House That Jack Built.*

Students of the folktale are primarily concerned with problems of two kinds: (1) the origin and dissemination of tales and (2) the folktale as an art. The latter problem has hardly been more than touched. It concerns the conditions of folktale telling (the kinds of people that tell tales, the circumstances of the telling, the reception by the audience, the way they are handed down), as well as the stylistic effects characteristic of this oral art.[7] There is a fundamental stylistic difference between the literary tale (G. *Kunstmärchen*), designed for readers, and the oral tale (G. *Volksmärchen*), which must make its appeal to listeners and which depends for its preservation entirely upon memory. Oral narrative art of this kind abounds in repetitions, formulas, and other well-known conventions. Sometimes, long passages recur, which must be recited again without the change of a word; most often they occur in threes and lead to a climax with the success of the youngest son or daughter. In some tales are "runs," conventional passages, largely nonsense, which ornament the tale at appropriate places and are anticipated by the listeners. Cumulative series further interest teller and hearer because of the virtuosity required in exact telling of the tale. Not only are these devices invaluable aids to memory but they come to be thought indispensable parts of folktale structure.

The first serious scholars to work on the problem of the origin and dissemination of tales were the brothers Grimm. They saw the problem clearly enough: The same folktale types are scattered over most of Europe and Asia and often far beyond; how is this situation to be explained? They thought of the tales as an inheritance from the Indo-European past and were convinced that, in their present form, they were broken-down representatives of ancient myth. A later school, founded by Thedor Benfey in 1859, saw the original home of all these tales in India. Later, anthropologists tried to discredit these theories by showing the universality of most of the ideas and by insisting upon the independent origin, at least of the details of the stories. Attempts at a single explanation of folktale origins still engage certain scholars, who find all tales coming from dreams, or from rituals, or else think of them as telling the adventures of the moon or the stars.

Later folktale scholarship has given up the attempt to find short and easy answers to its problems. Instead, it has recognized that every tale has its own history and that only by assiduous collecting, classifying, cataloguing, and by exhausting comparisons can any scholar hope to trace the history of a folktale. Though there may be criticism of it in detail, the most significant recent contribution has been the historical-geographical method (*q.v.*). Research has been fostered by recognition of the complementary concepts "type" and "motif." The motif is the smallest recognizable element that goes to make up a complete story; its importance for comparative study is to show what material of a particular type is common to other types. The importance of the type is to show the way in which narrative motifs form into conventional clusters.[8]

[1] Bolte and Polivka, *Anmerkungen zu den Kinder und Hausmärchen der Brüder Grimm,* 1913–31, v. 5. [2] Bibliog. and comparative study of American Indian tales: Thompson, *Tales of the N. Am. Indians,* 1929. A similar treatment of Indonesian tales: Jan De Vries, *Volksverhalen uit Oost Indië,* 1925–28, v. 2. [3] Bolte-Polivka, *op. cit.,* v. 4. [4] *Le Piacevoli Notti,* 1550. [5] N. M. Penzer, *The Pentamerone of Basile,* 1932. [6] *Travaux du Ier Congres International de Folklore,* 1938, p. 132 f. [7] For the conditions of folktale telling, see M. Azadovsky, *Eine Sibirische Märchenerzählern, FF Com.* 68, 1926; W. Wisser, *Auf der Märchensuche,* 1926; H. Grudde, *Wie ich mein* "Plattdeutsches Volksmärchen aus Ostpreussen" *aufschrieb, FF Com.* 102, 1932. Most studies of folktale style are based upon Axel Orik's *Nogle Grundsætninger for Sagnforskning,* 1921, or his *Folkedigtningens episke Love, Folkelige Afhandlinger,* 1919. [8] Aarne-Thompson, *The Types of the Folktale,* 1928, 1961; S. Thompson, *Motif-Index of Folk-Literature,* 1932–37. STITH THOMPSON.

folly literature (G. *Narrenliteratur*) developed 15th–17th c., using the conventionalized "fool" in tales, based on Christian ethics, for the masses. Sebastian Brant (1458–1521) combined slapstick satire with the travel tale (popular since Lucian) in *Narrenschiff* (*The Ship of Fools*), 1494. Trans. into L., then expanded in Eng. by Alexander Barclay (ca. 1475–1522), it spread into humanist works: Erasmus' *The Praise of Folly,* 1509, and many illustrated emblem-books. Combined with elements of common folks' jest-books (*Eulenspiegel,* 1483) and developing Brant's St. Grobianus (Friedrich Dedekind, *Grobianus,* 1549, L.; *Grob,* G., boor, booby) into an inverted patron of good manners—whose descendants run through *The Gull's Hornbook* (1609), to the recent *Do You Want to Be a Goop?* of Gelett Burgess. It helped in the movement from allegory to "characters," and the lively flow of the picaresque fiction. Katherine Anne Porter, in her novel *Ship of Fools* (1945, 1962), states that she read Brant's book, and that "the image of the ship of this world on its voyage to eternity . . . suits my purpose exactly. I am a passenger on that ship." *Cf.* Grobianism.

foot. A unit of rhythm in verse or prose; a segment of a passage measured in terms of syllable variation (long and short; stressed and unstressed) for analysis of the structure. Much modern prose is written without thought of such pattern; syllable-counting poetry (romance); Semitic; Germanic beat-verse; recent free verse, are not measured by this system; but to some extent classical prose, and the great body of western poetry, follow more or less rigidly set patterns or systems of recurring feet. The variation of feet within a passage determines its rhythm; the repetition of feet within a poem establishes its meter. There are 3 general groups of feet: falling, with the stress first; rising, with the stress last; rocking, with the stress in the middle. The scansion of classical versification (*q.v.*) and the still more complex problems of prose rhythm (*q.v.*) have led to the naming of feet with more than one accent. For most analysis, a few feet suffice: the dactyl is dominant in classical verse; the iamb, in modern, esp. Eng.; frequent also are the trochee and the anapest. The various foot names and patterns follow:

(— means long or accented; ∪ means short or unaccented.)

amphibrach ∪ — ∪

amphimacer — ∪ —

anapest, anapaest ∪ ∪ —

antibacchius — — ∪

antispast ∪ — — ∪

bacchius ∪ — —

choree (trochee) — ∪

choreus (by resolution) ∪ ∪ ∪

choriamb — ∪ ∪ —

cretic: amphimacer

dactyl — ∪ ∪

di-iamb ∪ — ∪ —

dibrach ∪ ∪

dispondee — — — —

ditrochee — ∪ — ∪

dochmiac, any combination of 5, esp. ∪ — — ∪ —

epitrite ∪ — — — (called 1st, 2nd, 3rd, or 4th, according to the position of the unaccented syllable)

iamb ∪ —

ionic
a majore — — ∪ ∪
a minore ∪ ∪ — —

mollossus — — —

paean — ∪ ∪ ∪ (called 1st, 2nd, 3rd, or 4th, according to the position of the stressed syllable)

palimbacchius: antibacchius

proceleusmatic ∪ ∪ ∪ ∪

pyrrhic: dibrach

spondee — —

tribrach ∪ ∪ ∪ (*see* choreus)

trochee: choree
See Prosody.

foreshadowing. The arrangement of incidents in a narrative so that "coming events cast their shadows before them." Presentation, early in a story, of the two opposing forces and their goal, and establishing the receptor's sympathy with one force; also, setting the tone of the story, *e.g.,* to prepare for a happy or sorrowful ending. Important events within the story may also be foreshadowed, as by the proffer of a promise, *q.v.*

form. The character of an object as experienced, or the structure into which the elements of an experience or a thing are organized (G. *Gestalt; cf. "Gestalt psychology"*). The concept of form, or obvious analogues, is older than the earliest documents of critical theory, and occurs in the East as generally as in the West, esp. in speculation about the process of creation (*par excellence,* creation of the world by God or gods), in which the mental notion or image of a thing-to-be-produced is regarded as the form or formal principle of that thing. (W. F. Albright, *From stone age to Christianity,* 1940, p. 130: "a precursor of the Indo-Iranian *arta* and even of the Platonic idea is found in the Sumerian *gish-ghar,* the outline, plan or pattern of things-which-are-to-be, designed by the gods at the creation of the world and fixed in heaven in order to determine the immutability of their creation.") Plato so conceived the forms or ideas of all things, even trivial human artefacts, to have an eternal and absolute preexistence apart from the accident of their mundane production, which was thus an *imitation,* more or less feeble, of their being (*Rep.* X). For Aristotle (*Met.* 1032b1) the human mind is the immediate source of the forms or characters which we perceive in works of human art; but since the mind derives forms from the external reality it experiences, the form of a work of art may "imitate" that of some objective reality. Modern use of the word *form* in analysis or description of works of art is in part a survival of long established Platonic and esp. Aristotelian terminology, in part an instance of a natural tendency, illustrated by that terminology, to refer to the character or structure of a thing or an experience as its *shape* or *form.*

In the Aristotelian system, the form is one of the four causes which account in full for the mode of being of any thing. Two of these causes (the efficient cause, or producer; the final cause, the purpose or end) are extrinsic to the thing. The other two, the formal and the material, are intrinsic; the matter is that of which a thing is made, the form that which makes it what it is. For Aristotle, therefore, form is not simply shape but that which shapes, not structure or character simply but the principle of structure, which gives character. So for the Aristotelian, form in a work of art is not structure (in a narrow sense) alone, but all that determines specific character; meaning or expressiveness, as well as structure, is a formal element. (But meaning, besides possessing structure and conferring it, since it involves relation is itself a kind of structure.) Actually, the Aristotelian will find in a work of art not one form but many, a complexity of formal elements or *formalities* (structures and meanings), the totality of which is the form (*the* structure, *the* meaning, *the* character) of the work as a whole. This total form will extend ideally throughout the work; the work will be all meaning, all structure. But it will equally be all that which is given meaning, that which has structure; matter, as well as form, will be everywhere in the work, though ideally the mind in beholding the object will know it not as matter, but only as what is formed, as what has structure and meaning. Where there is form there will be matter, informed; where there is matter there will be form, informing. To separate the matter and the form of the work will require a mental abstraction; in the actual thing the two will be a unity, since it is only by their union that the thing exists.

Such are the proper sense and implication of the Aristotelian terms *form* and *matter*. So understood, they are in full harmony with the results of modern analysis, and remain, if used with precision, valuable technical terms. The difficulties notoriously attendant upon their use in modern criticism are due to their not being always used with precision, to the use of other terms for reference to these concepts and to the use of these terms for reference to other concepts, esp. to elements in other dichotomies with which this one may be confused. Thus the *matter* of a literary work is commonly identified with its "subject," or with the thought or feeling about a subject to which the meaning of the work is a reference, or with this meaning itself; and *form* can then only be what is left of character in a work when its meaning has been subtracted, *viz.,* its bare physical structure, and esp. structure of sound. The word *content* often replaces *matter* in this opposition, and then *form* may be conceived as the accidental vehicle, trivial container, or frivolous wrapping, of a "content" regarded as alone significant and substantial; indeed, the word *substance* is then often used in turn to replace *content,* or in conjunction with it. These dichotomies are of course constantly identified with that of *thought* and *expression;* and the word *style* is freely used to replace either *expression* or *form.* So the alternative terms for reference to what purports to be a single distinction become so numerous, and the distinction so patently shifts with the terms, that what results may fairly be called chaos. What is needed to dispel or reduce the confusion is simply recognition of the fact that more than one distinction is implied in this collection of terms.

form and expression. To express anything it is necessary to impose a form upon a matter and conversely the imposition of a form upon a matter inevitably renders that matter expressive of something. Hence arises the confusion from which result most of the difficulties connected with the use of the word *form;* for, as expressiveness is a formal element in an object and so may be identified with form, the process of informing a matter may be identified with the process of expressing something by means of informed matter. From suggestions afforded by this identification modern æsthetic has learned much that it must not forget, and it is not the function of the present article to judge, but only if possible to clarify by providing a framework for such theories of poetry and fine art as (in opposition to Valéry and to most of the practitioners of the arts who have expressed an opinion) make expression the only operation of the artist and find in the whole constitution of a work of art nothing but expressiveness. But for such clarification it is essential at least in abstraction to distinguish the process of expressing a thought or other exprimend (*see* expression) from that of giving matter a form. The crucial difference between the processes lies in the fact that when matter and form are united their sum, as Hardy puts it, is unity; whereas no matter how perfectly any thing is expressed, what is expressed and what expresses it must always be distinct. Identity of the expressed with what expresses it is an impossibility, since it involves a contradiction; if an expression were identical with what it expresses it would be not the expression of that thing, but the thing itself. This necessary discontinuity of exprimend and expriment implies no inferiority in expression to the process of informing, by which a fusion is achieved; for, though romantic expressionism has perversely made an impossible fusion the goal of expression, there is nothing in fusion as such that requires admiration. In the simplest object, as long as it remains that object, matter and form are united; what we value in more complex things is not simply the union of matter and form in them, but the experience provided by the form. And in this expressiveness may be the most precious element. The true goal in the construction of a work of art is not some impossible identity of an exprimend with an expriment, but the consistent adjustment of individual formal elements into a perfectly harmonious whole. And it is the work of achieving this that constitutes the artist's informing. We admire in a perfect work not the fact that matter and form are united in it, but the admirable form that has been united with a matter. At whatever stage the artist leaves his work, it will have a matter and a form, and they will be united; the question is whether the form is that of a sketch or botch or of a finished and exquisite thing.

form and matter. The first of these, the traditional Aristotelian distinction, is a formula intended for analysis of objects as objects. To apply it with precision, as has rarely been done, it is necessary to keep this fact constantly in mind; and with it the fact that such a formula is useful only if we approach the object to be analyzed with a simplicity that some may feel amounts to crudeness. The questions posed by this formula are: What, in this thing, is material of which something is made, and what is that which is made of this material? To the first of these questions the general answer of objective analysis must be that in a literary work the matter out of which the thing is made is language; as Mallarmé is reported to have told Degas, "Ce n'est pas avec des idées qu'on fait des vers, c'est avec des mots." The matter out of which a poet makes his poem is a language as it exists in his time and place. But this language is by no means a wholly formless matter when the poet begins to work with it; it is itself the product of more or less art, of ages of human imposition of forms upon matter. In language the basic matter, a matter so solidly material as to fall within the province of the physicist, is sound. This is given form by selection, differentiation (*e.g.,* of consonant from vowel), and construction (syllable, phrase), by having significations, natural or conventional, attached to it (the word), and by conventional systematization of all these things (grammatical and syntactic "constructions"). When the writer begins to work, therefore, his material is already full of formal elements. But these, though they remain always formal elements and as such appear still in his finished work, are for him part of the matter which he is to inform; the form of his work is a form he imposes upon his mass of forms and purer matters by shaping it as a whole to a structure and a meaning determined by himself. The form he imposes is the peculiar total character of the speech he makes. Until the work is finished, this new form which he imposes upon his language is an idea, more or less dimly apprehended, in his mind; the idea of a thing (a speech) to be made. Such formal ideas are rather ghosts than ideas; they are not notions which can be signified or expressed. For them there is no sign, no translation possible. They are not concepts but conceptions, conceptions of a thing to be made; and they can be externalized only by the making of a thing. The impulse they generate in the mind is therefore not to expression, but simply to production, to making a thing. The difference, which is very important, is made clear by P. Valéry: "Si donc l'on m'interroge; si l'on s'inquiète (comme il arrive, parfois assez vivement), de ce que j'ai 'voulu dire' dans tel poèm, je réponds que je n'ai pas *voulu dire,* mais *voulu faire,* et que ce fut l'intention de *faire* qui a *voulu* ce que j'ai *dit.*" (*Variété* III, 68). So far is the poet from preoccupation with saying or expressing something that in fact what is said or expressed may originate within, and as a mere accident of, the process of composing a speech. Yet of course in a poem something is expressed. Therefore it has been easy for an incomplete analysis to suppose that in what is expressed the matter of the poem is to be found; that the matter out of which a poem, or any speech, is made is whatever is expressed in it, *viz.,* some thought or feeling about some reality or experience or that reality or experience itself. Actually we have here a confusion of related but by no means identical processes and things. Reality exists in the world round the poet, and he experiences it; this is one process (not peculiar to the poet). This reality comes to him as a more or less confused chaos, and his mind organizes, imposes order, form, upon this chaotic matter; this is a second process. Then, he may express in language, *i.e.,* use language to refer to, this order or form, his thought; this is a third process. But all these processes are distinct from that of making a poem, though in the process of making a poem the last (which occurs whenever *anybody* speaks) may incidentally be involved, and so the others be implied as preliminaries to it. In the poem, the expression of thought exists only as a structure of meanings. The meanings are there in the poem; the thought is not, nor is the reality about which the thinking is done. The poet makes his poem not of reality or his experience of reality, not of his thought or his ideas, but in part of the meanings he finds in words, because he makes his poems of words and words have meanings. (If words did not have meanings, perhaps he would not want to make poems of them; but as things are, words have meanings, and it is of words that poems are made.)

form and style. Style is a given way, or manner, or fashion, of doing anything, of going through any process; the concept of style cannot in practise be dissociated from that of some *process.* This is sufficient to distinguish it from the concept of form, since as we have seen form is a concept relevant only to objects as such, to things and not to processes. But what is a formal element in an object from the point of view of analysis of the constitution of that object may be an element of style from the point of view of analysis of a process in which the object is involved. Some formal elements in things are indeed simply suggestions of process. These may be, like the brushwork in a painting, themselves vestiges of the process that produced the thing; or they may, like the eccentricities of a pianist, be incidents in a process concomitant with and necessary to our apprehension of the thing. A Gothic arch has a form, and a Romanesque arch has a different form. If we think of both as performing the common function of arching a space, the difference between them, without ceasing to be a formal difference in the things, becomes the difference between two ways or styles of executing a process. So in all consideration of style there is something constant or common, the process, the thing that is done, and something variable and individual, the way of doing the thing, the style. To find a style in a literary work is impossible unless we conceive that something is being done in the work or with it, that it is not just an object but an element in or embodiment of a process; and is impossible unless we conceive that the thing done might be done or have been done otherwise, in some other way or style. But once we do conceive a process, and set the work within it, then formal elements become "stylistic" elements. In short, what is form in the object conceived as such is style in the process in which the object is conceived as being involved. Since it is harder to set poetry within process than prose, and less relevant to consider (even only theoretically) alternative executions of any process we associate with a poem, on the whole we use the word *style* rather of prose than of poetry.

"organic" form. No survey, however brief, of the idea of form can omit reference to the distinction, common in English criticism since Coleridge, between *organic* and *mechanic* (or abstract) form. "The form is mechanic," says Coleridge, "when on any given material we impress a pre-determined form, not necessarily arising out of the properties of the material; as when to a mass of wet clay we give whatever shape we wish it to retain when hardened. The organic form, on the other hand, is innate; it shapes, as it develops, itself from within, and the fullness of its development is one and the same with the perfection of its outward form. Such as the life is, such is the form." (*Lectures on Shakespeare,* i.) The intent of this passage is excellent, and the result of Coleridge's insistence upon this principle has been wholly good for criticism. But the terms of his statement involve a conflation of the distinction between form and matter with that between an expression and what it expresses, the ramifications of which it would take long to untangle. Fortunately the principle has been more accurately stated by T. S. Eliot in his Ker Memorial Lecture: "Some [structural] forms are more appropriate to some languages than to others, and all are more appropriate to some periods than to others. At one stage the stanza is a right and natural formalization of speech into a pattern. But the stanza—and the more elaborate it is, the more rules to be observed in its proper execution, the more surely this happens—tends to become fixed to the idiom of the moment of its perfection. It quickly loses contact with the changing colloquial speech, being possessed by the mental outlook of a past generation; it becomes discredited when employed solely by those writers who, having no impulse to form within them, have recourse to pouring their liquid sentiment into a ready-made mould in which they vainly hope that it will set. In a perfect sonnet, what you admire is not so much the author's skill in adapting himself to the pattern as the skill and power with which he makes the pattern comply with what he has to say. Without this fitness, which is contingent upon period as well as individual genius, the rest is at best virtuosity." (*Partisan Review,* IX, 463 f.) Mr. Eliot does well to invoke the principle by name: *fitness.* It is not a question of the form's "arising out of the properties of the material," which is impossible; it is not a question of the "innate" except as genius for perceiving relations and establishing them is innate. The problem is that of such perfect fitting together of structural elements and meanings as will produce for a mind that contemplates the completed structure a sense of perfect harmony and consistency: that is, of perfect *order. Cf.* Fitness; Expression; Expressionism; Imitation.

W. Pater, *Style,* 1888; A. C. Bradley, *Oxford lectures on poetry,* 1909; G. Santayana, *Sense of beauty,* 1896; W. P. Ker, *Form and style in poetry,* 1928; DeW. H. Parker, *The analysis of art,* 1926; J. M. Warbeke, "Form in evolutionary theories of art," *Journal of Philosophy,* (1941); V. M. Hamm, "Form in literature," *Thought,* XVII (1942); R. Wellek, "The mode . . . art," *Southern R.,* VII (1942). J. Craig LaDrière.

The word "form" applies directly in the visual, the plastic, arts. The physical elements of a book, its *format,* while they should be accordant, have the relationship to the work only of an external harmony. "Form" has been used as equivalent to "genre," or "kind"; as, the epic, the dramatic, form. Instead of the genus, it may refer to a species, as the farce, the sonnet. In still further specialization, it may indicate a particular framework or patterned structure of a work, such as the "merry-go-round" form of Schnitzler's *Reigen,* or the "hour-glass" form (Anatole France, *Thaïs*; Henry James, *The Ambassadors*): two lives crossing as one moves towards fulfillment and the other towards defeat. Of such formal patterns and devices, several types may be distinguished: (1) syllogistic progression: idea or situation A leads to B; (2) qualitative progression, by association or development of moods; (3) repetitive devices: the most obvious, rhyme; the subplot in the drama; the return of one principle under other guises; (4) conventional form: any form developed as an exercise, or for itself, as when one sets out to write a sonnet; (5) incidental forms, embodied in larger works, *e.g.,* figures: some of these (climax, change of meter) can be adapted to many moods and intentions; others (hyperbole; O. Henry ending) are more limited in their scope.

formalism. A Russian school developed in *Opoyaz* (Society for the Study of Literary Language) founded by Viktor Shklovsky, 1917. Its ideas can be summed up: Art is style, style is *métier,* technique, craftsmanship. Technique is not only the method but the object of art. "A work of art is equal to the sum of the processes used in it." Thus criticism is simply the objective study of technique. Dostoyevsky's work is viewed as a series of exalted crime novels, *romans à sensation.* "Pushkin's lyrics came from album verses, Blok's from gypsy songs, Mayakovsky's from funny-paper poetry . . . Novel technique creates characters; Hamlet was generated by theatrical technique." (Shklovsky, *Theory of Prose*; Zhirmunsky, *Rhyme*; *Tolstoi*; *Blok*; Eichenbaum, *Melody of Verse*; Grossmann, *Poetics of Dostoyevsky.*) Until 1927 formalism flourished; its concept of the man of letters as an artisan of words seemed to fit the Marxian ideology of the workers' state. Then Soviet cultural policy became suspicious of the artistocratic leanings inherent in any formalistic credo in literature and art; the group was dissolved, and the school decayed.

Not elevated as a school, the formalist attitude has been present in many periods of European literature, notably the neoclassic. Emphasis on form as opposed to content (or to the author's emotions and beliefs) appeared in the U.S. in Poe, Henry James, Santayana and his student T. S. Eliot, and esp. in the "new critics" of the 20th c., who have therefore also been called æsthetic formalist critics. *See* Criticism, the new; *cf.* Standard. B. M. Engelhardt, *The Formal Method in the Hist. of Lit.,* 1927; G. Struve, *Soviet Russ. Lit.,* 1935; L. T. Lemon and M. J. Reis, ed. *Russ. Formalist Criticism,* 1965; V. Zirmunskij, *Introd. to Metrics* (Formalist Poetics), Russ. 1924, trans. 1966. Renato Poggioli.

forms of discourse. *See* Composition.

four ages of poetry, the. (1820) essay by Thomas Love Peacock, provoked Shelley's *The Defence of Poetry.* Peacock's devastating thesis is: "Poetry was the mental rattle that awakened the attention of the intellect in the infancy of civil society; but for the maturity of mind to make a serious business of the playthings of its childhood, is as absurd as for a full-grown man to rub his gums with coral, and cry to be charmed to sleep by the jingle of silver bells." The four ages of poetry, according to Peacock, were (1) iron, (2) gold, (3) silver, and (4) brass. Poets of the iron age crudely sing of the rough, primitive life of their times; those of the succeeding age, stimulated by their predecessors, produce high, conscious art (Homer; Shakespeare); silver age poets palely rewrite the poems of the period before (Vergil; Dryden); their successors in the brass age (Peacock names the Eng. Romantics) reject "the polish and learning of the age of silver and, taking a retrograde strike to the barbarisms and crude traditions of the age of iron, profess to return to nature and in reality bring poetry to its second childhood." Peacock illustrates the die-hard conservative of 18th c. literary tastes, who disliked romantic poetry.

Much so-called "modern" poetry, especially since the 1920s, has deliberately sought the return to the primitive Peacock pictures. It may (1) turn to primitive models, American Indian or African tribal songs; (2) abandon the long tradition of regular verse (a) for free verse, (b) to break words into syllables and even letters (E. E. Cummings) on different lines; (3) seek to cast off the "limitations" of the intellect and reason by (a) spontaneous expression of immediate emotions, (b) immediate jotting down of whatever pops into the mind, (c) using sound patterns that have no meaning but may be expected to evoke feelings, if merely the pleasure of recognizing patterns of sound; or in other ways seek to return to the pre-intellectual and non-rational aspects of man's living. A similar movement is even more widespread in painting and sculpture. Rodin's *The Thinker,* forerunner of the school, is not a philosopher but a primitive man struggling into thought. Such poetry as Ezra Pound's *Cantos,* and such prose as James Joyce's *Finnegans Wake,* call for a wide range of resources and resourcefulness, using the accumulated treasures of language and culture for a sort of intellectual game, like a problem in chess. As mental gymnastics, they too belong in Peacock's age of brass.

four-beat verse. *See* German Versification.

fourteener. The long medieval Eng. line of 14 syllables. Its rhyming couplet, written as four lines, became the 8-and-6 meter, the common ballad stanza.

frame. 1. A story within which is presented either a series of tales (cyclical framed tale) or a single one. It can be subordinated to the story or stories it frames, motivating only the telling of that which follows, or it can have equal or greater significance, functioning as the main part of the text. Historically the form originated and was widespread in the Orient (*Arabian Nights*); westward the *Decameron,* Boccaccio, 1353; Chaucer, *Canterbury Tales,* c. 1387; Margaret of Angoulême, *Heptameron,* 1558.

In G. the first artistic instance, Goethe's *Unterhaltungen deutscher Ausgewanderten,* 1795, followed the tradition of Boccaccio; the romanticists, Tieck, Hoffmann, Hauff, adapted it to their individual ends. G. Keller, cyclical framed tale, *Das Sinngedicht,* 1881; Stevenson, *New Arabian Nights;* framed single stories, G. F. Meyer; T. Storm; P. Heyes.

2. As a picture is separated from the rest of the world by its frame so (some hold) all art is removed to a psychic distance (*q.v.*) from the receptor. Some of the framing (distancing) devices are basic conventions of the art: meter and rhyme; the "picture frame" stage. Others vary with the author and the work. In general, the more familiar the mood or theme, the greater the variation from the conventional form that may be ventured. The frame aids concentration on the work; the smaller the area to be centered upon (Shelley, *The Cloud*), the more elaborate the devices to fix it—the more intense the moment, the less marked the frame (as in Shakespeare's handling of blank verse). *Cf.* Story within a story.

freedom. Art paradoxically combines freedom with a sense of inevitability. The writer at every crucial point has an option, that is, a choice of two or more incompatible acts, so prepared that any one of them will seem reasonable. His choice destroys the alternatives, but opens a situation that offers new options. Thus the successive stages of a work, while not predictable, seem when we reach them to "click" into place. (The Abbé d'Aubignac, as far back as 1657, said that events in fiction must be prepared but not foreseen.) The author may choose, but he must choose within the limit of his options. His development of the work thus combines freedom and necessity. *Cf.* Determinism; Inevitability; Synaesthesis. A. M. Farrer, *The Freedom of the Will,* 1957, 1963; S. Morgenbesser and J. Walsh, ed. *Free Will,* 1962; K. Kolenda, *The Freedom of Reason,* 1964; S. J. Krause, ed. *Essays on Determinism in Am. Lit.,* 1964; B. Berofsky, ed. *Free Will and Determinism,* 1966.

free verse. A pattern of verse structure without meter and usually without rhyme. French *vers libre* (*q.v.*), which began with Hugo, was a gradual breaking free of the rules. In Germany, Novalis' *Hymns to the Night* was in verse in the manuscript but was printed (1801) as prose. Klopstock and Goethe (*Prometheus*) moved toward the form. Earlier in England (1760–63) Macpherson's "Ossian poems" were in richly rhythmed prose. The prose poem as a specific form was written by Aloysius Bertrand, in *Gaspard of the Night,* 1836, which Charles Baudelaire followed with his *Little Poems in Prose,* 1862. In America Walt Whitman, influenced mainly by the prose of the King

James *Bible,* wrote free verse in his *Leaves of Grass* (1855, repeatedly enlarged until 1892); but in his exhortatory criticism he referred to this as prose. Amy Lowell similarly referred to some of her work, with interspersed rhymes and other poetic devices, as polyphonic prose. The difference between free verse and prose may at times rest wholly in the intent of the author, or the arrangement of the words on the page. It has been noted that metrical verse may have a great range of rhythmical freedom within its form, whereas free verse within its formlessness tends toward regularity. English free verse, for instance, is very often iambic.

Free verse has been employed mainly by radical poets, of the schools that emphasize arbitrariness and irrationality on the one hand, and on the other social and collective forces. In many languages there has been a marked return to more regular, metrical forms; but the vogue of free verse served to challenge the arbitrary, mechanical use of meter, and to focus attention on the evocative values of words. *Cf.* Prosody.

A. Lowell, "The Rhythms of Free Verse," *Dial,* Jan. 1918; "Walt Whitman and the New Poetry," *Yale R.,* April 1927.

French versification. *See* Romance; Old Fr. . . . Forms.

Freytag's pyramid. GUSTAV FREYTAG (1816–95) G. novelist, in *Technik des Dramas,* 1863, presented the widely accepted pyramid construction of a (5-act) play:

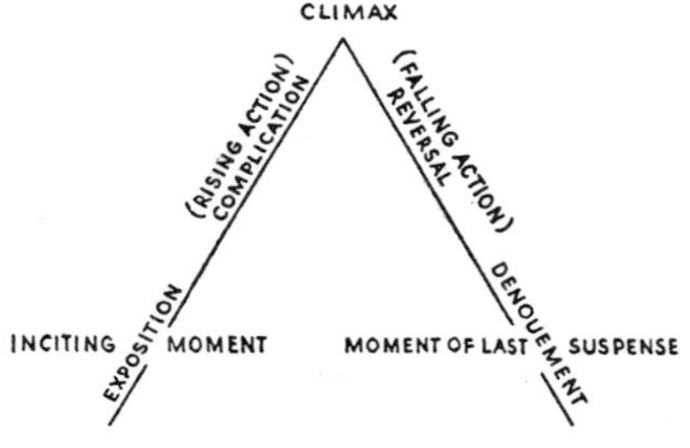

Fugitives, The. *See* Criticism, the new. J. M. Bradbury, *The Fugitives,* 1958, 1965; A. Karanikas, *Tillers of a Myth,* 1966.

futurism. Literary and artistic movement, founded 1909 by Filippo Tommaso Marinetti. Centered at first around the journal *Poesia* (Milan, 1910), later around *Lacerba* (Florence, 1914); but most of its manifestos were issued in the Paris daily *Le Figaro.* Marinetti defined its spirit as "modernolatry." The modern spirit was symbolized in the "praise of speed," already sung by D'Annunzio, and in urbanism, praise of the great industrial centers, which Verhaeren had celebrated as *villes tentaculaires.* These united in the engines that make modern life possible; Marinetti saw here the ideals and standards of a new beauty, the æsthetic of the American, an exaltation of war, as "the hygiene of the world," of the airplane—Marinetti sought in aerial acrobatics a new spectacle, the aerotheatre; hence also the reaction against what they called romantic or bourgeois sentimentalism, and their slogan *Uccidiamo il chiaro di luna* ("We will do away with the moonlight").

In literature, Futurism postulated the destruction of syntax and the dissolution of rhythm. The extreme manifestations (Marinetti, *La Battaglia d'Adrianopoli: Zang Tumb Bumb*) were fragmentary and chaotic successions of nouns and infinitive verbs, without conjunction or even the echo of a rhyme. "Typographical relief" replaced punctuation; all symbols were admitted, from the crudest representations of noises to chemical and mathematical formulæ.

In Russia, Futurism had the strongest influence, first in the Ego-Futurism of Severyanin, then in the work of Boris Pasternak, and of Vladimir Mayakovsky, who for a time made it the official school of Communist art. One group (Khlebnikov) stressed its irrationalist tendencies; as Cubo-Futurism it preached a meta-intellectual poetic language. Futurism also affected Yesenin's Imaginism and Selvinksy's Constructivism; and its ideas, diffused rather than directly caught, are one source of many of the avant-garde movements since its day (Vorticism, Imagism, in Am. and Eng.; Expressionism in G.; Ultraism in Sp.). *Cf.* Concrete verse; Automatic writing; Dadaism; Surrealism. C. Coquiot, *Cubisme, Futurisme, Passéisme,* 1914; F. Flora, *Dal Romanticismo al Futurismo,* 1925; C. Pavolini, *Cubismo, Futurismo, Espressionismo,* 1926; Luigi Russolo, *The Art of Noises,* 1913, trans. 1968. RENATO POGGIOLI.

G

GAELIC POETRY. The Irish Gaels, as well as the Scots Gaels who shared with them a common literary language and a common culture until the end of the 16th c., inherited with the Celtic language a social structure which had a special place for a learned class devoted to history and poetry. In pre-Norse Ireland there were two distinct classes of poets, the learned *filidh* and the less learned *baird*. Both classes seem to have undergone a long period of training. The Norse invasions, beginning in the late 8th c., destroyed the distinction between the two classes, but schools for the training of poets survived and continued until the Cromwellian invasion in the 17th c.

The social background of the poet probably accounts for the preoccupation with form characteristic of Gaelic poetry. Three distinct techniques followed one another: the pre-classical, the classical, and the post-classical. The earliest technique in its simplest form is characterized by a special vocabulary, extensive use of alliteration, a word-order less fixed and perhaps more archaic than that of prose, a rough, irregular rhythm and deliberate obscurity. The native word for this style is *retoric,* "rhetoric." Some conversational passages in the older sagas and a considerable body of gnomic material in *retoric* are extant. Fragments also exist in which a definite stanzaic form, usually of 2 long lines of 4 accents each, is discernible. Every accented word except the 1st must alliterate with a preceding or following word. Verses of this sort, in which rhyme is also employed, illustrate the transition between the pre-classical and classical technique.

Poetry in the classical technique (*dán díreach*), probably modelled upon the L. hymns of the Church, seems to have been introduced in the 7th c. Its root principle is the determination of the line according to syllables rather than accents. A type of rhyme peculiar to Gaelic is also regularly used, based on the Gaelic consonant-system in which a difference between the palatal and non-palatal and between the "aspirated" and "unaspirated" forms of consonants is functionally significant. The consonants may be divided, for the purpose of rhyme, first into 3 groups: (1) the stops *c, t, p, g, d, b;* (2) "unaspirated" liquids and nasals *l, r, n, m;* (3) the "aspirated" forms of these ten consonants. Each of these groups is subdivided into palatal and non-palatal. The consonant *s*, palatal and non-palatal, forms a class by itself. The consonants within each of these 7 groups are considered similar. Rhyme in *dán díreach* is constituted by identity of vowels and similarity of post-tonic consonants. *Cat, e.g.,* rhymes with *mac.* Alliteration (*uaimm*) and consonance are decorations frequently used but not required.

All poetry in *dán díreach* is stanzaic. By varying the length of line, number of lines, rhyme-scheme, and requirements for internal rhyme, the bardic schools developed a large number of different types of stanzas. One of the simplest and most frequently used was the *debide,* a quatrain consisting of 7-syllable lines, rhyme-scheme *aabb,* and with the last word of the 2d and the 4th lines one syllable longer than the last word of the 1st and the 3d:

> Messe ocus Pangur *ban*
> cechtar nathar fria *saindan;*
> bith a menma sam fri *seilgg,*
> mu menma cein im *saincheirdd.*

Other common types were quatrains of 7-syllable lines with rhyme-scheme *xbxb.* For example,

> Dom-*f*arcai *f*idbaidae *f*al,
> fom-chain *l*oid *l*uin—*l*aud nad-*cel*—
> huas mo *l*ebran ind *linech*
> fom-chain *trirech* inna n-*en.*

Here besides the rhyme *cel-en,* there is consonance between *fal* and the rhyme-words, alliteration, and junction between lines 3 and 4 by the rhyme *linech-trirech.* Such junction by internal rhyme (*uaithne*) is sometimes elaborately developed.

A very considerable body of poetry in the classical technique has been preserved. It was always sung or recited to harp accompaniment, though no music has survived. The poems dealing with Finn and his warriors are mostly in simple forms of *dán díreach,* and in these Gaelic poetry comes closest to success in narrative. The bard, however, was at his best in the brief lyric, where he often succeeded in combining simplicity of expression and depth of feeling with great complexity of form.

The destruction of the bardic schools in the wars of the 16th and 17th c. and profound changes in the pronunciation of Gaelic prepared the way for poetry in the post-classical technique, which by the year 1700 (earlier in Scotland) had entirely replaced the classical. Post-classical poetry is no longer syllabic; its main features are stress accent and assonance. It too was sung; many of its beautiful airs are preserved. In the strictest form of poetry of this type, the pattern formed by the accented vowels of the 1st line is continued through every line of the poem. In another favorite form (*caoineadh*), the line consists of 4 accents. In each line the 2d and 3d accented vowels assonate with each other. The final accented vowels in each line are identical throughout the poem. There are also freer forms where only the last accented vowel in the line enters into the pattern. In language and matter, post-classical poetry is more popular than bardic poetry; love is a more common theme, but political poems disguised as love poems form a considerable body of the new verse. Panegyrics, laments, and religious poetry continue. From the bards, the popular poets inherited the lyric gift and the passion for elaborate form, which in these native patterns persist today.

K. Meyer, *A Primer of Irish Metrics,* 1909; E. Knott, *Irish Syllabic Poetry, 1200–1600,* 1934. CHARLES DONAHUE.

galliambic. A catalectic verse of 4 ionic feet; usually altered by anaclasis and resolution of the long syllables.

gatha. A metrical hymn, frequent in the Buddha sutra, book of aphorisms. Also, a group of hymns, the oldest part of the Zoroastrian sacred writings, the Avesta. Usually 4, 5, or 7 words to the line.

gemells (twins). The paired lines of heroic couplets.

genre. Kind, or class, to which a work belongs. One of the most common sorts of criticism (now in disrepute) has been to judge a work according to the laws of its kind (Renaissance to the 19th c.). The quarrels of the Renaissance dealt often with *genres*—drama vs epic—or their intermingling, as in tragicomedy. A popular form of comparative literature has been (Brunetière) the study of the evolution of *genres;* and typology, the classification of works by psychological categories—naïve and sentimental; plastic and musical; Apollonian and Dionysian—is a return to the genre in other guise.

Georgian. Applied esp. to the reign of George V of Eng. (1910–36) and to the works in 5 volumes (1912–22) of *Georgian Poetry.* The writers, including Rupert Brooks, Masefield, de la Mare, and D. H. Lawrence, have little in common save perhaps a slightly conservative style and a preference for rural settings.

georgic (L.; Vergil, *Georgics,* 4 bks.). A poem dealing with rural life, esp. agriculture.

German versification (Early Germanic poetry: OE, Old English; OHG, Old High German; OS, Old Saxon). Although many forms of Germanic poetry were suppressed by Christian censorship, the meter, *i.e.,* the alliterative long line, survived the conversion and in OE remained the almost exclusive form, with its decorative devices: the kenning; synonyms and variations; uncommon compounds. The OE line has a smaller number of unstressed syllables than the G variant; thus the regular hemistichs became 4-beat verses that could be chanted, with alliteration marking at least the first, second, and fourth beats. Used mainly in the epic (*Beowulf*), this form survives in a few dramatic monologues, two of which (*Deor*; *Wulf and Eadwacer*) show stanzaic structure and refrain. The 4-beat alliterative form persisted in the 13th (Layamon, *Brut*) and 14th c., and in ME survives in Langland (1330?–1400?), *The Vision Concerning Piers Plowman,* 7,300 lines: "In a somer season, when softe was the sonne . . ." The OS epic *Heliand* often adds a stress in the line, and more unstressed syllables (*Schwellvers*). The OHG *Liber Evangeliorum* (*Krist*; Otfrid of Weissenburg, ca. 860) abandons the alliterative form, riming the hemistichs and combining a pair of long lines into a stanza. The hemistich has 4 accents, the 4th falling on the last syllable; the unstressed syllables are usually one to two for each accent. This form became the most popular for several centuries.

In the 10th and 11th c., the Saxon Emperors favored Latin. The chief forms were (1) the *Modi,* with irregular strophes, originally designed for the sequences following the *Alleluia* (invented by Notker Balbulus of St. Gallen, d. 912; *cf.* Hymn); (2) the Leonine hexameter (*Waltharius,* Ekkehard I, ca. 925; *Ruodlieb,* the first romantic novel of the Middle Ages, ca. 1040). A. Heusler, *Die altg. Dicht.,* 1923. Ernst Alfred Philippson.

German verse, later. Alliterative verse was later sporadically revived (Wagner; W. Jordan, *Die Nibelunge,* 1868), but the chief meter for later G. epic was the Gr. dactylic hexameter, freely used (Klopstock, *Messias,* 1748–73; Goethe, *Reineke Fuchs,* 1793; *Hermann und Dorothea,* 1797; G. Hauptmann; Thomas Mann). The dactyls are freely replaced by spondees and trochees, but the second and fourth accents are marked. Gradation of accents (*Reineke Fuchs*) produces a livelier melodic movement, in contrast to long sustained levels (*Hermann und Dorothea*).

Goethe broadly reflects the 18th c. development in G. versification. He uses, with occasional alexandrines, *Knittelvers* and *Madrigalvers.* The former, from Hans Sachs (1494–1576) is a rimed couplet of dipodic accent, with free variation of unaccented syllables within the foot (*Faust*; epistles; legends). The latter, iambic of 2 to 6 feet and free rhyme, combines with *Knittelvers* in *Faust,* but appears elsewhere (*Ilmenau,* 1783). Goethe carries on the anacreontic verse (Hagedorn, 1708–54), esp. iambic and trochaic tetrameters with 4th beat paused, and blends them with the *lied* forms of the folksongs (Herder; and *Wunderhorn,* 1806); also with those of the *Gesellschaftslied* (Reichardt, 1752–1814). From the classical tradition (Klopstock, 1724–1803) Goethe drew free rhythms (1772–83), dithyrambs fixed neither in time, accent, nor number of syllables, but increasingly metric. Klopstock's ode forms (mainly Alcaic, *An Fanny* and Asclepiadic, *Zürchersee*) sometimes lack a cogent sentence melody; this is mastered by Hölderlin (1770–1843) and Platen (1796–1835), who with Rückert (1788–1866) uses the ghazel; Rückert also the makame.

Two strains continue, not wholly apart: the more stately, monopodic, bisyllabic meter in larger structural stanzas with a tendency toward chanting (Platen; Hofmannsthal, 1874–1929; George, 1868–1933); and the lighter, *lied*-like verse with livelier speech melody and graded accents and a mixture of two- and three-syllable measures (Keller, 1819–90; Rilke, 1875–1926).

The critical theory of versification began with Karl Lachmann's ed. of OHG and MHG poetry in the first half of the 19th c. and with Westphal's *Theorie der Neuhochdeutschen Metrik,* 1870. Eduard Sievers, founder of *Schallanalyse,* proceeding from a motor reaction of the human body, paid foremost attention to the rhythmic and melodic constants of verse, which he came to use as a means of identification (*Rhythmisch-melodische Studien,* 1912). Andreas Heusler stresses predominantly the time element and denies the relevance of melodic factors (*Deutsche Versgeschichte,* 3 v., 1925–7). Franz Saran proceeds from the acoustic impression and strives for an exact description of time element, weight, accent, inflection of measure and verse (*Der Rhythmus des französischen Verses,* 1904; *Deutsche Verslehre,* 1907). A history of the use of metrical forms is still to be written. Jakob Minor, *Neuhochdeutsche Metrik,* 1902; W. Bennett, *G. Verse in Classical Metres,* 1963. Ernst Feise.

gesta [L., deeds; Fr. *geste;* Eng. jest, rarely gest (*Gest Historiale of the Destruction of Troy,* 14th c.)]. Tales of adventure, *Gesta Romanorum* (compiled 14th c., oriental and classical, printed 1472, widely used as a source book). The Fr. *chanson de geste,* fl. 11th–14th c., was a long epic poem, in lines (*laisses*) of 10 or 12 syllables, at first with assonance, then rhymed (lengthily on one rhyme). Three branches of the cycle: 1. The king (Charlemagne; Roland>Orlando Furioso), 2. William of Orange (*vs.* the Saracens), 3. Doon de Mayence (rebellious nobles). *See* jest-book.

Gestalt (G., form). The unified whole, with properties not explained by the sum of its component parts. Gestalt-thinking is said to underlie the organic unity of a work of art, as contrasted with the sequence-thinking that characterizes science. *Cf.* Form.

ghazel (Arab., spinning). Lyric form, used esp. by the Persian Hafiz (d. ca. 1390). In Persian poetry, of 4 to 14 lines; begins with a rhymed couplet, even lines throughout the poem repeat this rhyme, odd lines are unrhymed. In Turkish poetry, usually less than a dozen couplets, with, as in Persian, the author's name mentioned in the last couplet. In German (Goethe, etc.) up to 30 lines. The ghazel is usually in peaceful mood, mystical or erotic. *Cf.* Divan; Persian poetry; German versification.

ghost word. One created by error of scribe, editor, printer. By wrong letter: pernsal for perusal. By running two words together: whatno. Such compounding is a frequent method of word formation, in Eng., but esp. in G. A list of spurious words is given in *OED Supplement*, p. 333. *Cf.* Phantom; Telescope.

gierasa. Boasting poem among the Galla of Africa, of the powers and deeds of an individual hero. *Cf.* Farsa.

gloss (Gr. tongue, language; affected by MHG, hence lustre). Also glose. An explanation, from a marginal word to a lengthy note; hence, a list of explanations, a glossary. Thus E. K.'s gloss to Spenser, *Shepheardes Calender*, 1579; Coleridge's, 1817, to his own *Ancient Mariner*. Sometimes used of the foreign or obscure word that requires explanation. As effected by "to gloss over": a disingenuous explanation, a deceptive interpretation. The glose is also a fixed verse form (Sp.; rare in Fr. and Eng.), developing variations on a (usually quoted) theme, somewhat as the *rondeau redoublé*.

glyconic. A so-called logaœdic verse, ⏓ ⏓ — ⏑ ⏑ — ⏑ — widely used in early Gr. lyric and drama and L. lyric, origin and exact nature disputed. A series of glyconics often ends with a Pherecretean ⏓ ⏓ — ⏑ ⏑ — —: such a group is a priapean. Christ 517–37; Bowra, *Gr. Lyric Poetry*, 1936.

gnome (Gr. judgment). A maxim may be about (1) universals that are the objects of action, to be chosen or avoided in our doings; (2) men but not involving choice; (3) fate, death, the gods; (4) non-human subjects. Aristotle limits the term gnome to type (1); but all four appear in gnomic poetry.

gnomic poetry is widespread. Gnomes (type 3, above) occur occasionally in Homer; often (mainly type 1) in *Beowulf*; Hesiod's *Works and Days* (l. 214–47; 263–80) approach the type that consists only of gnomes (Theognis; many ancient and medieval collections, gnomologies). In Gr. the poems are continuous; likewise in A.S. (*Exeter Gnomes*; *Cotton Gnomes*, mainly type 4); in the Norse there is usually a stanza to a gnome. In the Norse *Hávamál* (types 1 and 2), the most artistic gnome poem, the god Othin speaks, the formula "ought to" (A.S. *sceal;* Norse *skal*) is frequent; the maxims are more practical than moral, *e.g.,* "He ought to rise early that plans to plunder his neighbor." *Cf.* Fable. E. Ahrens, *Gnomen in gr. Dichtung*, 1937.

god from the machine. *See Deus ex machina.*

Goliard (L. gula, glutton; *cf.* gullet). One of the educated jesters or wandering students, who wrote ribald and satirical verse, 12th–13th c., in G., Fr., and Eng. They attributed much of it to an imaginary Bishop Golias; some verses (*Apocalypse*; *Confession*) have been ascribed to Walter Map. Many are collected in *Carmina Burana*. They are the earliest works of a roisterous satire that reached its peak in Rabelais. Helen J. Waddell, *The Wandering Scholars*, 1927.

Gongorism (Sp., Don Luis de Góngora y Argote, 1561–1627). Style named from the Sp. poet, who ca. 1609 turned from his clear and simple works, to polish the language. He became obscure through complexity of verbal devices: inverted order; words coined from L., It., Gr., strangeness of diction and construction. Started a controversy, but for a time prevailed (Lope de Vega mocked it, but withdrew). Also called *cultismo, culteranismo*, from its appeal to the cultured. Akin to movements in other lands; *see Secentismo; cf.* Baroque.

good sense. The criterion of Fr. neo-classical criticism: Boileau; also Dryden, Johnson. Ability to recognize the fitness of things, according to an ordered understanding of past events and a reasonable anticipation of cause and effect. Common sense believes that evil begets evil and good generates good: it demands therefore a certain congruity in the development of characters in fiction. In the Fr. classical drama there was often a character, called by critics the *bon sens,* a bystander in whose mouth the author places his balanced ideas, in opposition to the error, or lack of balance, of the participants in the conflict. *Cf.* Point of reference.

Gothic. A term for aspects of medieval art first applied to pointed architecture in the early 17th c.: "Their very Uncomeliness ought to be exiled from judicious eyes and left to their first inventors, the Gothes, or Lumbards, amongst other Reliques of that barbarous age." (Sir Henry Wotton, *Elements of Architecture*, 1624). As Clark remarks, "For centuries the Gothic style had no name; it was the only way of building—architecture, simply. As soon as it was named it was a separate style, and when the word became widely used we may say that Gothic had become something artificial and peculiar."

It took nearly a century after Milton for the "Gothic spirit" to develop—until, in fact, the Renaissance products of Inigo Jones and

Christopher Wren had become smoke begrimed and the abbeys torn apart by Henry VIII had taken on the mossy patina of antiquity. The Gothic revival in its literary aspects was closely associated with the green copses, disordered stone piles, enchanting shadows and sweet melancholy of these ruined buildings. The late Augustans, searching for relief from their own calm reasonableness, found it in the distorted images of Gothicism. Horace Walpole built Strawberry Hill (1750–53) and wrote *The Castle of Otranto* (1764) in the same mood. Little Walpoles erected stucco ruins with pointed arches in their gardens, to shade them as they composed verses on fair damsels and ghostly visitations.

The Gothic novel grew into an established form. Thomas Leland (*Longsword,* 1762) wrote the first Eng. historical Gothic novel; *Otranto* is the first supernatural Gothic romance. Clara Reeve (*The Old English Baron,* 1778) introduced what Walpole called a "tame ghost," the seemingly supernatural naturally explained. Thus also C. M. Wieland's *Don Sylvio de Rosalva* (G. 1764, Fr. 1769, Eng. 1773) has all its apparitions, necromancies and wizardry, hauntings and horrors, explained in volume 4, with an *éclaircissement* harder to believe than a genuine ghost or actual diablene. The Gothic novel may be roughly divided into the historical, the sentimental, and the terror. Chief of the earlier writers are Ann Radcliffe (*Mysteries of Udolpho,* 1794), Matthew Gregory Lewis (*Ambrosio, or the Monk,* 1795), and the Rev. Charles R. Maturin (*The Fatal Revenge,* 1807; *Melmoth the Wanderer,* 1820). Edgar Allan Poe continued the mood in *The Fall of the House of Usher* (1839), with its poem showing the progress of insanity in "The Haunted Palace" of a crumbling mind. "Monk" Lewis (Prologue to *The Castle Spectre,* 1797) called Romance "the moonstruck child of genius and of woe." Poetry, in Gray and the Wartons, took a melancholy turn. Coleridge knew the inevitable scene:

> Oft in my waking dreams do I
> Live o'er again the happy hour
> When midway on the mount I lay,
> Beside the ruin'd tower.

In 1816, Lewis, in Switzerland with Byron and Shelley, set the company to composing goblin stories. Mrs. Shelley's contribution was *Frankenstein.*

The Gothic Revival can be conveniently divided into four periods: (1) that of spurious ruins and superficial medievalism, dominated by Barry Langley's architecture and Percy's *Reliques of English Poetry* (1765); (2) the Romantic Revival: Scott's poetry and historical romances; Wyatt's restorations; (3) National Gothic: Pugin's Gothic detail for the Houses of Parliament; the Oxford Movement; Carlyle's *Past and Present*; (4) eclecticism: Street's Law Courts; Ruskin; the Pre-Raphaelites.

The Gothic attitude of "the marvelous, trembling with passion" was later linked with surrealism (*q.v.*) in Breton's statement in the first Manifesto: "Only the marvelous is beautiful" and in such surrealist Gothic novels (*romans noirs*) as Julien Gracq's *Au Chateau d'Argol* (*Dung Castle,* 1938, 1961). In our time, the spread of literacy and the proliferation of paperbacks has brought a recrudescence of the Gothic novel, with all the apparatus of haunted houses, gloomy forebodings, grisly spectres, with new psychological and extrasensory pressures upon the harassed heroine, before the "natural" explanation and the hard-wrought happy ending. With such titles as *Ghostwind*; *Ravenscroft*; *Sarah Mandrake*; *The Haunting of Hill House,* the contemporary books are signed mainly with women's names: Shirley Jackson, Iris Murdoch, Charlotte Armstrong, Mary Stewart, Victoria Holt, Phyllis A. Whitney. Motion pictures were quick to follow the scent. *Frankenstein* (the man taken for the monster) has come in several versions, the 1931 with Boris Karloff being called "the most famous horror film ever made"; and the monster was brought back to life in such films as *The Bride of Frankenstein*; *The Curse of Fr.*; *Son of Fr.*; *Fr. Meets the Wolf Man*—updating the werewolf. Half a dozen vampire films (*Dracula*) continue the Gothic spirit. The books of two centuries ago are being reprinted, and one paperback house is currently issuing four new Gothic novels a month. Most recently, the Gothic spirit has been taken on space flights of fancy with science fiction. A curious combination of fantasy and shuddery Gothic is Mervyn Peake's "Gormenghastly" trilogy (1946, 1967) of the House of Groan. *Cf.* Short story; Novel, types; Melodrama; Detective story; Diabolism. John Ruskin, *The Stones of Venice,* "The Nature of Gothic," 1851–53; Kenneth Clark, *The Gothic Revival,* 1928; W. W. Watt, *Shilling Shockers of the Gothic School,* 1932; Montague Summers, *The Gothic Quest,* 1938, 1964; *The Gothic Spirit,* 1941; I. Malin, *New Am. Gothic,* 1962; R. D. Spector (Introd.) *Masterpieces of Gothic Horror,* 1963; J. H. Matthews, *Surrealism and the Novel,*

1966; D. Drake, *Horrors!*, 1967. Charles W. Jones and Montague Summers.

grace. 1. Circumstances under which rules may be ignored. "Snatch a grace beyond the reach of art" (Pope, *Essay on Criticism*, I, 141–157). Mentioned by Quintilian; Horace; Longinus; in the Renaissance, opposed to beauty (reason, regularity, restraint, conformity) as a product of imagination, irregularity, spontaneity, originality: "Beauty pleases by the rules only; grace, without them" (Roger de Piles, *L'Idée du peintre parfait*, 1699, Eng. trans. 1706). It is instant in effect. It defies analysis—to the It. (Firenzuola, 1541), it is *un non so che; un je ne sais quoi* to the Fr. (Bouhours, 1671, connects grace in art with grace in religion: both are mysteries: both were expressed in Gr. by the one word, *charis: Charites;* L. *Gratiae, the Graces*). The Ren. went so far as to say that beauty cannot charm without grace. But in the 18th c. the sublime replaced it as the transporting quality ranged against reasoned beauty; grace came to mean "the charm belonging to elegance of proportions"; and, now, an ease and lightness, or an ornament, of style. S. H. Monk, "A Grace Beyond the Reach of Art," *JHI*, 3, 1943. *Cf.* Correctness.

grace. 2. "There, but for the grace of God, go I." Expression supposedly indicating that the responses of the receptor match those of a character: under similar circumstances, the receptor would act as the character does. Thus the character is felt as real, lifelike. A successful work may even withdraw that grace; while its spell is on, "There go I!"

gradation. A series of statements so arranged that each succeeding statement marks an advance in thought, and usually so constructed that the concluding clause (or final word) of one statement is reiterated as the beginning of the succeeding statement. Thus: "Tribulation worketh patience, patience experience, and experience hope." In classical oratory, these are sometimes very elaborate. Similar to Eng. climax, *q.v.*, which is the ancient *incrementum*.

grammar (Gr. *grammatikós,* of or pertaining to letters or literature; *grámmata,* letters, literature, pl. of *grámma,* letter). *Meaning.* As the etymology suggests, the word was used in classical Gr. and L. for the methodical study of literature, including textual and æsthetic criticism, problems of literary history, as well as the study of language. During the Middle Ages, since the knowledge of Gr. was slight, and the vernacular languages were not deemed worthy of study, the term "grammar" came to mean study of L.; in Eng. the term "grammar school" was given to a type founded for teaching Latin. With logic and rhetoric, grammar was one of the subjects of the trivium, but again included the study of literature. As the study of the vernacular languages developed, the word "grammar" lost many of its wider implications; it meant in Eng. the art of speaking and writing correctly, that is, according to rule. In the early 18th c., the rise of the middle class to a position of authority was accompanied by a demand upon its part for guidance in cultural matters; in partial response there was developed a body of rules for the Eng. language. Such rules were often without any basis in actual usage; they not infrequently repudiated the practices of even the leading authors of the time. They were based upon rationalistic considerations or carried over from L. syntax. This idea of grammar is inherent in our present use of the word. We speak of "errors in grammar" or of "bad grammar," both of which are inconsistent with the scientific concept of the term. Grammar, when furnishing us with a guide to linguistic conduct, is often called Prescriptive or Normative.

With the development of the scientific study of language in the 19th c., a new concept of grammar arose, as set forth in H. C. Wyld, *Universal Dictionary of the English Language*: [Grammar is] "A branch of learning dealing with language and its analysis from several points of view; the term includes the study of the pronunciation of a language, its inflexions or other means used to express the relation of words to each other in sentences, syntax, and the principles of word formation; it is also applied (a) to the purely descriptive study of the phenomena presented by a given language at a given moment; (b) to the historical treatment of these, which exhibits the changes which take place in a language from age to age; (c) to a study based on a comparison of the phenomena existing in several languages sprung from a common ancestor." Grammar thus considered is usually spoken of as Descriptive in contrast to the Prescriptive attitude. The provinces of Historical and Comparative grammar are clear from portions *b* and *c* of Wyld's definition.

The terminology and basic categories of English grammar are unsettled. Until recently most grammarians were content to remain within the framework that had developed from a study of the classical languages, but in the present c. there has been a tendency to develop new concepts, categories, and terms. Jespersen uses a system of ranks (*i.e.,* primary, adjunct, subjunct). The greater preoccupation of present-day grammar with strictly linguistic considerations may be seen by comparing the divisions of the subject as given by Wyld (phonetics, morphology, syntax, word formation) with that prevailing until approximately the mid 19th c.: orthography (and sometimes orthoëpy), etymology, syntax, and prosody.

Philosophical Basis. From its beginning, grammatical speculation was philosophical in character, connected with the views of the philosophers concerning the origin of language and its place in the scheme of things. In the conflicting systems of Plato and Aristotle, we find the former apparently believing that language had arisen through some inherent necessity, whereas the latter maintained that it had arisen by convention or agreement.

The outstanding grammars of the late L. and early Christian era were those of Ælius Donatus (mid 4th c.) and of Priscian (Byzantium, early 6th c.). These became the type and source of the L. and Gr. grammars of medieval and Renaissance Europe. During the period of medieval scholasticism there was, however, another controversy concerning the existence of words: the realists maintaining that words and things were the counterpart of ideas; the nominalists, that they were only names arbitrarily assigned by man.

Utility. We have seen that the word "grammar" included in its meaning problems of literary criticism and history as well as the analysis of language; the underlying impetus to the study of grammar both with the Gr. and with the Hindus was to make intelligible the great religious and literary works of antiquity, such as the Homeric poems and the Veda, whose language had become archaic. (Panini had written a splendidly detailed analysis of the Sanskrit language as early as the end of the 4th c. B.C. He had many celebrated successors, but the grammatical speculation of the Gr. rather than the analysis of the Indians gave rise to a continuous intellectual tradition throughout the history of European thought.)

Later on, the Scriptures had to be interpreted. There was also need for a practical knowledge of the language of those to whom Christianity was to be carried; finally, the *Bible* was translated into the various vernaculars.

Grammar as a medium of interpretation is employed in connection with contemporary works as well as with earlier ones. Linguistic analysis of the devices employed by Cummings, Joyce, and the Sitwells may be as helpful as it is in connection with *Beowulf* or Chaucer. For in reading writers of earlier periods, it is imperative for readers of today to know the language conventions of the age, so that the text may be studied in their light. One critic, *e.g.,* through examining the use of the familiar and the formal second personal pronouns *thou* and *ye* in *Troilus and Criseyde,* was able to reach certain conclusions concerning Chaucer's conception of his characters in the light of the current courtly love tradition.

A detailed knowledge of the language of a period is often of aid in fixing authoritative texts, by enabling scholars to form judgments as to the authenticity of variant readings, to correct scribal or textual errors (the notes of Furnivall on Shakespeare; of Manly and Skeat on Chaucer).

Linguistic and grammatical criteria are also useful in dating, localizing, even in determining, authorship. Had 18th c. scholars known as much as we do about the inflexions and syntax of late Middle English, there could scarcely have been the slightest controversy over the genuineness of Chatterton's Rowley poems. Dialect criteria have been of immense value in determining where works (*Poema Morale*; *The Owl and the Nightingale*) were written, and in serving to distinguish (*King Horn*) between the language of the original and that of subsequent copyists. The proportions of *ye* and *you* as the nominative of the 2d personal pronoun constitute a test to distinguish the contributions of Beaumont and Fletcher in their joint plays. Such matters as the omitted relative, the use of *do* as a verbal auxiliary, the omission of *to* in the infinitive, have all been employed as tests of authorship for the post-Shakespearean drama.

The employment of grammatical criteria to serve in analyzing "the complex of style into its several strands" is illustrated in Edith Rickert's *New Methods for the Study of Literature* (1926). Her method is used chiefly to determine the effect upon the style as a whole, of an extensive use of one part of speech or type of construction, *e.g.,* of a high proportion of nouns to verbs, or of verbs of action to the total number of verbs. This method—though it must be employed with extreme caution, to prevent invalid generalizations—may be used for the relationship between sentence structure and rhythm, between tonal pattern and the normal phonetic repertoire of the language.

L. Bloomfield, *Language,* 1933; C. C. Fries, *What Is Good English?* 1940; L. H. Gray, *Foundations of Language,* 1939; O. Jespersen, *The Philosophy of Grammar,* 1924; *Essentials of Eng. Grammar,* 1964; A. H. Hill, *Introd. to Linguistic Structures,* 1958; A. G. Juilland, *Outline . . . of Structural Relations,* 1961; P. Hartmann, *Theorie der Grammatik,* 4 v., 1959–62. ALBERT H. MARCKWARDT.

Although the empiric study of language began in the 19th c., the burgeoning of "scientific linguistics" has come since 1940 and the publication of C. C. Fries' *Am. Eng. Grammar,* with its objective description of a large body of everyday prose. The term "grammar" became lost in the term "linguistics," which was aimed more at anthropology than at literature. The study of American Indian languages, esp. in the 1930's, had turned attention away from written language to the structures of spoken language, which became the base for scientific analysis. One of the immediate products was "structural linguistics," a method of analysis and description based almost entirely on sound structures, esp. on the so-called "suprasegmental" phonemes or morphemes accounted for by differences in pitch, stress, or juncture. These differences were treated as signals of meaning, even though questions of meaning were frequently relegated to the background by the structuralists while they tried first to define and describe the sound structures themselves. From *An Outline of Eng. Structure* by George Leonard Trager and Henry Lee Smith, Jr. (1951) a host of structural studies derived. C. C. Fries' *The Structure of Eng.* (1952), although less purely concerned with sound structures, was another seminal book in the development of structural linguistics. New branches of linguistic study came into being and flourished—phonemics, morphemics, morphophonemics, and tagmemics. However, a reaction to structuralism developed, and became significant with the publication of Noam Chomsky's *Syntactic Structures* in 1957. The result was a method of grammatical analysis leading to "generative" or "transformational" grammars. These are "depth," or "process," or "dynamic" grammars in contrast to the "surface," or "two-dimensional," or "static" grammars of either the structuralists or the traditionalists. What is stressed is the generation of complex structures out of basic or minimal structures and the precise transformations by which the complex structures can be accounted for. On the popular level, Paul Roberts followed the structuralist line in *Patterns of English* (1956) but turned to the transformational methodology in *Eng. Syntax* (1964). Although the connection is perhaps only accidental, transformationalism has been closely linked with computer mathematics and technology. "Constituent" and "string" analysis have also been explored. *Cf.* Syntax; Linguistics; Sentence. J. Sledd, *A Short Introd. to Eng. Grammar,* 1959; Zellig S. Harris, *String Analysis of Sentence Structure,* 1962; Martin Joos, ed. *Readings in Linguistics,* 1957, 1966; N. Chomsky, *Aspects of the Theory of Syntax,* 1965; W. Francis, *The Structure of Am. Eng.,* 1958; B. Hathaway, *A Transformational Syntax,* 1967. BAXTER HATHAWAY.

grand style, the. "Arises in poetry when a noble nature, poetically gifted, treats with simplicity or with severity a serious subject" (Matthew Arnold). Joshua Reynolds used the term of Raphael and Michelangelo. Walter Bagehot draws it to literature in his essay *William Cowper,* 1855, probably deriving it from Hazlitt (whose "gusto" was also drawn from art criticism). Ruskin (*Modern Painters,* v. 3, 1856) applies it to Homer. Arnold, *On Translating Homer,* 1858, distinguishes between the grand style severe (Milton) and the grand style simple (Homer); without the qualification, the term has had wide currency. Lowell calls it "at once noble and natural." *Cf.* Sublime. *See* Style.

Greek prosody. *See* Classical versification.

grobianism. A 16th c. effort to curb the indecency and crude manners of the period by pretending to glorify them. Rules of etiquette had been treated in didactic poetry since the age of chivalry; the Reformation, with its predilection for satire, converted the tradition. Grobianus (G. *grob,* coarse) is the patron saint in Brant's *Narrenschiff,* 1494. Dedekind's L. satire, *Grobianus* (1549) prescribed comprehensive rules for behaviour for all boors that would be worthy of their patron saint. Other versions and imitations (K. Scheidt, *Von groben Sitten,* 1551) sprang up in great number; while avowedly combating indecency, they take delight in the crudities they describe. In Eng., *The Gull's Hornbook* (T. Dekker, 1609). The influence extended to Swift (*Gulliver's Travels,* 1726) and has parallels in our own time. *See* Folly.

grotesque (It. *grotte,* grottoes, excavations of ancient buildings with murals of humans fantastically interwoven with animals and foliage). Hence, ludicrous from incongruity or distortion; fantastically absurd. Ruskin (*Modern Painters,* III iv, viii) says that by the bold conjunction of symbols it reveals truths otherwise difficult to express. Hazlitt applies the term to Gothic literature. W. Kayser, in *The Grotesque in Art and Lit.,* 1963, calls it an attempt to invoke and subdue the demonic aspects of the world. *Cf.* Gothic; Diabolism.

gusla. In Serbo-Croatian heroic verse, *q.v.,* a poem of the short line: 10 syllables, with a caesura after the 4th; no rhyme and no refrain. Still sung to the gusla (one-stringed fiddle), replacing the bugarstice. D. Subotic, *Yugoslav Popular Ballads,* 1932.

H

HAIKU. A Japanese poetic form now frequently used in English (sometimes as a school exercise). In 3 lines successively of 5, 7, and 5 syllables, it usually conveys a picture or a mood, often with deeper connotations. H. G. Henderson, *Haiku in English,* 1967; H. Stewart, *A Chime of Windbells,* 1969. *See* Japanese poetry.

hallelujah meter. Stanza of 6 iambic lines, 4 trimeter, then 2 tetrameter. So called from frequent use in hymns.

hamartia (Gr., error). Aristotle viewed the ideal tragic hero as "a man not preeminently virtuous and just, whose misfortune, however, is brought upon him not by vice and depravity but by some error (*hamartia*)." This error may be of judgment, or through ignorance, or by a moral fault, or due to inherent human frailty (as a family trait, *e.g.,* impetuosity of Oedipus) but whatever its cause, it usually provokes a specific action (Oedipus' marrying Jocasta; Antigone's defiance of civil law). S. E. Bassett, "The Hamartia of Achilles," *TAPA,* 1934; M. K. Flickinger, *The Hamartia of Sophocles' Antigone,* Diss. U. of Iowa, 1935; Richmond Lattimore, *Story Patterns in Gr. Tragedy,* 1964, 1969. *Cf.* Tragedy.

happening. A recently developed theatrical activity, in which events are spurred by audience and performer interaction. In this sense, the happening returns to the earliest stage of the theatre, the Gr. *comos,* which preceded classical comedy, and the *commedia dell'arte,* out of which modern comedy grew. Happenings are presented in cafés, discothèques, churches, and other gathering places. "Ideally a happening can occur only once," because it changes with location and audience, as was shown at the New York Times Square Recruiting Center on Oct. 28, 1967 at 2 P.M. and the Port Authority Bus Terminal on the same afternoon at 6. Applying new electronic devices, some happenings work in the intermedia, mixed media, or multimedia technique, using film, stroboscopic lights, colors, incense, as well as actors. They seek to "overload" the receptors by the multiplicity of stimuli, thus wiping out intellectual grasp, æsthetic appreciation, and objectivity, but pounding directly on the emotions. Happenings have employed such devices as microphones under the seats, through which the receptors' shiftings activate the stage lighting and provide cues for the actors. Historian A. L. Rowse described the Exhibition building at the Stratford-on-Avon Shakespeare quatercentenary (1964), with "a new way of assailing the visitors' senses, using light, sound, changing scales and levels, smell, and surprise: a technique elaborated and evolved by young artists on the other side of the Atlantic and given the name of Happening." As you walked along, you smelled pomander perfumes, you heard airs, madrigals, lute music, virginals, bird song, catches, street-cries, you saw books Shakespeare used, jewels of his Queen, and through latticed windows the Thames-side stretch of old London. The X 2 issue of the *Tulane Drama Review,* and the No. 4 issue of *New Writers* (1967, with 5 pieces by Allan Kaprow, who in 1958 first called such activity a happening) are devoted to the genre. *Cf.* Absurd; Modernism; Off-off-Broadway. M. Kirby, *Happenings,* 1966; J. Becker and W. Vostel, *Happenings,* 1965; M. Benedickt, ed. *Theatre Experiment,* 1967; Allan Kaprow, *Untitled Essay,* 1958, 1968; *Assemblages, Environments, and Happenings,* 1967; *Some Recent Happenings,* 1968; R. Kostelanitz, *The Theatre of Mixed Means,* 1968; W. Vostell, *Berlin and Phenomena,* 1968; A. Hansen, *A Primer of Happenings,* 1968; R. Schechner, *Public Domain,* 1969.

head rhyme. (1) Alliteration. (2) Rhyme at the beginning of the lines.

Hebraism. The attitude toward life and conduct based on obedience and high moral purpose. Opp. Hellenism, *q.v.,* in which the intellectual life is of primary importance. Discussed in modern times notably by Matthew Arnold in the 4th ch. of his *Culture and Anarchy*.

Hebrew poetry. *See* Canaanite.

hedonism. The doctrine that pleasure is the proper goal of action, developed by Aristippus (5th c. B.C.) and his Cyrenaic school; also urged in the *Bible*: "And I commend enjoyment, for a man hath no better thing under the sun than to eat, drink, and be merry" (*Ecclesiastes* vii, 15). A point of view found in writers of many periods, *e.g.* Anacreon; Herrick ("Gather ye rosebuds while ye may"); De Quincey (*Confessions*). The Cyrenaics sought the pleasures of the moment, but, as pictured by Epicurus (4th c. B.C.), the continuance of pleasure demands the guidance of reason; hence, prudence, honor, and justice are essential. Pleasure, note, rises from friendship, knowledge, art; the purely physical or "lower" pleasures (1) are ephemeral (2) involve prior or consequent pain. This distinction is not pressed in the "pleasure principle" of Freud, and the pursuit of pleasure often animates characters in recent novels. H. Spencer (*Data of Ethics,* 1879) distinguishes egoistic hedonism (one's own pleasure) and universalistic (the greatest pleasure of the greatest number). David L. Perry, *The Concept of Pleasure,* 1967; Godo Lieberg, *Die Lehre von der Lust . . . Aristoteles,* 1958.

Hellenism. To an ancient Greek, esp. a Stoic, purity of language: avoidance of solecisms, barbarisms, foreign expressions; use of an idiomatic style, free from excess. To later times, manner, language, culture, imbued with the Greek spirit. Addison (*Spectator* 285): "Vergil is full of the Greek forms of speech which the criticks call Hellenisms." (So also Latinity, Gallicism, Anglicism, etc.)

Matthew Arnold (*Culture and Anarchy,* ch. iv) contrasts Hellenism and Hebraism as two rival forces in the history of man: "The governing idea of Hellenism is spontaneity of consciousness; that of Hebraism is strictness of conscience." The one has a vibrant sense of being alive, of sensing through every pore, "seeing things as they are in their beauty"; the other stresses ideals of conduct and obedience to the will of God. Thus in the *Bible* Job, wronged to the utmost, still submits: "I abhor myself and repent in dust and ashes," whereas Prometheus under similar pressure still cries (the last words of Aeschylus' play): "Behold me, I am wronged!" The pagan heeds only the check of his own free nature; the puritan accepts an outer rule, of law or God. Note, however, that these terms by no means thus apply to actual primitive pagans; and by Arnold's distinction some Greeks are Hebraist: Euripides, "If gods do evil, then they are not gods"—but Sophocles, "Nothing is wrong that the gods command." *Cf.* Apollonian.

hemistich. Half a line of verse, usually to or from the caesura (*q.v.*). Also used of a shorter line in a stanza.

hendecasyllabic. A verse of 11 syllables; in classical poetry mainly ⏓⏓—⏑⏑—⏑—⏑—⏓, *e.g.,* (Tennyson) "O you chorus of indolent reviewers." In later poetry, the first 2 syllables are regularly long. Also called phalaecian. *Cf.* Glyconic. Bowra, *Gr. Lyric Poetry,* 1936.

hendiadys (Gr., one by two). "The figure of twins." The expression of one idea by two nouns and a conjunction, where one would suffice, or where in thought one modifies the other, *e.g.* (Vergil, *Georgics* II 192) "we drink from cups and gold." A favorite construction of Shakespeare's is such a linking followed by *of*: "The slings and arrows of outrageous fortune." E. A. Hahn, "Hendiadys, Is there such a thing?" *CW* 15, 1921–22.

hephthemimeral. Pause occurring within the 4th foot of a hexameter line. *Cf.* Caesura.

heptameter. Of 7 feet. *See* Meter.

heptastich. A group of 7 lines of verse. *See* Stanza.

heptasyllabic. Of 7 syllables. *See* Meter.

hero. The central figure or protagonist in a literary work; the character with whom the reader or audience sympathizes. If both forces contend within one person, he is usually referred to as the protagonist. For tragic hero, *see* Hamartia. The hero in Indian drama is conceived in 48 characters, of 4 main types: (1) the merry, careless: *Dhîralalita;* (2) the generous, virtuous: *Dhîraçanta;* (3) the brave but prudent: *Dhîrodâtta;* (4) the ardent, ambitious, zealous, proud: *Dhîroddhata. Cf.* Anti-hero; Story; Fiction; Opposition; Novel. Raglan, *The Hero,* 1936.

heroic couplet. In the Renaissance, heroic verse meant verse written in the high style of the epic. In the 18th c., from its use in translations of Homer, the term heroic verse or heroic couplet became affixed to the iambic pentameter in pairs of rhyming lines, continuous through a poem. As earlier used by Chaucer, the lines are not well knit, running often like a series of separate couplets; there is no regular caesura; the sense (sentence) usually ends at the line-end. Among the Elizabethans, two tendencies developed: (1) toward greater freedom: run-on lines; sense and sentence ending within the line; the rhyme pattern and the sense pattern playing upon one another; rhymes frequently of unimportant words (*to* with the infinitive on the next line; preposition; auxiliary verb), (2) toward the "closed" or "stopped" couplet: each couplet a clause or sentence; emphatic rhyme words; sense and metrical patterns coincide. John Beaumont (*Address* to James I, 1618) announced the pattern:

The relish of the muse consists in rime:
One verse must meet another like a chime.—

and with Waller (poems circulated in mss. ca. 20 years; pub. 1645) the heroic measure is fixed.

From this rigidity Cowley (*The Davideis,* 1656) sought variation by introducing Alexandrines. Dryden often has a decasyllable followed by a rhyming Alexandrine; also rhyming triplets and, for lighter moments (prologues; epigrams) feminine rhyme. These devices, however, are arbitrary; imported, not intrinsic; Pope swept aside this "rustic vein And splay-foot verse"; restored the closed couplet with a regular cæsura (after 5th or 6th syllable); divided the line or pair of lines in balanced repetition or antithesis—the same tune to every purpose: but with such polished elegance it became the standard and norm for 100 years. The Byron-Bowles quarrel, amidst the romantic freedom, is marked by Byron's defense of Pope's form, which (*The Corair, Lara*) Byron quickened but made almost monotonous. (Pope attained his variety not through meter but in timbre; contrast the delicate interplay of labials and sibilants, *e.g.,* for the sylph of *The Rape of the Lock* with the heavy words in ranks of double consonants in *The Dunciad.*)

Keats (prefixing to *Endymion* Shakespeare's line "The stretched metre of an antique song"), avoiding both the Popean mould and the Drydenesque variations, returned to the Elizabethan freedom, with sentences ending within the line, nine-tenths of his couplets unclosed, but with a rich and varied vowel music and an integrated flow. Browning ("My Last Duchess") and others have used the free form since, though the closed and balanced structure has continued, esp. in satire and light verse. *Cf.* Poetry; Meter; Eng. versification. R. M. Alden, *Eng. Verse,* 1903; John A. Jones, *Pope's Couplet Art,* 1969.

heroic poetry. The epic, *q.v.* Heroic verse: the form used for the epic; in Gr. and L. the dactylic hexameter; in Fr. the Alexandrine; in Eng. (Chapman, Pope, trans. Homer; Dryden, trans. Vergil) heroic couplet.

heterophemy. (1) Twisting of components of a word, so that one not intended is presented, *e.g.,* Calvary for cavalry. *Cf.* Spoonerism. (2) The use of a word or phrase in such a way as to show (by pause in speech, punctuation, or other device) that a different one is meant. A frequent device of euphemism, *e.g.,* "You go to—Heligoland!"

hexameter. A metrical line of 6 feet. In Gr. and L., esp. the dactylic hexameter, used in epic and widely elsewhere (save in lyric; it is not stanzaic); the first 4 feet may be dactyls or spondees, the last is a spondee with *syllaba anceps.* With a pentameter, it forms an elegiac distich. Christ 145–201.

hexastich. A group of six lines of verse. *See* Sextain; Stanza.

hiatus. (1) a gap, or section missing, in a manuscript. (2) A pause in writing or speech, for emphasis or other effect. (3) The slight pause between two successive vowels not separated by a consonant. English provides the article *an* instead of *a,* French *cet* instead of *ce,* etc. to make such flow smooth.

high comedy. The more graceful, urbane, and witty sort of comedy. Its shafts are driven by the bow of the intellect, with verbal play, often deft repartee, and mental agility. The pattern was set by Molière; among its practitioners have been Congreve, Wilde, Shaw. High comedy, when it deals with deft minds, often shows them at work to satisfy the desires of their bodies. Beyond the excesses that it mocks lies a world of basic values its characters assume. *Cf.* Comedy.

higher criticism. In biblical scholarship: lower criticism considers the text and mechanism of a work; higher criticism, its intellectual, æsthetic, and spiritual values.

hilarody. One of the forms of the ancient Gr. mime, a parody of tragedy. *See* Magody.

historical present. Use of the present tense in relating incidents of past occurrence. In L., Fr., Russ., this is an expected element of style. In Eng., rarely used, though recently more often (Hemingway; Komroff; in trans. *e.g.,* Ivan's poem in *Brothers Karamazov,*

Bk. V, 5) as giving immediacy, carrying the reader into the flow of the tale.

historical-geographical method (of folktale study). The oral tale may appear in hundreds of versions scattered over 2 or 3 continents, recorded, for the most part, within the past generation. The literary historian looks for a genealogical tree as the end of his researches. The historian of the oral folktale looks for a center of distribution; he attempts to follow the wave-like course from the center through all kinds of cross currents and disturbances to the farthest shore.

The term "historical-geographical method," though aspects of it have long been used, is applied to the technique developed in Finland by Kaarle Krohn and Antti Aarne (sometimes, therefore, the "Finnish method" *q.v.*). Recognizing that most folktales exist in both oral and literary forms, practitioners of this method arrange the oral versions in a geographical order and the literary ones in a chronological. Most successful studies have been based upon from 200 to 600 oral versions.

history. A play that fairly closely follows actual historical events; often loosely developed, like a chronicle, with pageants and battle scenes. Used esp. of plays dealing with royalty. The plays of Shakespeare are commonly divided into tragedies, comedies, and histories. M. Trotain, *Les Scènes historiques,* 1923; R. M. Smith, *Types of Historical Drama,* 1928; M. H. Golden, *The Iconography of the Eng. Historical Play,* 1965; I. Ribner, *The Eng. History Play in the Age of Shak.,* 1965; T. F. Driver, *The Sense of History in Gr. and Shakespearean Drama,* 1960, 1967.

history. Historiography. In the Western tradition, the writing of history emerges by the 5th c. B.C. in all the essential forms it has since taken. The 4th c. had the works of Homer (ca. 9th c. B.C.) in which, as in the *Old Testament* of the Jews and the similar traditional stories of other peoples, myth, legend and facts are inextricably mingled to inculcate religious beliefs, sound morals, and patriotic sentiments; it had Herodotus' (484?–425?) history of the wars of the Persians against the Greeks, in which that skilled lecturer tells with a thousand asides and anecdotes and with a fidelity to truth modern research has done much to confirm, the stirring tale of a conflict between two civilizations; and it had Thucydides' (471?–400?) history of the Peloponnesian War, in which that philosopher and soldier sought to diagnose from a dramatically clinical study of the recent past the evils of his own society. A body of religious, moral, and patriotic teachings; a story; a philosophic (or "scientific") study of the behavior of men in the past; these 3 elements have ever since gone into the writing of history.

The art of history attained a characteristic perfection in the 18th c. Gibbon's *Decline and Fall of the Roman Empire* (1776–88); Voltaire's *Siècle de Louis XIV* (1751) and *Essai sur les mœurs* (1756); Hume's *History of England* (1763); and Robertson's *Charles the Fifth* (1769) represent the serene and secure enlightenment of the age of reason turned to the contemplation of the past. Their tone is dignified, even when relieved by the wit of Voltaire or the skepticism of Hume, a bit patronizing—especially towards the Middle Ages—and steadily didactic. Bolingbroke, another child of the 18th c., aptly in their terms defined history as "Philosophy teaching by examples."

Sense of immediacy, feeling for the atmosphere of past times and remote places, emotional warmth, poetic strangeness, became the goals of the next generation of historians. The rising popular pride in the national and ethnic past, the generous hopes of Liberty, Equality, Fraternity, the romantic feeling for "old, unhappy, far-off things" stimulated especially by novelists like Sir Walter Scott, the mass of fascinating historical detail accumulated by the patient work of obscure researchers—all enriched Michelet's *Histoire de France* (1833–67), Thiers' *Histoire du consultat et de l'empire* (1845–62), Niebuhr's *Römische Geschichte* (1811–32), Sybel's *Geschichte der Revolutionszeit von 1789–1800* (1853–79), Treitschke's *Deutsche Geschichte im 19. Jahrhundert* (1879–94), Grote's *History of Greece* (1846–56), Macaulay's *History of England* (1848–61), Froude's *History of England* (1856–70), Prescott's *Conquest of Mexico* (1843) and *Conquest of Peru* (1847), Motley's *Rise of the Dutch Republic* (1856), Parkman's 10 v. on the rivalry between France and England in North America (1851–1892). These have a variety that marked their century, always eager for novelty, never quite attaining the unity and dignity of a single style. Some of these 19th c. historians write of the past, often by choice the mediæval past, in glowing colors; they regret the dull shopkeepers' times in which they live. Some ardently preach the gospel of progress and see their own age—and country—as the culminating point in the evolution of the human race. Some are first of all patriots.

Some use the broad sweep and the glittering generality; others draw with infinite detail the minutiae of daily life. Some are eloquent, some moving, others precise, sparing. But almost all tell a story well, make men and women come to life in their pages. Indeed, story and character are with them major concerns; there is little attempt to achieve sociological generalizations; their point of view is usually an obvious matter of patriotism or party. Most of them attained great popular success. The works of Macaulay, for instance, sold better than most novels. Many-volumed sets of histories, leather-bound, adorned the library of any man of culture.

In this century there also developed the claim that history is not art but science. The collection and assaying of historical materials, the development of technical disciplines in aid of research—diplomatics, the study of documents; palæography, the study of old forms of handwriting; epigraphy, the deciphering of inscriptions; sphragistics, the study of seals; numismatics, the study of coins —and the growth of such auxiliary sciences as archæology and anthropology, by the 19th c. demanded a long apprenticeship. No longer could these be dismissed as the antiquarian's concerns. Biological studies, moreover, were beginning to make the evolutionary or genetic approach to the study of human behavior seem inescapable. Historians came to feel that they could at last understand the real course of human events, as Sir Isaac Newton had come to understand the real course of celestial events.

History as a self-conscious science emerged most fully in Germany. In G. universities was first developed the seminar method, in which a teacher set his students to a series of cooperative and supervised researches on small points to be cleared up—and often made his own *opus major* out of the results. Mommsen (1817–1903) and von Ranke (1795–1886) set going the now familiar apparatus of *historismus*—professional academic history-writing: subdivision of labor into often extreme specialization in space and time, meticulous, richly footnoted monographs, learned journals, vast and carefully edited collections of source materials, and collaborative histories like the *Cambridge Modern History* (1902–12) or the *Histoire Générale* (1893–1901) edited by Lavisse and Rambaud, in which each specialist contributes his own special chapter. By 1900 the guild of professional historians was fully formed.

By 1900, also, only professional historians read the work of professional historians. The day of the Ph.D. writing to be read by other Ph.D.'s had come. Unlike their more impressive brothers in the natural sciences and in some of the other social sciences, the historians did not develop an esoteric technical jargon of their own. They were often quite successful in writing obscurely, but that was chiefly because they scorned to try to write well, and indeed rarely were trained to write at all. Except in the schools and colleges, for which the professional historians often wrote surprisingly good text-books, the general public no longer read the writings of contemporaneous historians.

Professional academic historical writing has continued to thrive, though in general outside the main stream of literature, in the 20th c. The historian strives to obey Ranke's dictum: "He will merely show how it really happened." (Ranke, *Gesch. der rom. und g. Völker von 1494 bis 1514, Vorrede.*) As the work of James Harvey Robinson (1863–1936) and the other "new historians" in America showed, however, it is possible by bringing in economic, social, and intellectual history to widen and deepen even the learned historical monograph.

History remains, however, no complete science of man. Science is not a collection of facts; it is a system of laws or uniformities the scientist finds in facts, which prove themselves useful under empirical tests. Such uniformities historians of the orthodox professional school did not even seek. Writers who sought them in history were known rather scornfully as "philosophers of history" and even the latest of them, (Oswald Spengler, *Der Untergang des Abendlandes,* 1918–22 trans. *The Decline of the West,* 1927–8; A. J. Toynbee, *A Study of History,* 6 v., 1934–40; P. A. Sorokin, *Social and Cultural Dynamics,* 1937–41) are clearly rather philosophers than scientists. At a less ambitiously philosophical level than this literature of "Whither Mankind?", professional historians of recent years have been turning to comparative history, even theoretical history, as witness two recently founded and presently thriving learned journals, *Comparative Studies in Society and History* (1958–) and *History and Theory* (1960–). There is a growing tendency towards mutual toleration between those for whom history is essentially literature and those for whom it is one of the social or behavorial sciences. Most anthropologists, sociologists, political scientists, and economists admit that there is, or should be, an important historical dimension in their work. Historians are increasingly willing to draw from their data tentative uniformities of human behavior, as for instance Crane Brinton, *The Anatomy of Revolution* (rev. ed. 1965). Economic historians and a few others even make use of computers.

Clio, a muse, is still thriving. Historical writing has benefited from the mid-century popularity of non-fiction over fiction. Romantic history is still written, especially in the form of the historical novel, which has seen new popularity as novelists like Bryher, Mary Renault, Zoe Oldenbourg, and MacKinlay Kantor make full use of modern historical scholarship. The unreadable but often very useful historical monograph or learned article is still turned out, but to such earlier readable yet professionally most respectable works as G. M. Trevelyan's *England under Queen Anne* (1931) and Elie Halévy's *Histoire du peuple anglais au 19me siècle* (1913–1933) there can now be added a great many in all the western languages. A sampling: G. Mattingly, *The Armada* (1959), Bruce Catton, *A Stillness at Appomattox* (1953), Barbara Tuchman, *The Guns of August* (1962), A. M. Schlesinger, *A Thousand Days* (1965), J. W. Wheeler-Bennett, *Munich: Prologue to Tragedy* (1946), B. Aron, *Histoire de la libération de la France* (1959), J. Chastenet, *Le siècle de Victoria* (1954), Fritz Fischer, *Griff nach der Weltmach* (1964). Marxist historians still disdain the human touch, though there is excellent contemporary history in a novel like Boris Pasternak's *Dr. Zhivago* (1958). Even Soviet historians, however, now take full part in international congresses of professional historians and, if they have not yet been able to achieve history as literature, have at least caught up with the standards of "scientific" history in the tradition of Ranke. Biography, autobiography, and memoirs all are thriving in the 1960's. At least two memoirs from World War II—of Winston Churchill and of Charles de Gaulle—have probably joined the list of great books. CRANE BRINTON.

It should be mentioned that some critics protest that history is inevitably both biased and partial. Macaulay, and the portrait of Richard III propagated by Shakespeare, come to mind. A comparison of the pictures of a "national hero" drawn by his compatriots and by historians of an enemy country, or a reading of the treatment of, say, Stalin in successive issues of Soviet encyclopedias and histories, makes one wonder where truth lies. School histories have been punningly yet pungently described as "rite words in rote order." No less an authority than the developer of the Ford car asserted that "history is bunk." More politely, it has been said that history is made by historians. *Cf.* Autobiography; Biography. J. H. Robinson, *The New Hist.,* 1912; J. T. Shotwell, *An Introd. to the Hist. of Hist.,* 1922; J. B. Black, *The Art of Hist.,* 1926; G. P. Gooch, *Hist. and Historians in the 19th C.,* 1913; J. W. Thompson, *A Hist. of Historical Writing,* 2 v., 1942, 1967; J. Barzun and H. F. Graff, *The Modern Researcher,* 1957; L. R. Gottschalk, ed., *Generalization in the Writing of Hist.,* 1963; F. E. Manuel, *The Shaping of Philosophical Hist.,* 1965; B. Mazlish, *The Riddle of Hist.,* 1966; Ernest A. Baker, *Hist. in Fiction,* 1907; D. Levin, *In Defence of Historical Literature,* 1967; A. G. Widgery, *Interpretations of Hist.: Confucius to Toynbee,* 1961; *The Meanings in Hist.,* 1967; G. Kitson Clark, *The Critical Historian,* 1967; R. Stover, *The Nature of Historical Thinking,* 1967; G. R. Elton, *The Practice of Hist.,* 1968.

hokku. Haiku, *q.v.*

holophrasis. The expression of a phrase or combination of ideas by one word, *e.g.* "man" in Kipling's line: "And what is more, you'll be a man, my son!"

homeosis (also omoiosis). The general term for comparison, but esp. implying action. The term in common use for the figure is simile: comparison of things of different classes, alike in at least one particular, *e.g.,* (Burns)

> Pleasures are like poppies spread—
> You seize the flow'r, its bloom is shed.

Placing two ideas in opposition is syncrisis (*cf.* Antithesis) *e.g. Proverbs* x, 1; xi, 1; xii, 1; xiii, 1; xiv, 1; xv, 1; xvi, 1; xvii, 1.

homeoteleuton (also homoioteleuton). (1) Occurrence of similar endings of words or lines, esp. as a source of error in copying. Chaucer asked his readers to blame faults on "Adam Scrivener"; Rabelais, accused of heresy, declared the offending passages were printer's errors. Proof-readers today know that the error is far from obsolete. *Cf.* Repetition. (2) Use of a series of words with similar endings. Applied today to occasional rhyme in prose. Aristotle applied it to rhyme in verse; his remark that it is to be used sparingly was frequently quoted in Renaissance controversy over rhyme. Formal classical prose might seek to avoid it; thus Cicero wrote *perangusto fretu* instead of *freto.* It is common in the plays of Plautus, and Terence used it for special effects (*Eunuchus*

287, *Taedet cotidianarum harum formarum,* I'm sick of these everyday sorts of shapes).

Homeric simile. One lengthily extended. It usually serves not only to clarify or strengthen the basic idea but to give pleasure in itself. First used by Homer, hence also called epic simile. In Eng. Milton, *Paradise Lost* (*e.g.,* III 431–441); Arnold, *Sohrab and Rustum. Cf.* Simile.

homonym. 1. Word of the same spelling as another, but different sound and sense, as *bow—bow.* Also called homograph. 2. Word of same sound as another, but different spelling and sense, as *bred, bread.* Also called homophone. These are sources sometimes of confusion, sometimes of humor. 3. Word of same form as another, but different sense, as *net.* The Latin sentence *Malo malo malo malo* may be translated, "I'd rather be in an apple tree than an evil man in adversity."

homonymbles, also nimbles. A parlor game, which builds upon homonyms and other verbal play. *E.g.,* the woman Susan whose husband calls her Peggy. Peggy is short for Pegasus; Pegasus is an immortal horse; an immortal horse is an everlasting nag.

hornbook. A printed sheet bearing the alphabet, combinations of consonants and vowels, and often the Lord's Prayer, mounted on a paddle-shaped piece of wood and covered with a sheet of transparent horn. Used in Eng. and the Colonies to the 18th c. A form on varnished cardboard was called a battledore. Succeeded by the primer. A. W. Tuer, *History of the Hornbook,* 1897, 1968.

hubris (Gr., overweening pride). Also hybris. Transgression of divine command or moral law, due to ambition, overconfidence, greed, lust, or other passion or flaw in character. Causal sequence in Gr. tragedy, esp. Aeschylus: (1) *hubris,* (2) *koros,* satiety, (3) *ate,* doom—*e.g.* in the *Oresteia* trilogy, Clytemnestra (1) murders her husband Agamemnon, (2) lives in adultery with Aegisthus, (3) is slain by her son Orestes. *Cf.* Hamartia.

huitain. A group of 8 lines of verse, usually as a complete poem. *Cf.* octastich.

humanism was the "renaissance" of classical literature and thought that was going on throughout the Middle Ages and, with increased momentum, in the 14th, 15th, and 16th centuries. Many neglected texts were rediscovered, many men learned Greek as well as Latin, and European culture underwent a reorientation. *Litterae humaniores,* the ancient poets, philosophers, historians, and orators who had dealt with human life and human values, were studied with unbounded ardor by men who were weary of degenerate scholasticism and theology. The humanists were the party of progress who saw classical civilization, with its moral wisdom, critical rationality, and great art, as the highest level man has reached; and their ideal was to re-create such a civilization in the modern world. Humanism from the first developed on two main lines: many men, like Erasmus, embraced the rational wisdom of antiquity as a helpmate of revelation; others, from Montaigne to militant extremists, found in the classics sanction for scepticism and naturalism. But humanism, whether religious or secular, became in general a comprehensive doctrine of order: ethical, social, political, and metaphysical; we meet this framework of thought at every turn in Renaissance writing, from Shakespeare down.

Literature was one of the areas in which the humanistic doctrine of order operated, since humanism led directly to neo-classicism, to the imitation of ancient authors and genres and the codification of principles derived from Aristotle, Horace, and others. Worship of the ancients could go to excess, as in the lifeless imitation of Cicero's style or of classical epics and dramas, and yet, if such zeal was often a liability, the gains were immense. The principles and practice of art were eagerly examined; literature was established as a realm of high activity; and both writers and readers everywhere had a common consciousness, both dynamic and stabilizing, of the rich tradition behind them.

Gilbert Highet, *The Classical Tradition: Greek and Roman Influences on Western Literature,* 1949; Julian S. Huxley, *The Humanist Frame,* 1961; A. Chastel, *The Age of Humanism,* 1963; Gilbert Murray, *Humanist Essays,* 1964; Sarah E. Herndon, ed., *The Humanistic Tradition,* 1964; A. A. Cohen, *Humanistic Education and Western Civilization,* 1964; W. M. Spackman, *On the Decay of Humanism,* 1967; S. Dresden, *Humanism in the Ren.,* 1968. DOUGLAS BUSH.

humanism, the new (U.S., phrase of Josiah Royce). Attitude of those who, led by Irving Babbitt (1865–1933) and Paul Elmer More (1864–1937), strove primarily through a study and emulation of the teachings of classical literature, to reassert the human will against the scientific-utilitarian (Baconian) or sentimental (Rousseauistic) naturalism of the day. Babbitt, quoting from Emerson's "Ode to W. H. Channing": "There are two laws discrete, Not reconciled . . . Law for man, and law for thing" (*Literature and the American College,* 1908), posited the dualism between man and nature and held that within man himself (very important to More) were to be found distinctive features of this opposition. With More (*Shelburne Essays,* 1904–1921, etc.) and Babbitt the new humanism had two basic principles: 1. to recognize within one and be guided by the controlled ethical imagination, the inner check or selective principle (*frein vital*) of the free will upon the naturalistic impulses (*élan vital*) also within one; 2. to recognize the existence of a superior, continuing reality, the element of immutability in a changing universe. Babbitt turned to Aristotle, Confucius, and Buddha; More sought inspiration in Hinduism, Platonism. Proceeding further than Babbitt (who recognized the necessity of humility as a control on the human intelligence), More saw that superiority in Jesus, thus merging the humanistic and religious traditions of Western civilization. To Aristotle's *Nicomachean Ethics* (decorum or sense of proportion is the supreme humanistic virtue to Babbitt), More added the Christian religion as a further bulwark against the plunge into animality.

Life (the new humanists affirmed) is experienced on three levels—naturalistic, humanistic, religious—which reveal fixity and diversity, change and universality: man must be truly critical, completely positivistic and through experience, not the acceptance of external authority, reach toward unity as a standard for life. The individualists who repudiate this outward control (as did Rousseau) without achieving an inner equilibrium are responsible for the chaos of modern times. As Edmund Burke said, modern man has no personality because in his eagerness to defend his right to self-expression, he has neglected to have a true self.

To be truly modern and critical, man, in art, politics, religion, etc., must utilize the best of the past as signposts for the present. Classical taste in æsthetics, the political aims of an intellectually aristocratic democracy, the humility of Socrates—with More, faith in Christ—were the guides of the new humanism.

Others in the movement were George Woodberry, W. C. Brownell—chief literary critic of the first generation of new humanists—Brander Matthews, Prosser Hall Fry, F. J. Mather, Robert A. Millikan. Stuart P. Sherman and Norman Foerster also joined, with varying echoes and emphases. Arousing considerable controversy in the late 1920's (*cf., The Nation, The Saturday Review of Literature, The New Republic, Forum, The Hound and Horn*), the movement, which had its own magazine, *The Bookman* (ceased publication in its 76th volume, March 1933), culminated in two symposia: *Humanism and America* (ed. Foerster) and the respondent *Critique of Humanism* (ed. C. Hartley Grattan), both 1930. The new humanism shortly lost favor, under the impact of Marxist critics and the New Critics. Alone among this latter group, Yvor Winters carried on the literary standards of new humanism by insisting that poetry, through a poem's structural strength or weakness, ought to manifest its moral attitude toward experience. The new humanism, which had attempted to bring over into the 20th c. the moral and metaphysical idealism of 19th c. American transcendentalism, dissolved (according to Howard Mumford Jones) into a "disillusioned neo-Calvinism." H. J. Muller, *Science and Criticism,* 1943, 1956; O. L. Reiser, *Man's New Image of Man,* 1961; N. Rotenstreich, *Humanism in the Contemporary Era,* 1963; Erich Fromm, ed. *Socialist H.,* 1965.

The "new humanism" of the 1960's rises as a protest against a computerized society. Calling itself "General Systems Theory," it includes literature and esp. linguistics, but emphasizes that in any human situation *all* relevant aspects must be considered. It recognizes in any human involvement the mechanistic (cybernetic) aspects, "the program," but insists upon the incalculable (humanistic) aspects, "the style." Between measurable input and measurable output moves the essential and non-measurable "computer" of the brain. Also, in the purely physical world one may speak of, and tally, cause and effect; with humans, a simultaneous reciprocal and mutual interaction grows. These human elements defy mechanical charting. There are already some 12 volumes of "General Systems" Archives, but the theory, although with applications in education and for creators, has not yet developed other than in expository writing. JOHN BURKE SHIPLEY.

humor (humour). First applied to the subject of laughter in 18th c. to distinguish the genial and affirmative forms of comic writing, then greatly in vogue, from satire, mockery and ridicule. Now widely used as a generic term for everything that appeals to man's disposition toward comic laughter. The change testifies to an increasing recognition, due largely to the influence of psychology and particularly the scientific observation of infants, that laughter is, in its simple biological form, genial and affirmative.

The word humor (from the L. meaning moisture, as still in *humid*) was used in the Middle Ages—following Hippocrates—to refer to the four humours of the body, the intermixture of which determined a man's mental qualities and disposition: blood, phlegm, choler (bile) and melancholy (black bile). Predominance of one of these made a person respectively sanguine, phlegmatic, choleric, or melancholic. A humoralist was one who believed in this humoral pathology. A humorist was a man subject to variations of these humors; hence, a fantastical or whimsical person. The word humour was used by Ben Jonson to mean the mood natural to one's temperament. It was not until the 18th c. that the current sense developed, with Shaftesbury, Dryden, Goldsmith. In 1854 H. Read in his *Lectures in English Literature* spoke of "the happy compound of pathos and playfulness which we style by the untranslatable term humour." Humor came to be balanced against wit as less purely intellectual, more a matter of the emotions, frequently sympathetic. Wit is likely to evoke a smile; humor, to provoke laughter.

Laughter, as Darwin observed, "seems primarily to be the expression of mere joy or happiness." It abounds especially in states of play. But in these states a secondary laughter seems to arise, associated not with joy or happiness in general, but with a specific emotional pleasure in experiences which would be frustrating or distasteful if taken seriously. This laughter and this quality of feeling are the kernel of what we call humor.

This was dimly apprehended by Plato, who opened the debate on this subject with the remark that "at comedy the soul experiences a mixed feeling of pain and pleasure." Aristotle's definition of the comic as consisting of "some defect or ugliness which does not imply pain" tends in the same direction. But his remark permits the inference that all laughter is a laughing at some other, putatively inferior, person, and is therefore in essence vainglorious and derisive. In this manner Cicero developed Aristotle's idea; and Thomas Hobbes revived the opinion in modern times with his celebrated remark that "sudden glory is the passion which maketh those grimaces called laughter." Descartes, Lamennais, Meredith, Groos, Bergson and others accepted this opinion. It has much apparent support, of course, in the prevalence and contagiousness of derisive laughter. Self-glory and hostility, however, are quite as prevalent in man's serious as in his laughing moods. These traits are of the essence of man, rather than of laughter.

This was understood by Voltaire, himself a master of derision, who stated that "Laughter always arises from a gaiety of disposition, absolutely incompatible with contempt and indignation." The German humanist, Jean Paul Richter, held a like opinion. Spinoza explicitly rejected the derision theory, insisting that "laughter and jest are a kind of joy"; likewise Kant: laughter arises "from the sudden transformation of a strained expectation into nothing." It is always his own disappointments, not yours, at which a baby laughs. Schopenhauer restricted Kant's idea to intellectual disappointments. Herbert Spencer, with his ingenious but easily disproved notion that we laugh only when we are prepared for a large perception and arrive at a small one, belongs to the same school. Hegel went even further: "Inseparable from the comic, is an infinite geniality and confidence, capable of rising superior to its own contradiction. . . ."

Hegel inferred from this that in the "highest" kind of comedy, the spectators laugh with the actor instead of at him. Inference either way is unjustified. It is important to recognize that comic laughter antedates, underlies, the distinction between self and others, finds its immediate stimulus in the playful frustration of the person who laughs; for without this understanding it is impossible to define wit, or explain the rather complex process called a joke. A joke is a playful disappointment of the listener's expectation—a destruction of his nascent pattern of perception, conception or emotion—combined with a fulfillment of some other interest or appetite. The "point" of a joke binds the collapse of one pattern with the satisfactory closure of another. Comedian and story-teller alike play continual tricks on their audiences, inventing ever new ways of tripping them playfully, and yet contriving that in their fall they alight upon some agreeable thought, image or emotion. The comic pleasure deriving from a fall is thus combined with innumerable other, often extremely serious, qualities of feeling. Contempt has its place here, but so also have pity and admiration. Hence arise the richness and infinite variety of humorous experience.

The derision theory still finds support, esp. among those who are not playful and that hate to be laughed at. But the classification of the kinds of humor, the definition of wit, and the analysis of a joke as a process, made possible by the play theory, have for the first time given theoretical disquisitions on this subject a practical value to humorists and comedians. It seems that our understanding of humor will advance along these fruitful lines. *See* Wit. Evan Esar, *The Humor of Humor,* 1954; S. Leacock, *Humor and Humanity,* 1938; E. M. Blistein, *Comedy in Action,* 1964; W. Blair, *Horse Sense in Am. Humor,* 1942, 1962; N. W. Yates, *The Am. Humorist,* 1964; W. F. Fry, Jr., *Sweet Madness,* 1963, 1968; G. Legman, *Rationale of the Dirty Joke,* v. 1, 1968. Max Eastman.

hybris. Hubris, *q.v.*

hymn; sequence; antiphon; chant. Odes in praise of the gods are sung at the festivals and services of all religions. The earliest Egyptian songs to Ra and Amen have a parallel structure, as later the Ugaritic and the Hebrew. Early Sanskrit hymns were collected ca. 1200 B.C., esp. in the Rig Veda. The Gr. hymns of Callimachus and Cleanthes, 3d c. B.C., were mainly in hexameters. Gr. *hymnos* is used in the *Septuagint* to denote various Hebrew musical forms and was adopted by the Church (Council of Toledo, 633) to mean any song of praise to God except the Psalms. *Hymn* thus denotes anthem, canticle, trope, sequence, and other religious compositions accompanied by music. In this sense hymnology prospered in the Gr. Church. Gr. renditions of Hebrew modes, as found in the Psalms, Alleluias, and Hosannas, largely made up the early Gr. liturgy; for instance, the antiphonal singing introduced by Ignatius of Antioch, presumably under divine guidance (Socrates, *Hist. Eccl.* vi. 8), seems to rest on a Hebrew mode. *Kyrie eleïson, Gloria in excelsis, Magnificat,* and *Nunc dimittis* are a few of the musical parts of the service adapted from the Hebrews. Whether the unique hymnody of the Eastern Church, based on the *troparion,* or rhythmical unit, developed in Constantinople during the 5th c. and associated with the name of Romanos, was really modulated prose or metrical verse is disputed. However, this hymnody flourished throughout the 6th and the 7th c. while Byzantine influence was felt in the West, and may have affected in some details the progress of Western hymnody, especially in the composition of tropes and sequences.

Hymn also has a more specific meaning in the West, denoting the metrical and strophaic compositions in the L. *hymnarium,* or hymnal. Together with other oriental ecclesiastical practices like asceticism, hymns set to Gr. music were introduced into the L. Church during the 4th c. One of the greatest, *Te Deum,* probably written by St. Nicetas (d. 415), and still used in the Office at the end of Matins, has many extra-liturgical uses as a hymn of thanksgiving; so Shakespeare, of the marriage of Anne Boleyn:

The choir
With all the choicest music of the kingdom
Together sang *Te Deum.*

Three names are especially associated with the new hymnody: Pope Damasus (d. 384), St. Hilary of Poitiers (d. 368), and St. Ambrose (d. 397). The last introduced hymns into his diocese at Milan as a means of combatting Arianism, and St. Augustine (d. 430), who heard them, composed a *Hymn Against the Donatists* in Africa. Ever since, Western hymns have tended to be inspirational, militant, and evangelical, as opposed to other liturgical music of the Church in repose; but they are also the product of the monastic life, to which Ambrose, Augustine, Gregory were addicted, for the monastic notion of a continually ascending praise of God led to the development of the Office and the *Hymnarium.*

In form, the Ambrosian hymn was made up of strophes of 4 iambic dimeters, with a sense-pause at the end of the 2d line, a stronger pause at the end of the strophe, and a definite change of thought at the end of every 2d strophe. Though the scansion followed classical rules (*see* Quantity), this new arrangement of lines according to sense, probably for the sake of antiphonal singing, hastened the development toward accentual metre and the modern strophe. In fact, the hymn is marked by its exceptionally strong accentual beat, by use of the strophe as a unit of thought, and by repetitive refrains that were originally the repeated Doxology. This important innovation in metres was not paralleled by innovation in melody; apparently Ambrose but slightly modified the 4 Greek modes in which he composed.

During the next 4 c., composition of hymns occupied the best poetical minds, *e.g.,* Prudentius (d. 413), Sedulius (5th c.), Fortunatus (d. 609), Paul the Deacon (d. 799), Hrabanus Maurus (d. 856). Later writers, under the influence of the Cluniac reform and the development of the sequence, turned their thoughts elsewhere. The fully developed sequences, being distinguishable from the hymns only by liturgical use, are often called hymns in this restricted sense of the word. Later hymns fell into a pattern of thought, treating subjects like the Passion, the joys of Paradise, the terrors of Judgment, and the compassion of Our Lady almost exclusively, although there were hymns that celebrated the virtues of individual saints. The inherent militant character of the hymns, however, reasserted itself with the Crusades, and Crusaders' Hymns, in the vernacular, spread a new and popular religious fervor over the western world. With the Reformation congregational singing developed, often (as with *Ein Feste Burg,* A mighty fortress is our God) with tunes from secular songs. G. hymns poured forth from Luther to Paul Gerhardt (1607–76). In Eng. there were many editions of the Psalter from 1558 to 1677, most hymns in the common meter (8.6.8.6 syllables, 2d and 4th lines rhyming). Isaac Watts, in 4 books of hymns, 1705–19, earned the title "Father of Eng. hymnody"; his best-known is "Our God, our help in ages past." Most prominent in the Evangelical revival was Charles Wesley (1707–88: "Hark the herald angles sing"; "Gentle Jesus, meek and mild"); James Montgomery (1771–1854; "Hail to the Lord's Anointed") was the greatest lay hymn writer before Robert Bridges. *Hymns Ancient and Modern* (1861) was the most widely used hymnary in Eng.; the 1906 Eng. Hymnal discarded hymns of too flexible musical idiom; it included some U.S. hymns, *e.g.,* Phillip Brooks' "O little town of Bethlehem." Gospel hymns were added by evangelist Dwight L. Moody, and Ira W. Sankey wrote naive, carol-like tunes. The hymn seeks less a literary quality than sincere and simple devotion in singable form.

Sequence. Whereas the Office is subject to change according to taste, the Mass has traditionally remained the same. Especially is this true of the parts of the Mass known as the Consecration and Communion. Although more freedom has been exercised in the Preparation, to which in the primitive Church catechumens were admitted, nevertheless the Mass gave comparatively little scope for the creative impulses of mediæval artists. Such variation as was allowed from earliest times was largely confined to a musical composition or intoning upon the *Alleluia* which followed the Epistle and Gradual. The final *a* was prolonged into a long musical score, called by various names such as *melisma, neuma, sequela, jubilus,* and *jubilatio;* to the long series was applied the name *sequentiae.* In the 9th c., words were added to these musical scores, largely to accommodate the memories of singers. The invention was first described in detail by Notker Balbulus of St. Gall (d. 912, Pref., *Liber sequentiarum*). At first these sequences were not arranged in regular strophes; frequently the full succession of 25 to 50 lines would end in the letter *a,* in imitation of the *Alleluia* upon which they were based. They came more and more to take on the form of hymns, which had long been a part of the Office. This extension of the liturgy was so abused in the later Middle Ages that in the revision of the Missal in 1570 only 4 sequences were retained: for Easter, *Victimae paschali* (attributed to Wipo, d. 1050); for Pentecost, *Veni, sancte Spiritus* (attributed to Pope Innocent III, d. 1216); for Corpus Christi, *Laude Sion* (St. Thomas Aquinas, d. 1274); for Requiem, *Dies Irae* (Thomas of Celano, 13th c.). *Stabat Mater* (attributed to Jacopone da Todi, d. 1306) was later added for the two Masses of the Seven Dolors. The sequence, distinguished by its position in the Mass from the hymn, is characterized by its deep solemnity, its tendency toward allegory and symbolism and its emphasis upon the Sacraments. In the 12th c. the school of St. Victor, esp. Adam, used the sequence to create a renascence of faith and devotion to the Virgin. The great sequences of the following c., *Stabat Mater* and *Dies Irae,* are "the supreme productions of the poetical genius of the Franciscan movement and the last authentic voices of Catholic hymnody." (Raby, p. 452.)

Antiphon (*antiphona,* whence *anthem*) basically denotes any practice of singing by statement and response, wherein the chorus is divided into separate choirs or cantors and choir. The practice seems to have originated with David (I Chron. 6, 31 ff.). Pliny (*Epist.* 10, 97) testified that the Christians sang their hymns *secum invicem. Antiphona* has been used to denote the Psalms themselves, or a sacred composition, or compilations from the Psalms or other Scripture, or any reading to which there is a musical response. But it eventually came to denote specifically a sentence sung alone as an interpolation or beginning or end.

Chant (*cantus*) denotes the musical arrangement in any hymnody. In ecclesiastical music, it has come more specifically to refer to the type of melodic composition used by the Church before the invention of polyphonic arrangements. This music is especially associated with the name of Pope Gregory I (d. 604), who developed a school of music at Rome where the Gr. modes imported by Ambrose two c. earlier were revised. The character of Gregory's personal contribution to this development is disputed.

Dreves and Blume, *Analecta Hymnica Medii Aevi,* 1866–1922, 55 v.; Karl Young, *The Drama of the Medieval Church,* 2 v., 1933; Father Britt's *The Hymns of the Breviary and Missal,* rev. ed., 1936, trans. the major hymns; G. Reese, *Music in the Middle Ages,* 1940; F. E. Raby, *Christian Latin Poetry,* 1927; L. F. Benson, *The Eng. Hymn,* 1962; M. W. England and J. Sparrow, *Hymns Unbidden,* 1966. CHARLES W. JONES.

hypallage. A figure of speech in which there is a reversal of the natural relation between two words or components of an idea, *e.g.* (Spenser) "Sansfoy's dead dowry" (instead of Dead Sansfoy's dowry).

hyperbaton. The inversion or transposition of idiomatic word order for emphasis, e.g., "roared the lion." Anteposition: using a word ahead of its normal place. A reversal of order, hysterology; if this creates a startling or preposterous effect, "the cart before the horse": hysteron proteron, *e.g.,* "when we had climbed the cliffs, and were ashore." (This is at times a fault; sometimes used to suggest tension or strong emotion.) If confined to two words, Anastrophe, *e.g., quibus de rebus, which things concerning.* If the transposition is intricately intermingled, synchysis, *e.g.* (Milton) "Is piety thus and pure devotion paid?"

hyperbole. Exaggeration for other ends than credence, *e.g.,* "virtues as the sands of the shore;" "But still fought on nor knew that he was dead!" *Cf.* Auxesis; meiosis. Sometimes considered as the general term, things made either greater or less; in such use, includes meiosis.

hypercatalectic. *See* Acatalectic.

hyperdochmiac. A trochaic tripody catalectic, — ∪ — ∪ —.

hypermetric. 1. A verse in which the final syllable is elided before the vowel that begins the following verse. 2. A verse with an additional syllable at the end, *e.g.* (Shak.) "Each substance of a grief hath twenty shadows."

hypobacchius. Antibacchius, *q.v.*

hypocorism. (Use of) a pet name, *e.g.* honeybunch. Not infrequent in lyric poetry.

hyporchema. Gr. choral lyric (Thaletas, ca. 665 B.C.) sung during pyrrhic dances in honor of Apollo.

hypostatization. A figure in which an abstracted quality or force is spoken of as an entity or human, *e.g.,* Virtue is its own reward; Honor compels me. Akin to personification.

hypotyposis. Representation of something as though present, *e.g.,* "Across the housetops of my native city I see the old tower . . ." Pragmatographia: an action as though witnessed. Vivid description of something as though present: diatyposis. Of a precise physical object: icon. Countenance of a real person: prosopographia.

hypozeugma. *See* Zeugma.

hysteron proteron. Putting before what should come after, *e.g.,* "My dame that bred me up and bore me in her womb." There is an herb called *filius ante patrem;* (Wordsworth) "The child is father of the man." *Cf.* Hyperbaton.

I

IAMBELEGUS. A form of Archilochian verse, *q.v.*

iambes, les. Fr. Used in the plural to indicate a bitter, satirical poem: 12-syllable alexandrines alternate with an 8-syllable line, the rhymes *croisés* (*abab*).

iambic. A metrical foot, a short syllable followed by a long, ◡ —. First used by Archilochus, 7th c. B.C. Used in Gr. in numerous verses and combinations. It is considered by Gr. writers to approximate more closely than any other the rhythm and character of ordinary speech, as it does in Eng.

iambic trimeter. A line of 6 iambic feet (*cf.* Syzygy), perhaps with a stronger stress on alternate feet. Used early for satirical or abusive effect (Archilochus, Semonides), it became the main meter of the episodes in Attic tragedy and comedy, as also in L. drama.

icon. Presentation of physical appearance, by direct description or imagery, *e.g.*

> Her bosom sleak as Paris plaster
> Held up two balls of alabaster.

Cf. Hypotyposis.

ictus. The stress on a syllable in verse; accent, *q.v.* It has been suggested that verse has a fundamental appeal (and in human history preceded prose) because the time from one stress to the next corresponds to the time between heart beats, while the length of a line corresponds roughly to the rhythm of breathing. This is manifest in the heave-ho songs of oarsmen and other workers.

ideal spectator. (1) A character in a play (the Shakespearean fool, the Gr. chorus, the Fr. *raisonneur*) who assumes the emotions or raises the questions the dramatist would like to have the audience feel or express. (2) The imaginary perfect audience or spectator of a work, at whom the author aims his work. The ideal spectator may be (a) the wide reading public, follower of fashion, target of the pot-boiler authors who hope for a hit or a best seller; (b) less greedily, but democratically, "the average reader," "the man in the street." Tolstoi appealed to the unspoiled moujik (who did not respond); Molière tried his plays on his pastry-cook; (c) the aristocrat of taste, whom Shakespeare (Hamlet's advice to the Players) called "the judicious . . . the censure of the which one must in your allowance o'erweigh a whole theatre of others." The best sellers may appeal to many for a few seasons; the best works may appeal to a comparative few for many generations. *Abie's Irish Rose* (1922) ran in New York for 2,237 consecutive performances; the longest single run of *Hamlet* (Sir Henry Irving's, 1874) reached 200. *Cf.* Reader, ideal; fame.

idealism. In philosophy, a metaphysics is said to be "idealistic" if it asserts that reality is, in the last analysis, a form of mind, or spirit, or something very similar to them. Idealism is thus opposed to naturalism (*q.v.*). Literary works are sometimes called "idealistic" when they express such a metaphysics, but in a more general sense a literary work is said to "idealize" human nature if it tends to emphasize the finer and nobler qualities of human beings, and to minimize or ignore their capacity for evil; in this sense "idealism" is opposed to "realism" (*q.v.*).

When the term "idealistic" is applied to literary criticism, it often means that the critic is concerned with the general ideas, or the Weltanschauung, of a literary work, and that in evaluating the work he takes into consideration its cognitive or revelatory aspect. *See* Truth.

idiolect. The sum total of the speech habits of an individual, his personal combination of the resources of his native tongue. *See* Language.

idyll (Gr., a little picture; image). Applied by scholiasts to the poems of Theocritus —mythological and epic as well as pastoral; to the odes of Pindar. The word had reference only to poetic form, short, descriptive, dramatic. As later distinguished from "eclogue," "idyll" was again extended to include epic, romantic, and tragic themes treated in verse (Tennyson, *Idylls of the King*; Browning, *Dramatic Idylls*). But like "pastoral," a word embracing content as well as form, "idyll" and "idyllic" came to suggest a mood of ideal quiet, content, and happiness, in verse or prose. Unlike "pastoral," "idyll" thus has not been subject to an orderly and logical evolution. For prose idyll, *see* Short story. M. H. Shackford, "A Definition of the Pastoral Idyll," *PMLA* 19, 1904.

illusion. Coleridge, in his declaration that the receptor grants a work of art "a willing suspension of disbelief," understates; we come to the work willing, but it must win our belief. Konrad Lange goes too far (*see* Æsthetics) when he says "the essence of æsthetic appreciation is conscious self-deception." Voltaire calls illusion "the queen of the human heart"; but she proves too oft deceiving. There are two sorts of illusion: fantasy creating a new world; realism leading the receptor to identify the world within the work and the world without. Occasionally, esp. in the drama, the illusion is deliberately broken. The slave in *Pseudolus* (Plautus, 191 B.C.) turns and talks to the audience about the play; so does the slavey in *The Skin of Our Teeth* (Thornton Wilder, 1942) as do many characters and "narrators" in recent drama. *Cf.* Escape; Truth; Narrator.

image, imagery. (1) Eliz. A figure of speech, esp. vision. (2) An expression evocative of an object of sensuous appeal. It usually serves to make an impression more precise; it may, on the other hand, carry the mind from too close a dwelling on the original thought. "Wealth," *e.g.,* may suggest millionaires and markets, may be glamorously "of Ormuz and of Ind," or be

beyond
The dreams of misers crouching on the hearth
And every spark a treasure . . .

and light a new lane of fancy. The number and variety of images, either figurative or direct, varies greatly in both poetry and prose. Shakespeare's song "When icicles hang by the wall" (*LLL*) is all literal imagery; his *Sonnet 123,* "That time of year thou mayst in me behold," is almost all figurative imagery; "Who Is Sylvia?" (*TGofV*) has virtually no imagery at all.

The value of an analysis of imagery in the elucidation of a work, even in establishing authorship, and esp. in understanding the author's nature, was indicated by the Rev. Walter Whiter (1793) and elaborated by Caroline F. E. Spurgeon (*Shakespeare's Imagery,* 1935) and her followers. Such absurdities in classifying, however, as listing "blanket of the dark" as an image drawn from 'Household Goods'; and the recognition that "Who's loony now!" may show in the speaker knowledge neither of water-fowl nor of moon-madness, indicates the extreme caution (*cf.,* L. H. Hornstein, "Analysis of Imagery," *PMLA* 57, 1942) with which the method must be applied. R. Tuve (*JHI* 3, 1942) pointing out that images may be conceptual as well as perceptual, maintains that the proper basis for their classification and analysis is their logical function. Susanne Langer (*Mind,* 1967) points out that "an image shows how something appears; a model shows how something works. The art symbol, therefore, sets forth in symbolic projection how vital and emotional and intellectual tensions appear, *i.e.,* how they feel." The purpose of an image is to intensify the feeling evoked with an idea. *Cf.* Symbolism. G. Hough, *Image and Experience,* 1960; A. K. Weatherhead, *The Edge of the Image,* 1967; Rosemond Tuve, *Elizabethan and Metaphysical Imagery,* 1947.

imagination has been variously defined: as a power responsible for visual images, singly or in association; as the capacity for making from these images ideal combinations of character and objects, on the one hand, and chimeras and castles in Spain, on the other; as a sympathetic projection of the artist into character and situation; as the faculty which creates the symbols of abstract conceptions; as the poetic equivalent of mystical intuition; and as creation itself, the "shaping power" inherent in man.

The meaning of the critical term has usually reflected its definition in philosophy and psychology. Plato distrusted *phantasia* (translated by *imaginatio* in late L.) as a function of the lower soul responsible for illusions and opinions; but in the *Timaeus* he recognized its capacity, transcending reason, for mystical vision. Aristotle, redefining it in *De Anima,* III, iii, in relation to other faculties, described its highest capacity as furnishing the schemata of thought. This account, with Plato's hints for a mystical view, determined the definitions in criticism for 2000 years. In the Middle Ages psychological description of a reproductive and combinatory function, often with distrust, prevailed, save in the views of some mystics who recognized a suprasensible imagination. Only in Dante's *l'alta fantasia* (as opposed to a lower capacity) was there full recognition of a transcendent poetic capacity.

The Renaissance, with a pervasive distrust of imagination and fancy (then synonymous terms) as disturbing to the life of reason, provided scattered materials for constructive views in poetics: in Mazzoni's *Difesa di Dante* (1572–1578), Fracastoro, Tasso, Sidney, Ronsard, Puttenham, and Huarte. Bacon (*Adv. Learning,* 1605), asserting that the poet's imagination may "at pleasure join that which nature hath severed," was repeating a commonplace.

Empiricism and rationalism, prevailing in the 17th c. (Descartes, Gassendi, Malebranche), provided an unfavorable milieu for critical definition. Hobbes described fancy as "decaying sense," and he shared with Davenant and Cowley the notion of a decorative function: "Judgment begets the strength and structure, and fancy begets the ornaments of a poem." In an age that stressed wit (*q.v.*) at the expense of imagination, Dryden alone extended the range of the critical term, asserting that after plot and character "the execution was the principal employment of the poet, as being the largest field of fancy; . . . 'tis fancy that gives the life-touches."

Addison's *Pleasure of the Imagination* (1712) was a retrogression from Dryden's insight: under the influence of associational psychology he confined his treatment to visual images in the fine arts and developed in terms of imagination an æsthetic of taste. He was followed by Gerard, Kames, Alison, Akenside, and Delille. L. A. Muratori (*Della Perfetta Poesia Italiana,* 1706) and A. Conti (*Trattato de Fantasmi Poetici,* before 1748), replying to French neo-classic attacks, and the Swiss æstheticians, Bodmer and Breitinger, stressing the imaginative nature of metaphor, made substantial contributions. Leonard Welsted (*Dissertation,* 1724) also asserted that "Imagination is as much a Part of Reason, as is Memory or Judgment, or rather a more bright Emanation from it."

With the Wartons the century approached views familiar among the Romantics: Joseph (*Essay on Pope,* 1756) preferred Spenser for his "creative and glowing imagination," and Thomas (*Observations,* 1754) found graces "where the force and faculties of creative imagination delight because they are unassisted by those of deliberate judgment." The grounds of preference of Hobbes and his contemporaries were thus reversed. Hurd (*Letters,* 1762) could demand "a *strong imagination* . . . enabling the critic to feel the full force of his author's excellence."

Romantic poets and critics found the grounds, both in mysticism and in the new German philosophy (Kant, Schelling) for a redefining of the imagination (*Einbildungskraft*), no longer a passive recipient of impressions, but an active agent conferring upon external nature its significance and unity. For the mystic Blake the imagination was "spiritual sensation," "the Eternal Body of Man." The material world of 18th c. empiricism had for him no existence, and Reason was a spectre and a negation. For Coleridge, influenced by both mysticism and German philosophy, the primary imagination was "a repetition in the finite mind of the eternal act of creation in the infinite I AM"; in this "esemplastic" process the thinking subject and its object "coalesce." Wordsworth accepted this view when describing imagination as

absolute power
And clearest insight, amplitude of mind
And Reason in her most exalted mood.

These views of a transcendental power are found also in Jean Paul Richter (*Vorschule der Aesthetik,* 1804), Schiller (*Naïve and Sentimental Poetry,* 1795), Goethe, Shelley, and Emerson (*Letters and Social Aims,* 1865).

The application of this new metaphysics of the imagination to criticism was revolutionary, especially in defining metaphor as the result of creative thinking rather than as superficial decoration. Coleridge and Wordsworth employed various verbs in describing the process of imaginative composition (unify, abstract, modify, aggregate, evoke, combine), and Hunt, Hazlitt, Ruskin, and others added to the vocabulary, not always in the service of clarity. Rejecting the notion that figurative language is adventitious decoration, they described poetic language as the result of the activity of the whole sentient being, involving processes which, in the absence of a more precise term, they called "imagination." This frequently involved distinguishing it from "fancy" (*q.v.*). Blake emphasized the "double vision" of the imaginative artist, as opposed to the scientist's blinkered concern:

Twofold always. May God us keep
From single vision, and Newton's sleep.

The task of the imagination is to grasp and make clear the "unity in multeity" of the objective world, and the "multeity in unity" of the subjective world.

In recent years there has been sporadic interest in defining this "seminal principle," both by elaborating and by supplementing romantic views. Ribot (*Essai sur l'imagination créatrice,* 1900) explains genius in many fields (mathematics, science, poetry) as the result of creative imagination. He pictures three levels: (1) *imagination ebauchée* (initial), the realm of the transient, the irrational: dreams, vague hopes; (2) *imagination fixée* (set) myth, speculative theories, art; (3) *imagination objectivée* (practical; the mature stage): invention; discovery of truth.

There have also been further attempts to contrast the roles of imagination and reason. Man's body, it is pointed out, is affixed to its present being; man's mind moves constantly to the future or the past. In youth imagination (expectation) colors the things to come; in age imagination (reminiscence) colors the things that have been. There is thus a constant incompatibility between human conceptions and human performance; reason would diminish this, but imagination will have it so. F. C. Prescott (*The Poetic Mind,* 1922) has made interesting use of Freudian psychology. Croce (*Aesthetic,* 1902) with his contrast of imagination (as intuition) and intellect has been perhaps the greatest contemporary influence. *Cf.* Wit; Genius; Spontaneity; Romantic. M. W. Bundy, *The Theory of Imagination in Classical and Medieval Thought,* 1927; "Invention and Imagination in the Ren." *JEGP* xxix, Oct. 1930; Coleridge, *Biographia Literaria,* ed. Shawcross, Introd.; I. A. Richards, *Coleridge on Imagination,* 1934; D. G. James, *Scepticism and Poetry,* 1937; R. D. Havens, *The Mind of a Poet,* ch. X, 1941; S. Chandra Sen Gupta, *Towards . . . Imagination,* 1959; J.-P. Sartre, *L'Imagination,* 1948, trans. 1962; J. Chiari, *Realism and Imagination,* 1960; E. J. Furlong, *Imagination,* 1961; A. W. Levi, *Lit., Philos. and Imagination,* 1962; S. Spender, *The Imagination of the Modern World,* 1962; H. O. Rugg, *Imagination,* 1963; N. Frye, *The Educated Imagination,* 1964; J. Bronowski, "The Reach of Imagination," *Am. Scholar,* Spring 1967. Murray W. Bundy.

imagism. Attitude of a group of British and Am. poets, whose aim was to restore to poetry the precise use of visual images. The intellectual background of the movement was supplied, indirectly, by T. E. Hulme, whose own poems, containing a dry precision of imagery, were Imagist models. Ezra Pound was the most important organizer of the movement, in 1912; Amy Lowell took charge in 1914, whereupon Pound seceded to Vorticism (John Gould Fletcher, Richard Aldington, Hilda Doolittle, F. S. Flint). They were influenced by Chinese and Japanese poetry, by Fr. and classical Gr.

Flint, writing in *Poetry,* March 1913, enunciated 3 Imagist rules: "Direct treatment of the 'thing,' whether subjective or objective; to use absolutely no word that does not contribute to the presentation; as regarding rhythm: to compose in sequence of the musical phrase, not in sequence of a metronome." *Des Imagistes: an Anthology* was published in 1914; Amy Lowell edited 3 anthologies, *Some Imagist Poets,* 1915–17. A backward-looking collection of poems of the dissolved Imagist movement was published at Richard Aldington's suggestion: *Imagist Anthology,* 1930; W. C. Pratt, *The Imagist Poem,* 1963.

imitation, in ancient theory, usually meant the rhetorical discipline of imitating literary models. Two of the most important events in ancient criticism were Plato's attack upon poets as imitators at the second remove from truth (*Rep.* 597 E) and Aristotle's vindication of poetry as an imitation (*i.e.,* representation) of the ends toward which cosmic Nature strives (*Phys.* 199a 15 ff.; *Poet.* 1451b 5 ff.). But Plato's attack had little effect on ancient literary practice, and Aristotle's *Poetics,* soon dropping out of notice, did not begin to exert its vast influence until the treatise was recovered in the 16th c. The rhetorical discipline of imitating models, however, first emphasized in the school of Isocrates (*Against the Sophists,* 18), fostered by the later Gr. schools of rhetoric, descended to Rom. times as a regular part of the training for writing either prose or poetry.

While most aestheticians today consider imitation at best a schoolboy's exercise, others saw it as the artist's essential task. Gr. painters esp. sought the illusion of actuality. A horse whinnied at Alexander's horse in Apelles' painting. Zeuxis was thought to have won a contest because birds flew down to peck at his painted grapes—until Zeuxis asked Parrhasius to draw back the curtain covering his picture: the curtain *was* the picture. Today, Resphigi had a nightingale's song recorded, for use in his music, *Pines of Rome.*

Throughout Rom. literary theory a fairly homogeneous idea of the methods to be used and the results to be striven for in imitating literary models prevailed. It is an error to regard this discipline as an exercise in plagiarism. Cicero recommends the imitation of Demosthenes because he wishes the orator to learn the methods, and, if possible, to master the literary tact (decorum) of this best and most versatile model in dealing with any theme or circumstance (*De Or.* I, 260; II, 90–92; III, 71; *Br.* 288; *Or.* 23 ff., 100 ff.). Horace requires that the poet steep himself in the normative tradition of poetic practice exemplified by the Gr. (*A.P.* 268–9); he holds that such imitative discipline is quite distinct from plagiarism (*A.P.* 133–35; 240–42; *Epist.* I, xix, 21 ff.) and perfectly compatible with the representation of empirical reality in the finished poem (*A.P.* 317–18). Longinus regards the imitation of great models as a means of developing habits of lofty thought, feeling, and expression through sustained study and emulative practice (XII, 2–4; XIV, 1–2). In the Renaissance, the writer's chief duty was held to be the imitation of nature, in one or more of its various senses; and such imitation was reconciled with the imitation of models either by regarding the latter practice as merely regulative of the major aim (*e.g.*, Petrarch), or by identifying the literary example and precepts of the ancients with the universal principles decreed by cosmic Nature (*e.g.*, Minturno, Scaliger). Renaissance theorists in general, however, regarded the practice of imitating models as a method subservient to the end of imitating (*i.e.*, reproducing the literary likeness of) universal Nature and Truth.

Though a few 19th c. writers reinterpret the idea of literary imitation in relation to such concepts as nature and imagination (*e.g.*, Coleridge repeatedly praises the literary imitation of *natura naturans* as the representation of life "raised and qualified by an imperceptible infusion of the author's own knowledge and talent" as distinct from the mere copying of *natura naturata, Biog. Lit.* ed. Shawcross, II, 30, 255 f.; cf. *C.'s Shaks. Crit.* ed. Raysor, I, 200 n.; cf. also Hazlitt, *Works*, ed. Howe, IV, 72 f.; XVI, 62 f.), the term imitation is gradually abandoned in literary theory and criticism as its suggestions of the second-hand or spurious become more prominent; and with the abandonment of the critical concept "nature" as well, the phrase "imitation of nature" yields to such terms as realism, naturalism. Stevenson drew the censure of critics by his acknowledgement of "playing the sedulous ape" to Hazlitt and others (though *cf.* George Sampson). The practice of imitating models has now few advocates; yet it is notable that T. S. Eliot ("Tradition and the Individual Talent") has described a discipline in a normative literary tradition in some ways suggestive thereof. *Cf.* Expression; Form; Mimesis; Narrator; Triad; Verisimilitude.

R. McKeon, "Lit. Crit. . . . Imitation in Antiquity," *MP* 34, 1936; G. C. Fiske, *Lucilius and Horace*, 1920; D'Alton; I. Scott, *Controversies over the Imitation of Cicero in the Ren.*, 1910; H. O. White, *Plagiarism and Imitation during the Eng. Ren.*, 1935; J. W. Draper, "Aristotelian Mimesis in 18th C. Eng.", *PMLA* 36, 1921; G. Sampson, "On Playing the Sedulous Ape," *Essays and Studies*, 6, 1920. HAROLD SOWERBY WILSON.

impressionism. An attitude that believes in conveying to the receptor the impression something has made upon the author, rather than an exact description from which the receptor can gain his own impression. It therefore is less concerned with particulars and details than with words that will directly induce a state of mind or mood. *Cf.* Subjective.

incremental repetition. Iteration with an advancing of the story; common (questions and answers; refrain) in early poetry, and ballad. For an example, *see* Canaanite poetry.

Indian drama, *nāṭya*, is an imitation (*anukṛti*) of an action (*avasthāna*). The mimetic dance (*nṛtya*) conveys the meaning of the words (*padārtha*), the mood (*bhāva*) and the flavor (*rasa*). Dramas are classified according to their subject (*vastu*), the nature of the hero, and the predominant flavor. The themes of the great dramas are derived from the epics, thus indirectly from the myths. Of the ten typical forms of the drama, the *Nāṭaka* is deemed best. The plot has 5 parts (seed, expansion, episode, incident, denouement); the action has 5 corresponding situations (taking hold, effort, promise of success, assurance of success, fruition) which may be dealt with in 5 acts (*aṅka*); and finally there are the 5 conjunctions (*sandhi*): the opening (*mukha*, protasis), counter-opening (*pratimukha*, epitasis), (*garbha*, that which is to be produced), delivery (*avamarśa, vimarśa*), and gathering-up (*saṁhṛti, nirvahaṇa*, catastrophe). The development of a plot is paralleled to that of a living organism; the denouement or catastrophe, in which "those meanings that had been scattered, in due place are reduced to one," corresponds to what takes place at an individual's death.

The chief writers of the classical drama were Aśvaghosa, Bhāsa, Kalidasa—often referred to as the Shakespeare of India—Harṣa, Bhavabhūti, and Rājaśekhara. The main surviving types of drama are the Kathakali (dance drama) of the South; and the Rās Līlāa Yātrās in the North, which are essentially mystery plays of the Krishna stories. These have been presented for at least two millennia; Patañjali (2d c. B.C.) speaks of those that "slay Kaṅsa before our eyes." The Indian shadow play (*chāya-nāṭaka*), found also in Burma, Siam, China, and notably in Java and Bali, projects shadows upon an upright canvas by means of a light behind; the audience watches the shadows (not the leather puppets) while the narrator roars out the battle scenes or chants the story. *Cf. Rasa.* A. B. Keith, *The Sanskrit Drama,* 1924; D. R. Mankad, *The Types of Sanskrit Drama,* 1936; Coomaraswamy and Duggirala, *The Mirror of Gesture,* 1936. ANANDA K. COOMARASWAMY.

Indian literary theory. There can be distinguished a Vedic period (ca. 1200–1 B.C.) in which *kavi* and *kāvya* are rather prophet and the prophetic art that finds expression in the verse forms of the liturgical incantations (*mantra*) than poet and poetry in the literary sense of the classical period (ca. 1–1200 A.D.). The incantations have a meaning (*artha*) to be understood. The Vedic seer is inspired by Fire or Sun or Indra; hence the designation of scripture as revelation, or more literally hearing (*śruti*), to be distinguished as such from tradition or memory (*smṛti*). At the same time the Vedic prophet takes a legitimate pride in the great skill with which he puts into words what it is given him to say.

The key word in the later rhetoric is flavor (*rasa, q.v.*). The Spirit is at once flavor of all existence, truth (*satyam*), and beatitude (*ānanda*), on which all life depends. Mind (*manas,* grammatically neuter but metaphysically masculine) the superior, and Voice (*vāc,* feminine) the inferior, form a syzygy of conjoint principles, celestial and terrestrial, sacerdotal and regal, inner and outer man, fiat and factor. Whatever is said truly is a concept (*saṁkalpa*) born of their sacred marriage and promulgated as science or art (*vidyā*). "The flower and fruit of speech is truth; the great litany, her supreme adaptation." The emphasis on truth as the last end of speech is carried over into Buddhist rhetoric. "Truth is the sweetest of flavors." There are 4 degrees of oratory (*vāda*): one who is in possession of the "four analytical powers" will be a master as regards both the correct enunciation of the text and the exposition of its meaning. These four powers are those of the ethical application (*attha*), spiritual doctrine (*dhamma*), hermeneutics (*nirutti*) and illumination (*paṭibhāna*). Illumination is the product of innate vision (*sahaja-netta*), arising as an afflatus (*udāna*). There are likewise 4 degrees of hearer: those that understand immediately, or upon reflection, or must be led, or never get beyond the words of the text.

Throughout the texts there is constant use of figures (*upamā*), teaching by means of metaphors and parables being called the parabolic path (*adhivacanam patha*); the style of the scriptures, as Clement of Alexandria says, being parabolic, but not for the sake of beauty of diction. But the Buddha foresees that his profound (*gambhīra*) discourses will some day be neglected and that only the work of poets (*kavi*) in the poetic style (*kāvya*), with decorated syllables (*cittakkhara*), will be heeded.

Rhetoric, so far, is implicit in the general principles of phonetics, metrics, and etymology, and their use in the communication of truth. Innumerable treatises discuss the true nature of poetry and the poetic drama; they are classed under the general heading of *Alaṁkāra-śāstra,* the science of the use of figures. Before discussing the later theory of poetic and dramatic expression we must premise that (1) poetic refers to a quality that may or may not be present in what is formally either prose or verse; *e.g.,* scientific treatises may be written in verse, but are not therefore poetry; (2) we are considering a spoken much more than a written language, and (3) the word *alaṁkāra* itself, although it often means ornament, originally meant equipment, a sense that is retained for the rhetoricians, for whom the function of the figures, whether of sound (*śabdālaṁkāra*) or meaning (*arthālaṁkāra*) is more demonstrative than æsthetic; as had been the case in the *Ṛgveda,* where many figures (*upamā*) are already employed; and the verb *alaṁ kṛ* means only to prepare or furnish.

The classical *Nāṭya-śāstra* of Bharata (4th c. A.D. or earlier) is the oldest extant separate treatise on poetic and dramatic expression. After Bharata, the rhetoricians are too many to be cited in detail. The most important include Bhaṭṭi (Bhartṛhari) author of the *Bhaṭṭikāya;* Daṇḍin, author of the *Kāvyadarśa* (*View of Poetry*); Udbhata, author of *Alaṁkārasamgraha* (*Conspectus of Ornament*); Vāmana, Bhāmaha and Rudraṭa, each the author of a *Kāvyālaṁkara* (*Ornament of Poetry*), all of the 8th c.: Rājaśekhara, author of the *Kāvyamimāṁsa* (*Remembrancer of Poetry,* ca. 900); Ānandavardhana, author of the *Dhvanyāloka* (*Contemplation of Suggestive-resonance,* ca. 850); Abhinavagupta, author of the *Locana* (*Illumination,* a commentary on the *Dhvanyāloka*) and of the *Abhinavabharati* (*Goddess of Speech,* 10th–11th c.);

Dhanaṁjaya, author of the *Daśarūpa* (*Ten Dramatic Types,* late 10th c.); Mammaṭa, author of the *Kāvyaprakāśa* (*Light of Poetry,* 11th c.); Kṣemendra, author of the *Aucityālaṁkāra* (*Propriety of Ornament,* 11th c.); Viṣvanātha Kavirāja, author of the *Sāhitya Darpaṇa* (*Mirror of Literature,* perhaps the masterwork of the whole list, 13th c.); and Nandikeśvara, author of the *Abhinaya Darpaṇa* (*Mirror of Gesture,* 13th c.). These are followed by others and by the vernacular authors, notably Keśava Dāsa, author of the *Kavipriyā* (*Poetical Endearment*) and the *Rasikapriyā* (*Endearment of Connoisseurship,* 16th c.); Jasvant Singh, author of the *Bhāṣa Bhuṣana* (*Ornament of Language*); Bihāri, author of the *Sat Sai* (18th c.) and his commentator Lāla Candrika (19th c.).

What is commonly understood by the expression "Indian rhetoric" is contained in this whole body of literature, from Bharata on. The 4 basic ornaments or figures (*alaṁkāra*) are those of simile (*upamā*), metaphor (*rupaka,* also meaning drama; *cf. rupakāra,* sculptor), illustration (*dīpika*), and alliteration (*yamaka*). Some authors regard these figures as the essential of poetry, but the consensus is that figures are rather the means than the spirit of poetry. Metaphor involves the notions of imitation (*anukṛti*) and likeness (*sādṛśya, sārupya*), the latter by analogy rather than verisimilitude. Figuration involves also the qualities (*guṇa*), *e.g.,* of clarity (*prasāda*), strength (*ojas*), sweetness (*mādhurga*), characteristic of different styles (*vṛtti, rīti*). The essential doctrine, that "Poetry is a statement informed, or animated, by flavor" (*vākyam rasātmakaṁ kavyam*) distinguishes the body (sound and meaning) of poetry from its very "self," an infused flavor; just as in the man, body and soul are distinguished as the vehicle from the immanent spirit.

The conditions conducive to the tasting of flavor (*rasāsvādana*) are (1) the component æsthetic surfaces of the work, its whole situation or extension (*vibhāva*), (2) the consequents (*aunghāva*), *i.e.,* the significant words and gestures of the characters, (3) the emotions or moods (*bhāva*), whether dominant or transient, and (4) the involuntary reactions (*sattvabhāva*) natural to the character under the given circumstances. It will be observed, of course, that our good or bad "taste" has nothing to do with this "tasting," but only with the distinction between what may be virtues (*guṇa*) or defects (*doṣa*) in the work of art itself. The flavor to be tasted, however it originates, is itself an invariable constant, and beyond analysis because it can be known only in the actual experience of tasting, just as many flavors are confused in the single taste of honey. In other words, the ultimate experience is not empirical, not a natural (*laukika*) emotion or pleasure, but supernatural, at once beatific and contemplative (*ānanda-cin-maya*), connatural with the tasting of God. That "the flavor is void of contact with things perceptible" is as much as to say that a catharsis of all æsthetic distractions and analytical interests is prerequisite to the tasting. Thus, while only madmen give expression to or take delight in sounds without meaning, the last end of poetry and drama does not lie in their logic but in the beatitude, to which sound and meaning are only the preamble and support.

A related approach is based on the analysis of meaning. In any poetic expression, there is a literal denotation (*abhidhā*), an intended connotation (*lakṣaṇā*), and a power of manifestation or suggestion (*vyañjanạ*) thought of as an inaudibly reverberant overtone (*dhvani, cp.* Chinese *yün*), with ultimate reference to the eternal syllable (*oṁ, akṣara*) enunciated by the Sun as a Word that may be called the single form of all words, and apart from which as an immanent principle the existence of separate words and meanings would be impossible. There is an almost universal agreement that a merely decorative poetry (*citra kāvya*), in which figures of sound or meaning are employed only for their own sake without suggestion or flavor, scarcely deserves to be called poetry. The "light of the creative power" (*kārayitrī pratibhā*) by which the poet works may be either innate (*sahaja*), acquired (*āhārya*), or dependent on instruction (*aupadeśika*). Finally, it must be mentioned that all of the rhetoric outlined above is not exclusively a matter of the verbal arts, but represents a general theory of imitation and expression that is also applicable, and is actually applied, to the interpretation of the plastic arts, in which the appeal is not to the ear, but to the eye, and to drama, which appeals to both. A. B. Keith, *Sanskrit Drama,* 1924; *A Hist. of Sanskrit Lit.,* 1928; A. K. Coomaraswamy, *Transformation of Nature in Art,* 2nd ed., 1935. ANANDA K. COOMARASWAMY.

Indian poetry (in Sanskrit. Prakrit poetry of medieval India, and the poetry of the modern vernaculars, in the main follow the old technique, content, spirit. The chief exception is Urdu poetry, which is based on Persian poetry and is the vehicle of the Mohammedan culture of India and Pakistan.)

The Vedas are the ritual-books of the earliest Indic period (ca. 2000—ca. 500 B.C.) from which we have literary records. Chief work is the Rigveda, a collection of over 1,000 hymns to the gods. Composition was oral, with traditional lines and tags. The essence of the form of this poetry is that each verse is a separate unit grammatically (it may be further subdivided into sentences), usually in thought as well. The meters are based on syllable-counting with syllabic quantities fixed, without too much rigidity, for the end-cadences of lines; usually stanzas consist of three or four lines. The language is an archaic Sanskrit, full of complexities of inflexion that allow a very free word-order, with a general effect similar to that of classical L. and Gr. lyrics.

The second great body of poetic material is in the two epics, the Mahābhārata and the Rāmāyaṇa (3rd c. B.C.). The epic technique is also marked by the use of traditional tags. For the most part, the meter is the *śloka* (*q.v.*), akin in its principles to the Vedic meters. A notable difference is that the stanza is not treated as a unit of grammatical construction and of sense, which may flow on. The *śloka* is suited to pedestrian narrative or exposition, when the subject is more important than artistic values; it has therefore been used almost to our time to present the myths and dogmas of Hinduism, and for technical treatises on philosophy, mathematics, literary criticism, medicine.

The third division of Sanskrit poetry consists of the *kāvya.* This stems in part from the Rāmāyaṇa and carries to an extreme the tendency seen there of attention to the embellishments of the verse. Form and ornament are more important than subject-matter. There is a long gap between the epic and the first extant *kāvya* work, that of Aśvaghoṣa (1st c. A.D.); during this gap Sanskrit ceased to be spoken except by men of learning, but remained the only language deemed fit to be a vehicle for Hinduism. Many attempts at the elaboration of the new style were made, but few survived the searching criticism that —along with difficulties of reproduction and preservation of mss.—winnowed out and preserved only what was regarded as the best. The works of the Buddhist Aśvaghoṣa survived precariously in Nepal; within India and Hinduism, the earliest preserved works are those of the greatest master of the style, Kālidāsa (4th or 5th c. A.D.); the other survivals virtually end in the 12th c., all later being imitative.

The *kāvya* is dominated by a conscious striving for flavor. This style tended toward display of cleverness, culminating in works where every syllable has two meanings, through which perhaps Śiva and Krishna are celebrated at once.

The *kāvya* continued from Vedic times the technique of treating the stanza as a sense-unit. Each stanza is independent in its production of flavor. This works havoc with the continuity demanded by narrative, but leads to neat epigrammatic statement. All is generality; the personality and life of the poet hardly appear. The language being dead, highly artificial linguistic effects were cultivated: long compounds; identification of synonyms; rare words; nominal instead of verbal sentences. All this makes much of the poetry hard to understand. The chief meters of *kāvya* verse, unlike those of the Veda and the epic, are quantitative, with the quantity of each syllable rigidly fixed; practically all have four identical lines to the stanza; syllables in the line run from 8 to 26. Keith describes 78 such meters. The *śloka* also is common. Not all *kāvya* is in verse; æsthetic theory recognized prose as a suitable vehicle for poetic effects. *Kāvya* has been used in Prakrit tongues. A. B. Keith, *A Hist. of Sanskrit Lit.,* 1928. M. B. Emeneau.

induction. Early term (Eng.) for introduction or prologue. Esp. of a framework; *e.g.,* Sackville's "Induction," *Mirror For Magistrates,* 1559. Shakespeare uses the "Induction" of *The Taming of the Shrew* as a device to set quick-tongued actors among the gay bloods onstage, so as to match their wit with impromptu rejoinder.

inevitability may mark the close of a literary work, from various points of view. To the childlike vision (of whatever chronological age; *see* Receptor) there is no other end for a villain than to be foiled, though this is esp. delectable when he is "hoist with his owne petar" or (fairy tales; *Arabian Nights*; *Bible, II Samuel* 12, Nathan to David: "Thou art the man!") pronounces his own doom. This poetic justice conversely with equal inevitability sets the youngest son upon the upmost peak of conquest. More mature works present an inevitability that grows out of character: given such an individual in such circumstances, the rest will logically follow. The tragedies of Shakespeare present a more life-like complexity. In them (*Romeo and Juliet; Hamlet*; *Macbeth*; *Lear*) the general movement is thus predetermined; but the instant and the avenue of doom are seemingly haphazard: the delinquent friar; the exchanged poisoned foil; death is implacable, but around any corner may reach his hand. *Cf.* Truth; Coincidence.

inkhorn (A portable vessel for carrying ink, 14th–18th c.). In the Elizabethan period, an inkhorn term was one drawn from the classics and thought to be bookish or pedantic. A person or work using many or lengthy neologisms was said to smell of the inkhorn.

in medias res (L., into the midst of things). The standard way of opening an epic. Used in fiction, also, to gain instant interest. Contrasted (Horace, *Satire* 1) with *ab ovo, q.v.*

innuendo (a medieval term used to make a reference explicit.) An oblique hint; esp., a derogatory meaning not literally in the words, but understood from them. A frequent device in satire, *e.g.* (Pope):

Now night descending, the gay scene is o'er,
But lives in Settle's numbers one day more.

inspiration (L. *in-spiro,* breathe into). A poet is said to be inspired when he is believed to function not in the same way as other workers, not depending on his own intellectual powers, but acted upon by a superior force that determines the quality of his work. Thus, Plato says in the *Ion,* a worthless poet may, if inspired, produce excellent poetry, while an able poet, when uninspired, may be unable to compose anything of value. A poet calls on the Muse—even though conventionally—because poetry is not a mere personal matter. A frequent misuse of the term might here be noted: when Sidney says "Stella behold, and then begin t'endite," when poets are prodded by external objects, they are stimulated, not inspired; inspiration is a possession within: thus Sidney again: " 'Fool,' said my Muse to me, 'look in thy heart, and write.' "

Some artists warn against yielding to inspiration; *e.g.,* the sculptor Rodin, the novelist Flaubert (ed. J. C. Tarver, 1895, p. 67): "You should mistrust everything that resembles inspiration, for it is often nothing more than a deliberate determination and forced excitement . . . Besides, Pegasus walks more often than he gallops; genius consists in knowing how to make him take the pace we require." Some sort of belief in inspiration seems nevertheless fairly constant, though its nature is modified in response to the prevailing doctrines of society. Thus the word cannot properly be used by a rationalist, as it implies a belief he does not share. After Freud, for whom inspiration wells from the "unconscious," the surrealists sought to create in the absence of conscious, or rational, control. It should be observed, however, that all that glisters in moments of "inspiration" is not gold; inspiration is what the receptor too must feel within the work. (Note that the word enthusiasm comes from Gr. *entheos,* the god within.)

The bohemian artist, lounging in the Latin Quarter or loafing in Greenwich Village, believes that inspiration (possession of the poet by a non-phenomenal being or force from outside of himself) is alone sufficient for the creation of art. The classical artist feels that education and training, knowledge of the rules, are essential, for the inspiration to work with and upon. This is a reason why some deem it important to determine whether the plays of Shakespeare could have been written by a cantankerous son of a glover with "little Latin and less Greek," or must be the product of a learned or noble spirit, as a Bacon or an Oxford. Much that is most felicitous in a poem seems just to "pop into the mind"; but the quality of that mind, and the scrutiny it takes of the "popped" material, must also be taken into account. *Cf.* Imagination. A. H. Gilbert, *Literary Criticism, Plato to Dryden,* 1940; K. Gilbert and H. Kuhn, *A Hist. of Esthetics,* 1939; J. Maritain, "The Dark Night of Poetry," *Kenyon R.,* 1942; G. B. Woodberry, "The Inspiration of Poetry," *The Torch,* 1920; C. M. Bowra, *Inspiration and Poetry,* 1955; R. Harding, *An Anatomy of Inspiration,* 1940, 1967. ALLAN H. GILBERT.

intensity. Under various terms (Gr. *tonos;* L. *vis,* vigor; Hazlitt, gusto, zest; Baudelaire was roused to *volupté*) intensity has been advanced as a criterion of great art—rather (says Peyre) "than sincerity, personality, or even profundity of ideas . . . The test of validity for a novelist or a poet should be not only 'Has he felt passionately what he has expressed?' but 'Has he felt or imagined intensely, and does his inner fire burn through his words?'." Peyre does not make clear the difference between feeling passionately and feeling intensely, nor explain how one can judge whether an author has "imagined intensely"—though he warns against confusing melodrama, vulgarity, and "hysterical art" with works truly intense. The criterion thus seems, like sincerity or integrity, to be wholly subjective. H. Peyre, *The Failures of Criticism,* 1967.

intention. *See* Literary criticism.

interior monologue: consciousness, stream of, *q.v.* *See* Monologue.

interpretation. I. To interpret a sign is to declare its meaning (*q.v.*), *i.e.,* to present another sign that has the same meaning. A complete interpretation of a literary work, considered as a complex linguistic sign, would be a different discourse that is identical to it in meaning, a paraphrase if it is in the same language, a translation if it is in a different language. Because complete interpretation is, in practice, nearly always impossible, it is customary to use the term "interpretation" in somewhat more special ways: (a) Exhibiting the ideas in a literary work, *i.e.,* the meanings of its symbols or the philosophical or social doctrines implicitly contained in it. This is not complete interpretation, but abstraction of part of the meaning of a work: its "message" or "ideology." The term "paraphrase" is used in a similar way, in the controversy over the "heresy of paraphrase" (*see* Cleanth Brooks, *The Well Wrought Urn,* 1946, ch. 11). (b) Explication, which involves analysis. The problems of interpretation, in the sense of explication, are of two sorts: (i) problems of discovery: such as finding the range of possible primary and secondary meanings of the words, construing the syntax, identifying the structural relationships among elements; and (ii) problems of choice, which arise from what is often called ambiguity (*q.v.*), when the critic must decide whether a certain possible meaning of a word can be assigned to the work (that is, to the word in that context) or not. In making such a decision, critics sometimes appeal to the intention of the author, sometimes to the coherence of the work; and they sometimes deny that there can be any appeal beyond the reader's association of ideas (impressionistic criticism). *Cf.* Sign; Language; Intention; Explication; Meaning. A. Kaplan, "On the So-called Crisis in Criticism," *JAAC* VII, Sept. 1948; C. L. Stevenson, "Interpretation and Evaluation," *Philosophical Analysis,* ed. Max Black, 1950; M. C. Beardsley, *Æsthetics,* ch. 3, 9, 1958; E. D. Hirsch, *Validity in Interpretation,* 1967; S. R. Hopper and D. L. Miller, ed. *Interpretation,* 1967. II. Developing a work along lines suggested by the original: (a) rendering or performing, as in the presentation of a play, or the reading aloud of a poem. (b) transforming a work from one form into another, as in the adaptation of a novel for the stage. MONROE C. BEARDSLEY.

introduction. *See* Speech, Divisions.

invention (Gr. *heuresis;* heuretic). (1) First of the 3 divisions of rhetoric (dispositio, elocutio), concerned with the finding of arguments. These (Aristotle; the middle ages) may be sought through reason, the morals, or the affections. (2) The term was expanded from oratory to include the initial survey or "discovery" of material in all literary forms. In Renaissance poetics it was redefined as a power of creating materials by new combinations of sensory experience, fiction, or the "fair feigned fable," and thus was loosely synonymous with wit, imagination, and fancy (Hawes, Ronsard, Daniello, Castelvetro, Gascoigne, Puttenham, Harvey). It was frequently coupled with elocution as comprehending both poetic substance and style. In the 17th c. also, invention was paired with wit, the prevailing critical term; but it sometimes reverted to its rhetorical signification: "The first happiness of the poet's imagination is invention, or finding of the thought" (Dryden, *Annus Mirab.,* 1666). Sometimes (Temple, *Of Poetry,* 1690) it was "the fruit of genius" and "the mother of poetry." In the 18th c. it gradually supplanted "wit" as a comprehensive term for poetic capacity (Pope, *Preface to the Iliad,* 1715: "It is Invention that in different degrees distinguishes all great geniuses."). Its synonym, imagination, predominated by the end of the c., relegating invention in Romantic theory to the function "by which characters are composed out of materials supplied by observation" (Wordsworth, *Preface,* 1815). The older meaning, the creation of fiction as opposed to fact, persisted throughout the 19th c. M. W. Bundy, *"Invention" and "Imagination" in the Renaissance,* JEGP, XXIX, Oct. 1930. MURRAY W. BUNDY.

inversion. A reversal of the normal order. Though frequent in poetry, it is as often attacked. Cowper says it gives dignity to English; Dryden: "We were whipt at Westminster if we used it twice together" (for rhyme); Wordsworth attacks it in Scott. Most frequently it consists in placing (1) an adjective after its noun (2) an object before its verb (3) a preposition after its noun. Pope's *Iliad* begins:

Achilles' wrath, to Greece the direful spring
Of woes unnumbered, Heavenly goddess, sing!

Homer's own first word is "wrath." In prose, inversion is the normal order in questions and exclamations; it occurs in conditional expressions (Had the plane left on time, it would not have been caught in the storm) and is frequent for emphasis. *Cf.* Hyperbaton; Zeugma.

invocation. Appeal (to the Muse; occasionally to a patron or the beloved) usually near the beginning of a long poem, for inspiration in its writing. Continued as a convention long after the belief in Muses. *Cf.* Inspiration.

ionic. A metrical foot of two long and two short syllables; *a majore* — — ∪ ∪; *a minore* ∪ ∪ — —. Found early (Alcman, 7th c. B.C.; Alcaeus, Sappho, 6th c. B.C.). Often with anaclasis; thus in Anacreon (late 6th c. B.C.). Two such feet usually became ∪ ∪ — ∪ — ∪ — —, the Anacreontic meter.

irony. I. (Gr. *eironeia,* originally applied to the manner of speech and behavior of a stock character of early Greek comedy, the *eiron.* He was the natural antagonist of another stock figure, the boastful *alazon,* who sought to achieve his ends by deception through exaggeration. The *eiron* was an underdog—small and frail, but sly and resourceful; he regularly triumphed over the bullying *alazon* by his ingenuity, his skill in dissembling his knowledge and his powers.) The term "irony" always preserves the essence of its original meaning. The Socrates of the Platonic dialogues, in his modesty, his profession of ignorance, his readiness to concede points of view at variance with his own in order to demonstrate their absurdity by assuming his opponents' very premises, shows his kinship to this comedy character. The originality of the *Socratic irony* consists in the adaptation to dialectical ends in the search for truth of the *eiron's* technique of self-effacement, understatement, and the encouragement of an opponent's excessive self-confidence.

Irony in Greek tragedy, while in no direct sense an outgrowth of this comic device, shows the same elements, but with an enormous enrichment of the concept. "Fate," or the "will of the gods," gives the fundamental direction to the movement of the play. The chief character of the play is frequently, like Œdipus, proud and willful, offends the gods by some excess in character, and from the beginning of the play is headed for a doom to which he remains blind up to the very end. Here can be seen most clearly the elements that are essential to irony: an ironic will, *i.e.,* a will (the gods or fate) that prepares the sudden disillusioning of a deluded character; a victim; and a spectator (the audience; sometimes, other characters within the play), for whom the reversal of fortune, the *peripeteia,* betrays an unmistakable "mocking" intent on the part of the powers that be. Irony in Greek tragedy may be seen as an aspect of the Greek moral view: it was the device by which the *lex talionis* operated, by which punishment was meted out to those who defied the gods. Irony was a heightened way of asserting the golden mean, of re-establishing an equilibrium, where a fault of character led to a wide breach between appearance and reality.

The frequent employment of the various devices of irony implies an attitude similar to that of a spectator at a Greek tragedy, an attitude of detachment and sophistication and a tendency to perceive life in terms of the incongruities that occur between appearances and reality. In Erasmus, Montaigne, Chaucer, Swift, Voltaire, Thomas Hardy, Joseph Conrad, Henry James, Anatole France, irony is more than a literary device; it may be said to inhere in their outlook on life, and their employment of its many technical devices is dictated by this outlook.

Verbal irony is a form of speech in which the words intentionally or unintentionally belie the real meaning, producing a sense of incongruity in the spectator and sometimes in one or more of the persons involved in the verbal situation. Thus the words of Lady Macbeth when Duncan's visit is announced:

He that's coming
Must be provided for . . .

may be understood at one level as referring to the performance of the duties of hospitality, but with sinister mockery actually express her resolve to have the king murdered.

Dramatic irony, also called *tragic irony,* is a device whereby ironic incongruity is introduced into the very structure of the plot, by having the spectators aware of elements in the situation of which one or more of the characters involved are ignorant. The words and actions thus have, in addition to their natural tragic impact and their value as furthering the action of the play, the peculiar relief which they derive from the contrast between the spectators' knowledge and the characters' ignorance. The supreme example of dramatic irony is Sophocles' *Œdipus Tyrannus,* in which the hero, all unwittingly, builds up the elaborate structure for his own undoing.

As suggested by the origins of the term, irony may be associated with comic as well as tragic effects. It is frequently found in the French farce (*e.g., Maître Pathelin*) and *fabliau,* in the tales of Boccaccio, the *Canter-*

bury Tales, the comedies of Molière and Shakespeare.

The phrase "irony of fate" figuratively assigns to fate the role of an ironic will that mocks men's plans, as pervasively in Thomas Hardy (*The Dynasts; Life's Little Ironies*). Renan and Anatole France tended to look upon life as an ironic spectacle contrived by a mock-god for his diversion; they portrayed the human tragi-comedy from the point of view of this putative god. Anatole France's linking of irony with pity (in *Le Jardin d'Epicure*) suggests that the ironic attitude is associated with tolerance and that its detachment may be tempered with sympathy. The extremely subtle effects to which irony may be put are perhaps best exemplified, among moderns, by Henry James.

Radical irony is a statement that contains its own ironic denial, as when a Cretan declares that all Cretans always lie. Thus Baudelaire both prays to the Lord and blasphemes.

Romantic irony is a term first used by Friedrich Schlegel to designate the objectivity of a romantic work (specifically Shakespeare's) which nevertheless reveals the subjective qualities of the writer, an idea suggested to him by an analogy of the author's relation to his work with God's relation to Creation. According to this conception the most objective work most adequately reveals the author's essential subjective qualities—his creative power, his wisdom, breadth; and the poet is at once creator and observer. This use of "romantic irony," however, is peculiar to Friedrich Schlegel. With Ludwig Tieck, Goethe, Heine, and subsequent writers, the term served to designate the attitude of the romantic writer deliberately destroying the illusion of objectivity in his work by the intrusion of his own personality, "hot baths of sentiment," as Jean Paul says of his own novels, being "followed by cold douches of irony." One of the most often-quoted examples is Byron's *Don Juan,* esp. Canto iii, cvii–cxi. J. A. K. Thomson, *Irony,* 1926; H. M. Chevalier, *The Ironic Temper,* 1932; C. G. Sedgewick, *Of Irony, Esp. in the Drama,* 1935; R. B. Sharpe, *Irony in the Drama,* 1959; N. Knox, *The Word Irony and its Context, 1500–1755,* 1961. HAAKON M. CHEVALIER.

II. *Surprise, suspense, dramatic irony,* form a climactic order of theatrical devices. Surprise has its effect but once; therefore Lope de Vega: "Keep your secret to the end. The audience will turn their faces to the door and their backs to the stage as soon as there is no more to learn." Modern mystery plays may bear a program request that the end be kept secret. Shakespeare, esp. in tragedy, seldom uses surprise (*e.g.,* Othello takes the "turban'd Turke" by the throat). Trollope objects: "Let the personages of the drama undergo for us a complete Comedy of Errors among themselves, but let the spectator never mistake the Syracusan for the Ephesian." Lessing is still more emphatic; but Edith Hamilton distinguishes two types of comedy: (1) (Terence; Molière) of ingenious plot, closely woven, built on surprise and suspense; (2) (Plautus) of loosely connected funny scenes, based on dramatic irony. Terence's *Mother-In-Law* ends "Don't let's have it like the comedies where everyone knows everything," and two characters keep the solution to themselves.

If in a melodrama a sleeper is roused by a stumbling in the next room, he is surprised. Grasping a revolver and awaiting a further footfall, he remains in suspense (poised expectancy). An uninformed audience may share his feelings. But if the audience knows that this intruder, who in a moment will face that revolver in the hands of a frightened man, is the man's own son, unwittingly stolen into the rooms of the man that had once driven him away, expectancy is keyed to a higher pitch. Thus dramatic irony sets the receptor in the flow of forces greater than the characters themselves, gives him a sense of participating in the determining drive, of being on a plane with destiny. Note that this power holds even with a known plot (Gr. tragedy told stories familiar to the audience); that knowledge may even strengthen the hold: when we hear Lady Macbeth's casual remark "A little water clears us of this deed" and we await the anguish: "All the perfumes of Arabia will not sweeten this little hand." III. P., "the dry mock." In irony, the receptor must be conscious of the dissembled meaning; the victim (sometimes even the speaker) is not. In sarcasm, the victim also is conscious of the double intent. Much irony works through understatement, meiosis, *e.g.* (Swift): "Last week I saw a woman flayed, and you will hardly believe how much it altered her person for the worse." Antiphrasis: by contrast: "See yonder giant!" of a dwarf. Asteism: polite banter. Charientism: a smoothing joke; intended as a slight, but glossed over so that it must be taken with a smile. Chleuasm: a jeer, a mock. Diasyrm: a reproach. Mimesis: a mimicking. Mycterism: a sneering expression. *Cf.* Sarcasm; Satire.

irrational. From the divine furor of classical inspiration and Socrates' *daimon* to the Freudian unconscious, to the surrealists and the literature of the absurd, there has been a persistent though usually minority claim that the creation of literature is an irrational process. From the notion that the poet is "possessed," some have moved to seek a deliberate discarding of reason, either by an act of the will or by the use of drugs or other stimulants. This denial of the intellect (as in D. H. Lawrence's "thinking with the blood"), said Bertrand Russell, "led straight to Auschwitz." *Cf.* Dream; Surrealism; Unconscious; Absurd; Rationalism. Wayne Chumaker, *Lit. and the Irrational,* 1960, 1966.

ithyphallic verse. Composed in the meter of the Bacchic hymns; priapean, licentious. Also applied to the form trochaic dimeter brachycatalectic (— ∪ — ∪ — ∪ × ×), by some called trochaic tripody. Used by Archilochus, early 7th c. B.C.; also in epode, or to conclude a series of other verses, as the phalaecian.

ivory tower (Sainte-Beuve, of Alfred de Vigny). The detached and aloof position from which certain artists are said to contemplate the world. Praised by some as a *sine qua non* of high achievement; attacked by others as a devitalizing withdrawal from the world. Thus it has been pointed out that "Goethe gave all his life to literature, but never lifted a finger to help a human cause." This, intended as condemnation, must not be inconsiderately regarded as such. The artist's products may be a gift greater than any participation in current controversy; some men may be able to combine writing and public affairs, but the life of Milton—not to mention such recent careers as of MacLeish and Sherwood—warns us to ponder; of some, it may be the condition of their art that they do not engage their sympathies in absorbing concerns of life.

J

JACOBEAN (reign of James I of England, "the wisest fool in Christendom," 1603–25; since some of the patterns of Elizabeth's reign continue, sometimes referred to as Jacobethan). James himself was a writer, of two books on poetry, of *Daemonologie,* 1599, which resulted in stricter laws against witches, of *A Counterblaste to Tobacco,* 1604, which did not stop the widening use of the weed. But he was a pedantic and unpopular ruler, insisting on the divine right of kings; and the split between the gay Cavaliers and the dour Puritans widened, toward Cromwell and the Revolution. In literature the period was rich. Drama grew more conscious of the problem of evil, in the late plays of Shakespeare, in the caustic comedies of Jonson, in the grim tragedies of Webster (*The White Devil, The Duchess of Malfi*), Tourneur, Ford, and esp. *The Changeling* of Middleton and Rowley. At the same time royal patronage encouraged the masque, with elaborate stage effects. In poetry came on the one hand the clarity of Jonson, on the other the metaphysicals with Donne. Prose was more concise and flexible in Bacon's essays, with Burton's *Anatomy of Melancholy,* and made its greatest gift to the language in 1611, the King James Version of the *Bible,* on which 47 ministers had worked for seven years. *Cf.* Elizabethan; Metaphysical. R. Ornstein, *The Moral Vision of Jacobean Tragedy,* 1966.

Japanese drama. The Nō are lyric dramas, popular for 600 years. They were all (about 300) written before the 16th c. Kiyotsugu (1355–1406) crystallized existing fragments of poetry, probably written by Buddhist monks, into the dramas now classical. He also availed himself of the *kagura* (pantomimic dances), a part of the Shinto festivals.

There are generally from 2 to 6 actors in a Nō drama: the hero (*shite*); his companion (*tsure*); a sort of deuteragonist (*waki*) who, representing the audience, wears no mask; and his companion; a child (*kokata*), and a supplementary actor (*ahi*). The stiff formality of their costumes, together with the beautiful masks and wigs, completely disguises the fact that all Nō actors are men. The ancient language of the Nō is difficult for any save the most cultured of the Japanese; until 1868, the Nō was the exclusive prerogative of the upper classes. When the Meiji Restoration abolished class distinctions, the common people found they could neither understand nor enjoy the Nō. Then the *kabuki,* long popular—though in its origin, first with women players, then with boys, it had been suppressed (1629; 1652)—became established. The word *kabuki* is formed of 3 ideographs: "singing," "dancing," "art." The form is rather like operetta; the dialogue is chanted, with many songs and dances. Intellectual appeal is subordinated to emotional. Make-up, costumes, scenery, technique of acting, text, are exaggerated to heighten the sensuous effect—in direct contrast to the technique of understatement of the Nō. The *bunraku* (puppet play) is also entertainment for the common people. Many of the plays (*jōruri*) in the *kabuki* repertoire follow the puppet style, which came into favor when the *kabuki* was temporarily prohibited on the ground of the actors' immorality. A. Wiley, *The Nō Plays,* 1921; Z. Kincaid, *Kabuki,* 1925; Y. Yoshikawa, *Jap. Drama,* 1935; Shoyo Tsubouchi, *Hist. and Characteristics of Kabuki,* 1960; L. C. Pronko, *Theatre East and West,* 1967. LA MERI.

Japanese poetry has been an integral part of Japanese culture throughout recorded history. There are millions of Japanese that not only read poems constantly, but also make a practice of composing them.

It is necessary to say a few preliminary words about the language. Japanese has five vowel sounds, *a, i, u, e,* and *o,* all short sounds, pronounced very much as in Italian. In poetry and in precise speech 2 vowels coming together are pronounced separately; the word *ookii* has four syllables *o-o-ki-i*. In ordinary speech there is some elision, esp. of the *u* sound, (as *imas'* for *imasu*) and, in the interior of words, of the *i* as well (*e.g., imash'-*

tai for *imashitai*). Every Japanese syllable ends in a vowel; it is thus obvious why rhyme has never been popular as a poetical device in Japan. Furthermore, there is no marked accenting of syllables in Japanese; rhythm consists in an alternation of shorter and longer word-groups.

The oldest extant Japanese poetry is found in the annals called *Kojiki* and *Nihongi,* from the early years of the 8th c. A.D. The first great written collection of poems was the *Manyoshu,* the "Collection of Ten Thousand Leaves," compiled in the early 9th c. and comprising over 4,000 poems. Most of these are *tanka,* short poems of thirty-one syllables. Practically all the rest are *nagauta,* "long poems." They are classified under the main heads of "The Four Seasons," "The Affections," "Elegies," and "Allegories." The *nagauta* is in alternating lines of 5 and 7 syllables, adding another of 7 to mark its end. Certain devices appear in early poems: balanced clauses; pillow words (conventional phrases, epithets); pivot words (related to the idea before and to that following; often making the shift by being used in 2 senses, as a pun). Gradually one length, 5-7-5-7-7-, became standard as the classic poem—so much that the word 'poem,' unqualified, means to a Japanese this form—the *tanka.* The *tanka* of the *Kokinshū* (ca. 922 A.D.) display an exquisite finish hovering on the edge of artifice, an emotion usually more delicate than powerful. Later *tanka* tried to preserve the delicacy, but in the hands of several poets the emotion grew somewhat more powerful. The following, (Saigyo Hōshi, in the *Shin-kokinshū*) retains the syllabic succession in translation:

Ima zo shiru
omoi-ide-yo to
chigirishi wa
wasuremu tote no
nasake narikeri

Now indeed I know
That when we said "Remember!"
And we swore it so,
It was in "We will forget!"
That our thoughts most truly met.

The writing of *tanka* has continued to the present, with annual imperial contests. The form, however, does not enjoy the same widespread popularity that it had in the Middle Ages, most of the recent work being somewhat formal and archaistic.

The *renga,* "linked poems," were a development from *tanka.* Their origin goes back to the traditional period, but esp. under Gotobain in the early 13th c. In these, 2 or more poets alternately compose in the 14 (7, 7) and 17 (5, 7, 5) syllable meter, the theme of each composition being suggested by its predecessor. The favorite number of a poetical team seems to have been 3, and the standard number of alternations, 10. They are, of course, a sequence, not single poems. The linkages should not be so obvious as to be dull, nor so esoteric as to be obscure. A team of poets usually worked, unrehearsed, surrounded by a discriminating audience. In time rules developed, *e.g.,* the successive seasons had to be referred to at stated intervals.

The *hokku* or *haiku* is the shortest form of Japanese verse. It consists of 17 syllables (5, 7, 5), like the 1st part of a *tanka.* It is, however, a complete poem by itself, and in its short compass can give a picture and a mood, and in the hands of a master, considerably more. The 1st extant *haiku* dates from the early 13th c.; *e.g.* of Fujiwara no Sadaiye, one of the compilers of both the *Shin Kokinshū* and the *Hyakunin Isshū*:

Chiru hana wo
oikakete yuku
arashi kana

A fluttering swarm
Of cherry-petals;—and there comes,
Pursuing them, the storm!

The form was constantly used, but chiefly at first for light inconsequential verse and word play. *Haiku* did not come into its own until the advent of Matsuo Bashō (1644–94). His *haiku* are mainly simple direct pictures of actual scenes, yet from them one gets not only the effect of a temporary mood, but also a companionship with a true and noble spirit. The so-called "second pillar" was Taniguchi Buson (1715–85). He was a master of technique, in love with novelty, and in spirit at opposite poles from the calm serenity of Bashō. Some idea of his quality may be obtained from the following pair, both dealing with spring rain. The first is in formal court language; the second is colloquial.

harusame ya
dōsha no kimi no
sasamegoto

Ah, the rains of spring
Dear lady driving with me here,
Your whispering!

harusame ya
kawazu no hara no
mada nurezu

Spring rain! And as yet
The little froglets' bellies
Haven't got wet!

Perhaps the best-loved of all the *haiku* poets is Issa (1763–1827). He had a sad life, and a consuming love for all living things:

katatsumuri
soro soro nobore
Fuji no yama

Snail, my little man,
Slowly,—oh, very slowly—
Climb up Fujisan!

When Issa died he left no school behind him, and Buson's followers fell more and more into an artificiality comparable to that before the advent of Bashō. A vigorous reform was started by Masaoka Shiki (1867–1902); *haiku* took on new life. He both preached and practised genuineness, was a merciless critic of all loose and slip-shod work. He popularized the purely objective *haiku,* the effect of which he likened to that of a painting.

Kumo no mine
shiraho minami ni
muragareri

Mountain-peaks of cloud;
White sails, in the south,
Crowded together . . .

It is doubtful what can be properly called poetry outside of the *nagauta, tanka, renga,* and *haiku.* It must be mentioned, however, that many of the *monogatari* (tales or novella) are at least akin to epic poetry. There is no other epic poetry in Japan; and some of them, such as the *Heike Monogatari* (*Tales of the Taira*) were for centuries chanted to accompaniment of musical instruments. There are chants connected with the popular theater, such as the *jōruri.* There are the Nō plays. There are the century songs, there are the humorous and semi-humorous "poems," some of which, like the *dodoitsu* (7-7-7-5), have special forms of their own. The *senryū* is a sort of comic *haiku,* as frequent (and as frequently unprintable) as the Eng. limerick. There is the great mass of "new" poetry, much of which has true poetic content, but most of which, partly influenced by western modes, has not yet crystallized into form. *Cf.* Haiku; Tanka, B. H. Chamberlain, *The Classical Poetry of the Jap.,* 1880; C. H. Page, *Jap. Poetry,* 1923; A. Waley, *Jap. Poetry,* 1919; K. Yasuda, *The Jap. Haiku,* 1958. H. G. Henderson.

jargon (originally, the chatter of birds). 1. Unintelligible combinations of words; often a term of contempt for something not understood. 2. Barbarous or debased expressions, esp. from a mixture of languages. 3. The special speech (cant) of a group or class, unlikely to be understood by outsiders; *e.g.,* when a man has a headache, his doctor may say: "You're suffering from cephalalgia." Esp. 4. Language more technical than is needed, as "verbal behavior" for "speech." *Cf.* Slang.

jest book. The *geste,* or exploit of the knightly romances, came for the middle-class townsman to be a realistic and often ribald anecdote. Collections of such jests became popular, esp. in G., after the *Hundred Merry Tales,* Eng. ca. 1526. Latin sources were the *Facetiae* of Poggio (1380–1459) and H. Bebel (3 v., ca. 1506). Sometimes the jests were attributed to a single man, as *The Gests of Skoggan,* ca. 1565. Sharp ridicule, practical jokes, on the whole range of bourgeois life. A popular form ever since.

Jesuitical writing. Verse (rarely, prose) in two columns, with opposite meanings according as you read down or across:

Who calls you shy, he tells the truth,
He's a lying youth who says you're sly.

It is sometimes written in successive lines, to be read 1, 2, 3, 4, then 1, 3, 2, 4, etc. In French, such verse is called *rime brisée. Cf.* Palindrome.

jeu parti (Fr. Prov., *juoc partitz; partimen*). A debate poem, fl. 13th c. Two persons, actual or represented; the argument proceeds in alternate stanzas. Usually in a final refrain the discussion is referred to some patron for judgment. Love problems were the most frequent topics. Such poetic contests are frequent in pastorals: Theocritus; Virgil, 3rd and 7th Eclogues. In Spenser's *Shepheardes Calendar, August,* the alternation is not by stanzas but by lines. See Old Fr . . . forms; *Débat.*

Johnsonian. Of the style of Samuel Johnson (1709–84), the "high style" of self-conscious utterance, with balanced phraseology and Latinic diction. When thought to be pompous or stilted, referred to as Johnsonese.

journal. *See* Autobiography.

judgment. The arrival at (or the faculty whereby we attain) a decision regarding a work. Two types: (1) æsthetic, "This poem is sublime"—spontaneous, involving one experience, the feeling blended with the work; (2) scientific, "This poem has sublimity"—meditated, two experiences intellectually joined, a relationship but not identity. The individual basis of opinion; thus Pope:

'Tis with our judgments as our watches, none
Goes just alike, yet each believes his own.

Cf. Taste; Wit; Value.

K

KABUKI. *See* Japanese drama.

karagöz. The traditional Turkish shadow-puppet play. Translucent colored puppets of camel hide (about 14 inches in height, save for Efe, who is twice as tall) are held against a translucent screen with a light behind. They are operated with a rod at the top of the spine, sometimes with a second rod at the base. A well equipped puppeteer may have 500 puppets, which are handed to him by assistants who, however, except for quick assertions or denials, do not work them behind the screen. The manipulator is also the narrator; he speaks in short rhyming lines, with quick interchange of remark and retort, and much verbal play. There is considerable improvisation on the basic story, with satire of current events and joking with the audience.

Some 30 of the traditional stories are extant, among them *Karagöz in the Bath, Karagöz Musician, Karagöz Public Letter-Writer,* and *Pleasures of Yalova Hot Springs.* The typical story begins with the lazy Hadjivat seeking amusement, and the earnest Karagöz (whose name was given to the plays) with a problem that Hadjivat tries to help him to solve. Hadjivat uses literary language, and the simpler Karagöz (who represents the common people) constantly misunderstands him. Efe (the Turkish Robin Hood) usually comes to straighten matters out. Sometimes a magician figures in the story; there are always songs, and most plays end with a dance.

In early times the shadow plays were called *kabartchuk* or *kolkortchak*. Hadjivat and Karagöz are said to be actual persons of the 14th century, when Shayh Küşterî fixed the form of the plays, adding a mystical element, which survives in the opening overture and monologue. Modern theatre and cinema, however, are making the *karagöz* less widely performed. NUREDDIN SEVIN.

kenning. A type of circumlocution, or metaphor, common in Old Germanic verse. Found in Old Norse runic inscriptions, in O Eng., in the Edda (*e.g., vágmarr,* horse of the sea: ship) they are most frequent in the literary (non-popular) verse of the skalds. *See* Periphrasis; Epic.

kind. Term used esp. in 17th and 18th c. Eng. for genre or class of work, *e.g.,* epic, tragedy. Criticism by kind determined into which class a work fell, then examined whether it obeyed the laws of its kind. Consideration today of earlier works must take this attitude into account. Thus Dryden in his prefaces indicates that a writer's first step was to consider the "kind" he wished, then to seek the appropriate style; Pope (letters to Spence) said that in going over his work he asked, *e.g.* of an elegy: "These lines are very good, but are they not of too historical a strain?" Such considerations, then common throughout Europe, were later condemned as establishing "the tyranny of the kind," from which the Romantic Revolution sought to break free.

Wittgenstein suggested that classification by kind be replaced by the notion of "family resemblances"; but however ill-defined the borders may be, each literary kind has its own aims, conventions, and satisfactions. If a critic does not judge, say, the farce *A Trip to Chinatown* by the same standards as the tragedy *Œdipus Rex,* he is practicing criticism by kinds; and in some manner, even today, this usually comes into account. *Cf.* Genre. Northrop Frye, *A Natural Perspective,* 1965; Graham Hough, *An Essay on Criticism,* 1966.

kitsch (G. kitschen, to throw together). Term used to dismiss a work as a potboiler, without æsthetic worth.

Knickerbocker group. Writers during the first half of the 19th c. in New York, then beginning to rival Boston as a literary center. Took its name from Washington Irving's *Knickerbocker's History of N.Y.* (1809); included James Fenimore Cooper, who founded the Bread and Cheese Club, 1822, with

Bryant and Halleck among the members. The monthly *Knickerbocker Magazine* (1833–65) began when the group was moribund; it was hastened to its death by Poe's satire, *Literati of New York City,* 1846. The linkage of the members was loose, geographical.

Knittelvers. G. 16th c. verse, popularized by Hans Sachs. Rhymed couplets, with four stresses and 8 (or 9) syllables. Frowned upon by Opitz, it was supplanted by Fr. Alexandrines until used by Goethe (opening of *Faust I*) and Schiller (*Wallensteins Lager*). *See* Gc. versification.

Kyrie eleison. *See* Hymn.

kyrielle. A Fr. form: usually 8 syllable lines in couplets; or quatrains rhymed a a b b; the last word (or line or part of line) is repeated from stanza to stanza as a refrain.

L

LAI. The Breton *lai* is a romantic tale of adventure, in O. Fr. The Prov. *lai* is a love poem (occasionally a religious poem) of varying verse lengths within the same strophe. At first the words were adapted to an already popular tune, hence the irregularity of form. *See* Old Fr. . . . forms.

laisse; *tirade.* Fr. Running lines (of 8 or 10 syllables) assonanced; later, rhymed; the verse form of the *Chanson de geste. See* Old Fr. . . . forms; *Chantefable.*

lament. A poem of more grievous woe than a "complaint," *e.g.,* Deor's *Lament,* AS. (with consoling refrain "That was o'erpassed; this may pass also"); *Complaint of Buckingham* (added, 1563, by Sackville, to *A Mirror for Magistrates,* 1559). *See* Pastoral.

lampoon. A scurrilous or abusive satire, usually brief. Johnson's Dictionary defines it as "censure written not to reform but to vex."

language may be defined as a set of habits, learned in childhood by each member of a speech-community, that consists in the utterance of typical sounds (phonemes) in recurrent patterns (morphemes, units of linguistic form; and tagmemes, features of arrangement). The function of these utterances is to relay stimuli from one person to another, so as to provoke reactions in the person who hears the uttered signals of linguistic form. Morphemes, whether free (such as may occur as minimal utterances) or bound (such as occur only in combination with other morphemes), and tagmemes, usually recur in certain situations or connections. The meaning of a word (minimum free form) or other morpheme may be defined as the sum of those features common to all situations in which the form occurs, and absent from all those in which it does not occur.

The main function of language is social, in that it serves to bridge the gap between individual nervous systems. So far as each individual is concerned, his language is almost wholly a social product, in that it is a result of his contact with other persons; the child learns to speak from his parents and others around him. In the sphere of meaning, those elements that are conventional, or common to all speakers of a given community, may be termed the denotation of a word or form. On the other hand, language is an individual phenomenon in that it exists only as a set of habits in each individual. These sets of habits are never absolutely identical for any two speakers. Each speaker has slight variations within the range of permissible variants in the phonemes of his language, also in his use of morphemes. In addition to any form's denotation, there are emotional associations and reactions to words and forms, according to one's personal experiences, that differ from one speaker to the next. These residual features of meaning that are peculiar to one speaker may be termed the connotation of a word or form for that speaker.

The use of language as an artistic medium depends largely upon the combination in varying degrees of the social and individual aspects of any given author's speech. The author's purpose is to arouse certain reactions in his auditor or reader, usually reactions similar to those which the author ascribes to himself or to other real or fictional persons in certain situations. He will choose the forms that, in his judgment, will call forth these reactions in his readers, *i.e.,* that have for him and for them the desired denotation and connotation. In realistic or in naturalistic writing, *e.g.,* the element of connotation is either reduced to a minimum or else directed towards producing in the reader a sense of particular reality; whereas in imaginative writing, the element of connotation is stressed, by the use either of accustomed forms in unaccustomed ways or meanings, or of unaccustomed forms in place of customary ones (*e.g.,* exoticisms, dialect borrowings, archaisms). In literary use, connotation plays a dominant role in giving special effect to morphemes and tagmemes.

It is sometimes thought that one language is superior to another or more suited to literary use. Thus, we are told that the sounds of Eng. or G. are unmelodic or harsh as contrasted with those of the Romance languages, especially It. or Sp.; or that Eng. is superior to other languages because of the greater extent of its vocabulary. In the Renaissance it was widely believed that the modern languages, because of their simpler morphological structure, were inferior to Gr. and L. On closer examination, however, it is apparent that in these respects all languages have some advantages and some disadvantages, which roughly cancel each other out. In the end, all languages may be regarded as approximately equal in merit for both practical and æsthetic purposes either in actuality or in potentiality. The morphological characteristics of any given language, for example, simply determine the nature of those aspects of experience that can find formal grammatical expression (others, of course, can always be expressed by periphrasis). By this are determined, not the total range of what can be said in any language, but the essential literary characteristics of grammatical and syntactical style in that language. Thus, Chinese receives terseness and concision from its ultra-analytical structure, L., a close-knit complexity from its highly-developed morphology and free word-order, and Eng. (morphologically between the two) a certain looseness and freedom of expression. In the matter of vocabulary, popular legends about savage tribes or illiterate speakers having only a few hundred words at their disposal are utterly unfounded; the normal speaker of any language or dialect has many thousands of words at his disposal, and, in case he is lacking in a term for any new object or concept, he can always either form one out of his already existing vocabulary (as the Gr. and G.) or borrow terms from some other language or dialect (as the L. and Eng.). The effective literary use of any language depends, therefore, in the long run, not upon its phonetic or morphological characteristics or on the extent of its vocabulary at any given moment, but upon the cultural level attained by its speakers (a totally unrelated phenomenon) and upon the appearance of an individual (*e.g.*, Dante) gifted and bold enough to realize the peculiar potentialities of his native speech. *Cf.* Communication; Linguistics; Signs; Meaning; Semantics. E. Sapir, *Lang.*, 1921; J. Vendryes, *Le Langage*, 1921; L. Bloomfield, *Lang.*, 1923; *Linguistic Aspects of Science,* 1939; H. Gray. *Foundations of Lang.,* 1939; R. Jakobson and M. Halle, *Fundamentals of Lang.,* 1956; S. Ullmann, *Principles of Semantics,* 1957, 1959; H. D. Lewis, ed. *Clarity is not Enough,* 1963; B. Malmberg, *Structural Linguistics,* 1963; J. Reiss, *Lang. Myth and Man,* 1963; A. Martinet, *A Functional View of Lang.,* 1962; J. H. Greenberg, *Universals of Lang.,* 1963; P. L. Garvin, *On Linguistic Method,* 1964; O. Jespersen, *Mankind . . . from a Linguistic Point of View,* trans. 1964; Y. Bar-Hillel, *Lang. and Information,* 1964; E. H. Lenneberg, ed. *New Directions in the Study of Lang.,* 1964; V. C. Chappell, ed. *Ordinary Lang.,* 1964; R. M. W. Dixon, *What is Lang.?,* 1965; J. Katz, *The Philosophy of Language,* 1966. L. Hjelmslev, *Prolegomena to a Theory of Lang.,* 1961; S. Saporta, *Psycholinguistics,* 1961; H. B. Allen, ed. *Readings in Applied Eng. Linguistics,* 2nd ed. 1964; J. A. Fodor and J. J. Katz, ed., *The Structure of Language,* 1964; J. O. Hertzler, *A Sociology of Lang.,* 1965; J. Casey, *The Lang. of Criticism,* 1966; Eric Auerbach, *Literary Lang. and its Public,* trans. 1965; S. Chatman and S. R. Levin, eds. *Essays on the Lang. of Literature,* 1967; R. W. Langacker, *Lang. and its Structure,* 1967, 1968; Max Black, *The Labyrinth of Language,* 1968; N. Chomsky, *Lang. and Mind*, 1968. Robert A. Hall, Jr.

A speech may be a specific address to a particular public. More generally, a language (Fr. *langue*) is the set of symbols and their organization common to a community, whereas speech (Fr. *parole*) is, within this, the pattern of individual use. The two interact: speech must be based upon the conventional forms and structure; language develops and changes by way of the individual variations from the norms of application and organization of the symbols. Linguists call an individual's personal way of speech an idiolect.

lay (by extension from the Prov. *lai, q.v.*). A short narrative poem, as Scott's *Lay of the Last Minstrel;* Macaulay, *Lays of Ancient Rome.* A song or ballad.

lectio difficilior (L., the harder reading). Principle of choice between two ms. variants apparently equal in authority, *e.g.,* if in the *Book of Common Prayer* an editor were offered "Till death us *do part,*" variant "depart," or in Gay's *Trivia,* "Spongy *morsels* in strong ragousts are found," variant "morells"—he would adopt the variant, since no copyist would have chosen "depart" or "morells" as a probable improvement. Therefore, *depart* is the author's original word. The principle is of great value, but the tradition of the variant should be thoroughly examined. *See* Criticism, textual.

legend (L., to read; LL. *legenda,* a book of saints' deeds to be read in church. *Golden Legend,* Jacobus de Voragine, 13th c., collection of saints' lives). 1. Title beneath an illustration. 2. A history or account, *e.g.*, Chaucer, *Legend of Good Women*. 3. Unauthenticated narrative, folk-embroidered from historical material, sometimes popularly deemed historical. The legend has been revived in Slovene literature (Francé Bevk; Ludvik Mrzel), mainly biblical themes given a modern interpretation.

Leitmotif (G., guiding motive. Coined by Hans von Wolzogen of a musical theme identified with a character, object, or emotion, in Wagner's operas, heralding the approach of that person or feeling). Applied by Thomas Mann (1907) to an expression that as a unit bears a particular significance, *e.g.*, the Homeric epithet, the folktale repetition; though usually applied to formulas used to recall previous situations. They thus help economically to build a unified work. Petténi, *D'Annunzio e Wagner*, 1923. Motif is the earlier term.

letter. The letter is usually a direct address from the sender in the 1st person to the receiver in the 2nd, but since the communication may be made by a messenger who in fact or by conventional pretense recites or reads the message, the voice of the letter may be that of an intermediary, using the 3rd person to refer to sender and receiver; or the direct address of the letter proper may, as in Babylonian letters of the 2d millennium B.C., be enclosed within an address of sender to messenger directing what shall be said and to whom. The significance of such physical factors in determining a basic rhetoric is evident; it is only when the letter is written and transmitted without the intrusion of an intermediary, that it can be substituted for intimate conversation, and so come in theory to be regarded as essentially informal and familiar. In the West this maturity of the letter may be dated near the end of the 5th c. B.C. (in Greece). The classical letter included no direction to a messenger, and the vestigial 3d person of its detached heading (*salutatio*) did not affect, much less control, its rhetoric; in ancient correspondence, as in modern, the implication of a messenger's address by use of the 3d person is preserved only in very formal messages.

The modern letter is ordinarily a manifestly written thing, no implication of a bearer appears inside its cover, and its tone is that of conversation. But even when the physical conditions for informality exist, not all letters are informal, since not all speech between two persons is so. It is convenient therefore with the later L. rhetoricians to distinguish (a) the private letter (*personalis*) from (b) the letter of affairs (*negotialis*). Within these classes we may distinguish various types according to the principal ends of the writers, as narrative, expository, hortatory, consolatory, amatory; in the most ancient treatises on letter writing we find such distinctions already more numerous than logical. There is also (c) the open public letter, ostensibly addressed to an individual but actually intended for general publication. Its species are those of the private letter, but its main use has always been expository and didactic. Like the dialogue (*q.v.*) it is an apt medium for presentation of tentative conclusions and the mind's exploration toward them; but its proper range is greater than the dialogue's, for though it permits the rhetorical and logical relaxations of casual talk it is not, even ideally, confined to them. The pretense of limited address is sufficient to assure the public letter a permanent rhetorical elasticity denied the formal treatise.

In ancient rhetorical theory the private letter of friendship is generally taken as the norm of all letter writing, and the easy informality of friendly conversation as the ideal of epistolary style. Demetrius, in the most important classical treatment of the letter (*On style*, 223–235), makes "friendly feeling" (*philophronesis*) its informing principle, and requires that it be sincere, simple, brief, and plain (yet graceful) in style; but since it is written it is not to be so casually composed as conversation or a dialogue, and decorum may require a heightening of style when the addressee is a public personage. Other notable ancient discussions of the letter, generally similar in doctrine, are those of a probably earlier Demetrius whose *Epistolary types* is the oldest extant manual of letter writing; of Cicero and Seneca in their own letters; of the late rhetorician Julius Victor in his *Rhetoric* (27). In the middle ages, when official correspondence was an important business, manuals of letterwriting were produced in great number; and since the letter then supplanted the oration as the characteristic product of rhetorical art, most of the many mediæval treatises on rhetoric (*artes dictandi* or *dictaminis*) are in fact treatises on letter-writing. The doctrine of these treatises is not the classical one of friendly feeling and plain style; they contain a universal rhetoric for letters of affairs as well as private letters, and they emphasize the distinctions in style prescribed by ancient decorum to fit the distinctions of persons addressed, so that letters are by no means confined even ideally to the plain style. Into this epistolary rhetoric the whole ancient rhetoric of the oration was finally absorbed. By the Renaissance, rhetoric was still conceived in terms of epistolography, and the reestablishment of oratory as ostensibly its primary concern came (so far as it did come) only gradually. In this process, the reduction of the letter to its ancient position as one form among many, and the reversion to the ideal of a plain style and general simplicity in its composition, are two aspects of a single response to increasing classical influence. Since the Renaissance the production of treatises on letterwriting, once a common employment of the chief humanists (*e.g.*, Erasmus), has descended to hands incapable of speculation; what theory there is in modern times corresponds generally to that of antiquity as outlined above.

C. H. Haskins, *The Ren. of the 12th c.*, 1928; R. W. Ramsey, "Some Eng. letterwriters of the 17th c.," *Essays by divers hands* (R. S. L.), 1936; A. Lyall, "Eng. letterwriting in the 19th c.," *Studies in lit. and hist.*, 1915; K. G. Hornbeak, *The complete letterwriter in Eng., 1568–1800*, 1934. *See* Epistolary fiction. J. Craig LaDrière.

letter in verse, though never considered a major was often (Horace; the Middle Ages; Ren.: 17th, 18th, 20th c.) a popular form, the Horatian familiar essay or the Ovidian sentimental epistle. Hence, from the latter's elegiac meter, association or confusion with elegy. Without abandoning a generally plain style, it can modulate at will to the highest registers of poetic speech. E. P. Morris, "The form of the epistle in Horace," *Yale Classical Studies* II, 1931.

lexis. *See* Computational stylistics.

liaison. Fr. 1. The binding together of two words, by the sounding of an ordinarily silent consonant before an initial vowel or mute *h, e.g.*, the *t* in *fait accompli*. 2. A principle of dramatic criticism, esp. 17th c., by which scenes of a play must be "linked." Various types of *liaison* were: *présence* (*i.e.*, one character remaining from the preceding scene); *vue* or *recherche* (*i.e.*, a person entering sees a person about to leave the stage, or vice versa); *bruit* (*i.e.*, a noise on the stage which brings in a character seeking its explanation); *temps* (*i.e.*, a character is unable logically to enter at a different moment); and *discours* (*i.e.*, when a character in hiding later speaks).

libretto. The "book," or words of the dialogue and songs, of an opera or musical comedy.

license. See Poetic license.

Lied. G. *See* Meistergesang.

light ending. *See* Ending.

light verse is poetry written in the spirit of play. Usually a short lyric, it may be of considerable length if this spirit is dominant. It often has a serious side, notably in its criticism of persons and manners, its often cynical tone. For the most part, the writer takes neither himself nor his poetic mission too seriously. Yet poets as profound as Milton and Goethe have written light verse, and Shakespeare's songs are clearly within the type. In origin it is as early as Aristophanes. Light verse ranges from highly meaningful satire to purposely meaningless nonsense; it includes songs, parodies, epigrams, *vers de société*, occasional verse. In certain of these, as the song, a mood of gaiety is accompanied by a lively metrical pattern which (Jonson; Burns; Béranger) may be set to music, or even (W. S. Gilbert; Cole Porter) be written in conjunction with a musical score. In satire, parody, and epigram, however, the leading characteristic is sharpness of wit, the epigram being marked also by verbal economy. The surprise ending is frequent. The play of wit is particularly noticeable in *vers de société*, which is satire concerned with the superficialities of polite society, written with technical facility in a tone of graceful and sometimes elegant badinage. Characteristically composed in times when society is stiff and regularized, *vers de société* was written by the Cavaliers; by John Gay and other Eng. and Fr. poets of the 18th c.; by such Victorians as Thackeray and Locker-Lampson, editor of *Lyra Elegantiarum* (1867), an anthol. of social verse. A similar variety is occasional or topical verse, so called because it arises from an occurrence of the day in which the poet detects absurdities or humorous implications. Contemporary light verse writers such as A. P. Herbert and Phyllis McGinley frequently employ a newspaper headline as their text. While light verse may be wittily intellectual (Swift, Pope; T. S. Eliot, Dorothy Parker), it may be naïve and fanciful as in nursery rhymes, folk ballads, children's verse (Belloc; Milne). Stress is usually laid upon novelty of form and dexterity in the handling (Charles Stuart Calverley). Puns and word play are common; slang and dialect may be used; by verbal deformations some poets (Léon-Paul Fargue) achieve phonetic caricature.

Rhymes are often humorous in their oddity. Byron in *Don Juan* and Gilbert in his ballads are masters of the unexpected and frequently polysyllabic rhyme. Browning, sometimes heedless of exactitude, employs mosaic rhymes (more than one word making one rhyme-sound): pooh-poohed it is, lewd ditties, nudities; from mice, promise. Lewis Carroll (two p—Ennyworth of beautiful soup) and W. S. Gilbert, followed by musical comedy lyricists, have rhymed by ripping letters off words. Calverley similarly, and frequently, tears apart familiar phrases:

> . . . . petal,
> Wherefore, Polly, put the kettle
> On at once.

Much of the humor of Ogden Nash's verse derives from the mating of seemingly unrhymable words, at times by bold alterations in orthography. Because of their challenge to technical virtuosity, such intricate Fr. forms as the ballade, triolet, and rondeau have long been favored. One form used almost exclusively in light verse, often with nonsensical content, is the limerick, *q.v.; cf.* clerihew; doubledactyl.

Recent literary schools have enriched the field. The futurist Palazzeschi's *La Passeggiata* (*The Passerby,* Windowshopper) is made up of names from store windows (several such verses have been made in New York's Chinatown): his *La Fontana Malata* presents phonetically the last drops of a drying fountain. Laforgue; Corbière (*Amours Jaunes*); Cros (*Hareng Saur*—which contributes the line-end repetition:

> Once there was a great white wall, bare, bare, bare,
> Against the wall a ladder, high, high, high,
> Below, a kippered herring, dry, dry, dry.)

and the Fantaisistes (Toulet, *Contrerimes*); Mayakovsky—have added individual notes. Morgenstern's *Fisches Nachtgesang* uses macrons and breves (—, ◡ ◡, — — —, ◡ ◡, —) in successive lines instead of words. Other typographical eccentricities, such as emblematic poems, shaped to resemble their themes, are older than print; favorite themes of these are religion and drinking. Words may be split (not necessarily between syllables) at line-ends for other effect than rhyme (e. e. cummings); letters may be added to words (Guiterman, *Complaint of the Camuel*). Being playful, light verse admits whatever in subject or form may hope to amuse; but it seldom wholly forgets its other role as sugar on the philosophic pill.

L. Untermeyer, *Play in Poetry,* 1938; W. H. Auden, ed. *The Oxford Book of Light Verse,* 1938; L. Kronenberger, ed. *An Anthology of Light Verse,* 1935; David McCord, *What Cheer,* 1945; Richard Armour, *Writing Light Verse,* 1947, 1958. Richard Armour.

limerick (? from the refrain "Will you come up to Limerick?" sung at groups that extemporized such verses; possibly influenced by "learic," coined by M. Russell, S.J., after Edward Lear, *Book of Nonsense,* 1846). Eng. verse form, used exclusively for light or nonsense verse (with a wide range of bawdry): 5 anapestic lines, a a_3 b b_2 a_3. In early examples, the last line repeats the 1st, *e.g.,* the Mother Goose jingle "Hickory dickory dock." In later varieties, the 1st (rarely 2d) line will recur with a slight variation, *e.g.,* "A smiling young lady from Niger." Now used with trick rhyme, surprise non-rhyme, and other devices. The form has invited noted writers, *e.g.,* O. W. Holmes of Henry Ward Beecher:

> There once was an eloquent preacher
> Called a hen a most elegant creature.
> The hen, pleased at that,
> Laid an egg in his hat,
> And thus did the hen reward Beecher.

See Light verse; *cf.* Clerihew; Doubledactyl. M. Wright, *What's Funny—and Why,* 1939; W. S. Baring-Gould, *The Lure of the Limerick,* 1967.

line. *See* Verse.

linguistics. The science of language. A. Mechanical: (1) Phonology, now usually divided into (a) phonetics: sounds, their formation and variations, and (b) phonemics: the basic units of language sound (phonemes). (2) Morphology: the grouping of sounds into sound-complexes of conventional meanings, *i.e.,* forms and formation of words (morphemes). B. Psychological: (3) Syntax: the organization of words into sentences and other structures of thought (tagmemes). (4) Semantics: evolution of meanings. (5) Etymology: variations of word forms from their earliest ascertainable base in the language group—that of English being the Indo-European. (6) Lexicography: often includes (4) and (5), plus the current pronunciation and other dictionary data. *Cf.* Grammar.

Another pattern distinguishes (1) descriptive linguistics: how language works; (2) historical linguistics: how language changes; and (3) institutional linguistics: varieties and uses of language. The first of these includes the study of literary works. Thus in *As You Like It,* a study of Rosalind's use of *you* and *thou, we* and *us,* of questions and imperatives, in talking to Celia, shows interesting variations in the degree of her involvement of her cousin in her own acts and feelings. Problems of linguistics have been complicated (perhaps ultimately to be lessened) by the use of computers; thus "A Four-letter Word in *Lady Chatterley's Lover*" (Angus McIntosh, *Patterns of Language,* 1966) considers how the computer can determine whether to use *savoir* or *connaître* in translating the 293 instances of the verb *know.*

Following Cassirer in adding to the animal receptory system and effector system the uniquely human symbolic system, Ragnar Rommetveit has developed the theory of psycholinguistics, in *Words, Meanings, and Messages* (1968, with extensive bibliography). *Cf.* Etymology; Semantics; Semiotics; Value theory; Signs. F. de Saussure, *Course in General Linguistics,* 1906, trans. 1959; R. H. Robins, *General Linguistics,* 1965; M. Joos, ed. *Readings in Linguistics I,* 1957, 1966; E. P. Hamp, ed. *Readings in Linguistics II,* 1967; J. J. Waterman, *Perspectives in Linguistics,* 1963; Noam Chomsky, *Current Issues in Linguistic Theory,* 1964; *Cartesian Linguistics,* 1966; D. E. Hayden . . . ed., *Classics in Linguistics,* 1967; L. G. Heller and J. Macris, *Parametric Linguistics,* 1967; D. T. Langendoen, *The London School of Linguistics,* 1968; Max Black, *The Labyrinth of Language,* 1968. For further bibliography, *see* Language.

linked sonnet. A sonnet with the rhymes intertwined: a b a b b c b c c d c d e e. Also called Spenserian, from its use by Edmund Spenser (1552?–99).

lipogram. Writing (listed by Addison as false wit) in which a specific letter is omitted. Pindar wrote an ode without *sigma;* the many works of Lope de Vega include 5 novels, each lacking a different one of the 5 vowels. A play, *Pièce sans A* (not using the letter *a*) by Ronden, was presented at the Paris Théâtre des Variétés in 1816. The Persian Jami, shown a poem without *a,* remarked: "It would have been a great improvement if you had also left out the other letters." The following lines use every letter of the alphabet but the most common, *e:*

> A jovial swain should not complain
> Of any buxom fair
> Who mocks his pain but thinks it gain
> To quiz his awkward air.

litany. A prayer consisting of a series of petitions (usually led by the clergy with lay response). Hence, a lengthy and repetitive enumeration, *e.g.,* Remy de Gourmont, *Litanies de la rose.*

literacy—the ability to read and write—is assumed in our day to be an unqualified good and an indispensable condition of culture. Here as elsewhere we fail to distinguish means and ends. We should ask whether the things likely to be read or written are worth reading or writing, either in themselves or to the persons concerned.

In civilisations other than ours—in ancient India and China, in mediæval Europe—the matter has been very differently viewed. The man of letters has been of a class apart, one for whom books and writing are the tools of apprenticeship and mastery in his own calling, the natural means of fulfilling his function according to his own way of life. Other classes have other tools, functions and ways of life; the knowledge that reaches some through reading reaches them from elsewhere, the visual arts specially providing richer means of communication than we now imagine. Nor does the lack of literacy imply the lack of what now we call literature, which is partly received by oral tradition, partly created by the unlettered classes themselves. In such conditions memory is vigorous and the spoken language resists decay. Even now, the older peasants in Tuscany (officially styled *analfabeti*) keep a sensibility to pure idiom envied by professional writers; and there are still some of them that have cantos of Dante by heart.

Popular schooling today enforces on men in general a convention of book-learning aping the apprenticeship proper to a clerical class. In a non-functional society with slight intellectual foundations, it is natural that the bookish education imposed should be largely irrelevant to a man's future life, standardised so as to fit no one well, and undirected by general principles based on the nature and hierarchy of knowledge. Few are concerned over this; there is no doubt of the quantitative increase in literacy of a kind, and amid the general satisfaction that something is being multiplied it escapes enquiry whether the something is profit or deficit.

Mass-produced learning for the people has had its influence among the still privileged classes of scholars, men of letters and "well-read" folk of leisure. The inorganic aridity of research, the presumption of 'cultured readers' ignorant of the greater part of the world's thought, the confusion of good and fashionable in the literary judgments of the genteel

—these things, though they have their counterparts in the past, are now more pronounced.

But the worst effects of enforced literacy have been on those for whom it was first designed—the poor who have been "compelled to come in" but are offered little better than a Barmecide feast—biased history, cheap science and a smattering of national classics soon erased. The few natural students are no better off than those of their ancestors who were schooled at some benefactor's expense or who bought their own knowledge of letters to read the Bible and *Pilgrim's Progress.* With the majority, their new accomplishment serves no ultimate end. For some it helps commercial advancement; for most it facilitates exploitation by political propaganda and business advertisement. Society at large is not intellectually enriched meanwhile. Learning and wisdom have often been divided; perhaps the clearest result of modern literacy has been to maintain and enlarge the gulf. WALTER SHEWRING.

On the other hand, since wisdom must be based upon some measure of understanding of the world, the complexity of which the scientific disciplines have made clear, without widespread literacy there can be little hope for a wider spread of wisdom. This can come but slowly. It is a recognized phenomenon that each new field of wide human response involves an opening period of a juvenile and elementary level; as Fenimore Cooper reminded his fellow-Americans, democracy entails government by the average, and the average is low. Motion pictures began with such a shallow-witted appeal; still in their early days, they only occasionally rise above this level; radio and television repeat the process. It is no easy task for humanity to lift itself by its own bootstraps. Mortal men are in a greater hurry than mother nature, and often rail at the present stage of a continuing process. The wiser are more patient. Although the achievements of the enforcedly literate remain dim, literacy remains the surest broad way to ultimate light.

literary criticism. The description, interpretation, and evaluation of literary works. The presentation of principles and theories underlying such works, and the application of these or other considerations to the judgment of such works and their discrimination. To describe these principles and considerations is the general purpose of this volume.

Literary criticism may be conceived as (1) a theoretical discipline or science; (2) a skill guided by feeling and developed through experience; (3) an "art" in the sense of the Aristotelian *techne, i.e.,* a methodical purposive production.

(1) *Criticism as a theoretical discipline or science.* It is the purpose of theory to provide knowledge. Criticism, however, subserves a practical purpose: it is instrumental in carrying forward the process of artistic creation and appreciation. Theory must therefore minister to criticism, affording the information it needs. The following types of such auxiliary information may be distinguished: (a) Knowledge of the techniques and materials of artistic creation; (b) Knowledge of the subject-matter, *i.e.,* the objects of artistic representation—a virtually unlimited field of study; (c) Knowledge of the artist and his activity—psychology of artistic creation, biography of the artist, history of art. There is a tendency to misconstrue each of these as criticism proper (F. Brunetière, "La critique scientifique," *Questions de Critique,* pp. 297–324). Thus (a) the expert in materials and techniques, *e.g.,* the linguist and metrician, may arrogate to himself the right of measuring artistic perfection by linguistic and metric values. Criticism is misunderstood as an appraisal of virtuosity. In like manner, (b) the knowledge of the subject-matter may be overrated; and anatomy may be expected to furnish a code for sculpture; sociology and psychology, rules for novel writing (Hippolyte Taine, *Philosophie de l'art,* 1865–69). Criticism, by this naturalistic error, is mistaken as a comparison of the artistic "imitation" with its model in nature. The most common error today consists in (c) substituting an interest in the artist for the critical interest in art. Much of our contemporary "criticism" is actually psychological, anthropological, and sociological analysis (Kenneth Burke, *Philosophy of Literary Form,* 1941, reviewed, *Philosophy and Phenomenological Research,* II, Dec. 1941). Historiography, however, instead of furnishing a factual basis for criticism, may be conceived and executed as a kind of criticism, emphasizing the historical context of works of art rather than the single work. T. S. Eliot has expressed the view that the work of art should be evaluated in terms of the totality of monuments of the past, which constitute the "simultaneous order" of tradition ("Tradition and the Individual Talent" in *The Sacred Wood,* 1920): "No poet, no artist of any art, has his complete meaning alone.

His significance, his appreciation, is the appreciation of his relation to the dead poets and artists." It must be observed, however, that the "order of tradition" is itself not a traditional datum but must be defined in terms other than tradition.

(2) *Criticism as a skill guided by feeling and developed through experience.* Critical evaluation, like all evaluation, must be made in accordance with norms. To allow instinct or feeling to determine our preferences would result in artistic anarchy. Many an eminent critic, it is true, never formulated his notions of art. Yet ineffable knowledge is still knowledge. Criticism is neither a "knack," nor an "art" in the sense of "fine art" or poetry. The latter error occasionally deflected the brilliant achievements of the Romantic critics (F. Schlegel; Sainte-Beuve; Ruskin). It was characteristic of the Art for Art's Sake movement, and reached a climax in the "impressionistic" idea of criticism (F. Brunetière, "La critique impressioniste," *Essais sur la littérature contemporaine,* 1881). For such "artistic criticism," the work becomes the material for a fresh creation. Walter Pater's lines on *La Gioconda* (*Renaissance,* 1935, p. 115 f.) tell us more about Pater than about Leonardo's art. (P. E. More, "Walter Pater," *Shelburne Essays,* VIII, 1913). The measuring-rod and the measured object cannot be of the same nature. True criticism subordinates itself to the work of art which it tries to understand.

(3) *Criticism as "art" in the sense of techne, i.e., a methodical purposive production.* Criticism is methodical in the sense that it proceeds in conformity with rules and principles developed in complex fashion through many centuries of tradition. Criticism is purposive in the sense that it subserves an end: to foster the creation and enjoyment of beauty. Criticism is production in the sense that it participates in the process of creation, though not by contributing works of art. Recognizing art as art and discriminating it from non-art, interpreting the created work and paving the way for fresh creations, it mediates between artist and receptor, furthering the interests of both. It nourishes the medium in which art may grow; it represents the æsthetic memory of mankind deciding what and how to remember. As the beauty or artistic perfection that criticism aims to recognize and foster lies in the domain of æsthetics, and as all rules of critical procedure are ordered toward this goal, criticism may be termed applied æsthetics. HELMUT KUHN.

A significant part of æsthetic inquiry in recent years has focussed on the nature of the reasoning by which judgments, or evaluations, of literary works can be supported. The problem is to identify and characterize the criteria of judgment, *i.e.,* the grounds that can relevantly and cogently be appealed to in arguing that a poem is good or poor, or that one play is better than another. Some criteria have almost universally been acknowledged to be relevant to critical judgment: *e.g.,* most critics would say that if a literary work is highly unified, its unity can legitimately be cited as a merit, because it helps to make it a good work—though that degree of unity may be neither a necessary nor a sufficient condition of its being a good work. On the other hand, whether originality or sincerity or success in fulfilling the author's intention is relevant to evaluation has been debated by critical theorists.

An effort has been made to provide an exhaustive classification of all relevant critical reasons under three headings: (1) those that bear upon the unity of the work, (2) those that bear upon the complexity of the work, and (3) those that bear upon the intensity of the work's regional qualities (*see* M. C. Beardsley, *Aesthetics,* ch. 10, 1958). But this scheme is not universally accepted (*see* Morris Weitz "Reasons in Criticism," *JA* Spring 1962; Beardsley, "On the generality of critical reasons," *JP* 1962). The principal issues under current discussion concern (1) the relevance of genetic reasons (*e.g.* sincerity, intention) and cognitive reasons—*i.e.,* whether the truth of the work's implicit doctrines counts toward its *æsthetic* worth—and (2) the intelligibility and applicability of general critical terms like "unity" (*see* Catherine Lord, "Organic unity reconsidered," *JA* Spring 1964). MONROE C. BEARDSLEY.

Judgments about the author's intention appear in the processes of interpretation and evaluation of literary works. The present article examines the meaning of such judgments, their role in criticism, and their mode of proof.

In referring to the meaning of a literary work, one should distinguish between (1) the meaning of the work itself, and (2) the meaning that the author intended to express in the work. These two meanings are called "actual" and "intended" respectively.

Evidence that the work has a certain actual meaning is derived from a study of the work itself, the words in which it is written and their syntax. Included in the meaning of the words will be their whole history as far as determinable, and all the uses and associations of the words that went to make up their value when the work was produced. The meaning of the work is all that the ideal reader can find in it; and the ideal reader is the one fully aware of the accepted value of the words and least influenced in his interpretation by idiosyncratic associations. Since no two readers will ever read the work in exactly the same way, it must be said that the meaning of the work lies within an area of readings, and is, like the pronunciation of language sounds, a norm (*cf.* René Wellek, "The Mode of . . . Art," *Southern R.,* VII, 1942). (In the course of years a work may undergo a shift of meaning in some of its words, so that one may have to distinguish between the work "then" and the work "now." It is obvious that in most cases the meanings of words "then" will have more relevance to the total work than the meanings "now.") The author must be admitted as a witness to the meaning of his work, and one may even grant special validity to idiosyncratic associations of the author, since at least they will be relevant to the total design. This kind of evidence, however, must be distinguished from the author's "intention." Even though it were known, for example, that a given author intended the word "glory" to mean a "knock-down argument," the word "glory" in his work could not be said to have that meaning in any sense valid for the reader or the work itself. The work after being produced must continue to exist independently of the author's intentions or thoughts about it. The idiosyncrasies of the author must not be repugnant to the norm (but *cf.* Joseph Wood Krutch, *Experience and Art,* 1932, p. 180–9).

Evidence that a work has a certain intended meaning may be distinguished as "internal" or "external." But this distinction is not one that can always be applied with certainty. (1) The normal meanings of words as determined in an historical dictionary or by other historical study constitute internal evidence—even though one must go outside the work itself to find the meanings. (2) But information about an author's intention acquired through his letters, diaries, or conversations (such, for instance, as the fact that a given poem is addressed to a given lady) is likely to be in the fullest sense external evidence, in that the intended meaning revealed will lie outside the meaning of the words as far as normally determinable. (3) A kind of middle ground is occupied by certain types of information regarding the author's life and work. The fact that he habitually attaches a certain meaning to a word may not be external evidence (if the meaning does not lie fantastically beyond the norm), for the author's biography is part of the whole history that makes up the meaning of the word. Again, even more particular associations which may be learned through a study of the author's reading or sources may fall within a reasonable extension of the norm. Professor J. L. Lowes's *Road to Xanadu,* 1930, is a classic exploration of just these types of borderline evidence. The distinction between (2) and (3) will always be difficult, but the drift toward (2) will in the long run produce a vastly different sort of criticism from that which is concerned with (1) and moderately with (3).

To infer the author's intention from internal evidence presupposes that the actual and the intended meanings coincide; but where there is no external evidence the critic cannot determine whether they coincide or not. He may argue that, since the author is a reader of his own work, he will probably not publish it if it actually means what he does not intend it to mean, but the author may supply as highly individual an interpretation to his words when he reads them as when he writes them. To infer the author's intention from external evidence, however, presupposes either that the external evidence is corroborated by the internal evidence (in which case the latter is made the ultimate verification) or, where there is a conflict, that the external evidence supplies a more convincing indication of the author's intention than the work itself. This can never be the case, since such external evidence (consisting of reports of what the author said at some time before or after, or in pauses during, the composition of his work) cannot, in the first place, be as specific and concrete a revelation of the author's state of mind during composition as the work that issues from that state of mind, and may, in the second place, be utterly misleading where the author's avowed intention is not his real one.

These considerations are ignored by critics that speak of a disparity between intention and result ("In every work regard the writer's End/Since none can compass more than they intend," Alexander Pope, *Essay on Criticism,* II, 255; *cf.* I. A. Richards on "defective communication," *Principles of Literary Criticism,* 1934, ch. 25). The widely-held theory that literary works should be judged with respect to their success in carrying out the author's intention has been called by H. L. Mencken the "Spingarn-Croce-Carlyle-Goethe Theory" ("Criticism of Criticism of Criticism," *Criticism in America,* 1924, p. 181). But it is significant that, though Spingarn, in his lecture on "The New Criticism," 1910 (in *Criticism in America,* p. 43), called this "the only possible method" of criticism, he later modified his position (in "The Growth of a Literary Myth," 1923, *Creative Criticism,* 1931, p. 167–8) by adding that the work itself is the "intention," and that the author's aim can be detected internally in the work even where it is not realized. This is surely a self-contradictory proposition (*cf.* Croce, *Æsthetic,* trans. Ainslie, 2d ed. 1922, p. 20–24, 111–12; Landor, *Imaginary Conversations,* Southey and Porson II, *Works,* ed. T. E. Welby, 1927–36, V, 207; P. H. Frye, *Romance and Tragedy,* 1922, p. 14). It would be less misleading to speak of the "intent of the work." A judgment in which the term "intention" is used in this sense is likely to mean that certain parts of the work could be changed, and conceivably might have been changed by the author, so as to improve the work as a whole. What is "intended" in a given detail is, then, what, on grounds of relevance to the whole meaning, ought to be said. It is what the work itself ought to say at a given point, or, if we like, what the author ought to say.

Such value-judgments often take the form: this technique (stanza-form, device of prose-style, bringing two characters together in a novel, letting a certain character be murdered) is good (or bad) in that it helps (or does not help) to secure the effect as a whole. And such judgments often appear to assume a distinction between elements of the work that are to be called "means" and others that are to be called "ends," between the "how" and the "what" (*cf.* Julian Symons, "Obscurity and Dylan Thomas," *Kenyon R.,* II, 1, 1940; I. A. Richards, *Practical Criticism,* 1935, pt. 3, ch. 8). This distinction is a very slippery one.

We may be tempted to say, for example, that the solemnity of a certain elegy is marred because the poem is written in a certain meter, and that, since the effect of the meter interferes with the solemnity, the meter is a bad means of achieving the solemn effect. Yet since the quality of the meter is just as much an element of the whole meaning as the solemnity of certain words, what we have distinguished are not really means and ends but two aspects of the whole or end (because we feel a conflict between them), and we have judged one with respect to the other. We may have good reasons for selecting one quality as the essential quality of the work, with respect to which other qualities are to be called subsidiary: the solemn elegiac quality may predominate, despite the meter, and it may seem sensible, in judging how the whole could be made a more effective unity, to wish altered that aspect which may be more easily altered. Nevertheless, the ends and means in poetry are never actually distinguishable from each other, as are the things in the physical world which are usually and literally called ends and means (*cf.* Cleanth Brooks, *Modern Poetry and the Tradition,* 1939, ch. 1).

The point becomes clearer when the problem is approached from the side, not of technique, but of what is called "subject-matter" (*cf.* A. C. Bradley, "Poetry for Poetry's Sake," *Oxford Lectures on Poetry,* 1934, p. 3–34). A commonly occurring type of judgment implies that two works have the same "subject," while one expresses it better than the other. It is possible to compare two lyrics expressing a lover's melancholy, to abstract this common characteristic, to express it in prose, and to call this the "common subject" of the two lyrics. The fallacy arises if we then proceed to take the abstraction as the "what" of the poems and to treat everything else in them as the "how" to be judged with reference to the "what." For the point at which we have here drawn the line between the "matter" and the "manner" is even more arbitrary than that in the preceding paragraph: for it does not here, as it did there, mark a distinction between a set of elements that conflict with the poetic unity. We might think of the same poems as expressing simply melancholy, and then we should have a more general "what," and more of the meaning of the poem would go into the "how"; we could say that the poet used a good means of symbolizing melancholy when he chose the case of the lover. In like manner, if we were to compare only poems that express melancholy of adolescent love, we should have a more specific "whatness" and a more restricted "howness." For particular purposes of focussing attention on different "whatnesses," it is convenient to draw the line at different points on different occasions —though the more general the classification, the less illuminating will be the comparison. It would be fruitless to compare a lyric and a novel insofar as their common subject is conflict, and then to ask which expresses conflict the better. At the extremes we have to admit, on the one hand, that all poems express experience of some sort, and on the other, that the "whatness" of each poem is unique, and there is no residue of "howness." If we have two poems that differ in only one word (as in two editions of a poem), we must say that, taken as a whole, we have two "whatnesses," and what we may call a technical judgment about the change of the word is really a judgment that one "whatness" as a whole is better than the other.

In summation: (1) It is difficult to distinguish between internal and external evidence of the author's intention, but it can be said that to rely on certain types of evidence is to go in the direction of biography and to rely on other types is to stay close to the actual meaning of the work. (2) For the meaning of a work resides within the work; no judgment of intention has relevancy unless corroborated by the work itself, in which case it is supererogatory. It is therefore circular and misleading to speak of judging the work with respect to its success in carrying out the author's intention. (3) The word "intention" is often used as an abbreviation for "whole actual meaning," so that in some instances a judgment about the disparity of "intention" and result is really a judgment about the whole meaning or plan of a work as seen in the work itself. These are judgments of evaluation, and (4) such judgments refer not to the relation of means to ends, or of manner to matter, but to the relation of parts to whole.

A. K. Coomaraswamy, "Intention," *The American Bookman*, I, 1944; W. K. Wimsatt, Jr., and M. C. Beardsley, "The Intentional Fallacy," *Sewanee R.* LIV, 1946; R. Jack Smith, "Intention in an Organic Theory of Poetry," *Sewanee R.* LVI, 1948; R. W. Stallman, *Critic's Notebook*, 1950; M. C. Beardsley, *Aesthetics*, ch. 1, 3, 10, 1958; T. M. Gang, *Essays in Criticism, VII*, 1957; H. D. Aiken and I. C. Hungerford, "Intention and interpretation in art," *JP*, 1955; P. Cioffo, "Intention and interpretation in criticism," *Proceedings of Aristotelian Soc. XLV*; G. Hough, *An Essay on Criticism*, 1966; W. K. Wimsatt, Jr., "Genesis," vol. in honor of René Wellek, ed. L. Nelson et al., 1968. MONROE C. BEARDSLEY and W. K. WIMSATT, JR.

A further limitation of the theory of intention is caught in André Gide's preface to his *Paludes*: "Before I explain my book, I want to wait for others to explain it to me. To elucidate it too soon would be restricting its meaning too soon. For, if we know what we intended to say, we never know whether we have said *that alone*. One always says *more than that*."

It should also be pointed out that, while a poem or other work may be self-contained and self-sufficient, the judgment of it is not contained in the work. All literature exists in a social and historical context, and an author's statement of his intention (as Spenser's letter to Raleigh about *The Faerie Queene* or Wordsworth's Preface to the *Lyrical Ballads*) is part of that context. And obviously if an author writes a sonnet or an elegy, or a satire, the conventions of the form are to be weighed in examining his work. Insofar, then, as criticism is comparative, and the work is to be placed in its period or its genre, intention has some relevance and valid claim. This must be kept in mind while weighing all earlier writing; Pope, *e.g.* (Preface to *Odyssey, II*) states that "in every design which a man deliberately undertakes, the end he proposes is the first thing in his aim, and that by which he governs the whole work and all its parts."

Recent discussion in the field of literary criticism has been enormous; a selected bibliography follows: Saints; Ship; L. Venturi, *Hist. of Crit.*, trans. 1936; C. M. Gayley, *An Introd. to the Methods and Materials of Lit. Crit.*, 1901; G. Boas, *A Primer for Critics*, 1937; T. M. Greene, *The Arts and the Art of Crit.*, 1940; I. A. Richards, *Principles of Lit. Crit.*, 1925; T. S. Eliot, *The Use of Poetry and the Use of Crit.*, 1933; J. E. Spingarn, *Creative Crit.*, 1917; L. Abercrombie, *Principles of Lit. Crit.*, 1932; H. Hazlitt, *The Anatomy of Crit.*, 1933; T. M. Greene, *The Arts and the Art of Crit.* 1940; R. Wellek, *The Rise of Eng. Lit. Hist.*, 1941, 1966; B. S. Oldsey, ed. *Visions and Revisions in Modern Am. Lit. Crit.*, 1962; G. J. and N. M. Goldberg, *The Modern Critical Spectrum*, 1962; P. Ramset, *The Lively and the Just*, 1962; Leon Edel, ed. *Lit. Hist. and Lit. Crit.*, 1965; D. Daiches, *Critical Approaches to Lit.*, 1956; M. Levich, ed. *Aesthetics and the Philos. of Crit.*, 1963; W. Righter, *Logic and Crit.*, 1963; N. K. Basu, *Lit. and Crit.*, 1963; N. Frye, *The Well-Tempered Critic*, 1963; R. Wellek, *Concepts of Crit.*, *A. Hist. of Modern Crit.*, 4 v., 1955–68; W. K. Wimsatt, Jr., *Explication as Crit.*, 1963; W. Sutton, *Modern Am. Crit.*, 1963; R. E. Scholes, *Learners and Discerners*, 1964; K. Burke, *Terms for Order*, 1964; *Perspectives by Incongruity*, 1964; L. S. Hall, ed. *A Grammar of Lit. Crit.*, 1965; O. Cargill, *Toward a Pluralistic Crit.*, 1965; A. Gomme, *Attitudes to Crit.*, 1966; K. C. Hill, *Interpreting Lit.*, 1966; R. Ruland, *The Rediscovery of Am. Lit.*, 1967; M. Krieger, *The Play and Place of Crit.*, 1967; H. Levin, *Why Lit. Crit. Is Not an Exact Science*, 1968.

literature. Written productions as a collective body. The total preserved writings belonging to a given language or people; that part which is notable for literary form or expression, "belles-lettres." Body of writing having to do with a particular subject—*e.g.,* the literature of art. A. Guérard, *Lit. and Society,* 1935; E. Vivas, *The Artistic Transaction . . . Theory of Lit.,* 1963; D. Daiches, *Critical Approaches to Lit.,* 1965; G. Watson, *The Study of Lit.,* 1969.

literature and society. The psychological factors which have made literature both an individual and a social need for man are obviously varied and complex, for literature serves a great variety of functions. It is connected on the one hand with magic and ritual and on the other (though at a much later stage in civilization) with the desire for individual self-expression. Literature is stylized, traditional, following accustomed forms and formulas; it is also invented, created, the product of original insights. Certain kinds of folk song are involved in their origins with both the rhythms of work and the movements of dance. The interplay between individual inventiveness and community response in certain kinds of folk literature, in orally-transmitted heroic poetry, in the early stages of some kinds of European drama, is often of the most intimate kind. The earliest definable need served by literature is a communal one: communal dance and song, communal ritual, communal listening to the recital of a professional bard. And even the most self-expressive of romantic poets, committed to the theory that the object of poetry is simply to give vent to the poet's feelings in the way that best satisfies himself, concedes by the very fact that he uses the communicative medium of language the desire to communicate. The creator of literature is never, in fact, solitary. However isolated or alienated he may feel, or claim to feel (and such a claim is a very recent one in the history of civilisation), he produces his literary work for a community of some kind.

This does not mean that the relation between the producer of literature and his public is static. Far from it. That relation varies between society and society; it constantly changes throughout history; and in many kinds of society there are different kinds of producers of literature each of whom has a quite different relation to the public. He can be anything from priest to entertainer, and indeed sometimes combines elements of these two apparently quite contradictory functions. The Athenian audience in the fifth century B.C. who watched a performance of three tragedies and one satyr-play during the Great Dionysia festival were in some sense participating in a ritual and in some sense enjoying an entertainment. The "tropes," or dramatic actings out of parts of the Christian liturgy, with which post-classical European drama began, represented both acts of worship and a kind of entertainment, and both elements are also present, though in different proportions, in the medieval miracle plays.

In conjecturing about the place of the producer of literature in primitive societies, we use whatever aids anthropology and psychology can provide and also make use of analogies provided by still existing relatively primitive societies. Our task becomes easier when we come to written literature. Although the bulk of literature about which we know anything at all is written, it must be remembered that an enormous amount of oral literature as well as a great deal of written literature has not survived. There are something like 2,800 languages in use among the world's population of some three billion people, and in only about fifty of these does their exist a literature of any real significance. The great majority of the languages of the world have produced no written literature. So again, when we talk of the place of the writer in society we must remember to what a small proportion of societies the question is relevant. We must distinguish, however, between the large number of languages which have produced no written literature and the proportion of actual people among whom a written literature exists. After all, thirteen of the world's languages are each spoken by over fifty million people, and Chinese, Russian and English by very many more than that, so that the majority of the world's population speak a language in which a literature exists even though many of them may themselves be illiterate.

The nearer we come to our own time the more we know about the place of literature in a given society, about the status, role and function of the writer, about the effect of technological change on the nature, distribution and reception of literature, about the nature of the audience (or audiences) for literature, about the reasons why people read, about the relation of literature to other arts and activities, about the ways in which literature reflects or helps to produce social change, about the motivation of writers and readers—in short, about the sociology of literature. There is therefore more to be said about the relation between literature and society in more recent than in more distant centuries. This is not only because we know more about recent times; it is also because some of the most interesting problems involved in a study of literature in its social context only begin to emerge with the wide spread of literacy. Mass literacy brings into being all sorts of new and fascinating areas of research, which go far beyond the accepted worry about the relation between "classics and commercials" to embrace some of the most fundamental questions of human behaviour in industrial democratic society and the location and transmission of the values of a civilization. From the crude query, "How does this writer make his living?" to the subtler one of "What is the relation between exercising a profession, giving form to an original insight, and helping to transmit the traditions of a culture to be found in the work of this writer?" an investigation into the social history of literature can cover an enormous and an exciting field.

The question of *why* man is a literature-producing and literature-consuming animal is at bottom a psychological one, but it also has its sociological aspects, and we certainly get very near the answer if we ask about the status and function of the producer or transmitter of literature, whether he be a professional minstrel partly handing down and partly re-creating traditional material or a priestly scribe formulating or re-formulating or guarding the religious documents of a community (or doing something of all three), or a man of private means and leisure writing for the amusement or pleasure of himself or his friends, or a dependent of a patron or of the government or of the Church, or a professional author living off publishers' royalties, or any of the innumerable intermediate types of literary composer. The status and function of those engaged in ancillary activities (the rhapsodist, the ballad singer, the copyist, the printer, the bookseller, the publisher, the actor, the theatrical manager), the development of new materials on which to write (clay tablets, papyrus, parchment, paper), the introduction of printing and the development of more rapid and efficient techniques not only of printing letter-press but also of reproducing graphic designs and illustrations, the emergence of different kinds of libraries (royal and religious archives, centres for accumulating and preserving manuscripts or books or both, private libraries, national and civic libraries, circulating libraries), the emergence and role of periodicals and of literary middlemen such as teachers, critics, reviewers, the development of physical facilities to make domestic reading easier (glass windows, improved methods of indoor lighting), the influence on literature of ideology, censorship, education, degree of social mobility, techniques of communication other than printing such as radio and television—all these represent only some of the many factors which anyone concerned to investigate the relation between literature and society will have to take into consideration. The question of why man functions as a literature-producing animal is bound up with the ways in which he so functions, so that an enquiry into the "how" gives us part at least of the answer to the "why" question.

But a writer is not merely someone who is at the mercy of social and economic forces, although those forces do of course continuously affect his status and function. He is also himself an influence on society. The kind and degree of influence will depend not only on the general structure of society but also on the writer's place in it. He may be a member of what we call today the Establishment, concerned to consolidate and transmit accepted values, or he may be a member of a dissident minority. He may be part of a minority that is not dissident, or his dissidence may be of a marginal or oblique kind. And dissidence may vary in kind and degree between the reformist and the revolutionary. What part, for example, did literature play in the English Civil War or in paving the way for the French Revolution? Was the authoress of *Uncle Tom's Cabin* really "the little lady who started this big war" as Abraham Lincoln said to Harriet Beecher Stowe with reference to the influence of her book on the American Civil War? What part does literature play in the twentieth century in the national assertiveness of emergent countries in Asia and Africa? Is it true, as has been claimed, that in some sense all literature is propaganda? And if it is true, how should we distinguish the degrees and ways in which and the contexts within which literature so functions? In any case, literature has other central functions, including entertainment (of different kinds), the communication of information, the directly educational. These functions are rarely single. The complex relation between entertainment and more solemn cultural functions is clearly illustrated in the history of the drama, whether in Greek tragedy, the Japanese Nō play, or the modern European theatre.

One could write the history of literature in terms of the autonomous development of different literary *genres,* but such a history would have to ignore social factors which helped to determine the demand for different types of work. The rise of the novel in Europe, for example, is clearly related to developments in the class situation, while the difference between the medieval fabliau and romance clearly reflects a difference in social origin and purpose. In conventional literary histories social factors are mentioned only in the most obvious cases. But if they are relevant at all, they are always relevant, even though the relevance may not always be apparent to the superficial observer. The popularity of the three-volume novel in nineteenth-century England, for example, and the pressure on novelists to produce novels in three volumes whether this suited their creative needs or not, was the direct result of the power and influence of "Mudies Select Library," the great chain of circulating libraries which lasted as an independent concern from 1842 to 1894. And Mudies Library was itself a response to as well as a creator of social needs. The development of the railway in Britain produced the so-called "railway novel," designed to provide relaxing entertainment during a train journey. The publishing of novels in instalments in periodicals, a common practice in nineteenth-century Europe, is the result of specific social demands that are bound up with a variety of social and economic factors; this way of publishing novels in turn affected the structure of fiction, just as the specific requirements of editors determined the length of short stories first published in periodicals, even for such a sensitive literary artist as Henry James. The related demands of publishers, editors, and public interact continuously with the æsthetic demands which the author makes on himself. The balance between the Establishment and the individual and between external social and internal technical factors is always shifting, from the "socialist realism" demanded by official Soviet culture in the 1930's, where the influence of external factors on the writer's choice of themes and treatment is patent for all to see, to the development in Chinese poetry during the T'ang period of the *t'zu,* explicable in the first instance as purely technical response to the need to produce words to fit particular existing tunes but at the same time involving social factors, as its employment of a language closer to speech and its fondness for a tone of sentimental melancholy would suggest.

A writer's evaluation of his own work is not always that of the public, nor is the evaluation of one generation necessarily the same as that of the next. Changes in literary taste—which are bound up with a variety of social factors—not only produce new literary fashions and movements; they also bring earlier writers from obscurity to fame and consign famous writers to temporary or permanent oblivion. Sometimes a work has great influence and is forgotten when that influence has been absorbed. Sometimes a writer sets out to exert influence and is remembered by later generations for reasons which have nothing to do with the writer's original purpose. Only scholars are now familiar with Swift's intention in *Gulliver's Travels,* although the work remains a European classic while the same writer's pamphlet *The Conduct of the Allies,* which had immediate political influence, is now known only to a handful of specialists. Changes in a writer's reputation naturally affect the sales of his work, which may vary enormously during and after his lifetime. The complete version of Lawrence's *Lady Chatterley's Lover* was banned in most European countries and in America throughout Lawrence's lifetime, although in a short period after the book was legally freed from the charge of obscenity in 1960 it sold 3,500,000 copies in Britain in a paperback edition. Flaubert's *Madame Bovary* brought on him a prosecution for producing an immoral work, but the novel has now long been established as a European classic and it has had great influence on both the theory and the practice of fiction. Similarly, the plays of Ibsen, once regarded with outrage, are now standard reading in universities. Changes in social and moral attitudes which have so strikingly manifested themselves in releasing works such as *Lady Chatterley's Lover* and Joyce's *Ulysses* for publicly approved general reading are only the most glaring examples of the kind of shift in taste and point of view which is constantly at work in moulding the history of literary reputations and determining the parts played by different literary works in a given society. These changes are themselves bound up with a whole concatenation of social and economic causes, with the consequences of wars, with technological change, with the relation between the generations, with the quantity and quality of literacy, with the acceptance by large segments of society of certain scientific and especially psychological notions which at one time had been accepted only by a small minority of specialists.

Literature has both causes and effects; it is in some degree a mirror of society and in some degree a perpetual influence on society. That influence can be good or bad or neutral. Literature can certainly change individual lives; its social effects are less immediately discernible and often less direct, but they are none the less real. To consider literature in its social context is not only to gain a new perspective on literature: it is also to gain a new perspective on the history of man. *Cf.* Propaganda; Naturalism; Fame. Q. D. Leavis, *Fiction and the Reading Public,* 1932; H. D. Duncan, *Lang. and Lit. in Society,* 1953 (includes "A Bibliographical Guide to the Sociology of Lit."); Lucien Goldmann, *Le Dieu Caché,* 1951; Leo Lowenthal, *Lit. and the Image of Man,* 1957; *Lit., Popular Culture, and Society,* 1961, 1968; G. Lukács, *Studies in European Realism,* 1964; *The Historical Novel,* 1962; L. Schücking, *The Sociology of Literary Taste,* 1931, trans. 1944; Bernice Slote, ed. *Lit. and Society,* 1964; Diana Spearman, *The Novel and Society,* 1966; J. Dunner, ed. *Handbook of World Hist.: Concepts and Issues,* 1967. DAVID DAICHES.

litotes (Opp. of hyperbole). Understatement, often ironical; esp. the expression of an affirmative by denying its opposite; *e.g.,* "He's not a bad sort." Dr. Watson calls Sherlock Holmes "a composer of no mean merit." *Cf.* Meiosis; Hyperbole.

livre à clef. A work in which actual persons are presented under fictitious names. The genre developed esp. in 17th c. France and has flourished since. Many works (La Bruyère, *Caractères,* 1688) were later furnished with keys. In the theatre, a notorious recent instance is *MacBird* (1966) which under the guise of a travesty of *Macbeth* presented American public figures at the time of the assassination of President Kennedy. The N.Y. Public Library has published some keys, to *romans à clef* in the *Branch Library News* of Sept. 1924, to *drames à clef* in the *Bulletin* of April, 1956. These were built into books by E. F. Walbridge, *Literary Characters Drawn from Life,* 1936, supplement, 1953; *Drames à Clef,* 1956. J. Sandoe, in *Murder, Plain and Fanciful,* 1948, gives stories and plays based on actual crimes. Georg Schneider, *Die Schlüsselliteratur,* 3 v., 1951–53; I. Wallace, *The Fabulous Originals,* 1955.

loa (Sp., praise). A flattering address to an audience, to gain sympathy and support. Hence, a prologue.

local color. The use of environmental details in a story, differs from regionalism (*q.v.*) in its mainly picturesque intent. Its interest lies in exploring a new or unfamiliar setting (Kipling, 1865–1936; Bret Harte, 1836–1902, the U.S. West), or in preserving the record of a changing or dying locale (Joel Chandler Harris, 1848–1908; Thomas Nelson Page, 1853–1922; Mary N. Murfee, 1850–1922: the Old South before the War Between the States). While the regionalist sees in each region different conditions that operate profoundly in the lives of its people and thus develop different patterns of culture and character, the local colorist takes rather the tourist's view of a countryside; so that Francis Hopkinson Smith (1838–1915) *e.g.,* wrote local color novels about many parts of the U.S. Local color thus presents superficial elements of setting, dialect, costume, customs, not as a basic element of the story but as decoration. In the U.S., however, esp. 1875–1914 (George Washington Cable, 1844–1925; Sarah Orne Jewett, 1849–1909; Mark Twain: Samuel Langhorne Clemens, 1835–1910) local color helped Am. fiction away from Victorian forms and topics. Since then, a more serious regionalism has grown. *Cf.* Description; Short story.

logaoedic (Gr., speech and singing). A modern term indicating a rhythm between poetry and prose, applied to Gr. meters in which dactyls are combined with trochees or iambs. Now largely replaced by the term aeolic, *q.v.* Christ, 508–68. *See* Classical versification.

logo- (Gr. combining form, meaning word). Logodaedalus, one cunning in the use of words, an inventor of words; logodiarrhea; logofascinated; logographer: (1) Gr. chronicler, transitional from epic poetry to prose, and from legend to history. Cadmus and Hecataeus of Miletus were early; Helanicus of Mytilene came just before the historian Herodotus (b. 484 B.C.). (2) At Athens, a professional writer of speeches for litigants. Antiphon (d. 411 B.C.) was in demand for cases of homicide; Lysias (b. ca. 458 B.C.) wrote over 200 such speeches, 34 extant and well-organized. Logography, writing (*e.g.,* Chinese) in which each symbol is a complete word. Logogriph, an anagram, or a verse from which anagrams or other verbal puzzles are to be guessed. Logolatry, excessive fondness for words. Logomach, a disputer over words or verbal subtleties; logomachy, battle of words. Logopandocy, readiness to use words of any kind. Logopoeia: Ezra Pound (b. 1885) states that poetry, beyond its meaning, may be energized in three ways: (1) Melopoeia emphasizes the musical qualities; (2) phanopoeia, the visual images; (3) logopoeia, "the dance of the intellect among words"—the play of the mind upon all aspects of verbal manifestation.

long -syllable, *see* Quantity. -meter: a quatrain stanza used in hymns, iambic tetrameter, second and fourth lines (usually) rhyming. To "long-and-short" (Byron): to write Gr. or Latin verses.

low comedy. The more boisterous, active, elemental sort of comedy, playing with buffoonery for the belly-laugh. If it is the dominant mood, we call the play a farce; usually it appears in a short skit—the frequent afterpiece in the 19th c. theatre—or as an element in a more serious drama, as with the Porter in *Macbeth*. Such moments may provide comic relief by breaking the emotional tension, while at the same time commenting on, reiterating, and reenforcing the serious action. The obvious centers of low comedy are the viscera or below, finding fun in man's concern with food and sex. The *Bible* speaks seriously of one whose bowels are loosed with fear; in Aristophanes' *The Frogs* the frightened Dionysus exclaims:

> I seem to have soiled myself . . . Bring me a sponge, and apply it to my heart.
>
> Here you are. Apply it yourself . . . Good heavens, is *that* where your heart is?

Two thousand years later, in *Never Too Late* (1966) the characters jest lengthily about a toilet bowl set down in the living room; the next morning it adorns the lawn of the mayor's house.

By pinpricking the balloons of pretentiousness and pretense, or blowing these balloons until they are ready to burst, low comedy gives us a sense of reality, a norm for the honest facing of life. *Cf.* Comedy; Farce; Absurd, theatre of the.

lower criticism. *See* Higher.

lyric (Gr., a poem to be sung to the lyre, by one person, monodic, or by several, choral). Dorian lyric, with dancing; Ionian, expressing the author's feelings. Horace and Catullus wrote Latin imitations of the Gr. monodic lyric, but to be read in the study; hence the general use of the word: a (usually) short, personal poem. In its earliest days the lyric may have been a succession of meaningless sounds to accompany dance and music; this aspect survives in the refrain, esp. of Elizabethan songs, *e.g., with a hey nonny nonny*. There has been a recent revival of the lyric as a poem to be sung (Vachel Lindsay; Alfred Kreymborg, and later poets who chant their verses in cafés). C. M. Bowra, *Gr. Lyric Poetry,* 1936, 1962; E. Rhys, *Lyric Poetry,* 1913; C. Day Lewis, *The Lyric Impulse,* 1965; D. L. Peterson, *The Eng. Lyric from Wyatt to Donne,* 1967; W. E. McCulloh, Introd. to W. Barnstone, *Gr. Lyric Poetry,* 1962, 1967.

lysiody. *See* Magody.

M

MACARONIC. A mixture of two or more languages in a poem, or the verse thus formed. Esp. Latin and a modern tongue. Begun as a burlesque of the hodgepodge of Latin and the vernacular in the sermons of monks in the Middle Ages. Usually for humorous purposes; often the vernacular words are given Latin endings. *Cf.* Fatrasie. J. A. Morgan, *Macaronic Poetry,* 1872.

macrology. P. "long language." Unnecessary repetition in lengthy phrases and clauses, *e.g.,* "returned home into their own country from whence they had come." *Cf.* Periphrasis, Repetition.

madness, poetic.

The lunatic, the lover, and the poet
Are of imagination all compact.

Long before Shakespeare, Plato associated the divine afflatus and the poetic furor. An uncritical acceptance of a close bond between "possession" and inspiration ("the poet's eye, in a fine frenzy rolling") paved the way for Max Nordau's *Degeneration* (1893) and Cesare Lombroso's *Genio e degenerazione* (1898), an attitude that brought response in Shaw's *The Sanity of Art* (1895). Two main counter-considerations arise. (1) The insane believes and lives his fantasies; the poet frees himself from his fancies by setting them down (and therefore apart from himself, as separate objects of contemplation); (2) insanity (and the dream) present imagination disorganized, following every whim or emotional impulse; art presents imagination most fully organized —emotion the steed, perhaps, but the artist holding the reins. Not only the majestic order of *The Divine Comedy,* with its intricate number-plan and fourfold symbolism, but the emotional outcry of Shelley's *Ode to the West Wind* shows synthetic, unifying power beyond any madman's phantasmagoria. It must none the less be observed that, just as the work of art itself is a delicate balance of opposites, a blend of unity in variety; just as it may rouse in the receptor a poised stimulation of opposite tendencies (*see* Synæsthesis), so in the artist it demands an arousal of intellect and emotion beyond their usual concordant range. This is manifestly difficult to maintain, *a fortiori* in the Romantics, pledged to indulgence; it may, in their non-creative hours, lead to excess. While there are always cases where extremes may seem to meet, it is perhaps of value to declare (Laura Riding and Robert Graves) that insanity and genius are both beyond mediocrity, hence linked by the mediocre; but insanity is below mediocrity in the direction of chaos, whereas genius is above it in the direction of cosmos, order. In creation, psychoanalysts emphasize an *abaissement du niveau mental* (Pierre Janet). Freud (letter to Fliess, May 31, 1897) compares creative writing to hysterical fantasying, and adds: "Shakespeare was right in his juxtaposition of poetry and madness." Jung goes further in his essay on *Ulysses,* speaking of Joyce's "conversation in and with his own intestines," his transformation of eschatology into scatology . . . "It is all too familiar, those interminable ramblings of the insane who have only a fragmentary consciousness and consequently suffer from a complete lack of judgment and an atrophy of all their values. Instead, there is often an intensification of the sense activities." From this "perversion of sense into nonsense, of beauty into ugliness," this "art in reverse, the backside of art," it is (as Genêt puts it) "a crab's jump" to the anti-novel and the school of the absurd. *Cf.* Unconscious; Psychoanalysis; Inspiration; Dream; Beat; Hippie; Anti-hero; Absurd.

madrigal. Originally a pastoral; now, any short love poem, esp. one to a tune. (Petrarch, *Canzoniere,* 52, 54, 106; D'Annunzio). Usually 2 or 3 tercets followed by 1 or 2 couplets; many rhyme schemes, *e.g., abc, abc, dd; aba, bcb, cc.*

magic. "Art is magic, not logic" (Edith Sitwell, in *Tradition and Experiment,* 1929). She declares that an irrational spirit in logical form is manifest in a Shakespeare, Da Vinci, Beethoven; a logical spirit in irrational form sprouts the poetasters and the surrealists. *Cf.* Supernatural; Inspiration; Madness.

magody (*lysiody, hilarody, simody*). Gr. literary forms variously defined as types of the mime, or akin to the lyrics of the variety-theatre. According to Aristoxenus of Tarentum (cited by Athenæus), the magodist took his plots from comedy, played both masculine and feminine roles, though all his garments were feminine; the lysiodist, with flute accompaniment, played women's roles in masculine dress. *Hilarody* was written in sober diction; the hilarodist wore masculine dress, a golden crown, even buskins, since he parodied tragedy. According to Strabo, *simody* was the later name for *hilarody,* from Simos, the melic poet. *See* Mime.

malaprop, malapropism. (Mrs. Malaprop, in Sheridan's *The Rivals,* 1775). Substitution of one word (usually polysyllabic) for another of somewhat similar sound, so as to produce a ludicrous incongruity. Dogberry (Shak., *Much Ado About Nothing*) is an addict; Cervantes' Sancho Panza speaks of crickets (critics). Mrs. Malaprop prides herself on her "nice derangement of epitaphs." The immediate suggestion for Mrs. Malaprop came from Mrs. Winifred Jenkins in *Humphrey Clinker,* 1771, a novel by Tobias Smollett.

mal mariée. An old Fr. lyric, classified as *chanson dramatique* (Jeanroy), *chanson à personnages* (G. Paris), or *son d'amors* (Gröber). A dance song of the May festival, in which the poet describes the complaint of a woman against her unloved husband. A variant presents a nun sorrowing because she does not feel her vocation.

manner. 16th–18th c., character as revealed in a work, or its portrayal. Later, the general way in which the work is developed, the style as opposed to the substance (manner vs. matter). One's manner reflects one's attitude toward life: gay, whimsical, sprightly; or cynical, or melancholy. Such an attitude may become a habit or mark a temperament; it thus does not necessarily reflect the mood of a writer at the time of a certain book. Indeed, manner can be artificial, following a school to which the artist adheres.

mannerism. Peculiarity, or sum of peculiarities, that enters into or constitutes an author's style. Often derogatory, denoting superficial or affected peculiarities (easily selected for parody) *e.g.,* the regular almost sing-song cadences of Gibbon; the fluid alliterative lines of Swinburne (self-parodied in the last poem of *Heptalogia*).

mantra. Ind. Pantomimed religious chant, probable origin of Indic *Natya,* dance drama. The *Mantrapatha* (prayer-book) contains 590 mantras for domestic rites and ceremonials.

maqāma. Arabic. Romance and anecdotes in rhymed prose. First used by Abu al-Fadl Ahmed ibn al-Husain al-Hamadhani (967–1007), known as Badi al-Zaman "wonder of the age." Developed by Abu Mohammed al-Qasim al-Hariri (1054–1122), one of the great masters of Arabic style, whose 50 *maqāmāt* rank next to the Koran as a model of Arabic writing. In subject the maqāmāt are akin to the picaresque tales, recounting the adventures of the rascally Abu Zayd. Their dialogue marks the closest Arab approach to drama. Both al-Hamadhani and al-Hariri are available in English; their form was imitated in the German *Makame. Cf.* German versification.

marinism. The exaggerated, artificial, bombastic style of G. B. Marino (It., 1569–1623). *Cf.* Secentismo; Baroque.

marivaudage. Affected manner of writing in the style of Pierre Carlet de Chamblin de Marivaux (1688–1763), Fr. dramatist and novelist. Seeking to sift the human heart, Marivaux expressed his psychological insights in nice but affectedly phrased nuances. He utilized a prose conversation esoteric and subtle—*recherché*—in an incisive examination of the human psyche under the stress and strain of love in a cultivated society. His chief comedies are *La Surprise de l'amour* (1722), *Le Jeu de l'amour et du hasard* (1734), *Les Fausses confidences* (1737): delicate analyses of the female heart—Marivaux being the first dramatist to do this—in which the action is motivated by chicanery in the "war between the sexes." The originality of expression lies in the mixture of the ordinary or natural with antitheses, subtle witticisms, and finely-spun thoughts. In *La Vie de Marianne* (1730–41), his best novel, can be found the same sensitive analysis and expression of the sentiment of love. Contemporary writers—Grimm, Diderot, d'Alembert, Beaumarchais—were united, with the notable exception of l'abbé Prévost, in condemning Marivaux for hair-splitting, undue straining for originality, and the like; Voltaire said of him that he spent his life weighing nothing in scales of spider webs. Despite this, Marivaudage has had its imitators, the most successful being Alfred de Musset (*La Caprice*);

and more recently the critics Sainte-Beuve, Richard Aldington, and Edmond Jaloux have recognized its psychological validity, while the Fr. dramatist Giraudoux has noted its influence upon his work. F. Deloffe, *Marivaux et le marivaudage,* 1955; E. J. H. Greene, *Marivaux,* 1965. JOHN BURKE SHIPLEY.

masculine rhyme. Single, monosyllabic rhyme; also called male rhyme. Correspondence of final syllable, accented, of two or more words, differing in the initial consonant, *e.g.,* blow, snow, owe, dough. This is the most common form of rhyme in English. In French, it often alternates with feminine rhyme (the Fr. feminine rhyme made so by the final *e,* which in prose is silent). *Cf.* Rhyme; Feminine rhyme.

masochism. Pleasure, esp. sexual, derived from the acceptance of humiliation or pain. *See* Pornography.

masque, the. (Rather a theatrical than a literary genre; it flourished mainly in Eng. during the career of Ben Jonson. Folk plays and elaborate court entertainments in It. and Fr. paved the way; also the Ren. pastoral drama and the early opera). The masque was characterized by elaborate machinery, capable of striking changes, as from "an ugly hell" to the House of Fame in Jonson's *Masque of Queens,* by a turning machine, *machina versatilis,* designed by Inigo Jones; the apparel of the actors was richly designed, attempting historical accuracy or allegorical significance; the noble masquers, including Queen Anne, were costumed as 12 famous queens of antiquity. In contrast were the characters of the anti-masque, witches as in *Macbeth*; one of them had vipers in her hair and bore a torch made of a dead man's hand.

The masquers performed spectacular dances, also with men and women from the audience; one of these in the *Masque of Queens* occupied almost an hour. These dances, survivals from the predecessors of the Jonsonian masque, remain a feature of the form, as in the spectacular entrance or revelation of the masquers.

Jonson demanded, in addition to the spectacular, that the whole, masque and anti-masque, be brought into a unity. His insistence on the poet as leader in the preparation of masques led to a quarrel with Inigo Jones, who stood for the primacy of spectacle and costume, and was willing to sacrifice intellectual quality, unity, for visual attractiveness. Shirley, Carew, Davenant were more amenable to Jones' desires. Milton called his *Comus* a masque, yet it must have seemed more drama than masque to its first beholders, despite the dance of Comus' rout—which serves as a sort of anti-masque—the country dances, and the dance of the three chief actors with members of the audience. Davenant's *Salmacida Spolia,* 1640, is generally considered the last important masque. With the reopening of the Eng. theatres after the Restoration, the stage techniques and devices of the masque greatly influenced the production of plays; the flexibility they displayed has developed in the treadmills, moving platforms, and revolving sections of current stage productions.

In the 20th c. there was a revival of the masque, esp. in the work of the Am. Percy Mackaye (1875–1956). H. A. Evans, *Eng. Masques,* 1897; A. Nicoll, *Stuart Masques and the Ren. Stage,* 1918; R. Withington, *Eng. Pageantry,* 1918. ALLAN H. GILBERT.

meaning. The nature of meaning—what it means to say that an expression has a meaning or means such-and-such—is still subject to philosophical inquiry and dispute (*see* Sign; Language). But, without taking a premature or dogmatic position, it may be said that there is substantial agreement that an adequate account of meaning must include two ingredients, though the exact relationship between them is undecided: meaning involves both *regularities* and *rules.*

The first point is that for a word or a sentence to have a specific meaning, there must be some general causal connection between its utterance under certain conditions and the responses of members of a linguistic community. This point is emphasized by C. L. Stevenson (*Ethics and Language,* 1944, ch. 3), who construes the meaning of a sign as a dispositional property of the sign, *i.e.,* its tendency to produce certain responses under certain conditions. This does not imply that a verbal expression can be tied to specific invariant mental or physical behavior (the word "cow" will arouse different images and feelings in different listeners; people may react to the imperative "Look out!" in different ways); but it does imply that unless there is some limited range of responses which is connected with the use of an expression that appears in the context of a given language, then that expression has no meaning (makes no sense) in that language.

The second point is that for a word or a sentence to have a specific meaning, its use in a linguistic community must be governed by rules, in terms of which the expression may be said to be correctly or incorrectly applied on a given occasion, and correctly or incorrectly combined with other expressions in that language. This point has been emphasized by William Alston (*Philosophy of Language,* 1964), following the work of J. L. Austin (*How to do Things with Words,* 1962) and other philosophers strongly influenced by Ludwig Wittgenstein (*Philosophical Investigations,* 1953). Austin classifies the various things that a language-user does in using sentences: *e.g.,* stating, exhorting, requesting, promising, warning, advising. He calls these "illocutionary acts," to distinquish them from "perlocutionary acts," or what the language-user does *by means of* language, the results he obtains: *e.g.,* informing, sentencing, convincing, inspiring, moving. What defines a particular illocutionary act is a set of "conditions" for which the speaker "takes responsibility"; for example, a person cannot promise to do something yesterday, nor can he promise to do what no one wants him to do, nor can he promise that someone else will do something. These are among the rules for promising—not moral rules governing the rightness or wrongness of acts of promising, but rules that determine whether an act of promising has actually been performed (if a person says "I promise to take you to the movies last Saturday" he is not really promising; he has violated the rules governing the use of the term "promise," and what he says is unintelligible). Alston's proposal is to define the meaning of sentences and parts of sentences in terms of their "illocutionary act potential," or capacity to serve in specific ways in the performance of illocutionary acts.

Students of language often distinguish certain types of meaning according to the type of response involved: the main distinction here being that between "emotive meaning" and "cognitive (or descriptive) meaning" (the latter is also called "referential meaning" by Ogden and Richards in their pioneer treatise, *The Meaning of Meaning,* 1923, 1966). Some writers speak also of "pictorial meaning"—the tendency of a sign to evoke images in the hearer (Virgil Aldrich, "Pictorial Meaning and Picture Thinking," in Feigl and Sellars, *Readings in Philosophical Analysis,* 1949). Emotive meaning, according to Stevenson, "is a meaning in which the response (from the hearer's point of view) or the stimulus (from the speaker's point of view) is a range of emotions," in contrast to meaning in which the relevant response and stimulus are "cognitive" states and processes, such as thinking, believing, supposing, doubting. Thus, for example, the *cognitive* meaning of the word "formalism" (as employed by opponents of the "New Criticism") consists, roughly, in its tendency to call attention, loosely, to a special concern with the structure and unity of poems; its *emotive* meaning consists, in part, in its tendency to arouse a feeling of disapproval in the hearer, as, in turn, its utterance evinces a feeling of disapproval on the part of the speaker. It is to be noted that the word "disapproval" does not have "emotive meaning," though it *refers* to a feeling.

An important problem raised by this distinction lies in the connection between the emotive meaning of words and their cognitive meaning. Stevenson, like many other contemporary empiricists, argues that to a significant extent the emotive meaning of words is independent of their cognitive meaning, so that a word may have emotive meaning without having cognitive meaning; a word may vary in either type while the other remains unchanged; and two words may have the same cognitive meaning but very different emotive meanings. Others have urged a much closer connection between the two types (see the symposia in the *Philosophical Review,* March 1948 and July and October 1950), especially in the case of poetry; many critics, either in theory or practice, hold that the emotional effect of poetry depends in large part upon its cognitive meaning. Though much debated, and very important, this issue is still far from clear (I. A. Richards, "Emotive Language Still," *Yale R.* XXXIX, 1949; W. K. Wimsatt and M. C. Beardsley, "The Affective Fallacy," *Sewanee R.,* LVII, Autumn 1949).

Under the heading of cognitive meaning, it is customary to distinguish between two relations: (1) The relation between a word and the things it *names,* or denotes; these things are then called the "extension" or "denotation" of the word. (2) The relation between a word and certain characteristics, or properties, of things; these characteristics constitute the "intension" of the word, or are said to be "signified" by it; logicians, however, following the usage of J. S. Mill, call these characteristics the "connotation" of the word. Thus the word "man" is said to mean (that is, denote) George Washington and any other individual man; and it is said to mean (that is, to have as part of its intension) such characteristics as *being an animal* and *having two legs.*

In dealing with a natural language, and esp. with poetry, it is usual to distinguish two levels of intension in verbal meaning. There are certain characteristics that form the standard meaning of a word; and when the word is used so that in a great many contexts it regularly refers to a certain set of characteristics, and its meaning is therefore felt to be relatively fixed by rules of usage, the word may be said to "designate" those characteristics (as, *e.g.*, "fox" designates the characteristics that define the species). What is here called "designation" is commonly called "dictionary meaning"; literary critics often misleadingly use the term "denotation" for it; Stevenson calls it "descriptive meaning." With most common words, certain characteristics become associated, in such a way that the word can suggest those characteristics to users of the language; thus, *e.g.*, the word "fox" carries the idea of *cunning*, though this is not part of its designation. Such associated characteristics are said to be "connoted" by the word, or to be part of its "fringe meaning" (in contrast to its "core meaning"), or to be part of its "cognitive suggestion" (Stevenson; *see* Connotation; Symbolism). Despite the bewildering variety of terminology, and the difficulties that remain in giving a clear account of the relation between designation and connotation, this distinction appears to be widely assumed and employed in the analysis of poetry. *Cf.* Ambiguity; Obscurity; Etymology; Language; Linguistics; Emotive; Literary Criticism. C. L. Morris, *Signs, Lang. and Behavior,* 1946, ch. 1; W. Empson, *The Structure of Complex Words,* 1951; Roger Brown, *Words and Things,* 1958; J. Ciardi, *How Does a Poem Mean?,* 1960; E. T. Gendlin, *Experiencing and the Creation of Meaning,* 1962; M. C. Beardsley, "The Metaphysical Twist," *Phil. and Phenomenological Research XX,* 1962; C. L. Stevenson, *Facts and Values,* 1963; H. D. Lewis, *Clarity Is not Enough,* 1963; L. Antal, *Questions of Meaning,* 1963; *Content, Meaning, and Understanding,* 1964; G. Stern, *Meaning and Change of Meaning,* 1931, 1964; K. C. Hill, *Interpreting Lit.,* 1966; S. I. Hayakawa and W. Dresser, *Dimensions of Meaning,* 1967; G. H. R. Parkinson, *The Theory of Meaning,* 1968. MONROE C. BEARDSLEY.

meaning, change of, may take place in several ways. A. Apart from the quite different senses that one word may have (*e.g.* plain: clear; not good looking; a stretch of land), the same combination of letters may at times take less noticeably different meanings. This is a source, occasionally of poetic power, frequently of all too prosaic confusion. The most frequent such changes are: (1) Part-whole shifts, from a general range to a specific application, *e.g.*, "Argument is often fruitless"; "Your argument is invalid." (2) Content change: "That" (a 5-dollar bill) "is a potent argument." In addition the meaning of a word may be modified by its associations: *e.g.*, "the 13th" takes on a sinister significance if preceded by "Friday." A sign has meaning (*i.e.*, a sign is a symbol) only if it signifies something, *e.g.*, "square" as opposed to "square circle." Of course, no word (no symbol) *is* the thing it signifies. Some words (*e.g.*, "argument," above) are multiordinal, have meaning within many orders of abstraction. Some words have meaning within one order, but in another are meaningless; *e.g.*, "unicorn" in heraldry and fancy, and in zoology. *Cf.* Hypostatization. B. More permanently, in the history of the language, words may change by (1) substitution, as customs or devices change, *e.g.* "ship" of the 17th c. and "ship" of the 20th are quite different. (2) analogy, *e.g.*, "quick," living, as in "the quick and the dead," comes to mean lively. (3) shortening, as the principal teacher becomes the school's "principal." (4) nomination, by metaphor, *e.g.*, "cow's lip" becomes cowslip. (5) transfer, "leaf" of a tree to "leaf" of a book. (6) permutation, *e.g.*, "beads," prayers, becomes the rosary balls by which the prayers are counted. (7) adequation: animal's "horn" becomes the musical instrument. *See* Etymology; *cf.* Language; Signs; Symbol. W. Empson, *Seven Types of Ambiguity,* 1929; G. Stern, *Meaning and Change of Meaning,* 1932, 1964; I. A. Richards, *How to Read a Page,* 1942.

meaning, four kinds of. I. The Middle Ages saw four levels of significance in all valid writing, as in Dante's *Divine Comedy,* and most notably in the *Bible.* (1) Historical: the literal or actual story. (2) Allegorical: truths relating to mankind as a whole. (3) Tropological: a moral lesson. (4) Anagogical: the spiritual or mystical vision of ultimate and eternal truth. II. Most human utterances can be regarded from four points of view, viz.: Sense, Feeling, Tone, Intention. (1) Sense. We use words to direct our hearer's attention upon some state of affairs, to present some items for consideration and to excite some thoughts about these items.

(2) Feeling. But we also, as a rule, have some feelings about these items, about the

state of affairs we are referring to. We have some special bias of interest towards it, some personal coloring of feeling; and we use language to express these feelings, this nuance of interest.

(3) Tone. The speaker has ordinarily an attitude to his listener. He chooses or arranges his words differently as his audiences vary, in automatic or deliberate consequence of his relation to them. The tone of his utterance reflects this relation, his sense of how he stands towards those he is addressing.

(4) Intention. Apart from what he says (Sense), his attitude to what he is talking about (Feeling), and his attitude to his listener (Tone), there is the speaker's intention, his aim, conscious or unconscious, the effect he is endeavoring to promote. Ordinarily he speaks for a purpose; this modifies his speech. The understanding of it is part of the whole business of apprehending his meaning. Unless we know what he is trying to do, we can hardly estimate the measure of his success. He may purpose no more than to state his thoughts, or to express his feelings about what he is thinking of, *e.g.,* Hurrah! Damn!, or to express his attitude to his listener as in the case of endearments and abuse.

Frequently intention operates through a combination of other functions, but it has effects that are peculiarly its own. It may, *e.g.,* govern the stress laid upon points in an argument, shape the arrangement, and even call attention to itself in such phrases as "for contrast's sake" or "lest it be supposed." It controls the "plot" in the largest sense of the word, and is at work whenever the author is "hiding his hand."

Contrast, *e.g.,* the case of a man writing a scientific treatise with that of a man writing an election campaign speech. The former will put the sense of what he has to say first; the latter will subordinate sense and give priority to the furtherance of intentions (of all grades of worthiness). The scientist will subordinate his feelings about his subject and be careful not to let them interfere to distort his argument or suggest bias. The politician will implement the furtherance of his intentions by expressing his feelings about causes, policies, candidates and opponents. The scientist's tone will be more or less settled for him by academic convention; the politician's will be calculated for the establishment of favorable relations with the audience. The scientist's intention will normally be confined to the clearest and most adequate statement of what he has to say. *Cf.* Narrator. I. A. Richards.

measure. (1) Meter (*q.v.*); *e.g.,* long measure in hymns; Poulter's measure. (2) Control, or the proportion attained by the exercise of control; the mean.

mechanism. The structure of a work; the skill of execution, or the system of mutually adapted parts in the work, considered purely from the point of view of its construction. Opp. to expression and style as well as to content and meaning.

medievalism. Accenting themes or patterns popularly regarded as medieval. First recorded use, by Ruskin, 1854. In literature, concern for European national folklore and emulation of primitive literary form is one aspect; another is accentuation of romantic themes such as castles, fair ladies, chivalric codes. In religion, medievalism accents sacerdotalism and ritual (as in the Oxford Movement); in the state, dictatorship of the "man on horseback"; in social welfare, craftsmanship and communal economics; in teaching, dialectics, etc. The most important manifestation of medievalism was the Gothic Revival which readily united with the Romantic Revival, though the leading Romantics were not so directly interested in recapturing the medieval imagery as in creating a veil of beauty or melancholy such as shrouded the medieval ruins that they knew. The "discovery" of the *Song of Roland* and the *Nibelungenlied* is typical medievalism; the pre-Raphaelite movement is more extreme. H. B. Parkes, *The Divine Order,* 1969.

meiosis. P. "the disabler." Presenting something as less than it really is; the irony of understatement. Sometimes colloquial: "I rather think so"; sometimes endearing: *"mon petit chou";* sometimes poetic: "The Hound of Heaven." Sometimes homely: (*David Copperfield*) "Barkis is willin';" opposite of hyperbole (*q.v.*) *Cf.* Amplification; Litotes; Irony.

Meistergesang. G. Poetry written to be sung to melodies; reached its height in the 16th c. with Hans Sachs. The *Meistersinger* were for the most part artisans and tradesmen; they eschewed the love themes of the earlier *Minnesinger*; their songs were didactic, trying to maintain moral standards in an age that was lax, and to bring to the middle class the heritage of the past. Esp. characteristic is the tri-part strophe, called *Lied* or *Gesätz.* The first two parts, *Stollen* and *Gegenstollen* (strophe and antistrophe) were alike; the third, the *Abgesang,* though related in structure, was longer. *Meisterlieder* helped spread the doctrines of the Reformation, and were included in Protestant hymnals. *Cf. Minnesinger;* Ode. A. Taylor, *The Lit. Hist. of Meistergesang,* 1937; Taylor and Ellis, *A Bibliog. of Meistergesang,* 1936.

melic poetry (Gr. *melos,* song). Was written to be accompanied by music of lyre or flute. It had many subdivisions (dithyramb, pæan, hymn); of practically any meter. The golden age of Gr. melic poetry was from the 7th to the 5th c. B.C.; from this period the scholars of Alexandria drew their canon of 9 melic poets; Alcman, Alcæus, Sappho, Stesichorus, Ibycus, Anacreon, Simonides, Pindar, and Bacchylides, to whom Corinna is sometimes added. By the Alexandrians and after them the term lyric was applied to this type of poetry. H. W. Smyth: *Greek Melic Poetry,* 1900, 1963.

melodrama (Gr. "song" + Fr. *drame*). Originally a piece of declamation accompanied by music (Rousseau, *Fragmens d'observations sur l'Alceste italien de M. le Chevalier Gluck,* 1767). Begun in It. (Rinucinni, *Dafne,* 1599, music by J. Pieri and Caccini) as an effort to recapture the methods of classical drama; for 100 years synonymous with opera: G. F. Händel (1685–1759, lived in Eng. after 1710) called his works by both names. (Laurent Garcin, *Traité du Mélo-Drame; ou, Réflexions sur le Musique dramatique,* 1772). Rousseau's *Pygmalion* (Paris, 1775) has been called "the first example of this Monster which so delights the mob, and which is so justly despised by men of taste and culture" (Gaiffe). Many writers (de Larive, Florian, Mayeur de Saint Paul) multiplied the characters, hence elaborated the dialogue, augmented the spectacle giving more importance to the music, and in less than 20 years we have full-blooded melodrama, with sensational incident, violent emotional appeal, happy ending (*L'Auto da-Fé,* L. Gabiot; prod. Ambigu-Comique, Nov. 1790). For villainy and thrills this can hardly be paralleled until we reach the convulsive horrors of *Isaure; or, the Maniac of the Alps* and the evergreen "shudderful sanguifulminous" *Alone in the Pirates' Lair* of Victorian days.

Many influences went to the making of melodrama. The sombre and loudly applauded tragedies of Crébillon père: *Atrée et Thyeste* (1707); *Rhadamiste et Zénobie* (1711), had already pointed the way. A master of the form is René-Charles Guilbert de Pixerécourt (1773–1844), the *"Corneille du Boulevard,"* who wrote 63 melodramas. His most famous is *Cælina; ou, l'enfant du mystère* (prod. Ambigu-Comique, Sept. 1800). The first full melodrama on the Eng. stage was an adaptation of *Cælina* as *A Tale of Mystery,* by Thomas Holcroft (prod. Covent Garden, Nov. 1802). The spirit and essence of melodrama, of course, are present in many Eng. plays from the beginnings (*e.g., The Jew of Malta*) and scores in the late 18th c. approximate the type. It is rooted in most tragedy, being to that form as farce is to comedy, a cruder and more popular kin.

In many of these melodramas (Chas. Somerest, *The Mistletoe Bough,* at the Garrick, 1843), as now in the motion pictures, the action was sustained by the orchestra: soft music for the heroine's sorrows; all emotions deftly fortified with concordant strains. An element of the supernatural is never amiss: skeletons in a moonlight churchyard, Milner, *Alonzo the Brave*; a lovely rose-garlanded nymph changed to a skeleton, Grattan, *Faust*; apparitions, Lewis, *The Castle Spectre,* Mark Lemon, *The Ancestress*; astrologers and visions of the future, Farren, *The Field of Forty Footsteps,* Wilks, *The Red Crow*; books of fate, Walker, *The Wizard Priest*; witches, forest demons, vampires, kobolds—the library of occult lore. At the opposite pole are the purely domestic melodramas, stories of everyday life, in which the spectators could see themselves. In fact, the audiences asked for and got an adroitly mixed bag. The metropolitan minor theatre might open with a piece of sensational, even sordid, realism, and finish a long program with some wizard legend or tale of diablerie. *Scamps of London* (with "new Flash Medley Overture and Slang Dramatic Music") by W. J. Moncrieff, 1843, gives us the thriller technique, building toward a big scene, usually a rescue: "Louisa Placed Upon the Rails. The Mail Approaches Nearer and Nearer. Louisa Saved by Fog. The Express Train Dashes Along." A similar incident occurs in Augustin Daly's *Under the Gaslight* (prod. N.Y. Theatre, Aug. 1867); in *After Dark* (Princess's, London, 1868); *The Streets of London* (Princess's, 1864; adapted by Boucicault from the Fr.; played in the U.S. as *The Poor of New York.*)

Melodrama, though obvious, was theatrically effective in the highest degree. Its technique was borrowed by more "refined" writers (Hugo, Dumas, the "well-made" play of Scribe) and thus influenced the regrowth of the dramatic art, from Ibsen to the expressionists. A factor that contributed to the great number of English melodramas was the monopoly of the patent theatres, Drury Lane and Covent Garden. While the minors were allowed "burlettas," and a vagueness let many things slip by, their safest line was with spectacle and melodrama. The acting of melodrama is a tradition, almost lost today. Nothing finical, nothing mealy and mincing, nothing half-hearted; forceful acting, with breadth and power. It seeks not æsthetic detachment but emotional identification, the villain hissed, the hero hailed along. Its scripts are difficult to read; stage direction must be transposed into action; the stage visualized in movement and meaning from the printed page. Barrymore's *Manfred, e.g.,* Act II, Sc. 2, has its climax in a page and a half of stage directions with scarce a couple of dozen spoken words. Leopold Lewis, a less than indifferent literary lounger, tinkering at and spoiling *Le Juif Polonais* of Erckmann-Chatrian, produced a hack-work piece he called *The Bells.* The script is not easy to read; the dialogue is often awkward and flat, or stilted and mouthy. With the acting genius of Henry Irving it held theatres enthralled. . . . Founded on primal human emotions, on a universal sense of right and wrong, melodrama endures. The longest continuous run in all dramatic history is that of Agatha Christie's melodrama *The Mouse Trap,* which has been running in London since 1952.

Melodrama carries into a world that no longer believes in hellfire deeds that might deserve it; it is a secular presentation of the demonic mode, with the horned devil replaced by a human villain. *Cf.* Diabolism; Opera; Gothic; Drama. P. Ginisty, *Le Mélodrame,* 1919; Carados (H. Chance Newton), *Crime and the Drama,* 1927; M. W. Disher, *Blood and Thunder,* 1949; R. B. Heilman, *Tragedy and Melodrama,* 1968. MONTAGUE SUMMERS.

melopoeia (Aristotle: the musical element in Gr. tragedy). *See* Logo-.

memoir. *See* Autobiography.

merde, mystique de la. Term used (first by Robert E. Fitch, 1956) to mark the obsessive preoccupation of some recent writers with "mud, blood, money, sex, and merde," as merging in the basic reality of life. Of mysticism—the direct contact, without intermediaries, between an individual and his god—Fitch neatly distinguishes two types. In the Biblical mysticism of confrontation "the individual and God always remain two distinct personalities and God confronts man with an ethical imperative." In the pagan mysticism of identification, the individual and the deity blend, "the self disappears, and the ethical requirement evaporates. The mystique de la merde belongs to the pagan tradition." It takes sustenance if not origin in Freud's dictum that "embryologically the anus corresponds to the primitive mouth." Freud goes on to link the faeces, the merde, with the penis, and with gold and money. Thus if sex is the prime symbol of the cult, merde is its terminal symbol. Writers of this school reject God because he has not made men happy. They proclaim a passion for honesty; but, like Papa Hemingway, they feel that truth is best apprehended when intoxicate.

In Hemingway's *A Farewell to Arms* (1929), Catherine wishes that she could have shared Frederic's gonorrhea. The French writer Jean Genêt (*Notre Dame des fleurs,* 1949) cherishes the crab in his pubic hair because no doubt it came from his (male) lover. In the theatre, Tennessee Williams is the chief exponent of this mystique, although an important element in a number of recent plays is the presence or the audible flushing of the toilet. These writers take as their realm what Shakespeare (*King Lear,* IV, 6) says is the devil's: "But to the girdle do the gods inherit; Beneath is all the fiend's." *Cf.* Slice of life; Low Comedy; Black Comedy.

meronym. A term midway of a polarity, the mean between two extremes, as convex, *flat,* concave; theism, *agnosticism,* atheism.

mesode. Part of an ode, independent in structure, between the strophe and antistrophe.

mesostich. *See* Acrostic.

mesothesis. A reconcilement; an idea suggested to link two apparently contradictory thoughts or principles. *Cf.* Antithesis.

metalepsis. (1) "The far-fetched." Substitution of an idea distantly related, *e.g.* (Medea) "Curse the mountain that bore the pine that first caused all my care!" (The mast of the ship that brought us together.) (2) A form of metonymy: substitution in which the original word would be figurative, *e.g.,* "His thirst for life that bottle will never quench!" ("bottle" for its contents; but the context may show the reference is not to liquor).

metamorphic word. One created by change to a more familiar form; *e.g., chestnut* from *castnut; frontispiece* from *frontispice; sweetheart* from *sweethard. See* Etymology.

metanoia. P. "The penitent." Making a remark, then at once retracting or softening it, *e.g.:*

"... in rage he shook,
Not rage, but righteous wrath ..."

metaphor (L. *translatio;* "the figure of transport"). The substitution of one thing for another, or the identification of two things from different ranges of thought, *e.g.* (Shak.) "Thou art the grave where buried love doth lie." Though often loosely defined as "an implied comparison," "a simile without like or as," metaphor is distinct, logically and probably phylologically the prior symbol. Myth and metaphor, says Susanne Langer (*Mind,* 1967) "seem to have preceded our sober literalmindedness." This may *seem* to be so, but more probably what we now call myth and metaphor were themselves originally literal. (*Cf.* Symbolism as a literary device.) Metaphor is considered by many the basic poetic figure: Quintilian calls it the commonest and most beautiful; Aristotle claims it is the best gift of the poet, the ability to find resemblance in seemingly disparate things. Shelley said "Language is vitally metaphorical." I. A. Richards (*The Philosophy of Rhetoric,* 1936) stresses that thought works basically through metaphor—which he analyzes into the tenor (idea) and the vehicle (image): together they constitute the figure; their interaction provides the meaning. Their relation is various; at one pole the vehicle may be a mere decoration of the tenor; at the other the tenor may be a mere excuse for introducing the vehicle. Richards suggests a division of metaphors according as tenor and vehicle (A) have a direct resemblance ("the winter of my discontent") or (B) are bound by the maker's attitude (one's enemies are rats or gargoyle grotesques). The thought that rises from the figure, he feels, is influenced by the differences as well as the resemblances. The most common type, the compound or loose metaphor, catches the mind with several points of similarity; *e.g.,* "He has the wild stag's foot" (*Sohrab and Rustum*) suggests grace and sureness as well as speed, and daring, too, of hazardous attainment. So also "She's a peach!" A simple or tight metaphor is one in which there is but one point of resemblance—often called the focus of the figure—between tenor and vehicle, *e.g.,* "Thou art the grave ..." above. So also "Cool it!" A complex metaphor mounts one identification on another, *e.g.,* "That throws some light on the question," wherein (1) "throwing" light is a metaphor and (2) there is no actual light. A mixed metaphor leaps, in the course of a figure, to a second identification inconsistent with the first one; sometimes a fault, this may be an indication of perplexed or tumultuous feeling, as in Hamlet's soliloquy: "To take up arms against a sea of troubles." Some expressions, *e.g.,* "a wooden leg" are at once literal and metaphorical.

Linguists point out that most words were originally metaphors (indeed, all words identify a thing intended and a sign), so that what we now call metaphor is actually a figure imposed upon another (forgotten) figure. When we can trace the original pattern, we call it a dead metaphor, one in which the sense of a transferred image is not present, *e.g., money,* so called because first minted at the temple of Juno *Moneta.* A root metaphor is one basic or pervasive in human thought, *e.g.,* the thread or cord (spun and cut by the Greek Fates, worn by Parsi and Hebrew; Sanskrit *sutra,* aphorism in the holy books, actually means thread. *Cf.* Archetype). In Sanskrit, what we may express as a metaphor was expressed as a negative, *e.g.* Eng. "The king is a loving father"; Sansk. "The king is loving, not a father"—where "although" seems understood before the "not." A submerged metaphor is one in which the vehicle is implied, or indicated by one aspect, as "my winged thought" leaves us to supply the bird. An absolute or paralogical metaphor, sometimes called antimetaphor, is one in which there is no discernible point of resemblance between idea and image. This type is common in today's poetry, *e.g.,* "the sounds of silence"; "the hungry mollusc moon"; "We are the eyelids of defeated caves." A conceit is a far-fetched simile or metaphor. The suggestion that poetry and humor are allied draws support from the fact that the metaphor is the obverse of the joke: the one unites two ideas that had seemed distinct; the other breaks asunder what had seemed one: sudden recognition of congruity, or of incongruity.

Metaphors may also be divided (Helen H. Parkhurst, *Beauty,* 1930) on the basis of the concreteness of their terms: (a) both from the same sense domain, *e.g.,* ruin'd choirs where late the sweet birds sang" (aural); (b) from different sense domains, *e.g.,* "Heavy with bees, a sunny sound"; (c) the "imageless realm of mind and spirit"—the abstract —endowed with sensory qualities, *e.g.,* "Custom came to take me in her arms"; "cool fingers of oblivion"; (d) the reversal of the preceding: personification; sensory things caught into the abstract: (Parkhurst calls this the "most momentous" type), *e.g.,* "The moving waters at their priest-like task of pure ablution round earth's human shores." Beyond this (not listed in the Parkhurst grouping) is the fifth level, of symbolism, in which the whole image gains a further application to transcendent values. The use of metaphors was attacked by the expressionists and the futurists; the *roman nouveau* tends to eschew the figure.

One cause of obscurity in contemporary verse is the treatment of metaphor. Many of the metaphors are simple—and if the one point of resemblance does not prick the attention, the figure fails: "the skylight of an hypothesis"; firs topped with "an emerald turkey-foot"; such identifications stand on a single pillar. Beyond this, many metaphors suppress the literal term. Hugo, in "the fleece of the sinister sheep of the sea," makes known, with "sea," the whitecaps of the rounded waves; Valéry (*Cimetière marin*) in

This tranquil roof where pigeons peck
Vibrates between the pines, between the
tombs—

lets us surmise that he means the sea and the dipping sails. When T. Roethke writes "her quick look, a sidelong pickerel smile," it seems a fishy figure. *Cf.* Meaning; Simile; Figure; Symbol. H. Konrad, *Etude sur la métaphore,* 1939; M. C. Beardsley, *Æsthetics,* 1958; "The Metaphorical Twist," *Phil and Phenomenological Research,* 1962; L. C. Knights and B. Cottle, ed. *Metaphor and Symbol,* 1960; P. Wheelwright, *Metaphor and Reality,* 1962; J. A. Mazzeo, *Ren. and 17th C. Studies,* 1964; Christine Brooke-Rose, *A Grammar of Metaphor,* 1965; W. Embler, *Metaphor and Meaning,* 1966; N. A. Brown, *Love's Body,* 1966; S. R. Hopper and D. L. Miller, ed. *Interpretation,* 1967; James Dickey, *Metaphor as Pure Adventure,* 1969.

metaphrase. Through the 18th c., a translation, esp. one in verse. Later, a literal version; opp. to though sometimes confused with paraphrase.

metaphysical POETS: John Donne (1572–1631) and poets of the 17th c. whose style (though influenced also by Jonson) is similar to his (*e.g.,* Herbert, Vaughan, Crashaw in the sacred line; in the profane, Marvell, Cleveland, Cowley). The epithet is now misleading, for none of these men was a philosophical poet like Dante or Milton, expounding a view of man's relation to the universe. When first used (by Dryden) it carried another meaning which, barring the derogatory estimate, is applicable to most of this poetry. Donne, he said, "too much affects the metaphysics; . . . and perplexes the minds of the fair sex with nice speculations of philosophy, when he should engage their hearts . . . with the softnesses of love." In short, Donne is given not to the expression of feeling, but to its analysis: the philosophy, rather the psychology, of love, which was then a part of metaphysics. These poets are psychological poets exploring the recesses of consciousness. But they are also concerned with ethical and religious persuasion, and with sheer technical virtuosity. In all 3 categories their poetry has the same distinctive character: the blend of emotion with intellectual ingenuity. The two most famous quotations from Donne—"For Godsake hold your tongue, and let me love" and the comparison of two parted lovers to the legs of a draftsman's compass—isolate the opposite extremes of passionate spontaneity and calculated subtlety.

From the blending of these strains comes the dual form of metaphysical poetry: on the one hand, the dramatic medium in which diction, imagery, and rhythm are based closely on living speech, and on the other, the rhetoric of wit, both dialectic and conceit. The dialectic is the pattern of argument, often intricate and paradoxical, which underlies the structure of metaphysical poems. The conceit is the prominent use of a figure where major and minor terms are sufficiently far apart to cause a break in the normal intuitive perception and therefore the substitution, momentarily, of logical analysis. But these poets favor a special type of conceit which starts not from any common resemblance, but from an unsuspected analogy between physical and psychological action: *viz.,* the two lovers influence or "work" on one another in the same way as a compass works. It is because the major and minor terms have no past association but are a newly observed connection between disparate worlds that the metaphysical conceit may seem far-fetched.

After 1660 this poetry stood condemned before the standards of clarity and order decreed by classical canons and Baconian science. It was not until the 1920's that the social temper was in tune again with metaphysical sensibility. The distaste for both romantic idealism and Victorian preaching, in forms that seemed too loose and sensuous, with the complementary demand for a hard, intellectual verse, compressed and idiomatic in technique and in content, following the vogue of Freud, a detached and ironic analysis of mental phenomena—these are the factors, analogous to those of the Jacobean age, that produced the Donne revival, and under his ægis, that of the other metaphysicals. *Cf.* Baroque.

H. J. C. Grierson, introd. *Metaphysical Lyrics & Poems of the 17th c.,* 1921, repr., *Backgrounds of Eng. Lit.,* 1926; T. S. Eliot, "The Metaphysical Poets," and "Andrew Marvell," 1921; G. Williamson, *The Donne Tradition,* 1930; Rosamond Tuve, *Elizabethan and Metaphysical Imagery,* 1947; J. E. Duncan, *The Revival of Metaphysical Poetry,* 1959; F. J. Warnke, *European Metaphysical Poetry,* 1961; Helen L. Gardner, ed. *The Metaphysical Poets,* 1967. WALTER E. HOUGHTON.

metastasis. (Gr. "a changing"). Passing over a matter with scant attention as though it were unimportant. *See* Apophasis.

metatheater. Term suggested by Lionel Abel for serious plays that are not tragedies. Steiner declared that the Christian promise of salvation rendered tragedy impossible. Then Abel added that self-consciousness destroys tragedy, calling *Hamlet* and serious plays thereafter, *e.g.,* Arthur Miller's *Death of a Salesman,* Tennessee Williams' *A Streetcar Named Desire,* metatheater. Kerr, stating that such plays moved via Ibsen, Strindberg, and Pirandello to Beckett, Genêt, and black comedy, declared that tragedy depends upon a belief in man's freedom of choice and action. Thus Darwin, Marx, and Freud have swelled the number of those that cry tragedy is dead. Metatheater, Kerr goes on to say, is not a third form, but a new name for a subdivision of comedy; and since comedy requires the prior presence of tragedy, it is not the tragic form but creative theatre itself that calls for resuscitation. *Cf.* Theatre; Tragedy; Comedy; Drama; Melodrama; Black comedy. George Steiner, *The Death of Tragedy,* 1961; Lionel Abel, *Metatheater,* 1963; Walter Kerr, *Tragedy and Comedy,* 1967.

metathesis. (1) Change of word order. (2) Change of order of sounds or letters, or an instance thereof: (a) within a word, as an element of language growth, *e.g.,* "fringe"< *frimbia*<*firmbia* (b) between two words; Spoonerism, *q.v.*

meter (Gr. *metron,* measure). The recurrence of a rhythmic pattern within the line, and in corresponding lines, of a poem. Impassioned speech tends to be metrical. All continuous activity tends to assume a regular rhythm, an alternation of effort and relaxing —the intent or effect of which is to render the action more mechanical, thus to postpone fatigue. Similarly, meter may (Coleridge; Yeats) lull the mind into "a waking trance." It may also serve as a frame, to provide psychic distance (J. M. Murry): "There is a background of metrical sameness separating us like a curtain from the practical world; there is a richness of rhythmical variation to make the world in which we are, worthy of attention." Thus lulled into the poem's mood, our sensitivity to the poet's ideas and images is increased.

Meter may either flow with the meaning, or by its movement challenge the sense. Thus Browning, in *How They Brought the Good News From Ghent to Aix,* gives his steeds a gallop every school-boy stamps along:

I sprang to the stirrup, and Joris, and he;
I galloped, Dirck galloped, we galloped all three;
"Good speed!" cried the watch, as the gate-bolts undrew,
"Speed!" echoed the wall to us galloping through;
Behind shut the postern, the lights sank to rest,
And into the midnight we galloped abreast.

Thomas Campbell, against the sad home-thoughts of *The Soldier's Dream*:

Then pledged we the wine-cup, and fondly I swore
From my homes and my weeping friends never to part;
My little ones kiss'd me a thousand times o'er,
And my wife sobbed aloud in her fullness of heart.—

sets the ironic reality of the same meter, the soldier (not in dream) galloping to battle. Milton presents two falls from heaven, that of Lucifer:

Him the Almighty Power
Hurled headlong flaming from the ethereal sky
With hideous ruin and combustion, down—

and that of Mulciber:

flung by angry Jove
Sheer o'er the crystal battlements; from dawn
To noon he fell, from noon to dewy eve,
A summer's day; and with the setting sun
Dropped from the zenith like a falling star
On Lemnos, the Ægean isle: thus they
Relate, erring.

The first of these pours with an awesome tumult of reality; the second (subtly within the one pattern) by its dallying makes redundant the final word.

Meter and metrical form have been used to refer both to the foot-pattern and to the line of so many feet; usually, to the simple unit of the foot, composed of a certain number of syllables in a given order. The line is then described as a given number of feet of a specific pattern, the stanza as a given number of lines of uniform or varying length.

The function of quantity in verse has been a subject of much controversy among prosodists. The problems arise from conceiving the patterns of speech to be simpler than, in fact, they are, and a consequent imposing upon a metrical line of a rigid measure of long and short that does not exist in normal speech. The sharply defined "long" and "short" constitute an approximation that permits the formulation of prosodic rules, adequate for the scansion of Gr. and L. verse. How closely this quantitative measure approaches the spoken form of the dead languages we have no way of knowing. But even in the Germanic languages, which probably rely more upon stress than do any of the South European, the conception of long and short provides a rough and ready guide to the metrical pattern.

Stress, energy, accent, loudness, through phonetic necessity, are likely to coincide with quantity. In Eng., stress is commonly mistaken for quantity in the subjective judgment of a verse pattern. Since Coleridge, the importance of stress in establishing the meter has had proper attention from the prosodists. But his "new principle," of number rather than regular sequence of stresses, was not new. And all that can be said for it can be said with equal pertinence for quantity, or for any other physical factor that might establish a metrical pattern within the line. In experience, no feature of meter is more distinctive than the iambic-trochaic or the anapæstic-dactyllic opposition. For metrical variation within the line, substitution is easier within the pattern than across. The common exception to this is the first foot, where a trochee is very often found in an iambic line. A. R. MORRIS.

Pitch is a significant element in Chinese poetry; quantity, in classical Gr. and L.; exact number of syllables regardless of accent, in Japanese; in Eng., various emphases conveniently grouped as "stress." While other theories have been put forward—linguistic (G. L. Trager and H. L. Smith, *An Outline of Eng. Structure,* 1951); and musical (Northrop Frye, *Anatomy of Criticism,* 1957, suggesting an isochronic recurrence, an approximate equality of time for successive passages or lines)—most English verse seems to fall into either of two categories: strong stress or syllable stress. (Efforts to distinguish various degrees of stress have been unfruitful.) Strong stress verse (*Beowulf*; *Piers Plowman*; *Christabel*; G. M. Hopkins; *The Cocktail Party*) has a definite number of stressed syllables, usually four, with an indefinite number of unstressed between. Syllable stress verse has a definite number of syllables, with variations in the stress, and often an interplay of sense stress and meter. Thus in Milton:

Rocks, caves, lakes, fens, bogs, dens, and
  shades of death . . .
Immutable, immortal, infinite—

there are 8 strong syllables in the first line, 3 in the second, but in each there are 5 metric stresses, and ten syllables. These, of course, are extreme instances; but with T. S. Eliot and after there has been greater interweaving in one poem of the strong stress and the syllable stress patterns. In one way or another, T. S. Eliot remarked, "There is no escape from metre, there is only mastery." *Cf.* Foot; Distance; Rhythm; Prosody. Wimsatt and Beardsley, "The Concept of Meter," *PMLA* 74, Dec. 1959; John Thompson, *The Founding of Eng. Metre,* 1961; Paul Russell, Jr., *Poetic Meter and Poetic Form,* 1965; S. Chatman, *A Theory of Meter,* 1965; Harvey Gross, ed. *The Structure of Verse,* 1966; V. Zirmunsky, *Introd. to Metrics,* Russ. 1924, trans. 1966.

method (Gr., pursuit of knowledge). (1) (16th c.) Branch of rhetoric concerned with arrangement of ideas. (2) The planned procedure followed by a literary artist in the composition of his work. Too detailed method makes for rigidity, dampens inspiration. Some artists in most periods decry method; but even the "madness" of genius profits by this control. Whatever its emphasis, natural sanction is claimed; thus Pope:

Those rules of old discovered, not devised,
Are Nature still, but Nature methodized.

metonymy. (Gr., "the misnamer.") A form of synecdoche in which one word is used, with the intention that another be understood: the inventor for the invention, possessor for the thing possessed, etc., *e.g.,* Neptune (for the sea); Some skirt! (for a girl); Go fight City Hall! A multiplied or farfetched metonymy is metalepsis, *q.v. See* Synecdoche.

mezzozeugma. (Gr., "the middle

marcher.") Setting a word between two expressions to which it equally refers, *e.g.,* "Either the truth or speak nothing at all." *Cf.* Zeugma; Pivot word.

middle comedy. Gr. comedy burlesquing mythological stories and introducing typical characters. No pure examples of this type of comedy (fl. 388–338 B.C.) have survived.

Milesian tale. A short picaresque or erotic story (Aristides, ca. first c. B.C.). Popular in ancient Rome (in Petronius' *Satyricon*; Apuleius' *Metamorphoses*).

milieu (Fr., environment). With the *race* and the *moment,* presented by Hippolyte Taine (Fr. 1828–93; *Hist. of Eng. Lit.* 1865–69) as the determining factor in the production of art. Although mechanically pressed ("Vice and virtue are products, like vitriol and sugar"), his points are driven by later sociologists. The influence of environment is esp. stressed by those who would radically change it. *See* Description.

mime. A short dramatic spectacle (or an actor therein), imitating everyday life, in solo scenes or duologues. The action was largely improvised. Sophron of Syracuse (5th c. B.C.) gave it artistic form. (Theocritus; the *Mimes* of Herondas). Closely associated with buffoonery and wandering players, it developed special forms; *cf.* magody. It was characterized by slapstick and coarse humor; its license was continually denounced by Christian writers.

mimesis (Gr., imitation, *q.v.*) (1) Considered by many a basic principle in the creation of art, (a) as representation of nature (opp. symbolism); (b) as emulation of earlier work, esp. of the Gr. and Roman authors (opp. spontaneity, originality). (2) The imitation of another's idiosyncrasies or ways of speech, dress, behavior. (3) The second mode of presentation of a story; *see* Narrator; *cf.* Irony III. E. Auerbach, *Mimesis,* 1957; Göran Sörbom, *Mimesis and Art,* 1966; J. D. Boyd, *The Function of Mimesis and its Decline,* 1968.

minnesang (G., ca. 1150– ca. 1300). The courtly lyric, opp. the didactic *Spruchdichtung.* The poet, a knight, sang of *hohe Minne,* courtly love, esp. at Thuringia and Vienna. The earlier poets (The Danubian group: Kürenberg; Dietmar von Eist; Meinloh von Sevelingen) had pictured the woman as not only loved but loving, in contrast to "my lady" of the *Minnesang.* This flowered with Friedrich von Hausen; Reinmar von Hagenau; Wolfram von Eschenbach, Walther von der Vogelweide. Walther also sang of *nidere Minne,* uncourtly love, *e.g., Unter den Linden.* But he wrote much of his best work in the *Spruch,* which was the vehicle of the wandering minstrels and clerics. By his time, the decline of the *Minnesang* had set in; the idealism sank to realism and coarseness; the style became increasingly artificial and over-refined. *Cf. Meistergesang.* Lachmann-Vogt, *Des Minnesangs Frühling,* 1920; Bartsch, *Deutsche Liederdichter . . .* 4th ed., 1920; Olive Sayce, ed. *Poets of the Minnesang,* 1967; C. M. Lancaster, *Two Moods of Minnesong,* 1944.

miracle. Medieval religious drama in which a divine miracle plays a part. Sometimes on the life of a saint, but frequently a problem in contemporary life, solved by divine intervention. The most numerous and interesting examples are in 14th c. France. The Fr. miracle play is distinctly superior to the mystery play, both in dramatic value and in literary quality. In Eng. the two types were not clearly distinguished.

mock-heroic. Ludicrously imitating the heroic; applying formal style and dignified language to a trivial theme. *E.g.,* in epic: the Homeric *Batrachomyomachia* (*Battle of the Frogs and the Mice*; rewritten as a contemporary satire by Thomas Parnell, 1717); Pope, *The Rape of the Lock*; in lyric: Gray, *Ode on a Favorite Cat, Drowned . . . Fishes*; in drama: Fielding, *Tom Thumb.*

mode of discourse. *See* Signs.

modern poetry. The *Concise Oxford Dictionary* defines *modern* as "after the Middle Ages"; *modern English,* "from 1500 on." Critical use often limits the term to the almost contemporary. As applied to poetry, it generally refers to the fashions that took root in Eng. and the U.S. in the late 19th c., and flowered in the second and third decades of the 20th. In addition to its special use of metaphor, modern poetry may seek deliberate obscurity; it may present only a suggestion, with multiple possible interpretations, hoping that the ambiguity will result not in confusion but in enrichment; it may seek to reinforce its powers by slipping in lines from earlier poets (sometimes with footnotes to make sure the reader recognizes the borrowing, as with T. S. Eliot's *The Waste Land*). Modern poetry may also (1) break the syntax: It may invert the order; jumble the sequence; omit connectives; omit or play with punctuation; (2) break the words: reverse letters; end a line with one letter of a word, the rest on the next line; separate letters with marks: all esp. in e. e. cummings, *e.g.,* : *a*) *s w* (*eloo*) *k* ; (3) break the prosody: with very long lines (Marianne Moore); prosaic lines; free verse (recently less frequent); (4) break the language barrier (as esp. Ezra Pound, using Latin, French, Italian, Provençal, Chinese); also using technical terms, and the usually avoided four-letter words; (5) break the contact with the reader, drawing references from a private world (Edith Sitwell: "With eyes like Mary's when she smiled," asked which of the Marys, replied that she meant a maid the family had when she was a young girl). In the 1960's poets were beginning to show less tendency to turn from the traditional stream. *Cf.* Prosody; Poetry and Prose; Ambiguity; Obscurity; Metaphor; Free verse. S. Coblentz, *The Poetry Circus* (roundly iconoclastic), 1967; H. Nemerov, ed. *Poets on Poetry,* 1966; Irving Howe, ed. *Literary Modernism,* 1967; M. L. Rosenthal, *The New Poets,* 1967; John Hollander, ed. *Modern Poetry,* 1968; James Dickey, *Babel to Byzantium,* 1968.

modernism. An attitude that rises in rebellion against what has preceded, seeking to escape tradition. Of our time, Irving Howe (Introd. *Literary Modernism,* 1967) lists nine heterogeneous characteristics, including nihilism, the challenge to belief, belief in the self-sufficiency of the work, the neglect of nature and of æsthetic order, the quest of primitivism and of perversity. Any of these, of course, may itself become a tradition.

A sympathetic, if not persuasive, discussion of modernism distinguishes it from the purely and gloatingly destructive "absurd," from the *nouveau roman,* which "abdicates both intellect and feeling," and from the inane "happening" (as when a cellist at a concert dives into a tank of water). Three stages are traced in the development of drama: (1) Traditional: from Aeschylus up to Ibsen. The traditional accepts basic ethical standards, seeks to reconcile the individual to society, to justify the ways of God to men; it is for the status quo. (2) Naturalistic: Ibsen and his followers. The naturalistic challenges the basic tenets of society; it is against the status quo. (3) Modernistic, which bids the individual spectator to re-examine not only his values but his very being; to find new connections with the world. The modernistic seeks to involve the audience in reality, hence, to break the frame between the receptor and the work, and between the work and life. It is therefore non-æsthetic and has no regard for form, rules, motives, character development, or other ploys and patterns of the traditional works of art. Instead of presenting or containing values (traditional or revolutionary) the modernistic may manifest what Kampf calls a "humane anarchism"; it sets up a situation that challenges us to find our own values; to ponder; and by our own thoughts and actions to take a path it may not even indicate but only make us feel has to be found. Baudelaire said that art is morality put into a form; the modernist by the formlessness of his work hopes to get us to function without binding codes, or at most to fashion a more flexible morality in this confused and fumbling world. *Cf.* New; Absurd; Antihero; Happening. R. Kostelanetz, ed. *On Contemporary Lit.,* 1964; A. B. Kernan, *The Modern Am. Theatre,* 1967; Louis Kampf, *On Modernism,* 1967; Irving Howe, comp. *The Idea of the Modern,* 1967, 1968; Irving Howe, ed., *Literary Modernism,* 1967.

molossus. A metrical foot, of three long syllables. *See* Foot.

moment. Decisive moment: *see* Climax. Poetic moment: term opposed by Saintsbury to the poetic subject. Many (Aristotle, Arnold, John Erskine) discuss the subjects "suitable for poetry," setting various criteria; magnitude; high seriousness; remoteness (Troy, Anatolia rather than Troy, New York). Others (partly Longinus; Patrizzi, 1529–97; the Romantics) state that any subject is suitable for the poetic moment of "passionate interpretation, in articulate music"—of inspiration. *See also* Psychological moment.

monodrama. 1. A dramatic play or sketch for one player, as popularized in the 20th c. by Yvette Guilbert, Ruth Draper, Cornelia Otis Skinner. Usually called monologue; the player is called a monologist; Fr. *diseuse.* 2. A play in which all the characters and action are viewed as through the mind of one figure within the play. Occasionally conventional, as Arthur Richman's *Ambush,* 1921; more often expressionistic or otherwise tensely shaped by the mind of a character under great stress, *e.g.,* Georg Kaiser, *From Morn to Midnight,* 1920. (Ellen Glasgow stated that she wrote her novels, *e.g. Barren Ground,* 1925, similarly, through the eyes and mind of one character. Stories told in the first person do the same; *cf.* Narrator.) 3. A poem, a dramatic monologue: Tennyson called his *Maud* a monodrama.

monody (Gr. melic poem intended for solo presentation). Esp., a mourning poem, an elegy presented by one person. Arnold called *Thyrsis* a monody.

monogatari. Chanted tales or legends of Japan. *See* Japanese poetry.

monologue; soliloquy (Gr. *monos,* one, alone, +*logos,* speech; L. *solus,* alone, + *loqui,* to speak). In everyday usage the two words are interchangeable, designating almost any kind of extended individual utterance. In literary usage a distinction is customary: monologue is the broader category, the genus; soliloquy is one of its species.

A monologue is speech by one person. In this literal sense, of course, all speech except a chorus is monologue. But monologue is distinguished from one side of a dialogue by its length and relative completeness, and from the soliloquy (except in the case of the "interior monologue") by the fact that it is addressed to someone. It may be a prayer, a hymn, an apostrophe, a lament, a lovesong. It may be an independent unit, a whole work of art (*The Banished Wife's Complaint,* O. Eng.; Strindberg, *The Stronger,* trans. in *Poet Lore,* 1906), or it may be part of a larger whole (Tonio Kroeger's outbursts to Lisabeta in Thomas Mann's short story, 1903).

A soliloquy is spoken by one person that is alone or acts as though he were alone. It is a kind of talking to oneself, not intended to affect others. ("The dialogue of the mind with itself": Matthew Arnold, Pref., 1853.) St. Augustine coined the word (*Liber Soliloquiorum*) to characterize a series of discussions between himself and his Reason. In his sense the soliloquy is a private debate, a posing of moral alternatives; it has its origin in doubt. Kierkegaarde's *Entweder-Oder* carries on this tradition. And the element of privacy has been increasingly emphasized; the soliloquy now expresses all sorts of thoughts and desires. It often employs the first person, is allied to the confessional, the *journal intime.* As a dramatic convention it may also function in a technical way, as a means of exposition or narration, to open, close, or join scenes, to identify characters, to summarize plots. Like the monologue it may be either a whole or a part (Browning, *Soliloquy in a Spanish Cloister*; the "To be or not to be" of Shakespeare's *Hamlet*).

The soliloquy has been popular only since the Middle Ages. In classical drama soliloquies are very few; the chorus or confidant is always present. The presence of the confidant in Seneca, it is true, is rather mechanical and arbitrary, and plays of Plautus and Terence exploit the comic possibilities of the overheard soliloquy. But in the Eng. Renaissance the soliloquy becomes an integral part of the dramatic structure, as well as a means of character revelation and a medium for introspection. In the early 18th c., and again with the 19th c. realist playwrights, the soliloquy was felt to be inadequate to the artist's themes. But the romantic poets and closet dramatists, and later the symbolists, used it widely. Mallarmé, *e.g.,* developed from a consideration of Hamlet's soliloquies his *drame avec Soi,* in which only one character holds the stage, soliloquizing for 5 acts; the revelation of different aspects of this one personality is supposed to replace the variety of events and characters of the old stage action.

There are other types of monologue besides the soliloquy. The aside or *à parte* has a strictly dramatic function within a play. This is a brief speech, whispered or spoken aloud, conventionally heard only by the audience, or the one or ones within the play for whom it is intended. It may be as brief as Polonius' remark, "Still harping on my daughter," or as long as Shylock's speech of 12 lines beginning, "How like a fawning publican he looks." Perhaps the most elaborate use of aside, in line with the psychological development of the soliloquy, is the device used by Eugene O'Neill (*Dynamo*; *Strange Interlude*) to convey the gathering thoughts of a character, as they lead toward an action.

Another special type is the dramatic monologue. Robert Browning was not the first to write one, but produced the most successful, combining dramatic immediacy with psychological penetration. The dramatic monologue is a character sketch, or a drama condensed into a single episode, presented in a one-sided conversation by one person to another or to a group, *e.g., My Last Duchess*; *Andrea del Sarto.* Browning's conception of the genre was a union of lyric form with a dramatic principle; he discarded "the simulation of the painted scene, Boards, actors, promoters, gas-light, and costume" to "take for a nobler stage the soul itself" (*Aurora Leigh*).

The most recent development in monologue form is the stream of consciousness or interior monologue. William James popularized the first phrase in a lecture on psychology, Valéry Larbaud originated the second in an essay on Joyce. Edouard Dujardin first hit upon the form in his novel *Les lauriers sont coupés* (1877; *Le Monologue intérieur,* 1931); James Joyce in his *Ulysses* and Dorothy Richardson in her 12 novels (1915–38) grouped as *Pilgrimage* have used it to most advantage. Much controversy has turned about the veracity of the technique and its artistic utility. It seeks to give the reader a direct impression of the continuous flow of ideas, sensations, feelings, and memories as they come into consciousness. *Cf.* Dialogue; Narrator. R. Langbaum, *The Poetry of Experience,* 1957. ROBERTA MORGAN.

monometer. A stanza, or poem, of the same meter throughout. Also, a line one foot in length.

monopody. A line consisting of one foot.

mono-: *-rhyme,* a long passage, or a poem, all in one rhyme. *-stich,* a poem one line long. *-strophic,* of a poem (a) one stanza long or (b) with every stanza of the same form.

mora. Unit of quantitative measure: The duration of a short syllable in classical verse. Although in theory its length varies with the meter, it is usually taken as equal to an eighth note in music; half a long syllable. The basis of substitution (of one foot for another), by equivalence; thus a dactyl and a spondee are equal, having 4 *moræ* each. When anapests or dactyls, *e.g.,* were substituted in iambic or trochaic verse, their short syllables were hastened to a half *mora* each; the foot was then called cyclic.

G. M. Lane, *Latin Grammar,* 1898. *See* Prosody.

moral. The lesson to be drawn from a work. It is generally assumed that, if not every work, surely the fable should press home a moral. It should be observed, however, that (whether or not the "moral" as an appended apothegm—*e.g.* Persuasion is greater than force—is a later addition of the grammarians) *as art,* the moral is not after the fable, but in it. In poetry, more widely, the moral, if present, is not to be extracted. Applied literally to life, it may be excessive (Coleridge, the Ancient Mariner's punishment) or otherwise inappropriate. It is deliberately held in its place, as proper in a child's story, by the closing triviality of rhyme in Browning's *Pied Piper of Hamelin*; Burns similarly shows that (like Tam O'Shanter's mare) it is caught in the tale. For the basic problem of morality in art, *see* Didacticism. *Cf.* Epimythium.

moral play. Old name for morality, *q.v.*

morality. Late medieval drama, esp. 15th and 16th c. In origin, an attempt to bring to the stage didactic material which had been handled in other forms by earlier satirists and moralists. Great variety in type, ranging from serious, pseudo-historical dramas resembling the miracles, to light, satirical sketches that differ little from *sotties.* The typical morality is a long debate between allegorical characters representing virtues and vices, usually accompanying a man on his march toward the grave. In the 16th c., under the double influence of the Renaissance and the Reformation, it became an ethical drama or a political pamphlet. The earlier examples sometimes run to more than 20,000 lines, but the later ones are not likely to exceed 1,000. *Everyman* (first in Dutch ca. 1495) has had numerous recent revivals, as Reinhardt's production of the G. version, *Jedermann,* by Hugo von Hofmannsthal, at Salzburg in 1913, and there annually from 1920 into the 1960's.

morology. Foolish discourse, intentionally assumed, as by Pierre Pathelin (15th c. farce of that name) when the draper tries to secure payment of his bill. *Cf.* Folly.

morpheme. A minimal unit of linguistic form, a word or meaningful part of a word, as *-ed,* marking past time. *Cf.* Language.

mosaic rhyme. A rhyme of two or more syllables, with more than one word making one of the rhyming group, usually in humorous or satiric writing, *e.g.,*

> In such calm fashion ate
> As though she were not passionate.

Ogden Nash's verse is the outstanding modern example.

mosaic verse. Poem made up of lines from other poems. *See* Cento; *cf.* Light verse.

mot (Fr., word). (1) *Bon mot:* a clever remark, a witticism. (2) *le mot juste,* the precise word, sought (Gautier; Flaubert) as the one, inevitable word for the unique and particular occasion. (3) *le mot propre,* the exact term: calling a spade a spade. Opp. to circumlocution (*périphrase*). Thus Hugo, saying simply (*Hernani,* 1830) *"Minuit bientôt,"* shocked the classicists, who wished a less direct, but, they thought, more elevated, style.

motet. *See* Old Fr. . . . forms.

motif. A word or pattern of thought that recurs in a similar situation, or to evoke a similar mood, within a work or in various works of a genre. Lucretius, *e.g.,* repeats theme words at regular intervals. *See* Folklore; *Leitmotif.*

motivation. (Sometimes applied to an entire work, more usually separately to characters or incidents therein): the combination of circumstances (or the art of their combining) that makes plausible the actions of a character by supplying them with a reasonable basis in past events. The inciting cause of the struggle or of an episode therein, as acting upon and refashioned by the person's nature. It has been said that in serious works "every character is in the right"; this means that the motivation is valid: the reader recognizes that, given this person and these circumstances, the actions that follow are a natural consequence. Except in playful works, the receptor desires—demands—a feeling that the main movement of the story has been properly motivated. ("Motived" was the term used until mid 19th c.)

motivator. *See* Signs.

motive. (1) Motif, *q.v.* (2) Inciting cause or purpose of an action. "A great composition always has a leading emotional purpose, technically called its motive" (Ruskin). *See* Motivation.

motoria. *See Fabula.*

mummery. Eng., 15th c., a mummer's play. Folk-drama of humor, boasting, and sword-play, rising from the sword-dance (widespread among tribal folk, still danced by the Turks, Scots etc.) and the legends of St. George. Usually with duels, and a doctor reviving the dead; perhaps a survival of the nature-myth ritual of the death of the year and its Spring rebirth—of which Gilbert Murray (*The Classical Tradition in Poetry,* 1927) finds more than a trace in *Hamlet. Cf.* Mime; Tragedy. R. J. Tiddy, *The Mummers' Play,* 1923; Zinzow, *Die Hamlet Saga . . . ,* 1877.

musical comedy. The current form of a development from It. *opera buffa,* Fr. vaudeville, Eng. ballad opera. On a light thread of plot (with spoken dialogue) jokes, comic situations, and songs are strung, with a singing and dancing chorus and often lavish spectacle. Light opera, operetta—the terms are interchangeable—implies more emphasis on the musical structure (*e.g.,* sung dialogue) and music more classical than popular in tone. Musical comedy is distinguished by its thread of plot from the revue, which is a series of skits connected only by having the same actors and chorus. The vaudeville of the 1940's had a Master of Ceremonies (M.C.) and usually a continuing chorus; it differed from the revue in having animal and acrobatic numbers, and less extravagant settings and costumes. All three may contain travesty of current figures and events; clowning; word play, double entendre; exposure of pulchritude in slight but gay costume and lively movement.

Folk opera appeared in 1935 with *Porgy and Bess* (from the novel *Porgy* by Du Bose Heyward); in 1947 came the musical version of Elmer Rice's *Street Scene. Oklahoma!* (1943) struck oil with its solo opening, "Oh, What a Beautiful Morning!", instead of the conventional opening chorus. Most musical comedies have been adapted from plays or novels, notably *Show Boat,* 1927, from Edna Ferber's novel; *South Pacific,* 1949, from James A. Michener's *Tales of the South Pacific*; *My Fair Lady,* 1956, from Shaw's *Pygmalion* (earlier *The Chocolate Soldier,* operetta from Shaw's *Arms and the Man*); *Fiddler on the Roof,* 1964, from stories by Sholem Aleichem. *Cf.* Opera; Comedy. S. Green, *The World of Musical Comedy,* 1960; L. Engel, *The Am. Musical Theatre,* 1967; David Ewen, *The Story of America's Musical Theatre,* 1968.

mycterism (Gr., "turning up the nose). Sneering derision, dissembled but not wholly concealed.

mystery. I. (L. *ministerium,* church office, service. Formerly supposed associated with mystery<mastery<L. *magisterium,* Fr. *métier,* craft, since it was presented by the craftsmen of the guilds). Religious play of the Middle Ages, given at Easter, Christmas, and other church festivals. Found in all important European centers in the 11th c. (somewhat earlier in Eng.) in the form of dialogue interpolations (tropes) in the Easter mass, but reached its height in the late 15th c., followed by rapid absorption into the Renaissance theatre.

In its heyday the mystery play was a vast spectacle, with many of the characteristics of the pageant and the circus, formless and often grotesque, an incoherent mixture of drama and low comedy, intended to represent (in its central theme) a Bible story, esp. the life of Christ, or the biography of a king, saint, or hero. Sometimes there were processions through the streets with floats; sometimes the mystery was enacted on a wagon platform stage, with the gate of Heaven at one end and yawning mouth of Hell at the other. A mystery given by the burghers of Valenciennes, 1547, attempted to represent in 25 *journées* (daily installments) the whole of the New Testament and much of the Old. One ms. version of this play has more than 67,000 lines.

In Eng. the comic elements in the mystery rose naturally from the theme; in Fr., they were mainly unrelated interludes, monologues, farces, horseplay. This paved the way for (1) the rich Fr. late medieval comic theatre; (2) the sharp separation of comedy and tragedy in the Fr. classical theatre, as opposed to Eng. tragicomedy; (3) the early secularization of the Fr. theatre—developed in the 13th c., as the plays of Adam de la Halle. *The Confrerie de la Passion* had a monopoly for production of mystery plays in Paris as early as 1402. *Cf.* Morality play. H. C. Gardiner, *Mysteries' End,* 1946, 1967. II. (Gr. *mysterion,* secret religious rite, as the Eleusinian mysteries, <*myein,* to close, to initiate). A play or story or film in which a problem is posed, its solution—the finding of an object (Poe, *The Gold Bug*; *The Purloined Letter*); the preventing of a crime or capture of the criminal—providing the climax. While the conflict may be seen in the work, *e.g.,* thief versus detective, it may also be viewed as between author and receptor: all essential information should be provided, with no irrelevant false trails, in such a way that the solution is not guessed (far) before it is given, yet when presented will seem natural, almost obvious. The Poe and Conan Doyle (Sherlock Holmes) pattern is the presentation of (1) the crime or the danger; (2) shortly thereafter, the detective's success; (3), then, step by step, the ratiocination that led him to his goal. More frequently today, after (1), the receptor accompanies the detective on his quest, sharing the clues if not their interpretation as they arrive, and reaching the goal toward the very close. The usual mystery play has been skeletonized: Act I, No one suspected; Act II, Everyone suspected; Act III, Caught! *See* Detective story.

mysticism. The belief in the spiritual intuition of truths beyond the reach of reasoned understanding; direct contact with supernal powers without the intervention of the reason or of an officiating priest. By virtue of its meaning, mysticism itself defies reasoned exposition. It has been facetiously defined as "I" surrounded by mist and schism. Yet almost every artist hopes for its functioning. *See* Merde. D. Knowles, *What is Mysticism?,* 1966.

myth is essentially a religious term: it is something said, as distinct from ritual, something done. Regardless of its appearance in modern idiom, no proper myth is meaningless, ridiculous, or obscene. It is metaphysic in its primary and purest form, the closest verbal approach to an immediate intuition of reality. It is antecedent to theology, as the terms and statements of a myth are prior to their exegesis.

As a product of the poetic faculty, myth is a thing in itself, single, whole, complete, and without ulterior purpose. The use to which it may be put is secondary. Although much can be learned by studying the applications and occasional distortions of myth to practical ends (whether ethical, to sanction tribal custom, or political, to endorse the doctrines of the state), the essential fact is that, as the evidence of every great religion shows, to the believer, myth is actually identical with truth (*cf.* the opening sentence of the Apostles' Creed).

Neither the ultimate origin nor the precise original structure of any myth whatever is known. Comparison of similar myths in related languages shows that not even the most scrupulous care for tradition (as in the case of the Indian Vedas) preserves a myth in—or even nearly in—its pristine form. The problem of myth is considerably perplexed by this fact, and by the complementary evidence (collected notably in Sir J. G. Frazer's *The Golden Bough*) that remarkably similar myths (*e.g.,* of the origin of fire) exist in all parts of the earth.

The Gr. word *mythos,* from which "mythology" is derived, was frequently used to designate tales of any kind. It was the regular word for folklore or fairy tale.[1] A specialized use, however, was early recognized; Plato and Euhemerus, *e.g.,* employed the word in much the same sense as we.

Myths have usually been differentiated from other tales on account of their subject matter rather than because of any stylistic quality. They have to do with superior beings and with origins. This definition is adequate for the great historical mythologies such as the Greek, the Norse, the Irish, or the Egyptian. Students of primitive peoples, however, do not find such a differentiation helpful in classifying the narratives that they collect. Most primitive peoples seem to recognize as a special category the tales of a previous world before the present one was formed. Such narratives are usually spoken of by ethnologists as mythical tales, though the concepts "tale" and "myth" are continually merging.

Most theoretical discussion of myth has concerned the great historical mythologies. The primary interest has been to account for the stories of the gods and for creation tales. While Plato speculated about the Greek myths, it was Euhemerus (4th c. B.C.) who first attempted a theory: that the gods of Gr. mythology were originally human beings who, because of their famous deeds, were deified (like the kings of Egypt and emperors of Rome). Euhemeristic explanations of some mythical stories are plausible, as anyone who has observed the growth of legends about such a figure as Charlemagne will recognize. But that real human actions are depicted in all the extravagant stories of Zeus and Heracles is so improbable that Euhemerism has long been abandoned. Another school thought of myths as purely allegorical, as always designed to teach. A modification of this theory reduced the myths to representations of the forces of nature, spring overcoming winter, sunlight conquering storm, and the like. Although the latter school flourished a century ago, these explanations are now generally considered conflicting and lacking in real foundation. The attempt by such scholars as Ehrenreich[2] to apply the nature explanation to myths of all parts of the world in order to account for their resemblances forced him and his school into an even narrower interpretation, *viz.,* that all myths are, in the last analysis, stories of the heavenly bodies, primarily the moon.

Myths are often used to explain natural phenomena. Whether they were originally made up for this purpose or whether the explanatory element is secondary has been much studied by folklorists. Certainly for the N. Am. Indians the tale is of primary importance, and the explanation may be attached almost anywhere. It is clearly not the reason for the tale.[3]

No generally satisfactory explanation of mythology has thus far appeared. The difference between myth and tale has probably been overemphasized, and the role played by priests and shamans not sufficiently recognized. Nor do we yet know about the processes of the making and borrowing of myths among primitive peoples. The function of myth in directing the lives and regularizing the rituals of people who tell them has recently been the subject of much study.[4] But the functional approach has a tendency to neglect the problems of parallels between the various mythologies. Only by a proper understanding of the ways in which the incidents of myth are borrowed and adapted, of the ways in which these incidents are related to the life of the people who use them, of the role of priests and other gifted persons in changing tales to religious or didactic ends, and by a rigorous study of the myths of peoples with the most diverse cultures—can the problems presented by the study of mythology be resolved.

Most persons have enjoyed myths with very little thought of such theoretical questions. The great historical mythologies have been read for sheer pleasure. They have formed a weighty part of the training of our poets, who, particularly in the Renaissance, loaded their lines with allusions to obscure tales from Gr. mythology. Recently there has been a deliberate avoidance of such allusions, though occasional references are made not only to the gods and heroes of Greece, but to those of Ireland, Iceland, India, and less familiar parts of the world. *Cf.* Fable; Fiction; Folklore.

[1] Johannes Bolte has assembled many hundreds of these references: Bolte und Polîvka, *Anmerkungen zu den Kinder und Hausmärchen der Brüder Grimm,* 1913–31, IV; [2] P. Ehrenreich, *Die allegmeine Mythologie,* 1910; *e.g.,* [3] T. T. Waterman, "The Explanatory Elements in N. Am. Mythology," *J. Am. Folklore,* XXI, 1908; [4] C. Kluckhohn, "Myths and Rituals: a general Theory," *Harvard Theological R.,* XXV, 1942.

J. L. McCulloch and L. H. Gray, ed. *Mythology of All Nations,* 13 v., 1933; T. A. Sebeok, ed. *Myth,* 1955; N. Frye, *Fables of Identity,* 1963; K. S. House, ed. *Reality and Myth in Am. Lit.*; G. W. Cox, *Introd. into the Science of Comparative Mythology and Folklore,* 1883, 1968; T. E. Porter, *Myth and Modern Am. Drama,* 1969; D. S. Norton and P. Rushton, *Classical Myths in Eng. Lit.,* 1952.

Murry Fowler and Stith Thompson.

N

NAIV UND SENTIMENTALISCH. G. Antithesis developed by Schiller in what has been called the greatest G. essay in the field of æsthetics, *"Über naive und sentimentalische Dichtung"* (1795), based on Kant and Hemsterhuys. A poet is *naiv* whose personality is in full harmony with nature (the Greeks, Shakespeare, Goethe), while the *sentimentalische poet* (Schiller himself and most moderns) has lost his immediate contact with nature, yet longs to return to it. Thus, the "naïve" poet is a realist, while the "sentimental" poet is an idealist: they complement one another.

Schiller's essay is an attempt at self-justification before the majestic serenity of Goethe's work. Later typological undertakings have used other terms: antique vs. romantic or modern (Schlegel); Dionysian vs. Apollonian (Nietzsche); classical vs. baroque (Wolfflin); classical vs. romantic (Strich); puritan vs. pagan. *Cf.* Apollonian; Romantic; Baroque; Classical.

narrative. The general term for a recital of events, true or fictitious. *See* History; Biography; Novel; Truth; Fiction. R. Scholes and R. Kellogg, *The Nature of Narrative,* 1966.

narrator. Who talks in a poem? Who tells the story in a novel? in a play? What voice is speaking, or is supposed to speak? And who is supposed to listen? To whom is the poem, the story, the play addressed? In the analysis of a speech or literary composition, nothing is more important than to determine precisely the voice or voices presented as speaking and the precise nature of the address (*i.e.,* specific direction to a hearer, an addressee); for in every speech reference to a voice or voices and implication of address (*i.e.,* reference to a process of speech, real or imagined) is a part of the meaning and a frame for the rest of the meaning, for the interpretation of which it supplies an indispensable control.

To generalize these notions as technical devices for analysis involves no commitment concerning the communicative or merely expressive, or other, nature of human speech as such, or concerning the origins of speech; the concepts are universally applicable to all speech-constructs, normal or eccentric by whatever standards, whether the indication of specific address in them be obviously explicit (as when, in a letter or apostrophe, a vocative is used) or only implied or wholly lacking.

The significant distinctions as to voice are those made first by Plato (*Rep.,* III, 392 D–394 C) and Aristotle (*Poet.,* 1448a20–24) and regularly applied by critics throughout subsequent antiquity, according to which a speaker (poet) may (1) speak in his own person, or (2) assume the voice of another person or set of persons and speak throughout in a voice not his own, or (3) produce a mixed speech in which the basic voice is his own, but other personalities are at times assumed and their voices introduced, *i.e.,* directly quoted. The first of these forms of presentation, called by the ancients *diegesis* or *apangellia,* produces pure exposition (where the meaning is reference to ideas of static reality or of process statically abstracted, *i.e.,* a logical discourse) or pure narration (where the meaning is reference to events or actions as such, to dynamic reality or reality envisaged as dynamic, *i.e.,* a story). From speech of this kind direct quotation is excluded; in it quoted matter ("He said, 'I will'") must be cast into indirect discourse ("He said that he would"), for the characteristic of this mode is that the speaker assimilates the speech of all other cited voices into his own, so that his voice is the only voice heard. The second mode of presentation was by the ancients called "imitation" (*mimesis*); it produces dialogue (as where there is a story or action, in drama) or, if there be only one assumed voice, "dramatic" monologue. (Plato and Aristotle used the same word, "imitation," to designate both this mode of voice in a composition and the relation to reality of the fictions in the poetry they chiefly discuss; these two senses of the word in ancient texts, though related, should not be confused.) These 2 modes, with the mixed 3d that needs no separate comment, provide in fact 4 basic types of structure as to voice, *viz.* (a) one in which a single voice is heard throughout, and this is the voice of the speaker himself (as in the speech of ordinary conversation or a letter in which there is no quoted matter), (b) one in which a single voice is heard throughout, not that of the speaker but that of a personality assumed by the speaker in imagination (as in a monologue of Browning, or most lyric poetry), (c) one in which a single basic voice (that of the speaker in his own person or of an assumed personality, *e.g.,* that of one of the characters in a story) speaks, but the speech of this voice is interrupted by direct, verbatim quotation of other voices as their speech is reported (as in most narrative), and (d) one in which a dialogue of two or more voices, which in narration would be quoted, is heard directly without the intrusion of a narrator's voice (as in drama, where of course action and a setting are added to speech). The progression through these types of structure is formally a progression from the extreme of subjective assimilation of objective reality to the extreme of objectivity; and, though of course the things referred to within the framework supplied by any of these modes will have their own relative subjectivity or objectivity which may not seem to correspond to that of the modes employed for their presentation (so that, *e.g.,* Chekhov or Maeterlinck may use the drama to present reference to reality far from "objective," or Joyce the most objective mode of narrative for presentation of the interior of a mind, and even the interior of an unconscious mind), yet obviously either to understand such incongruities or to penetrate to the insights necessary for their resolution if that is possible, some such system of distinctions is required. And the notion of such a progression, which though its demarcation of types is definite enough nevertheless presents as a whole a kind of continuum, provides not the crude and obviously incomplete compartmentalization of narrative, dramatic, and lyric that embarrasses much criticism, but flexible categories that exhaust the possibilities of both prose and poetry, and modes among which modulation is as easy in theory as it evidently is in practise. For the various types of voice-structure, and of address, are in literature what the basic colors of a palette are in painting, or keys in music; the whole tone and character of a composition is set by the writer's choice among them, and changed by any variation from one to another within the work. The advantage of such a system of conscious distinctions is that it provides a sure technical foundation for discussion of all that concerns the "point of view" in a piece of writing, and a clear view of some of the major technical relations among works as disparate as, *e.g.,* the novels of Fielding, Jane Austen, James, Proust, and Joyce, or *Widsith, The Seafarer, Prufrock,* and Yeats' *I am of Ireland.* Perhaps the most important thing to remember in analysing the voice of a composition is that the basic voice need not be the author's, and may even be that not of a person but of an abstraction or a thing; the voice may be a wholly imagined voice, and the process of speech involved an imagined process in an imagined situation. (Here, perhaps, is the best handle for a practicable distinction between poetry and prose; it seems possible at once to reconcile and to illuminate nearly all the historic characterizations of poetry if we define it as speech that is not the instrument of any actual speech-process, or more briefly as "detached speech," *i.e.,* actual speech detached, by whatever mechanisms of meaning, sound, or structure, from any actual speech-situation.)

The phenomena of *address* in literature include all that part of literary meaning which is reference to specific direction to a hearer and to the relations between speaker and addressee established or presupposed by such direction, or rather by the social situation which occasions and environs it. The mechanisms of address furnish a necessary framework even for poetic form and, since the character of a speech is powerfully affected by the speaker's consciousness of a relation between himself and the addressee, what is usually called the "style" of a composition is in large part a function (in the mathematical sense) of its address. Here the question of first importance for analysis is that of the precise identity and character of the addressee or grammatical second person in a speech (as in the matter of *voice* it is the identity and operation of the *first* person). The addressee may be ontologically as well as grammatically a person. In this case, one will naturally distinguish between a singular and a plural addressee, and discriminate further according to what may be roughly called the definiteness of the address (address to somebody, address to anybody, address to everybody). With these varieties of address may be classified that in which so little personality is felt in the addressee (and so, correlatively, in the speaker) that the address may be conceived as impersonal (address to nobody), and thus minimal. But the address may be not to a person, but to a thing or an abstraction; and of address to persons an eccentric variety is that in which the person addressed is the speaker (soliloquy). Since, as Aristotle observed (*Rhet.*, III, 1358 a–b), the speaker's end in ordinary speech is in the addressee and the addressee therefore largely determines the character of the speech, each of these varieties of address has its inevitable effect upon the attitude of the speaker, which, reflected in the details of the speech, becomes either explicitly or implicitly a part of its meaning. This part of the meaning, *viz.* all reference to the attitude of the speaker toward his addressee, is commonly called "tone" (*cf.* Meaning, the four kinds). The relation between speaker and addressee cannot of course be adequately seized in isolation from the relation of both speaker and addressee to the agencies represented in grammar by the third person, whether conceived as the "subject"-reference of the speech or as a true personality present to hear or overhear it. This latter third person, though it be excluded physically in private dialogue, can perhaps never be eliminated psychologically; it is the sum of all the social pressures of the community that provides the environment in which a speech occurs. The difference in rhetoric between private speech and public is partly the difference between a singular and a plural addressee (second person), partly a function of the relative consciousness of the presence and pressure of a third person, definite or vague (the smaller or larger community or group, linguistic, national, international; society at large; humanity at large, or in the West, through its whole history). For distinctions such as that by which J. S. Mill differentiated poetry from prose ("Eloquence is heard, poetry is overheard. . . . All poetry is of the nature of soliloquy." *Thoughts on poetry and its varieties,* 1859) these schemes provide a useful frame of reference, within which one may pass from such insights to a plainer view of their implications and difficulties than is possible without such a system. And of course, it is within such a systematic framework that the problems concerning the relation of poetry to communication generally are to be worked out, or at any rate made practically intelligible.

I. A. Richards, *Practical criticism,* 1929. *See* Rhetoric and poetic. J. Craig LaDrière.

The equivocal position of the author in regard to the persons in his story has been considered in various recent works. Luigi Pirandello in *Six Characters in Search of an Author* (1921) shows persons started on their way, then abandoned but refusing to fade away. In *Tête-de-Nègre* (Maurice Fourré, 1960) the author enters the story, and toward the end commits suicide, leaving the other characters at loose ends, losing belief in their own lives. Other attitudes appear in various *romans nouveaux,* or anti-novels. Some Fr. thinkers (J.-P. Sartre, *Saint Genêt,* 1951; M. Proust, *Contre Sainte-Beuve,* 1954) say that as he writes, the author creates another being, distinct from himself, a fictional figure that is the writer himself. Wallace Fowlie, *Climate of Violence,* 1967.

naturalism. In philosophy, the doctrine that everything that exists is a part of nature. "Nature" commonly means the sum-total of events in space-time, or what can in principle become known by scientific method, in the broadest sense. Though the naturalist is committed to the denial of a supernatural deity, a supernatural element in man, and a supernatural basis of æsthetic and ethical value, he is not necessarily a materialist in his metaphysics or an egoist in his ethics, though some forms of evolutionary naturalism are associated with ethical systems that reduce all motives to self-preservation or will to power.

In literary criticism, the term "naturalism" has been used in three very different ways. (1) It refers to works that exhibit a marked interest in and love of natural beauty; for this characteristic, the word "naturism" would be preferable. (2) It is often loosely used as synonymous with "realism." (3) It refers to, and should be reserved for, works of literature, esp. since Zola, that utilize realistic methods and materials to embody a certain form of philosophical naturalism.

Broadly speaking, naturalistic writing (*e.g.,* Zola, Hauptmann, Dreiser, Farrell) presents, explicitly or implicitly, a view of experience that might be characterized as pessimistic materialistic determinism. It emphasizes the strength of external forces (social and natural) that obstruct human freedom, and the strength of internal forces (genetic and unconscious) that limit human rationality and moral responsibility. There is a tendency in naturalistic writing to look upon life as a downhill struggle with the only outcome in quiescence or death. Since they assert man's kinship with the lower animals, writers in this mode are likely to take a behavioristic or epiphenomenal view of mind and to show the primacy of tropistic or "instinctive" behavior, assigning a large part of human motivation to sex, hunger, and other basic drives. This reductionist view is frequently reinforced by the use of animal symbolism, as with the horses in Zola's *Germinal,* or the battle between the squid and the lobster in Dreiser's *The Financier.*

From the beginning, naturalism has been under attack as being sordid, gloomy, and subversive, notably by the New Humanists (*q.v.*). Its preoccupation with the less cerebral functions of human behavior has led many writers to sensationalism and has helped produce the popular confusion that identifies anything "raw," "stark," or "sordid" as naturalistic. *Cf.* Nature; Mystique de la merde; Literature and Society; Determinism; Realism; Materialism; Idealism. G. J. Becker, ed. *Documents of Modern Literary Realism,* 1963; C. Beuchat, *Hist. du naturalisme français,* 1949; G. Boas, *Courbet and the Naturalistic Movement,* 1938; P. Cogny, *Le Naturalisme,* 1953; Y. H. Krikorian, *Naturalism and the Human Spirit,* 1944; C. C. Walcutt, *Am. Literary Naturalism,* 1956; E. Zola, *The Experimental Novel,* 1880; S. P. Lamprecht, *The Metaphysics of Naturalism,* 1967; R. N. Stromberg, *Realism, Naturalism, and Symbolism,* 1968; D. Madden, ed. *Proletarian Writers of the Thirties,* 1968. G. J. BECKER and MONROE C. BEARDSLEY.

nature. In Pindar, the distinction between the poet "that knows many things by nature" and those that have merely acquired their poetic art through "learning" (*Od.* II, 86–88) is an application of his view that all human excellence is innate and hereditary (*cf. Od.* IX, 100 ff.; *Pyth.* VIII 44–45; *Nem.* III, 40–42). "Nature" is the divinely appointed motivating and ordering power in things, thought of as reflected in the aristocratic order of society in Pindar's day, by virtue of which "the poet is born, not made." Subsequent Gr. literary theory, however, reconciles the elements in literary activity and achievement that are given ("nature") with those that are acquired through study and practice, in the various formulas for attaining any kind of human excellence ("nature, practice, knowledge"; "nature, exercise, art"; "nature and art"; etc.), formulas that became commonplace at least as early as the 5th c. B.C. Nature comes first in these formulas, as applied in rhetorical theory by Plato (*Phædrus,* 269 D), Isocrates (*Ag. the Sophists,* 14–18), and in poetic theory as well by a host of others during the next two millennia, to indicate that "native endowment" is the indispensable and prime requirement for literary excellence; the other components indicate that native literary ability can be brought to full fruition only through some intellectual discipline and experience in writing. With Aristotle, poetry first attains a philosophic vindication against such attacks as Plato's, in the conception of the poet as one that represents the entelechy cosmic Nature strives toward through the union of form and matter (*cf.* Phys. 194^{a} 12 ff.; 199^{a} 15). The poet's activity is thought of as an imitation of the creative processes of Nature, and his successful achievement as a representation of the universal actions and passions of men (*Poet.* 1448^{a} 1 ff.; 1451^{b} 5 ff.).

The reciprocal functions in literary achievement of nature (native endowment) and art (what is learned) are emphasized throughout Roman times. Thus the imitation of the literary methods and skills of Homer, Demosthenes, or others becomes a means of disciplining and bringing to fruition the artist's nature with the help of art, according to the cosmic design of things. While a republican like Cicero holds that cosmic Nature supplies a tribunal of literary taste by endowing all men with spontaneous power to discriminate what is essentially beautiful or harmonious in the use of language (*De Or.,* III, 195 ff.; *cf. Br.,* 183 ff.; *Tusc. Disp.,* I, xiii, 30), the characteristic view of critical authorities under the Empire is that the appreciation of literary excellence is largely confined to the intellectual and cultivated few who have learned how to improve merely natural taste by the discriminations of art (*e.g.,* Dion. Hal., *De Comp. Verb.,* cc. 12, 25). This view is transmitted to the Renaissance and prevails among literary theorists into the 18th c.

Boccaccio defines poetry as a "fixed science" that expresses the eternal and uniform operations and effects of cosmic Nature, thus anticipating the main ground for the "defence of poetry," to be re-echoed throughout the Renaissance in the contention that the poet rivals the philosopher by representing truth enhanced by the moving power of beauty (*De Gen. Deorum,* XIV; *cf.* Petrarch, *Fam.* X;

Invect., bks. i, iii. Students of Aristotle's *Poetics,* somewhat later, maintain that the poet represents Nature's ideal aims and exalt the poet's function even above the philosopher's, *e.g.,* J. C. Scaliger, Sidney). The culminating expression of Renaissance literary theory in the authority of such critics as Minturno and Scaliger—whose influence was not fully developed until the 17th c.—marks the yielding of the more flexible art to a dogmatic formulation of the "laws" prescribed by "nature" for literature and expounded from the theory and practice of the ancients by their Cinquecento interpreters.

17th c. Fr. classicism inherited from the Cinquecento humanists, and further systematized, the view of literary art as regulated by the laws cosmic Nature prescribes for literary methods, forms, aims, and, the Fr. critics add, taste. From Chapelain on, these regulative laws are thought of as embodied in ancient precept (especially the rules of Aristotle) more than example, and as ascertainable above all through the exercise of reason, itself an aspect of cosmic Nature, *i.e.,* the means cosmic Nature provides for man's finding out its designs (*cf.* R. Bray, *La Doctrine Classique,* p. 53 f., 359 f.). The literary artist that follows nature represents truth by a process of selecting from and idealizing actual human experience and behavior according to nature's rational ends; appreciation of his art is therefore restricted to the cultivated few (*honnêtes gens*) whose rationally formed taste qualifies them to discern and enjoy the literary portrayal of nature thus idealized.

The traditional idea of an ordered universe that impresses its natural canon of uniformity and regularity upon literary art remains prominent in the critical doctrine of such writers as Rapin, Dryden, Pope, Johnson; but these critics usually distinguish between the unchanging laws of Nature for literary art, and accidental literary conventions. Thus Johnson reserves the privilege of discarding a received rule that does not square with the practice of Shakespeare, whom he praises as "the poet of nature," whose disregard of the unities of time and place he defends on the ground that these requirements are authorized not by nature and reason but simply by accident or custom (*Pref. to Shak.; cf. Rambler,* No. 156). The external limits of nature's canons for literature are weakening. About the same time, some critics, following current fashions in theological, philosophical, and other fields of speculation, begin to think of nature in another way. In harmony with the growing rationalistic criticism of received theological dogma, the orthodox Christian conception of the imperfection of human nature when unredeemed by Divine Grace or undisciplined by supernaturally imposed authority begins to yield, notably in the teachings of such a popular philosopher as Rousseau, to a more optimistic view of the innate goodness of human nature and a distrust of rules, conventions, or supernaturally imposed laws designed to regulate spontaneous human impulses. Correspondingly, in literary theory, the view that the literary artist's nature is imperfect and relatively unfruitful when not disciplined and completed by art gradually yields to a tendency to exalt the independent value of the artist's nature—interpreted especially as an organism fitted to receive direct intuitions of cosmic Nature's forms, substance, purposes, or laws—and an accompanying distrust of conventional authority, traditions of formal propriety, rules, all that may be summed up as art. Hence derive the various primitivistic conceptions of the untutored genius and of the importance of spontaneity in human art (Lovejoy, *MLN,* XLII). Whereas the traditional Aristotelian doctrine of the Renaissance and the 17th c. had taught that the artist attains truth in his representation of nature by selecting and idealizing the data of his experience according to universal rational principles crystallized by literary tradition, under the influence of the revised opinion of the goodness of human nature and of the external world uncontaminated by art there is a growing tendency to exalt the practice of realism (conceived as the literary representation of the artist's experience) with the aim of fidelity and completeness, independent of any regulative principle of selection not inherent in the artist's own temperament. For Wordsworth, the poet universalizes his sense experience through the agency of imagination—a faculty assumed from experience rather than explained; and this mystical process is regarded as resulting in a faithful representation of the humanly fathomable part of cosmic Nature's purpose or essence (*cf.* Garrod, *Wordsworth*). The inward norm of the artist's own intuition, sensibility, or imagination, operating upon his individual experience, replaces the outward norm of the canons of literary tradition as embodying the laws of nature for literary art.

The cult of literary realism during the 19th c. in turn fosters the doctrine known as naturalism. In the light of scientific speculation, however, it becomes increasingly difficult to identify the literary artist's experience and activity with cosmic Nature's purpose, processes, or substance. As the purposiveness of cosmic Nature seems less easily reconcilable with human claims and desires ("Nature, red in tooth and claw") or the very concept of purposiveness in cosmic Nature eludes speculation, literary values come to be dissociated from participation in a natural design. The link between man's nature and cosmic Nature is broken, and the once potent ambiguity of the norm of nature vanishes. Literary critics, under the influence of modern psychology, become cautious of generalizing even concerning human nature. The norm of nature no longer figures seriously in literary theory and criticism. *Cf.* Method; Art; Aesthetics, J. W. Beardslee, Jr., *The Use of "Physis" in 5th C. Gr. Lit.,* 1918; A. O. Lovejoy, *The Great Chain of Being,* 1936; H. S. Wilson, *Some Meanings of "Nature" in Ren. Lit. Theory, JHI* 2, 1941; J. W. Beach, *The Concept of Nature in 19th C. Eng. Poetry,* 1936; "Reason and Nature in Wordsworth," *JHI* 1, 1940; W. O. Clough, *The Necessary Earth* (Am. Lit.), 1964; J. W. Dixon, Jr., *Nature and Grace in Art,* 1964; A. Young, *The Poet and the Landscape,* 1962. HAROLD SOWERBY WILSON.

natya (Sanskrit). Indian dance-drama, plots drawn mainly from the two great epics, the *Ramayana* and the *Mahabharata.* Usually the actor presents pantomime (*abhinaya*) while the narrator (*bhagavatar*) chants the lines; but in popular (*deśi*) performances the actor also speaks. *See* Indian drama.

negation. Affirmation by denial; inclusion by limitation, *e.g.* (Shak. *Hy. IV,* Pt. I, Act II, iv, 144) "There live not three good men unhanged in England, and one of them is fat, and grows old." Negative metaphor is common, esp. in early poetry, *e.g.,*

It is not a whirlwind rolling along the valley,
It is not the grey feather-grass bending to the earth,
It is the terrible wrath of God. (Chad. II, 73, 156)

Negative description occurs throughout poetry; the evocation of images contrasting with the basic thought, from a line (Kalidasa, ca. 500 A.D., *Winter,* "The bloom of tenderer flowers is past") or a passage (Milton, first 10 lines of *L'Allegro,* "Hence, loathed Melancholy . . .") to an entire poem lamenting vanished things (*see Ubi sunt*). Sometimes the negative reenforces the main idea, as in the 1st stanza of Keats' *Ode On Melancholy*:

"No, no, go not to Lethe, neither twist
Wolf's-bane, tight-rooted, for its poisonous wine . . ."

neo-classicism. A movement towards the recovery of the spirit of ancient classical literature, in the Renaissance and 18th c. Strictly speaking, only that modern work which succeeds in recapturing the spirit of the ancients is properly called neo-classical; work that fails to recapture that spirit is pseudo-classical. *See* Part Two, Eng. Criticism. M. S. Røstvig, *The Background of Eng. Neo-Classicism,* 1961; Hugh Honour, *Neo-Classicism,* 1969.

neologism. A recently coined word; usually, one not yet accepted as standard English. There was much argument in Elizabethan days as to which neologisms should be retained. *Cf.* Nonce-word.

neoteric (Gr., newer). A writer or thinker along new lines. The word was very common in the 17th c., used first of those who went to the Gr. classics for new stimulation. McKeon today says that "the neoteric approach is to discover the new and the stimulating even in the familiar and the forgotten." R. K. McKeon in *The Knowledge Most Worth Having,* ed. W. C. Booth, 1967.

new. *See* Criticism, the new; *cf.* Originality; Novelty.

new comedy. Gr. comedy without supernatural or poetic elements, with emphasis on realistic observation of life. Flourished in 4th and 3rd c. B.C.; chief exponent Menander (342–291). Imitated by the Romans, Plautus (ca. 254–184); Terence (ca. 190–159). *See* Comedy.

new wave. *See* Nouvelle vague.

Nibelungenstrophe. G. The stanza (first used by Kürenberg, fl. 1160) of the MHG epic *Nibelungenlied*: four lines, each of 6 stressed syllables except the last, which has seven. Marked by a regular feminine caesura with a secondary stress. The rhymes, almost always masculine, are *aabb.*

Nō drama. *See* Japanese drama.

noema. P., "figure of close conceit." A statement that seems to say its opposite, *e.g.,* "I thank the Lord that in our forty years together never any neighbor patched up our quarrel" (they lived in harmony); "I would you were a saint" (I wish you were dead).

nonce-word. One employed on a single occasion. (1) A word deliberately invented for a unique use, as the nonsense words (Lewis Carroll, *Jabberwocky*). (2) A new word not accepted in the language. Thus

Coleridge, 1825, coined *tautegorical* to balance *metaphorical.* New words flowered in the Elizabethan age; Puttenham defends as essential, *e.g., majordomo, audacious, metrical, prolix, implete,* of which the last did not survive.

nonsense. Writing which may lapse from meaning in several ways. (1) The host of utterances in which the lapse is unintentional, and perhaps remains unwitting; in many such cases, the receptor also is unaware. (2) Material not intended to make sense. (a) Experiments in sound patterns (esp. in the 20th c.) as in the pure poetry of Hugo Blümner, *e.g.*:

Oiai laéla ssisalu
Ensúdio tresa sudio mischnumi . . .
Ua sésa masuó túlû
Ua sésa machiató toro.—

and in most of the writings of Gertrude Stein, which (reversing the usual poetic process) use meaning as an overtone to patterns of sound. (b) Typographical designs, games, eccentricities, whimsies, Rabelaisian cranks such as the contest of signs between Panurge and Thaumastes (*Pantagruel,* Bk. II, 19). These may often be allegorical or satiric, in which case they are not nonsense; in any event, all the varieties thus far are negative nonsense. (3) Positive nonsense; material intended to make no sense. (a) Earnest nonsense, which follows logically the initial pattern of its absurdity, as many limericks, as *Alice in Wonderland* and *Through the Looking-Glass,* where mathematics and chess control the world of rigamarole. This nonsense (the off-with-her-head Duchess; shelves full all around, but whichever you look closely at is always bare; Alice in the wood surrounded by mad folk; Humpty Dumpty's business dealings with his words) has a topsy-turvy bearing on real life; just step again through the looking-glass. Some of Carroll's poems are direct parodies. Nonsense here is achieved through logic, reason on a holiday—which is not much of a contrast, "for, after all," (Chesterton) "mankind in the main has always regarded reason as a bit of a joke." (b) Playful nonsense, that flashes away on the wings of its own creations. This variety often leads us along familiar paths until we look up in a nonsense world where we are nonetheless surprisingly at home:

For his aunt Jobiska said "Everyone knows
That a Pobble is better without his toes"
(Edward Lear).

Emotions have entered here, and a mystic sense of supra-rational importancies:

Far and few, far and few,
Are the lands where the Jumblies live.

This variety of nonsense, with no bearing on life, is an almost completely Eng. achievement. Chesterton (*A Defence of Nonsense,* in *The Defendant,* 1901) exalts it: "This simple sense of wonder at the shapes of things, and at their exuberant independence of our intellectual standards and our trivial definitions, is the basis of spirituality as it is the basis of nonsense. Nonsense and faith (strange as the conjunction may seem) are the two supreme symbolic assertions of the truth that to draw out the soul of things with a syllogism is as impossible as to draw out Leviathan with a hook." *Cf.* Fantasy; Absurd; Black Humor. E. Cammaerts, *The Poetry of Nonsense,* 1925; L. W. Forster, *Poetry of Significant Nonsense,* 1962.

norm. *See* Rule; Correctness. For sense of the normal within a work, *see* Point of reference.

nouvelle, (*la*) Fr. A kind of short novel or novelette, not so tight in plot-structure as the short-story or *conte. See* Novelle.

nouvelle vague (Fr., new wave). A vogue term, employed to designate a new group or trend in the arts; esp., the Fr. and It. motion pictures of the early 1960's. It has been applied to some Eng. writers who appeared at about the same time: John Osborne, John Arden, Arnold Wesker, Robert Bolt, Brendan Behan, most continuingly Harold Pinter. Pinter's *The Birthday Party,* 1958, was produced in New York in 1967, after his *The Caretaker,* 1960, had won attention and his *The Homecoming* was the Critics Circle prize play for 1966. A Pinter play has been described as "an X-ray touched up to suggest it is a snapshot"; his characters have no discernible motives; life remains a mystery. The author seems to seek maximum tension with minimum fact. The "new wave" writers range from the angry through the traditional (Bolt's play *A Man for All Seasons,* 1960) to the vague and the absurd; they are linked by contemporaneity and current vogue. The fullest theoretical justification of current trends has been developed by the structuralist group around the periodical *Tel Quel* (Paris, 1960—): Jacques Lacan divides experience into the real, the imaginary, and the symbolic; Philippe Sollers (*Logiques,* 1968; *Nombres,* 1968) seeks to combine applied linguistics and Marxism, to "demythify" current notions, and attain a richer awareness of multiform reality. *Cf.* Absurd; Black Comedy; Structuralism.

nova rimada. Prov. A narrative genre of poetry, generally written in lines of 8 or 10 syllables arranged in rhymed couplets. Usually a brief tale of courtly love.

novel. An extended fictional narrative in prose. The most protean of literary forms, the novel is the least amenable to formal definition. At various stages of its development, it has assimilated the characteristics of other ways of writing—essays and letters, memoirs and histories, religious tracts and revolutionary manifestoes, sketches of travel and books of etiquette, all the popular varieties of prose. Since it has never had to face the circumstances of public performance, or even of oral recitation, it has managed to evade the stricter conventions of drama and poetry. Since, in contradistinction to these more conventional forms, the novel is based upon a more private relationship between reader and writer, it opens up wider possibilities for the direct communication of experience.

Hence it is all too easy to overstress the experience communicated at the expense of the mode of communication, to disregard the form of the novel by over-emphasizing its content. The uncritical reader is chiefly concerned with the emotional identification between himself and his reading. The mediocre novelist is willing to hinge his books on the adventitious interest of their subject-matter. Even the critic frequently discusses works of fiction as if they were amorphous products, the result of a haphazard growth, the very negation of deliberate craftsmanship. But the novel could scarcely have accommodated itself to so many different subjects, or have been a vehicle for such varying purposes, if it had not developed a body of technique that is characteristically fluid and resilient, increasingly subtle and complex.

The word that designates the novel in other languages than Eng., *roman,* points to its remote origins in medieval romance. Our word, stemming from the Italian *novella* and roughly equivalent to "news," suggests a new kind of anecdotal narrative that claims to be both recent and true. Thus the development of the novel touches heroic legend at one extreme and modern journalism at the other. Historically, it coincides with the educational diffusion of literacy, the technological perfection of printing, the economic ascendancy of the middle classes. Today the predominance of the novel over other kinds of literature is amply demonstrated by the nearest library or bookshop, with its classification of all books into two categories, "Fiction" and "Non-Fiction."

The point of departure for the modern novel is the actual contrast between truth and fiction. *Don Quixote*—to consider the primary example—is a realistic commentary upon *Amadis de Gaule* and other romantic fiction: Cervantes tests the chivalric ideals of a waning feudalism and finds them contrary to bourgeois standards of common sense. As times change, and new facts of experience clamor for literary expression, conscientious novelists must challenge, or even repudiate, the fictive and conventionalized world that previous novels have established. Fiction is constantly disclaiming the fictitious. It is no accident that many of the great realists have begun with parodies on their predecessors—from Rabelais' burlesque upon the Arthurian romances to Jane Austen's ridicule of the Gothic novel.

Realism, in literature, therefore, may be viewed as a continuous effort, from one generation to the next, to adjust the techniques of literature to the changing conditions of life. Of all the techniques of literature, the novel has been the most accessible to such readjustments. Having supplanted the epic and the romance, it has always been committed to the criticism of obsolete ideals and false ideologies. The significant title of Furetière's *Roman bourgeois* and Fielding's conception of "a comic epic in prose" are no longer regarded as paradoxes, but they still betray the antiromantic and mock-heroic bias of the early novelists. Thackeray's subtitle for *Vanity Fair, A Novel Without a Hero,* describes all realistic novels, if the presence of a hero implies the hero-worship of an earlier idealism.

Modern novelists are less interested in high exploits and marvelous adventures than in familiar routines and quotidian episodes. Their works, comparatively uneventful, are more often contrived by internal motivation than by external incident. Consequently, they shy away from farcical coincidence and melodramatic surprise. The less they depend upon plot, the more they concentrate on characterization. "What is character," Henry James has asked (*The Art of Fiction,* 1888), "but the determination of incident? What is incident but the illustration of character?" Characters need no longer be highly placed in the social hierarchy or the moral order: Victor Hugo celebrates the escaped convict and Dostoevsky venerates the patient prostitute. Heroic figures are rediscovered among the victims of society, and society itself—condemned by its own changing values—becomes the villain.

If character is the determination of plot,

plot is the determination of background. Most of the 18th c. novelists, manipulating a set of comic types through a series of stock situations, followed the random and picaresque highroad that leads from the countryside to scenes of city life. Scott and Cooper took the same pedestrian course, but went in the opposite direction and guided their followers back to the landscapes of romantic nationalism and the bypaths of local color. Under the sterner compulsions of naturalism, these backgrounds are shifted to the foreground, and the characters themselves—whether through the cosmic irony of Thomas Hardy or the social determinism of Theodore Dreiser —are viewed as the creatures of their environment.

Scott was much more than a regionalist, though he was at his best on his own northern terrain. His most influential novels were those that treat the more remote past. For he conceived the historical novel not as an avenue of romantic escape but as a method of antiquarian realism; he introduced his fictitious heroes not merely to the courts of real kings but to the cottages of real peasants; he felt a historian's obligation to survey the whole society of a given time and place. It only remained for the Fr. realists to systematize his methods and apply them to the contemporary scene: for Stendhal to write a "chronicle of the 19th c." and for Balzac to cite the *Waverley Novels* as his precedent for the *Comédie humaine*.

But Balzac, who cited a further precedent in the biological experiments of Geoffroy Saint-Hilaire, set out to be a naturalist of the human species as well as a historian of his own times. The whole of the *Comédie humaine* is greater than the sum of its component novels, since these are held together by a network of human relations—the connections between his metropolis and the provinces, the *liaisons* between his women of the world and his young careerists, the cash nexus that enchains his characters to his plots. When Zola set out to chronicle the natural and social history of a family under the Second Empire, his scientific apparatus was far more elaborate than Balzac's; yet his experimental novels prove less about the laws of heredity than *La Cousine Bette* demonstrates about the wages of sin.

Zola's more ambitious efforts to document his cases, by compiling *dossiers* and working up material, have never quite convinced his readers, because such methods are necessarily as strong or as weak as the perceptions of the observer. Ultimately he was persuaded to make due allowance for the angle of observation, and to define a work of art as "a nook of life visualized through a temperament." His successors have abandoned the promiscuous documentation, the all-inclusive catalogues and mechanical panoramas, of the naturalistic school. They prefer artistic selection to photographic reproduction. They prefer to focus their observation upon a single significant detail, a slight but typical incident, or what Maupassant called "a slice of life." Their approach, which is common today, has been more successfully applied to short stories than to full-scale narrative.

At this point, the transition from realism to impressionism, it is convenient to turn from the sociological to the psychological aspects of the novel, from the narrative to the narrator. The novelist himself, if he is as indifferent to the progress of his story as Sterne, may be an omnipresent and discursive master of ceremonies. In the interests of plausibility, however, he may take the position of his own protagonist, like Dickens in *David Copperfield*; or perhaps assign the narration to a minor character, like the choric figure that echoes the housekeeper's tale in *Wuthering Heights*. Obviously he can gain freshness and intensity from this use of the first person, but he may also find that it limits his field of action and increases the difficulties of characterization. His alternative is a more or less Olympian impersonality.

Dickens, cheerfully accepting the limitations of the novel, embraces both alternatives in *Bleak House*: the naïve impressions of his heroine's journal are amplified by the cold-blooded omniscience of his impersonal narrative. The most viable compromise, while maintaining the detachment of the third person, would attach the sensibilities of the novelist to the point of view of his central character. This approach enables him to reduce the diverging elements of his story to a flexible and comprehensive pattern, by integrating them within a unified experience and orientating them against a single standard. And it still leaves room for the ironic inference, which the examples only confirm, that life itself is much broader than the horizons of those characters with whom the author has chosen to associate himself.

In recent years this association has been even closer. The author, not content with assuming the characters' point of view, has evolved a style that, by various devices of verbal impressionism, approximates their stream of consciousness. Indeed, it almost seems as though truth had finally overtaken fiction, and confined the novel to such themes and situations as could be verified by the immediate responses of the novelist. The consequences of so much objectivity are quite subjective. With Proust, self-portraiture is cultivated to the point where all the other portraits are obscured; *A la recherche du temps perdu* constitutes a sustained apology for the novelist's career. With Joyce, though his nook of life is as broad as the city of Dublin, it is refracted through the temperament of the artist; *Ulysses* is as remarkable for its psychic fantasy as for its social realism.

The effect of these autobiographical tendencies has been to make our most serious contemporary novels seem, to the general reader, morbidly preoccupied with the personal problems of the artist or unduly elaborated by the technical virtuosity of his art. Yet the novelist who is still unwilling to meet the mass-production requirements of the larger public is perforce restricted to a decreasing audience and a specialized vein. A hundred years ago, when Flaubert would turn out forty pages in a year and Trollope could toss off the same number in a week, there was already a distinction between artistic achievement and popular success. Now, with the triumph of what Sainte-Beuve considered "industrial literature," distinguished craftsmanship survives mainly as a curiosity. The current industrial product has few pretensions to originality or realism; it conforms to conventional models and encourages its tired readers in a romantic escapism.

At a time when the middle-class society that found its critical mirror in the realistic novel is being rapidly altered, we must look for a parallel alteration in the forms of fiction. What new forms will make their appearance we cannot precisely predict; but we can observe some progression—in Thomas Mann's terms—"from the bourgeois and individual to the typical and mythical." It is true that primitive types of narrative, tales of the supernatural and the didactic, have been strongly felt in American literature: our great tradition is not the self-conscious naturalism of Howells and Norris but the moral allegory of Hawthorne and Melville. We should be prepared, then, to see more novelists adopting symbolic techniques and idealistic attitudes, to read more novels that take us back to the fable and the epic.

Whatever the future of the novel may be, it has produced some of the most revealing and enduring monuments of past civilization. It has combined, both in vaster proportions and with more minute detail than the other literary forms, the qualities of a human document and a work of art. Accordingly, a novel may be judged by the twofold canon of truth and beauty; by its closeness to life, its depth of insight, its range of observation; as well as its integration of life, its breadth of treatment, its reduction of experience to a pattern. Both canons have seldom been better satisfied than by Tolstoy's *War and Peace*. Here the novelist is able to show individual lives involved in a common destiny, to place history itself within the wider orbit of nature, and thus to give significance to the tangled events and crowded sensations of the modern world. *Cf.* Document; Narrator; Fiction; Science fiction; Detective story; Anti-hero. J. Dunlop, *The Hist. of Fiction,* 1842, 1906; P. Lubbock, *The Craft of Fiction,* 1921; A. Comfort, *The Novel and Our Time,* 1948; E. Auerbach, *Mimesis,* 1953; Ian Watt, *The Rise of the Novel,* 1957; W. E. Buckler, *Novels in the Making,* 1961; Miriam Allott, ed. *Novelists on the Novel,* 1959, 1966; Wayne C. Booth, *The Rhetoric of Fiction,* 1961; Henry James, *The Future of the Novel,* ed. Leon Edel, 1954; Harry Levin, *The Gates of Horn* (5 Fr. realists), 1963; A. Robbe-Grillet, *For a New Novel,* 1965; V. S. Prichett, *The Working Novelist,* 1965; M. Raimond, *La Crise du roman,* 1966; R. Paulson, *Satire and the Novel,* 1967; R. Scholes, *The Fabulators,* 1967; R. Rabinovitz, *The Reaction Against Experimentation in the Eng. Novel, 1950–1960,* 1967; P. Stevick, ed. *The Theory of the Novel,* 1967; A. Burgess, *The Novel Now,* 1967; J. H. Raleigh, *Time, Place, and Idea,* 1968; R. Alter, *Fielding and the Nature of the Novel,* 1968; D. I. Grossvogel, *Limits of the Novel,* 1968; R. M. Davis, comp., *The Novel,* 1969; W. Allen, *English Novel,* 1955. HARRY LEVIN.

novel, Types of. The concern of the novel for empirical reality, as well as the comparative indifference of its readers to questions of form, is implicit in the terms under which fiction is commonly classified, *e.g.,* sociological, bourgeois, psychological, local color, crime, sentimental. These may be subdivided as—like everything else—the novel has become specialized. The *sociological novel* studies the effect of economic and social conditions at a given time and place upon human conduct. Although problems of society appeared in the works of Delony, this type first flourished during the Industrial Revolution. Balzac, perhaps first picturing the importance of money, paved the way; Kingsley's *Yeast,* Mrs. Gaskell's *Mary Barton,* Disraeli's *Sybil,*

Dickens' *Hard Times* are but a few of the novels that reflected the hungry forties. Because of its restricted subject matter and extraæsthetic purpose, the sociological novel may have only a temporary and local reference and a mere historical interest to later readers. Within this type: The *problem novel* deals with a specific social question, such as divorce or race prejudice; if the author writes to a thesis by upholding one class or institution and indicting another, his work may be more properly called a *propaganda novel.* The *proletarian novel* treats sympathetically the problems of laborers. In the *novel of the soil,* the environment is not a man-made economic system but the blizzard, drought, barren soil of some usually remote or primitive locality.

The concern of fiction with actual events recurs in the *historical novel,* which has been defined simply as one in which the characters, setting, and events are drawn from the past. But such a definition is something less than adequate until it has been sharpened by such questions as these: How many of the characters are historical? Are these principal or secondary figures? How important is the setting, and does it stress period detail or permanent elements in the national life? What is meant by the past?—the remote past of documents or the recent past of living tradition? These questions reveal 3 kinds of historical fiction. (1) The period novel, written in the spirit of historical research or antiquarianism, is a detailed re-creation of a past society. The characters may be expository illustrations of the period rather than living people. This group includes some of the early attempts in historical fiction (Barthélemy, *Anacharsis in Greece,* 1788; Strutt, *Queenhoo Hall* 1808). (2) The historical romance is an escape from the tedium and perplexity of the present to the historical exploits of rulers and adventurers of the distant past—*e.g.,* the works of Dumas; Lytton; some of Scott. (3) The historical novel proper (*The Heart of Midlothian, Henry Esmond, Romola*) does not evade reality but sharpens and increases it. The events of the past may be, more or less explicitly, related to the present. Such a novel disengages the essential and enduring problems and motives from mere contemporaneous circumstantiality. Inasmuch as the writer with a true historical sense does not favor the past over the present, he is likely to avoid the remote past and to make small use of historical persons and recorded events. Often (*War and Peace*) the scene is but a generation away from the author, so that recollection of childhood tales is a potent creative force. In most historical novels, the important historical figures play a minor part; the main characters are fictitious. There has been a recent tendency, however, as in the Greek scenes of Mary Renault (*The Bull from the Sea*; *The King Must Die*) and the Arthurian *The Once and Future King* of T. H. White, to retell old legends with modern psychology; also, as in *I, Claudius* of Robert Graves and *Herod* of S. Sandmel, to make the main figure an important person of ancient times, and to try to bring his story, his nature, and his times, to life today.

To these types should perhaps be added the confessional novel, *q.v.* Dreiser and others have used case-histories for their fabrications, building newspaper stories into novels while the public still remembers the notorious, scandalous, or tragic real events. *Cf. Livre à clef*; Gothic; Detective Story; Science-fiction; Novel; Document. E. Bernbaum, *Guide Through the Romantic Movement,* 1930; "Views of the Great Critics on the Historical Novel," *PMLA* XLI, 1926; J. R. Kaye, *Historical Fiction,* 1920; A. T. Dickinson, *Am. Historical Fiction,* 1963; G. Lukács, *The Historical Novel,* trans. 1965; P. M. Axthelm, *The Modern Confessional Novel,* 1967.

With respect to structure it is helpful to distinguish between two overlapping but recognizable types of fiction—the panoramic (or epic) and the dramatic (scenic or well-made). The panoramic novel is loose in plot and does not center in a single issue. The events are only partially bound by causality, the temperaments of the actors, the situations. The ending is a tapering off, or an interruption of what could go lengthily on, rather than a decisive resolution. In short, the panoramic plot is not so fateful, logical, and tragic as the dramatic. The characters are numerous, typical rather than individual, with a single person less often monopolizing the attention.

The dramatic novel is focused in a single issue that is resolved logically from the premises, *i.e.,* the initial situation and the natures of the actors. Thus the plots of *Pride and Prejudice* and *The Egoist* have the inevitability of a syllogism. The tension created by such a plot is released by a decisive ending; the characters are closely integrated with the action. The dramatic novelist seeks an immediacy, even in expository matter—which Richardson had in mind when he prided himself on his "instantaneous descriptions and reflections." In the interest of intensity, this type is likely to observe the unities more closely, with (*Wuthering Heights*) lapses few and unobtrusive. Thus the dramatic novel excludes wide areas in order to scrutinize a narrow segment of life; the panoramic embraces and orders great expanses of human experience. J. W. Beach, *The 20th C. Novel,* 1932; E. M. Forster, *Aspects of the Novel,* 1927; H. James, *The Art of the Novel,* 1934; P. Lubbock, *The Craft of Fiction,* 1921; E. Muir, *The Structure of the Novel,* 1928; W. Booth, *The Rhetoric of Fiction,* 1961; C. Brooks and R. P. Warren, *Understanding Fiction,* 1959; B. Hardy, *Appropriate Form,* 1964; R. Scholes and R. Kellogg, *Nature of Narrative,* 1966. ROYAL A. GETTMANN.

novelette (earlier, novelet). A work of fiction longer than a short story but shorter than a novel. *Cf.* Short story. R. Paulson, *The Novelette Before 1900,* 1968; *The Modern Novelette,* 1965.

novella. It. Short prose narrative, sometimes moral, usually realistic, satiric (women, clergy). Developed by Giovanni Boccaccio, *Decameron,* pub. 1471; Tommasa Guardati (pseud. Masuccio), *Novellino,* 1467; Matteo Bandello (1480–1561), 214 *novelle.* The term was used in Ren. Eng. (Painter, *Palace of Pleasure,* 1556) before the novel.

novellat. *See* Folktale.

novelle (G.) Prose narrative shorter than a novel (3 pages, Kleist, *Das Bettelweib von Locarno,* to 300, Ludwig, *Die Heiterethei*) developed in G. in 19th c. Defined by A. W. Schlegel, 1804, Goethe, 1827, as a single incident, strange yet actual; by Tieck, 1829, as marked by a *Wendepunkt,* an unexpected turn. Heyse, 1871, developed the "silhouette and falcon" theory: a compact outline and a climax. T. Storm, 1871, brought it toward the then developing concept of the short story. *Cf. Falkentheorie.* E. K. Bennett, *Hist. of the G. Novelle, Goethe to Thomas Mann,* 1934.

novelty. A change from the old. Novelty attained fullest recognition as an æsthetic concept in 18th c. Eng. (Addison, Akenside, Kames, Johnson). Addison, placing the new on a virtual equality with beauty and greatness as sources of æsthetic pleasure, makes little distinction between novelty and variety, or between novelty and the surprising and the wonderful. Johnson regards a deliberate search after novelty, such as he finds in the metaphysical poets, as wholly bad (*Cowley*). Equally bad, however, was the use of the outworn in form and image: thus he condemns "Lycidas" on the ground that "whatever images it can supply are long ago exhausted" (*Milton*). What he demands of art is genuine newness or the effect of freshness in presentations of permanent truth: "either to let new light in upon the mind, and open new scenes to the prospect, or to vary the dress and situation of common objects, so as to give them fresh grace and more powerful attractions" (*The Rambler,* No. 3). Reynolds (*Fifteen Discourses,* V, VI, VII, VIII, XIII, XIV) was in essential agreement with Johnson.

Writers of the Romantic period have a good deal to say of novelty; but the representative Coleridge differs little from Johnson; he approves Shakespeare for preferring expectation to surprise; he is quite as severe as Johnson in condemning a craze for mere novelty (*Biographica Literaria,* ed. J. Shawcross, I., 15; II, 21, 23, 24, 160). On the other hand, Coleridge maintains that one of the certain marks of genius is the production of "the strongest impressions of novelty" in rescuing "the most admitted truths from the impotence caused by . . . their universal admission" (Shawcross, I, 59, 60). There must, however, be a nice balance between sameness and variety. (Coleridge does not maintain clear distinctions between variety and novelty.) Too much variety ends in the effect of sameness; the proper goal is "unity in multeity" (Shawcross, I, 15; II, 21–24, 160, 262).

Later writers generally have shown comparatively little theoretical interest in novelty. The chief exceptions were the interest shown in "artificial originality" by Poe and Baudelaire and the emphasis on strangeness added to beauty by Pater and others of his group. The position of Johnson and Coleridge is essentially that which prevails today. Novelty for the sake of surprise or shock or astonishment may be the ideal of some few writers of the secondary sort, but the test applied by substantial critics, *e.g.,* Eliot, is whether the impression of novelty has been created to surprise or shock as an end in itself, or whether it is the product of true originality, of the genuinely new or of the expression in fresh and arresting ways of permanent and universal truths.

M. Akenside, *The Pleasures of the Imagination,* 1744; T. S. Eliot, "Tradition and the Individual Talent," *The Sacred Wood,* 1920; C. D. Thorpe, "Addison and Some of His Predecessors on Novelty," *PMLA* 52, 1937. *See* Originality. CHARLES DEWITT THORPE.

number. Conformity to a regular beat or measure, esp. of counted syllables in a line of verse. (Plural): periods or feet; hence, verses. Usual sense from Shakespeare (L.L.L.): "These numbers will I tear, and write in prose" through Pope (Essay on Criticism):

But most by numbers judge a poet's song,
And smooth or rough with them is right or wrong.—

into the 19th c. (Wordsworth; Longfellow: "Tell me not in mournful numbers Life is but an empty dream"). *Cf.* Prose and Poetry; Meter.

O

OBJECTIVE. (1) A goal or purpose, toward which the author, or a character in a work, is striving. (2) Applied to writing in which the personality, and particularly the emotions, of the author are uninvolved or at least unobtrusive; or to a consideration of an object as it is in itself. Opp. subjective, *q.v.* Whatever is felt as impact (coming from outside oneself) is objective; whatever is felt as action (moving from within oneself) is subjective. The term "objective" is sometimes applied to criticism that is purely descriptive rather than normative; in this sense "objective criticism" consists of statements about the more clearly identifiable and reportable elements of literature (*e.g.,* meter, stanza form), excluding both interpretations of meaning and judgments of value. *Cf.* Narrator.

objective correlative. "The only way of expressing emotion in art is by finding an 'objective correlative'; in other words, a set of objects, a situation, a chain of events which shall be the formula of that *particular* emotion; such that when the external facts, which must terminate in sensory experience, are given, the emotion is immediately evoked" (T. S. Eliot, *Hamlet,* 1919, in *Selected Essays,* 1932). This skimps acting and music, at least; but any emotion (pity; horror; amusement; love) can be evoked by countless formulæ. If by emphasizing "particular" Eliot means the complex of feelings summoned by the unique set of external facts, he is remarking merely that in art as in life each individual set of circumstances is attended by concordant feelings. It is no novelty to state that the artist must create the combination that will produce the effect he desires—though Eliot confuses expression of an emotion in the work with its arousal in the receptor. The same combination may evoke different emotions in persons of different backgrounds and experiences. Susanne Langer (*Mind* v. 1, 1967, p. 215–6) indeed, shows the advantage that rises from the flexibility Eliot would deny: "As there are many uses for one and the same device, so there are many possible means to the same end . . . The fact that a desired quality may be achieved by more than one means allows a good artist to reinforce his created elements by using one chosen device to establish a particular impression but letting others incidentally serve the same purpose." Such development may provide not merely reinforcement but refinement. Earlier (p. 115–17) Dr. Langer points out the "subtle yet crucial" error in Eliot's "famous" formula. Eliot is concerned with an "emotion presented in the work, not by the work." Dr. Langer's most cogent point is that a work of art does not reproduce in us the author's feelings, nor the character's feelings—we do not feel sad, let us say, because Vergil was sad, nor because Dido is sad; and to feel sorry for Little Nell is sentimentality: both empathy and sympathy are irrelevant—what the work does is to make us more fully aware of the essence, of the nature and the depth, of sadness. (It might be more accurate to say that, while we may weep with or for Dido, if the work is not a mere "tearjerker" but is true art, it lastingly enriches us in this deeper way.) The work of art is the feeling given form. As a result, instead of being saddened, we are enriched, exalted. But Eliot's term has been widely used. *Cf.* Connotation; Emotion.

obscurity. A condition of a work, in which it is difficult to discern the meaning. To be distinguished from ambiguity, wherein it may be difficult to determine which meaning (of more than one possible) is pertinent. In figures, puns, and pivot words (*q.v.*), more than one meaning may belong. Obscurity may be intentional, to demand close attention, or for other effects; but deliberate obscurity, which is obfuscation, should not be mistaken for wisdom. Profundity lies in the thought; obscurity is tangled in the expression. There is, however, a tendency to acclaim a work as profound just because it is obscure—satirized in Gilbert's *Patience*:

If this young man expresses himself in terms
too deep for me,

Why, what a singularly deep young man this
deep young man must be!

Henri Peyre (*The Failures of Criticism*, 1967) discusses various types of obscurity, from the complete absence of meaning (in deliberate nonsense, in a revolt against logic, in ineptitude), past the verbal experiments of a Rabelais or a Joyce, to subtlety and complexity of thought and the presentation of many-level meanings. Many writers who seemed obscure to their contemporaries (Wordsworth, Browning, Hugo's poems, Mallarmé) have become less so to more accustomed generations. *Cf.* Clearness; Ambiguity; Meaning; Metaphor. T. J. (Baron) Horder, *Obscurantism*, 1938; Yvor Winters, *In Defense of Reason*, 1947.

Occam's razor (Wm. Occam, fl. 1340). The principle of parsimony: "entities must not be unnecessarily multiplied." Interpreted as implying that, unless a compelling reason dictate otherwise, the simplest way of saying a thing is the best, this is deemed by many a basic principle in writing.

occasional verse. Verse written because of some immediate incident in life, as (for a poet laureate) a royal anniversary, a great victory (or defeat, *e.g.*, Tennyson's "Charge of the Light Brigade"). Often spurred by a newspaper item, which may be reprinted atop. *Cf.* Light verse.

octameter. A measure, or line, of 8 feet, *e.g.*, Swinburne, *March.* Also octonarius.

octastich. A group or stanza of 8 lines of verse. As a complete poem, also called *huitain.*

octave. A stanza of 8 lines, esp. *ottava rima.* Also (octet), the first 8 lines of an Italian sonnet, the last 6 being the sestet.

octet. A group of 8 lines of verse, as the two quatrains of an Italian sonnet.

octonarius. (1) L. A line of 8 feet, as in L. comedy. (2) A stanza of 8 lines, esp. of *Psalm 119* (which has an 8-line stanza for each letter of the Hebrew alphabet).

octosyllable. A line of 8 syllables. The octosyllabic couplet, rhymed, was frequent in medieval poetry (Fr. romances; Chaucer, *Romaunt of the Rose*); it has been less common since (Scott, *Lady of the Lake*; *Marmion*), having lost popularity to the It. *endecasillabo*, the Fr. *alexandrin*, and the Eng. pentameter (heroic couplet; blank verse).

ode (Gr. *ode*, song; tragedy is Gr. *tragos ode*, goat song). Originally simply a poem intended or adapted to be sung to instrumental accompaniment. The G. melos or song led in two diverse streams: through Alcæus, Sappho, Anacreon to the lyric, while Alcman first gave to the choir-song of the drama that strophic arrangement which has become an important element in the ode: strophe, antistrophe, epode. Pindar and Bacchylides were masters of this poetic style, the former having created the heroic ode, composed in consciously elaborate, intricate measures that used Alcman's prosodic pattern. Their harmonics were incomprehensible to the Latins who (Horace; Catullus) returned to the monostrophic lyrics of Sappho, etc.

The English ode has coursed along three runnels, merging at times with the stream of the lyric. (1) Poems of uniform stanzas (monostrophic lyrics) each comprising lines of varied length (Jonson; Randolph; Herrick), but tending toward regularity in later practice (Gray in short odes; Keats; Collins; Swinburne). (2) *Vers irreguliers*, those stemming from Cowley's, introduced as "Pindaric" in 1655, with stanzas more or less regularly varied and consciously constructed on solemn themes. After the Restoration, this form became very popular; Dryden ("Alexander's Feast") wrote several of the best of this style in the language. Gray ("Pindaric Odes"), Wordsworth ("Intimations of Immortality"), Coleridge, and Tennyson likewise employed this irregular (and freer) form. Shelley, who desired to revive the pure Greek manner, began "Ode to Naples" with 2 epodes, followed by 2 strophes and the 4 antistrophes. G. M. Hopkins ("The Wreck of the Deutschland"), Sir W. Watson, Laurence Binyon have written memorable odes in *irreguliers*. (3) Poems written in the tripartite scheme of Pindar's heroic odes, on themes of praise, patriotic sentiment, reverence, reverie, commemoration, etc. Congreve published in 1705 his *Discourse on the Pindarique Ode*; then wrote unpoetical odes in strophe, antistrophe, epode. Few true Pindarics may be discerned until those of W. S. Landor, who understood his Gr. model probably better than any other Eng. poet ("Ode to Shelley"; "Ode to Miletus"; interludes in *Pericles and Aspasia*). Landor had little influence. Only Swinburne in his political odes ("Birthday Ode for the Anniversary Festival of Victor Hugo") cultivated the prosody of Pindar and Bacchylides.

Some critics maintain that variants from Pindar are lyrics, not odes. Yet this diversity within the modern ode led L. Binyon to describe the form as consisting merely in a "poem of address written about a theme of universal interest," usually in exalted language and feeling. John Burke Shipley.

off-Broadway. Term referring to drama produced in New York City away from the Broadway area, usually characterized by experimental and low-budget offerings. Sometimes gives pale imitations of Broadway material, but more often presents experimental or sexual or sharply satirical pieces which the audience of the commercial Broadway theatre might resent. Frequently imaginative in conception and staging; their weakest element often is the acting. (Arthur Kopit, *Oh Dad, Poor Dad, Mamma's Hung You in the Closet and I'm Feeling So Sad,* 1962; *The Day the Whores Came out to Play Tennis,* 1965). Sometimes a play unsuccessful on Broadway (the APA repertory company) plays successfully off, but several off-Broadway plays have had long runs, *e.g., Hair, The Fantasticks. Cf.* Absurd; Cruelty; Off-off-Broadway. Julia S. Price, *The Off-Broadway Theatre,* 1962.

off-off-Broadway. Term referring to the happenings (*q.v.*) and other skits presented in churches, cafés, and lofts, esp. in New York's Greenwich Village, with little cost, considerable improvisation, and much audience participation. The players are usually amateurs, the subjects topical, the productions ephemeral. The pieces are often, as Michael Smith says, "clear to the point of perfect mystery." S. Richards, ed. *Best Short Plays of 1968*; *Best Short Plays of the World Theatre,* 1968; E. Parone, ed. *Collision Course,* 1968; R. Gard, M. Balch, and P. Temkin, *Theater in Am.,* 1968; Michael Smith, ed. *The Best of Off Off-Broadway,* 1969; R. Schechner, *Public Domain,* 1969; R. J. Schroeder, ed. *The New Underground Theatre,* 1968; R. Brustein, *The Third Theatre,* 1969.

old comedy. Gr. comedy (Aristophanes, 5th c. B.C.), characterized by the appearance of the Chorus, the use of specific personal in-invective, and frank physiological realism as well as absurd fantasy. *See* Comedy.

Old French and Provençal forms. In the period 850 to 1300 nearly all Fr. and Prov. literature was verse, chanted aloud. Before 1100 the prevailing types were dance poetry, saints' lives, and the *chansons de geste* (or epics). Probably because of censure from the Church no Prov. lyrics earlier than William of Aquitaine (d. 1127) and no Fr. lyric poetry before 1147 have survived.

The hey-day of new forms was the 12th c. The rhymed chronicles came as a further step after the epic, flourishing best in Normandy (the *Brut* and the *Rou* of Wace). The 8 syllable rhymed couplet was the preferred verse scheme of these chronicles. A new form arose with this same versification before the middle of the 12th c.: the romance, perhaps imitated from the L. art epic. It celebrates the deeds of individual knights, against a background of love and marvelous adventure. At first pseudo-classic themes were exploited: the youth of Alexander was sung in Prov. by Alberic of Pisançon; in Fr. the Thebes story, the Æneid, the Fall of Troy, the life of Alexander. The form was then used for legends of Arthur's court in southwestern Britain and Brittany. A pioneer was Chrétien de Troyes (in Champagne). Folk themes, and stories brought from Byzantium and southern It., were also retold in this manner. The Prov. brought the form to a new height in the 13th c. romance of manners, *Flamenca.* While the romance was taking shape, episodes were being adapted into Fr. from the *Metamorphoses* of Ovid, in the same octosyllabic rhymed-couplet meter. These were the *contes,* on such themes as Pyramus and Thisbe, Narcissus, Hero and Leander. When such short tales were written on more knightly themes, as by Marie de France, they were called *lais.* Stories of a moral type were now known as *dits.* Often a *dit* (*e.g.,* the Prov. *Castia-gilos*) bordered on the fabliau, which had a folk-tale plot, humorous, often disrespectful, briefly handled in rhymed couplets. A popular theme, developed after 1170 in northern Fr., was the *Roman de Renart,* which probably grew from imitation of animal references in the Bible and in moral *exempla.* At first the individual poems were animal folk-tales; social satire gradually seeped in. The main characters are Renart, the fox, and his victim Ysengrim, the wolf. The fable, with a moral lesson, was also popular in northern Fr., based on the *Romulus,* an early L. imitation of the Phædrus collection; its richest expression is by Marie de France. From the early 12th c., didactic poetry flourished in both Fr. and Prov., though with a tendency in Prov. toward prose: lapidaries, bestiaries, calendars, sermons, moral works. Often the familiar octosyllabic couplets were used; but in Normandy there were poems for the *simple gent* in shorter verse lengths. In the epics, assonance gave way pretty generally to rhyme by 1200.

In the 13th c. the most influential of medieval works was created in the *Roman de la Rose,* a combination of allegory and didactic material in the Romance form. Starting then, but not maturing till the 14th c., were the Fr. lyrics of fixed form, first the ballade, a poem with the strophe form ababbcC. In the 14th c. the *ballade* was a poem of 3 strophes, often octosyllabic with rhymes ababbcbC, with an envoi. The *chant royal* was similar, but of 5 strophes. The earliest rondeau was originally either AAaA aaAA or AbaAabAA. Charles d'Orléans, in the 14th c., wrote many rondeaux, usually of the type ABbaab-ABabbaA. By the 16th c. this repetition of refrain was much reduced. Marot's rondeau is a poem of 5, 3, and 5 line stanzas (rhyming aabba aab aabba) with the 1st 4 syllables of the 1st stanza repeated extra, as a refrain, after the 2d and 3d stanzas. The *bergette* (15th c.) was a rondeau of one strophe without refrain. The *virelai* was a series of bergettes with the refrain repeated once, at the close of the last strophe. The *motet* corresponded to a musical form known by that name. A *lai* was a poem, of varied meter, set to a current popular tune. The 14th c. developed the *dit* until it became a very long poem, partly narrative but mostly debate.

In the 19th c. some of these, now known as "fixed forms," were revived in the vogue of *vers de société* and light verse, *q.v.* Some more recent inventions are described in C. Wood, *Poets' Handbook*, 1940, p. 395–9.

A. Jeanroy, *La poésie lyrique des troubadours*, 2 v., 1934; *Les origines de la poésie lyrique en France*, 1904; W. P. Jones, *The Pastourelle*, 1931. URBAN TIGNER HOLMES, JR.

Old Norse poetry comprises the folk-poetry of the Elder Edda and the highly contrived courtly verse of the skalds. The Eddic poems were composed in the Viking period (ca. 800–1000); they were written for the most part in Iceland, ca. 1300. Skaldic verse developed at the same time, declining in the 14th c.; the tradition continues, however, until today.

Eddic poetry shares the ancient stock of Old Germanic lore and the structure of the primitive Germanic measured line. The Edda contains lays of gods and heroes; there are 37 complete poems, and fragments.

The Eddic meter is accentual. Of word-accent there are 3 grades: a primary stress on the first syllable, a secondary on the subordinate element in compound words, and a tertiary on inflectional endings. In the sentence, nouns, adjectives, and adverbs bear the primary stress, the verb is secondarily accented, and other parts of speech are weak. Quantity is also measured. The rhythm of Eddic verse consists in the regular alternation of strong and weak sentence elements, now commonly called "lift" and "sinking." A strong element, or lift, is both long and accented. Unlike O. Eng. and most W. Germanic poetry, which is stichic, the poems of the Edda are strophic: the normal stanza contains 4 lines, but the unit of metre is the half-line, itself called a *visa* (pl. *visur*) or verse. The half-lines are bound together by alliteration of accented words. Any vowel alliterates with any other. Alliterating letters are called staves (*stafr*, pl. *stafir*). The principal or head staff (*hofuðstafr*) is in the 1st lift of the 2d half-line; to it are fitted in the preceding *visa* either 1 or 2 supporting or "prop" (*stuðill*, pl. *stuðlar*) staves. In the 2 following *visur, e.g.*, from the 3d stanza of *Voluspá*,

gap var ginnunga   en gras hvergi

gras, an accented, monosyllabic noun, the 1st lift in the 2nd visa, provides the *hofuðstafr*, *g*; the *stuðlar* are the initial consonants of *gap* and *ginnunga*.

Scansion of Eddic poetry according to the foregoing rules reveals the existence of several regular stanzaic forms. Of these the most common are named *fornyrðislag*, *ljoðaháttr*, and *malahattr*. *Fornyrðislag* consists of 8 *visur* of 4 parts each, 2 lifts and 2 sinkings arranged according to 5 principal modes; a decided break in the sense marks the middle of the stanza. *Ljoðaháttr* has 1 long line (2 *visur*) and a short line of 3 stresses, without cæsura and having interior alliteration. This grouping is a unit; 2 of these units make up the *ljoðaháttr* stanza. The *malahattr visa* is of 5 parts, with 3 lifts and 2 sinkings; 8 *visur* make the stanza. *Fornyrðislag* is the oldest type: it is undoubtedly close to the primitive Germanic stanza-form, which, in turn, may be the rhythm of the sword-dance (*barditus*) mentioned by Tacitus (*Germania* 24). The further suggestion has been made that primitive Germanic metre is utimately related to Latin Saturnians and the metres of the Indian vedas.

The greatest difference between skaldic and Eddic verse is that in skaldic convention slight variations often developed into independent forms; whereas in the Edda the old types remained dominant above all variants. Thus, Snorri Sturluson (1178–1241) lists 100 distinct types of skaldic metre, nearly every one of great complexity. The favorite *drottkvaett* stanza will serve as an example. It consists of 8 lines of 3 stresses each, the last word being invariably of the shape — ⏑. The remainder of the line is constructed according to the accepted skaldic arrangement of *fornyrðislag. Drottkvaett* also has a complex system of rhyme. The beauty of *drottkvaett,* as of other skaldic metres, is in the adaptation to this rigid, artificial form of fine distinctions in quantity, accent, and tone.

The diction of the skalds is as strict as their metres and quite as artificial. The kenning is developed to the point of unintelligibility for all save the initiated skald. Snorri, for instance, quotes a dozen accepted kennings for the sky and elsewhere lists 14 doubtful ones. Hardly one of these is now transparent; yet it is certain that a great part of skaldic skill lay in precision of epithet and in the delicate employment of figures such as these. The poetry of the skalds is highly artificial professional verse written for a critical courtly audience, many of whom were themselves practicing poets.

Skaldic and Eddic verse complement each other: the former is part of the great court-poetry of the world; the Edda is at the other extreme of folk creation. In this radical purity, indeed, the Edda parts company with even its closest congener, for the introspection, the note of sadness, even the thinking twice which figurative language implies—all these qualities of O. Eng. verse are spare indeed in the poetic Edda. The style of this peripheral folk-poetry of the Middle Ages is lean, hard, intense, and vigorous; its chief virtue is conciseness. *Cf.* Germanic versification; Kenning. *Edda,* ed. Gustav Neckel, 2 v., 1936; *Younger Edda* (Snorri Sturluson's Edda) ed. Finnur Jónsson, 1931; Trans. Am. Scand. Found., 1929; B. Phillpotts, *Edda and Saga,* 1931. MURRAY FOWLER.

one-act play. The growth of the experimental and "little theatre" movement—*Théâtre Libre,* 1887, Paris; *Freie Bühne,* 1889, Berlin; *Independent Th.,* 1891, London; *Th. de l'Œuvre,* Lugné-Poë, 1839, Paris; *Little Th.,* 1899; the *Abbey,* 1904, Dublin; *New Th., Hull House Th.,* 1906, Chicago; *Th. du Vieux Colombier,* Jacques Copeau, 1914, Paris; *Provincetown Players, Neighborhood Playhouse, Washington Square Players,* 1915, became *Theatre Guild,* 1919, N.Y.—brought the one-act play, which until then had been no more than an afterpiece or a vaudeville skit, into a rich growth. Although some recent full-length dramas have been divided into scenes or episodes instead of acts, the usual one-act piece is to the play as the short story is to the novel: it can stress but one aspect—character, action, background, emotion—of the many in a full and rounded work. But this gives it great flexibility and variety; the new companies (and hundreds of eager amateur groups after them) staged programs made up of several one-act plays, which attracted the whimsey of J. M. Barrie, the wit of G. B. Shaw, the evocation of horror of Lord Dunsany (and many Fr. writers esp. for the *Grand Guignol*); Hauptmann; Schnitzler; Galsworthy; O'Neill. These works were produced in a great variety of styles, and have been a prominent factor in the recent development of the theatre. An esp. brief form, known in Fr. as the *quart d'heure,* is in Eng. a "curtain-raiser" (*10 Minute Plays,* ed. P. Loving, 1923). In the Theatre of the 1960's both on and off Broadway, the one-act play returned to favor, often presented in groups of three. *Cf.* Drama. P. Wilde, *Craftsmanship of the One-Act Play,* 1923; F. Shay and P. Loving, ed. *50 One-Act Plays,* 1920.

onomatopœia. (1) The formation of words in imitation of natural sounds: bang; growl; hiss; swish; also called an echoic word. *See* Language. (2) The use of words so that the sound fortifies the sense. Sometimes the normal word for an idea supports it with the sound; the physical contraction of the jaw for *gh* in ghastly, ghost, ghoul; dastardly; sly. Sometimes the sound belies the sense, as when one joins the *k* of kick and the *iss* of hiss, for kiss; the most sound-accordant use of "peace" is in Patrick Henry's bitter outburst (borrowed from the *Bible: Jeremiah*); "Peace! Peace!—but there is no peace!" Hence it is the writer's problem so to select and associate his words that the aural aspect (even if heard only through silent reading) will harmonize with the meaning and the mood. The frequency of the word "golden" as opp. to "yellow" *e.g.,* may have auditory as well as monetary cause. Onomatopœia thus may rise from word groupings (Tennyson):

> The moan of doves in immemorial elms
> And murmur of innumerable bees.

June Downey (*Creative Imagination,* 1929) lists "onomatopoetic" appeal to other senses: taste (Keats, "And lucent syrups tinct with cinnamon"); touch; to which might be added the kinæsthetic appeal, sound (and rhythm) rousing one to muted motion. Such efforts have been pursued by the symbolists. That other poets have not sought them in vain is indicated by experiments, where lines of syllables pied from poets' lines have roused, in the receptors, moods congruous with those evoked by the originals, *e.g.*,

Shun dole ow rod thu nark blore o land eep

"Roll on, thou dark and deep blue ocean, roll." This notion, however, is challenged by many; *cp.* J. C. Ransom, *The New Criticism,* 1941; *PMLA* June 1932. For a more basic union of sound and meaning, *cf.* A. K. Coomaraswamy *"Nirukta-Hermeneia," Visva-Bharati Q.,* Aug. 1936.

opera. As a modern art form, a drama whose language is music, opera was first produced in 1594, Rinuccini's *Dafne* at the Palazzo Corsi, Florence, as an attempt to revive the classical Gr. tragedy. Opera was thus first a chanted tragedy, with solemn recitative replacing the tragic declamation. This sense of opera as drama, filled with the spirit of Gr. tragedy, has persisted throughout its history; it dominates the work of Gluck (18th c.) and (19th c.) the "total theatre" of Wagner. In opera the voices not only sing the dialogue but (like the strings, the winds, and the percussions) they are instruments of the music—quite unlike musical comedy, in which they speak the dialogue and, musically, just follow the tunes.

Rome, Naples, and esp. Venice between 1637 and 1700 produced some 300 different baroque operas, which in the 18th c. flooded Europe. Effects were now the primary quest: arias were interlaced with coloraturas, castrati sang the heroic roles with feminine voices. In addition to these It. operas, which dazzled the spectators in the halls of princes and the public theatres (first public opera house, Venice, 1637), the Fr. court opera of Louis XIV under the influence of Racine's tragedies returned—despite modern stylization and numerous ballets—to the serious spirit of Gr. tragedy. This was transmitted to Gluck, whose followers (Salieri; Sacchini; Cherubini; Spontini) similarly modernized the Fr. musical tragedy.

By the mid 18th c. baroque opera had lost its vitality, dying with the courtly and feudal society that had carried baroque culture. In It. *opera buffa* (Logroscino; Gazzaniga; Anfossi; Piccini) supplanted the *opera seria,* taking many liberties with musical form, and introducing more realism. In Fr. composers such as Gretry, Lesueur, Cherubini, expanded the comic opera into sentimental and realistic works; and in G. (Schweitzer; Holzbauer; Dittersdorf; Hiller) the development of serious opera was everywhere associated with popular opera and *Singspiel.* Mozart's chief operas are written either in the style of the *opera buffa* (*Don Giovanni*; *Cosi fan tutte*; *Nozze de Figaro*) or in that of the *Singspiel* (*Elopement from the Seraglio*; *Magic Flute*). Beethoven's *Fidelio* continues the realism of Cherubini, and the great works of G. romanticism (esp. Weber's *Freischütz*) are *Singspiele.*

The Romantic Movement contributed new subjects and forms. During the troubled period of the July Revolution Rossini's historical opera *Wilhelm Tell* appeared in Paris, 1829; and the first naturalistic opera, Auber's *Stumme von Portici,* 1828. Romantic folk-operas were produced in G., ghost operas, knightly and oriental works (Weber, *Euryanthe*; *Oberon*; Marschner; Spohr). In It. the movement progressed from Rossini to Bellini and Donizetti, until Wagner in G. and Verdi in It. employed in consummate fusion all the resources of romantic opera.

Later literary movements had counterparts in opera. Naturalism appears in Mascagni's *Cavalleria Rusticana,* 1891; Kienzl's *Evangelimann,* 1895; E. D'Albert's *Tiefland,* 1903. Richard Strauss drew creative strength from naturalism for *Salomé,* 1905, *Elektra,* 1909, and the new comic style of his *Rosenkavalier,* 1911. Fr. impressionism, Mallarmé, Verlaine, may be felt in Debussy's *Pelléas et Mélisande,* 1902; the constructivism of Arnold Schoenberg's *Erwartung* in Stravinsky's *Œdipus Rex* and Berg's *Wozzek.* Thus throughout its history, in style or presentation, in combination of all the resources of music and the theatre, opera has been an effective expression of the artistic and spiritual forces of the time. *Cf.* Tragedy; Operetta; Musical Comedy; Baroque; Drama. H. Kretschmar, *Gesch. der Oper,* 1919; W. Brockway and H. Weinstock, *The Opera,* 1941; H. Graf, *The Opera,* 1941; J. Kerman, *Opera as Drama,* 1956; W. W. Weisstein, *The Essence of Opera,* 1964; E. J. Dent, *Opera,* 1940, 1965; *Foundations of Eng. Opera,* 1928, 1965. MAX GRAF.

operetta (It. *opera buffa*; Fr. *opéra bouffe*; *opéra comique*: G. *Singspiel*). Light drama with spoken dialogue and musical interludes. It rose in popular reaction to stilted, aristocratic grand opera. In Naples *intermezzi* had been inserted between the acts of the *opera seria* since the early 18th c. Gradually an independent genre emerged (Pergolesi, *La serva padrona,* 1733; Rousseau, *Le devin du village,* 1753; John Gay, *The Beggar's Opera,* 1728, a parody of grand opera using popular ballads and folk song. The form was very popular in Austria and Germany; Hiller; Mozart. Goethe wrote several libretti.) In the 19th c. the tradition grew into the comic opera of Gilbert and Sullivan in Eng., the romantic opera of von Weber in G., the popular Fr. operetta, and the Am. musical comedy of today. *Cf.* Opera; Musical comedy.

opposition. (1) A milder term than conflict, seen by some as the basic element in a novel or play. The opposition may arise from difference in personality, but usually involves opposing forces in a struggle for a goal. *Cf.* Story; Conflict; Novel. (2) A state explicit or implied in many figures. Thus a simile is starker when the one point of resemblance is opposed by many points, or a great gulf, of difference, as when a man is called a cockroach, or a square. This is so basic that I. A. Richards declares: "All living use of language depends upon the user's discernment of how what is being said differs, *significantly,* from other things that might be said instead. Perception of oppositions is thus the active principle of language." *Cf.* Metaphor.

Various types of direct opposition may be distinguished, *e.g.*: (a) opposing sides: left and right; open and closed; plus and minus; (b) mirror image, enantiomorph: helix or swastika turned clockwise and counterclockwise; a pair of shoes; (c) polar, extremes of a scale: hot and cold; good and evil; (d) directional: up and down; bring and take; to and from (also with extremes, as top and bottom, full and empty); (e) by definition: town and country; man and brute; heaven and hell; (f) balanced: half and double; masculine and feminine. Note that enantiosis is a figure of speech: saying one thing and meaning the opposite. C. K. Ogden, *Opposition,* 1932, 1967.

oration. *See* Rhetoric.

oratory. The art or act of public speaking, esp. of formal speech. A major concern of classical rhetoric, taught in the schools until recent times. Now largely confined to international bodies, legislatures, courts, and congresses, though drawing attention once more as audiences widen with radio and television. *Cf.* Rhetoric; Persuasion; Proof; Argumentation; Propaganda.

organic. The terms "organic form" and "organic unity" are sometimes employed, to press an analogy between a work of art and a living organism. (Susanne Langer in *Mind,* 1967, uses the term "living form.") The notion, though in recent vogue, is found as far back as Plato; Socrates in Phædrus states that a speech "should be put together like a living creature." The terms imply a systematic arrangement of parts into a unified whole, which has a special value precisely because of this structure, the whole being greater (more significant, more beautiful) than the sum of its parts. *Cf.* Gestalt; Form.

originality. Ability to express oneself (or the expression) in a fresh, independent, and individual manner. "Novelty" usually refers to a more superficial quality, perhaps with unexpectedness; or to an item or event different from previous ones, as time moves on. Originality resides rather in the point of view or in the style than in the basic idea. The desire for originality, though recently spurred by many considerations including copyright, is "no new-fangle singularitie." It is of course encouraged by public eagerness; John Webster declared (early 17th c.) that "most of the people that come to the playhouse resemble those ignorant asses who visiting stationers' shops, their use is to inquire not for good books but for new books." Today there are book-selling "clubs" to provide them. Longinus rebuked writers that have a horror of the obvious. On the other hand Marivaux is but one of those that had rather "be humbly seated in the last row of the little troop of original authors, than proudly placed in the front rank of the vast herd of literary apes." Others that prize originality make similar attack upon borrowing, plagiarism, until in reaction Laurence Sterne plunders from Robert Burton a diatribe against such plundering; Horace Smith defines originality as "unconscious or undetected imitation"; and Tennyson cries out "As if no one had heard the sea moan except Horace!" There being nothing new under the sun, Seneca boldly pronounces "what anyone has well said is mine"; Molière: *"Je prends mon bien ou je le trouve"*: Shakespeare without discussion appropriates all his plots. John Donne after him warns borrowers:

For if one eat my meat, though it be known
The meat was mine, the excrement is his
own.

Many saw not only no sin, but an advantage in admitting debt. The continent complimented Chaucer as "the great translator"; Cervantes—who apologized for inventing instead of drawing upon ancient sources—published *Don Quixote* as from the Arabian of Cid Hamet Ben Engeli. Gascoigne, Drant, Whetstone, among the Elizabethans, called some of their own works translations from the Italian; Walpole similarly labeled his *Castle of Otranto* (1764). The names of those that have freely used the Trojan themes would make a lengthy list.

Originality, then, seems seldom to reside in the subject. As Scott said, it "consists in the mode of treating a subject"; so Dryden before him. Basic themes are few, esp. in popular fields: the novelist in *Beggar on Horseback* (Kaufman and Connelly, 1924) is writing his 16th best seller by dictating his 15th. Forms are many, and (Roger Fry) "what never grow less or evaporate are the feelings dependent on the purely formal elements." Even of the forms of art, however, there is a repetitive range, beyond which one ventures at the risk of the eccentric, the freakish, the frigid. Originality lies deeper, and beyond questing. Any dauber may hire the artist's model. Manner and matter may both be of a long tradition; what a man feels and thinks, what he stands for, what he is, lies at the heart of the work. The personality dictates the procedure. The message, the style, is the man: fundamental—but by him taken for granted, like the sun, like breathing. Each personality thus presses the subject and the form—sonnet, novel, drama—into the unique mold. It is in this sense (not of any outer design; *cf.* Intention) that the form is inseparable from the work; and it is in this sense, in the measure of the author's personality, that the work is original. *Cf.* Plagiarism; Novelty. H. M. Paull, *Literary Ethics,* 1928.

orismology. Explanation of technical terms —the student's demand and the scholar's despair.

orismus. Defining by denying things that are close. Thus Shaw in the "Don Juan in Hell" act of *Man and Superman*. Sometimes used in humor as explaining what a thing is not, but thereby only seeming to make clear what it is.

ornament, now implying a decoration added to a work for æsthetic purposes, originally referred to the proper ordering or arrangement of its parts with a view to efficient operation. St. Augustine lays down that "any ornamentation exceeding the bounds of responsibility to the content of the work is sophistry". Sometimes what one selects as "mere" ornament has underlying hold: "the collective memory preserves, in the form of "ornament" or "decorative" element, archaic symbols of purely metaphysical essence" (A. K. Coomaraswamy, *Art Bulletin* 21, 1939). *Cf.* Symbolism.

orta oyunu. Turkish folk drama. After the abolition of the janissaries in 1825, Turkish traveling players borrowed stories from the shadow-puppet play, the karagöz (*q.v.*). The chief character of the *orta oyunu,* Kavuklu, wears the traditional red coat (*aba*) of the janissary and the 18th c. officer's hat (*kavuk*). The all-male companies use somewhat old-fashioned language for improvisation and criticism of contemporary life and events, with rhymed dialogue in lines of irregular length, and frequent word play. Usually but two characters are onstage at a time; there is constant horse-play, the simple Kavuklu often cudgeled by his companion Pisekar. The form is giving way before the cinema and western style theatre.

orthotone. A word normally unstressed that, because of its metrical use or other importance, takes an accent in the verse.

Oscan fables. *See Fabula Atellana.*

ottava rima. It. verse in stanzas of 8 hendecasyllabic lines, rhymed *abababcc*. It appeared in the religious and minstrel poetry of the late 13th c. (Schiller, describing the form, says it was born in love); then was used in the sacred representations and the songs of chivalry or of the classical cycle. Boccaccio raised it to literary dignity (*Teseida*; *Filostrato*; *Ninfale Fiesolano*). It became (Poliziano; Pulci; Boiardo; Tasso) the exclusive meter of epic and other narrative. Ariosto achieved in it the richest harmony of thought and meter, so that his verse is called the *ottava d'oro,* the golden octave. Naturalized in G., Fr., and Eng., the form was used by Byron in his trans. of Pulci and in *Don Juan*. *Cf.* Spenserian; Romance versification.

oxymoron (Gr. "pointedly foolish"). A figure of speech (rhetorical antithesis) which combines two seemingly contradictory or incongruous words for sharp emphasis or effect. For example, "darkness visible" (Milton); "make haste slowly" (Suetonius); "Eternity! Thou pleasing, dreadful thought!" (Addison); "loving hate" (*Romeo and Juliet*). *Cf.* Antisyzygy, Opposition, Antithesis.

oxytone. A word, or a line of verse, with the accent on the last syllable.

P

PAEAN (Gr. *ie Paian,* cry with which the chorus punctuated its leader's song; perhaps from Paian, name of Apollo as physician). A song to implore Apollo's aid; then of thanks and praise for deliverance; then, a song of triumph. Probably the oldest Gr. lyric. The sympotic paean is sung as an introduction to a symposium, and at its close. In battle, the martial paean followed the prayer and preceded the war-cry to Enyalius (Mars). The Paean was usually in the meter (— ◡ —: 2 shorts may be substituted for either long) that took its name. Plato called the paean of Tynnichus the most beautiful song in existence. (Sometimes used for paeon, *q.v.*)

paeon. A metrical foot, one long and three short syllables: 1st pæon — ◡ ◡ ◡; 2d: ◡ — ◡ ◡; 3d: ◡ ◡ — ◡; 4th: ◡ ◡ ◡ —. *See* Prose rhythm.

palimbacchius. Antibacchius, *q.v.*

palimpsest. Writing surface of vellum, parchment, etc., which has been used twice or more, the previous text having been removed to make room for the final one. Modern chemical methods make it possible to recover the earlier texts.

palindrome. Word, sentence, or verse, that reads the same, letter for letter, backwards and forwards, *e.g.,* Able was I ere I saw Elba. L. (a lawyer speaking): *Si nummi, immunis:* Give me a fee and you go scot-free. In 1802 a Gr. poem signed Ambrose Pamperes had 416 lines, every line a palindrome. Found throughout the early Christian world; scratched on a Roman wall at Cirencester, England, is the square palindrome

```
S A T O R
A R E P O
T E N E T
O P E R A
R O T A S
```

which reads the same right or left, up or down. Various translations of this palindromic magic square have been suggested, *e.g.,* Arepo the sower holds the wheels at work. But the square was used on amulets and for charms, and a neat suggestion is that, like the fish (*cf.* Acrostic), it made a sign by which the early Christians hiding from persecution could recognize one another. Note that TENET, "he holds," makes a cross in the square, its ends surrounded by A O A O. And all the letters in the square form an anagram, rearranged in the form of another cross:

```
          P
          A
          T
          E
          R
P A T E R N O S T E R
          O
          S
          T
          E
          R
```

—with four letters left over: A O A O. Put these at the four ends of the big cross; they represent alpha and omega: "I am the Alpha and the Omega, the first and the last, the beginning and the end," *Bible, Revelation* 22, 13. Thus the cross and the first two words of the Lord's Prayer combine with alpha and omega to give the magic palindrome a trinity of divine reference. Although palindromes, acrostics, and other word play were frequent among the early Semitic peoples, this is the only palindromic square; its purport may be an accident, but it seems to be an intricately devised symbol of esoteric significance. Magic power has, in many parts of the world, been attributed to verbal combinations and to names.

A recurrent palindrome is one that, read backwards and forwards, makes different words, *e.g.,* trap, emit. The strict form (level; Madam I'm Adam) is also called a reciprocal palindrome; in L. *echoici versus.* Palindromes are also called sotadics, after Sotades, a Gr. poet of the third c. B.C. *Cf.* Pun. G. R. Clark, *Palindromes,* 1887.

palinode. A recantation. A poem retracting or counterbalancing something said in an earlier work. Chaucer's *Legend of Good Women* begins with a dream in which the god of Love berates him for picturing evil women in *Romance of the Rose* and *Troilus and Criseyde,* then permits him to do penance by writing of women good and true.

palinodic. Applied to verse wherein 2 similar stanzas or stanzaic groups (*e.g.,* strophe and antistrophe) are separated by another matched pair, different from the first set.

palliata. *See* Fabula.

pantoum (A Malayan form, introduced into Fr.: Hugo, *Les Orientales* and Eng.: Austin Dobson). A chain verse: quatrains, *abab,* any number of stanzas, with the second and fourth lines of each stanza used as the first and third of the next—except the last, in which lines two and four are lines three and one of the first stanza, ending the poem with its opening line.

parabasis. Gr. A long speech (generally in anapestic tetrameter) spoken probably by the chorus leader, in the person of the poet: a feature of Attic Old Comedy. Near the middle of the play, the actors left the stage and the chorus with its leader addressed the audience. Flickinger 41 f.

parable. The three most common of the short moralistic literary types, allegory, parable, and fable, are often distinguished but vaguely if at all. A parable is a short narrative, whereof the characters are usually human beings; the incident has little point without the moral, which is always closely attached. In the fable the characters are animals or plants or even inanimate objects, but the incident is self-sufficient without the moral; in the allegory the names of the participants are abstract qualities, and the application is always evident. The best examples of parables are those of Jesus in the New Testament. *See* Fable.

paradiastole. (1) Euphemism, esp. by synonym that softens the tone, as "clever" for "shrewd"; "liberal" for "spendthrift"; "thrifty" for "niggardly." (2) *See* Repetition.

paradigm. A model or pattern. Resemblance pointed up by examples, *e.g.,* "The elephant is strong, yet death did it subdue; the bull . . . ; the lion . . . ; —you!"

paradox. A statement seemingly self-contradictory or absurd that on examination proves to be well-founded. As its unexpectedness catches attention and adds force to a statement, paradox has always been used; by the Greeks and Romans, esp. in encomiums. In the Renaissance, Erasmus' *Praise of Folly,* its title (*Encomium Moriae*) itself a paradoxical pun on his host, the wise Sir Thomas More. Donne wrote *Paradoxes and Problems.* Hazlitt called works of Pope "the poetry of paradox"; G. K. Chesterton has been called a paradoxmonger. Such critics as F. Schlegel, De Quincey, and recently Cleanth Brooks have stated that paradox is vital if not inevitable in poetry, which develops by indirection and contradiction.

Paradox may be verbal—"The more I think of you, the less I think of you"—or of ideas, *e.g.,* "Agnostics are the most dogmatic men I know"; Shakespeare's Sonnet 138, beginning:

When my love swears that she is made of truth
I do believe her, though I know she lies . . .

C. Brooks, *The Well Wrought Urn,* 1947; D. Daiches, *Critical Approaches to Lit.,* 1956; R. L. Colie, *Paradoxia Epidemica,* 1966.

paragoge. *See* Epenthesis.

paragram. A play on words by alteration of a letter or letters; a verbal pun, *e.g.,* "The druggist is a piller of society." *Cf.* Pun.

paragraph. The basic unit of a composition, conveying a single distinct point in the progression of the work. *See* Composition.

paralepsis. *See* Apophasis.

paralipomena. Items omitted in the body of a work, and appended.

parallelism. (1) Balanced return of structure, as in Hebrew verse; *cf.* Canaanite. (2) A species of repetition, *q.v.* It may be of sound, or structure, or of meaning; usually the several segments are of approximately the same weight or length.

paraphrase. The process (or its product) by which each successive idea in a work is reproduced, usually in a simplified form. Sometimes, also, a summary. *Cf.* Periphrasis; Metaphrase.

pararhyme. The repetition of the same consonantal sounds with different vowels between, *e.g.,* slim, slam; draining, drowning. *Cf.* Rhyme.

parasiopesis. *See* Apophasis.

parataxis. The coordination of clauses without conjunctions; opp. hypotaxis. The oldest form of clause connection is parataxis with asyndeton, *e.g., tacent: satis laudant* (they are silent; that is praise enough—Terence, *Eunuchus* 476). This developed into coordination with connecting particles and finally into subordination. Gr. never advanced so far in the direction of subordination as did classical L., and non-literary L. maintained parataxis as the favored type. Hypotaxis developed from parataxis, *e.g.,* Gr. *deidō mē elthes* (I fear that you will come; originally, I fear; do not come); L. *timeo ne venias;* Fr. *J'ai peur que tu ne viennes* with the vestigial negative. Eng. is far more paratactic than L.; although the trend may be toward subordination. In common speech esp. strings of clauses loosely held together by "and" do service for the more intricate subordinations of formal discourse.

Meillet et Vendryes, *Grammaire Comparée des Langues Classiques,* 1927.

parodos (Gr. Passageway along the side of the *skene,* the stage structure). The chorus entered singing, along the parodos on the spectators' right; hence the opening song of the Gr. drama was called the parodos.

parody. Using the words, thought, or style of an author, but by a slight change adapting them to a new purpose or ridiculously inappropriate subject; the imitation or exaggeration of traits of style so as to make them appear ludicrous.

Aristotle named Hegemon (*Gigantomachia, Battle of the Giants,* 5th c. B.C.) as the inventor of parody; but Hipponax of Ephesus and the author of the Homeric *Batrachomyomachia* (*Battle of the Frogs and Mice*) wrote parody earlier; and it is frequent in folk verse. Aristophanes (*e.g., The Frogs*; *The Acharnians*), parodying Æschylus and Euripides, made parody an effective form of judicial criticism. Lucian (*Dialogues of the Gods*; *The True History*) parodied Homer; the form was so frequent in L. that Cicero listed its varieties. The Roman practice of satirizing enemies in wills gave rise to the parody testament (as late as Villon, *Petit Testament, Grand Testament*; and Goldsmith, *Retaliation*); and as offshoots the animal testaments popular throughout the middle ages; and parody epitaphs (Villon, *Ballade des pendus*), which still appear. From the 12th c. on, parodies abound on the Bible, the mass, the litany (Jonson, in *Cynthia's Revels*).

In the early Ren., Chaucer's *Rime of Sir Thopas* and Cervantes' *Don Quixote* parodied the long-winded manner and grandiose style of the medieval romance. With the Ren., harsh personal invective was more richly supplemented by a gentler literary parody. Epic was a fertile field: John Philips (Eng., 1676–1709) *The Splendid Shilling,* 1705, of *Paradise Lost*; Paul Scarron (Fr., 1610–60) *Vergile Travestie.* J. Racine (Fr. 1639–99) in *Les Plaideurs* parodied the exalted sentiment and rolling rhythm of Corneille; John Hookham Frere (Eng., 1769–1846) in *Whistlecraft,* the Arthurian romance; in *Loves of the Triangles,* E. Darwin's *Loves of the Plants.* But Dr. Johnson thought even the best parody of slight merit: "The Style of Billingsgate would not make a very agreeable figure at St. James's."

In Victorian Eng., parody flourished, mainly in short poems. James (1775–1839) and Horace (1770–1849) Smith wrote *Rejected Addresses* (for the reopening of the *Drury Lane Theatre* after the fire of 1812). "Bon Gaultier" (W. E. Aytoun and Sir Theodore Martin); C. S. Calverley (1831–84; *Fly Leaves,* 1872, some of the best); J. K. Stephen (1859–92, *Lapsus Calami,* 1891); *Alice in Wonderland*—have parodies of the romantics and of the sentimental poems popular with the Victorians. In America the parody gained favor more slowly, but is now widely popular.

Parody of the novel began with the very first work; *Pamela* was victim of several besides Fielding's *Joseph Andrews.* Thackeray's *Burlesques* range from Scott to Goethe (*The Sorrows of Young Werther;* parodied in G. also, *e.g.,* by B. Nicolai). Bret Harte (*Condensed Novels,* 1867), Stephen Leacock (*Nonsense Novels,* 1911; *Frenzied Fiction,* 1918), esp. Max Beerbohm (*A Christmas Garland,* 1913) continue this variety. Parody of the theatre is less frequent, but is found in most periods: Aristophanes; in and of Shakespeare; Molière; *The Rehearsal,* 1672, of the heroic tragedy; *Der Frosch* (D. E. Hartleben, in G.) of Ibsen. On Broadway at the turn of the 19th c. parody often trod on the heels of its victim. Thus Clyde Fitch's *The Stubbornness of Geraldine* opened in November, 1902; before the end of the year Weber and Fields, with Fay Templeton, were a hit in Edgar Smith's parody *The Stickiness of Gelatine.*

A recent development (J. C. Squire, *Tricks of the Trade,* 1917) is the rewriting of a poem "how they would have done it," *e.g., Casabianca* in the style of various other authors; Carolyn Wells, *Diversions of the Re-Echo Club*; of critics, F. C. Crews, *The Pooh Perplex,* 1963.

Three types or levels of parody have been distinguished: (1) Verbal, in which the alteration of a word makes the piece trivial, *e.g.,* "the short and simple flannels of the poor" (Gelett Burgess<Gray's *Elegy*: "annals."). (2) Formal, in which the style and mannerisms of a writer are used for a ludicrous subject. These two levels are humorous only. (3) Thematic, in which the form, usually a typical subject, and the spirit of the writer are transposed, *e.g.,* Lewis Carroll (Cowper) "You are old, Father William"; J. K. Stephen (Wordsworth) Sonnet; Shakespeare (the blood and thunder bombast as of Marlowe, in Hamlet's recital to the players, "The rugged Pyrrhus, he whose sable arms"). The quick spontaneity of Touchstone's parodies of Rosalind's tree-verses (in *As You Like It*) should not hide the fact that parody demands both finished craftsmanship and keen appreciation: admiration as well as laughter. On its third level, it is searching and effective criticism of a poet by a poet. *Cf.* Burlesque;. Satire; Travesty; Spoof. W. E. Hope, *The Language of Parody* (in Aristophanes), 1906; C. R. Stone, *Parody,* 1915; G. Kitchen, *A Survey of Burlesque and Parody in Eng.,* 1931; H. Richardson, "Parody," *Eng. Assn. Pamph.* 92, 1935. John Olin Eidson.

paronomasia. A play on words of similar sound; a pun, wherein a word (Pope, *The Art of Sinking,* 1727) "like the tongue of a jackdaw, speaks twice as much by being split." Some would limit paronomasia to play based upon sound, which does not survive in translation; and use pun for play upon ideas, which does. Thus when we read in the *Bible* (Matthew, 16) "Thou art Peter, and upon this rock I will build my church," we see no word-play unless we know that *petra* is the Greek word for rock. When, on the other hand, Cicero sees a neighbor ploughing the family graveyard, we do not lose the play when we translate: "He is cultivating his fathers' memory." *Cf.* Pun.

paronym. A word from the same root as another. Esp., a word taken over into another language with only a slight change, as of termination, *e.g.,* Gr. *paroxysmos,* L. *paroxysmus,* Fr. *paroxysme,* Eng. paroxysm.

paroxytone. A word, or a line of verse, with accent on the penult. In Fr. verse, this is produced by a final *e* (mute in prose), which creates a feminine rhyme. *Cf.* Romance versification.

partimen. *See* Tenson.

paso (Sp., passage). Procession representing one of the passions of Jesus. Then, a short dramatic piece (Lope de Rueda, ca. 1510–65, *Las Aceitunas*) in Sp. marketplace, or a comic interlude or extraneous episode in a longer play (Lope de Vega, 1562–1635).

passion play (L. *pass-,* suffer). A religious presentation, epic in dramatic form. The enacted life, or episodes from the life, of a god. In Egypt ca. 2000 B.C., of Osiris. In Persia called *ta 'ziya.* In Mohammedan countries (Hassan and Fatima) played for ten days in the month of Muharran, since the 10th c. In Christian Europe, mainly 14th–16th c. (*Confrèrie de la Passion, Paris,* 1402). Reached its widest spread in G. where a few (esp. at Oberammergau) are still presented as civic spectacles.

K. Young, *The Drama of the Med. Church,* 1933.

passus (L. step). A chapter or other division of a story; canto of a poem.

pastiche (It. *pasta,* paste). A work patched together from various sources (esp. all from one author) as a parody. Hence, an imitation of another's work. *Cf.* Cento.

pastoral poetry, as a literary genre, may claim only one constant feature: contrast implicit or direct between town and country. Not to be confused with popular rustic song and other naive expressions of folk life, the pastoral began as a presentation of shepherds in characteristic and usually happy moments. From his recollections of Sicily or Cos, Theocritus (fl. 280 B.C.), a city man longing for the country, created character in monologue or dialogue, seeking artistic realization of actual herdsmen in the setting that he knew and loved. Every later pastoralist imitated either Theocritus or another imitator.

Theocritus perfected three forms of the pastoral which were later varied only to suit the demands of the age. (1) The singing-match owes its ultimate origin to contests held during early folk festivals. Two shepherds meet, engage in light-hearted banter, decide to settle their differences by a singing-match. A third shepherd is named judge, and the alternate singing tells the joys and woes of lovers; the contest often ends with an exchange of wagers, the judge being unable to choose between the singers' merits. (2) A single shepherd pictures in song his mistress' charms and laments his own hard case. In its earlier form, the singer directly apostrophizes the mistress. Later the poet first describes the scene and the singer, whose song is separate and, sometimes, incidental to the whole piece. (3) The elegy, or dirge, has proved the most lasting form of the pastoral. Theocritus' first idyll, *The Lament for Daphnis,* established most of the conventions that were repeated through the centuries. Here the setting for the song is laid as a goat-herd, meeting Thyrsis, promises him gifts if he will sing the old song about mythical Daphnis, who scoffed at love. The song then follows as an incidental but elaborate part of the idyll. The refrain, the address to the woodland nymphs, the visits of various deities, the prayer that Nature revoke her laws in token of sorrow: to these chief devices in elegy should be added the innumerable turns of phrase first used in this poem. Long after the decease of the pastoral as a genre, the metaphors and the traditional devices of elegy continued, as poets paid tribute to their departed fellows. Conventions characteristic of the pastoral elegy include: a pastoral setting, the invocation of the muses, all nature joins in the mourning, an expression of grief, a procession of mourners, bewilderment caused by grief, use of flower symbolism, and a closing consolation (grief becomes assurance, belief in immortality).

In the process of its transfer to Rome by Virgil (70–19 B.C.) the pastoral lost its appeal as an immediate image of actual rural folk in an actual setting. Once and for all it became an art of imitation. Except for the addition of the panegyric, the forms remained essentially unchanged as they became the mould for personal aims, from expressing gratitude to the emperor for restoring the poet's property (*Eclogue* 1) to consoling a friend who had lost his mistress (*Ecolgue* 10). As the pastoral was becoming the city man's dream of the country, the realities of rustic manners gave place to pleasant rustic pictures of the Golden Age; coincident with this emphasis, esp. notable in the famous 4th eclogue, pastoral settings came to be identified with a fanciful Arcadia.

The Renaissance saw three ramifications of the classical eclogue which, assuming new forms, absorbed new matter foreign to the genre. The pastoral romance was introduced by the Neapolitan Sannazaro in the popular *Arcadia* (1504), which combines verse with prose; also, Port. Montemayer (*Diana,* 1558), Eng. Sidney (*Arcadia,* 1590), and Fr. d'Urfé (*Astrée,* 1610). Perhaps taking his cue from Theocritus, Sannazaro invented the piscatory eclogue, the shepherds replaced by fishermen. This form, which despite substitutions followed Virgil closely, did not become widely popular, and after a brief vogue on the Continent and in Eng., is remembered now chiefly for reminiscences in Milton's *Lycidas* (1637), though Hazlitt says "perhaps the best pastoral in the language is that prose-poem, Walton's *Compleat Angler*" (1653). Analogous is the vogue of another ephemeral offshoot, namely, the pastoral drama; in It. esp. the *Aminta* (Tasso, prod. 1573) and the *Pastor Fido* (Guarini, prod. 1590). Already pastoral personages have absorbed the courtly code of manners, and these plays, intricately constructed, bear all the marks of Petrarchism. The Eng. *Faithful Shepherdess* (John Fletcher, 1602) is the best in this kind.

Spenser's *Shepheardes Calendar* (1579) comprised older types and new additions—lover's lament, singing match, elegy, panegyric, and church allegory. His eclogues, closely imitated in the 16th and 17th c., remained the best in the Virgilian tradition. Pastoral drama was assimilated by the masque; the prose pastoral, *e.g.,* Sidney's *Arcadia,* with its chivalric accretions, borrowed from the epic while moving toward the novel. The pastoral lyric remained the natural medium for the city man's longing for rural content and simplicity. With such variety, the word "pastoral" came gradually to be associated more with content than with form. *Cf.* Eclogue; Idyll. W. W. Greg, *Pastoral Poetry and Pastoral Drama,* 1906, 1959; E. K. Chambers, ed. *Eng. Pastorals,* 1895, 1925; W. Empson, *Eng. Pastoral Poetry,* 1938; Andrew Young, *The Poet and the Landscape,* 1962. THOMAS PERRIN HARRISON, JR.

pastorela. Prov. A genre of courtly lyrical poetry, No. Fr. *pastourelle.* A debate between a knight and a shepherdess, with her usually winning the verbal duel. In the Prov. examples, courtly love requires that the shepherdess always reject the knight and retain her virtue. Later, various types were distinguished according to the girl's occupation: *cabreira* (of a goatherdess); *aqueira* (of a goose girl); *vaqueira* (of one that keeps cows); *porqueira* (of one that tends pigs); *hortolana* (of one that keeps a garden).

pathetic fallacy. (Ruskin, *Modern Painters,* v. 3, Pt. iv). The presentation of the inanimate world as having human feeling. "Natural subjectivity"; a type of personification. It may range from a brief phrase (Homer: ruthless stone; ship that joys in the breeze) to an entire poem (Moschus, *Lament for Bion*). It may be limited to (*Christabel*):

The one red leaf, the last of its clan,
That dances as often as dance it can

or see all things as (Pope):

. . . one stupendous whole,
Whose body Nature is, and God the Soul.

This panpsychism extends from Plato (*Timaeus*) through Johannes Kepler (1571–1630) to the romantics (Wordsworth), sometimes as a basic philosophy, sometimes as a figure; often it appears as hylozoism (the earth is an animal), *e.g.,* Shak. *Henry IV, Pt I,* iii:

> . . . oft the teeming earth
> Is with a kind of colic pinch'd and vex'd
> By the imprisoning of unruly wind
> Within her womb.

The usual meanings of the two terms that Ruskin wrings to special use, make many suppose he is condemning where he but characterizes. He indicates four types of men: (a) those that feel weakly and see truly; to these, the primrose by the river's brim is nothing more; (b) those that feel strongly, but think weakly, therefore see untruly; to these the primrose is a fairy's shield, or a forsaken maiden; (c) the poet, who feels strongly, thinks strongly, sees truly; and (d) the seer—for there are subjects "by which his poor human capacity for thought should be conquered . . . so that the language of the highest inspiration becomes broken, obscure, and wild in metaphor, resembling that of the weaker man, overborne by weaker things." Thus pathetic fallacy produced by (b) is objectionable; that welling from (d) is inspired. It is manifest that Ruskin's categories are subjective. The passage he dislikes from *Christabel* (above) is highly praised by George Moore (*Pure Poetry*); Tennyson objected to Kingsley's "cruel, crawling foam," which Ruskin also cites; if we prefer Milton's "remorseless deep" we must note that the figure is the same in both; Hazlitt praises (Shak.) Iachimo's remark, of Imogen:

> The flame o' the taper
> Bows towards her, and would underpeep her lids
> To see the enclosed lights—

which may seem to others as artificial (consciously elaborated) as Donne.

Poets (lengthily, *e.g.,* Lowell, the two Preludes to *The Vision of Sir Launfal*), dramatists, novelists, have frequently set the moods of nature in accord with the events or emotions of their tale.

Some recent writers have declared that Ruskin's term stresses material differences but neglects structural anologies. Thus Riesser: "Pathetic fallacy reveals itself to be poetic truth, for in aroused æsthetic contemplation the feelings reanimate what the scientific intelligence has killed." *Cf.* Truth; Nature; Personification. Max Riesser, *Analyse des Poetischen Denken,* 1954.

pathopoeia. A figure, passage, or scene, that seeks to work upon the receptor's feelings. *Cf.* logopoeia.

pathos. A sense of distress, that awakens pity or tenderness in the receptor. Usually associated with the sentimental, with melodramatic rather than tragic situations and moods. Shakespeare sometimes (*Hamlet, Lear*) uses pathos to lighten the strain of the tragic; *cf.* Comic relief. *Cf.* Tragedy; Bathos; Social comedy; Catharsis.

patter song. A lengthy comic lyric, half spoken half sung as rapidly as possible, by one of the characters in a musical comedy. In ancient Gr. comedy called the *pnigos, q.v.* The most challenging in recent times is the "nightmare song" in Gilbert and Sullivan's *Iolanthe* (1882).

pattern (L. *pater,* father, model; ME *patron,* which still in Fr. means pattern and patron).

In literature, (1) an archetype or model: the *Odyssey* of Homer as that of the epic; Mendoza's *Lazarillo de Tormes* as that of the picaresque novel. Petrarchan sonnets were the "pattern" for Wyatt. Signifies here more than a mere influence, rather a fairly faithful imitation. (2) Within any one work, the part or segments that reveal the figure or quality of the whole, such as the strophe, antistrophe, epode of the Pindaric ode. In this sense the term can be applied to those works whose "construction" follows a regularly recurring form. Yet it can also be used to describe parts of such as certain essays of F. Bacon in which are revealed not the figure, but the quality or thought-content. For example, the phrase "He that hath Wife and Children, hath given Hostages to Fortune; For they are Impediments to great Enterprises, either of Virtue, or Mischiefe" ("Of Marriage and Single Life," No. 8, 1625 edit.) announces the thoughts to follow, thus sets the pattern. (3) Finally, the manner—on the premise that content and style are interdependent—in which any one literary work is constructed or achieved. Herein one examines the piece complete as to figure and quality to ascertain its total "plan." In the determination of symbolic referents, *e.g.,* the Persian rug in Maugham's *Of Human Bondage,* one finds a plain linkage between thought and style that demonstrates the "how and what" of the work as completely as possible. Such an examination covers a poem as simple as Wordsworth's "I wandered lonely as a cloud" and prose as complex as the stream-of-consciousness writings of Joyce.

The term "archetypal pattern" has been coined by modern criticism based on the psychological theories of Jung, to refer to the primordial, atavistic symbols that are to be found in literature. Melville's *Moby Dick*, amongst other works, has been discussed from this point of view. *Cf.* Symbolism; Archetype. JOHN BURKE SHIPLEY.

pause. (1) In fiction, a point of rest, esp. to prepare for and give contrast to the climax. It is necessary in moving the reader from one scene to another to come to such a point of rest. During this quiet interval the author may indicate a lapse of time, or he may for contrast use his pause to heighten description or for a long piece of explanation. The pause allows the reader to think back and join the loose threads, thus providing a more intense awareness of what is going on. (2) Cæsura, *q.v. Cf.* Prosody.

penny dreadful. *See* Dime novel.

pentameter. A verse of 5 feet; in classical poetry esp. dactylic pentameter, — ∪ ∪ — ∪ ∪ — || — ∪ ∪ — ∪ ∪ — (a long may replace either of the 1st 2 pairs of shorts). A marked cæsura exactly bisects the verse. It is generally the 2d line of an elegiac distich. The most common verse in Eng. is the iambic pentameter, the line of the sonnet, the heroic couplet, most blank verse.

pentapody. A sequence of 5 feet, or a verse of that length.

pentastich. A group of 5 lines of verse; as a stanza or entire poem, also quintain. *Cf.* Cinquain.

penthemimer. A unit of 5 half feet in a line, esp. in dactylic pentameter, thus regularly broken by the cæsura. In hexameter, the first section when the cæsura comes after 2½ feet.

period, in literature: a section of its development in which one system of literary norms is dominant. This definition rejects the view (common among G. scholars) that a period is a metaphysical entity; also, that a period is merely a linguistic label. The view that the literary process moves in a continuous directionless flux leaves us with a chaos of isolated events on one hand and purely subjective labels on the other. In practice, most histories of literature assume that periods can be delimited. Usually the division, however, is based on criteria taken over from some other human activity; our current division of Eng. literature is a hodge-podge of periods whose distinctions are derived from the most varied fields. Some refer to distinct political events (Restoration); some are derived from the reigns of the sovereigns (Elizabethan, Caroline, Victorian); others (baroque) are drawn from art history. The usual defense of this confusion is the alleged fact that the contemporaries spoke of their own times in these terms. In most instances, this is not true; the term "Romanticism," *e.g.*, was introduced in Eng. in 1844; "Renaissance," in 1840. More systematic attempts have derived sequences from art history: Gothic, Renaissance, Baroque, Rococo; or construct some psychological development of the national mind; thus Cazamian conceives of Eng. literature as a series of oscillations between the poles of reason and sentiment. Such theories make literature dependent on some other cultural activity or on the evolution of some abstraction such as the national mind or the *Zeitgeist* (time-spirit). If we assume that literature has its own development, coordinate with and not a passive reflection of the political, social, intellectual, or linguistic evolution of mankind, we must conclude that literary periods should be determined by purely literary criteria. Only after we have ascertained a series of literary periods should the further question arise, how far these periods coincide with those determined by other criteria.

The individual periods will be distinguished by the dominance of distinct literary norms. The many futile attempts to define "romanticism" or the "baroque" show that a period is not a concept similar to a logical class. An individual work of art is not an instance of a class, but a part, that, together with other works, makes up the concept of the period, thus itself modifies the whole. The history of a period will thus consist in the tracing of the changes from one system of norms to another.

The unity of a period is relative; during this time, a certain system of norms has been realized most fully. Survivals of preceding norms, anticipations of subsequent ones, are inevitable. The obvious difficulties in determining the actual date of the prevalence of a certain system of norms, and the persistence of undercurrents, explain the frequent disputes as to the limits of periods. Exact dates, such as the publication of the *Lyrical Ballads*

(1798), are rather signposts than divides, but the fact of the continuity does not destroy the value of tracing the emergence, dominance and final decline of systems of literary norms in the actual process of literature.

M. Foerster, "The Psychological Basis of Lit. Periods," *Studies for William H. Read,* 1940. R. Wellek, "Periods and Movements in Lit. Hist." *Eng. Inst. Annual,* 1940. RENÉ WELLEK.

peripeteia. Reversal; in drama, the sudden change of fortune, usually from prosperity to ruin. Aristotle states that the three basic elements of tragic plot are recognition, reversal, and suffering. *Cf.* Recognition; Tragedy.

periphrasis. Circumlocution; saying in many words what might be expressed in few, or roundabout what might be put directly. An instance of this is a periphrase (not a paraphrase, *q.v.*). Propriety in the verbal sense—calling things by their right names—may conflict with propriety in the social sense, when the matter is beneath the dignity of the speaker, is obscene, or otherwise unseemly. In the 18th c. esp., such expressions were avoided by periphrasis, or by euphemism; the habit lingers, *e.g.* "gone to his rest"; "the deceased." Periphrasis may also amplify the thought or embellish the language. To such ends, the 18th c. made frequent use of general terms, *e.g.,* "the scaly breed"; "the feathered kind," akin to the Gc. kenning, "foamy-necked floater." Without such justification, roundabout expression is an impropriety: perissology. (*See* Occam's Razor.) Similarly, overdelicacy of euphemism is acryology. The use of more words than are required to express a thought is pleonasm, *e.g.,* "With mine own ears I heard his voice." When not an embellishment but a flaw, this is macrology. Other faults are: tautology, needless repetition of the idea in different words; prolixity, unnecessary rambling or detail; verbosity, floundering in a sea of words; verbiage, excess beyond meaning; ambage, circumlocution, especially for deceit or delay.

An inexact word, or a periphrasis, may sometimes be unavoidable; as when there is a linguistic gap, *e.g.,* L. *lapidare* 'to throw stones' used for the throwing of clods; such a use is called catachresis. There are many such gaps in Eng., as will be seen on seeking the extremes and the means of a polarity, *e.g.,* what is the mean between "loud" and "soft"? "Soft," indeed, perforce does double duty, for hearing and for feeling. The same term, catachresis—a gap even here!—is applied to avoidable improprieties of all sorts, such as exaggerated or distorted figures: to call the base of a mountain its foot is metaphor; to call the foot of a man his base is catachresis. *Cf.* Abstract; Repetition.

peroration. The concluding section of a speech. It usually recapitulates the main points or arguments, and adds an emotional appeal. *Cf.* Rhetoric.

Persian prosody existed in Iran before the time of Zoroaster (7th c. B.C.). The Gāthās (hymns) contain rhythm that depends upon the number of syllables in each verse. Most metrical stanzas of the Avestan Yašts (praises) are octosyllabic. The earliest specimens of poetry in Modern Persian date from the 9th c. A.D., since which time the language has changed little. A variety of meters and structural forms have developed, mainly modified from the Arabs.

A *miṣrā'* or verse is composed of *arkān* (feet) and *uṣul* (syllables). *Uṣul* are of three types: *sabab, watad,* and *fāṣila,* each of which is divided into *ḫafif* (soft) and *thaqil* (hard). A soft *sabab* is a syllable in which an accented consonant is followed by a consonant that is quiescent (with no following vowel), as *kām.* A hard *sabab* is one in which two accented consonants occur in succession, as *farā.* A soft *watad* is composed of 2 accented letters and 1 quiescent letter, as *caman.* In a hard *watad* the quiescent letter occurs in the middle, as *pārsā.* A soft *fāṣila* is composed of 2 accented letters followed by a quiescent with the sign of *tanwīn* (nunnation), as *jabalin.* A hard *fāṣila* is composed of 3 accented letters followed by a quiescent with the sign of *tanwīn,* as *barakatin.*

The *arkān* are either *sālim* (perfect) or *ğayr-i sālim* (imperfect). The perfect foot is that in which no alterations or adaptations have been made. The imperfect foot is that in which something has been added or taken away. The imperfect foot is called *muzāḥaf* and the alteration is called *ziḥāf.*

A *bayt* generally cannot consist of less than a distich, formed of 2 hemistichs, each called a *miṣrā'.*

All the forms of meter are named from the root *f'l* (*see* Arabic Poetry), and every type of metrical foot is modeled after the following 8 standards:

fa'ulun ◡ — —
fā'ilun — ◡ —
mafā'ilun ◡ — — —
mustaf'ilun — — ◡ —
mufā'ilatun ◡ — ◡ ◡ —

mutafā'ilun ∪ ∪ — ∪ —
fā'ilātun — ∪ — —
maf'ulātu — — — ∪

There are 19 *buhūr* or meters: *ṭawil, madid, basiṭ, wāfir, kāmil, hazaj, rajaz, muqtaḍab, ramal, munsarih, muḍāri', mujtathth, sair', jadīd, qarīb, hafīf, muśākil, mutaqārib,* and *mutadārik*. These are subdivided into further variations, of which about 80 have been recorded. Of these 19 metres, the first 5 are peculiarly Arabic; very few Persian poets have used them. The 14th, 15th and 17th are peculiar to Persian poetry:

(*jadīd*): *fā'ilātun fā'ilatun mustaf'ilun*
— ∪ — — — ∪ — — — — ∪ —

(*qarīb*): *mafā'ilun mafā'ilun fā'ilatun*
∪ — — — ∪ — — — — ∪ — —

(*muśākil*): *fa'ilātun mafā'ilun mafā'ilun*
— ∪ — — ∪ — — — ∪ — — —

The remaining 11 varieties are common to Persian and Arabic.

Qāfiya, rhyme, occurs at the end of distichs and hemistichs. The basis of the *qāfiya* is the *rawī* or the last quiescent letter of the rhyming word. 8 letters, 4 antecedent and 4 subsequent, are united with *rawī* to form different kinds of rhyme.

Persian poetry may be divided into 2 principal groups, that in which the rhyme is external or one-rhymed, and that in which the rhyme is internal or many-rhymed. In the former, the same rhyme is used throughout the whole poem, at the end of each *bayt.* In the latter, the *miṣrā's* of the bayts rhyme together.

The 2 important non-rhymed verse forms are: *qaṣida* or elegy (a long poem of 30–120 lines) and *gazal* or ode (not over 15 lines). The same metres are used in both and the *maṭla's* or opening verses of both have internal rhyme. The *qaṣida* may be a panegyric or satire, or it may be didactic, philosophical, or religious. The *gazal* is generally erotic, or mystical, and contains the *taḫallus* or pen name of the poet in its *maqṭa'* or final verse. Other one-rhymed verse forms are: *qiṭ'a* (fragment) and the two strophe-poems *tarkīb-band* (composite-tie) and *tarjī'band* (return-tie).

The many-rhymed form is represented only by the *matnawī* or couplet poem, of epic, romantic, didactic, or ethical themes (*Śahnama,* Firdawsī; *Panj Ganj,* Niḍāmī; *Haft Awrang,* Jāmi). The *matnawī* and the *gazal* are both of Persian origin. Another form originated by the Iranians is the quatrain. It consists of 2 *bayts* (hence called *dū-bayt*) or 4 hemistichs (hence called *rubā'i*). Fitzgerald's renderings of the quatrains of "Omar Khayyām" have made this form of verse familiar to the Western world.

E. G. Browne, *A Literary History of Persia,* v. 1–2, 1902–06; U. M. Daudpota, *The Influence of Arabic Poetry on the Development of Persian Poetry,* 1934. MEHMED A. SIMSAR.

personification. (Gr. prosopopeia). 1 Speaking through the lips of a person not present, or deceased, or of institutions or ideas. Demosthenes, *e.g.* (first *Olynthiac*) has "the present opportunity" speak. 2. The endowment of abstract qualities, general terms, inanimate objects, or other living things, with human attributes, esp. feelings. Frequent in all literature, *e.g.,* "The dish ran away with the spoon"; (Blake) "Little sorrows sit and weep"; (Boccaccio, *The Falcon,* 5th day, 9th Tale) "as often as the weather would permit"; (Shak., *Macbeth*) "confusion now hath made her masterpiece." *Cf.* Pathetic fallacy; Anthropopathia.

persuasion. The art, or the act, of moving to action. Often confused with convincing, which is the art or act of winning to belief. (Thus "persuade" is normally followed by "to"; "convince," by "that.") To a rational mind, conviction is the prior step; as one believes, so one will behave. In the heat of controversy, however, a speaker may seek, not the establishment of proof and properly founded belief, but direct emotional incitement to action. If one says "He persuaded them that John was guilty," the implication is that their belief has been attained by specious or emotional appeal rather than by rational and logical argument; and the fact of John's actual guilt is still questionable. To persuade and to convince are the two purposes of argumentation, *q.v.;* its devices depend upon which purpose is major in the speaker's mind. *See* Proof; Oratory; Rhetoric; Discourse; Question of Fact. M. E. Bonney, *Techniques of Appeal,* 1936; W. C. Winnick, *The Art of Persuasion,* 1957, 1968; R. L. Rosnow and E. J. Robinson, ed. *Experiments in Persuasion,* 1967.

pessimism. The view that the universe is intrinsically bad and that life in it is consequently futile. The pessimist usually holds that there is an inevitable preponderance of unhappiness over happiness in human life, but two types of pessimism may be distinguished according to whether this preponderance is regarded as constant or increasing. (1) Cosmic pessimism conceives of the universe either as being at the mercy of a malignant or at least careless spirit (as in some of the *Rubaiyat* of Omar Khayyam, and in the words of Gloucester, *King Lear,* IV. 1, 36), or as driven by a blind, directionless, and irrational will (the view expounded by Eduard von Hartman in *Zur Geschichte und Begründing des Pessimismus,* 1880, and, more fully, by Arthur Schopenhauer, in *Die Welt als Wille und Vorstellung,* 1818, and *Parerga und Paralipomena,* 1851). The latter type of cosmic pessimism appears in the "drift" of Thomas Hardy, and pervades the poetry of Leopardi, Chateaubriand, Heine, Byron (*Manfred,* parts of *Childe Harold*). (2) Retrogressive pessimism (also called "pejorism") is the doctrine that the world is undergoing an inevitable degeneration; this doctrine appears in the 16th and 17th c. theory of the world's decay (Richard Foster Jones, *Ancients and Moderns,* 1936); in the views of Mr. Escot, the "deteriorationist," in Thomas Love Peacock's *Headlong Hall*; in Edna St. Vincent Millay's *Epitaph for the Race of Man*; in Oswald Spengler's thesis (*The Decline of the West,* 1918–22) that Western Culture, and perhaps all culture (*Man and Technics,* trans. C. F. Atkinson, 1932, p. 78) is nearing the exhaustion of its creative possibilities; Spengler denies, however (*Pessimismus,* 1921), that his view is pessimistic.

To a certain extent, pessimism is an ingredient in two complex attitudes that have frequently been expressed in literature. (1) In romantic melancholy (Irving Babbitt, *Rousseau and Romanticism,* 1919), it is combined with *Weltschmerz,* longing for the unattainable ideal, and the feeling that the sensitive artistic genius is bound to be destroyed by the materialistic crowd. In this form, pessimism runs through the romantic poets, and appears in D. H. Lawrence, Baudelaire, George Moore, Senancour, Vigny, Thomas Mann. (Ernest Seillière, *Le Mal romantique,* 1908). (2) In one type of stoicism, it combines with emphasis upon the irony of life, and a certain pride in suffering (William James, "Is Life Worth Living?" in *The Will to Believe,* 1897); some of this appears in A. E. Housman, Thomas Hardy, James Thompson; R. L. Stevenson, *Pulvis et Umbra,* 1888; Bertrand Russell, "A Free Man's Worship," *Mysticism and Logic,* 1918; Miguel de Unamuno, *The Tragic Sense of Life,* trans. 1926.

J. Sully, *Pessimism, a History and a Criticism,* 1877; E. M. Caro, *Le Pessimisme au XIXe siècle,* 1878; H. Fierens-Gevaert, *La Tristesse contemporaine,* 1904. Monroe C. Beardsley.

Petrarchism. Poetic style developed in the *Rime* (to Laura) of Francesco Petrarch (1304–74); humanized the theological ecstasies of his Tuscan predecessors, but in a mannerism marked by artificial diction, intellectual casuistry: a play of words and ideas (later called *concetti,* conceits) and forced antitheses (the pun or Fr. *pointe*) with purely intellectual opposition of elements. Its forerunners lie in Prov. poetry (*see* Old French): the language, literary and conventional; the prosody, complex and difficult; the style, obscure and enigmatic (the *trobar clus, q.v.,* hermetic versifying). Petrarch brought the *dolce stil nuovo* (*q.v.*) of Dante, Guido Cavalcanti, Cino de Guinicelli to a mould that was long employed. 15th c. court poets followed his love casuistry in madrigals and *strambotti* (erotic love epigrams), and many blazons, celebrating in detail various parts of the feminine body. Michelangelo (1475–1563) and his lady, Vittoria Colonna, were amongst the last to feel the influence of Petrarchism, which died about 1600. The foreign influence, lasting somewhat longer, extended from P. Ronsard, J. du Bellay (1524–60) of the Pleiade and Louise Labé (1526–66) of the Ecole Lyonnaise in France to Boscan, Camoens, and esp. Herrera (1534–97) in Spain and Portugal, to poets from Wyatt (1503–1542) to Donne (1572–1631) including Spenser and the early Shakespeare (*Sonnets*) in England, and to Opitz and other exponents of *Schwulst* (grandiloquence) in Germany. What is sometimes called Anti-Petrarchism was the attempt (often by fervent disciples: du Bellay, *Contre les Pétrarchistes*) to lop off excesses. Petrarchism not only broke the dominance of Latin, but introduced new forms (sonnet), and esp. in It. and Sp. regulated and standardized the new poetic powers.

J. M. Bertan, "A Definition of *Petrarchismo,*" *PMLA* 24, 1909; T. F. Crane, *It. Social Customs of the 16th c . . . ,* 1920. Cornell U. has an excellent Petrarch collection.

phantom word. One that exists through lexicographer's or other error. Thus Chatterton's "slug-horn" (Celtic *sloggorne,* slogan, battlecry), was later used, by Browning also, as a musical instrument. Also, ghost word, *q.v.*

Phébus (Fr. Phœbus Apollo; from Gaston de Foix, 14th c. *Miroir de Phébus*). Bombastic and precious style; esp., the diction of the characters in 17th c. fiction. High-flown speech. Tallemant (1618–92, *Historiettes*): "The heroes are as like as two drops of water, they all talk *Phébus* . . ."

philology. The study of literature and literary scholarship or learning in general, *i.e.*, knowledge of literary phenomena and the methodic techniques and apparatus for acquisition of this knowledge. The Gr. ancestor of the word is obviously an analogue of *philosophia* (love of wisdom); as such it was applied to his professional work by Eratothenes (3d c. B.C.), who called himself *philologos*. In Eng. esp. through the 19th c., it has been much used to designate the study of language (now, *linguistics*). Philology includes the two disciplines of literary *theory* (or the science of literary phenomena in general) and literary *history* (or the record of particular literary phenomena, singly or as related together, with all that has to do with their transmission and interpretation). It is to be distinguished on the one hand from literary *practise* or art, the production of literary works, and on the other hand from literary *criticism* strictly so called (for this is evaluation in the light of relevant knowledge, not the knowledge itself). Since to be effective, however, or indeed intelligible, evaluatory discrimination must be founded upon knowledge, theoretical and historical, criticism is impossible without philology. (*Cf.* Scientific method in criticism.) One can, indeed, distinguish the philologist or literary scholar (the pure knower) from the critic (the pure evaluator) only by an abstraction, since the distinction is in fact not of persons but of operations, and of operations that can be successfully performed only by the same person. The critic is ideally a scholar who does not stop at knowing, but goes on to judgment in the light of his knowledge. (The scholar likewise must ideally be a critic, for knowing demands discrimination, and all selection implies evaluation.) Logically, therefore, there can be no conflict between philology or scholarship and criticism. The assertion of such conflict in recent controversy between partisans of "criticism" and of "literary history" has been due partly to confusion concerning the real issues contested, which are not reducible to the simplicity implied by the unfortunate opposition of these two terms, and partly to wayward and uncritical use of the terms chosen to designate the contending ideals. If the literary departments in the universities, the function of which is to provide society and the practising critic with an adequate philology, have neglected the theoretical part of their work in a (historically intelligible) temporary excess of emphasis upon the historical, and especially if they have in this allowed other kinds of history to usurp the place of literary history, any other exclusive emphasis would equally jeopardize the satisfactory performance of their total function. The fact that neither history nor criticism can ever actually appear in isolation suggests that the only satisfactory ideal is the common and equal development of both, in an ordered general system that relates them to each other and to the whole of which they are parts.

Sandys, I, 1–13; A. S. Cook, "The Province of Eng. philology," *The higher study of Eng.*, 1906; T. C. Pollock, *The nature of lit.*, 1942, p. xiii–xxiv. *See* Criticism, textual. J. Craig LaDrière.

phoneme. A basic unit of sound in a language. Phonemes vary from language to language (and sometimes linguist to linguist), from 20 to 60. Thus in Eng. *p* and *b* are separate phonemes, but *ph* and *f* are not. *See* Language. W. F. Twaddell, *On Defining the Phoneme,* 1935; D. Jones, *The Phoneme,* 1950.

picaresque (Sp. *picaro,* rogue). A work that tells the life story of a rogue or knave. It is usually first-personal and episodic. Serving in some menial position, the picaroon through his experiences as a social parasite satirizes the society he has exploited. Although the rogue has been a favorite character in story from earliest times, the picaresque novel originated in 16th c. Sp. As a reaction against the fantastic romances of chivalry, it showed that everyday life could offer situations as interesting as the imaginary careers of magicians, giants, knights, dragons. The earliest specimen is the anonymous and ever-popular Spanish story, *La vida de Lazarillo de Tormes* (ca. 1554). This set the pattern, in and out of Sp.; most of the Fr. writers (*e.g.*, Le Sage, *Gil Blas*) set their tales in Sp. After Thomas Nash's *The Unfortunate Traveller* in 1594, the type gained importance in Eng. in the novels of Daniel Defoe (*Moll Flanders*), Tobias Smollett (*The Adventures of Roderick Random*), and Henry Fielding (*Tom Jones*). The type underwent many modifications. Feminine characters were used as the picaroon, who was placed in every position imaginable; the episodes grew more and more extravagant.

Blending with the Robin Hood and the Tyl Eulenspiegel tradition of the idealistic or patriotic brigand, outlaw, rogue, another variation—esp. the Räuberroman in G., growing through Goethe, *Götz v. Berlichingen,* 1773; "Veit Weber" (L. Wächter) *Sagen der Vorzeit,* 1787, 98; Schiller, *Die Räuber,* 1781; Zschokke, *Abällino,* 1793; Vulpius, *Rinaldo Rinaldini,* 1798; but popular elsewhere, transmuted as the sentimental *Pirates of Penzance,* 1879, the philosophical brigands of Shaw's *Man and Superman,* 1903; and in narrative poems Scott's *Lochinvar*; Noyes' *The Highwayman*—pictures an outlaw hero battling for the good, or with good-hearted gallantry. These, however, often leave behind the essential picaresque quality, which is that of the merry rogue wandering, through various social levels, into a succession of escapades. Such contemporary novels as Mark Twain's *Huckleberry Finn* and Saul Bellow's *The Adventures of Augie March* have been loosely described as picaresque.

F. W. Chandler, *The Lit. of Roguery,* 1907; E. M. W. Tillyard, *The Epic Strain in the Eng. Novel,* 1958; R. Alter, *Rogue's Progress,* 1964; R. W. B. Lewis, *Picaresque Saint;* A. A. Parker, *Lit. and the Delinquent,* 1967. John Olin Eidson.

pitch. *See* Meter.

pivot word. A word or phrase that may be construed as modifying both what precedes it and what follows (called *apo koinou* by the Greeks). This may add complexity and richness to a passage. In the Japanese Nō drama, pivot words are frequent. If such a double possibility of linking is a grammatical error, the construction is called a squinter. *Cf.* Ambiguity.

plagiarism. The conscious and unacknowledged repetition of another man's words was condemned in antiquity as it is today. Although it was even more prevalent then, partially because of the absence of copyright laws, the literary historians and grammarians prided themselves on discovering it. Hardly a great name escaped attack; Herodotus, Aristophanes. Sophocles, Menander, and Terence were accused, and the *furta Vergiliana* were the delight of the Roman poet's enemies. Rigorous though the judgments against plagiarism were, imitation, particularly of a reputable model, was encouraged. Milton, for example, said that copying without improving was plagiarism. H. M. Paull, *Literary Ethics,* 1928. *See* Originality; *cf.* Imitation.

plain style. Simplest of the three ancient types of style. Cicero (*Orator*) remarks that its simplicity makes it sound much easier than it actually is. It is a style not trammelled by cadences; free, but not rambling. *Cf.* Style; Clearness.

plateresco (Sp. *platero,* silversmith; filigreed; applied to house-façades in Sp. Ren. architecture). The style of writing in Sp. 16th c. romances, before Cervantes; in the 17th c. ornaments grew even more frequent and elaborate, as on the buildings of Churriguera (*estilo churrigueresco*).

play. Mimic action; stage performance, or a piece to be performed. *See* Drama. An "acting play" is one that is "actor-proof," succeeds when given merely competent performance; opp. the literary play, which requires consummate direction and playing. Unlike both these is the closet-drama, intended not for playing but for reading. *Cf.* Tragedy; Comedy; Dark Comedy; Low Comedy; Absurd, theatre of the. T. Cole, ed., *Playwrights on Playwriting,* 1960; Ivor Brown, *What is a Play?,* 1964; G. C. Weales, *A Play and its Parts,* 1964; W. Wager, ed. *The Playwrights Speak,* 1967; E. Bentley, ed. *The Theory of the Modern Stage,* 1968.

Pleiad (Pleiades, the 7 daughters of Atlas, transformed to a group of stars). A cluster of 7 "stellar" poets: (1) in Hellenistic Alexandria, third c. B.C., included Aratus, Lycophron, Theocritus; (2) in Paris, 1549 (*see* below); (3) with Pushkin and Lermontov, in 19th c. Russ.; (4) self-styled in 20th c. Fr. with Pierre Camo, Comtesse de Noailles, Paul Valéry; (5) 20th c. Provence, around T. Aubanèu, G. Roumaniho, Fr. Mistral. The most influential was (2), *la Pléiade*: Pierre de Ronsard; Joachim du Bellay; Baif; Belleau; Jodelle (all under 24 years); Thuard; Dorat, Ronsard's teacher. They sought the *enlustrement,* "illustration" of the language; cleared away the "confectionery," *épiceries,* of the rhetorical school; spread love of the classics; introduced new forms (the sonnet); freshened Fr. poetry.

plot is that framework of incidents, however simple or complex, upon which the narrative or drama is constructed; the events of the depicted struggle, as organized into an artistic unit. In the *Poetics* Aristotle names plot as the first essential of drama or epic. The elements of plot are a beginning that presumes further action, a middle that presumes both previous and succeeding action, and an end that requires the preceding events but no succeeding action. The unity of the plot is thus the result of necessary relationship and order among the events, not that they center upon a single character. The epic requires the same unity and completeness of plot, due allowance being made for the greater magnitude and complexity of the epic form.

The reverence for Rom. drama and the critical neo-Aristotelianism of the Ren. created a demand for strict plot unity (of time, place, and action) that found wide expression among critics and acceptance among playwrights of Europe, *e.g.*, Racine; Corneille. In the meantime, however, there had grown the more rambling romance and picaresque plot, that sought critical justification by analogy with the epic, and found frequent practice, as in Shakespeare and Lope de Vega. Plots since then (in Fr. drama not until 1830) have increasingly broken from rigid limitations. In 19th c. Fr., Scribe, Sardou, Labiche, and Feydeau developed the "well-made play," with a plot so neatly patterned, its effects so prepared for and spaced, that the audience is kept expectant from start to finish. Robertson, Henry Arthur Jones, and Pinero did the same in Eng. Such plays, however, mainly melodrama and farce without depth of characterization or distinction of dialogue, came to be scorned, with such terms as Sardoodledum and Pinerotic, and plot became decreasingly a basic concern. Yet despite the widest ranging in novels and plays, every narrative still presents, psychologically or somehow logically, a basic unity of plot—except that in the 1960's, some works have abandoned plot (in the sense of consecutive and logically sequential events) for haphazard happenings, or indeed the thoughts and words of characters, without action. Such unity as these works present is not of story structure, but of character, or style, or mood, or intention. Most plays and novels continue to present a coherent plot. *Cf.* Unity; Coherence; Form. R. G. Moulton, *Ancient Classical Drama,* 1890; J. R. Taylor, *The Rise and Fall of the Well-Made Play,* 1967. JOHN HICKS.

plurisignation. Term recently introduced (Philip Wheelwright, *The Burning Fountain,* 1954) to indicate that a word, passage, or work, may have various meanings, or levels of "semantic thrust." *See* Ambiguity; *cf.* Clearness; Obscurity; Pivot Word; Symbolism.

pnigos (Gr., strangler). In Attic Old Comedy, a part of the *parabasis,* in anapæstic dimeter, which was to be recited without a pause for breath, *e.g.*, Aristophanes, *Thesm.* 814–29. Comparable to the patter song (*q.v.*) of modern musical comedy.

poem. *See* Poetry. J. Ciardi, *How Does a Poem Mean?,* 1960.

poème (le). Fr. In addition to the general sense (Eng., poem), used by Alfred de Vigny (Pref. *Poèmes antiques et modernes,* 1829) and to some degree since, to signify a poem in which a philosophical thought is presented in epic or dramatic form.

poetic justice (Thos. Rymer, *Tragedies of the Last Age,* 1678; dramatic justice; G. *poetische Gerechtigkeit;* It. *giustizia poetica;* the equivalent term does not occur in Sp. or Fr., although the 17th c. Fr. developed the idea extensively, using the term "immanent justice." There are two related though clearly distinguishable meanings attached to the term. The literary scholar uses it to refer to the doctrine that all conflicts between good and evil, whether in the drama, the epic, or the novel, must be concluded with the reward of the virtuous and the punishment of the evil, in order that good persons may be encouraged to persevere in their good works, and that evildoers may be frightened from a persistence in evil courses. [Thus S. H. Butcher refers to that "prosaic justice, misnamed 'poetical,' which rewards the good man and punishes the wicked" (*Aristotle's Theory of Poetry and Fine Art,* 4th ed., 1927).] To the non-literary scholar, or a lay person, poetic justice means a reward or a punishment (more frequently the latter) which is somehow peculiarly appropriate to the good deed or the crime; it may be of a sort that occurs rarely in life; but it is gratifyingly concrete, and it somehow ironically "fits the crime," as when the villain is overwhelmed by the catastrophe he had planned for others.

Although Aristotle rejected the prevalent opinion of his day that the tragedy which observes the doctrine is the best, nevertheless poetic justice was almost universally required by Continental critics until Corneille's attack on it in 1660; Addison led the English attack in 1711 (*Spectator,* No. 40). The doctrine went out of favor with both critics and audience with the developing taste for the pleasures of pity. As a practice, however, it persists in the motion picture, as well as in many novels and plays. THOMAS A. HART.

poetic license. "Poets, being slaves to their meter, are pardoned for their faults by giving names to them; we call them metaplasms and schematisms, and praise as a virtue what was really a necessity" (Quintilian). The license is not for the marriage of true minds; it is, simply, for bad workmanship, a flaw that we suffer for the sake of greater virtues in the work. If the poet takes too many liberties, his license is revoked. Note, however, that what seem flaws to some may be natural to the poet's time, or intentional (and perhaps justified) deviations.

poetry, oral, found everywhere in early times, and still persisting among tribes and the folk, falls into 6 main types. (1) Narrative poetry for entertainment is widespread, but not universal; there is little among the Hebrews, the African tribes, the Irish and Welsh. In prose saga, narrative is more abundant. (2) Speech or dialogue in character; often in longer works, but usually an independent poem, is found almost everywhere (esp. Eng., Russ.; India; in Hebrew; Africa; also in medieval poetry and the ballad). (3) Didactic poetry (and saga) relating to individuals abounds in Sanskrit and Hebrew; in some degree, is found everywhere. (4) Literature of appeal and celebration, prayer and praise, is universal, to "whatever gods may be." (5) Poetry of diversion, relating to the poet and his surroundings, is universal, though less abundantly extant (rich, in Gr. and in Norse). This type is ephemeral, unless it is set down at once, or incorporated in a saga or a poem of general interest (*e.g.,* Hesiod) or preserved by quotation in a book on meter (Gr. and Norse) or attached to a famous person, *e.g.,* the poems of King Harold the Fair-haired of Norway. (6) Popular song and ballad. Usually short narrative, often sentimental verse, frequently prompted by a recent event (*e.g.,* 17th and 18th c., execution) or attitude (*e.g.* civil rights) and consequently often moralistic or propagandistic, these are continuously fashioned, recorded in national archives, and now sung by "rock and roll" and other concert hall and radio-television groups. *Cf.* Folksong.

poetry and prose. "It is nearly impossible," wrote Ezra Pound in 1913, "to write with scientific preciseness about 'prose and verse' unless one writes a complete treatise on the art of writing, defining each word as one would define the terms in an essay on chemistry. And on this account all essays about 'poetry' are usually not only dull but inaccurate and wholly useless." (*Pavannes and divisions,* 1918, p. 231). R. Whately, writing a century earlier of definitions of rhetoric, had put the general problem in much the same way: "Various definitions have been given by different writers; who, however, seem not so much to have disagreed in their conceptions of the nature of the same thing, as to have had different things in view while they employed the same term." (*Elements of rhet.,* Introd., 1.) When, in the third part of the same work, Whately deals with poetry, after protesting that "Any composition in *verse* (and none that is not) is always called, whether good or bad, a Poem, by all who have no favourite hypothesis to maintain," he adds that his purpose is only to "explain and vindicate" the conception of poetry "which is the most customary among all men who have no particular theory to support. The mass of mankind often need, indeed, to have the meaning of a word (*i.e.,* their *own* meaning) *explained* and *developed,* but not to have it determined *what* it shall mean, since *that* is determined by their use." The procedure thus suggested is an excellent one; but unfortunately, historic use of the words *poetry* and *prose* is not reducible to the simplicity suggested by Whately. The "mass of mankind" has shown less uniformity in this matter than Whately observes; and it has been constantly influenced by the—in itself more interesting—use of the words by men who have in fact had a "particular theory to support." What is attempted here is only the briefest survey of some of the more significant and influential of these.

In all distinctions between poetry and prose there is one common element implied or explicit: prose is ordinary speech, poetry speech that is somehow extraordinary. The problem of defining poetry is the problem of defining its extraordinariness. A scientific formulation of the distinction, such as Pound suggests, would involve a complete analysis of ordinary speech into its elements, and a precise enumeration of possible deviations from the ordinary in terms of each of these elements. We should at the end of such study be equipped for an enlightened inductive account of the actual deviations found in existing speeches that are called poems, and thus for generalizations, about deviation from the ordinary in general and about specific deviations, which would in practise replace existing "definitions of poetry," since these with few exceptions are all more or less hypothetical generalizations of this kind. At present such analysis is far from complete. But two broad statements can be made. (1) A principal problem here is to determine the value of deviation in general as distinct from that of any specific deviation (peculiar kind of diction, or sound-structure, or meaning, etc.); for if what is required for the title *poetry* be not any specific deviation, but simply deviation from the ordinary as such, then existing definitions of poetry in terms of specific deviations or combinations of them may be unsatisfactory, as partial and inadequate, without being erroneous. And (2) in a general way we can systematize existing distinctions between poetry and prose, as we can other distinctions which produce literary classes, upon some such set of principles as is outlined under classification, *q.v.*

The view of Whately, that the difference between prose and poetry is a difference simply as to structure of sound (*i.e.,* identification of this distinction with that between prose-structure and verse) is as old as any, and as common at all times. It perhaps arises from, and certainly in many of its forms it is sustained by, the association of poetry with music; for one of the most obvious directions in which speech can deviate from the ordinary is that of song. Gorgias (*Helena* 9) says simply, "I consider and call poetry every speech in meter"; and there are suggestions of a like notion in Plato (*e.g., Rep.* 601B, *Gorgias* 502C) and even Aristotle (*Rhet.* 1406b, 1408b). But Aristotle in the *Poetics* (1447b) clearly distinguishes poetry from verse; and by the time of Horace (*Sat.* 1, 4, 39 f.) the distinction was well established (*cf.* Cicero, *Orator* 66–7) if not universally accepted, so that Horace could regard his writing in hexameters as a kind of prose in verse-structure. Since the Renaissance this distinction has been much insisted upon. Du Bellay (*Art poét., au lecteur*) wants to see *"ou moins d'escrivains en ryme, ou plus de Pöetes François"*; Ronsard (*Franciade,* pref.) writes, *"Tous ceux qui escrivent en carmes, tant doctes puissents-ils estre, ne sont pas poëtes"*; Sidney (Smith, *Eliz. crit. essays* I, 159), that for poetry verse is "but an ornament and no cause"; Jonson (Spingarn, *Crit. essays 17th c.* I, 53), that "A Rymer and a *Poet* are two things." General dissemination of this idea in the English Renaissance may be deduced from Jonson's using it for comic effect, *Epicœne,* II, ii: "Every man that writes in verse is not a poet . . . They are poets that live by it, the poor fellows that live by it." A tradition of this kind is behind the distinctions drawn by Wordsworth in his *Preface* (1800), making the opposite of poetry not unmetrical structure of sound but "matter of fact or science"; it seems natural enough that in 1828 De Quincey's review of the work of Whately that has been quoted should contest its identification of poetry and verse, and that five years later J. S. Mill (*Thoughts on poetry*) should speak of a definition "which confounds poetry with metrical composition" as "a wretched mockery." In 1926 Sir P. Hartog, concluding a survey of the problem (*On the relation of poetry to verse*), could write, "We may then regard the view that all verse is poetry as entirely obsolete, and grant that there is some common characteristic of content [*i.e., meaning*] which is essential to all poetry, and which is not to be found in all verse." Yet the word *poetry* is still occasionally used as a synonym of *verse,* and there are some apparently even today who, despairing of alternative criteria, would agree with Scaliger and Casaubon, the chief defenders of this view in the Renaissance, that *"illud verum certumque est: omnem metro astrictam orationem et posse et debere poema dici"* (Casaubon, *De sat.,* p. 352). But of course, many who do not consider that all verse is poetry nevertheless believe that all poetry must be written in verse, *i.e.,* regard verse as an indispensable accident, though not the *differentia,* of poetry; so, *e.g.,* Hegel, Arnold, and many today.

What precise *differentia* for poetry Aristotle had in mind in rejecting that of verse it is perhaps not so easy to discover as has usually been supposed. Aristotle nowhere explicitly defines poetry, and his characterization of the poetry treated in his *Poetics* as *imitation* may not be truly susceptible of the generalization it has usually been given, since the *Poetics* deals only with dramatic and narrative forms, and it is impossible to be sure that Aristotle would or would not have regarded the lyric as imitation. In later antiquity the Stoics generally identified poetry with imitation; in the 16th c. the Italians revived this conception, as Aristotelian, and it remained the commonest, though not the only, one in vogue through the Renaissance and the classical period. In general, to conceive poetry as imitation is to identify it with *fiction;* and perhaps of all ideas in the history of theory of poetry the idea that poetry is fiction is the commonest and the hardiest. It was widespread in antiquity, and appears frequently during the Middle Ages; at the Renaissance, fiction becomes the most generally accepted *differentia* of poetry and, though confusion of poetry with verse often obscures the fact, it has ever since been very commonly so applied. Jacques Le Grant, at the opening of the 15th c., defines *poetrie* as the *"science qui aprent a faindre et a faire ficcions"*; Philemon Holland might be translating this when in 1601 he writes that poetry is the art of "faining and devising fables." It is "because he wrote not fiction," says Drummond, that Jonson "thought not Bartas a Poet, but a Verser" (Spingarn, I, 211); Jonson himself writes, "Hee is call'd a Poet, not hee which writeth in measure only, but that faineth and formeth a fable . . . for the Fable and Fiction is, as it were, the forme and Soule of any Poeticall work or *Poeme*." (*Ib.*, 50.) Marston (*Sat.* 4) says, "For tell me, critic, is not fiction The soul of poesy's invention?" So Donne (*LXXX Sermons*, p. 266) explains, making the connection between this fiction and the idea of *creation* which has had such a history since, and was already a commonplace (Tasso, Sidney): "Poetry is a counterfeit Creation, and makes things that are not, as though they were." For Dryden (*Essays*, ed. Ker, II, 128), "Fiction is of the essence of poetry." In our own time, F. C. Prescott (*The poetic mind*, 1922, p. 8) writes, "Poetry, then, may appear in prose as well as in verse . . . The essence is the myth, the fiction, or the poetry—the three . . . come to the same thing."

The *differentia* for poetry that Horace had in mind in distinguishing it from verse was not this one of fiction or imitation. For Horace the difference is the rhetorical one of eloquence, of a grand style. The poet is to have *ingenium, acer spiritus ac uis*, as well as an *os magna sónaturum*, so the requirement is not only of "style" in the usual narrow sense (Johnson's "manner of writing with regard to language"); but in its subsequent history this *differentia* is often reduced to this alone. In the middle ages esp. poetry was often so conceived; the extraordinariness of poetry was that of speech extraordinarily figured and ornate. In the dictionary of Vincent of Beauvais (13th c.) we find indeed a combination of this with the idea of fiction, which produces a very interesting definition of poetry: *"Officium . . . poetae in eo est, ut ea quae uere gesta sunt, in alias species, obliquis figurationibus, cum decore aliquo conuersa transducat"* (*Spec. doct.*, 3, 110); and Dante, about the same time, defined poetry as *"fictio rethorica in musica posita,"* combining even more with rhetoric. But in the Middle Ages generally the poetic process was a species of the rhetorical, not another process distinct from it; so the poets were called *Rethoriqueurs*, and the art of verse was treated as a *seconde rethorique* (the first being that of prose), in French rhetorical manuals of the early Renaissance. This conception has never wholly died, of course, though it has been assimilated to others and in various ways refined. M. Arnold, the apostle of the grand style to his time, required this style, conceived as he conceived it, of poetry: "There are two offices of poetry—one to add to one's store of thoughts and feelings—another to compose and elevate the mind by a sustained tone, numerous allusions, and a grand style." (*Letters to Clough*, p. 100.)

Modern theory, in its effort to explain the extraordinariness of poetry, has in general addressed itself to the problem of understanding the mental processes (*e.g.*, imagination) involved in the production of a poem or reported in the poem produced. It has conceived poetry on the whole not, as the Renaissance did, in terms of story (fiction, imitation) so that drama and narrative are its most natural forms and provision for the lyric may occasion discomforts, but rather (somewhat as was done in the Middle Ages) in terms of statement or direct speech, so that the lyric is the very type of poetry, and drama and narrative seem in fact less purely poetic than an ode. This is partly due perhaps to the modern descent of drama and novel from verse to prose; but it is due still more to complementary developments in psychology and general æsthetics that have characterized the modern period. These developments cannot here be followed in detail, and in any case their results have not been uniform and are not easily reducible to simple categories. But some of the principal elements of characteristic modern views of poetry can be briefly summarized.

There are three more or less divergent conceptions today of the nature of the poetic process. Some conceive it is a process of expression. Of these a few, like Croce, verbally at least identify poetry and expression, so that a speech is poetic in the degree in which it is expressive. But generally such theories assimilate so much into the concept of expression that in fact the *differentia* they propose is not in the act of expression, but in the nature of what is expressed (imagination, feeling, etc.). Others conceive the process as one of communication (I. A. Richards, *et al.*). Since prose is evidently also communication, these too tend actually to place the *differentia* rather in the nature of what is communicated (an "organisation of impulses," some kind of "experience" or knowledge, etc.), than in the process itself. But many critics make the *differentia* intensity or exactness of communication, as others make it intensity or exactness of expression. Prose communicates (or expresses) only roughly and cumulatively and without finesse; in poetry, there is more precise, more compressed and more highly charged, expression or communication, wherefore poetry can express or communicate much that prose cannot. A third conception of the poetic process makes it simply the production or making of an object or thing, the speech or poem. This conception does not preclude the possibility of expression, or indeed of communication, though in such theories this is usually not stressed; in practise, what differentiates this view from the others is more recognition of other elements than meaning as important in the constitution of the poem.

In general, whatever view they take of the process and whatever significance they attach to meaning, critics today regard the character of the meaning in a poem as unlike that of the meaning in a piece of prose. Since the romantic movement it has been common to consider the total meaning of a poem as necessarily affective; in general, feeling is today considered as essential to the reference of a poem as to its effect upon a reader. But the most striking development of modern theory as to poetic meaning is its distinction between the purely cognitive reference of prose and that of poetry. In general it may be said that the modern critic insists much more than the critic of former periods (who usually nevertheless made some provision for the fact itself) upon the fact that poetry exists not to give information or practical direction, but to present a meaning the value of which may consist precisely in its not being informative and its abstention from practical concerns. Reference to the concrete or the particular rather than to the abstract or general became in the 19th c. a usual requisite of poetic meaning; some critics have disapproved of this, but it is still common doctrine. Related to this though not identical with it is the notion that the meanings of poetry are irreducible to concepts, whereas prose exists only to present concepts. (Since immediate intuition of individual reality is commonly regarded as non-conceptual, this means that the reference of poetry is to experience as experience rather than to experience reflected upon and abstracted from; thus too an explanation is afforded for the connection of poetic meaning with strong feeling and with the concrete and the particular.) Much speculation has been devoted to the problem whether there is not presented in poetry, or apprehended in the poetic process, a special kind of knowledge, not otherwise available. In recent discussion of this problem one does not hear much of imagination; but in the 20th c. as throughout the 19th the imagination has regularly been regarded as the specifically poetic faculty, by which such knowledge is obtained and understood. It is in any case usual to contrast such knowledge (imaginative or non-conceptual) with the knowledge of science or technics which is conceptual or practical, *i.e.,* concerned with action with or upon things rather than with contemplation of them; and it may be said that for most modern critics as for Wordsworth the opposite of poetry is science. Scientific speech may not seem to be ordinary speech; but it is conceived as the ideal implicity accepted by ordinary speech, which is on the one hand conceptual or abstract and on the other hand practical in intent. The extraordinariness of poetic speech thus consists in the radical abandonment of the practical and conceptual ideal of prose, and perhaps of its whole social orientation, for an ideal which, whether it be conceived as expression or communication or simple production of a thing for contemplation, results in speech whose total meaning is non-conceptual and whose function is not to systematize the actual or to direct action but, at least in the extreme case, simply to present speech or its meanings for contemplation. It must be noted finally that this general conception of poetry has made modern critics often insist upon the utility of verse, and of regular meter, as an instrument toward the poetic end. For a structure of sound that is highly patterned may itself operate to control meaning so as to keep its total effect from being conceptual and prosaic; and thus, while it remains true that few would list rhyme among the essentials of poetry, traditional critics assumed that typical poetry would be written in verse, and regarded verse as, if not indispensable, a most convenient accident to poetry.

It is clear from what has been said that the *end* of poetry, even when it is assimilated to a process generally rhetorical, is universally conceived as different from that of prose. It remains to be noted that distinctions between poetry and prose are very commonly phrased in terms of their diverse ends alone, esp. of ends conceived as effects upon a reader or hearer. Of such definition in terms of effect as end the most famous example in English is that of Coleridge, *Biog. lit.,* ch. 14, "A poem is that species of composition, which is opposed to works of science, by proposing for its immediate object pleasure, not truth . . ." This type of distinction is as old as criticism. Ancient rhetoric afforded a frame for it by providing the orator three major *officia* or functions, as his appeal was cognitive (*docere,* to teach, present information) or affective or volitional (*delectare,* to delight or please; *mouere,* to move). Ancient theory of poetry at times required of the poet both instruction and delight, but more often delight alone. Partly from a misreading of Horace, *AP* 333–4, partly from prejudices and needs of its own, the Renaissance generally insisted upon a conjunction of delight with teaching, delight usually being regarded as a mediate end or means toward the more ultimate end of moral profit or instruction. Gradually a more truly Aristotelian, or Horatian, position was arrived at. Aristotle seems to conceive the end of poetry in terms solely of pleasure and enthrallment (*ecplexis*): its *catharsis,* though at least in tragedy an inevitable effect (of the pleasure and *ecplexis*), is not presented as in itself an end. For Horace the end of poetry is to give joy to the mind (*animis . . . iuuandis, AP* 377); his view differs little from that of earlier theorists who had minimized or wholly excluded didactic ends, conceiving the effect of poetry as a sweet abstraction of the mind (*psychagogia*). Longinus (15, 2) says, "In poetry the end is *ecplexis* (enthrallment); in prose, clarity." The excitement of *ecplexis* or *psychagogia* has from early antiquity been associated with the wonderful, the astonishing; since Minturno in the 16th c. protested that wonder (*admiratio, meraviglia*) is the true end of poetry, the association has been common in modern theory. In general, modern notions are very similar to these older opinions, and the quotation from Longinus might be from one of our contemporaries; but the recent emphasis among psychological critics upon the volitional, upon satisfaction in poetry of impulse and desire, may perhaps be regarded as peculiarly modern.

F. N. Scott, "The most fundamental diff. of poetry and prose," *PMLA* XIX (1904); I. A. Richards, *Science and Poetry,* 1926; O. Barfield, *Poetic Diction,* 1928; J. Bronowski, *The Poet's Defence,* 1939; S. Buchanan, *Poetry and Mathematics,* 1928; G. Boas, *Philosophy and Poetry,* 1932; F. X. Roellinger, "Two theories of poetry as knowledge," *Southern Rev.,* VII (1942); P. Valéry, *Introd. à la poétique,* 1938; T. Gilby, *Poetic experience,* 1934; W. J. Ong, "The prov. of rhet. and poet.," *Modern Schoolman,* XIX (1942); P. Hartog, *On the Relation of Poetry to Verse, Eng. Assn. Pamph.* 64, 1926; Ship.; G. Hughes, *Imagism,* 1931; George Boas, *Philosophy and Poetry,* 1932; E. Drew, *Discovering Poetry,* 1933; *Discovering Modern Poetry,* 1961; Melville Cane, *Making a Poem,* 1953; S. Spender, *The Making of a Poem,* 1955; 1962; R. Thomas, *How to Read a Poem,* 1961; C. Norman, *Poets on Poetry,* 1962; T. Roethke, *On the Poet and His Craft,* 1965; H. W. Wells, *New Poets from Old,* 1940, 1964; H. Nemerov, ed. *Poets on Poetry,* 1965; R. Whittemore, *From Zero to the Absolute,* 1967; John Hollander, ed., *Modern Poetry,* 1968. J. Craig LaDrière.

Modern theory of poetry thus accords in large measure with the perception theory of æsthetics, according to which the work of art is one viewed without other end, solely for its resident, undetachable qualities. When one has absorbed the values of prose, the speech may be discarded, the values put to use or re-presented in other forms; the poetic values, residing in the work, require its remaining intact: Prose, the Sphinx, that dies with its enigma; Poetry, the Phoenix, reborn of its consumption. Some therefore, continue to insist that poetry is magic: verse, says Mallarmé, is "an act of incantation." *Cf.* Prosody; Verse; Meter; Eng. versification; Narrator; Power, literature of.

point of attack. The moment in a play or story when the direct action begins. Thus in *Hamlet* all is preparatory—exposition of past events; introduction of characters; creation of mood—until in Scene v the ghost gives Hamlet his commands. Epics usually begin *in medias res* (*q.v.*), going back later for preliminary events.

point of honour (Sp. *pundonor*). A word or deed that seems an affront and therefore requires a gentleman's requiting, despite all odds and consequences. Introduced by Torres Naharro, *La Ymenea,* ca. 1525. The catastrophe in many Sp. plays (Vega, 1562–1635, Calderon, 1600–81, *El medico de su honra;* in Fr., Corneille, *Le Cid,* 1636; Hugo, *Hernani,* 1830; *Ruy Blas,* 1838) is precipitated by a stain on one's honour that must be avenged—though one's love, one's life, fall to ruins. More fundamental than the Fr. *noblesse oblige.*

point of reference (L. *punctum indifferens*). Idea of Coventry Patmore (*Principle in Art,* 1889), applied first to painting, developed by A. T. Quiller-Couch (*Shakespeare's Workmanship,* 1917), that in many great works there is a figure that gives the receptor a sense of the normal, a balance against the excessive weights of passion that sway the characters and determine the events. Thus in *Hamlet,* Horatio stands as a human figure between the two excesses: the over-reasoning inaction of Hamlet; the unreasoning action of Laertes. In *Macbeth,* Banquo stands like most honest men, tempted but controlled; in *Lear,* Kent is like the eye of the storm that rages round.

point of rest. *See* Pause.

point of view. *See* Viewpoint; Narrator.

point, turning. *See* Climax.

poised expectancy. Suspense, *q.v.*

policy. *See* Question of fact.

polyphonic prose. A free poetic form developed in 1914 by Amy Lowell (1874–1925), named by John Gould Fletcher (b. 1886). The idea for the form was derived (Pref. *Sword Blades and Poppy Seed,* 1914) from the Fr. poet Paul Fort, who wrote verse (*Ballades fr.,* 1886) printed as prose. Amy Lowell felt in Fort a very imperfect union; she sought to develop an "orchestral form"—a blending of meter, free verse, rime, assonance, alliteration, and the return (*i.e.,* repetition of a dominant image). The result in *Can Grande's Castle* (1918), her most ambitious attempt in this form, is a many-voiced (polyphonic) poetry, free enough to use prose rhythms. "Its only touchstone is the taste and feeling of its author."

Fletcher, who employed this form in *Breakers and Granite* (1921), thought of polyphonic prose as a medium far different from Fort's; it bears an affinity to the elaborate rhythms of Sir Thomas Browne, De Quincey, Melville (Fletcher, *Life is My Song,* 1937, p. 201). It is part of a conscious effort, noticeable in Eng. and Am. after 1914, to enrich poetry by modifying old forms and inventing new ones. *See* Free Verse; Imagism.

polyptoton. Repetition of a word in another case or inflection. *Cf.* Repetition.

polyrhythmic. Of a poem with lines of different metrical patterns, *e.g.,* Cowley's *Odes.*

polyschematic. In Gr. and L., variable combinations of trochee and choriambus verse, esp. Eupolidean (choriambic trochaic tetrameter) and variants of the glyconic.

polysyllabic rhyme. Rhyme of more than three syllables, seldom used save for humor, as in the more sophisticated musical comedy lyrics, *e.g.,* emphatically, ecstatically. Often such rhymes are formed by repeating words, *e.g.,* throw me a kiss, blow me a kiss; this can go on for 6 or 7 syllables: Clink! till the moon has met the sun; Drink till . . . sun. *Cf.* Rhyme.

polysyndeton. *See* Asyndeton.

popular antiquities. The earlier name for folklore, *q.v.*

pornography (Gr. *porne,* prostitute). Writing about prostitutes (as the posted advertisement in front of the ancient harlot's house); then, in general, treatment of obscene subjects. Both "obscene" and "pornography" are so hard to make specific, esp. for legal purposes, that the term "hard-core" or "high" pornography has come to be applied to writing or pictures that seem intended solely to inflame sexual desire. Leslie Fiedler, defining it as "material sold under the counter," states that pornography is dead; while this may be an overstatement, it is true that reputable publishers now issue books that a decade ago would have been instantly suppressed—and are still, in many communities, banned or subject to prosecution.

Masochism, the term for pleasure in suffering, is drawn from the name of Leopold von Sacher-Masoch (1836–1895), a German novelist, whose best-known work is *Venus in Furs,* although the fullest picture of a masochist appears in *Story of O* (1954), a French work signed Pauline Réage. Sadism, the term for pleasure in inflicting pain, is taken from Comte Donatien Alphonse François de Sade, called the Marquis de Sade (1740–1814), whose novels—*Justine* (1791), of an innocent woman subjected to every humiliation and defilement, and *Juliette* (1798), of her evil sister, finding sexual ecstasy in every crime: arson, torture, murder, even parricide—are still the major sadistic writings, although the British have written many books that specialize in flagellation. Ultimately, the definition of pornography is subjective: writing or picture that arouses the concupiscence of the bibliovoyeur. *See* Censorship.

Erotic writing, which prudish persons or periods may label pornographic, has appeared in the prose and verse of every age. In some works, as Ovid's *Amores* and Shakespeare's *Venus and Adonis,* the love element is basic; in others, as Rabelais' *Pantagruel* and Herrick's *Hesperides,* it is occasional and subordinate. The moods of erotic writing are many, including the woodland freshness of the lesson in love given the young innocent in Longus's *Daphnis and Chloe,* the satirical stories of Boccaccio, the sophisticated smile of Restoration comedy, the smirk of Mark Twain's Elizabethan conversation piece, *1601*, and the direct delight of the Biblical *Song of Songs*. Innocence and experience both perk up at the thought of love, and increasingly since Freud erotic writing has overflowed from poetry into prose fiction, with physical detail or psychological probing. A comprehensive verse collection is the 3 vol. *Poetica Erotica*, ed. T. R. Smith, 1921–22. E. Partridge, *Shakespeare's Bawdy*, 1948; H. S. Ashbee, *Index Librorum Prohibitorum*, 1877, 1962; R. S. Read (Alfred Rose), *Registrum Librorum Eroticum*, 1936; Stephen Marcus, *The Other Victorians*, 1966; P. G. Gillette, *An Uncensored Hist. of Pornography*, 1966; R. H. Kuh, *Foolish Figleaves?*, 1967; R. G. Reisner, *Show Me the Good Parts*, 1968; Ch. Rembar, *The End of Obscenity*, 1968; P. S. Boyer, *Purity in Print*, 1968.

portmanteau word. One formed by "pressing two words together," *e.g.* (Lewis Carroll's *Jabberwocky*), *chortle*, at once a chuckle and a snort. Usually for humor, such words have been coined for other effects. Colloquial speech also has formed them, *e.g.*, slantindicular; brunch. Also called telescope, *q.v. Cf.* Etymology.

poulters measure (from poulterer's practice —Gascoigne, *Steele Glass*, 1576—of giving 14 eggs as the second dozen). A rhyming couplet, the first line of 12 syllables; the second, 14. Used in Eliz. poetry (Wyatt, Surrey, Sidney). Used later in the form of an iambic quatrain, x a_3 x_4 a_3, the short meter of hymns.

power, literature of. Opp. to literature of knowledge by Thomas De Quincey (Eng. 1785–1859). The latter teaches—carries us farther in the same plane; the former moves —exalts us; the latter is superseded, and perishes; the former endures as long as its language. *See* Poetry and prose.

pragmatics. *See* Signs.

praxis. Aristotle's term, usually translated "action," for "the first principle and soul of the tragedy." G. Murray (*The Classical Tradition*, 1927) says it includes "the way people fare, the things they do, and the inner life they lead." It is not character that drama "imitates," but human action, which in the work of art must be "one and complete." *Cf.* Tragedy.

precious. Giving the sense of affected fastidiousness, or over-refinement in organization and language. If in a work it seems that the idea came first, we call it didactic; if it seems that the form was of prior concern, precious; in great (if not in all true) works of art, the two seem one.

préciosité (*la*). Fr., Refinement of manners and language, extending at times to the excessive and the ridiculous. The constructive aspects of the movement, which have made a permanent contribution to the French language, are associated with the Hôtel (mansion) of Mme de Rambouillet (1588–1665). The extravagances of *préciosité* are satirized by Molière in his farce *Les Précieuses ridicules* (1659). *Le Grand Dictionnaire des Précieuses* (1661) of Saumaise is a contemporary authority on *précieux* language. The movement had its counterparts in the *Marinismo* of Italy, the *Gongorismo* of Spain, and the Euphuism of England. *See Secentismo*; *cf.* Bluestocking; Baroque.

Pre-Raphaelite (Brotherhood). A group of young artists in London (the painters Holman Hunt, Dante G. Rossetti, and John E. Millais, aged respectively 21, 20, and 19, and the slightly older sculptor Woolner) united (1848–51) by their enthusiasm and aims: to have genuine ideas to express; to study Nature attentively, so as to know how to express them; to sympathize with what is direct and serious and heartfelt in art, to the exclusion of what is conventional, self-parading, and learnt by rote; and to produce good works, as those of the Italian painters before Raphael. *The Germ* (4 numbers, 1850) contained some verse with the same artistic aims. Six years later Rossetti met Morris and Burne-Jones, and then Swinburne at Oxford, and pre-Raphaelitism was reborn. In poetry this combined realism with medievalism and a taste for archaic diction, thus harking back to Spenser, the 18th c. ballad revival, and the early Tennyson (whose *The Lady of Shalott*, 1832, was already pre-Raphaelite). Another quality, its tendency to richness and elaboration of accessories, was an offset to its marked attention to literal detail. Thus what began as strict truth to nature became almost a cult of unreality, with a deliberate remoteness from actual life. Rossetti's *The Blessed Damosel* is the purest example of these traits. *Cf.* Gothic; Baroque. W. H. Hunt, *Pre-Raphaelitism and the Pre-Raphaelite Brotherhood*, 2 v., 1905; F. L. Bickley, *The Pre-Raphaelite Comedy*, 1932; W. Gaunt, *The Pre-Raphaelite Tragedy*, 1942; D. S. R. Welland, *The Pre-Raphaelite in Lit. and Art*, 1953; W. E. Fredeman, *Pre-Raphaelite*, 1965; G. H. Fleming, *Rossetti and the Pre-Raphaelite Brotherhood*, 1967. PAULL F. BAUM.

priamel (L. *praeambulum,* preamble). A type of short G. folk verse, 12th–15th c. One verse presents an idea, followed by illustrations, then an epigrammatic close.

priapean (from the usual theme, Priapus). A classical meter, logaoedic: a glyconic catalectic and a pherecratean.

primitive, the. Beyond the conscious quest of the spontaneity, sublimity, free expression of powerful feeling, or paradisiac virtues supposed to reside in primitivism (*q.v.*), some scholars declare that all literature is, unconsciously, a return to the primitive. The language of literature, says Shumaker—fortifying himself with quotations from anthropologists, psychoanalysts, and aestheticians—is "psychically regressive." He lists many points of similarity in primitive and literary expression, among them: (1) language more concrete, specific, sensory; (2) perception by grouping, configuration; (3) association by contiguity, conjunction alogical; (4) ideas often (*Iliad, Bible*) linked by parataxis (and . . . and); (5) part taken for the whole: man bewitched by use of his nail-paring; synecdoche, which Kenneth Burke calls the basic process of representation; (6) emphasis on the visual and motor; (7) frequent animism, personification; (7) fusion of what is perceived with what is fancied, as in eidetic imagery; (9) metaphor; (10) ambiguity: Donne, Eliot; its types analyzed by Empson; (11) handling of time; (12) dreams, omens, the marvelous; (13) animals: Homer, Circe's swine; Orwell's *Animal Farm*; Æsop, and Uncle Remus; the "comics": "an archaic attitude toward animals has been established as a convention in literature"; (14) initiation and conversion: Goethe, *Wilhelm Meister's Apprenticeship*; Joyce's epiphany. Shumaker, with many illustrations of these and other points, concludes that "during æsthetic creation the mind falls back into archaic perceptual habits." Chase declares that "the artist and the neurotic and the dreamer have much in common both with one another and with the primitive magico-mythical psychology." We have returned to Shakespeare's lunatic, lover, and poet.

As Voltaire objected to Rousseau's return to primitive man, so the 20th c. new humanists opposed this "surrender to the irrational," protesting that man's greatest achievements spring from his intellectual powers, that art does not result from dominance of feeling but from a simultaneous intensification of both emotional sensitivity and intellectual awareness. The glory of art, in both creator and receptor, is its faculty of stimulating together what in other aspects of life are the often opposed arousal of reason and emotion. (*Cf.* Synaesthesis).

In line with this linkage of art and the primitive is such a thought as in Bernard Shaw's *Back to Methuselah*: in the far future, man discards the "childish toys" of art. As long, however, as there are ranges of the universe (of space or thought) still to be explored, art will survive; for art is the arrow of imagination shot flame-tipped into the dark, science the bulldozer that clears a road to where the arrow has flown. Feeling may more legitimately be claimed as a basic element in painting and music; but literature uses words, and willy-nilly words have meaning. Any basic reliance of a writer on feeling, therefore, is a regression from man's higher levels of attainment. Eric Fromm nevertheless speaks of the "irrational symbolism" of art, and says that "the language of fiction is at bottom the same as the regressive language of dreams." Such expressions describe not the literature woven of the "golden thread" through the ages, but the deliberately distorted writing of recent times, springing from or simulating the phantasmagoria of artificially induced psychedelic states and paranoic dreams. *Cf.* Symbolism; Madness; Dream; Unconscious. Richard Chase, *Quest for Myth,* 1949; Eric Fromm, *The Forgotten Language,* 1951; B. Ghiselin, *The Creative Process,* 1954; E. G. Ballard, *Art and Analysis,* 1957; Wayne Shumaker, *Lit. and the Irrational,* 1960, 1966; Kenneth Burke, *The Phil. of Literary Form,* 1951, *Language as Symbolic Action,* 1966; R. E. Mueller, *Inventivity,* 1963; *The Science of Art,* 1967.

primitivism: The L. *primitivus,* emphasizing little more than priority in time, took on the stress of a qualitative superiority in the 17th c. (J. Evelyn: "a maiden of primitive life"; Bossuet: *"La grandeur primitive et essentielle"* of God). Not extensively used before 20th c.; as a literary school (Fr., 1911) opposed to futurism, and as a term of censure by the Am. humanists.

Primitivism is the glorification (and proposed imitation) of an earlier stage of human development. Every period seems to have preserved the memory, or developed the legend, of an earlier time of uncorrupted, vigorous, genuine expression of life. The *Bible* begins with a lost Paradise; the *Iliad,* with praise of the warriors gone by; later times exalt the nobility of the Homeric age; the prophets and the psalmist turn for inspiration to the patriarchs. Aristotle and the Roman critics reverted to the ideals of 5th c. Attic majesty and simplicity; Aristophanes, attacking (*Knights*; *Clouds*) his own degenerate days, looked back to the spiritual health and intellectual balance of the Athens of Miltiades. The notion of progress has always been counterbalanced by the idea of spiritual degeneration from a primitive *saturnia regna,* a golden age of the past. Progress itself, indeed, on any other than material ground, was often represented as little more than the messianic or dream journey toward this lost earthly paradise. Ages of restlessness have sought to reconstruct this realm of pristine virtue and beauty. The entire Renaissance is a quest of the glory that was Greece and the grandeur that was Rome; the artificial nymphs and shepherds of the 18th c. voiced the nostalgia for an earlier simplicity and joy; an Arcadian parade is staged in Goethe's *Faust* (II 3). Rousseau's desire to have man once more "walk on all fours," Nietzsche's blonde beast, are phases of an idealization of the barbarian, the noble savage, that has never ceased from the writings of ancient Greece and Rome through the widening world of the Renaissance to the recent "happy isles" of the south seas (Tahiti; Bali: Stevenson; Gauguin; the motion pictures).

The quest has moved in 3 directions. (1) Distance has always held a lure: the isles of the blest, the Hesperides, the abodes of strength and virtue (since each age knows they are not at home) must be found afar (Homer's Ogygia; Thule; Tacitus' Germania; Prévost, Chateaubriand and the new world; De Foe, Bernardin de St. Pierre; the growth of anthropology; the legend of Atlantis, which sprang ca. 1580 from passages in Plato, *Timaios, Critias*). (2) The wistful desire for the good old days (journey to times past) may rise in part from the individual's regret for his vanished youth, and from the urge of the elders to maintain their prestige. In the pastoral and agricultural ages, indeed, paternal authority was strongest. (3) Along with and partly out of these impulsions is a journey within: a tendency to idealize the child and the childlike, the simple even unto the simpleton (Goethe; Wordsworth; Dostoevsky). Allied to this is the idea (Vico) of poetry as sheer spontaneity, embraced by the romantics; and the notion that the folk mind is more fertile than the scholar's brain. These 3 directions meet in such finds as the It. primitives, the pre-Raphaelite movement; even more fully, in the cults of archaism, of Chinese, Am. Indian, and African Negro art, as by the school of *les primitifs.* It is the primitive that Freud found in the realm of the unconscious, in endless conflict with the later impressed and repressing patterns of society and its law. In literature, the urge of the primitive may be regarded as a freshening impulse, which may prevent tradition from encrusting to stagnation. *Cf.* Primitive; Spontaneity; Medievalism. G. Boas and A. O. Lovejoy, *A Documentary Hist. of Primitivism* ("the record of civilized man's misgivings about his performance"), 1935; C. B. Tinker, *Nature's Simple Plan,* 1922, 1964; Y. Winters, *Primitivism and Decadence,* 1937; L. B. Wright, "The Noble Savage . . . 1640," *JHI,* 1934; G. A. Borgese, "Primitivism," Encyc. Social Sc.; R. Gonnard, *La Légende du bon sauvage,* 1946; Hoxie N. Fairchild, *The Noble Savage,* 1928, 1961. G. A. Borgese.

proceleusmatic. A metrical foot, a resolved anapest, ◡ ◡ ◡ ◡. *See* Foot.

prochronism. Setting something into a period before its time, as the Connecticut Yankee in King Arthur's Court (Mark Twain). A form of anachronism, *q.v.*

prolepsis. (1) Assuming a future act as already bearing consequences, or applying now an attribute that will have relevancy later, *e.g.* (Browning, *Incident of the French Camp*): 'You're wounded!" "Nay, I'm killed, Sire."; Gay: "Shall strike his aching breast against a post." (2) Forestalling an argument; raising an objection in order to remove it. The objection, hypophora; the answer, anthypophora. (3) A summary presented, of a detailed account that is to follow.

promise. Offering foretoken of things to come; a device in fiction comparable to expectancy in poetry, foreshadowing in drama. Thus, more than once J. R. R. Tolkien, when he pictures Bilbo Baggins (*The Lord of the Rings,* 1965) at the approach of danger longing for the comfortable chair before the fire in his hobbit-hole, adds "Not for the last time"—thus readying the reader for further perils.

To avoid a let-down of reader interest when one promise is fulfilled, the author may interlink one promise with another. Many chapters in exciting novels (esp. Dumas) end with a new promise. Balzac and Dostoevsky, as opposed to Conrad, show restraint in the promise, which may be a mere suggestion, with the reader rewarded by more delivered than promised.

promythium. A maxim; esp. the concise

statement of the moral of a fable, formerly put before the story as a subject-listing. *See* Fable; Epimythium.

proof. The establishment of something as a fact. Basic to the first type of argumentation; *see* Question of fact. Apart from scientific experiment (physical proof), five steps are involved: (1) statement: the presentation of something as true; (2) assertion: a statement vouched for by the one who makes it; (3) testimony: an assertion offered as helping to establish a fact; (4) evidence: testimony accepted as helping to establish a fact; (5) proof: evidence accepted as establishing a fact. *Cf.* Argumentation; Persuasion; Communication; Meaning; Propaganda.

propaganda. (1) The spreading of a specific idea, or that activity (including writing) which aims at spreading a particular belief, esp. (L. *Congregatio de propaganda,* 1622, to supervise foreign missions) the Catholic faith. Recent wide use makes distinction essential. (2) The presentation of a point of view. In this sense, as the expression of the author's personality and outlook on life, "all art is propaganda." Such an application, however, widens the word beyond usefulness—save to mask the next sense. (3) The partial, or not impartial, presentation of a point of view. Claiming that one must take sides (that consciously or unconsciously all art does take sides, and it is better to be aware), that art is a weapon in the class struggle, the advocates of art for life's sake may write a work from the point of view of the attorney for the prosecution, not the unbiased judge. Many admit and seek to justify this attitude; others gloss it with the cry that "all art is propaganda." What validates this definition is, however, not the author's intention but the receptor's discernment. If the work seem impartial, it may be art; if the finger is felt tipping the scales (Galsworthy's *Justice* and *Loyalties* are disputed cases) it is propaganda.

The work may still be art. The frequently asserted dichotomy between art and propaganda (even in sense 3) is not real, it needs no more than Aristophanes and Bunyan, Dickens and Shaw, to attest. Of the many impulses toward writing, an overflowing indignation is as worthy as an empty purse. It may affect the product, but (like fly in amber) need not be a blemish; after the contemporary concerns have lapsed, the work—for any of many reasons—may remain as art. Yet the distinction between art and propaganda holds in this wise, that a work may be both, but not at the same time. If the receptor is sensitive to the "resident" functions of art, if his attention is bound to the work's intrinsic values, he has barred out the extrinsic concerns of propaganda—which at another time may be his only thought. *Cf.* Literature and Society; Didactic. E. W. Doob, *Propaganda, Its Psychology and Technique,* 1935; L. M. Fraser, *Propaganda,* 1957; A. L. Huxley, *Tyranny Over the Mind,* 1958; J. T. Klapper, *The Effects of Mass Communication,* 1960.

prophecy, in fiction, esp. drama, serves not only as promise but as a suggestion of the universality of the forces involved, an implication of powers beyond the human. It may take 1 of 4 forms: (1) simple warning of future fact, which is then arranged to occur, *e.g.* (*Julius Caesar*) "Beware the Ides of March!" (2) announcement of fact already accomplished, the gradual revelation of which provides the drama's movement, *e.g., Œdipus.* (3) promise "fair in words but false in hope": the type of the Sibylline oracle; *e.g.,* (*Macbeth*) the witches' word that no harm will come to Macbeth from "man born of woman," nor until "Birnam forest come to Dunsinane." (4) foretelling that makes itself come true; *e.g.,* given the characters of Lady Macbeth and Macbeth, the words of the witches set moving events that make them sooth. The last type is the most dramatic, and the most rare.

proportion. The accordant interrelationship of the various elements and aspects of a work, so that each receives due measure of stress, space, attention, while contributing duly to the harmony and balance of the whole. *Cf.* Form.

propos (Fr., chat). Brief essay, informally polishing a nugget of thought; raised almost to a new critical genre in *Les propos* of Alain. Ca. 800 words; as opp. to the ca. 2,500 words of the *causerie* (Fr., talk) similarly distinguished by Sainte-Beuve.

proposition. 1. The part of a poem in which the author states his theme, or his intention. 2. In medieval rhetorics, the third step in the Disposition, *q.v.,* presenting the affirmative case for the speaker. 3. A form of speech in which something is affirmed of a subject. Propositions may be divided accord ing to quality, into affirmative and negative; according to quantity, into universal and particular; according to substance, into categorical and hypothetical. A hypothetical proposition is one that deals with the logically possible; it is essentially an implication—"If this, then that"; the validity of its *forms* is to be established; its postulates constitute the realms of logic and mathematics. A categorical proposition is one that deals with the actual world; it is essentially a statement—"This is the case"; the validity of its *content* is to be established; its subjects constitute the realms of history and science.

The basic distinction between a proposition and a propositional function (indicated by Bertrand Russell and elaborated by Cassius J. Keyser in "The Meaning of Mathematics," *Mathematics As a Culture Clue,* 1947), though of tremendous importance in discourse, is widely unknown and commonly ignored. A propositional function is a statement consisting of a variable connected with one or more other variables in such a way that the values of the former depend upon the values of the latter; the values are expressed as propositions. Thus of the three statements (1) John L. Higginbotham is a man. (2) Platinum is a plant. (3) x is a y., (1) is a true proposition, (2) is a false proposition, (3) is a propositional function, its truth or falsity dependent upon the values of x and y.

The importance of this distinction becomes apparent when we examine such a statement as "God is love." If, as frequently happens (Keyser), "that statement occurs in a discourse containing no indication of the senses in which the terms *God* and *love* are to be understood, then, in and for that discourse, the statement is exactly equivalent to the statement that x is y and, in the interest of clarity, might as well or better be replaced by it. Even if, as also frequently happens, the discourse affords *some* indication of the senses in question but not sufficient indication to identify them, then the two terms are still variables, quite as genuinely though not quite so obviously as before . . . A little reflection suffices to show that the books of the world's libraries are mainly filled with statements that, though asserted by their authors as propositions and taken for such by readers, are not propositions, whether true or false; they are, that is, neither proper nor improper values of propositional functions, but are indeed propositional functions themselves. That fact goes far to account for the endless disputations of men." In no fields is this basic distinction more frequently and fatally overlooked than in political science, æsthetics, and criticism.

propositional function. *See* Proposition. Note that every proposition is a value of a propositional function, expressed or understood.

propriety. *See* Correctness; Wit; Periphrasis; Fitness; Decorum; Diction, poetic.

prose. 1. A sequence (often of L. accentual rhymed verse) sung in church between the epistle and the gospel. Among such prose works are the *Veni Sancte Spiritus,* the *Dies Irae,* and the *Stabat Mater.* Originating as words extending the *jubilatio* of the *alleluia,* the prose is one of the sources of medieval drama. 2. Ordinary speech or writing, as distinguished from verse or poetry. The usual patterns of prose progression are narrative, description, commentary, and dialogue. To these should be added the interior monologue, with its various non-syntactic devices. Such patterns, however, have recently been challenged, as when the (London) *Times Literary Supplement* called for a "reordering of prose to fit the modes of autocentric and allocentric perception." Note that the adjective is *prosal* or *prose; prosaic* is now used to mean commonplace or dull. *Cf.* Poetry and Prose; Composition; Style. W. Gibson, *Tough, Sweet, and Stuffy,* 1966; Ian A. Gordon, *The Movement of Eng. Prose,* 1967; R. Adolph, *The Rise of Modern Prose Style,* 1968.

prose poem. *See* Polyphonic prose; Free verse.

prose rhythm. Ancient tradition attributed to Thrasymachus the sophist the introduction into Gr. prose of consciously constructed rhythmic patterns, the use of which became in later antiquity a regular convention of artistic prose, excluded only from the plain style (Cicero, *Orator,* 77; cf. 168–236). Aristotle (*Rhet.,* 3, 8) recognizes and approves the practise, as a means of achieving structural order and avoiding unpleasant indeterminateness; for determination, he says, is by number, and rhythm is the number of speech. The extreme of number, continuous measure or meter, Aristotle considers unfit for prose, since its evident art reduces persuasiveness and so defeats the rhetorical end; he recommends in prose only a pattern, the pæonic (1st, — ∪ ∪ ∪, or 4th, ∪ ∪ ∪ —), which is not adapted to metrical sequences and so may achieve its effect unnoticed. Such rhythm, he says, should occur at the beginning of a period (where the 1st pæon is best) and at the end (where the best form is the 4th). Definitely marked cadences in positions other than final do occur in ancient as in later prose, and are often explicitly prescribed even by mediæval precept, which like ancient and modern is theoretically designed to assure pleasing movement through the whole of a composition; but subsequent theory and practise are mainly concerned with end-patterns (L., *clausulae* or *cursus*), which were reduced in ancient times to a relatively small number. In Cicero's prose there recurs with remarkable frequency a type roughly reducible to a cretic (— ᴗ —) followed by some variation or extension of the trochee (— ᴗ), and to a few variations upon the accentual equivalent of such a pattern the medieval *cursus* was generally restricted. It did not allow a stress on the last syllable of a sentence or member, and provided regularly at least 2 unstressed syllables between the last 2 stresses (W. Meyer's "law," formulated originally for Gr. *clausulae,* in which the last syllable may bear stress). Thus the typical *cursus planus* has a word accented on its penult followed by a trisyllable accented on its penult (. . . . ó o / o ó o, *vincla perfrégit*); the *cursus tardus,* a word accented on its penult followed by a tetrasyllable accented on its antepenult, or a rhythmical equivalent (. . . ó o / o ó o o, *vincla perfrégerat*). Where more than 2 syllables intervened between the last 2 stresses, a secondary stress was permitted to arise, but only on a syllable not adjacent to a stress; so commonly in the *curus velox,* in which a word accented on the antepenult is followed by a tetrasyllable accented on the penult, or the equivalent (. . . ó o o / ò o ó o, *vinculum frègerámus*). The most general law of the medieval L. cursus, observed in all these forms, is simply that stresses must never fall upon adjacent or upon final syllables. The important aspect of the pure *cursus* is its polar structure, however achieved; and the rhythmic grouping determined by the breaks between words (the arrangement of which is now called the "typology") gives the typical conclusion even of the *tardus* not a falling but a (simple or extended) circumflex or rolling (amphibrachic) movement.

The influence of the L. *cursus* in the production of similar rhythmic patterns in modern vernacular prose, and the actual characters of native vernacular prose rhythms, have not been sufficiently studied. In L. the favored rhythms, as we have seen, are smooth, avoiding strong endings and juxtaposition of accents. In Eng. such smooth rhythms occur abundantly, esp. in the OE. period when the usually falling cadence of the inflected words made weak or feminine endings natural; but the profusion of monosyllables in modern Eng. makes avoidance of adjacent and final stresses impossible, if it were desired. That it has not generally been desired is established by the preliminary studies so far made; in Eng. prose strong cadences are as much favored as smooth, and are probably commoner. But there has been in Eng. no general effort or tendency to restrict the rhythmic patterns of prose to a set number of approved formulas; even the law, recurrent in theory since Aristotle, that prose rhythm must avoid the regularity of verse has not always been followed. In general one may say that in Eng., though the end of the sentence provides here too an intensification of the rhythmic impulse, the clausula appears to be less often than in L. a relatively independent rhythmic structure; it is usually a series, not a system, and often detached only by the recessive force of the final pause from the larger rhythmical series of the sentence, or even paragraph, as a whole. *See* Prosody.

A. C. Clark, *The Cursus in Mediæval and Vulgar L.,* 1910; *Prose Rhythm in Eng.,* 1913; N. Denholm-Young, "The cursus in Eng.," *Oxford Essays in Med. Hist. Pres. to H. E. Salter,* 1934; M. W. Croll, "The cadence of Eng. oratorical prose," *SP,* XVI, 1919; G. Saintsbury, *Hist. of Eng. Prose Rhythm,* 1922; W. M. Patterson, *The Rhythm of Prose,* 1917; N. Tempest, *The Rhythm of Eng. Prose,* 1930. J. Scott and Z. Chandler, *Phrasal Patterns in Eng. Prose,* 1932; A. Classe, *The Rhythm of Eng. Prose,* 1939; E. K. Brown, *Rhythm in the Novel,* 1950; Huntington Brown, *Prose Styles,* 1966. J. Craig LaDrière.

prosody. The most convenient general name for analysis of the rhythmic structure of sound in speech, esp. in verse. The elements out of which spoken rhythms are constructed are of course those of the physical constitution of speech, a flow of vocal sound against silence in time, in which differentiation is produced on the one hand by the interruption of sound by silence, and on the other hand by variations in the sound as to character or quality, pitch, length or temporal duration, and intensity or force of utterance. All these elements are emphasized and different relations are established among them. These distinctive characteristics of utterance are in any language the immediate potential material of verse, which simply carries further (prompted, it may be, by an extraneous influence like that of accompanying music or dancing) the natural emphases of a language by making rhythmic patterns of the obvious recurrences and contrasts that they afford. Rhythm may be generally defined as recurring alternation, in temporal series of perceptual data, of an element or elements relatively more conspicuous for perception with elements relatively less conspicuous. In all but the simplest rhythms three factors are involved. (1) the recurring alternation of stronger and weaker elements as such, and the pattern created by their disposition in relation to each other, (2) a division more or less marked of the whole series into sections occasioned by this recurrent alternation and disposition of the elements and by the tendency of weaker elements to group themselves for perception round stronger elements, and (3) the temporal relations among all such perceived divisions in the series. The first of these may conveniently be referred to as the *cadence,* the second as the *grouping,* the third as the *measure.* These affect and involve each other so that they are at times distinguishable only by difficult abstraction. Yet this abstraction must be made, for as D. S. MacColl has said of two of them, "Till these separate entities . . . are distinguished, there will be confusion in prosody." (*What is Art?* Pelican ed., p. 148.) Prosodic analysis, esp. of Eng. verse, has suffered much from confusion of the three and from attempts to interpret all the phenomena of rhythm in terms of one alone, with consequent controversy as to which best deserves to be singled out for this emphasis. One cause of such confusion is failure to distinguish properly between the ends of what may be called *preceptive* prosody (*i.e.,* systematic recognition of what concerns a poet in actual composition of a rhythm or a reader in scanning, where simplification is a practical necessity) and those of a truly *analytical* prosody, which attempts to account for whatever occurs in the rhythm. The obvious fact that the former must depend upon the latter, and that adequate analysis when it has been made will automatically provide adequate precept, has perhaps always been recognized; not so the danger of oversimplification that attends analysis undertaken with a primarily preceptive end, as in most prosodic study of all but the very recent past. In any case, a complete analytical prosody must provide impartially for the three factors here called cadence, grouping, and measure. The rhythm of speech is a structural order of relative magnitudes of sound and silence as such, *i.e.,* an ordered play of units of more sound or silence against units of less. (The units of sound thus ordered are syllables; but the syllable is not to be conceived as isolated from other such units by an intervening cessation of sound, for syllables may run together without any silence between them. A syllable is a single perceptible massing of vocal sound round a central peak. It is thus itself a miniature rhythmic group or phrase.) Every actual prosodic system is simply a specific technique for thus ordering the flow of speech in time by some marked distribution of varying magnitudes of sound and silence within it. The primary principle of distribution or arrangement is always that of perceived quantity of sound; the considerable differences among the various prosodic systems of the world result from the fact that in different languages the various quantifiable properties of sound (pitch, force, and duration) have different values for perception, and different properties are therefore chiefly considered in estimating relative magnitude or prominence. (In some systems qualitative differentiation, as in assonance, is employed as an adjunct to quantitative; but it appears to occur in none as a principal factor, whereas every quantifiable property of sound serves as the basis for some system. *Cf.* in this connection the ancient application of the word *number* to the rhythm of speech. Slight rhythmic effects are perhaps attainable by ordering qualitative difference in sounds, but if this is possible the effects are probably due not to qualitative variation as such but to the quantitative variation that is inseparable from it.) In a language like Japanese, in which no single property of sound is conventionally much emphasized, the mere recurrence of the syllabic peaks naturally assumes great importance and furnishes a structural principle for verse in which the syllables are counted, and one verse-group of a certain number balanced against another; but the art of such verse also includes subtle distribution of the slight variations in pitch, force, and duration that inevitably complicate the alternation afforded by the rise of the syllabic center from the surrounding flow of sound and silence. The Chinese, whose natural utterance is characterized by much variation in pitch, make differences of pitch a foundation for the structure of their verse; this is a rhythmic structure, not a melodic, since its principle is recurring alternation of varying magnitudes in pitch simply as such, not continuous phrasal organization of intervallic relations among the magnitudes. The ancient Greeks made duration, or temporal quantity, the foundation of their verse, and the L. poets abandoned a native syllabic or accentual prosody to adopt the Gr. system. In this system the unit of measurement was theoretically a fixed quantity, the *mora,* supposed to be equal to that of an average short syllable and half that of a long. Rhythms were composed by arranging long and short syllables in simple cadence-groups (*feet*) the succession of which provided a division of time into approximately equal periods. Of verse so composed there were two kinds, one for recitation, in which a single basic cadence or foot was continuously repeated with little variation, and one for song, in which different feet were variously combined. Quintilian (9, 4, 45–54) gives the name *metrum* (meter) to the former only, calling the latter simply *numerus* or rhythm; with Cicero (*Orator,* 183–84), he regards the rhythms of the lyric poets as occupying a middle ground between the more regular schemes of recited verse and the still looser patterns of rhythmic prose. In the middle ages this system of temporal quantities was superseded, in both Gr. and L., by one founded upon a "stress" or "accent" due mainly to the relative force or intensity rather than the duration of syllables. The classical versification continued its artificial life through the middle ages (during which it was called *metrum,* and distinguished from *rhythmus,* the more common accentual composition), into the Renaissance and beyond; but though several attempts were made, esp. in the 16th c., to impose it upon the vernaculars (including Eng.) as it had been imposed upon L., none was successful, and in modern Europe only the analysis or interpretation, not the composition, of verse has been significantly influenced by classical prosody. In the Romance languages verse is constructed by grouping set numbers of syllables in verses defined and linked by assonance or full rhyme; but the main rhythmic effects of Romance verse are produced by varied placing of pauses and the distribution of stronger and weaker syllables within the smaller groupings thus created. In the Germanic languages evident contrast of stressed and unstressed syllables is the most prominent and constant characteristic of verse as of prose, and the primary constituent in rhythmic structures. Though intensity or force of utterance seems normally to contribute more than the other properties of sound to the constitution of this stress in Eng., duration is also usually involved, and often pitch; so that the variation upon which rhythms are based is not in Eng. that of any single property or aspect of sound, but more or less general quantitative variation as such.

In modern Eng. this variation in stress is partly free and partly predetermined. Every word of more than one syllable has a conventional "accent" on one of its syllables, and in long words there may be a secondary accent on another. But the amount of stress involved in this accent, or in the utterance of any monosyllable, is not conventionally fixed; it varies with the degree of logical or rhetorical emphasis proper to the word in its context. In ordinary speech or typical prose, the stress of accented syllables is weak in words that are logically or rhetorically unimportant; there is a tendency to subordinate these to one main stress (the "centroid"), which corresponds to a logical or rhetorical emphasis. Eng. prose is characterized by the formation in this way of relatively large groups of syllables, separated usually by pauses and each dominated by one major stress; as a whole it has rhythmically a broken effect, and within the groups there is the effect of huddling of sounds together round the centroid. In typical verse, on the contrary, generally speaking every syllable truly capable of acting as a centroid (*i.e.,* of resisting attraction and subordination in stress to a syllable nearby, and of attracting and so subordinating other syllables) is allowed centroidal weight; so that on the whole the only weak, completely subordinated syllables are those that are "naturally" weak, *i.e.,* those that have no conventional accent and, in monosyllables, no rhetorical or logical emphasis to supply the lack of it. The resulting groups in verse are therefore smaller than those of prose; in each fewer syllables are concentrated together, and often a single strong syllable stands alone. The effect of their succession is also more continuous than that of the larger groups in prose. For (1) the rhythmic groups in verse are separated usually not by true pauses but only by quasi-pauses (brief hesitations or mere dilation of sound to give the effects of pause; *cf.* A. Snell, *Pause,* 1918); they are constituted apparently rather by the solidity and attraction of the centroid than by actual breaks in the flow of sound. And (2) the attractive power of the centroid, like that of a center of magnetism, is exercised in more than one direction and over varying distances, so that a weak syllable may be subjected more or less equally to the opposite attractions of two centroids between which it falls, and thus offer for perception a choice of groupings or even (more rarely) a stable indeterminacy.

Within each rhythmic group the distribution of weak syllables round the centroid establishes a definite cadence, rising, falling, or undulating. Sometimes a single cadence is repeated in several successive groups, as in Milton's *And swims or sinks or wades or creeps or flies* (o ó / o ó / o ó / o ó / o ó); more often the cadences in succeeding groups differ: *As killing as the canker to the rose* (o ó o / o o ó o / o o ó), *Die of a rose in aromatic pain* (ó / o o ó / o ò o ó o / ó). But in either case, apart from the natural grouping of weaker syllables round stronger, a more general pattern of continuous cadence is established by the mere recurrence of stresses and their alternation with weak syllables. This general pattern of cadence may be irregular, *i.e.,* a succession of varying smaller or unitary cadences; or it may be regular, *i.e.,* constituted by continuous repetition of a single unitary cadence. (Where within the natural groups there is such continuous recurrence of the same cadence, the total pattern of cadence is simple, and emphasized by the coincidence of group-pattern with general pattern. The total pattern is simple again where there is variation in the group-patterns from group to group and no regularity in recurrence of unitary cadence in the general pattern. But a complex total pattern arises when variation in the group-cadences co-exists and is counterpointed with regular repetition of a single cadence in the general pattern, as in *The curfew tolls the knell of parting day,* where the cadences in the groupings [o ó o / ó / o ó / o ó o / ó] are crossed by the recurring iambic unitary cadence of the general pattern [o ó o ó o ó o ó o ó].) We may describe as *metrical* any such approximation to regularity in general cadence, whether produced by the repetition of one cadence through all the centroidal groups or only by the alternation of stress and slack considered in abstraction from such grouping; but strict use of the word *meter,* conformed to ancient (as above), mediæval, and careful modern usage, would reserve it for structures expressly designed to present this regularity, in which a single unitary cadence (or *foot*) recurs with little variation throughout the general pattern, and the line or single verse is constructed by combining a given number of such cadences or feet, so that every normal line contains the same number. It should be remarked that in the creation of the general pattern of cadence in any verse, metrical or only rhythmical, since the grouping is ignored, not only the centroids but all stresses, including those of secondary accents, operate equally: and that the regularity of meter requires only that there be some regular alternation of stress and slack, not that all the stresses be of even approximately equal strength. Where, as in metrical verse, there is general uniformity of unitary cadence, the established expectancy may in fact bestow upon even a syllable naturally quite weak sufficient weight to assure a felt continuance of the pattern. So, *e.g.,* the last syllable of *necessity* (o ó o o) may without undue emphasis be so weighted—most naturally rather by slightly extended duration than by increased force—that in this word the 3d and 4th syllables seem to stand in the same relation as the 1st and 2nd, and distinctly if more faintly to repeat their plainly iambic cadence (o ó o ó); and so likewise *necessary* may be read as two trochaic feet (ó o ò o) without the crudity of equalizing the stress of the 3d with that of the 1st syllable.

As we noted in beginning, the phenomena of measure or temporal relation are in any actual rhythm inseparable, except by abstraction, from these phenomena of grouping and cadence. Indeed, though the word *meter* has come to refer in common usage primarily to cadence, its first denotation remains that of a measure of something entirely continuous, and though there has been (esp. during the past c.) much disputing about this, prosodists now seem increasingly to agree (with Quintilian; 9, 4, 48, *"tempus enim solum metitur"*) that what is measured in rhythm is time. (The chief practical effect of this is a provision for explicit measurement of silence as well as, and along with, sound, and thus for the possibility that silence in a given measure may replace expected sound.) Time in the rhythmic structure of speech is measured by the occurrence of stresses or of pauses (or quasi-pauses), alone or in combination, or by the repetition of cadences or rhythmic groups. Thus we may measure from stress to stress, from pause to pause, or from the beginning to the end of a given cadence or group; and each of these measurements provides some useful descriptive information about the constitution of any verse, whether all equally reveal a principle of its structure or not. The periods into which the time of a rhythm is thus divided are either unequal or isochronous (of equal or approximately equal length). To regularity of general pattern in cadence evidently corresponds regularity, or approximate equality, in temporal measures; and though many prosodists assume the necessity of the latter (isochronism) as of the former, since it does not occur in all verse and is rare in rhythmical prose we must conclude that regular temporal measure is no more necessary for the constitution of rhythm as such than is metrical regularity in cadence. The rhythmic impulse clearly tends to regularity, and we may perhaps even say that regular rhythms are more truly rhythmical than irregular; but the two species belong to the same genus. In point of regularity generally we may distinguish three broad classes of rhythmic phenomena in Eng.: the rhythms (1) of prose, characteristically irregular because composed of large units not related together by any continuous general pattern; (2) of metrical verse, which present a continuous pattern of approximately strict regularity; and (3) of non-metrical verse and of occasional (esp. terminal) sequences in artistic prose (*see* Prose rhythm), which occupy an intermediate position because, though constructed of minimal unitary cadences like those of metrical verse, they do not like those present a regular continuous pattern throughout.

The many systems that have been proposed for analysis of Eng. verse rhythm cannot here be discussed individually (*cf.* Omond), but their variety may be related to that of the methods of construction (and so of conceptions of the constitution) of the line or single verse. Lines may be constructed in Eng. by combining (1) a determined number of syllables (without regard to cadence or grouping), or (2) a determined number of centroidal stresses (without regard to number of syllables or to any regularity in general cadence), or (3) a determined number of repetitions of a given cadence, or feet (without regard to centroidal grouping, and without explicit concern for the number of syllables), or (4) an indeterminate number of centroidal groups, with varying but harmonious cadences. (Lines composed by this 4th method lack the evident individual demarcation afforded by some of the others, and their rhythms tend to run over and produce the effect of a larger continuous series; this effect in less extreme form is possible in all but the first.) Any of these may involve, and it may be a writer's primary concern to produce (5) a determined number of approximately equal periods of time. These principles of construction are of course freely combined, and rarely occur in the exclusive purity of this enumeration. In general, the 2d is the basis in OE verse, occurring again notably in the 19th c. (Coleridge, *Christabel*; Hopkins' "sprung rhythms") and in some more recent verse. After the Conquest the 1st (in more or less combination with the 3d) began to operate significantly in Eng. verse, in which by the 18th c. it came to be accepted as the cardinal (though not the only) principle (Bysshe, Pope, Kames); in recent times it has been so used again, often but not solely in imitation of Japanese forms (Crapsey; Bridges, Daryush). The 3d, or metrical, system is of course exemplified consciously or unconsciously at all periods since the Conquest; the 4th, esp. in the "free verse" of the 19th and 20th c. Of the schools of prosodic analysis that have professed to explain all the phenomena of all Eng. verse in terms largely of one of the principles, that which applied the principle of meter, variously interpreted, has produced the greatest number of studies and its influence is still, after its ascendancy in the later 19th c., strongly felt. Reinterpretation of the metrical principle in terms of the 5th principle noted above, the temporal, and initiation of experimental researches aided by mechanical instruments have since the beginning of this c. opened the way to a broader, less Procrustean scheme. *Cf.* Rhythm; Meter; Poetry and Prose. W. L. Schramm, *Approaches to a Science of Eng. Verse,* 1935; G. Saintsbury, *Hist. of Eng. Prosody,* 1906–10; 1923; T. S. Omond, *Eng. Metrists,* 1921; L. Abercrombie, *Principles of Eng. Prosody,* 1923; V. V. Nabokov, *Notes on Prosody,* 1963; J. Scully, ed. *Modern Poetics,* 1964; H. Gross, ed. *The Structure of Verse,* 1966; T. R. Barnes, *Eng. Verse,* 1967; D. Geiger, *The Dramatic Impulse in Modern Poetics,* 1968. J. Craig LaDrière.

prosonomasia. (Gr., "the nicknamer.") (1) Use of a jesting name that resembles the real one, *e.g., Caldius Biberius Mero* (immoderate imbiber of wine: Claudius Tiberius Nero). (2) Balance of repeated sound in a pithy saying, *e.g.,* Prove me ere you reprove me; *Qui s'excuse s'accuse.*

prosopopoeia. (Gr., "counterfeit impersonation.") Giving human action to non-human things, *e.g.,* in Spenser's *Prosopopia or Mother Hubberd's Tale* are presented the human disguisings of the ape and the fox.

prosthesis. Addition of a letter or syllable at the beginning of a word, as beloved, yclad. *Cf.* Epenthesis.

protagonist (Gr. *protos,* first; *agonistes,* contender, actor). The earliest Gr. drama seems to have been enacted by a chorus and its leader; Thespis (ca. 535 B.C.) is said to have added one actor, the protagonist, to allow greater dialogue and action. A second actor, or deuteragonist, was added by Aeschylus; a third, or tritagonist, by Sophocles (ca. 470 B.C.). Gr. drama was traditionally limited to these three actors, who by change of mask might assume several roles. The second actor usually played the chief adversary or antagonist.

Today the term protagonist is applied not to the actor, but to the chief character within the play or (by extension) novel, esp. when there is no sharp personal opposition of hero and villain, but the conflict is of irreconcilable urges and needs within the main individual or between him and natural or social forces. *Cf.* Tragedy; Opposition; Hero; Novel. K. Rees, *The So-called Rule of Three Actors . . .*, 1908.

protasis. (1) The subordinate clause in a conditional sentence, *i.e.,* the "if" or "although" clause. *See* apodosis. (2) the introductory part of a play.

protatic character. A figure introduced (esp. by Terence and Plautus) in the beginning of a play solely to avoid development of the exposition in a monologue. A stage in the transfer of the exposition (*q.v.*) from the prologue into the play. In 19th c. Eng. drama, this function was frequently assigned to a butler and housemaid. "Inorganic Roles in Rom. Comedy," *CP* 15, 1920.

prothalamion (Spenser's poem, 1597). A song heralding Hymen. *Cf.* Epithalamium.

prothetical. Of a figure (prothesis, rare) in which the image not only embodies the spiritual but is one and the same with it, *e.g.,* the water that is wine that is blood of the Christ. *See* Symbol.

protozeugma. *See* Zeugma.

protreptic. A hortatory or persuasive discourse. A common ancient literary type. Aristotle's *Protreptikos,* in Cicero's paraphrase, the *Hortensius,* converted Augustine to Christianity. T. C. Burgess, *Epideictic Lit.,* 1902.

Provençal verse forms. *See* Old French.

proverb. (Gr. *paroimia*). A gnomic form of folk literature; a short pregnant criticism of life, based upon common experience, as (*Bible*) *The Book of Proverbs.* Quite generally the product of the popular mind, it was important as reflecting prevalent attitudes. In Gr. and Rome, it often served as a vehicle of literary and dramatic criticism. In longer works, it brought vividness, color by compression and boldness of imagery. Collections of proverbs (compiled as early as Hadrian, Emperor 117–138 A.D.) served as medieval texts. When Sancho Panza began a tale, Don Quixote: "Leave off your proverbs; go on with your story." Sancho: "All tales must begin in this way." Don Q.: "The whole race of Panzas come into the world with their paunches stuffed with proverbs." B. J. Whiting, *Proverbs in the Earlier Eng. Drama,* 1938; M. P. Tilley, *Eliz. Proverb Lore . . .*, 1926. *Cf.* Fable; Epigram.

proverbe. Fr. A comedy in which the idea expressed in a proverb is developed with grace and fancy. Written by Mme de Maintenon (ca. 1690, pub. 1829) and esp. by Alfred de Musset (1810–57), *e.g., On ne badine pas avec l'amour,* 1834.

pseudo- -classic; -naturalistic; -Shakespearean, etc. Falsely attributed to the author, period, school; having some characteristics but not in essence belonging.

psittacism (L. parrot). Speech that is repetitive and meaningless. Criticism is too often psittacism.

psychic distance. The awareness in the receptor (or the fact, or the device ensuring it) that he is in the presence of a work of art, that the actions, characters, emotions displayed are not there involved in practical, urgent living. Opp. illusion. By thus setting the work apart from utilitarian concerns, it makes possible the unique effects of art. Improper distancing (its success is subjective) may make a work seem a tract (impelling some to sign a check, some to rail upon realism or propaganda) or on the other hand far-fetched, artificial. Because of the presence of living players, distancing devices are important in the theatre (*e.g.,* the ravishing of Lucrece, in the Obey-Wilder-Katharine Cornell presentation, was set off by pantomime with a narrator); then the skill of the author and actor must reach across to bind the receptor to the play's concerns. (Some recent critics have preferred the term "æsthetic distance.") In comedy from the earliest days (Aristophanes) there have been occasional instances—and in recent drama frequent cases—of the deliberate bridging of this "distance" gap, to draw the audience into the action and emotions of the play. In the novel likewise, the author may stop the flow of the story to address the "dear reader." *Cf.* Narrator; Estrangement; Happening.

psychoanalysis brought a boon to the artist and the critic. Developed by Sigmund Freud (1856–1936), it posits (1) an unconscious mind, wherein lurk and moil basic impulses of the race, also thwarted personal desires; (2) an inner censor that, recognizing society's ban on these impulses, forcing their repression, seeks to sublimate them in more allowable forms of expression (one of which is art) (3) a basic libido or sex-drive (*cp.* Shaw, the life-force) which, when checked, may produce (Œdipus complex; mother fixation) distorted if not broken lives. Thus it sets love (the chief topic of modern poetry, novel, drama) at the root of all human action. To these new ideas and terms and avenues of character analysis Alfred Adler added the inferiority complex and the superiority complex; C. G. Jung, the concepts of the introvert and the extrovert, as well as the notion of the "collective unconscious," where the surrealists graze.

The Bohemian was quick to seize what he took to be the new psychoanalytical justification of the old romantic freedom. Shake out of repressions, suppressions, inhibitions, he cried; refrain from nothing, withhold nothing, or your art is falsified. Joyce wove this into a symbol; he, Lawrence (*Women in Love, Sons and Lovers, Lady Chatterley's Lover*) and younger writers (Erskine Caldwell; James Farrell) sought full freedom in expression. But Freud has not only acted as a liberating force. He has also deepened and made more complex the writer's insight into human nature. Proust, Romains, Gide—with virtually every other writer of our time—have used the Freudian system of analysis to probe within their characters. It has given force to the "new biography," which seeks beyond the surface for the hidden motifs and motives (*e.g.*, Van Wyck Brooks, *The Ordeal of Mark Twain*, 1920, which helped establish the pattern). In the drama, though the freedom-seeking Freudians were often mocked (S. Glaspell and C. C. Cook, *Suppressed Desires*, 1915), the method was soon appropriated, from plays of thwarted love and of incest on the farm (Virgil Geddes) to reconstructions of Gr. tragedy (O' Neill, *Mourning Becomes Electra*) or the bringing to light of hidden impulses—in serious study (Bourdet, *The Captive*; Shairp, *The Green Bay Tree*) or bland acceptance (Coward, *Design For Living*). Eugene O'Neill has made the fullest dramatic use of the Freudian analysis; it is significant, therefore, that in his longer plays the synthesis is lacking. For, as Stuart Sherman points out ("The Point of View in Am. Crit." *The Genius of Am.*, 1923) what people today require is not liberation of impulses, but an integrating force. Obey your impulse! was the cry many heard in the Freudian ranges; but the control of impulse and the ordering of emotions have marked the growth of civilization and culture. This is the chief line of attack on the Freudian attitude, by the few that oppose it on other than logical or psychological ground. In poetry, its influence appears widely (in the intellectual autopsies of E. A. Robinson; the juxtapositions and implications of T. S. Eliot; the *omnium gatherum* of Ezra Pound—and all their brood). In criticism, its tenets have been hailed. Gilbert Murray (*The Classical Tradition*, 1927, p. 56 f.) finds in the notion of repression and release a parallel with the Aristotelian catharsis. The work of I. A. Richards, T. S. Eliot, the reawakened interest in semantics, owe much of their probing, of their direction if not their energy, to psychoanalysis. In men like Kenneth Burke, (*The Philosophy of Literary Form*, 1941) it has produced a new school of criticism, which claims that only if art is approached as "a strategy" to "encompass a situation" is the interrelationship of matter and form intelligible. (Thus the suggestion is made—Clifton Fadiman, *Reading I've Liked*, 1941, lxi—that the chief figures in a great novel are "unconscious projections of unreconciled factors in the author's own character.") It has also produced a new æsthetic (DeWitt Parker, *The Analysis of Art*, 1926). Far beyond any fiat of other psychologists, Freudianism has been a factor in this period every writer has had to face. So widespread has it become that there is pertinence in the remark that psychoanalysis is the disease whose symptoms it purports to cure. Antony Starr (quoted in Rycroft) says: "To every man his own delusional system is a likely principle of human existence; and the evidence that psychoanalysis is more than yet another delusional system is slender." Thomas Mann, on the other hand, calls it "one of the foundation stones of a structure of the future that shall be the dwelling-place of a free and conscious humanity."

Freud's emphasis on sex may be a concentration on the creative urge (the physical apex of which is followed by the "little death") as opposed to the ultimate fear of dying. Tennessee Williams links these when he declares that a man's greatest fear is of impotence; a woman's, of her loss of beauty and appeal; out of these Williams states that he builds his plays. The exposing of "unconscious" impulses, as towards homosexuality or incest, is also frequent in recent fiction and drama. Along with Marx (with whom some, *e.g.* Kenneth Burke, have built him into a synthesis) Freud has been a major influence in our time. *Cf.* Dadaism; Surrealism; Absurd; Modern Poetry; Aesthetics, C. Baudouin, *Psychoan. and Aesthetics*, trans. 1924; O. Rank, *Art and Artist*, 1925, trans. 1932; A. R. Martin, L. Trilling, and E. Vivas, "The Legacy of Freud," *Ken-*

yon R., 1940; E. Bergler, *The Writer and Psychoan.,* 1954; L. B. Fraiberg, *Psychoan. and Am. Lit. Crit.,* 1960; H. M. Ruitenbeek, *Psychoan. and Existential Phil.,* 1962; *Psychoan. and Lit.,* 1964; E. Kris, *Psychoanalytical Explorations in Art,* 1962, 1964; Harry K. Wells, *The Failure of Psychoan.,* 1963; H. J. Eysenck, *Fact and Fiction in Psychology,* 1965; H. Marcuse, *Eros and Civilization,* 1956; L. and E. Manheim, ed. *Hidden Patterns,* 1966; F. J. Hoffman, *Freudianism and the Literary Mind,* 1945, 1967; C. Rycroft, *Psychoan. Observed,* 1967, 1969; N. N. Holland, *The Dynamics of Literary Response,* 1968; Claudia C. Morrison, *Freud and the Critic,* 1968; Ernst Becker, *Angel in Armor,* 1969.

psychography. Term applied (G. Saintsbury) to Sainte-Beuve, who called himself "a naturalist of souls"; widened by Gamaliel Bradford to cover recent biography (*q.v.*). It emphasizes the importance of (1) the author's life in the work of art; (2) apparently trivial elements (a shoulder shrug; a "casual" remark—no remark is casual) in the life of the author.

psychological moment. (G. *das psychologische Moment,* the psychological momentum; mistaken for *der psychologische Moment,* the psychological instant). The moment at which, because of the preparation within the work, the receptor is expectant of a particular event—which then occurs.

puff. A verbal gust of wind to help a book sail along. Term used from the 17th to the mid-19th c. The earliest analogue is the case of Psapho's birds (told by Erasmus, *Adagia*): the Libyan Psapho trained many birds to say "Psapho is a god"; then he released them, and was worshipped among the Africans. For the gales of puffery today, *see* Blurb.

pun (Gr. *paronomasia;* L. *adnominatio*) called by many the lowest form of wit, listed by Addison as false wit, is probably the earliest type of word-play. Its primary use was not for humor but in earnest, in the form of names of double import, as in Sanskrit, Hebrew, Gr., culminating in the pun that established the Catholic Church. (Peter=petra=rock). The idea that the name held power, the principle of *nomen et omen,* was fortified by the fact that early literature was intended for the ear, so that all phonetic effects were prominent. The serious and thoughtful prologues of Terence are much richer in puns than his comedies themselves. Of course the device was also (Plutarch) amply used for humor, though to be controlled by decorum. The play was preferably on words of slightly different sound; an exact pun (called *traductio*)—*e.g., Amari iucundum est, si curetur ne quid insit amari:* To be loved is sweet, if you don't let it grow bitter—was frowned upon by Quintilian. Shakespeare's puns range widely in mood. Sometimes for fun only, often they bear a bitter tang. The dying Mercutio (*R and J*) says "Ask for me tomorrow and you shall find me a grave man." Cassius (*JC*): "Now it is Rome indeed and room enough, When there is in it but one only man." The song in *Cymbeline*: "Golden lads and girls all must, As chimney sweepers, come to dust." Hamlet's first two speeches are puns. Such uses were attended to, not for themselves, but as part of the general flow, for the total effect.

So ancient a device has developed variations. (1) The equivoque, *e.g.,* when the reporter, trying to discover whether the young Sarah Bernhardt was wife or mistress, asked where she had been married: she (divining his intent) gave in one sound two answers: *"A l'autel." ("A l'Hôtel").* (2) The conundrum, which often asks the cause of a resemblance: Why are pretty girls like hinges? Because they are things to a door (to adore). (3) Play on one word in different senses: A Frenchman boasted he could pun on any subject. Someone called "The king." "The King is not a subject." (4) Play on double meaning in one use: Odd about a debt: the more you contract it, the bigger it grows! (5) Play on the one sound with different meaning:

On s'enlace;
Puis, un jour,
On s'en lasse.
C'est l'amour. (V. Sardou)

Or, in schoolboy parlance, as Macbeth's sentry cried when he saw Birnam wood marching on Dunsinane, "Cheese it the copse!" (6) Different words, nearly alike: *Tibi erunt parata verba, huic homini verbera:* there's a scolding for you and a scourging for me. In this group falls the boner: most schoolboys' boners are made by teachers; Brian de Bois-Guilbert (*Ivanhoe*) asked Rebecca to be his mistress, and she "reclined" to do so. (7) By development: "If a swallow cannot make a summer, it can bring on a summary fall" (G. W. Carryl, *Red Riding Hood.*) More seriously, as in the prayer:

God loving me
Guard me in sleep
Guide me to Thee.

This is ablaut punning: by vowel change. (8) By a slight change in a well-known saying. In effective use of the pun, for comic or serious effects—as with all else in art—familiarity breeds contemplation. (9) By splitting words: since *pro* means *for* and *con* means *against,* obviously the constitution is against prostitution—and congress is against progress.

James Brown calls "bad puns" those that twist words by (1) malaprop, as *Ivanhoe,* above; (2) distortion: Much science fiction offers a horrorscope. Brown ("Eight Types of Pun," *PMLA,* March 1965) classifies puns according to the interrelations of meanings with the syntax and sense of the passage. He also mentions triple context puns, the one word bearing three meanings; and the pun phrase, of two puns in close relation, as when Juliet says "Learn me how to lose a winning match," where *winning* means both victorious and appealing, and *match* means both a contest and a marriage. There is further pun complexity when two situations are implied. Thus the poet Hood complained that an anticipant undertaker wanted to "urn a lively Hood"; a man being shown a place by an attractive real estate saleswoman inquired: "Are you to be let with the apartment?" and she responded; "No, I am to be let alone." Brown concludes that the accomplishment of the pun, "context linking and consequent expansion of the whole context," is basic in all literary use of language. *Cf.* Bull; Paronomasia; Low Comedy; Humor; Black Humor. C. J. Fordyce, "Puns on names in Gr." *CJ* 28, 1932–33; E. S. McCartney, "Puns and Plays on Proper Names," *CJ* 14; A. Koestler, *The Art of Creation,* 1964.

punctuation is used to aid intelligibility, through pitch, stress, time and pause. Various marks have come to be used to satisfy these needs, their success determined by considerations of grammar, rhetoric and rhythm. The practice of the past reveals two important principles, often concurrent: marks used to clarify the logic of a sentence; pauses used to mark off rhythms. A scheme of punctuation formed to clarify logic and structure is apparent in the Authorized Version of *Mark* IV. 1:

> And he began again to teach by the seaside: and there was gathered unto him a great multitude, so that he entered into a ship and sat in the sea; and the whole multitude was by the sea, on the land.

Punctuation guided chiefly by metrical considerations is employed in the original printing of Shakespeare's 25th sonnet:

> Then happy I, that loue and am beloued
> Where I may not remoue, nor be remoued.

These lines are printed in modern editions with punctuation that is worked out (with unfortunate results) to clarify the grammar and logic:

> Then happy I, that love and am belov'd,
> Where I may not remove nor be remov'd.

In Donne's poem *The good-morrow,* commas are used for both metrical and rhetorical reasons:

> And now good morrow to our waking soules,
> Which watch not one another out of feare;
> For love, all love of other sights controules,
> And makes one little roome, an every where.

The separation of words by spaces was not fully developed (and first in L.) until the 11th c. Paragraphs, however, were divided by spaces or dividing strokes as early as the 4th c. B.C., and later by the use of enlarged or ornamental initial letters. Works such as the *Psalms,* intended for public reading, were early divided into sense lines of a sort. Two noteworthy divisions were invented: the colon, a clause of from 8 to 17 syllables, and the comma, a clause of less than 8 syllables. A period was originally a rhythmical division composed of two or more cola.

A system of pointing designed to support grammatical structure, using commas, inverted semi-colons, question and quotation marks, developed as early as the 9th c.; its fullest and most nearly modern use in Eng. is in Wyclif's translation of the Bible (ca. 1382). Alfred's paraphrase of Gregory's *Cura Pastoralis,* however, employed different marks in an extremely effective way, to translate into the vernacular something of the logic and precision of the L. The loss of inflection in Eng. was partly responsible for the development of an exact punctuation that would help clarify grammatical relationships and prevent confusion of meaning.

The development of a rhetorical punctuation to solve the problems indigenous to vernacular phrasing was complicated by the Renaissance fashion of imitating the style of various L. writers. The 1625 edition of Bacon's essays well illustrates this complexity. The influence of such punctuation persists, so that most modern prose and verse is punctuated by the structural system. But occasionally (in the poems of E. E. Cummings and Marianne Moore and the prose of James Joyce and Gertrude Stein) punctuation is used more in accordance with the rhythmical principle, with little regard for considerations of grammatical structure. The first new punctuation mark in recent years was set in type in 1967: the "interrobang" (*bang* is printers' cant for an exclamation point). The mark, of combined interrogation and exclamation, is to be used for expressions of double meaning or dubious intent, as "How about that‽" or "What the hell‽". T. F. and M. F. A. Husband, *Punctuation, its Principles and Practice,* 1905; P. Simpson, *Shakespearian Punctuation,* 1911; L. Riding and R. Graves, *A Survey of Modernist Poetry,* 1927; G. V. Garey, *Mind the Stop,* 1939; Richard Armour, *On Your Marks,* 1969. JOHN ARTHOS.

pure poetry is a fictional property of rhythmic expression which, according to certain theorists and critics, embodies the peculiar and untranslatable essence of a poem. This vague counter has gone through periodic fluctuations of currency and credit and a variety of interpretations since 1857, when Charles Baudelaire employed it in his *Notes Nouvelles Sur Edgar Poe,* probably guided by Poe's *The Poetic Principle* (1850). In Fr. ca. 1884 the theory underlying this term came into literary fashion as a reaction against romanticism. For its advocates of this period, it signified liberation from eloquence and rhetoric, and the supremacy of music in poetry. A. C. Bradley in his lecture *Poetry for Poetry's Sake* (1901) equated the term with identity of form and content:

> "When poetry answers to its idea and is purely or almost purely poetic, we find the identity of form and content; and the degree of purity attained may be tested by the degree in which we feel it hopeless to convey the effect of a poem or passage in any form but its own. Where the notion of doing so is simply ludicrous, you have quintessential poetry."

The most zealous advocates of pure poetry in the 20th c. have been George Moore in Eng. and the Abbé Bremond in Fr. Moore in his introduction to an anthology of *Pure Poetry* (1924) indicates his standard of selection in a reference to Poe:

> "His poems are almost free from thought, and that is why we have gathered so many in his tiny garden for our anthology."

The Abbé Bremond in *La Poésie Pure* (1926) relates poetry to prayer; his conception of pure poetry is an elaboration of Bradley's, with a mystical emphasis. The concrete poem is, in his opinion, composed of miscellaneous elements, thoughts, images, sentiments, all of which may be susceptible of prose expression. The abstraction pure poetry is ineffable; it does not exist in the nature of things but is nevertheless the potent factor that transmutes the "impure" or prose-susceptible elements into poetry. The Sp. poet Jorge Guillen, in his *Letter to Fernando Vela,* dismisses the Abbé Bremond's thesis because it discusses pure poetry in terms of a poetic state rather than in terms of the poem. Guillen contends that there is no poetry except as realized in a poem; he defines pure poetry as all that remains in the poem after the elimination of everything that is not poetry.

(A phonetic excrescence of "pure poetry" lies in such work as of Gertrude Stein, who uses meaning merely as an overtone—as most poets use sound—and of Hugo Blümner, whose assemblages of syllables are not intended to make sense at all.) *Cf.* Poetry and Prose.

purism. (1) Care, precision, observance of the rules of expression. Often derogatory, as overniceness of language, or a correctness inappropriate to the audience or the occasion. Its practitioner may be called a precisionist. (2) Historically, the effort to preserve a supposedly pure state of the language, esp. from the use of foreign terms. Sometimes older native forms (archaisms) were enlisted against the invaders (Edna St. Vincent Millay in 1927 wrote *The King's Henchman* with only words from Anglo-Saxon); sometimes these too were regarded as the foe. Found in many periods: the Gr. Atticists; the Romans versus coinages from the Gr.; the medieval L. Ciceronians; Wordsworth's plea for the language of common speech. *Cf.* Correctness.

puritan and pagan. *See* Apollonian.

purple patch (L. *purpureus . . . pannus,* Horace, *Ars Poetica, Epistles* 2, 3, 15–16). A florid passage of description incongruously inserted in a work; now, any ornate passage that stands out from the body of a text.

pyrrhic (Gr. war dance). A metrical foot of two short syllables, ⏑ ⏑. Rejected by most modern scholars, who attach the two syllables to an adjacent group.

pythiambic verse. A dactylic hexameter followed by an iambic dimeter (Horace, *Epod.* 14, 15) or trimeter (16).

pythian meter. The dactylic hexameter. (Pythias, Apollo of Delphi.) Perhaps named from its use in the oracles; explained in ancient times as named from Apollo's song of triumph on defeating the python.

Q

QASIDA. A poem (Arabic; in Persian, 30 to 120 lines; in Turkish, often longer) usually in praise of someone. An elegy or eulogy. The two hemistichs of the first line rhyme; this rhyme is repeated at the end of all the other lines. The classical form of Arabic poetry, *q.v.*

quality. Degree of excellence; especial kind or character of a work. Quality and value (*q.v.*) are subjective terms, to be assayed by a jury—the jury being the public (present and to come) for whom the work exists. The critic serves as judge, to see that the "laws" are observed, but the public delivers the verdict. *Cf.* Expression.

quantity. The duration of the sound of a syllable, the basis of the scansion of Gr. verse and (perhaps after the Saturnian) consequently of Latin. Syllables are counted as long or short (*cf.* Mora), but attempts to measure various degrees of length have been unfruitful. Bridges' theory that "syllables in English have fixed quantity" is challenged by Frost's contention that length varies with the context, but that the sentence-sound is a unit, sentence-sounds being "definite entities . . . apprehended by the ear." *Cf.* Classical versification; Prosody.

quartet. Four lines of verse, as a stanza (quatrain), or (esp.) as one of the first three (four-line) groups of a Shakespearean sonnet.

quatorzain. A poem of 14 lines. Loosely, a Shakespearean sonnet, but usually a poem of 14 lines deviating from the sonnet pattern.

quatrain. A stanza of 4 lines. The most common form of stanzaic verse; used with every possible rhyming pattern, though rarely with the last line left unrhymed. An alternate quatrain is one rhymed *abab;* an enclosed quatrain, *abba.* Another common form (as in Fitzgerald's *Rubaiyat*) is *aaxa.* An interlinked quatrain is one in which one or more lines rhyme with lines in the next stanza or stanzas, as *abab, bcbc, cdcd,* etc. (Dante's *terza rima* is of three lines, thus interlinked).

question. An expression intended to elicit an answer. A rhetorical question, however, is one the answer to which (the speaker assumes) is self-evident; it is thus a literary device, a statement put in the interrogative form for emphasis. The listener, framing the desired answer in his mind, may think he has come upon it by his own reasoning and thus hold more firmly the opinion the speaker desires to evoke. Epic question: early in heroic poems, after the theme is announced, the Muse is asked what started the action; the answer sets the story on its way.

The advice or practice of dialecticians from Socrates on has been to question all things, to submit all ideas to rigid scrutiny. There are, in general, three sorts of questions, those concerned with (1) basic ends; problems of human significance, of human destiny and the gods. These have engaged thinkers of every age, and have not been capped with final answers; (2) means and ends; the validity and pursuit of goals; and (3) means; practical problems of how to go about specific actions. Earlier, Aristotle divided questions into forensic, for the court, and deliberative, for the legislature. These are also called question of fact and question of policy. A question of fact deals with a specific incident or phenomenon, usually in the past. It is answered through the methods of proof, *q.v.* A question of policy deals with the advisability of conduct, thus usually in the future. Hence proof is inapplicable; the answer hangs upon less reliable devices: authority, statistics, example, analogy, inference. Because of this weakness, there are usually sought basic questions of fact (called issues) upon which the question of policy can be made to depend. A model of this development is Burke's speech *On Conciliation with the Colonies,* 1775.

Questions of policy are sometimes (*e.g.,* Thos. Wilson, *Art of Rhetoric,* 1552) divided into definite and infinite. The former deal with specific or limited cases (*e.g.,* should Eng. priests today live celibate?); the latter, with general (*e.g.,* is it better to marry or live single?).

questions for narrative, seven. Since Pierre Abelard (1079–1142) rhetorics have emphasized 7 questions a narrative should answer in its opening: Who? What? Where? Why? How? By what means? In what way? Substituting When? for the last two (which may be subsumed under How?), modern schools of journalism teach the same series. Condensing the seven questions into "a pentad of terms," Kenneth Burke (*A Grammar of Motives,* 1945) projected a 3-volume study with these as a "generating principle": act, scene, agent, agency, purpose. *Cf.* Plot; Novel.

quinary. A metrical line of five syllables, usually as combined with lines of other lengths.

quintain. A stanza, or verse group, of 5 lines. A special form, as a complete poem, is the cinquain.

quintet. A 5-line stanza. The most common is rhymed a b a b b, of various line lengths.

quinzain. A 15-line stanza.

quod semper quod ubique (L., St. Vincent, d. 304. The test of great literature: *quod semper, quod ubique, quod ab omnibus,* what always, what everywhere, what by everybody). Longinus (first c. A.D.) in the treatise *On the Sublime* states that "lofty and true greatness in art pleases all men in all ages"; he was anticipated by Horace, *Ars Poetica* 365. This principle for determining greatness is akin to "the test of time."

R

RAISONNEUR. *See* Ideal spectator; Comedy.

rasa. Sanskrit. One of the nine "flavors" to be induced by a work of art. They are the: erotic, heroic, furious, piteous, comic, fearful, repulsive, marvelous, peaceful—with basis in the emotions (bhāva) of love, courage, anger, distress, mirth, fear, disgust, wonder, calm. Conditions for the tasting of flavor (rasāsvādana) are (1) the component æsthetic surfaces of the work (vibhāva); (2) the significant words and gestures of the characters (anubhāva); (3) the appropriate emotions, as above, either dominant or transient; and (4) the involuntary reactions (sattvabhāva) natural to the character under the circumstances. In addition to the most tasty work (rasavat), there must be the capacity of the receptor who, if not an authentic taster (rasika) will not properly grasp the qualities of the work. *Cf.* Indian literary theory; Taste.

rationalism. (1) The doctrine that reason can furnish *a priori* knowledge, derived from "natural light" without the necessity of inference from the data of sense-perception. It is in this sense that the "Cartesian" rationalism of the 17th c. continental philosophers is contrasted with empiricism. (2) The doctrine that reason has a certain autonomy in seeking truth for its own sake, and is capable of disinterested search. This is intellectualism. (3) The belief that reality exhibits a natural and rational order which enables it to be understood; or that in understanding reality, reason constructs an order and imposes it on reality. (4) "Rationalist" is often used in a specifically religious connotation, as equivalent to "critical," "free-thinking," or "skeptical" (Henri Busson, *Les Sources . . . du rationalisme dans la lit. fr. de la renaissance,* 1922). In this sense the 18th c. deists are called rationalists. It is important in discussing elements of rationalism in such writers as Montaigne or Shelley or irrationalism in such writers as Dostoevsky or D. H. Lawrence, to keep these distinctions in mind. *Cf.* Romanticism; Spontaneity; Absurd. George Boas, *Rationalism in Gr. Philosophy,* 1961; *The Limits of Reason,* 1961.

rationalization. Self-justification in the guise of reason. J. H. Robinson ("On Various Kinds of Thinking," *The Mind in the Making,* 1921) suggests the wide spread of this, as an influence beneath philosophy, the social sciences, and literature. Freud deemed rationalization the usual activity when we think we are using our reason. *Cf.* Psychoanalysis; Truth.

Räuberroman. *See* Picaresque.

reader, ideal. (1) A character in a work, representing the receptor, experiencing the feelings—wonder, excitement, admiration—the author hopes the work will evoke. *E.g.,* the wedding guest in *The Ancient Mariner.* Dr. Watson, in the Sherlock Holmes stories, is at once narrator and ideal reader. In ancient drama, the chorus played an analogous role. (2) An imaginary person, who appreciates in totality what an author hopes will be found in his work. *Cf.* Receptor; Ideal spectator.

realism. A primary distinction must be made among (1) the accurate reproduction of detail for purposes of incidental embellishment; (2) realism as a guiding principle or absolute æsthetic goal presiding over the entire work of literature; and (3) the movement that developed in the last half of the 19th c. under the impetus of (2).

The first has appeared at all stages of literary history, being associated particularly with the depiction of low-life characters in comedy, with the cult of local color (*q.v.;* and *see* Regionalism), and with the use of life-giving details drawn from common experience. In this sense, Falstaff and his companions, or the persons of Ben Jonson's *Bartholomew Fair,* are realistic characters; Smollet's London scenes show a zeal for accuracy of milieu; and Wordsworth's "never lifted up a single stone" is a touch of nature of realistic cast.

The second is characterized by an over-all faithfulness in the rendition of actuality, especially in terms of the relationship of individual to environment, the nature of the events in which he is involved, and the whole shape of his life and personality. It rests upon a "realistic" theory of knowledge, according to which the objects revealed by sense-perception, and the unobservable objects inferred from sense-perceptions by physical science, exist independently of being perceived or known. In realistic writing, the author assumes an objective attitude toward the events he relates; he claims to report, to give the "facts," to conduct an "inquest" (Taine) over the situation. Thus he rigorously excludes his own feelings, normative judgments, philosophical interpretations, and recommendations for action. And he aims to give the reader a strong sense of participation by circumstantiality and relative fullness of detail. (*See* Verisimilitude; Vraisemblance; Slice of Life; Truth in Fiction.)

The *realistic movement* consists of a various group of writers, from the time of Flaubert to the present, who have avowed or practiced realism. They have in common a tendency toward objectivity, toward "letting the facts speak for themselves," and toward stressing the ordinary aspects of experience (Flaubert: "Yonville is just as good as Constantinople" as subject-matter for literary treatment). Some, like Howells, exploit the "realism of the commonplace" and are reluctant to transgress moral taboos; others, like Maupassant, prefer to move into areas of sensationalism. Some develop a life history in the manner of Maugham's *Of Human Bondage*; others give a cross-section centered around an institution or a crisis. "Invention," praised by the romantics, gives way to observation and documentation, to *petits faits vrais* (Stendhal and Taine); fine writing and rhetorical device are played down as likely to obscure the main issue, which is "the bare and explicit truth of human life and human character" (W. L. Courtney). One achievement of realism is its persistent seeking out of new subject-matter for literature, especially situations and language that have previously been excluded by religious or sexual taboos.

The most significant development in this direction is what may be called "psychological realism," a tendency springing from the example of Dostoyevsky and the findings of the 20th c. "depth-psychologists," such as Freud. Since the chosen data of the realist are directly observable, and the contents of the mind are not, this aspect of the movement is somewhat anomalous. Nevertheless the crude materialism (*q.v.*) that usually underlay the thinking of the earlier realists has given way to a more comprehensive portrayal of human nature, as of Leopold and Molly Bloom, in Joyce's *Ulysses.*

The advance of realism as a movement has been somewhat uneven. It became full-fledged in France through the efforts of Flaubert, the Goncourts, Zola, and Maupassant. A brand of native Russian realism was developed by Tolstoy and Turgenev. This second current came to be influential particularly as an avenue of escape from what were considered the excesses of the French example. Realism in England has rarely gone as far as in other countries, while in the United States, in spite of the example and doctrine of Howells, it fell almost still-born in the nineties, only to be revived after the first World War into a vigorous torrent.

Sometimes realism is confused with sensationalism, and authors attempting to achieve realism have been accused of sensational writing. For example, some of the post World War II novels, *e.g.,* Norman Mailer's *The Naked and the Dead* (1948), and James Jones' *From Here to Eternity* (1951), used harsh, violent, graphic descriptions of battle, of personal relationships, of sex, to convey a true picture of war. In the 40's and 50's, there was a growing freedom among writers in their use of detailed, graphic (often pornographic) descriptions of sex and sexual aberrations (along with a lessening of censorship). Such works as Tennessee Williams' *A Streetcar Named Desire,* (1947); Edmund Wilson's *Memoirs of Hecate County* (1946); J. D. Salinger's *The Catcher in the Rye* (1951); Vladimir Nabokov's *Lolita* (1958) reflect the increasing use of clinical descriptions and realistic details, culminating in the best-selling novels, *Couples* (1967), by John Updike, and *Portnoy's Complaint* (1969), by Philip Roth.

Realism must be distinguished from literary tendencies with which it has been closely associated and with which it mingles. First, the term "Naturalism" (*q.v.*) is often used synonymously with "realism," but, strictly speaking, the naturalistic novel is one that interprets its events in terms of a particular philosophy, so that it exceeds the strict bounds of realism. Second, the realistic portrayal of ordinary human beings in their severest circumstances (the soldier in the army; the worker in the factory) may cause the reader to draw ethical or political conclusions. If the author himself draws the conclusions, and condemns injustice or suggests social remedies, his novel may shade off into social criticism.

Under attack from the start, the realistic movement has been frequently misunderstood and misrepresented. It has in various quarters been accused of betraying the prime purpose of literature (to uplift the hearts of men); of degrading human nature by ignoring exceptional and admirable persons, and consequently of being unable to achieve the sublimity of tragedy; of cultivating the structureless plot, and thereby of failing to provide the sort of æsthetic experience that would distinguish it from ordinary journalism. Nevertheless realism continues to be a vital current of contemporary literature, as is evident in the so-called *nouveau roman* of Alain Robbe-Grillet and others in France; in the documentary, such as Anatoly Kuznatsov's *Babi Yar,* or Truman Capote's pretentious category of the "non-fiction novel." E. Auerbach, *Mimesis,* 1953; G. Lukács, *The Meaning of Contemporary Realism,* 1957, trans. 1962; G. J. Becker, ed. *Documents of Modern Literary Realism,* 1963; "Realism: an Essay in Definition," *MLQ* 10, 1949; J. H. Bornecque and P. Cogny, *Réalisme et naturalisme,* 1958; Mary Colum, *From These Roots,* 1937; A. McDowell, *Realism: A Study in Art and Thought,* 1918; A. Tertz, *On Socialist Realism,* 1960. GEORGE J. BECKER and MONROE C. BEARDSLEY.

Realism in any literal sense as reproduction of life is unattainable. As the realist Maupassant points out, in the Preface to *Pierre et Jean*: "To give an account of everything is impossible, for we should need more than a volume for each day . . . Selection is therefore necessary." As a consequence, "the realist will seek to give us not a photographic reproduction of life, but a vision of it that is fuller, more vivid, and more compellingly truthful than reality itself." Another, perhaps unwitting, deviation from literal truth is indicated by James Branch Cabell (*Beyond Life,* 1919, p. 268): "The serious artist will not attempt to present the facts about his contemporaries as these facts really are, since that is precisely the one indiscretion life never perpetrates . . . In living, no fact or happening reveals itself directly to man's intelligence, but is apprehended as an emotion, which the sustainer's prejudices color with some freedom. Thus, were you to hear of your wife's sudden death it would come to you not, I hope, as an interesting fact, but as a grief. All the important happenings of life, indeed, present themselves as emotions that are prodigally conformed by what our desires are willing to admit . . . In life no fact is received as truth until the recipient has conformed and colored it to suit his preferences: and in this also literature should be true to life." *Cf.* Truth; Novel; Naturalism; Propaganda; Document; Anti-hero; Imitation.

recension. A critical revision of a work. *See* Criticism, textual; Emendation; Part Two, Fr. Criticism.

receptor. Term used (20th c.) comprehensively, for one contemplating a work of art. Includes listener, spectator, reader, any one or the whole audience. The term suggests a fusion between receiving and responding or reacting to a work. In the discussion of current works, various levels of consideration are essential; the reviewer cannot balance the latest farce, the newest best-seller, on the scales that he holds for Aristophanes and Dostoyevsky. In terms of the receptor, three rough levels have been suggested, as the work appeals (whatever the chronological age) to the mental and emotional child, adolescent, or adult. (1) To the child, all natures are black or white. This satisfies the child; he demands his villains black, knows only the happy ending. (2) To the adolescent, all things are black or white; this, however, troubles him; he wants to make the world better. To him, says Aristotle, all things are didactic. The adolescent leads all revolutions. But he has learned that the happy ending is often false. Hence may come a sense of impotence, of romantic melancholy, and an attempt to withdraw from the contemporary world; or, conversely, a cynical acceptance of the wicked world and a plunge for one's share of its baubles. Satire, propaganda; idealistic stories, utopias; sordid realism; escapism —crowd this most popular range, the haunt of the violent rebel and the withdrawing hippie. (3) To the adult, all characters are shades of gray. He has less faith in the fury and speed of revolutions; he may move to destroy obstacles, but without moral judgments or self-deluding slogans. Tragedy and high comedy are his mettle; the maturity of an age may be measured in terms of what it deems tragic. Few persons, of course, are mature, save at moments; within each, and ready to respond to the other appeals, linger the adolescent and the child. Some works (*Abie's Irish Rose*) rouse only the undeveloped aspects in us; others (*Idylls of the King*) make almost exclusive appeal to the adolescent; the best (*Don Quixote; War and Peace*) reach out to every level of the receptor's capacities, building upon the child's delight in triumph with the adolescent desire for justice and the adult concern to see life steadily and see it whole. *Cf.* Reader, ideal; Ideal spectator.

recognition. In tragedy, the (moment of the) protagonist's becoming aware of the doom that is closing in upon him. Thus Oedipus' discovery that he has killed his father and married his mother; Macbeth's awakening when Macduff says he was from his mother's womb untimely ripped. Tensely in melodrama, as when the woman in *Kind Lady* (E. Chodorov, 1934, from the short story *The Silver Mask*, by Hugh Walpole) suddenly becomes aware that the strangers in her house have made her prisoner. The same device is used in comedy, as in the transformation scene when Rosalind discards her male attire in *As You Like It*. *Cf.* Comedy; Tragedy; Peripeteia; Catharsis.

recoil, tragedy of. That in which the protagonist's own failings work inevitably to his doom. (*Lear* V, 3):

The gods are just, and of our pleasant vices
Make instruments to plague us.

Opposed (by F. L. Lucas, *Tragedy*, 1928) to the tragedy of circumstance, *q.v.*

reference, point of. *See* Point.

refrain. A phrase or verse recurring at intervals in a poem, esp. at the end of a stanza. It occurs as repetition in unrhymed poetry, the Egyptian *Book of the Dead*, the Hebrew *Bible*; in the Gr. idyls of Theocritus and Bion, the LL. *Vigil of Venus* (though rare in Gr. and L., and in AS. only in *Deor's Lament*); more frequent in primitive tribal verse, as the songs of the Am. Indian. It abounds in the set forms of Provençal; in Renaissance verse; in modern poetry even into free verse, *e.g.*, Carl Sandburg "in the dust, in the cool tombs"; Remy de Gourmont "Hypocrite flower, flower of silence." It may be an aid in establishing meter, and mood. Sometimes the refrain has a meaning that grows with the poem—perhaps with slight changes in the wording, as the echoes of "O sister swallow" in Swinburne's *Itylus*; sometimes it is a nonsense jingle or an irrelevant phrase that carries the tune and the spirit: "hey down a down derry"; "bend your bow, Robin"; "as the dew flies over the mulberry tree" (the last two from Eng. ballads. *Cf.* Poetry and Prose; Repetition; Old Fr . . . forms).

regionalism (G., *Heimatkunst*). (1) The tendency of some writers to set their works in a particular locality, presented in some detail as affecting the lives and fortunes of the inhabitants (Balzac; Hardy; Bennett, the "five towns" tales; J. P. Hebel, the upper Rhine; Hauptmann; many Am. *See* Local color). (2) A specific movement "back to the soil," of agrarianism in reaction against the industrialism of life and the naturalism of literature. In G. esp. Adolf Bartels and F. Lienhard (journal *Heimat*, 1900–04) developed a conservative program later linked with National Socialism. In the U.S. some of the group that in Tenn. issued the poetry magazine *Fugitive*, 1922–26 (John Crowe Ransom), emphasized the South in *I'll Take My Stand*, 1930; developed an increasingly conservative tone (Allen Tate, *Reactionary Essays*, 1936). Regional fiction (Erskine Caldwell, b. 1903; James T. Farrell, b. 1903) frequently realistic and far from conservative, has continued vigorously in many lands. *Cf.* Short story; Realism; Description; Local color.

rejet. Fr. When the sense of a line of poetry is completed in the following line, the part run over is the *rejet*. The act or fact of thus carrying over the grammatical structure and the sense is *enjambement*.

Il neigait, il neigait toujours! La froide bise
Sifflait; sur le verglas, dans les lieux inconnus,
On n'avait pas de pain et l'on allait pieds nus.
(Hugo, *L'Expiation*, 1852)

Sifflait constitutes *le rejet*. It may sometimes be used for more startling effects, as in T. S. Eliot's *Burbank with a Baedecker; Bleistein with a Cigar*, 1920:

Princess Volupine extends
A meagre, blue-nailed, phthisic hand
To climb the waterstair. Lights, lights,
She entertains Sir Ferdinand

Klein. Who clipped the lion's wings
And flea'd his rump and pared his claws?

It was with a *rejet: escalier—Dérobé*, that Hugo brought down the house on the first night of *Hernani* (25 Feb., 1830), the "Bastille Day" of the French romantic revolution. *Cf.* Run-on.

relativism in æsthetics (in the strict sense) is the metacritical thesis that it is logically possible for both of two verbally contradictory value-judgments to be true and known to be true. This can happen according to some proposed interpretations of critical judgments: for example, if when critic A says "This poem is good," he can only mean "This poem will be enjoyed by those who share my tastes," and if when critic B says of the same poem "This poem is *not* good," he can only mean "This poem will *not* be enjoyed by those who share *my* tastes," then the apparent dispute is unreal; both A and B may be saying what is true. Since relativism, in this philosophical sense, is an important position, which evidently places limits on critical argument by resolving many critical disputes into merely verbal ones, it should be kept clearly distinct from other positions that are sometimes also called "relativism."

The view that critics' judgments, or readers' tastes, differ fundamentally and unchangeably from individual to individual or from group to group may be called "descriptive relativism" (one form of it is defended by F. A. Pottle, who in *The Idiom of Poetry,* 1941, holds that critical evaluations express the "sensibility" of the period in which they are made, and that "shifts of sensibility" from period to period make changes in judgment inevitable; *cf.* Cleanth Brooks, *The Well-Wrought Urn,* 1946, Appendix). This is not a philosophical position, but a psychological or sociological one; however, it has often been used as an argument for strict relativism. Yet even if there is considerable variability in literary enjoyment or preference (and the extent of this variability, as well as its irremediableness, is also disputed), it is logically compatible with some nonrelativistic theories of literary value. For example, if to say that a poem is good is to say (among other things) that it has the capacity to provide considerable æsthetic enjoyment, it does not follow that every reader will in fact enjoy it, since successful readers are qualified by training and temperament.

Cf. Standards; Taste; Subjective; Value. M. C. Beardsley, *Aesthetics,* 1958, ch. 10; George Boas, *A Primer for Critics,* 1937, ch. 6. Monroe C. Beardsley.

relief. *See* Comic Relief.

Renaissance. Originally applied to the rebirth of Gr. and L. studies, the "revival of learning" that began in 14th c. Italy and spread through Europe in the next two centuries, the term came to be used of the outburst of creative activity in the various new tongues, which followed the rediscovery of the classics. Petrarch and Dante set the pace in Italy, followed by Boccaccio, Machiavelli, and Sannazzaro (the pastoral, *Arcadia*). The humanist emphasis was carried on in the north by such 16th c. figures as Erasmus in the Netherlands; Budé and the Scaligers and after them the poets of the Pléiade in France; Thomas More in England. After the humanists came the creative writers, in Spain (Lope de Vega, Cervantes) and in England (Sidney, Shakespeare) paying less heed than in France to "rules" derived from the classics; and in a surge that swept through every phase of life—politics, religion, painting and architecture, invention, exploration, cosmology, social change—bringing the fullest flow of literature any period has produced. *Cf.* Elizabethan.

The term Renaissance has also been applied to earlier impulses: the scholastic 12th c. Ren.; the 10th c. Ottonian Ren.; the 8th c. Carolingian Ren. under Charlemagne.

T. Cox, *The Ren. in Europe,* 1933; H. Hauser and A. Renaudet, *Les Débuts de l'age moderne,* 1929; H. S. Lucas, *The Ren. and the Reformation,* 1934; J. E. Spingarn, *Lit. Crit. in the Ren.,* 1899, 1966; J. C. Burckhardt, *Die Kultur der Ren. in It,* 1860, trans. 1878, 1960; J. A. Symonds, *Ren. in It.,* 1875–86; L. Einstein, *The It. Ren. in Eng.,* 1913; S. Lee, *The Fr. Ren. in Eng.,* 1910; J. W. H. Atkins, *Eng. Lit. Crit.,* 1951; P. O. Kristeller, *Studies in Ren. Thought and Letters,* 1956; Hiram Haydn, *The Counter-Ren.,* 1950; F. M. Schweitzer and H. E. Wedeck, *Dictionary of the Ren.,* 1967; D. Hay, ed. *The Age of the Ren.,* 1967; Douglas Bush, *Prefaces to Ren. Lit.,* 1965; R. R. Ergang, *The Ren.,* 1967; Diane Kelder, *Pageant of the Ren.,* 1969.

repetend. Loosely, a refrain; spec., irregularly placed repetition of a word, a phrase entire or partially changed, in the flow of a stanza or a poem. Sometimes called echo. Frequent in Coleridge; Poe; Swinburne; Meredith's *Love In The Valley.*

repetition. (1) In the sense of an aroused expectancy that must be echoed in its satisfaction, repetition has been deemed a basic principle in art. Linked with variation, it exemplifies in the material of the work what is commonly sought as unity with variety in the spirit. (2) In poetry esp., as a recurrence of rhythmic flow or pattern of sound, it is a most frequent aspect of verse. Meter, rhyme, alliteration, assonance, consonance, the stanza or strophe itself, are all based upon repetition; refrains, repetends, are common, esp. in popular verse:

> Hot cross buns, Hot cross buns,
> One a penny, two a penny,
> Hot cross buns.

Metrical repetition satisfies an expectancy set in the first line; sometimes this is held in suspense, with partial satisfactions, before the full return. In Shelley's *To Night,* the shortened 2d line is matched in rhyme by the longer fourth line, but not in both length and rhyme—though expected again at the sixth—until the seventh: a_4 b_2 a b a a_4 b_2. The repetition, even when immediate, often gives a different emphasis or even significance to the term, *e.g.* (G. M. Hopkins, *Carrion Comfort*): "I wretch lay wrestling with (my God!) my God." (3) As a type of verbal play or figure, repeated patterns are very common; their value in oratory has led to the naming of many varieties: Tautotes: frequent repetition of the same word, *e.g.,* Jacques (*As You Like It,* II, 7): "A fool! a fool! I met a fool i' the forest" uses *fool* 8 times in 8 lines, and 6 times more in 8 lines at the end of the speech; Celia (III, 2) "O wonderful, wonderful and most wonderful wonderful! And yet again wonderful, and after that, out of all whooping!" (When this is not a figure but a bore: tautology; though this may also mean taking too many words to say a thing once. Puttenham, however, defines tautologia as excessive alliteration.) Paramoion: any likeness of sound at beginning of words. Parechesis: like-sounding syllables in different words, *e.g.* (Cicero): *Fortunatam natam me consulam Romam;* also called, when definitely bad, tautophony. Anaphora: first word of lines or clauses. Epanaphora: regularly at the beginning. *Kings* II has 23 of 25 verses beginning with "And." Epistrophe: last word of lines or clauses. Epiphora: regularly at the end, *e.g., Psalms* cxv 9, 10. Symploche: at beginning and end; *Psalms* cxviii 2, 4. Mesarche: at beginning and middle. Mesoteleuton: at middle and end. Mesodiplosis: word in middle of successive lines or sentences. Mesophonia: sound in middle of successive lines or sentences. Epizeuxis, or the redouble: immediate repetition, *Psalms* xxii 1. Hypozeuxis: of what might be understood, *e.g.* "Unto the King she went, and to the King she said . . ." Epanalepsis: last word repeats first word, *1 Cor.* iii 21. Anadiplosis: end of one clause, beginning of next, *Rom.* viii 16–17. Epanadiplosis: last word of one, first word of next: "Howling they heard the heralds of the storm Storm down the archways of the darkening sky." Epanodos, balance: second half iterates first, *Ezek.* vii 6; xxxv 6. Quintilian uses this more generally of the reiteration of things so as to draw distinctions between them: "John and Henry came forward; John with head hung low, Henry head high and eyes flashing; John. . . ." This may carry the thought through a progression, *e.g.,* Touchstone (*AYLI* 3, 2): "Why, if thou never was at court thou never sawest good manners; if thou never sawest good manners then thy manners must be wicked; and wickedness is sin, and sin is damnation." Antimetabole: an intricate or poised balance. Antimetathesis: a deferred balance, *2 Cor.* xii 14; *John* xv 16. Paradiastole: counterbalance, as with antonyms, *1 Cor.* vii 10, 11; iv 18, 20. Ploche: repetition with variations. Antistrophe: (a) in reverse order; (b) successive clauses, not at end of lines, end with same word. Synonymy: with words of like meaning. Exergasia: with synonymous sentences. Epexergasia, with elaborate structure of synonyms, including figures; *Prov.* i 20–22; ii 2; Rabelais *passim*; Lamb, *Poor Relations.* In *Tristram Shandy,* ch. 13 of vol. 8 consists of an alphabetical characterization of love (including galligaskinish, iracundulous, ninnyhammering, obstipating) breaking off at the R and after S as an instance of hypallage, with the Widow Wadman harnessed and caparisoned. Polyopton, polyptoton: with different forms (case, number, etc.) of the same word, *Ecclesias.* xii 8. Metagoge: ringing the changes on a word; Lyly, *Euphues*: "This lovely beloved dove of love whom I most lovingly love"; *Rom.* xi 36. Antanaclasis: same word with other sense or implication, *Matth.* viii 22. Antistasis: with sharp shift in sense, *Matth.* x 39. Paronomasia: like sound with different meaning (*cf.* the modern pun); "Pray for them? He'll prey on them!" Paregmenon: words of one root. Homeoteleuton: rhyme (which in classical verse and prose was a rare figure). Homeoptoton: rhyme of like forms (cases, tenses). Epimone: lengthy repetition, as of a sentence in dialogue. Theocritus, *Idyl* 1; Gen. xviii 24; *As You Like It* III, 4; V, 2 (70–115). Battology: unnecessary and burdensome repetition (as above).

Repetition of any element at regular intervals (which intervals are thus themselves repeated) produces a design. Some of the various units in a work may be repeated while others are not, giving the effect of "irregular regularity." In modern prose, repetition may be endlessly fertile. Pearl Buck (*The Good Earth,* 1931, ch. 19) begins four clauses in one sentence "He had suffered"; begins and ends a paragraph "If one had told him, he would not have believed it." It was in despair at the ubiquity of repetition that the cry burst out, as early as *Ecclesiastes*: "There is no new thing under the sun." André Gide went on: "Everything's been said. But nobody listens." Hence our unending repetition. *Cf.* Metaphor; Figure.

reputation. *See* Fame.

resolution. (1) The substitution, in quantitative verse, of two short syllables for one long. *Cf.* Mora; Classical versification; Foot (choreus). (2) The clearing away of the complications in a story; the final adjustment. (3) The balanced fusion of opposite impulses in, or wrought by, the work of art. *Cf.* Synaesthesis.

Restoration. The period of the return of Charles II to the English throne (1660); often extended to include his whole reign (—1685) or beyond through that of James II (—1688) and of James's daughter Anne (1702–14). Restoration comedy, in particular (Congreve, Etherege, Wycherley, Vanbrugh, Farquhar) is marked by the pleasure-loving, sophisticated attitude of Charles himself, neatly turned in Shaw's play (1939) *In Good King Charles's Golden Days. Cf.* Elizabethan. F. W. Bateson, *Eng. Comic Drama 1700–1750,* 1929; M. Summers, *Restor. Theatre,* 1934; ed. *Restor. Comedies,* 1921; V. de Sola Pinto, *Restor. Carnival* (poets), 1954; C. Camden ed. *Restor. and 18th C. Lit.,* 1963; E. Rothstein, *Restor. Tragedy,* 1967.

retroencha. Troubador song, with refrain. Richard Coeur de Leon was found (according to legend) by his faithful troubador Blondel, through his singing a retroencha in prison.

revelation. Benedetto Croce declares (*Aesthetics as the Science of Expression,* 1901, trans. 1909) that if art is anything more than expression, "no one has been able to indicate of what the something more consists." The "something more" is revelation. Art does not merely express, it reveals.

When T. S. Eliot states ("Tradition and the Individual Talent," *The Sacred Wood,* 1920) that "poetry is not a turning loose of emotion but an escape from emotion, it is not an expression of personality but an escape from personality," he is echoing the age-old æsthetics of the orient; but he is picturing only the preliminary step. After the escape, what use is made of the freedom? An angry man is likely to express himself by a burst of indignation; a lover, by an amorous plea or plaint. Emotions are so fluid in all of us that their intense or deft expression by another may touch a deep responsive chord. But the artist quickens more. He sees and shows not only the emotion's vent, but its self, its causes immediate or basic, the pity and the pride of its evocation, the absurdity or havoc of its excess, the counter-drive of other cosmic forces, the pattern of earthly time, and the heavens that encircle our sins. Thus we are not merely caught into the author's or the characters' emotion, but we become richly aware of its essence, potentiality, and depth. Expression rouses us; revelation exalts. *Cf.* Feeling; Triad; Exaltation. Susanne K. Langer, *Mind,* 1967.

reverdi. Old Fr. dance song celebrating the beauties of spring: the singing of the nightingale, the green vegetation. In later variants, the poet meets the God of Love or other allegorical figure.

revenge play. Beginning as early as the Oresteia of Aeschylus (458 B.C., the only Greek trilogy of which all three plays are extant) the revenge play followed two main courses. In the Spanish-French tradition of Calderon and Lope de Vega (*The Star of Seville*) continuing in Hugo's *Hernani* and *Ruy Blas,* it emphasized the *pundonor* (point of honor), the conflict between love and duty, as when the Cid, in Corneille's drama, to avenge an insult to his father kills the father of Chimène whom he loves. In the English tradition, revenge became fused with the "blood and thunder" play, as Kyd's *The Spanish Tragedy* (ca. 1589) with its mingling of murders, ghosts, madness, and love became the most popular English play for a century and drew scores of imitations, including Shakespeare's *Hamlet.* In some of these the settings (and even the speeches) grew stereotyped: night with its ravens, mandrakes, ghosts, and yawning graves gave cover to the plotters, as they besought the powers of hell to give fire to their revenge. In Anthonie Copley's *A Fig for Fortune* (1596) Revenge is hailed as "the pith of tragedies." The avenger is usually pictured as a villain; yet the plays drew power and appeal from a double drive in the Elizabethan: the knowledge that private revenge is a sin against God, a crime against the state, and "a cancer that could destroy mind, body, and soul," countered by the natural impulse of the individual to take into his own hands the righting of a personal wrong. This battle of the mind with the passions still courses in the human breast, and gives power to recent revenge plays such as *Blood Wedding* (1933) of García Lorca. *Cf.* Pundonor; Melodrama; Tragedy. Fredson Bowers, *The Elizabethan Revenge Tragedy,* 1940; Eleanor Prosser, *Hamlet and Revenge,* 1967.

review. A brief discussion of a current work. Reviewing and criticism overlap; the terms are often used indiscriminately; yet there is a distinction. Reviewing is primarily a news function; the Fr. call reviewers *critiques du boulevard.* In criticism the emphasis is on appraisal; in reviewing, on information. A review should present, clearly and interestingly, the scope and theme of the work in question. It should indicate the degree of interest and power the author has achieved, and the importance of his subject, or the skill with which he has woven lighter designs or fantasy into his fabric. It should also, at its best, place the work in relation to other work in the field. Actually, the distinction between reviewing and criticism is of degree rather than kind. Reviewing can be criticism, and sometimes is. *Cf.* Criticism, types. W. Gard, *Book Reviewing,* 1927; L. Jones, *How to Criticize Books,* 1928; Ship. ch. 1; S. S. Smith, *the Craft of the Critic,* 1931; Symposium, "Front-Line Reviewing," *Saturday Rev.* 10, 1934; H. E. Haines, "Book Reviewing in Review," *Library J.* 59, 1934; 61, 1936; F. A. Swinnerton, *The Reviewing and Criticism of Books,* 1939; J. E. Drewry, *Book Reviewing,* 1945. J. Donald Adams.

revision. *See* Emendation; Criticism, textual.

rhapsody. (1) A song sung by a rhapsode (in one session), *e.g.,* one book of an epic. (2) A work unified not by coherent organization but by exalted or extravagant emotion; an effusive outburst.

rhetoric is the art and science of composition in words. The term has at least 8 restricted meanings. In various modern contexts it carries almost all of the senses which it (or its Gr. original) has borne during the past 24 c. It may denominate: (1) a body of principles concerning the composition of persuasive or otherwise effective public speeches, or (a) the speeches themselves, or (b) the skill of an orator; (2) a body of principles applicable in prose composition in general, whether designed for publication or for oral delivery, or (a) the technique of a master of prose style, or (b) artificial prose tinged with insincerity. (3) any classified and systematized body of doctrine about artifices or verbal composition, whether prose or poetry, or (a) the use of such artifices or devices in either prose or verse.

Medieval handbooks of rhetoric followed ancient authority in recognizing 3 principal styles of writing, strong, mediocre, and weak, or high, middle, and low. Theoretically, the high style required not only more decoration but also the employment of those figures or "colors" of rhetoric which are most difficult and hence most dignified.

In the Renaissance, theoretical rhetoric received new impetus from the general revival of classical studies. Manuals of the 15th and 16th c. continued to treat of rhetoric as the art of preparing and delivering a public address, according to the classical steps in the process from *inventio,* through *dispositio, elocutio,* and *memoria,* to *pronunciatio.* An early *Art of Rhetorique* in Eng. (Thomas Wilson, 1533), included a memorable protest against pedantic "inkhorn terms" but followed the ancient tradition in identifying rhetoric with oratory. By the mid 17th c. Samuel Butler was ridiculing the pedantic futility of the modern sophist:

For all a rhetorician's rules
Teach nothing but to name his tools.

Nevertheless, textbook emphasis on the technicalities of ancient rhetoric continued until the mid 18th c. George Campbell (*Manual of Rhetoric,* 1776) enlarged the field of his discussion by announcing that "Poetry is properly no other than a particular mode or form of certain branches of oratory." G. M. Hopkins (*Correspondence,* 1935) said: "By rhetoric I mean all the common and teachable elements in literature."

Many Am. textbooks on the art of writing, among them several still current, bear the word *rhetoric* in their titles although they deal chiefly with composition for readers rather than for listeners and their catchwords are "unity, coherence, and emphasis" rather than *elocutio* and *pronunciatio.*

Although I. A. Richards refers to rhetoric as "the dreariest and least profitable part of the waste that the unfortunate travel through in Freshman English," he has given a traditional title, *The Philosophy of Rhetoric* (1936) to one of his studies of the difficulties of verbal communication. Presumably he means by rhetoric not merely the old art, which, in his phrase, was "an offspring of disputation," but the whole subject of communication by means of words. Yet the rhetoric of our day is not far removed from the fundamental principles of Plato and Aristotle, and when S. I. Hayakawa warns his readers that "the meanings of words are not in words; they are in us," we hear an echo of the sophist of Abdera who declared that "Man is the measure of all things."

C. B. Baldwin, *Ancient Rhet. and Poetic,* 1924; *Medieval Rhet. and Poetics* (to 1400), 1928; D. L. Clark, *Ren. Lit. Theory and Practice,* 1939; *Rhet. and Poetry in the Ren.,* 1922; S. I. Hayakawa, *Language In Action,* 1941; R. F. Howes, *Historical Studies of Rhetoric and Rhetoricians,* 1961; W. C. Booth, *The Rhetoric of Fiction,* 1961; M. H. Nichols, *Rhetoric and Criticism,* 1963, 1967; M. Steinmann, Jr., ed. *New Rhetorics,* 1967; R. A. Lanham, *A Handbook of Rhetorical Terms,* 1968. Robert C. Whitford.

rhetoric and poetic. In the experience of western civilization, the two primary forms of discourse. Rhetoric deals primarily with practical effectiveness, poetic with beauty.

The distinction between the forms of discourse is not the conventional one between prose and poetry. The familiar essay, for example, is likely to be poetic, while a satire in blank verse may be primarily rhetorical. Neither does the relation of the two forms of discourse depend upon the medium of presentation. Originally both rhetoric and poetic were oral, and their use of the written word is simply an adaptation. The rhetorical problems of the pamphleteer and the persuasive orator are essentially the same; likewise, the related materials of character, plot, and movement must be employed by the creator of poetic discourse whether his vehicle be the written or the spoken word. Furthermore, although the self-expressionism of modern romantic poetry has emphasized the poet rather than his audience, the characteristic difference between poetic and rhetoric is not to be found in the presence or the absence of an audience. In the older and more enduring traditions of poetic, a poet sings to his hearers as well as for himself; the orator speaks likewise.

The essential distinction between the forms of discourse is to be found in the intention of the creator of discourse at the moment of composition and delivery; this shapes his product, and is reflected in differing types of receptor response. Whereas the creator of poetic discourse is concerned primarily with portraying life, the creator of rhetorical discourse is concerned primarily with influencing it. The end that the creator of poetic discourse seeks to achieve is the stimulation of the receptor's spirit and imagination. He endeavors to entertain, divert, quicken, enthrall. The end that the creator of rhetorical discourse seeks to achieve with his audience is belief or action. He endeavors to instruct, impress, persuade, or convince. (Kenneth Burke, in what he calls "the new" rhetoric, would replace the term *persuasion* with *identification.*)

This difference has profound significance for both the poet and the orator. The requirement of action or acquiescence shapes the mold and limits the scope of oratory. The liberation from the claims of a single immediate audience together with the lack of urgency involved in his message may free the poet from the handicaps of the orator and permit him to develop less parochial themes.

Although the distinction between poetic and rhetoric here set forth has been useful in many generations of western culture, its usefulness will be impaired if the forms of discourse be conceived as mutually exclusive categories. Neither should one be subsumed within the other. Perhaps they may best be regarded as a single continuum with beauty at one end of the scale and power at the other. Probably no discourse can be purely rhetoric or purely poetic. A powerful oration may have elements of striking beauty all its own, and the oft-told saga of ancestral heroes will doubtless mold the character of a people. Even so, the essential character of the oration is lost if the immediate hearers become aware primarily of its beauty. Likewise the essential character of the tale is lost if the receptors consider it propaganda. The distinction is one of intent, direction, degree. *See* Narrator.

G. Campbell, *The Philosophy of Rhet.,* 1851; A. Korzybski, *Science and Sanity,* 1933; C. K. Ogden and I. A. Richards, *The Meaning of Meaning,* 1923; D. N. Smith, *The Functions of Criticism,* 1909; D. L. Clark, *Rhet. and Poetry in the Ren.,* 1922. Bower Aly.

rhetorical question. *See* Question.

rhétoriqueur. Fr. One of the 15th c.

school of formal poetry, in the late medieval blend of rhetoric and poetics. Intricate rhymes and meters, Latinized diction and complicated allegory made the poems obscure to the point of meaninglessness (Jusserand: *"Leur art de bien dire devient . . . un art de rien dire"*). The school included Chastellan; Molinet; St. Gelais *père;* Marot *père;* their "sovereign poet" Guillaume Crétin, who gave his name (Crétinism) to the style. Their "groceries" were attacked by the Lyons school and the Pléiade; Rabelais uses a rondeau of Crétin (*Pantagruel* iii, 21) for his satire.

rhopalic verse (Gr. *rhopalon,* cudgel). Wedge verse, in which each word is one syllable longer than the preceding one. Occasionally, of a stanza in which each line is a foot longer than the preceding line, as Crashaw's *Wishes To His Supposed Mistress.*

rhyme; rime. *nature and function.* Rhyme has been variously defined as a "correspondence of terminal sounds," as a "repetition of identical or closely similar sounds arranged at regular intervals," as a "device by means of which the extreme words of two periods are rendered like each other" (Aristotle), as *"similis duarum sententiarum vel plurium finis"* (Quintilian), as a "return of corresponding sounds" (H. Blair), as a "similar sound of two syllables at the end of two verses" (Schütze), as a "correspondence which exists between syllables containing sounds similarly modified" (Edwin Guest). All these definitions, easily supplemented indefinitely, are purely verbal; they denote what the word rhyme means without indicating its reason or its nature.

What could be the reason for repeating the same sound at the end of two periods? What is the æsthetic nature of such arrangement, which, if practiced indiscriminately, would result in sheer monotony? According to most writers on the subject, rhyme fulfills a double function. (1) It is beautiful in itself. Language is a fascinating thing. Every fragment of it has its own peculiar charm. By being repeated, within appreciable distance, such fragments attract our attention to the inherent beauty of words, which, in the practical business of language, is usually forgotten. In ordinary speech our words are aurally transparent; we pay no attention to their sound, eager to comprehend their meaning. But poetry, not disregarding meaning at all, adds the joy in the sound itself. The mechanism by which this is accomplished is repetition, rhyme. Hence rhyme is primarily a lyrical device, closely akin to music. (2) Secondly, in the structure of the verse, rhyme fulfills a rhythmically constructive function. It serves as a signal, audibly defining the end of each verse whatever its actual duration. It is a "time-beater." Like the beats of a tympan (L. Becq de Fouquières) rhyme helps to organize versicles into larger units, stanzas. Thus *terza rima* can be distinguished from ordinary triplets only by its specific rhyme-scheme. Hence rhyme is defined as an "acoustic repetition that carries an organizing function in the metrical composition of the verse" (Zhirmunski).

This rhythmic function of rhyme is not confined to the end-rhymes. It is often accomplished by inner rhyming, esp. by alliteration (*e.g.,* Anglo-Saxon verse). Modern Eng. is highly sensitive to alliteration; Sp. versification is based on assonance. Fr. versification is practically unthinkable without rhyme: the difference between accented and unaccented syllables in Fr. is far less than in either G. or Eng.; hence the measure of the verse lines is clearly defined for the ear only by the "tympan-beats" of rhyming. For such a purpose, "perfect" form is inessential. Rhythmic effects can be obtained by incomplete rhymes, by assonance or alliteration. "Remember" can be used as a rhyme for "ember" or for "temper"; the dissonance may be desired, having indeed become an important factor in modern music as well as in poetry. An important variety of imperfect rhyme, which retains the identity of consonantal arrangement, but changes the vowel, is called suspended rhyme, sprung rhyme, sometimes false or tangential rhyme, (*e.g.,* ready-study; many in Shelley, *Adonais*). The gamut of tonal effects, and the range of expectancy, may thus be greatly extended.

theories. The phenomenon of rhyme as an acoustic repeat at the beginning or end of corresponding rhythmic or semantic groups early attracted the attention of philosophers and rhetoricians. In the Western world, it was first taken into account by Aristotle in the *Rhetoric.* Under the name of homœoteleuton, a variety of paromœosis, it is here defined (iii, 9) as "making the extreme words of both members of a period like one another"; the function and purpose of such an arrangement, to facilitate grasping and retaining ideas by the mind. Similiarly Quintilian mentions a poetic device by means of which two or several sentences receive identical endings. Such a figure began to be deliberately cultivated in the Christian L. hymns, whence it was transferred to the early It. Dante was the first to suggest that rhyme has an organizing function in the rhythmic composition of a verse. This idea was developed by the Eng. prosodists of the 16th and 17th c. Beginning with George Puttenham (*The Art of English Poesie*) and William Webbe (*Discourse of English Poetrie*), through Milton and Dryden, to Edwin Guest and G. Saintsbury, they regard rhyme as an auxiliary of rhythm. "It marks and defines the accent, and thereby strengthens and supports the rhythm." It is not merely ornamental; it is organic and functional. For, as Saintsbury sums up this theory, "when accepted by any language, it gradually . . . breaks up prosody by sections merely, and substitutes prosody by feet, that is to say, by minor internal divisions which are batched and brought to metrical correspondence by the rhyme itself."

Fr. prosodists are inclined to regard rhyme largely as an ornamental device. On that basis they justify even purely visual rhymes. Marmontel (1723–99) explains the pleasurable effect of rhyme by the vividness and grace it adds to the expression of thought. It is more beautiful in proportion as it is more difficult: *le beau c'est le difficile*. Marmontel's classical tradition dominated Fr. prosody till modern times. Fr. prosody has never fully freed itself from visual implications. Even though Quicherat (*Traité de versification fr.*, 1850) insists that "logically" all acoustically perfect rhymes, "whatever their spelling may be," ought to be acceptable for partnership; even though Grammont emphatically says that "rhyme exists for the ear, not for the eye," and Bellanger in his *Études hist. et phil. sur la rime fr.* declares the classical tradition "unsound," —nevertheless such visually imperfect though phonetically correct rhymes as *quet* and *égaie* have never attained general approval.

G. accounts of rhyme are based largely on its musical or acoustic value, with roots in the Eng. tradition. For alongside the rhythmological explanations of rhyme (Webbe, Guest, Saintsbury) there is a strong undercurrent of Eng. prosody that identifies rhyme with its musical effect. Sir Philip Sidney says that "rhyme strikes a certain musicke to the ear," and he points out (as later, Hegel) that this musical factor recompenses modern poetry for the loss of the ancient quantity. He also strikes the pragmatic note that later reappears in G. theories (Schütze, Schlegel) by saying that rhyme is a device assisting memory. In 1802, J. S. Schütze, a student of Kant, in *Versuch einer Theorie des Reimes nach Inhalt und Form*, attempts to explain the relation of rhyme to the meaning. On the basis of Kantian æsthetics, he maintains that the identity of sound (constituting the formal definition of rhyme) can have an æsthetic significance only when, and only because, it covers a variety of meaning (*Morgen, Sorgen*). The principle of diversity in unity is here applied to explain the æsthetic effect of rhyming, which otherwise (Schütze maintains) would result in unbearable monotony. According to Schlegel, the æsthetic function of rhyme is to attract our attention and compel our mind to appreciate and to compare words as such. Similarly Hegel maintains that rhyme preserves the physical aspect of words by attracting attention to them *qua* words, regardless of their meaning. This physical factor appeals to the senses, springs from the heart (Goethe: *es muss von Herzen gehen*) not the intellect. In Am. Sidney Lanier (*Music and Poetry*, 1898), and Henry Lanz (*The Physical Basis of Rime*), have tried to show that poetry is a variety of music, Lanz on the basis of analysis of vowels as clusters of overtones. His conclusion is that rhyme plays the same part in the structure of a verse as the key or tonality plays in musical composition.

T. W. Rankin, *Rime and Reason*, 1929; Ch. F. Richardson, *A Study of Eng. Rime*. HENRY LANZ.

technique. "Rhyme" may signify rhyming verse, as "a tale in rhyme"; or a composition in rhyming verse, as *The Rime of the Ancient Mariner*. It may signify one of a group of words having the correspondence of true rhyme (*see below*), as " 'love' and 'dove' are well worn rhymes"; or the sound felt to be in common to two or more words, as, "the meanings of the last words in the lines of a couplet are as important as their rhymes." It may signify, generally, pleasantness or correspondence in the sound of words, as in the phrase "rhyme or reason."

Rhyme may signify any or all of the specific types of sound correspondence in the language, though many have special designations of their own.

Head, beginning, or initial rhyme (for another use, *see below*) or alliteration occurs when one or more syllables of different words begin either with consonant sounds or with vowel sounds felt to be identical, *e.g.*, Peter Piper picked a peck of pickled peppers.

Assonance occurs when the vowel sounds of one or more syllables of different words are felt to be identical, but the adjacent consonants are different, *e.g.,* road, home, cold.

Consonance occurs when the consonant sounds following the vowels of one or more syllables of different words are felt to be identical, but the vowels are different. The consonant sounds preceding the vowels may be but are not necessarily the same, *e.g.,* road, bed, bid, rood; wild, weld, bald, cold. The Fr. unanimists (Romains; Chennevière, *Petit traité de versification,* 1923) list varieties of consonantal matching, which they call *accord.*

Pararhyme is that in which the consonants coincide before and after different vowels, as (Wilfred Owen) falling-feeling, escaped-scooped.

Rime riche (Fr., *see below*), rich rhyme, perfect or identical or echo rhyme occurs when the sounds of one or more syllables of different words are felt to be the same both in vowels and in adjacent consonants, but the meanings are different, *e.g.,* rain, rein, reign; raid, arrayed; mistaken, taken. *Cf.* Echo.

Some of the special designations for rhyme in its most common meaning are true, complete, full, or perfect (for another use of perfect, *see above*), final or end rhyme (for another use of end, *see below*). In this usual sense, rhyme occurs when two or more words are felt to be identical in sound from the last accented vowel to the ends of the words, but different in whatever consonants or consonant groups within the accented syllable may precede that accented vowel, *e.g.,* ache, sake, steak, mistake, lake, slake.

The words just mentioned exemplify the one-syllable rhyme, also called single (-ending), masculine, or male rhyme.

Two-syllable rhyme is also called double (-ending), feminine, or female rhyme, *e.g.,* garter, barter, self-starter.

Three-syllable rhyme is also called triple (-ending), feminine, or female rhyme, *e.g.,* slenderly, tenderly.

Deliberate sound correspondence has appeared occasionally in prose, in the Gr. decline; in marinism, euphuism; polyphonic prose. Numerous frozen phrases are characterized by alliteration (purse-proud, sink or swim), by rhyme (might is right, helter-skelter), or by comparable organizations of sounds (ods bodkins, pitter-patter, punch drunk).

The special province of all kinds of rhyme is verse. Therein rhymes serve as adornments, as means of reinforcing or completing the poetic expression, or as integral parts of delimiting artistic forms. When a poet employs rhymes for this third function, he accepts in some degree the restraints of a convention. To describe these is to describe whatever rules of rhyme exist.

In OE poetry the device was alliteration. Each typical long line contained 4 heavily stressed syllables; the 1st 2 and 1 other, usually the 3d, regularly began with a common alliterative sound. Rarely in Eng. poetry assonance, occurring at the latter end of the lines, has characterized a whole poem, as George Eliot's *Maiden Crowned with Glossy Blackness.* More frequently it has been interspersed among rhymes, as in E. B. Browning's *Casa Guidi Windows.*

Though *rime riche* is sanctified by one famous Chaucerian couplet—

The hooly blisful martir for to seke
That hem hath holpen whan that they were seeke—

it occurs but rarely in Eng. poetry.

True rhyme, overwhelmingly the most widely used structural sound device in middle and modern Eng., usually occurs at the end of a line, in which case it is called end rhyme:

There was a young girl from St. Paul
Wore a newspaper dress at a ball, . . .

Normally a line of poetry ends with a whole word; broken rhyme occurs (usually for humorous effect) where a word is divided between two lines:

If you chose to compare him there are two per-
Sons fit for a parallel: Thompson and Cowper. (Lowell)

When one or both of the rhyming partners are made up of more than one word (sometimes a word and a fraction), it is mosaic rhyme; *cf.* light verse:

Unqualified merits, I'll grant, if you choose, he has 'em,
But he lacks the one merit of kindling enthusiasm. (Lowell)

Internal rhyme usually occurs in a poem with lines marked by a regularly placed cæsura: the sound at the end of the first section (member) of the line corresponds to the sound at the end of the line (leonine rhyme, esp. in LL.), or wholly within the line, or in the middle of the next line:

I bring fresh showers to the thirsting flowers
From the seas and the streams. (Shelley)

Say that health and wealth have missed
me. (L. Hunt)

It may, however, designate rhyming sounds that occur anywhere except at the end of a line.

Vainly might Plato's brain revolve it;
Plainly the heart of a child might solve
it. (Lanier)

—though such concord of first words is also called initial or beginning rhyme.

The question, what constitutes a good rhyme in Eng. poetry, can be answered with slightly greater precision than what constitutes a beautiful woman. The necessary degree of correspondence in sound is undetermined. The definition of true rhyme given above may be called the orthodox requirement, supported by the unquestionable fact that by far the largest part of rhymed poetry fits the convention. Lanier the poet did not feel that Lanier the critic was crabbed when he said, "If the rhyme . . . demands any the least allowance, it is not tolerable, throw it away." Against this rigid position, however, is arrayed a multitude of exceptions. Besides instances of assonance and consonance and weak rhyme (also called unaccented rhyme): correspondence of final unaccented syllables (*see below*), there are such pairs as rivalry, sepulchre (Campbell); river, ever (Tennyson); refined, ashamed; could, world; time, ran (Dickinson. The last pair is from *A Day*; the other rhymes are begun, sun; stile, while; gray, away). Though some prosodists condemn all these phenomena as faults of carelessness or of defective ear and call them false or imperfect rhymes, others have devised "laws" that by classifying purport to justify some types. Another treatment, resisting the temptation to legislate, simply affixes a comprehensive but noncommittal label: a "near rhyme" occurs when two words not rhyming are recognizably similar in their final sounds.

For serious Eng. poetry the 1-syllable rhyme is most common; but those of 2 and 3 syllables may also be appropriate, especially when the rhyme does not tend to distort normal pronunciation.

Rhyming conventions are by no means universally the same. In many languages, including classical Gr. and L., rhyme is a rare figure. In the early poetry of Romance languages, particularly OFr., OSp., and Prov., assonance as a structural device was more prevalent than rhyme; it remains important in Gaelic. In modern Romance languages rhyme has so completely displaced assonance that poets in these tongues exhibit a predilection for more exact correspondences than Eng. ears enjoy. In It., *e.g.,* feminine rhymes are so generally employed that a masculine rhyme may produce a grotesque effect; in French the *rime riche,* in disfavor with us, is frequent and valid (though the final consonants must give the same sound when *liaison* is imagined, *e.g., parlais* and *allaient* do not, save in recent freer verse, form a normal rhyme). Among medieval Persians and Arabs, indeed, rhyme was elaborated to an even greater degree, producing instances of exact correspondence extending back for as many as 5 syllables.

A number of other terms are employed for various rhyming devices.

Analyzed rhyme begins with any two words ending successive lines; at the end of the next two lines the same sounds occur, but with final consonants interchanged, *e.g.,* down, trees; drowse, scene.

Eye rhyme is visually, but not aurally, true rhyme, *e.g.,* love, move—but when the poem was written, pronunciation may have justified the coupling, *e.g.* (18th c. Eng.) join, divine; obey, tea.

Riding rhyme: (from the canter of the pilgrims in *The Canterbury Tales*) decasyllabic rhyming couplets. (Perhaps, from the lilt of the lines as read without sounding the final "e," the value of which was unrecognized from the Elizabethans to Tyrwhitt, 1775.)

Synthetic rhyme: words artificially altered to create the rhyme, *e.g.,* stile-a, mile-a (Autolycus' song, *Winter's Tale*). Unless for humor, this is usually to fit the lilt of a measure.

Unaccented rhyme, minor accent rhyme, "misplaced" or "strained" accent rhyme: a word ending in an accented syllable paired with one that ends with an unaccented syllable, *e.g.,* dead, disinherited; agree, symmetry. Sometimes the spelling is changed to suggest the rhyme: sea, countree. This rhyme is frequent in Shakespeare's sonnets (*e.g.,* 16, 18, 32, 125); often with words ending in "ing." Unaccented rhyme, without such strains, is a normal element in Welsh: meadow, blow.

The Fr. also employ several more specific terms. *Rime couée;* tail(ed) rhyme: in a group of 3 or more lines, the last is shorter, rhyming either with one before or with a similar short line in a following group. *Rime léonine:* word at cæsura rhymes with word at end of line; *rime batelé:* word at end of line rhymes with cæsura word of next line.

Rime annexée: word at end of line (in addition to the usual rhyme) rhymes with the 1st word of the next line:

Dieu gard' ma maîtresse et régente
Gente de corps et de façon
Son cœur tient le mein dans sa tente
Tant et plus. . . . (Marot)

Rime enchainé: a sound (or root) in each line is repeated within the next:

. . Dieu des amans, de mort me garde,
Me gardant donne-moi bonheur,
Et me le donnant. . . . (Marot)

Rime couronnée: repetition of sound within the line:

Toujours est en vie envie,
Qui, le jour et la nuit, nuit.

Rime équivoquée rhymes one word with the same combination broken into two words of different meaning; *rime brisée* is Jesuitical verse (*q.v.*). The Fr. set rhymes in a scale of fulness: *rime très riche* or *rime richissime:* disyllabic, all consonants and vowels, *e.g., vaillant, travaillant; rime riche:* all consonants and vowel, *e.g., eternel, solennel; rime suffisante:* vowel and following consonants, *e.g., faire, téméraire; retard, hasard; rime pauvre,* also *rime faible:* vowel only, *e.g., ami, defi; rime défectueuse* (imperfect rhyme): both words from one root, a simple word and one of its compounds, *e.g., faire, défaire,* and other faults as in Eng.

Rhymes of any type are expertly employed when they occur in words that are the best available in the language for the other effects intended. The excellence of the rhyme is therefore proportional to the excellence of the thought or feeling and the appropriateness of the words in which this is lodged. At times, however, the quest for a rhyme has also revealed a fresh or fertile figure. For the system of notation of rhymes, *see* Scansion. *Cf.* Meter. R. MacD. Alden, *Eng. Verse,* 1903; G. W. Allen, *Am. Prosody,* 1935; G. Saintsbury, *Hist. of Eng. Prosody,* 3 v., 1906–10; H. C. K. Wyld, *Studies in Eng. Rhymes from Surrey to Pope,* 1923. Thomas Walter Herbert.

rhyme royal (named from its use in *The Kingis Quair,* 1423, by James I of Scotland). Stanza of 7 decasyllabic lines, rhymed *aba bbcc.* Used first in Chaucer's *Complaint unto Pity,* it is sometimes called Chaucer stanza; it is the pattern of ca. 2,000 of his stanzas; used also by Shakespeare, *The Rape of Lucrece*; Masefield, *Dauber.* Widely varied in *The Mirror for Magistrates,* 1559, 1563, it indicates the experimentation that led to the Spenserian stanza, *q.v. Cf.* Septet.

rhyme scheme. The pattern of rhymes in a stanza or poem. For the system of noting this, *see* Scansion.

rhythm in language is the natural "swing," or alternation of some quantitative differences (stress, duration, pitch, silence) that accompany all flow of meaningful sound. As emotion is manifested, the rhythm tends to grow more pronounced; the contrasts become more noticeably accentuated or more regular in their recurrence, tending toward meter, *q.v.*

The patterned alternation and repetition of rhythm is within our bodies in systole and diastole, inhalation and exhalation, the flex and relaxing of muscle. It surrounds us in the alternation of day and night, the tidal ebb and flow, the succession of the seasons. It is in our consciousness in the interplay of identity and diversity, the self and the world without. It thus inevitably characterizes our speech. If the succession of alternations involves the balancing of contraries, the rhythm is a dialectic. The movement of tension, building to a crisis then subsiding until the flow turns toward a new crisis, is essentially rhythmic. Strophic rhythm, frequent in free verse, marks the flow of units larger than a line or stanza. *See* Ictus; *cf.* Prose rhythm; Prosody; Dialectic; Tension. E. A. Sonnenschein, *What is Rhythm?,* 1925; S. Lanier, *The Science of Verse,* 1898.

riddle comprises a variety of literary forms that have never been clearly separated. The true riddle compares one object to another and entirely different one; its essence is the surprise that the disclosure of the answer occasions. *E.g.,* the Humpty-Dumpty riddle describes a fall with a shattering that cannot be put together again, then resolves the contradiction in the answer "Egg." In the tradition of unsophisticated peoples, riddles of this sort are abundant; in more sophisticated literatures the knack of coining such riddles is almost lost. They are usually presented through an introductory element (a scene, a summons to guess), a descriptive core (which may include a descriptive name like "Dick Redcap"), a contradictory core, suggesting the act or aspect to be reconciled, and a concluding element (a summons to guess, a promise of reward or punishment). Literary riddles often develop the contradictory at the expense of the descriptive details; they may represent the object as speaking in the first person. Such literary riddles were very popular in Byzantine, early medieval and Ren. L. literature; they have been written by Dean Swift, Goethe, Schiller, Winthrop M. Praed, and continue to be a minor genre.

Many varieties of puzzling questions are called riddles. There are arithmetical questions, which may be seriously or whimsically intended. Among the riddles exchanged by Solomon and the Queen of Sheba, she asked: "What is it that has ten openings; when one is open, nine are closed; when the one closes, the nine are open?" Solomon looked at her, and answered: "The human body" (the navel closes at birth). Questions about Biblical figures may also appear in serious and whimsical forms, *e.g.*, "Who was born and did not die?" (Enoch). Many of these are ultimately of catechetical origin and may be traced far back in medieval and patristic tradition, as may many of the punning questions and wisecracks that abound today.

There are several specific types of riddle. The Gr. *ainigma* (enigma) presents in obscure wording what must be solved through grasping associations or similarities; the *griphos* seems obvious but hinges upon a verbal play or other trick. Decapitation: *e.g.* Take away one letter, I destroy; take two and I die, unless my whole saves me (Ans: Skill). Addition, as with the story compressed in *he, her, hero.* A rebus is a riddle in pictures, representing phonetically the answer or the syllables of the answer, through the meanings of the separate pictured sounds. The charade is an enigmatic description (written or acted) of a word and its separate syllables. The popular or traditional riddle is ordinarily in prose, although simple rhymes and other stylistic embellishments are readily introduced. The literary riddles usually employ highly sophisticated devices. Riddling is a form of popular entertainment; it amuses the natives of Africa or Asia as it once amused the Greeks and Romans and Anglo-Saxons at their banquets (Athenaeus, *Deipnosophistæ*; Petronius, *Cena Trimalchionis*). Efforts to use riddles in mythological studies, however, have been largely fruitless. The description of a snowflake as a bird without wings devoured by a maiden without hands (the sun) is probably no more than a riddle; but the picture of the year as a tree with twelve branches probably has mythological and cosmological antecedents. *Cf.* Humor.

A. Taylor, *A Bibliog. of Riddles, FF Communications, 126,* 1939; F. Tupper, *The Riddles of the Exeter Book,* 1910. ARCHER TAYLOR.

rime. From Gr. *rhythmos.* In LL. *rithmi* was used of accentual verse, as opposed to quantitative verse, *metra.* As most medieval accentual verse was marked by similarity of terminal sounds, this feature drew to itself the name *rithmus,* which (perhaps influenced by OHG. *rim,* number, reckoning) became *rime.* The influence of classical learning in the 16th c. brought various spellings, and in the 17th c. the distinction between *rhyme* and *rhythm* was established. The spelling *rime,* however, has again found considerable favor in the past hundred years. *See* Rhyme.

rococo (Fr. *rocaille,* grotto; shell-work). Applied to Fr. scroll-work decoration in architecture; without utilitarian end or classical restraint. In G. applied to the poetry produced at and for the courts of absolutism and the aping bourgeoisie (*Rokokodichtung,* fl. 1720–70). Erotic and cynical, interested only æsthetically in ethical problems; attacked by *Sturm und Drang.* Excelled in lyrics (Brockes; Haller; Hagedorn; Gleim; Gessner; Wieland; the early Goethe). *Cf.* Baroque; Gothic. E. Ermatinger, *Barock und Rokoko,* 1926; G. Bazin, *Baroque and Rococo,* 1964.

roman à clef. *See* Livre à clef.

roman noir. *See* Gothic.

romance. A narrative of heroic or marvelous achievements, of colorful or unusual events; a story of gallant love; distinguished from the more realistic novel. *See* Novel.

romance. Sp. Ballad, corresponding in many features to the Eng. There are historical, sentimental, biblical ballads, *romances fronterizos* (of the border), relating fights and love-stories between Sp. and Moors. Some *romances* are old, popular, anonymous; others are learned. Collections, called *Romanceros,* since the 16th c. (*Romancero de Sepúlveda* 1551; Wolf, *Primavera y flor de romances,* 1856). *See* Romance versification.

romance-six. Line of 6 syllables, tail to the 8 syllable couplet of the OFr. romance.

romance versification includes the Prov. Fr., It., Sp. and Port. metrical systems. Its basic characteristic is the tonic or accentual nature of its rhythm. The cellular unit of a Romance verse (*i.e.,* the element from which the rhythm is built up, but which, alone, produces no sense of rhythm) consists of a stressed syllable, either preceded or followed by one or more unstressed; two or more such units have rhythm. Thus every Romance verse has at least two accents; of these, the main one is the last, which is fixed; to some extent the other may be shifted.

This flexibility was not evident in the earliest forms, which grew from the imitation of the patterns of medieval L. (liturgical) poetry. In this, the sense of "quantity" was gradually lost; the poets replaced long and short with stressed and unstressed syllables. These forms, in distinction from the classical meters, are called rhythms. *Cf.* Rime. Many of them were long; a medial cæsura divided them into two hemistichs. The first of these was often felt to be weak; as a rhythmic compensation, its last word was made to accord in sound with the word similarly placed in the next line; hence rhyme. This internal rhyme, with strong cæsura, led to the breaking of the long line.

Verse (Prov.<L. *vertere,* to turn) indicated a part of the stanza of the canzone. By the early It. poets it was given its modern sense, a rhythmical series complete in itself. In Romance versification, the addition of one or more unstressed syllables after the last accent does not change either rhythm or verse, *i.e.* Romance verse may have an oxytonic, a paroxytonic, or a proparoxytonic ending (accent on the last syllable, the penult, or the antepenult, respectively). The typical scheme of Fr. verse is oxytonic, paroxytons existing only through poetic pronunciation of final *e muet.* It. and Sp. have proparoxytonic words; but in these tongues and in Prov. the typical verse is paroxytonic. Hence, with a predominantly numerical nomenclature, the Fr. *décasyllabe* corresponds to the hendecasyllable of the other Romance languages, and the other verses accordingly.

Internal phonetic laws govern the counting of the syllables. Most important of these is elision, which is the reduction to 1 syllable of the 2 that end and begin adjacent words, when the 1st ends and the 2d begins with a vowel. The separate sounding of such vowels, hiatus, is far less frequent. The cæsura occurs only in long verses, such as the alexandrine and the hendecasyllable, the two most important Romance verses. In the alexandrine (to the 19th c.) it is always symmetric, dividing the verse into identical hemistichs; in the hendecasyllable, it is asymmetric and variable.

The phonetic consistency of Sp. and It. produces an almost invariable orthographic identity in the rhyming syllables; and a frequent quest of complicated rhymes. Such virtuosity was denied the Fr., who often, especially in academic periods, employed *rime pour les yeux,* eye rhyme; lacking proparoxytonic words, they sought phonetic identity also for one or more letters preceding the final stressed vowel, developing the *rime riche* and the *rime richissime.* (*See* Rhyme.)

Verses are built into strophes and stanzas, according to certain patterns; *e.g.,* verses of different rhythmic structure, *i.e.,* imparisyllabic verses, may not always be combined. All forms created before the Renaissance, *i.e.,* developed naturally in Romance growth, are called stanzas; all later forms (imitations mainly of the classical), strophes. Many stanza types were invented by the Provençals, perfected and canonized by the Italians; they use many combinations of rhyme. The most characteristic development of the rhyme scheme in the strophe is the Fr. *alternance,* imposed by Ronsard, codified by Malherbe, and—with the recent exception of a few advance-guard experiments—universally respected. In this system a masculine rhyme alternates invariably with a feminine one (ending, as it must in French, with *e muet*).

"Meter," as used in Romance versification, indicates the relationships that govern a complex poetical form, larger than stanza or strophe. Of the many meters of the learned poetry of the Middle Ages and the early Renaissance, the best known is the sonnet.

The earliest Romance poems were in popular forms, epic or lyrical. Most important of these were the Spanish *romance,* later used in academic poetry: stanzas of four eight-syllable verses, with one assonance alternating with unrhymed verses throughout the poem; and the Fr. epical *laisse*: a series of decasyllables all ending in the same assonance. These forms were supplemented by many highly refined stanzas (Arnaut Daniel added the sestina) by the Provençals, the masters of Dante and Petrarch who developed, respectively, the *terza rima* and the sonnet. The prestige of It. literature in the Renaissance imposed many of its verse forms on all Europe; especially on Sp. Petrarchism gave vogue to the sonnet; the It. chivalric poems spread the use of the *ottava* as a narrative meter (Camoëns). Even as the It. influence began to decline, it passed on another form, the *endecasillabo sciolto,* invented by Trissino for tragedy and epic, consisting of a series of unrhymed hendecasyllabic lines, which was adopted in Eng. as blank verse. It. influence was strong only at the beginning of the Fr. Renaissance; the Hellenism of the Pléiade led to imitations of the free strophic combinations of Gr. poetry, especially in the ode. The alexandrine and *alternance* triumphed; verse became more rhythmical and symmetrical, in final systematization by Malherbe and Boileau. In the Golden century, a few standard forms were almost exclusively employed.

Romanticism, in the Romance countries as elsewhere, provoked the multiplication of metric forms, some rediscovered through study of popular poetry; but the basic structure of the verse remained unchanged. The only fundamental changes were the *alexandrin ternaire,* imposed by Hugo; where a double and variable cæsura destroyed the parallel symmetry of the 2 hemistichs; and in It. the *metrica barbara,* an attempt to imitate in tonic verse the prosodic schemes of Gr. and L. versification, successful only in the hands of Carducci. The dominant æstheticism of the advance guard movements of the 3d quarter of the c. (*Parnasse,* Decadence, Symbolism) emphasized the value of metrical tradition and of formal virtuosity. Only after 1880, with the invention of free verse, the natural development of a flexible tonic versification, was there a truly basic innovation in the forms of Romance poetry. *Cf.* Meter; *Vers libre;* Old French . . . Forms; Alexandrine; Cæsura; Sonnet; *Terza rima.* F. D'Ovidio, *Versificazione Romanza,* 1932; F. Zambaldi, *Il Ritmo dei Versi It.,* 1874; M. Grammont, *Le Vers fr.,* 1913; Hugo P. Thieme, *Essai sur l'hist. du vers fr.,* 1916; Henriquez Ureña, *La Versificación irregular en la poesia castellana,* 1920. Renato Poggioli.

romanticism, *the word.* The adj. "romantic," from which the modern noun "romanticism" is derived, comes from OFr. *romanz,* a romance, or novel; but its first attested uses are in Eng. ca. 1654. The meaning is "like a romance," usually with the derogatory connotation of fanciful, chimerical. Increasingly in the 18th c., the word was used in a favorable sense, and came to be applied to places with the additional meaning of agreeably melancholy. In Fr. there is an example of *romantique* in 1675, in the then current Eng. sense, but without apparent effect upon usage; then as now the French word for this meaning was *romanesque. Romantique* does not appear again until 1776, when Letourneur, in a *Discours* prefatory to his translation of Shakespeare, used it in italics, with a capital R, relating it to the English word and explaining in a note that neither *romanesque* nor *pittoresque* contained the "tender affections and melancholy ideas" conveyed by the English word. In the closing years of the century the word became very popular, and was officially recognized by the Academy in 1798. In G. *romantisch,* which had been used since the 17th c. in the sense of the Fr. *romanesque,* came, toward the middle of the 18th c., probably through translations and imitations of Thomson's *Seasons,* to be applied increasingly to natural scenes, in the new Eng. sense. It was the G. word that was first applied to a literature contrasted to classicism; by Friedrich Schlegel in the *Athenäum* (1798–1800). Mme. de Staël, who came to know the Schlegels in two visits to G., is chiefly responsible for popularizing in Fr. the literary connotation of *romantique.* By 1800, in her *De la littérature,* she had made the distinction between "the literature of the south and the literature of the north"; in *De l'Allemagne* (suppressed 1810; pub., London, 1813) she spoke clearly of "classic" and "romantic" poetry. To this work and to A. W. Schlegel's *Dramatic Art and Literature* (pub. in Eng. trans., 1815), is largely due Eng. adoption of "romantic" to designate literary tendencies already well recognized.

Definitions of romanticism, begun by the Schlegels, were by 1836 so numerous and so inconclusive that Musset satirized them in *Lettres de Dupuis et de Cotonet*; despite the warning, they continued to multiply; they are still without definitive result. Without preliminary limitations and distinctions, it is impossible to isolate the essence of a word that has been so diversely used. First we must distinguish "romantic" in the sense of adventurous, emotional, or fanciful (the Fr. *romanesque*); such meanings antedate literary romanticism. Second there is "romantic" as applied to a many-sided literary movement and its immediate forerunners. Finally we note that "romantic" is applied to any or all of the vast implications of the literary movement—to its remote antecedents and its posterity, to allied arts, to politics, religion, morals, philosophy, history, nations, human nature.

the literary movement. Even within these limitations literary romanticism cannot be exactly defined in character nor precisely limited in time. It is a comprehensive term for a large number of tendencies toward change in the later 18th and earlier 19th c., that vary with times, places, authors, from a mere search for new directions within the framework of older traditions to an open revolt. The tendencies may be roughly classified by subject matter, attitude, and form. Romantic subject matter includes scenes and culture of non-classic lands, the Middle Ages, the national past; the exotic, local color, the particular in preference to the general; nature (especially in its wilder moods) as an immediate personal experience; Christianity and transcendentalism; the supernatural; night, death, ruins, graves, the macabre, the Satanic; dreams and the subconscious. The most characteristic romantic attitude is individualism; the romantic hero is either an egocentric devoured by melancholy or boredom, or a fiery rebel against society, in either case often a man of mystery; the poet is a seer; the emotions are preferred to the reason, the ideal to the real, aspiration to compromise with necessity. In expression romanticism proclaims freedom from rules and conventions, emphasizes spontaneity and lyricism, and tends to reverie, vagueness, synæsthesia, an overlapping of the functions of the arts. To no national literature, period, or author can all of these aspects of romanticism be applied; some of them are in contradiction to others. The critical writings of the romantics themselves give the impression that they are chiefly concerned with combatting classicism.

The frequent division of the movement into preromanticism and romanticism proper involves the difficulty of finding a date that is applicable to all countries. On the whole the turn of the century as a dividing line has a justification lacking to other dates, in that, with the literary connotation of the word "romantic," attention began to be focussed, not only in G. but elsewhere also, on differences between classic and romantic.

Lacking a definite school, Eng. had many romantic writers and a particularly rich and influential preromanticism. From the late 17th c. through the 18th, sensibility enjoyed an increasing vogue, finding expression in the theatre, poetry, prose fiction, criticism, even philosophy. Anticipating Rousseau, Shaftesbury, in *The Moralists* (1711), urged a natural religion that man could find in response to his own instinctive goodness, with sanction and support in the "Genius of Nature." James Thomson's *Seasons* (1726–30), with its direct observation and genuine emotion, gave nature poetry a new turn. The poetry of melancholy, night, and the grave is represented by Edward Young's *Night Thoughts* (1742–44) and Blair's *Grave* (1743). Return to the poetry of the past, particularly of northern lands, appears in ballad collections from 1719 on (Macpherson's *Ossian* 1760–63, Percy's *Reliques* 1765); the Gothic vogue is exemplified in Walpole's prose extravaganza *The Castle of Otranto* (1764). Greater naturalness in poetic diction is long urged, though ineffectively practised before Blake and Wordsworth.

The great Eng. romantics were poets, or writers of both poetry and prose. They did not tend to form groups, differed sharply in theory and practice, and in some instances disliked one another heartily. But they have resemblances in spite of themselves: they show more freedom and spontaneity than pseudoclassic poets, their works are more charged with emotion; they exhibit more individualism; many of them have a mystical quality. Visionary Blake, Tory Wordsworth, radical Shelley, alike believe in the Poet's Mission.

In G. the preromantic and romantic periods, considered as a whole, paradoxically coincide with the classic age of G. literature. Thomson's *Seasons, Ossian,* Percy's *Reliques,* found enthusiastic reception and stimulated new efforts in parallel directions. The movement of the Göttingen poets (1772), the *Sturm und Drang* period, to which belong Goethe's *Werther* (1773) and Schiller's *Räuber* (1782), are romantic before the name. A movement calling itself romantic did not come until 1798; it was then characterized by a preponderance of criticism and philosophy over original artistic creation.

Fr. literature's greatest contribution to preromanticism is unquestionably Rousseau. Antecedents may be found for his major literary, social, philosophic, and religious ideas; but his style, his personality, and the exact period at which he lived combined to give his works an unprecedented influence. But neither they nor the important contributions of Chateaubriand and Mme. de Staël in the first decade of the 19th c. sufficed to launch an immediate movement. The years 1820–30, culminating in the uproarious first night of Hugo's *Hernani,* are in France the great period of battle and debate between classic and romantic. In no other country was romanticism so openly anticlassic, or the effort to define and justify it more extreme. Although the theatre was the chief battleground, Fr. romantic drama had little of permanent value; the plays of Hugo, the chief standard bearer, are redeemed only by passages of magnificent verse. Under the influence of Walter Scott, the historical novel achieved some success, but the most lasting accomplishments of the period were in poetry.

Geographically the home of one of the classic literatures of antiquity, It. nevertheless furnished over several centuries many literary examples of what can, in retrospect, be called romantic attitudes; but what is usually called the romantic movement did not begin until about 1815, after the fall of Napoleon's empire. Literature and politics were combined to a degree unexampled in other countries; "romantic" came to be practically synonymous with "liberal." To Sp., romanticism came still later and in a still more confused form; except in a few extreme cases it involved no complete rejection of classical and pseudo-classical principles. Elsewhere, its challenge to reason has led to an extreme in surrealism, and is manifest in such works as the anti-novel and the theatre of the absurd.

implications. Among the many semantic accretions of the word romanticism, two closely related ideas are the most fertile sources of implications: liberty and the emotions. Liberty covers individualism and rebellion against rules, authority, and tradition; the emotions seem to involve spontaneity, the subconscious, the springs of action and of artistic creation, and other human characteristics that are non-rational, such as "life force," intuition, the mystical faculty.

During the romantic period and since, painters, sculptors, and musicians, particularly in Fr., often made common cause with literary romantics in the name of rebellion against rules and tradition, or of spontaneity and emotional expression. The music dramas of Wagner were in line with G. romantic theories favoring the breaking down of divisions between the arts; the Fr. Symbolists of the late 19th c., who made a cult of Wagner, accentuated the same trend, and recognized their kinship with romanticism.

We should logically expect liberalism in politics to correspond to romanticism in literature, and so, in the main, it does. In religion the idea of individual liberty led some romantics (Shelley) to atheism, others (Baudelaire) to blasphemy; still others, however, were good Catholics, or otherwise devoutly religious. Certain aspects of the philosophy of Nietzsche can be called romantic, as can the vitalism of Bergson, Eucken, Driesch.

Early in the 20th c. Lasserre made a celebrated attack on romanticism for "usurpation by the sensibility and the imagination of the hegemony of the intelligence and of the reason." For Babbitt, similarly, Rousseau's "return to nature" involved a flaccid yielding to emotional reverie, at the expense of the specifically human virtues of reason and self-control. Imagination and emotion, said Babbitt, must be subordinated to intelligence; balance must be maintained by the will in accordance with the dictates of reason. Neo-romantics (Middleton Murry; Fausset), while admitting that a return to a dubitative primitive innocence by the abandonment of self-conscious intelligence is neither desirable nor possible, maintain that contact between rational man and spiritual forces must be re-established by a fusion of human faculties, rational and non-rational. The surrealists, however, "go the whole hog" in abandoning reason.

In its narrower literary connotations romanticism is an outworn quarrel; the greatest writers have always eluded classification as romantic or classic. That debates continue and the word retains its vitality is due to the immense philosophical implications of liberty, reason, and the emotions.

The term negative romanticism or antiromanticism has been applied to the presentation of an ironical or cynical acceptance of human limitations, of the influence of unreason or absurdity in human affairs. At its best, this may lead to polished satire, as in Anatole France and James Branch Cabell; at its worst, to withdrawal from the concerns of life to amorality or immorality, indiscriminate striking out for oneself, or defeatism, self-indulgence, drifting into drugs. These attitudes are common in current fiction. *Cf.* Classicism; Humanism; Individualism; Primitive; Expressionism; Da-da; Feeling; Surrealism; Gothic; Spontaneity; Anti-hero; Apollonian; Absurd; Symbolism. W. Graham, "The Romantic Movement: a selective and critical bibliog." *ELH* March, 1940; F. Baldensperger, "Romantique, ses analogues et équivalents," *Harvard Studies and Notes in Philol. and Lit.* XIV, 1937; I. Babbitt, *The New Laokoön,* 1910; *Rousseau and Romanticism,* 1919; F. L. Lucas, *The Decline and Fall of the Romantic Ideal,* 1936; George Boas, *Romanticism in Am.,* 1940; P. L. Thorslev, *The Byronic Hero,* 1960; H. A. Beers, *Hist. of Eng. Romanticism in the 18th C.,* 1899, 1966; *Hist. of Eng. Romanticism in the 19th C.,* 1901, 1966; P. Courthion, *Romanticism,* 1961; G. Cottier, *Du romantisme au Marxisme,* 1961; M. Peckham, *Beyond the Tragic Vision,* 1962; L. Abercrombie, *Romanticism,* 1926, 1963; N. Frye, *Romanticism Reconsidered,* 1963; A. Rodway, *The Romantic Conflict,* 1963; P. Hodgart, ed. *Romantic Perspectives,* 1964; I. Fletcher, *Romantic Mythologies,* 1967; A. Thorlby, *The Romantic Movement,*

1967; J. P. Houston, *The Demonic Imagination* (Fr. Romantic poetry), 1969. HAROLD M. MARCH.

rondeau. OFr. form: 15 lines (of usually 8 syllables each) in 3 stanzas; the opening words of the poem become the refrain: rhymed *aabba, aabC, aabbaC*. A frequent light verse form. *Cf.* Ballade; Virelais.

rondeau redoublé. A quatrain, followed by four more, each using a successive line of the first as its own last line; followed by one more that ends (sometimes as an extra line, unrhymed) with the opening words of the poem. The whole poem uses two rhymes only.

rondel. Usually 13 lines in 3 stanzas, rhymed *aBba, abAB, abbaA* (the capitals indicate repeated lines; sometimes *B* is repeated as a 14th).

rondelet. Usually 7 lines in one stanza, *abCabbC;* the refrain may be the first words of the poem.

roundel. Poem in 11 lines (varying in length in different poems, 4 to 16 syllables), *abaC, bab, abaC*. The refrain, which repeats the first words of the poem, may rhyme as B, *e.g.* (stanza 1):

A roundel is wrought as a ring or a star-bright sphere,
With craft of delight and cunning of sound unsought,
That the heart of the hearer may smile if to pleasure his ear
A roundel is wrought.

Swinburne wrote *A Century of Roundels.*

roundelay. 1. A simple song, with refrain, such as was danced to in medieval times. 2. Any of the fixed forms with frequent word repetition or refrain, as the rondeau or the villanelle.

roundlet. A shortened roundel.

rubáiyát (pl. of rubai, Arab., quatrain). Popularized in Eng. through the Edward Fitzgerald trans. (1859, 1868) of the *Rubáiyát* of Omar Khayyám (d. 1123). *See* Arabic poetry.

rule. The formulation as a precept of a principle supposedly derived from nature. Classical theory balances natural endowment (*ingenium*) with training in the rules (*ars*). Horace and Longinus pardon minor violations of rule, as poetic license, in otherwise great works. Pope, in his *Essay On Criticism* (1711) makes similar allowance:

If, where the rules not far enough extend
(Since rules are made but to promote their end),
Some lucky license answer to the full
Th' intent proposed, that license is a rule . . .
Great wits may sometimes gloriously offend,
And rise to faults true critics dare not mend;
From vulgar bonds with brave disorder part
And snatch a grace beyond the reach of art.

Increasingly since the romantics, rules have been considered irrelevant, if not impertinent. *Cf.* Grace; Correctness; Standard; Spontaneity; Surrealism. F. Gallaway, *Reason, Rule, and Revolt in Eng. Classicism,* 1940.

rune. 1. A letter of the alphabet of the early Scandinavians and Anglo-Saxons; specif., as a magic charm. 2. A Finnish poem; esp. one of the songs of the *Kalevala* (medieval epic, pub. 1822). Ancient Scandinavian poems are sometimes called runic poems.

running rhythm. The common Eng. rhythm, measured by feet of 2 or 3 syllables (falling, if the stress first; rising, if the stress last; rocking, if the stress is between two slacks). Opp. by G. M. Hopkins to sprung rhythm, *q.v. Cf.* Rhythm; Meter.

run-on. Of a line of verse that flows without pause in rhythm or sense into the line that follows. Opp. end-stopped. Also called enjambment; *cf.* Rejet.

rupaka. In Indian literature, a metaphor in which two different things are assimilated, *e.g.,* Love, the hunter. Hence, in the drama, an actor's impersonation of a character. *Cf.* Indian literary theory.

S

SABER. *Prov.* Originally, wisdom; then, poetic talent or skill. *Gai saber, gaia sciensa,* in the early 14th c.: the art of the troubadour as codified in the Toulousian treatise *Leys d'amors,* which influenced the poetry of Sp. and Catalonia, where these terms lingered.

sadism. Sexual satisfaction and excitement from inflicting pain or humiliation. *See* Pornography.

saga, the Icelandic, was born in exile and loneliness and pride. During the 50 years after 874 A.D., Iceland was settled by violent and aristocratic men fleeing the attempt of Harold Fairhair to unify Norway by breaking the power of the nobles. On the isolated farmsteads of their descendants, in the long winter evenings, there was created an epic literature in prose, at once an entertainment, a history, and an *Almanac de Gotha.*

The word "saga" means simply something said; until the 12th c. the sagas were oral, memorized to be recited at the fireside and the *Thing.* But Christianity, come to Iceland in the year 1000, had gradually spread knowledge of a written literature in L. To the Icelander, whose runic characters were used chiefly for magical purposes, the idea of writing down his stories seemed strange, and by the time he was ready to begin that practice, the style and idiom of the genre had been set.

During those years of oral transmission, the form had developed its distinctive charm. Saga prose style stands apart from all other vernacular styles of the Middle Ages, in freedom from L. influence, in terseness and colloquial simplicity. It is, of course, anonymous, and it tends towards complete impersonality; which, with a conscious understatement, and a presentation of psychological states only by external gesture, creates the peculiar reticence of saga sytle, making the more terrible the impact of the implicit violence and passion.

There are 3 styles of saga. The earliest was the Family Saga, with its accounts of the individual exploits and continued feuds of the old Icelandic families, loosely bound together by the blood relationships of the protagonists. The Historical Sagas turn back to the homeland of their exiled authors, and because of their Norw. subject matter were once considered earliest. The Lying Saga, purely fictional, came latest, as the Icelander slowly realised that prose can be used for more than fact; it did not reach full development until Icelandic culture had begun to decay.

With the loss of Iceland's independence, mid 13th c., the creative impulse declined. The fierce individualism and the pride of blood that inform the sagas could not survive the freedom that produced them. As the Icelandic writers turned more to fictional subjects, so also they turned to foreign models. They had never been entirely immune to outside influence; the 12th c. Renaissance, spreading from Fr., had helped bring the written saga to full flower, and Celtic influences had been felt from the first; but only with the decline of their own civilization did they come to depend upon foreign sources. More and more exclusively the Icelandic artist turned to trans. Fr. Romance, as the values of the heroic age, the love of vengeance, the ironic gesture in the face of death, gave way to imported codes of chivalry. The age of the saga was past. *Cf.* Folktale; Epic. A. W. Craigie, *The Icelandic Sagas,* 1913; E. V. Gordon, *An Introd. to Old Norse,* 1927; W. P. Ker, *Epic and Romance,* 1908; H. Koht, *The Old Norse Sagas,* 1931. LESLIE FIEDLER.

Sanskrit. *See* Indian.

sapphic meter. A strophe of 4 verses, the first three of the pattern — ∪ — ⊻ — ∪ ∪ — ∪ — ⊻, while the last is an adonius, — ∪ ∪ — ⊻ (Sappho; Alcaeus, early 6th c. B.C.). In Horace the 4th syllable is always long, and the 5th usually ends a word, making the caesura. Used in Eng. by Swinburne; Ezra Pound; in G. (trans. Horace) by Voss. *Cf.* Adonic.

sarcasm. (L. or Gr. "to tear flesh.") A cutting remark; a verbal sneer. Sarcasm pretends to disguise its meaning, but does not intend to be misunderstood. Satire makes no pretense. Irony blandly affects directness, without veiled intention; it works so that the person being "ironed out" is hardly aware of the fact. The receptor should grasp the ironic intention; that he does not always do so is shown by the Irish wrath at Swift's *Modest Proposal* that the poor Irish raise their children to be eaten at the English tables. *See* Irony III.

satire [L. *satira*<*satura,* the "stuffing" of a roast. (*Cf.* Farce).] The etymology is traced to a hypothetical (*lanx*) *satura,* a full dish, a platter of mixed fruits as an offering to a rural god. The root sense of mixture or medley, of farrago or apparent disorder, still helps quicken the meaning of the word today. Roman critics extended the definition of *satura* by exploiting the Greek *saturos* (satyr), so that modern Eng. *satirize* and *satirical* stem from the Greek. In Renaissance Eng. *satire* was held to derive from the ancient satyr plays, with their rough language and pranks; the false etymology was both reflected in and aided by the Ren. spelling *satyr* or *satyre.* Since John Dryden's *Discourse On the Original and Progress of Satire* of 1693, there have been no serious attempts to define the term until this century, more particularly within the last generation.

Satire remains an elusive, protean term, escaping easy definition. Traditionally it has been defined in terms of technique and purpose, the emphasis falling on its moral or even reformative function. Today, scarcely any two writers on the subject agree on definition, though the emphasis seems now to be on technique or form. Yet despite all shifts in meaning from Quintilian to Northrop Frye and since, certain characteristics have remained constant: satire as attack to expose folly or vice, dullness or evil—or even to advance some amoral position (e.g., H. L. Mencken) or an immoral stance (e.g., Machiavelli)—whether by gentle rebuke or scarifying verbal onslaught, by ridicule or invective, whether direct through burlesque or indirect through irony. Satire as attack, the single most important generic trait, has traditionally implied, and still implies today, a public, extra-literary role for the form.

Satire arose out of ritual and magic. Among pre-Islamic Arabs the poet led his tribesmen into battle to hurl his satires—imprecations and curses—like so many spears at the enemy. And the pre-Christian Irish lived in fear, hatred, and awe of their poets (*filid*) who for many generations exercised power with their death-dealing ability with words. In Greek fertility rites, the leaders of the Phallic Songs broke through the festivities with occasional outbursts of invective and curses, usually directed against a particular person who stood for the evils—blight, drought, disease—being exorcised. The magical power of such abuse remained to give potency to later, nonritualistic curses.

It is this potency that attaches to the first satirist known by name, Archilochus (7th c. B.C.). According to legend, when his intended bride Neobule and her father Lycambes refused to honor the marriage contract, Archilochus publicly shamed them by his angry invective and drove them to hang themselves. This killing power, this black magical force of words, has remained potent among some present-day primitive cultures. And even in the Western world one recognizes the power of satire in such phrases as "to murder a reputation" or "to rhyme someone to death." American school children continue to chant the refrain

Sticks and stones may break my bones
But names will never hurt me

precisely because it deflects, or is intended to deflect, the satiric shafts of the "hard-attacker." Two recent Eng. satirists, novelist Wyndham Lewis and poet Roy Campbell, sought to instruct a truculent and nasty authoritarianism in satire as "magic," as "curse and malediction."

In Greece, some time between Archilochus and the 5th c. B.C. comic playwright Aristophanes, satire shed its magical powers to develop as an art form. The formal satires, however, were composed in Latin. Lucilius (d. 103 B.C.) created the specific kind of satire since called formal verse satire, *satura,* or Lucilian satire: a long poem (as distinct from an epigram), usually with dialogue in hexameters between a first-person narrator and an *adversarius,* a frame device, and an underlying design of attack on vice and praise of opposing virtue, with the emphasis on attack. Horace (d. 8 B.C.), Persius (d. 62 A.D.), and Juvenal (d. ca. 140 A.D.)

worked within the Lucilian pattern to establish the type of verse satire of which Quintilian (d. 95 A.D.) was the ablest critical expositor. It is to this type that Quintilian referred when he said *"Satura . . . tota nostra est"*—satire is wholly ours. The Augustan poet Horace chose a plain and familiar style, ridiculed rather than excoriated his victims, and established the socially (as distinct from the morally) corrective function of satire. In his turn, Juvenal adopted the stance of satirist as upright, commonsensical man, essentially conventional in his moral posture, driven to frenzy by the degeneracy of his times. His darkly pessimistic view of life—the source of his satiric style with its invective at once ample, luxuriant, and grand—he laced with a stoicism that the very heat of his anger belied. Horace set the model for a genial and general satire, whereas Juvenal became the standard of satirical severity. Just as these two different modes of satire carried over into Renaissance critical theory, so did Lucilian satire form for centuries one of the two species of the genre.

The other species, Menippean satire (or Varronian satire), originated with the Greek cynic Menippus (3rd c. B.C.), whose satires, long lost, apparently mixed various forms of verse or prose and poetry. He is known to us almost wholly through Lucian, his admirer and imitator, and through the *Saturae Menippeae* of Marcus Terentius Varro (1st c. B.C.), of which only fragments survive. Quintilian, describing the characteristics of Menippean satire as the blend of prose and verse, colloquialism, and parodies of the grand style, was the only one before Northrop Frye to attempt to fix its formal qualities. (Dryden defined it so loosely as to put forward his own verse *Absalom and Achitophel* and Spenser's *Mother Hubbard's Tale* as examples of the species.) Frye replaces the term *Menippean satire* by the word *anatomy,* taken from Robert Burton's *Anatomy of Melancholy* (1621), and defines it as "a form of prose fiction . . . characterized by a greater variety of subject-matter and a strong interest in ideas. In shorter forms it often has a *cena* or symposium setting and verse interludes." More important in Frye's view than its prose medium is its matter, in that it "deals less with people as such than with mental attitudes." In its exposure of man's occupational approach to life, it uses stylized characters as mouthpieces for abstract ideas presented in a loosely-hung narrative whose pattern results from the free play of the intellectual fancy. Menippean satire is seen to have several sub-species: pure fantasy (e.g., *Alice in Wonderland*); all moral vision (e.g., William Morris's *News From Nowhere*); a dialogue or colloquy or an encyclopedic farrago (e.g., *Anatomy of Melancholy*). Works in this tradition range from *The Satyricon* of Petronius Arbiter and *The Golden Ass* of Apuleius, through Boethius' *Consolation of Philosophy,* Erasmus's *The Praise of Folly,* Rabelais' *Gargantua and Pantagruel,* and Swift's *Gulliver's Travels,* to Samuel Butler's *Erewhon* and Aldous Huxley's *Brave New World.* Yet other contemporary critics (e.g., Alvin Kernan) do not restrict Menippean satire to prose fiction, defining it as "any satiric work obviously written in the third person, or . . . where the attack is managed under cover of a fable"—a definition admitting whole poems (e.g., *Don Juan*), as well as works entirely in prose. The term *Menippean satire* or *anatomy,* it has been suggested, should be reserved for prose works, and *Varronian satire* used for those in verse (conventionally termed burlesque poetry; e.g., Dryden's *MacFlecknoe*).

In the middle ages there was no lack of indigenous satire, whether in prose or verse. Twelfth and 13th-c. goliards mocked the princes of the Church in lyric parodies—while François Villon mocked everyone—and sang the joys of a zestful life to upset the proper clergy. Beast-fables, such as *Reynard the Fox* and the foolish fowls of Chaucer's "Nun's Priest's Tale," and the bourgeois *fabliaux* displayed social criticism in earthy, realistic, often crudely sexual terms. Beneficed clergy and friars delivered countless sermons holding up the Eternal Woman as main object of scorn and abhorrence. Vision literature, too, was surcharged with the satirist's intent; and William Langland's *Vision concerning Piers the Plowman,* commencing with a dream of a field full of folk, an image some critics consider the typical "satiric scene," progresses to an encompassing examen of the ways of medieval man. The medieval sermon, it has been claimed, actually served as seed-bed for Eng. satire.

Beginning with the Renaissance, all types of satire written in most European languages have poured from the presses. First of the verse-satirists in Eng.—for this we have his own word—was Joseph Hall who in his *Virgidemiarum* (1597, 1598) flailed at his victims in what he thought was the Juvenalian manner of rough verse, rough language, darksome meaning. Notable for their satires among his contemporaries were John Marston and, somewhat later, the better poet John Donne. In Italy, there were Lodovico Ariosto (1474–1533) and Pietro Aretino (1492–1556), self-styled "scourge of princes." In Clément Marot (1496–1544) France had an early satirist, against whose *coq à l'âne* tales members of a later group of poets, the Pléiade (esp. Ronsard and Joachim du Bellay) reacted with more polished satires of their own. But it is the names of Marthurin Regnier (*Satires,* 1608–09), Nicolas Boileau-Despréaux (esp. the period 1660–1669), and Voltaire that represent the evolution of satire in the history of French classical literature.

Another established vehicle for caustic criticism of humanity was the mock-heroic (or mock-epic) narrative poem, a form of burlesque (e.g., Alessandro Tassoni, *La Secchia Rapita*; Boileau, *Le Lutrin*). In Eng., the pattern for mock-heroic treatment of the small behavior of great folk is Pope's *The Rape of the Lock,* but the true masterpiece of epic burlesque is Butler's *Hudibras* (1662, 1663). Among Am. poems of satirical intent, the most notable is James Russell Lowell's *Fable for Critics* (1848). (It is these mock-epics and the like that come under the rubric of Menippean or Varronian satire.) The tradition of dramatic burlesque can be traced all the way from Aristophanes' *Frogs* through the commedia dell' arte down to the Ziegfeld *Follies* and *Pins and Needles.* Dramas by master playwrights (Ben Jonson, Molière, Shaw, O'Neill, Brecht) have been heavy with satire, and the theater of the absurd now attacks man's comfortable illusions about self and inner self, self and universe, to lay bare the grim joke that is his life.

The most significant satirical writings of modern times, however, have been in the guise of prose fiction—the Menippean satire. Lucian's witty subtlety as revealed in his dialogues and above all in his *True History* set a precedent for Erasmus and other humanists impatient with humanity. Among such skeptics of romance Cervantes occupies high, if not highest, place. The element of mockery of weak and wicked humanity is found in varying degrees in the best novels of Fielding, Thackeray, Anatole France, Stephen Crane, Sinclair Lewis, Evelyn Waugh, Günter Grass, William Golding, and on and on; the list of names is legion. Indeed, the names of satirists in verse and prose appear thick as crab apples in studies of the genre. Literary satire ranges in time and space across the world, from the *Bible* to the U.S.S.R.'s humor magazine *Krokodil*; from Fu Hsuan to Sp. satirist Quevedo (1580–1645).

Coursing through the chronological development of satire generally, and Eng. satire specifically, has been an evolutionary change in satiric approach from the direct to the indirect, from invective to irony. What may be described as the four ages of satire—or the four seasons, to imitate Frye—are invective, burlesque (first low and then high), comic irony, and tragic irony including the cosmic. We live in an age of an all-corrosive irony, when to the statement that "God is dead," the absurdists reply, "When did he live?" Ours is an age in which form has subsumed meaning—a process begun not by critics of satire, but by the satirists themselves.

Though 17th and very early 18th-c. Eng. verse satire preferred the Juvenalian mode and Pope and his followers opted in theory for Horace, these Eng. writers (and their counterparts in France and Italy) were united in declaring for the moral, even the socially reformative, function of satire. But such writers as Juvenal himself and Dryden, Pope, and Swift really knew better. They were charged with being foul-minded or obscene, misanthropic or proud; and against such charges they had nothing for it but to declare themselves doers of good, reformers. Critics have come increasingly to view such protestations as dodges, as tubs tossed out to divert their detractors. Ever since Byron's *Don Juan*—and the distance can be measured from his earlier *English Bards and Scotch Reviewers*—Eng. satire (and satire as a whole) has moved far from what has traditionally purported to be its role. While sentimentalists antipathetic to satire still decry its savaging, its destructive enterprise, only recently have critics come around to questioning, if not denying, that it relies at all on moral norms or on ameliorative intent. Even if the writer seek *ridens dicere verum,* joking in earnest, the reader is likely to be less indignant than amused.

Others, to be sure, still suggest that satire always contains an implicit or a fragmented moral which the reader must work to obtain, or that it evokes a "satiric emotion" (*e.g.,* Highet: amusement plus contempt or hatred; Patricia Meyer Spacks: uneasiness versus complacency) in the reader causing him to act, if only within himself. Yet Highet, who finds (in addition to the "satiric emotion") two elements characteristic of satire—the author's statement of his purpose, and the specific diction and literary devices associated with it—emphasizes in his analysis the formal aspects of satire. Satire, he discovers, is trichotomous: consisting of parodies, non-parodic monologues, and non-parodic fiction (dramatic and narrative). Frye, who also refers explicitly to the moral intent of satire, in effect resolves the moral vision into a function of technique. Satire forms, according to Frye, one of the four great myths (of comedy, romance, tragedy, and irony-satire) that like the seasons unfold in some sort of cyclical pattern, an ever-recurring dance of life mythologized by literary kinds in which satire-irony corresponds to winter. In his anatomy of the genre, he finds that it contains six phases (the last three of which are of irony and thus impinge upon tragedy), the first three: satire of low norm; intellectual satire, the quixotic phase; and satire of the high norm. In the first of these, an *eiron* (a self-deprecating, commonsensical man, *e.g.* Chaucer in his *Canterbury Tales*) confronts a mighty *alazon* (an impostor) in a world of follies and crimes against which the *eiron* appeals to conventional wisdom and morality. The second phase sets theoretical views, ideas, dogmas about life over against the actuality of life they pretend to explain, and as in *Don Quixote* reduces theory to absurdity. Satire of the high norm is the most subversive of the three; it inverts the normal, commonsense perspective (appealed to by satire of the low norm) and achieves the ridiculous by all manner of violent devices—the obscene, the sadistic, the revolting, and the ugly. Alvin B. Kernan in his book, *The Cankered Muse,* is equally concerned with satire as technique and equally committed to a view of satire as essentially unchanging. He analyzes the essence of satire as composed of three parts: "the satiric scene," the satirist in his public personality or persona and his private role, and the plot of satire. Density, disorder, grossness, decay, and "a hint of an ideal" characterize the satiric scene, peopled by masses of dullards and sinners, by "dense knots of ugly flesh."

The satirist (within the work) ranges from a speaking voice to a name and distinct personality (as Colin Clout or Lemuel Gulliver), who usually becomes the satirist satirized, and fades away to let the fools and villains expose one another (*e.g., The Birds*). It is dullness (as in Pope's *Dunciad*) that the satirist attacks, and the plot of satire erupts out of the conflict between dullness and the reality opposing it. Everything works by threes: dullness acts by degrading or diminishing, by self-inflating or magnifying, by jumbling or the mob tendency. And the plot of satire dramatizes the conflict in three corresponding ways: by scrambling everything and nothing (*e.g., The Dunciad*), by rising and falling (*e.g., Volpone*), and by running in circles (*e.g.,* Waugh's early novels). Incongruity, exaggeration (invective, *reductio ad absurdum,* caricature), understatement, contrast, disparaging comparison, and irony are among the major weapons in the attack of the satirist.

There is, then, a "satiric view of life," just as there are a comic view and a tragic one, that inhere in the condition of life as it is. The world as recreated in satire takes different forms. There is the madhouse world of Grass's *The Tin Drum* and of *Dr. Strangelove,* of Kafka, Ionesco, and Beckett, of *The Madwoman of Chaillot* and of *Alice in Wonderland.* Or there may be a puppet-show world, which as in Swift's "Mechanical Operation of the Spirit," Karel Čapek's *R.U.R.,* or O'Neill's *Hairy Ape* is peopled by automata. The world of satire may also be made up of a mob of fools and rascals (*e.g.,* the plays of Plautus or Molière; the fiction of Smollett or Joyce Cary; the poetry of Rochester or Burns). It may be a menagerie, as in Æsop, Joel Chandler Harris, Saki, or Orwell's *Animal Farm*; a pseudo-utopia, as Zamiatin's *We* or Stephen Leacock's *Afternoons in Utopia.*

Yet whatever the world of satire, it criticizes, unmasks, subverts the world we know. Satire attacks because man is, or at least some men are, engaged in a ceaseless battle against evil or dullness or (Frye) against some "form of romanticism or the imposing of over-simplified ideals on experience." Man may not win, but he must go on fighting: in the fight is life. Thus from mockery to despair—and by the very battle proving hope—directly or indirectly satire wages war against Chaos, the mighty Anarch. Its effect on the rest of us? We laugh. *Cf.* Sarcasm; Irony; Fiction; Narrator; Triad. D. Worcester, *The Art of Satire,* 1940, 1969; R. C. Elliott, *The Power of Satire,* 1960; L. Feinberg, *The Satirist,* 1963; *Introd. to Satire,* 1967; N. Frye, *Anatomy of Criticism,* 1957; Ian Jack, *Augustan Satire,* 1952, 1966;

Alvin B. Kernan, *The Cankered Muse,* 1959; *The Plot of Satire,* 1965; Ellen D. Leyburn, *Satiric Allegory,* 1956; G. Highet, *The Anatomy of Satire,* 1962; E. M. Rosenheim, Jr., *Swift and the Satirist's Art,* 1963; Sheldon Sacks, *Fiction and the Shape of Belief,* 1964; issues of *The Satire Newsletter,* 1963—; James Sutherland, *Eng. Satire,* 1958; W. O. S. Sutherland, *The Art of the Satirist,* 1965; Patricia Meyer Spacks, in *Genre* I, 1; R. Paulson, *The Fictions of Satire,* 1967; *Satire and the Novel in 18th C. Eng.,* 1967; anthologies: Edgar Johnson, ed. *A Treasury of Satire,* 1945; C E. Vulliamy, ed. *The Anatomy of Satire,* 1950; J. Russell and A. Brown, eds. *Satire: A Critical Anthology,* 1967. JOHN BURKE SHIPLEY.

Saturnian verse. An archaic L. verse, employed chiefly by Livius Andronicus and Nævius. A strong break (diaeresis) occurs in the middle, and alliteration is more frequent than in other classical forms. Some scholars maintain that Saturnians, prior to Greek influence, are to be scanned not by quantity but by accent. Lindsay, *Early L. Verse,* 1922.

satyr play. The earliest Greek drama was usually presented as a tetralogy: a trilogy of serious plays—a tragic story working toward its resolution in a final illumination or reconciliation—followed by a satyr play, a burlesque of the tragic theme, with a chorus of satyrs. The satyr, mixture of god and goat, gave the ribald tone to this mockery of the serious dramas; its sexual reveling led the way to the Old Comedy of Aristophanes. The one extant satyr play is Euripides' *Cyclops,* which draws its fun from the episode of Odysseus and the Cyclops Polyphemus, and with wordplay and horseplay makes light of the serious story. Thus comedy is both offspring of and commentary on the tragic outlook, reducing it from its high seriousness to a more realistic or riotous fronting of human values. *Cf.* Tragedy; Comedy; Burlesque; Farce.

Savoyard. Originally, natives of Savoy, in France near the Lake of Geneva, were well known in the 18th c. as itinerant musicians with hurdy-gurdy and monkey. Also, the Savoy Palace in London was a sanctuary for criminals until the right was abolished in 1679. Today, a Savoyard is one connected with or enthusiastic about the Gilbert and Sullivan operas, for which D'Oyly Carte in 1881 built the Savoy Theatre in London, opening with *Patience* transferred from the old Opéra Comique. *Cf.* Operetta; Patter song.

scansion. The act or system of analyzing the form of a verse or a poem; describing the organization of a poem in lines, feet, syllables, or dividing it into these units; or the method and symbols employed for such an indication. Each letter represents a line; for each recurrence of a rhyme the same letter is used, unrhymed lines being indicated by *x;* if there is no other statement of line-length, the number of feet (or, if made clear in the context, syllables) is indicated by a subscript numeral at the last line (last line for each length, if the lines vary), *e.g.,* the Rubaiyat quatrain is $a\ a\ x\ a_5$. A refrain (repetition of a whole word, phrase, or line) is indicated by a capital. Rarely, numbers are used, instead of letters, to indicate the rhyme-scheme. For the details within a line, — or ′ marks a long or accented syllable, ∪, sometimes ^{0}, a short or unstressed one. The feet may be separated |, cæsura indicated by || or /. Thus, in the lines:

Thy voice from inmost dreamland calls;
The wastes of sleep thou makest fair;
Bright o'er the ridge of darkness falls
The cataract of thy hair.

The sun renews its golden birth;
Thou with the vanquished night doth fade;
And leav'st the ponderable earth
Less real than thy shade.

the general pattern is $a\ b\ a_4\ b_3$. A stanza is scanned by either of two principles: (a) Some indicate the metrical scheme strictly, in which case every foot of stanza 1 above is an iamb save for the 2d in line 4, an anapest ∪ ∪ —. Over this basic metrical regularity are felt the normal stresses of the words as their sense and the feelings conjoin them. (b) Others attempt to scan the lines in feet as determined by the interaction of the basic metrical pattern and the sense-and-feeling flow. As the latter is subjective, there is considerable dispute as to the scansion of many passages in well-known poems. One pattern for the first stanza above would be:

∪ ′ ∪ ′ ∪ ′ ∪ ′
∪ ′ ∪ ′ ∪ ′ ∪ ′
′ ∪ ∪ ′ ∪ ′ ∪ ′
∪ ′ ∪∪ ′ ∪ ′

The last line, because of the heavy stress on "falls," might also be scanned: ∪ ∪ ∪ ′ ∪ ∪ ′. *See* Meter; Rhythm.

scazon. *See* Choliamb.

scholasticism (L. *doctores scholastici,* the teachers of the liberal arts in the medieval schools; later, the teachers of philosophy and theology). During the Renaissance, the whole medieval period was dismissed with the contemptuous term "scholastic." Scholasticism now designates in a vague way the philosophical and theological thought of the middle ages. Within that time, however, the Aristotelian logic had been brought (Scotus Erigena; St. Thomas Aquinas) into harmony with Christian theology; the chief works are commentaries on "the philosopher." There was, moreover, a remarkable agreement on fundamental principles, a universal assurance that truth was attainable, an attitude of respect for divine revelation; there was at the same time no smothering of individuality and freedom of thought within the limits of a faith that had been freely accepted. Those who bear the name scholastic (or neo-scholastic) today see in the fundamental principles of medieval thought valid truths that can be applied to our own problems, including those of literature and criticism. M. Grabmann, *Geschichte der scholastichen Method,* 1909; M. de Wulf, *Scholasticism Old and New,* 1910; F. Pelster and A. C. Little, *Oxford Theology and Theologians* (Pref.), 1934; L. Wencelius, *La philosophie de l'art chez les néo-scolastiques de langue fr.,* 1932.

science and literature. C. P. Snow has recently (*The Two Cultures,* 1959, 1964) restated the old opposition of intellect and imagination, as producing respectively science and the humanities, each now so expanded that he fears their mutual exclusion. More frequently they are seen as two applications of the same elements in man's nature, as artist, inventor, and scientist all use, in the pursuit of their several goals, imagination tempered by reason. R. E. Mueller considers both fields as "communication phenomena": science uses structured communication to describe the reality of nature; art, to create a new reality. Mueller finds four main ways in which science and technology may influence art: by providing (1) new or altered media, as motion pictures, television, electronic musical instruments; (2) new subjects, as the microscopic world and outer space; or new points of view, as evolution, the Freudian postulates; (3) new ways of communicating, as by telephone, satellites, magnetic tape; and the new devices of staging; and (4) increased understanding, as through psychology and techniques of criticism. One might add new printing methods, as microfilm, coded tape; visiophone and other electronic processes, to which Mueller refers in a footnote. The advances of science also require new words, as laser, quasar, which poets and other writers may draw to their various ends. *See* Cultures, the two; *cf.* Apollonian; Romanticism; Classicism; Literature and society. H. Brown, ed. *Science and the Creative Spirit,* 1958; R. E. Mueller, *The Science of Art,* 1967.

science fiction (SF) is that branch of literature which deals with the response of human beings to advances in science and technology. More broadly, it can be a tale set against any fanciful background (however implausible or even impossible) that is widely different from any existing in the past or present. Thus, in the broad sense, Tolkien's popular *Ring* series is science fiction.

At its broadest, science fiction is as old as literature, for tales of ghosts, demons, and other manifestations not subject to human sense-perception are a primitive analogy. The earliest well-known work of intentional science fiction is *True History,* by Lucian of Samosata (ca. 150 A.D.). Lucian's hero visits the sun and the moon, and takes part in interplanetary warfare. In the 17th c., Cyrano de Bergerac also wrote stories of the "states and empires" of the sun and the moon.

In its narrow sense, however, science fiction could not serve a function until men came to realize that there is a continuous change in the state of science and technology, which is bound to affect human life and elicit new human responses. Prior to such a realization, science fiction was merely fantasy intended to entertain or moralize. In the 19th c. the rate of change in technology grew rapid enough to force itself upon the general attention, and real science fiction began to be written. Edgar Allan Poe is frequently referred to as the first science fiction writer as well as the first mystery writer. Science fiction grew popular with the stories of Jules Verne (1828–1905), which were at once highly romantic and filled with respect for science. He was the first writer to make science fiction the major part of his output, rivalled in popularity only by H. G. Wells (1866–1946).

These were exceptions. Science fiction lacked a popular base for writers until, in

1926, Hugo Gernsback introduced *Amazing Stories,* the first magazine devoted entirely to science fiction. Other magazines followed; aspiring science fiction writers had a market toward which they could aim, and within which they could experiment. Much of the magazine science fiction through the 1930's was written in the style of the Gothic novel. *Frankenstein* (1818) was the prototype: scientific advance was dangerous, and scientists were often mad. Another variety closely resembled the ordinary adventure story, thinly plastered over with futurism. The spaceship and disintegrator gun took the place of the horse and revolver, but much of the "Western" aura remained. Tales of this sort were known as "space opera," after the Western "horse opera."

In 1938 John W. Campbell, becoming editor of *Astounding Stories,* encouraged a return to the principles of Verne and Wells, placing emphasis on the scientific content, and demanding that his writers have some knowledge of science and scientists. Full-length books, also, were written by men with scientific backgrounds, such as Arthur C. Clarke and Isaac Asimov. Science fiction had earlier entered the theatre, notably in Karel Čapek's *R.U.R.* (1921; Russum's Universal Robots), which pictured robots wiping out mankind, and gave our language its word for a manlike automaton. The emphasis on *science* fiction ("scientifiction") marked the beginning of the "Golden Age" of the early 1940's. This plausibility and scientific realism led to emphasis on the nature of the society built in response to the scientific advances. A new form of science fiction became common ("social science fiction"); in this, not the characters in the foreground but the society in the background is important. This form expanded into the 1950's. Magazines increased. *Astounding* (its name changed to *Analog*) remained pre-eminent, but two others in particular, *Galaxy* and *Fantasy and Science Fiction,* printed much good work.

Because the authors of the Golden Age tried to view the future realistically, it is not surprising that in many ways they foresaw what actually came to pass. Nuclear weapons, rocketry, moon-trips, robots, computers, all passed from the science fiction pages to the newspaper front page. The most significant consequence of Campbell's work is that the real world of the 1960's is much like the science fiction world of the 1940's. As technology advances, obsolete techniques, becoming laughable, may take their books with them into oblivion.

As a result, the style of the 1940's is passé. To write level-headed plausible science fiction is still possible, but risks competition with reality, and may give the reader a non-science-fiction feeling. Therefore seeking new paths, science fiction has turned toward the murkier corners of knowledge as yet untouched by hard-and-fast scientific advance, to stories involving extra-sensory perception and other "wild talents" as well as controversial subjects such as flying saucers and magic. Another tendency takes advantage of the greater freedom now allowed the exploration of hitherto taboo subjects. Since World War II, the readership has grown older, partly because individual fans have aged and partly because adults are now attracted to a field which scientific advance has freed of the stigma of being "crackpot." The sex content of science fiction can therefore now be high indeed, and sometimes is. Science fiction is thus broadening into a new form of social commentary, which makes free use of all the experimental writing styles that have developed in literature generally.

In the 1920's and 1930's science fiction dealt primarily with the exploits of the individual or adventurer, often in battle for the existence of mankind against inimical inhabitants of other worlds, and the background was dimly seen. In the 1940's and 1950's, it dealt chiefly with the scientific aspect of the background, with the foreground serving only as the immediate excuse for the story. In the 1960's, it deals with all aspects of the background, with the total society of the future; the scientific content merely accounts for differences in detail from our own day. It may be that science fiction, as such, is therefore dying; or, rather, that all fiction is becoming science fiction. As scientific advance becomes more rapid, as it fills life more completely, it will be difficult to write any significant work of fiction set in the present that does not take science into its account. Thus, while the earlier sorts survive in magazines and TV serials, the best science fiction and the best general fiction tend to merge. *Cf.* Literature and society; Imagination; Fiction; Novel; Short story. R. J. Healy and J. F. McComas, *Adventures in Time and Space,* 1946; L. Sprague de Camp, *Science Fiction Handbook,* 1953; R. Bretnor, *Modern Science Fiction,* 1953; Isaac Asimov, *The Hugo Winners,* 1962; Sam Moskowitz, *Explorers of the Infinite,*

1963; *Seekers of Tomorrow,* 1967; A. Rogers, *A Requiem for "Astounding",* 1964; H. Ellison, *Dangerous Visions,* 1967; H. B. Franklin, *Future Perfect,* 1966; Kingsley Amis, *New Maps of Hell,* 1967; D. F. Knight, *100 Years of Science Fiction,* 1968. Isaac Asimov.

scientific method in criticism. The question whether there is or can be a scientific method for criticism is at least as old as Plato's *Ion* (532 C). Explicit discussion of it has naturally increased since the general scientific advances and conscious refinements of method in recent centuries, but a scientific ideal for the theory and a generally scientific procedure in the practise of criticism did not, of course, have to await the development of modern science. In later antiquity both were well established if not universally agreed upon in detail, and admirable progress was made (most notably by Aristotle) in scientific investigation of literary phenomena. The attempt of medieval teachers to retain the ancient knowledge, and their efforts and those of Renaissance scholars to recover what had been lost or obscured in it, were largely frustrated by historical ignorances; and though some significant developments occurred in the Middle Ages and the Renaissance, it is fair to say that in those periods, and generally during that of classicism which they prepared and determined, there was less appropriation of the permanently valid general method of the ancients than of its temporally conditioned particular results. So in 1751 Dr. Johnson (*Ramb.* 158) wrote, "Criticism . . . has not yet attained the certainty and stability of a science." For "certainty and stability" in criticism Johnson seems to have had a desire perhaps in excess of the temperate demands of a truly scientific spirit. The romantics were more moderate in this respect, but the critical part of their reaction too was a drive, however misdirected, toward surer knowledge and sounder method; and one of the directions in which the criticism (like the literature itself) of the later 19th c. turned to recover the objectivity it had lost was that of the developing natural sciences. Fr. criticism, the most influential of the period, was indeed then as a whole simply a succession of attempts to apply to literature formulas supplied by contemporary science, and includes more discussion of the possibilities and requisites of scientific method in criticism than we have from any other period or place. Into our own time such discussion has continued; but though one young critic (Bronowski, *The Poet's Defence,* 1939) can declare, "I have tried to write criticism as reasoned as geometry," it is the "considered opinion" of another (C. Brooks, *Kenyon R.* II) that literary studies in general "will have to forego the pleasures of being 'scientific.' " We can hardly say that the question of Plato's Socrates has been finally answered.

Its answer will depend, of course, upon the definition given its terms. Science may be defined as systematized conceptual knowledge that is directly or indirectly verifiable; all questions of its method are questions of the means proper in a given case to the attainment and verification and systematization of conceptual knowledge, or to its communication. If criticism is conceived as response to a work of art simply, the adventure of a soul among masterpieces (A. France, *La Vie lit.,* I, 1888, Pref.; *cf.* Santayana, "Enjoyment, which some people call criticism"), it can hardly be scientific, for the operation of the critic is then wholly or principally affective-volitional (or "affective-motor"), whereas science is as such wholly cognitive. It is now generally agreed that this view of criticism, which fails to distinguish it from ordinary reading, is wrong; for such simplification is in practise impossible, and approximation to it produces results unsatisfactory precisely because deficient in cognitive value. Criticism is not simply affective response, however sensitive or intense. But neither is it mere cognition of the object or stimulus, however acute. Arnold's account of the "endeavor" of criticism, "to see the object as in itself it really is," though admirably (if in strict epistemology extravagantly) expressive of one primary aim of both criticism and science (which it practically identifies), is as incomplete as the impressionist's; for the critic must not only "know the best that is known and thought in the world," but be able also as far as possible to determine the meaning and validity of its claim to be best. It is not, to be sure, judgment or evaluation alone that criticism adds to the acute cognition of an object and sensitive response to it which are required of both critic and lay reader; for the lay reader also judges or evaluates. Evaluation is truly the ultimate function of criticism, one which it cannot subordinate to any other or, in a pseudo-scientific effort toward the scientific, replace by mere description; to eliminate judgment is to eliminate criticism. But critical judgment is not the direct and spontaneous evaluation in which all reading naturally culminates. It is a reflex operation by which this evaluation, or any other proposition about a literary work or process, is itself evaluated, in the light ideally of everything that can be known about it and about its occasion. (In practise the primary and the reflex operations may be concomitant, the latter controlling the former as it proceeds; the complete critical process is usually not a separate recapitulation of the normal process of reading but simply an expansion and deepening of it by addition of concurrent cognitive acts, so that when the final evaluation emerges its critique is provided with it. A given criticism, however, may and usually does involve only a part of this full process, and may evaluate not the final judgment but only prior incidental evaluations or propositions not evaluatory at all but simply descriptive or classifying.) The specifically differentiating operation of criticism is thus not evaluation but discrimination among evaluations, actual or possible, explicit or implied; *"krinein"* meant "to discriminate" before it meant "to judge." And the principle of this discrimination is cognitive; for the only criterion by which evaluations can in any sense be tested is that of relative consistency with all the relevant reality that is securely known. Criticism thus adds to lay reading a greater cognitive curiosity and more relevant knowledge and its work is to bring this knowledge methodically to bear upon judgment. But it is evidently absurd to use for discrimination means selected and applied without discrimination; the knowledge and the method used by the critic must themselves be critically evaluated by the criteria appropriate to them. This is to say that they must be scientific. Criticism is not a science, because its concern is with the particular, thing or value, whereas science is by definition concerned only with what is general; but it realizes itself and achieves its own ideal only in the degree to which it appropriates and assimilates science and scientific method. Criticism is simply the application to a particular judgment of as much science and as scientific a method as possible.

Scientific method is not attained in criticism by adopting the jargon or the formulas or data that have resulted from its application elsewhere, as those of biology were adopted by French critics (esp. Taine, Brunetière) in the 19th c. or as those of various inchoate systems of psychology or sociology have sometimes been adopted in the 20th. Nor is it the application to literature without modification of the specific method of any of the exact or natural sciences; for every science has its own method, determined by its objects, and the literary datum must determine the peculiar method by which it is to be investigated. Scientific method in criticism means simply bringing to bear upon literary judgment every item of relevant knowledge (conversely excluding from consideration everything that is not relevant knowledge) and restricting judgment to what is warranted or permitted by the sum of this relevant knowledge. The knowledge required for criticism, though all susceptible of scientific scrutiny, is not all science, for much of it is particular (of the particular data immediately concerned, and of other similar or related particulars and their relations, *i.e.,* of literary history); but a large part of it is or should be science, for continuous discourse in terms of the particular alone is impossible and the critic's determinations concerning the particular must rest upon some systematic generalized knowledge of the nature and categories of literary phenomena. The ideal of such a science or general literary theory is to provide accurate observation of the literary object and the processes of its production and reception (including evaluation), analysis of these into their elements, and exact description and classification of them in terms of these elements and their combinations.

In the practise of criticism, to be scientific or truly critical is to say nothing that is not somehow grounded in strictly relevant knowledge, and to make this grounding clear. This means in general to avoid merely affective or volitional exclamation, which, though legitimate in itself and for the lay reader often a convenient means of summarily indicating an unanalysed reaction, is not criticism; in criticism feeling should appear only as a datum for cognition, object of analysis or item of evidence. It means to avoid also multiplication of purely evaluatory propositions on the way to the final judgment; for these, unless only parenthetical, interrupt and embarrass the progress of logical argument and create rather than dispose of critical problems. In constructing the descriptive and classifying propositions that should preponderate in critical discourse, to be scientific is to be careful of one's terms, using them as exactly and as univocally as possible and choosing those with plain denotations and without compromising connotations; it is to make all crucial statements as obviously verifiable as possible, presenting or suggesting the means used or the sources relied upon by the critic himself for verification. (For the analytic and comparative observation upon which these statements are based should be as systematic and as controlled as the critic can make it. The findings and the techniques of all the sciences should of course be used wherever they are relevant and applicable; those of physical and physiological phonetics for examination of sound-structures, *e.g.,* those of well certified experimental or clinical psychology or psychiatry for analysis of a meaning or of a creative process or a response. The great controls of modern scientific observation, measurement and experiment, are not often subtle enough for use upon the object of literary criticism. But though strict measurement in literature is possible only with data that it is generally not very important to measure, in matters of very specific detail at least the critic can often profitably contrive a kind of measurement by comparing two data with the same third; and simple experiment is not denied him, with the processes of production and reproduction and reception, by imitating or repeating them under varying conditions, and with the object, by such devices as translation and alteration of structure—insertion, omission, rearrangement. These procedures were all in common, if not always systematic, use in classical antiquity.) But to be scientific is above all to accept the established fact always, whatever its character or one's disposition toward it; and it is sometimes to acknowledge that the fact cannot be established. The critic must not shrink from noting the subjective and the relative as such where they occur, or from confessing that a given object of his attempted scrutiny eludes it, or that in a given case the inadequacy, perhaps the inaccessibility, of reliable knowledge makes evaluation of a judgment impossible. What is unscientific and uncritical is not to observe and report subjectivity, relativity, and ignorance, but to mistake these for or to pretend that they are their opposites.

The ideal suggested by this account of method is not often realized. Most criticism is, perhaps all criticism must always be, partial and imperfect. But it is something to recognize the ideal, and to understand that we are truly critical only in so far as we approach its realization. *Cf.* Value; Criticism, the new.

J. M. Robertson, "The theory and practice of crit.," *New Essays Toward a Crit. Method,* 1897; E. P. Morris, "A science of style," *TAPA,* XLVI, 1915; T. Munro, *Scientific Method in Æsthetics,* 1928; M. R. Cohen and E. Nagel, *Introd. to Logic and Scientific Method,* 1934; O. Neurath and others, *Foundations of the Unity of Science,* 1938. H. J. Muller, *Science and Criticism,* 1943, 1956. J. Craig La Drière.

Secentismo. A reaction against classicism: The taste for conceits prevalent in It. literature of the 17th c. (the *Seicento*). Designated, sometimes, by the more general term of *Concettismo,* it is akin to *culteranismo* or Gongorism (from L. de Góngora y Argote, 1561–1627) in Sp., *préciosité* in Fr. (imported from It. and Sp. by Théophile de Viau; spread by Voiture, 1598–1648, at the *Hôtel de Rambouillet*), and Euphuism (from J. Lyly's novel, *Euphues,* pub. 1579–80) in Eng.

In It. *secentismo* is synonymous with Marinism. G. B. Marino (1569–1625), author of *L'Adone,* a poem of more than 5000 strophes in 20 cantos, gave it greatest vogue. The *Adone,* in content and style, reflects an epoch cloaked with false religion and morality, an era of political servitude and national decadence for It. in the clutches of her Sp. rulers. With abuse of metaphor, the cult of the unexpected and extraordinary; with subtle artificialities, ingenious antitheses, witticisms, conceits, bombast, the *Adone* embodies all the traits of *secentismo,* in the literary aim of the *secentisti:* to dazzle and astonish the reader.

The artistic form most suitable to *secentismo* was the epigram, greatly favored by the 17th c., and often imbedded in other metrical forms. Marino's longer poems, although in *ottava rima,* are epigrams; so too his sonnets and madrigals and those of the *marinisti* (*e.g.,* R. Crashaw, *The Weeper*). The popularity of the epigram, derived from Martial, whom Baltasar Gracián (*Agudeza y arte de ingenio,* 1648) called the ancestor of the *agudeza* (*conceit*), spread with the wide diffusion of *concettismo.*

Secentismo, like *baroque,* its counterpart in art (by which term it is sometimes designated), used to have only a derogatory meaning. Recent studies have done much to rehabilitate the taste of the *Seicento*; so that, although its extravagances are admitted, *secentismo* is regarded as having made a valid contribution to literature. *Cf.* Baroque; Romanticism; Classicism. Mario Praz, *Studies in 17th C. Imagery,* 1939. Angeline Helen Lograsso.

seguidilla. Sp. Improvised song of 4

verses, usually x_6 a_5 x_6 a_5, the long lines of sometimes more than 6 syllables. The name dates from the 16th c., probably meaning "song of the way-faring people" (*gente de la vida seguida*).

sej. A stylistic characteristic of Turkish prose, consisting in the rhyming of the last words of clauses of a sentence. The Koran, esp. the early chapters, is written in the *sej* style.

self-expression. The author may keep his personality out of the work, or enter his story. The distinction between these two approaches (objective and subjective) arose with the Romantic movement. Fielding, for instance, objectified his affective states and intellectual representations, whereas the Romantic Hugo merely projected them. Authors naturally "expressed their personality" prior to the Romantic intoxication with the self, but did so through the creation of characters whose sole existence lay within the story itself. Stemming from this or that fact within the range of the author's experience, each facet of the characterization helps make complete an individual for whom the tale is the unique home. The subjective writer (*e.g.,* Thomas Wolfe), on the other hand, deliberately or unwittingly creates a central character who presents the psychological states of the author, sometimes as faithfully as the screen returns the image of an illuminated slide.

James Joyce emphasized the importance of the artist's revealing himself fully. When in the *Odyssey* the Cyclops asks Odysseus his name, Odys-Zeus replies that his name is *Odys* ("No man"). "Exactly!" Joyce exclaimed (in conversation): "If an artist seeks to withhold any part of himself, it is inevitably the *Zeus,* the divine in him, that is sloughed, and no man indeed that remains." On the other hand there is the teacher of art who asked a pupil what she was doing, and when she replied, Expressing her personality, told her: "La personnalité de Mam'selle n'intéresse qu'à Maman!" The surrealists gave formulæ for automatic writing, without any smudge of conscious self-expression: "If thought intervenes, stop, and begin at once with the letter M."

"Subjective" and "objective" of course mark a polarity. The personality of a writer pervades his work, determines toward which of these poles he tends, and gives his work its lasting value. *Cf.* Narrator; Da-da; Subjective; Surrealism; Expression. Wylie Sypher, *Loss of the Self in Modern Lit. and Art,* 1962; C. I. Glicksberg, *The Self in Modern Lit.,* 1963; R. S. Lazarus and E. M. Opton, Jr., eds. *Personality,* 1967. John Burke Shipley.

semantics. (1) The study of the relation between words and things, later extended into the study of the relations between language, thought and behavior, that is, how human action is influenced by words, whether spoken by others or to oneself in thought; significs. The word was originally used to mean (2) in philology, the historical study of changes in the meaning of words; semasiology.

Since the publication in 1923 of *The Meaning of Meaning* by C. K. Ogden and I. A. Richards, interest in semantics has become widespread. The term "semantics," in spite of its original use by Michel Bréal to designate historical inquiries into changes in the meanings of words, is now used more widely to refer to the kind of inquiry initiated by Lady Viola Welby under the name "significs." Significs was to her "the science of meaning or the study of significance, provided sufficient recognition is given to its practical aspect as a method of mind, one which is involved in all forms of mental activity, including that of logic." The study of "significance" was to her far more than the study of words; it was also the study of acts and situations; "significance" itself was more than lexical "meaning"; it included both insight into motives and moral judgment. The object of her study, then, was the total interpretative act, the reaction of the individual to signs and sign-situations. Out of such study, she urged, would develop general principles of interpretation and evaluation, a "method of mind." This "method of mind" should be applied generally in all intellectual endeavors and especially in education, in order to escape the "hotbed of confusion," the "prison of senseless formalism," and the "barren controversy" which are the result, first, of the defects of our inherited languages ("The leading civilizations of the world have been content to perpetuate modes of speech once entirely fitting but now grossly inappropriate"), and secondly, of defects in our habits of interpretation. She proposed, therefore, systematic revisions in both.

Support for Lady Welby's contentions has gathered from many quarters since her time, and the word "semantics" is now generally used to indicate the speculations and findings in many fields of knowledge which throw light on the problems she raised. Mathematicians and logicians of the "logical positivist" and "physicalist" points of view, by making sharp discriminations between the different functions of language and the conditions under which utterances may be said to be meaningful, have demonstrated, at least to their own satisfaction, that metaphysical problems, being by nature incapable of empirical solution, had best not be discussed at all. Other philosophical problems, they maintain, are translatable in "analytical" form, and when translated reveal themselves to be problems not of "reality," but merely of vocabulary. That is to say, the "necessary propositions" of logic and mathematics give us information not about the universe but about our use of words. In the light of an adequate theory of signs, or *semiotic,* we shall have a basis, according to leading members of this group (Rudolf Carnap, Charles Morris, Bertrand Russell), not only for the solution of problems previously held to be insoluble, but for the unification of knowledge, by the discovery of the relationship of the languages of ethics and poetry to that of science.

From the point of view of the proponents of "semiosis," then, many crucial problems which have disturbed practical men and philosophers are not problems at all, and usually disappear on linguistic analysis. Among those who urged this view was Alfred Korzybski (1879–1950), who made the further contribution of showing that many problems arise from unconsciously held assumptions about language and its relationship to whatever words stand for—these assumptions in turn being the result of ignorance of how language works and what its limitations are. C. K. Ogden and I. A. Richards were also extremely influential in advancing semantics, or, as they called it, the science of symbolism. They addressed themselves vigorously to the problems Lady Welby had regarded as fundamental, and pointed out that since "New millions of participants in the control of general affairs must now attempt to form personal opinions upon matters which were once left to a few," we must cease to look upon linguistic inquiry as "purely theoretical," but must rather "raise the level of communication through a direct study of its conditions, its dangers and its difficulties." They attempted to show the linguistic difficulties, the unconscious intrusion of verbal superstitions, the unconscious belief in word-magic, that underlie many of the problems of æsthetics and philosophy.

Anthropological researches have further contributed to semantics. Bronislaw Malinowski (1884–1942), in his study of primitive languages, found that "to regard (language) as a means for the embodiment or expression of thought is to take a one-sided view of one of its most derivate and specialized functions." Language is rather a "mode of behavior." Linguistic events are therefore not to be studied in terms merely of their lexical content or logical coherence, but in relation to the social institutions, activities, and rituals of which they are a part. His suggestion that this contextual approach to interpretation be applied toward the study of the utterances of civilized man was carried out, notably by Thurman W. Arnold, with provocative results. Anthropological linguists (*e.g.,* Benjamin Lee Whorf, 1897–1941) studying languages outside the Indo-European family have performed a further service to semantics, in showing the variety of structures that languages may possess, and in so doing have demonstrated that "laws of thought" are by no means as universal as they were once believed to be.

The "operationalism" of P. W. Bridgman, who holds that the meaning of scientific statements resides in the "operations" involved in testing their validity, has done much to eliminate unconscious metaphysical assumptions from scientific thought. Excellent semantic observations have also been contributed by social psychologists and students of propaganda (Lasswell, Doob), by psychologists (Piaget, Koffka), while the literature of psychoanalysis is crowded with information about human linguistic and symbolic functioning.

The most ambitious attempt to synthesize and make usable such linguistic observations as are here called "semantic" was the work of Alfred Korzybski. In *Science and Sanity* (1933), he proposed a system called "general semantics," which discarded "theories of meaning" (which he regarded as leading inescapably to verbal and terminological hair-splitting) in favor of a study of "evaluations," *i.e.,* the responses of the human organism-as-a-whole to signs and sign-situations. Underlying our "evaluations," or "semantic reactions," Korzybski said, are neurologically channelized epistemological and linguistic assumptions. These assumptions, when infantile, primitive, or unscientific, lead not only to confusions and perplexities in discourse, but also to misevaluations in everyday life. Such misevaluations are systematic and widely shared; education and social institutions often perpetuate harmful semantic reactions; in such cases cultures, like individuals, may be compulsively driven into a persistence in those very acts or policies most certain to bring about their destruction.

In order to safeguard against the false notions about the world inevitably conveyed by faulty linguistic systems and response patterns inherited from our primitive ancestors, in order to force the nervous system to take into account the necessary "refraction" of the linguistic medium, in order that men should be masters of their linguistic instrument rather than its slaves, Korzybski formulated what he termed "non-aristotelian" laws of thought, designed to overthrow the tyranny of prescientific habits of evaluation. To evaluate habitually in "non-aristotelian" ways, Korzybski claimed, is to make effective the assumptions underlying modern science as foundations for day-to-day thought and action. To think scientifically is to think sanely.

The foregoing semantic ideas, especially those of Richards and Korzybski, have had considerable influence on the teaching of English in the United States. Richards showed, especially in *Practical Criticism* (1929) and *Interpretation in Teaching* (1938) that students, even advanced students in literature courses, could by no means be trusted to understand poems or to agree as to their interpretation. His revelation of the barriers to accurate interpretation existing in the minds of most readers led to a marked revival of interest in the explication of texts. Two methods of study were widely used, both urged by Richards: the first was the comparison of prose paraphrases; the other, the translation of poems into a simplified form of the language, Basic English. A monthly magazine called *The Explicator,* devoted to the interpretation of well-known English and American poems, was founded in 1942. The so-called "New Criticism" was on the whole hostile to semantics, especially because semanticists placed a high value on scientific modes of thought; however, the interest of the New Criticism in "the poem as such" reinforced the interest in accurate explication urged by semanticists.

The teaching of composition was influenced by semantics even more than the teaching of literature. Courses in writing in American colleges and universities had often been, both for the teacher and the student, arid and relatively futile exercises in traditional rhetoric and prescriptive grammar. Semantics, especially as presented in nontechnical language by such writers as Stuart Chase, S. I. Hayakawa, Irving J. Lee, Hugh R. Walpole, and F. A. Philbrick, offered the teacher of composition a new discipline to impart which would have the effect, it was felt, of sharpening the student's capacity for self-criticism and self-expression, and simultaneously increasing his awareness, as a citizen, of the traps that lie in the words in which public affairs and politics are ordinarily discussed. Composition courses influenced by semantics dealt less with the question, "Have you said it correctly?" and more with, "Have you said anything meaningful and verifiable?" This interest in semantics on the part of teachers of English, public speaking, and the social sciences led, from about 1946 on, to the appearance in many colleges and universities of courses in "communication," which combined instruction in writing, speaking, critical reading, and critical listening (including appraisal of the press and radio); insights provided by semantics often formed the theoretical basis upon which the many matters studied in such courses were united.

The contributions of semantics to literary criticism and theory were slower to mature. This was to be expected, since the original purpose of semantics was to eliminate meaninglessness from discourse purporting to be scientific; semanticists of scientific background were often content, therefore, to describe the conditions under which scientific and logical utterance could be said to be meaningful, and to ignore the problems presented by poetic, ritualistic, and imaginative uses of language. Nevertheless, Richards saw clearly, in his *Principles of Literary Criticism* (1924) that a scientific account had to be given of the poetic functions of language. He therefore attempted to formulate a psychological theory of value, and to show how the arts, including poetry, are the special instruments for the transmission of value. He was curious, too, as to the way in which literary form is determined by facts of psychology. Thomas C. Pollock, in his pioneering work, *The Nature of Literature* (1942), gave a detailed theoretical study, from a semantic point of view, of the ways in which the evocative symbols of literature perform tasks incapable of being performed by the language of science. Herbert J. Muller, in *Science and Criticism* (1943, 1956), also sought to give a scientifically usable account of the literary process; he regarded art as "a consummation of the processes of adaptation by which living organisms seek constantly to maintain their integrity and equilibrium amid the stress of constant flux and change." Kenneth Burke, in his *Philosophy of Literary Form* (1941) and *A Grammar of Motives* (1945) proceeded, as did the semanticists, on a clear recognition of the complexities of human symbolic behavior; defining poetry as "equipment for living," he analyzed the symbolisms of human behavior and of poetry to show how they derive from common origins. Susanne K. Langer, foremost expositor in the United States of the philosophy of Ernst Cassirer (1874–1945), was also much concerned, in her *Philosophy in a New Key* (1942), with the functions performed by the uses of symbols in art, religion, poetry, and myth. Her analysis of the symbolic process has been developed in *Form and Feeling,* 1953, and in *Mind,* vol. 1, 1967.

In so far as semantic theories of literature can be briefly characterized, they have in common the following features. First, they regard literary and scientific uses of language not as opposed, but as complementary and equally necessary to human existence. In this they differ sharply from those theories of literature that rest upon a disdain of science. Secondly, they think of art as a form of symbolic activity, not unrelated to all the other forms of symbolic activity in which man engages. Third, they tend to account for art in terms of biological function, as in Burke's statement that art is "a remarkably complete kind of biological adaptation." Fourth, they take into account as central data the response of the reader to a work of art. The "poem as such, apart from the reactions of particular readers," which some contemporary schools of criticism seek to study, has, from a semantic point of view, no existence except as black marks on paper which constitute potential stimuli. Lastly, semantic theories of literature tend to relate art to the culture as a whole, and hence to morality. Art is, to the semanticist, not for art's sake, but for life's. *Cf.* Signs; Criticism, the new; Language; Linguistics; Symbolism; Communication. V. Welby, *Sense, Meaning, and Interpretation,* 1896; *What is Meaning?,* 1903; *Significs and Language,* 1911; T. W. Arnold, *The Symbols of Government,* 1935; *The Folklore of Capitalism,* 1937; A J. Ayer, *Language, Truth, and Logic,* 1936; L. Bloomfield, *Language,* 1933; *The Linguistic Aspects of Science,* 1939; P. W. Bridgman, *The Logic of Modern Physics,* 1927; R. Carnap, *Logical Syntax of Language,* 1937; W. Empson, *The Structure of Complex Words,* 1951; J. Frank, *Law and the Modern Mind,* 1930; P. Frank, *Relativity, a Richer Truth,* 1950; S. I. Hayakawa, *Language in Thought and Action,* 1949, 1964; W. Johnson, *People in Quandaries,* 1946; A. Korzybski, *The Manhood of Humanity,* 1921; I. J. Lee, *Language Habits in Human Affairs,* 1941; C. Morris, *Foundations of the Theory of Signs,* 1938; *Signs, Language, and Behavior,* 1946; A. Rapoport, *Science and the Goals of Man,* 1950; H. Walpole, *Semantics,* 1941; B. L. Whorf, "The Relation of Habitual Thought and Behavior to Language," in Hayakawa's *Language in Action,* 1941; P. Ziff, *Semantic Analysis,* 1960; D. E. Hayden, ed. *Classics in Semantics,* 1965; periodical *Etc: A Review of General Semantics,* 1943—. S. I. HAYAKAWA.

semiotic. The general theory of signs, *q.v. Cf.* Semantics.

sense; *bon sens; sensibilité;* sensibility; *sensiblerie;* sentimentality. Francis Bacon said "the office of the sense shall be only to judge of the experiment, and the experiment itself shall judge of the thing" (*Instauratio magna,* Pref.). It was in this meaning of the normal mental faculties that most subsequent critics used the term. In time, however, it came to be used loosely for soundness of judgment, and capacity for appreciation of beauty. Jane Austen (*Sense and Sensibility,* 1811), contrasts sense or "sensibleness" with sensibility, which she confuses with sentimentality. Sensibility is, as Edmund Burke defined it (*On Taste*), a "bent to the pleasures of the imagination"; it means fine feeling, "chords that vibrate sweetest pleasure through the deepest notes of woe" (Burns). This sensitivity to emotion is likewise *sensibilité* in Fr. A false degree of this is sentimentality, an exaggerated expression of sentiment.

The Fr. language contrasts *sensiblerie* and *bon sens;* both of these terms have been carried over into English with special flavor. *Bon sens* is that poised variety of the intelligence which we associate with the Fr. classical school of thought: it is a balanced judgment based upon universal understanding. On the other hand, *sensiblerie,* in 18th c. Eng., referred to that Fr. exaggeration of amorous sentiment which was portrayed in the novels of the day. When sense is properly cultivated æsthetically, Burke thought of it as the gateway to the sublime (*Inquiry into the Origins of the Sublime*). A variety of sense which adapts itself to the homelier side of life is common sense, which is a normal understanding of everyday life.

sentence. (L. *sententia,* maxim, opinion, *sentire,* to feel). A group of related words expressing a single thought as a statement, exclamation, question, command, or wish, usually with a subject and predicate and related modifiers (words, phrases, clauses).

sentimentality, applied to art, suggests that the social or sympathetic emotions have been excessively or otherwise wrongly used: tenderness, compassion, naive faith in human nature have pervaded the work in such a way as to produce a pathetic rather than an æsthetic experience. The expression of sentiment is not sentimental so long as it is thought to be proper, normal, or just. Wordsworth's *Idiot Boy,* Galsworthy's treatment of Jon in the Forsyte novels, Dostoievsky's *The Idiot,* may be thought sentimental insofar as idiocy or mere innocence is misrepresented as true human goodness. Such excess or misdirection of sentiment may be present in works of great literary power and charm, even when aggravated by self-conscious indulgence (in *The Sentimental Journey,* Sterne's luxuriating in his feelings about the donkey). When a character (Richard II; Queen Margaret in *King John*) is deliberately presented as sentimental, the total effect is of course far removed from sentimentality.

A skillful author can create an atmosphere or frame, moreover, in which the reader's values will be different from those in real life (the sonnet-sequence; *Arcadia, Euphues*; the dreamy adolescence of Kipling's *Brushwood Boy*). In all such reading there is possibly some of the self-indulgence that prompted Meredith to describe sentimentality as "fiddling harmonics on the strings of sensualism." But this indulgence on the imaginative level should be distinguished from sentimental literature that takes on a realistic tone and is confused with life. Such an excess of realism appeared in the drama of sensibility and the sentimental novel of the 18th c.; and Rousseauism supplied a sentimental philosophy that enabled 19th c. novelists to set up social outcasts as heroes and heroines. Even in naturalism and the hard-boiled school one may detect, in the manfully suppressed sobs of a Hemingway, or beneath the tough accents of a Broadway hit, (John O'Hara, *Pal Joey,* 1941), the presence of a pathetic rather than an æsthetic attitude toward life. *See* Sense. NORMAN E. NELSON.

septenarius. Gr. A verse of 7 feet; in L. (mainly comic) poetry, of 7½.

septet. A stanza of 7 lines, often used for long poems. Variously rhymed. Most common is rhyme royal, *q.v.*

sequence. 1. The order in which events occur, or words follow one another. *See* Coherence; Form; Organic. 2. A hymn sung before the gospel. *See* Prose; Hymn. 3. An episode in a story.

Serbo-Croatian heroic verse exists in two forms, poems of the long line and of the short line. The former (*burgarštice*) have a line of 15 syllables, usually with a cæsura after the 7th syllable, sometimes with a refrain of 3 trochees. The poems are no longer sung. Those of the short line (*guslar songs*) are of 10 syllables unrhymed, with a cæsura after the 4th syllable and without refrain. These survive, usually sung to the *gusla* (one-stringed fiddle). Both types treat the same general themes of combat, especially with the Turks. The *burgarštice* are usually considered the older, with the 16th c. the latest date for the origin of both types. Dragutin Subotic, *Yugoslav Popular Ballads,* 1932. *Cf.* Gusla.

serpentine verse (the snake swallows its tail). A line (or stanza) of poetry that begins and ends with the same word, *e.g.*, *Ambo florentes aetatibus, Arcades ambo,* Both at life's spring, Arcadians both.

sestet. (1) Loosely, a stanza of six lines; also sextet; sextain; sixain; hexastich. The most common form is rhymed *a b a b c c.* (2) The last six lines of an It. sonnet.

sestina. A fixed poetic form: 6 stanzas, 6 lines each, envoy of 3 lines. Usu. unrhymed, but repeating as final words those of the first stanza, in the following order:

Stz. 1	A	B	C	D	E	F
2	F	A	E	B	D	C
3	C	F	D	A	B	E
4	E	C	B	F	A	D
5	D	E	A	C	F	B
6	B	D	F	E	C	A
Envoy	B	D	F or	A	C	E.

Often the envoy uses all the final words, 2 to a line: B E; D C; F A. Invented by Arnaut Daniel; frequent in It., Port., Sp.: Dante; Petrarch; also—not always following the order above—Swinburne (also with rhyme); Kipling.

sextain. A group of six lines of verse as a unit: (1) as a separate poem; (2) as a stanza or other grouping within a poem.

sextet. A six-line stanza. Also sestet.

shock. Pressing hard and with attempted surprise upon the sensitivity of the receptor, a frequent practice in recent writing. The trouble with attempts to shock is that one quickly grows used to them, so that (as with drugs) the doses have to be made increasingly powerful. Thus violence, sex, and the end-processes of metabolism tend to run riot. Their influence on the receptor has not been scientifically gauged, but is emphasized, for instance, by those who blame delinquency in part on motion pictures and television. The satirical play *Little Murders* (1967) shows a family victimized by, and then so accustomed to, random shooting in the city streets, that they get a gun and casually take turns sniping from their window. The shock technique builds up a counter resistance. *See Epater le bourgeois.*

short measure. (1) Hymn stanza: A quatrain, 1st, 2d, 4th lines of 6 syllables; 3d of 8. (2) Poulter's measure (couplet) written as 4 lines.

short story. [Has a definite formal development, focussing on a single aspect of the many elements of the novel. Character, however, is revealed, not developed as in the novelette, which is simply a short novel. A tale is any short narrative, usually loosely constructed; it is not limited to reality, but may take place in fairyland or on Mars. The Fr. term *conte,* and the G. *Novelle,* may be used for either the tale or the short story. A sketch lacks the depth of the short story; narrative may be subordinated, psychological atmosphere may be stressed. A prose idyl is a brief, delicate romance or love theme. A tall tale emphasizes irreality, usually hyperbolic; it often deals with outdoor experiences (fishing, hunting, fighting) and with legendary or folk heroes (Hercules; Paul Bunyan).]

A collection of short prose narratives bequeathed to us by the ancient Egyptians (*Tales of the Magicians*) contains stories from approximately 4000 B.C. Many other ancient collections have been left us, by the Hindus, the Hebrews, the Greeks, and the Arabs. The Middle Ages and the Renaissance, with their Beast Fables, Picaresque Tales, the *Gesta Romanorum,* the *Decameron* and its imitations, have made a rich contribution. But it is in the 19th c. that the narrative form currently known as "the short story" emerged.

Edgar Allan Poe, in 1842, first formulated some critical and technical principles that distinguish the briefer form from the long narrative. Reviewing Hawthorne's *Twice-Told Tales,* he digressed into generalizations upon the nature and structure of the "short prose narrative." By short, he meant any story "requiring from a half-hour to one or two hours in its perusal." This brevity dictates the structure. The writer conceives a certain unique or single effect that he wishes to create, and proceeds to invent such incidents and to clothe them with such words as will produce it. Totality of effect is the objective. Appropriateness and economy of incident and style are the technical means.

Despite Poe's precepts, most short stories of the 19th c. continued to be loosely constructed. The very term 'story' was seldom employed, short narratives being generally called "tales," "sketches," "vignettes," or even "essays." Brander Matthews (*The Philosophy of the Short-story,* 1885) emphasized the 'story' and distinguished the short-story from the story that merely is short. He hyphenated the two words into one term designating a specific genre.

Poe's theory has stood up rather well; yet the development of the short story has been in directions that he could not possibly foresee. His own practice contributed the Gothic story (terror, revenge, crepuscular adventure) and the detective story (ratiocination, M. Dupin serving as a model for Conan Doyle's Sherlock Holmes). But the realistic and naturalistic movements in literature have tended to emphasize substance rather than artistic effect, the photographic and the documentary rather than the extravagantly imaginary, truth to life rather than truth to an artistic principle.

Poe himself was somewhat influenced by European practices. The G. romantic Gothicists, especially Hoffmann, left their impress upon the early 19th c. short story. In the main, however, the G. preferred the *Novelle* (*q.v.*), popularized by Goethe and Keller and Ferdinand Meyer. The influence of the Fr. has been much greater. The *conte* developed lightness and flexibility in Musset, dramatic logic in Mérimée, sentiment—sometimes verging on sentimentality—in Daudet, subtlety, along with powerful compression, in Maupassant.

In the U.S., where the short story for various reasons [(1) lack of international copyright; (2) rapid growth of periodicals; (3) tradition of the "tall tale"; (4) speed and mechanization of life] has had its greatest development, expanding interest in geography helped to create the local color story. [Bret Harte: pioneer California (*The Luck of Roaring Camp and Other Sketches,* 1870); George Washington Cable, Kate Chopin, Grace King: Creole Louisiana, esp. New Orleans; "Charles Egbert Craddock" (Mary Noailles Murfree): the Tennessee mountain region; Joel Chandler Harris: the Negro folklore of Georgia; Sarah Orne Jewett, Mary E. Wilkins Freeman: the remote rural corners of New England]. Interest in foreign locale, powerfully stimulated by Kipling's phenomenal success with his Indian stories, encouraged the extension of regionalism *q.v.,* to Alaska and the South Seas.

Early in the 20th c. the Am. short story, in the hands of O. Henry (William Sydney Porter), crystallized into a characteristic form. From the local color tradition it retains an interest in the regionally picturesque (*e.g.,* stories of Texas, Latin America, or New York City); from the tall tale it absorbs a hyperbolic and anecdotal style; from the Fr. (possibly through Thomas Bailey Aldrich: *A Struggle for Life; Marjorie Daw*) it borrows dramatic compression and the ironic twist at the end (*Cf.* Maupassant, *The Necklace* with O. Henry, *A Municipal Report; The Gift of the Magi*); from journalism it imbibes an air of topicality and rush; from Poe it derives a striving for single effect.

A major influence in shaping the modern short story has been the Russ. Anton Chekhov. His creed of objectivity, his practice of presenting a slice of life with little complexity of plot, have stimulated a whole school of storytellers (Katherine Mansfield, Eng.; Sherwood Anderson, U.S.). Effect for its own sake is replaced by effect for life's sake. Significance of material, sociological or psychological, becomes the dominant emphasis. The compression of a maximum of life within a minimum of space is the ideal of such short-story writers.

A more recent influence has been James Joyce (*Dubliners,* 1914). His practice of leading to a moment at the end (an epiphany, *q.v.*) that suddenly lights up the entire story and gives it significance has been widely emulated.

The divergence between the artistic or literary story and the merely clever or popular story has in recent years been diminished. The Gothic element, as in Shirley Jackson's "The Lottery," probably owes much to the influence of Kafka; it has modified the Poe tradition of the arabesque by emphasizing, either symbolically or by implication, the existence of evil and the faces it assumes. What Poe called the grotesque has now assumed a new form, loosely called the absurd. While the realistic story is still popular, the fantastic and the absurd are the vogue among younger writers, currently often moving into science fiction or a concentration on sex. In general, however, the short story in the Sixties has lost much of its appeal. Reality has proved stranger than fiction, and there is a tendency to fictionize it. *Cf.* Fiction; Novel; Novelle; Detective Story; Science Fiction. H. S. Canby, *The Short Story in Eng.,* 1909; N. B. Fagin, *Am. Through the Short Story,* 1936; Fr. Newman, *The Short Story's Mutations,* 1924; Sean O'Faolain, *The Short Story,* 1948; F. L. Pattee, *The Devel. of the Am. Short Story,* 1932, 1966; Michael O'Donovan (pseud. of Frank O'Connor) *The Lonely Voice,* 1963; Whit and Hallie Burnett, ed. *Story Jubilee,* 1965. N. BRYLLION FAGIN.

Sicilian octave. An 8-line stanza or poem, iambic pentameter, rhymed *abababab.*

significatum, significs. *See* Signs; Semantics.

signs, *General Theory of.* A discipline (also, semasiology, semiotic, semantics, significs, sematology) that studies all forms of sign-processes ("meaning"-processes), linguistic and non-linguistic, animal as well as human, natural as well as conventional. In this article, "semiotic" will be used as the general name of the discipline, "semantics" *q.v.* being restricted to a subdivision of semiotic.

"Semiotic" has a long history. The term was used by the Greek physicians to refer to that portion of medicine which dealt with diagnosis and prognosis. In the Stoic philosophy semiotic (*semeiotike*), which included logic, theory of knowledge and rhetoric, was regarded as one of the three branches of philosophy, co-ordinate with physics and ethics. John Locke continued this usage (*Essay*

Concerning the Human Understanding, Bk. IV, Ch. 21); Charles Peirce employed "semiotic" as the most comprehensive term for the general theory of signs (*Collected Papers*, vol. II). The Hellenistic schools of Stoicism, Epicureanism, and Scepticism oriented their philosophic disputes around the question as to the limits of reference of signs. In the late Middle Ages, due to the influence of Platonic, Aristotelian, Stoic, and Augustinian sign analyses, logic, grammar, and rhetoric were regarded as branches of the general semiotical discipline, *scientia sermocinalis*. The theory of signs was later prominent in representatives of diverse schools of philosophy (Leibniz, Hobbes, Locke, Berkeley, Hume, Condillac, Mill, Bentham, Peirce) as well as in Chinese and Indian cultures. The vigorous contemporary development of the subject is being enriched by students of animal behavior, psychiatrists, linguists, sociologists, anthropologists, and logicians. A semiotical orientation is prominent in pragmatists, is characteristic of the writers led by C. K. Ogden and I. A. Richards, and dominates the contemporary Unity of Science movement.

There is as yet no well-defined and widely accepted set of terms for discussing sign processes. Outside of merely terminological differences, the main divergences in approach arise from the fact that most theories of signs are developed within the framework of a particular school of psychology or in terms of a particular system of metaphysics. Thus Eng. thinkers have been partial to a psychological terminology (thought, idea, image); the followers of Aristotle and Aquinas to a philosophical terminology (substance, accident, concept). The relational approach considers semiotic as an objective science. In this point of view, the various modes of signifying, and functions that signs perform, are distinguished.

A sign-process (such as occurs when someone reads a newspaper article about China) is any process in which something (x) allows something else (y) to take account of a third something (z) through reacting to x. Thus the reader y of the article x takes account of China (z) through taking account of the printed marks of the article. The y's are called "interpreters," the x's "signs," and the z's "significations." Whenever what is signified exists it is said to be "denoted" by the sign (or to be a "denotatum" of the sign). A sign may signify without denoting, as in the case of the word *centaur*.

Signs have different dimensions (or modes) of signifying. A sign is "designative" to the extent that it signifies without appraising what is signified or prescribing action with relation to it; a sign is "appraisive" to the extent that it sets a value (positive or negative) upon what is signified; a sign is "prescriptive" to the extent that it signifies a certain action which is to be performed. Thus the statements "That is a large book," "That is a very fine book," and "You ought to read that book" are in turn primarily designative, appraisive, and prescriptive.

In addition to the dimensions of signifying, semiotic studies the various functions that signs perform and the various uses to which signs may be put. Signs function or operate in many ways in the behavior of the individual and the group, and may be used for various purposes. Signs facilitate the thinking of an individual and make possible complex organized social behavior. A prescriptive sign is ordinarily the dimension used to cause a person to perform a certain action, but a designative sign (such as the statement that a given brand of cigarette has low nicotine and tar content) may be used instead. The functions and uses of signs are very numerous and very complex.

Types of discourse (scientific, poetic, legal, mathematical, moral, religious, etc.) may be analyzed in terms of their main dimensions of signification and the characteristic uses to which they minister. Thus scientific discourse is primarily designative and is used primarily for the purpose of giving information; moral discourse is primarily prescriptive and is used to induce certain modes of action with respect to persons; and so forth.

"Semantics" is that portion of semiotic which studies the significations of signs; "pragmatics" is that portion of semiotic which studies the uses and functions of signs; "syntactics" is that portion of semiotic which studies the interrelations of signs in a system in abstraction from their significations and functions. These disciplines and their interrelationships constitute semiotic.

Semiotic has wide relevance to linguistics, logic, philosophy, the unification of science, propaganda analysis, psychiatry, and the interpretation of the language of law, politics, and religion. Insofar as a work of art can be regarded as a sign, æsthetics includes that part of semiotic which deals with æsthetic signs—however these be analyzed in terms of dimensions and uses of signs. Aesthetic criticism (as opposed to æsthetic analysis) is an appraisal of works of art, and semiotic can be of value by the light it throws upon the general nature of critical discourse. Semiotic has extensive educational implications in providing a basis for the interpretation, integration, and teaching of the humanities, and for the understanding of the complementary relation of the humanities and the sciences. The study of signs in all their forms and in all their uses and functions is a major intellectual enterprise of the present time. If man is, as Ernst Cassirer, George Mead, and Charles Peirce have maintained, the essentially "symbolic animal," then the study and understanding of man should gain much from the extensive contemporary developments in the theory of signs. *Cf.* Language; Linguistics; Semantics; Cultures, the two; Diction; Grammar; Symbolism. Charles Morris, *Signs, Language, and Behavior,* 1946, 1955; *Signification and Significance,* 1964; Charles S. Peirce, *Collected Papers* v. 2, 1932; George H. Mead, *Mind, Self, and Society,* 1934; Rudolf Carnap, *Introd. to Semantics,* 1942; John B. Carroll, *The Study of Language,* 1953; Ludwig Wittgenstein, *Philosophical Investigations,* 1953; Ernst Cassirer, *The Philosophy of Symbolic Forms,* trans. 1953–57; I. A. Richards, *Speculative Instruments,* 1955; R. Carnap, *Meaning and Necessity,* 2nd ed., 1956; Colin Cherry, *On Human Communication,* 1957; Charles Osgood et al., *The Measurement of Meaning,* 1957; P. Henle, ed. *Language, Thought, and Culture,* 1958; Roger Brown, *Words and Things,* 1958; T. A. Sebeck, ed. *Style in Language,* 1960; *Approaches to Semiotics,* 1964; J. Ruesch, *Therapeutic Communication,* 1961; Ch. Osgood et al., *Psycholinguistics* 2nd ed. 1965; K. Burke, *Language as Symbolic Action,* 1967. CHARLES MORRIS.

simile. The comparison of two things of different categories (thus "John is as tall as Henry" is not a simile; but "John is as tall as a lamppost" is) because of a point or points of resemblance, and because the association emphasizes, clarifies, or in some way enhances the original, *e.g.,* "Fair as a star, when only one Is shining in the sky" (Wordsworth); "Two wasps so cold they looked like bark" (R. Eberhart). An epic, or Homeric, simile: (a) one that suggests heroic qualities or proportions: in *Paradise Lost* the shield of Satan "hung on his shoulders like the Moon"; (b) one in which the image is lengthily developed (as in Arnold, *Sohrab and Rustum*).

Some similes are balanced, *e.g.,* (*Prov.* xxvi): "As a thorn goeth up into the hand of a drunkard, so is a parable in the mouth of fools"; in such, the figure is called the protasis; the literal return, the apodosis.

In modern poetry, it is often hard to find the relation between the image and the object, *e.g.* (T. S. Eliot):

When the evening is spread out against the
 sky
Like a patient etherised upon a table—

on which C. S. Lewis comments:

For twenty years I've tried my level best
To see if evening—any evening—would
 suggest
A patient etherised upon a table—
In vain. I simply wasn't able.

Or this, from "The April Rain," by Edith Sitwell:

Upon your wood-wild April-soft long hair
That seems the rising of spring
 constellations—
Aldebaran, Procyon, Sirius . . .

in which, beyond the difficulty of seeing long hair as a seasonal rising, not one of the three stars named is a constellation. Sometimes, however, what the poet seems to be seeking to evoke is not an image but an emotion or a mood. *Cf.* Conceit; Homeosis; Figure. T. H. Svartengren, *Intensifying Similes . . . ,* 1918; S. A. Coblents, *The Poetry Circus,* 1967.

simplicity, says Quintilian (8, 3,87) has about it a certain chaste ornamentation of the sort much admired in women. Roman simplicity: plain, blunt, straightforward discourse. Rude simplicity: (a) the naïve speech of the rustic (pastorals; Wordsworth); (b) the rough and coarse speech of the uncultured (realistic fiction; Masefield, *The Everlasting Mercy*). "Simplicity—shallowness," "complexity—profundity" are ideas that should be dissociated. For *simple* should not be confused with (though it has been defined as) *clear,* easy to understand. In the following famous problem, every word is simple (in fact, save for one name, one plural, and one number, every word is a familiar monosyllable): Mary is twice as old as Anne was when Mary was half as old as Anne will be when she (Anne) is three times as old as Mary was when Mary was three times as old as Anne. The sum of their ages is 24. How old is Anne?

single rhyme. Of one syllable; masculine rhyme. Esp. of monosyllabic words, *e.g.,* core, gore, store.

single-moulded line. An end-stopped line, esp. in early blank verse.

Singspiel (G., musical comedy). *See* Opera, Operetta; Musical Comedy.

sirventes. Prov. A satirical subdivision of the lyric. Usually in the same form as the *canson,* which dealt with love, praise, all pleasant and courtly themes; whereas the *sirventes* attacked political, moral, or personal foes. The *planh* (plaint), a lament for a dead patron, is of this type, for it extols the deceased by flaying the vices of the living. The *sirventes* has also been used for literary criticism.

Its form is not fixed. One variation, supposed by some to have suggested Dante's *terza rima,* is in quatrains: 3 rhymed hendecasyllables followed by a quinary rhyming with the next three: $a\ a\ a_{11}\ b_5$; $b\ b\ b_{11}\ c_5$; $c\ c\ c_{11}\ d_5$ . . . *Cf. Canson; Terza rima.*

situation. The conjunction of circumstances at a particular moment in a story. While this may be any point in a narrative or drama, most frequently considered are the basic or initial situation, from which the struggle springs, and the critical or climactic situation, toward which the events drive. Many have attempted to classify the basic situations available (or hitherto used) as plot material; most elaborately Georges Polti, in *Les 36 Situations dramatiques* (1895, 1912, trans. 1924). *Cf.* Plot; Theme; Climax.

skaldic verse. The courtly poetry composed by skalds, ancient Scandinavian poets, in the Old Norse language in the late 8th c., reaching its highest development in Iceland during the 10th and 11th c. (the Viking period). At once "more melodious, more ornate, and more artificial" than any other Germanic poetry, skaldic verse is notable for its metrical virtuosity, its elaboration of the *kenning,* its free word order. To some modern critics it has seemed an example of "false wit," but there is in it an extraordinary richness and concentration, above and beyond any pursuit of obscurity. The saga and the poetry of the skald represent the poles of prose and poetic expression. *Cf.* Saga; Kenning; Obscurity; German versification. Leslie Fiedler.

skazka. A Russian folktale in verse, akin to fairy tales in prose, as it treats of the wonderful. The folk form has had literary imitators (Alex. Pushkin, *Tsar Saltan; Le Coq d'or*).

Skeltonical verse (John Skelton, Eng. ca. 1460–1529). A dashing, tumultuous doggerel (*q.v.*) with rapid rush of rhyme.

sketch. *See* Short story.

slang (Norwegian *slengja kjeften,* to sling the jaw). At first not to be distinguished from cant or argot, slang today denotes a popular speech without limitation of class or sect. It varies from the norm more than does the colloquial, which is the loose enunciation, diction, and structure of casual talk. (1968: standard, "He is well informed on current affairs"; colloquial, "He keeps in touch with what's going on"; slang, "He's hep.") Speakers with limited vocabularies seek picturesqueness and force by using words in farfetched connotations, with colloquial grammar. Now it has become the vogue for writers whose vocabulary is not necessarily small to spread the use of such expressions in their newspaper columns. Short stories may be written in slang, esp. in a metropolitan atmosphere. Periodicals (the weekly *Time*) may seek to be striking with a mixture of slang and pertness, although colloquial syntax may be eschewed in this racy mixture, which is occasionally referred to as slanguage. A colorful expression may "catch on" and be used widely for a time, or even become a part of the standard vocabulary.

Slang expressions vary regionally. Am. slang, *e.g.,* used to some degree by all classes, is essentially different from Eng. slang, although the motion pictures, radio, and television help it to leap the Atlantic. It should not, however, be confused with the American koine or standard American dialect of English. Most slang, worn by over-use, dies quickly; some of it is absorbed into accepted usage [*e.g.,* pluck. Pluck originally meant the part of a fowl the farmer plucked out when cleaning it; slang, when the word pluck (meaning "courage") lost its color, went right back to the viscera: "That guy's got guts!"]. Thus slang serves (Lounsbury) as a "source from which the decaying energies of speech are constantly refreshed." F. Sechrist, *The Psychology of Unconventional Language,* 1913; Farmer and Henley, *Slang and its Analogues,* 7 v., 1890–1904; H. L. Mencken, *The Am. Language,* 4th ed., 1936;

Supplement I, 1945, II, 1948; Eric Partridge, *Slang Today and Yesterday,* 1933, 1950; *Chamber of Horrors,* 1952; *Dictionary of Slang and Unconventional Eng.,* 1937, 1961; *Dictionary of the Underworld,* 1949, 1961; L. V. Berry and M. van den Bark, *Am. Thesaurus of Slang,* 1942; R. Bridgman, *The Colloquial Style in Am.,* 1966; H. Wentworth and S. B. Flexner, *Dictionary of Am. Slang,* 1960, 1967; M. J. Leitner and J. R. Lanen, *Dictionary of Fr. and Am. Slang,* 1965. Urban Tigner Holmes, Jr.

slapstick (The cudgel of Harlequin in the *commedia dell'arte*: two slats attached to a handle, so that when swung against nearby posteriors a loud report is heard). Farce, or an incident therein, in which physical pranks predominate.

slice of life (Fr. *tranche de vie,* phrase of the playwright Jean Jullien). Applied to the work of Zola and other naturalistic writers, suggesting that it is neither creation nor selection, but direct presentation of reality itself, life "in the raw," uncolored. Usually, the slice is taken through the viscera, or just below. *Cf.* Realism; Naturalism; Verisimilitude; Truth.

slipslop (Mrs. Slipslop in Fielding's *Joseph Andrews,* 1742). The ludicrous misuse of one word for another, *e.g.,* "When he's had one drink, he gets all erotic" (erratic). *Cf.* Malaprop.

šloka. Sanskrit. A verse-form, of two hemistichs, each consisting of 16 syllables organized in 4 units of 4 syllables each, the last unit being a diiambus, and the other units showing certain favorite arrangements of long and short syllables. This is the meter of a very large part of the epics and of many later Sanskrit works. *Cf.* Epic; Indian Literary Theory.

social criticism. Related to but to be distinguished from *satire* and *comedy of manners* (*q.v.*), which for the most part treat of more general or more trivial matters, social criticism is a recognizable genre, with some economic, political, or social malfunctioning as its subject. It shades into the multitudinous popular discussions of current problems on the one hand and into the timeless depiction of the human condition on the other, but primarily it deals with current problems that because of the changing nature of society are galling for a time until they either reach solution or diminish in importance.

The genre may use any of the established literary forms (a surprising amount of the poetry of the Romantic Movement falls into this category), but it is most likely to be found in prose fiction and in the essay. It may be speculative, as in the *utopia* (*q.v.*), which usually by implication is as concerned with present evil as with future perfection. It is often analytical, seeking to do no more than to expose, to make plain the plight of a group, the workings of an institution, the implications of social change. An excellent instance is Winifred Holtby's novel *South Riding,* which seeks merely to show how local government in England functions in human terms. In its most familiar form it is polemic, mobilizing all the power at the author's command to spur the reader to action against some evil, with or without a proposed remedy. The most famous American novels in this category are generally said to be *Uncle Tom's Cabin, The Jungle,* and *The Grapes of Wrath.*

While the utopia is a vehicle which dates from classical antiquity, this genre generally could not undergo full development until there was a widespread belief in a dynamic society whose forms are not immutable but capable of amendment. The philosophy of progress popular in the 19th c., the severe social dislocations brought about by the Industrial Revolution, and the enlargement of subject matter encouraged by the Realistic movement are largely responsible for the phenomenal growth of social criticism in the last hundred years or so. Since the author is usually more concerned with a sense of wrong than with a desire to create timeless literature, few works of this type are likely to be immortal masterpieces, though occasionally a deeply-probing analysis such as *The Education of Henry Adams,* or a balanced and carefully-wrought novel like *Cry The Beloved Country,* may prove the exception. *Cf.* Propaganda; Satire; Literature and Society; Comedy of Manners. E. Bloch, *Freiheit und Ordnung,* 1946; R. Escarpit, *Sociologie de la littérature,* 1958, trans. 1965; C. A. Madison, *Critics and Crusaders,* 1947; F. E. Manuel, *Utopias and Utopian Thought,* 1966; C. Walsh, *From Utopia to Nightmare,* 1962; L. Trotsky, *Lit. and Revolution,* 1925; E. Manheim and P. Kecskemeti, ed. *Essays on the Sociology of Culture,* 1956. George J. Becker.

sociometry. Measurement of attitudes and other aspects of groups. In literature, there have been studies of what sorts of readers buy certain books; also, the extent to which popular books are popular because of structure rather than subject or sentimentality. (Avant-garde writing, *e.g. Ulysses,* makes use of diction and structure to parody social groups.) Hermann Broch has discussed the sociology of kitsch; Dwight Macdonald has found Hemingway to be the chief exponent of "midcult." *Cf.* Literature and society. R. Barthes, *Le Degré zéro de l'écriture,* 1953; H. Rosenberg, *The Tradition of the New,* 1959; R. Escarpit, *Sociologie de la littérature,* 1958, trans. 1965.

Socratic irony (favorite method of Socrates, ?470–399 B.C.). Pretended ignorance in discussion; esp. the asking of questions that may gradually entrap the answerer into recognition of error and acceptance of the questioner's view. *Cf.* Irony.

solecism. (Fr., L., or Gr., "speaking incorrectly"). A violation of the rules of grammar, or grammatical structure, or idiom. *E.g.,* "between him and I", "he don't".

soliloquy. *See* Monologue; Narrator.

sonata form. In literature, a three-part form (similar to the A B A form in music, in which the first and last movements are usually lively, and the middle movement is slow). In short stories, there is often a lull, or a dream, between two sections of action; it may be a fantasy, or a scene of the supernatural. The object is to give deeper meaning to the story. In Dickens' *Christmas Carol,* the section in which Marley's ghost and the three spirits appear thus comes between two realistic sections. The last part of *Christmas Carol* is lively and happy. In general, the parallel to the musical form is of mood and tempo rather than of structural detail.

song. A poem (*e.g.* in Shelley: "Our sweetest songs are those that tell of saddest thought"), or poetry in general. Spec., a composition in regular metrical form, intended for singing. Many poems have been set to music; perhaps even more (among them—*e.g.,* Burns—the most popular) were written to fit existing tunes.

Songs are frequent in the drama, esp. in the Elizabethans. Shakespeare uses them often for romantic mood (*As You Like It, Twelfth Night*), but sometimes, as with the mad Ophelia in *Hamlet,* for more dramatic effects; they are thus used by Heywood (*The Rape of Lucrece*).

At the other theatrical extreme are the songs of musical comedy, which are introduced with sometimes intricate rhyme but little reason. *Cf.* Lyric; Musical Comedy.

sonnet (<It. "a little sound"). A lyric of fourteen lines, with a formal rhyme scheme; during its early history, the number of lines varied. Apparently this verse form was devised in Italy during the 1220's. Our earliest specimens are hendecasyllables by Giacomo da Lentino of the Sicilian school, usually rhymed *abab abab cde cde.* The accepted theory is that the Sicilian *strambotto,* consisting of two quatrains, was lengthened by a double refrain, of six lines, thus forming the sonnet. The early Italian name for the tercets is *volte,* meaning "returns." Often a group of poets would contribute to a *tenzone* (poetic argument) phrasing their points, in succession, in separate sonnets—occasionally with a *canzone* interspersed. Thus grew a custom of using the sonnet structure for stanzas of a longer poem. Durante (late 13th c.) retold the first part of the *Roman de la Rose* in a sequence of sonnets, giving it the title of *Il Fiore.* Guitone d'Arezzo was the first to prefer the quatrain order *abba abba.* Dante was the first great poet to use the sonnet (*Vita Nuova, Canzoniere*); he preferred *abba abba*; his usual tercets were *cdc dcd; cdd dcd; cde cde; cd cd cd; cde ede.*

In 1332 a learned judge of Padua, Antonio da Tempo, wrote a treatise on vernacular poetry, listing 16 possible forms of the sonnet, with sub-varieties. Petrarch, in his *Canzoniere,* the first great sonnet cycle, avoided complicated forms. His quatrains resemble those of Dante; his tercets were mostly *cde cde; cde dce; cdcdcd.* In the 15th c. the Marquis de Santillana introduced the Petrarchan sonnet into Sp.; it became the usual Sp. form. In 1529 Clément Marot wrote some sonnets that lay buried among his epigrams. At this time the favored sonnet meter (Mellin de Saint-Gelays; Louise Labé) in Fr. was decasyllabic. Ronsard experimented with the alexandrine line. Du Bellay revived the Petrarchan sonnet sequence (*Olive,* 1549).

In Eng. Sir Thomas Wyatt wrote sonnets after his return from Italy (1527), most often *cdd cee.* This idea of a final couplet was carried much further by the Earl of Surrey, who thereby fixed the Elizabethan form: *abab cdcd efef gg* and *abba cddc effe gg.* The 14-line sonnet was then forgotten in England for a few decades. Spenser dabbled with the idea as early as 1569, but in 12 lines, or in blank verse. In 1573, 30 fourteen-line sonnets were published, reviving interest; of 11 by Gascoigne, 7 were in one sequence, linked by repeating the last line of one as the first line of the next. The Eng. sonneteers preferred the iambic pentameter. Sir Philip Sidney's *Astrophel and Stella* (1580) fixed the 14-line sonnet cycle. In such a cycle, or sequence, there is a unity of ideas, but no interlocking of the verses or direct stanzaic flow of the thoughts (Daniel; Drayton; Spenser, *Amoretti*). Shakespeare's sequence was published in 1606, but the passion for writing love sonnets was already on the wane in England. (He also has a few in his plays.) Milton returned to the Italian model. The form then lost popularity until the late 18th c.; Gray, Cowper, Thomas Wharton—esp. Bowles, who stimulated Coleridge; and, above all, Wordsworth. Since him, it has flourished.

In France, Malherbe fixed as the standard rhyme *abba abba ccd ede* and *ccd eed* in alexandrine meter. But interest in the form did not last. Sainte-Beuve revived it in the early 19th c.; the Parnassians (Leconte de Lisle, Heredia) brought the form once again into its own. In G., G. R. Weckerlin and Martin Opitz (*ccd eed; ccd ede; cde ded*) introduced the sonnet from Fr. models early in the 17th c. The vogue died; renewed in the late 18th c. (G. A. Bürger: *cdd cee; cdd cdc*). Note the *cdd,* which appears to have been a favorite in G. The Romanticists gave the sonnet a place of honor [A. W. Schlegel, Goethe (*cde cde*), Arnim, Heysel]. In Port. (where the sonnet is hendecasyllabic) the first great sonneteer was Luiz de Camões (16th c.), who deserves a place not far below Petrarch. In his 354 sonnets, Camões favors *cde cde; cde dce; cdc dcd; cdc cdc.*

The sonnet has frequently been attacked: "He is a fool which cannot make one Sonnet, and he is mad which makes two" (Donne); "Oh for a poet. . . . To put these little sonnet-men to flight" (E. A. Robinson); but it continues to be nobly practiced.

A number of more specific terms have developed, with the varying forms. The Italian or Petrarchan sonnet, esp. if there is a run-on of structure and thought at the end of the octave, is also called the Miltonic. The linked sonnet, *abab bcbc cdcd ee,* is the Spenserian. Sometimes a Wyatt(ian) is distinguished: *abba abba cc dd ee.* The English Elizabethan, or Shakespearean (*see* above) often has a sharp shift of thought with the final couplet. In addition to the loose linking of the sonnet cycle or sequence (each sonnet of which is a separate poem, the unity being of mood or general theme), there are also poems in which the sonnet is used as a stanza. It may be thus in continuous flow (Wm. Ellery Leonard, *Two Lives,* 1922) or interlinked in a fixed form: (a) the *sonnet redoublé:* 15 sonnets; each of the lines of the first sonnet becomes, in order, the last line—rarely, the 1st line—of a sequent one (except for which repetition no rhyme word may be used twice); (b) the *crown of sonnets:* 7 sonnets; the last line of each becomes the first line of the next; the 7th sonnet ends with the first line of the poem. Here too, no rhyme word may be repeated. John Donne uses this form in *La Corona,* heading the *Holy Sonnets* (after 1617, pub. in *Divine Poems,* 1633). Occasionally a quite irregular form appears, as in Shelley's *Ozymandias, abab acdc edef ef;* Edna St. Vincent Millay's 17 "Sonnets From An Ungrafted Tree" (*Collected Sonnets,* 1941) all have the last line of 7 feet.

E. H. Wilkins, "The Invention of the Sonnet," *MPhil* 13, 1915; W. L. Bullock, "Genesis of the Eng. Sonnet Form," *PMLA* 28, 1923.
Urban Tigner Holmes, Jr.

soraismus. "mingle-mangle." Indiscriminate mixture of terms from various tongues, *e.g.,* the pretended delirium of Pierre Patelin (in the med. Fr. farce, *L'Avocat Pathelin*) when the tailor presents his bill for the cloth.

sotadean; sotadic. (Sotades, Gr. poet, 3d c. B.C.). (1) A coarse satire. (2) A palindrome. Sotadean verse: An Ionic *a maiore* tetrameter catalectic,

— — ∪ ∪ — — ∪ ∪ — — ∪ ∪ — ⏓

Used in L. by Ennius (late 3d c. B.C.)

sottie (Fr. sot, sotte, fool). Farce, 14th–16th c., on the principle that this world is the kingdom of folly. The performers dressed as fools, in pied yellow and green, with long-eared bonnets. Free-spoken under Louis XII, it mingled social and political satire with its tomfoolery. Many of the sotties were written in elaborate combinations of intricate verse forms. Henri IV (reigned 1589–1610) forbade their performance. *Cf.* Folly.

sound is a most potent element in literature, whether it strikes the actual eardrums or beats only upon the inner ear. The writer esp. the poet, whose work is always intended to be heard—has always utilized the effects of sound. Manifest in rhythm and meter, its power is subtlest within the word. Onomatopoetic words and phrases announce their linkage with the thought, as do the clang associations—"green seas meet fleet the beaked boats, where between . . ."—of such superficial sound painting (G. *Lautmalerei*) as in John Gould Fletcher's color symphonies. A deeper binding is claimed in Richard Paget's theory of speech as grown gesture, or mouths and throats incipiently moving as in the emotion or the deed (*ghost, ghastly, ghoul*). Kenneth Burke thus emphasizes that the explosive *p* (*pest*) esp. *pf*, suggests repulsive, repugnant things, as though we were spitting: G. *pfui;* a columnist's coinage, *phfft.* Such declarations others might deem subjective; Stevenson after a wide survey concluded that the most beautiful consonantal chord is *p v f. See* Onomatopoeia.

Some combinations of sound seem discordant to the sense. Thus the explosive *p*, the inner squeak, and the final hiss of *peace* seem hardly placid. Poets, esp. symbolists (G. *Lautsymbolik*) have worked with many intertwinings of sound. Coleridge's *Kubla Khan* weaves intricately the elements *k a n d l s r*. Beyond the familiar patterns of rhyme, alliteration, assonance, consonance, at least 5 types of sound repetition (Burke) have been traced: (1) cognate variation: *b p m; th d t n.* (2) scrambling (acrostic): tyrannous$_{1\,2\,3\;\;4}$ and$_{3}$ strong.$_{412\,3}$ (3) chiasmus: (with vowels) dupes$_{1}$ of a deep$_{2}$ delusion;$_{2\,1}$ (with cognates) beneath the ruined$_{1\;2}$ tower;$_{2\;1}$ the ship drove$_{1\;2}$ fast.$_{2\;1}$ (4) augmentation: gentle sleep$_{12}$ from heaven that slid$_{12}$ into my soul.$_{1\;2}$ (5) diminution: but silently,$_{1\,2}$ by slow$_{12}$ degrees. The last instance illustrates also a subtle vowel pattern: the *ah-ee* of the initial diphthong (si) lapses to the unaccented *ee* (*ly*), is repeated as an unaccented diphthong (*by*), then its second element concludes the flow with a long stress (*grees*). Doubtless, no poet consciously works out all such intricacies; the language bears its dower; study of them, none the less, may increase both the receptor's appreciation and the writer's command.

Considered as part of the total effect of sound must be the values of the interspersed intervals of silence. Further study of such sequences and of phonotactics, sound arrangement, has been facilitated by computational stylistics, *q.v.* Poets have always been alert to sound values, as Swinburne recognizes his excessive use of alliteration in his self-parody in *Heptalogia.* Besides the 5 types of sound repetition noted by Burke (whose *augmentation* and *diminution* have also been called *loosening* and *tightening*), two more may be mentioned: (6) the bracketing of one sound between two occurrences of a pair (in the following example, reversed repetition): *h*i*nd*ering *h*ills u*nd*er *h*igh-blown clouds; and (7) a consonantal frame enclosing different vowels: *fil*thy, *f*ou*l*, and *f*u*ll* of *v*i*l*e disdain. E. Rickert, *New Methods for the Study of Lit.*, 1927; R. A. S. Paget, *Human Speech*, 1930; Ship; M. M. Macdermott, *Vowel Sounds in Poetry*, 1940; A. Oras, *Pause Patterns in . . . Drama*, 1960; S. Chatman and S. R. Levin, ed. *Essays on the Language of Lit.*, 1967.

speech, divisions of a. The ancients variously named the component parts of an oration. Aristotle, Cicero (*De Oratore*), Quintilian (Bk IV pref. 6) allow four: (1) introduction (proem; exordium); (2) statement of the case (diegesis, *narratio*); (3) argument (*agon*)—often divided into (a) proof (*pistis;* apodeixis; *probatio*) and (b) refutation (*lysis*); (4) conclusion (*epilogos; peroratio*). Some add, after (2), a further *divisio* or *partitio*, which includes (a) points agreed upon, (b) points in controversy (issues) and (c) points the speaker intends to establish. Some introduce a digression (*parekbasis*) or excursion, before the conclusion. These divisions are in the main still taught today. R. L. Irwin, "The Classical Speech Divisions," *QJS* xxv, Apr. 1939. *Cf.* Language.

Spenserian stanza. A nine-line stanza rhymed *ababbcbcc;* 8 iambic pentameter lines with a final alexandrine. First employed by Edmund Spenser in *The Faerie Queene* (1590, 1596), which begins:

A gentle knight was pricking on the plain,
Yclad in mighty arms and silver shield,
Wherein old dints of deep wounds did remain,
The cruel marks of many a bloody field;
Yet arms till that time did he never wield.
His angry steed did chide his foaming bit,
As much disdaining to the curb to yield:
Full jolly knight he seemed, and fair did sit,
As one for knightly jousts and fierce encounters fit.

This stanza form has been used, for long poems, by several later poets: *e.g.*, Burns (*The Cotter's Saturday Night*, 1786); Byron (*Childe Harold's Pilgrimage*, 1812, 1816); Keats (*The Eve of St. Agnes*, 1820); Shelley

(*Adonais,* 1821). *Cf.* Alexandrine; *ottava rima*; Rhyme Royal; Eng. versification.

spondee, spondaic. A metrical foot of two long syllables. Rare in accentual verse. *See* Quality; Foot.

spontaneity. The fact or quality of leaping into the mind (thence, into speech or onto paper) without premeditation. Prized by the romantics—though even Byron, who boasted that he'd rather destroy than revise, did try and try again. With the surrealists spontaneity, which seems the denial of method, has a method for its own attainment: various deliberate ways of removing deliberation from the expressive act. It cannot be denied that many (if not all) ideas, and esp. poetic phrases, however sought, come at last with a leap as of inspiration into the mind. Since reason cannot control these, the surrealist tries to remove reason and leave the ground free for spontaneity to play. Its consequences, however, have a long antecedent trail—as J. L. Lowes showed, tracing *The Road to Xanadu* (1927). Nor should "spontaneity" be confused with ease for the writer; as Pope declared (*Essay on Criticism,* 1711):

True ease in writing comes from art, not chance,
As those move easiest who have learned to dance.

And, as surrealist writings show, "spontaneity" often results in great difficulty for the receptor. *Cf. Ars est celare artem*; Dadaism; Form; Surrealism; Self-expression.

spoof. A presentation that, while on the surface literal or factual, is actually poking fun. It is related to, and uses most of the devices of, parody, satire, and burlesque. Its characteristics are playfulness and irreverence with respect (or disrespect) to facts, ideas, and words. It employs such techniques as wordplay, sentence play, exaggeration, and understatement. Like burlesque, it points up inherent absurdities, but unlike satire it is rarely bitter. Its aim is laughter rather than anger or indignation.

As with parody, the spoofer must have a close knowledge of whatever he is spoofing, and an ear for the nuances of language and style. The spoof often involves scholarly research, however light and frolicsome the result may appear. By exaggerating defects and mannerisms, it can have the effect of literary criticism, with sense showing through the nonsense.

The spoof is probably as old as parody and satire, and therefore has its roots in the writings of ancient Greece and Rome, such as the banquet of Trimalchio in the *Satyricon* of Petronius. There are elements of the spoof, though probably more of parody, in Chaucer's *Tale of Sir Thopas,* which further exaggerates the overblown elements of the medieval romance. Shakespeare does some spoofing in *A Midsummer Night's Dream,* Pope in his mock heroic *The Rape of the Lock,* and Byron in *Don Juan* and *English Bards and Scotch Reviewers.* Swift's works sometimes combine spoof and satire, though satire predominates. Mark Twain's *1601: Fireside Conversation as it Was in the Days of Queen Elizabeth* is a mixture of spoof and burlesque, with a touch of the Rabelaisian.

Of recent years there has been a narrowing of the spoof into an independent and definable form. Though it is likely to be prose, it can be verse, as in Newman Levy's *Opera Guyed* (1923), a rollicking retelling of the plots of operas. The acknowledged prototype of the modern prose spoof is *1066 and All That* (1931), by W. C. Sellar and R. J. Yeatman. This spoof of British history, with its sly footnotes and zany test papers, set a new style. The principal device of *1066 and All That* is the actual or simulated schoolboy boner, involving malapropisms and miscomprehension.

Will Cuppy, in *How to Tell Your Friends from the Apes* (1931) and especially in *The Decline and Fall of Practically Everything* (1950), brought scholarship, or at least a knowledge of minutiae, into his spoofs of natural and unnatural history. He also, in his stacks of footnotes, raised fine print to a fine art.

With *It All Started with Columbus* (1953), Richard Armour began a series of *It All Started with* books spoofing American history, European history, Russian history, famous women of history, and the history of medicine, as well as spoofs of literature such as *Twisted Tales from Shakespeare* (1957), *The Classics Reclassified* (1960), and *American Lit Relit* (1964). These combine the techniques of Sellar and Yeatman with those of Cuppy and add the Swiftian device of "looking through the wrong end of the telescope," wherein the large becomes small and the small large; sometimes the absurd is looked at seriously and sometimes the serious is looked at absurdly.

Though the spoof makes fun of anything, it seems to find its best material in literature and history. In addition to the works already mentioned, note should be made of Robert M. Myer's survey of English literature *From Beowulf to Virginia Woolf* (1952) and Frederick C. Crew's *The Pooh Perplex* (1963), a spoof-parody of critics and schools of literary criticism. There is also Robert Nathan's simultaneous spoof of archæology and of American civilization, *The Weans* (1960). Perhaps because of its playful irreverence, perhaps because it combines information with fun, the spoof is especially enjoyed by students and those seriously familiar with its field. *Cf.* Parody; Satire; Burlesque. RICHARD ARMOUR.

spoonerism (Rev. W. A. Spooner, New College, Oxford; dean 1876–89; warden 1903–24). Transposition, usually unintentional, of initial letters of words, with comic effect: "I'll sew you to a sheet"; or the famous spoonerism attributed to Spooner himself: "The queer old dean" for The dear old queen. *See* Metathesis.

sprung rhythm. A type of poetic meter, described by poet Gerard Manley Hopkins (1844–1889), in which the rhythm of the line is measured by the number of stressed syllables. This often creates lines of varying length, since the unstressed syllables are not taken into account, making scansion difficult. Found in nursery rhymes ("One, two, buckle my shoe"); in the Middle English poem, *Piers Plowman*; Shakespeare ("Tomorrow, and tomorrow, and tomorrow,/ Creeps in this petty pace from day to day"); and, of course, frequently in Hopkins ("The heart rears wings bold and bolder," or, "Of silk-sack clouds! Has wilder, willful-wavier/ Meal-drift molded ever and melted across skies?"), and used as a device by many other poets.

standard. Thing serving as a basis of comparison or estimation; a model for imitation or (esp.) by which to judge other works. Standards of judgment may be divided into external standards, those that appeal from the poem to the real or ideal world it represents, or to some perfect model, or to some irrefragable authority, and internal standards, based upon the psychological or "æsthetic" experience of the receptor. Some claim a third kind of standard, drawn from or intrinsic to the work itself: its inner consistency or autonomous unity. Since, however, it is impossible for a thing to provide the standard by which it is judged, this "intrinsic" standard must actually be determined by either of the methods mentioned above.

Standards have been derived from any of 5 main sources. (1) Persons. (a) "What pleases all men, at all times, everywhere." (b) What pleases properly qualified men: Milton's "fit audience, though few"; Hamlet's ". . . make the judicious grieve; the censure of the which one must, in your allowance, o'erweigh a whole theatre of others." (c) What pleases the critic himself: "the adventures of a soul among masterpieces." This is manifestly the most subjective source. (2) Acknowledged masterpieces. These may serve (a) for imitation, as has been urged in every neo-classic age. This may lead to slavish reproduction, as of those medievalists who wrote no word not used by Cicero; or of disciples who (as Goethe warned) copy the cough of genius. (b) as touchstones, enabling us to recognize other great works. (c) as containers of principles to be extracted from them and applied to other works: thus Reynolds: "Instead of treading in his footsteps, endeavor only to keep the same road." (3) Formal qualities. Seeking objectivity, critics have tried to discern elements of form and technique, not in the individual work, but in all of its genre. This may lead to Procrustean criticism, "the tyranny of the kind." Such qualities may be specific (the three unities; the epic opening *in medias res*) or general (significant form). (4) Psychological effect on the receptor. Here lie problems of intensity, duration, Longinus' transport. "The test of a work is that it repeat its thrill." Again, these effects may be general desiderata from all works; or specific: that each genre (Aristotle) give its "proper pleasure," as tragedy "effects a catharsis." (5) Philosophy of the author. Henry James, speaking of Turgenev, declares that in all great works we seek this most. It may be as specific a question as of his party allegiance, his sympathy with labor or (Macaulay) with Tory politics; it may be a wider but still specific attitude: his tolerance, cynicism, irony and pity (A. France); or the rounded range of his consideration of the world. Most persons employ a set of standards derived variously from several if not all of these sources.

Many today deny the applicability, if not the existence, of standards. The "historical school" believes that it has done away with standards when it reminds us that one age produces a Pope and appreciates him; another, a Tennyson and appreciates him. But this relativism does not account for the presumption that both for his own day and for all time Pope produced better poems than

Samuel Garth and Ned Ward. It is perhaps fortunate that men who construct extensive theories to demolish values and standards cannot in fact live without them. *See* Æsthetics; *Cf.* Value; Criticism; Propaganda. W. C. Brownell, *Standards,* 1917. NORMAN E. NELSON.

stanza. A group of lines of verse (any number; most frequently four) with a definite metrical and (usually) rhyming pattern, which becomes the unit of structure for repetition throughout a poem; also, the pattern thus employed. Earlier Eng. terms for stanza are batch (amount baked at one time) and stave (back-formation from staves, plural of staff). While the stanza sets the general pattern for the poem, there are often minor variations; most frequently, the substitution of a different foot (*e.g.,* trochee for an iamb at the beginning of a line); occasionally the shortening of a line, or the addition of an extra line or two, as in Spenser's *Epithalamion* or Coleridge's *The Ancient Mariner. Cf.* Strophe; Prosody; Free verse.

stasimon (Gr., sung in position). Ode sung and danced by Gr. chorus in the course of the play, after the parodos, *q.v.* Kranz, *Stasimon,* 1933.

statement. Any expression in words; esp. the presentation of something as a fact. The basic form of all communication, as well as the beginning of argument. *See* Proof; *Cf.* Question of fact; Argumentation.

stave. Stanza, *q.v.*

stichos. Gr. A line of verse. Poetry is called stichic when composed in a series of homogeneous lines (*e.g.* dactylic hexameter); opp. stanzaic. *Cf.* Canaanite Poetry.

stichomythia. Gr. Dialogue, usually disputatious, in which each person speaks one line or so at a time. Characterized by antithesis; repetition of the opponent's words; sharp retort. Frequent in classical drama; used by Elizabethan playwrights (*e.g.* the opening of Hamlet's interview with his mother, III iv; *King Richard III,* IV iv, beginning: Q. Eliz: "Shall I be tempted of the devil thus?" K. Rich: "Ay, if the devil tempt thee to do good."). Molière tends to employ the device in pairs of lines, instead of single. Lowell calls it the battledore and shuttlecock of drama.

stock (A supply of items constantly used, and therefore kept on hand). Stock character: a frequently recurring type; *e.g.* the boastful soldier, from ancient drama (*miles gloriosus*) through *commedia dell'arte* (in which virtually all the figures are stock) and Shakespeare (Pistol; Sir Toby Belch) to such stereotypes in modern plays and motion pictures as the typical politician, domestic, the bumbling British aristocrat, the straight man, gangster. Stock company: one that uses the same players in successive plays. Stock situation: one frequently recurring, either as the general pattern of a play (the eternal triangle) or in details (confusion of relationship: Plautus' *Menaechmi,* repeated in Shakespeare's *Comedy of Errors*). Such characters and situations, though in essence constantly repeated, may of course be given individuality by the dramatist. Polti, in *Les 36 situations dramatiques,* lists playwrights from many lands from Æschylus to the stage of 1922, with their plays sorted according to their stock types. *See* Situation.

storm and stress. *See Sturm und Drang.*

stornello (It. *tornare,* to return). A short popular lyric (esp. among Tuscan peasants); sometimes improvised; usually playing upon one or two words that constantly recur in different order or emphasis.

story. The general term for a narrative or recital of events. In fiction, a story is usually regarded as the presentation of a struggle, involving two opposing forces in conflict, and a goal. If the two forces are not embodied in a single character, we have a hero (leader of the approved force) and a villain; often the heroine is the goal. If the two forces are within one person (*e.g.,* love vs. duty; personal ambition vs. social good) we call him the protagonist. R. Lattimore, *Story Patterns in Gr. Tragedy,* 1964, 1969. *See* Short story; Novel.

story within a story. A pattern of narrative, esp. in the long-winded romances: interrupting one tale to tell another, which may even be interrupted by a third. A feature of the *1,001 Nights*; found in Fr. 17th and 18th c. fiction (Scudéry; Marivaux); Smollett; Dickens' *Nicholas Nickleby.* Not to be confused with the story within a frame, as the *Decameron; The Canterbury Tales.* (The *1,001 Nights* employs both devices.) *See* Frame.

stream of consciousness. The supposed unending and uneven flow of the mind (Wm. James), a man's "interior monologue," presented in recent fiction. (Ed. Dujardin,

Les lauriers sont coupés, 1887; J. Joyce, *Ulysses,* 1922). Donne complained that his prayers were disturbed by "a memory of yesterday's pleasures, a fear of tomorrow's dangers, a straw under my knee, a noise in mine eare, a light in mine eye, an anything, a nothing, a fancy, a Chimera in my braine." The novelist permits many seemingly irrelevant ideas, drawn in by loose association, to bob up in the main stream of the story—which may seem rather a Sargasso Sea (as in the last 42 pages of *Ulysses,* in the mind of Mrs. Bloom: one sentence with one punctuation mark). The technique may be less exhaustively applied: tentatively by Henry James; in all the novels of Dorothy Richardson (*Pilgrimage,* 13 v. 1916–57; 1967); long before it was given the name, in Sterne's *Tristram Shandy.* Interest is less in event than in speculation upon life, and in character revelation.

Recent critics have used *stream of consciousness* to name a type of psychological novel, and *interior monologue* to name one, the main one, of its techniques. The type may (1) exploit the element of incoherence in our conscious processes; (2) ignore the boundaries of space and time, or set new patterns in place of the wakeful movements of our days; (3) seek internal analysis of motives and drives; (4) esp. stress sensory impressions. R. Humphrey, *Stream of Consciousness in the Modern Novel,* 1954; M. J. Friedman, *Stream of Consciousness,* 1955.

stress. Usually interchangeable with accent. Sometimes distinguished from it, accent being used for the forceful syllable in a word by itself, and stress for the emphasis given the word by its position in the sentence or the metrical scheme or by its value in the thought. A foot (some now call it a stress-unit) is made up of one stressed syllable and one or two (rarely more; *see* running rhythm) unstressed (unaccented; slack) syllables. *See* Prosody; Sprung rhythm; Prose rhythm. Also *cf. Sturm und Drang.*

stringency. The limitation of a word or passage to one specific meaning (enforced by sense and context). *See* Ambiguity; Clearness; Obscurity.

strophe. Gr. A group of lines of various lengths. Usually more than two lines, one line being a monostich; two, a distich. In choral lyric the strophe is often combined with an answering antistrophe (identical in structure) and an epode (different in structure), forming a triad. In monody, the lyric is usually monostrophic; *i.e.,* strophes are repeated without variation; in this sense the word is equivalent to stanza. In free verse, "strophe" is sometimes used to denote a paragraph or unified group of lines within the poem. *See* Quantity; Romance versification.

structure. The sum total of the elements that make up the form of a work. A structure may have such diverging elements that it does not satisfy any logical or critical estimate, in which case it is called formless. G. Murray, *The Classical Tradition in Poetry,* 1927, esp. 165 f.

From G. *Gestalt* and from linguistic emphasis, structuralism has developed, emphasizing the organized whole, which transcends its parts. *Cf.* Form; *Nouvelle vague.* M. Foucault, *Les Mots et les choses,* 1966; J. Piaget, *Le Structuralisme,* 1968.

structural linguistics. *See* Grammar.

Stuart. Of the period of the royal family that ruled in England from 1603 to 1714 (with time out for Cromwell). *See* Elizabethan.

Sturm und Drang (G., storm and stress). A G. literary movement during the 1770's in violent protest against the precepts of *Aufklärung,* Enlightenment. The first emergence in G. literature of a definitely young generation with consciousness of a common program. They worshipped feeling and passion; they proclaimed vitality and uniqueness; they sought truth in inspiration and intuition. Freedom, considered by Enlightenment to be man's ultimate achievement, was proclaimed by *Sturm und Drang* as his original possession and innate nature. Hence the cult of the great man, *der grosse Kerl,* or of any phase of forceful vitality, even at the expense of moral or æsthetic harmony.

Pride in individual selfhood and independence, recklessness of behavior, passionate sensualism tempered by brooding melancholy, have invited the verdict of immoralism, irresponsibility, or, at best, lack of balance. However, this very shift from the rational to the irrational, from thinking to experience, produced a lasting stimulus to the development of literature as art. It sought, not to imitate nature, but to reproduce it, by appealing, in a pantheistic fervor, to the original genius in man. Literary criticism, therefore, which now purported to stimulate rather than to clarify, abandoned the formulation of rational rules in favor of the study of the character of artistic productivity. The nature of expression was investigated: the origin of language, of gestures, symbols, and other means of communication (Herder). Thus, the movement, following Shaftesbury and Young (esp. *Conjectures on Original Composition*) is aptly called the *Geniezeit,* the Genius Time. The shift in æsthetic criteria was considerable: art became paramount instead of reason: the artist instead of the critic; expression instead of taste; the subjective, the characteristic, the miraculous instead of the objective, the typical, the clear. The sublime was the favored æsthetic category. Tragedy was a natural means of expression for this activistic generation, in emulation of its literary idol, Shakespeare. Refinement of style and precision of form were frequently neglected. Most genuinely this movement asserted itself in its fervent religious pantheism, its quest of historical origins, its evocation of personality in national literatures. Its main representatives were Hamann, Herder, Möser, the younger Goethe, Lenz, Klinger, the Göttinger Hain, young Schiller. The name is from Klinger's play, *Sturm und Drang,* 1776. *Cf.* Enlightenment; Classicism; Romanticism. HELMUT REHDER.

style [L. *stilus,* an instrument used to write with upon waxed tablets. He who manipulated this instrument firmly and incisively to make a clear, sharp impression was deemed praiseworthy (*stilus exercitatus*); his opposite, worthy of blame (*tardus, rudis, et confusus*). When in late Latin the word passed from a specific term describing penmanship, it merely extended its meaning; and it still serves to mark the critic's approval or disapproval of the quality of a writing].

Although our modern critical word "style" is derived from Latin, the Greeks (using other terms) had well developed theories about it. Their schools of rhetoric and their treatises on æsthetics laid the groundwork for all subsequent discussion of the subject. The two major concepts of style go back to Plato and to Aristotle (and beyond them). Members of the Platonic school regard style as a quality that some expression has but that other expression has not; those of the Aristotelian school regard it as a quality inherent in all expression. Thus the one school speaks of a work as having style or as having no style; the other school speaks of a superior or inferior, strong or weak, good or bad style. These two concepts are so far apart that only a broad definition is possible: Style is a term of literary criticism, viewed as specific by some and as generic by others, used to name or describe the manner or quality of an expression.

The Platonic concept of style is a natural outgrowth of the Greek concept of the *logos,* wherein every idea is perfect both in substance and in form. When a thought is invested with its essential form, style results. The thought and the form are an indivisible one. St. John's opening verse "In the beginning was the Word" powerfully expresses this point of view. The characteristic and necessary attribute of style is its inevitability; the idea would cease to be itself were it expressed in any other way. Any change in form creates a change in substance. Flaubert's struggle for *le mot juste* stemmed from his belief that the essential word existed and was discoverable. In prose, style is the result of the union of beauty and truth, "the finer accommodation of speech to that vision within" (Pater). In poetry, the afflatus, the poetic madness or frenzy, the inspiration, must be present before style can be. M. Arnold says that when Wordsworth has style, "Nature [the *logos*] herself seems . . . to take the pen out of his hand, and to write for him with her own bare, sheer, penetrating power." When this happens, the result is "inevitable," "unique and unmatchable."

These critics have terms to name the absence of style or the presence of "no-style." The commonest are manner, mannerism, and rhetoric. When inspiration departs, style also disappears. The presence of manner shows that an author is trying to achieve a state of inspiration by imitating the inspired writing (the style) of himself or others. Again, a critic will point out passages that have style and passages that have only "rhetoric."

Stendhal's definition ("Style consists in adding to a given thought all the circumstances calculated to produce the whole effect that the thought ought to produce") points to the problem facing the critic: how is he to know "the whole effect that the thought ought to produce"? The "touchstone" method of recognizing style is the best known. Since style is an essence, a quality, it cannot be known by a logical, analytical process; it must be perceived directly in terms of its effect upon the trained perceptions of competent judges. Competence is acquired by experiencing the "whole effect that the thought ought to produce." The critic comes to know style by having made a series of appreciations, each of which becomes a precedent or a touchstone by which style in other writings may be recognized.

A critic of the Aristotelian school regards style as a generic term. He conceives it to be not an essence but a product of many elements. To him, there are as many styles as there are writings. Styles differ both in kind and in degree. Under his hand, the genus style is broken down into species and subspecies until it terminates in the individual. "The style is the man himself" (Buffon), or "The style is the physiognomy of the mind" (Schopenhauer), or "Style is a thinking out into language" (Newman) are popular definitions reflecting this point of view. Because the Aristotelian conceives of style as genus, he usually precedes the term with a classifying epithet, a term stating what species of style he is discussing, as Miltonic, British, 18th c., familiar, forensic, ironic style.

An examination of these epithets reveals that they may be grouped under 7 headings or species, each of which may be broken down into sub-species. These species represent the 7 large elements that enter into communication, hence affect style. A style may take its epithet (species) from (1) its author, Homeric style; (2) its time, mediæval style; (3) its language or medium, Germanic style or lyric style; (4) its subject, philosophical style, (5) its geographical place, Billingsgate style; (6) its audience, popular style; (7) its purpose, humorous style. The Aristotelian critic considers one or several or all of these elements in his analysis of style.

Species 1: The style that takes its epithet from an author is known by the way in which the author put a trademark on what he wrote. Thus we have Homeric, Miltonic, Shakespearean, Dantean, but Euphuistic instead of Lylyan, the book instead of the man. A powerful writer may so impress his characteristics upon his contemporaries and followers as to create a school, the members of which imitate him and each other. Ciceronianism is admiration for or imitation of the style of Cicero and may be traced in all modern tongues. Sometimes a special word is coined to name an author's style, as Jeremiad, prophecy in the style of Jeremiah. At times two epithets develop: one denoting the style as a whole (Johnsonian; Carlylean); the other, its eccentricities or peculiar characteristics (Johnsonese; Carlylese).

Species 2: The style that takes its epithet from time (day, decade, century, historical event, or epoch, literary epoch) is known by the way in which time affects style, as modern style, pre-Shakespearean style, the style of the Golden Age of Latin Literature.

Species 3: The style that takes its epithet from its medium is known by the way that a medium affects expression. A work written in German will have a style different from that of a work written in French. The "genius" of the one differs from the "genius" of the other; the "second intentions" or connotation of synonyms differ from tongue to tongue. So also is it with literary media, as in poetry: lyrical, ballad, epic, dramatic style and in prose: essay, epistolary, novelistic style. In both poetry and prose, the verbal medium leads to epithets, as florid, metaphorical, ungrammatical, tautological style.

Species 4: The style that takes its epithet from its subject is known by the way in which subject affects expression, as legal, historical, scientific, philosophical, comic, tragic, elegiac, didactic style.

Species 5: The style that takes its epithet from its geographical location is known by the way in which place affects expression, as urban, provincial, Bronx, New England, midwestern, forensic, pulpit. In ancient rhetorics all styles are classified as Attic, Rhodian, or Asiatic. Place creates dialects, idioms, metaphors, superstitions—all of which affect the manner of expression of an author who is subject to their influence.

Species 6: The style that takes its epithet from the audience addressed is known by the way in which the audience affects expression, as popular or demagogic style, appropriate to the populace; courtly or genteel style, appropriate to the court or to the refined; familiar style, appropriate to the family or one's familiars.

Species 7: The style that takes its epithet from the aim, purpose, intention, mood of its author is known by the way in which these affect expression, as sentimental style in which the author seeks to induce a flow of sentiment, sarcastic style in which he seeks to set the reader's teeth on edge, disarming or diplomatic style in which the author is so suave that the reader lets down his mental guards, the grand or sublime or majestic style in which the author seeks to create the appropriate effects in his reader, technical or informational style in which the author seeks to impart knowledge.

Some of the preceding epithets may be listed under more than one species, by reason of the several meanings of the same word.

Likewise, hybrids and combinations of terms are numerous.

It is important that the critic recognize whether he is viewing style as essence or as genus, for confusion often results when the term is used now in one sense, now in another, without warning to the reader and without due regard to the wide difference between the two concepts. For instance, M. Arnold sometimes defines style according to one concept and sometimes according to the other, thus: (Platonic) "Style . . . is a peculiar recasting and heightening, under a certain condition of spiritual excitement, of what a man has to say, in such a way as to add dignity and distinction to it" (*On the Study of Celtic Literature*); (Aristotelian) The Corinthian style "has glitter without ease, effectiveness without charm. Its characteristic is, that it has no soul; all it exists for, is to get its ends, to make its points, to damage its adversaries, to be admired, to triumph. A style . . . so far from classic truth and grace, must surely be said to have the note of provinciality." (*The Literary Influence of Academies*).

Because of the ambiguity latent in the term style, careful critics set it in an unmistakable context or eschew its use. For style in the Platonic sense, they use the terms mind or soul or spirit; and for style in the Aristotelian sense, they use manner or fashion. Our critical vocabulary would be strengthened if we had not one but two words to name and differentiate the two concepts. Until someone invents these words, style will remain an equivocal term. EDWARD A. TENNEY. Criticism today, however, tends to discredit Aristotle's picture of style as "sweetened language," the cake-and-icing notion that style is a decoration laid upon the thought, detachable and manipulable, independent of the meaning. Rather, style is felt as the organization of implicit meaning, and good style is no more (but no less) than "logical congruity of explicit and implicit meaning." Faults of style, therefore, are basically faults of logic; to change the style of a passage is to change its meaning. L. Cooper, *Theories of Style . . . Essays . . .*, 1907; D. W. Rannie, *The Elements of Style,* 1915; J. M. Murry, *The Problem of Style,* 1925; H. Read, *Eng. Prose Style,* 1928; B. Dobree, *Modern Prose Style,* 1935, 1964; W. K. Wimsatt, Jr., *Prose Style of Samuel Johnson* (Introd.), 1941, 1963; J. Ullman, *Language and Style,* 1964; J. V. Cunningham, ed., *The Problem of Style,* 1966; M. W. Croll, *Style, Rhetoric, and Rhythm,* 1966; H. C. Martin, ed. *Style in Prose Fiction,* 1959; Huntington Brown, *Prose Style,* 1966; T. E. Sebeck, ed. *Style in Language,* 1960, but *see* review in *Language,* xxxvii, 1961; G. Hough, *Style and Stylistics,* 1969. *Cf.* Form; Prosody; Surrealism; *Dolce stil nuovo.*

For style in the more practical sense of usage, appropriate diction, grammatical and idiomatic form, there are many handbooks, *e.g. U.S. Govt. Printing Office Style Manual*; E. D. Seeber, *A Style Manual for Authors* (based on the MLA style sheet), 1965; H. W. Fowler, *Modern Eng. Usage,* 1965; Wilson Follett, *Modern Am. Usage* (ed. J. Barzun), 1966; Rudolf Flesch, *The ABC of Style,* 1964; T. M. Bernstein (of the N.Y. *Times*) *Watch Your Language,* 1965; University of Chicago *Manual of Style,* 12th ed., 1969.

stylize. To (endeavor to) give to a work that quality known as style or the manner of a particular period or writer or school. Style may be spoken of as conscious or unconscious. If unconscious, it shows traits of the writer that he is not concerned to bring to attention. Conscious style (stylization) is the result of a deliberate seeking after logical or æsthetic effects by choice of diction, form, devices. In thus referring to style as natural or artificial, however, it is wise not to assume that simplicity implies unconscious style. There is artifice only when detected; Quintilian pointed out that the art consists in concealing the art.

subject and expression and their relative importance have been lengthily and futilely argued. Though the "what" and the "how" of a work of art are one (*see* Intention), the theme or topic may be announced or considered in theoretical detachment, as Milton long pondered a "subject" for his *magnum opus,* and chose the most majestic. Aristotle posits a 'subject' of some magnitude; he gives precision (*Poetics,* 7) to the terms beginning, middle, and end. Arnold sets in quotation marks what he thinks sums up ancient opinion: "All depends on the subject: choose a fitting action, penetrate yourself with the feeling of its situations; this done, everything will follow." Cato had declared *"Rem tene, verba sequentur"*; or, as Alice's Duchess remarks, "Take care of the sense, and the sounds will take care of themselves."

The truth of all this, however, depends upon the organization, the organism, that is taking care of the sense: its depth, its ability to "penetrate itself" to that depth, and its control. The "subject" may seem predominant, because it is often the more conscious or the greater concern; but the personality that chose the "subject" in advance makes it actually the subject only as it fuses with, as it takes shape in, the form. Indeed, it may be argued that in every work, as Anatole France says of every critical work, the real subject is the author himself, as the story and the form fuse in the expression of his inmost self. It is for the essential author that a work is reread.

Since Aristotle, many critics have pondered the "subjects proper to art." John Erskine has urged a remoteness: Ithaca, Greece, rather than Troy, New York. Manuel Komroff points out that much of the greatest fiction deals with the generation before that of the novelist, neither his own (too close) nor those far away, but that of which in his childhood he heard stories and saw survivors (*e.g., War and Peace*). Whatever the general topic with which a work deals, it should be noted that the only true statement of the subject is the work itself. *Cf.* Situation; Objective; Theme.

subjective. Though this term, and its opposite "objective," are very loosely applied to literary works and literary criticism, they may occasionally be useful if certain major distinctions are observed. (1) Most commonly, perhaps, "subjective" is applied to literary works in either of two broad senses. (a) It may mean that the work in question is in some degree autobiographical; that the incidents in the work or the emotions felt by its characters (including the dramatic speaker) conform to the author's actual experience (Thomas Wolfe; James Jones). (b) It may mean that the emotions and reflections of the dramatic speaker are a central and obtrusive element in the work: that the story is told in the first person, and the speaker tells the story from his own point of view, showing how he feels about it and what conclusion he draws from it (Dostoyevsky, *Notes from Underground*; *Moby Dick*). In a narrower sense (c), "subjective" can mean personal or individual, and may be applied to works of literature (*e.g.,* some of Baudelaire's lyric poems) in which the dramatic speaker's attitudes are rare or eccentric, rather than ones shared, or shareable, by a large section of humanity. In this sense Tolstoi (*What is Art?*) objected to the subjectivity of romantic literature. Finally, in sense (d), "subjective" may be applied to literary works in which the language, syntax, symbols, or external references are such that the work can be understood only by a small audience of initiates (coterie literature) or by personal friends (occasional verse). (2) When applied to criticism, the term "subjective" generally means that the criticism in question is impressionistic, an expression of individual taste, or a report of the critic's emotional response to the work. Subjectivism, as a theory about criticism, is the view that, when properly understood, all critical evaluations ("This is a good poem") involve a reference to actual or possible states of mind—to what some one or some group approves, likes, enjoys, wants; or the reverse. *Cf.* Surrealism; Self-expression; Objective; Narrator. M. C. Beardsley, *Aesthetics,* 1958, ch. 11. MONROE C. BEARDSLEY.

sublime (Gr. *hypsos,* elevated; G. *Erhabenheit*). The sublime consists in a certain consummateness and eminence of words, not calculated but "opportunely outflung"; its effect being not persuasion but transport; its test, the power to repeat the upsurging thrill. This is the statement of an anonymous Greek, who taught rhetoric at Rome in the 1st or 2d c. A.D., in his answer to another author's now lost treatise. Through a confusion with Cassius Longinus, the author is often referred to as the Pseudo-Longinus. His work, *Peri hypsous,* has been called *aureus libellus,* the golden booklet. Edmund Burke reopened speculation in the field, with *A Philosophical Inquiry into the Origin of our Ideas of the Sublime and the Beautiful,* 1757. His ideas were developed by Emmanuel Kant (1766; 1790), who linked beauty with the finite; the sublime, with the infinite. This naturally made "the sublime" a favorite quest (and term) of the Romantics. The term, conveying a sense of grandeur or the awe-inspiring, has now, with these feelings (except for descriptions of nature: sky, sea, or mountain) largely lapsed from use. *Cf.* Romanticism; *Sturm und Drang*. S. H. Monk, *The Sublime,* 1935.

subplot. A repetition on another plane of the main conflict, present occasionally in tragedy: Gloucester and his sons, Edgar and Edmund, repeating the opposition of the sisters, in *King Lear*; more frequent in comedy. A Restoration version of *The Tempest* provides Miranda, who has never seen a young man, with a sister beloved of a youth who had never before seen a maid. Such devices are mocked in Gilbert's *The Pirates of Penzance,* wherein the hero, Frederic, has seen no woman save his nurse. The subplot is esp. frequent in Fr. and Eng. farce and comedy of manners, as caught in the title of James Townley's *High Life Below Stairs* (1759). Sometimes, instead of echoing the main story, the subplot may contrast with it, or indeed be introduced to supply further action with little relevance to the main movement of the play. *See* Plot; Comedy.

substitution. In poetry, the use of a type of foot other than that for which the meter calls. This may occur only at places, and with feet, fixed for each kind of meter. Where allowed, the substitution is effected on the basis of equivalence (one long syllable equals two short; though a dactyl or anapest may be substituted for a trochee or an iamb on the theory that then the two short syllables will be read in double-quick time). *See* Mora; Resolution; *cf.* Foot; Scansion; Prosody.

succès (Fr. success): *succès d'estime,* critical but not popular favor. *succès fou,* a great hit; most enthusiastically welcomed. *succès de scandale:* popular because of some notoriety or scandalous attribute, sometimes for its impinging upon important current events, sometimes because of a performer rather than of the play.

suggestion. Beyond the sense and the sound of words, the ideas, feelings, impulses that they evoke are considered by the artist, who seeks to choose and to use words—with an eye also to their effects in combination—so that they will be enriched beyond their meaning with whatever may serve his purpose. He will regard not only their usual connotations, but their special literary associations (as T. S. Eliot indicates in the notes to *The Waste Land*), also any linkage that may be in the minds of the particular receptors for whom the work is intended. He may leave such suggestions for the receptor to discern, or point them with allusion or reference. In many works, through figures or pervasive symbolism or allegory, the most important element is the suggestion. *Cf.* Allegory; Symbol; Figure.

supernatural. Applied to (1) Any literary treatment of the major mysteries of existence, hence any literature metaphysical, religious, or mystical, *e.g.,* Lucretius, *De Rerum Natura*; St. Augustine, *Confessions;* parts of Wordsworth, *Tintern Abbey*.

(2) More usually, treatments of gods, demons, ghosts, talismans, marvels of magic, and the like—things outside the usual order of nature, *E.g.,* the section on demons in Burton, *Anatomy of Melancholy*. (Coleridge, using the term "preternatural," allowed a suspension of disbelief for physical, but not for moral, miracles. All the fairy tales abide by this law.)

(3) Narratives that convey the sense of supernal powers. This is not necessarily given by the discussion or even the presentation of phenomena—Pope's *Rape of the Lock* has the machinery but is foreign in aim to any effect of the supernatural; and it may be achieved without the phenomena—Melville's *Moby Dick* arouses the awe and terror that are the characteristic effects of supernatural mystery, yet has no ghost or other phenomenon unexplainable within nature.

The effect of the supernatural may be achieved in biography, as in Plutarch's life of Dion, or in history, as sometimes by Herodotus, or in personal memoir, as in Cellini's *Autobiography* with its noted conjuring episode, or in sacred writings, as in the Biblical story of the Witch of Endor. But most often and most artfully it is in fiction: epics, dramas, satires, prose narratives of all sorts, even lyrics that have a narrative skeleton, as Heine's *Die Lorelei* and Hugo's *Djinns*.

Although wonder and awe or terror, the primary responses to mystery, are the customary effects of the supernatural, there is also the pleasant escape of fantasy, as in *Midsummer Night's Dream*. Sometimes associated with the other two is the elation that comes with a vicarious sense of power: hence, in part, the appeal of the stories of Aladdin's lamp and Fortunatus' purse. At times the goal seems to be mere sensationalism, as in Heywood's *Late Lancashire Witches*.

The kind and degree of these effects, particularly of the great and serious effect, depend largely on the belief the author has in what he writes. The superstition behind the saga of Grettir, the simple religion behind the *Chanson de Roland,* even the tone that the 16th c. lent Marlowe's *Dr. Faustus,* give these works in the handling of the supernatural a certain simplicity and force missing from the *Æneid* and from Goethe's *Faust*. The successes of these latter are products of a more deliberate art, laden with unexpressed but evident reservations. Not that *Faust*—much less the *Divine Comedy* and *Paradise Lost*—is ultimately skeptical, or intends the supernatural chiefly as ornament, like the *Faerie Queene*. But whereas Marlowe's Mephistopheles is literally a devil, Goethe's is a symbol. A symbol too is Dante's Lucifer, with his three sets of jaws punishing equally Judas and two betrayers of a Cæsar; so, too, is Milton's Satan, begetter of Death on Sin. There is here a quality of demonstration from which the *Chanson,* with its fixed chivalric faith, and the sagas, with their primitive conviction of trolls and witch-wives, are free. The great art epics are less pure too in this than such a poem as *The Ancient Mariner* of Coleridge; for although Coleridge, like them, uses the supernatural with deliberate art and purpose, that purpose is almost altogether the imaginative impact, where Goethe, Dante, and Milton use it largely to get a special purchase on their philosophical themes.

In this they resemble the satirists. Anatole France, in *The Revolt of the Angels, e.g.,* and Voltaire, are but slightly concerned with the emotions of awe and terror. Like them is Mark Twain in his *Mysterious Stranger,* the title character of which is Satan, introduced primarily for the bitter demonstration he can give of cosmic evil. In such works, supernatural figures are but hypothetical; they do not commit the author or invite the reader save to the pleas of which they are instruments.

Unlike them except in its non-commitment to the phenomena is that literature which implies the supernatural but does not establish it. Hawthorne in *The Scarlet Letter* recites for the reader an almost perfect balance of evidence on events that, however taken in the end, are certainly weird enough to produce the effect of the supernatural. In Synge's *Riders to the Sea* is the report of a drowned man walking, but it comes from the mouth of a person fatalistic and terrified, and—as an apparition at least—it is not insisted upon. Sigrid Undset seems to bend rather toward the natural explanation for some passages of her *Kristin Lavransdatter*; but again there is no insistence. This kind of work merges by imperceptible degrees with another, represented by Ibsen's *Master Builder,* which cannot perhaps be said to contain the supernatural because the mysteries it hints seem those of the personality in a psychopathic sense, not of the larger universe. This atmosphere forms an aura about the incidents in many current Gothic romances and other recent fiction, cloaking their effects under the shrouded authority of parapsychology, "the science of the future."

Finally, a mechanical and indirect use of the supernatural appears in such works as Mrs. Radcliffe's. Each of her Gothic novels has its ghost or seems to, but in all save one the wraith is revoked in the end by an unequivocal natural explanation.

It has been said that the effect of the supernatural depends largely upon indefiniteness. Not upon vagueness certainly, but upon a kind of dogmatism, an abstinence from rationale, a shrouding of the antecedents of an event that in itself may be starkly clear: the Lady Ligeia's black eyes living again in the sockets of her pale, dead successor; Grendel in Hrothgar's hall at midnight; the cackling malice of Macbeth's nemeses. Whenever there is history or explanation it detracts from the mystery, and awe fades. The battlements of Elsinore are awesome before the ghost's colloquy with Hamlet. In *Macbeth* the awe and the terror grow to the end—when we know no more about the weird sisters than the first scene presented.

The proportion of the supernatural to its vehicle ranges from the fullness of *The Eumenides* to mere isolated allusions. Its importance and place vary from its highly integral function in *Macbeth* to the exterior and largely conventional status of the Senecan ghost. Sometimes, too, artists have used it as an incidental technical instrument to keep the action moving or to resolve the plot. Thus Webster (*The White Devil*) and Chapman (*Bussy D'Ambois*) lug in conjuring scenes that merely give information to the audience and to some of the characters. Galdos closes his *Electra* with the shade of the heroine's mother as *dea ex machina.* Since these uses are principally for decoration and dramaturgical utility rather than for the effect, they ought only in a literal sense be classed with the supernatural. *Cf.* Gothic; *Deus ex machina.* E. E. Whitmore, *The Supernatural in Tragedy,* 1915; D. Scarborough, *The Supernatural in Modern Eng. Fiction,* 1917; E. Birkhead, *The Tale of Terror,* 1921; Montague Summers, *The Hist. of Witchcraft,* 1926; P. M. Spacks, *The Insistence of Horror,* 1962. Robert H. West.

surprise. 1. A comic effect obtained by ending a statement or quotation with something that does not belong in the context; much used by Aristophanes. 2. As a plot device, *see* Irony II.

surrealism aims to transcend the accepted limitation of reality, to bring into literature material hitherto unused, the dream and the automatic association, and to synthesize the experiences of the conscious and unconscious minds. The surrealist permits his work to organize itself non-logically, so that its pattern may approximate that of the unconscious itself.

To Herbert Read, romanticism tends "naturally and inevitably" toward surrealism. To others, surrealism is rather a *reductio ad absurdum* of romanticism. At any rate, they have in common a preference for the diversitarian rather than the uniform, the associational rather than the logical; a distrust of the rational; a desire *"épater la bourgeois."* But if surrealism represents the romantic spirit, it is that spirit chastened by the World War I's revelation of the decay of values, and the postwar revolt against reason, nurtured by the new relativist science, esp. by the findings of Freud, who saw beneath the presumed rationality of our lives the working of the uncontrolled and irrational. Indeed it is Freud who, together with Hegel and Marx, is chiefly responsible for surrealist theory. From Freud came the exploration of the subliminal mind; from Hegel, the concept of synthesis by negation, creation through destruction; from Marx a rationale for the hatred of contemporary values and a political program of action.

The parent of surrealism is *dada,* a movement initiated by Tristan Tzara in 1916, named with a word picked at random and dedicated to the destruction of all standards of morals or taste. The work of *dada* was marked by an elaborate absence of literal sense; its meetings, by speeches given in diving helmets to the clanging of bells, and displays in public urinals. In this school of abuse many future surrealists learned contempt for art and society, while longing for new values and a new art to which they could give allegiance.

The new values they found in Marxism; the new art in automatic writing. André Breton, trained as a psychologist, began in 1920 with the help of Phillipe Soupault a series of experiments in writing under hypnosis and in collective composition which mark the beginning of surrealism proper. Breton issued the first *Manifeste* in 1924. The history of the movement has been stormy, with personal and political disputes and desertions to everything from Catholicism to Socialist Realism.

The growth of the movement falls into 3 periods. The years 1920–24 are marked on the æsthetic side by the development of techniques for exploiting the unconscious, and on the political level by the search for a positive program. During the 5 years ending in 1930 the surrealists became officially identified with the Communist International, while producing literature in accord with theories of "pure automatism."

During the late 30's their politics gradually separated from those of Moscow, which seemed to be reverting to the hated institutions of patriotism, religion and the family; and the æsthetic theories of the movement expanded to permit some degree of conscious control in writing. This expansion under the name of the "paranoic method" or "estrangement" (the simulation within a work of art of certain forms of insanity to create a new view of reality), together with "objective hazard" (a fortuitous conjunction in the world or mind the significance of which is greater than its apparent lack of causes would indicate) and "black bile" (the grim surrealist humor, "the irony of irony"), makes up the æsthetic triad of surrealism.

Early in the surrealist mood was Raymond Roussel (*Impressions d'Afrique,* 1910, 1963: wholly imaginary and fantastic things, described as actual and commonplace in realistic detail; discussed in *Comment j'ai écrit,* 1963, and in *L'Afrique des "Impressions"* by Jean Ferry), who uses the device of "fatherwords" (Breton: "Words have finished playing games. Words make love."). Taking, *e.g., billard-pillard* Roussel begins a story: *Les lettres du blanc sur les bandes du vieux billard,* and ends it: *Les lettres du blanc sur les bandes du vieux pillard.* The expressions mean: "The letters in chalk on the cushions of the old billiard table"; and "The letters of the white man about the hordes of the old bandit." *Billard* suggests cue (*queue*), which becomes the (*queue*) train of a gown. (*Cf.* J. H. Matthews, Introd. *Péret's Score,* 1965; P. Dhainaut, *Machines à écrire, L'Esprit créature* VI, Spring 1966.).

Surrealism seeks to take advantage of the fortuitous, "beyond the paltry discrimination of good and evil." Raymond Queneau in *Cent mille millards de poèmes* gives 10 sonnets, cut into one-line strips so that they can be rearranged in every possible combination (a total of about 567, 497 followed by 24 zeros). His *Exercises in Style* (1947) tells an insignificant episode—a man complains of being jostled on a bus and later is told to sew a button on his coat—in 195 different styles, *e.g.,* as a blurb, in alexandrines, with rhyming slang, with onomatopœia, litotes, epenthesis, polyptotes, Spoonerisms. The technique of pure chance was renewed in the

1960's, as in the "shuffle novel" of Marc Saporta, who bids each reader write his own by shuffling a deck of word cards. Such a *Language Box,* by Bici Hendricks, was printed by the Black Thumb Press of New York (1966), and has been proffered at the Judson Memorial Church in Greenwich Village, where absurdities abound. Or you may proceed by cutting a page of printed matter into shreds of words and phrases, and picking them up severally, with your eyes closed.

The Gothic mood is caught in surrealist terms in Julien Gracq's *Au Chateau d'Argol* (*At Dung Castle,* 1938, 1961). Joyce Mansour (*Les Gisants satisfaits,* 1958) links the surrealist lack of motives with cruelty, the erotic, and the scabrous (an old man urinates every morning into his neighbor's letter-box) along the avenues of the absurd. Meanwhile surrealism found its way to America, where it continues to exist as an influence in poetry and drama (Thornton Wilder, *The Skin of Our Teeth,* 1942), esp. in the theatre of the absurd (*q.v.*), lending a freedom to fancy, and to imagery a freshness and affective violence, which are perhaps the most enduring contributions of the movement. It may be pertinent to note Northrop Frye's remark (*The Morality of Scholarship,* 1967): "In the long run, subjective art is as impossible as subjective science." The opposite view is put as bluntly in the final words of Wallace Fowlie's *Climate of Violence* (1967): "A work of art is the expression of a subjectivity that is addressed to the subjectivity of the reader-critic." *Cf.* Futurism; Alienation; Anti-hero; Cruelty, theatre of; Subjective. André Breton, *Manifestos of Surrealism,* trans. 1969; M. Nadeau, *Hist. du surréalisme* 1945; with *Documents surréalistes,* 1964, partly trans. 1968; G. Brée and M. Guiton, *An Age of Fiction,* 1957; Yves Duplessis, *Surrealism,* trans. 1962; H. Behar . . . ed. *Cahiers dada surréalisme* I, 1967; H. S. Gershman, *The Surrealist Revolution in Fr.,* 1968; J. H. Matthews, *Introd. to Surrealism,* 1965; *Surrealism and the Novel,* 1966, but *see* review in London *Times Lit. Supp.,* Nov. 9, 1967; F. Alquié, *The Philosophy of Surrealism,* 1955, trans. 1965. Leslie Fiedler +.

suspense, or poised expectancy in which the receptor is held, lies between surprise and dramatic irony, as a device for rousing and sustaining interest. It is of two main types: of uncertainty; and of anticipation, both found from earliest times. Events may be foreshadowed by the atmosphere, or by specific allusions to what lies ahead; but Euripides sometimes plays on the element of uncertainty by foreshadowing falsely. Ironic suspense is that during which the receptor anticipates a doom of which the victim is wholly unexpectant; this is a halfway stage toward dramatic irony. Even when the fate seems sealed, however, there is often a last loophole (as Macbeth's assurance that "no man born of woman" would bring him death) that even in the crack of the catastrophe leaves a final moment of suspense. *See* Irony II.

N. T. Pratt, *Dramatic Suspense in Seneca* . . . Diss. Princeton U., 1939; D. C. Stuart, "Foreshadowing and Suspense. . . ." *N. N. C. Stud. in Phil.,* 1918; G. E. Duckworth, *Foreshadowing and Suspense . . . Vergil,* Diss. Princeton U., 1933. For suspense as a rhythmic device in poetry, *see* Rhythm.

sūtra. Sanskrit. (1) A mnemonic rule, usually with commentary. (2) A poetic treatise; an expository comment in meter. (Most of the Sanskrit treatises on the Veda,—including all the dictionaries—are in verse.) Spec., a treatise of the late Vedic period, *smriti* (of the authoritative tradition) but not *śruti* (of divine revelation).

sweetness and light. The basic contributions of the artist, as stated by Arnold (*Culture and Anarchy*), who credits the phrase to Swift (*Battle of the Books*). Swift has Æsop contrasting the dirt and poison of the spiders (modern writers) with the product of the bees, that "fill our hives with honey and wax, thus furnishing mankind with the two noblest of things, which are sweetness and light." Philo Judæus (fl. 40 A.D.), symbolically interpreting the manna the Jews ate in the wilderness as the word of the Lord brought by Moses, says "this Divine ordinance imparts both light and sweetness to the soul."

syllaba anceps. L. A "doubtful" syllable, esp. at the end of a line in classical verse, that may be read either long or short, as the meter requires. *Cf.* Meter; Rhythm; Scansion.

syllepsis. *See* Zeugma.

symbol. (1) A formal authoritative summary of the belief of the Christian church; esp. the Apostles' creed. (2) A sententious statement, a motto or maxim. Most common today, (3) something that stands for something else ("not by exact resemblance, but by vague suggestion, or by some accidental or conventional relation." *OED*). A sign has only one meaning; a symbol "is characterized not by its uniformity but by its versatility" (Ernst Cassirer, *An Essay on Man,* 1944). Symbols provide us with an alternative mode (to sense perception) of apprehending the universe. Thus the symbol of Christianity is the Cross. E. Cassirer, *The Philosophy of Symbolic Form,* 1933, trans. 1953; Roland Barthes, *Critique et Verité,* 1966; Y. R. Chao, *Language and Symbolic Systems,* 1968. *See* next item.

symbolism. Though words can be used irrationally, for merely æsthetic and for non-artistic purposes, they are by first intention signs or symbols of specific referents. However, in any analysis of meaning, we must distinguish the literal and categorical or historical significance of words from the allegorical meaning that inheres in their primary referents: for while words are signs of things, they can also be symbols of what these things themselves imply. For what are called practical (shopkeeping) purposes, the primary reference suffices; but when we are dealing with theory, the second reference becomes the important one. Thus, we all know what is meant when we are ordered, "Raise your hand": but when Dante writes "And therefore doth the scripture condescend to your capacity, assigning hand and foot to God, with other meaning. . . ." (*Paradiso* IV, 43), we perceive that in certain contexts 'hand' means 'power.' Language is thus not merely indicative, but also expressive, and we recognize that, as St. Bonaventura (*De red. artium ad theol.*) says, "it never expresses except by means of a likeness" (*nisi mediante specie*).

"Likeness," however, does not mean visual resemblance; for in representing abstract ideas, the symbol is imitating (in the sense that all art is mimetic) something invisible. Just as when we say "The young man is a lion," so in all figures of thought, the validity of the image is one of true analogy, rather than verisimilitude; it is, as Plato says, not a mere resemblance (*homoiotes*) but a real adequacy (*auto to ison*) that effectively reminds us of the intended referent (*Phaedo* 74 d).

Symbolism may be defined as the representation of a reality on one level of reference by a corresponding reality on another: *e.g.,* Dante, "No object of sense in the whole world is more worthy to be made a type of God than the sun" (*Convito* III, 12). No one will suppose that Dante was the first to regard the sun as an adequate symbol of God. But there is no more common error than to attribute to an individual "poetic imagination" the use of what are really the traditional symbols and technical terms of a spiritual language that transcends all confusions of tongues and is not peculiar to any one time or place. "A rose by any name (*e.g.,* English or Chinese) will smell as sweet," or considered as a symbol may mean the same; but that it should be so depends upon the assumption that there actually are analogous realities on different levels of reference, *i.e.,* that the world is an explicit theophany, "as above, so below." The traditional symbols, in other words, are not "conventional" but "given" with the ideas to which they correspond; there is, accordingly, a distinction between *le symbolisme qui sait* and *le symbolisme qui cherche,* the former the universal language of tradition, the latter that of the individual and self-expressive poets who are sometimes called Symbolists. Hence also the primary necessity of accuracy in our iconography, whether in verbal or visual imagery.

It follows that if we are to understand what the expressive writing intends to communicate, we cannot take it only literally or historically, but must be ready to interpret it "hermeneutically."

The problem presents itself to the historian of literature whenever he meets with recurring episodes or phrases. The "true" or "original" form of a given story cannot be reconstructed by an elimination of its miraculous and apparently "fanciful" or "poetic" elements. It is precisely in these "marvels," *e.g.,* in the miracles of Scripture, that the deepest truths of the legend inhere; philosophy, as Plato, whom Aristotle followed in this respect, affirms, beginning in wonder. The reader who has learnt to think in terms of the traditional symbolisms will find himself furnished with unsuspected means of understanding, appreciation, and delight, and with a standard by which he can distinguish the individual fancy of a litterateur from the knowing use of traditional formulas by a learned singer. He may come to realize that there is no connection of novelty with profundity, that when an author has made an idea his own he can employ it quite originally and inevitably, with the same right as the man to whom it first presented itself, perhaps before the dawn of history.

Thus when Blake writes, "I give you the end of a golden string, Only wind it into a ball; It will lead you in at heaven's gate Built in Jerusalem's wall" he is using not a private terminology but one that can be traced back in Europe through Dante (*questi la terra in se stringe, Paradiso* I, 116), the Gospels ("No man can come to me, except the Father . . . draw him," John VII, 44; cf. XII, 32), Philo, and Plato (with his "one golden cord" that we human puppets should hold on to and be guided by, *Laws* 644) to Homer where it is Zeus that can draw all things to himself by means of a golden cord (*Iliad* VIII, 18 f.; *cf.* Plato, *Theatetus,* 153). And it is not merely in Europe that the symbol of the "thread" has been current for more than two millennia; it is to be found in Islamic, Hindu, and Chinese contexts. Thus we read in Shams-i-Tabrīz, "He gave me the end of a thread . . . 'Pull,' he said, 'that I may pull: and break it not in the pulling' " and in Hāfiz "Keep thy end of the thread, that he may keep his end": in the *Śatapatha Brāhmaṇa* that the Sun is the fastening to which all things are attached by the thread of the spirit, while in the *Maitri Upaniṣad* the exaltation of the contemplative is compared to the ascent of a spider on its thread; Chuang Tzu tells us that our life is suspended from God as if by a thread, cut off when we die. All this is bound with the symbolism of weaving and embroidery, the "rope trick," rope-walking, fishing with a line and lassoing; and with that of the rosary and the necklace, for as the *Bhagavad Gītā* reminds us, "all things are strung on Him like rows of gems upon a thread."

We can say with Blake too that "if the spectator could enter into these images, approaching them on the fiery chariot of contemplative thought . . . then he would be happy." No one will suppose that Blake invented the "fiery chariot" or found it anywhere else than in the Old Testament; but some may not have also remembered that the symbolism of the chariot is likewise used by Plato, and in the Indian and Chinese books. The horses are the sensitive powers of the soul, the body of the chariot our bodily vehicle, the rider the spirit. The symbol can therefore be regarded from two points of view: if the untamed horses are allowed to go where they will, no one can say where this will be; if they are curbed by the driver, his intended destination will be reached. Thus, just as there are "two minds," divine and human, there are a fiery chariot of the gods and a human vehicle, one bound for heaven, the other for the attainment of human ends, "whatever these may be" (*Taittirīya Saṁhitā* V, 4, 10, 1). In other words, from one point of view, embodiment is a humiliation, and from another a royal procession. Let us consider the first case only here. Traditional punishments (*e.g.,* crucifixion, impalement, flaying) are based on cosmic analogies. One of these punishments is that of the tumbril: whoever is, as a criminal, carted about the streets of a city loses his honor and all legal rights; the "cart" is a moving prison, the "carted man" (*rathita, Maitri Upaniṣad* IV, 4) a prisoner. That is why, in Chrétien's *Lancelot,* the Chevalier de la Charette shrinks from and delays the step into the cart, although it is to take him on the way to the fulfillment of his quest. In other words, the Solar Hero shrinks from his task, which is that of the liberation of the Psyche (Guenevere) who is imprisoned by a magician in a castle that lies beyond a river that can only be crossed by the "Sword Bridge." This "bridge" itself is another traditional symbol, by no means an invention of the story-teller, but the "Brig of Dread" and "razor-edged way" of Western folklore and Eastern scripture. The "hesitation" corresponds to that of Agni to become the charioteer of the Gods (RV, X, 51), the Buddha's well known hesitation to set in motion the "Wheel" of the Law, and to Christ's "May this cup be taken from me"; it is every man's hesitation, who will not take up his cross. And *that* is why Guenevere, even when Lancelot has crossed the sword-bridge barefoot and has set her free, bitterly reproaches him for his short and seemingly trivial delay to mount the cart.

Such is the "understanding" of a traditional episode, which a knowing author has retold, not primarily to amuse but originally to instruct; the telling of stories only to amuse belongs to later ages in which the life of pleasure is preferred to that of activity or contemplation. In the same way every genuine folk- and fairy-tale can be "understood," for the references are always metaphysical; the type of "The Twa Magicians," for example, is a creation myth (*cf. Bṛhadāraṇyaka Upaniṣad* I, 4, 4 "She became a cow, he became a bull"), Snowwhite's apple is "the fruit of the tree," it is only with "seven-league boots" that one can traverse the "seven worlds" (like Agni and the Buddha), it is Psyche that the Hero rescues from the Dragon, and so forth. Later on, all these motifs fall into the hands of the writers of "romances," litterateurs and in the end historians, and are no longer understood. That these formulas have been employed in the same way all over the world in the telling of variants and fragments of the one Ur-mythos of humanity implies the presence, in certain kinds of literature, of imaginative (iconographic) values far exceeding those of the belle-lettrist's fantasies, or the kinds of literature that are based on "observation"; if only because the myth is always true (or else is no true myth), while the "facts" are only true eventfully. *Cf.* Myth.

We have pointed out that words have meaning simultaneously on more than one level of reference. All interpretation of scripture (in Europe notably from Philo to St. Thomas Aquinas) has rested upon this assumption: our mistake in the study of "literature" is to have overlooked that far more of this is really scriptural and can be "criticised" only as such, than we supposed; an oversight that implies what is really an incorrect stylistic diagnosis. The two-fold significance of words, literal and spiritual, is well illustrated in the word "Jerusalem" being (1) an actual city of Palestine and (2) Jerusalem the "golden," a heavenly city of the "imagination." And in this connection, too, as in the case of the "golden" thread, it must be remembered that the traditional language is precise: "gold" is not merely the element *Au* but the recognized symbol of light, life, and immortality.

Many of the terms of traditional thinking survive as clichés in our everyday speech and contemporary literature, where like other "superstitions" they have no longer any real meaning for us. Thus we speak of a "brilliant saying" or "shining wit" without awareness that such phrases rest upon an original conception of the coincidence of light and sound, and of an "intellectual light" that shines in all adequate imagery; we can hardly grasp what St. Bonaventura meant by "the light of a mechanical art." We use the word "beam" in its two senses of "ray" and "timber" without realizing that these are related senses, coincident in the expression *Rubus igneus* and that we are here "on the track of" (this itself is another expression which, like "hitting the mark," is of prehistoric antiquity) an original conception of the immanence of Fire in the "wood" of which the world is made. We say that "a little bird told me" not reflecting that the "language of birds" is a reference to "angelic communication." We say "self-possessed" and speak of "self-government" without realizing that (as was long ago pointed out by Plato) all such expressions imply that "there are two in us" and that in such cases the question still arises which self shall be possessed or governed by which, the better by the worse, or vice-versa. In order to comprehend the older literatures we must not overlook the precision with which all such expressions are employed; and if we write ourselves, may learn to do so more clearly (again we find ourselves confronted by the coincidence of light with meaning,—to "argue" being etymologically to "clarify").

It is sometimes objected that the attribution of abstract meaning is a later and subjective reading into symbols that were originally employed either only for purposes of factual communication or only for decorative and æsthetic reasons. Those who take up such a position may first be asked to prove that the "primitives," from whom we inherit many of the forms of highest thought (the symbolism of the Eucharist, for example, being cannibalistic) were really interested only in factual meanings or were influenced only by æsthetic considerations. The anthropologists tell us otherwise, that in their lives "needs of the soul and body were satisfied together." They may be asked to consider such surviving cultures as that of the Amerindians, whose myths and art are far more abstract than most story telling or painting of modern Europeans. They may be asked, Why was "primitive" art formally abstract, if not because it was required to express an abstract sense? They may be asked, Why, if not because it is speaking of something other than mere facts, is the scriptural style always parabolic?

It is no more suggested that the interpretation of symbols be left to guesswork than that we should try to read Minoan script by guesswork. The study of the traditional language of symbols is not an easy discipline, primarily because we are no longer familiar with, or even interested in, the metaphysical content they are used to express; again because the symbolic phrases, like individual words, can have more than one meaning, according to the context in which they are employed, though this does not imply that they can be given any meaning at random or arbitrarily. Negative symbols, in particular, may bear contrasted value, one "bad," the other "good"; "nonbeing," *e.g.*, may represent the state of privation of that which has not yet attained to being, or on the other hand the freedom from limiting affirmations of that which transcends being. Whoever wishes to understand the real meaning of these figures of thought that are not merely figures of speech must have studied the very extensive literatures of many countries in which the meanings of symbols are explained, and must have learned himself to think in these terms. Only when it is found that a given symbol—*e.g.,* the number "seven" (lands, seas, heavens, worlds, gifts, breaths) or the notions "dust," "husk," "knot," "eye," "bridge," "ship," "ladder"—has a generically consistent series of values in a series of intelligible contexts widely distributed in time and space, can one safely "read" its meaning elsewhere and recognize the stratification of literary sequences by means of the figures used in them. In this universal language, the highest truths have been expressed. But apart from this interest, alien to a majority of modern writers and critics, without this kind of knowledge, the historian and critic of literature and literary styles can only by guesswork distinguish between what, in a given author's work, is individual, and what is inherited and universal. ANANDA K. COOMARASWAMY.

Symbolism as a literary device depends on the pliability of language, which may be exercised at 4 levels of expression. A. Animism: "the sea rages"—because it is a monster. B. Metaphor: the belief lapsed to symbol; but the form retained. C. Simile: the symbol analyzed to analogy; the sea is like a monster. D. Concrete image: the figure rejected for the fact; not "the raging sea" but "the stormy sea," Homer: "the wet sea."

"Symbol" (Gr. *symballein,* to cast together) is thus, in 2 quite different senses, a sign of something else. I. Scientifically, literally: of a specific object or idea that the symbol (word) denotes, a sign of what it means. This symbolic use is distinguished from the emotive (*q.v.*) use of a word, and is tantamount to intending the dictionary definition of the word. Thus Santayana says man's "simian chatter becomes noble as it becomes symbolic." II. By implication, of something beyond the object or idea that it denotes, of another level of significance that somehow reaches forth to embrace the spirit, mankind, the mysteries words cannot otherwise capture that underly and determine the universe and human destiny. It is in this sense that the term "symbolism" is commonly employed: in this sense Roger Fry protests that "in proportion as an artist is pure, he is opposed to all symbolism"; but Browning answers:

> Art—wherein man nowise speaks to men,
> Only to mankind—Art may tell a truth
> Obliquely, do the thing shall breed the thought,
> Nor wrong the thought, missing the mediate word.
> So you may paint your picture, twice show truth,
> Beyond mere imagery on the wall—
> So, note by note, bring music from your mind,
> So write a book shall mean beyond the facts,
> Suffice the eye and save the soul besides.

Using language applicable to either of these two senses, Kenneth Burke states that "a symbol is the verbal parallel to a pattern of experience." As such, it is marked by power or complexity: power, as the symbol is held to simplicity, reenforcing the theme (monotony must here be avoided); complexity, as the symbol's own pattern is developed (here, the danger is diffusion). The symbol may serve (a) to interpret a theme; (b) to make it acceptable; (c) as escape; (d) to awaken dormant or suppressed experience; (e) as adornment or exhibition.

Symbols themselves, however, may be of various orders. Perhaps most detailed use was made of them in the middle ages, culminating in the symbolic interweaving of *The Divine Comedy* where, in addition to the many symbolic creatures introduced, and the very structure and number of the verses themselves, there are 4 patterns of interpretation on each of 4 levels of symbolism: the literal level gives against the background of *natura* the fourfold story of Dante's life; the allegorical level gives against the background of *scriptura* the fourfold story of humanity; the tropological level gives against the background of reason the ways of progress in insight; the anagogical, reached by grace alone, brings all to fuse in union of the soul with God. Each level is fully understood only when inspired by the one next higher.

More generally, Paul Elmer More has indicated that all symbols fall into 1 of 4 levels (each including all below it): (1) Significative: the arbitrary, conventional sign (often with all emotion removed): H_2O; πr^2; "rally round the flag." (2) Metaphoric: the first, plus a natural association still felt: "pure as the lily." (3) Commemorative: adds the recollection of a literal occasion: "For each man has his cross to bear." (4) Sacramental: the symbol is the thing symbolized: "to eat of the bread." The first two, says More, are primarily literary; the third and the fourth, primarily religious—yet every great work wins apotheosis. Below these four levels is the Accidental or personal, with significance to one individual because of a memorable association (agreeable or disagreeable) in his own life; such symbols are prominent in Proust's *A la recherche du temps perdu*. *cf.* Figure; Signs. C. Feidelson, *Symbolism and Am. Lit.,* 1953; C. C. Jung, ed. *Man and His Symbols,* trans. 1964.

Symbolism, as a school, was announced in a manifesto in the *Figaro* of 1886, by a group of writers known for 20 years as "Decadents," to describe a mode of literary expression in which words are used to suggest states of mind rather than for their objective, representational or intellectual content:

". . . symbolist poetry seeks to clothe the Idea with a sensory form which, however, would not be its own end, . . . Thus, in this art . . . all concrete phenomena are mere sensory appearances destined to represent their esoteric affinities with primordial Ideas."

This movement, contemporary with impressionism in painting and in music, and with the philosophy of the subconscious culminating in Bergson, coincides with the idealism of the late 19th c., and is an offshoot of romanticism to which it is connected by an almost uninterrupted, if sometimes underground, current and, more generally, to a mystical conception of the universe, derived more or less remotely from neo-Platonism.

Plato used symbols only because "it is easier to say what a thing is like than what it is"; the neo-Platonists of Alexandria tended towards a more formal and esoteric use. The rather obscure symbolism of medieval romances may, according to M. Denis de Rougemont, be a Celtic illustration of the same tradition of Indo-European Manichæism, which holds that the world, first created in spiritual form, had been given material form by the demon, so that concrete phenomena are only the symbols of a lost spiritual universe. The neo-Platonists of the Renaissance followed both Plato and his Alexandrian disciples, and their use of symbols was confined generally to those consecrated by these sources: fire, the sun, wings. It is only with the Illuminati of the 18th c., particularly through Swedenborg's theory of correspondences, popularized by Baudelaire's sonnet, *Les Correspondances,* that the converting of all known objects into symbols—as distinguished from myths which retain a collective character, and from allegories whose meaning is extrinsic and conventional—came to be regarded as a legitimate means of individualistic expression, and that the poetical possibilities of the neo-Platonic tradition were consciously elaborated into a new lyrical language.

Baudelaire's sonnet alluded to the theory of synæsthesia, according to which visual, auditory and other sensations may correspond to each other, and to the notion of correspondences, which made him see man walking "through a forest of symbols" where all material things dissolve themselves into the "dark and confused unity" of the unseen world. Baudelaire's poetry illustrated the advantage of this system by attaining a certain subjectivity, either through juxtaposition of corresponding symbols, or opposition of conflicting symbols, in a time that had become hostile to romantic lyricism.

Following Baudelaire, Arthur Rimbaud, in an effort to transcend immediate reality and to become a seer untrammeled by space or time, told his spiritual history through a succession of visions where logical sequence was completely abolished. Through Rimbaud, Verlaine may have acquired some of his qualities: use of words for their suggestive value and for the creation of atmosphere, disregard of clarity, stress on the musical quality of the verse to reproduce the very movement of his mind, which seldom rises above the plane of spontaneous feeling. Another follower of Baudelaire, Mallarmé, by further insistence on the clash of images through dislocation of syntax, by veiling and expressing at once through ingenious analogies and complicated thought, brought a certain preciosity as well as the obscurity that in the past had distinguished similar esoteric schools of poetry. Mallarmé wished to make every term "a plastic image, the expression of a thought, the stir of a feeling, and the symbol of a philosophy."

Ca. 1886, young writers looking for leadership discovered Mallarmé and Verlaine. The symbolists may therefore be roughly divided into two groups: the followers of Verlaine, melancholy or eccentric but characterized by a general trend towards simplicity and directness in the transposition through appropriate symbols of vague states of mind or subconscious ideas: Le Cardonnel, Samain, Mikhaël, Rodenbach, Maeterlinck; and the followers of Mallarmé, "Harmonistes" or "Vers-libristes," distinguished by a more conscious, intricate and synthetic art: Ghil, Dubus, Mockel, Mauclair, Merrill, Verhaeren, Kahn, Laforgue, Vielé-Griffin, Dujardin, Retté, Henri de Régnier.

The influence of the symbolist movement was widely felt outside of Fr. (the Eng. *Decadents,* the Am. *Imagists* and *Symbolists,* R. M. Rilke and Stefan George in G., the *Modernistas* in Sp. Am. and Sp.). Other currents had flowed into symbolism. Wagner's music; Paul Valéry stated: "We are nourished on music, and our literary heads dream only of winning from language almost the same effects as pure sounds produce on the nervous system." While Valéry sought this in mathematical constructions of his verse, Paul Claudel turned symbolist mysticism towards the more orthodox channel of prayer. The symbolism of the later Ibsen, drawn from these sources, in its turn affected Maeterlinck, as well as (often with Catholic emphasis) Yeats, Synge, Paul Vincent Carroll, of the Irish theatre; Anton Chekhov, Eugene O'Neill, Philip Barry. Symbolism, indeed, not only in the drama, but in fiction (Joyce; Jules Romains; Richard Beer-Hofmann; Hemingway, in poetry (Eliot) and through its strain in expressionism, surrealism, and other subjective trends, is one of the strongest forces in art today. Susanne Langer, indeed (*Mind,* 1967), defines all art as "the symbolic expression of an artist's knowledge of feeling." *Cf.* Archetype; (root) Metaphor; Romanticism; Surrealism; Allegory; Myth; Synesthesia; Synesthesis; Expressionism; Correspondence of the arts. A. Symonds, *The Symbolist Movement in Lit.,* 1911; Remy de Gourmont, *Decadence,* trans. 1921; E. Wilson, *Axel's Castle,* 1931; R. Taupin, *L'Influence du symbolisme fr. sur la poésie am.,* 1929; O. Maslenikov, *The Frenzied Poets,* 1952; P. Wheelwright, *The Burning Fountain,* 1954; Sir Cecil M. Bowra, *The Heritage of Symbolism,* 1943, 1962; Anna Balakian, *The Symbolist Movement,* 1968; R. N. Stromberg, *Realism, Naturalism, and Symbolism,* 1968. JACQUES L. SALVAN.

symmetry. Harmony within the work, of part to part and parts to the whole. Sought by most; but a too regular correspondence is felt by many to destroy a certain quality of life (as in handicraft, but lost in the machine-made); hence even races have been marked by symmetrophobia (Egyptian temples; Japanese art), and artists occasionally (Browning) prize a ruggedness or roughness above a smooth and rounded symmetry. *Cf.* Grace; Propriety; Form.

synæsthesia (Gr., feeling together): the concurrent appeal to (or action of) more than one sense; the response through several senses to the stimulation of one. Occurring in pathological states and under the influence of drugs, such acts as hearing color or savoring (tasting) sound are claimed by some (Tieck; Baudelaire; Huysmans) as possible through art. Emphasized in the 1960's by the "mixed media," or multimedia, attempt to rouse the emotions through simultaneous pressure—even to "overload"—upon several senses, as in the happening, *q.v. Cf.* Correspondence. E. R. von Erhardt-Siebolt, "Harmony of the Senses in Romanticism," *PMLA* June 1932; S. Hartman, "In Perfume Land," *Forum* Aug. 1913.

synæsthesis. The harmonious and balanced concord stimulated by art, as posited in the definition of beauty advanced by Ogden, Richards, and Wood in *The Foundations of Aesthetics,* 1925. Harmony is produced by the work of art in that it stimulates usually opposed aspects of being: keen thought yet strong feeling; fear (as at a tragedy) yet calm. Balance, equilibrium, among these is maintained, in that there is no desire for action, only a poised awareness, a general intensification of consciousness, exercising all a man's faculties richly and together. This test of beauty is subjective: to each man, that is beautiful which affords him the greatest and most rounded stimulation of which he is capable. The value of a work depends, in this theory, upon the level of intellectual and emotional complexity to which the work raises the receptor.

Susanne Langer seems to go beyond Freud, suggesting (*Mind,* 1967) that the supposed dichotomy of reason and emotion may be unreal, that intellect is actually a "high form" of feeling. Then all reasoning is seen as a subtler process of rationalization, hiding its passional basis and motives under the veneer of "higher" aims and logical plans. George Eliot indicates another sort of reconcilement: "To be a poet is to have a soul . . . in which knowledge passes instantaneously into feeling and feeling flashes back as a new organ of knowledge." *Cf.* Aesthetics.

synchoresis. Concession. If yielded directly: epichoresis. Epitrope: granting the adversary's point, or his desire, as though it is unimportant, or will prove his downfall. Also, shrugging one's shoulders, and leaving it to the receptor, *e.g.* "You call me puny. True. I am no taller than Napoleon." Paromologia: accepting an objection, then pointing out that it holds more strongly against the adversary.

syncopation. Shifting of accent in a line of verse, as when the rhetorical (or natural speech) stress differs from the metrical stress; esp. beginning with a heavy beat where normally a slack would occur. Thus in iambic pentameter lines, the first foot is often trochaic. *Cf.* Rhythm; Sprung rhythm.

syncope. The cutting short, reducing, or slurring over a word. Esp., the practice (or an instance thereof) of using dots, dashes, or asterisks in place of letters, in names or words the writer does not wish to (or dares not) give in full.

syncrisis. *See* Homeosis.

synecdoche (Gr., understood together). A figure wherein another thing is understood with the thing mentioned, as "fifty sail" and therewith fifty ships; "Give us this day our daily bread" and therewith three square meals. Some (K. Burke) extend the figure as including the basic process of representation; Hegel: "everything is its other." Gr. rhetorics listed 13 forms: the part for the whole, the genus for the species, the material for the thing made of it, the container for the contents, etc. *Cf.* Figure, Metonymy.

syneciosis. The linking of opposites (as when extremes meet):

> Niggard and unthrift are as one,
> Neither knows how to use his own.

Cf. Oxymoron.

synizesis. The process (common in Gr. and L. verse) whereby two vowels, keeping their separate sound, are pronounced with the time value of one; or the fact of such rapid pronunciation. Sometimes called synaeresis, but this term may also be used for contraction.

synonym. Although many a word means the same as another within one range of their significance, so that they are synonyms, usually each word has different connotations (bold, brave, fearless, courageous, reckless, foolhardy) or diverse senses (burden, load; stall, stop). The language is thus enriched with possibilities of precision and association. A sense of the danger of elegant variation (*q.v.*), however, and of the value of repetition, should temper the desire for variety.

A synonym is often proffered as a quick, loose definition, which will hardly suffice in rigorous discourse. The most effective use of synonyms is in the discrimination of closely allied meanings.

syntactics. *See* Signs, general theory of.

syntax. The organization of language into meaningful structure, or the pattern of relationship between words when so organized. Also, the pattern characteristic of a particular writer, as in "His syntax is involved." *See* Grammar. N. Chomsky, *Syntactic Structure,* 1957; *Aspects of the Theory of Syntax,* 1965; P. Postal, *Constituent Structure,* 1964.

synthesis. The building up of separate but related elements into a unified whole. Opp. analysis. The dialectic process presents a thesis opposed by its antithesis; the two are then united in a "higher" synthesis. *Cf.* Dialectic. E. Auerbach, *Literary Language and its Public,* 1965.

synthetic rhyme is that created (usually in humorous verse) by altering a word or by other distortion, *e.g.* (Ogden Nash) "Conundrum . . . clean out from undrum." Synthetic rhythm (frequent in ballad and folksong) is that established by repeating a word, adding syllables, or using nonsense words, *e.g.,* "As I have done before, O."

systrophe. A heaping up of definitions of a thing; repetition by definition; *e.g.,* Macbeth's lines (II ii 34–38) beginning:

> Sleep that knits up the ravell'd sleave of care,
> The death of each day's life, sore labour's
> bath. . .

There are 18 references to sleep in that scene, 31 in the act. *Cf.* Repetition.

syzygy (Gr., yoke). A joined pair of terms. A pair of feet considered as a unit (also called dipody); hence, *e.g.,* iambic trimeter instead of hexameter. Esp., the complete epirrhematic agon in Gr. Old Comedy. Phonetic syzygy (Lanier) is complex alliteration, *e.g.* (G. M. Hopkins): Those lovely lads once, wet-fresh windfalls of war's storm.

T

TAG. Something added, or tucked in: (1) for adornment, or emphasis, as a familiar quotation or proverb; hence, a trite parenthesis or closing remark; (2) as a refrain, or a nonsense line repeated for the rhythm; (3) as the closing words of an exit speech, when specially phrased (in blank verse drama often rhymed, hence tag rhyme) to catch attention and allow the player to take off with a flourish amid applause.

tagmeme. The smallest unit of grammatical form. *See* Language.

tail rhyme (tailed, caudate rhyme; L. *versus caudati,* Fr. *rime couée;* G. *Schweifreim*). Rhyme of two (sometimes more) short lines, each coming after and as a "tail" to several longer lines in the stanza pattern, *e.g.,* in Shelley's *To Night*: a_4 b_2 a b c c_4 b_2, the b_2 lines are the tail rhyme. Sometimes such a line is used to link successive stanzas.

tale (to tell, to count; *cf.* recount). Any relation or spoken story. As a form: a narrative, usually loosely woven and told for entertainment; in verse or prose (Chaucer, *Canterbury Tales,* ca. 1387; Swift *A Tale of a Tub,* satire, ca. 1696; Dickens, *A Tale of Two Cities,* 1859; Irving, *Tales of a Traveller,* 1824; Longfellow, *Tales of the Wayside Inn,* 1863; Poe, *Tales of the Grotesque and Arabesque,* 1839. The "tales" of Poe present a more tightly knit form, that came to be called the short story). Sometimes presented as truth, but not to be credited (*e.g.,* traveler's tale; fish story). Tall tale: realistic Am. frontier scene, with fantastic occurrences, usually of the prowess of a pioneer, riverman, cowhand, railroader, lumberjack (*e.g.,* Paul Bunyan); or gossipy and long-winded (old wives' tale). Fairy tale: of supernatural, potent though often diminutive beings, some bringing harm, but always with ultimate happiness, to pretty maids and patient heroes. *Cf.* Folk tale; Short story.

tanka. Jap. A poem of 31 syllables, in lines of 5, 7, 5, 7, 7. It is esp. a court poem, in elevated and traditional diction. Note that the first three lines constitute the haiku form, which has been more influential in the West. *Cf.* cinquain; haiku; Japanese poetry. E. Miner, *The Jap. Tradition in Brit. and Am. Lit.,* 1958.

tapinosis. Expression (or the fact of its use) lacking in propriety; undignified epithet, that demeans or belittles the subject, *e.g.* "a wart of a mansion, on the mountainside." Thus (J. Joyce) "Joepeter" at once summons and dethrones the god. *Cf.* Hyperbole.

taste [It. and Sp. *gusto;* Fr. *goût;* G. *Geschmack*. It. and Sp. Renaissance used the word metaphorically, to mean pleasure, amusement, inclination. Used first to designate a special faculty by the Sp. thinker and moralist Balthasar Gracián (mid 17th c.); but his phrase *hombre de buen gusto* meant simply a tactful person. Systematic adoption of the term in the æsthetic field probably took place in Fr., thanks to Bouhours. La Bruyère affirms (*Caractères,* 1688) that one may or may not have the sense of perfection in the arts: *il y a donc un bon et un mauvais goût;* therefore, despite the old proverb *de gustibus non est disputandum, l'on dispute des goûts avec fondement.* Discussions centred about 'good' and 'bad' taste; the term grew into wide use, and by the beginning of the following c. established itself in G. and Eng.]

Such phrases as "critical taste," "judicial criticism," "taste and judgment of the critic" indicate the intimate associations of these terms. Yet their exact interpretation, either singly or in conjunction, is frequently elusive: first because they have been given varied and interlocking meanings; secondly, because they are frequently employed in a careless, imprecise way. An early definition of taste (Baldinucci, 1681) is the "mode of working of each artist"; this is approached today in Lionello Venturi's idea of taste as "the sum of the elements of a work of art." This use of "taste," however, seems exceptional and would now ordinarily be indicated by the word "style."

More significant are the widely varying meanings all of which connect taste with intuitive experience and appraisal of works of art. Two of these meanings should be carefully distinguished: taste as (1) "the fact or condition of liking or preferring something"; (2) "discernment and appreciation of the beautiful in nature or art." Both of these senses are used, *e.g.,* in one short essay by Addison. (1) "Our general Taste in England is for Epigrams, turns of Wit, and forced Conceits—"; (2) Taste is "the Faculty of the Soul, which discerns the Beauties of an Author with Pleasure, and the Imperfections with Dislike" (*Spectator,* 409).

The first of these general meanings regards taste primarily as unreasoned preference or liking. The second makes taste to some extent a rational activity (most emphatically so, *e.g.,* for Hume and Coleridge); it is in some sense to be considered good or bad, true or false, better or worse. This meaning is closely connected with most senses of judgment and criticism. Thus T. S. Eliot: "Criticism . . . must always profess an end in view, which, roughly speaking, appears to be the elucidation of works of art and the correction of taste." Delicate problems of interpretation arise over the precise implications in terms of value of most statements about excellence or improvement in matters of taste. Goodness or badness in taste, *e.g.,* may be considered to have a subjective basis yet to be universally valid (as with Kant); or may be considered relative to different psychological types of people and in no way absolute; or may be considered to depend upon eternally fixed principles (as with Neo-Classic criticism).

Judgment is frequently identified with taste or with its findings (*e.g.,* Hume: "If [taste] pronounce the whole in general to be beautiful or deformed, it is the utmost that can be expected; and even this judgment. . . .") To the aforesaid two meanings of taste thus correspond two meanings of judgment: (1) A sensuous æsthetic activity unregulated by reasoned thought (*e.g.,* Kant: "The judgment of taste is therefore not a judgment of cognition, and is consequently not logical but æsthetical, by which we understand that whose determining ground can be no other than subjective.") When Croce and his followers refer to taste as a "judicial activity" or "faculty of judging," the judgment intended is "of the senses" and has nothing to do with cognition. Such judgment plays a vital role only in subjective types of criticism; it is at most a preliminary stage when criticism is regarded as reasoned estimation. (2) A serious reasoned discrimination between good and bad, better and worse (*e.g.,* Burke: "A rectitude of judgment in the arts, which may be called good taste,—"). Judgment and taste, according to this view, are primarily cognitive, intellectual activities; and they are essential to all kinds of criticism that stress the need for standards.

Both types of association between taste and judgment fail to distinguish between immediate, sensuous æsthetic likings and æsthetic satisfactions that are based in part upon thoughtful reflective inquiry. This useful distinction is brought out in the definitions that dissociate taste and judgment, confining the meaning of "taste" to the immediate and the meaning of "judgment" to the reflective. The difference in meaning might then be elucidated (following John Dewey) by contrasting certain words in pairs, the 1st word indicating the preference of taste, the 2d, the conclusion of judgment: "desired" and "desirable," "satisfying" and "satisfactory," "admired" and "admirable."

The diverse interpretations of taste and judgment, it has been noted, help to determine types of criticism; conversely, types of criticism will in large measure determine the sort of taste and judgment involved and the relationships between all three. If critical theory is impressionistic (*i.e.,* if the aim of the criticism is wholly to record in writing sensations experienced in the presence of a work of art), neither taste nor judgment can reasonably be defined in other than highly subjective terms; certainly judgment cannot be interpreted as intelligent, thoughtful inquiry. If, with the Croceans, critical theory inquires solely: "What has the artist tried to express and how has he expressed it?", taste and judgment tend to become critical tools for re-creating the artist's aim; they become similar to, if not identical with, genius. If, on the other hand, criticism is based upon cognitive judgment, taste is likely to assume a subordinate position; judgment becomes a tool which the critic must decide for what end to employ.

Thus the interrelations of these terms must be considered in the light of at least 6 major problems of criticism: (a) What is the place of precepts, principles and postulates? (b) What is the relative value of the following sorts of standards: technical, æsthetic, historical, sociological, metaphysical? (c) What is the comparative significance of elucidation and appreciation, of interpretation and evaluation? (d) What is the worth of distinctions between form and content? (e) What merit lies in the concepts of artistic greatness and artistic truth? (f) What effect should ethical beliefs have upon æsthetic evaluations?

From the foregoing comments upon taste, judgment and criticism, it becomes clear that those who naïvely demand to know what taste or judgment or criticism 'really' is, or what the true relationships between them 'really' are, cannot be answered. *Cf.* Rasa; Judgment; Value; Criticism, types. F. P. Chambers, *The History of Taste,* 1932; George Boas, *A Primer of Critics,* 1937; John Dewey, *Art as Experience,* 1934; D. W. Prall, *Aesthetic Judgment,* 1929. BERNARD C. HEYL.

taxis. *See* Computational stylistics.

telescope word. A coined word formed by combining two other words, *e.g.:* infanticipating. Sometimes they are run together by a printer's error (*see* Ghost word). The rebels in the magazine *transition,* led by James Joyce, sought the "revolution of the word." Thus "viterberation" packs the double violence of a quarrel. Often used by pundits (*e.g.,* Walter Winchell), and esp. *Time* magazine. B. Crémieux, *transition,* June 1930. Also called portmanteau, *q.v.* Cf. Etymology.

telestich. A poem in which the last letters of successive lines form a word or other special meaning. *Cf.* Acrostic.

tema con variazioni. Term borrowed from music to denote a form of humorous verse, or parody. A poem is taken, *e.g.,* a quatrain: each line of the original becomes, in order, the first line of a new quatrain (in the same meter) ludicrously developing the original idea—*e.g.* Lewis Carroll, "I never loved a dear gazelle" (from Thomas Moore).

tenor. (1) The thought running through a passage, the purport. (2) The subject or idea named in a metaphor (I. A. Richards, who calls the image the vehicle; the two together constitute the figure).

tension. Strain, excitement or suspense, caused by a movement in many poems, novels, and perhaps all plays: an initial promise and expectancy, the inception of action, followed by acceleration (with keyed-up anticipation) until the resolution or consummation, and a decline or "cadential finish." Except for the final tension of a work there is usually, within the decline of one tension, the roused expectancy of another. Thus the organization of tensions is a basic technical element in the projection of the artist's feeling and tone. This rhythmic balance of tightening tension and relaxation helps to maintain the receptor's interest. It is inaugurated at the very beginning of a work, even by the rising of the curtain on an empty stage.

Another sort of tension, in poetry, is created by the interplay of meter and sense, or by the counterposing of the syllable-counting stress (of, *e.g.,* the iambic pentameter) and the normal stress of the words. Thus we may have the subtle contrast of an iambic meter formed with trochaic words: "It little profits that an idle king," or such a varied flow as (Reed Whittemore):

Waking was wisdom, ungodly, civil,
Wrapped in the shawl of the commonplace.

Allen Tate uses the word (which he derives from *ex*tension and *in*tention) to refer to the range and interplay of literal and figurative elements in a work, the organization of the abstract and the concrete, of denotation and connotation. Psychoanalysts speak of psychic tension, the constant strain and delicate balance of the energy of the *id* and the control of the *ego;* the subtlety of this balance, they assert, is indicated by the ambiguity in art. *Cf.* Suspense; Ambiguity. Allen Tate, *Reason in Madness,* 1941; Susanne Langer, *Mind,* 1967.

tenson. Prov. From the L. debate, developed in So. Fr. in the 12th c. Often amorous (*see pastorela*): a poetic disagreement or debate between two poets (often then called *tenzone,* from its popularity in It.) or with a poet imagining his opponent—his patron, his lady, an allegorical figure; both contenders may be allegorical. Its subject might also be politics, or literary criticism; it admits a familiar tone, malice, realism (hence gives vivid glimpses of the times). Sometimes sung to music. *Partimen,* or *joc partit:* a tenson in which one term of the discussion excludes the other, *e.g.,* Which is more valuable, knowledge or love? Is it wiser to marry a widow or a maid?

tercet. Triplet in verse: a group of 3 lines, variously associated: (a) as a stanza. (b) as one of a series of stanzas interlinked by rhyme, *e.g.,* in *terza rima.* (c) as one of the pair of triplets that often makes the sestet of a sonnet. (d) as 3 successive rhyming lines (commonly called a triplet) in a poem rhymed mainly as a series of couplets.

term. A word or group of words intended to convey something to a receptor; the unit of comprehensible discourse. "The source of bad criticism, as universally of bad philosophy, is the abuse of terms" (Hurd). Hence, the common cry "Let us define our terms." To this it is countered that "Definitions are not set *a priori,* save perhaps in mathematics. In history it is from the patient study of reality that they emerge." As the writer is seldom so patient, it is wise that at least he know in what sense he employs his terms, and usually helpful that he share this knowledge with the receptor. J. W. Bray, *A Hist. of Eng. Crit. Terms,* 1898.

terminology, technical, for validity demands: (1) that each of its terms denote with economy and precision one and only one thing, (2) that the terms imply as few fixed relations among themselves as possible and as little association as possible with any general hypothesis concerning the mutual relation of the ideas or things they denote or the relations of these to other things; so that on the one hand adjustment to new developments is easy, and on the other hand communication, and thus agreement upon report of fact and mutual comprehension of differing interpretations of it, are possible between men who subscribe to different general hypotheses. The terminology of literary theory and criticism is at present far from satisfying either of these requirements. It is not, like that of modern chemistry, a special nomenclature created originally for the purposes it serves, but simply lay vocabulary adapted for technical use. Then, a large part of it is inherited from a more or less remote past (mainly classical, esp. Greek antiquity), and the vicissitudes of its often agitated transmission have modified and complicated its reference, and sometimes compromised its utility, more than we in practise recognize. Such words, *e.g.,* as *lyric, ode,* and *romance,* which once referred to distinctions "as simple as the difference between cricket and football" (W. P. Ker, *Form & Style,* 1928, p. 105), are in their modern use almost incapable of exact definition; and words like *beauty, poetry,* and *expression* are so ambiguously weighted with complicated theoretical associations that it is hardly safe to use them in simple descriptive situations. The intelligent critic must abandon (if he has entertained) the assumption that the existing critical terminology is as a whole a true technical language, and treat its terms exactly as he treats all the words of his lay or general vocabulary, using commonly only those that are immediately intelligible in the sense he intends, and defining all others in terms of these or referring, explicitly or by implication, to such definition of them. Where no explicit definition is furnished by the critic, the implied reference is to a standard dictionary of the general language. (In Eng. the best of these for the critic's purposes is of course the *Oxford English Dictionary*). It is a function of the present work to supplement and order (not to supplant or replace) the information furnished for literary terms by such a dictionary, and so to provide at least rational starting-points toward the approximation to uniformity in the use of these that is necessary, but distressingly lacking in much contemporary criticism.

J. C. C. Ernesti, *Lexicon technologiæ Gr. rhetoricæ,* 1795; *Lex. tech. L. rhet.,* 1797. J. Craig LaDrière.

tern. A group of three stanzas; esp. in a ballade, consisting of a tern and an envoi. Also, tercet, *q.v.*

ternaire. Fr. *See trimètre.*

terza rima. The metrical scheme invented by Dante for the *Divine Comedy*: a continuous series of hendecasyllable tercets in which, at the beginning, line 1 rhymes with line 3, line 2 of each tercet rhymes with 1 and 3 of the next until the series closes (at the end of the canto) with a single line rhyming thus: *aba, bcb, cdc . . . mnm, n.* Many modern scholars, following the ideas of the old commentators, attribute its source to the *serventese;* others suggest the Sicilian sonnet. The appropriateness of the *terza rima* for the *Divine Comedy* is evident when one considers not only the emphasis it gives to the symbolical number 3, all-important for the poem, but the harmony it achieves while maintaining a structural solidity that in its closely-knit interlacing reminds one of the Byzantine mosaics of Ravenna and Palermo. So strong and compact is the interweaving of fine detail into a vast design that it has been argued, even, that Dante used it in order that no one might tamper with his masterpiece by altering a verse here and there.

The *terza rima* was immediately used by the imitators of Dante in the 14th c. and by

Boccaccio and Petrarch in their allegorical poems. Its use was revived in the later 18th c.; Vincenzo Monti (1754–1828) became known as "a new Dante" because he used it for his most important poems. But no poet has been able to reproduce Dante's precision, compactness, lucidity, or vigour, to say nothing of the beauty and harmony of his verse. Milton, Shelley (*Ode to the West Wind*), Byron, experimented with the *terza rima,* but it has proved even less adaptable to Eng. verse. ANGELINE HELEN LOGRASSO.

terzina. A stanza of three lines, esp. in the *terza rima.* Also, a continuous (nonstanzaic) poem rhymed *aba, bcb, cdc . . . mnm;* common in early Romance languages. Introduced into Eng. (in iambic pentameters) by Surrey, but not often used.

tetralogy. The traditional set of plays submitted for tragic competition by the Athenian poets: a trilogy of tragedies followed by a satyr play. *Cf.* Trilogy; Tragedy.

tetrameter. A verse of four feet. In classical verse, usually four dipodies or eight feet; commonly iambic, anapaestic, or trochaic, and normally catalectic. *Cf.* Classical versification.

tétramètre. Fr. The normal division of the 12-syllable alexandrine line into four rhythmic beats, *e.g.* (Lamartine, *Le Lac,* 1820): *Un soir, / t'en souvient-il? / nous voguions / en silence. Cf. Trimètre;* Prosody; Romance versification.

tetrapody. A group or line of four feet.

tetrastich. A group or stanza of four lines. *See* Quatrain.

textual criticism. *See* Criticism, textual.

theatre. *See* Drama; Play; Comedy; Tragedy; Absurd; Cruelty; Anti-theatre. H. Hartnoll, *Oxford Companion to the Theatre,* 1951, 1967; J. Cleaver, *Theatre Through the Ages,* 1967; Allardyce Nicoll, *The Development of the Theatre,* 1966; G. Freedley and Reeves, *A Hist. of the Theatre,* 1941, 1955, 1968; E. Bentley, ed. *The Theory of the Modern Stage,* 1968.

theme. The subject of discourse; the underlying action or movement; or the general topic, of which the particular story is an illustration. Themes may be divided (Dahlstrom) into (1) Physical, man as molecule; (2) Organic, man as protoplasm; (3) Social, man as *socius:* (4) Egoic, man as individual; (5) Divine, man as soul.

(1) Physical forces may be a main theme, personified: Scylla and Charybdis; the seasons quickening life (esp. in poetry): Vaughan, *The World*; Milton, *On Time.* Time or place may dominate, in novels (Verne, *Around the World in 80 Days*; Hamsun, *Growth of the Soil*; Buck, *The Good Earth*) and documentary films (*The Wave*; *The River*). They may also "cradle," or frame, the action. (2) Organic forces play in the attraction and repulsion of the sexes; the incest dramas; in the keeping and breaking of faith (Turgenev, *Fathers and Sons*). (3) Social forces include the feral (organic) broadened beyond individual concerns (H. G. Wells, *Marriage*); education, politics; propaganda. (4) The egoic represent individual responses, mainly to social forces—these two groups being the most crowded: the individual risen from instinct to thought (Goethe, *Faust*; Ibsen, *Brand*). (5) Divine forces may be within the human, as in the vision of Dante, or as in Æschylus' *Prometheus Bound*; Jacob wrestling with the angel.

Recognition of such basic themes permits fresh analysis of a work. Thus *As You Like It* is cradled in opposition of kin: banished duke vs. the usurper his brother; Rosalind vs. her uncle; Orlando vs. Oliver—with an aspect of the physical: wrestling match; the forest; lion and snake. Its main opposition is of the sexes; note Shakespeare's variety: Orlando and Rosalind, romantic dalliance, love at first sight and at its dearest; Touchstone and Audrey, love's caricature, any wench an she come smiling; Silvius and Phebe, at odds, mated by a trick; Oliver and Celia: everybody's doing it; here we are, come along! C. E. W. Dahlstrom ("The Analysis of Literary Situation," *PMLA* 51, 1936) seeking to distinguish theme from subject, situation, plot, limits it to "guiding idea, moral, lesson, pronouncement." *Cf.* Subject, Situation.

thesis. (1) The unstressed syllable of a foot; however, *see* Arsis. (2) The first of an opposed pair; *cf.* Antithesis. The thesis is the proposition to be proved. Hence, thesis play: one that presents a social problem, perhaps with the dramatist's solution (Ibsen; Shaw; Brieux, *Damaged Goods,* 1903). Usually not so specific as a propaganda play, endeavoring rather to inculcate an attitude that will not tolerate the evil than to urge a particular program for its eradication. *Cf.* Propaganda; Dialectic; Literature and society.

threnody, threne. A type of Gr. melic, a choral dirge, later monodic; usually an encomium. Strophic in form, various meters. Not widely used until the spread of the Doric choral lyric, 6th c. B.C.; then esp. by Simonides of Ceos, but continuing (many in J. C. von Zedlitz, *Totenkränzen,* 1827). *See* Dirge.

time. I. The sense of the movement of time underlies man's thinking. From so flippant a consideration as Arnold Bennett's *How To Live On 24 Hours a Day,* through Paul Claudel's characterizing of the universe as a machine for marking time, to the second law of thermodynamics, which tells us that the world is running down, man has a death's-head reminder at the banquet of life. Thus "time is the chief character of every tragedy": while Lady Macbeth dreams, time brings her the royal guest; while Hamlet hesitates, while Faust tastes life, time hurries them to their doom. "The passing of all things is the theme of every poem." Basic in man's view of nature is the knowledge that everything is transitory. "And," says Goethe, "art is the exact opposite: it springs from the individual's effort to maintain himself against the destructive power of the all." (Hence, perhaps, the poet's frequent promise, or claim, of immortality.) II. Time, as the chronological extent of a work, in its handling permits the compression of almost instantaneous action, or the rambling inclusion of several lives' range. Most epics present their stories in a comparatively short time (Odysseus relates the longest stretch of his adventures at the Phæacian court) or in a few major episodes, with intervening years leapt in a phrase. The unity of time in the drama is still often observed, with action continuous throughout the play. Against the "scars healed in the tiring room" of Elizabethan drama, there was more than one protest, *e.g.,* Sidney: "For ordinary it is that two young Princes fall in love; after many traverces, she is got with child, delivered of a fair boy; he is lost, groweth a man, falls in love, and is ready to get another child, and all this in two hours' space: which how absurd it is in sense, even sense may imagine, and art hath taught, and all ancient examples justified." Plays that survive on the stage have had to cope with Sidney (*see* III, below). The majority of motion pictures, of novels, spread but a short span: *Silas Marner* jumps 16 years in a sentence; *Ulysses* (Joyce) crams a Dublin day. Whatever the time extent, devices are usually employed to make the receptor feel its pressure rather than its duration. Sidney's protest recalls the dramatic unity of time (binding in Fr. for 300 years, seldom observed in Eng.), which prescribes that no more shall transpire on stage than can occur in the time it takes to enact the play (usually stretched to allow 24 hours). Jacqueline de Romilly, *Time in Gr. Tragedy,* 1968. III. Time as the gait, the pace, the "tempo" of the work is the predominant temporal aspect, determining the receptor's consciousness of the others. A manifest method of its control is the meter in poetry, which, even within the adopted pattern, can be considerably varied. In narratives, the tempo can be controlled by such devices as (1) space. Dwelling longer upon an incident may either (a) make it seem important or (b) give it an unhurried aspect: fainéant leisure; calm; deliberate calculation; enshrouding doom—according as the (2) variation of diction suggests precipitate weight, onrush of events and emotions; or a more protracted spread. A preponderance of action-words and short sentences, *e.g.,* suggests speed (Vernon Lee, *The Handling of Words,* 1923; E. Rickert, *New Methods For the Study of Lit.,* 1927). The rush of Shakespeare's plays makes astounding a calculation of the time actually involved. Dispute over Hamlet's age, and the play time-span, has led Christopher North to speak of Shakespeare's "two clocks"; others of his "protractive" time and "accelerating" time; his "long" time, emphasizing its passage, and his "short" time, its pressure. James M. Manly protests that there is but one; that the events are to be viewed not in actual temporal progression but in logical growth, with time but sustaining their reality, propriety, or force. *Macbeth, e.g.,* covers 9 days in the scenes onstage; but between Act II and Act III come long and wretched years of Macbeth's reign. Yet the first words spoken in Act III, Banquo's "Thou hast it now—king, Cawdor, Glamis, all, As the weird women promised," and Macbeth's own words (III, end of iv) explaining his terrors: "We are yet but young in deed," suggest that but a few days have passed since the first murder. In Act IV the news of Lady Macduff's murder follows Macduff to Eng.; in Act V, ii, Malcolm is in Scotland again; from this point to the end (V, viii) there is no check on time. Thus over the actual passage of days is a pressure of imminent action.

The same apparent heedlessness of chronology prevails in Russ. fiction. Turgenev's *Rudin* presents the chief figure as a young man in 1845; many years pass, he dies an old man on the barricades—in 1848. There is a sense, whatever the time, that the action is present. At its best, this gives an immediacy and vividness to events and characters, an instant urgency to the flow. *Cf.* Unities; Prosody; Meter; Quantity. A. A. Mendilow, *Time and the Novel,* 1952; H. Meyerhoff, *Time in Lit.,* 1955; G. Poulet, *Studies in Human Time,* 1956; *The Interior Distance,* 1959; I. Morgenstern, *The Dimensional Structure of Time,* with *The Drama and its Timing,* 1960; H. and A. Thornton, *Time and Style. . . in Classical Lit.,* 1962; M. Church, *Time and Reality . . . in Contemporary Fiction,* 1963; T. H. Bell, *The Riddle of Time,* 1963; J. B. Priestley, *Man and Time,* 1964; J. H. Buckley, *The Triumph of Time* (distinguishes private time and public time), 1966; Joost Meerloo, *Along the Fourth Dimension,* 1969.

tirade. 1. A vehement harangue, esp. of abuse or denunciation. 2. A passage of verse (in a longer poem) dealing with one subject; esp., in the *chanson de geste,* a passage bound by a single assonance or rhyme (in this sense pronounced as in Fr. and equivalent to *laisse*).

tmesis. Diacope, *q.v.*

tone, tone color. (1) The attitude of a work, as revealed in the manner, rather than stated. (2) The mood, or the creation of a mood, or the devices that create it, as rising from the manipulation of the materials of the art. E. Rickert (*New Methods For the Study of Lit.,* 1927) lists as "tone patterns" repetition, rhyme, alliteration, assonance, consonance; she analyzes these in detail, *e.g.,* alliteration may be (1) surface, of stressed syllables; (2) submerged, stressed and unstressed; (3) crossed; (4) eye, same letter but not same sound; (5) close; (6) loose; (7) complex. This is but an indication of the many devices that help establish tone—punctuation, figures, choice of words, condensation or amplification: the entire and not always or altogether consciously manipulated set of symbols that comprise the work reveals the author's intention, hence establishes his tone. *See* Meaning; Narrator; Alliteration.

topic (Gr., place). Subject of a work; originally, the field from which invention might draw its themes. "Places" (efficient, material, formal, and final cause; effect; species; adjunct; relatives; differences: repugnancies, adversatives, contraries) were detailed in most Renaissance rhetorics, *e.g.* Thos. Wilson, *Art of Rhetoric,* 1552; P. Ramus, *Logike,* 1574. *Cf.* Theme; Subject.

tornada. Prov. The *envoi* of a lyric, usually with half as many lines as the stanza.

tradition in its broadest sense denotes all the conventions, literary devices, and habits of expression handed on to a writer from the past. We can speak of the tradition of a specific device, as of the happy ending; or, of a particular literary form, as of the pastoral elegy; or of a period, as the Victorian tradition; or of a culture, as the French tradition; or—using the term in its largest and most honorific sense—we can speak of *the* tradition, whereby we mean the essential line of development coming to us out of the past, the main current as distinguished from the accidental and peripheral. In this sense, also, we may use the term in order to praise a writer: he is "full in the tradition," we say, or, he "represents the great tradition." But the term may be used for damnation as well, not only by connecting the writer with a "bad" tradition, but by asserting that the writer is "merely" traditional.

The differing inflections with which critics use the term call for a re-inspection of the relation of the practising craftsman to his past. The relation is subtle and complex, and varies from writer to writer; but two points should be obvious. (1) Every writer, even the humblest, even the so-called illiterate writer, begins with a tradition. The very fact that he inherits a language means that he cannot start from scratch. His own compositions, written or oral, will reflect what he has read or heard. (2) No writer, on the other hand, no matter how imitative, can repose passively in his inherited tradition; of necessity, he will modify it. The shifting, dynamic nature of language involves this in its every use.

These two points should be kept in mind, if we are to understand a writer's relation to the tradition. For the meaning of the relation resides in a tension between the two principles—the inescapable sense of the past, and the neccessity for relating the inherited past to the present.

In *Tradition and the Individual Talent,* T. S. Eliot says: "[Tradition] cannot be inherited, and if you want it you must obtain it by great labour." Inherited forms, used without modification by new perceptions, lose the sharpness that they originally possessed and become *clichés,* or mere conformity to arbitrary "rules."

The literary historian constantly treats the tradition as though it were a great river whose course he traces from its beginnings to the present. We are in the habit of viewing it chronologically, of seeing it as a continuity of cause and effect, of moving downstream with the current. But new writers do not float idly upon the current like so much driftwood; rather, like salmon, they fight their way upstream. The active attempt to master the past, to see it in terms of the present, to solve present problems in line with the solutions and achievements of the past—these make the writer "traditional" in the best sense. An uncritical imitation of the past can at best result in the construction of "period pieces," not vitally connected with the present—hence, except for outward semblance, not really connected with the past.

The creation of any new work is, thus, paradoxical in that the author always claims that he is getting back to "the tradition." Thus, the Romantic poets, in repudiating their immediate heritage, the neo-classic period, claimed that they were re-establishing connections with the main stream. The Imagists, in announcing their credo, claimed that they were reasserting principles native to the tradition but fallen into abeyance.

Cleanth Brooks, *Modern Poetry and the Tradition,* 1939; T. S. Eliot, "Tradition and the Individual Talent," *The Sacred Wood,* 1920; J. L. Lowes, *Tradition and Revolt,* 1930; G. Murray, *The Classical Tradition in Poetry,* 1927; F. L. Pattee, *Tradition and Jazz,* 1925; *Tradition and Experiment* (10 writers; R. H. Mottram states: "The tradition of the Eng. novel is experiment"; Ashley Dukes says more shrewdly: "Tradition is surely no more than the fruit of successful experiment"), 1929. The Greeks recognized that Memory is the mother of the Muses. *Cf.* Augustan; Classicism. R. F. Livingston, *The Traditional Theory of Lit.,* 1962. CLEANTH BROOKS.

tragedy. The origins of tragedy are closely related to primitive ritual in the form of vegetation, tomb or ancestral, totemic and initiation rites of importance in the economic and social life of the community. Characteristic was the theme of conflict between the hero (mythological, ancestral, semi-historical) and an antagonist, culminating in the former's death and resurrection, thus paralleling the cycle of death and resurgence in nature. The first religious tragedies known to us were the Passion Plays of Egypt and Syria, revolving around the mythological characters Osiris, Attis and Adonis. (In the Far East there is little evidence of tragedy, except in the medieval Noh plays of Japan, mostly ghost plays or dramas of reminiscence.) In Europe, tragedy developed first in Greece, chiefly out of ritual centred upon the nature-god Dionysus (the *dithyramb,* or leaping dance, enacted events from his life or Passion), supplemented by tomb rites in worship of tribal heroes and totemic rites. (Note the survival in Euripides' *Bacchae* of the *sparagmos* or tearing of the sacrificial victim into pieces). Literally, tragedy means goat-song (*trag oidia*); it seems to refer to totemic ritual, the sacrifice of a goat. (The goat was apparently also given as a prize, in early dramatic contests). Aristotle traced tragedy to the satyr plays in which the characters were half-man, half-goat. The term was applied to all plays of high seriousness, with or without (*e.g.,* Sophocles, *Philoctetes*) an unhappy ending. The choruses, which comprised a large portion of the play, gave the tragedies not only reflective dignity and philosophic content, but great scope, since the reflections and comments of the chorus recall the active past that caused the present action. In the work of Æschylus, dimension was given to the tragedy by the trilogy form—three plays devoted to the development of a single theme. Compression and the custom of writing single tragic plays did not greatly reduce the dimension of Sophocles' and Euripides' tragedies, because the action was extended at the expense of the chorus, the choral odes being considerably abbreviated. The subjects were always exalted, because of the heroic stature of the characters, the heroic myths from which the plot was taken, and the formal poetic style. Later, in the work of Euripides, realistic detail was introduced into the drama, some romantic plots were employed (*Helena*), some heroes and gods were deflated (*Orestes, Ion*); but even then the intention and the execution remained noble.

Aristotle's definition of tragedy in his *Poetics,* some 70 years after the death of Euripides, substantially fits extant Greek tragedy: "A Tragedy, then, is an artistic imitation of an action that is serious, complete in itself, and of adequate magnitude." The term magnitude may be applied to other features of tragedy, as Aristotle sensed in his stress on "embellished" or poetic language, in his finding a correspondence between tragedy and epic ("epic poetry has much in common with tragedy; it is an imitation, in a lofty kind of verse, of serious events"), and in his opinion that tragic characters must have stature or importance. Magnitude is also ensured by *ethos* (the moral decisions of the characters) and *dianoia* or intellect ("the power of the agent to say what can be said, or what is fitting to be said, in a given situation").

Important, too, in Aristotle's theory was the place of suffering: "an incident of a destructive or painful sort, such as violent death, physical agony." This encompasses not only a classic idyl like *Philoctetes* but modern plays like *The Cherry Orchard,* in which the physical incident is the loss of the family estate and the suffering is mental. For the suffering to evoke pity, moreover, Aristotle recommended a hero neither superlatively good and just nor wholly vicious and depraved, but "brought low through some error of judgment or shortcoming." This flaw (*hamartia*) is a lack of insight within the character that results in some catastrophic action. *Hamartia* is widely applicable as a dynamic factor in both characterization and plot; in modern social drama, however, the tragic flaw often exists more strongly in the milieu or in society than in the hero, who becomes the victim of external circumstance. (It is also questionable whether Œdipus' *hamartia* isn't disproportionate to his suffering, in which the "crass causality" of Fate plays the major role, so that the balance of poetic justice trembles.)

As a result of these attributes, the effect of tragedy, according to Aristotle, is "to arouse the emotions of pity and fear in the audience; and to arouse this pity and fear in such a way as to effect that special purging and relief (catharsis) of these two which is characteristic of tragedy." Success in effecting catharsis Aristotle related especially to the action or plot, which carries the story progressively forward, involving the audience through the force of the progression. This is assured by the proper construction of the plot, which, like any whole, has a beginning, a middle, and an end; and also by the special dynamics of reversals and discoveries. The reversal or *peripeteia* is a "change at some part of the action from one state of affairs to its precise opposite"—*e.g.,* from good fortune to ill—in a necessary or probable sequence. A discovery or *anagnorisis* is a "transition from ignorance to knowledge" and a consequent emotional reaction—such as a character's recognition of the identity of a person or discovery of facts concerning a person's past behavior. Pity and fear in tragedy are aroused, then, not merely by the complete action but by salient incidents in the plot—provided, however, that they are part of the design of causality.

Concerning tragic catharsis there has been considerable debate. It is probable that the Aristotelian view was related to Greek medical thought. Pity and fear are present in human nature, and may be troublesome to the psyche. Tragedy provides experiences that enable the spectator to discharge these emotions, thus relieving the soul. Lessing's view was that the spectator feels himself filled with pity for those "whom a fatal stream has carried so far," and with terror "at the consciousness that a similar stream might also thus have borne ourselves" (*Hamburgische Dramaturgie*); this in turn purifies our passions. Gustav Freytag, in his *Technique of the Drama,* 1863, held the view that the catharsis comes from the spectator's aloofness from the tragic events, his sense of security. Modern psychoanalysis provides an explanation in the patient's reliving unconscious experience, bringing it into the open, and evaluating by the intellect (Aristotle's *dianoia*) consciously what had been unconscious and therefore inhibiting and painful (John Gassner, *Catharsis and the Theory of Enlightenment*). Tragic irony, the spectator's knowledge of tragic imminence unknown to the dramatic character until the moment of the catastrophic event, can also promote catharsis as Lessing views it.

Although some of Aristotle's observations on tragedy have a special reference to Greek drama, magnitude, plot, reversal, discovery, catharsis, *ethos* and *dianoia* may be found in fully devoloped tragedy in any age. Another feature, unity of plot (originally unified action, "the structural order of the incidents being such that transposing or removing any one of them will dislocate and disorganize the whole") has also been found essential to later tragedy, with at most minor divergences. After the classic period, the concept of tragedy underwent a variety of changes and amplifications, without, however, vitally affecting the validity of the Aristotelian formulation.

During the Renaissance, scholars, led by Lodovico Castelvetro (1570), arrived at a stricter definition of unity than Aristotle intended and 5th c. Athenian tragedy exemplified. They made unity of time, and unity of place (not mentioned in the *Poetics*), incumbent on all tragic writers. This resulted in the imposition on tragedy, during the neo-classic period, of the three unities (time, place, and action), a feature of the work of Corneille, Racine and their followers in France and the rest of Europe.

In the golden age of the Spanish theatre and the Elizabethan period, the unities of time and place were disregarded, and the unity of plot was only loosely observed. Subplots were employed in Elizabethan drama, and comic and tragic incidents commingled, as in tragicomedy or romance (the later Shakespeare; Beaumont and Fletcher). The same freedom prevailed in the romantic drama; since then, the unities have no longer been considered essential to tragedy. The principle of causality, which requires that the main incidents of the plot be organically related, is still generally observed.

Since the 18th c. (with Diderot; George Lillo; Lessing) the principle of magnitude has been modified to include the common people among the *dramatis personæ* of tragedy. The tragic hero—always an aristocrat in classic and neo-classic drama and with rare exceptions (*Arden of Feversham; A Yorkshire Tragedy*) in Elizabethan drama—can now be of any social level. Magnitude is defined in terms no longer of rank but of spirit and intellect. The self-assertion of the middle-class in the 18th c. and later democratic tendencies made the life of the common man even preferred as subject for tragedy. (Diderot, *De La Poésie Dramatique à M. Grimm,* pref. to his middle-class drama *Le Père de Famille,* 1758; Lessing, in his criticism and his middle-class tragedies, *Miss Sarah Simpson, Emilia Galotti.*) Beaumarchais summed up the argument: "The true heart-interest, real relationship, is always between man and man, not between man and king. Thus, far from increasing my interest in the characters of tragedy, their exalted rank rather diminishes it. The nearer the suffering man is to my station in life, the greater is his claim upon my sympathy." (*Essai sur le genre dramatique sérieux,* 1767). This emphasis on the common man was related to the development of social realism, and led to the growth of the tragedy of social conflict.

Realistic drama has, however, also presented situations and characters that lack true tragic dimension, although the circumstances are serious, even socially or psychologically important, and although the conclusion may be catastrophic. For this type of play (*e.g.,* C. Odets, *Rocket to the Moon*) the term "serious drama" may be preferable to tragedy. It was first used by Denis Diderot as descriptive of a play that falls between tragedy and comedy, like his own dramas *Le Fils Naturel* (1757) and *Le Père de Famille.* This type has also been called "social drama," "problem play," and more recently "metatheater."

Different philosophical concepts have appeared in the tragic literature of different ages. The Greek concept of Fate (*ananke*) appears as a causal factor in Greek dramas. In its simplest aspect, Fate resembles Thomas Hardy's "crass causality," but a conscious design appears in the Oresteian and the Promethean trilogies, and in Sophocles' resolution of the Œdipus story (*Œdipus at Colonus*). *Hubris* or pride, regarded as a sin offensive to the gods, is also a cause of the downfall of characters; this added to acts of extreme violence creates a fatefulness or curse—a domestic *Até* that dogs successive generations of a family. Æschylus saw the domestic *Até* revived afresh by the more or less voluntary deeds of individuals, so that Fate may be called a predisposition (*The Seven against Thebes;* the Oresteian trilogy). In Elizabethan tragedy, the dominant principle is the individual will, which leads to acts of violence and conflict. Spanish tragedy, wherein the conflict is often between the dictates of honor and the demands of love, gives emphasis to Hegel's thought (also illustrated in Joyce's *Exiles*) that tragedy is a struggle between two "rights." In modern realistic tragedy, the causal tragic factor is often the individual's conflict with society, its traditions, prejudices, representatives, laws (Ibsen, *A Doll's House,* Hauptmann, *The Weavers,* Sudermann, *Magda,* Shaw, *Saint Joan*). The naturalists add such causal factors as heredity (alcoholism; venereal disease: Hauptmann, *Before Sunrise*; Ibsen, *Ghosts*) and biological impulses (Hauptmann, *Rose Bernd*). Zola attributed tragedy to "the beast in man," to blind instinct or a largely sexual drive, which acts like Fate and leads to evil and suffering (*Thérèse Raquin,* 1867). The old concept now received a new meaning; Fate, in modern realistic terms, was nothing but instinct and heredity. Modern psychology, especially psychoanalysis, placed the first of these two tragic factors in the foreground by stressing the Unconscious. Tragedy is thus seen as produced by conflict between the conscious and unconscious forces of the psyche (O'Neill, *The Great God Brown, Days Without End*), and by conflict with society or other individuals caused by a character's inner, unconscious drives, like homosexuality (Mordaunt Shairp, *The Green Bay Tree*; Edouard Bourdet, *The Captive*). Finally, in the era of intensified class-struggle, drama added the struggle between capital and labor, or class-war, to its stock of tragic forces.

Two diametrically opposed conceptions of tragedy appear in the critic Ferdinand Brunetière's definition of drama and in the practice of Chekhov and his school. The latter leads to a view of tragedy as defeat by frustration and attrition, by a decadence and failure of the active will (*Uncle Vanya*; *The Three Sisters*; *The Cherry Orchard*). Brunetière, in *The Law of the Drama,* makes tragedy stem from the will of man that leads to conflict. Man's conflict may be against "the mysterious powers or natural forces that limit and belittle us," against "fatality, against social law, against himself, if need be, against the ambitions, the interests, the prejudices, the folly, the malevolence of those that surround him." Brunetière insisted that fatalism (as in 19th c. naturalism) makes drama impossible, that man's belief in the freedom of will "is of no small assistance in the struggle that we undertake against the obstacles that prevent us from attaining our goal."

Fatalism nonetheless cropped up in the symbolist and neo-romantic drama that arose as a reaction to naturalism in the last decade of the 19th c. (Maeterlinck, *The Intruder*; *Interior*; *The Blind*; Andreyev, *The Life of Man*). This fatalism led to the development of static tragedy, consisting of subjective presentation and the denial of action as a factor in drama, upheld by Maurice Maeterlinck in *The Treasure of the Humble* (1896): "the true tragic element of life only begins at the moment when so-called adventures, sorrows and dangers have disappeared." Maeterlinck wanted to have even "psychological action" suppressed, until "the interest centers solely and entirely in the individual face to face with the universe." (A. W. Schlegel: tragedy leads us to "contemplate the relations of our existence to the extreme limit of possibilities . . . the contemplation of infinity.") This view led to few achievements of even minor importance.

In the 20th c., marked by continually intensified national and class struggles, and by corresponding intellectual and emotional conflicts, tragedy naturally remained securely wedded to the Aristotelian theory of the primacy of action. The philosopher Hegel, applying his dialectic method to the drama, found the most apt description of its moving force in the term "tragic conflict": "the action is driven forward by the unstable equilibrium between man's will and his environment: the wills of other men, the forces of society and of nature." This dialectic definition of tragedy found support in dramatists influenced by Marxism, emphasizing economic and class conflict as a tragic factor, virtually creating a new form of heroic tragedy (Hauptmann, *The Weavers*; Toller, *The Machine-Wreckers*; Sklar and Peters, *Stevedore*) with the masses as protagonist. The threat of mechanization is emphasized in such plays as Karel Čapek's *R.U.R.* (1921), which gave our language the word *robot.* The field of tragic drama has thus widened until F. L. Lucas maintains that all definitions must be reduced to the "bare tautology: Serious drama is a serious representation by speech and action of some phase of human life." Exception may, however, be taken to this statement, since many serious representations of human life are not tragic, owing to lack of magnitude and will in the characters and of exaltation in the effect of the play. A distinction between tragedy and mere serious drama is necessary for both critical discernment and theatrical practice. Many contemporary plays fail to impress critics or to attract audiences because of their tepidity; they fall between two stools, insufficiently amusing to be comic, insufficiently stirring to be tragic. In the 1920's Joseph Krutch went so far as to claim (*The Modern Temper*) that tragedy cannot flourish in the present age, with its complex anti-heroic conceptions of character. The exacerbations of class struggles and national conflicts—and the eternal quest of man—do not support this generalization.

Despite declarations that tragedy is dead (*see* Metatheater), tragedy will be written so long as man, acting as with freedom of choice, elects to strive toward goals beyond his grasping, toward an existence better than he has known. It need not, often does not, end in disaster; there may be cleansing or transfiguration, as in *Oedipus at Colonus*; there may be illumination, even with death, as in Lear. Awakening from *hubris* may lead to sanctification, but *hubris* is no essential element in tragedy; Indeed, John Jones points out that *The Persians* is "the one play in the entire extant literature that is genuinely and fully founded upon *hubris*." But always, somewhere in the course of the tragedy, comes the stage direction (actual or implicit) "Enter the gods." It is man's reaching toward the heights that makes possible the tragic fall. Schlegel said that the distinctive aim of tragedy is "to establish the claims of the mind to a divine origin." And in the audience, this sense of man's worth, of his indomitable will, produces the final effect of tragedy, which is not so negative a movement as catharsis, but the positive upward urge of exaltation. In varying degrees the theatre may give us entertainment and enlightenment; the greatest drama adds the third gift, the gift of exaltation. *See* Drama; Comedy; Melodrama; *cf* Ode. A. H. Thorndike, *Tragedy,* 1908; A. Nicoll, *The Theory of Drama,* 1931; Ship; T. H. Gaster, *Thespis,* 1950; H. J. Muller, *The Spirit of Tragedy,* 1956; Cleanth Brooks, ed. *Tragic Themes in Western Lit.,* 1955; G. W. Knight, *The Wheel of Fire,* 1930, 1957; F. L. Lucas, *Tragedy,* 1958; D. D. Raphael, *The Paradox of Tragedy,* 1960; Elder Olson, *Tragedy and the Theory of Drama,* 1961; John Jones, *On Aristotle and Greek Tragedy,* 1962; W. Barrett, *Irrational Man,* 1962; L. Michael and R. B. Sewall, ed. *Tragedy: Modern Essays in Criticism,* 1963; G. Steiner, *The Death of Tragedy,* 1963; R. W. Corrigan, ed. *Tragedy: Vision and Form,* 1965; Raymond Williams, *Modern Tragedy,* 1966; B. H. Clark, ed. (enlarged by H. Popkin), *European Theories of the Drama,* 1966; C. Benson and T. Littleton, *The Idea of Tragedy,* 1966; Lionel Abel, ed. *Moderns on Tragedy,* 1967; Walter Kerr, *Tragedy and Comedy,* 1967; W. Kaufman, *Tragedy and Philosophy,* 1968; G. Brereton, *Principles of Tragedy,* 1968. For a challenge to Aristotle, *see* W. M. Spackman, *On the Decay of Humanism,* 1967. JOHN GASSNER.

tragicomedy. A play combining tragic and comic elements; esp. one of deeply serious tone but with a happy ending. Used with other combining forms, *e.g.,* (Hawker, 1729) *The Wedding,* "A Tragi-Comi-Pastoral-Farcical Opera" and the list Polonius gives (II ii) in *Hamlet. Cf.* Metatheater. M. T. Herrick, Tragicomedy, 1955; A. Hoy, *The Hyacinth Room,* 1964.

tragic flaw. That "error of judgment" in a man which occasions his misfortune is called by Aristotle the "tragic flaw" (hamartia, *q.v.*). The change from happiness, from the enjoyment of great reputation and prosperity, to misery is effected not through innate depravity but through a weakness or lack of insight within the character itself. Such an individual is the proper subject of the tragic plot, whose action logically follows from the characteristics of the persons involved: "within any series of actions, the characters have as two causes of these actions, Thought and Character, . . . the second (being) that which denotes certain moral qualities of the agents."

It is essential that the characters be "like us"; it is equally necessary that they be consistent. And from this inner consistency must come the unity of plot action. Aristotle found this dramatic relationship in the plays of Sophocles, in whose works we see into the mind of "one like us" undergoing a process of destruction. The stages of this process, the Greeks described as *kairos* (tempting opportunity), *hubris* (presumption against the gods), and *ate* (retribution). Yet in order that pity and terror be aroused in the audience as a result of this process, the tragic hero or heroine, as are those of Aeschylus and Euripides, must be many-sided, complex; and it is the defect in the character that makes it tragically imperfect. The "certain moral qualities of the agents" must be several in number in order to conform to the Aristotelian ideal: one weakness, *hubris,* among many honorable traits is sufficient to bring the hero and perhaps other, dependent persons to ruin. Sophocles' dramas are basically those of character portrayal, so that the plot turns on a series of dramatic events, consistent within themselves, which are a logical consequence of the characterizations. The Sophoclean hero undergoes change, generally in the direction of a more complete understanding of himself, and with coincident spiritual nobility. Shakespeare's *King Lear* presents a romantic extreme of this Sophoclean-Aristotelian tragic hero, the person well-intentioned, but blinded by his hamartia, who in the process of spiritual growth and self-illumination brings ruin upon others as well as upon himself. *Cf.* Hubris. JOHN BURKE SHIPLEY.

transcendentalism. New England transcendentalism was the result of the impact of post-Kantian idealism, as transmitted through such middlemen as Cousin, Coleridge, and Carlyle, on a liberal Puritanism in crisis. It affected chiefly Harvard-trained Unitarians and reached its height in the decade 1835–45. Transcendentalism—a name coined by its opponents, but soon accepted, as in Emerson's lecture "The Transcendentalist" (1841), which cites the supposed authority of Kant—was never a school or a doctrine, and resists accurate definition. Unitarians had rejected the Calvinist doctrine of total depravity; transcendentalists in turn rejected the truth of the Christian miracles and so found themselves believers who had unwillingly lost any revealed belief. They were therefore ripe for the idea then in the air of a divine principle in the "interior consciousness" of each man, an idea which carried them to an internal sanction for faith. Thus they stressed the adequacy of intuition for truth, of conscience for moral guidance, and of inspiration for literary creation. They turned for inspiration and support, on the one hand to nature, after the example of Wordsworth and his predecessors, on the other to their natural affinities in world literature—Plato and the Neo-Platonic tradition, Christian mystics like Boehme, contemporary literature, notably Goethe, and at a later date, Oriental literature.

Although their discovery of "the infinitude of the private man" led logically to a stress on the trustworthiness of impulse as a guide to action, in practice their inbred moral code filtered out impulses not acceptable to it and kept New England's *Sturm und Drang* innocent. Potentially, however, asserting as it did the right of the private conscience to pass judgment on all institutions, transcendentalism was profoundly revolutionary. Its drive toward reform took two directions: toward the individual's emancipation from society, and toward the reconstitution of society itself. The first reached its clearest expression in Emerson's "Self-Reliance" and Thoreau's "Civil Disobedience" and was the guiding aim not only of Thoreau's life, but of the Brook Farm experiment in its first years. The second contributed its powerful zeal to major agitations (by no means due solely to transcendentalists) such as those for temperance, women's rights, public education, and against war, government, and slavery, as well as a host of more ephemeral crusades, against money, for beards, for Graham bread. With time, transcendentalism became respectable and vaguely commonplace, and the crusading zeal that survived in this group was finally focused on anti-slavery and spent in the Civil War.

Some of the chief figures connected with this movement are: Ralph Waldo Emerson, whose *Nature* (1836) was as close to a manifesto as the group ever had, and who memorably voiced the transcendentalist challenge in *The American Scholar* (1837) and the Divinity School *Address* (1838); Theodore Parker, preacher and crusader, whose sermon on *The Transient and Permanent in Christianity* (1841) is the most explicit statement of the transcendentalist religious position; George Ripley, founder of the Brook Farm community (1841–47); Orestes Brownson, most pugnacious, restless, and acute of the group, whose stress on union in his *New Views of Christianity, Society, and the Church* (1836) foreshadowed his later conversion to Catholicism; Margaret Fuller, whose *Woman in the Nineteenth Century* (1845) was a pioneer statement of feminism in the United States; Bronson Alcott, teacher, talker, and seer, founder of the ill-starred Temple School (1834–36) and the ill-starred community at Fruitlands (1844); the poets Jones Very and Ellery Channing; Frederic Henry Hedge, Unitarian minister at Bangor, Maine, whose visits to Boston were the occasion for meetings of the discussion group variously known as Hedge's Club, the Transcendentalist Club, or "The Club of the Like-Minded," so-called, Emerson remarked, "because no two of them thought alike"; James Freeman Clarke, Convers Francis, and Charles King Newcomb. The chief transcendentalist periodical was *The Dial* (1840–44), edited first by Margaret Fuller and then by Emerson, preceded by Brownson's *Boston Quarterly Review* (1838–42), and succeeded by Parker's *Massachusetts Quarterly Review* (1847–50). The most lasting literary result of transcendentalism is Henry David Thoreau's *Walden* (1854).

O. B. Frothingham, *Transcendentalism in New England,* 1876; C. Goddard, *Studies in New England Transcendentalism,* 1908; H. D. Gray, *Emerson,* 1917; Perry Miller, *The Transcendentalists: An Anthology,* 1950. Stephen Whicher.

transferred epithet. One applied to a term with which it is not literally associated (*e.g.,* Shakespeare, "dusty death"). *See* Catachresis.

transition. (1) A shift from one topic, or phase of a work, to another; or the devices that carry the thought from one stage of its development to the next. The technical machinery that bridges gaps in the flow of a work, so as to maintain coherence. Also, metabasis. *Cf.* Composition. R. D. Elliott,

Transition in the Attic Orators, 1919. (2) A stage between two contrasted states, stages, periods, possessing characteristics of each. "Every age deems itself an age of transition." *See* Period; Progress.

translation. There are masterpieces in more languages than even a professional scholar can hope to command. Literary translation is therefore indispensable. It is folly to deprive oneself of *Crime and Punishment* because one cannot read Russian, or of *The Book of Job* because one has not mastered Hebrew. Not everyone will learn to read the language of an admired work. Translation will destroy the author's precise balance of thought, feeling, written word, sound: the loss is undeniable; but it has been greatly exaggerated. The Italian proverb, *Traduttore, traditore* (translator, traitor) is a victim's hyperbole. The merit of books lies in the beauty, richness and adequacy of their symbols, rather than in the sound of their language. The greater the work, the less will it suffer from transplanting. The punning of Thomas Hood, the alliterations of Swinburne, the lilt of *Ulalume,* the jangle of *The Bells,* the rich orchestration of Edward Lear's *Yonghi-Bonghi-Bo,* defy translation. The majesty of *Genesis* (as Longinus remarked many centuries ago), the intensity of the *Divine Comedy,* survive the ordeal. A Count d'Orsay needs perfection of attire; a hero, like Lincoln, remains heroic in ill-fitting clothes.

Every man translates what he reads in terms of his own experiences. Shakespeare is not the same in the mind of Coleridge, Kittredge, George F. Babbitt, or a high school sophomore. Of the many planes of reference, the intimate, colloquial, vernacular use of words is not the highest. An American with the soul of a poet and the training of a scholar may appreciate Dante in translation better than a Florentine cab driver in the original.

Every translation is inevitably an adaptation. It may attempt to 'naturalize' the foreign work, substituting images that will give the new readers the same idea and feelings the original work gave native readers; or it may offer a literal rendering (sometimes called transliteration) of the foreign text. The balance between the spirit and the letter shifts with every book, every translator, every reader.

Much translation is hackwork, ill-rewarded in money and prestige. But great writers have not disdained the modest and difficult art (in G., Goethe, Schiller, Herder; in Eng., Chaucer, Milton, Dryden, Pope, Fielding, Coleridge, Carlyle). The tradition is still alive; among 20th c. translators are Maeterlinck, Claudel, Gide, Proust, Larbaud, Romains; Santayana, Van Wyck Brooks, Scott Moncrieff.

Among translations that have proved of commanding influence, primacy belongs to the various renderings of the *Bible,* esp. the *King James Version.* Also: Jacques Amyot, *Plutarch*; Florio, *Montaigne;* O. W. von Schlegel, *Sp. drama, Shakespeare*; Baudelaire, *Poe.* The translator's delight, in the neoclassical age, was Horace; in the 19th c., Heine; yesterday, Heredia. Some writers have translated their own work: Oscar Wilde wrote *Salomé* first in Fr., for Sarah Bernhardt (with the help of Pierre Louys). Beckford wrote *Vathek* in Fr.; the translation by the Rev. Samuel Henley achieved a permanent place in Eng. literature. Beckett wrote both French (1952) and English (1955) versions of *Waiting for Godot.* The alternatives Croce sets, of faithful ugliness or faithless beauty, do not bind the successful translation. K. W. H. Scholz, *The Art of Translation* (G. to Eng.), 1918; J. M. Cohen, *Eng. Translators and Translations,* 1962; E. Cary and R. W. Jumpelt, ed. *Quality in Translation,* 1963; G. Mounin, *Les Problèmes théoriques de la traduction,* 1963; *La Machine à traduire,* 1964; E. A. Nida, *Toward a Science of Translating* (esp. the *Bible*), 1964; P. Selver, *The Art of Translating Poetry,* 1966; T. Savory, *The Art of Translation,* 1968. There is now a Translation Institute at the University of Indiana. ALBERT GUÉRARD.

travesty (from the same root as transvestite, one who changes dress to that of the opposite sex). A work "re-dressed" so as to be made ridiculous; a ludicrous alteration of the theme, form, style, or tone of a serious work. *See* Burlesque; Spoof.

triad. The most frequent grouping in literature and in criticism is a triad, a linking of three. Poets turned as often to the three Graces (Aglaia, Thalia, and Euphrosyne) as to one of the nine (3 times 3) Muses. Classical lives were determined by the three fates; the northern Norns had names meaning "What Was," "What Is," and "What Shall Be," the three aspects of time. Early writers sought the good, the true, and the beautiful, linking these with the body, the mind, and the spirit; psychoanalysts talk of the ego, the superego, and the id. Within a work of art, the formal elements and the moral elements rest on the fulcrum of the artist's personality, as the intellect and the emotions teeter on the fulcrum of the will. The work itself, said Taine, is a product of the race, the milieu, and the moment. And every work, said Aristotle, must have a beginning, a middle, and an end, which rhetoricians call the introduction, body, and conclusion. The work should be marked by unity, coherence, and emphasis.

In the drama, there was long insistence on the three unities of time, place, and action. An idea should be clear, concise, correct; if it is dialectical, it moves from thesis past antithesis to synthesis. The modes of knowing are enactive, iconic, and symbolic. The processes of thought are abstracting, imagining, generalizing; the laws of thought are Identity, Excluded middle, Contradiction (A is A; a thing is either A or not A; nothing can be at once A and not A). The narrator of a work must be the first person, or second, or third: I, you, he—there are plurals, but there is no fourth. The fact that Cinderella had two sisters, that it is the youngest (not younger) son that wins the prize, is given deeper significance by Freud in his study of *King Lear* and *The Merchant of Venice,* "The Theme of the Three Caskets." The Hellenic trinity of beauty and laughter and love is counterbalanced by the Christian faith, hope, and charity, while in the Christian Trinity (Hooker, *Ecclesiastic Polity,* 1594) three is "the mystical number of God's unsearchable perfection within Himself."

A work may picture aristocrats, middle class (plebeians) or workers (proletarians); it may appeal to the highbrow ("egghead"), middlebrow (average man), or lowbrow. A vogue or fashion in art passes through the three phases of innovation, imitation, irritation; while a great work inspirits the receptor with entertainment, enlightenment, exaltation. There is an old saying that all good things come in threes. The ancient Persians taught three useful things: To draw the bow, to ride, and to tell the truth. The ancient Chinese (Lao Tsze, 604–351 B.C.) held precious gentleness, frugality, humility. Caesar noted that *Gallia est omnis divisa in partes tres;* Benjamin Franklin averred that three may keep a secret . . . and "what I tell you three times is true." II In Gr. Lyric poetry, a triad is a set of three strophes, called *strophe, antistrophe,* and *epode*. The strophe and antistrophe are metrically identical, the epode different: this constitutes the form of an ode, *q.v.* The term is also applied, in Welsh literature, to groups of maxims, traditions, poetic rules, arranged in threes, probably as mnemonic. The practice is alluded to in Peacock's parody of the Arthurian legends, *The Misfortunes of Elphin,* 1829.

tribrach. A metrical foot of three short syllables (stress uncertain), usually a resolved iamb or trochee.

trilogy. A group of three tragedies which, with the addition of a satyr-play, makes up the traditional set of plays presented by each contestant at the dramatic festivals in Athens. The Aeschylean trilogy was usually composed of three tragedies dealing with successive stages of the same legend (the *Oresteia,* 456 B.C.). After Aeschylus, this practice was dropped.

trimeter. A verse of three feet. (Often, short for the commonest, iambic trimeter. In classical scansion iambs were counted as a dipody, so that iambic trimeter consists of three pairs of feet.)

trimètre. Fr. Twelve-syllable line divided by three rhythmic beats. Thus the medial cæsura is considerably weakened or disappears altogether, *e.g.* (Hugo, *Le Parricide*):

Il fut héros,/il fut géant,/il fut génie.

This three-part (*ternaire*) division characterizes the romantic alexandrine, which was used sparingly, however, in order to give contrast and variety by comparison with the normal *tétramètre, q.v.*

triolet. Medieval No. Fr. form, still used (Austin Dobson; H. C. Brunner; W. E. Henley) for light verse. One stanza of eight (usually short) lines, rhymed (the capitals indicate repeated lines) A B a A a b A B. Called by Eustace Deschamps (*Arte de dictier,* 1392) the simple rondeau.

triple measure. A metrical foot of three syllables; or a series of lines of three feet each.

triple rhyme. A rhyme of three syllables (one or more words); *e.g.,* irascible-passable; I'll say she ate-ingratiate. Almost nonexistent in Fr.; found in It.; rare in Eng. except in comic verse.

triplet. A succession of three lines in the same pattern, as a stanza, as a separate poem, or in a poem of another basic pattern; esp., three successive rhyming lines in a poem of rhyming couplets. Swift both illustrates and ridicules the last form, at the end of his "Description of a City Shower" (with the last line an alexandrine):

Sweepings from butchers' stalls, dung, guts, and blood,
Drowned puppies, stinking sprats, all drenched in mud,
Dead cats and turnip-tops come tumbling down the flood.

Irregular triplets have been used by recent poets, as William Carlos Williams (*The Desert Music*). In It. called *terzina.*

tripody. Three metrical feet considered together; usually, a line of three feet.

trobar (Prov.; L. *tropare,* to make tropes, thus stressing the inventive faculty of the troubadour or *trobaire*). The profession or art, or the act, of writing poetry.

trobar clus. The more obscure school of Prov. poetry which, stemming from the early poetic riddles (Count de Poitiers, 1071–1127), developed through the rhetorical hermeticism of Arnaut Daniel and his followers into the metaphysical mysticism of the later troubadours and of the It. *dolce stil nuovo.* The more popular and simple lyric was sometimes called *trobar clar. Cf.* Petrarchism; Troubadour.

trochee. A metrical foot, a long syllable followed by a short, — ᴗ. Used (Aristotle, *Poetics* 1449a) in early tragedy, as trochaic tetrameter; replaced by iambic trimeter (save often for excitement and swift action). Common stichic forms are trochaic dimeter catalectic, and trochaic tetrameter catalectic (Schiller, *Ode to Joy*; Tennyson, *Locksley Hall*; Longfellow, *Hiawatha*). Koster, *Traité de métrique gr.,* 1936.

trope (Gr., turning). (1) A conversion of a word to use for another. Distinctions contradictory or without difference have been drawn between trope and figure of speech. "Trope" was earlier popular; associated in the 18th c. with flowery language and conceits, it fell into disrepute, and has gradually been supplanted by the other term. (2) Early in the history of western liturgy, individual churches introduced verbal amplifications, or tropes, into particular passages in the authorized service. Where, in the Roman rite, *e.g.,* the Mass closes with the announcement of the deacon, *Ite, missa est,* to which the choir responds, *Deo gratias,* the church might interpolate as follows:

Ite *nunc in pace, spiritus sanctus super vos sit, iam* missa est.

Deo *semper laudes agite, in corde gloriam et* gratias.

"Their purpose is to adorn the liturgical text, to enforce its meaning, and to enlarge its emotional appeal." (Young, *The Drama of the Medieval Church,* 2 v., 1933, I, 178). Though creation of tropes was not favored by Rome, it did not, in the Middle Ages, openly condemn this practice of decoration. Considerable effort at creation was expended, but limitations of space and control of meaning often led to affectation and sheer verbal manipulation. Many of the tropes contained short dialogues, but apparently only the *Quem quaeritis* (which immediately preceded the *Introit* of the Mass of Easter) developed into dramatic action. To the expansion of this trope is generally traced the inception of medieval drama. *Cf.* Hymn; Figure. CHARLES W. JONES.

troubadour (Prov. *trobaire, trobador,* fem. *trobairitz*). One of a class of lyric poets of So. Fr. and No. It., 11th–13th c., who sang in *langue d'oc,* the language of Provence, verses chiefly about love and chivalry, addressed to some noble lady, the patron. Experimented in verse technique, created many fixed forms. William, Count de Poitiers; Bernard de Ventadour; Arnaut Daniel; Bertran de Born. *See trobar clus.* R. Briffault, *The Troubadours,* 1965.

trouvère. Corresponds in No. Fr. to So. Fr. troubadour, 11th–14th c. Themes chiefly love lyrics, chivalric romances, chansons de geste. Chrétien de Troyes (late 12th c.) wrote the influential Arthurian romances.

truncated. Of verse lacking a syllable of the meter established for the line. Initial (headless verse); or final (catalectic, *q.v.*).

truth in art. Two questions rise from a consideration of truth in relation to art. (1) Is the question of truth relevant? (2) If so, has "truth" when applied to art the same meaning as when applied to life?

(1) There are two points of view from which truth seems irrelevant to a work of art. (a) Truth or falsity, it is averred, may be affirmed only of propositions, of statements made as references; the work of art is not concerned with presenting propositions, language has other functions than reference. Thus Plato's statement that poetry is falsehood and the later concurring "all art is but feigning," Sidney counters with the observation: "Poetry nothing affirmeth and therefore never lies." A work of art rouses emotions or attitudes; these should have, not

truth, but value. (b) When an object is beheld æsthetically (*see* Æsthetics) the question of its truth or falsity does not arise, as when one watches the winged beauty of an airplane in the sky, free from all thought of bombs. All the aspects of the work combine to center our attention upon the work itself, as a worth-while unit. Assuming the technical competence of the work, if not merely our capacity for enjoyment but our judgment be exercised, the relevant polarity is not "true . . . false" but "important . . . trivial." This distinction is æsthetically pertinent; in its light each person more or less crudely constructs his own scale, ranging, say, from limericks and like bagatelles to Sophocles and Shakespeare.

In what may the "importance" of a work be said to consist? The problem of value is as complex as that of truth. Yet in formal, in technical and structural values, *The Rape of the Lock* may be as rich as *Paradise Lost*; indeed, an admittedly "trivial" work often displays great skill of execution. The importance of a work (Vivas) depends upon "the constellation of moral and/or religious values that it embodies."

Such values manifestly depend upon their truth. There may be danger, but not importance, in a false value. Despite any words to the effect that "the value of the work" lies in its organization of the complex of values it presents, we seem thus, for the test of these values, thrust back to life. Certainly belief in the ideas of a work (*e.g., The Divine Comedy*) increases its effect. (While some authors deliberately seek this advantage, it may be irrelevant to æsthetic consideration, as was shown by the enthusiastic American and Russian reactions to crude political plays after their respective revolutions.) Applying the criterion of "truth," however, brings us again to the word. (2) There are three main senses in which "truth" has been used of a work of art. (a) Loosely, agreement with one's beliefs. The widely gathered and seldom examined set of feelings-and-ideas that with many passes for a world outlook has been crystallized in various terms, from "common sense" to "the code of a gentleman." To an unexpressed credo of this sort, the work may be expected to conform; *e.g.*, it must express (Johnson) "sentiments to which every bosom returns an echo." (b) Truth as correspondence to life is the basis of the theory of imitation (*q.v.*), persistent from earliest times. This has ranged through a polarity of its own, from crude copy (Aristotle speaks of the pleasure of recognition) through the naturalist "slice of life" and the mirror held to nature, to a purely symbolic correspondence, which the receptor must discern, or link with reality through an *als ob.* (c) Truth as self-consistency is the interpretation offered by those who declare the work of art is not a document. Does the work hang together? Is it a unity of integrated parts? Do the values within the work arrange themselves in a coherent and concordant scale? "The criterion of truth" (Vico) "is to have made it."

The words of Vico suggest the obverse consideration. Works of art, it may be maintained, are signposts of the human spirit; they point the way of human aspirations and ideals. If, therefore, we look upon them as documents, we should regard their characters and actions not factually, as occurring in life, nor naturalistically, as efforts at exact copies of life, but as ideal imitations, as documents of mankind's upward march. Thus works of art are not to be checked by any outer criterion of actuality, of truth as in life; rather they establish (or at least display) the criteria by which men's actions may be judged. It is this interpretation that gives dignity to the thought (Baudelaire, Remy de Gourmont, Pater) that life should imitate art.

The discerning Greeks named truth *aletheia*, "away from Lethe," out of oblivion: the uncovering of what is hidden or concealed. Only recently (Ortega y Gasset, 1914; Heidegger, 1927) has their thought been recaptured in terms of art, with the declaration that "reality becomes creative when we discover it." Truth may be eternal, as it is external, but it has no human value until man lays it bare. Science may elaborate its patterns, but the first gleam of it shines in art. *Cf.* Illusion; *Als ob*; Value; Realism; Science Fiction. George Boas, *An Analysis . . . Truth,* 1921; E. T. Bell, *The Search for Truth,* 1934; Bertrand Russell, *An Inquiry into Meaning and Truth,* 1940; A. E. Wright, *Prolegomena to . . . Truth,* 1941; Ship; H. K. Khatchadourian, *The Coherence Theory of Truth,* 1961; G. J. Warnock, *Truth and Correspondence,* 1962; T. J. J. Alitzer, ed. *Truth, Myth, and Symbol,* 1962; S. L. Bhyrappa, *Truth and Beauty,* 1965; A. Hofstadter, *Truth and Art,* 1965; R. Barthes, *Critique et verité,* 1966.

Tudor. Relating to or during the time of the royal family that ruled England from 1485 to 1603. *See* Elizabethan.

Turkish prosody. Turkish verse-forms belong either to court (*divan*) literature or to popular (*halk*) literature. Those of the former category are borrowed from Arabic and Persian literature, while those of popular poetry are indigenous.

Turkish court poetry from the 13th c. onwards has used 10 of the 19 meters, called *bahr,* common to Arabic and Persian (*see* Persian prosody); namely the 5th–7th, 9th–13th, 16th, and 18th *bahr*. Several variations are introduced in arranging the feet in each of these meters. The 8th (*hezec*), e.g., which is *mefâilün mefâilün* may become *mefâilün faûlün mefâilün faûlün* or *mefûlü mefâilü mefâilü faûlün*. Court poetry, following Arabic prosody (*arûz*), has, strictly speaking, no caesura. Pauses occur after each foot, and therefore two or three times in a line; and these frequently break a word in two. Court poetry has remained faithful to all the rules of the *arûz,* and has adopted most of its verse-forms; particularly popular have been the *kit'a, rubaî, gazel, kaside,* and the *mesnevi.*

Turkish court poetry (completely out of practice for almost two hundred years) had strained the language to fit it into the accented measures of Arabic poetry. Popular poetry is quantitative, and its measures are natural to the Turkish language, which is unaccented and polysyllabic. These syllabic meters of popular poetry vary from 3 to 16 syllables. The most common syllabic units in the Turkish language being 3, 4, and 7, the most popular meters are 3+4 (or 7); 4+4 (or 8); 4+4+3 (or 6+5); 4+3+4+3 (or 7+7); and 4+4+4+3 (more often as 8+7). As this analytical presentation of the meters indicates, caesura (*durak*) does exist in popular Turkish poetry. It often divides the line into two symmetrical halves, and it must fall at the end of a word. Though rhyme (*ayak*) is important in popular poetry, the chief characteristic of this poetry is that it is written to be sung, and the melody chosen determines the verse-form—much as with the songs of Robert Burns. The forms most frequently used are *mâni* (four-line stanzas of 7 syllables rhyming *aaxa*); *koşma* (four-line stanzas of 6+5 syllables rhyming *abab*); and *destan* (rhyming couplets of 6+5 syllables).

Since the mid-19th century, not only have syllabic measures been universally replacing accented measures in Turkish poetry, but European forms, too (such as the epic, drama, and various types of the lyric) have been introduced into the language and have won great currency. ORHAN BURIAN.

turning point. A figurative term, drawn from Gr. peripeteia, or from Freytag's pyramid (*q.v.*), indicating the moment when the tide of fortune changes, and the movement begins that is to carry the story to its end. Also called the decisive moment; when manifest as a specific event, it is the climax. *Cf.* Peripeteia; Climax; *Falkentheorie.*

twisting (Aristotle, Gr. *desis;* with unraveling, denouement, Gr. *lusis,* the two main stages of tragedy). The intertwining of the threads of the events of the dramatic conflict. Corresponds to the rising action; *cf.* Freytag's pyramid.

type. A person (as in novel and drama) not rounded and uniquely human, but exhibiting the characteristic of a class. Usual in the morality, in *commedia dell'arte*; also called stock character. Often in the theatre (18th c. Fr.; 20th c. U.S.), even more in the motion pictures, actors are cast to type; *i.e.,* chosen originally perhaps because of a physical resemblance to the role, they are engaged again and again to play the same sort of person. The more competent (or more successful) victims of this method of choice are called character actors (in the sense of the "special" character they constantly present). Also, a representative of a class; by extension, a class or kind. *Cf.* Novel, types of; Genre; Folktale; Stock.

U

UBI SUNT (L., "where are—"). Frequent opening words of medieval L. poems, now used as a term to identify such works. They emphasize the transitory nature of all things. The mood is widespread; *e.g.,* the AS. poem *The Wanderer*; outstanding in early Fr. is François Villon's ballade *"Mais ou sont les neiges d'antan?"* trans. by Dante Gabriel Rossetti, "But where are the snows of yester-year?" The *ubi sunt* motif usually opens the poems, perhaps begins every stanza, often re-appears as a refrain. It persists today mainly in the fixed forms, *e.g.,* Edmund Gosse, *Ballade of Dead Cities.*

Ugaritic poetry. *See* Canaanite.

ugliness in life may be an element of beauty in art. (1) Aristotle credits this to the pleasure of recognition—which the camera now supplies. (2) The pleasure has therefore been attributed to recognition of the artist's skill, appreciation of the technique. Yet many who do not grasp this (often well concealed) art enjoy the product. (3) The artist may (a) by distancing devices avert the judgments of life, (b) infuse a spirit that opens to the receptor a richer realm below the surface; perhaps clearest pictorially, *e.g.,* Rembrandt's *Old Woman Paring Her Nails.* (4) Ugliness is often used for contrast. This is a major method in poems of T. S. Eliot (*Sweeney Erect*; *The Waste Land*); Masefield (*Cargoes*). Swift, in *Gulliver's Travels,* sets the Yahoo to serve the Houyhnhnm.

ultraism. General term for the basic attitude of many of the radical literary schools of the 20th c. Opp. to humanism (which posits three levels, natural, human, divine, and sets man with free will and common consciousness of the good to chart his own path), it sees man in one flow with all things and bound by the same laws; it seeks the essence, the universal, rather than the unique and individual. Embraces expressionism, surrealism, abstract art.

After World War II, the deliberate fortuity of surrealism and other ultraistic quests was dismissed by a generation that at first seemed largely composed of "angry young men," but it soon returned with the bitterness, or hopelessness, or deviant drift of the "absurd." The meaninglessness such persons contemplate is no longer mainly verbal. *Cf.* Expressionism; Dadaism; Surrealism; Absurd.

Unanimism. A vision of the world born from the consciousness that man is not only an individual but a member of a group, each group evolving with all the attributes of life, including diseases and death. Thus the story of humanity is a story of groups in relation with other groups and of individuals in relation not only with one another but with the groups that they have formed and that they may destroy.

Already in germ in writers like Baudelaire, Verhaeren, Walt Whitman, in philosophers like Le Bon, Tarde and Durkheim, unanimism, greatly increased by the development of big cities, was formulated and applied to literature by Jules Romains. This conception of man in connection with the universe gave scope to Romains' poetry: *La Vie unanime* (1908), *Ode Gênoise* (1923), *L'Homme blanc* (1937); to his plays: *l'Armée dans la Ville* (1911), *Cromedeyre-le-Vieil* (1920), *Knock, ou le triomphe de la médecine* (1923); to his novels: *Mort de quelqu'un* (1911), *Les Copains* (1913), *Les Hommes de bonne volonté,* a novel in 27 volumes (1932–46). Volume 1 is entitled *Le 6 Octobre*; vol. 27, *Le 7 Octobre.* The preface to this work keenly analyzes earlier novels that seek to picture large social groups; in the story itself, characters appear and disappear with the apparent casualness of life, but gradually take their places, in their intertwining groups, in the single flow of humanity. Unanimism lost something of its appeal in the individualism that marked the post-war period, but in recent years has regained strength, esp. in its social and political applications, with the concept of all humanity as "one world." Ship. MAURICE EDGAR COINDREAU.

unconscious, the. Those mental processes that do not emerge into consciousness; distinguished by Freud from the "preconscious" (*The Interpretation of Dreams,* trans. A. A. Brill, rev. ed., 1933, ch. 7, esp. pp. 560–70). In the usage of some other psychologists, the "unconscious" consists of neural processes, and is, along with the "co-conscious," one of the subdivisions of the "subconscious" (M. Prince, *The Unconscious,* 2d ed. rev., 1929, chs. 6–8; *cp.* W. L. Northridge, *Modern Theories of the Unconscious,* 1924). The conception of unconscious mental activity has been criticized and rejected by some psychologists (*e.g.,* W. James, *Principles of Psychology,* 1890, I. 162–76; C. D. Broad, *The Mind and Its Place in Nature,* 1925, 1962, ch. 8–10). Susanne Langer (*Mind,* 1967) declares even that "there is no such entity as 'consciousness' directing the course of behavior. 'Consciousness' is not an entity at all . . . It is a condition built up out of mental acts." The unconscious has nevertheless been regarded by various creative writers, esp. the surrealists (*q.v.*), as (1) the abode of the universal symbols and longings of the race (C. G. Jung, *Psychology of the Unconscious,* trans. B. M. Hinkle, 1916), and (2) the ultimate source of æsthetic inspiration (Freud, *Wit and its Relation to the Unconscious,* trans. A. A. Brill, 1905; A. Smith, *Art and the Subconscious,* 1937; R. Fry, *The Artist and Psychoanalysis,* 1924; J. M. Thorburn, *Art and the Unconscious,* 1925). Consequently these writers have consciously sought to explore the unconscious and to express its contents through dream-symbols. Some critics speak of a "creative unconscious." Arthur Koestler (*The Act of Creation,* 1964) says this works by a "bisociation of matrices," a linkage of previously separated fields or forms, in a fruitful conjunction. This seems obfuscating jargon for one's hitting on a good metaphor—which Aristotle too calls basic in creation, but not unconscious. The notion of creation by the unconscious, says Forrest Williams, gives us an implausible explanation "reached by a *non sequitur* based on a confusion." *Cf.* Hypostatization; Psychoanalysis; Self-expression. F. H. Hoffman, *Freudianism and the Literary Mind,* 1945, 1957; S. O. Lesser, *Fiction and the Unconscious,* 1957; L. and E. Manheim, *Hidden Patterns,* 1966; Forrest Williams, in *Creativity and Learning,* ed. J. Kagan, 1967.

unities, the three. The problems of dramatic unity were first considered by Aristotle. He clearly announced the first unity, of action: "that the fable should be the imitation of one action, and of the whole of this, and that the parts of the transactions should be so arranged, that any one of them being transposed, or taken away, the whole would become different and change" (*Poetics* 8). He also indicated the unity of time (*Poetics* 5): "Tragedy endeavors to confine itself to one revolution of the sun, or but slightly to exceed this limit." His statement (*Poetics* 17) that, as contrasted with epic, tragic episodes are short and (*Poetics* 26) "confined in less extended limits . . . crowded into a narrow compass" is the nearest he comes to any utterance regarding a unity of place. Yet almost as soon as Renaissance attention is turned to the Poetics, in 1570, the three unities were categorically set forth and defined, in the *Poetica* of Castelvetro. His fellow scholars in It. and shortly thereafter in Fr. assumed that Aristotle had not only described three unities but had insisted upon them as regulations to be followed by all playwrights. In 1572 the playwright Jean de la Taille, in the *Art of Tragedy,* announced as laws the unities of time, place, and action, for Fr. to follow for 250 years. The Fr. called them *les unités scaligeriennes,* though Scaliger (*Poetices Libri Septem,* 1561) had not enjoined the rules, insisting only on verisimilitude, which pointed toward them.

Briefly, the classical school declared that Aristotle's requirements were that the action of a play be a unified whole; that the time be limited to 24 hours (though some conceded 36); and that the scene be unchanged, or at least within the limits of a single city. With some initial grumbling (*e.g.,* of P. Corneille) the rules were accepted for tragedy, save in Eng. and Sp. The Eng. allude to the problem, but do not lengthily seek to justify their free practice. The Sp. Lope de Vega proclaimed (1609): "When I have to write a comedy I lock the precepts with 6 keys . . . and write in accordance with that art which they devised who aspired to the applause of the crowd." Not many years later (1663) Molière in Fr. asked whether the "great rule of all rules is not to please." In Fr., however, freedom was not wholly won until Hugo's 1827 preface (*Cromwell*) and 1830 production (*Hernani*).

The observations of Aristotle were basically sound and his conclusions, granted the the limitations of the play material with which he was concerned, wholly logical. The principle of artistic unity is, of course, known or sensed by all artists, and even the rigid three unities form a useful rule of thumb; yet, mankind is apt to agree with Molière who, in his critical skit *School for Wives Criticized* (1663), has a character say: "For my part, when I see a play I look only whether the points strike me; and when I am well entertained, I do not ask whether I have been wrong, or whether the rules of Aristotle would forbid me to laugh." Remember, however, that the three unities were not Aristotle's rule. *Cf.* Plot; Form; Tragedy. S. H. Butcher, *Aristotle's Theory of Poetry and Fine Art,* 4th ed., 1911; B. H. Clark, *European Theories of the Drama,* 1929, 1966. Barrett H. Clark.

unity. The concept of artistic unity was first propounded by Plato (*Phædrus* 264 C) and by Aristotle. It involved chiefly the unity of action and of character-portrayal; but by Horace (*Ars Poetica* 1–37) it is extended to the entire composition, by analogy with the organic aspect of Nature. Horace's warning against the purple patch is indicative of his emphasis on the principle of unity, which is linked in his theory of literature with the law of decorum. In the effort to accredit various works with the principle, several sorts of unity have been described: of action; of form; of intent. Dramatic unity, achieved through organization (*see* Unities, the 3) has been contrasted with epic unity, wherein the central character holds together many episodes. *Cf.* Aesthetics.

universality. That quality of a work of art whereby its significance is made to exceed the limits of the particular (incident, situation, place, time, person) and to extend itself throughout the universe. The effect of this quality is to make the work of art tend to stir the souls of all men of all time.

A writer may, for instance, see material for a play in a news item from the morning paper, recording that John Jones, 33, alderman, of 1234 Jones Street, Jonesville, suspecting his wife, Mary, 28, of adultery with his gardener, Jack Jackson, 27, on evidence of gossip set in motion by Bill Williams, 32, a rival in small-town politics, shot his wife in their home on the night of May 22, 1968, at 11:20, and then shot himself. Using these particulars, even somewhat disguised and shorn of much detail, the playwright may compose, not high tragedy, but *John Jones, the Jonesville Alderman.* Its significance will remain within the limits of the particular. Jonesville and points adjacent may be interested; beyond these, perhaps only a research student in 1990 studying the faded 60's. Using essentially the same materials, Shakespeare wrote *Othello*; and the heart of the world is moved by its beauty. *Othello* presents neither an actual, historical event nor an abstract consideration of adultery, murder, and suicide. It is sufficiently particular to be of this earth; it is sufficiently lifted above this earth to carry us to the heady atmosphere where humanity still breathes vigorously, to see life whole. It disengages itself just enough from a man to involve Man.

To produce this effect is the work of poetic genius; esp. of its power to create a literary organism and its use of imagery, the point of contact by which the poet reproduces in us his own wide, deep, and altitudinous experience, intellectual, emotional, sensitive. Other means we can more easily discern: remoteness of place and age in scene and character; high social rank (the fate of the king involves the kingdom), majestic moral stature in the hero; subplot showing the same or contrasting pattern of events on another plane; impossibilities made probable; the supernatural; dramatic irony; the use of verse as a vehicle, a rhythm and language somewhat removed from and lifted above those of everyday speech.

The great distinction between *Othello* and *The Jonesville Alderman* is in this quality of universality; wherein is also that between the Sistine Madonna and a snapshot of Mrs. Jones and the baby; wherein, in general, the distinction of all great art. Atkins; Butcher; M. Dixon, *Tragedy,* 1925; R. A. Scott-James, *The Making of Literature,* 1929. *Cf.* Distances, the three. William H. McCabe, s.j.

university wits. Applied esp. to the group in London, 1585–95: Christopher Marlowe, Robert Greene, Thomas Kyd, Thomas Lodge, Thomas Nash, George Peele—some add John Lyly. Their bohemian lives, their eager discussions of the concerns of the time (as at the Mermaid Tavern) bore fruit in poetry, fiction, and esp. the drama, for which they developed blank verse and explored the range of subjects from the tragedy of blood to the romantic comedy. They were a rich part of what Shakespeare found in London. (The term has also been applied to a recent Eng. group, in William Van O'Connor's *The New University Wits,* 1963.) *Cf.* Elizabethan; Wit.

usage. A practice, or mode of expression, established by general adoption; the body of words and system of word relationships developed through the years and currently widespread. Considered—esp. as in the speech and writing of the cultured; though here the quarrels begin—the basic sanction of diction and forms. Horace, as Gabriel Harvey roundly reminds Spenser (in his *Letter* on the use of the Gr. verse forms, 1579) says the guide is *Penes usum* and *norma loquendi.* Usage, being a fluid element of society's movement, is never more than tentatively prescribed; the works that record it (dictionaries; grammars) are always in the rear of its flow. For bibliography, *see* Style.

utopian literature. Since Plato, the description of Ideal Commonwealths has been one of the standard byways of literature. The conception of these commonwealths was not confined to Plato originally, for Aristotle in the *Politics* mentions other essays, notably by Hippodamus, the city planner; but the form itself derives from the Platonic notion that every earthly phenomenon has an ideal form; and therefore a description of society in its ideal moment of perfection would not merely throw a light upon its real nature but indicate the possibilities of development.

Among the classic utopias, Plato's *Republic* is by far the most important, for it deals with every aspect of the common life including its ultimate ends in religious and philosophic insight. The *Republic* set the pattern for a good part of the utopias since, in its emphasis upon communism. Plato's first great successor was Sir Thomas More, the Renaissance humanist; and More gave a name to this whole literature: "utopia" is a pun: *outopia,* no place, and *eutopia,* the good place. These two modes of utopia divide the whole literature, more or less, into utopias of escape and utopias of reconstruction. Both aspects of utopia are present in More's work. In presenting Utopia as a newly discovered country on the other side of the planet, More allied his account with the many travelers' tales of distant lands, like those that Hakluyt and Purchas were to gather from real life; but in *Utopia* the narrator, Raphael Hythloday, opened an even wider door for the reader's imagination to escape through. On the other hand, More's utopia, with its reasonable spirit and its reliance upon wise laws and sensible social institutions, gave encouragement to the great movement of social reform from the 15th c. on, beginning with the Anabaptists and the Cromwellian Diggers, gathering strength in a succession of utopian communities, some of them as successful as those at Amana, Iowa and the Mormon community in Utah, and supplying concrete images of the future to the 19th c. socialist movement, not least to the non-utopian followers of Karl Marx. Though neither innovation nor reform, still less reconstruction, was a popular term in More's day, he gave strength to both tendencies by his mordant introduction, which pictured the miseries and injustices that prevailed in his own country. The reader needed no special invitation to draw the proper conclusion: if a better social order can exist in Utopia, why not in England, or in any other country?

The escape mode is a fantasy, or a dream-projection, close to the heart of the writer, no matter how remote from realization: into this class falls the imitative utopia, *The City of the Sun,* by Tomasso Campanella, or *The Coming Race,* by Bulwer-Lytton. Since the 18th c., however, the utopia of reconstruction has become the more common form: witness such influential utopias as Cabet's *Voyage to Icaria* (1845) and Edward Bellamy's *Looking Backward* (1888). These utopias are attempts to provide a plan and a program of living for a better society.

There is of course no clear dividing line between these two forms; for though William Morris's *News from Nowhere* is a pure idyll of rural felicity, it contributed almost as powerful an impulse to the Garden City movement as James Silk Buckingham's *National Evils and Practical Remedies,* one of the conscious sources of Ebenezer Howard's practical proposals in *Garden Cities of To-morrow* (1898). Similarly the more fantastic story of *Looking Backward,* with its young Bostonian awakening into a better world, begun by Bellamy as a romance in the style of Hawthorne, probably contributed more to practical reform than the detailed and conscientious prescriptions of his supplementary treatise, *Equality.*

Few utopian writers, however, have dared follow the logical steps by which Plato builds up his ideal society from the most elemental premises: most writers have sought to make perfection credible by projecting voyages to far countries or voyages through time that were bridged by sleep. The fantasy usually so lacks any robustness of imagination that the reader of utopias sometimes feels a little like the citizens of Morris's imaginary England, who read the morbid novels that treated of 19th c. unhappiness in order to add a little pepper and vinegar to the flat and savorless happiness of utopia. This in general points to another weakness of the utopian psychology; most of the golden ages of the future are conceived as being without struggle, imperfection, or crisis: therefore without any of the essential drama of personal and collective life. Hence a tendency toward substituting ritual for drama, and a regimentation, benign but nevertheless despotic, for the unseemly conflicts and tense cooperations that characterize actual life.

Plato, Cabet, Bellamy, conceive their ideal world as a sort of militaristic, totalitarian paradise: utopias that are uncomfortably close to the infantile societies that the fascists have sought to force into existence. On the other hand, the statesmanlike mind of Theodor Herzl, in describing his Utopia of *Altneuland,* stood so close to the needs and purposes of our own day, that he outlined both the possibilities and the inherent dangers in erecting a Jewish commonwealth in Palestine.

Along with the comprehensive description of ideal commonwealths, two other forms of utopian literature must be noted. The first is one in which imaginary episodes in an imaginary state serve as vehicles of satire and criticism: in this class stand Swift's *Gulliver's Travels* and Butler's *Erewhon.* The other is a strain of utopian daring in imaging better forms of society that has gone into otherwise sober essays in politics, education, and sociology. Though Fourier, for example, wrote no single utopia, his prolific volumes conjured up a whole world, entirely reconstructed on his principles, and his conception of industrial armies and the conservation movement long antedated practical political proposals. So too with Robert Owens' plans for a new society.

Though Engels, in his *Socialism: Utopian and Scientific,* poured scorn on utopian thinking because of its remoteness from current realities and its reliance upon verbal persuasion, utopian writers have often been the first to point out the social mutations and emergents that were already dimly discernible in their social order: they lifted their contemporaries out of the ruts of habit and familiar associations and gave them a clearer view of the forces working around them. Thus, while only a handful of utopias now deserve serious reading, the freedom of imagination that characterizes the utopian writers will always be a useful check against a pedestrian realism that goes along with a pedestrian acceptance of life as one finds it. Many of the voyages pictured in the works of science fiction take their readers to various sorts of utopias. Samuel Johnson (*Rasselas* XLIV: *Life of Swift*) said that Utopia was a persistent but futile dream. Oscar Wilde (*The Soul of Man Under Socialism*) was emphatic: "A map of the world that does not include Utopia is not worth even glancing at."

Recent works have pictured an anti-utopia, or dystopia, showing the dreaded consequences of authoritarian control or of the mechanization of society. Among these are *We* (E. Zamyatin, trans. 1934), which influenced *1984* (G. Orwell, 1949); *Darkness at Noon* (A. Koestler, 1940); *Ape and Essence* (A. Huxley, 1948). Such pictures warning of evil to come have largely superseded pleasant prospects of the future (as still in N. O. Brown's *Love's Body,* 1966) or the indirect attacks of a *Gulliver's Travels* or a *Penguin Island. Cf.* Social Criticism; Literature and Society. J. Hertzler, *The Hist. of Utopian Thought,* 1923; L. Mumford, *The Story of Utopias,* 1922; K. Mannheim, *Ideology and Utopia,* 1934; F. T. Russell, *Touring Utopia,* 1932; G. Negley and J. M. Patrick, ed. *The Quest for Utopia,* 1952; G. A. Kateb, *Anti-Utopianism,* 1960; Buell G. Gallagher, *A Preface to the Study of Utopias,* 1960; G. Walsh, *From Utopia to Nightmare,* 1962; R. Boguslaw, *The New Utopians,* 1965; C. A. Doxiadis, *Between Dystopia and Utopia,* 1966; H. B. Franklin, *Future Perfect,* 1966; M. R. Hillegas, *The Future as Nightmare,* 1967; N. Eurich, *Science in Utopia,* 1967; A. Sachs, *Passionate Intelligence,* 1967; M. I. Finley, in *The Critical Spirit,* ed. Kurt H. Wolff and B. Moore, 1967. LEWIS MUMFORD.

V

VAGUENESS. Certain terms are vague in themselves, in that they lack definite boundaries, *e.g.,* middle-aged, simple, cold, strong. These are often of value in art, as well as in diplomacy. They should not be confused with terms that are merely unspecific (also frequent in diplomacy), such as "Immediate steps must be taken"—when no planned steps are mentioned. Less valuable vagueness may result from combining inadequate terms. *Cf.* Ambiguity; Clearness. W. P. Alston, *Philosophy of Lang.,* ch. 5, 1964.

value. The fact that an object, work of literature or art, has pre-eminence or is deserving of special attention, care, or regard. The question that rises is, by what criteria do we determine value?

Value theory (axiology) as it is pursued today is not a very old discipline, and therefore it is only recently that some critics have come to see, with I. A. Richards, that criticism is grounded on value presuppositions, whether of an explicit or an implicit nature, since a meaningful assertion that an object is æsthetically adequate assumes knowledge of what makes it adequate. A frequent reason for the failure of criticism is to be traced to confusion and inconsistency in the principles that guide its judgments. But while it is probably a fair statement that criticism, particularly in our day, has suffered chiefly from a hand-to-mouth pragmatism, it would be fatal to forget also that there are many serious errors and defects involved in too rigid theoretical guidelines. The critic wedded to a rigid theory all too often buys clarity and consistency at the price of narrowness and insensibility. The ideal approach would recognize that our critical standards have an empirical source. They are drawn from the practice of the artist and the changing taste of his public. Because they are standards, they serve to correct the present by the authority of the acknowledged excellences of the past; but because they are empirical, they themselves are responsive to modifications in terms of new experience and of the technical changes demanded by its expression. This view, however, is not compatible with the two traditional theories of value.

We perceive an object's value in the same way we perceive its color or its size. But it is widely acknowledged that somehow value is related to interest or desire. Disagreement among philosophers stems from the question as to whether the interest accounts for the value or the value for the interest; in other words, are things beautiful (in the case of æsthetic value) because we are æsthetically interested in them, or are we æsthetically interested in them because they are beautiful? The question calls for a somewhat abstruse answer, but it is not a "mere academic question" for the practical critic, for with the former alternative value depends upon ourselves, and is in so far subjective; while with the latter our interest depends upon the value's preexistence, and hence it is in some sense objective. But neither of these two positions, though mutually exclusive, is without inherent difficulties. Consider first the objective theory: If value is objective, whence the almost bewildering confusion of opinion regarding its presence in an object? The variability, the inconstancy of value judgments is a commonplace. But regarding truly objective qualities—length or volume, for example—no such disagreement exists.

On the other hand, the subjective theory is confronted with the fact that when a man deems an object beautiful it is not about himself or his feelings that he is talking. The subjectivist explains this away by saying that he *projects* his feelings into the object (*see* Empathy) or imputes value to it. But this is a metaphor that cannot be made literal; he has never explained by what means this projection or why this imputation takes place.

Mediating between these two contending and mutually incompatible theories, an alternative theory of value has recently been proposed, according to which an object is said to have value because we evince interest in it; but we evince interest in it because it actually possesses objective features that are capable of eliciting our interest. According to this point of view, usually referred to as "objective relativism," the presence of value in an object and our interest in it are correlative, or polar, neither of the two being prior to the other. We have to assume neither that we project or impute value to objects; nor that the value, pre-existing, arouses our interest. The interest is aroused by an object because it possesses a structure capable of arousing it; and the value emerges in an object, as a result of our interest. Both are products of the interaction of organism and object; but they have been made possible by a preceding process of mutual adjustment. The structure of the object in which the value appears is, considered by itself, a physical structure, just as, considered by itself, the organism is a mere physiological organism. Value then is objective, being a quality of an object. But while objective, mark that it depends on the subject that apprehends it as much as on the structure of the object in which, on apprehension, it appears. Beauty thus involves two sets of determinants, the objective, for which we hold the creative artist responsible, and the subjective, which we contribute as receptors. But this theory must not be interpreted individualistically. Since our interests are obviously at least partially determined by social factors, our conceptions of what is beautiful will change *pari pasu* with social changes. Thus rules and principles are as fluid and as continuous as human society. And thus it is irrational to hold artists to principles educed from objects created to satisfy interests that are no longer alive; but also it is absurd to imagine—as revolutionaries do—that one can cut one's nexus with the past and free oneself from its authority. It follows that no man has a right to call "beautiful" an object in which no one but himself can find æsthetic satisfaction. *Cf.* Meaning, Truth; Standards; Æsthetics; Beauty; Signs. John Dewey, *Theory of Valuation,* 1939; H. O. Eaton, *The Austrian Philosophy of Values,* 1930; C. E. M. Joad, *Matter, Life, and Value,* 1929; W. Kohler, *The Place of Value in a World of Facts,* 1938; C. I. Lewis, *An Analysis of Knowledge and Valuation,* 1946; R. B. Perry, *General Theory of Value,* 1926; *Realms of Value,* 1954; W. M. Urban, *The Intelligible World,* 1929; Eliseo Vivas, *The Moral Life and the Ethical Life,* 1950; R. Lepley, ed. *The Language of Value,* 1957; Charles Morris, *Varieties of Human Value,* 1956; *Signification and Significance,* 1964; C. L. Stevenson, *Facts and Values,* 1963. Eliseo Vivas.

value theory. The range of value language is quite extensive. It embraces the moral, the æsthetic, the pathological, the therapeutic, the economic, the practical, the religious, and the theological. It is often assumed that only one value term is basic and that the distinctive value use of all the others can be explicated in terms of it. "Good" and "ought" are the two most likely candidates. Theories that choose "good" are called *teleological,* for they explicate "ought" in terms of the means to or the conditions of the good. Those that take "ought" to be basic are called *deontological.* Some would explicate both "good" and "ought" in terms of imperative sentences.

Value language is closely related to and in some way grounded in affective and in conative experience; the former being a matter of enjoying and suffering, liking and disliking, favoring and disfavoring, approving and disapproving; the latter a matter of desiring, wanting, preferring, feeling constrained or obligated, and the like.

Naturalists in value theory subscribe to the subjectivistic view of value experience, claiming that it is not itself knowledge-yielding or a mode of gathering data. Thus they contend that value judgments are only about value experiences themselves, or that they express and excite value experiences, or some combination of these, without bearing upon actuality or truth. A subjectivist with regard to value experiences, however, may be an objectivist about value judgments. He may believe that they have truth-values or that they can be backed by good reasons, so that they have relevance in actual situations. Realists within the empiricistic tradition believe not only that value judgments are true or false, but that experiences of liking, desiring, etc. do enable us to discern values as part of the objective life-situation. Rationalistic realists have contended that reason performs this function. For both sorts of realists, value judgments make truth-claims about objective values inherent in the human situation. *Cf.* Linguistics; Æsthetics; Value; Language. C. L. Stevenson, *Ethics and Language,* 1944; R. M. Hare, *The Language of Morals,* 1952; E. M. Adams, *Ethical Naturalism and the Modern World-View,* 1960; E. W. Hall, *What is Value?,* 1952; *Our Knowledge of Fact and Value,* 1961; P. W.

Taylor, *Normative Discourse,* 1961; H. Feigl and W. Sellars, ed. *Readings in Ethical Theory,* 1952; G. H. von Wright, *The Varieties of Goodness,* 1963. E. M. Adams.

values in a work may be: (1) hedonic: it gives direct immediate pleasure. (2) artistic: it manifests sound workmanship. This may be a source of further enjoyment. (3) cultural: it has significant bearing upon a society or a civilization. (4) ethical, moral, religious. (5) practical.

Any or all of these values may be present in a work; different ones are emphasized by different critics. The term "æsthetic" is usually limited to the first, or the first two.

variation. *See* Elegant variation.

vaudeville. [In 15th c. Fr. light satirical songs were composed by Olivier Basselin in the valley (Vau) de Vire; under Basselin's name Jean Le Houx wrote and published some in 1610. Such songs were later interspersed in Fr. comedies; hence, "comedy with vaudevilles," usually plots of intrigue and love, with erotic verses (*"Cela ne se dit pas, Mais cela peut se faire";* Such things are not spoken of, But they may be done). In the 19th c.—esp. of the plays of Scribe and Labiche—the term was shortened to vaudeville.] In the U.S. late 19th and early 20th c., vaudeville was a show consisting of a number of individual acts—a joking couple, singing, dancing, impersonations, juggling, acrobatics, ventriloquism, and the like—in Eng. called variety (show). It lapsed with the growth of the cinema, but has returned (without the name) on radio and esp. television, now with a Master of Ceremonies (an M.C.). *Cf.* Farce. D Gilbert, *Am. Vaudeville,* 1940; A. McClean, Jr., *Am. Vaudeville as Ritual,* 1965.

Veda. Sanskrit (knowledge). A sacred book of the Hindus, one of the 4 looked upon as *śruti,* divinely inspired: *Rig-veda* (hymns); *Atharva-veda* (prayers, curses, incantations); *Sāma-veda; Yajur-veda.* Vedic science (*Vedanga*) has 6 branches: (1) *Śikshā,* phonetics (esp. in the *Pāniniya śiksha*); (2) *Chhandas,* meter (*Chhandah-sūtra* of Pingala is the first work on prosody; for Vedic meters, esp. *Nidāna-sūtra*); (3) *Vyākarṇa,* Grammar (also Pāṇini); (4) *Nirukta,* etymology (word lists—often by homonyms and/or synonyms—with commentary; esp. Yāska); (5) *Jyotisha,* astronomy; (6) *Kalpa,* ceremonial (*Śrauta-sūtras,* based on the *śruti; Smārta-sūtras,* based on the *smṛiti: see sūtra*).

vehicle. Name given by I. A. Richards to the image in a metaphor, *q.v.;* the idea to be caught in the image he calls the tenor. *Cf.* Figure.

verisimilitude. A degree of likeness to truth that induces belief that the action and characters in an imaginative work are probable or possible. In both ancient and modern criticism it is generally agreed that some element of actual or idealized reality contributes toward making an imitation verisimilar and credible. In discussing the kinds of narrative, Cicero *De inventione* (I.21,29) and the *Ad Herennium* (I.8–9) defines verisimilitude as likeness to a truth that may be verified by experience, history, or common opinion. According to Plutarch (*Moralia,* 25 B–C) an imitation is pleasing when it is likely; closeness to nature, comments Horace (*Ars poet.,* 338), is necessary in a fiction intended to please. In Aristotle's opinion (*Poet.,* IV. 2–6) even the exact imitation of horrible things is delightful because of our immediate awareness that the imitation is a true one. The delight experienced in exact imitation is abundantly illustrated by Pliny the Elder (*Nat. Hist.* XXXV. 36) and Herodas (Mime IV) in their descriptions of art works so life-like as to be mistaken for the reality. Of late years, photography and the cinema have largely taken over this delight, which wax figures in museums had taught us to question.

What an audience is willing to accept as verisimilar is always a problem. Aristotle remarks (*Poet.,* IX. 6–7) that the tragic poets reworked familiar subjects accepted as true, for what is believed to have happened is likely to be convincing. But Aristotle—despite the Renaissance idea attributed to him that tragedy requires historical reality—saw into the nature of fiction as an art aiming to develop characters and situations logically from premises the audience is asked to accept; the "logic" of fiction may involve the telling of lies artistically (*ibid.,* XXIV. 18–19). His view may have been close to that of Giraldi Cinthio (*De i romanzi,* 1554, p. 55–56), who refers to impossibilities in imaginative literature as acceptable by a convention established by poets themselves.

The loose use of the term verisimilar and the awareness that things like ghosts are improbable but not impossible—at least not to the popular imagination—led French critics (Chapelain, D'Aubignac, Batteux), to make a distinction between *vraisemblance extraordi-*

naire (what rarely happens) and *vraisemblance ordinaire* (what usually happens), a distinction probably derived from Castelvetro (*Poetica d'Aristotle,* 2d., 1576, p. 400). English critics recognized this distinction in the definition of the romance and the novel; the romance, says Clara Reeve (*Progress of Romance,* 1785, I, 111), "describes what never happened nor is likely to happen," but the novel deals with everyday life in a manner "so probable, as to deceive us into a persuasion (at least while we are reading) that all is real." In drama, and particularly in tragedy, such persuasion was considered necessary; for the object of the dramatist is "so to deceive the mind, that the Spectator may forget the representation, and consider the action real" (John Newberry, *Art of Poetry,* 1762, II, 156)—a view, incidentally, that is at the basis of the dramatic unities. As a general rule, critics since the Renaissance have assumed that the mind, which is made for truth, does not willingly accept improbabilities and must therefore be deceived. But a few (John Mottley, essay appended to Thomas Whincop's *Scanderbeg,* 1747; George Colman the Elder, *Critical Reflections,* 1761) pointed out that an audience will allow anything within the framework of a fiction provided the whole is self-consistent. These critics were anticipating Coleridge's remarks (*Biographia Literaria,* chap. XIV) on supernatural fiction which nevertheless secures "that willing suspension of disbelief for the moment, which constitutes poetic faith."

Much of the speculation on the nature of verisimilitude virtually neglects to consider that in all probability the majority of readers do not expect fiction to have any rapport with actuality; "we want a story," says Mortimer Adler (*How to Read a Book,* 1940, p. 306), "that must be true only in the sense that it *could have happened* in the world of characters and events which the novelist has created." *Cf.* Imitation; Truth; Vraisemblance; Realism; Naturalism; Romance; Novel. R. M. Alden, "The Doctrine of Verisimilitude in Fr. and Eng. Criticism of the 17th C.," *Matzke Memorial,* 1911. G. Giovannini.

vers de société (Fr., society verse). A sophisticated and polished form of light verse, *q.v.,* usually gently satirizing the ways of the man-about-town and his bosom friends.

vers libre (Fr., free verse, *q.v.*). *Vers libre* is distinguished from both *vers régulier* (classic and romantic alexandrines) and *vers libéré* by: (1) the formal interior unity of the individual line; (2) freedom from any fixed number of syllables; (3) freedom from certain special rules, such as hiatus, caesura, rhyme. One fundamental characteristic unites it with the earlier forms: the presence of regularly recurring accents that create the rhythm. Three factors are present in accent: pitch, intensity, and duration; it is the accent of duration that determines rhythm, thus is the basis of Fr. verse. Thus the *vers librists* are squarely in the tradition of Fr. poetry, merely arranging their rhythms in different accentual schemes.

verse (L., turning). (1) A line, esp. of metrical writing (the earlier sense). (2) A stanza in a poem; in a song, one of the differing stanzas (alike in metrical form) as distinguished from the chorus repeated after each of them. (3) Poetry in general. The distinction between verse and poetry, though Aristotle (*Poetics* I 14476) seems to have been aware of the problem, was first made by Horace (*Sat.* I, 4, 54). General agreement among Gr. and L. critics held that verse (meter), at any rate, was necessary in poetry. Later opinions differ; *see* Poetry and Prose. *Cf.* Prosody; Meter; Rhythm. Harvey Gross, ed. *The Structure of Verse,* 1966.

versification. *See* Arabic; Canaanite; Chinese; Classical; English; Gaelic; German; Indian; Japanese; Old French and Provençal; Old Norse; Persian; Welsh; Romance; Prosody; Rhythm; Rhyme. P. F. Baum, *Principles of Eng. Versification,* 1922; O. C. de C. Ellis, *Poetic Technique,* 1949; D. Davie, *Articulate Energy,* 1955.

verso sciolto. The unrhymed It. hendecasyllabic line. As used by Trissino (1478–1550) in epic and tragedy, it served as a source of Eng. blank verse. *See* Romance versification.

Victorian. Of the era of Queen Victoria's reign (1837–1903), when the sun never set on the British flag. Usually denoting the brashly insular, materialistic, complacent, hypocritical, moralistic, censorious. Dickens' Mr. Podsnap (*Our Mutual Friend,* 1864–5) lampoons the typical Victorian. Victorianism served as a sort of censorship, exerting a silent suppression of what was not genteel, respectable, proper. Thus Thackeray rejected one of Mrs. Browning's poems because it had in it the word "harlot": "You see, our magazine is written not only for men and women but for boys and girls, sucklings, almost." The concentration of solemn respectability and complacent self-sufficiency is labeled mid-Victorian. *Cf.* Elizabethan. R. Langbaum, ed. *The Victorian Age,* 1967; Gertrude Himmelfarb, *Victorian Minds,* 1968; for the obverse of the coin, Steven Marcus, *The Other Victorians,* 1966. Note that the many excellent qualities of the period are neglected; the term is usually employed as denigration.

viewpoint. The relation in which the narrator stands to the story, considered by many critics to govern the method and characters of the work. It may be either internal or external. In viewpoints that are internal, the person who is telling the story is one of its actors; hence the story is a first-person story. The external viewpoint presents a mind outside, one that has not taken part in the story; in this case the story is usually third-person.

Internal viewpoints have several variations, the first being that in which the story is told by the leading actor; a pretended autobiography. This has several advantages: (1) If the tale is strange, wild, supernatural, or otherwise hard to believe, it is easier to communicate such adventure to the reader and the reader will be more apt to accept it, if the tale is told by one who has experienced the adventure (*Robinson Crusoe*; *Moll Flanders*; Conrad). (2) The emotional experience in a first-person tale is told from the heart, thus is usually more intimate and intense than one told from outside. The "I" promotes intimacy; "He" is already one step removed. Vividness is gained by intimacy. (3) A first-person story has a simple coherence; the capital "I" serves as a cement between the blocks that build the story unity.

But this internal viewpoint also has disadvantages: (1) The hero can speak his own thoughts only; he has no way of making known the thoughts of others in the tale. (2) The hero can analyze himself only from inside out, not from outside in. He can say that he feels hot, but cannot possibly describe how he looks to other actors in the story. This is why the psychological story demands the external or third-person point of view. (3) There is difficulty in characterizing the narrator. A hero cannot tell you what a fine man he really is; he must lead you on to believe that he is fine by his actions and his thoughts. Therefore the reader must form his opinion of the narrator through an indirect method—which may, however, be so skillfully handled that the reader has the sense of not accepting but judging for himself: this binds him more firmly. (4) If a narrator should tell a fine tale, the reader may question how a simple boy or engineer or whoever he happens to be is so good a teller of tales. This may weaken credibility in some readers' minds; but it seems an accepted convention, so that the reader is usually ready to believe that a shipwrecked sailor, such as Robinson Crusoe, is a pretty good story-teller.

There is also an internal, or first-person story, that is told by a minor character, not the hero. This at once presents a great advantage. This minor character is able to describe the hero from outside, and also to work with the hero and relate the adventure. Where the hero is a wonderful person, *e.g.* Lord Jim, this viewpoint is almost necessary, for it would be egotistical and quite unlike Lord Jim to tell the reader how wonderful he is. In the police mystery novel, the Dr. Watson serves the same purpose. The story may also be told by several characters, each taking a different part in the adventure. The advantages in this type of tale are obvious. The disadvantage is a weakening of the unity, unless the drama is strong and the sequences of the various experiences natural.

The external point of view, in its fullest sense, is omniscient in scope. A superior mind outside the story views the characters, all from an equal distance. The narrator is godlike. He knows the past, present, future. He knows the secret thoughts and feelings of all his characters. He need never account to the reader how this information came to him. His ears can hear things before they are spoken, his eyes can look through locked doors and darkness.

The main disadvantage of the omniscient (sometimes called Olympian) point of view is the loss of a certain nearness to the scene. Vividness is sacrificed and a definite sense of intimacy is surrendered. To overcome these obvious disadvantages, there is an external point of view that limits the Olympian powers of the narrator. This brings the reader closer to the stage of action. The limitation can be carried further, with the external story told as though seen by a single mind of one of the characters within the tale. Such a restriction has almost the full advantage of the internal viewpoint with many of the advantages of the omniscient. One more step is possible: the narrator may surrender all godlike powers and tell only what might have been seen externally by a witness of the events. He would not interpret or record opinions of his own, nor what went on in the minds of his characters. As in a tale by Maupassant, he would allow the reader to draw his own conclusions from the events of the story.

A personal note is added and a friendly relationship established between author and reader when the writer admits at once that it is he who is relating the tale and that the opinions and side-remarks are his very own.

The shifting viewpoint makes use of a number of viewpoints within one book or story. Sometimes this is done unconsciously by the writer; often the shift is not noticed by the casual reader. E. M. Forster points out, in *Aspects of the Novel,* that with an effective shift in viewpoint, the writer has "the power to bounce the reader into accepting what he says." In *Bleak House* by Dickens, Chapter I is written from the omniscient point of view, as though some God in Heaven were describing all the people in the courtroom. Chapter II is partly Olympian; there is a limitation in visual penetration. Chapter III is told mostly from the first person or internal point of view. But the reader does not notice this shift, for Dickens "bounces" his reader breathlessly along. The same is true of *War and Peace.* While *Dr. Jekyll and Mr. Hyde* is told from the external point of view, the last chapter, which is a confession, shifts the viewpoint to the first person. To add intimacy is to reinforce credence.

It is sometimes a relief to the reader to have a change in viewpoint; this relief is often accomplished by the introduction of a letter or a message within the text. Such a device adds another voice; if the tale is external, it introduces a first-person note of relief.

A shifting point of view has also the power to expand or contract perception and take the reader closer to or further from the scene. Such movement at once adds life to the writing. The reader may feel himself actually taking part in the tale, or standing aloof from the parts where he would rather not be present. Rarely does the reader notice where the shift takes place. Like most devices, it works best unseen. *Cf.* Narrator; Monodrama; Novel. MANUEL KOMROFF.

villain. The figure whose evil nature, designs, and actions form the chief opposition to the hero, in stories and plays in which such figures appear. They are absent from Gr. tragedy; in most great works the conflict is within the main character—commonly now called the protagonist. Shakespeare has few unmitigated villains, such as Iago in *Othello.* But from fairy tale to melodrama the villain has always been a favorite figure for shudders and hisses. Often he is more vigorous, more human, than the hero, who may be a puppet, or may (like Ulysses, with the gods battling for him) be destined to triumph. There is genuine majesty, *e.g.,* in the greatest of all villains—Lucifer—as pictured in Milton's *Paradise Lost. Cf.* Hero; Tragedy; Novel; Anti-hero.

villanelle. Fr. pastoral round, originally of various forms, fixed after Jean Passerat (1534–1602). Five 3-line stanzas *aba,* and a final quatrain; all on two rhymes. The first and third lines are alternately the last lines of the remaining tercets, and together are the last lines of the quatrain. Used by Oscar Wilde; W. E. Henley; sombrely by E. A. Robinson, *The House on the Hill. Cf.* Old Fr. . . . forms.

vireli (Prov. By false analogy with *lai,* also *virelai, virelais*). A verse form; varies in length and number of lines and stanzas. (a) *Vireli ancien:* Two rhymes in each stanza; the second becomes the initial rhyme of the next stanza; the last rhyme (but other words) repeats the very first. (b) *Vireli nouveau:* Two rhymes throughout; the first two lines alternately are the end of successive stanzas, and together in reverse order end the poem. Used by Austin Dobson; not frequent. *Cf.* Ballade; Rondeau; Old Fr. forms. N. Wilkins, *100 Ballades, Rondeaux and Virelais from the Late Middle Ages,* 1969.

vísa. The half-line unit of Old Norse poetry, *q.v.*

vocabulary. *See* Diction.

vorticism. A movement in the arts begun by the painter and writer Wyndham Lewis (ed. *Blast: Review of the Great Eng. Vortex*; two issues, June 1914, July 1915, carrying the vorticist manifestos of the Am. poet Ezra Pound and the Fr. sculptor Henri Gaudier-Brzeska). The principles of the movement are not clear; it opposed naturalism, impressionism, and futurism: "The new vortex plunges to the heart of the present." Pound thought of poetry as essentially a matter of images; the image is the unifying element and the form, "a vortex from which, and through which, and into which, ideas are constantly rushing. . . . The vorticist will use only the primary media of his art. The primary pigment of poetry is the image." Thus, with regard to poetry, vorticism is virtually another name for imagism, *q.v.* Pound's vorticist poem "In a Station of the Metro" is illustrative, in its brevity and directness, of poetry in which the image constitutes the form:

The apparition of those faces in the crowd;
Petals on a wet, black bough.

The movement was short-lived, but is important as an instance of the preoccupation with form and the passion for experiment in modern literature (parodied in the Pref. and poetry of *Spectra,* 1916). E. Pound, *Gaudier-Brzeska, a Memoir,* 1916; "Vorticism," *Fortnightly Rev.,* Sept. 1. 1914; S. A. Coblentz, *The Poetry Circus,* 1967.

vraisemblance. Fr. Verisimilitude or probability in a literary work, a measure of artistic convincingness. 17th-c. Fr. criticism distinguished between *vraisemblance* (1) *ordinaire* and (2) *extraordinaire.* (1) included appropriateness of the actions of characters to their social level (decorum) and to their expressed motives (internal probability). (2) covered supernatural action (*i.e.,* of the gods), all surprising outcomes, and sometimes any unusual richness of expression. (1) was deemed indispensable to art; (2) was an extra "delight" which might or might not be present. *Cf. Bienséances;* Verisimilitude; Truth; Realism.

W

WARDOUR STREET ENGLISH (From the London street lined with shops of—often imitation—antiques). A style that affects archaisms, *q.v.*

weak ending. Feminine, *q.v. Cf.* Ending. Weak syllable: one that is unaccented. *Cf.* Accent; Prosody.

Welsh versification. I. The strict metres. All Welsh poetry in the native tradition (*y mesurau caethion*) is measured by the number of syllables in the line. From the beginning, end rhyme has been the rule, and multiple internal rhyme, including *cynghanedd lusg* (*see* below), is common. Identity of terminal syllable makes rhyme (going: coming), and a word may rhyme with itself repeated if in one case it makes part of a compound word (man: woodman). Sometimes instead of rhyme we find assonance, sometimes *proest* (*cf.,* Icelandic "half-rhyme"), in which the final consonants are the same but the vowels preceding them differ (man: sin: run). In the early period we find also "Irish rhyme" in which the vowels are the same and the consonants differ but belong to the same phonetic class, the commonest being the "clear," d.l.r (awr: nawd; aer: mael; olt: ort). Alliteration is common, and in the early poems follows the Irish rule that a consonant may alliterate with its mutated form (b:v:m; t:d:n, etc.). Often there was a sort of rudimentary *cynghanedd.* By the time of the *Gogynfeirdd* (the court poets of the 11–13 c.) the Irish forms of rhyme and alliteration had lapsed, but the other features had hardened into a formal aristocratic poetry, suggestive rather than definite, and often obscure. It was marked by an extensive vocabulary of nouns and adjectives, many of them compound, by the infrequent use of verbs, and by the almost complete absence of the article. Other features were the frequent use of the *gair llanw,* a parenthetical word or phrase introduced chiefly to fill out the *cynghanedd,* and the employment of elaborate metaphors after the fashion of the Teutonic *kenning;* this practice is known as *dyfalu.*

After the loss of national independence, toward the end of the 13th c., this elaborate court poetry was replaced by simpler and more popular domestic forms. The metres most commonly used were the *cywydd* (*see* below) and the *traethgan,* which is much the same but without the rigid rules governing the length of the lines and the use of *cynghanedd* and unequal rhyme.

Cynghanedd (Symphony). The simplest form is *cynghanedd lusg* (trailing symphony), or penult internal rhyme. The line must end in a paroxytone, and the last syllable before the cæsura (which may or may not be accented) must rhyme with the accented penult of this. (In the following schemes, *a* represents the *prifodl* or chief rhyme, which links the line to others but should have no counterpart within the line itself; other letters indicate the other rhymes; numbers, the consonantal correspondences; ′, accented; °, unaccented.)

```
          ′              ′  °
He may frown | on thy crowning
          b              b  a
```

All the consonants that follow the rhyming vowel must be counted, even though some may be in the next syllable or the next word. (The rhyme below is on *ardn.*)

```
     ′                 ′   °
The bard n|ever knew hardness
     b                 b   a
```

Since *cynghanedd lusg* is so easy to make, its use is restricted; in general it may not be used in 2 successive couplets, or in the last line of any metre. The other forms of *cynghanedd* all involve consonantal correspondences between the parts of the line. The most complete is *synghanedd groes* (transverse symphony). In this, the line divides into two parts and all the consonants in the first half must be repeated in the second half, and in the same order, but with different vowels:

To the arch | tie the urchin
1 2 3 4 1 2 3 4

Various modifications of the *croes* are permitted. Considered the best (and obligatory in some metres) is the form (*rhymwiog*) in which the two halves of the lines may be interchanged without destroying either sense or *cynghanedd:*

If now he throws | a fine thread
1 2 3 4 1 2 3 4 a

A fine thread | if now he throws
1 2 3 4 1 2 3 4 a

Cynghanedd sain (sonorous symphony) has the line divided into three parts; the ends of the first and second parts rhyme; and the second and third parts form a *croes* or a *traws* whose cæsura coincides with the end of the second part:

Quickly, | I'm angry, | mongrel
b 1 2 3b 1 2 3 a

In *sain* it is sufficient if only the last consonant before the rhyme is repeated:

What cheer! | A can of beer, | boy
b 1 b 1

This form of *sain* is very common. In all the forms, the words may be run together so as to make a hidden rhyme (*odl gudd*) by conjunction (*o gysswllt*):

For thee l | et him feel | afar
b 1 b 1 a

The Four and Twenty Measures, or the **Venedotian Code (Dosbarth Gwynedd).**

In the middle of the 15th c. the old metrical rules were codified by Dafydd ab Edmwnt; although all but 2 of his 24 metres were very old, the bards of Glamorgan rejected his system and proceeded to compile one of their own (*Dosbarth Morgannwg*). The Venedotian code is, however, generally accepted as the standard today. Many of the metres in each code are so exceedingly complex that their use displays more virtuosity than poetry, and some can be used only as part of an ode. Modern poets tend to ignore these and to concentrate on a few of the simpler forms. Some, like the *cywydd* and the *englyn,* have a history of extensive use.

There are two standard forms of *cywydd,* the lines having respectively 4 and 7 syllables. The latter, the *cywydd deuair hirion* (*cf.* Irish *debide scāilte*) is the common form. It is written in couplets (called stanzas); the final syllables of each pair of lines rhyme, but with the proviso that one of the rhyming syllables must be accented and one must not. Each line must contain one of the forms of *cynghanedd,* but *llusg* may not be used in the second line of any stanza, or in any two consecutive stanzas:

Night may dare | not, my dearest,
1 2 3 4 5 1 2 3 4 5 a

Shadow throw | where) she doth rest;
1 2 3 4 1 2 3 4 a

Daylight | round her shall | dally,
1 2 1 2 b

As sunshine | on) snow is she.
1 2 3 1 2 3 b

When amid | the gree)n meadow
1 2 3 1 2 3 c

Asphodels | and blue | bells | blow,
e 1 2 e 1 2 c

If to the grove | she roveth
f f d

Life's a dance | laughs away death.
1 2 3 4 1 2 3 4 d

T. Gwynn Jones
(from *Dafydd ap Gwilym*).

In the earlier poetry it was usual to link together the two lines of a stanza, and sometimes successive stanzas, by *cymeriadau* (resumptions). This resumption might be by sense—the thought of the 1st line not being complete without the 2d—or by sound—the two lines beginning with the same consonant, or with vowels (the same or different), or being connected by *cynghanedd.*

There was an early form of *englyn* which contained 3 lines instead of 4 as the modern ones do. This is called by some the *warrior's englyn* and by others *englyn penfyr;* these latter then use the name *warrior's englyn* for what others call the *warrior's triplet,* which lacks the *gair cyrch.* The Venedotian code contains 3 forms of *englyn,* but when the name is used without qualification it usually means the *englyn unodl union,* by far the commonest form in modern times. In this, the 1st line is of 10 syllables; the second is of 6, and must end in an unaccented syllable. The 1st line is divided into 2 parts, the break coming after the 7th syllable, or, less often, after the 8th or 9th. The 1st part of this line contains some form of *cynghanedd* and its final syllable rhymes with the ends of the other lines. The remaining 3 syllables (or less) form the *gair cyrch* and are linked with the 1st part of the 2d line by either *cynghanedd* or rhyme. In the former case no further *cynghanedd* is used in the 2d line; but in the latter, the 2 halves of this line must be joined by *cynghanedd.* The 1st 2 lines form the "shaft" (*paladr*) of the *englyn;* the last 2, the "wings" or "feathers" (*esgyll*), are the same as a couplet of the *cywydd,* and carry on the rhyme of the shaft.

Now her flouting | ne'er flatter—and even
Endeavor | to conquer:
In a grave way | now grieve her
For leaving | her) fair lover.

When 12 consecutive *englynion* have the same rhyme they are called a *gosteg* (introduction) *o englynion* because they were often used as an introduction to the *awdl;* when they are linked by having the last word of each one repeated at the beginning of the next they are a *cadwyn* (chain) *o englynion. Awdl* (ode): 1. Originally, a poem with a single end rhyme throughout. 2. A class of metres in the Venedotian code. 3. Today, usually, a poem written in *cynghanedd* and containing a number of the classical metres: until recent times poets often employed all the 24 metres in a single poem. II. The free metres. Besides these native strict metres the Welsh also employ the free metres (*mesurau rhyddion*), which are imitated from foreign models. Rhyme is usual, but *cynghanedd,* when used, is apt to be informal and irregular. The Glamorgan code recognizes the *dyrïau,* a class of metres based upon the accentual system. This was used esp. for poems like the psalms or carols, which were sung in unison by a group. Because of the Anglicization of the Welsh gentry, which took place under the Tudors, the professional poets lost their patrons and a new group of poets, catering to the simpler taste of the peasantry, took their place. A folk poetry (*pennillion*) also developed in the 16th c. There is a modern school of poets who, besides experimenting with modifications of their own strict metres, have introduced many foreign forms, so that Welsh poetry has taken on a cosmopolitan character. One form very popular in the 17th c. is the *tri thrawiad,* so called because there are only three accents in the last line. It consists of dactylic half lines of 6,6,6,5; 6,6,6,3 syllables rhyming *aaab; cccb* (or *aaab*), the fourth ending in a masculine and the others in unaccented rhymes. The *a* rhyme is repeated in the middle of the fourth half line. T. Edwards, "Characteristics of Welsh Poetry," *Transact. Nat'l Eisteddfod of Wales,* 1886; J. M. Jones, "The Rules and Metres of Welsh Poetry," *Zeitschrift für Celtische Philologie,* 4, 1903; T. Gwynn Jones, "Welsh Poetic Art," *Y Cymmrodor,* 36, 1926; J. G. Davies, *Welsh Metrics,* 1911. John J. Parry.

will. Considered by some as a sort of fulcrum, balancing reason and emotion in the artist. Tragedy is said by many to depend upon the idea of the freedom of the will, as it is the free choice of the main character that must make him deserving of his doom. *Cf.* Determinism; *Als ob;* Tragedy; Metatheater.

willing suspension of disbelief. Coleridge's term for what the receptor "must grant" the work of art when he approaches it. *See Als ob.*

wit. Originally the 5 senses, later the 5 internal senses (usually *communis sensus, imaginatio, phantasia, aestimatio, memoria*) and in the Renaissance mental capacity, aptitude, "genius," as opposed to learning (*cf.* L. *ingenium,* It. *ingegno,* Sp. *ingenio,* and Fr. *esprit,* J. E. Spingarn, *Critical Essays of the 17th C.,* 1908, I, xxix). It was soon identified with "quick wit," intellectual liveliness (*cf.* Ascham, *Scholemaster,* 1570; Lyly, *Euphues,* 1579), and it specifically denoted an aptitude for poetry in Sidney (*Apology,* c. 1583), Meres (*Palladis Tamia, or Wit's Treasury,* 1598), and Jonson (*Timber,* 1620–35), who also deprecated its exuberance, as in Shakespeare.

The vogue of wit as a critical term extends from Davenant and Hobbes (1650) to Pope and Addison (1711). As opposed to false wit (*see* next entry), true wit was "dexterity" or "celerity" of thought, fancy, or imagination (Davenant, *Preface to Gondibert,* 1650; Hobbes, *Leviathan,* 1651) which, "like a nimble spaniel beats over and ranges through the field of memory" for its poetic materials (Dryden, *Annus Mirab.,* 1666; *cf.* Boyle, *Reflections,* 1665, Locke, *Essay,* 1690, and Addison, *Spectator,* No. 62, 1711). Boyle, Addison, and Welsted added the element of surprise, as essential. As desirable poetic activity, it was native capacity for observing similarities in materials apparently unrelated, sometimes extolled as indefinable, "being somewhat above expression and such a volatil thing as 'tis altogether volatil to describe" (Flecknoe, *Discourse,* 1664; *cf. A Farrago,* 1666, and Cowley, "Of Wit," 1656). More often it was described in negative terms in the attacks upon its superficial manifestations as false and sheer wit. Hobbes took an extreme position in regarding judgment rather than fancy as the chief ingredient: "Judgment without fancy is wit, but fancy without judgment not" (*Lev.* 1651). In 1675, recognizing that "men more generally affect and admire Fancy than they do either Judgment or Reason . . . and . . . give to it alone the name of Wit," he warned that unless it be held in check by Discretion, "their delight and grace is lost." Others were content to censure the failure of judgment to control fancy in the excesses of the "wits": far-fetched metaphors or conceits, clenches, epigrams, anagrams, and acrostics. This is the point of view in Dryden's characterization, "a propriety of thoughts and words," *i.e.*, appropriateness in both the materials compared and their expression (*Apology*, 1677; *Albion and Albanius*, 1685), dominant also in Cowley, Pope (*Essay on Criticism*, 1711), and Addison (*Spectator*, 58–61). (Addison misunderstood Dryden's meaning in his censure in No. 62). This emphasis upon propriety, an aspect of neo-classic decorum, led to the distinction between wit and humor. Exponents of repartee as wit had denied wit to Jonson. Shadwell (*Pref. Sullen Lovers*, 1668) replied that wit enabled the dramatist to discover appropriate speeches for his characters in lieu of the display of cleverness in smart dialogue. This attack upon sheer wit was coupled with the censure of profaneness and obscenity, "bawdry, that poor pretence of wit" (Sheffield, *Essay on Poetry*, 1682).

The exponents of true wit (dexterity and subtlety in detecting resemblances, properly controlled by judgment) lost their battle against conceits, clenches, and repartee. This led in the 18th c. to a condemnation of wit in general and a preference for other critical terms. Pope in his youthful *Essay on Criticism* (1711), using the term 46 times in 5 or 6 senses, sided with those who stressed propriety:

"True wit is Nature to advantage dressed,
What oft was thought, but ne'er so well expressed"—

but he soon turned to "invention" in extolling Homer (*Preface*, 1715). Joseph Warton (*Essay on Pope*, 1756) preferred the "creative and glowing imagination" of Milton to the wit of Dryden and Pope. Johnson—attacking Cowley (*Lives*, 1779), the idol of the exponents of true wit—found in "*discordia concors*, a combination of dissimilar images," the grounds of censure of "heterogeneous ideas . . . yoked by violence together, . . . nature and art . . . ransacked for illustrations, comparisons, and allusions." Wit was an inadequate designation of poetic capacity because its practitioners "were not successful in representing or moving the affections." This points to Hazlitt's contrast of wit as the discovery of apparent similarities in things totally opposite, and imagination as finding comparisons in things alike or in things "with like feelings attached to them" ("Wit and Humour," *English Comic Writers*, 1819). In subsequent comparisons of wit and humour the former connotes intellectual brilliance; the latter, imaginative sympathy. *Cf.* Humor; Bull; Pun; Brevity. R. E. Lane, *The Liberties of Wit*, 1961; D. Judson Milburn, *The Age of Wit*, 1968. Murray W. Bundy.

wit, false. Addison in several issues of *Spectator* (58–62) attempts to distinguish "false" from "true" wit. He concludes that wit may rise not only from resemblance, but from opposition as well; if from resemblance, it should add surprise, *e.g.* "My mistress's bosom is as white as snow—and as cold." In true wit, the association is of ideas; in false wit, merely of words. Of false wit, he lists 12 main types: (1) shaped verse. (2) lipogram. (3) rebus. (4) echo-verse. (5) A poem ringing the changes of a word. (6) anagram. (7) acrostic. (8) chronogram. (9) bouts-rimés. (10) double rhyme (2 words making 1 rhyme-sound). (11) Pun that is *vox et praeterea nihil* (vanishes in translation). (12) Witches' prayer (*rime brisée*). Verse read one way has one meaning (*e.g.* blessing); read otherwise—backward; alternate lines—another (*e.g.* curse). This is also called Jesuitical writing, *q.v.*

word. *See* Language; Diction; Etymology.

word analysis, detailed study of an author's use of words, is one aspect of the "new" methods in criticism. It includes: (1) word-proportions: of content words to structural words; of image-bearing to non-image-bearing words; of the various parts of speech; (2) word lengths: proportion and succession of words of different numbers of syllables; (3) extent and variety of vocabulary: *e.g.*, of rare words; words in rare senses, in unique sense; coined words; words borrowed from foreign languages, from technical fields; non-literary words: slang, dialect words and forms. Perhaps a list of his most frequently used words will reveal a basic strain in an author's nature. (4) use of words for their associational value, *i.e.,* in such a way as to add to their meaning the memory and emotional impact of earlier use. (5) combination of words; phrasing habits; dependence on the context, interplay of words, cumulative effect; *e.g.,* "for old, unhappy, far-off things," where each adjective means more because of the others; or the exquisite adjustments in Horace, *e.g.* (*Odes* I, ix, 21):

Nunc et latentis proditor intimo
Gratus puellae risus ab angulo.—

as analyzed by G. Murray, *The Classical Tradition,* 1927, p. 170. *Cf.* Explication; Linguistics; Semantics. E. Rickert, *New Methods for the Study of Literature,* 1927.

word order in languages in which the relationships are expressed by inflectional forms, as in Gr. and L., is in general free and lies within the realm of stylistics rather than of grammar. Thus in Latin, *e.g., Romulus Romam condidit, Condidit Romulus Romam, Romam Romulus condidit* indicate varied stress and intonation, roughly equivalent in spoken English to *Romulus* founded Rome, Romulus *founded* Rome, Romulus founded *Rome,* and in written English (as in French) to syntactical variation: It was Romulus that founded Rome; The founding of Rome was the work of Romulus; It was Rome that Romulus founded. In a few instances in both Gr. and L., order is indifferent (*e.g.* L. *mea causa* or *causa mea*) and, again in a few instances, obligatory, so that a change in order will produce a change in denotation: L. *praetor urbanus,* praetor of the city; *urbanus praetor,* a witty praetor; yet in general, factors of rhythm, psychological prominence, or other effects may be served at the author's will by varying the order of the words. Two rhythmic principles inherited from Indo-European are, however, well known and accurately described: Wackernagel's law that an unaccented word tends toward the second position in the phrase (noticeable particularly with weakly accented particles and forms of the verb "to be"); and Behaghel's law, that of two members the shorter tends to come first (as in Eng. "gold and precious stones"; L. *res publica;* Gr. *Troes kai euknemides Achaioi*—Trojans and well-greaved Achaeans). Beyond this, however, Gr. and L. tend to regularize order in different ways. The Gr. verb, *e.g.,* comes usually to stand in the interior of the clause, while the L. verb regularly closes a subordinate clause and usually takes that position in a principal clause. Both languages are, however, very free as compared to Fr., G., and Eng., which must work through rephrasing (as with Romulus, above) to effect shadings that the classical tongues produce with word order. Hence the abundance of passive and causative verbs in the modern tongues. Fr. and the other Romance languages in general prefer a "descending order," the main word, then the modifier: subject, object; noun, adjective; verb, adverb. In Eng., a fixed order is usually necessary to maintain the meaning: a green deep, a deep green; "The boy hit the man." *Cf.* Style; Grammar. Murray. KENNETH MORGAN ABBOTT.

word play. *See* Pun.

work. (1) The work of art: the product. Obviously in the case of a musical score, but truly in all works of art, the finished product is a signal, an aid to the reproduction in the receptor of a complex of ideas, emotions, impulses, intended by the work. The expression of the author, made visible in the work, produces expression in the receptor (Croce). (2) The work at the art: the process. Reverie, planning, may help or delay; what matters is the actual activity, the work. As this goes on, changes suggest themselves: the feel of the tools, the response of the materials (words, phrases, images; the need of a rhyme) help in the patterning: beauty does not exist in the prior dream or vision, but takes shape with the forming of the work (Alain).

writer. Various classifications of writers have been suggested. A frequent division is in two: (a) the man who has a story or emotion to convey, and takes the words for it; (b) the man who rouses to the feel of words, the use of language, the challenge of expression, and finds a tale to clothe with his delight. Thus T. S. Eliot (*For Lancelot Andrewes,* 1929) pictures Donne as "constantly finding an object which shall be adequate to his feelings," whereas Lancelot Andrewes "is wholly absorbed in the object and therefore responds with the adequate emotion." Another grouping seeks less subjective discriminations: (1) the trailblazers (bards before Homer); (2) the masters (Homer; Shakespeare); (3) the diluters (imitators; *cp.* Peacock's silver age; Vergil; Pope); (4) the representatives: minor writers who acceptably reflect their age (Wyatt; Hunt); (5) belles-lettrists, who bring a specific mode to a high development (Longus; Pater); (6) the starters of crazes (Góngora; Joyce). *Cf.* Four ages of poetry.

Z

ZANY (It. zani, zanni<Giovanni). Servant-clown of the *commedia dell'arte, q.v.* Loosely, any jester or clown; spec., a clown's comic assistant, the butt of the comedian's jokes; what the 20th c. theatre calls a stooge.

Zeitgeist. The spirit of the time; the general trend or state of culture or taste characteristic of a period or era.

zeugma. The linking (or the construction that effects it) of two or more words to one, *e.g.,*

Her beauty pierced mine eye, her speech my woeful breast,
Her presence all the powers of my discourse.

This instance is, more specifically, protozeugma: the one word preceding its various ties. If it comes in the middle, mezzozeugma; if at the end: hypozeugma. Syllepsis is such a linking when the one word is used in two constructions or senses, either (a) as a faulty construction or (b) as a figure, *e.g.,* "My lady laughs for joy and I for woe." It is a frequent device in satire, as in the fear (Pope, *Rape of the Lock*) lest Belinda "stain her honour or her new brocade." *Cf.* Figure; Word Order.

PART II

CRITICAL SURVEYS

Note

For a fuller discussion, from the Greeks through the 19th c., George E. B. Saintsbury, *A Hist. of Crit. and Lit. Taste in Europe,* 3 v., 1900–04, 1929–34. Also, Joseph T. Shipley, *The Quest for Literature,* 1931; *Trends in Lit.,* 1949. Of more limited range; Joel E. Spingarn, *Hist. of Lit. Crit. in the Renaissance,* 1899, 1966; G. G. Smith, *Elizabethan Crit. Essays,* 2 v., 1904, 1964; O. B. Hardison, *Modern Continental Lit. Crit.,* 1962; R. A. Foakes, ed. *Romantic Crit.,* 1968; René Wellek, *Hist. of Modern Crit.,* 4 v., 1955–65. Concise surveys of the literature of more than a hundred countries are in *Encyclopedia of Lit.,* ed. Joseph T. Shipley, 1946.

AMERICAN CRITICISM, TO 1919, was dominated, roughly speaking, by five successive ideals. The first was essentially neo-classic, echoing current British criteria and sobered by the American inheritance of Puritan moralism and utilitarianism. This criticism, mainly in periodicals, may be studied in Lyon Richardson's *History of Early American Magazines, 1741–1789*. Pope and Swift represented the ideals of poetry and prose. Critical criteria derived esp. from such widely used textbooks as Lord Kames' *Elements of Criticism* (1762), Hugh Blair's *Lectures on Rhetoric* (1783), and Archibald Alison's *Nature and Principles of Taste* (1790). Beyond conventional neo-classicism, however, two trends were esp. important in America in the later 18th c.: these resulted from the influence on literary theory of Newtonian science, fostering nature-analogies, orderliness, and "perspicuity"; and esp. after the Revolution, of nationalism and the consequent revolt against imitation and tradition. Franklin, Jefferson, Paine, and Freneau owed many of their literary ideals to science. Even the conservative Presbyterian Rev. Samuel Miller, in his 2 v. *Brief Retrospect of the 18th c.* (1803, II, 101, 234), which includes much literary criticism, concludes that "the scientific spirit of the age has extended itself remarkably, in giving to our language that precision, spirit, force, polish, and chaste ornament" in which he thought his age excelled. "The discoveries in science . . . have also conferred some peculiarity on the poetic character of the age, by furnishing the poet with new images, and more just and comprehensive views of nature." As early as 1770 John Trumbull's *Essay on the Use and Advantages of the Fine Arts* had attacked "luxurious effeminacy" and "false taste" which he fathered on "pedantry," "admirers of antiquity," and "servile imitation" of European writers. He urged a "common and natural expression" and expressed confidence that a native Shakespeare would soon appear. Neo-classicism is represented by three influential college lecturers: Yale's Timothy Dwight; Princeton's John Witherspoon (*Lectures on Eloquence,* 1803); and Harvard's John Quincy Adams (*Lectures on Rhetoric and Oratory,* 2 v., 1810). In journalism it is represented by C. B. Brown, whose yardsticks were correctness, elegance, propriety, moralism, and nationalism; and by Joseph Dennie, ed. *Portfolio,* 1801–09, who was even more reactionary, except for the fact that he favorably introduced Wordsworth and Coleridge to American readers. W. C. Bryant's *Early American Verse,* 1818, attacked "a sickly and affected imitation" of the English neo-classicists; his 4 *Lectures on Poetry,* 1825, urged the harmonious combination of imagination and emotion rigorously restrained by judgment; but being transitional he praised Wordsworth, advocated originality, nationalism and prosodic flexibility. The weighty *North American Review,* founded in 1815 as essentially neo-classic, helped to prepare for romantic transcendentalism by elaborate discussions of German literary trends and their eloquent interpreter, S. T. Coleridge. Criticism from 1810–1835 is dominated by social principles; the critic must be the watch-dog of society; he attacks whatever savors of rebellion, of immorality, of pessimism, of mysticism, of the egocentric, says Charvat. This neo-classical ideal was gradually superseded by a 2d, essentially romantic or transcendental, prepared for by James Marsh's persuasive and elaborate introd. to Coleridge's *Aids to Reflection,* 1829, and *The Friend,* 1831, and by the essay on Coleridge in the *Christian Examiner,* 1833, by F. H. Hedge. The latter's work in introducing the critical ideas of German writers (of whom Coleridge and Carlyle were interpreters: Kant, Fichte, Schelling, the Schlegels, Goethe) was strongly reinforced by such widely influential journalistic critics as George Ripley (for 31 years reviewer of the New York *Tribune*) and by Margaret Fuller (ed. of the transcendental *Dial* and Ripley's successor). Broadly speaking, transcendentalist criticism revolted against neo-classicism as over-stressing external form and the judicial application of rules and substituted a concern for the inward spiritual power of the individual. The Unitarian W. E. Channing, friend and follower of Coleridge, suggested the new criteria in urging "a poetry which pierces beneath the exterior of life to the depths of the soul, and which lays open its mysterious working, borrowing from the whole outward creation [nature] fresh images and correspondences, with which to illuminate the secrets of the world within us." Among those who held up this ideal, in varying degrees, were R. H. Dana, Sr., George Bancroft, Henry Reed (ed. and disciple of Wordsworth), J. S. Dwight (ed. who related music to literature), W. G. T. Shedd (ed. 1852, and trenchant interpreter, of Coleridge), Bronson Alcott, Theodore Parker, G. H. Calvert; critics who used Coleridge's approach to Shakespeare such as E. P. Whipple, Julian Verplanck, Jones Very, and H. N. Hudson; and leaders of the St. Louis School of Transcendentalism such as Denton Snider (who tempered transcendentalism with Hegel's views in long critical books on Homer, Dante, Shakespeare, Goethe). Noah Porter, Pres. of Yale, in *Books and Reading,* 1876 (pp. 265–284) summed up the "new criticism" (which he thought to be of German origin): it has "a more enlarged and profound conception of literature itself"; it is catholic, liberal and appreciative in spirit; it is more philosophical in its methods; it is "more generous and genial . . . , for its cardinal maxim is, the critic cannot be just to an author unless he puts himself in the author's place"; it strives to re-live the author's vision rather than to judge; to interpret "the times of the author by means of his writings," and "the secrets of their hearts, and to open to us the hidden springs of their character."

The man who gave this transcendental ideal its most commanding vogue in America, by virtue of his character, personality, and style, is R. W. Emerson, esp. in his *Representative Men,* 1850. Believing that "beauty is the mark God sets upon virtue" and that "expression is organic" and will take form as the spontaneous by-product of an inspired idea, Emerson disregarded the mere mechanisms of literature. Critics should be poets, dealing with "the order of . . . thoughts and the essential quality of . . . mind" of writers. A post-Kantian idealist, Emerson judged literature by its approach to archetypes existing in the highest imagination of man, calling criticism legitimate only as it sought the "text in nature" with which poems must "tally." The "fundamental law" of criticism was to teach the reader to partake at first-hand of "the same spirit which gave . . . forth" the timeless work of the great genius. Hence it should be not destructive, but "guiding, instructive, inspiring."

"America is a poem in our eyes," he announced, calling for geniuses to write it down and use the common, wholesome facts of its existence to symbolize the universal spiritual laws. Emerson dealt with the broad ethical contributions of an author, esp. exploring his use of the world's variety to show forth the One, the unity of mankind's spiritual power. Stylistic beauty and optimism gave him inspirational power and charm.

The excessive appreciative sympathy and spirituality of the transcendentalists doubtless helped to stimulate a reaction against them toward a 3d critical ideal, that of rigorously evaluating literature in the light of absolute æsthetic standards. Of this, the best representative is E. A. Poe, who used the "tomahawk" methods of sensational journalism as a reviewer of mostly minor current authors, to save criticism from what he regarded as provincial sins of moralism, chauvinism, and a neglect of conscious artistic craftsmanship. In "Exordium," 1842, he said the critic should be concerned with opinions in a book only to judge how artistically they are handled. Poe would "limit criticism to comment upon *Art.*" Apart from its rules, the critic should be "absolutely independent." He thought E. P. Whipple was our best critic. His emphasis on rationality, form, and unity was of the 18th c., as were his interest in melancholy, graveyardism, horror, and desire (*Eureka*) to model art upon the symmetrical unity of the Newtonian universe. Coming ever more under the influence of the Schlegels' critical ideas as he matured, he sought to write in terms of the divine creativity and idealistic immortality of the higher imagination interpenetrated by the higher Reason. Like Coleridge, he insisted upon "particular and methodical application" of his rules to each work, maintaining that pleasure through beauty, not truth, was the essence of "The Poetic Principle." Deeply concerned with prosody, he equated poetry and music, holding melody essential to verse. He first formalized the technique of the short story, seeking totality of effect through compression, immediacy, verisimilitude, and finality. The critic's primary task, he said, was "in pointing out and analyzing defects."

The New England common sense in Lowell came as a mediator between these two extremes. Although Lowell admired Emerson personally, especially as a decorous and urbane banquet speaker, he ridiculed transcendentalists such as Thoreau for their mystical attempts to live off "the internal revenues of the spirit." To Emerson's ethical earnestness (which Poe deemed irrelevant) Lowell added a much more scholarly and extensive knowledge of literature, and an ability to handle strictly literary matters such as philology, style, and form. He developed through three phases, emphasizing humanitarianism to about 1850, nationalism to about 1867, and thereafter the self-conquest of the individual guided by the long experience of humanity embodied in great literature (such as *The Divine Comedy*), which he thought should be "judged . . . absolutely, with reference, that is, to the highest standard, and not relatively to the fashions and opportunities of the age." Among his major contributions was his helping to found American regionalism with the *Biglow Papers,* which exalted rustic good sense, attacked bookish writing, and (Pref.) urged a native and indigenous literature in earthy dialect. As a founder of the *Atlantic Monthly,* 1857, he gave both opportunities for publication and high sanction to this sort of writing. On the other hand, his rich critical essays did much to open the minds of an æsthetically starved and chauvinistically narrowed people to the treasures of their cultural past. Lowell strove to follow the Greeks in "absolute" judgment of literature in terms of organic, harmonized form and permanent, universal ethical values. He was the most rounded and scholarly American critic. Originality, sympathy, insight, and imaginativeness redoubled his influence.

Another practitioner of judicial criticism of wide influence was E. C. Stedman, the Wall Street broker, who answered the question "What is criticism" by defining it as "the art . . . of declaring in what degree any work . . . conforms to the Right." This he measured by traditional standards of the unity and parity of "verity, æsthetics, and morals," which he held could be intuitively apprehended and checked against the teachings of the past. If in this he resembled Emerson, he was even more like Poe (whom he edited and loved) not only in his judicial approach but in his hostility to didacticism; Stedman's *Nature and Elements of Poetry,* 1892, develops the idea that poetry is the creation of pure beauty independent of moral considerations. Indeed, "a prosaic moral is injurious to virtue by making it repulsive." To him beauty is "absolute and objective," and genius alone produces poetry. These were the criteria, involving a good deal of attention to form, that Stedman applied in his *Poets of America,* 1885, and *Victorian Poets,* 1887. He is perhaps most forward-looking in his discussion of the "approaching harmony of Poetry and Science," in his plea that criticism be a constructive agent of literary evolution, and in his recognition of Whitman.

Nevertheless, Stedman's general diffuseness, rhetoric, timidity, and air of vague impressionism encouraged the turn to a 4th critical ideal, inspired by evolutionary science and equalitarian democracy, which emphasized realism considered as the quest of the average and which (following Hippolyte Taine) regarded literature as determined by the author's time, place, and race and hence as an index to the nation's social history. Of this ideal the most famed spokesman is Walt Whitman, who sought to be a revolutionist in criticism as in poetry. His *Democratic Vistas* proposed to announce "a native-expression spirit" for America, independent, and inspired by "science . . . and the principles of its own democratic spirit only." Literature he would have "the divine mirror" of the "People"; he attacks all writing not favorable to democracy. Thus, while he admires Shakespeare as "the loftiest of the singers," he warns against his "feudalism." Scott, Tennyson and Carlyle are similarly held up as writers subversive of "progressive politics." Burns won praise for championing the downtrodden; but he had too "little spirituality" to be a model for the New World. In later age Whitman came to temper this early conclusiveness with internationalism and a desire for universality of spirit. He saw the democratic ideal embracing all mankind in spiritual as well as physical comradeship and he sought literature to "celebrate the divine idea of All." A literary theorist urging new ideas, to be embodied by himself and others, Whitman stands historically as a powerful seminal figure. His actual criticism, however, suffered from misplaced emphases and a failure to see beyond his peculiar yardstick.

As a critic of fiction the high priest of realism in America was William Dean Howells, who owed his widely influential theories to a conjunction of native democracy with science and its subsidiaries, Tolstoian evolutionary ethics and Taine's determinism. Realism was simply "fidelity to experience and probability of motive," he wrote. It was democracy in taste, and its sole artistic duty was to "interpret the common feelings of commonplace people." The realist must regard the world with the same objective utilitarianism as the scientist, neither idealizing nor selecting but representing life itself "without a plan." Since Victorian ethics, particularly in Tolstoi, recognized ethical growth as part of scientific evolution, Howells believed that factual presentations of literature must be ethically constructed and æsthetically good; for the perfect æsthetics result from the perfect ethics. Science, too, supported the determinism of Taine, and Howells besought the critic to become like the botanist; "observing, recording, and comparing . . . analyzing the material . . . then synthesizing its impressions" was to be his non-judicial, objective job. Howells' own best criticism was broad appreciation of *Literary Friends and Acquaintances* (1900), such as Mark Twain, from a personalized standpoint. He is also noteworthy for having secured public favor for Emily Dickinson, Garland, Crane, and Norris.

Henry James had deeper roots in tradition and idealism than his friend Howells, but what has been most influential in his work is not without kinship with the realistic and scientific age. He continued the symbolism of Hawthorne, the idealism of Emerson, and the cosmopolitanism of Lowell; on these 3 men he wrote discerning and appreciative essays. He thought the novel should be "both a picture and an idea," that it should "represent life" rather than merely please; censuring Fr. writers such as Maupassant for creating characters without "the reflective part which governs conduct and produces character," he valued fiction for its representation of life as made up of the physical, intellectual, and spiritual properly proportioned. "Art is essentially selection, but it is selection whose main care is to be typical, to be inclusive," to avoid merely artificial "rearrangement" which might militate against "the illusion of life." In his essay on *Criticism,* however, as elsewhere, he follows his master Sainte-Beuve, in seeking merely to steep himself, "sentient and restless," in the writing concerned until he understood and appreciated it fully. His expressionism in criticism, and the inconclusiveness of many of the ethical conclusions of his novels (*The Ambassadors*), seem the counterpart of his admiration for his brother William's Pragmatism which, with its denial of absolutes and its espousal of empiricism and relativity, did much to provide sanction for realism and naturalism. How far he departed from Holmes' Cambridge is apparent in James' extended appreciations of Zola, high priest of "scientific" naturalism. His modernness is most apparent, however, in his absorption in psychology and the study of motives, and his anti-transcendental and very self-conscious delight in experimentation in all the subtleties of form and construction (use of "reflectors," etc.). In later years, as Mrs. Wharton complained, he came close to criticizing the novel solely as a technician.

More typical of indigenous realism was Hamlin Garland, whose *Crumbling Idols* (1894) illustrates the way in which Darwinism inspired a revolt against tradition and "the statical idea of life and literature." He adopted "two great literary concepts—that truth was a higher quality than beauty, and that to spread the reign of justice should everywhere be the design and intent of the artist." H. H. Boyesen and H. W. Mable emphasized the manner in which new interpretations of life inspired by science led to new techniques in fiction and criticism. C. D. Warner summed up *The Relation of Literature to Life* (1896) in the thesis "that all genuine, enduring literature is the outcome of the time that produces it, . . . and that consequently the most remunerative method of studying a literature is to study the people for whom it was produced." Perhaps the most representative signpost in 1900 is W. M. Payne's "American Literary Criticism and the Doctrine of Evolution" (*International Monthly,* II); science is said to have transformed criticism, and since Taine's deterministic method is "unsurpassed," we should be relativistic rather than judicial and study the time, place, and race that "produced" the books being criticized.

This brings us to what may be called the 5th general movement in American criticism: to the growing conflict after 1900 between those who rely on some aspect of tradition, emphasizing the good life and conventional literary form, and those who would describe or express gusto or "disgusto" on the basis of an author's being nationalistic, indigenous, or frankly naturalistic. Among the 1st group are G. E. Woodberry, exalter of "the race-mind" and lover of Lowell; George Santayana, who loved form and hated Whitman; W. P. Trent, defender of *The Authority of Criticism*; W. C. Brownell, austere judge of *Victorian Prose Masters* (1901) and of *American Prose Masters* (1909), emphasizing "the criterion of reason"; P. E. More, whose *Shelburne Essays* (1904–35, 14 v.) sought "to temper the enthusiasm of the living by the authority of the dead" and the yardstick of dualism; and Irving Babbitt, More's fellow

Humanist, whose *Masters of Modern French Criticism* (1912) and *Rousseau and Romanticism* (1919), sharply judicial, did most to provoke the anti-traditionalists. Among the 2d group are John Burroughs, loving interpreter of Whitman, whose relativistic *Literary Values* (1902) emphasized sympathy, personality, and naturalism; Brander Matthews, devoted to Mark Twain, to the indigenous, and to criticism as sympathetic appreciation; Frank Norris, preacher of *The Responsibilities of the Novelist* (1903) to tell the naturalistic truth about the victims of an *Octopus* capitalism; T. R. Lounsbury, scholarly critic of Chaucer, Shakespeare, and Cooper, and apologist for a racy dialect literature; F. L. Pattee, dean of American literature professors whose main criterion was nationalism; John Macy, impressionist and nationalist; James Huneker, whose many *Promenades of an Impressionist* (1910) explored the exotic in foreign lands and related music and literature; Van Wyck Brooks, whose *America's Coming of Age* (1915) provoked wide discussion by its attack on "Our Poets" as being, except for Whitman, lacking in "Americanism"; and H. L. Mencken, whose frank identification of criticism as extreme impressionistic *Prejudices* (1919 f.), coming in the same year as Babbitt's *Rousseau and Romanticism,* did much to establish the polarity of critical debate during the next two decades.

H. H. Clark's "Lit. Crit. in the *N. Am. R.,* 1815–1835," *Transact. Wisc. Acad.,* XXXII, 1940, provides summaries; Norman Foerster's *Am. Crit.,* 1928, has incisive essays on Poe, Emerson, Lowell, and Whitman, with a final chapter explaining The New Humanism; J. P. Pritchard, *Return to the Fountains,* 1942. Harry Hayden Clark.

Recent. Joel Elias Spingarn's *The New Criticism* (1911, 1931) came out at the right time to challenge the complacency of the "old order." Spingarn (1875–1939), a disciple of Croce, insisted upon æsthetic standards and a consciousness of literature as art; and it is hardly too much to say that without his pioneer work, the new school of "critical realism" which centered in *The Seven Arts* and *The Masses* could not have been born. Although Van Wyck Brooks' *America's Coming of Age* (1915) and Randolph Bourne's *The History of a Literary Radical* (1920) are concerned with the social milieu of American writing, these two pioneer books ask a leading question that owes much to the influence of Spingarn: What are the limiting and frustrating influences in American life, which have prevented the growth of a literature that in scope and maturity, and in æsthetic disinterestedness, can challenge the literatures of Europe?

With this question the recent American critical movement was born. Two other writers of considerable talent added to its power: Waldo Frank (b. 1889), whose *Salvos* (1924) and *The Rediscovery of America* (1928) set forth a mystical vision of a better America, although not based upon wide American experience, and Lewis Mumford (b. 1895), whose *The Golden Day* (1926) and *The Brown Decade* (1931) followed closely the main thesis of Van Wyck Brooks, that our narrow Puritanism and pioneering had betrayed the early promise of the great New Englanders: Hawthorne, Melville, Emerson. These critics were more or less unconsciously concerned not with judging the merit of works of literature but with Matthew Arnold's more general idea of "culture." They performed a great service in exposing the cultural defects of a society dominated by industrial capitalism; but weakness of specific critical judgment, a facile nationalism (even a whooping it up for the American article), and an intolerance of the unpopular are the marks of this school in its decline, in writers like Bernard de Voto (1897–1955) and Howard Mumford Jones (b. 1892). A powerful support for this movement came late in the twenties in Vernon Louis Parrington's *Main Currents in American Thought* (1927–30), which also influenced the Marxists of the next decade.

Meanwhile an expatriate in England, T. S. Eliot, had been reexamining the basis of the European traditions of literature. His first collection of essays, *The Sacred Wood* (1920), also owes much, in its insistence upon cosmopolitan culture, to Matthew Arnold, but it broke the Victorian domination in poetry, and opened to the imagination a range of subject and method that the immediate Victorian past could not provide. As editor of *The Criterion* Eliot wielded vast influence, even upon writers who opposed his growing religious interests, for he more than any other critic of the period set the limits and the subjects of discussion. His *Selected Essays* (1932, 1950) is probably the leading critical achievement of our age.

Around the example of Eliot the "younger generation" rallied, in opposition (though it still owed a debt) to the school of Van Wyck Brooks. These younger men felt that their interests could not be represented in the established journals, *Harper's, Scribner's, The Atlantic Monthly, The Yale Review*; so beginning with the First World War a succession of "unpopular" magazines has run down to the present: *The Little Review, Secession, The Dial* (the chief organ of the Eliot influence, 1921–28), *Hound & Horn, The Symposium, The Southern Review, Partisan Review, The Kenyon Review,* and *The Sewanee Review*. Those magazines that survived public indifference were joined, in the years after the Second World War, by an increasing number—founded by university literature departments—that have become more and more institutionalized and academic, even as has the critical movement they reflected. Although great variety of political bias was exhibited by these reviews, they nevertheless form a single tradition from the literary point of view: they all hewed to the critical line in assuming the value and even the autonomy of works of the imagination.

While these two forces, the historical-patriotic under Brooks and the critical under Eliot, were struggling for supremacy, an older school of critics, the Humanists, headed by Paul Elmer More and Irving Babbitt, had, at the end of the twenties, a brief resurgence. A Humanist symposium, *Humanism and America* (1930), edited by Norman Foerster (b. 1887), reaffirmed traditional morals and moralistic critical standards. It was immediately attacked by a counter-symposium, under the editorship of Hartley Grattan (b. 1902), *The Critique of Humanism* (1930), in which for the occasion collaborated critics of many views. (The confusion of the issues involved is betrayed by Eliot's appearance in the Humanist volume, while many of his school were in the opposition.) A violent controversy ensued, but quickly subsided after a year, in which no issues were decided. The defects of More and Babbitt as literary critics were tellingly exposed, but in the heat of controversy their value in another direction was ignorantly dismissed. Both men were primarily informal historians of ideas; both were concerned, Babbitt as a non-religious moralist, More as religious moralist, with the forces and ideas that have made for the decay of the modern world. The prime failure of both men lay in their inability to understand the creative imagination, which must be concerned with what is, not with what ought to be. The 11 volumes of More's *Shelburne Essays* are a distinguished critical achievement, while Babbitt's *Literature and the American College* (1908) and *On Being Creative, and Other Essays* (1932) will in time win recognition of their lasting value.

The collapse of the stock market in 1929 and the Humanist controversy marked the end of a critical era and the rise of the Marxist school of critics, of whom Kenneth Burke (b. 1897), James T. Farrell (b. 1904), Newton Arvin (b. 1900), and Edmund Wilson (b. 1895) were the most conspicuous. (Wilson had formerly been "without politics," had written for *The Dial,* and was conceded to be our best expositor of the new writers, Eliot, Pound, Joyce.) Wilson's *Axel's Castle* (1934) and Burke's *Counter-Statement* (1931) and *Permanence and Change* (1935) are probably the ablest criticism from the Marxist point of view in this period. Farrell's *A Note on Literary Criticism* (1936) corrected many of the grosser errors of his fellow Marxists who supposed that "proletarian" literature could be fundamentally different from other literature; and that was the value of many occasional essayists of this school: Horace Gregory (b. 1898), Malcom Cowley (b. 1898), Philip Rahv (b. 1908), William Phillips (b. 1907), Joseph Freeman (b. 1897).

While the Marxist ideologues like Bernard Smith (b. 1906) in *Forces in Am. Crit.* (1939) were as dogmatic as the humanists, and even narrower, what is sound in the best Marxist writers fuses with the traditional body of common sense about literature in all times: literature must come out of life. Towards the end of the thirties the Marxist group began to break up; an expansion of interest and a greater objectivity marks their later writing (*e.g.* Burke, *The Philosophy of Literary Form,* 1941). Under the threat of the coming war these men began to appear in journals like *The Southern Review* and *The Kenyon Review,* and the contributors to these journals in *Partisan Review,* a Marxist journal—being moved to collaborate, no doubt, by the awareness of the growing menace of the war to all schools of critical thought. *The Southern Review* (1935–42) and *The Kenyon Review* (1938–) brought to a limited public the work of a group known as the "intellectualists." The former of these journals during the Marxist thirties took the regionalist line; but it nevertheless published some of the best Marxian criticism; and many of its regular contributors came down from *The Dial* and *Hound & Horn.* This group later came to be called the "new critics," the name derived not from Spingarn's use of the term but from John Crowe Ransom's borrowing of it for *The New Criticism* (1941). With this work, with his earlier *The World's Body* (1938), and by his career as teacher at Vanderbilt University and Kenyon College, Ransom (b. 1888; founding editor of *The Kenyon Review*) established himself as leader of the movement. It seemed to be a school to the extent that its members shared a concern to justify poems as objects in their own right by claiming for them an indispensable function and an irreducible meaning. Associated with Ransom as an editor of *The Fugitive* [Tenn. 1922–25; prominent among poetry magazines that followed Harriet Monroe's *Poetry* (Chicago, 1912–) in the resurgence of Am. verse], Allen Tate (b. 1899) has maintained a defense of poetry against positivism and sociologism, concerned with principles rather than individuals. Cleanth Brooks' (b. 1906) *Modern Poetry and the Tradition* (1939) is a valuable, if extreme statement of the case for modern poetry, based upon a synthesis of the views of Eliot and the Eng. I. A. Richards. His *The Well Wrought Urn* (1947) though it springs from the same critical position, tries to attain a more catholic and inclusive view of English poetry. R. P. Blackmur (b. 1904), who after the demise of *Hound & Horn* came to be associated with this group, in his early work (like *The Double Agent,* 1935) provided our closest analysis of the language of certain modern writers. His later works showed an increasing complexity and difficulty, together with an increasing richness and profundity, as he expanded his literary concerns to broad cultural issues. Yvor Winters (b. 1900) has much in common with the "intellectualists," but the influence of the humanists on him gives his criticism—despite its brilliant observations of technical detail—a strongly moralistic flavor, often leading to an eccentric violence of statement.

Archibald MacLeish (b. 1892; *The Irresponsibles,* 1940) and Van Wyck Brooks (1886–1963; *What is Primary Literature?,* 1941) led a reaction against criticism in favor of a patriotic nationalism; these men repudiated modern literature as decadent and called imaginative writers to action and propaganda. Brooks' *The Flowering of New England* (1936) and *New England: Indian Summer* (1940) had dissolved literature into its historical backgrounds, a procedure from which could have been predicted a loss of confidence in the creative imagination and its supporting activity, rational criticism. This anti-critical, liberal social impulse has recurred from time to time, notably in the late 1940's when the *Saturday Review* tried to raise a furore over the Bollingen award to Ezra Pound. But it has never struck a major note in our most serious critical community.

Also on the outside of the new-critical movement, though far more faithful to literary values, has been a series of social and psychoanalytical critics. Their distinction arises from their special powers as critics rather than from revolutionary approaches, since their approaches are mainly adapted from those of 19th c. cultural historians. The most distinguished of these are Edmund Wilson and Lionel Trilling (b. 1905). Alfred Kazin (b. 1915) is somewhat more derivative. Irving Howe (b. 1920) has a more central social and political interest, and Leslie Fiedler (b. 1917) a more central psychoanalytical interest, although he joins with it a mythic bent.

In this period academic scholars entered the critical arena, with distinguished and urbane work of which their predecessors seemed to be incapable. Attitudes toward literature of the ensuing generation of teacher-scholars were revolutionized in the new-critical directions by the undergraduate text of Cleanth Brooks and Robert Penn Warren (b. 1905), *Understanding Poetry* (1938, 1950) and by the more advanced *Theory of Literature* (1949, 1956) of René Wellek (b. 1903) and Austin Warren (b. 1899). Thus the new criticism entered the university and became firmly established in the literature classroom as it was being established in the increasing number of journals created by universities in imitation of the reviews that ushered in the movement. But, thus institutionalized, it turned programmatic at the cost of its vitality. Newer approaches had to win the support of younger minds, although this fact meant that they would once again have to turn from the study of literary works in their own right, as uniquely closed systems of meaning.

Northrop Frye (b. 1912) of the University of Toronto, with his *Anatomy of Criticism* (1957) became the next center of academic critical system-making. Frye supplied a rallying point for the anti-classicist impulse that had long been suppressed by the impersonal tradition from Eliot through the new criticism. (Frye's first major work, *Fearful Symmetry,* 1947, was a brilliant exposition of Blake.) Instead of the contextualist concern with the discrete work as a self-sufficient, closed system, Frye centered on all literature as an entity, a mythic unity fed by the open society of all its members. These members, the no longer isolated works, together form the single, many-faceted construct, the world as dream, the world as envisioned—as willed—by the human imagination, all human imaginations. The visionary system according to Blake—or, as Harold Bloom (*Shelley's Mythmaking,* 1959; *The Visionary Company,* 1962) might prefer it, according to Shelley too—supersedes the single work as a *fiat* of the wishful imagination supersedes the existential world. The increasing interest in vision did much to return the work to its author, to allow a renewed interest in biography as a comment upon the free flow between life and art.

Others reacted even more strenuously, in the romantic service of vision, against what they saw as the critical establishment descended from Eliot. Some, like the poet Karl Shapiro (b. 1913) in *In Defense of Ignorance,* 1960, attacked formalism by trying to found a prophetic, anti-æsthetic tradition of anti-poems. Or, more recently, a critic like Ihab Hassan (b. 1925) looking toward an apocalyptic poetry, can countenance the total destruction of the Word to reach the silence of immediacy. The cultivation of immediacy, with its visionary consequences, was abetted also by those who, after many years of our theoretical self-sufficiency, looked once more to Continental influences. Georges Poulet left several imaginative followers, like J. Hillis Miller (b. 1928) and René Girard (b. 1923) behind him after his stay at the Johns Hopkins University. These, and other critics like Geoffrey Hartman (b. 1929) concentrated on the role played by the author's consciousness in his work as they pursued what has come to be called "phenomenological" criticism. Or, influenced by other Continental critics like Roland Barthes, they have begun to turn to a more general structuralist method.

The interest in vision that broke open the literary object in the direction of its creator was matched by the renewed interest in history and existence that broke open the object in the direction of the world outside. Usual complaints against "formalist" criticism (often springing from misunderstanding) led to attempts to re-invoke the social criticism of the thirties (as, *e.g.,* with Walter Sutton). But other theorists (*e.g.* Eliseo Vivas, b. 1901, and Murray Krieger, b. 1923), more faithful to new-critical attitudes and just as concerned with the existential consequences of literature, want to return the object to its historical moment without allowing it to lose its uniqueness and authenticity. Clearly, the critical situation is in flux, with so many competitors for dominance that no single figure or movement can claim a wide allegiance. Norman Foerster, ed. *Am. Crit. Essays,* 1930; *Am. Crit.,* 1962; W. Charvat, *The Origins of Am. Crit. Thought, 1810–35,* 1936; S. E. Hyman, *The Armed Vision,* 1948; H. M. Jones, *The Theory of Am. Lit.,* 1948, 1966; C. I. Glicksberg, *Am. Lit. Crit., 1900–50,* 1951; M. D. Zabel, *Lit. Opinion in Am.,* 1951; E. Vivas, *Creation and Discovery,* 1955; Murray Krieger, *The New Apologists for Poetry,* 1956; C. W. Moulton, *Library of Lit. Crit. of Am. and Eng. Authors,* 8 v., 1901–04, 1959; 4 v., 1966; J. P. Pritchard, *Crit. in Am.,* 1956; R. Foster, *The New Romantics,* 1962; L. T. Lemon, *The Partial Critics,* 1965. ALLEN TATE and MURRAY KRIEGER.

ENGLISH CRITICISM. Renaissance. In contrast to Italy, 16th c. England was not fertile in critical writing. Most of such work listed in anthologies is incidental to writing for other purposes. Sir Thomas Elyot's *Governour* (1530) was intended to give advice on the training of boys likely to hold high political office, part of whose education should consist of the reading of poetry. Hence Elyot is led to the "defense of poets," and attempts "to show what profit may be taken by the diligent reading of ancient poets, contrary to the false opinion, that now reigneth, of them that suppose that in the works of poets is contained nothing but bawdry (such is their foul word of reproach) and unprofitable leasings." He points out the "commendable sentences and right wise counsels" to be found even in "dissolute" poets, and insists that "no ancient poet would be excluded from the lesson of such a one as desireth to come to the perfection of wisdom." Elyot's theory is wholly didactic, as indeed his subject demands, but his love for poetry appears between the lines. Since there were 8 editions of his work, it may well have influenced later English writers. The didactic theory of Elyot and his successors is not to be thought of as especially Puritan or even English, but as normal in European literary theory in the age. Attacks on poetry and the stage such as those of Gosson in his *School of Abuse* (1579) and Prynne in his *Histrio-mastix* (1633) have little critical importance, though it has been suggested, without proof, because of his dedication, that Gosson—not a complete obscurantist—stimulated Sidney to write his *Defence of Poesie.*

Writers on English criticism commonly mention the rhetoricians—chiefly, it seems, in default of authors really critical. Thomas Wilson's *Art of Rhetoric* (1553) is what its name indicates. He gives less than three pages to poetry, considering, in medieval fashion, only its power to teach allegorically. The theory of rhetoric obviously influenced the theory of poetry in the Renaissance, as in the belief that poetry had as one of its functions to move the reader.

Roger Ascham's *Scholemaster,* 1570, deals in part with literature; his discussion of Sallust has some elements of critical estimate. With Sir John Cheke and Watson, he compared "the preceptes of Aristotle and Horace *de Arte Poetica*" with the examples of Euripides, Sophocles, and Seneca. Of the tragedies of his own time he found but two "able to abyde the trew touch of Aristotles preceptes and Euripides examples," viz., Watson's *Absolom* and George Buchanan's *Jephthes.*

Qualities and even ideas derived from Elyot, and the classical spirit of Ascham, powerfully reinforced by study of Italian critics, appear in the only critical work of the first rank produced in England, the *Apology for Poetry* or *Defence of Poesie* by Sir Philip Sidney, published posthumously in 1595. It is the work of a man about 27, a poet indeed, but still more a courtier, aspiring to public office and military command. Without the learning of his Italian teachers (Scaliger, Minturno), he surpasses all of them in the charm of his writing and in his manifest disinterested love for poetry. His *Defence* is no pedantic treatise, but a vigorous presentation of the case for poetry. The personality of the author appears, and his delight in humour, so that the strictly planned work has some of the qualities of the familiar essay. Altogether it is something new among works of criticism. Poetry for Sidney is primarily didactic, "full of virtue-breeding delightfulness." But he always remembers his own delight in it, and conveys this to the reader. This preserves him from judging by rules alone, and enables him to recognize poetry when he meets it. Though Scaliger, whose words of wisdom he revered, was wholly a classicist, Sidney, partly perhaps because his mind was not primarily analytic, received Ariosto's Orlando, who "will never displease a soldier," into the company of Æneas. The poet's word is "golden":

> "Poetry ever setteth virtue so out in her best colours, making Fortune her well-waiting handmaid, that one must needs be enamored of her. Well may you see Ulysses in a storm, and in other hard plights; but they are but exercises of patience and magnanimity, to make them shine the more in the near-following prosperity. And of the contrary part, if evil men come to the stage, they ever go out (as the tragedy writer remarked to one that misliked the show of such persons) so manacled as they little animate folks to follow them."

Such liberation from fact enables the poet also to show his creative power by presenting "formes such as never were in Nature, as the Heroes, Demigods, Cyclops, Chimeras, Furies, and such like: so as hee goeth hand in hand with Nature, not inclosed within the narrow warrant of her guifts, but freely ranging onely within the zodiac of his owne wit."

Partly because of his Italian training, partly because he had seen no modern tragedy that had stirred him as did the *Orlando Furioso,* Sidney is more classical in his demands on the dramatist than on the epic poet, requiring brevity of action:

> "Of time they are much more liberal, for ordinary it is that two young princes fall in love. After many traverses, she is got with child, delivered of a fair boy; he is lost, groweth a man, falleth in love, and is ready to get another child; and all this in two hours' space; which how absurd it is in sense even sense may imagine, and art hath taught, and all ancient examples justified."

Seneca rather than the Greeks, however, furnishes his ideal of tragedy, something of which he saw in *Gorboduc,* "as full of notable moralitie, which it doth most delightfully teach, and so obtaine the very end of Poesie." Yet we must record to his credit—he calls it his barbarousness—that "I never heard the old song of Percy and Douglas that I found not my heart moved more than with a trumpet."

If we may judge from Spenser's *Faerie Queene,* with its letter to Sir Walter Raleigh, he expressed in his *English Poet*—now lost—views like those of Sidney. Though for his long poem he borrowed much from Virgil, Ariosto is his chief guide, but even the Italian is no dictator. The *Faerie Queene* exemplifies a theory of structure freshly, originally formed.

Ben Jonson's critical work, an Aristotelian commentary on Horace, has also perished; we can infer its nature only from scattered bits in his other writings. His chief emphasis is on invention, the finding of suitable matter for the intellect to grapple with; his comedy in this respect is rather of Aristophanes than of Plautus. He maintained the liberty of the modern poet, who "should enjoy the same license or free power to illustrate and heighten" his invention as his predecessors had enjoyed; we know that in his lost work he defended *Bartholomew Fair,* which is not a classical comedy, and the non-classical features of his tragedy of *Sejanus.* Classical rule and example were in his eyes to be followed only as they made plays better; they were not to cramp and hamper the dramatist in presenting his abundant and varied material.

One of the critical problems of the age was that of religious poetry. Giles Fletcher, in the address *To the Reader* prefixed to his *Christ's Victory* (1610), says of pious objectors: "It may bee, they will give the Spirit of God leave to breathe through what pipe it please, & will confesse, because they must needs, that all the songs dittied by him, must needs bee, as their Fountaine is, most holy; but their common clamour is, who may compare with God? true; & yet as none may compare without presumption, so all may imitate, and not without commendation." The remainder of his argument has in it something of Sidney, and looks forward to Milton.

The latter held the didactic theory to the full. In his *Reason of Church Government,* he speaks of celebrating "in glorious and lofty hymns the throne and equipage of God's almightiness," and of "teaching over the whole book of sanctity and virtue," with "delight to those especially of soft and delicious temper." In *Paradise Lost* itself he announces his purpose to

assert Eternal Providence,
And justify the ways of God to men.

Milton, however, is not to be charged with a crude didacticism; he knew that the truth must be "elegantly dressed," whereas George Wither spoke of a poetry "which delivers commodious truths, and things really necessary, in as plain and in as universal terms as it can possibly devise . . . This is not so plausible among the witty as acceptable to the wise; because it regardeth not so much to seem elegant as to be useful for all persons, in all times" (*Haleluiah, To the Reader*). Even in theory Milton conceded much of the secular to poetry. He allowed, for example, that it might deal with the "changes of what is called fortune from without," and exemplified such action in *Paradise Lost* 2, 935, when he said that Satan owed his successful voyage against man to "ill chance." Fortune (Sidney, above) was important in Renaissance theory, especially that of the drama, though not acceptable to Milton's theology (*Paradise Regained* 4, 317). Yet even Milton's classicism was not unyielding; in his 34th year he gives for the epic the alternative "whether the rules of Aristotle herein are strictly to be kept, or nature to be followed, which in them that know art and use judgment is no transgression, but an enriching of art." Inveighing against the mingling of comedy and tragedy on the English stage, he yet presented in the giant Harapha of *Samson Agonistes* a comic figure from Plautus and the Italian 16th century.

In addition to the general questions of literature, English critics of the Renaissance discussed more detailed matters. Much was said on the nature of English vocabulary; Nash, for example, objected to "inkhorn" words, the creations of affectation, usually of foreign derivation. Meter was also discussed, as by Campion in his *Observations on the Art of English Poesie* (1602), where he presented and exemplified a theory of unrhymed verse, which Samuel Daniel shattered in his *Defence of Ryme* (1603). There was little criticism in the sense of an endeavor to set forth the characteristics of an author, though Chapman approached it, in the dedication of part of his Homer, by preferring Homer to Virgil in opposition to Scaliger; the essence of his work is the exclamation: "Thou soule-blind Scaliger!"

R. P. Cowl, *The Theory of Poetry in Eng.,* 1914; A. H. Gilbert, *Lit. Criticism: Plato to Dryden,* 1940; F. E. Schelling, *Poetic and Verse Crit. of the Reign of Eliz.,* 1891; Smith; J. E. Spingarn, *A Hist. of Lit. Crit. in the Ren.,* 1930; ed. *Crit. Essays of the 17th c.,* 1908; G. A. Thompson, *Eliz. Crit. of Poetry,* 1914. ALLAN H. GILBERT.

Neo-Classical Criticism. "Dryden," wrote Johnson in the *Lives of the Poets,* "may be properly considered as the father of English criticism, as the writer who first taught us to determine upon principles the merit of composition." Unfair as this judgment may now seem to the efforts of earlier authors, it points nevertheless to the undoubted fact that it was in the period from Dryden to the end of the 18th c., and to some extent under the influence of Dryden's example, that criticism of poetry, painting, and the other fine arts became, for the first time in the history of Eng. literature, an important branch of learning, considered worthy of cultivation, for both practical and theoretical ends, by some of the most distinguished minds of the time. Beginning with the essays and prefaces of Dryden himself and the treatises of Thomas Rymer, the output of critical writings continued rapidly to increase in volume through the next two generations until, in the middle and later years of the following c., it is hard to name any author of consequence, poet, dramatist, novelist, philosopher, historian, or scholar, who did not attempt in some medium—treatise, essay, dialogue, lecture, preface, didactic poem, history—either to formulate the principles of one or more of the arts or to pronounce on the merits of artists and works.

In terms of the scope or primary locus of their subject-matter, the many products of this movement fall into at least six characteristic groups. There were many works, to begin with, in which the dominant concern was to reduce to some kind of method the rules or precepts peculiar either to one of the various arts considered as a whole or to some one of its branches or genres; *e.g.,* Dryden's *Essay of Dramatic Poesy* (1668), the Earl of Mulgrave's verse *Essay upon Poetry* (1682), John Dennis' *The Grounds of Criticism in Poetry* (1704), Joseph Trapp's *Praelectiones Poeticae* (1711–15), Jonathan Richardson's *Essay on the Theory of Painting* (1715), Charles Gildon's *The Complete Art of Poetry* (1718), Richard Hurd's commentary on Horace, with its annexed essays (1749–57) and his later dissertation on "The Idea of Universal Poetry" (1765), several of Johnson's contributions to the *Rambler* (1750–52), the *Art of Poetry on a New Plan* (1762), sometimes attributed, erroneously, to Goldsmith, Sir Joshua Reynolds' *Fifteen Discourses delivered in the Royal Academy* (1769–90), Percival Stockdale's *Inquiry into the Nature and Genuine Laws of Poetry* (1778).

With these, because of their common concern with the principles of art, may be associated a series of works, of which Dryden's *Parallel betwixt Poetry and Painting* (1695), James Harris' *Three Treatises* (1744), Daniel Webb's *Observations on the Correspondence between Poetry and Music* (1769), James Beattie's *Essays on Poetry and Music* (1776), and Thomas Twining's "Two Dissertations on Poetical and Musical Imitation" (1789) are characteristic examples, in which the major problem was the discovery of a basis both for clarifying the likeness among the various arts and for making intelligible their differences. Something of the same interest in discovering unifying principles was present also in Hugh Blair's very popular *Lectures on Rhetoric and Belles Lettres* (1783), though Blair's mode of treatment lent itself more easily to an emphasis on the differences among the arts of language—oratory, history, philosophy, and poetry—than to an exhibition of their fundamental analogies.

In both of these classes of writings problems involving either the nature and functions of the creative artist in general or the genius and accomplishment of individual poets or painters were treated in subordination to a systematic exposition of the ends and rules of arts or genres. But a more specialized discussion was also possible and was in fact attempted, especially after the first quarter of the 18th c., in works that either, like Edward Young's *Conjectures on Original Composition* (1759) or the treatises on genius of William Duff (1767) and Alexander Gerard (1774), approached the question in general terms, or, like Thomas Blackwell's *Enquiry into the Life and Writings of Homer* (1735), Joseph Warton's *Essay on the Genius and Writings of Pope* (1756), and Johnson's *Lives of the English Poets* (1779–81), introduced their principles in a context of biography and particularized critical evaluation.

In a fourth class of works, also more characteristic of the 18th c. than of the 17th, the center of attention was shifted from the rules of art or the traits of artists to the qualities of individual productions or of particular, historically determined, styles of composition. Of this mode of criticism the most important early examples were Rymer's *Tragedies of the Last Age* (1678) and Dryden's *Dedication of the Æneis* (1697); among many that followed after 1700 may be mentioned Addison's papers on *Paradise Lost* (1712), Pope's preface to the *Iliad* (1715) and postscript to the *Odyssey* (1726), Joseph Spence's *Essay on Mr. Pope's Odyssey* (1726–27), Johnson's essay in the *Rambler* on Milton's versification and on *Samson Agonistes,* Joseph Warton's appreciations of the *Odyssey* and of Shakespeare's *Tempest* and *King Lear* in the *Adventurer* (1753–54), Thomas Warton's *Observations on the Fairy Queen* (1754, 1762), Hugh Blair's *Critical Dissertation on the Poems of Ossian* (1763), John Scott's *Critical Essays on Some of the Poems of Several English Poets* (1785). Robert Lowth's *De sacra poesi Hebraeorum praelectiones* (1753), Richard Hurd's *Letters on Chivalry and Romance* (1762), and the critical portions of Thomas Warton's *History of English Poetry* (1774–81) differ from the others chiefly in that their writers chose to bring together in one context several or many works the qualities of which were dependent at least in part on common conditions of time or place.

The 18th c. also saw the rise to popularity and importance of a species of criticism of which few models, in the form of extended works at any rate, are found earlier. Its distinguishing feature lay in the fact that it was concerned less with the rules of art (though these might enter by way of final deductions) or with the nature and achievements of artists (though these might be alluded to) than with the emotions and tastes by which art is judged and found either beautiful or deformed. The earliest significant contribution to this kind of inquiry was Addison's series in the *Spectator* (1712) on the pleasures of the imagination; this was followed by Francis Hutcheson's *Inquiry into the Origin of our Ideas of Beauty and Virtue* (1725), William Hogarth's *Analysis of Beauty* (1753), Hume's essay on tragedy and on the standard of taste (1757), Burke's *Philosophical Enquiry into the Origin of our Ideas of the Sublime and Beautiful* (1759), Gerard's *Essay on Taste* (1759), Lord Kames' *Elements of Criticism* (1762), Archibald Alison's *Essays on the Nature and Principles of Taste* (1790), to say nothing of a host of less distinguished or familiar attempts.

With these works, lastly, may be grouped a number of writings that dealt with the question of criticism itself—its nature, its utility, its kinds, its history: the most notable of these were Pope's *Essay on Criticism* (1711), Goldsmith's *Enquiry into the Present State of Polite Learning in Europe* (1759), Gibbon's *Essai sur l'étude de la littérature* (1761).

In spite of the diversity of interests reflected in these various classes of productions, and in spite also of the many conflicts or apparent conflicts of doctrine and taste that separated their writers, it is nevertheless possible, without undue simplification, to tell the story of the development of criticism in England from Dryden to the death of Johnson in terms of a single dominant and unified conception of the art, in relation to which even the more seemingly revolutionary changes in the latter part of the period can be interpreted as so many shifts of emphasis within the framework of a common intellectual scheme. The conception was a sufficiently flexible one to permit the integration into it of terms, distinctions, topics of argument, and doctrines drawn from a great variety of earlier critical systems, ancient and modern. "Aristotle with his interpreters, and Horace, and Longinus," Dryden confessed, "are the authors to whom I owe my lights"; but the list of preferred authorities, both for Dryden himself and for his contemporaries and successors, included many more than these three names: Plato and certain of the Neo-platonists, Cicero, Dionysius of Halicarnassus, Demetrius, and Quintilian from antiquity; Scaliger, Sidney, Ben Jonson from the Renaissance; Boileau, Rapin, Bossu, Bouhours from the France of Louis XIV; and, as time went on, most of the distinguished figures in the continental criticism of the 18th c.—all these and others, in varying proportions for different writers, were made to yield quotations or arguments, examples or schemes of analysis, suitable to the uses of contemporary debate. The number of such borrowings, however, and the range of philosophically very disparate sources from which they came, should not be allowed to obscure the fact that, if Restoration and 18th c. Eng. criticism was highly eclectic in its choice of authorities, it was far from being merely so in its selection of the ruling principles of method by which these authorities were interpreted or its own original efforts controlled. With respect to such principles, at any rate, it constituted, from the beginning of the period to the end, a distinct and fairly consistent school, which can be characterized most simply by saying that its basic historical affinities were Roman rather than Greek, that its favorite masters were Horace rather than Aristotle (for all its many debts to the *Poetics*) and Quintilian rather than Longinus (for all the enthusiasm many of its adherents felt for the treatise *On the Sublime*), and that its typical devices of analysis and evaluation owed more to the example of rhetoric, in at least one conception of that art, than they did either to philosophy or to poetics in any senses of these terms that warranted a treatment of poetry or one of the other arts either in a context of universal human values or as a uniquely definable subject-matter with principles of its own.

As determined by these influences and preoccupations, neo-classical criticism may be described, in comparison with the Greek tradition, as being at once broader in its scope than the criticism of Aristotle and more restricted than that of Plato. Like Plato and unlike Aristotle its invariable concern was with what poets or artists ought to do rather than with what they have done and hence may do; but unlike Plato its characteristic appeal, on all issues that involved the end or good of art, was not (as in the *Republic* or the *Phædrus*) to the knowledge of philosophers or (as in the *Laws*) to the sagacity of statesmen, but rather to the trained taste and sensitive judgment of men expert in the enjoyment of poetry, painting, or music. Its frame of reference, in short, tended to be not the republic but the republic of letters, and although the larger context of morals or civil philosophy was seldom left entirely out of view, and although, as we shall see, the statement of criteria for works of art involved the use of terms applicable to values beyond the limited realm of taste, it still remains true that the utility of criticism in this tradition was normally conceived in terms of the needs of men, not as moral beings or as seekers after truth, but as poets and artists, readers and spectators, listeners and connoisseurs. In the formula of Addison and of many others in the 18th c., its special domain was the pleasures of the imagination; but though this was generally so, the result was never, on the other hand, any such concentration on the formal aspects of poems or paintings isolated from the real objects or thoughts that they embody, the genius and productive activity of their makers, or the natural or habitual demands of the men who read or view them as had constituted, for Aristotle, the distinctive principle of poetics as the science of imitations. Instead, both of these extremes were avoided, in the arguments of the neo-classical critics, through the almost universal preference for a scheme of terms, inherited from such Romans as Horace and Quintilian, in which the problems of any of the fine arts, like those of rhetoric, could be treated in a fourfold context of the art itself, the artist, the work, and the audience, in such a way as at once to preserve its distinctness from other human activities or from things and to give to its peculiar aims and rules a clear justification in the nature of man.

Such was the flexibility of this scheme that any one of the four terms—art, artist, work, or audience—might be taken as a primary frame of reference for a particular discussion and the other terms subordinated to it; much of the variety of 18th c. criticism, as has been suggested, was due precisely to contextual shifts of this sort. No single statement, therefore, of the meanings or distinctions that might be attached to each of the four main topics can be expected to do exact justice to the structure of any one argument in which they appear. But on the whole it may be said that the special problems of art were those of ends and rules either for the art as a whole or for one or more of its distinctive species or genres; of the artist, those of the aims he ought to pursue and of the natural and acquired powers he must have in order to attain them; of the work, those of style or quality as determined by the art and the artist; of the audience, those of its particular composition or standards and of the demands it makes on the artists who would serve it. For each of these sets of problems an abundance of terms was available in the ancient traditions of rhetoric and poetics or in the more recent attempts to formulate, by analogy, the precepts of the other arts, and their use persisted, with relatively few additions from other sources, throughout the period, until in the early 19th c. a new vocabulary of criticism, philosophical rather than rhetorical in origin, began to replace the old in the writings of Coleridge and others.

Thus in the analysis of an art the major terms were commonly derived from the rhetorical distinction of invention, arrangement, and expression—a distinction which, though signifying primarily the parts of the art, might also be applied in discussions of the artist, when invention was often referred to natural genius and the other parts to judgment, or in treatments of the work, when invention was correlated with the actions, thoughts, and images, expression with the style, and arrangement with both. The systematic statement of an art, however, was seldom considered complete without a section, usually a long one, on its various kinds; and here again the richness of the terminology bequeathed to the neo-classical critics by their predecessors in antiquity and the Renaissance for whom the question of genres was the central question of art, coupled with the possibility of obtaining criteria for definition and classification not only from distinctions of artistic matter and means but from differences in the natural faculties of artists and audiences, permitted a mode of analysis that was often (as in Boileau and Dryden) elaborate and subtle to a degree. The typical schematism for at least the major poetic kinds, such as drama and epic, came ultimately, though with many dialectical modifications, from the *Poetics,* but the influence of Roman rhetoric was also important, if not in determining the details of the discussions, at least in orienting them toward a conception of artistic genres as resting not so much on inductively ascertained differences among existing works as on distinctions of purpose, subject-matter, and style that derived from the nature of the art itself. In general, the realm of art was the locus of differentiations: the final end was perfection or excellence or writing or painting well, but though, as Reynolds pointed out, there is only one beauty, the means by which beauty may be achieved are many, and in consequence the special pleasures that may be sought in an art are as numerous as the subjects that may be treated, the combinations of stylistic devices that may be employed, or the powers and dispositions of the mind that may be appealed to.

For their discussions of the poet or artist, as distinct from the art, the neo-classical critics also drew, in the main, on topics long familiar in the tradition to which these critics belonged. Whether the immediate task of the argument was the statement of rules for an art or a genre or the appraisal of work already done, it was still appropriate to consider the comparative importance of nature, genius, or imagination on the one hand, and of art, judgment, imitation, or culture on the other, in the formation of the artist or in the determination of his success or rank; questions might be raised concerning the specific natural powers he must have or the knowledge he needs for the achievement of special effects such as delineating character or moving the passions; and the particular ends of an art in relation to the public might be stated, as in Quintilian and Horace, as so many interests or duties devolving on the artist—to instruct, to move, to please, or (as in most 18th c. critics) simply to please. Again, all these terms and distinctions, as well as those pertaining to art as such, might be shifted from their original contexts and applied to the work considered as the product of both the art and the artist; apart from such considerations discussion of the work tended to turn chiefly on distinctions of style relative to times and places or the tastes and ideals of individuals. The audience, finally, which functioned in this criticism as a distinct element related in various ways to all the others, was generally treated in terms either of propositions and definitions concerning the passions and temperaments of men (prominent in the tradition of rhetoric from the time of Aristotle) or of distinctions (such as Horace often introduced) of education or taste, nationality, social status, or, as in the frequent appeals to posterity, simply position in time.

Such, very briefly, was the apparatus for the analysis of poetry or painting inherited by 17th and 18th c. critics from the Roman tradition of rhetoric as a fine art or of poetics rhetorically conceived. In the main, and with due allowance for certain apparently radical variations that appeared in the middle of the 18th c., the four terms were related, by the writers of this school, in much the same fashion as in Quintilian or Horace. In the first place, both the artist and the work were normally subordinated to the art, the artist as the agent by which excellence in art is achieved only if his natural powers are cultivated in conformity with the precepts and great examples given by the art itself, the work as the product of both art and artist, and hence as somethng to be analyzed or judged primarily by reference to these two more inclusive topics. Art, in this tradition, was thus conceived as an impersonal ideal of excellence to which artists must subject themselves if their works are to be praiseworthy or useful to mankind; it was thought of, in short, as a species of virtue, and its standard was the universal criterion, common to art and morals alike, of the mean. In the second place, however, in spite of the fact that an art was treated commonly as more universal than the artist and as independent both of him and of any particular body of readers or spectators, it was nonetheless consistently subordinated to the audience in the triple sense that its origins and reason for existence are in the natural instincts of human beings to take pleasure in imitations or in eloquent and rhythmical language, that it achieves its effects, however artificial, by administering the natural sources of pleasure in the mind of man, and that its value is necessarily measured, in the long run at any rate, by the approval of the public. Art was accordingly at the same time something distinct from nature and even superior to it—a set of particular rules and standards by which nature was to be imitated—and something intimately dependent on nature as the "universal light," in Pope's phrase, that constituted at once its source, and end, and test.

The complications of the dialectic that resulted from the efforts of neo-classical critics to reconcile what Reynolds called the "demands of nature" and the "purposes of art" can be no more than indicated here. When the issue arose in a context of the rules of art or of the praise or blame to be bestowed on individual artists or works, a resolution could be effected by one or the other of two devices or (as more often happened) by their combination. On the one hand, the whole problem could be subsumed under art on the strength of the simple assumption that those things that have actually delighted all ages in the works of poets or painters must be proportioned to human nature and hence capable still of giving delight when they are imitated in modern production: it was thus, according to Pope, that Virgil came to identify Nature and Homer; it was thus that the rules of Aristotle, founded, as they were, simply on observation of those traits in which Euripides, Sophocles, and Æschylus pleased, acquired the authority which is rightfully theirs as "Nature still, but Nature methodiz'd." The appeals to example and precedent that this assumption seemed to warrant formed one of the distinctive marks of neo-classical criticism throughout its long history, even in critics, like Johnson or Blair, *e.g.*, whose primary emphases were very different.

It was seldom, though, that the case for the harmony of artistic standards and the demands of nature was allowed to rest merely on a recourse to authority however venerable. "He who is ambitious to enlarge the boundaries of his art," declared Reynolds, "must extend his views, beyond the precepts which are found in books or may be drawn from the practice of his predecessors, to a knowledge of those precepts in the mind, those operations of intellectual nature, to which everything that aspires to please must be proportioned and accommodated." This was written in 1778, but the expedient here recommended of basing the rules or verdicts of criticism on premises in which particular artistic techniques or qualities were referred directly to their natural effects on the minds of men had had a long and significant history in the tradition to which Reynolds belonged. It was in terms of such "natural reasons," stated sometimes as mere factual probabilities, sometimes as explicit deductions from psychological causes, that Horace had vindicated the importance of vivid sentiments and truthful characters, that Quintilian had urged the effectiveness of a temperate and timely use of metaphor, that Dryden had argued for the unities of time and place, that Hume had accounted for the delight we receive from tragedy in spite of its painful images, that Johnson explained why Butler's *Hudibras,* wanting that variety which is the great source of pleasure, is likely to weary modern readers. The principles thus brought into the criticism of a particular art, it was widely recognized, applied equally to all the arts, and hence could be made the warrant of analogies between poetry and painting or poetry and music of a more than merely methodological import: we have already noted the vogue of "parallels" of this kind between Dryden and the end of the 18th c. The importance, in short, of this direct appeal to nature, considered as the constant wants and desires of the mind to which artists must administer if their works are to give satisfaction, cannot be exaggerated, but the "demands of nature" in this sense could be reconciled with the "purposes of art" only by means of additional premises derived from a consideration, not of "what pleases most" in the productions of an art, but of "what ought to please." The function of artists, it is true, is to delight audiences, and to this end, both to avoid errors and to realize fresh opportunities, they need to know, if only instinctively, the "natural sources of pleasure in the mind of man." But at the same time, if they are to achieve excellence, they must attempt to please on terms dictated not by the actual preferences or passions of particular men but by the proper standards of the art or genre—its ideals as reflected concretely in the great works of past artists or as expressed abstractly in the precepts of criticism.

When made explicit in writings on the theory of art or on the performances of artists, these standards could be formulated in terms either of the art itself or of the audience. Viewed in relation to the work, artistic excellence was invariably found to consist, like moral excellence, in a mean between two extremes, or, what amounts to the same thing, in a just mixture, relative to the kind of work or the nature of the audience addressed, of opposite qualities; and faults, conversely, were identified with excesses or defects in any of the traits determined as virtues or with an exclusive emphasis on one extreme, of style or treatment to the neglect of its corresponding opposite. "It is allowed on all hands," wrote Hume, "that beauty, as well as virtue, always lies in a medium," and the most superficial acquaintance with the writings of the neo-classical critics is sufficient to verify the truth of his generalization. The model again had been set by Horace and Quintilian (*cf.* the *Ars poetica, passim,* and the *Institutio oratoria,* esp. X. i. 46–49, and XII. x. 79–80); and both the form of the argument in the neo-classical writers and many of the particular terms they employed show how powerful still was the influence of the ancient tradition. "A play ought to be a just and lively image of human nature, representing its passions and humors, and the changes of fortune to which it is subject, for the delight and instruction of mankind"; "True Wit is Nature to advantage dress'd, What oft was thought, but ne'er so well express'd"; "Their thoughts are often new, but seldom natural; they are not obvious, but neither are they just"; "The skilful writer *irritat, mulcet,* makes a due distribution of the still and animated parts"; "In this work [*The Rape of the Lock*] are exhibited, in a very high degree, the two most engaging powers of an author. New things are made familiar, and familiar things are made new"; "The same just moderation must be observed in regard to ornaments; nothing will contribute more to destroy repose than profusion. . . . On the other hand, a work without ornament, instead of simplicity, to which it makes pretensions, has rather the appearance of poverty"—it was by such manipulations of contraries or of positive and privative terms that the critics of this school achieved their characteristic formulations of artistic ideals or applied them in the judgment of artists and works. In the best critics such statements were reinforced by constant appeals to examples and illustrations from the history of art and hence to the feelings of audiences whose natural love of truth or delight in liveliness and variety were, along with other passions and affections, the ultimate sources from which, as Reynolds said, "all rules arise, and to which they are all referable."

But the formulation of standards could also be made more directly in terms of the audience by means of devices designed to effect a qualitative separation between readers or spectators in general and those select minds whose judgment could be considered as in some degree equivalent to the reasoned verdict of true criticism itself, or at least as a confirmatory sign of the presence of merit. Frequently, when it was a question either of justifying traditional precepts or of assigning degrees of excellence to older artists, the "best" audience was identified with posterity, on the principle often quoted from Cicero that "time effaces the fictions of opinion, and confirms the determinations of Nature": such, for instance, was Johnson's procedure at the beginning of the *Preface to Shakespeare,* though he hastened to buttress the judgment of time, which is never infallible, with arguments based on the critical premise that "Nothing can please many, and please long, but just representations of general nature." Sometimes, again, the selection was made in terms of tastes, as evidenced in the preference of the chosen public for particular past artists, or in terms of a proper balance and cultivation of mental faculties, or simply of freedom from habits likely to interfere with a correct judgment: examples of the three possibilities are, respectively, Dryden's definition of the best public as "those readers who have discernment enough to prefer Virgil before any other poet in the Latin tongue"; his remark that true comedy, as distinguished from farce, requires for its appreciation spectators "who can judge of men and manners" and who are moved by both fancy and reason; and Johnson's statement, in his critique of Gray's *Elegy,* that he rejoices "to concur with the common reader; for by the common sense of readers uncorrupted with literary prejudices, after all the refinements of subtilty and the dogmatism of learning, must be finally decided all claims to poetical honors."

By an easy transition, finally, warranted by the assumption that the public, as Blair said, is "the supreme judge to which the last appeal must be made in all works of taste," the focus of critical interest could be shifted from a preoccupation with guiding artists to a concern with educating the audience they address; and when this was the case, as it was, *e.g.,* in Hume's essay on "The Standard of Taste" and in parts of Blair's *Lectures,* the problem of values was commonly solved by a dialectic that followed a direction the reverse of that taken by the writers on the rules of composition: the issue was still the reconciliation of nature and art, but whereas in the criticism of art the effort was to find principles for the artist which accorded with the highest or most permanent demands of audiences, the criticism of taste was characteristically oriented toward finding principles for audiences which accorded with the true purposes and the best achievements of art. The two inquiries, however, though opposed in aim, were yet closely related as complementary aspects of the same general question; and it is not strange, therefore, that in most critical writings of the 18th c. the line separating them is somewhat hard to draw.

With this general view of neo-classical criticism as a background, it is possible to account for certain of the more striking changes in critical practice that took place esp. after 1700 and that serve to distinguish the age of Johnson, Goldsmith, and Young from that of Rymer and Dryden. In particular three main lines of development may be traced within the tradition, each of them involving a more or less pronounced shift of emphasis with respect to one of the major determinants of the system as a whole.

One important line of evolution had to do with the source and guarantee of the natural principles on which, it was universally admitted, the rules of art in general and of all particular arts are founded. Were they to be sought, whether by artist or critic, directly in the mind as known by common observation or philosophy, or indirectly through study of the great works of art which owed their permanent appeal to conformity with them? There were few, if any, writers on criticism from the beginning to the end of the period who did not, as we have seen, think it essential to combine the two approaches. In this respect, except for the distribution of their emphasis, Johnson and Reynolds writing in the 1770's were no different from Dryden writing a hundred years before, so that if Johnson, *e.g.*, could accuse Cowley, in 1779, of "not sufficiently enquiring by what means the ancients have continued to delight through all the changes of human manners," Dryden could conversely insist, in 1679, that a dramatist who would move the passions must, in addition to possessing a lofty genius, be skilled "in the principles of Moral Philosophy." Nevertheless, between the two dates represented by these quotations, a significant change of emphasis did take place, and its character may be indicated by contrasting another statement of Dryden, written in 1677, with typical declarations of critics in the middle of the following c. It requires philosophy as well as poetry, Dryden had remarked in the preface of his *State of Innocence*, "to sound the depth of all the passions: what they are in themselves, and how they are to be provoked." But, he added, "in this science the best poets have excelled," and their authority, as codified in the rules of critics like Aristotle, is, for the modern writer, "the best argument; for generally to have pleased, and through all ages, must bear the force of universal tradition." For Reynolds, on the other hand, in 1786, the ambition of criticism must be to rise from a study of the beauties and faults in the works of celebrated masters (a narrow and uncertain mode of investigation), through a comparison of the principles of painting with those of the other arts, to a comparison of all the arts with the nature of man—and this, he says, "as it is the highest style of criticism, is at the same time the soundest; for it refers to the eternal and immutable nature of things." Burke, in 1757, had been even more critical of the position represented by Dryden. A consideration of "the rationale of our passions," he wrote, "seems to me very necessary for all who would affect them upon solid and sure principles." In this inquiry, however, we can learn little from the artists themselves, and "as for those called critics, they have generally sought the rule of the arts in the wrong place; they have sought it among poems, pictures, engravings, statues, and buildings. But art can never give the rules that make an art"—only the observation of nature can do that. To Lord Kames, again, whose *Elements of Criticism* (1762) was founded on an elaborate analysis of the causes of the emotions and passions in relation to various kinds of natural and artificial objects, the history of criticism in modern times stood in direct opposition to that of the other philosophical sciences; whereas they had abandoned authority for reason, criticism "continues to be no less slavish in its principles, nor less submissive to authority, than it was originally." And he went on to speak of Bossu, "who gives many rules; but can discover no better foundation for any of them, than the practice merely of Homer and Virgil, supported by the authority of Aristotle." In spite of the somewhat exaggerated contrast these manifestoes draw between the new ideal of criticism and the old, they are indicative of an important shift of emphasis in the critical writing of the mid 18th c.—a shift that exalted the philosopher (in the current sense of an inquirer into the operations of the mind) over the artist or the mere critic as the expert best qualified to determine the rules of art, and that served hence to bring about, within criticism, a sharper separation between criticism itself, considered as a codification of past artistic experience, and the "demands of nature" on which its precepts and judgments, if they are to be valid, must ultimately rest.

The consequences of the change were most marked in those writers from Addison on to Hume, Burke, Gerard, Kames, and Alison who had acquired most completely what Hume called a "tincture of philosophy"; it was in them that the search for "natural reasons," which had been from antiquity an essential part of the critical tradition inherited by the 18th c., assumed most clearly the form of an explicit and systematic inquiry into causes. The majority of contemporary critics, including such representative figures as Johnson and Reynolds, were not "philosophical" in this strict sense, but were content for the most part to rely on such knowledge of the operations of the mind as could be obtained by introspection or as was available in the common psychological wisdom of educated men. For both groups alike, however, the problem of the relation between the rules of art and nature presented itself in much the same light. It was no longer, as in the mid 17th c., a question primarily of vindicating the great traditions of art against contemporary artists whose reliance on their own natural powers had seemed to lead only to irregularity or excess; what was at issue now was rather the authority of criticism itself as a body of rules not all of which could be assumed, without examination, to be equally binding or essential. When Johnson remarked, in the *Preface to Shakespeare,* that "there is always an appeal open from criticism to nature," he stated a principle that would not, indeed, have been denied by any of his predecessors in the tradition but that led, in his own writings and in those of many contemporaries, to a new attempt, sometimes carried out with great shrewdness (as in his remarks on tragi-comedy and on the unities of time and place) to distinguish between those established precepts of art that could be seen as necessary consequences of man's nature and those that, like Horace's rule of five acts, must be regarded as only "the arbitrary edicts of legislators," to be observed or not as the artist may choose. To appeal to nature in this sense was inevitably to give greater prominence to the generality of the audience than to the particularity of the art, and it is not surprising, accordingly, that in much of the criticism of the period the problem of genres became relatively less important than it had been for the critics of an earlier generation: it is noteworthy, for example, that Johnson tended to discuss pastoral, comedy, and tragicomedy chiefly in terms of reasons common to all poetry or even all discourse and derived from his characteristic distinction between general and particular nature and his insistence on resolving all poetic value, whatever its species, into a union of truth (in the meaning of "sentiments to which every bosom returns an echo") with novelty and variety. The same preoccupation with the universal psychological basis of artistic effects also accounts for the increased popularity of inquiries, like those of Harris, Webb, Beattie, and Twining, into the analogies between the arts, and for the widely prevelant interest in the definition and distinction of such general qualities, peculiar to no art or species of art, as the sublime, the beautiful, the pathetic, the romantic, the picturesque. Finally, all these developments, in which the dependence of art upon the nature of readers and spectators and hence on philosophy became the starting-point for new or at least more elaborate investigations, had their appropriate counterpart and completion, during the same period, in numerous attempts to bring the problems of the standard of taste and of the psychological principles operative in critical judgments within the context of one or another of the various contemporary sciences of human nature.

A second group of changes, running parallel to these, likewise involved considerations of the audience but from a point of view that emphasized its relation rather to the work of art than to the art itself. The question at issue was one that Quintilian had touched on briefly (XII. x. 1–2) when, in speaking of the kind of style the orator should aim at in his discourses, he had remarked that the forms of style are many, "not merely because some qualities are more evident in some artists than in others, but because one single form will not satisfy all critics, a fact due in part to conditions of time or place, in part to the taste and ideals of individuals." The point indeed was sufficiently obvious not to have escaped the attention of many writers before the 18th c., but for the most part, except for incidental passages (such as Dryden's explanation of the differences between Eng. and Fr. plays in terms of the contrasting temperaments of the two peoples), the principle of relativity it implied was subordinated, in the earlier neo-classical critics, to an emphasis on the universal traits of audiences—witness the frequently reiterated assertion that "Nature is still the same in all ages"—and hence on the necessary obligation of the artist to the general rules of his art. In the 18th c., however, though this obligation was seldom if ever rejected entirely, the consequences drawn from it by critics like Rymer, or by Dryden himself in most of his statements, were often treated as of somewhat minor importance in comparison with the natural tendency or even duty of artists to produce works adapted to the peculiar tastes and manners of their own generation or country. There are only a few really universal rules, declared Goldsmith in 1759, and these few are likely to be obvious to all; what is needed, therefore, he insisted, is "a national system of criticism," which will take account of the differences between peoples and adjust its precepts and judgments accordingly.

As manifested in discussions of individual artistic monuments in the 18th c., the tendency to supplement an absolute consideration of works or styles in terms of the universal principles of the art of which they were products by a qualified or relative consideration in terms of the particular audiences to whom they were addressed owed its chief incentive to the need many writers felt of overcoming prejudices against certain productions of the past which had been conceived in an idiom different from the prevailing mode, or of doing fuller justice to esteemed poets or artists who, when viewed apart from circumstances of time and place, had been blamed for faults not properly theirs. This species of critical apologetics was a dominant or at least an important motif in an increasing number of writings from the end of the 17th c. on through the 18th: in various defenses of the Scriptures published before and after 1700, in which the "Oriental" style of the sacred books and in general their departure from the poetic and rhetorical canons of the ancients were both explained and justified by reference to the climate, manners, and peculiar genius of the Hebrew people; in several notable works on Homer, especially those of Thomas Blackwell (1735) and Robert Wood (1769), which attempted to explain historically those traits of the *Iliad* and *Odyssey* that had seemed to many earlier critics merely signs of Homer's artistic inferiority to Virgil or even to certain of the moderns; in the efforts of Thomas Warton (*Observations on the Faerie Queene,* 1754 and 1762), Richard Hurd (*Letters on Chivalry and Romance,* 1762), and others to account for the "Gothic" character of Spenser in the light of medieval manners and the vogue of chivalric romances in his time; in numerous discussions of Shakespeare, including the final section of Johnson's great *Preface* (1765), in which the admitted irregularities or stylistic faults of the plays were, if not entirely vindicated, at least made to appear consequences not so much of their author's failure in judgment as of the demands imposed on him by the audience of his age; lastly—not to prolong the list—in such writings as those of Hugh Blair on Ossian and of Thomas Percy on the romances, wherein the critical problem of winning favor or attention for works of supposed or undoubted antiquity that yet were written in an unfamiliar style was solved partly by insisting on their essential conformity to the rules of Aristotle and partly by relating them to the background of primitive manners and sentiments that they reflected. In many of these writings, critical argument or appraisal, based on the dictum that it is unfair to judge works by rules of which their authors were ignorant or which they did not intend to observe, was combined with erudition in such a way as to form a species of literary history much more common after the middle of the 18th c. than before. Of this sort of history the most imposing monument was Thomas Warton's unfinished *History of Eng. Poetry* (1774–81).

To complete the story of shifting emphases within neo-classical criticism it is necessary, finally, to consider what happened after 1700 to the traditional conception of the artist. In the general scheme of this criticism, as we have seen, the work of art had been usually interpreted as the product at once of the artist and the art, and the artist had been said to depend for such perfection as he might achieve on nature or genius first of all and then, as equally important conditions, on art (which included invention, arrangement, and expression), on exercise, and on imitation of models. The chief possibility of variant emphasis, therefore, had to do with the relative importance attached by critics to nature on the one hand and to the various terms associated with art on the other. For reasons that have been partly indicated, the disposition of most critics before 1700 or a little later was to place the main stress on art and hence on the judgment of the artist in contrast to his genius or imagination or natural powers of invention.

The bias was particularly evident in Rymer, and it was never entirely absent even from the pages of Dryden, since both these critics were principally occupied with the problem of educating poets and playwrights to what seemed to them a more civilized standard of art. Even so, however, it would be an error to assume, because the improvement of art was the primary concern of writers like Dryden, Dennis, Addison, or Pope, that the natural sources of artistic perfection were regarded by them as of little moment. For the most part their necessity was taken for granted, but no estimate of Dryden's critical system would be adequate that did not make clear his constant insistence on the need of imagination in poets and of "liveliness" as well as "justness" in works or that overlooked his assertion, in the *Parallel betwixt Poetry and Painting,* that no rules can be given for invention since that is the work of genius and "a happy genius is the gift of nature," without which, as all agree, nothing can be done; and equally it would be unfair to Pope not to recall his words about "a grace beyond the reach of art" or his enthusiastic praise of Homer's "invention" in the preface to his version of the *Iliad.*

In the treatment of the problem of the artist the majority of critics after Pope and Addison in the 18th c. differed from their predecessors, if at all, only in a somewhat more equal distribution of emphasis as between genius and art or imagination and judgment and (with notable exceptions, such as Hurd and Reynolds) in a somewhat more skeptical view of the importance of imitation; in many of them the influence of Longinus was evident, but, as in the criticism that Dryden wrote after his discovery of *On the Sublime,* the effects were apparent rather in incidental borrowings of passages, terms, and distinctions, than in any serious dislocation of the traditional critical scheme. The same period, however, saw the publication of a series of writings in which, also in part under the stimulus of Longinus, the question of the relative importance of the natural and acquired qualities of the poet or creative artist was discussed in a considerably more radical spirit. The starting point of much of this literature was Addison's essay in the *Spectator* (No. 160, 1711) in which he distinguished two classes of great geniuses, the one comprising those that have "formed themselves by rules, and submitted the greatness of their natural talents to the corrections and restraints of art," the other those that "by the mere strength of natural parts, and without any assistance of art or learning, have produced works that were the delight of their own times, and the wonder of posterity." The opposition of the two types continued to be a favorite topic throughout the century, but whereas Addison had been careful to leave their comparative rank undecided, many of the later writers did not hesitate to assert the necesary precedence of the "natural genius" over the genius formed by art and imitation. One of the most eloquent of these was Edward Young, whose *Conjectures on Original Composition* (1759) effected a fairly thorough-going reduction of all the traditional distinctions to a simple pattern of literary values in which everything in art is resolved into invention and invention identified with a quasi-scientific discovery of new subject-matter, in which imitation of the classics is at times denounced and at times recommended in the form of a reproduction of the creative activity of the artist chosen as model, and in which genius is exalted as a natural force whose operations need be checked by nothing external save the verities of the Christian religion. In other writings—for example, in William Duff's *Essay on Original Genius* (1767) and occasionally in Blair—support for a similar thesis was drawn from a consideration of the superiority of primitive society before the rise of arts, as a setting favorable to genius, to the modern state of enlightenment. It will not escape notice that, in sharp contrast with both the first and second of the main lines of evolution in 18th c. criticism that have been sketched here, the inevitable effect of this increased stress on the natural powers of the artist was to minimize rather than to enlarge the significance of the audience as a determinant in the production and evaluation of art. The exaltation of the poet or painter as the chief if not indeed the only lawgiver for art was to be carried much further after 1800 than it had ever been before, but the extent to which the tendency had gone even by the middle of the 18th c. may be seen by anyone who will compare Boileau's dictum, in the preface to the 1701 edition of his works, that the poet achieves excellence by expressing justly the thoughts already possessed by a majority of his readers, with the statement of an anonymous writer for Dodsley's *Museum* in 1747 to the effect that the greatness of the major Eng. poets,

Chaucer, Spenser, Shakespeare, and Milton, lies precisely in their immense superiority to the times in which they lived.

Cambib; bibliog. also in W. H. Durham, ed., *Crit. Essays of the 18th C.*, 1915; J. W. Draper, *18th C. Eng. Æsthetics: A Bibliog.*, 1931. S. H. Monk, *The Sublime: A Study of Critical Theories in 18th C. Eng.*, 1935; René Wellek, *The Rise of Eng. Lit. Hist.*, 1941. Ronald Salmon Crane.

Nineteenth Century. 19th c. English criticism may be viewed in three main phases: (1) the Romantic, 1800–32; (2) Victorian, 1832–67; and (3) Late Victorian, 1868–1900. During the first period, writers revolted against 18th c. rules and criteria and subscribed to no laws except those of "genius," manifested in feeling and imagination: though resisted by conservatives, they were aided by sympathetic critics who supplied rationalizations of transcendental insights. By the time of the passage of the 1st Reform Bill (1832) they had won sufficient public response. The main movement of criticism during the second period (until the agitations for the 2nd Reform Bill triumphed) coincided with political and social efforts to adjust English conditions to realities caused by a rampant industrialism which threatened the foundations and fabric of England. Earnestly, Victorians struggled to reconcile discordances transmitted by their romantic predecessors: to harmonize "duty" and "beauty." In 1867, Matthew Arnold published *Culture and Anarchy*, a palliative for the turbulence aroused by agitations for the 2nd Reform Bill, discerning in the English mind too much "Hebraism" (or "strictness of conscience") and too little "Hellenism" (or "spontaneity of consciousness"). His analyses disturbed the precarious balance of the Victorian Compromise, whose dissolution was heralded by John Morley's *On Compromise* (1874). During the last third of the century (1867–1900) creative effort, and the criticism which accompanied it, sharply broke into (1) an ethical rationalism which sustained the hospitable intellectualism of John Stuart Mill; and, (2) æstheticism, or the cult of "art for art's sake," which, developing from the insights and dogmas of John Ruskin, worked into a rationale of criticism through the exquisite devotions of Walter Pater. Significant as many of the 19th c. poems and novels are as works of art, criticism itself became a form of *belles lettres*, as in Byron's *English Bards and Scotch Reviewers*, Peacock's novels, Shelley's *Defence of Poetry*, Keats's *Sleep and Poetry*, Macaulay's miscellaneous essays, Carlyle's *Dandiacal Body*, Pater's *On Style* and *Studies in the Renaissance*, and Arnold's *Sweetness and Light*.

Improvements in paper-making, printing, binding, publishing, and modes of circulation hastened the manufacture and distribution of books and periodicals, so that commentary in the form of reviewing tended to provide ready pabulum of opinion for those who were unable or unwilling to see literary productions in decent perspective. Both before and after Arnold's challenging essay, 19th c. English criticism was predominantly nationalistic; but critics were primarily concerned with a condition not elsewhere matched in Europe. They could no longer address only the culturally élite—beneficiaries of an aristocratic order—who had been educated at the grammar schools and universities in which exposure to Aristotle's *Poetics* and Horace's *Ars Poetica* assisted in some understanding and agreement upon the nature and function of literary criticism. Because of the rapid extension of literacy among enfranchised lower middle classes and masses, English critics were moved to attract and hold eager minds of the newly-literate, who were either indifferent to classical canons or unable adequately to understand them. In the immediate foreground, therefore, throughout the century, criticism ranged from the merest journalistic chit-chat to memorable items of lasting quality later collected and issued in book form. Much of this commentary, especially during the first half of the century, was subverted to propaganda of religious sect or political party: when critical norms were not so determined, this ephemeral criticism was a strange melange: *a priori* judgments revealing decaying notions of 18th c. rules of taste; rhapsodic, lauding ancient classics or established authors like Spenser, Shakespeare, Milton, Dryden, Pope in conventional deference; tedious textual commentary, remotely resembling what is today called "close reading"; the puff (or slightly disguised paid-advertising); the savage onslaught (which attacked the book "puffed"); and the timidly appreciative, usually mildly sentimental. "For what," asked Matthew Arnold in 1865, "at present is the bane of criticism in this country? It is that practical considerations cling to it and stifle it. It subserves interests not its own. Our organs of criticism are organs of men and parties having practical ends to serve . . . so much play of mind as is compatible with the prosecution of those practical ends is all that is wanted." Shortly after he uttered these words, a new periodical, *The Fortnightly Review* (May 15, 1865) appeared on the stands, having for its purpose what Arnold wanted: ". . . to understand and utter the best that is known and thought in the world, existing, it may be said, as just an organ for the free play of mind."

Arnold did not dismiss the romantics because they were romantics; ". . . poetry of the first quarter of this century," he said, "with plenty of energy, plenty of creative force, did not know enough. This makes Byron so empty of matter, Shelley so incoherent, Wordsworth even, profound as he is, yet so wanting in completeness and variety." He believed that "the creation of a modern poet, to be worth much, implies a great critical effort behind it; else it must be a comparatively poor, barren, short-lived affair." But, in criticizing the romantics, Arnold failed to consider them in their historical setting. Revolutionary violence in France and the French threat of invasion cut off England from the Continent; hence the romantic poets, with their apologists among the critics, found themselves driven to an individualism that stressed solipsistic feeling and imagination. Intuitively grasping a new principle of creativeness, while simultaneously revolting from stereotyped dicta of 18th c. criticism, they ventured experiments in literary expression stimulated by a concept of the uniqueness of the individual in harmony with cosmic forces manifesting themselves in nature and in mankind. They were moved, in some instances, to verbalize in fugitive expositions their vision of the poet as seer and sage. They intuitively created, without benefit of systematically arranged critical principles, so that each, according to his individual urge, imperially expressed his sovereign consciousness in forms revived from the Elizabethans. Romantic critics like Hazlitt, De Quincey, Lamb, and Leigh Hunt rediscovered neglected Elizabethans and, with an enthusiasm varying by the critic's temperament, suffused their comments with warmth, achieving an impressionistic criticism which persuaded increasing numbers of readers, and so created a sensibility that sapped prevailing critical dicta of the previous century.

But they tended also to divert the office of criticism to the exhumation of extractable beauties of particular passages, characters, and scenes that satisfied their sentiment for beauty and truth in terms of immediate impression. What their generation needed, a directing clue to their aspirations, was supplied by Samuel Taylor Coleridge whose analytical and fecund mind, "acting as the arbitrator between the old school and the new school," they failed to grasp, nor until after the mid-century was his work as critic duly sensed. Matthew Arnold singled out Coleridge as one whose critical action he himself sought to have his own Victorian contemporaries emulate. ". . . that which will stand of Coleridge is this; the stimulus of his continual effort," Arnold wrote in *Joubert* (1865), ". . . crowned often with rich success, to get at and to lay bare the real truth of his matter at hand, whether that matter were literary, or philosophical, or political, or religious; . . . Coleridge's great usefulness lay in his supplying in England, for many years and under critical circumstances, by the spectacle of this effort of his, a stimulus to all minds capable of profiting by it, in the generation which grew up around him. His action will still be felt as long as the need for it continues."

Coleridge's profound learning, his diligence in scrutinizing the dark depths of the conscious and subconscious, aided by his thoughtful readings of British psychologists and German philosophers, as well as his violinic responsiveness to modes of thinking and expression, which enabled him to retrieve and activate attitudes that resisted shifting fashions of taste and values, made him the most significant critic in England since Dryden. His encyclopedic vision was too vast and too intricate for him wholly to set forth; his own bodily and mental distresses distracted and prevented him from fully writing out what he glimpsed so clearly for himself. His publications, even today, are too fragmentary and discursive for any but the most intrepid and persistently attentive to see as related parts of a well-conceived whole. Nevertheless, he supplied an organon which has but recently, in the 1920's and 30's, been re-discovered and expounded by the boldest of scholars and critics. Out of a philosophy which accrued from his criticism of English thinkers of the 17th and 18th centuries and from his sympathetic assimilation of techniques of contemporary Germans like Kant and Schelling, Coleridge steadfastly retained Edmund Burke's insistence upon the necessity of principles in the shaping of society through tradition, religiously directed by a pious sense of Divine Immanence accessible through the Church and its sacraments. In scrutinizing the human mind in its struggle for truth, he found in the reciprocal principle of resistances transformed by willed action (by thinking, which substantiates intuition) the creative issuances of existence. "Every power in nature and in spirit must evolve an opposite, as the sole means and condition of its manifestation; and all opposition is a tendency to re-union." He found polar repulsion between Reason and Understanding and, in modes of transcending that tension in poetry, he indicated the conflict between Imagination and Fancy. Had 19th c. English criticism grasped his distinctions, it would have been more of a dialectical astringent and perhaps less of an educative effort towards propriety and gentility in a troubled era of social, economic, and political contentions.

Beneath the shift of criticism during the middle third of the century (1833–1867) to political and social purposes, a steady undercurrent of development of Romantic criticism continued. Devotion to the austere concept of "duty," celebrated by Wordsworth in his *Ode to Duty* and in his own prudent life, tended to issue in a strict ethical criterion that steadied the rapidly increasing reading public recruited from Evangelistical classes. Minor critics, chiefly in periodicals, elected themselves custodians of public manners and severely condemned literary productions that did not minister to edification, frowning upon writings dedicated to joy and beauty. They remembered De Quincey's opium-eating, Shelley's "atheism," and Keats's unholy sensuousness. Coleridge had his disciples; but they were, like John Henry Newman and Frederick Maurice, applying his ideas to Church revisionism. Literary criticism lapsed into periodical reviewing for immediate practical ends.

Four great stylists, each an exponent of a critical attitude, converted literary criticism to social purposes in their efforts to shape and direct the mind of the age: Macaulay, Carlyle, John Stuart Mill, and Ruskin. Macaulay, champion of the successful middle classes, rationalized British prosperity resulting from manufactures and commerce, and exercised his critical gifts in making literature subserve the idea of autotelic progress. Carlyle, viscerally mystical and ill at ease in Zion, a voice crying in the wilderness, denounced complacency that rested on material satisfactions, turning criticism to hortatory exclamations. The younger Mill, tough-minded analyst of society and its institutions, utilized the critical essay for austerely reasoned expositions of social and ethical necessities which the changing age demanded and emphasized the imperative of a morally-based individualism. Ruskin, persistently agitating for correction of artistic taste, evolved his philosophy of a society whose monuments would visibly disclose the religious piety of Christian architects, painters, and workers. These four critics, each according to his vision and belief in the efficacy of criticism as an agent in the formation of beliefs, were less attentive to the demands of criticism as an act of analyzing modes and devices of literary expression than as a socially educative force.

This was the situation in criticism when Matthew Arnold, in 1865, published his *Essays in Criticism, 1st Series,* with its opening essay "Function of Criticism at the Present Time" criticizing the provincialism of English criticism, its addiction to practical politics, its disposition to premature adjudication: conversely, urging the necessity of criticism as the theatre of a free play of ideas, inspired by a disinterested endeavor to know the best that has been thought and said in the world. "Judging," he said, "is often spoken of as the critic's one business; and so in some sense it is; but the judgment which almost insensibly forms itself in a fair and clear mind, along with fresh knowledge, is the valuable one; and thus knowledge, and ever fresh knowledge, must be the critic's great concern for himself. And it is by communicating fresh knowledge, and letting his own judgment pass along with it,—but insensibly, and in the second place, as a sort of companion and clue, not as an abstract lawgiver,—that the critic will generally do most good to his readers." Arnold, demonstrating the Victorian Compromise at its best, converted criticism into the activity he called "culture." He demonstrated this in *On Translating Homer, Essays in Criticism, On Celtic Literature,* and especially in *Culture and Anarchy,* in which he disclosed the delicate balance of Hebraism and Hellenism in English dispositions: reconciling, for cultural contemplation, the tensions between the prevailing sense of duty, manifested in the earnestness of his four great contemporaries, and the importunate call for beauty, manifest in contemporary French critics like Sainte-Beuve and in the German Heine.

Arnold's balanced truce between duty and beauty was destined to remain a solitary gesture. It appeared in a year which was exercised by a heated controversy over the neo-paganism of Swinburne's *Poems and Ballads* (1866), a book that shocked earnest moralists by its musical adorations of fleshly beauty. Thereafter, the issue was clear for the rest of the century. English criticism split into two contending camps: (1) critics who sympathized with the new hedonistic school, including FitzGerald of *Rubáiyát of Omar Khayyám* (1859), Swinburne, Rossetti, Morris, Lionel Johnson, Ernest Dowson, and Oscar Wilde; and, (2) critics, disciples of Mill, Comte, or Darwin, who austerely and vigorously applied rationalistic standards in the office of literary criticism.

Hedonistic criticism evolved into a rationale of æstheticism with Walter Pater and John Addington Symonds. Both were Oxonians, influenced by Benjamin Jowett who had enriched the Oxford mind by his diligent discourses on Plato and Hegel. As critics, they provided a theoretic program for the cult of beauty, or "art for art's sake." Their essays, wrought with consummate art and almost painful attention to stylistic effect, contributed a new "aid to reflection" to youth who sought a career of joyous experience, supplying an anodyne for the growing scepticism of the times, caused by Darwinian agnosticism, in a deliberate and discriminative cultivation and refinement of sensuous dispositions. Their thought affectionately played, with almost a feline subtlety, with contraries, continually busy in harmonizing superficially antipodal conceptions. Symonds displayed his passion for beauty in his essays on Greek poets and in the sustained *The Renaissance in Italy* (1875–1886). Pater, in his *Studies in the History of the Renaissance* (1873), *Plato and Platonism* (1893), and in *Appreciations, with an Essay on Style* (1889), tenderly advocated his gospel of beauty, calling it "the new Cyrenaicism," a vision that exquisitely heightened expectation and realization of the poignancy of life. The concluding chapter of his *Renaissance* delicately proposed this as a creed summarized in the phrase, to live as "a pure, hard, gem-like flame." He elaborated it as a critical clue to the appreciation of the foremost living exponent of the creed, Dante Gabriel Rossetti. "To Rossetti, life is a crisis at every moment. A sustained impressibility towards the mysterious conditions of man's everyday life, towards the very mystery itself in it, gives a singular gravity to all his work. . . ."

Liberal principles that pervaded the contemporaneous rationalist group of critics inhibited their antagonism to the æsthetic school. Though John Morley, the most persuasive of the rationalists, caustically attacked Swinburne's *Poems and Ballads* on its first publication, he later modified his opinion and generously recognized the significance of the æsthetic critics. "There is no more hopeful sign for that general air of intellectual activity which is now slowly making itself visible in this country," he wrote in 1873, "than the rise among us of a learned, vigorous, and original school of criticism. . . . The speculative distractions of the epoch are noisy and multitudinous, and the first effort of the serious spirit must be to disengage itself from the futile hubbub which is sedulously maintained by the bodies of rival partisans in philosophy and philosophical theology. This effort after detachment naturally takes the form of criticism of the past, the only way in which a man can take part in the discussion and propagation of ideas while yet in some sort aloof from the agitation of the present." Rationalist critics (Morley, Frederic Harrison, and Leslie Stephen), whose thought was shaped by scientific and moral positivistic themes of man's development and by the newer evolutionary methods of interpreting history, dealt with great ideas as historic forces, expressing "the hopes and energies of the human mind in its mightiest movements." This naturally produced a biographical type of critical exposition (John Morley's series of *English Men of Letters,* 1877).

Criticism, operating as intelligence, fulfilling Arnold's call for it as a free play of ideas—the "criticism which regards Europe as being, for intellectual and spiritual purposes, one great confederation, bound to a joint action and working to a common result; and whose members have, for their proper outfit, a knowledge of Greek, Roman, and Eastern antiquity and of one another"—supplemented tentative and ephemeral reviewing of English books as they poured from the press. Much of it was revisionary, in large part stabilized by scholarly activities which, through fresh translation and incisive comment, secured contacts with great critical minds of classical antiquity, the renaissance, and of modern Europe. This was at its best in Higher Criticism of the *Bible,* in the revision of Gr. and L. texts and commentaries on classical literature, in the incessant examination of Shakespeare's plays and poems, in impressive historical researches in the lives of authors and their works, from earliest Anglo-

Saxon times to the age of Victoria. S. H. Butcher's *Aristotle's Theory of Poetry and Fine Art* (1895) and Ingram Bywater's *Poetics* (1909) owed much to the 19th c. British scholars. Critical scholarship in Hebrew and Gr. texts established a rationale that, while it sapped earlier pietistic attitudes towards Scriptures, supplied the grounds for a more adequate understanding. Revisionary criticism also provided the basis for a more adequate interpretation by its extensive explorations in linguistics and philology. Etymological study (Henry Sweet, F. J. Furnivall, J. M. Kemble, W. W. Skeat) contributed not only to *The Oxford English Dictionary* but to the formation of organizations like the Early English Text Society (1868). New critical methods for biography, manifested in Lockhart's *Life of Scott* (1837–38), Dowden's *Life of Shelley* (1886), and Masson's *Milton and his Times* pointed the way towards *The Dictionary of National Biography* (63 v., 1882–1900). Continual efforts were made to discover fundamental, even abstract, principles or laws of literary processes, to which George Saintsbury gave the name, "metacriticism": the form of intellectual inquiry which goes beyond specific literary works to define general concepts like "What is Poetry?", "What is Biography?", "What is the Novel?", "What is Comedy?" Notable instances were E. S. Dallas's *The Gay Science* (1866) and Meredith's *Essay on Comedy* (1877). Appreciative, or impressionistic, criticism followed the general tone of the familiar essay and while it may have wanted much in giving light it surely emanated sweetness in graceful disquisitions on literary subjects and authors. Practitioners of this mode who were eminently charming were Arthur Symons, Sir Arthur Quiller-Couch, Andrew Lang, Sir Edmund Gosse, Edward Dowden, A. C. Benson, Sidney Colvin, Arthur Clutton-Brock, and Saintsbury. These gentlemen-critics of highly sensitive taste were the beneficiaries of revisionary and metacritical efforts by their predecessors and contemporaries, eschewing polemics and refraining from too searching investigation of mere facts of literary or critical history. They continued the elegant attitude and tone, as they conceived them, of Arnold and Pater, even though they may have eviscerated the intellectual content of those rigorous-minded critics. Had 19th c. criticism engaged more in the dialectical criticism of criticism itself, following the pattern set by Coleridge at the beginning and by Arnold in the middle of the century, it might have left fewer impure forms and lessened the responsibilities of 20th c. critics like Eliot, Richards, and Tillyard in making their revolutionary turns upon the products of criticism which the 19th c. transmitted.

Cambib; R. M. Alden, *Crit. Essays of Early 19th Cent.*, 1921; G. Saintsbury, *Hist. of Eng. Crit.*, 1911; L. J. Wylie, *Studies in Evol. of Eng. Crit.*, 1903; B. E. Lippincott, *Vict. Critics of Democracy*, 1938. William S. Knickerbocker.

Twentieth Century. At all times contemporary observers of the literary scene have repeated that all was confusion around them and that no single critic or trend in critical thought was dominant. This was doubtless always true, especially in a country like Britain, which distrusts groups, schools, doctrinaire manifestos and set labels. "Everything has always co-existed," as the French critic Rémy de Gourmont used to assert. With the passing of time, however, and the more selective, if far from infallible, perspective which is that of posterity, some names eventually emerge as significant; the influence of some critics may become broad and fecundating long after their death; others, who enjoyed fame in their lifetime and occupied a position of prestige, may cease to hold out against the tide of changing taste.

The average level of critical writing, in Britain as in America and in France, is considerably higher than ever before; the critical production is more abundant, and seldom as dogmatic and cocksure as it was when the most influential quarterlies stood in implacable opposition to most of the romantic literature; fewer gross mistakes are committed by appraisers of living writers, probably because critics have grown more prudent and more timorous. The surprising phenomenon is that the enormous mass of book reviewing and of critical writing now accumulated in the most sophisticated countries has not succeeded in stifling original creation. Still, since 1935 or so, a certain loss of vigor has been diagnosed, and deplored, in the fiction and poetry of England and of other Western countries. Powerful successors to Yeats, Joyce, Lawrence, Eliot appear to be lacking. Talents which might have been, in other ages, drawn to the novel, the drama, the epic, have gone to social and political thought, to history, to philosophy. The passing of the literary avant-garde has been mourned and the famous epitaph on literary creativeness, which Edward Gibbon once wrote in his *Decline and*

Fall, has been ominously and repeatedly applied to our own mid-century: "The name of poet was almost forgotten . . . A cloud of critics, of computers, of commentators darkened the face of learning, and the decline of genius was soon followed by the corruption of taste."

Quarterlies and monthly reviews, which once used to address themselves to the cultural élite, have all but disappeared; the share granted in those reviews to critical appraisals of past or present literature has dwindled to very little. Professional journals, subsidized by University Presses and written chiefly by academic critics for other academic readers, are, on the other hand, more numerous. But they are far more specialized, more pedantic in tone, and have been likened, by those who refuse to be absorbed by the increasingly tentacular power of the universities, to a mutual exchange of dirty linen by dons. They have tended to accumulate repetitious and ever more ingenious essays on an unhappy few books: *Ulysses, Women in Love, Four Quartets.* The *Adelphi* and *New Adelphi* (1923–30), the *Criterion,* first a quarterly (1922–27), then a monthly (1928–1939), to a lesser extent the *Calendar of Modern Letters* (1925–1927) and its successor, *Scrutiny* (1932–1953), enjoyed a far-reaching influence on living literature. The lively articles appearing now and then in *The New Statesman, The Spectator,* and other weeklies like *The Observer,* the *Sunday Times,* are far from uninfluential. *The Times Literary Supplement* enjoys a prestige second to none in English speaking countries: it has been far from broad-minded or imaginative in its reception to the most significant early works of T. S. Eliot, D. H. Lawrence, J. Joyce, J.-P. Sartre or to the first claims of "the American imagination" to take over the leadership of the fiction and poetry written in English. Its criticism of recent novels has been conspicuously perfunctory and the would-be "smart alec" titles given to its articles often border on a levity which can be that of an awkward pachyderm. But, in the nineteen sixties, the *T.L.S.* has devoted a number of important articles, often requested from occasional contributors signing their names, to the theory and philosophy of criticism. Its great superiority over the periodicals of America or of continental Europe has lain in its cosmopolitan approach to literature: books from France, Germany, Italy, Russia have been granted intelligent attention. The insularity long branded as the bane of English criticism is certainly not one of the faults of that versatile and remarkably well-informed weekly which is, when all is said, second to none in the world today. One of the English critics who has climbed to eminence since the middle of the century, Graham Hough, remarked in *The Dream and the Task* (1964) that "there appears to be something about the study of English literature as a separate subject that leads inevitably to a boring provincialism." British universities have long evinced a distrust of comparative literature as a separate discipline, as they have of sociology: but the practitioners of criticism and even the book reviewers of Britain are far more widely read in the classics and in at least one continental literature, that of France, and far more aware of the relations between literature and history, than their counterparts in the United States. Provincialism is rather a feature of literary life in the European capital on the other side of the Channel.

Universities have grown markedly in number, in affluence provided by government funds, and in prestige, since 1930 or so. Still their departments of literature have not monopolized criticism as they have in other countries; English criticism has not yet become what Stephen Spender called American criticism: "the substitute muse of the universities." Writers of fiction, of verse and of essays have less often than in the United States been enticed by university faculties as writers in residence. Critics have more seldom isolated themselves from life and from what Wordsworth termed the "language really used by men." They have been less afraid of passion and of ardent partiality. More so than the critics of other lands ensconced in the idyllic peace of a campus, they have evinced sympathy for what may be vulgar but throbbing with life in Rabelais, Balzac, Dickens, Zola, H. G. Wells, Joyce. Speculations on the theoretical aspects of criticism and search for an anatomy of genres or modes, defined with fearful symmetry, have been less rife in England than in France, Germany, Switzerland or the United States. Tocqueville had shrewdly remarked early in the last century that the Americans were more addicted to general ideas than the English.

Few genres of writing age faster than criticism; great critics, able to challenge the wreckage of time, are more of a rarity than the practitioners of any other art or than philosophers or historians. T. S. Eliot is perhaps the only one between 1920 and 1950 who reached a position of eminence even remotely comparable to that once occupied by Dr. Johnson, by Sainte-Beuve and by Matthew Arnold. There has arisen no such pontifical figure after him. The critics of the first two decades of the century have lost much of their lustre. Walter Pater, the finest writer of prose among them and the most exquisitely sensitive to beauty, had died in 1894 but his influence outlived him. Arthur Symons (1865–1945) had pioneered in introducing the French Symbolists and Decadents to the English public; but his critical appreciations were lacking in acumen. Little remains of the essays written during the decade of the *Yellow Book*; Oscar Wilde's paradoxes, often arresting, fail to earn for him a place, as a critic, comparable to that of Gide in France or that of Thomas Mann in the Germanic world. George Saintsbury (1845–1933) was an indefatigable reader, catholic in taste, immensely broad in range, unconcerned with rigor or uninterested in a methodical system of critical views. His books are very uneven; his taste was erratic or, at the least, personal and impressionistic. But he had a genuine zest in relishing literature and assimilating it. He fulfilled Hazlitt's definition of the critic as a taster for the public or, as Virginia Woolf wrote of Hazlitt himself, he loved books and the men behind them, and took the liberties of a lover. His lack of a reasoned philosophy of literature and his distrust of any objective standards of taste have aged him, and other British critics of those early years of the twentieth century, in the eyes of a more austere generation which distrusts its pleasure. Not many, however, among the critics who have written after the sobering experience of two world wars, have matched the catholicity, the leisurely discursiveness, the naïve but contagious enjoyment of literary works rather than of systems erected à propos of them which were the merits of Saintsbury and of several of his contemporaries. For more substantial pronouncements on the symbolism of poetry and on the examples then provided by the innovations attempted by the French "fin de siècle" poets, one would have to go to some of the essays of W. B. Yeats and occasionally to reminiscences and paradoxes interspersed in George Moore's volumes of charmingly insolent impressions and mercurial opinions.

The persistence of a civilized tradition of enjoyment of literature as a source of refined pleasure is perhaps among the most original features of English criticism throughout the first half of the twentieth century. To affix upon such independent and often casual writing a label like "hedonistic" or "impressionistic," in the sense which, on the continent, Anatole France and Jules Lemaître gave to the adjectives, would be a distortion. Walter Pater's cult of beauty and of sumptuous and fluid prose found fewer adepts in England, after the Yellow Decade, than overseas, where George Santayana, Bernard Berenson and even the more iconoclastic James G. Huneker pursued the search for fullness of life in art, even at the risk of challenging too genteel a tradition of conformity. Much of the writing done, with gracefulness and lightness of touch, by polished commentators of literature, particularly of poetry, provided students and a broader public with a pleasant means of forming their taste. Little in the output of such critics is destined for survival: Like actors, musical performers and journalists, few literary critics, after all, must entertain the ambition to outlive their own age and to mold imaginative production for years to come.

Lafcadio Hearn (1850–1904) and, much later, Edmund Blunden (1896–1967), who both initiated Japanese students to English poetry, may be ranked among the amiable commentators of the poetry of the romantics and of the Victorians. Sidney Colvin (1845–1927) lacked boldness in taste and decisiveness in judgment, as did, to an even greater degree, Edmund Gosse (1849–1928) who, for a time, appeared (at any rate on the continent) as the chief legislator of letters and a polished interpreter of John Donne, of Swinburne and of Scandinavian authors. A. C. Bradley (1845–1933), in his *Oxford Lectures on Poetry* (1909) and in his widely influential *Shakespearean Tragedy,* published five years earlier, spread a romantic, mostly Coleridgean, approach to literature. Edward Dowden in Dublin (1843–1913), J. W. Mackail (1859–1945), H. W. Garrod (1878–1960) blended biography, psychological insight and æsthetic enjoyment in their various essays and volumes, most of them devoted either to the classics of antiquity or to the romantic poets. Without bitterness or bellicose irony, they reacted against the moralizing and the high seriousness of the Victorians. Ungratefully, no doubt, H. W. Garrod railed at Matthew Arnold's solemnity, which had treated "the criticism of literature as though it were a part of the church service." Sir Walter Raleigh (1861–1922) wrote admirable and concise volumes of initiation to Shakespeare, Milton, the English novel; W. P. Ker (1855–1923), who made the vast field of English and of continental medieval literature his province, wrote with similar urbanity and deserved T. S. Eliot's praise (in 1942) that he never forgot "that the end of scholarship is understanding, and that the end of understanding poetry is enjoyment, and that this enjoyment is gusto disciplined by taste."

An enumeration of the many critics who recorded casually their subjective reactions to works of the past revisited or to the few contemporary works which they found congenial would include most of those who acquired some influence in the present century. Some were men of the world and diplomats who enjoyed a cosmopolitan bird's eye view of several cultures and treated foreign literatures, especially those of Russia and of France, with eclectic sympathy but without any intent to say what had not been said and thought before them: such were Maurice Baring (1874–1945), also a pleasant novelist and poet, and Harold Nicolson (1886–), who, after his retirement, penned agreeable volumes on Sainte-Beuve and on the Age of Reason. Gilbert Murray (1866–1957), like Mackail and Richard Livingstone primarily a classical scholar, is one of the distinguished company of Australian-born essayists who have contributed penetration, breadth and fervor to English criticism. His translations from Euripides, and his views on that poet and on Greek religion, have been attacked: the criticism of ancient writers proves to be even less lasting than that of English authors. But there are admirable pages on positivism, stoicism, satanism and on "literature as revelation" in his *Humanist Essays* (1964). G. Lytton Strachey (1880–1932) won fame as a biographer and as a witty, often brittle, historian of individuals; but few compact histories of any literature can match the masterpiece of his youth, *Landmarks in French Literature* (1912). Ifor Evans (1899–) and V. S. Pritchett (1900–) wrote on a much greater variety of topics, often with some brilliance, and played one of the roles of the critic, that of intermediary between authors and the public: they did not strive for depth or for high seriousness and were content with mixing the useful with the pleasant.

Among those critics, whose versatility and casualness appear eminently British, because they wrote as gentlemen fearful of ponderousness and always anxious to share their own refined pleasure with their readers, three or four stand out between the years 1920 and the middle of the century. John Middleton Murry (1889–1957) belonged to the same gifted age group as D. H. Lawrence, Richard Aldington, Aldous Huxley, Virginia Woolf, and his wife, Katherine Mansfield. He appeared in his youth to be destined for the critical leadership of his generation when he published, in 1916, an amazingly precocious essay on Dostoevsky, then others on "The Function of Criticism," in *Aspects of Literature,* 1920, and in *Countries of the Mind* (1922). Murry's critical credo, in the latter of those volumes, set high standards both for book reviewing and for the more lengthy and more thoughtful essays which any critic is called upon to write; the critic, according to Murry, should "convey the whole effect of the work he is criticizing," work back and define the unique quality of the sensibility which produced it, establish the determining causes of that sensibility, analyze the means by which this sensibility was given expression, and lastly prove his point through the close scrutiny of a characteristic passage. In his *Discoveries* (1924), Middleton Murry offered samples of highly readable and never shallow critiques of dead and living writers. Throughout, he remained modest and pliable, and refused to "erect his personal impressions into laws," in Rémy de Gourmont's phrase which he quoted. At a time when T. S. Eliot and some others, influenced by T. E. Hulme, felt inclined to some pontification, Murry blandly confessed, in *Discoveries*: "After all, I believe that criticism is a personal affair, and the less we critics try to disguise this from ourselves, the better." That very pliability, however, in Murry as in Herbert Read (1893–), became a peril. It induced both of them to shift their standards every few years, to espouse one cause after another, and to arouse distrust in readers bewildered by an excessive versatility. "Better be imprudent moveables than prudent fixtures," Keats had exclaimed; but mutability driven too far turns the chameleon critic into a plaything of passing vogues or of his own contradictory enthusiasms.

Stephen Spender (1909–), like Murry a poet, a biographer of himself wavering between two worlds of space and time (Europe and America, the modern and the romantic tradition), appeared for a time likely to become the apostle of a new romanticism and an advocate of resolute courage in formulating an æsthetics for a new avant-garde. His volumes, however, have remained disconnected, hasty, lacking in a firm substratum of thought: they range from *The Destructive Element,* 1935, to *The Imagination and the Modern World* (1962). Through his editorship, for several years, of *Encounter* (1953–), he provided English critics with an opportunity to write serious articles of evaluation of contemporary works, at a time when *Horizon* (1940 to 1949), *Life and Letters* (1928–1950), the *London Mercury,* had perished and when *The Twentieth Century* had practically excluded literature from its pages. Cecil Day-Lewis (1904– now Poet Laureate), like Spender, MacNeice and Isherwood, appeared, in the middle thirties, as one of the musketeers who might escort and perhaps challenge the literary kingship of W. H. Auden. As a poet, he failed to fulfill his promises; but his small volume, *A Hope for Poetry* (1936), was a striking plea for the new spirit and techniques in poetry, after Yeats and Eliot; and *The Poetic Image,* his Clark lectures at Cambridge in 1946, eschewing pedantry, but learned, precise and polished, felicitously blended remarks on the poets of the past and on the moderns. George Orwell (1903–1950) lacked the time to apply himself to criticism with much steadiness of purpose; but he was less afraid than some of his countrymen, who had also gone through Eton and Oxford, of what Aldous Huxley contemptuously called, à propos of E. A. Poe, "vulgarity in literature," and, in an era which was fascinated by the study of style and the problems of linguistics, he dared denounce "language as an instrument . . . for concealing or preventing thought" (in "Politics and the English Language," 1946, published in *Shooting an Elephant,* 1950).

The pleasant and affable, but at times also jejune urbanity of English criticism, envied in other English speaking countries as a triumph of culture, may also detract from its audacity: criticism, around the older universities, may also become too genteel, too friendly toward the secure "déjà vu," slightly fastidious in its abhorrence of Joyce and Lawrence at their most brutal, or of their successors today (usually American émigrés in Paris) who question the "Establishment." Such is probably the weakness of a critic of talent and refinement, Lord David Cecil (1902–). He is judicious and lucid in his revaluations of the early Victorian novelists, of Jane Austen and of Thomas Hardy (the latter so unjustly treated by George Moore, D. H. Lawrence and, most cruelly of all, by T. S. Eliot); he never forsakes pleasure and grace, even more than sweetness, as literary values. Unfashionably, in his *Fine Art of Reading* (1957), he submitted that "art is a subjective, sensual, and highly personal activity in which facts and ideas are the servants of fancy and feeling; and the artist's first aim is not truth, but delight. . . The primary object of a student of literature is to be delighted. His duty is to enjoy himself."

Names could be added *ad infinitum.* The primary and very eminent merits of the group of critics here lumped together in a succinct characterization are clear enough: none of them will reach posterity once this century is gone, not any more than most political writers, than the majority of historians or than performers, whose function and fate it is to address themselves to their own age and to serve it. But they have conceived their task modestly, and not assumed airs of superiority to the books on which they comment, as their nineteenth century predecessors had often done. They have been amateurs in the better sense of the word, loving literary works of quality and attempting to impart their enjoyment to others, true to Wordsworth's admonition at the end of the *Prelude:* "What you have loved, others will love,/ And you will teach them how." They have taken risks in assessing contemporary works, more hardily than many academic critics, who prefer to descry new and subtle secrets in the works of the past which they spend their lives elucidating for their students. They have as a rule possessed artistic sense and written a clear and elegant prose, refusing to deserve the sarcasm of an American scholar, himself an expert stylist (Harry Levin) who summed up most criticism as "bad writing about good writing." They have generally held the authors whose works they were assessing in some respect, a notable achievement in an art in which most critics of the nineteenth century had displayed singular obtuseness when judging the output of their contemporaries: Goethe, who had not suffered as much as other writers of the romantic age from lack of recognition at the hands of critics, had wisely warned evaluators of contemporary works against the most insidious pitfall ever open in front of them: to prefer mediocrity to greatness when greatness is accompanied by novelty: "All great excellence in life or art, at its first recognition, brings with it a certain pain arising from the strongly felt inferiority of the spectator. . . Mediocrity, on the other hand, may often give us unqualified pleasure; it does not disturb our self-satisfaction. . ." Implicit in the attitudes of those critics who may be termed "descriptive" or "analytical" (but without any claims to scientific thoroughness) is a healthy respect for the author or the artist, and a wish to let him write or create as truthfully to himself as he can. That is what so-called "creative writers" have always most earnestly yearned for in their loudly voiced impatience with critics.

To a much greater extent than in the United States and almost as frequently as in France, creators in Britain have at some time or other become critics. Thomas Mann, himself an admirable essayist (on Schopenhauer, Wagner, Chekhov) and a master of artistic irony in his fiction, penned the famous formula: "Kunst wird Kritik." Baudelaire had posited it as a law that creators inevitably become critics—often, he omitted to add, at the cost of their creative faculty. That criticism by creators, because of the personality of those who practise it, because it enlightens their own works, is the most valuable of all. It was that of Dryden, of Dr. Johnson, of Wordsworth, of Matthew Arnold and of Swinburne. It was also that of Henry James, of D. H. Lawrence (whose *Studies on Classic American Literature,* 1923, have renovated our perspective on half a dozen American authors). T. S. Eliot is the only one whose eminence as a poet matches his importance as a critic. But W. H. Auden, Aldous Huxley, George Orwell gained much weight for their occasional critical essays from the experience and the prestige which they had acquired as poets or novelists. Sometimes the most expert dissector of other writers' output is one whose own imaginative power was weak or derivative: William Empson, for example, more original in his critical prose than in his verse, or, earlier, Percy Lubbock (1879–1965), whose *Craft of Fiction* (1921) remains the most searching volume of criticism of the novel, from a Jamesian point of view, in the English language, while his semi-fictional *Roman Pictures* are pallid. It is not impossible that E. M. Forster himself (1879–) may survive as a master of the essay longer than he will as a novelist, and so will the lively but less searching and eclectic reviewer that Victor S. Pritchett (1900–) was. Many a reader of Iris Murdoch (Mrs. J. D. Bayley, 1919–) cannot help wishing she had written more sketches such as the one she gave of J.-P. Sartre in 1953, and fewer of her novels of strained acerbity; and some critical essays or small books by John Wain (1925–) or Angus Wilson (1913–) instill into us further curiosity for their judgments on past masters or on today's problems. The most delicately felicitous balance was achieved by Virginia Woolf (1882–1941). Her *Common Reader* (1929 and 1932), her assault on the realism of Arnold Bennett, her perspicacious remarks on feminine literature and on other topics collected in posthumous volumes like *The Death of the Moth* (1942) or *Granite and Rainbow* (1958) have helped alter the taste of her contemporaries: they will live, in anthologies of English essays, as long as any by Addison or Lamb.

The advantages enjoyed by creators who apply themselves to criticism are naturally immense: they write only on those authors or themes which they choose to comment upon and which stimulate them, and do not have to be sifters for the readers of a certain magazine or newspaper. They feel instinctively more respect for other authors, whose doubts and pangs and touchiness they sympathize with, than hardened critics may. Their thrill of excitement in the presence of a work which they reinterpret or love is more intense; their response is warmer and more imaginative. Their awareness of precedents and of sources does not have to be as broad, and as constricting, as in academic critics who, for years, have taught the great masters of the past and are cool to an apparent novelty which may be hardly new. Finally, in Schiller's words, these artists, composers, novelists, or poets are liable to be less distrustful than the cool professionals of criticism, of "the momentary madness of all creators."

A mention of even a few of the many literary historians whom Britain has counted in the present century could only amount to a dull list of names. Most of them have laid no claim to the label, judged at times hardly honorable, of "critic." The line that separates critics and historians is a tenuous one. There are some historians or researchers who have elected as their task the gathering of documents (on the Elizabethan stage, or social life under Queen Anne, or fiction and the reading public), and their devoted work offered to future scholars and to interpreters of their data is invaluable. It does not exclude the formulation of value judgments; indeed, it implies them. The broadest among these historians of literature have not balked at attempting syntheses which draw a balance sheet of already extant knowledge and stimulate further research. In the early decades of the twentieth century, the best known and most respected among these men were Oliver Elton (1861–1945), E. K. Chambers (1866–1954), Herbert Grierson (1866–1960). They did not endeavor to pass judgment on the literature being produced in their lifetime and they were not, by nature, open to vanguard innovations. But, by their reassessment of the Victorians, or of the Elizabethans, or of John Donne and the Metaphysical poets, they helped the younger writers acquire a more vivid awareness of a period in the past with which they felt congenial. They were not cold, lifeless recorders or mere authors of manuals of literary history. As one of them, E. K. Chambers, declared in *A Sheaf of Studies* (1942), the danger of the historical spirit is to induce us to spend too much time on mediocrities. "No criticism is worth much which is . . . not based upon actual personal impressions."

Among the most brilliant successors to those historians who were also prudent critics, since 1940 or so, stands a scholar of vast knowledge and independence of judgment and a prolific writer, who has striven for versatility rather than for profundity, David Daiches (1912–); he has been prompt to denounce pretentiousness, "misguided ingenuity" and excessive subtlety in young critics. On Walter Scott, Richardson, and others, he has put into practise his ideal of "the best appreciative criticism, . . . which enables the reader to get a glimpse of the real life in a work; having glimpsed it, he can proceed to enter into all its rich vitality."

Graham Hough (1908–) is almost as encyclopedic and certainly just as eclectic, ranging from reexamination of Aristotelian and Thomistic standards to a judicious discussion of the dogmatic approach to poetry in the "new" American criticism. Unity, inner coherence, clear radiance, added to a prudent distrust of the ethical and of the social emphasis advocated by Marxists or by moralists, are the values he sets above all others in his courageous *An Essay on Criticism* (1966). He is less abstract, more flexible and, on particular authors (Spenser, the romantics, Ruskin, Yeats, *et al*) more illuminating in the five or six more modest volumes which had preceded that one. Helen Gardner (1908–) reinterpreted texts from the Christian tradition, others by the Metaphysical poets, some modern ones, with incisive acumen. Like most practitioners of the elusive and subjective art of criticism, she has been concerned about the underlying postulates of her judgments. In *The Limits of Criticism* (1956), then in *The Business of Criticism* (1959), she maintained that interpretation and evaluation are inextricably bound together, as are the historical approach and the psychological and formal one. In the face of some arrogant dogmatism in the midcentury critics of America and of France even more than of Britain, she advises humility. Critics should not be carried away by neat labels or convenient hypotheses, like "the Elizabethan mind" or "the Elizabethan world-picture," mere phantoms of our generalizing brains: neither in the sixteenth nor in the twentieth century did the people of the same country think alike. "All critics should acknowledge that the provision of information, analysis and description can defeat the interpreter's true end, if he does not realize that, after a certain point, silence may well be the best service he can render his author and his reader." ("The Historical Sense," in *The Business of Criticism.*)

In a younger generation of critics, born around or after 1920, talent is plentiful, but, as usual, assessment of the importance or of the depth of those who evolve original ideas on and around literature can only be attempted once the fecundity of those ideas has been proved by time. Kenneth Tynan (1927–) succeeded in instilling lasting significance into the branch of critical writing least likely of all to reach greatness and to endure: criticism of plays. His big volume of collected pieces on the theatres of five countries, entitled *Curtains* (1956), followed by a new volume in 1967, is lively and refreshingly combative. John Holloway, (1920–) in his studies of *The Victorian Sage* (1953) and in *The Lion Hunt: A Pursuit of Poetry and Reality* (1964), and the Australian A. D. Hope, in *The Cave and the Spring* (1966) are at one and the same time refined poets and lucid interpreters of poetry and of poetics. Norman Jeffares (1920–) has done important work, notably on Yeats, proving that biography, when it probes into the psychology of a great writer, can immensely enrich critical interpretation. Frank Kermode (1919–), in remarkable critiques in *Encounter* and in his *Romantic Image* (1957), showed that he can be both a philosopher, a cosmopolitan interpreter of several European literatures and the most lucid mind judging literature in the nineteen sixties. Alfred Alvarez (1929–) is his closest rival, both being keenly sensitive and shrewdly analytical. In *The Shaping Spirit* (1958), he writes as an elegant master of style and as a theorist of criticism who is so intelligent that he can afford to distrust the claims of the intellect to understand and explain everything in a work of art: the physicists, he submits, have long accepted the element of irrationality which they call entropy, the role of chance or probability. Likewise, in our attitude to literature, "to be intelligent does not mean simply to be rational. It means the ability to make one's reason supple and subtle enough to include the irrational without being overwhelmed by it" ("The Professional Critic," in *The New Statesman,* September 24, 1960).

Through a mischievous irony of fate, those critics are discussed longer and loom most considerable in subsequent histories of letters who spurned humility, a pliable eclecticism and the modest duty of trying to meet each creator half way through sharing his vision before passing judgment upon it; instead, they chose (or felt temperamentally constrained to choose) a system, easily remembered for its slogans, formulas and theorems, and proposed it to others as a "summit of sovereignty" from which to utter their oracles. France used to be the home of such lovers of rigorous logic, from her neo-classicists, Auguste Comte to Taine, then Brunetière to, more recently, critics in love with linguistics or with structural anthropology. Twentieth century America, with the theorists of "new criticism," the new Aristotelians, Kenneth Burke, has had more than her share of those imperious doctrinaires. In Britain, the tradition of empiricism and the distrust of the intellectual comfort provided by a system have kept most practitioners of criticism in our time from imprisoning themselves in a theory. Freudian criticism has not conspicuously flourished after Ernest Jones (1879–1958); the Jungian myths which Maud Bodkin skillfully applied to literature in her *Archetypal Patterns in Poetry* (1934), after having tempted a few younger critics, hardly appear to have effected a breakthrough. Marxist criticism has indirectly impressed able minds which, however, refused to let themselves become the captives of that dialectics: William Empson to some extent and, with more ardent conviction on his part, Christopher St. John Sprigg who, under the name of Christopher Caudwell (1907–1937), ingeniously applied Marxist analysis to the elucidation of English poetry in *Illusion and Reality* (1937).

The two most powerful tendencies under which the more dogmatic English critics may without artificiality be classified are those which have always played a conspicuous part in the British national temper: the scientific one and the moralistic one. Of the former, the two chief representatives are I. A. Richards (1893–) and the brilliant and provoking writer who began as his disciple, William Empson (1906–). Richards, who found his starting point in Coleridge, rather belongs to the family of minds of which Aristotle is the progenitor. His earliest works, published before he set up residence in America in 1939, wielded an enormous influence on a generation that yearned to replace a romantic sentimentality in its approach to works of art by a more rigorous and more uniform attitude. His *Foundations of Aesthetics* in 1921, and especially his *Principles of Literary Criticism* (1924) and his *Practical Criticism* (1929) represent the most scientific attempt in English to blow up "the chaos of critical theories" of the past and to set in its place techniques founded upon experimental psychology. Richards deliberately rejected the scrutinizing of the mental processes of the poet and the surrender to the emotional world of feelings. The distrust of sensual enjoyment of poetry and of historical approaches to literature, and even of any exploration of the historical context of the works constitutes Richards' greatest shortcoming. But, on a less central problem, that of communication, "the only goal of all critical endeavors," and even more on the elimination of stock responses in students which prevent them from actually reading, Richards has thrown much light and been a master of perspicuity and rigor.

Empson, first a student of mathematics, became a disciple of Richards at Magdalene College, Cambridge; he soon amazed his teacher by his prodigious facility, then took his distances from him. His books are exasperating with their sophomoric display of ingenuity and his affectation to treat poems, including his own, as verbal puzzles. He has done his best to antagonize even those who most admired his gifts of verbal analysis and his uncanny talent for detecting and cataloguing ambiguities, impressively styled "stages of advancing logical disorder." *Seven*

Types of Ambiguity, first published in 1930, was recast and altered in 1947. *Some Versions of Pastoral,* in 1950, was less provoking but more sensitive; and *Milton's God* (1965), while still deliberately paradoxical, is rich in insights and in humane sensibility. Empson's magazine essay on *Tom Jones* showed that, unlike other scientific or engineering minds at work on the dissection of poetry exclusive of other genres, he could also admire and appraise novels, loose as one of the greatest of them may be. As Richards and Leavis ceased being active forces in criticism, Empson, as the year 1970 drew near, was the most unpredictable but also the most dazzlingly acute critic in the English language. Less than some French linguistic and structuralist critics who, tardily, have come to admire him, he does not take it for granted that an author writes mostly in order to express a coherent structure; unlike Richards or American adepts of the hackneyed motto of Archibald MacLeish that "a poem must not mean, but be" ("It is never what a poem says which matters, but what it is," had contended Richards), Empson does not pretend to neglect the content or the emotional and intellectual force latent in poetry.

The methods, the precision and the alleged objectivity of science have been the butt of much envy from the group of critics dissatisfied with either the timorous historical approach or the emotional subjectivity of the romantics. Different from them, often opposed to them, are the critics who, blandly disregarding the prestige of scientific doctrines (be they Freudian, Marxist, psychological or semantic), stress above all others the ethical, and even the religious, values inherent in literature. Their ancestors were many in the last century; in the forefront of them (even when, as T. S. Eliot, they have questioned his religious elusiveness, or ambiguity) stood Matthew Arnold. "The sea of faith was once too at the full," he had mourned in his most famous short poem; but it had ebbed. "Most of what now passes with us for religion and philosophy will be replaced by poetry," Arnold submitted in "The Study of Poetry." "The strongest part of our religion today is its unconscious poetry." Henry James had, more plausibly, in his *French Poets and Novelists,* argued that "to count out the moral element in one's appreciation of an artistic total is exactly as sane as it would be to eliminate all the words of three syllables . . . Morality is simply a part of the essential richness of inspiration . . ." Neither the vogue of art for art's sake in the eighteen nineties nor the later sarcasms at the Victorian complacency have succeeded in weakening the deep strain in the English character which stresses the ethical values in a work of literature.

C. S. Lewis (1898–1963) has written wittily and pungently on Christian apologetics, but his most significant works as a literary historian, *The Allegory of Love* (1936), *English Literature in the Sixteenth Century* (1954), *An Experiment in Criticism* (1961) are those of a committed, but objective scholar. His ethical outlook on life added vigor and breadth to his treatment of Spenser and of Milton, the latter in his view a respectable Christian and not a rebel obsessed by Satan. Frank R. Leavis (1895–   ) has been more bellicose in asserting blandly that "works of art enact their moral valuations." If Shakespeare thought and felt morally, he did not have to state moral judgments: his poetic use of language more than sufficed. Keats, likewise, is far more than sensuous and, in a higher sense, moral. D. H. Lawrence is moral throughout and, to boot, "the great creative genius of our age." But Milton and Shelley are found deficient. Spiritual vitality, sincerity, energy of intelligence, the submission of the emotions to a basically moral and universalized purpose are the guiding formulas of Leavis' criticism. He has had the courage, rare among the critics of his generation, to take his stand not only on poetry (where detailed analysis can be neater and subtle to one's heart's content) but also on the novel. *The Great Tradition* (1948) and *D. H. Lawrence Novelist* (1955) deeply influenced taste in Britain and America: strangely, Leavis concluded that the novelist of *Women in Love* has a more religious sensibility than the poet of *Ash Wednesday.*

The religious strain in Eliot's critical and semiphilosophical works became most conspicuous in the works he wrote after his fortieth year. Born in St. Louis, Missouri, in 1888 (he died in 1965), he then published *For Lancelot Andrewes* (1928), *Dante* (1929), *After Strange Gods* (1934) and *Essays ancient and modern* (1936). He subsequently appeared, or pretended, to dismiss his early, and most influential work as a critic; his later collections of essays are indeed disappointing and very uneven, many of them being pieces delivered as lectures or written in response to occasional requests. He has contradicted himself more than once, and at times made amends to authors (the Elizabethans, Shakespeare, Milton) on whom his earlier pronouncements had been summary. Yet it is not unfair to hold him to some of his more dogmatic assertions on the close links binding literature and ethics, or even literature and religious orthodoxy. He distrusted most heresies of his century (Marxist, Freudian, plainly agnostic as in Thomas Hardy, or sexual, as in D. H. Lawrence seen by him), but he clung to his pontifical statement in "Religion and Literature" (*Essays ancient and modern*) that "literary criticism should be completed by criticism from a definite ethical and theological standpoint . . . The 'greatness' of literature cannot be determined solely by literary standards."

Eliot seldom attempted analytical criticism (the precise dissection of a poem dear to the American "new critics") or the criticism that prospects uncharted lands and evaluates new talents. On several of his contemporaries (T. E. Hulme, Djuna Barnes, even Saint John Perse) and on Shakespeare in his relation to Seneca, on Milton, Baudelaire, probably even on Laforgue, he was patently and dogmatically wrong, or grossly partial. He overvalued T. E. Hulme (1883–1917), a mediocre poet, a militant anti-romantic and a champion of classicism (distorted as the recognition of original sin) who enjoyed for a time a prestige out of proportion with the scant merit of his *Speculations*. He multiplied austere generalizations, at times novel and illuminating, at times flying in the face of all that is known about the contradictions in the views of life held by the Fifth Century Greeks, the medieval Christians or the French classicists. Like the priest of the "sacred wood" of Nemi whom Renan, before J. G. Frazer, had conjured up in an ironical philosophical drama, he could slaughter some of his predecessors if they appeared to him to have worshipped "strange gods." His "rage for order" often drove him to cryptic and challengeable assertions, such as "the function of criticism seems to me essentially a problem of order," or a poet must accomplish "a continual extinction of personality," far less original than they seem at first sight to be: Rémy de Gourmont, André Gide, even Charles Maurras had advanced similar propositions. Some acerbity in his early critical essays, a narrow obscurantism in the writings of his middle age on orthodoxy or on a culture distrustful of the masses, have alienated many of his admirers and offered an exposed flank to dissenters and adversaries who, after he wrote some poor unpoetic dramas, rushed in to topple his statue from its pedestal.

Posterity will brush aside many of the peremptory assertions of Eliot, on classicism as the recognition of "the fact of original sin," on Racine's *Bérénice* as "a Christian tragedy," *Hamlet* as "most certainly an artistic failure," on the objective correlative and on the mysterious formula of the "dissociation of sensibility" in the Metaphysical poets. Enough that is significant remains in Eliot's early criticism to have made him, a nostalgic romantic dreaming of an impossible return to the past, the greatest apostle of tradition in our time and the most cogent exemplar of what criticism at its highest could be. Alone in the twentieth century, and more profoundly than Dryden whom he at times resembles (even though he judged Dryden's mind "commonplace") and than Arnold whom he upbraided as not Christian enough, he stands as the critic whom future generations will find it impossible to ignore, equally masterful in his prose and in the best of his poetry.

Cleanth Brooks and W. K. Wimsatt, *Lit. Crit.: A Short Hist.*, 1957; Vincent Buckley, *Poetry and Morality: Studies in the Crit. of Arnold, Eliot, Leavis,* 1959; R. S. Crane, *Critics and Crit., Ancient and Modern,* 1952; George Watson, *The Literary Critics,* 1962.

J. W. H. Atkins, *Eng. Lit. Crit., The Medieval Phase,* 1943; *The Renascence,* 1947, 1951; *the 17th and 18th C.,* 1951; Aisso Bosker, *Lit. Crit. in the Age of Johnson,* 1930, 1953; Leah Jonas, *The Divine Science* (17th c.), 1940; Edmund D. Jones, ed. *Eng. Critical Essays* (16th, 17th, 18th c.), 1922; Phyllis M. Jones, ed. *Eng. Critical Essays* (20th c.), 1935; C. W. Moulton, *The Library of Lit. Crit. of Eng. and Am. Authors,* 8 v., 1901–04, 4 v., 1966. Henri Peyre.

FRENCH CRITICISM, Renaissance. From the Middle Ages, literary theorists of the 16th c. inherited two distinct traditions: (1) rhetorical, stemming from the Roman rhetoricians and from Horace, concerned primarily with the ornaments of verse style and the decorum of persons (E. Faral, *Les Arts poétiques du XIIe et XIIIe* siècles, 1923); and (2) prosodic concerned with the rules for rhyme and rhythm of the various verse forms (E. Langlois, *Recueil d'arts de seconde rhétorique,* 1902). Moreover, they fell heir to a group of prejudices, essentially clerical, which regarded literature as sinful or frivolous and insisted that it could be made acceptable only by a moralizing intention. These traditions and prejudices were obviously inadequate for an age becoming enamored of the beauties of poetry and discovering the masterpieces of classical antiquity. Hence theorists found themselves faced with these problems: (1) the defence of poetry; (2) the discovery of its nature and essence; (3) the distinction of the ends, subjects, and means of the various literary genres; (4) the decision as to the language (L. or the vernacular) to be used; and (5) interpretation of the dicta of the Ancients on all of these points. The solutions, found in treatises, essays, and prefaces, derive from the antecedent traditions, from the works of ancient and Italian theorists, and from the independent adaptation of such theories to the special case of the French Renaissance.

In the early years of the c. the old justification on grounds of morality was still prevalent; *e.g.*, the anonymous preface to the *Roman de la rose* (1527; once attributed to Clément Marot) distinguished between the pleasure to be found in the literal meaning of the work and the profit to be derived from its allegorical interpretation. But from mid-c. new bases of defence prevailed; the arguments were essentially those of Boccaccio's *Genealogia deorum*. Sebillet, in his *Art poétique françoys* (1548), defended poetry because of its divinity, its antiquity, its early use for religious purposes, and the great esteem in which good poets have always been held. Jacques Peletier du Mans in his *Art poétique* (1555), pointed to its civilizing function, to the instruction in morals and virtue which it gives, to the fact that even great emperors have practiced it. Thenceforth, these arguments were commonplaces; but morality still dominated: tragedy, *e.g.*, furnishes lessons to kings and the great for their conduct of government, to all men for the moderation of their passions. It was in connection with this line of thinking that the Aristotelian catharsis was later interpreted as meaning a purging of the wicked passions of the audience. Likewise, comedy exposes vice to ridicule and instructs in the ways of men (J. Grévin, Preface to *Théâtre,* 1562).

The fact that poetry was defended as morally profitable to its audience is an indication of the current conception of its nature. Throughout the c. poetry was regarded as a kind of rhetoric; hence, attention must be paid to the character of the poet and the exigencies of the audience as well as to the work itself. Treatises differed from one another largely in the placing of emphasis on the three considerations. Poetry is unlike oratory (1) in using verse (Sebillet; Du Bellay, *Deffence et illustration de la langue françoyse,* 1549), (2) in exploiting the fictional and the *vraisemblable* rather than the factual and the *vrai* (Peletier; Ronsard, Pref. *Franciade,* 1572, 1587), (3) in demanding divine inspiration in the poet (Du Bellay). Otherwise the poet, like the orator, is a product of nature and of art—a long debate centered about their relative importance—and he must have the three special faculties of invention, disposition, and elocution. He must also have great erudition (Du Bellay) and moral goodness (Ronsard, *Abrégé de l'art poétique,* 1565). The audience, on the other hand, is an elite familiar with the works of the ancients, cognisant of the rules of decorum and of certain conventional precepts, and susceptible of moral improvement through pleasurable forms.

The means by which this effect is accomplished on the audience is the poem itself. Under the influence of Plato and Aristotle, as interpreted by the It. and such humanists as Scaliger, the poem was defined as an imitation of nature in verse. Both terms must be taken with caution; for both acquired new meanings in the light of the audience. If this audience is to profit, it must first be convinced of the truth of the poem, *i.e.*, the resemblance of the poem to nature. The nature to be imitated included "the Ideas and forms of all things which can be imagined, celestial as well as terrestrial, animate or inanimate" (Ronsard, *Abrégé*); but essentially it consisted of the actions and the characters of men (Jean Vauquelin de la Fresnaye, *Art poétique français, ca.* 1574–90; 1st ed. 1605). As early as Du Bellay, however, it is clear that this nature was to be discovered and imitated not from the world of reality, but from the writings of the Ancients. This theory led to the concept of imitation as copying, widely current in the Renaissance.

From the practice of the Ancients, the theorists of the Renaissance rationalized a complicated theory of the literary genres. Each form was distinguished by its subject matter, its style, its verse form, its general character or effect, its models in antiquity, its particular precepts or rules. The earliest distinctions were prosodic (Sebillet); these continued to the end of the c. (Pierre de Laudun, *Art poétique français,* 1597); they were an outgrowth of the medieval tradition, as was the determination of styles. But the rest of the theory, especially insofar as it was preceptual, stemmed largely from Horace's *Ars poetica*. The genres recommended were those practiced by the Ancients and the It., while those of the Middle Ages and the Rhétoriqueur school were disdained (Du Bellay, Peletier, Vauquelin). The epic was regarded as the greatest of all genres, largely because of the admiration for Vergil, while tragedy and comedy were recommended among the dramatic forms, the ode and the sonnet among the lyric. The question of the language to be used was regarded as a subsidiary problem for poetic theory. The main document here is Du Bellay's *Deffence,* which was derived from Sperone Speroni's *Dialogo della lingua*.

The *Poetics* of Aristotle came increasingly into prominence as the century progressed, but was probably the least understood of all the texts; none of the Renaissance treatises is Aristotelian in method or conclusions. For the texts represent a growing effort to relate poetry to other considerations rather than to single it out for special study: to grammar, prosody, history, nature, classical models, and especially rhetoric. These tendencies are to be accounted for by a growing Platonism of method and a dominance of the influence of Horace and the rhetoricians, especially Cicero and Quintilian.

Saints; J. E. Spingarn, *Hist. of Lit. Crit. in the Ren.,* 1899 f; C. S. Baldwin, *Ren. Lit. Theory and Practice,* 1939. BERNARD WEINBERG.

Seventeenth Century. The critical treatises of the Renaissance dealt for the most part not with specific works but with abstract problems of literary æsthetics. The approach was philosophical (pseudo-Aristotelian in the main), and envisioned possible literary works, relating them to the needs of hypostatized audiences. In the 17th c. this theorizing tradition of the Renaissance, increasingly active, was joined by a new type of criticism directed at individual authors and works (*Dissertations, Réflexions, Entretiens, Examens*). Criticism became a complex amalgam of general principles (*la doctrine classique*), discussions of particular genres (*e.g.,* Le Bossu's *Traité du poème épique*), quarrels over the application of principles to a given work (*e.g.,* the quarrel of the *Cid*), and purely technical regulations of all kinds (*e.g., liaison des scènes*). Intricate overlappings among these categories resulted inevitably from the 17th c. conception of literature and its forms as a mathematically demonstrable, unified result of "nature" and "reason." A number of outstanding individuals (Malherbe, Boileau, etc.) gained enormous critical reputations, and were personally credited with the elaboration of critical systems and principles.

Classical Doctrine. The first critical "treatise" of the 17th c. was not an organized argumentation like the *Deffense* of the Pléiade, but a series of laconic marginal notes to the works of the poet Desportes, composed by Malherbe, 1605 f. As practical criticism, this *Commentaire* has been charged with inconsistency, hair-splitting, envious quibbling, and blindness to essential poetic qualities (Brunot). Its underlying principles, however, became standard practice, except in the case of a few incorrigible oppositionists (Régnier, Théophile de Viau). Essentially rationalistic, Malherbe's "common-sense" approach outlawed the emotional and the imaginative, applauded tight-knit structure, coherence, sobriety, clarity, syntactical precision, exactitude of word usage, use of antitheses. Deeper than Malherbe's effect on subsequent grammatical practice and choice of poetic vocabulary was the impetus he gave to literature away from the imaginative free-play and Petrarchian emotionalist tradition of the Renaissance, towards a basic "reasonableness," and the severe censorship of the "inspirational" that formed part of the classical strait-jacket of self-imposed rigors. To his contemporaries he was the lawgiver of a new literary era, the founder of practical criticism.

Ideologically, the classic doctrine acquired principles from foreign sources (Sp. theorists, It. thinkers, Vida, Scaliger, Castelvetro) and domestic (especially Renaissance Aristotelianism). Prime concerns were: the ends of art (chiefly utilitarian and moralistic), art as an imitation of nature (but a selected, idealized imitation, not to be termed true realism), the nature of the poet and his "génie," the necessity of rules and of imitation of ancient models, and the role of reason as the censor of art. From these bases may be traced the construction of the general classical system as it was applied to all the genres, though the chief data are from writings on dramatic theory.

The foundation of the doctrine was *vraisemblance.* Although the concern over probability within the structure of a work of art (as in Aristotle) was frequently neglected in favor of the principle of the agreement between art and life, the former reappeared in the principle of unity of action and preparation of events, and *vraisemblance* thus sometimes meant internal convincingness. Many rules were derived from the principle: *e.g.,* history in the drama might need alteration in its details in order to achieve *vraisemblance,* but it could not be changed in its important, well-known events. The criterion for *vraisemblance,* vague at best, remained the opinion of audiences and critics, and the creators of art sought to put themselves in the place of the spectators, anticipating their judgment in order to flatter it.

Corollary to *vraisemblance* were the *bienséances,* which determined both the appropriateness of personality-traits and actions within plays and their similarity to the *mœurs* of the age in which the play was written, two standards which were often at variance. In the quarrel over the *Cid,* Rodrique's request to Chimène that she stab him, after his slaying of her father, was said to violate *les bienséances internes,* while the marriage of the two implied at the end of the play was called an insult to *les bienséances externes,* since the action was deemed nonpermissible in real life.

Frequently contrasted to *vraisemblance,* but paradoxically dependent upon it, *le merveilleux* was the subject of extended theoretical debate. It included not only the intervention of gods and the use of machines, but any surprising turn of plot, and sometimes any unusual richness of expression or ornamentation. The *merveilleux,* however, must be produced by *un enchaînement des choses qui arrivent d'ordinaire* (Chapelain), and the intervention of a god (as in *Phèdre*) must be *préparé* so that there exists *une attente vraisemblable de son assistance* (d'Aubignac).

Unity of action, most closely followed of all the classical unities, worked to concentrate the movement of the plot, esp. in tragedy, around the central action, or crisis; critics and dramatists alike argued for the postponement of the play's beginning until the last possible moment in the action. All the incidents must be, in d'Aubignac's standard formula, prepared but not foreseen: the "telegraphed" outcome was, then as now, received with protest and derision. A closed determinism of cause and effect, gradually divulged to the audience, represented the goal: gratuitous acts and even free will (except when rationalized as the deciding factor in a multiple choice, as between honor, duty, love) disappeared. The unities of time and place, held to be required for *vraisemblance,* became a "French mania," invading even the heroic novel (Scudéry, pref. to *Ibrahim,* set the duration of a novel at one year), and completely dominating the theatre. The classical concentration of effect praised by modern critics as a result of these unities was ignored by the 17th c., which saw in them abstract truths like the laws of geometry or logic.

Criticism of Genres. (1) Tragedy, the classical genre *par excellence,* was a subject of major critical activity. Aside from the general principles of *vraisemblance,* the most discussed rules of the tragedy were those of the unities. The first important codification of these appeared in the preface to Mairet's *Silvanire* (1631), written less under the direct influence of the It. theorists (who had begun to resurrect the unities) than under that of the It. pastorals and L. comedies (Lancaster). The practice of adhering to the unities of place, time (24 hours), and action ("causal relationship between the subordinate and main plot") became fixed relatively late, and was a self-imposed convention agreed upon by dramatists, rather than a burden forced upon them by critics or pedants. The quarrel of the *Cid,* though primarily concerned with the *bienséances,* evoked much critical discussion and support of the unities (*e.g.,* Chapelain). One critic (Ogier) dared point out that the unities may sometimes work against, rather than for, *vraisemblance.* The last word on dramatic rules was d'Aubignac's *Pratique du théâtre,* published in 1657, but known in large part 10 or 15 years before. Racine, whose tragedy has been termed the embodiment of d'Aubignac's system (Bray), owned an annotated copy. It endorsed the severest interpretation of the unities, and prescribed in detail how each scene must be linked with the next (by *liaison de présence, de recherche, de bruit*); when the chief characters should appear; what kinds of plots are best; how effects of rhetoric must be handled.

Corneille's three *Discours* (1660) on dramatic construction and the pamphlets and polemics provoked by his later plays were the chief works of dramatic criticism after d'Aubignac. Most important departure was Corneille's endorsement of the "historical guarantee" (*i.e.,* the *vrai* rather than the *vraisemblable*) and his emphasis on the aim of drama as the arousing of pleasure in the audience, a doctrine also subscribed to by Molière in his prefaces.

Towards the end of the c. Saint-Evremond (living in Eng.) produced a quantity of dramatic criticism, expressing "modern" preferences for French and English drama as opposed to classical, but maintaining an Aristotelian insistence on the supremacy of plot over character (a principle that he accused Racine of repeatedly violating). Boileau reiterated in quotable couplets the standard classical amalgam of Aristotle and Horace as compounded by d'Aubignac and others; his clear, pithy phraseology made his *Art poétique* a useful and popular summary of critical and technical principles of all the literary genres.

Several dramatic prefaces of the last years of the c. contain passages of critical interest (Racine, Hauteroche, Boursault), and some minor critics of the drama flourished (Lamy, Bouhours, Rapin, Le Bossu). The periodicals of the late 17th c. contained much would-be dramatic criticism, most of it on an inferior plane (*cf.* Mélèse, *Le théâtre et le public à Paris,* 1659–1715). It is probable also that oral criticism played a considerable role in the formation of public opinion and exerted some influence on the actual composition of plays (Lancaster).

(2) Tragi-comedy. A mixed genre, tragicomedy formed during the early 17th c. a refuge for anti-classical writers who opposed the rules, especially the rules of the unities. Its chief characteristic was its happy outcome, which followed an *intrigue* with tragic possibilities. Though many critics discussed the genre (Vauquelin, Chapelain, La Mesnardière, d'Aubignac), none esteemed it greatly and it was never subjected to the vigorous technical scrutiny given to the tragedy (*cf.* Lancaster, *The Tragi-comedy*).

(3) The dramatic pastoral. It. in origin, this genre was at first deemed anti-classical, but soon fell in line with classical rules, was merged with comedy, and thus considered by the critic (Chapelain, Scudéry, d'Aubignac).

(4) Comedy. Few critical writings dealt exclusively with comedy, but most theoreticians gave "rules" for the genre. Corneille saw the difference between comedy and tragedy solely as a difference between kinds of actions (that of the comedy being invented, that of the tragedy historical), and envisioned a "comédie héroïque" which has been called an anticipation of the 18th c. *"drame bourgeois."* Molière, concurring with Corneille's general principle that the pleasure received by the audience is the end of comedy, saw in the genre an opportunity to make humor of man's faults, generalized and impersonalized, but recognizable as the shortcomings of his own age. Critics of Molière accused him of repudiating the comedy of intrigue, of creating too complex characters, and of ignoring *vraisemblance* in many details (*cf.* Lancaster). One (Robinet) even protested at his ending *L'Ecole des femmes* on the unhappy note of a disappointed lover's outcry of distress. In general (*cf.* Boileau) comedy followed the rules of tragedy, but its characters were required by the critics to be of *petite condition,* its subject non-historical, and its ending happy.

(5) Poetic genres. The epic or heroic poem, praised by the critics of the Pléiade, suffered with the failure of Ronsard's *Franciade* and the general 17th c. disregard for Renaissance poetry. It reappeared in France after 1650, however, accompanied by an outburst of critical argument and discussion. Godeau, Desmarets, Peletier, Vossius and others placed it above tragedy in rank, despite the cautions of Rapin and Bussy. Critics (Chapelain, Marolles, Scudéry, Huet, d'Aubignac), argued over the suitability of an unwarlike subject, the introduction of love, the "heroic fault" of the hero (*cf.* Boileau), whether the hero might be a woman (Chapelain had written *La Pucelle*), the historicity of the subject. Most important documents were Scudéry's preface to *Alaric,* Le Bossu's and Le Moyne's *Traités* on the epic poem. Technical considerations (*e.g.,* whether the poet should follow the "natural" or the "historical" order in the proposition, invocation, narration, and dénouement) held considerable place. Most critics held for a happy ending, and insisted on as strict an observance of *vraisemblance* as in tragedy. Admission of Christian subjects was a debated point, settled more or less permanently by Boileau's banning of *le merveilleux chrétien* from literature on the ground that it brought up theological consideration inappropriate to the æsthetic effect.

Lyric poetry in the 17th c., although not one poem has survived from the period as a masterpiece, was a much-practised if little-debated genre. The numerous pastoral poems, odes, elegies, and the like written at the time were mentioned by critics only *en passant.* Rapin defined an elegy as a lover's complaint; Colletet considered the epigram in a brief *Discours.* Boileau mentioned the various types, praising especially his own genre, satire. Toward end of the c. verse and the theory of lyric poetry had sunk to such a level that the characters of a popular novel by Mme. de Villedieu were able to agree that the only difference between prose and poetry was the presence in the latter of livelier thoughts (*des pensées vives*).

(6) Prose genres. The novel, considered a secondary genre, was discussed in prefaces, brochures, letters, a few rare essays (*e.g.*, Chapelain's *De la lecture des vieux romans*). Huet's *Traité de l'origine des romans* contained mainly superficialities. The novel and prose story, though *mondain* and inferior in importance, were nevertheless held subject to *certaines règles* (Huet), and d'Urfé in *L'Astrée* was credited with having saved the novel from barbarism by first applying rules to it. Perhaps by analogy with the romanesque action of the *Æneid* and Tasso's *Gerusalemme liberata,* the novel was considered an offshoot of the epic and subjected to the rules thereof, as well as criticized by comparison with well-known epics (Boisrobert, La Calprenède, Scudéry, Chapelain). D'Aubignac, speaking of his own novel *Macarise,* stated that the sole distinction between a novel and an epic was verse. At one time or another critics insisted that the novel follow all the unities (except that of time, which was always modified), observe *vraisemblance, bienséances,* and the rules of the *merveilleux.* Scudéry and Rapin thought historical subjects essential to the novel, and as the century progressed a new genre of historical fiction developed, beginning with the "historical" backgrounds of d'Urfé, La Calprenède and the authors of heroic novels, and culminating in the historical-psychological novels and stories of Mme. de La Fayette, Mme. de Villedieu, and Saint-Réal. Bussy and others criticized *La Princesse de Clèves* (1678) because they found the confession of Mme. de Clèves to her husband a violation of *vraisemblance;* Valincour objected because its events did not always appear well-motivated within the traditional scheme of unity of action. Mme. de Villedieu in her prefaces claimed that historical fiction could show the hidden motives behind historical events, and limited the novelist's invention to private interviews and other unrecorded but possible episodes. Saint-Réal practised documentation and research (*Dom Carlos*), envisioning the novel as a sort of historical tool (*cf.* Dulong). Much critical attention was provoked around 1660–80 by the introduction into fiction of psychological studies of the *honnête femme* and *honnête homme* (*cf.* Dallas). An entire special issue of the *Mercure galant* was consecrated to amateur opinions concerning the *vraisemblance* of the actions of the most-debated *honnête femme,* Mme. de Clèves.

Some criticism of prose forms occurred in the shape of burlesque and satire (*e.g.*, Sorel's *Berger extravagant,* Boileau's attack on the precious *Héros de roman*). Occasionally a novel was discussed in brochures (*Dom Carlos*) or in a collection of varied essays (Sorel's *Bibliothèque françoise,* Baillet's *Jugemens des sçavans*). "Reviews" appeared in the rhymed columns of the *Mercure galant* and other periodicals. Most thorough of the journalistic critics was Bayle, who in the *Journal des sçavans* and the *Nouvelles de la république des lettres* sought to give serious accounts of new *contes, nouvelles,* and *romans.* Considerations of prose style in general appeared in Balzac, Voiture, Boileau (*Longin*), and in La Bruyère's *Caractères,* which contained variegated criticism in many genres.

Critical Quarrels; Individual Critics. The tenor of 17th c. criticism was clearly reflected in several notable literary quarrels. Foremost was that of Corneille's *Cid* (1637), "the first literary discussion in the 17th c. of large proportions in which the general question of the rules of art. . . [was] brought out" (Lancaster). The details and chronology of the quarrel are complex (*cf.* Gasté), but the chief documents may be described briefly. Scudéry's examination attacked the *vraisemblance* of the play, as well as the ethics of the characters. The unity of action was deemed violated by the role of the Infanta, and that of time forced by an improbable series of events all occurring within 24 hours. The anonymous pamphlets written in reply defended Corneille on most of the counts, and claimed that not rules, but pleasure, constituted the aim of drama. Richelieu then approved an undertaking of the Académie to judge the work (*Sentimens de l'Académie sur le Cid*). Therein the critics (chiefly Chapelain) laid down their interpretation of Aristotle, defined *vraisemblance* and the unities, and measured Corneille's achievement by their formulæ. The chief criterion was *bienséances,* and on this ground the morality of the *Cid* was denounced. Better no play at all, they argued, than one in which a girl intends to marry her father's slayer. The real struggle in the *Cid* (the attempt of its protagonists to fulfill the requirements of the code of honor even when their actions seemed destined to be fatal to their love) was overlooked, and it was even suggested that some trick of plot by which the Count might turn out not to be Chimène's father, or be resuscitated, would reconcile the play with the rules. When Corneille later wrote his *examen* of the *Cid* (1660) he replied to criticism of form and of ethics or decorum without distinction, making with equal contriteness the admissions that the arrival of the Moors was unprepared (formal), and that Rodrigue should not request Chimène to take his life (decorum). The failure of the age to distinguish between matters of construction and conceptions of traditional ethics was thus apparent from its first great critical debate.

Echoes of the impact of Malherbe's system and the protest against it by such men as Régnier and the libertine Théophile de Viau were found in the pronouncements on style, vocabulary, and syntax made by such critics as Vaugelas and Balzac. The latter figured also in the critical battle over the relative merits of Voiture's *Uranie* and Bernserade's *Job,* two sonnets that roused a disproportionate amount of comment. Everyone then, as now, set himself up as a critic: witness the presence of literary judgments in a private journal like Tallemant des Réaux' *Historiettes,* in the polite conversations of novels, in letters (Bussy), in plays (*cf. Le Misanthrope; La Critique de l'Ecole des femmes, etc.*), in the mouths of figures satirized in handbooks of mores (*Les Caractères*).

Corneille was again the center of a critical storm during the years following 1660. Always much concerned with literary theory, the playwright composed 3 *Discours* on tragedy, revealing his conversion to a stricter interpretation of the unities and rules than he held during the *Cid* quarrel. His *examens* of his own plays, also published at this time, constitute an outstanding example of applied criticism; with remarkable detachment, the author-critic praises, condemns, explains, compares, comments. The new quarrel arose over the plays *Sertorius* and *Sophonisbe.* The journalist de Visé and the critic d'Aubignac both attacked Corneille, and several anonymous writers published polemics. De Visé in a *volte-face* issued a *Défense de Sophonisbe.* The upshot of the discussion was another victory for the rules, and a tightening of the method of their critical application (Bray, *La Tragédie cornélienne devant la critique classique*).

Documents of some importance, most of them patterned on Chapelain's neo-Aristotelian essays, appeared by Sarrasin, Scudéry, La Mesnardière, Mambrun, Desmarets. All concerned topics discussed above. Saint-Evremond wrote capable and learned critical papers: comparing Racine and Corneille (preferring, as did Mme. de Sévigné, the latter), setting forth a theory of catharsis, criticising the opera, philologically investigating the word *vaste.* Scattered in the *-ana* collection of mss. of the time (Huetiana; Ménagiana) are many critical observations, though few were ordered compositions or reasoned discourses.

Most widely known of 17th c. critics was of course Boileau, whose influence was felt over all Europe. Untrustworthy in the extreme in his historical portions (*e.g.,* his account of the development of French poetry and drama), Boileau contributed no original ideas (his borrowings from Horace were extensive). He helped reinforce the classic rejection from poetry of anything beyond sentiments and thoughts dictated by common sense. His attacks on bad poets (Chapelain, de Pure) were justified, but hardly necessary, and hardly compensate for his blindness to the poetic merits of, *e.g.,* Ronsard. Boileau's reputation, which has been enormous, has elevated him to a critical rank for which the true justification is indeed scanty.

Not primarily a critic, La Bruyère nevertheless included in his work some critical passages worthy of note (*Les Caractères,* especially the section *Des ouvrages de l'esprit*). Treating wittily in a few pages what writers like Father Bouhours took volumes to discuss (Bouhours, *La Manière de bien penser dans les ouvrages de l'esprit,* 1687), La Bruyère argued aphoristically for the superiority of ancient literature ("*Tout est dit*"); passed a variety of judgments on such authors as Corneille, Molière, Malherbe, Rabelais; lauded *le mot juste.* He used no method, applied no rules, stated that a work is good when it exalts the mind: a step ahead of Boileau's narrow common sense. Another part-time critic, Fénelon, wrote a treatise on religious eloquence, and an important *Mémoire sur les occupations de l'Académie,* proposing the joint composition of an official Rhetoric and Poetic, and uttering comments on literary principles, many of which are among the most striking dicta of post-Boileau criticism: reversion to the Pléiade's admission of word borrowings and coinages, depreciation of the stilted syntax and impoverished vocabulary of his age, insistence on judgments based not on rules but on understanding of the particular work.

Better known perhaps in Eng. (through Rymer's trans.) than in France, Rapin produced several critical *Comparaisons:* Homer and Virgil, Plato and Aristotle. They were, however, superficial, and Rapin's system was dominated by conceptions of *bienséances externes* which rendered his observations almost wholly moralistic.

Of the practising critics of the end of the c., Pierre Bayle was the most prolific. For the first time criticism took on, with Bayle, the journalistic cast it was destined later to display on the popular level. Bayle's accounts in his *Nouvelles de la république des lettres, e.g.,* were "book reviews" *avant la lettre,* with biographical comments on authors, pat evaluations of books, generalizations on works of the type considered. Some of the literary items in his *Dictionnaire historique et critique* were also of a critical nature.

The Quarrel of the Ancients and Moderns, famous in literary annals, was a polemic episode in the history of the idea of progress (natural and cultural) rather than in the history of literature or of criticism. That old and new writers were praised and blamed was largely incidental, indicative of the general position of the critic and of little else. Two modern studies (Rigault, Gillot) trace in detail the genesis and chief chapters of the quarrel in Fr.; its spread to Eng. has been dealt with separately (R. F. Jones, *Ancients and Moderns*). The quarrel of the *Cid* and the debate over the suitability of Christian subjects in the epic are regarded as early stages in the battle. Arguments over Fr. versus L. inscriptions for public buildings filled several polemics (Le Laboureur, Charpentier). Formal beginning of the quarrel was the reading before the Académie of Perrault's pro-modern *Siècle de Louis le Grand.* Answers were made by La Fontaine, La Bruyère, Boileau. Fontenelle sponsored Perrault. For the first time the abstract principles of 17th c. criticism were laid aside and a cultural, "scientific" approach adumbrated: Fontenelle argued a relativistic stand for judging art, with such factors as climate and *milieu* taken into consideration. Last stage of the quarrel was the debate over the merits of poetry (verse) and those of prose, with Houdar de la Motte proposing the total rejection of verse, and writing a prose tragedy to illustrate his point. When Voltaire replied in favor of verse, his defense praised chiefly the rationalistic neo-classical versification, which prevailed in Fr. until the end of the 18th c., with the appearance of the "first lyric poet since Ronsard," André Chénier.

R. Bray, *La Formation de la doctrine classique en* Fr., 1931; F. Brunot, *La Doctrine de Malherbe d'après son Commentaire sur Desportes,* 1891; D'Aubignac, *La Pratique du théâtre,* ed. Martino, 1927; D. F. Dallas, *Le Roman fr. de* 1660–80, 1932; A. Gasté, *La Querelle du Cid,* 1898; H. C. Lancaster, *Fr. Dramatic Lit. in the 17th c.,* 9 v., 1929–42; M. Magendie, *Le Roman fr. au XVII*e *siècle de l'Astrée au Grand Cyrus,* 1932; Ship.
Bruce A. Morrissette.

Eighteenth Century. A second phase of the Quarrel of the Ancients and the moderns ushered in the 18th c.

In 1711, Mme. Dacier (1654–1720) published her translation of the *Iliad,* with a Preface in which she modestly stated that no copy, however accurate, could do justice to the poetic harmony and cadence of the original. The manners and customs depicted by Homer might be crude, but this was no defect. Indeed, they could not but be different from those of modern times. *"Pour moi,"* she said, *"je trouve ces temps anciens d'autant plus beaux qu'ils ressemblent moins au nôtre."* The principle of the relativity of taste is here definitely posed.

Two years later, however, Houdar de La Motte (1672–1731) brought forth his verse translation of the *Iliad,* shortened to 12 books and "improved" by omission of the "crudities" of the ancient Gr. poet. In the prefatory *Discours sur Homère,* La Motte asserted that there was no reason why Homer's Gr. (which La Motte did not know) should sound better than a Fr. version. He emphasized his belief in the "barbarousness" of Homeric manners and customs, shocking, in his opinion, to cultivated modern taste. Though respecting the ancients, we should hope to equal them, perhaps to surpass them, in literary achievement. Thus the question of progress came again to the fore.

Mme. Dacier replied (1713) with some asperity in her *Des causes de la corruption du goût.* La Motte continued the dispute, but with persuasive urbanity, in *Réflexions sur la critique* of the same year. More definitely than La Motte, the Abbé Terrasson (1670–1750), in his *Dissertation sur Homère* (1715), gave expression to his theory of progress, of "perfectibility," though this aspect of his thought did not in his time draw the attention it deserved. *"Les progès de l'esprit humain dans le cours des siècles,"* he confidently asserted, *"sont une suite d'une loi naturelle."* Literary principles, like those of science, should be constantly open to reexamination in the light of Cartesian reason.

Thus this *esprit géométrique,* though himself dogmatic and naïvely certain of the rightness of literary taste in his own time, laid down principles of independent thinking and change that would lead far. Fénelon (1651–1715), the aged Archbishop of Cambrai, in his *Lettre sur les occupations de l'Académie* (1716), took a characteristically moderate position between the two extremes of the Quarrel, which had laid the groundwork, however, for a saner appreciation of the real merit of the Ancients, while opening the door to the development of new literary forms and style.

La Motte took sides on one more question. Too narrowly rationalistic, like many in his age, he was fundamentally unable to appreciate poetry, which could say nothing, he held, that could not be said better, more accurately, in prose. Many another 18th c. critic [Fontenelle (1657–1757); Montesquieu (1689–1755)] agreed. *"En prose on dit ce qu'on veut,"* said the Abbé Trublet in his *Essais,* 1760, *"et en vers ce qu'on peut."* On the basis of contemporary Fr. poetry, these critics were largely right. Voltaire (1694–1778), however, though definitely rationalistic, came forward as a vigorous defender of poetry. The Abbé Du Bos (1670–1742) is more important than is generally recognized. In his *Réflexions sur la poésie et sur la peinture* (1719), which went through numerous editions, Du Bos, in contrast to Terrasson, distinguished between the sciences, which develop with accumulating knowledge, and the arts, including literature, which depend upon insight, feeling, intuition, for much of their power and excellence. In science, the moderns have a definite advantage. In literature and the arts, the ancients early attained outstanding and in many cases unsurpassable excellence. In appreciating literature and the arts, *le sentiment,* feeling, is more important than *la raison.* Climate, which works on the physical organs of the body, hence also on the brain and the feelings, may be more favorable to achievement in some countries and in some ages than in others. Thus relativity again appeared, but with more emphasis. This important doctrine was expounded by Du Bos, on a semi-scientific basis; Montesquieu gave it the prestige of his great name in the *Lettres persanes* (1721) and the *Esprit des lois* (1748). Du Bos did little in criticism of individual works, but his basic principles opened the way to a more liberal outlook than the rigid canons of Fr. classic taste generally permitted. If climate and physical surroundings explain the varied literature of different countries and ages, then these variations are evidently necessary and legitimate. The relativity of taste and a cosmopolitan viewpoint are natural consequences.

Since the Revocation of the Edict of Nantes in 1685, French Protestant refugees across the Channel had increasingly encouraged interest in English literature. [*Les Lettres sur les Anglais et sur les Français* (1725), by the Swiss Béat-Louis de Muralt (1655–1749) had influence on Rousseau among others.] The Abbé Prévost (1697–1763), though not the *anglomane* he has been called, discussed Shakespeare and in 1738 analyzed some of the plays in a literary journal of his editorship, *Le Pour et Contre* (1733–40), echoing, however, the opinions of the English critics, Rowe and Gildon. Voltaire, who had gone to Eng., 1726, staying over two years, commented vigorously upon Shakespeare, notably in his *Lettres philosophiques* of 1734. But Voltaire, naturally a classicist at heart, influenced too by Addison, Bolingbroke, and the general trend of cultivated opinion in Eng. at the time, though he thought Shakespeare a genius *"plein de force et de fécondité,"* emphasized also that the great English dramatist was *"sans la moindre étincelle de bon goût, et sans la moindre connaissance des règles"* (18th *Lettre philosophique,* 1734). Discussion of Shakespeare waged hotly in Fr. through the 18th c. Voltaire, who claimed in his early years that he had revealed Shakespeare to the Fr., attacked his "dangerous" influence violently in his *Lettre à l'Académie* of 1776. Shakespeare's obscenities, his "monstrous irregularities," his tragedies, half in verse, half in prose, with their *mélange des genres,* all shocked Voltaire, who saw that the triumph of Shakespeare would threaten the very existence of French classical tragedy.

Meanwhile there was much discussion of the 3 unities, and some tendency (La Motte) to call them in question. General practice remained timid, however; even Diderot in the last half of the c. hesitated to take a clear-cut position.

La Chaussée (1691 or 2–1754), unable to write amusing comedies, wrote verse plays on serious bourgeois themes; these *comédies larmoyantes* were another threat to classical tragedy with its insistence upon extraordinary and aristocratic characters. Lillo's mediocre, melodramatic, and moralizing bourgeois drama, *George Barnwell, or the London Merchant,* had been seen by the Abbé Prévost in

London in 1731. He wrote appreciatively of it, trans. some scenes in his *Pour et Contre* in 1734. A complete trans. by Clément of Geneva appeared in 1748; Rousseau praised the work. Edward Moore's *Gamester* of 1753 interested Diderot and drew the attention of others that were looking for a dramatic preachment dealing with bourgeois life.

Hence it is no matter for surprise that Diderot (1713–84), in his *Entretiens sur le Fils naturel,* 1757, and in his *De la poésie dramatique,* 1759, called for a new type of tragedy, *la tragédie domestique et bourgeoise.* This tragedy of ordinary middle-class life, *das bürgerliche Trauerspiel* of G. admirers and followers of Diderot, will be in prose. The author will portray *les conditions,* that is, men and women as affected by their social status or profession, *"l'homme de lettres, le philosophe, le commerçant, le juge, l'avocat, le politique, le citoyen, le magistrat, le financier, le grand seigneur, . . . le père de famille."* More naturalness of dialogue and acting is needed, cried Diderot, though in his own practice he did not escape melodramatic exaggeration. Classic declamation is to be avoided. The *confident* should give way to a more convincing technique of exposition. The importance of stage setting was emphasized. Diderot himself did not hesitate to preach; he wanted the new bourgeois drama clearly to point its moral. His own dramatic achievement, *Le Fils naturel* (1757) and *Le Père de famille* (1758), fell far behind his stimulating theories; yet points toward the success of Augier and Dumas *fils* nearly 100 years later. The democratization of tragedy, the opening of the doors of serious drama to all forms of human experience, is the natural result of his original and challenging essays.

Diderot is notable for his breadth of interest, in opera, interpretative dance, painting, sculpture, new forms of literature, the classicism that is passing, or the unknown romanticism that is to be. Reason and feeling in him both are on the *qui vive.* His mind is in continual incandescence, striking off new ideas or illuminating old ones. Sometimes he is chaotic, often *touffu,* a man who for lack of discipline and control never perhaps gave the full measure of his capacities, but better known (through posthumous publication) and better appreciated today than in his own time.

Grimm (1723–1807), in his *Correspondance littéraire* from 1753 until he withdrew in favor of Meister twenty years later, is no doubt the outstanding example of the professional reviewer of books during the 18th c. Since his work was not for publication, but circulated confidentially among subscribers, Grimm could be frank. As the intimate of Diderot, in the very center of Paris literary activities, he knew most of what was going on. Since his judgment was generally balanced and sane, he is more notable for a certain hard-headed rightness in most of his evaluations than for any newness or originality or forward-looking impulse in his semi-monthly letters.

The *Encyclopédie* (1751–72), directed by Diderot and D'Alembert (1717–83) and its *Supplément* (1776–77), with a *Table raisonnée et analytique de l'Encyclopédie* in 1780, reacted against excessive admiration of the ancients and did much to stimulate interest in modern foreign literatures. There are even articles on Arabic, Chinese, and Hebrew literature. The *Encyclopédie* called for a relaxation of the rigid rules of versification, for more emotion (*sensibilité*) in poetry. Marmontel sought to liberalize the three unities, attacked *les confidents,* advocated reforms in conventional staging, costumes, and declamation. He accepted bourgeois tragedy, but in verse. The *Encyclopédie* praised the newly developing *genre* of the novel for its realistic reflection of life. The most important contributors are not in general those best known today. La Harpe (1739–1803), as might be expected from his intransigent classicism, was the most conservative, the German Sulzer (1720–99), the boldest in his literary views. Marmontel (1723–99), though far from an intellectual mastodon, comes next in suggestion of reforms. The Chevalier de Jaucourt (1704–79) was hard-working, devoted to the *Encyclopédie,* but with hardly a spark of originality. In short, the *Encyclopédie* in many ways sums up the criss-cross of ideas in this intellectually active period. The *Encyclopédie* gathered these diverse ideas together, codified them, put them before the public in a single great work of reference, impressive and influential by its very bulk and by its semi-official character as a summation of knowledge and opinion in its day.

Jean-Jacques Rousseau (1712–78), important in his general influence, hardly counts as a literary critic. He prepared the way, however, for Romanticism and a new literary criticism with Mme. de Staël (1766–1817) and Chateaubriand (1768–1848) at the beginning of the 19th c. An early significant work of Mme. de Staël is her *Lettres sur les ouvrages et le caractère de J.-J. Rousseau* (1788). Her emphasis upon relativity and literary relationships (*les rapports*) in the important *De la littérature* (1800) goes back to such works as Montesquieu's *Esprit des lois* (1748). Much pre-Romanticism, unconscious naturally, developed at this time. André Chénier (1762–94), a victim of the guillotine under Robespierre, again shows the clash of the old and the new. His admiration for Greek literature was intense and vivid. Yet he was shocked, like Voltaire, by *"ces convulsions barbares, . . . ces expressions monstrueuses, . . . ces idées énormes et gigantesques, . . . ces disparates bizarres, ces incohérences sauvages"* (Paul Dimoff, *André Chénier*, II 341 f.) of Shakespeare and *"les poètes du Nord."* Chénier is *le dernier des classiques,* not *le premier des romantiques,* but he is a classicist of original and vigorous genius.

This, however, was a dying gasp of the old order in literature. The 18th c. had undermined classicism as a dominant and unyielding system. Relativity and cosmopolitanism would soon appear more clearly than ever in Mme. de Staël's *De la littérature* (1800). Reason could play a role, but not a reason based upon fixed canons of taste. Feeling and intuition must have their place. For a new age swept by Revolution, Mme. de Staël can demand a new literature.

Vial and Denise, *Idées et doctrines littéraires du XVIIIe siècle,* 4th ed., 1926; H. Rigault, *Hist. de la querelle des anciens et des modernes,* new ed., 1859; J. Rocafort, *Les doctrines litt. de l'Encyclopédie,* 1890; D. Mornet, *"La Question des règles au 18e siècle," Rev. d'Hist. litt. de la Fr.,* 1914; P. Chaponnière, "Les critiques et les poétiques au 18e siècle," *Ibid.,* 1916; J. R. Miller, *Boileau en Fr. au 18e siècle,* 1942. George R. Havens.

Nineteenth Century. (1800–1914). Three figures dominate this period: Sainte-Beuve, Renan, Taine. The latter two enjoyed in their maturity a prestige extending far beyond literary criticism, comparable to that of Voltaire and Rousseau. Their credit has waned since, whereas Sainte-Beuve, their predecessor and teacher, continues to be widely consulted and quoted even by those whom his reputation or temperament or occasional lapses annoy. All three represent with significant variations aspects of relativism, appraisal in terms of circumstances, one of the main trends of the age and intimately connected with new views of history and science.

The pioneer relativist of the sequence is Mme. de Staël (1766–1817); the first document, her *De la littérature considérée dans ses rapports avec les institutions sociales* (1800). Her proposition, literature the expression of society, had already been suggested by Bonald in 1796; some of her views recall Montesquieu. Her faith in progress and enthusiasm for chronology made her place L. literature above Gr. Exuberant generalizer (inspiring Hugo in *Préface de Cromwell,* 1827) she somewhat simply divided literature in two, Southern and Northern, classical and romantic, transplanted and indigenous. Her preference is for the North with its subjectivity and "sense of the infinite"; her masterpiece in criticism, *De l'Allemagne* (1810) set before Fr. a new model; her Teutonism and interest in *Kulturgeschichte* were influential at home and abroad (*e.g.,* in Am. Ticknor; Prescott). She was a brilliant, genuinely cosmopolitan spirit.

Another innovator, somewhat in spite of himself, Chateaubriand (1768–1848), started in criticism as a champion of the old order; he wanted selection, and no monsters (*Atala,* 1801, Pref.), insisted in one mood that literature was sinking into barbarism. He was close to Joubert (1754–1824), Platonic idealist of delicacy and strength, definitely unsympathetic with moderns, and published a selection of Joubert's *Pensées* (1838). But the enchantment of his style (Augustin Thierry relates in a famous passage how *Les Martyrs,* 1809, made history come alive to him), and a plea for "the great and difficult criticism of beauties rather than the petty criticism of faults" (echoed in the *Préf. de Cromwell*) stimulated the new school, allied him to it. He wrote of the relation of Christianity to art and literature in *Le Génie du christianisme* (1802).

Lesser personages took fairly definite stands as the century advanced, for or against the new tendencies. Villemain (1790–1867) continued Mme. de Staël, played a role in the founding of comparative literature and in giving the previous century its place in the history of ideas (*Tableau de la litt. fr. au XVIIIe siècle,* 1828). On the other side stood Gustave Planche (1808–57), purist, harsh, displeased with his contemporaries (many articles in the *Revue des deux mondes,* 1831–57); and Désiré Nisard (1806–88), full of nostalgia for the good taste of the 17th century, unwilling to consider literature in terms of the local and temporal and later esteemed by the dogmatic Brunetière for precisely that reason (Nisard, *Histoire de la litt. fr.*, 1844–61). Jules Janin (1804–74) was superficial and jovial enough to be called for a while, no doubt chiefly by readers of similar temper, the "prince of critics." But the depth, as well as the occasional acerbity, of his almost exact contemporary Sainte-Beuve (1804–69) was early recognized by the discerning; his mastery has, however, not remained unchallenged. Sainte-Beuve was for a few years close to Fr. Romanticism and intimate with Hugo, whom however at the very beginning of their careers he charged amicably with abuse of the colossal. His *Tableau historique et critique de la poésie fr. et du théâtre fr. au XVIe siècle* (1828) was meant to provide the Romanticists with a distinguished heritage. Even as a poet Sainte-Beuve is dubious of *spectacles sublimes,* treads the common path, is something of a Wordsworthian realist. He turned more and more toward objective appraisal of Romanticists; his *Chateaubriand et son groupe littéraire* (lectures in Belgium, 1848–49) questioned the magician without denying his magic; it is headed by an epigraph from Chateaubriand himself: "The writers of our epoch have in general been placed too high." Ernest Seillière (1866–1955), a later, fecund commentator who hated Romanticism and all its works, produced a book about Sainte-Beuve as "agent, judge, and accomplice" of the Romantic evolution; the critic clearly passed through the first two stages but the final charge is highly debatable. Sainte-Beuve is frequently called the great doctor of relativity, speaks himself of metamorphoses, numerous adaptations to new circumstances. There is indeed a bewildering variety in the thousand articles about some 500 authors, artists, and statesmen now collected in more than 50 volumes (of which the most frequently consulted are the work of his full maturity: *Causeries du Lundi,* 15 v., 1848–61; *Nouveaux Lundis,* 13 v., 1861–69). This record is entirely in keeping with the century's interest in details and may seem a good example of "surrender of essence to miscellany" (Santayana). Certainly Sainte-Beuve was distrustful of system, said the word *synthétique* is not French, refused to compose a History of French literature. His method required, first of all, scholarly scientific exactitude in the investigation of all particulars of an individual writer's history. But the ultimate result is a gallery of portraits where technique becomes art and where the moralist, in his wisdom, seems a 19th c. Montaigne. It is commonly admitted, however, that Sainte-Beuve was least wise about some of his contemporaries, and conspicuously misunderstood Balzac, Flaubert, Baudelaire. (Baudelaire himself was an understanding and brilliant critic, even though not a practicing professional.)

Port-Royal (first presented in lectures at Lausanne, 1837–38, constantly revised during the author's lifetime) is Sainte-Beuve's *magnum opus.* He turns back from Romanticists and other contemporaries to study patiently, exhaustively, a group of men and women, the Jansenists of 17th c. France, to whom modern relativism could have been nothing short of sin. His interest is double: that of the scholar-critic; that of a man hoping to discover for his own benefit, even salvation, a way to wisdom. From the point of view of strictly literary criticism the most important parts of *Port-Royal* are those that deal with men like Pascal (by contrast Montaigne) and Racine; Sainte-Beuve once referred to his book as *"une méthode pour traverser l'époque."* His preference is for Montaigne even though Montaigne represents "nature without grace"; he is far from a convert, but he writes with anguish of the disappearance from France of a Jansenist element that might have anchored to some kind of stability "nos mobiles et brillantes générations françaises."

The influence of Sainte-Beuve has naturally been various and extensive. The new edition of his letters (*Correspondance générale,* 1935; prepared by Jean Bonnerot) which is the last word of scientific literary scholarship of the Sainte-Beuve canon, shows the critic's multitudinous relations with contemporaries. Edmond Schérer (1815–89), writer for *Le Temps,* great admirer of his colleague Sainte-Beuve, who actively sponsored him, was outside the main tradition but important in his own right: a Protestant theologian who had turned to literature, he was effective as critic of ideas (*Etudes crit. sur la litt. contemporaine,* 10 v., 1863–95). Harking back to Romanticism was Barbey d'Aurevilly (1808–89), brilliant virtuoso. Also against mid-century tastes was J. J. Weiss (1827–97), author of a famous article, *De la litt. brutale* (1858). Sainte-Beuve's direct and great successors were his close friends Renan and Taine.

Ernest Renan (1823–92), trained for the priesthood, became passionately devoted to scientific learning, remained something of a mystic. It was in one of his less mystic moods that he spoke of the *Corpus Inscriptionarum Semiticarum* as his major achievement. He did not engage in much strictly literary criticism (*cf.* however *De la poésie des races celtiques,* 1854, and numerous contributions to the *Histoire litt. de la France par les Bénédictins,* 1862–93) but he helped set the tone for historical and literary studies for a generation. His great historical works (*Hist. des origines du christianisme,* 1863–81; *Hist. du peuple d'Israël,* 1887–93) apply relativism to religion; the famous *Vie de Jésus* (v. 1 of the first series) places the founder of Christianity in his environment so picturesquely that one realizes the scientist in Renan has yielded to the gifted artist. The quality of his imagination and his genius for multiplying distinctions are already evident in his youthful *Patrice* (1849, fragment of a novel); Faguet, addicted to affirmations, later called him the most intelligent man of the century. The book that contains his scientific creed *in extenso* is *l'Avenir de la science* (1848, pub. 1890) upon which he frequently drew for subsequent writings; in the preface he makes the often quoted reference to a time when literary history will replace literature (he was too much the artist himself to mean this in the bald sense in which Lanson and others have criticized it).

The writing of Hippolyte Adolphe Taine (1828–93) is colorful and dynamic, but he had little of the sensitivity of Renan and Sainte-Beuve; he is determinedly scientific. His first work (*Essai sur les Fables de la Fontaine,* 1853, extensively revised later) is not a book about poetry, he says, but "a study of Beauty and what is worse, a Sorbonne thesis." In the *Essai sur Tite-Live* (1856) he contrasts a modern, scientific, German concept of history with the artist's point of view of Antiquity (Livy is the *"historien-orateur"*). At a very early age he took an oath with himself constantly to reexamine his own first principles; if he did so he constantly found them good—whence certain weaknesses and impressive strength. Full of the Hegelian idea of "becoming," scrupulous investigator of "conditions," he launched himself upon a career of energetic generalizations, notably about English literature and about the evolution of modern French. The Introduction to the *Hist. de la litt. anglaise* (1864–69) was first (1863) an essay on the present and future of history; here he offered the often quoted deterministic analogy about "vice and virtue being products like vitriol and sugar" (a formula he later regretted because he felt it was misunderstood to mean identity of spirit and matter), and outlined his method for studying literature as a resultant of circumstances (*race, milieu, moment*). Most commentators (including Sainte-Beuve) are sure he goes much too far, but most modern scholars and many critics still make extensive use of the method (*cf.* in Am. in the 20th c. critics like Edmund Wilson and Harry Levin). His studies of Eng. writers are stimulating, although Taine often exemplifies his own apothegm that any fixed idea becomes a false idea. The critic made other applications of his theories in his *Philosophie de l'art* (1882) and in his *Origines de la France contemporaine* (1875–94), an indictment of the French Revolution. Renan was accused, too lightly, of having turned dilettante in his later years; no such charge was heard against Taine, who remained the stern and often effective crusader.

Emile Zola (1840–1903) applied determinism to literature in his own way, with plans for the reform of human nature (*Le Roman expérimental,* 1880, heralding naturalism). He considered himself a disciple of Taine as well as of the physiologist Claude Bernard, but Taine said he did not care to recognize his "son." Scientific methods were continued more soberly and more authentically in the works of the great Fr. medievalist Gaston Paris (1839–1903) and of the indefatigable and discriminating Gustave Lanson (1857–1934) whose important *Hist. de la litt. fr.* was first published in 1894, and his *Manuel bibliographique de la litt. fr. moderne* in 1909–14. For some two generations Lanson's methods prevailed among professional students of French literature. Emile Faguet (1847–1916), also a university professor, was much less a forthright scientist; he was a vigorous and lucid manipulator of clear ideas, actively against the *philosophes* (*Dix-huitieme siècle,* 1890), definitely for the classical age, and for some of his contemporaries (*Politiques et moralistes du dix-neuvieme siècle,* 1891–99), not enthusiastic about democracy (*le Culte de l'incompetence,* 1910).

Paul Bourget (1852–1935) put Taine into a novel (Adrien Sixte in *Le Disciple,* 1889) in which he attacked extremes of determinism, but he was a disciple himself and shared Taine's objections to the Revolution. Gifted as a critic, he now seems more significant in that field than in fiction. His first *Essais de psychologie contemporaine* (1883) are probably his best; his practice of analysing authors as "signs" of a mood current in society relates him to Taine and Mme. de Staël. Fernand Brunetière (1849–1906) seemed to establish the union of 19th c. science and art by becoming a literary Darwinian and studying a *genre* as though it were an organism (*l'Evolution de la poésie lyrique en Fr.*, 1894; *Les Epoques du théâtre fr.*, 1892). But after a trip to Rome he wrote (1895) of the "bankruptcy of science" and became more and more the eloquent polemicist dedicated to social and religious causes (*Discours de combat*, 1900–07). He attacked Renan and the toying with fine distinctions: "*pas de nuances, il faut choisir*" (*Cinq lettres sur Ernest Renan*, 1903). His oratory and his asperity were famous. Brunetière was long the editor-in-chief of the conservative and slightly Olympian *Revue des deux mondes*. Other faithful collaborators of the *RDM* were René Doumic (1860–1937), lucidly caustic, and Victor Giraud (1868–1953), critic of critics (valuable study of Taine, 1900; he considered Sainte-Beuve a "secondary" nature, over-refined, and has himself been called somewhat without subtlety).

Brunetière once engaged in lively controversy with two men who represented another consequence of relativism and delicate shadings, the impressionistic group: Anatole France (1844–1924) and Jules Lemaître (1853–1914). France felt that a critic cannot be objective; in his own criticism (*La Vie litt.*, 1887–93) he describes the entirely specific, circumstanced, and spontaneous adventures of his own soul. But underneath there is a steady, classical humanistic taste; his impressionism is far from whimsical although there may be a touch of whimsy in his remark that criticism will finally absorb all other literary genres. Lemaître took for an epigraph Sainte-Beuve's image of the critical spirit as a river winding through and reflecting various landscapes. His studies (*les Contemporaines*, 8 v., 1885–95; *Impressions de théâtre*, 10 v., 1888–98) have the grace and strength of the French tradition of genteel culture. Whatever the first appearances, neither man wanders very far from certain French standards of good taste.

Remy de Gourmont (1858–1915), called "ultra-æsthetic" by Irving Babbitt (who did not have that weakness), has not always been credited with his real importance. He was fascinated by æsthetics but also by almost every problem of civilization. For 25 years chief editor of the *Mercure de France*, he examined current tendencies with tolerance, bound himself to no group, proved himself heir to a long French tradition of perspicacity (*l'Esthétique de la langue fr.*, 1899; *la Culture des idées*, 1901; *Epilogues*, 1903–10; *Promenades litt.*, 1904–13).

A belligerent standard-bearer of another order was Charles Maurras (1868–1962), guiding spirit of the royalist newspaper *Action Française*. Maurras had three hates: the Reformation, the Revolution, Romanticism; he brought all the resources of his brilliant mind to bear upon vulnerability in these movements, and was widely read by people who had no part of his politics (some of his chief articles of 1898–1904 are reprinted in *Romantisme et Révolution*, 1922, pub. in a series of which the title is a program: *Les Ecrivains de la Renaissance fr.*). Associated with Maurras for a time was Pierre Lasserre (1867–1930), author of a doctoral thesis that provoked much discussion, *Le Romantisme fr.* (1907), a hostile survey of this "revolution in sentiments and ideas in the 19th century."

This whole period of criticism (1800–1914) has a kind of pattern: Romanticism; historical relativism; scientific dedication to assembling innumerable facts which would then speak for themselves—with sharp reactions in favor of one or another set of permanent values. The fluctuations elude any bare summary, partly because the best of these critics are consummate artists in discrimination. There is no adequate and objective book on the period.

F. Brunetière, *l'Evolution de la crit. depuis la ren. jusqu'à nos jours*, 1890 (through Taine only); I. Babbitt, *Masters of Modern Fr. Crit.*, 1913; L. Levrault, *La Crit. lit.*, 1910; A. Belis, *La Crit. a la fin du 19e siècle*, 1926. HORATIO SMITH.

Twentieth Century. Literary history received a great impetus after 1900, when the French reorganized their universities and adopted many features of the German scholarship which, in philology, in exegesis, in history of ideas and culture, had displayed, on one side, far more precise rigor, on the other, a more philosophical bent for ambitious hypotheses than had any other European nation. Most of the Sorbonne professors would have to be enumerated if one were to mention the outstanding representatives of that historical scholarship. The fields most sedulously tilled were the French eighteenth century, which earlier neo-classical critics like Faguet and Brunetière had slighted, and foreign literatures, which then drew a number of the finest scholar-critics of France: Henri Hauvette on Italian letters, Charles Andler, Henri Lichtenberger, Edouard Spenlé on German literature and culture, Emile Legouis, Louis Cazamian on the literature of Britain. After 1920, as the dream of a culturally united Europe drew crowds of foreign students to Paris, Fernand Baldensperger and Paul Hazard gave much prestige to comparative literature. The characteristics of the works published by those French scholars between 1900 and 1940 are: a strong orientation toward a philosophical and sociological interpretation of literature, under the influence of Henri Bergson (1859–1941) and of Emile Durkheim (1858–1917): also a meticulous scrutiny of the texts themselves and of their historical milieu, as practised by the master of literary history, Gustave Lanson (1857–1934). The latter's most seminal essays have been collected posthumously in *Essais de Méthode, de Critique et d'Histoire littéraire,* 1966. A reaction has since set in against some excess of positivism and of historical perspective in the work of these scholars. French criticism has remained to this day the almost exclusive preserve of professors: those trained in philosophy have lately replaced the men of an earlier generation who had been firmer believers in biography, in "explication de textes," and in history.

The most perceptive critics of the first three decades of the century were, however, men of letters who, unprofessionally, expressed themselves occasionally on authors of the past with whom they felt strong affinities, or brilliant free-lance writers who, discarding any pretence of objectivity, championed a cause or a group. The first category includes almost all the luminaries of French literature, who verify the famous statement of Baudelaire that every poet has a critic in himself and fatally turns critic. A poet and dramatist like Paul Claudel, a novelist like Marcel Proust, a fanciful playwright like Giraudoux, an adventurer like André Malraux, even the impetuous founder of Surrealism, André Breton, have all been at some time remarkable critics. The most incisive, but also the most negative, of these "critiques-créateurs" was Paul Valéry, both in his abstruse poetics and in his onslaughts on Pascal, on Baudelaire, on the laxness of some romantics. André Gide's literary judgments, often inconsistent and whimsical, but rich in insights, have also wielded much influence on his group of the *Nouvelle Revue Française,* founded in 1909.

The two most profound critics of the years 1910–1930 had been, for a time at least, close to Gide: Jacques Rivière (1886–1925) and Charles du Bos (1882–1939). The former left thoughtful studies of Rimbaud, of Proust, and diverse essays gathered in *Etudes* (1912) and *Nouvelles Etudes* (1947). His pliability enabled him to espouse successive, even opposite, causes. At a time when Brunetière and critics of the political right (Charles Maurras, Pierre Lasserre, Ernest Seillière) had been misled by their dogmatism into colossal errors of judgment, Rivière's flexibility allowed him to advocate the new post World War I authors. Charles du Bos was likewise a very personal, often profound reader, not only of French authors, but also of Goethe, Keats, Pater, Rilke. His early *Approximations* have stood the test of time remarkably well: he lost much of his vigor after his conversion to Catholicism, when he based his judgments on moral criteria.

Albert Thibaudet (1874–1936) started his career around 1910 with the first solid study on Mallarmé, then with volumes on Bergson, Barrès and Maurras. He became the regular literary commentator in the *Nouvelle Revue Française.* He practised a descriptive criticism, pleasantly rambling, animated with zest and fond of grouping authors according to geographical and historical data. His racy Epicurean enjoyment of letters recalls George Saintsbury: he seldom undertook to discover new talents.

The influential names of the reviewers and critics in the monthlies and weeklies were Paul Souday (1869–1929) in *Le Temps,* Emile Henriot in *Le Monde* (1889–1961), Edmond Jaloux (1878–1949) in *Les Nouvelles Littéraires,* the latter at his best when appraising foreign literatures. P. H. Simon, more recently in *Le Monde,* and André Rousseaux are more heavy-handed and not strikingly open to innovations. The Jesuit Father André Blanchet, in *Etudes* and in three volumes entitled *La Littérature et le Spirituel,* shows more independence of views, as does, in *Le Figaro Littéraire,* the eclectic, Belgian-born Robert Kanters.

New breezes blew across French criticism in the years immediately preceding World War II. Three philosophers inspired the new trends: Gaston Bachelard (1884–1962), J. P. Sartre, and Claude Lévi-Strauss. Bachelard came to criticism after having made his reputation as a philosopher of science. His own taste is often unsure: he resorts to very mediocre poets to illustrate his theories. He is better when he speculates on imagination as a function of perception itself. He attempts to return to prescientific categories and to the four basic elements of earth, air, fire, and water. Phenomenology became to him, in his later years, even more fecund than psychoanalysis as a principle of elucidation of poetic imagination. His suggestions, even when arbitrary, have impressed Poulet, Richard, Barthes and others among the critics of 1950–1970.

Sartre's early critical essays on Faulkner, Dos Passos, Mauriac, Ponge, collected in the successive volumes of *Situations,* were unusually keen. They formed an integral part of his existentialist system and constituted what the French call a "critique de combat," militant and ironical. His *Qu'est-ce que la littérature?* (1948) is the most significant redefinition of the purpose and of the duties of literature in the modern world, hostile to art for art's sake and to the dilettantism of Gide, Valéry, and Proust. Sartre then became blatantly unfair and acrimonious in his semi-psychoanalytical analyses of Baudelaire and of Flaubert; he descried in those authors, afflicted with a mother-complex, the very bourgeois features that he hated in himself. Lévi-Strauss, a philosophical anthropologist, has not actually written literary criticism, but his stress on the structures that underlie even the most primitive cultures has impressed his admirers among the structuralists of the middle sixties.

Other theoreticians of criticism have failed to impress their judgment on literature as lastingly as Bachelard or Sartre. Charles Mauron (b. 1899), a chemist who came late to literary studies (after a laboratory accident that made him blind) undertook to rest his approach to poetry upon Freudian views. His volumes on Baudelaire, Mallarmé, but especially on Racine (1957), while diffuse and pedestrian, may well be the most cogent application of psychoanalysis to French authors. Marie Bonaparte had treated chiefly of E. A. Poe, and Jean Delay uses Freudian concepts merely as an adjunct in his biography of Gide. Mauron formulated his doctrine in his *Introduction à la Psychocritique,* shortly before his death. Maurice Blanchot (b. 1907) matured slowly and has remained a solitary figure. To him, as to some Germans, literature is a process of creative destruction. To know an object is to annihilate all else, abstracting it from the other objects and replacing it with a sign. A writer aims at destroying the clichés of language, hence at incommunicability. His logical refuge would be silence, or death. Blanchot owes much to Hölderin, Nietzsche, Kafka, Heidegger. His best essays in his early, and not yet over-obscure, volumes, *Faux-pas* (1943), *La Part du Feu* (1949), and "La Littérature ou la Droit à la Mort" in *L'Espace Littérature* (1955) are the most pregnant, the most anguished of our age. Since then, like many other philosophical critics, he has tended to lose sight of the æsthetic and sensuous qualities of the work of art.

The Catholic critics have not as a rule proved quite so doctrinaire. None since 1930 has fallen into such gross errors as had Maurras, Lasserre, and Massis. Jacques Maritain (b. 1882) has written little criticism, except on aspects of modern poetry in *Situation de la Poésie,* 1938, and *Creative Intuition in Art and Poetry,* originally published in English in 1953. His point of view is broadly Thomistic. Etienne Gilson (b. 1884), a great specialist of medieval philosophy, has, with combativity and wit, written brilliant volumes on Dante, on Descartes, and on modern artists (*L'Ecole des Muses,* 1951). Albert Béguin, a Swiss who became a convert to Catholicism, did much to promote a keener insight into German romanticism among the French. He then reinterpreted with warmth and passionate partiality Pascal, Nerval, Bernanos, and guided the important review *Esprit.* Among the philosophical minds that were drawn to literature, none has been so open, so judicious, so careful to eschew systems, as Gaeton Picon (b. 1915). His books on Malraux, his essays on Balzac, Retz, Proust, Camus, and others collected in *L'Usage de la Lecture* (3 vols. 1960–63) are among the most modest and the most lucid to have come out of France, at a time when the French seemed bent on beating the Germans at their game of abstruse and cloudy philosophizing. His rival might have been Claude-Edmonde Magny (1912–1966), whose early works on French and American fiction were highly promising, but were not followed up.

Most French critics in the past, Taine and Brunetière excepted, had considered their muse as a mere handmaid to imagination and bowed to the creators, even when, like Sainte-Beuve, they were jealous of them.

Since the middle of the present century, perhaps due to some flagging of inventiveness in the creators, probably also because of the irruption of philosophy into every walk of life, critics have displayed an assurance bordering on arrogance. They seldom condescend to review and assess current books, to assist the writers or to rally an audience around them. They prefer to analyze abstrusely their favorite authors of former days (Racine, Laclos, Stendhal, Mallarmé *et al.*) and the few foreign writers naturalized in France and, à propos of them, to erect ambitious theories on consciousness, on structure, on language, on "the contestation" of literature or on the "unveiling of being." Their criticism has become an autonomous creation: its practitioners seem anxious to show how much more obscure, or profound, than the artists they can be. Their métier has become a very technical one, relying upon epistemology, anthropology, linguistics, and theoretical æsthetics. Several of their most significant works have come from Switzerland, and that "new criticism" is sometimes designated as "the Geneva School." Sarah Lawall, in an excellent book on them, calls them *Critics of Consciousness* and characterizes them thus: "They look upon literature as an act, not as an object." Their primary interest is philosophical and psychological, and they have little in common with the more analytical "new critics" of the 1940's in America, who unravelled ambiguities, hidden symmetries, and alleged symbolic secrets in the works. The oldest and least dogmatic among them was Marcel Raymond (b. 1897), whose interests embraced Renaissance poetry, the baroque, Rousseau, and modern poetry. His successors at the University of Geneva have refined his method: Jean Starobinski, trained in medicine and psychiatry, on Montesquieu and Rousseau, and Jean Rousset, in his provocative studies on the French baroque. George Poulet (b. 1912), Belgian by birth, successively attached to the universities of Edinburgh, Johns Hopkins, and Zurich, is more abstract and scholastic. In his *Etudes sur le Temps humain* (1949 to 1964), he embraced almost every major French writer, showing him as revealed best in his grasp of space and time. Chronology is disregarded in the process. Quotations, often out of context, are used to present a view of the author that is somewhat arbitrary, but illuminating. Jean-Pierre Richard (b. 1922) followed along the line of Bachelard and Poulet, but less arbitrarily, in his attempt to define the manner in which a writer seizes and transforms reality, his creation passing from a shapeless to a formal state.

The critics upon whom the label of Structuralists was affixed around 1960–65 are more bellicose. They reject uncompromisingly all inquiry into sources and influences, any dwelling upon the historical perspective. Through key-words, metaphors, symbols, they detect a system of imagery and patterns of thought in a creative writer. They are not interested in the finished work, but in the structure that underlies it. Sensuous and voluptuous enjoyment seems banished from their approach. They rebuild each author according to a pattern which they superimpose upon him and thus tend to negate the fluidity of the work and to imprison the creator inside a structure once and for all established. Roland Barthes is the most talented of these structuralist critics, with his *Degré Zéro de L'Ecriture* (1953), if not in his rather erratic *Racine* (1963). Lucien Goldmann (b. 1913) has more warmth and has revealed an original view of Pascal and Racine: his later excursions into the sociology of the novel, inspired by George Lukacs, are more adventurous and expressed in turgid prose. Serge Doubrovsky has no less philosophical profundity, but far more pliability and fairness even when he is polemical, as in his *Pourquoi la Nouvelle Critique?*. Jacques Derrida and Gérard Genette, respectively in *L'Ecriture et la Différence* (1967) and in *Figures* (1966) are the most promising among the doctrinaires of structuralism. Their methods, inspired by linguistics at its most scientific and by symbolic logic, are austere and forbidding, their style abstruse. But they fulfill one purpose of criticism that the French have never ceased pursuing: to arouse lively debates around the work of art.

Serge Doubrovsky, *Pourquoi la Nouvelle Critique?*, 1966; Mikel Dufrenne, *Pour l'Homme*, 1968; Michel Foucault, *Les Mots et les Choses*, 1966; Sarah W. Lawall, *Critics of Consciousness*, 1968; Henri Peyre, *The Failures of Criticism*, 1967; *Quatre Conférences sur la Nouvelle Critique* (Studi Francesi, Torino), 1968; W. Fowlie, *The Fr. Critic, 1549–1967*, 1968. Henri Peyre.

GERMAN CRITICISM. To the Age of Enlightenment. In the last chapter of his *Gospel Book* (*Liber evangeliorum*, c. 870) Otfrid of Weissenburg (ca. 800–70) rebukes, as envious, future critics of his work. He identifies his plight with that of St. Jerome (ca. 340–420). Then, with an expression of confidence in the good will of the more sensible part of his audience, Otfrid presents the prototype of those innumerable prefaces and postscripts in which authors of all kinds and ages practice a sort of anti-critical prophylaxis. It is worthy of note that Otfrid cannot conceive of anything but envy as motivating a critical attitude toward his work. This, too, is a primitive view that persists through the centuries and remains discernible in ages of an otherwise more constructive conception of the task of the critic. With the constitution of a literature-minded social stratum, first knightly and then bourgeois, partly conditioning and partly conditioned by the increased æsthetic subtlety of *MHG* minnesong and epic, more refined standards of taste evolved, *e.g.,* as seen in Gottfried von Strassburg's discussion of contemporary poets in his epic *Tristan* (ca. 1210).

The Renaissance brought no blossoming of G. literary criticism comparable to that of It. and Fr. The *Meistergesang* went on elaborating the complex critical canons and doomed the tradition to stagnation in a cul-de-sac. Expressions of a critical attitude must be sought in contemporary poetics like H. Bebel's (1472–1518) *Ars versificandi* (1506). Indeed, the *Poetice* (1561) of Scaliger, which marks the consolidation of pseudo-Aristotelian dictatorship in European letters, was from a G. point of view, although a foreign, by no means an alien factor.

Throughout the 17th c. the domains of criticism and poetics remain largely undifferentiated. Criticism was a prescriptive force regulating matters of linguistic usage, style, versification. The age of the baroque, of Marinism, in G. mainly of the 2d Silesian School, offered more than enough material for this approach, which joined forces with the richly developed contemporary satire to produce works like Johann Balthasar Schupp's (1610–61) *Ineptus Orator*; the 4th of the *Scherzgedichte* (1652) of Johann Lauremberg (1590–1658); G. W. Sacer's *Reime dich oder ich fresse dich* (1665). There also appeared what might be called the defense and "illustration" of the G. language, esp. among the *Sprachgesellschaften.* Nonetheless, the dependence of G. letters on foreign models became still more pronounced. Earlier, the *Buch von der deutschen Poeterey* (1624) by Martin Optiz (1597–1639) had urged the closest imitation of antiquity. It had rejected the autochthonous verse tradition in favor of the French Alexandrine; its doctrine involved a science of expression and description, which was the prerogative of men of learning. Hence the achievements of the Fr. invested their principles with absolute validity. Their emulation in G. signified not so much an imitation of foreign models as an expression of belief in immutable standards. It is in this sense that Fr. influence was definitely established by the turn of the century (Friedrich von Canitz, 1654–99; Christian Wernicke, 1661–1725).

The heir of this development was Johann Christoph Gottsched (1700–66). From the university at Leipzig his rule extended virtually undisputed over all of G. letters. His verdicts and decrees were published in a number of critical journals, *e.g., Vernünftige Tadlerinen* (1725–27). In 1730 he published his code, the *Versuch einer kritischen Dichtkunst vor die Deutschen.* This has been called a cookbook of literature, which (if we disregard the slur upon its merits) indicates the normative purpose of all of Gottsched's criticism. It was a vulgarization of the Wolffian vulgarization of Leibnitz' thought. Since poetry is an imitation of nature and since nature is eminently plausible, everything must be banned from poetry that is not believable, in the naïvest sense of the term. Thus the absurd, but potentially highly poetic, *Hanswurst* must go from the German stage. In a similar vein, Gottsched insisted on the strictest adherence to the 3 unities.

Gottsched's school produced one critic of note, Johann Elias Schlegel (1719–49), one of the *Bremer Breiträger, i.e.,* those who contributed to the *Neue Beiträge zum Vergnügen des Verstandes und des Witzes* (Bremen, 1744–57). Schlegel's comparison of Shakespeare and a 17th c. G. dramatist (*Verleichung Shakespeares und Andreas Gryphs,* 1744) marks him a precursor of Lessing; his appreciation of the absurdity of transplanting the principles of Fr. Neo-Classicism to G. soil, his experiments with Shakespearean blank verse, his general grasp of the potential significance of Shakespeare for G. letters make him, indeed, the most promising opponent rather than a faithful disciple of Gottsched.

A noisier (not therefore more significant) sign of impending revolt was Gottsched's quarrel with the Swiss critics Johann Jakob Bodmer (1698–1783) and Jakob Breitinger (1701–76). In 1732 Bodmer had presented his prose translation of Milton's *Paradise Lost*; in 1740 by his essay on the miraculous in poetry (*Von dem Wunderbaren in der Poesie*), he justified his claim that this sort of literary production could be called poetry although not within the narrow limits of Gottsched's classicism. Gottsched retorted; but the Swiss were unexpectedly re-enforced by the appearance of a G. Milton, Friedrich Gottlieb Klopstock (1724–1803) whose epic *Der Messias* began to appear in 1748. The opponents did not mean the same thing by "poetry"; their conception of the task of criticism was likewise of a fundamentally different nature. The Swiss taught appreciation and enjoyment of literary values where Gottsched explained the tricks of the trade. In a way this quarrel played in G. letters the same role as the *Querelle des anciens et des modernes* in Fr. It was symptomatic of a slow transition from *la critique par les règles* to *la critique de sentiment*.

1750–1830. It is customary to see the beginnings of modern G. criticism in Gotthold Ephraim Lessing (1729–81). He should also be understood as presenting a climactic summary of the preceding age. Among his precursors, Christian Liscow (1701–60) must be mentioned. Furthermore, Lessing's first major critical contribution, the *Briefe die neueste Literatur betreffend* (1759 f.), was an enterprise organized by Friedrich Nicolai (1733–1811), who continued on a somewhat higher level where Gottsched was being forced to leave off. Lessing's aim in these letters is not in basic disagreement with the prescriptive dogmatism of the older tradition, nor is his best-known work, the *Laokoon, oder über die Grenzen der Malerei und Poesie*, 1766. The epoch-making character of this work does not lie in the incomparable cogency of its argument nor in its lucid conclusions about the inviolable limits of the individual arts. Indeed, their non-existence was to become an essential assertion of the romantic dogma. Lessing's major contribution was that he derived his conclusions from an analysis of what he knew to be great works of art, that he did not apply previously conceived criteria to the works. Here we recognize the lessons taught by Johann Joachim Winckelmann (1717–68).

In the *Hamburgische Dramaturgie* (1767–68), planned as a series of critical essays on the performances of the Hamburg National Theatre but actually elaborated into a basic analysis of dramaturgy, Lessing proceeds not by showing what one should enjoy in a given drama but rather by presenting the drama in its essence and clarifying its intention. Criticism before Lessing was prescriptive and dogmatic; criticism after Lessing was descriptive and appreciative. His own was neither and both. It was æsthetic and thus philosophical. A work of art was for him a microcosm animated by the same manifestations of supreme rationality as the world of our ideas and beliefs. *Die Erziehung des Menschengeschlechts* (*Education of the Human Race*), published *in toto* in 1780, is, with its declaration of faith in universal reason and human progress, the testament no less of a critic than of a deeply religious thinker.

The polar complement to Lessing's critical aggressiveness is the contemporary insistence on the empathetic element in criticism. This trend was marked in Heinrich Wilhelm von Gerstenberg's (1737–1823) so-called Slesvig Letters on Literature (*Briefe über die Merkwürdigkeiten der Literatur*, 1766), but its major impetus probably came from the East, through Johann Georg Hamann (1730–88) and his disciple Johann Gottfried Herder (1744–1803). These men were the critical god-fathers of *Sturm und Drang*. Deeply as the *Stürmer and Dränger* were (and felt) indebted to Lessing, their attitude toward criticism seemed to rebel against everything he stood for. Their reviews are manifestos. Critical ardor found its outlet in attacks on contemporary social and cultural conditions, *e.g.*, in the dramatic satires and farces of young Goethe. The Storm-and-Stress was a youth movement. Its excesses were bound to give way to more moderate views as its representatives attained a more responsible maturity. Yet not one ever abandoned the conviction that criticism must take art as an expression of a given cultural state, that the individual work must thus be considered in its ethical, basically its metaphysical, significance. Schiller's (1759–1805) reviews, *e.g.*, the devastating one of Bürger's collected poems of 1791 (Gottfried August Bürger, 1747–94), are applications of these æsthetic theories (*Briefe über die æsthetische Erziehung des Menschen*, 1793). Goethe's (1749–1832) attitude was more comprehensive and consequently more liberal: works of art, for him, were not basically different from works of nature; both have to be understood simultaneously as self-sufficient organisms and as integral parts of the chain of being. This explains on the one hand how Winckelmann's classicism of antiquity could bear modern fruit in Goethe and on the other how Goethe, in his later years, came to elaborate his critical concept of *Weltliteratur.*

Herder's basic demand was that a work of art be appreciated empathetically in its organic structure and setting. With him, the romantic *Organismusgedanke,* the idea of the organism, attains critical potency. An almost morbid irritability induced Herder to present many of his thoughts in seeming opposition to Lessing. The *Fragmente über die neuere deutsche Literatur* (1776) complement Lessing's *Briefe*; the *Kritische Wälder* (1769), his *Laokoon.* Yet the *Ideen zur Philosophie der Geschichte der Menschheit* (1784 f.) show the basic coördination of Herder's and Lessing's endeavors. They form, together with Lessing's *Die Erziehung des Menschengeschlechts* and Schiller's *Briefe über die æsthetische Erziehung des Menschen,* the triune declaration of faith in humanity of German classical idealism.

G. Romanticism is in its beginnings a purely critical movement. As such, however, it did not originate as a break with the tendencies of the preceding generation. On the contrary: romantic criticism, particularly that of the *Frühromantik,* is best characterized as a synthesis of Lessing and Herder. Friedrich Schlegel (1772–1829) began as a student of Gr. classicism, in Lessing's spirit seeking eternal values. Yet the yield of this search was the wisdom that the historian Herder had never tired of preaching: that works of art are organic representations of a specific genius. Thence Schlegel came to the discovery that we, whose genius is different from that of the Gr., must create differently, to a declaration of independence of the modern creative genius from classical antiquity. This is the gospel that he preached together with his brother August Wilhelm (1767–1845) in the romantic journal *Anthenaeum* (1798–1800).

The all-inclusiveness of the romantic conception of art (Friedrich speaks of a scale of art from a system embracing several vast systems to the naïve sigh of a child) frees the critic from judging. He is an historian and a philosopher; his task is to characterize. The romantic critic has been called the priest of poesy, just as the romantic poet is the priest of mankind. If we add that conversely the romantic poet, at least in theory, never ceased to be a critic, we have the conceptual background of the romantic irony.

Friedrich Schlegel's most representative productions are his characterization of Lessing the critic (1797) as the philosopher, the Spinozist; and his discussion of Goethe's *Wilhelm Meister* (1798) the symptomatic importance of which he felt to be on a par with that of the Fr. revolution, in a different sphere of human endeavor.

August Wilhelm Schlegel's most important contribution to the romantic theory lay in his lectures. After the dissolution of the Jena circle of early romanticists, he expounded the new dogma in his Berlin lectures *Über schöne Literatur und Kunst* (1801 f.). His Viennese lectures *Über dramatische Kunst und Literatur* (1808 f.) are historically more important; they were translated into Fr., Dutch, Eng., It., and they, as much as the book *de l'Allemagne* (1813) by Mme. de Staël, August Wilhelm's disciple, determined the foreign appreciation of G. romanticism. From a G. point of view, however, these lectures show a decline of the romantic spirit. "The history of art," says August Wilhelm, "teaches what has been done. The theory of art explains what should be done." Between them, he reasons further, a third factor is needed if history and theory are not to remain equally barren. "It is criticism that clarifies the history of art and makes the theory of art fruitful." The danger of his principle becomes apparent in its application. The great achievement of romantic criticism had been its emancipation from dogmatic prescription. But when Schlegel imposes his theories on history the result is often something that it is hard not to call *a priori dogmatism,* not necessarily any better than the opposite dogmatism of a Gottsched.

Thus in its later phases Romanticism (the infinite) seeks new bounds. In the elder Friedrich Schlegel, in Adam Müller (1779–1829), in Joseph von Görres (1776–1848), the most remarkable critical mind among the latter romanticists, and in Joseph von Eichendorff (1788–1857) these standards are supplied by political and religious convictions. In them we discern the utilitarian pragmatism of the following generation. ALEXANDER GODE-VON AESCH.

1830 to the present. The year 1830 marks a turning point in the history of German criticism as it does in the history of the literature. A differentiation of functions begins: general literary criticism (*Literaturkritik*), literary history (*Literaturgeschichte*), and literary theory (*Literaturwissenschaft*) become separate disciplines, practiced by different persons. Literary criticism, ranging from the casual book review to the polished literary essay that deals with a book, an author, or a whole period, is henceforth produced largely by writers, journalists, and professional critics; literary history becomes principally the preoccupation of academics; and a new science of literary theory develops in the 20th c., replacing the older rhetoric and poetics but dealing with literature in much broader scope than its forerunners. This too is a product of the universities. The explosion of knowledge that characterizes the 20th c. brings about a division of labor in this new discipline itself: whereas formerly one man wrote a whole poetics, which treated the entire subject of literature as it was conceived at the time, the literary theorist now explores some one aspect of the vast, complex theoretical structure that comprises the science of literary study today.

Actually these three aspects are interdependent. Worthwhile literary history cannot be written without a knowledge of the results obtained by literary theory, and any critic worth his salt knows both literary history and *Literaturwissenschaft.* "In every good book review," wrote Jean Paul Richter, "a good æsthetic is concealed or revealed." Moreover, there is to this day a considerable divergence of opinion about the proper scope of each of the three fields of study and even on the definition of the three terms. And, of course, several functions often converge in the same person; there are academic scholars who are excellent critics and essayists (Ernst Robert Curtius, Walter Jens, Walter Höllerer). On the other hand, most of Paul Ernst's or Bertolt Brecht's criticism is really literary theory, though it seems incongruous to associate these most unacademic writers with so academic a subject. The late Paul Fechter was a literary essayist of distinction; he wrote one of the better histories of German literature and a history of the European drama; and he published two volumes dealing with the theory of literature. Walter Benjamin was a critic, literary historian and literary theorist of rare originality, imagination and depth, as close to a seminal mind as German criticism has produced since its great era. But on the whole, the dissociation of functions has held: the separate disciplines have been cultivated by professional specialists.

A few generalizations:

1.) The period under discussion cannot compare with the great eighteenth century; there are no seminal minds of the stature of a Lessing, Herder, Goethe, Friedrich Schlegel. Modern criticism has revealed much about the nature of literature, has refined many of the ideas of the previous age and staked out new territory to be explored. But this has been the work of lesser minds.

2.) There has been a gradual movement to the view of literature as a purely æsthetic phenomenon, as an art of words rather than a branch of theology or philosophy. This has been carried to the point of proclaiming that literature creates a world of its own by means of language. (Ingarden, Kayser). But there have been many challenges to this view. The æsthetics of content has many persuasive champions, who insist that literature is more than words, that it is about life, embracing political and social life, individual and collective striving. The disciples of this "mimesis" may be social realists of the Marxian persuasion or they may take the view that art does depict life, but not with the eye of the camera.

3.) The influence of philosophy on all branches of criticism has been strong: Hegel, Schopenhauer, Nietzsche, Husserl, and Heidegger have affected critical theory in important ways.

4.) All three branches of criticism have followed the general development of German literature in the period, as represented by the currents *Junges Deutschland* (1830–1850), realism and naturalism (1850–1890), and the idealistic reaction against the positivist spirit that marks German literature and thought after 1890. Those students of the literary scene who view the course of German literature in the twentieth century as a fragmentation into many small movements (impressionism, neo-romanticism, neo-classicism, expressionism, *Neue Sachlichkeit,* etc.) will find the same fragmentation in the development of critical theory.

5.) Throughout the period German criticism is well aware of what is being thought and written elsewhere. And there is reason for believing that German critical ideas have been influential abroad, as they were in the early nineteenth century.

Historical Survey. During the years between the Revolutions of 1830 and 1848 German criticism was vigorously revolutionary in mood. The age of Goethe was seen as the end of an "æsthetic" era. Goethe was criticized for his indifference to contemporary events and social ideals, and the romantics were condemned for their medievalism and their reactionary outlook. Schiller and Jean Paul Richter were lauded as liberals. Criticism was accordingly valued as a vehicle for the promotion of liberal ideals. Journalism became a force in German life; the prominent writers of *Das junge Deutschland* wrote for newspapers or edited journals (Börne, Heine, Gutzkow, Laube). The æsthetic yielded to the ethical as a basic criterion for literary excellence; emphasis shifted from classical beauty to the characteristic and effective, from form to content. Poetry lost ground to prose.

The failure of liberal aspirations after 1848 brought an end to this ferment. The next period (1850–1890) is characterized by a confusion of intellectual currents: scientific materialism and neutral positivism exist side by side with stale, imitative idealism, free thinking with Victorian prudery. The Munich circle of writers hankered again for the Weimar ideal of classical beauty and perfection of form. In this spirit Gustav Freytag (who was certainly not without political concern) wrote his *Technik des Dramas* (1865) and Otto Ludwig his *Shakespeare Studien* (1874) with their polemic against Schiller. But the earlier liberal ideology is found in the writings of Hermann Hettner and Gottfried Keller. And in these years the theory of realism was developed by Stifter and Spielhagen, while Hebbel defended his dramas, which represent a synthesis between classicism (in their form) and the new spirit of realism (in their psychology and problems).

The criticism and literary history of the naturalists (1880–1890) was ideological again, but social rather than political. Once more there was a call for interaction between art and life. The writer was to be the photographer of life and he was to direct his camera at the mean and sordid aspects of modern existence—to reform them. The novel was felt to be the genre best suited for giving a scientifically exact picture of life. The most original contribution to naturalistic criticism came from Arno Holz, the theorist of "consistent naturalism" and the "Sekundenstil" (the technique of describing minutely a scene or event—*e.g.,* a leaf as it falls to the ground).

The European revolt against the spirit of positivism and materialism found an echo in Germany. A revival of idealism (symbolism, neo-romanticism) manifested itself in many forms, both in creative literature and in the various branches of criticism. The great efflorescence of literary theory now began, but neither in general criticism nor in literary history are there any outstanding triumphs to record. The widening breach between liberals and conservatives that was a mark of the Wilhelmine era and the Weimar Republic may be seen in criticism as well. After 1900 Marxian criticism, which had its beginnings in the mid-19th c. with Marx, Engels and Lassalle, grew in importance. The strident, often ugly nationalism that was fostered by Treitschke and others spread in criticism and created the mental atmosphere for literary criticism in the Third Reich.

From 1933 to 1945 German criticism was, like all intellectual life, government controlled; it was assigned the task of promoting National Socialist ideology. The government favored art—heroic, "German" art, anti-democratic, anti-intellectual, anti-Western, anti-individualist. When the National Socialists seized power they found enough writers and critics (including Germanists) to carry out the new ideals. National Socialist criticism was a development of a tradition that goes back at least to the romantic era. At the beginning of our period Wolfgang Menzel was already writing nationalistic, anti-liberal, anti-Semitic literary history. Treitschke (who, though not primarily a critic, exerted considerable influence on literary opinion) sharpened the strident nationalism of German intellectual life. The early literary history of the 19th c. was dominated by political ideology. When this ceased to be liberal-progressive and became chauvinistic, a segment of German criticism took on the same political coloration. Thus the concept "deutsch" became the highest literary (in fact, artistic) criterion, synonymous with spiritual, metaphysical, mystical, Faustian, genuine, deep, beautiful. What the Nazis did was to develop this attitude with a systematic fanaticism undreamed of by the earlier chauvinists.

When intellectual life resumed after 1945, criticism took a new orientation. Practical criticism revived first. The Group of 47 was essentially a mutual society of critics who happened to be professional writers and who practiced pre-publication criticism. The older literary journals, like the *Neue Rundschau,* supplemented by new ones like *Akzente, Neue deutsche Hefte, der Monat, Merkur, die Zeit,* fostered critical writing at a high level, from the book review to the literary essay, without demanding any special bias, literary or political, except opposition to the Nazi past. In recent years the Hamburg newspaper *Die Welt* established a literary supplement, *Die Welt der Literatur,* on the model of the *Times Literary Supplement* and the *New York Times Book Review.* A new type of literary history was written by the novelist and classical scholar Walter Jens. His erudition sits very lightly on him and his broad knowledge of foreign literature gives his writing a cosmopolitan tone that was much needed in Germany. A sprightly, almost racy, style is among his many virtues. Other general critics, like Friedrich Sieburg, Theodor Adorno, Günther Blöcker, and Marcel Reich-Ranicki, have contributed regularly to the literary journals. The juxtaposition of these names indicates that opinion in Western Germany has not been monolithic.

But again it is in the field of literary theory that contemporary Germany has been most productive and original. The publication of such outstanding books as E. R. Curtius' *Europäische Literatur und lateinisches Mittelalter,* Erich Auerbach's *Mimesis* (which must be counted among the fruits of German scholarship), Wolfgang Kayser's *Das sprachliche Kunstwerk* (all three appeared immediately after World War II) and Walter Höllerer's *Zwischen Klassik und Moderne* testifies to the vigor of German scholarship.

To these achievements must be added the work of great scholars like Friedrich Beissner and Friedrich Sengle, who have produced monuments of scholarship in an older philological tradition and have demonstrated an open mind to the latest developments in the world of literary ideas.

Literary criticism in Communist Germany has followed the orthodox Marxian line. Anyone deviating from the party line has incurred the wrath of the official censors. For instance, when the government objected to the pacifist thesis of Brecht's play, *Das Verhör des Lukullus,* the author obligingly added two passages that satisfied the party views on war and peace. Scholarship too has been harnessed to the chariot of party ideology. Eminent critics like Ernst Bloch and Hans Maier have left the DDR and settled in Western Germany. But there is much scholarly activity in the East and some of it is on a high intellectual plane. There is even a measure of collaboration with West German scholars in the editing of important scholarly projects.

It is not surprising that after twelve years of government-directed intellectual life, scholars in Western Germany turned away from anything that smacked of ideology and welcomed investigation of the purely literary qualities of the work. This movement, which actually began as early as the thirties, represents a radical rejection of historical scholarship and of all attempts at genetic explanation. Some advocates of this formalism went so far as to detach art from life and assign to it—even to literature—an autonomous realm. "Literature conjures up, through imagery, a shifting reality which is self-sufficient, and it would be meaningless to inquire beyond this reality" (Johannes Pfeiffer).

However, after some years this extreme position began to be modified in favor of a more historical approach to literary study. Some advocated a fusion between historical background research and precise interpretation (Benno von Wiese, Friedrich Sengle, Fritz Martini). There was a movement to revive the study of literature in relation to the other arts; this had been in disfavor because of the excesses to which it had been carried. At present (1969) individual textual interpretation in the manner of the new criticism is most widely practiced. Even general studies of writers give detailed interpretations of individual works. But the first retreat from over-formalism has already been made. The outlook is for a more balanced method of literary analysis in the future.

Literary Criticism. While it is true that Germany in this period has no critics to compare with those of the eighteenth century or with critics in other countries (Sainte-Beuve, Arnold, Croce, T. S. Eliot, Edmund Wilson), distinguished and important literary criticism has been produced in Germany. There is, first, the contribution made by creative writers: reviews of single works, of the total work of an author, essays on their own work (Hebbel: "Mein Wort über das Drama," 1843; Stifter: "Vorrede" zu *Bunte Steine,* 1853), reflections on problems in æsthetics. The following major writers have left a critical oeuvre of substance: Heine, Grillparzer, Hebbel, Otto Ludwig, Fontane, Thomas Mann, Hofmannsthal, Paul Ernst, Döblin, Arnold Zweig. A list of important critics who were not primarily men of letters would include: Herman Grimm, Kurt Hillebrand, Josef Hofmiller, Karl Kraus, Alfred Kerr, Hermann Bahr, Herbert Ihering, Bernhard Diebold, Oskar Loerke, Max Rychner, Georg Lukács (a Hungarian who wrote in German and who is indissolubly bound up with German letters), Friedrich Sieburg, Theodor Adorno, Günther Blöcker, Marcel Reich-Ranicki, Franz Mehring, Paul Rilla.

From the beginning of our period German criticism has been associated with the press, with literary journals and the *feuilleton* section of the daily newspaper. Theater criticism has of necessity been written hurriedly, without adequate time for reflection, reviewing, comparison. But these features have been characteristic of literary criticism everywhere; and there is no evidence that German criticism has suffered especially through the conditions under which it was produced.

Marxian writers have accused the professional critics in the West of being unfree to speak their minds because of the compulsion to conform to the policy of the newspaper or journal that employs them. While this may hold for minor critics, it is certainly untrue of the eminent men of the profession. In the period between 1830 and 1850 the writers of *Das junge Deutschland* ran afoul of the censor repeatedly. But thereafter a critic was free to say what he felt. Fontane hailed Hauptmann's radical naturalist drama *Vor Sonnenaufgang* in the capitalist Berlin press, at a time when the atmosphere in Prussia was very hostile to the new literature. Alfred Kerr championed the moderns in the teeth of philistine opinion. The reactionary pre-Nazi publicists screamed that the *Kulturbolschewisten* had taken over the press and were poisoning the German collective mind with their un-German (*i.e.,* liberal-socialist) writings: Where were the capitalist bosses who employed them? It is rather an obvious case of the pot calling the kettle black. For it is clear that the Marxian critics have been controlled from outside by the press for which they wrote, before 1933, and by the government of the East German Republic (DDR) since 1945.

German literary criticism has been as varied as that in other countries. It is sometimes described as "impressionistic," by which is meant that it is not tied to any specific theory of literature. Some critics have encouraged this naïve notion that they sing their native woodnotes wild. Thus Günther Blöcker has insisted that the critic should not concern himself with the results of modern literary scholarship. But it is idle to pretend that the better critics are not aware of what is being written in the academies. Virtually all of them have studied German literature at the university.

The principal question that literary critics have debated is the problem of values. Should literary criticism be normative, legislative, or should it strive to maintain strict neutrality and confine itself to mere description? Unless a critique confines itself to a retelling of the story, it cannot escape making value judgments. Literary history, too, cannot escape evaluation if only through its inclusions and omissions and its relative allotment of space as between two authors or two works. The subject is discussed at length in Beriger's study *Die literarische Wertung* and in Max Wehrli's published lecture *Wert und Unwert in der Dichtung*. What is important, as Horst Oppel has pointed out, is that the set of values one brings to literary criticism should not be extraneous or highly subjective. Schopenhauer's condemnation of all optimistic literature is as wrongheaded as the insistence of the soap-box public on the happy ending.

German critics have been berated for their polemical manners. The critics of the extreme right and left have been abusive beyond the bounds of decency; a look at the writings of Adolf Bartels or Will Vesper's journal *Die neue Literatur* from 1930 to its end will shock the Anglo-American reader. But the large body of literary criticism has been serious, responsible, and urbane.

It seems to be a fact that literary criticism in Germany has been more willing than academic criticism to use that non-literary body of knowledge which, according to Stanley Edgar Hyman, is the distinguishing mark of modern criticism: the tools and techniques offered by psychoanalysis and other branches of psychology, anthropology and sociology. German *Literaturwissenschaft,* as we shall see, has been almost exclusively philosophical or purely literary. Practical criticism has shown a greater readiness to interpret literature in the light of what we can learn about man from the social sciences and other sources.

Literary History. The nineteenth century believed in causality and order in human affairs; it accepted the existence of mental forces behind physical events. And this holds even for the Marxists, whose adherence to the dialectical principle as a motive force in history constitutes a recognition of a spiritual factor directing phenomena. The literary history of the nineteenth century is therefore no mere cataloging of names and titles but an attempt to trace development and connection and to discover leading ideas and motifs in literary documents.

The first important literary history of the age was written by G. G. Gervinus, whose *Geschichte der poetischen Nationalliteratur der Deutschen* (1835–1842) indicates his bias in its very title. German literature is no longer viewed, as it was by the Enlightenment, as a segment of world literature, but in the spirit first suggested by Friedrich Schlegel: as the expression of a people's soul. Gervinus shared the belief of *Das junge Deutschland* that the æsthetic age was a thing of the past and that German intellectuals must henceforth concern themselves with political progress. He therefore judged the literature of the past by political-ethical criteria. Heine's brilliant essay *Die romantische Schule* (1833) had shown the way. The example was followed also by Theodor Mundt, Julian Schmidt, and Gottfried Keller. Political conservatism had its champions too: in Wolfgang Menzel, August Vilmar, Karl Goedeke, and Eichendorff; and there were historians of literature who were politically neutral (Koberstein, Kurz, Wackernagel). Common to them all was a concern with the matter of literature rather than its form.

At about the middle of the century the spirit of positivism made itself felt in the writing of literary history. The six volumes of Hermann Hettner's *Literaturgeschichte des 18. Jahrhunderts* (1856–1870) may be reckoned among the great achievements in the genre. They depict the development of literature in England, France, and Germany during the period of the Enlightenment, the age whose ideological position was closest to Hettner's. But the political bias in Hettner is a benign one; it does not intrude itself to an objectionable degree, as it does in Gervinus or Goedeke. This is rounded history of literature, concerned with both history and literature. Hettner's notable achievement was matched by others: by Justi's *Winckelmann* (1860–1872), by Haym's *Die romantische Schule* (1870) and his biography of Herder (1877–1885) and by Wilhelm Scherer's famous *Geschichte der deutschen Literatur* (1883), justly celebrated for its clarity of presentation.

Scherer is the principal representative of the positivist spirit in German literary scholarship. He used Taine's formula in his analysis of literature: *das Ererbte, das Erlernte, das Erlebte* (heredity, culture, experience). The emphasis was on genetic factors (external influences), the study of sources, the detailed accumulation of facts—all the facts—the exclusion of subjective and metaphysical bias. The positivists were not as objective as they fancied themselves to be. The national bias is there (in Scherer and some others, at least); there is a strong ethical slant too, as in naturalistic literature, which was flourishing at the same time. The novel was favored over the drama as the modern art form, and the lyric was wholly disparaged. Standard monumental critical editions of the German classical writers were published; academic literary periodicals were founded. The influence of these models has extended into the twentieth century.

The reaction against positivism is reflected in the subsequent writing. Oskar Walzel, H. A. Korff and others worked within the tradition of *Geistesgeschichte*. Josef Nadler, following a suggestion of August Sauer, published a comprehensive history of German literature: *Literaturgeschichte der deutschen Stämme und Landschaften* (3 volumes, 1912–1918), in which literature is seen as shaped by the forces of racial origin and landscape, an adumbration of the later Nazi slogan "blood and soil" (*Blut und Scholle*). In subsequent revisions under different titles (4 volumes 1923–1928; 1938–1941) Nadler adjusted himself easily toward National Socialist ideology. Friedrich Kummer depicted the evolution of German literature by generations (*Deutsche Literaturgeschichte des 19. Jahrhunderts dargestellt nach Generationen, 1909*). A group of scholars, led by H. O. Burger, published a volume *Annalen der deutschen Literatur* (1952), in which literary works are depicted in strict chronology of appearance. Julius Wiegand produced a history of German literature by motifs, themes and ideas rather than men and works (*Geschichte der deutschen Dichtung nach Gedanken, Stoffen und Formen in Längs- und Querschnitten,* 1922). Apart from the scarcely remembered writings of Samuel Lubinski (*Literatur und Gesellschaft im 19. Jahrhundert,* 4 vols., 1899–1900; *Die Bilanz der Moderne,* 1904; *Der Ausgang der Moderne,* 1909) this is the only sociological treatment of literary history. A Marxian history of literature is being written by a group of East German scholars, planned to comprise ten volumes, of which the first two appeared in 1960.

A characteristic of literary history written a generation ago was the elaborate division of the literature into periods. More and more subdivisions were made on the basis of style or *Weltanschauung,* many of them according to criteria borrowed from other arts. To describe the literature of the late 19th and 20th c. a proliferation of divisions was invented, which justifies the epithet "fragmentation" used above. Since 1945 literary historians have become more and more skeptical about the value of such labels; there is a literature on the subject. While no one denies the validity of a term like "Enlightenment," there have been several attempts to counteract the traditional breakdown of the period from 1750 to 1830 into movements and sub-movements. Korff suggested the term *Goethezeit* to characterize the complex of *Sturm und Drang, Klassik,* and *Romantik.* More and more this era has come to be spoken of as the age of "German idealism." The new edition of Soergel's *Dichtung und Dichter der Zeit,* edited by Curt Hohoff, recognizes only two basic movements: naturalism and expressionism. Karl August Horst, in his survey of German Literature of the 20th c., *Strukturen und Strömungen,* dispenses with periodization altogether; his divisions are by theme and genre. His longer study *Kritischer Führer durch die deutsche Literatur der Gegenwart* (1962) is composed on the same principles.

Related to this problem is the exploration of periods in literary history to arrive at a more scientific definition and understanding of their true essence. Terms like "Barock," "Biedermeier," "Manierismus," "Jugendstil" stirred lively debate among German scholars; recently the term "realism" has been subjected to considerable discussion. André Jolles' *Einfache Formen* (1930) and Ernst Robert Curtius' suggestion of the "topos" indicate other avenues of literary research.

Literaturwissenschaft. The term first occurs in 1852; not until 1897 does it appear as the title of a book (Ernst Elster: *Prinzipien der Literaturwissenschaft*). Of course the discipline had been practiced by the great critics of the eighteenth century, by Friedrich Hebbel, by Freytag (*Technik des Dramas,* 1865), by Paul Heyse (theory of the novelle). The older poetics were *Literaturwissenschaft*; but they dealt largely with the formal side of literature and had only a secondary interest in the many other facets which literature offers for exploration: the philosophical, historical, psychological, mythological, sociological, and its relation to the other arts. All these relationships are the concern of *Literaturwissenschaft* as it has developed in the twentieth century. Even the whole complex of philology—bibliography, editing of scholarly texts, the study of sources and influences, the biography of the writer—is part of this discipline.

1. The emergence of *Literaturwissenschaft* as a discipline may be said to date from 1883, with the publication of Dilthey's *Einleitung in die Geisteswissenschaften,* in which it was argued that the mental sciences (*i.e.,* the social sciences and the humanities) have a goal and method of their own, basically different from those of the natural sciences. That goal is not explanation through causality, but understanding based on personal experience and insight (*Erlebnis*). Dilthey regards literary interpretation as an art which is the product of a special talent; this talent is a function of an affinity that is cultivated through immersion in the life of the author and his work. The method is divinatory, but the procedures of the inspired interpreter can be stated in the form of rules and principles for the guidance of the less gifted. These rules constitute the science of hermeneutics.

The publication of Dilthey's volume of essays *Das Erlebnis und die Dichtung* (1905), coupled with the new intellectual atmosphere created by the work of Nietzsche, Bergson, Simmel, and the neo-Kantians, produced a strong reaction against the rationalist-positivist current in criticism. Dilthey's method came to be known as *Geistesgeschichte*; for several decades after 1900 it was the most popular of all the critical approaches. As it developed, *Geistesgeschichte* tended to neglect the specifically literary qualities of the work and to concentrate on its intellectual, philosophical features, especially on the relation of the work to the *Zeitgeist.* This is the opposite of what Dilthey had intended; for he insisted that the history of the mind cannot be deduced from political and social phenomena but must be divined subjectively, through an intuitive process, and described with sensitivity and without passing judgment from the critic's subjective point of view. But the application of Dilthey's principles by German scholars tended to encourage the native propensity for abstract thought. Many of the outstanding scholars between 1900 and 1930 worked in this tradition (Unger, Cassirer, Korff, Cysarz, Strich, Ermatinger, Rehm, Kluckhohn, Kindermann, Böckmann). Rudolf Unger introduced a special branch of *Geistesgeschichte* which he called *Problemgeschichte.* The task of criticism, he argued, is to examine the fundamental problems of existence as depicted in literature; these problems are: destiny, religion, the I-world conflict, nature, civilization, love, death, family, marriage, etc.

The spell of positivism had been broken. In liberating the humanities from their tutelage to the natural sciences Dilthey had freed the creative mind from its dependence on environmental forces. The watchword now was: away from facts to ideas, generalizations, *Weltanschauung*. Analysis yielded to synthesis; unity of spirit was sought in the various intellectual disciplines; the slogans were: Ganzheit, Epoche, Wesen, Dynamik, Stil, Struktur—all pointing to the goal of discovering a unified pattern of development for all mental activity in the sphere of the humanities and social sciences. At the end of World War II the influence of *Geistesgeschichte* was still strong enough to warrant an attack that was launched by Karl Viëtor in a celebrated article in *PMLA*. The great scholar and critic E. R. Curtius, too, raised his voice in opposition to the methods of *Geistesgeschichte*.

2. The search for a synthesis naturally led to a crossing of the boundaries between the various arts. It was assumed that the same æsthetic principles underlie all the arts and that the spirit of the age manifests itself in all of them. The Baroque style, for instance, must be embodied in the literature and music, as well as in the architecture and painting, of the 17th c. Bach in music, the late Shakespeare, Donne and Milton, Corneille and Racine, were all classified as Baroque artists. If the same principles underlie all the arts, one should be able to apply stylistic criteria from one art to another (*Wechselseitige Erhellung der Künste*). Thus Oskar Walzel (and later Fritz Strich) used Wölfflin's famous categories to differentiate between Renaissance and Baroque art and between classic and romantic styles in literature. Literary movements were named after similar currents in the sister arts (impressionism, *Jugendstil,* mannerism). Jost Hermand has written an instructive monograph on this subject. Untenable generalizations and the Procrustean stretching of historical facts to fit theory however, aroused much scepticism.

3. The attempt to classify artists and art according to general psychological categories has a long tradition in German thinking, from Schiller's polarity of naïve and sentimental to Nietzche's Apollonian and Dionysian. Dilthey added to the tradition by dividing all thinkers into three types (positivists, objective idealists, and subjective idealists). Various sets of polarities were announced and exploited by literary scholars.

4. Throughout its history German æsthetics has been divided between the champions of content and the devotees of form. The art for art movement at the end of the 19th c. furthered the interest in structure, imagery, style. Style or form ceased to be regarded as an ornament imposed on the matter of art. More and more scholars assumed that literature is its form, structure, style. Again it was Oskar Walzel who was a leader in the movement. His book *Gehalt und Gestalt im Kunstwerk des Dichters* (1925) was built on the premise that literature was essentially *Wortkunst.* Influential contributions to this point of view were made by Karl Vossler, Leo Spitzer, Karl Viëtor, Hermann Pongs, Robert Petsch, Günther Müller, Paul Böckmann, and Emil Staiger.

5. The problem of style was approached from another angle by some scholars, who were dissatisfied with the conventional division of literature into periods or literary currents. About 1920 Karl Viëtor and Günther Müller proposed a series of historical studies of the various literary types: including the minor genres such as the ode, ballad, sonnet, novelle. Viëtor and Müller themselves wrote on the ode and the ballad respectively. This preoccupation was part of a wider concern with the theory of the genres, which had remained unchanged since the days of Aristotle. Modern German literary theory has devoted much attention to the problem of the genres, as in Emil Staiger's *Grundbegriffe der Poetik* (1946). Proclaiming his indebtedness to the philosophy of Heidegger, Staiger works out an elaborate poetic based on Goethe's characterization of the three genres as existential or ontic forms of experience. In other words there is an epic way of experiencing reality and of depicting it as literature; there are also a lyric and a dramatic way. What Staiger says is quite cogent; but he introduces other elements that strain the credibility of the reader. It is difficult to accept his rapprochement between the genres and the three modes of time or his symbolic list of correspondences between the genres and the elements of grammatical speech.

6. Staiger is a master of the new school of "interpreters." In Germany, as elsewhere, the time came when scholars turned away from both the fact collecting of the positivists and pale abstractions of *Geistesgeschichte* to the kind of close textual reading that we know as "the new criticism." Germans call it

werkimmanente Interpretation and derive it from the old Biblical hermeneutics. Dilthey's concept of *Verstehen* was influential in turning attention to this method of literary study; so was Husserl's phenomenological method, filtered through Heidegger's modification of it and applied in Heidegger's own exercises in literary interpretation. In philosophy the phenomenologists had advocated an intuitive (*anschaulich*) description of the phenomenon, without reference to its antecedents or its environment. Applied to literary criticism, this called for a close reading of the text without reference to the historical background out of which it had arisen. Such a reading would yield a "neutral," i.e. unbiased interpretation leading to a penetration of its essential character (*Wesensschau*). Friedrich Schlegel's earlier dictum: criticism means understanding an author better than he understood himself, was interpreted as a proposal to rely on absolute, intuitive, divinatory interpretation. Only the poet's words matter, not what lies behind them or under or above them. Literary analysis should deal with particular words, sounds, rhythms, images. It is the uniqueness of each literary work that the interpreter explores, not general philosophical ideas which precede or surround it. While this procedure may be conceived as a perfectly rational, pragmatic operation (as our own "new critics" hold), German *Literaturwissenschaft* has tended to associate it with a level of mind that is connected with emotion, the unconscious, and the irrational. The masters in this type of interpretation are Max Kommerell, Emil Staiger, Fritz Martini, and Richard Alewyn.

A related approach to this was the method made famous by Erich Auerbach in his *Mimesis* (1946). Auerbach, too, submitted a series of texts to minute stylistic analysis. But he went further; he claimed that each text examined by him contained the whole author *in nuce*. His performance is a tour de force, sometimes more brilliant than convincing. It has been used with equal brilliance by Walter Höllerer in his book *Zwischen Klassik und Moderne* (1958).

7. A final approach to *Literaturwissenschaft* in the twentieth century might be called the totalitarian; it is the method favored both by National Socialist Germany and the Communist East. The emphasis in criticism falls heavily on ideology. Literature exists and should be fostered in order to promote the welfare or transformation of a) the nation or race, or b) the worker's state. Art is created by productive forces rather than by individuals; these forces are a) ethnic (Nadler) or b) "social groups" (Hauser). Literature should be judged primarily by biological (for the Nazi) or sociological (for the Marxian) criteria. Does the work of art promote the welfare of the state? then it is good. In the view of the National Socialist critic, Heine could not write good poetry because he was not an Aryan and lacked the true Aryan soul; the Marxist admires Heine's poetry because he sees Heine as almost a Marxian. There is, of course, a fundamental difference between the two approaches: National Socialism sees artistic talent as a function of biological and ethnic forces; the Marxians are willing to accept converts. The Marxists, too, conceive of literature as an objectification of historical-materialistic processes which determine the development of society itself. But the two groups are at one in curtailing the role of the individual artist in favor of the community. Both are oriented toward content rather than form; both favor "social realism" as opposed to avant garde experiments in highly individualistic, esoteric expressions of a personal artistic vision. Both are anti-bourgeois (*i.e.*, anti-liberal). National Socialism wants literature to glorify the noble peasant; Marxian criticism wants it to extol the noble proletarian. Both have developed the art of double talk to a high degree of perfection.

W. H. Friedrich and W. Killy, *Literatur*, 3 v. (Fischer Lexikon) 1964–65; Merker-Stammler, *Reallexikon der deutschen Literaturgeschichte*, rev. ed. 1958f; W. Stammler, *Deutsche Philologie im Aufriss*, I, 1957; René Wellek, *Hist. of Modern Crit.* III and IV, 1965; Gero von Wilpert, *Sachwörterbuch der Literatur*, 1964; Horst Enders, *Die Werkinterpretation*, 1967; W. Benjamin, *Illuminations*, trans. 1968; L Beriger, *Die literarische Wertung*, 1938; W. H. Bruford, *Lit. Interpretation in G.*, 1952; K. O. Conrady, *Einführung in die neuere deutsche Literaturwissenschaft*, 1966; J. Hermand, *Literaturwissenschaft und Kunstwissenschaft*, 1965; R. Ingarden, *Das Lit. Kunstwerk*, 1960; W. Kayser, *Das sprachliche Kunstwerk*, 12th ed., 1967; B. Markwardt, *Geschichte der d. Poetik*, 5 v., 1960; K. Otto, *Kritik in unserer Zeit*, 1960; H. Pongs, *Das Bild in der Dichtung*, 2 v., 1939–60; H. Seidler, *Die Dichtung*, 1965; E. Staiger, *Grundbegriffe der Poetik*, 1966; O. Walzel, *Gehalt und Gestalt im Kunstwerk des Dichters*, 1923;

M. Wehrli, *Allgemeine Literaturwissenschaft,* 1951. HARRY STEINHAUER.

GREEK CRITICISM, deliberate and systematic, emerges after some centuries of creative activity. It is preceded by many pronouncements that imply, or even formulate, standards and principles. Such remarks are scattered through epic, lyric, and dramatic poetry, philosophy, history, and oratory. Homer, *e.g.,* enunciates the principle of inspiration (*Iliad* II, 484–493), and distinguishes two styles of oratory (*Iliad* III, 203–224). The persistent problem of inspiration vs technique was raised by Pindar. Moral judgment (not, in the Gr. field, wholly separable from æsthetic) is pressed on individual writers by philosophers (Heraclitus, Xenophanes) in the late 6th and early 5th c. Again, Thucydides' strictures on his predecessors are not only individual judgments, but raise the important question of final purpose: pleasure or instruction. Scattered remarks bear on the nature of composition [Corinna's advice to Pindar on the sparing use of myth (Edmonds, *Lyra Græca* III, p. 6); Simonides' definition of painting as silent poetry and poetry as painting that speaks (*op. cit.* II, p. 258)]. Parody, which is implied criticism, occurs in Homer and Hipponax (6th c. B.C.).

Such remarks continue throughout Gr. literature; they represent the creative writer's sensitivity to the standards of his craft (Demosthenes' censure of the style and purpose of Æschines; the judgments of Polybius on his predecessors; Meleager's characterization of the lyric and epigrammatic poets).

Deliberate, theoretical criticism begins with Aristophanes and the other comic poets of the 5th c.; with Socrates and Plato. The writers of Old Comedy took as their field the life of contemporary Athens; literature received its due share of (mostly hostile) attention. Apart from the well-known assessments of poets and philosophers of the day of Aristophanes, the very titles of lost plays testify to their strong literary interest: *e.g., Archilochi,* Cratinus; *Hesiodi,* Teleclides; *Muses,* Phrynichus; *Poet, Sophists,* Plato Comicus; and there is much about literature, esp. poetry, in the fragments that have been preserved. Such criticism is mainly from the point of view of ultimate moral values; Euripides and Socrates are attacked, as are Pericles, Cleon, Alcibiades, because they contribute to the political and moral decline of Athens. Yet at the same time, the necessary connection between content and style is apprehended; there is much incisive criticism of diction, meter, construction: a concrete analysis scarcely matched for centuries to come. Plato also is primarily ethical and educational in his concerns. By Plato's time, however, systematic criticism of literature had already begun. Before mid 5th c. the Sicilians Croax and Tisias, and after them the early sophists, had laid the lasting foundations of a systematic rhetoric. Its beginnings are linked with the advancing recognition of the fact that prose, as well as poetry, is an art; that in it also the effects of rhythm, sound, and structure are matters of rule. Critical rhetoric, like Plato's æsthetic, is theoretical rather than practical, is much concerned with classification, division, distinction of ends. The essential difference is that, for critical rhetoric, literature is no longer a mere facet (and no very considerable one) of the science by which we strive to apprehend beauty, truth and the good; but an autonomous activity of the intellect, treated in its own right without hostility or apology. Such a critical rhetoric was taken up, on the theoretical side, by semi-philosophical rhetoricians (Isocrates) and philosophers sympathetic (as Plato was not) to rhetoric (Aristotle; Theophrastus). On the practical side it influenced the early authors of that oratory which, once delivered, was to be written, or which was never to be delivered at all (Antiphon; Thucydides). Thereafter, we have as practitioners, and occasionally as theorists, the grand series of the major 4th c. orators. The main creative literature of the 4th c. is oratory, with developments in philosophy, New Comedy, and history, the last much influenced by Isocrates. This tendency had its effect on criticism. Thus Aristotle treats epic and tragedy from the point of view of rhetoric, and almost entirely ignores lyric, which would not have answered to such treatment, and which was at the time neglected.

The main contributions of 4th c. criticism are along general and theoretical lines: (1) classification, the division of literary styles and techniques into types; (2) anatomical analysis of literary forms, a systematic interpretation of structural principles that had been observed in practice (how consciously is debatable) by writers as early as Pindar and Æschylus. Other advances are the study of the parts played by natural endowment and application, respectively; a recognition of the value of literary history; and some redefinition of the final purpose of literature.

In the Alexandrian period, once more, history affects creative literature, and both affect criticism. Democratic government declines, the numerous wars are fought by mercenary rather than citizen armies; the narrow and intense Hellenic patriotism, with its great virtues and vices, passes away, replaced by a cosmopolitanism of broader horizons and more varied activities. Oratory passes with Demosthenes and Hyperides; but lyric and epic poetry, philosophy, and criticism live on or are revived. Textual criticism, the methods of which are determined by æsthetic as well as other considerations, is developed by the great librarians of Alexandria, Zenodotus, Aristophanes of Byzantium, Aristarchus. Grammar (which then had a wider sense) was treated systematically and with authority by Dionysius Thrax. Many of the tendencies of the 4th c. continue. An influential division of poetics into poetry, poem, and poet is offered by Neoptolemus of Parium, as well as various other classifications of poetical material and style. Many critical antitheses are debated, *e.g.,* Asianism vs. Atticism; style vs. content (Heracleodorus); instruction vs. entertainment as the end of art (Crates of Mallos); authority (Callimachus) vs. originality (Apollonius Rhodius). The conflicting claims of genius, skill, study, luck, and helpful criticism are all recognized by Simylus. The Alexandrian age was one of innovation, of great creative, antiquarian (study of Homer), and scientific activity; much critical work known to have been written is lost.

In the last important epoch, the Roman, the scholarly activities of the grammarian, the metrician, and the scholiast were still vigorously carried on; the tradition of classification continued, as did controversies over antithetical schools or concepts. Yet between the Alexandrian and the Roman periods there is a fundamental difference. For Greek literature, the Roman period is an age of exile in an alien though sympathetic world. No new forms developed in Greek, save the romantic novel and the romantic biography (anticipated by Xenophon). With the loss of political autonomy and creative vigor, confidence and self-assurance were gone. The ancient writers were thus contemplated as from a great distance and with a new respect, not only by Gr. critics (Dionysius of Halicarnassus, Demetrius, Longinus), but also by such gifted creative authors in L. as Cicero and Horace. To them, respect for antiquity, critical though it may be, brought a sense of inferiority that amounted at times to defeatism. This may be illustrated in the changed significance of the term imitation (*mimesis*). To Plato and Aristotle, this meant the imitation, or representation, of man in action; to the Roman generations, it meant the use of great classical authors as models of method and sources of inspiration.

Despite—and in a way because of—this position, the Rom. period produced some of the best literary criticism of antiquity, and of all time. The various elements of classical literature fell into their true pattern and focus, and made possible a more nearly objective study. In individual judgment there is less unevenness, there are fewer gaps, than at any preceding stage. Thus the archaic lyric came back into its own; a product of the remote age of local tyrannies and aristocracies, neglected or misunderstood for centuries, the superb poetry of Archilochus, Alcæus, and Sappho was better appreciated by Demetrius, Dionysius of Halicarnassus, Longinus, Quintilian, than it had been by Plato and Aristotle.

Certain old, bewildering controversies were at last settled. Thus the clash between Asianism and Atticism (this last based on the standard of correctness exemplified by Lysias) seems to be resolved by Longinus, who sets the high style between bombast (Asianism) on the one side and over-leanness or insignificance (Atticism) on the other. Both Dionysius and Longinus go beyond rigid classicism in recognizing a factor in literature, making for beauty and power, that eludes scientific analysis. Such recognition carries Longinus beyond the negative standards of correctness and purity and enables him, *e.g.,* to establish Plato, once for all, as greater than Lysias. At the same time it disowns the age-old hostility toward emotion. One other great advance made in this period (Demetrius, Longinus, Dio of Prusa, esp. Dionysius) is concrete, thoroughly documented analysis and interpretation of individual styles and writers, seen nowhere to better advantage than in Dionysius' appreciation of Homer. In such senses, the Roman period, even towards its close, is the great age of Gr. criticism. By its end, most of the important problems of criticism had been intelligently raised, and many of them settled with authority. Atkins; Schmid; Saints; I. Bywater, *Aristotle on the Art of Poetry,* 1909; J. D. Dennison, *Gr. Lit. Crit.,* 1924; R. Roberts, *Gr. Rhetoric and Lit. Crit.,* 1928; G. M. A. Grube, *The Gr. and R. Critics,* 1965. Richmond Lattimore.

ITALIAN CRITICISM. *The Renaissance.* Criticism after Dante was insistently concerned with problems his work raised, *e.g.*, of the use of the vernacular or the continued imitation of the classics in their own tongue. Rather an erudite and connoisseur than a critic, Petrarch (Francesco Petrarca, 1304–74), despite his vast learning, made no special contribution to the movement of ideas and the change in values. By his discoveries, however, by his enthusiastic comments, he brought a great part of classical literature from the heights of cold veneration to a warm familiarity in artistic and cultured taste. His evaluations of new or unknown poets were on the whole faulty; his judgment of Dante was belittlingly moderate. Less egocentric and more amenable to discipline, Boccaccio (1313–75) admired Dante unqualifiedly; and although his good judgment and the traditional allegorical method formed rather an amalgam than an integration, his commentary furthered the interpretation and the popularity of the *Divina Commedia;* while the eloquent and persuasive effusions of his Latin works spread the love, or rather the cult, of poetry.

By this cultivation of poetry, this vigor of æsthetic consciousness, the great writers of the late Middle Ages were also the initiators of the Renaissance. For while Humanism must in one sense be interpreted as a continuance of the Middle Ages, in it, as in the Reformation and the Counter-Reformation, are the seeds of the literary criticism that the later years brought to harvest. It continued, and further systematized, medieval thought insofar as it demanded universal Latinity and an equally universal orthodox pedagogy: hence its aloofness from the national language movements into which the medieval unity had dissolved, its general lack of understanding and of sympathy for the pre-Dante movement (which was perhaps more strongly imbued with actual or virtual heresy than has been usually considered), its very frigidity towards Dante who, Roman and Catholic though he was, could not bring himself to write his poem in the language of the Empire and the Church. Humanism remained always chiefly concerned with L. literature, the sanctification if not deification of which continued from Politian (1454–94) to Scaliger (1434–1558), and beyond. On the other hand, it manifested new characteristics of the new era: a more discriminating and tasteful love of poetry; a desire to interpret and justify poetry at an extremely high level of the spiritual life; in the very field of L. literature a greater concreteness of style and precision of taste, a new perspective on such figures as until then had been seen in distortion or bias, and an eminence conferred upon Cicero as the Virgil of prose, the model of eloquent elegance, which persuades us to the good; finally, a relatively rapid advancement of Gr. literature and the progressive direct discovery of Homer (whom Petrarch himself, father of the Humanists, read—in a bad L. trans.—at 63), even though understood as a sort of primitive Virgil.

Politian, in the *Sylvae* (a sort of university course in verse, sketching the first outline of literary history), though in the 3d part continuing the glorification of Virgil, in the 4th part elevated Homer also, as a master of wisdom. Unheedful of Dante, who had suggested the canzone as the highest of vernacular forms, he renewed the exaltation of the epic, sustained for many centuries. In the *Poetica* of Vida (1527; largely echoing Horace) the epic is the crown of all literary activity: it dominated the unsuccessful life of Trissino (*Poetica,* ca. 1515 pub. 1563), the tragic life of Tasso (*Discorsi,* 1594), and still it prevailed in the thought of the Fr. Rapin (1674), though by then the Fr. classical drama was at its peak.

Critical polemics or controversies are usually a sign of great creative periods, or indeed mark their end. In the It. Renaissance the more clamorous disputes were over the romances or poems of chivalry and the conjoined controversy regarding the *Gerusalemme Liberata.* Granted that the supreme form is the epic; granted—against the invertebrate formlessness of medieval works—that the basic characteristic of form is unity (so much so that Trissino disapproved of the octave as a narrative form, for its break between stanza and stanza, which the unity of the epic poem would not tolerate) granting these principles, what rank should be assigned to the poems of chivalry? Granting that Tasso sought the perfection of the ancient epic, what degree of success did he attain?

Prominent among these polemists are Giraldi Cinthio (1504–73), defending the romances, and Minturno (*Poetics* of 1559, 1563), holding firm for classical form. During the struggle two fundamental concepts were made clear. In the 1st place, the principle of the unity of the work of art was fixed more firmly; in the 2d, it was finally established that there had been developed new forms and types unknown to antiquity, for which the old laws must be revised, if new ones were not framed. Thus, through the breach effected by the romances, the concept of modern literature made its way: almost as at a lightning stroke there ended the darkness through which for centuries the critical consciousness had stood before the budding, flowering, and withering away of new styles and structures in the arts of space and time, without discerning that something different from the styles and structures of antiquity had been born.

In this awakening contrast—which did not prevent the *commedia dell'arte* and other spontaneous forms from passing without leaving any important trace on literary criticism —were the first tracings of what were later called the "fortunes" of the poets: vehement evaluations pro and con, impassioned upsettings of values. While taste began to acclaim the romances and what we should call the Gothic, the possibility of understanding and appreciating Dante also increased: Varchi (1570) set him above Homer; Iacopo Mazzoni (1573, 1587) wrote his *Difesa*. In the dispute over the *Gerusalemme,* Tasso was preferred to Homer, to Ariosto, to Virgil—or was criticized mercilessly; and—paradoxical result of an effort at restoring in their integrity the classical poem and the classical poet —from the sorrows and errors of Tasso sprang the legended prototype of the romantic poet.

The most important incident in literary criticism, however, was the discovery of the *Poetics* of Aristotle. This little treatise, not widely circulated in antiquity, coming to the new period as a fragment across the silence of three epochs, was brought to light in 1498 in the L. of Giorgio Valla; in the original Gr. in 1508; more widely in 1536 in the edition of Trincavelli and the L. version of Pazzi—just at the time when the philosophical authority of Aristotle was declining, in the very year in which the humanist Ramus successfully defended at the U. of Paris a doctoral thesis maintaining that all the opinions of Aristotle are erroneous. The first commentary, that of Robortello, appeared in 1548; the trans. of Segni in 1549; then (1550) a significant interpretation by Vincent Maggi, called *pius Madius,* who, forcing the celebrated Aristotelian passage on catharsis into the sense that tragedy liberates the human soul not only and not so much from terror and pity as also and esp. from violent and sinful passions, impressed upon criticism a religiously intransigent direction, such as the Counter-Reformation was to seek, such as might be called medievalistic, an anticipation of the concept of poetry of the Latin Catholic romanticism and Alessandro Manzoni. Castelvetro's extensive commentary (1571) emphasized the function of poetry "solely to delight and recreate the minds of the crude multitude and the common people"; though in his demand for verisimilitude he forged the links of the three unities.

A large body of work in exegesis and in popularization accumulated around the brief Aristotelian text; from which, in diverse and often opposite directions, are sprung the main currents of modern literary thought. The doctrine of *mimesis,* and that of the unity of the work of art (more or less rightly understood) reinforced the concepts of fidelity to truth and of the organism (*simplex dumtaxat et unum*) that constituted the basis of the traditional classicism resting upon the *Ars Poetica* of Horace. The preference for tragedy—due in some part to the chance mutilation that gave greater prominence to the pages devoted to this genre—shook the primacy of the epic and gave a first impulse to the exaltation of the theatre that was to dominate the entire romantic period. Consideration of catharsis, *i.e.,* of the purification of feelings through the tragic catastrophe, induced the moralistic, pedagogic—redemptive—concept of art. Finally, the Aristotelian thought that distinguishes poetry from history, assigning the universal to the former and the particular to the latter and above all that other thought which places the plot above the other constituent elements of a tragedy, produced notions not merely different from but even opposite to those induced by the concept of catharsis. They freed poetry from the domination of morals and truth, stimulating in Riccobono (1584) the æsthetic doctrine that poetry is dream, that it must detach itself from life; they confirmed the triumph of the *Pastor Fido* and of the pastoral genre; decided in favor of the *antidantisti* the dispute over the value of Dante; opened the way to *Secentismo* with the doctrine that art and morality are two distinct worlds which must not be commingled; that poetry is, in fine, a "superb tapestry."

Diverse forces worked in seeming contrast, through the Renaissance, toward the same end. Among the most apparent is the Protestant Reformation which, by exalting Grace and Faith above good works and the rationality of dogma, induced a similar elevation of the spontaneity of genius over the disciplined observance of rules and the acquisition of technique. The Catholic Counter-Reformation was similarly influential in various ways: whether by relegating art, for fear of contamination, to the realm of tolerated toys, subtleties, dexterities, ornaments, tapestries, and thereby disengaging, releasing—unleashing—it; whether instead by seeking to make it the exclusive interpreter of religious and holy things, a divine minister, thus strengthening its power and its aim; whether, finally, by spreading everywhere through Jesuitic pomp stylistic tendencies of a far from classical taste. The Protestant aversion from Italy and France, the Spanish, English, and Prussian revolt against French rule, prepared the way for other assaults upon the citadels of classicism. The rapid swelling of the middle-class public (*cf.* Castelvetro), rather, the first real forming of what in the modern sense can be called the public, began to challenge the courtly standards of artistic taste. The very style of the *Bible,* now increasingly studied and venerated, set in highest repute an anticlassical form. Thus out of the romances and throughout the Renaissance a mixture was prepared, in which through all the restrictions and observances of the neo-classical period there was working the yeast of the romantic age.

D. L. Clark, *Rhetoric and Poetic in the Ren.,* 1922; J. E. Spingarn, *A Hist. of Lit. Crit. in the Ren.,* 1930; R. C. Williams, "It. Crit. Treatises of the 16th C." *MLN* 35, 1920, bibliog. G. A. Borgese.

Since the Renaissance. The 17th c. in It. was a period of relative decadence. The prevailing style in poetry was Marinism; criticism was correspondingly ineffectual. Nevertheless, search for novelty replaced submission to the authority of the ancients, marked a new phase in critical theory.

The most influential critical work was *Ragguagli di Parnaso* by Traiano Boccalini, 1612. It satirizes pedantry, plagiarism, and other current faults, in the form of conversations supposed to take place in Parnassus among great writers of past ages. Widely imitated, its form became the conventional vehicle for criticism of literature and politics. The style is vivacious, the criticism clever, but superficial. Other writers (Tassoni, Salvator Rosa, Pallavicino) show more originality. Galileo Galilei, the best prose writer of the century, brought into literary discussions the same intelligence that is shown in his scientific works.

In 1690 the Arcadian Academy was founded to counteract the bad taste of the prevailing school of poetry. Its historian was G. M. Crescimbeni; its lawgiver G. V. Gravina, whose critical works marked a partial reaction against the prevailing Cartesian rationalism, and anticipated later ideas (Vico; Montesquieu).

The first half of the 18th c. was dominated by Muratori and Vico. With monumental erudition L. A. Muratori laid the foundation of modern historical method, based on the study of documents. Publishing and interpreting the records of the Middle Ages, he contributed to the awakening of national consciousness. G. B. Vico, with his epoch-making *Scienza nuova* (1725), originated the philosophy of history and the modern science of æsthetics. In his view, based on the humanistic tradition, history is the development of human activity from primitive ages, through the heroic period when poetry arises spontaneously, to modern civilization. Poetry is to be judged intuitively as a product of the human mind; æsthetic judgment is a fundamental form of knowledge, distinct from logic and natural science. Vico thus anticipated modern idealism as applied to the study of literature; but he was so far in advance of his time that his system was not fully appreciated in Italy until adopted by De Sanctis.

The second half of the 18th c. saw a marked improvement in literary production, with increased knowledge of the literature of other countries. Criticism flourished, and frequently led to polemics, but was journalistic rather than philosophical. Giuseppe Baretti helped the flow of literature between Italy and England. He published a review, *Frusta letteraria* (*Literary Scourge,* 1763–65), lashing not only mediocre writers, but Dante and Goldoni; Shakespeare, however, he defended against the strictures of Voltaire. Another attack on Dante was made in the *Lettere Virgiliane* (1757) of Saverio Bettinelli, to which a spirited reply, *Difesa di Dante,* was made by Gaspare Gozzi, who also published several journals that contain effective criticism. The modern appreciation of Dante as poet rather than as philosopher really began with Vico, who like other critics of the time preferred Dante and Ariosto to Petrarch and Tasso, the idols of the preceding century. Girolamo Tiraboschi wrote (1772–82) the first systematic history of Italian literature, much used by later historians.

Romantic discussion began, 1816, with an article in the *Biblioteca Italiana* by Mme. de

Staël, urging the study of foreign literature. In the same year Giovanni Berchet published his *Littera Semiseria di Grisostomo,* a satirical attack on the classicists, manifesto of the Romantic movement. To oppose the reactionary *Biblioteca Italiana* a group in Milan started (1818) *Il Conciliatore,* which until its suppression a year later (for political reasons, by the Austrian government) was the organ of the Romanticists. Edited by Silvio Pellico, it contained book reviews and critical articles (Ermes Visconti on the dramatic unities and on Romantic poetry; Pellico; Berchet; Romagnosi). Romagnosi, *e.g.,* declared that to maintain the exclusive dominion of the classical rules was to desire the death of Italian poetry. Leadership of the movement came into the hands of Alessandro Manzoni. He had produced, 1820–22, two thoroughly romantic tragedies; in 1823 he wrote a letter to defend his procedure in disregarding the rules of the unities, and a general statement of his literary principles, his central idea expressed in the famous phrase: "poetry, and literature in general, should have as its purpose the useful, its subject the true, and its means the interesting." He believed that rules for writing should not be arbitrary and conventional, but should follow the dictates of the writer's individual judgment. These principles he exemplified in his great historical novel, *I Promessi Sposi* (1827).

Political unity absorbed much of the energy of most writers. Ugo Foscolo, an exile in England, wrote excellent articles on Dante, Petrarch, Boccaccio. Giuseppe Mazzini, the spiritual hero of the Risorgimento, an exile for much of his life, published in the *Foreign Quarterly Review,* 1844, a significant essay *On the Minor Works of Dante*; he wrote on Carlyle and other Eng. authors, on Fr. and G. literature, combining literary considerations with patriotic exhortation. G. A. Borgese, *Storia della critica romantica,* 2nd ed. 1920; H. Quigley, *Italy and the Rise of a New School of Criticism in the 18th c.,* 1921; Saints.; J. G. Robertson, *Studies in the Genesis of the Romantic Theory in the 18th c.,* 1923; R. A. Foakes, ed. *Romantic Criticism,* 1968; Bernard Weinberg, *Hist. of Crit. in the It. Ren.,* 1963. KENNETH MCKENZIE.

Recent. The æsthetic doctrines of Francesco De Sanctis (1817–83), generally regarded as Italy's greatest literary critic and historian, anticipate Croce's position on the autonomy of art and the concept of form. Yet De Sanctis was not so much a forerunner as a synthesizer who fused Hegelian history with romantic dialectic æsthetics and translated both into a new context in which the positive and realist spirit of the later 19th c. supplanted Hegel's metaphysics. For De Sanctis, the work of art is organic, concrete, and individual; its form and content are ideally indistinguishable. This æsthetic is accompanied by a theory of criticism which recognizes three stages in the critical act: surrender to the spontaneous impression produced by the work of art; recreation of the work by analysis of the impression, *i.e.,* the translation of the unconscious into the conscious, or the acting out of the poet's words; and judgment of the work, aimed at establishing its intrinsic value, "not what it has in common with the times, a school, or with its predecessors but what it has that is peculiar and untransferable." In De Sanctis' critical practice this scheme is vivified by a typically romantic view of the high social mission of literature and the successful union of a historical vision with in-depth analysis of the poet's "world." With few exceptions, such as the study on Zola, De Sanctis devoted himself exclusively to Italian literature: his *History of Italian Literature* (1870–71) is supplemented by a series of studies which grew out of his teaching activities, principally during the period of his 1856–59 exile in Zurich and later in his 1872–74 lecture courses at the University of Naples. The *History* and its sequel *La letteratura italiana nel secolo XIX* trace Italian literature from the genres of the Middle Ages through the liberal and democratic schools into which De Sanctis divides the followers of Manzoni and Mazzini respectively. Essentially it is a history of the Italian "conscience," understood as intellectual and moral awareness. Art is thus subordinated to the totality of man's striving for ideals, and the "hero" of the work is a unitary national mind whose bearer is the total man, who, if he is an artist, has the high imagination necessary to express this consciousness. De Sanctis assumes that Italian literature constitutes the very essence of Italian history and that it enacts the great spiritual drama of the fall and redemption of Italy.

De Sanctis had no immediate successors. The literary scholars active in the last decades of the 19th c. (Adolfo Bartoli, 1833–94; Alessandro d'Ancona, 1835–1914; Domenico Comparetti, 1835–1927; Pio Rajna, 1847–1930; Francesco D'Ovidio, 1849–1925) devoted themselves to the study of sources and influences, editing, biography, and erudition.

Their positivism finds evident expression in the frequent biological, social, racial, and psychiatric analogies of their writings. Their organ was the *Giornale storico della letteratura italiana,* founded in 1883, with a program of "studying the facts" rather than aiming at interpretation and critical judgment. The solid achievement of Italian positivist literary scholarship is the series of the *Storia letteraria d'Italia,* the cooperative effort of a group of scholars, the first edition of which was published between 1898 and 1913, and which has since gone through a number of revisions.

Giosuè Carducci (1835–1907) was the one dominant figure of the late 19th C. His authority as poet and for over forty years professor at the University of Bologna gave his work an impact on his contemporaries which was denied to De Sanctis. Carducci was a first-rate editor (especially in his 1876 variorum edition of Petrarch's *Rime*) and a fine research scholar. The main interest of his comprehensive interpretation of the development of Italian literature (contained not in a single work but in scattered writings) lies in his defense of Humanism, of that cult of form and the word, that imitation of the classics, to which romantic criticism attributed the lack of popularity of Italian literature among the masses, but which Carducci saw instead as the true Italian tradition deriving from ancient Rome and by and large bypassing Christianity. Carducci's practice of poetry made him particularly sensitive to poetic diction, and his concern with rhetorical devices and metrical schemes has made him an ancestor of modern stylistic criticism.

The critical theory and practical criticism of Benedetto Croce (1866–1952) must be viewed against the total systematization of human intellectual experience and behavior which he elaborated in the four volumes of his *Filosofia dello spirito* (1902–1917, with subsequent editions to 1958). A theory of knowledge in which the cognition of the particular by intuition is sharply distinguished from the cognition of the universal by logic stands at the basis of Croce's recognition of the autonomous nature of æsthetic activity and his formulation of the doctrine of intuition as expression (*Estetica come scienza dell'espressione e linguistica generale,* 1902). The 1908 Heidelberg lecture, *Intuizione pura e il carattere lirico dell'arte,* added the concept of *liricità,* "true poetry" (*i.e.,* the successful union of a poetic image and an emotion), as a standard of judgment. In *Breviario d'estetica* (1913) and *Aestetica in nuce* (1929, originally written as the article on "Aesthetics" for the 14th ed. of the *Encyclopaedia Britannica*), Croce explored the relation between "personality" and work of art, and defined the universal, "cosmic" character of artistic expression. In *La poesia* (1936) Croce turned more resolutely to the vast area of literature (as distinguished from poetry), which he had formerly intentionally neglected and which he now declared to be a high expression of civilization, an important institution in the cultural refinement of mankind, but which must not be confused with poetry, "the unscheduled, unprogrammatical, spontaneous creation of genius." The critical essays that in a dynamic relation of mutual conditioning accompanied these theoretical statements number in the hundreds, range from book length studies to short notes, and cover all Western literatures. Croce's earliest essays, later collected in the four volumes of *Letteratura della nuova Italia* (1914–15), were devoted to contemporary figures and began appearing in *La Critica* in 1903, the year in which that most important periodical was founded. There followed the book on Goethe (1919), the triptych *Ariosto, Shakespeare, Corneille* (1920), Croce's recognized masterpiece, and the highly controversial *La poesia di Dante* (1921), which in its radical distinction between the "theological-political romance" of the *Commedia* (*i.e.,* the structure as an abstract scheme) and the poetry which grows around it like a luxuriant vegetation challenged the unity of that great work. Croce's essays generally follow a pattern in which a brief review of existing criticism serves to clear the ground of errors and unnecessary problems before the critic moves to his principal concern: the characterization and thereby the evaluation of the artist's imagination and work. Extremely important in Croce's method is the exposition of the work of art, where time and again the critic's range of human and cultural experience, his psychological finesse, historical knowledge, and æsthetic sensitivity are revealed. In his writings on æsthetics and in his critical essays Croce carried on an overt and a latent polemic against both the survivals of positivism in criticism (*i.e.,* the extrinsic approaches to literature) and the Romantic view of the history of literature as an expression of the political history of a nation. But while Croce's criticism is æsthetic in its uncompromising emphasis on the æsthetic fact, it is also strongly ethical, even psychological, in its recognition of the "poetic personality" as the basis of art.

The sway Croce held over Italian intellectual life in the first half of the 20th c. did not inhibit the revision of his thought either by himself or by his disciples and followers. Though most academic critics during his lifetime were Crocean, they were so in different ways and with differing emphases. All, however, shared belief in the principle of the autonomy of art and in value judgment as the critic's ultimate goal and responsibility. The principal reason for dissatisfaction with orthodox Croceanism—and it is natural that this should be especially so in the academic environment—was Croce's rejection of the relevance of history to criticism. Thus, for instance, Luigi Russo (1892–1961) attempted to reestablish a view of the "complex, historical reality" of the poet by shifting attention from the *stato d'animo lirico,* the perfect union of intuition and expression, to *generazione lirica,* the *stato d'animo* in its becoming. Walter Binni (b. 1913) took up and developed Russo's genetic view by reinserting the poet's "active awareness of inspiration," his poetics, into a discussion of his poetry, and "the vital tensions and cultural thrusts of a literary epoch" into the consideration of the history of the literature of that epoch. More resolutely than either, Natalino Sapegno (b. 1901), the great literary historian of the *Trecento* (in the series *Storia letteraria d'Italia*), pleaded for a new historicism which he epitomized in the phrase, "a return to De Sanctis." Mario Fubini (b. 1900), too, whose faith in positivistic scholarship never wavered, measured himself against Croce: his awareness of the relationship between historical context and work of art led him to a pluralistic, as opposed to Croce's monistic, approach to criticism. His two contributions to the important volume *Tecnica e teoria letteraria* (1951; part of the series "Problemi ed orientamenti critici di lingua e di letteratura italiana" which for academic literary studies in Italy has had a normative function similar to that exercised in America by the Modern Language Association pamphlets and Wellek and Warren's *Theory of Literature*) state his conviction, contrary to Croce, that critical judgment is both absolute and relative and that genre studies are legitimate even though they contribute nothing to an understanding of the uniqueness of great works, of *poesia.* Attilio Momigliano (1883–1952) and Francesco Flora (1891–1962) in their widely used student manuals, both entitled *Storia della letteratura italiana,* successfully combine (though in different degrees) æsthetic analysis with historical exposition in a manner that clearly marks the change from romantic and positivist studies of literature.

In the period immediately following the second World War Marxist criticism enjoyed a fair measure of success. At its best, it allied itself with the new historicism and looked back to De Sanctis and Antonio Gramsci (1891–1937), rather than to Marx and Engels, as its forerunners. In the notes posthumously published as *Letteratura e vita nazionale,* Gramsci, though deeply concerned with the intellectual and sociological aspects of Italian literary life, never really confused poetry with ideology nor based æsthetic judgment on ideological conformity. Marxist critics, such as Gaetano Trombatore (b. 1900), Carlo Salinari (b. 1919), Carlo Muscetta (b. 1912), and Giuseppe Petronio (b. 1909), have preferred certain periods of Italian literature to others and have reached the most satisfactory results with authors who worked in the realistic tradition (Boccaccio, Goldoni, the *veristi,* the neorealists) in which the mimetic theory of art is least in conflict with the critical assumptions of Marxism.

Stylistic criticism is easily the most important development since Croce. Together with the phenomenological approach of Luciano Anceschi (b. 1911) it has opened the way to structuralism which, with its substitution of the concept of structure for that of evolution and the consequent displacement of interest to the internal relationships of the work, stands at the very antipodes of the new historicism. Though Croce rejected stylistic criticism as the study of words, rhythms, sounds, lines, or colors apart from the *stato d'animo lirico* which gives these meaning and unity, he may be said on the other hand to have given central importance to style when he made intuition and expression equivalent. Critics of fundamentally Crocean persuasion, such as Cesare De Lollis (1863–1928) and his disciple Domenico Petrini (1902–1931), who had a strong training in philology and were particularly sensitive to stylistic values, in practice did little more than substitute characterizations in terms of language and style for characterizations in terms of psychology in what remained essentially æsthetic criticism. The new stylistics instead, which Leo Spitzer helped to introduce to Italy (a selection of his writings, *Critica stilistica e storia del linguaggio,* was published by Croce in 1954), moved further and further away from psychological biography and *Geistesgeschichte* and closer and closer to the scientific formulations and methods of linguistics. The two major stylistic critics are Gianfranco Contini (b. 1910) and Giacomo Devoto (b. 1897). Like Curtius, Auerbach, and Spitzer, Contini is primarily a Romance philologist with training in Provençal, Old French, and Italian literature of the 13th and 14th centuries. His principal contributions have been to Dante and pre-Dantean studies. He has a parallel interest in modern writers, especially in the *scapigliati,* the Lombard and Piedmontese linguistic and narrative experimenters of the late 19th C. whom he helped to rediscover. Devoto was trained in comparative philology and linguistics, and though he has made some important contributions to literary criticism (specifically in his study on the style of *I Malavoglia,* now in *Nuovi studi di stilistica,* 1963), he is essentially a linguist. The distinction between linguistics and literary criticism lies in the latter's continued emphasis on value judgment, while the former is concerned with identifying linguistic "institutions" and departures from these norms in literary language.

Given the importance of the critic's role with regard not only to the explication of works of literature but to the social influences which one explication as against another may have, it is no wonder that the new techniques of criticism should be applied more and more frequently to the works of the critics themselves. Contini himself is often quoted on the importance of reaching a critic's thought through the systematic study of his language. Roland Barthes' view that a critic is not someone who clarifies the objective nature of a work of art, but a secondary writer who recreates the work as he discusses it (just as the primary writer starting from the phenomena of the world had created the pattern which is the work) is gaining greater and greater currency in Italy. R. Wellek, *A Hist. of Modern Crit.,* v. 4, 1965; "Benedetto Croce," *Comp. Lit.* v, 75–82, 1953; G. N. G. Orsini, *Benedetto Croce,* 1961; M. E. Brown, "It. Crit. after Croce" and "Recent It. Crit." *PhQ* xlvii, 92–116, 253–279, 1968; H. Hatzfeld, "Recent It. Stylistic Theory and Stylistic Crit." in *Studia . . . in honorem L. Spitzer,* 1948; O. Ragusa, "It. Crit. since Croce" *Contemp. Lit.* ix, 1968; M. Sansone, "La critica postcrociana," "La critica stilistica," "La critica marxista," *Cultura e Scuola,* Oct. 1961-April 1962; "Benedetto Croce critico," Jan. 1967; A. Scaglione, "Croce's Definition of Lit. Crit.," *J. of Art and Aesthetic Crit.,* xvii, 447–456, 1959; "Lit. Crit. in Post-War It.," *It. Q.* Spring-Summer 1960; R. Montano, "Crocean Influence and Historicism in It." *Comp. Lit. Studies,* I, 273–86, 1964; C. Santelli, "Lit. Hist. and Lit. Crit. in 20th C. It.," *Comp. Lit. Studies,* II, 71–78, 1965. OLGA RAGUSA.

LATIN (ROMAN) CRITICISM is deeply influenced by Gr. theory and example. Plautus and esp. Terence begin Rom. criticism, the latter with prologue comments on the style of his predecessors and detractors. The circle of Scipio fostered the study of Gr. ca. 155 B.C.; its influence familiarized the more cultured Romans with literary principles and styles. Ennius, epic poet; Lucilius, father of Rom. satire; Accius, dramatist, contributed to the development of criticism.

The Rom. prejudice against things Gr. and insistence upon the practical value of the arts served as checks upon the growth of critical theory, as did the constant emphasis upon morality. As a practical art that led to public office, oratory assumed prime importance; the professional teachers of grammar and oratory created the first formal critical theories at Rome. The *grammaticus* and the *rhetor,* the elementary and the secondary teacher of the Romans, studied etymologies, archaisms, word-order, and the sounds of words. Varro, a wide-ranging scholar (116–27 B.C.), wrote on grammar, drama, poetry, style; he also established the canon of the plays of Plautus. His *De Lingua Latina,* of which Books v-x have been preserved, is a valuable source of knowledge of the L. language.

The Gr. philosophical schools influenced Rom. critics. Varro profited from Stoic linguistic and critical studies. The Peripatetics had a strong charm for Cicero and Horace, the two most eminent Roman critics; Horace developed their doctrine of the mean in the *Ars Poetica.*

In the *Auctor ad Herennium,* long attributed to Cicero but now ascribed to a certain Cornificius (ca. 86 B.C.), appears the first Roman classification of oratorical styles. Cicero, upon whom the influence of the *Auctor* was considerable, gave the first genuine impetus to the systematizing of criticism. In the *Brutus* he presented a history of oratory and a brief analysis of the styles of various Roman orators. In the *Orator* and the *De Oratore* he analyzed the principles and objectives of oratory. While earlier critics had confined their investigations to poetry since prose had not yet been created at Rome in the literary sense, Cicero discussed oratorical and historical prose. In the oration *Pro Archia* he delivered an eloquent eulogy of Gr. literature and culture. He also created a L. critical terminology.

With Horace, Rom. criticism turns again to poetry and to earlier Gr. doctrines. Whether or not Horace read Aristotle's *Poetics,* he shows many parallels with it in his *Ars Poetica* and in his entire body of literary criticism in the *Epistles* and *Satires,* as well as with Hellenistic theorists like Philodemus of Gadara and Neoptolemus of Parium. The 476 lines of the *Ars Poetica,* longer a source for later critics than even the *Poetics* (which were unknown to Europe in the Middle Ages), follow the Gr. in treating literature under the headings of the poem, poetry, and the poet. Not as full a body of principles as the *Poetics,* it shows more clearly a personal experience of the art of poetry, and is rich in memorable phrases.

Post-Augustan critics of note are the elder Seneca (who defends the writers of his day in the literary quarrel, so dear to the Romans, as to the relative merits of the ancients and the moderns); Petronius; Tacitus (*Dialogus de Oratoribus*); Quintilian (*Institutes of Oratory*). Later writers, from Aulus Gellius to Martianus Capella (early 5th c. A.D.), show further dogmatism and elaboration of principles already laid down.

Rom. literary criticism as a whole shows a fondness for categories, canons, formulæ, with a tendency to set up objective standards in criticism without sufficient regard for individuality or inspiration; poetic inspiration was accepted, however, as a convention, although Horace, for example, seems to give it small importance. Few critics—only Cicero and Quintilian—reveal any historical perspective. The objects of Roman criticism embrace such questions as the oratorical styles: plain, middle, grand, as applied to the types of oratory: forensic, deliberative, epideictic. Theophrastus had formulated the four virtues of style: correctness, clearness, ornateness, and appropriateness, from which the Rom. critics did not deviate. Another matter of criticism was the controversy between the Atticists and the Asianists, *i.e.,* between the followers of a simple style in oratory and those who preferred a florid style. This quarrel stirred Cicero to some of his best critical writing. Horace lays stress upon the golden mean and upon the related principle of decorum or taste in literature; other critics are much exercised by puristic scruples, by conscious archaism (as in the Silver Age of Latin literature).

The genres of literature were regarded as forming a definite hierarchy, each with its own law of organic development and, for poetry, its characteristic meter; but Horace himself, who speaks of the *lex operis* (*Sat.* 2, 1, 2; *Ars Poetica* 135) does not consistently observe the latter rule. Much attention (Cicero) was paid to prose rhythm, the sounds and order of words, figures of speech —to form in general.

The emphasis upon form helps to explain, even for the Renaissance, the attitude toward imitation. This was not regarded as plagiarism unless it was slavish; it was the method in which a writer handles his borrowings that made all the difference. So exclusively rhetorical was the nature of much Latin literature that few writers dared to break the conventions and to strike out upon new paths; perhaps the most daring were Lucretius, Tacitus, and Fronto; Petronius is noteworthy as strongly opposed to the excessively florid rhetoric that was the style of his day.

Rom. criticism, like Gr., was confined chiefly to the epic and the drama in poetry, and to oratory and history in prose. On the verbal side, its merits were a steady emphasis upon moderation in language, exactness of words, aptness and euphony of phrase; in the larger sphere of literary æsthetics, it maintained a unity of composition, a sense of appropriateness among thoughts and emotions expressed and the character of the genre and the individual composition in which they were conveyed. The faults of Rom. criticism are its neglect of psychology, too great willingness to abide by established conventions, a tendency to objectify criticism into a set of standards that became too abstract and divorced from reality. The virtues of clearness of expression, unity of conception, moderation in choice of words and phrase, however, the entire classical balance that governed the best Rom. literature, have never been more necessary than they are today. Saints.; D'Alton.; Atkins; R. K. Hack, *The Doctrine of Literary Forms,* 1916; M. A. Grant and G. C. Fiske, *Cicero's "Orator" and Horace's "Ars Poetica,"* 1924; G. M. A. Grube, *The Gr. and R. Critics,* 1965. L. R. LIND.

MEDIEVAL CRITICISM. The few formal critical works of the Middle Ages are mainly imitative. That millennium formed our drama, our lyric patterns, our fables and romances, our historical and dialectical prose, our liturgy. Its greatest poem (*the Commedia*), its greatest epic (the *Nibelungenlied*), its greatest satire (the work of Chaucer) are preeminently expressions of the age. In the 5th-12th c., during which the medieval pattern was formed, men faced the Herculean task of creating a new economic, social, political, and moral order. The old union of race and soil that had formed the Latin or Hellenic or Semitic temper was swept away; a new mixture had to be stirred together before it could harden into form. In the medieval mixture that is our calendar, *e.g.,* the contradictory elements—Germanic, Hellenic, Latin, Hebraic, Arabic, even Celtic—were fused, but by a long and bitter process. By the time of Norman feudalism, the new economy that could support a leisure class, new forms of literature were entrenched. To supply the belated criticism, the dry bones of classicism were exhumed, to be erected into standards for literature to which they never could apply. Medieval criticism was 500 years behind before it started. This fact must be understood before one looks at such criticism as there was.

The critical statements fall primarily into two main groups: (1) the writings of the theologians, long the arbiters of taste; (2) the schoolbooks.

(1) The Fathers made ethical judgments as to which books should be read. Tertullian, Augustine, and Jerome debated whether the literature of the pagan world adversely affected men's religious sensibilities. Boethius banned the Muses from the presence of a Philosophy that promised to lift him out of his soul's prison. Jerome's famous dream ("Thou art a Ciceronian, not a Christian; where thy treasure is, there is thy heart also." *Epist.* xxii, 30) echoes throughout the Middle Ages. Yet the commonplace that patristic criticism determined the course of mediæval reading must be doubted. Diatribes against the stage, for instance, are only echoes in the tomb; classical drama would have disappeared had there been no Christianity (Chambers, *Mediæval Stage,* Ch. I). Macrobius and Martianus Capella flourished, whereas Varro, whom Augustine praised, disappeared. The vast library written by the famous Bishop Hippolytus was never transmitted, but three works of an unknown author were so revered as to place Dionysius high in Dante's Heaven. Yet though the Fathers did not determine what was read, they did determine the language of criticism. After Jerome and Gregory, a classical work was "pagan." Bede, who loved Pliny's *History* and quoted at length from it, prefixed the words, "Though worldly literature, it should not be contemned." Patristic criticism, which established a mode of thought extending to our time, did center attention on ethical content.

Yet theologians often transmitted the classics with loving care. Alcuin, Charlemagne's schoolmaster and intellectual mentor, in a poem praising his native York, listed among other authors represented in the York library Virgil, Statius, Lucan, Cicero, and Pliny the Elder. Before the 12th c. Livy, Sallust, Terence, Suetonius, Caesar, Horace, Ovid, and Quintilian were restored to favor and frequently imitated. Early medieval commentaries on the classics first were glosses on the popular textbooks (Macrobius, Capella, Donatus, Priscian); the schools of Auxerre and Fleury at the time of Heiric and Remigius were especially active in this form of criticism. Though such glosses helped to accumulate an amazing erudition, the nature of composition precluded critical accuracy or proportion. From the time of Gerbert (d. 1003), the famous teacher of Reims who became Pope Sylvester II, the cathedral schools of northern France became centers of humanism. "The moderns are to the ancients as dwarfs on the shoulders of giants," is the classic remark of Bernard of Chartres (12th c.). Although the work of John of Salisbury (who became Bishop of Chartres, 12th c.) was continued by 16th c. scholars, none surpassed him in breadth of outlook or in freedom from pedantry.

In Italy, Anselm of Bisate (fl. 1050) admitted an allegiance divided between the saints and the muses, and Abbot Desiderius of Monte Cassino, under whom the study of the classics flourished, became Pope Victor III. By mid-12th c., when William of Moerbeke translated the *Rhetoric* and *Politics* of Aristotle, a more precise and selective critical doctrine began to emerge; for Roger Bacon (d. 1294) it was not enough that a classic be discovered, translated, and circulated—the work of translation must be performed with an accuracy at which no modern scholar would carp, and the content must then be tested against nature for its validity. Bacon's *Greek Grammar* (first pub. Nolan and

Hirsch, 1902) is clearly based on a knowledge of the language derived from contemporary Greeks.

The notion that Biblical diction was universally true, *i.e.,* true in every sense, made the Fathers attach a moral and typical as well as a literal meaning to texts; an allegorical interpretation was often included. Cassian (ca. 400) maintained that the Scriptures yielded historical, allegorical, tropological, and anagogical meaning. This method of exegesis was especially developed and popularized by Gregory I's ingenious and voluminous *Moralia on the Book of Job.* The method was later extended to other literature, so that secular poetry of the later Middle Ages was deeply glossed by scholars and interpreters. Dante claimed that all good poetry was polysemous (*Epist.* x; *Convivio* ii, 1); but he reiterated that "the literal sense should always come first as the one in the meaning whereof the others are included." (*See* Meaning.)

(2) Before the founding of the universities, the chief schools were occupational—largely training-schools for priests. The teachers talked a great deal about the liberal arts, but their curricula were specialized. The several works that treat the 7 or more liberal arts as a whole—by Capella, Cassiodorus, Isidore, Alcuin, Alain of Lille, Henri d'Andeli, Vincent of Beauvais, Brunetto Latini—supply crumbs of critical doctrine, dogmatic enough for the classroom, but hardly inspirational for the reader. Of the literary arts, grammar and rhetoric long held the field alone because to the Germans of the north, for whom Church-Latin was a second tongue, these studies were necessary tools. Grammar, primarily from Donatus, taught them how to scan a line with moderate rectitude. A voluminous commentary on Virgil, attributed to Servius, 4th c. (ed. E. K. Rand), and in part his work, preserved for the Middle Ages their most substantial knowledge of classical criticism and notably opposed the current overemphasis on allegorical interpretation. As the vernacular tongues strayed farther from mother L., "grammar" came to denote the learned language, the second tongue of literary L. For Dante, grammar was the stabilizing force that slowed inevitable change (*De Vulg. Eloq.* I, i, 9). Rhetoric, based in great part on the New Sophistic, though no doubt studied to obtain flowers for homilies, preserved traditions of ancient oratory. With Abélard (1079–1142) dialectic introduced the method that has since marked mediæval thought (*cp.* Henry Adams, *Mont St. Michel and Chartres,* xii). At the same period, technical studies of *dictamen* (the art of letter-writing) and *cursus* (prose-rhythm) provided a lively criticism of prose form and organization. The primary effect of rhetorical teaching was to fasten disproportionate attention on stylistic ornament, though even the most stylized of the teachers (*e.g.,* Matthew of Vendôme) professed a love for the "natural" style.

Poetic, which suffered initially by exclusion from the sacred 7 arts, suffered yet another way. For the ecclesiastic, the highest and truest poetry must be Biblical; *e.g.,* Isidore (7th c., *Etymologiae* I) attributed to Moses the invention of hexameters and maintained that the Hebrews invented the important classical lyric forms. Since the Hebrews left no criticism, there was no accepted basis for new theory; perforce, poetry had to be regarded as grammar, *i.e.,* scansion, or as morality—to be treated by the pedant or the theologian. True, as early as the year 700, Bede (*De Arte Metrica*) described the syllabic rhythm that was turning into the new accentual verse, but no one noticeably developed his discussion during the next 500 years. In the 12th and 13th c. a series of versified poetics appeared (Geoffrey of Vinsauf, John of Garland, Matthew of Vendôme, Eberhard of Bethune); although Manly (*Chaucer and the Rhetoricians*) showed that criticism was too hackneyed to influence deeply the vital poetry of the Middle Ages. They are interesting chiefly for the judgments they recorded about traditional poetry, and for their long lists of ornamental devices and figures of speech.

In criticism as in creation Dante is at once the ideal and the typical writer of the age. His critical doctrine, hinted at throughout his encyclopædic *Convivio,* is detailed in the unfinished *De Vulgari Eloquentia.* Dante considered what kind of vernacular was suitable for poetry; he did not explicitly recommend the vernacular in preference to L., though he did call it "nobler"—*i.e.,* more natural or less artificial and more human or uncontrolled by grammar. Although the tract did not circulate widely during the subsequent century, it carried the theories of the workers in the "sweet new style," and Dante's own choice of the vernacular for his greatest poem (though not wholly conforming to his own doctrines) gave additional import to his words. By a series of distinctions he concluded that the highest type of vernacular poetry is the *canzone* of tragic style written on the worthiest subjects in the illustrious vernacular. *Canzone* he defined as a series of stanzaic verses without refrain, written to be accompanied by music, though music is not essential; it is dominated by the hendecasyllabic line with end-rime. Tragic style is the highest, or elevated, style, as differentiated from comic (the middle style), and elegiac (the style of the wretched). The worthiest subjects are three: *salus* (safety or war), *venus* (love), and *virtus* (virtue or religion); these are, be it noted, the subjects of medieval romance. The illustrious vernacular is the *si* dialect of the Romance tongue, imperfect in nature, but more nearly perfected in Bologna and other northern municipalities not too near the borders of Italy. It is *illustrious* in being exalted and in exalting its users. It is *cardinal* in being the basis of all local dialects; *courtly* in being the language of rulers; *curial* in being the language of courts of justice. This language should never be used for mean, lowly, or vulgar themes.

The notion of tragic style as lofty and serious, though subscribed to in the later Middle Ages, conflicted with the notion of tragedy (its application to drama long forgotten) as a story with an unhappy ending. In his letter to Can Grande (*Epist.* x), which criticizes in some detail his own *Commedia* (so-called because of its happy ending), Dante explicitly states: "[Comedy] differs from tragedy in its content, in that tragedy begins admirably and tranquilly, whereas its end or exit is foul and terrible. . . . Comedy introduces some harsh complication, but brings its matter to a prosperous end. . . . Hence certain writers, on introducing themselves, have made it their practice to give the salutation, 'I wish you a tragic beginning and a comic end.'" Dante here repeated the century-old words of Uguccione; he was in turn paraphrased by Chaucer nearly a century later; the tragic tales of the Monk, "so piteous," are in the "wretched" style that Dante called elegiac.

Saints; C. S. Baldwin, *Mediæval Rhetoric and Poetic,* 1928; H. O. Taylor, *The Classical Heritage of the Middle Ages,* 1901; E. Lobel, *The Medieval L. Poetics,* 1932. CHARLES W. JONES.

RUSSIAN CRITICISM. Although earlier Russian literature contains examples of evaluation by one writer of another's writings, *e.g.* Prince Andrey Mikailovich Kurbsky's (1528–1583) scathing remarks about the style of the epistles of Tsar Ivan IV (1530–1584), literary criticism in Russia really begins only in the 18th c. Initially critical evaluations concerned chiefly word usage, since the newly established contacts with the West at the turn of the 18th c. brought with them new ideas and concepts, for which Russia had no terminology. Peter I (1672–1725) himself felt obliged to admonish his translators to revise their work and use ". . . not (Church) Slavic words, but simple Russian," thus making the new, secularized culture more accessible to a wider mass of readers.

Literary theory and criticism began when Russian literature entered its new, European, phase, based first on the French classical tradition. Vasily Kirillovich Trediakovsky (1703–1769), Mikhail Vasilievich Lomonosov (1711–1765) and Aleksandr Petrovich Sumarokov (1718–1777) are the three important figures of the first period. Their chief concern was with questions of language and style, as well as literary theory.

Through treatises on Russian prosody Trediakovsky (in 1735) and Lomonosov (in 1739) brought about a replacement in Russian versification of the then current syllabic system by a syllabo-tonic system. Trediakovsky also published translations of Boileau's *L'Art poétique* (1752) and Horace's *Ars poetica.* Lomonosov's treatise "On the Use of Sacred Books in the Russian Tongue" (1757), reflecting classical views on the three styles of literature ("high," "middle," "low") was the first essay in a Russian guide to stylistics, in which Lomonosov defined the limits of Slavonicisms in Russian usage. Another handbook on Russian usage and prosody is Sumarokov's *Instructions to Those Desiring to Become Writers* (1772). In the literary interchange among the writers of this period, opinions were limited chiefly to a critical evaluation of language and style.

Toward the end of the 18th c. sentimentalism began to replace classicism as the leading literary mode. Nikolay Mikhailovich Karamzin (1766–1826), the leading proponent of the new literary current, effected the replacement of Lomonosov's three styles by one ("middle") style, based on the speech of the educated nobility. In vocabulary and syntax Karamzin oriented himself largely on the example of the French, rather than on that of the traditional Greek, Latin, and German. In the *Moscow Journal* (1791–1792) which he published, Karamzin established the first Russian regular section devoted to bibliography and criticism. Still newer trends were exploited in the 19th c. by the poet Vasily Andreevich Zhukovsky (1783–1852), a remarkably gifted translator, who introduced European romantic poets to the Russians. In the subsequent struggle between defenders of the old and champions of the new in questions of language, a conservative group upholding the "purity" of the older literary language formed the "Society of Lovers of the Russian Word" (1811–1816) under the leadership of Admiral Aleksandr Semyonovich Shishkov (1754–1841) and the poet Gavrila Romanovich Derzhavin (1743–1816). The proponents of the new trends banded together in the literary circle "Arzamas" (1815–1818) with Karamzin and Zhukovsky as their guiding lights.

During the 1820's and 1830's the Russian romantic school was reflected in the critical writings of Nikolay Alekseevich Polevoy (1796–1846), Dmitry Vladimirovich Venevitinov (1805–1827), Vladimir Fyodorovich Odoevsky (1804–1869) and Nikolay Ivanovich Nadezhdin (1804–1856). Attacking the Karamzinian concept of criticism as judgment based essentially on the æsthetic "good taste" of the critic, they proposed instead an historical evaluation of a writer's work.

Also among the important literary critics of the period was Aleksandr Sergeevich Pushkin (1799–1837), who criticized the lack of discipline of the romantics and the growing moralizing subjectivism of the late 1820's and early 1830's, and moved Russian literature on its first steps away from both classicism and romanticism, toward a realistic mode. Several of Pushkin's personal friends also left their mark as critics—Prince Pyotr Andreevich Vyazemsky (1792–1878), Baron Anton Antonovich Delvig (1798–1831), the Decembrist Vilgelm Karlovich Kyukhelbeker (1797–1846).

During the 1830's the notorious journalistic "triumvirate"—Nikolay Ivanovich Grech (1787–1867), Faddey Venediktovich Bulgarin (1789–1859) and Osip Ivanovich Senkovsky (1800–1858)—wielded considerable influence in establishing the literary taste of the reading public. In their popular periodicals (*Son of the Fatherland, Library for Reading*) they praised political allies and their works and condemned those whom they regarded as adversaries.

The most important and influential Russian critic of the 19th c. was Visarion Grigorievich Belinsky (1811–1848), a commoner by birth. Belinsky began as a disciple of Schelling, and the influence of German romantic idealism is seen in his *Literary Reveries* (1834). By the 1840's, however, Belinsky became absorbed in social problems, and his writings take on the "civic" aspect that characterizes his subsequent criticism, as seen in his evaluation of Gogol's fiction. Famous also was his "Letter to Gogol," a scathing denunciation of Gogol's political and social views as set forth in his "Selected Correspondence with Friends" (1847). Belinsky's position is that literature must be "faithful to life" (and therefore to its national character) and progressive and liberal in its view of life and thus of service to the betterment of social conditions. Belinsky's "civic" criticism was further developed by the "radical" critics Nikolay Grigorievich Chernyshevsky (1828–1889), Nikolay Aleksandrovich Dobrolyubov (1836–1861) and Dmitry Ivanovich Pisarev (1840–1868). Chernyshevsky in his *Essays on the Age of Gogol* (1855–56) and in his M.A. dissertation, *The Esthetic Relations of Art to Reality* (1855), discusses the relation between literature and life. To him, literature, being merely a copy of life, and therefore inferior, can be justified only when it shows a progessive social awareness. Dobrolyubov appears as a disciple of Chernyshevsky. His "What is Oblomovism? (1859)—an examination of the "Superfluous men" among the heroes of Russian fiction, and "Dark Kingdom" (1859) a study of the dramas of Ostrovsky—analyse literature as a reflection of society. Pisarev, a nihilist by inclination, came to a complete denial of æsthetic value in literary judgment. Poetry that had no civic worth seemed useless to him and he accordingly downgraded Pushkin's work. The influence that these three critics had in the 1850's and 1860's cemented the position of a utilitarian approach to evaluating literature in Russia.

Essentially an æsthetic approach to literary criticism during the middle of the 19th c. may be seen, however, in the essays of Aleksandr Vasilievich Druzhinin (1824–1864), Vasily Petrovich Botkin (1811–1869), Pavel Vasilievich Annenkov (1812–1887) and Valerian Nikolaevich Maykov (1823–1847). Druzhinin, better known for his novel *Polinka Saks* (1847), was among the first Russian critics to challenge the demand that art must serve society. Annenkov is now best remembered for his memoirs *The Remarkable Decade, 1838–1848*. Another opponent of a purely civic literature was Apollon Aleksandrovich Grigoriev (1822–1864), whose "Organic Criticism" reflects an idealistical view of reality and demands that Russian literature display those elements of life that are indigenously Russian. His volume of reminiscences, *My Literary and Moral Wanderings* (1864), is still regarded as an outstanding portrayal of his age.

Many Russian literary figures of this period successfully combined critic with artist, as Ivan Sergeevich Turgenev (1818–1883) had pointed out in a letter to Flaubert. Thus Turgenev himself wrote a number of essays, such as "Hamlet and Don Quixote" (1859); Ivan Aleksandrovich Goncharov (1812–1891) has a penetrating essay (*A Million Torments,* 1872) on Aleksandr Griboedov's (1795–1829) masterpiece *Woe from Wit.* Fyodor Mikhailovich Dostoevsky (1821–1881) in his "Pushkin Speech" (1880) makes a complete break with the Pisarev tradition in evaluating the poet.

Nikolay Konstantinovich Mikhailovsky (1842–1904), the leading populist literary theoretician and critic of the last quarter of the 19th c., continues the tradition of social protest in criticism. His essay on Leo Tolstoy "The Right Hand and the Left of Leo Tolstoy" (1875), analyzes some basic contradictions in Tolstoy's art. In "The Cruel Genuis" (1882) he examines the works of Dostoevsky; in "On Maxim Gorky and his Heroes" (1898) Mikhailovsky reveals the ideological differences between the populists and the Marxists.

Leo Nikolaevich Tolstoy's (1828–1910) *What is Art?* (1897–1898) is his best known work on the theory of art. It shows his later ("post-conversion") æsthetic position. Its influence can be seen even in some tenets of Soviet literary criticism of our day. Tolstoy insists that the best literature must be morally inspiring and intelligible to the broad mass of potential readers. He, therefore, criticized all *avant-garde* movements, because they could appeal only to a few select readers.

A growing opposition to the tendentiousness of civic criticism developed from the forerunners of the symbolist movement. A. Volynsky (pseud. of Akim Lvovich Flekser, 1863–1926) in *The Struggle for Idealism* (1900), *Russian Critics* (1896) and various studies on Dostoevsky attacked the social utilitarianism of the Russian radical critics and defended an idealistic approach in criticism, which might bring about a religiously oriented contemplation of art. Other early modernist critics included: Vasily Vasilievich Rozanov (1856–1927), Lev Shestov (pseud. of Lev Isaakovich Shvartsman, 1866–1938); and Dmitry Sergeevich Merezhkovsky (1865–1941), whose essay *On the Causes of the Decline and on the New Currents of Contemporary Russian Literature* (1893) can be regarded as the first manifesto of Russian modernism. Also important was Merezhkovsky's study *Tolstoy and Dostoevsky* (2 v. 1901–1902) and his collected essays *Eternal Companions* (1896), which interpret the great writers of the past as being essentially symbolist.

With the flowering of the symbolist movement in Russia, especially in the first decade of the 20th c., the entire group of young symbolist writers began a reevaluation of literature from their anti-materialist viewpoint. Outstanding among them were: Zinaida Nikolaevna Hippius-Merezhkovsky (1869–1945)—*A Literary Diary* (1908); Vyacheslav Ivanovich Ivanov (1866–1949)—*By the Stars* (1909), *Furrows and Boundaries* (1916); Innokenty Fyodorovich Annensky (1856–1909) —*Book of Reflections* (2 v. 1906–1909); Valery Yakovlevich Byusov (1873–1924)—"Keys of Mysteries" (1904), *The Near and the Far* (1911); Andrey Bely (pseud. of Boris Nikolaevich Bugaev, 1880–1934)—*Symbolism* (1910), *Green Pastures* (1910), *Arabesques* (1911); Konstantin Dmitrievich Balmont (1867–1942)—*Mountain Peaks* (1905), *Poetry as Magic* (1916). Post-symbolist criticism is seen in the *Letters on Russian Poetry* (1923) by Nikolay Stepanovich Gumilev (1886–1921), leader of the Russian "Acmeists."

At the turn of the 20th c. Dmitry Nikolaevich Ovsyaniko-Kulikovsky introduced the psychological approach to literary criticism in his studies on Turgenev and other Russian classics. An exponent of Freudianism in Russian criticism was Alfred Lyudovigovich Bem (1886–1947?), most of whose studies on Dostoevsky were published in emigration, abroad. A leading disciple of the sociological approach was Ivanov-Razumnik (pseud. of Razumnik Vasilievich Ivanov, 1878–1946)—*History of Russian Social Thought* (2 v. 1907), *On the Meaning of Life* (1908), *Leo Tolstoy* (1912), *Pinnacles* (1922).

The Marxist camp of critics was best represented in the pre-revolutionary period by Georgy Valentinovich Plekhanov (1856–1918), Anatoly Vasilievich Lunacharsky (1875–1933), Vatslav Vatslavovich Vorovsky (1871–1923), A. Bogdanov (pseud. of Aleksandr Aleksandrovich Malinovsky, 1873–

1928). D. S. Mirsky, *A Hist. of Russian Lit.*, 1960; René Wellek, *A Hist. of Modern Crit.* v. III, IV, 1965; B. P. Gorodetsky, ed. *Istoria Russkoy Kritiki*, 2 v., 1958; W. E. Harkins, *Dictionary of Russian Lit.*, 1957.

Soviet Literary Criticism displays little of the oppositional fervor that had characterized the writings of such 19th-century critics as Belinsky, Chernyshevsky, Dobrolyubov, Pisarev. Oriented on principles of Marxist-Leninism, Soviet literary criticism reflects largely the thinking of the political theoreticians of the Communist Party of the U.S.S.R. Although stemming from the views of Belinsky and his followers, it has its more immediate roots in the writings of Plekhanov, Lunacharsky, Lenin and Gorky.

Soviet literary criticism passed through various shifting stages before it accepted the current official doctrine for Soviet literature: Socialist Realism. The struggle reflected the political orientation of the various factions, with critics representing the party line polemicising with its opponents.

Inasmuch as Socialist Realism assumes that Soviet writers accept the Communist Party's views on art, it prescribes that literature be expressed in "forms intelligible to the broad masses of readers," and it therefore cannot escape a strong political and social flavor.

From the outset of the revolutionary era, party-oriented literary criticism has stressed the need for art to take an active part in the state's struggle to build a new society. It therefore opposed such dissenting currents as the apolitically oriented Formalism (represented by B. Eikhenbaum, V. Shklovsky, B. Tomashevsky, V. Zhirmunsky and others) and other groupings.

Attempts to adhere too closely to political doctrines of the time led such critics as V. F. Pereverzev to insist that a writer's output was irrevocably determined by the world-view of his class and that every work of literature reflected only the class origins and economic background of its writer. This view is now condemned as "vulgar sociologism."

Though evident since the beginning of the revolution, by the 1920's Soviet literary criticism had clearly split into two basic factions: writers representing the proletariat, who saw themselves as the sole true standard bearers of the new revolutionary culture, and all others—their ideological foes.

The mid-1920's saw a bitter polemic arise between the proletarian writers, centered about the periodical *On Guard* (G. Lelevich, S. Rodov, B. Volin, eds.) and such groups as the "Fellow Travelers" (*Red Virgin Soil*, A. K. Voronsky, ed. and chief theoretician).

Seeking to establish a purely proletarian literature, the On Guardists, just as the Proletkultists had done before them, claimed hegemony, as representatives of the new ruling class, over all cultural activity of the new state and dismissed all literature and art of prerevolutionary tradition.

Voronsky, chief spokesman of the *Divide* group and of the Fellow Travelers, *i.e.* writers not claiming proletarian origin, but willing to live with the new order, insisted on continuing the traditions of the cultural past. The struggle became increasingly intense and was temporarily resolved by a Party decree (June 6, 1925) on "The Party's policy in the realm of fine literature." The resolution stressed that literary criticism was to profess a didactic orientation and directed Fellow Travelers to act accordingly in order to become absorbed into the main stream of Soviet literature.

Within a short time the All Russian Association of Proletarian Writers, VAPP (L. Averbakh, V. Ermilov, A. Fadeev & others) resumed with renewed vigor their campaign for a strictly proletarian hegemony over all Soviet literature. Their attacks on their opponents—Fellow Travelers, Formalists, the *Divide* group (D. Gorbov, A. Lezhnev and others), even some of the Futurists—increased in intensity and virulence, since they saw the Soviet literary world only as partisan allies or as enemies. Averbakh became virtually a dictator in his sphere and was instrumental in having a number of writers purged as enemies of the state.

On April 23, 1932, the Central Committee of the Communist Party issued a decree "On the reconstitution of literary organizations." It declared that all writers who were willing to uphold the Soviet regime and to take part in the "building of Socialism" were free to unite in a single Union of Soviet Writers (1934), which accepted the Gorky sponsored "Socialist Realism" as the principal literary method of Soviet literature.

Throughout the early 1930's Gorky remained one of the most influential voices in the U.S.S.R. in matters of literature. He opposed the extreme views of the On Guardists and advocated instead the importance of the Russian classical tradition and propagandized Socialist Realism (journal *Literary Studies*).

Present day Soviet literary historians see certain evils in the Stalin era of Soviet literature and criticism: the "Cult of the Individual," demanding flattering references to Stalin; a simplified depiction of only the positive aspects of Soviet life and characters, which leads to an omission of conflicts between protagonists ("theory of Conflictlessness").

During the years of World War II, Soviet literature willingly devoted itself almost exclusively to the heroic war effort against the invaders and enjoyed a period of relative freedom from restrictive directives from without.

With the end of the war, however, Andrey Zhdanov, Secretary of the Central Committee of the Communist Party, reasserted the Party's control over all cultural activity in the Soviet Union, his policy demanding complete adherence to party ideology. This was continued even after his death (1948) and effectively paralyzed dissent in Soviet literature until after Stalin's death in 1953, when Soviet literature entered a new phase of alternating "Thaws" and "Freezes."

After the 20th Congress of the Communist Party of the U.S.S.R. (1956), literary criticism was permitted to modify its views on the essence and function of Socialist Realism—especially as regards its excessively romantic idealization of Soviet life.

During the 1960's Soviet literary criticism has been allowed to display a rising tendency toward treating works of literature as works of art. Much effort is currently being devoted to poetics and stylistics in attempts to have literary studies approach the sciences in their methodology.

Ever since the death of Stalin a vocal opposition to political domination of Soviet literature has been growing within the U.S.S.R. The Communist Party, while allowing some expression of dissent, is permissive only to within certain limits after which it clamps down on the illusory newly acquired freedom of Soviet writers. The fate of Boris Pasternak (after his writing of *Dr. Zhivago* and his subsequent award of the Nobel Prize); then of Yuly Daniel and Andrey Sinyavsky; and more recently, the troubles of Ivan Solzhenitsyn are cases in point.

At present the liberal faction of Russian letters seems to have centered about the journal *New World* (A. Tvardovsky, ed.) as its chief outlet, while the traditionalist wing centers about *October* (E. Kochetov, ed.).

Edward J. Brown, *Russian Literature since the Revolution,* 1963; Herman Herman Ermolaev, *Soviet Literary Theories, 1917–1934,* 1963; *Kratkaya Literaturnaya Entsiklopedia,* vols. I–V, 1962–1968; William E. Harkins, *Dictionary of Russian Literature,* 1957; Marc Slonim, *Soviet Russian Literature,* 1967; Gleb Struv, *Soviet Russian Literature, 1917–1950,* 1951. Oleg A. Maslenikov.

SPANISH CRITICISM. Through the Renaissance. The history of Sp. criticism begins with Saint Isidore of Seville (560–636). His Summa of 20 books, *Etymologiæ,* quotes 160 Pagan and Christian authors, displacing the pagan authors Vergil, Horace, Ovid, Persius, Lucanus, with the Christian poets Ambrose, Prudentius, Juvencus, Sedulius. Behind Isidore's religious justification for his choice, there are also æsthetic reasons. The pagans, he says, "glitter by their eloquence, but are innerly empty, without virtue and without wisdom." Wherever he finds substantial virtue and wisdom, there he acknowledges harmony, rhythm, and metre as the appropriate vehicles for persuading good actions. He uses the word "art" for the treatment of "verisimilitudes," and follows Cassiodorus and Quintilian in asserting that historical facts achieve poetry when they rise to a general scope (*"Ea quae vere gesta sunt in alias species conversa transducat poeta"*). Thanks to his wrong etymologies Isidore established a sort of *Kalokagathia* as æsthetical ideal, deriving *bonus* from *venustas;* thanks to his moralistic raging against the theatrical performances of his time, he gave a definition of comedy (anticipating Lope de Vega) as dealing with the acts of private persons, raping of girls and love-tales of low women.

The philosophically æsthetic basis for literary criticism came to Sp. through the Arabs. The physician Avempace (1085–1138), declared (*Guidance for the solitary thinker,* 1119) that arts and poetry belong to a higher order of things because, being neither sensible nor abstract forms, they pave the way to the pure forms. The Jewish philosopher Avicebron (1021–70), in *The Source of Life* explained that "the sensible forms are to the soul as the written book to the reader when the eye perceives the letters and the signs: the soul perceives the actual sense hidden under those forms, the bodily forms being only a picture of the psychic forms." Maimonides (1135–1204) emphasized that the outside is silver only and the inside gold. His "inborn oriental incapacity to understand the artistic side of the Greek" (Menéndez y Pelayo) was redeemed by the critical comprehension of æsthetic principles *a posteriori,* by observation of the artist's work in order to find out the rules he has followed (*The Guide to those that doubt,* 1190). Similar ideas made the Arabian commentator Averroes (1126–98) misinterpret Aristotle's Poetics (*Paraphrase of the Rhetoric*; *Paraphrase of the Poetics,* 1152). Rhetoric, according to Averroes, is designed to persuade those that philosophy cannot convince. For them are needed the enthymeme instead of the syllogism, exemplum instead of induction, oratory instead of logic. Averroes replaced Aristotle's Gr. examples with Arabian ones, and achieved the relativistic statement: "Beauty varies according to the diversity of men." The principles of this relative beauty are put by Nature into the hearts of the poets, who try to imitate the living model for the sake of truth, use verses (*numeros*) for beauty's sake, hence have to avoid certain figures of style (*e.g.* hyperbole) which are perforce at odds with truth.

Full of such oriental ideas was the Catalan theologian Raymond Lull (1235–1315), who in his *Ars magna* (1311), however, gave more æsthetic flashes of literary criticism. His mysticism was aware of a realm between knowledge and faith, to which poetry belongs; he called the magic element in rhetoric *Alchimia verborum,* as do the modern symbolists. Lull was also a sober literary analyst, saying that rhetoric must teach "how to join beautiful subjects with beautiful predicates." In spite of his confusion of word and thing, he recognized emotional connotations: "April" and "May" are wonderful words "because they carry with them the remembrance of flowers, leaves, and bird's song." He sought unshakable æsthetic principles, convinced that particular beauties must shine and reappear in a general and unifying law. He was the first Sp. to set literary criticism in the general system of his rational philosophy. Criticism is, he thought, a mixed art, between the art of speaking and the art of interpreting; it belongs consequently to grammar.

Western influences now began to appear. In contact with Fr. and Prov., Don Enrique de Villena (1384–1434) in his fragmentarily preserved *Arte de trobar* (1433) tried to imitate such collections of rules for meter and rhyme as the Prov. *Leys d'amors* and Ramon Vidal's *Dreita maniera de trobar.* He describes a literary tournament in Barcelona, where the *capitul* judges the competitors according to pedantic master-singer rules. A much better critic, the first literary historian, was Iñigo López de Mendoza, Marqués de Santillana (1388–1458); *Prohemio e Carta al Condestable Don Pedro de Portugal* (between 1445 and 1449) is a preface to his own poems, dedicated to the prince. Poetry means "useful things painted or veiled with a beautiful mantle," fruits from gardens called poets, imbued with the loftiest science. Their eloquence may flow in verse or prose. The difference of quality lies in the style, which may (following the ancients) be very low (*infimo*) as in the popular ballads, mediocre as in the Provençals and Italians, or sublime as in the Greeks and Romans. He considered the art of the troubadors as an integral tradition of the neo-Latin peoples, and, although he admired the technical knowledge of the French, he preferred the ingenuity of the Italians, whom he imitated.

The pedantic speculations of Alfonso de la Torre fill his clumsy allegory: *Visión delectable de la Filosofía y artes liberales* (1485). Rhetoric appears here with the inscription *Ornatus persuasio,* and boasts of having converted many men and women from vile and beastlike life to virtue and honesty, as well as of making sisters of science and art. This jargon was cut short by the first great humanist, Antonio de Nebrija (1441–1522). Half a century before Vida and Trissino, he persuaded the learned world that only close imitation of the ancients can be the basis of literary art. He provided rich material in his *De artis rhetoricæ compendiosa coaptatione ex Aristotele, Cicerone et Quintiliano* (1481) and showed how the cultivation of the Spanish language can profit from good examples (*Arte de la lengua Castellana,* 1492). Juan de Valdés, in his *Diálogo de la Lengua,* opposed Nebrija, with no sharply defined position in the Aristotelian struggle, but showing the best taste among his contemporaries as to purity of language and just appraisal of the great Castilian writers. From Nebrija's *Arte* sprang the first practical handbook for the Spanish poet, by Juan del Encina (1469–1529), *Arte de la Poesía Castellana* (1496). Rhyme is an important It. invention for the aid of memory. The technique of assonance, consonance, metres, feet, must be learned even by the genius, otherwise the poet would be a fertile but not well cultivated field. The born poet must become a learned troubadour, although the two are related as master and slave, captain and private, composer and singer. The man not born as a poet is as a sterile field, which the rules of agriculture can hardly aid. There is, however, one fertilizer: reading good poets.

Interest in dramatic criticism was shown by Bartolomé de Torres Naharro (d. 1531) in the *Proemio* to his comedies and poems. He defines comedy as "an ingenious arrangement of noteworthy and finally joyous events played by different persons," restricting the characters to between 6 and 12. He distinguished realistic comedy, *a noticía,* from romantic, *a fantasía.*

Luis Vives (1492–1540) in *De Arte dicendi* (1532), which appeared some years before the complete and correct text of Aristotle's *Poetics,* comments vigorously on ancient rhetoric. Vives objects to the exclusive following of ancient patterns, defends the value of new experience. No one would construct buildings in Spain according to the rules of Vitruvius. Quintilian, says Vives, cannot distinguish between ethics and æsthetics. Aristotle's *partes rhetoricæ* do not belong exclusively to rhetoric. The three styles of the ancients he discards for an infinite variety of styles, according to the circumstances. The external division of literature into prose and poetry must be replaced by a deeper one, Plato's dialogues being obviously more poetical than a rhymed comedy. The new principle should be not to imitate, but to surpass the classical models. Spanish comedy, through its themes alone, arouses more interest than the plays of the Greeks and Romans.

Sebastian Fox Morcillo (b. 1526) continued the break from It. ideas, in his *De imitatione seu de informandi styli ratione* (1554). This Platonist put his thoughts into the mouth of Gaspar Núñez, in a Socratic dialogue with a student of Louvain. He sought the solution of the problem of style in the connection between matter and form. "Style is a certain character, genius, or form of speech, derived as well from the type of the writer as from the question treated." "Is the knowledge of the liberal arts anything else than the understanding of their history?" The Aristotelian Padre Juan de Santo Tomas Poinsat (1589–1644) in *Artis logicae* (1631) worked out new points of æsthetics, perhaps more fundamental than those of Minturno, Scaliger, and Castelvetro in Italy. On the basis of Saint Thomas Aquinas, he severed æsthetics from morals. In morals the final goal of man is always to be kept in mind; in art, the immediate aim is decisive, namely that the work of art correspond to the idea of the artist. If the artist, though he fall short in the ultimate aim of life, achieves this, he creates a valid work. This theory, however, was counterbalanced by the Tridentine and the National Spanish *Indices librorum prohibitorum,* established with the help of Juan de Mariana, whose taste for decency is also clearly expressed in his treatise on the theatre, *De Spectaculis.*

The discrepancy between Sp. and It. Renaissance criticism is due to the persistence of scholasticism as a leading force in Sp.; also, to a reenforcement of the oriental trend by the speculation of León Hebreo (Judá Abrabanel, b. 1460): *Dialogues of Love* (1535), highly esteemed by Cervantes. León's æsthetics are relativistic, denying the existence of an ontological beauty, which was the starting point of the Aristotelians. Beauty depends "on the love for the artistic object in the contemplating subject." Material objects are in themselves ugly; "formed," it is true, they become beautiful, through parti pating in the spiritual world. Even then, however, only their "lover" finds them beautiful. The critic then must recognize, not the beautiful forms as such (*lo hermoso hermoseado*), but their immanent idea of beauty (*hermosura*), as far as this emanates from God, the Beauty creating beauty (*lo hermoso que hermosea*). On the line from León Hebreo to the Spanish mystics, Luis de Granada was most insistent on æsthetic questions. In 7 passages of his ascetical treatise *Guia de Pecadores,* he underscores the fact that natural beauty compared to its principle God is nothing but ugliness; he adds in his *Memorial de la vida cristiana* the reason for this statement: God possesses infinite beauty that he does not communicate to his creatures. Fray Luis explains, in his *Simbolo de la Fe,* that all earthly beauties are only imperfect letters somewhat illuminated by God, but lacking essential beauty. This reasoning induced an overestimation of abstract antirealistic art, as correcting the imperfections of Nature by classical idealization. In the field of literature, rhetoric consequently leads man nearer to Beauty than plain speech, or, as he puts it in his L. *Rhetorica Ecclesiastica* (Sp. trans. 1770), Art is a safer guide (to perfection) than Nature. These spiritualistic principles represent one blow against Italy and antiquity, the Quixotic one; the other attack comes from Sancho Panza, from the popular side. Juan de Mal

Lara (1525–71) in his *Filosofía vulgar* (1568) defends a *refran,* stating: "There is no art and no science secluded in books, which the people themselves have not enriched."

This popular trend in Renaissance criticism paved the way for the Baroque. Even the humanist Benito Arías Montano (1527–98) who competed (4 bks. of *Rhetorica,* 1569) with Gerónimo Vida, replaced the ancient examples of Aristotle with modern Sp. ones. Dr. Francisco Sánchez, El Brocense (1523–1601), who tried, in accord with his other scientific innovations, to raise rhetoric to the rank of a linguistic philosophy, wrote comments (1574) on the Sp. poet Garcilaso de la Vega, before writing his *Organum dialecticum et rhetoricum* (1579). Similarly, the criticism of Fernando de Herrera (1534–97): *Anotaciones a las obras de Garcilaso de la Vega* (1580), starting from the words of the different sonnets, sought the essence of æsthetic conceptions. Beauty, says he, commenting on Sonnet 22, is that grace which the Greeks call *charis* and the Tuscans *leggiadria.* The intelligence of the poets has to work out new forms of beauty. Meanwhile the Jesuits serving the Counter-Reformation combined æsthetics and religion. So did Juan Díaz Rengifo, who learned a lot from It., in his technically excellent *Arte poética Española* (1592). A profound critic was the physician and admirer of the Arabs Alonso López Pinciano: *Philosophia antigua poética* (1596), a considered imitation of Aristotle. The book consists of 13 epistles in dialogue: the 6th and 7th on style, the 8th and 9th on tragedy and comedy. He is one of the neatest interpreters of Aristotle's catharsis, balancing pity and fear so that a momentary anguish is followed by a lasting and deeper calm. He extends catharsis to the epics, as Cervantes declared that novels are epics, too. An innovator in hermeneutics and analysis was Baltasar de Céspedes, at the end of the 16th c., in his *Art of Rhetoric* with the important epilogue *Discurso de las letras humanas,* called *The Humanist* (ca. 1600). He proposed the study of poems first for the genesis of the poet's thought, then for the anatomy of the finished work: grammatically, logically, rhetorically, ethically. A partisan of Aristotelian poetics was Spain's greatest author, Miguel de Cervantes (1547–1616), who adopted "Pinciano's theory that verisimilitude, æsthetic pleasure and encyclopedic culture were elements of beauty" (S. Shepard). Constructing his comedies according to classical pattern, and without success, he maintains his point of view through the long critical exposition of the canon of Toledo in *Don Quixote,* I, 48 (1605).

The Sp. popular taste was more nearly approached by the Jesuit Luis Alfonso de Carvallo (d. 1630), who in his rhymed poetics *Cisne de Apolo* (1602) casts aside unity, and purity of genres, recommends 3-act comedies that intermingle men and allegories and spread through the childhood, maturity and old age of a Saint. The playwright Juan de la Cueva (1550–1610) in his *Ejemplar poético* (1616) praises the 4-act tragicomedy with metrical variety according to the persons and their moods. This became the ideal of Lope de Vega Carpio (1562–1635) in his *Arte nuevo de hacer comedias* (1609). Lope explains that he knows all the rules as well as the Italians, but that he does not dare inflict them upon the Spanish people, who wish to see, in 3 acts played in a few hours, the whole of history from the creation of the world to the day of judgment. He is willing "to mix up Terence with Seneca, and produce the dramatic Minotaur." As in nature, so in art variety causes delight, and modern customs impose new artistic forms.

Lope, of course, provoked attacks of scholars remote from theatrical practice. Francisco Cascales (1567–1642) in his *Tablas poéticas* (1617) and *Cartas filológicas* (1634) protests that the unity of truth demands unity in art. A dramatist who reproduces the actions of a historical hero instead of drawing general ideas from them, confuses the poet's task with that of the historian. One may extend the unity of time reasonably, even to 10 days, but it is absurd to show a Saint staying in Paradise 200 years. The blending of comedy and tragedy is an hermaphroditic monstrosity. But the majority of scholars agreed with Lope. Don Carlos Boyl (1577–1617) buttressed his theories in *A un licenciado que descaba hacer comedias* (1616). Ricardo de Turia (1578–1638) in *Discurso Apologético sobre el juicio de las comedias españolas* (1616) went so far as to declare that Sophocles' *Oedipus* is really a *comedia* and that the Sp. nature must determine style in the theatre as well as in dress. Don Francisco López de Aguilar Coutiño (d. 1665) in *Expostulatio Spongiae* (1618)—written against an anti-Lope pamphlet by Pedro de Torres Rámila, called *Spongia,* now lost—declared Lope superior to any other dramatist. Lope's most objective defender was Tirso de Molina (1571–1648). In *Los Cigarrales* (1621) he pits Lope's moral verisimilitude against the physical verisimilitude of the Aristotelians, explaining, as to the unity of time, that an honest lover cannot fall in love and marry in 24 hours, but needs months, even years, to examine and prove his love.

The popular trend in æsthetics had become so strong that the *culteranismo* of Góngora (1561–1627) seemed doomed from the beginning. Its learned allusions and picturesque ornaments were opposed by Pedro de Valencia (1555–1620), in *Censura de las Soledades, Polifemo y obras de Don Luis de Góngora* (1613). Valencia rejected all poetry not based on grand thoughts (*bedeutend,* as Goethe later termed it), and declared the outer ornament a ridiculous blown-up vacuity. Juan Martinez de Jaúregui (1583–1641) presented a similar antibaroque criticism, in the *Introducción a las Rimas* (1618), *Discurso Poético* (1624), *Antídoto contra las Soledades* (1624). Distinguishing in poetry soul, body, and ornament, he objected also to the *Conceptismo* of Francisco de Quevedo y Villegas (1580–1645), in which the concepts are not real ideas forming the soul but odd formulations giving only deformity to the body and leaving poetry without any soul at all (*unas poesías desalmadas*). Quevedo (pref. to ed. of the poems of Fr. Luis de León and Francisco de la Torre) ridiculed Góngora, but sustained his own *conceptos* in opposition to vulgarity in language. A more significant compromise between the ancients and the moderns was attempted by Bartolomé Leonardo de Argensola (1562–1631), in his two *Epístolas* (1634) treating with poetics. The modern poet must be not merely a sailor on the Ancients' sea, but a pilot; he must also eschew levity in serious works, in order not to vulgarize noble minds.

With the replacing of Lope's taste by Calderón's in drama, the artificial and the baroque began nevertheless to prevail. Sheltered by the new atmosphere of artistry, Joseph Pellicer de Salas delivered *Lecciones solemnes a las obras de D. Luis de Góngora* (1630). The second champion of the baroque taste was Cristóbal Salazar y Mardones (b. 1570) in *Illustración y defensa de la fábula de Pyramo y Tisbe* (1636). The reasons given in such defences are baroque themselves, as proved by the statement of the Peruvian Juan de Espinosa Medrano (*Apologético en favor de Don Luis de Góngora,* 1694): "It belongs to the Spanish genius to glide on the waves of Latin poetry with the ease of oil over water." It was in vain that Juan Eusebio Nieremberg, S.J. (1595–1658) in his *Tratado de la hermosura* (1641) recalled the scholastic principle that beauty appeals to the power of distinguishing and understanding. Even Baltasar Gracián (1601–58), who in *Criticón* regards all of life as an æsthetic-moral problem, did not (*Agudeza y arte de ingenio,* 1642) free himself of the conceptist belief that ideology and well-expressed oddity are the same thing: "An intelligence without flashes of spirit and concepts is a light without beams." What these critics did for Góngora and Quevedo was undertaken by Guerra y Ribera (1638–92) for the *Churriguerismo* of Calderón in his *Apelación al tribunal de los doctos, justa defensa de la aprobación a las comedias de D. Pedro Calderón* (1682). Diego de Saavedra Fajardo (1584–1648) in his *República Literaria* (1655) added some eclectic aspects to Sp. criticism. But on the whole it had reached such a state of decay that new values could spring only from another æsthetic world, in this case, France.

M. Menéndez Pelayo, *Historia de las ideas estéticas en Esp.,* 1883–91, v.2; E. Díez Echarri, *Teorías métricas del Siglo de Oro,* 1949; A. Vilanova, "Preceptistas esp. de los siglos XVI y XVII" (en *Hist. Gral. de las Lit. Hisp.,* ed. Díaz-Plaja, III, 1953); S. Shepard, *El Pinciano y las teorías lit. del S. de Oro,* 1962; E. C. Riley, *Cervantes' Theory of the Novel,* 1962; H. J. Chaytor, *Dramatic Theory in Sp.,* 1925; M. Romero-Navarro, *La preceptiva dramática de Lope de Vega,* 1935; M. Newels, *Die dramatischen Gattungen in den Poetiken des S. de Oro,* 1959; E. K. Kane, *Gongorism and the Golden Age,* 1928; D. Alonso, *Estudios y ensayos gongorinos,* 1955; T. E. May, "An Interpretation of Gracián's *Agudeza,*" *Hispanic Rev.,* 1948. HELMUT A. HATZFELD.

1700 to 1900. The change from a degenerate Hapsburg dynasty to the Bourbon line gave hope for an artistic renewal. The founding of the Royal Academy of the Language (1714) was one of the first constructive moves; its dictionary (6v., 1726–39) was the greatest work of its kind, till then, in any language. Ignazio de Luzán (1702–54) was the first great critic of this period. His close contact with It. scholars, his thorough knowledge of It., Fr., and G., prepared him to accept and promulgate the neoclassical doctrines. His *Poética* (1737), the most important critical document of the 18th c., is based on Aristotle and Horace and their followers. It deemed the Spanish Golden Age drama destructive of good taste. This direct attack on one of Spain's greatest claims to glory, *la comedia,* concentrated the fight between the nationalist and the neoclassical schools on the drama. According to Luzán, literature ought to teach as well as entertain. He follows the It. Muratori in listing 3 primary subjects for artistic presentation: Nature, Man, and the Celestial World. Luzán's style makes his *Poética* good reading even today and has given him more importance than the rehashing of old doctrines justifies.

Luzán's *Poética* had its detractors and supporters. Juan de Iriarte (1702–71) attacked it in the famous *Diario de los literatos de España,* 1737. Blas Antonio Nasarre (1689–1751), in his *Discurso sobre la comedia esp.,* 1749, in his edition of the plays of Lope de Vega and Calderón, went further than Luzán and called them "pestilent corruptors of our theatre." Agustin de Montiano (1697–1764) joined Nasarre in his *Discursos sobre las tragedias esp.,* 1750–53. Luzán excluded prose from the discussions in his *Poética*; it is roundly considered from the classical point of view in the *Retórica* (1757) and *Orígenes de la lengua castellana* (1737) of Gregorio Mayans (1699–1781). The novel of Padre Isla (1703–81), *Fray Gerundio. . . ,* 1758, may be considered a satirical fictional treatment of sacred oratory.

Nicolás Fernández de Moratín (the elder, 1735–80), a writer of moderate merit, was a leader in critical thought. His *Desenganos al teatro esp.,* 1762, praised French neoclassical drama. Lyric poetry was left almost undisturbed by the arguments on neoclassicism, although some slight Italian influence was felt. Among the many meetings of writers, Moratín the elder led the informal reunions in the Fonda de San Sebastián, where neoclassicism was the accepted standard.

But a spirit of national pride inspired writers to publish or republish masterpieces of the 15th, and 16th, and 17th c., which, more than any theories, prepared the way for more romantic literature. Francisco Nifo (Nipho, 1719–1803), in *El Caxon de sastre,* 1760, 1781–82, a literary review, attacked the neoclassicists, sometimes bitterly. Vicente de los Rios (1736–79) in his ed. of the works of Manuel Villegas, and García de la Huerta (1734–87) in his *Teatro esp.*, 1785, did much to popularize almost forgotten works of truly Spanish spirit. The middle-of-the-road critics were the most influential. Vicente de los Rios recommended, as basic criteria, brevity, clarity, and simplicity. Antonio Capmany (1742–1813) in his *Filosofía de la elocuencia,* 1777, and *Teatro histórico-crítico de la elocuencia,* 1786–94, did much to hasten the return to national models. He insisted on the need of a wide variety of types and models for the development of literature. The hold that neoclassicism had gained on Spanish letters declined rapidly after the death of Moratín the elder. Spanish literature and Spain's contribution to world literature were defended in Italy by Padre Lampillas (1739–98), *Ensayo apologético de la lit. esp.,* 1778–81; in France by Abbot Cavanilles (1745–1804) in his *Observaciones,* 1784; and in Germany by Carlos Denina (1731–1813), *Riposta all domanda: che si dee ala Spagna?.* Esteban de Arteaga (1747–99), *Investigaciones filosóficas . . . imitación,* 1789, warned against servile imitation. He came very near to concluding that all nature is legitimate material for artistic imitation.

Leandro Fernández de Moratín (the younger, 1760–1828), even before his father's death, exercised considerable influence in favor of neoclassicism. His *Comedia nueva,* esp. the prol. to the 1792 ed., ridicules those who write plays *sin reglas de arte,* insists on the didactic value of literature.

Eng. influence was felt through an adaptation of Hugh Blair's *Lectures on Rhetoric* by Sánchez Barbero (1764–1819), who also wrote a treatise *Principios de retórica y poética,* 1805, in which he listed attributes of art: clarity, order, simplicity, symmetry, unity, variety, contrast, suggestion—thus giving less emphasis to formal rules than to basic general criteria. Félix José Reinoso (1772–1841), in his *De la influencia de las bellas letras,* approaches the art for art's sake ideal. Gaspar de Jovellanos (1744–1811) combined with a sincere respect for the Moratíns and their neoclassic doctrines a love for all artistic expression; he advised copying directly from nature rather than from other artists. Manuel José Quintana (1772–1857) wrote labored criticism, but his *Colección de poesías selectas castellanas,* 1807, did much to turn Spaniards back to a consideration of the merits of their *Romances* and other early native forms.

The occupation of the Peninsula by the French, though almost bringing literary production to a halt, made the following generations more eager to cultivate their own literary gardens. The first important writer to reawaken an abiding interest in the Sp. classical theatre was Juan Nicolás Böhl von Faber (1770–1836): *Floresta de rimas antiguas castellanas,* 1821–25; *Teatro anterior a Lope de Vega,* 1832. A protesting *Poética* (1827) by Francisco Martínez de la Rosa (1787–1862) reaffirmed neoclassicism, as did José Joaquin de Mora (1783–1864). Martínez de la Rosa later became a moderate and produced the first great Sp. romantic play which, although apparently modeled on Victor Hugo's *Hernani,* was quite like the Sp. Golden Age drama. Before this, however, Javier de Burgos (the elder of the two men of this name, 1778–1848) had spoken, at his reception into the Academy, in favor of a romantic approach to letters.

The Sp. exiled intellectuals, the *emigrados,* after contact with Ossianism, Sir Walter Scott, Victor Hugo, and Goethe, returned to renovate Sp. letters with native literary forms. They put into practice the almost forgotten *Ejemplar poético* of Juan de la Cueva. The basic manifesto of romanticism was by Antonio Alcalá Galiano (1789–1865; the introd. to the Duque de Rivas' *Moro expósito,* 1834). This return to native, romantic types and manners was evident in poetry and the drama. At first the novel did not receive the serious attention of the critics; but Böhl von Faber's insistence on the use of local color and folklore soon bore fruit in the earliest works of his daughter, Cecilia Böhl von Faber (pseud. Fernán Caballero, 1796–1877). Eugenio de Ochoa (1815–72), in the journal *El Artista* (1835–36), and the brilliant though destructive Bartolomé José Gallardo (1776–1852), attacked 18th c. neoclassicism while strongly urging greater study of Spain's Golden Age masterpieces. An outstanding work is the *Biblioteca des autores esp.* (1846–80) begun by Buenaventura Aribau (1798–1862) and Manuel Rivadeneyra (1805–72). The inclusion of biographies, studies, and criticisms of the individual entries, makes this more than an anthology. Criticism became more firmly linked with careful scholarship with the appearance of Agustín Durán (1793–1862), who carried on the work of Böhl von Faber in his *Romancero* (vols. X and XVI of the *Biblioteca*) and in his *Discurso sobre el influjo de la critica moderna en la decadencia del teatro antiguo esp.* (1828). Durán, as well as Eugenio de Ochoa, Ventura de la Vega (1807–65) and José Espronceda (1808–42), was greatly influenced by Alberto Lista y Aragón (1775–1848), who headed the rather reactionary Sevillian School.

Mariano José de Larra (1809–37), as journalist, dramatist, novelist, and critic, upheld romanticism as the partner of political liberalism. His criticism of *La conjuración de Venecia* and many other contemporary plays set a new standard. José Amador de los Ríos (1818–78), besides his criticism of art, manifests, in *Historia crítica de la lit. esp.,* a thorough scholarship. Cañete, a periodical essayist, found beauty in all schools of literature.

Cayetano Alberto de la Barrera's *Catálogo del teatro antiguo esp.* (1860), because of its interesting classifications of types of dramatic works, is more than a mere listing of plays; it is a *sine qua non* for the specialist in this field.

Because of his own work and even more because of his ability to stimulate others, Manuel Milá y Fontanals (1818–84) is often considered the most important Sp. critic of the later 19th c. His *De los trovadores en España,* 1861, and *De la poesía popular castellana,* 1874, are well documented, and set the pattern for subsequent studies. His pupil Marcelino Menéndez y Pelayo (1856–1912) was the critics' critic. In his *Ideas estéticas* he traces the development of western æsthetics from the Greeks to the 19th century. He elevated the literary establishment of Spain with monumental works on lyric poetry, the theatre, and the origins of the novel. He was Platonic and catholic. He described with great animation the historical process of letters, and evaluated authors and their works with incomparable good taste.

Another historian of critics and criticism was Francisco Fernández y González (1833–1917), whose *Hist. de la crit. lit. desde Luzán hasta nuetros días,* 1867, is exceptionally well organized and, though brief and unsympathetic toward neoclassicism, gives valuable insight into mid-19th c. views.

The optimistic critic of the 19th c. was Juan Valera (1824–1905), whose criticisms were based on moderation and middle-of-the-road attitudes, *e.g.,* his chiding of Emilia Pardo Bazán (1852–1921, *Cuestión palpitante,* 1883) because of her acceptance of naturalism. Another novelist-critic was Clarín (pseud. of Leopoldo Alas, 1852–1901), with a tendency toward fiery diatribes and acceptance of extremes. He attempted with his criticism (defined as "an æsthetic judgment") to orient public taste, and to exert a sound influence over literary professionals.

He occupied himself mainly with the novel. Among many critics, Gómez de Baquero (pseud. Andrenio, 1866–1929) made serious attempts to analyze the novelists of the years 1875–1925.

Although Emilio Cotarelo y Mori (1857–1936) in his *Bibliografía de las controversias sobre la licitud del teatro en Esp.* was interested primarily in the older periods, this book is important even in the present day, because of its estimate of the prejudice against the theatre in Spain.

M. Menéndez Pelayo, *Ideas estéticas,* v. 3; R. E. Pellissier, *The Neo-Classic Movement in Sp.,* 1918; J. Cano, *La Poética de Luzán,* 1928; J. L. McClelland, "The 18th c. Conception of the Stage and Histrionic Technique," *Estudios Hispánicos* (Homenaje a A. M. Huntington), 1952; J. A. Cook, *Neo-Classic Drama in Sp.: Theory and Practice,* 1959; M. Nerlich, *Untersuchungen zur Theorie des klassizistischen Epos in Sp.,* 1964; J. L. McClelland, *The Origins of the Romantic Mov. in Sp.,* 1937; E. A. Peers, *A History of the Romantic Mov. in Sp.,* 1940; F. Fernández y González, *Historia de la crítica literaria en España desde Luzán hasta nuestros días,* 1867; J. Martínez Ruiz ("Azorín"), *La crítica literaria en Esp.,* 1893; J. Entrambasaguas, "Panorama histórico de la erudición esp. en el s. XIX," *Arbor,* 1946; A. Carballo, "Los estudios de Preceptiva y de Métrica esp. en los siglos XIX y XX," *Rev. de Lit.,* 1955; E. Fishtine, *D. Juan Valera, the Critic,* 1933; W. E. Bull, V. A. Chamberlin, *Clarín: the Critic in Action,* 1963; M. Olguin, "M. Menéndez Pelayo's Theory of Art, Aesthetics, and Criticism," 1950, *Univ. of Calif. Publ. in Modern Philology*; D. Alonso, *Menéndez Pelayo, crítico literario,* 1956; P. Sainz Rodríguez, *M. Pelayo, historiador y crítico literario,* 1956. JAMES O. SWAIN.

20th Century. Three areas can be distinguished: a) judgment of contemporary literature; b) interpretation of literature worthy of current concern; c) study of earlier literature.

a) In judging contemporary works, critics like "Andrenio" and Andrés González Blanco (1886–1924), author of *Los Contemporáneos* (1907–1910), abandoned the educational aim of "Clarín" and its satirical tendency, inclining rather to subjective commentary. This expansive and enthusiastic criticism, of impressionistic character, reached its extreme in *La nueva literatura* (1917–1927) of Rafael Cansinos-Assens (1883–1964), but is counterbalanced by the penetrating sketches of dramatic literature, collected in *Las Máscaras* (1917), of Ramón Pérez de Ayala (1880–1962), who urged the æsthetic education of the Spanish, and by the serious journalistic work of Enrique Díez-Canedo (1879–1944), weighty and cosmopolitan critic, with great capacity for relating and defining values (*Conversaciones literarias 1915–1930,* 1964). The Vanguard spirit, incipient in Cansinos, produced a show of novelty in *Carteles* (1927) of E. Giménez Caballero (b. 1899). However, the finest of the Vanguard spirit was assimilated by Guillermo de Torre (b. 1900). His liberalism, his love of all new experience, and his insatiable curiosity for contemporary art, manifest themselves in several miscellaneous volumes and in two major works: *Problemática de la Literatura* (1951) and *Historia de las literaturas de Vanguardia* (1965). To situate the works and the intellectual phenomena in their historic time and literary space, and to evaluate their essence and qualities, are the bases of his method. After the Civil War (1936–39) criticism of current literature decayed notably; its best examples are found in the review *Insula.*

b) Interpretative criticism, usually in essay form, was of decisive importance among the writers of the generation of 1898. J. Martínez Ruiz (pseud. "Azorín," 1873–1967) reacted against positivism and, influenced by Taine, Guyau and Nietzsche, as well as by Impressionism, understood literary criticism as a revalidation of forgotten works and a reassessment of values from the point of view of life. His criticism, of inner erudition and poetic shadings, sought to discover in the past the "truth" of Spain, and embody it with modern sensitivity (*Lecturas españolas,* 1912; *Al margen de los clásicos,* 1915). A poetic work springing from another poetic work was *Vida de Don Quijote y Sancho* (1905) by the existentialist thinker Miguel de Unamuno (1864–1936). Ramiro de Maeztu (1874–1936) also understood art as a function of life when he interpreted the values Love, Power, and Wisdom as the three Spanish literary symbols: *Don Quijote, Don Juan y la Celestina* (1926).

"To give the reader a more perfect visual organ" was the objective of José Ortega y Gasset (1883–1955), in *Meditaciones del Quijote* (1914), *La deshumanización del Arte* (1925) and other essays, as lucid as they are elegant. His reflections on the tragicomic essence of the novel, and on the antisentimental tendency of the new art, were of widespread influence. Founder of the *Revista de Occidente* (1923), he acquainted Spain with psychoanalysis (Freud), phenomenology (Husserl) and philosophy of life (Dilthey). His own philosophy (vital reason, perspectivism) taught the recognition of the specifically artistic values of a literary work, with a rather adverse attitude toward realism and the alleged excellence of popular poetry. This teaching was reinforced from another angle by Eugenio d'Ors (1882–1954), who preached the interpretation of artistic phenomena in the light of their structure: stylistic constants, rhythms, order, symbolic content of all the forms (*Las ideas y las formas,* 1928; *Lo Barroco,* 1944). From these two masters, there was derived a current of profound attention to the morphologic values, which fertilized idiomatic (A. Alonso, D. Alonso), thematic (P. Salinas), and structural (J. Casalduero) stylistics. Other historians (A. Castro, J. F. Montesinos) remained more interested in the personal attitudes, the experiences, and the ethical as well as æsthetic ideas of the artist.

Although the formal criteria gave strength to interpretative criticism and are still applied (Carlos Bousoño: *Teoría de la expresión poética,* 1952; Juan Ferraté: *La operación de leer,* 1962), recently existentialist criteria have appeared: *La Generación del Noventa y Ocho* (1945) of P. Laín Entralgo; *Crítica y meditación* (1957) of J. L. Aranguren; *La voluntad de estilo* (1957) of Juan Marichal; *Introducción a la poesía española contemporánea* (1960) of L. F. Vivanco; and of socialist base: *La hora del lector* (1957) of J. M. Castellet; *La novela española contemporánea* (1958–62) of E. G. de Nora; *La tragedia y el hombre* (1962) of J. M. de Quinto; *Anatomía del realismo* (1965) of A. Sastre. These last critics reveal the influence of Karl Marx and G. Lukács.

In general, interpretative criticism reveals the predominance of five guiding concepts: Life, Reason, Form, Existence, and Society. The wealth of perspectives as well as the expressive dignity of this type of criticism has greatly benefited the other two types: the scholarly and the journalistic criticism.

c) The direct or indirect disciples of Menéndez Pelayo were the Cervantists F. Rodríguez Marín and N. Alonso Cortés; J. Cejador, author of *Historia de la lengua y literatura castellanas* (1915–1922); A. Bonilla, scholar of Humanism; the aforementioned Cotarelo, and more. The major disciple was undoubtedly Ramón Menéndez Pidal (1869–1968), master of almost all Spanish linguists, historians, and critics of this century. Author of the first critical edition of *Poema del Cid* (1908) and of fundamental works of linguistic and political history, he studied especially the origins of poetry, epic as well as lyric, the Romancero, and the theater of the Golden Age. His view of Spanish literature may be condensed as follows: the historical and realistic character of epic poetry; formation of the romances from the epic narratives, and the national theatre of Lope de Vega from the romances and chronicles; potency and survival of the literature recreated by the people and destined for the masses. The basic concept of his criticism is tradition: the transmission of the message of the spirit, sometimes patent, sometimes latent, throughout the generations; a chain of vital variations on the theme of something their own, in which the people feel united in language and circumstances. Menéndez Pidal indicated the primordial characteristics of Spanish literature (1949) and studied primitive lyricism (1951), the life of the romances (1954) and the origins of the French epic (*La "Chanson de Roland" y el neotradicionalismo,* 1959). He founded the *Revista de Filología Española* and to his mastery is owed the consolidation of various disciplines: phonetics (T. Navarro), history of thought (A. Castro), history of language (R. Lapesa), stylistics (A. Alonso, D. Alonso), dialectology, and linguistic geography.

Amĕrico Castro (b. 1885) was primarily a linguist and historian of ideas (*El pensamiento de Cervantes,* 1925). He moved to the United States after the Civil War, and in 1948 published *España en su historia,* rewritten in 1954 as *La realidad histórica de España.* He returned to the study of Cervantes (1957, 1966) and the importance of honor in the Spanish theater (1961). His new point of view consists in inserting himself into the functional structure as seen in conduct, work, personality, and text. This form of criticism enhances the "situation," and explains the peculiarity of Spain's history through the conflicting coexistence of Jews, Moors, and Christians, which was of decisive importance for literature, in creating a horizon of possibilities and obstacles both intimate and general. (C. Sánchez Albornoz, in *España, un enigma histórico,* 1956, discussed Castro's theories).

Spanish stylistics springs from the influence of Menéndez Pidal, Ortega and D'Ors, combined with foreign doctrines (linguistics of Saussure and Bally, æsthetics of Croce, neo-idealism of Vossler, Spitzer, and Hatzfeld). Amado Alonso (1896–1952), director of the Instituto de Filología of Buenos Aires since 1927, founded the *Revista de Filología Hispánica* (1939) and was Professor at Harvard (1946). He expounded and practiced stylistics, understood as the study of expressive systems and their æsthetic efficacy (*Poesía y estilo de Pablo Neruda,* 1940; *Ensayo sobre la novela histórica,* 1942; *Materia y forma en poesía,* 1955). A similar vigor of intellectual and beautiful exposition is seen in the works of Dámaso Alonso (b. 1898): *La lingua poética de Góngora* (1935), *La poesía de San Juan de la Cruz* (1942). In *Poesía española: Ensayo de métodos y límites estilísticos* (1950) he distinguishes, besides the impressive knowledge of a reader and the synthetic and orientating vision of a critic, a third approach to understanding a work of art (his own), namely, a quasi-scientific analysis of the connections between word and meaning. Stylistics is defined as the science of the momentary use of creative language in a work of poetry which is always both of the present and eternal. Dámaso Alonso is editor of the "Biblioteca Románica Hispánica" (Ed. Gredos, Madrid), which publishes the finest philological studies of the Spanish-speaking world.

Both Alonsos understand stylistics principally from the point of view of linguistics. This is also prominent in the monographs of Rafael Lapesa (b. 1908) on Garcilaso de la Vega (1948) and on Santillana (1957). Thematic stylistics, on the other hand, is practiced by the poet Pedro Salinas (1891–1951), author of *Reality and the Poet in Spanish Poetry* (1940), *Jorge Manrique* (1947), and *La poesía de Rubén Darío: Ensayo sobre el tema y los temas del poeta* (1948). Structural stylistics is best represented by Joaquín Casalduero (b. 1903), who has studied all the works of Cervantes (1943–1951), the *Vida y obra de Galdós* (1943) and the poetry of Jorge Guillén (1946) and of Espronceda (1961). His method consists of describing the structure of a work of art from intuition of the essence of the structure, and discovering the functional symbolism of the elements of the work, in order to penetrate it vitally. The common denominator of these critics is their harmonizing of poetic intuition and scientific rigor. They hope to increase delight in the work of art by making explicit its immanent virtues.

José F. Montesinos (b. 1897), although also an essayist educated by the study of Ortega, has always given equal value to the artistic result and the historical and social circumstances. Exiled, in Berkeley, California, he embarked on a history of the Spanish novel in the 19th century, and in the volume which serves as its introduction (1955), he attempts to raise, in front of "the criticism of pure Beauty," a literary sociology attuned to the ideas and anxieties of the creator, the problems of the undertaking, and the reaction of the masses of readers.

The Academic critics of Spain count many valuable representatives: Emilio Alarcos, Fernando Lázaro, Martín de Riquer, J. M. Blecua. In the USA Federico de Onís (1885–1966), founder of the *Revista Hispánica Moderna* (New York), and Angel del Río (1901–1962), author of an excellent manual *Historia de la Literatura Española* (New York, 1948) have reached notable stature. Well known in Spain and of major proportions is the *Historia de la Literatura Española* (1937) of Angel Valbuena Prat (b. 1900), a work of interpretation, as contrasted with the scholarly manual of J. Hurtado and A. González Palencia (1921). Here, one sees once again the principal characteristic of criticism of this century: the predominance of the personal "æsthetic" interpretation over the "ethical" judgment of ideas, and over the "historical" investigation of the facts.

E. de Zuleta, *Hist. de la crít. esp. contemporánea,* 1966; A. Carballo, "El saber literario" (in *Hist. Gral. de las Lit. Hisp.,* ed. G. Díaz-Plaja, VI, 1967); M. E. Buffum, "Lit. Crit. in the Essays of the Generation of 1898," *Hispania,* Calif., 1935; J. A. Maravall, *Menéndez Pidal y la Historia del Pensamiento,* 1960; E. I. Fox, *Azorín as a Literary Critic,* 1962; G. Correa, "Últimas tendencias de la crítica literaria española," Symposium, 1953. GONZALO SOBEJANO.

PART III

Selected list of Critics and Works from other countries

ARABIC

C. Landberg, *Crit. Arabica,* 3 v., 1886; Ahmed Deif, *Essai sur la lit. crit. chez les Ar.,* 1917; Gustave von. Grunebaum, *Ar. Lit. Crit. in the 10th c.,* 1941; *Krit. und Dichtkunst,* 1955; Amjad Trabulsi, *La Crit. poétique des Ar. jusqu'au 5e s. de l'Hégire* (11th c.), 1955; Franz Rosenthal, *Hist. of Muslim Historiography,* 1952; M. H. ‹Abd al-Razig, *Ar. Lit. Since the Beginning of the 19th c.,* 1922; ‹Abdin ‹Abd al-Majid, *Hist. of Ar. Culture in the Sudan,* 1953; As ‹ad Daghir, *A Short Hist. of Ar. Civilization,* 1918; J. M. Abd-el-Jalil, *Brève Hist. de la litt ar.,* 1943; L. Cheiko, *La Lit. ar. au 19e s.,* 2 v., 1924–26; J. W. Fück, *Arabiya . . . du style ar.,* 1955; H. A. R. Gibb, *Ar. Lit,* 1963 (good bibliography); Anis E. Khuri, *Devel. of Ar. Prose,* 1935; R. A. Nicholson, *A Lit. Hist. of the Arabs,* 1930; G. T. Adler, *The Poetry of the Ar. of Spain,* 1867; C. Almuly, *Poésie ar. sous le ciel andalou,* 1956; A. Kh. Kinany, *The Devel. of Gazal in Ar. Lit.,* 1951; A. R. Nykl, *Hispano-Arabic Poetry . . . Troubadours,* 1946; H. Ringgren, *Studies in Ar. Fatalism,* 1956; al-Bakillani (10th c. document of Ar. Lit. theory), trans. G. E. von Grunebaum, 1950.

BRAZILIAN

Martins Wilson, *A Crit. Lit. no Brasil,* 1952; Amoroso-Lima, A., *O Crit. Lit.* 1945; *A estetica lit.,* 1954; Anderson Imbert, Enrique, *La Crit. Lit. Contemporánea,* 1957; Coutinho, Afranio, *Da Crit. e da Nova Crit,* 1957; *A Crit.,* 1958; Herrera, Lucilo Pedro, *Sugestiones Crit.,* 1938; Portilla, Eduardo, Dimensões I, II, 1959; Cayetano Raurich, Hector, *De la Crit. como Creación,* 1965; Jobim, Renato, *Crit.,* 1960; Congresso Brasileiro de Crit. (assis), 1963.

BULGARIAN

Paisi Hilandarski, *Hist. of Slavenko-Bulgarians,* 1772; V. Aprilov, 1789–1847, *Morningstar,* 1841 on contemporary writers; Nesho Bonchev, 1839–78, on Russ. lit.; Kristo Kristev, 1866–1919, ed. journal *Thought,* æsthetics; Todor Trayanov, b. 1882, j. *Hyperion,* moderns, symbolists; L. Stoyanov, b. 1888, j. *Hyperion,* moderns, symbolists; Vladimir Vasilev, j. *Zlatorog*; j. *Archer,* German influences; j. *Zora,* Irodan Badev *vs* propaganda; realist; Georgi Tsanev, *Pisatelli i Problemi,* 1965; D. Shishmanov, *Survey of Bulgarian Lit.,* 1932.

CHINESE

Three Periods I 249 B.C.—589 A.D. (Chin Dynasty—Southern and Northern D.) emphasized form; II 581–1911 (Sui D.—Ching D.) emphasized substance; III 1912–1945 (Republic) western influences; analysis and evaluation.

P'i P'ing: criticism is picking flaws; therefore scholars wrote little; Liu An (literary name Huai-nan Tzŭ) d. 122 B.C. standard work on Taoism; Liu Pen Ping 6th c. *Wen Hsin Tiao Lung* (*Carving a Dragon in the Heart of Lit.*) exalts emotion and natural impulse; Li Li Weng *Ch'u P'ing* of drama; Chin Sing T'an (Ching D.) of the novel; Evan Morgan, *A Guide to Wenli Styles and Ch. Ideals,* 1912; Georges Margoulies, *Evolution de la prose artistique Ch.,* 1929; Chung Chao, *The Communist Program for Lit . . . ,* 1955; Liu Hsieh (465?–522?) *The Literary Mind,* trans. 1959; *The Chinese Classics,* 5 v., 1960; T. A. Hsia, *Enigma of the Five Martyrs* (Leftist), 1962; Liu, Ts'un-jen, *Buddhist and Taoist Influences on Ch. Novels,* 1962; Cyril Birch, ed. *Ch. Communist Lit.,* 1963; F. S. Drake, ed., *Chung-kuo wen hsuan* (Selections from Ch. Lit.), 1955; Jos. Schyns, *1500 Modern Ch. Novels and Plays,* 1948; Kate Buss, *Studies in the Ch. Drama,* 1922, 1930; Ch'êng, Hsiu-ling, *Secrets of the Ch. Drama,* 1937; H. A. Giles, *A Hist. of Ch. Lit.,* 1901, 1929; A. C. Scott, *An Intro. to the Ch. Theatre,* 1958–59; John L. Bishop, ed. *Studies in Ch. Lit.,* 1965; Ch'en, Shou-I, *Ch. Lit.,* 1961; E. D. Edwards, *Ch. Prose Lit. of the T'ang Period* (618–906) 2 v., 1937–38; D. W. Fokkema, *Lit. Doctrine in Ch. and Soviet Influence,* 1965; Jas. R. Hightower, *Topics in Ch. Lit.,* 1950; R. G. Irwin, *The*

Evolution of a Ch. Novel, 1953; Ming Lai, *A Hist. of Ch. Lit.,* 1964; Yun-Shan Tan, *Hist. of the Ch. Lang. and Lit.,* 1952; I. Ting, *A Short Hist. of Modern Ch. Lit.,* 1959; Burton Watson, *Early Ch. Lit.,* 1962; A. Wylie, *Notes on Ch. Lit.,* 1902, 1964; Jo-'Yü Liu, *The Art of Ch. Poetry,* 1962; Chih Wei Luh, *On Ch. Poetry,* 1935; R. E. Teele, *Through a Glass Darkly: a Study of Eng. Trans. of Ch. Poetry,* 1949.

CZECHOSLOVAKIAN

Jan Hus 1370–1415, established standard language and orthography; Comenius 1592–1670, *Dictionary* (lost); Josef Dobrovsky 1753–1829, *Hist. of Cz. Lit.*; Josef Jungmann 1773–1847, continued Hist.; introduced Romantic movement; Králov Dvur and Zelená Hora, Manuscripts, purporting to be 13th c. Cz. works. Dispute over these forgeries (1880's) quickened criticism; František Palacky 1798–1876, prosody; Pavel Josef Safărik 1795–1861, prosody; Karel Havliček-Borovsky, journalist critic; Jaroslav Vrchlický 1853–1912, j. *Lumír*; Julius Zeyer 1841–1901, turned from G. to Fr. and Russ. lit.; Thos G. Masaryk 1850–1937, j. *Athenaeum* (1883) *Essay on Concrete Logic,* 1885; František Xavier Salda 1876–1937, emphasized rules; foreign lit.; Jiři Karasek ze Lvovic b. 1871, decadence, j. *Moderní Revue*; Jan Máchal, scholar critic (Charles U.); Arne Novák, scholar critic (Charles U.); Dušan Jeřábek, *Vítězslav Hálek,* 1959; F. Chaboda, *A Short Survey of Cz. Lit.,* 1924; Otokar, *Slovo o Krit.,* 1947; René Wellek, *Modern Cz. Crit.,* 1954.

DUTCH

Van der Schueren, *Teuthonista of Duytschlender,* 1475–77; Lambrecht, *Nederduitsche spellinghe,* 1550, rhetoric; Van der Werve, *Tresor der Duitscher talen,* 1553; Van Mussem, *Vocabularius,* 1553; Plantijn (with Kornelius Kilianus), dictionaries, by 1600; Mattijs de Castelain, *Const von Rhetoriken* (Flemish), 1555; 1584 oldest Chamber of Rhetoric (Amsterdam: *In Liefd Bloeyende*) pub. *Twee-Spraack van de Nederduitsche Letterkunst*; Daniel Heinsius, 1580–1655, *De Tragoediae Constitutione,* 1616, from Aristotle; Gerhard J. Vossius, 1577–1649, *Ars Rhetorica,* 1620; Grotius (Huig de Groot), 1583–1645, Prolegomena to trans. of Euripides; Sidney's *Defense of Poesie,* 1619 (adapted by Rosenburg); Joost von den Vondel, 1587–1679, *Aanleidinge ter Nederduitsche dichtkunste,* 1650; Jan Vos, Pref. *Medea,* 1667, *vs.* Aristotle, for nature; Samuel Coster, 1579?–1665?, Pref. *Isabella* 1618, for nature, but later joined Lodewijck Meyer and Andries Pels, Lit. Society *Nil Volentibus Arduum,* advocating Fr. classicism; Meyer, *Verloofde koninckxsbruid*; Pels, *Q. Horatius Flaccus' Dichtkunst*; Michael de Swaen, 1700, pro Fr.; Justus van Effen, ed. *De Spectator* 1731–35, modeled on Eng.; Van Alphen, *Pref. Theorie der schoone Kunsten* (by Riedel, 1778–80, trans. from G.); *Digtkundige verhandlingen,* æsthetics; Jan D. Macquet, *Proeven van dichtkundige letteroefningen* 1780 conservative; Jeronimo de Bosch, 1783 pro rules, *vs.* Van Alphen; W. de Perponcher, *Goonbeginselen van de . . . schoone,* theory; Rijnvis Feith, poet-critic, *Bijdragen ter . . . kunsten,* 1781–96; *Brieven*; Bellamy, *Proeven voor . . . smaak en het hart,* 1784–85, reason plus taste; J. Kinker, *Post van den Helicon,* (1789–), *vs* sentimentality; Bilderdijk, *Het Reveil,* helped introduce romanticism; J. H. van der Palm *Over het versmaden . . . kunst,* 1810, *vs* rules; N. G. van Kampen, 1823, pro ancients; Potgieter j. *De Gids,* ed. 1837–65, mouthpiece of romanticism; Bakhuizen van den Brink, *Vondel met Roskam en Rommelpot,* 1837, romantic; C. Busken Huet, *Fantasiën en Kritieken* (25 v.) 1868–88, romantic; Jacob Geel, *Onderzoek en fantasie,* 1838, æsthetics; Nicholas Beets (popular romantic poet), *Verpoozingen . . . gebied; Versheidenheden*; J. *Nieuwe Gids,* "Men of the 80's": Kloos, individual emotion; Verwey, mystical union of poetry and life; van Deyssel, symbolism; van Eeden, social concern; H. Heijermans, 1864–1924, ed. j. *De Jonge Gids* 1897– ; Guido Gezelle 1830–99, Flemish revival; Karel van de Woestijne, 1878–1929; I. Querido 1874–1932, realism.

Journals: *Het Getig,* 1916; *Vrije Bladen,* 1925, Marsman; *De Stem* 1921, Dirk Coster, humanist; *De Gemeenschap,* 1927, Catholic; *Opwaartse Wegen,* cultural Protestant.

ESTONIAN

F. R. Faehlmann, 1798–1850, scholar, collector of folk poetry; F. R. Kreutzwald, 1803–82, scholar, collector of folk poetry; 1871 Society of Estonian Writers; Oskar Kallas, national revival; *Noor Eesti* 1905– (Young Estonia) neo-romantic; Gustav Suits, b. 1883, poet-critic; 1917, Siuru Group, realistic; Friedbert Tuglas, nationalism, tradition; J. Semper, world literature.

Greek (Modern)

Adamantios Koreas (of Chios), 1748–1833, combin. classical and modern diction; Iakovos Polylas, 1824–96, *Our Philological Lang.*, 1892, comparative; Emanuel Roïdies, *Contemporary Lit. Crit. in Gr.*; John Apostolakis, *Poetry in Our Life,* 1927, advocates strong (negative) attack; Kostes Palamas, *My First Critiques,* 1913; *My Poetic Work,* 1933, analytical; Photos Polites, austere; A. Vlahos; Pavlos Nirvana; Spyros Melas; Gregorios Xenopoulos; Alkis Thrylos (*Critiques,* 1925); Kleon Parashos; P. Haris; Petros S. Spandonides, *To Thema tes Krit.*, 1959; G. Hatzidakis, *Hist. of the Modern Gr. Lang.*, 1915; P. Marks, *Emanuel Roidies,* 1938.

Hungarian

Trailblazers (1770–1817): George Bessenyei, Joseph Pećzeli, Joseph Kármán, Francis Verseghy, Michael Czokonai, George Szerdahelyi, Gábor Dobrentei, Emil Buczy, Francis Bacsányi; *Romanticists* (1817–): Francis Kölcsey, Samuel Brassai, Paul Hunfalvy, Louis Schedius, Francis Toldy, Joseph Bajza, Michael Vörösmarty, Joseph Eötvös, Imre Henszelmann, John Erdelyi, G. Szontágh; *Idealists* (1849–): Agost Greguss, *Outline of Æsthetics,* 1849; John Arany, Pá Gyulai, Francis Salamon, Charles Szász, Jenó Péterfy; *Recent:* Zsolt Beöthy; Jenö Dóczy; Michael Babits; Frigyes Riedl (*Hist. of H. Lit.*, 1906); Geza Voinovich; Lászlo Ravasz; Lajos Kéky; Imre Kajlós; B. Janosi, *A Magyar Esztétika Története,* 1915; Aurél Kárpáti, *a búsképü lovag,* 1920; *Tanulmányok és Krit.*, 1964.

Indian

Bharata, 4th c. A.D., Nāṭya-śāstra, on poetic and dramatic expression; Bhaṭṭi (Bhartṛhari), 7th c., *Baṭṭikāvya; Vakyapadiya,* philosophy of grammar; Daṇḍin, 6th c., *Kāvyādarśa* (view of poetry); Udbhata, *Alamkārasamgraha* (conspectus of ornament); Vamana, 8th c. *Kāvyālamkara* (ornament of poetry); Bhamaha, 8th c., *Kāvyālamkara*; Rudrata, 8th c. *Kāvyālamkara*; Rājaśekhara, ca. 900, *Kāvyamimāṁsa* (remembrancer of poetry); Anandavardhana, ca. 850 *Dhvanyāloka* (contemplation of suggestive resonance); Abhimavagupta, end 10th c. *Locana* (illumination; commentary on preceding); *Abhinavabharati* (goddess of speech); Dhanamjaya, late 10th c. *Daśarūpa* (ten dramatic types); Mammaṭa, 11th c. *Kāvyaprakāśa* (light of poetry); Kṣemendra, 11th c. *Ancityākaṁkāra* (propriety of ornament); Viṣvanātha Kavirāja, 13th c. *Sāhitya Darpaṇa* (mirror of lit.), the masterwork; Keśava Dāsa, 16th c., *Kavipriyā* (poetical endearment): *Rasikapriyā* (endearment of connoisseurship); Jasvant Sing, *Bhāṣa Bhuṣana* (ornament of language); Bihari Lal, *Sat Sai* 1662; Lala Candrika, 19th c., commentary on preceding. Dittakavi Subrahmanya Sarma, *Lit. Crit. in Sanskrit and Eng.*, 1950; C. D. Narasimhaia, ed. *Lit. Crit.: European and Indian Traditions,* 1966; A. B. Keith, *Sanskrit Lit.*, 1928; Ananda K. Coomaraswamy, *Transformation of Nature in Art,* 1935; Ed. A. Shilo, *The Intellectual Between Tradition and Modernity,* 1961; Suniti K. Chatterji, *Langs. and Lit. of Modern India,* 1963; Gertrude E. Sen, *Cultural Unity of India,* 1965; Wm. T. De Bary, *Sources of Ind. Tradition,* 1958; Balwant Gargi, *Theatre in Ind.*, 1962; Manomohan Ghosh, *Contributions to the Hist. of Hindu Drama,* 1957; H. H. Gowen, *A Hist. of Ind. Lit.*, 1931; K. R. Srinivasa Iyengar, *Lit. and Authorship in Ind.*, 1943; G. Allana, ed. *Presenting Pakistani Poetry,* 1961; Bhandarkar Oriental Research Inst., *Commemorative Essays . . . ,* 1917; Sahitya Akademi, *Contemporary Ind. Lit.*, 1959; All-India Writers' Conference, *The Ind. Lit. of Today,* 1945, *Drama in Modern Ind.*, 1957.

Japanese

Pu Shang: Preface, *The Book of Songs* ca. 450 B.C.; *The Record of Ancient Matters,* 712 A.D.; Ki no Tsurayuki (868–946?) Preface, *Collection of Ancient and Modern Poems*; *The Tosa Diary*; Lady Murasaki (real name unknown, 978–1016), *The Tale of Genji* (Vol. 3, Ch. "The Glow-worm"); Nijō Yoshimoto (1320–88), *The New Rules of Linked Verse,* 1372, etc. linked verse: 100 stanzas, alternating 5-7-5 and 7-7 syllable lines, written successively by members of a group of poets; aiming at *Yugen* (elegance) and unity in variety; Zeami Motokiyo (1363–1443), *The Writing of the Nō,* 1423, etc.; Okura Toraaki (1597–1662), on the *Kyogen* (comic interlude; usually presented between two Nō plays); Jigu (early 17th c.), *The Remnants from the Western Sea,* on Heikyoku (narrative song); Matsuo Bashō (Munefusa, 1644–94), essays on the haiku; emphasized *sabishi* (loneliness) and impersonality. Followed by: Zushi Rogan, *The Record of the Seven Days,* 1693; Morikawa Kyoroku, *Dialogues on the Art of the Haiku,* 1698; Mukai Kyorai, *Kyorai's Writings,* 1775; Hattori Dohō, *Three Books on the Art of the Haiku,* 1776; Chikamatsu Monzaemon (Suginomori Nobumori, 1653–1725: "the Japanese Shakespeare"), Preface, *Souvenirs from Naniwa,* 1738, by Hozumi Ikan; on the puppet play, Motoori Norinaga (1730–1801, the major literary theorist), *Whispers in Favor of Ancient Poetry,* 1763; *The Precious Little Comb,* 1796 (study of *The Tale of Genji*); *Studies in "The Record of Ancient Matters,"* 1798, etc. Shintoism and lit. Nondidactic; seeks *mono no aware,* elevated human feeling; vs. Buddhism, which renounces feeling. F. V. Dickins, *Primitive and Medieval Jap. Texts,* 1906; Takeshi Ishakawa, *Etude sur la lit. impressioniste au Jap.,* 1909; Yuske Tsurumi, *Present-Day Jap.,* 1926; E. V. Gatenby, *The Cloud-Men of Yamato,* 1929 (Mysticism in Jap. Lit.); Yoshie Okazaki, *Jap. Lit. in the Meiji Era* (1867–1912), 1955; Wm. G. Aston, *A Hist. of Jap. Lit.,* 1937, 1966; Takamichi Ninomiya, *The Poetry of Living Jap.,* 1957; R. H. Brower and Earl Miner, *Jap. Court Poetry,* 1961; R. H. Blyth, *A Hist. of Haiku,* 1963; Ki Kimura, *Jap. Lit. . . . Meiji-Taisho Era,* 1957; Joseph Koshimi Yamagiwa, *Jap. Lit. of the Showa Period* (20th c.), 1959; Kokusai Bunka Shinkokai (Soc. for International Cultural Relations), *Introd. to Classical Jap. Lit.,* 1948; *Introd. to Contemporary Jap. Lit.,* 2 v., 1959; Makoto Ueda, *Literary and Art Theories in Jap.,* 1967.

Latin-American

Andrés Bello, 1781–1865 (Chile), humanistic; Miguel Antonio Caro, 1843–1909 (Colombia), academic, conservative; Antonio Gómez Restrepo, b. 1869 (Colombia), classical; Juan María Gutiérrez, 1809–78 (Argentine to Chile), *América poética,* 1846; José Enrique Rodó, 1872–1917 (Uruguay), formal beauty, *modernista*; Rufino Blanco-Fombona, b. 1874 (Venezuela), *Grandes escritores de Am.,* 1917, nationalist background; Ventura García Calderon, b. 1885 (Peru), *modernista*; aloof; Alfonso Reyes, b. 1889 (Mexico), comparative; Alba Herrera y Ogazón (Mexico), *Puntos de Vista,* 1920; Luis A. Sánchez, b. 1900 *Hist. de la lit. Am.* 1937, 1940, sociological; Ricardo Rojas, b. 1887, *La Lit. Argentina* 4 v., 1924, classical; Pedro Henríquez Ureña, b. 1884 (Dominican Rep.), *Seis ensayos,* 1928; Arturo Torres Rioseco (Chile), research; Alberto Ureta, b. 1887 (Peru), *El Parnaso y el Simbolismo,* 1915; Julio Planchart, *Temas Crít.* 1948; Emilio Bobadilla (Cuba), *Crít. y satira,* 1964; S. Morena Cora, *La Crit. Lit. en Mexico,* 1907; I. J. Barrera, *Lit. hispanoam.,* 1934; A. Coester, *Lit. Hist. of Sp. Am.,* 1928; E. H. Hespelt, et al., *An Outline Hist. of Sp. Am. Lit.,* 1941; C. Santos González, *Poetas y Crit. de Am.,* 1913; Alberto Zum Felde, *Estética del novecientos,* 1927; *Procesco intelectual del Uruguay,* 1930; C. M. Bonet, *Escuelas lit.* (Argentina) 1953; E. Anderson Imbert, *La Crit. Lit. contemporanea,* 1957; *La Crít. Lit. en la Argentina* (Encuesta, U. Nacional de Litoral, Rosario), 1963.

Latvian

Krišjānis Barons, 1835–1923, collected folk poetry (daina); Jānis Jansons, 1871–1917, realistic; Teodors Zeiferts, 1865–1929, literary historian; Pludons, b. 1874 (Vilis Lejenieks), impressionistic; Janis Sudrabkalns, b. 1894 (Arvids Peine), expressionistic; Uriah Katzenelenbogen, *The Daina,* 1935; M. Walters, *Le Peuple lettone,* 1926; W. K. Matthew, *The Tricolour Sun,* 1936.

Lithuanian

Jonas Basanavičius, 1851–1927, ed. j. *Anšra,* 1883 f. comparative; Adomas Jankštas (Bishop Alex. Dumbrauskas), 1860–1938; Vincas Kudirka, 1858–99; Juozas Tumas-Vaizgantas, 1869–1933; J. A. Herbačiauskas, b. 1876, symbolism; *after independence:* Julionas Lindé-Dobilas, 1872–1934; Vincas Krévé-Mickevičius, b. 1882 (scholar); V. Mykolaitis-Putinas, b. 1893 (scholar); Jean Mauclere, *Lit. Lithuanienne,* 1938; Antanas Vaiciulaitis, *Outline Hist. Lith. Lit.,* 1942.

Lusatian

Jan Arnošt Smoler, 1816–84, founded Mačica Serbska, 1847, for lit. studies; Jakub Bart-Cišinski, 1856–1909, comparative; Ota Wičaz, b. 1874; Józef Nowak, b. 1895, realism; Josepf Páta (Czech), 1866–1942, *Zawod do studija serskeho pismowstwa,* 1929.

Persian (Iranian)

James Darmesteter, *Les Origines de la poésie Pers.,* 1887; A. V. W. Jackson, *Early Pers. Poetry,* 1920; M. 'Abd al-Ghani, *Pre-Mughal Poetry in Hindustan,* 1941; Hādī-Hasan, *Mughal Poetry,* 1952; Mas 'ūd Farzād,

The Metre of the Robàà, 1942; Mohammed Ishaque, *Modern Pers. Poetry,* 1943; Helmer Ringgren, *Fatalism in Pers. Epics,* 1952; Ed. G. Browne, *A Lit. Hist. of Pers.,* 4 v., 1953–56; A. J. Arberry, *Classical Pers. Lit.,* 1958; Dhabīh Allah Safa, *A Hist. of Iranian Lit. of the Islamic Era,* 1954; Dinshāh Jȳibhai Irānī, *Poets of the Pahlavi Regime,* 1933; Umar Muhammad Daudpota, *The Influence of Arabic Poetry on the Devel. of Pers. Poetry,* 1934; F. Rieckert, *Grammatik, Poetik, und Rhetorik der Pers.,* 1874; Nizami al-ʿArūzi al-Samarkandi, trans. *Chahār Maqála* (4 discourses), 1921.

POLISH

Jan Kochanowsky, 1530–84, followed French Pléiade; Lukasz Opalinski, 1612–62, *Poeta* 1661, anticipated Boileau in France; Stanislaw Lubomirski, 1636–1702, *Conversations* (esp. "On Style"), imitation of ancients; St. Konarski, 1700–73, *De emendandis eloquentiae vitiis,* 1741; *vs* imitation; W. Rzewuski, 1706–79, *Art of Verse-Writing,* 1762; combine head and heart; Fr. Ksawery Dmochowski, 1762–1808, *The Art of Rhyme,* 1788 Boileau's rules; Fr. Karpinski, 1741–1825, *Eloquence,* 1782, pure poetry, toward romanticism; Al. Swietochowski, 1849–1938, *Hist. of the P. Peasant,* 2 v., 1925–28, positivist; Ig. Matuszewski, 1859–1919, *The Devil in Poetry,* 1893; *Our Own People and Others,* 1898, idealistic; St. Brzozowski, 1876–1911, *Legend of "Mlodo Polska"* (Young P.), social; St. Baczynski, *Art on the Warpath,* 1923, utilitarian plus æsthetics; P. Chmielowski, *Dzieje Krytyki lit. w. Polsce,* 1902; T. Grabowski, *Kryt. Lit. . . . ,* 1918; *w. epoce romantyzmu,* 1931; *w. epoce realizmu i modernizmu,* 1934; A. Brückner, *Dzieje kultury P.* 1931; K. Czachowski, *Obraz wspolczesnej lit. P.,* 3 v., 1934; W. Kubacki, *Krit. i tworca,* 1948; St. Wiykiewicz, *Sztuka i kryt . . . ,* 1949; H. Markiewicz, ed., *Teoria badan Lit. w. P.,* 1960; Maria Naksianowicz-Golaszewska, *Filozoficzne podstawy Kryt. lit.,* 1963; J. Z. Jakubowski, *P. Kryt.,* 4 v., 1959, 1966.

PORTUGUESE

F. de Figueiredo, *Hist. de la crit. lit. em P.,* 1916 (*See also* Brazilian).

RUMANIAN

Titu Maiorescu, 1840–1917, *About the Writing of the Rum. Lang.,* 1866; *Rum. Poetry,* 1867; *Word Intoxication,* 1873; *Criticisms,* 3 v., 1874, conservative; art for art's sake; Ivan Dobrogeanu-Gherea, 1855–1920, *Critical Studies,* 1890, 1891, 1897, social; Taine; Marx; Con. Stere, 1865–1936, j. *Viata R.,* 1906; *People in Art and Lit.,* 1893; Garabet Ibraileanu, 1871–1936, *Spirit of Crit.,* 1909, for peasantry; H. Sanislevici, b. 1875, *Critical Essays,* 1903, 1916; Taine; *Studies,* 1920; M. Dragomirescu, b. 1868, *Theory of Poetry,* 1906, personal, for nature; Ovid Densusianu, b. 1873, conservative; Fr. tradition; N. Jorga, ed. *Samanatorul* (The Sower), 1903; national, for peasantry; Ilarie Chendi, 1872–1913, middle-of-the-road; Eugen Lovinescu, b. 1881, ed. *Sburatorul* (The Incubus); Perpessicus (D. Panaitescu), b. 1891, *Critical Mentions* 1928–36, contemporary.

SCANDINAVIAN

Snorri Sturluson, 1178–1241, *Prose Edda,* oldest northern handbook for poets; Aarhus, ca. 1586, Dan. phonetics; A. P. Beyer; P. C. Fries; 16th c. Nor.; Bishop Michael Agricola, 1513–67, Finn. *Alphabet,* 1537; Anders Christensen Arrebo, 1587–1637, Dan. verse technique; Arvidi, Swe. poetics 1651; Skogekär Bärgbo, Swe. *Complaint,* 1658: alexandrines; S. Columbus, Swe. diction, 1670; L. G. Paulinus, ca. 1615, Christian revelation; J. Magni, ca. 1615, pro-Aristotle; T. Reenberg, Dan. *Ars Poetica,* 1701; S. V. Triewald, Swe. 1708, neo-classical; Olof von Dalin, Fr. rules of form; Hedvig Nordenflicht, 1718–63 French taste; first Swe. salon 1753; *A Woman's Play of Thoughts,* 4 v., 1744–50; Bergklint, 1761, pro form in poetry; N. V. Rosenstein 1793, Enlightenment; Gyllenborg 1798, reason and good taste; Ludvig Holberg, 1684–1754, Dan. the new and the useful; Knud L. Rahbeck, 1760–1830, pro sentimental comedy; ed. *Minerva* 1785–1809; P. C. Stenersen Nor. treatise on unrhymed verse 1752; J. H. Wessel, Nor. vs rules of form, pro natural feeling; H. G. Porthan, 1739–1804, Finn. folksongs; C. B. Tullin, Nor. pro pastoral poetry; J. F. Neikter, Swe. *De poesi tragica,* 1774, genius *vs* rules; G. Regnér, Swe. *Thoughts on the Swe. Theatre,* 1780, vs Fr. taste; Karl Gustav af Leopold, 1756–1829, Swe. *Genius and Taste,* 1786 pro order; J. H. Kellgren, 1751–95, Swe. *A Person is not a Genius because he is crazy,* 1787, rationalism; T. Thorild, Swe. opposed preceding, pro genius; 1786 Swedish Academy founded by King Gustav III; gives Nobel Prize for Lit.; B. C. H. Hoijer, toward romanticism; Henrik Steffens, 1801, romantic; P. D. A. Atterbom, 1790–1855, Swe. comparative; G. influence. *Swe. Seers and Poets,* 6 v., 1841–55; Lars Hammarskjöld, 1785–1827, Swe., *Belles Lettres* 1818–19; Livijn, Swe.; W. F. Palmblad, 1788–1852, Swe., trans. Gr. classics; E. G. Geyer, 1783–1847; A. A. Afzelius, 1785–1871 (*Svenska Folkvisor,* 1814–16); E. Tegnér, 1782–1846, national themes; collected Swe. folksongs; J. L. Runeberg, 1804–77, Finn., pro realism vs obscure Fosforists; B. E. Malmström, 1816–65, *Studies in Lit. Hist.*; *Elements of Hist. of Swe. Lit.* 5 v., 1866–68; Stiernstolpe; J. I. Braggesen 1764–1826 Dan. rationalism, vs romantics; A. G. Oehlenschläger 1779–1850 Dan. romanticism (vs. preceding); N. F. S. Grundtvig 1783–1872 Dan. nationalism; his son S. H. Grundtvig 1824–83 folklorist; Fredrika Bremer 1801–65 Finn. truth in lit.; A. V. Rydberg 1828–95 Swe. liberalism, *Faust,* 1867; J. H. Heiberg 1854–1928 Dan. sought unity of idealism and realism; Hierta Swe. j. *Aftonbladet* 1830– realism; P. C. Ploug 1813–94 Dan.; Sturzen-Becker Swe.: nationalism, realism; J. S. C. Welhaven, 1807–73, Nor., cosmopolitan, *Norges Daemring,* 1834; H. A. Wergeland, 1808–45, opposed preceding, nationalistic; F. Cygnaeus, 1807–81, Finn., democratic realism; I. A. Aasen, 1813–96; A. O. Vinje, 1818–70; A. Garborg, 1851–1924, Nor. pro landsmål vs literary diction, the riksmål; H. Ibsen, 1828–1906, founded j. *Andhrimer,* 1851; Georg Brandes (Morris Cohen), 1842–1927, *Main Currents in 19th c. Lit.,* 1871–90; trans 7 v., 1901–05, naturalism, *Æsthetic Studies,* 1868; H. J. Bang, 1857–1912, Dan.; Hr Pontoppidan, b. 1857, Nobel Prize 1917, Dan.; A. L. Kielland, 1849–1906, Nor.; Amalie Skram, 1847–1905, Nor.; Pálson, Iceland; Bukdahl, ca. 1890, Dan. vs Brandes; Rode, b. 1870, Dan. vs materialism, pro mysticism; V. von Heidenstam, 1859–1940, Swe. Nobel Prize 1916, neo-romantic; Selma Lagerlöf, 1858–1940, Swe. Nobel Prize 1909, neo-romantic; O. I. Levertin, 1862–1906, æstheticism; Ola Hansson, 1860–1925, symbolism; Nordal, Iceland, scholarly, romantic; H. Solander; G. R. Berg; A. Blanck; M. A. Castrén, 1813–52, Finn., ballads, philology; J. Krohn (Surmio), 1835–88, sketch of Finn. lit.; Tor Kedberg, 1862–1908; Lamm; Soderman; Sylwan; H. Schück, *Svensk Lit. Hist.* 1886–90; Sören Aabye Kierkegaard, 1813–55 faith and knowledge; Otto Manninen, b. 1872, Finn., neo-romanticism; B. Bergman; Böök; Fogelquist; Hirn; Landquist; W. Söderhjelm; Stolpe; Warburg; A. B. Benson, *Swe. Romanticism,* 1914; K. Elster, *Norsk Lit. Hist.,* 2 v., 1923–4; Th. Jorgensen, *Hist. of Nor. Lit.,* 1923; C. S. Peterson and V. Andersen, *Illusteret Dansk Lit. Hist.,* 4 v., 1924–34; R. Steffen, *Svensk Lit. Hist.,* 1919; Topsvë-Jensen, *Scand. Lit., Brandes to Our Day,* 1930; Ph. Durham, *Am. Fiction in Finland,* 1960; D. Andreae, *Liberal Litt. krit.,* 1940 (Swe.); ed. *Svensk Litteraturkritik,* 1966; B. Christoffersen, *Svenska Kritiker . . . ,* 1962; Fr. Schyberg, *Dansk Teaterkritik indtil 1914,* 1937; Sven Linner, *Litteraturhistoriska Argument,* 1964 (Swe.).

SERBO-CROATIAN

Andrija Kačić-Miošić, 1702–60, folksongs; Dositej Obradović, 1742–1811, enlightenment; Vuk Karadjić, 1787–1864, standardized language; L. Gaj 1809–72, romanticism; Bishop J. J. Strossmayer, 1815–1905, Yugoslav solidarity; Svetozar Marković, 1846–75 realism, pro Russia; F. Marković, 1846–1914; A. Senoa 1838–91: pro West; Bogdan, Fr. influence; Pavle Popović, *Pregled srpske Knjizevnosti,* 1921; Jovan Skerlić, *Istorija nova srpski Knjizevnosti,* 1921; *Hrvatski Književni kriticari,* 1958; Dorothea Kadach, *Die Anfänge der Literaturtheorie bei den Serben,* 1960.

SLOVENE

Matija Čop, 1797–1835, in Pavel J. Šafařík, *Geschichte der sudslavischen Lit.,* 1864; Fran Levstik, 1831–67, *Popotovanje iz Litije do Čedeža,* 1858, draw lit. from life and lang. of the people. Also, Anton Janežić; Josip Stritar; Janko Pajk; Anton Mahnić; Ivan Cankar; Ivan Prijatelj; Anton Debeljak; Tiné Debeljak; Francé Koblar; Božidar Borko; Jurij Bamberger, historian; Karol Glaser, 1st comp. hist. of Slovene lit.; Ivan Grafenauer, biographies; Anton Slodnjak, *Slovensko Slovstvo,* 1934, critical survey; Anton Ocvirk, Josip Vidmar, Fr. standards; Anton Oven, Marija Borštnik, Franc Kidrić, biographies; Etbin Kristan (drama), Fran Govckar, Bratko Kreft, Janko Oštir, dramatic criticism; B. Paternu, *Slovenska lit.,* 1960.

TURKISH

K. J. Basmadjian, *Essai sur l'hist. de la litt. Ottomane,* 1910; Edmond Saussey, *Litt. populaire turque,* 1936; Hasân Ali Yucel, *Ein Gesamtüberblick über die Turk. Lit.,* 1941;

G. Chaliand, ed., *Poésie populaire des Tur. et des Kurdes,* 1961; Derek Patmore, *The Star and Crescent* (anthology of poems), 1946.

Ukrainian

Al. Potebnya, 1835–91; M. Drahomaniv, 1841–95; V. Antonovich, folksong; V. Gratyuk; Katerina Hrushevska; Philaret Kolessa, sociology, philology; Mikola Kostomariv, 1817–85, *Molodik,* 1843, on written lit.; Taras Shevchenko, 1814–61 (poet), nationalism; Pantaleimon Kulish, 1819–97, comparative; Omelyan Ogonovsky, 1833–94, 1st hist. of Uk. lit.; Mikhay Vosnyak, 3 v. hist.; emphasized environment; Ivan Franko, 1856–1916, j. *Zhitta i Slovo,* realism *Lit. Naukovy Vistnik,* chief authority; Oleksander Konisky, 1836–1900; Oleksander Kolessa; Leonid Biletsky, comparative; Stepan Smal Stotsky, followed Potebnya; Stepan Baley, psychological; Vasil Shchurat (Western Uk.); Pavlo Zaytsev (Eastern Uk.) analytical; Mikola Evshan; Mikita Sriblyansky; Mikhaylo Rudnitsky, art for art's sake; Dmitro Dontsov; Ostap Hritsay; Evhen Malanyuk; Bohdan Kravtsiv, nationalism; Gavriylo Kostelnik; Mikola Hnatisek, Catholic ethics; Marxian: M. Zerov; V. Yurinets; O. Doroshkevich (*Hist. Uk. Lit.,* 4v.); V. Koryak; B. Yakubinsky; Mikola Khvilovy, Marxian: Ivan Franko, *Moloda Uk.,* 1910; M. Zerov, *Vid Kulisha do Vinnichenko,* 1929.

Yiddish

Bal-Makhsoves, 1873–1924 (Isidore Eliashev, Lithuania), *Selected Works,* 5 v., 1910–15, followed Taine; *Poland and Lithuania*: Nakhman Maisil, ideological; J. Rappaport, stressed pattern; J. I. Trunk, philosophical; Jacob Gottlieb; *Argentina:* Jacob Botoshansky, comparative; *U.S.*: Hillel Rogoff, social analyst; Joel Entin; Kalmen Marmor, 1879; Khaim Lieberman; Mordecai Jaffe, impressionistic; A. Almi; A Tabatchnik; A. Mukdoini; Moissaye Olgin, Marxist; Ab. Cahan (b. 1860) realism; *Soviet Union*: M. Litvakov; J. Dobrushin; A. Musinov; M. Winer; A. Gurshtein; J. Bronshtein; Nokhum Oislender, *Main Characteristics of Y. Realism,* 1919; S. Niger (Samuel Charney), b. 1883, *On Y. Writers* 2 v., 1912; j. *Der Tag* (N.Y.); B. Rivkin, (Borukh Ab. Weinrib), b. 1883, *Main Tendencies in Y. Lit.,* 1937; Nokhum Borukh Minkoff, (U.S.), *Y. Classic Poets,* 1937, analysis of form; Israel Zinberg, b. 1873, *Hist. of Jewish Lit.* 10 v., 1933–37; Nokhum Shtif, on Contemporaries; Max Weinreich, b. 1894, *Pictures of Y. Lit. Hist.,* 1928; Max Erik, b. 1898, *Hist. of Y. Lit.,* 1928; L. Wiener, *Hist. of Y. Lit. in the 19th c.,* 1899; Zalman Reisen, *Lexicon of Y. Lit.* 4 v., 1926–29; A. A. Roback, *The Story of Y. Lit.,* 1940; M. Waxman, *Hist. of Jewish Lit.,* 4 v., 1941; Samuel Niger, *Geklibene Verk,* 1958; *Krit. un Kritikers,* 1959.

Advisors and Contributors to the Original Edition

Kenneth Morgan Abbott
J. Donald Adams
Richard Alewyn
Bower Aly
Richard Armour
John Arthos
Emanuel S. Athanasiades
Julius Bab
Fernand Baldensperger
Adriaan J. Barnouw
Erik Barnouw
Charles Wisner Barrell
Iris Barry
Paull F. Baum
Monroe C. Beardsley
George J. Becker
Theodore Bedrick
Isadore Bennett (Reed)
Adolph B. Benson
Ernest Bernbaum
Edward M. Betowski
Shlomo Bickel
Otto Bird
Morris Bishop
Frederick Thomas Blanchard
Gabriel Bonno
G. A. Borgese
Louis I. Bredvold
C. D. Brenner
Crane Brinton
Cleanth Brooks
Calvin S. Brown, Jr.
Herbert Ross Brown
Murray W. Bundy
Orhan Burian
Oscar Carl Burkhard
Wayne Burns
Stanley Burnshaw
Harold Burris-Meyer
Douglas Bush
A. L. Campa
Henry Seidel Canby
John Leslie Catterall
Haakon M. Chevalier
Gilbert Chinard
Nicholas Chubaty
Barrett H. Clark
Harry Hayden Clark
Maurice Edgar Coindreau
Edward C. Cole
Arthur Prudden Coleman
Ananda K. Coomaraswamy
Lane Cooper
Katharine T. Corey
John Todd Cowles
Ronald Salmon Crane
David Daiches
Lloyd W. Daly
Nathan Dane II
Hallie Flanagan Davis
André Delattre
Angel del Rio
Marc Denkinger
Herbert Dieckmann
Otto Alvin Dieter
Charles Donahue
Gustave Dumas, S. J.
Max Eastman
Albert van Eerden
James Mark Egan, O. P.
John Olin Eidson
Stefán Einarsson
Lucius W. Elder
Roscoe B. Ellard
Frances H. Ellis
M. B. Emeneau
Martin Eshleman
M. Blakemore Evans
N. Bryllion Fagin
Ernst Feise
Leon Feraru
Albert Feuillerat
Leslie Fiedler
Chauncey E. Finch
William A. FitzGerald
Murray Fowler
Donald Frame
W. M. Frohock
Kwok-Ying Fung
John Gassner
Royal A. Gettmann
Allan H. Gilbert

Katherine E. Gilbert
Rosamond Gilder
G. Giovannini
Alexander Gode-von Aesch
Cyrus H. Gordon
D. W. Gotshalk
Max Graf
Gustave E. von Grunebaum
Albert Guérard
Carl W. Hagge
Robert A. Hall
Homer Halvorson
Marian Harman
Martin P. Harney, S. J.
Brice Harris
Thomas Perrin Harrison, Jr.
Thomas A. Hart
Howard Graham Harvey
Baxter Hathaway
Helmut A. Hatzfeld
George R. Havens
S. I. Hayakawa
Hubert C. Heffner
H. G. Henderson
Thomas Walter Herbert
Marvin Theodore Herrick
Ernest Herman Hespelt
Leonard L. Hess
Bernard C. Heyl
John Hicks
Urban Tigner Holmes, Jr.
Walter E. Houghton
Charles C. Hower
Glenn Hughes
Kenneth H. Jackson
Sam Jaffe
Mimi I. Jehle
Ernst Jockers
Cécile Juliette Johnson
Gerald White Johnson
Charles W. Jones
Frank W. Jones
William Robert Jones
Alexander Kaun
L. Clark Keating
Ruth Kelso
Walter F. Kerr
Robert E. Kingery
Anthony J. Klančar
David Klein
Frances Wentworth Knickerbocker
William S. Knickerbocker
Frederick H. Koch
Katherine Koller
Manuel Komroff
Samuel Noah Kramer
Alwin Kronacher
Helmut Kuhn
Harry Kurz
James Craig LaDrière
La Meri (Russell Meriwether Hughes-Carreras)
Henry Lanz
Richmond Lattimore
Rensselaer W. Lee
Harry Levin
L. R. Lind
Sol Liptzin
Angeline Helen Lograsso
Roger Sherman Loomis
Helge Lundholm
Carlos Lynes, Jr.
Curtis D. MacDougall
Robert B. MacLeod
Dougald MacMillan
Kemp Malone
Clarence A. Manning
Harold M. March
Albert H. Marckwardt
Berthe M. Marti
Dwight Marvin
Oleg Maslenikov
André Maurois
William H. McCabe, S. J.
Kenneth McKenzie
Paul McPharlin
Hubert J. Meessen
Harold G. Merriam
M. F. Ashley Montagu
Henry C. Montgomery
Nancy Moore
Bayard Quincy Morgan
A. R. Morris
Charles Morris
Bruce A. Morrissette
William J. Mulloy
Lewis Mumford
Norman E. Nelson
Allardyce Nicoll
Paul Nixon
Algy Smillie Noad
Marshall E. Nunn
William Abbott Oldfather
Revilo P. Olivar
Edd Winfield Parks
George B. Parks
John J. Parry
Wolfgang Paulsen
Lucien Dean Pearson
B. E. Perry
Henry Ten Eyck Perry
Ernst Alfred Philippson
Erwin Piscator
Renato Poggioli
Louise Pound
Franz Rapp

Daniel A. Reed
Helmut Rehder
Walter A. Reichart
John T. Reid
I. A. Richards
Edouard Roditi
Hyder E. Rollins
Winthrop H. Root
Harris Livingston Russell
J. L. Salvan
Paul Schubert
Nureddin Sevin
Jean Seznec
Walter Shewring
Emi Shimizu
John Burke Shipley
Mehmed A. Simsar
Sister M. Emmanuel, O. S. F.
Horatio Smith
Winifred Smith
Donald A. Stauffer
Kurt Steel
Grundy Steiner
Harry Steinhauer
S. Byron Straw
Frank Sullivan
Montague Summers
James O. Swain
John L. Sweeney
Joseph Szentkirályi
Allen Tate
Archer Taylor
Edward A. Tenney
Arthur A. Thompson
Stith Thompson
Clarence De Witt Thorpe
N. J. Tremblay
Claude P. Viens
Eliseo Vivas
Charles C. Walcutt
Hugh Walpole
Chi-Chen Wang
E. Bradlee Watson
Dan F. Waugh
Bernard Weinberg
René Wellek
Robert H. West
Phillip Wheelwright
Stephen Whicher
Helen C. White
Robert C. Whitford
Harold Sowerby Wilson
Lowry Charles Wimberly
W. K. Wimsatt, Jr.
R. E. Wolseley
Cuthbert Wright
Lawrence W. Wylie
Demetrius B. Zema, S. J.
Palmer Louis Zickgraf
Paul Zucker
Henry Zylstra